DISCARDED
—by—
Memphis Public Library

A CONCORDANCE TO
PERSONAE:
THE SHORTER POEMS OF
EZRA POUND

A CONCORDANCE TO
PERSONAE:
THE SHORTER POEMS OF
EZRA POUND

Edited by
GARY LANE

HASKELL HOUSE PUBLISHERS LTD.
Publishers of Scarce Scholarly Books
NEW YORK ■ 1972

Published by Haskell House Publishers, Ltd.
280 Lafayette Street, New York, N.Y. 10012

Copyright © 1972 by Haskell House Publishers, Ltd.

All rights reserved, including those to reproduce
this book or parts thereof in any form.

Library of Congress Cataloging in Publication Data

Lane, Gary, 1943-
　A concordance to Personae.

　1. Pound, Ezra Loomis, 1885-　　Personae--Concor-
dances. I. Pound, Ezra Loomis, 1885-　　Personae.
II. Title.
PS3531.082P429　1972　　　811'.5'2　　　72-6462
ISBN 0-8383-1613-1

This concordance is compiled from *Personae: The Collected Poems
of Ezra Pound,* copyright 1926 by Ezra Pound and published by
New Directions Books.

Printed and Bound in the United States of America

PREFACE

This volume is part one of what is intended to comprise a concordance to the collected poetry of Ezra Pound. Mr. Pound is of course still working on his epic *Cantos,* but as that enormous task has occupied him for many years and continues to do so, it seemed reasonable to begin the concordance now with a volume devoted to the shorter poems. This book includes, therefore, all poems except the *Cantos* that Pound wishes to preserve, those he chose for *Personae: The Collected [Shorter] Poems of Ezra Pound.*

The book was compiled on an IBM 360 computer, kindly made available to me by the Bethlehem Steel Corporation. It lists, on pages 1-491, all the words and numbers, and their occurrences, in *Personae*. It lists also, on pages 492-515, the separate components of Pound's many hyphenated words. This second listing will enable the user interested in simile, for example, to augment the ninety-two uses of "like" in the concordance's main body with eleven additional ones he might otherwise miss, from "net-like" to "faun-like" to "sky-like." A final section, pages 516-546, provides a frequency table.

The format lists the entire line wherein a usage occurs, and follows each line with its page number in *Personae,* its poem's title or an abbreviated version, and its line number within the poem. Most lines are listed in the concordance exactly as they appear in the New Directions text — including Mr. Pound's inconsistencies, "gray" and "grey," for example, "odor" and "odour"—but two cases necessitated special treatment. First, because the computer could neither read nor write Greek, where the text is in that language—a dozen or so lines in all — I have transliterated it. Thus the poem "Δόρια" appears as "DORIA," and "Παρὰ Θῖνα Πολυφλοίβοιο Θαλάσσης" is listed as "PARA THINA POLYPHLOISBOIO THALASSES." Finally, because of our computer program's limitations, I was forced to change "L"s and "X"s in "The Game of Chess" to 'L's and 'X's.

To save space, I have suppressed the full listing of the following words, including after each one only its frequency of occurrence. Such a procedure is justified not only by the considerable thickness of this book, but by the extreme unlikeliness that the omitted words might prove interesting to its users. While my list is less extensive than it might be, my principle has been to include in the concordance too much rather than too little.

Suppressed Words

a	hadn't	isn't	she	was
am	has	it	she'd	wasn't
an	hasn't	it'd	she's	we
and	have	its	that	we'd
are	haven't	it's	the	were
aren't	he	I've	their	we're
at	he'd	me	theirs	weren't
be	her	my	them	we've
been	hers	neither	these	with
but	he's	no	they	you
by	him	nor	they'd	you'd
can	his	not	they're	your
cannot	I	of	they've	you're
can't	I'd	on	this	yours
either	I'm	onto	those	you've
for	in	or	through	
from	into	our	to	
had	is	ours	us	

Many of Mr. Pound's poems have titles longer than the fourteen spaces available in this book. For them, I have tried to devise shortened versions evocative of the originals. The table that follows lists those poems whose titles in the concordance and in *Personae* are not identical.

Concordance	Personae	P Page
ABU SALAMMAMM	Abu Salammamm—A Song of Empire	237
AESTHETICS	The Study in Aesthetics	96
AGE DEMANDED	"The Age Demanded"	201
ALF'S EIGHTH	Alf's Eighth Bit	263
ALF'S ELEVENTH	Alf's Eleventh Bit	266
ALF'S FIFTH	Alf's Fifth Bit	260
ALF'S FOURTH	Alf's Fourth Bit	259
ALF'S NINTH	Alf's Ninth Bit	264
ALF'S SECOND	Alf's Second Bit	258
ALF'S SEVENTH	Alf's Seventh Bit	262
ALF'S SIXTH	Alf's Sixth Bit	261
ALF'S TENTH	Alf's Tenth Bit	265
ALF'S THIRD	Alf's Third Bit	258
ALF'S TWELFTH	Alf's Twelfth Bit	267
ALTAFORTE	Sestina: Altaforte	28
ANCIENT WISDOM	Ancient Wisdom, Rather Cosmic	118
ANOTHER BIT	Another Bit—And an Offer	268
AT TEN-SHIN	Poem by the Bridge at Ten-Shin	131
BEAU TOILET	The Beautiful Toilet	128
BEFORE A SHOP	Women Before a Shop	114
BLACK SLIPPERS	Black Slippers: Bellotti	111
BLANDULA	"Blandula, Tenulla, Vagula"	39
BOWMEN OF SHU	Song of the Bowmen of Shu	127
BREAD BRIGADE	The Charge of the Bread Brigade	257
CABARET DANCER	To a Friend Writing on Cabaret Dancers	161
CAKE OF SOAP	The New Cake of Soap	99
CANTICO SOLE	Cantico del Sole	183
CANTILATIONS	Come My Cantilations	146
CH'U YUAN	After Ch'u Yuan	108
CITY OF CHOAN	The City of Choan	138
COMING OF WAR	The Coming of War: Actaeon	107
CONTEMPORARIES	Our Contemporaries	118
DANS OMNIBUS	Dans un Omnibus de Londres	160
DIEU! QU'IL	Dieu! Qu'il la Fait	72
DOMPNA POIS	"Dompna Pois de me No'us Cal"	105
DORIA	Δώρια	67
DUM CAPITOLIUM	Dum Capitolium Scandet	96
E. P. ODE	E. P. Ode Pour L'Election de Son Sepulchre	187
EXIT' CUIUSDAM	In Exitum Cuiusdam	59
FAMAM CANO	Famam Librosque Cano	14
FAN-PIECE	Fan-Piece, for Her Imperial Lord	108

Concordance	Personae	P Page
FISH & SHADOW	Fish and the Shadow	166
FOR PSYCHE	Speech for Psyche in the Golden Book of Apuleius	39
FOR THIS YULE	Villonaud for This Yule	10
FORMIANUS LADY	To Formianus' Young Lady Friend	113
FRATRES MINORE	Fratres Minores	148
FROM HEINE	Translations and Adaptations from Heine	44
FROM HEINE: 1	Translations and Adaptations from Heine: I	44
FROM HEINE: 2	Translations and Adaptations from Heine: II	44
FROM HEINE: 3	Translations and Adaptations from Heine: III	45
FROM HEINE: 4	Translations and Adaptations from Heine: IV	45
FROM HEINE: 5	Translations and Adaptations from Heine: V	45
FROM HEINE: 6	Translations and Adaptations from Heine: VI	46
FROM HEINE: 7	Translations and Adaptations from Heine: VII	47
FROM HEINE: 8	Translations and Adaptations from Heine: VIII	48
FRONTIER GUARD	Lament of the Frontier Guard	133
GAME OF CHESS	The Game of Chess	120
GOODLY FERE	Ballad of the Goodly Fere	33
GUIDO INVITES	Guido Invites You Thus	25
HER MONUMENT	Her Monument, the Image Cut Thereon	41
HIMERRO	Ἱμέρρω	112
HIS OWN FACE	On His Own Face in a Glass	35
HORAE BEATAE	Horae Beatae Inscriptio	51
HUGH SELWYN	Hugh Selwyn Mauberley	185
HUGH SELWYN: 2	Hugh Selwyn Mauberley: II	188
HUGH SELWYN: 3	Hugh Selwyn Mauberley: III	189
HUGH SELWYN: 4	Hugh Selwyn Mauberley: IV	190
HUGH SELWYN: 5	Hugh Selwyn Mauberley: V	191
HUGH SELWYN: 10	Hugh Selwyn Mauberley: X	195
HUGH SELWYN: 11	Hugh Selwyn Mauberley: XI	195
HUGH SELWYN: 12	Hugh Selwyn Mauberley: XII	196
IDEA OF CHOAN	Old Idea of Choan by Rosoriu	141
IMAGE ORLEANS	Image from D'Orleans	111
IN THE METRO	In a Station of the Metro	109

Concordance	Personae	P Page
INSTRUCTIONS	Further Instructions	94
IONE, DEAD	"Ione, Dead the Long Year"	112
JACOPO SELLAIO	Of Jacopo del Sellaio	73
JEWEL STAIRS'	The Jewel Stairs' Grievance	132
LADY'S LIFE	Prayer for His Lady's Life	38
LANGUE D'OC: 1	Langue D'Oc: I	172
LANGUE D'OC: 2	Langue D'Oc: II	173
LANGUE D'OC: 3	Langue D'Oc: III	174
LANGUE D'OC: 4	Langue D'Oc: IV	177
MAUBERLEY: 1	Mauberley 1920: I	198
MAUBERLEY: 2	Mauberley 1920: II	199
MAUBERLEY: 4	Mauberley 1920: IV	203
MOEURS CONTEMP	Moeurs Contemporaines	178
MOEURS CON: 1	Moeurs Contemporaines: I	178
MOEURS CON: 2	Moeurs Contemporaines: II	179
MOEURS CON: 3	Moeurs Contemporaines: III	179
MOEURS CON: 4	Moeurs Contemporaines: IV	179
MOEURS CON: 5	Moeurs Contemporaines:: V	180
MOEURS CON: 6	Moeurs Contemporaines: VI	181
MOEURS CON: 7	Moeurs Contemporaines: VII	181
MOEURS CON: 8	Moeurs Contemporaines: VIII	182
MONUMENTUM AER	Monumentum Aere, Etc.	146
MOYEN SENSUEL	L'Homme Moyen Sensuel	238
MR. HOUSMAN	Mr. Housman's Message	43
MULBERRY ROAD	A Ballad of the Mulberry Road	140
NATIONAL SONG	National Song (E. C.)	272
NEAR SHOKU	Leave-Taking Near Shoku	138
OF AROUET	Impressions of Francis Marie Arouet (de Voltaire)	167
OF DEPARTURE	Four Poems of Departure	137
OF SPLENDOUR	The House of Splendour	49
OF THE DEGREES	A Song of the Degrees	95
OF THE GIBBET	A Villonaud: Ballad of the Gibbet	11
OF 600 M.P.'S	Song of Six Hundred M.P.'s	270
ON RIVER KIANG	Separation on the River Kiang	137
PAGANI'S NOV 8	Pagani's, November 8	161
PARACELSUS	Paracelsus in Excelsis	32
PHASELLUS ILLE	"Phasellus Ille"	63
PIERE VIDAL	Pierre Vidal Old	30
PORTRAIT FEMME	Portrait d'une Femme	61
POST MORTEM	Post Mortem Conspectu	147
PRAISE YSOLT	Praise of Ysolt	16
PROVINO DESERT	Provincia Deserta	121

Concordance	Personae	P Page
PSYCHOLOG HOUR	Villanelle: The Psychological Hour	158
QUINTUS SEPTIM	Homage to Quintus Septimius Florentis Christianus	164
RIVER-MER WIFE	The River Merchant's Wife: A Letter	130
SALUTATION 2ND	Salutation the Second	85
SALUTATION 3RD	Salutation the Third	145
SENNIN POEM	Sennin Poem by Kakuhaku	139
SEXTUS PROP	Homage to Sextus Propertius	205
SEXTUS PROP: 1	Homage to Sextus Propertius: I	207
SEXTUS PROP: 2	Homage to Sextus Propertius: II	210
SEXTUS PROP: 3	Homage to Sextus Propertius: III	212
SEXTUS PROP: 4	Homage to Sextus Propertius: IV	214
SEXTUS PROP: 5	Homage to Sextus Propertius: V	216
SEXTUS PROP: 6	Homage to Sextus Propertius: VI	218
SEXTUS PROP: 7	Homage to Sextus Propertius: VII	220
SEXTUS PROP: 8	Homage to Sextus Propertius: VIII	221
SEXTUS PROP: 9	Homage to Sextus Propertius: IX	223
SEXTUS PROP: 10	Homage to Sextus Propertius: X	224
SEXTUS PROP: 11	Homage to Sextus Propertius: XI	226
SEXTUS PROP: 12	Homage to Sextus Propertius: XII	227
SIENA MI FE	"Siena mi fe'; Disfecemi Maremma"	193
SOCIAL ORDER	The Social Order	115
SOUTH-FOLK	South-Folk in Cold Country	139
TAKING LEAVE	Taking Leave of a Friend	137
TEMPERAMENTS	The Temperaments	100
THE YOUNG KING	Planh for the Young English King	36
THREE POETS	The Three Poets	118
THUS NINEVEH	And Thus in Nineveh	24
TO KALON	Το Καλόν	96
TO WHISTLER	To Whistler, American	235
TOMB AKR CAAR	The Tomb at Akr Caar	60
TRANSLATOR	Translator to Translated	46
UNMOVING CLOUD	To-Em-Mei's "The Unmoving Cloud"	142

This book would be incomplete without an acknowledgment of two men who made possible its execution. Roland Dedekind, indefatigable Registrar of Muhlenberg College, developed the concordance program, and Robert Vogelsinger, Bethlehem Steel Corporation Systems Engineer, guided it through testing, proof-creating, and final runs. Their cheerfully given expertise made far easier a long and exacting task.

GARY LANE

A -- ABOUT

	PAGE	TITLE	LINE
A (683)			
A.			
WE WHO WENT OUT INTO THE FOUR A. M. OF THE WORLD	104	ANCORA	3
A STRAY GIPSY--A. D. 1912	119	THE GYPSY	EPI
STARTIN' IN ABOUT 6 A. M.	271	OLE KATE	11
A'			
THEY'LL NO' GET HIM A' IN A BOOK I THINK	33	GOODLY FERE	21
A-A-A			
A-A-A-A--A-MEN.	101	AMITIES	20
AB			
TAN QUE I PUOSCH' OM GITAR AB MALH.	151	NEAR PERIGORD	EPI
"ET ALBIRAR AB LOR BORDON--"	153	NEAR PERIGORD	90
ABANDONED			
ONCE MORE ARE THE NEVER ABANDONED GARDENS	90	SURGIT FAMA	18
SHE HAS ABANDONED THE VICAR	178	MOEURS CON: 1	9
ABASHED			
AND AT THIS I WAS MILDLY ABASHED.	97	AESTHETICS	22
ABBOT			
MABIE, AND LYMAN ABBOT AND GEORGE WOODBERRY,	239	MOYEN SENSUEL	28
ABDOMINAL			
THAT THE TWITCHING OF THREE ABDOMINAL NERVES	148	FRATRES MINORE	6
ABE			
YOU AND ABE LINCOLN FROM THAT MASS OF DOLTS	235	TO WHISTLER	18
ABELARD			
"OH! ABELARD!" AS IF THE TOPIC	181	MOEURS CON: 7	8
ABIDE			
ABIDE	69	THE NEEDLE	13
ABIDED			
BITTER BREAST-CARES HAVE I ABIDED,	64	THE SEAFARER	4
IDES			
ABIDES 'MID BURGHERS SOME HEAVY BUSINESS,	64	THE SEAFARER	29
BINDING			
WE WHO HAVE SEEN EVEN ARTEMIS A-BINDING HER SANDALS,	104	ANCORA	6
-BITIN'			
AND DON'T KNOW WHAT BUG IS A-BITIN'	269	SAFE AND SOUND	11
ABJECT			
SHAMEFUL IN SIGHT, ABJECT, ABOMINABLE	42	HER MONUMENT	36
DULNESS HERSELF, THAT ABJECT SPIRIT, CHORTLES	239	MOYEN SENSUEL	31
ABLAZE			
MY SONG WAS ABLAZE WITH HER AND SHE WENT FROM ME	17	PRAISE YSOLT	42
ABLE			
I WERE ABLE TO LEAD HEROES INTO ARMOUR, I WOULD NOT,	217	SEXTUS PROP: 5	38
ABODE			
PLACE AND ABODE,	249	DONNA MI PREGA	27
ABOMINABLE			
SHAMEFUL IN SIGHT, ABJECT, ABOMINABLE	42	HER MONUMENT	36
ABOUT			
OH I KNOW THAT THERE ARE FOLK ABOUT ME, FRIENDLY FACES,	20	IN DURANCE	2
AND HAVE NONE ABOUT ME SAVE IN THE SHADOWS	20	IN DURANCE	18
LO, I HAVE SEEN THEE BOUND ABOUT WITH DREAMS,	25	GUIDO INVITES	7
"WHY TOOK YE NOT ME WHEN I WALKED ABOUT	33	GOODLY FERE	11
OUT OF A TURMOIL OF SPEECH ABOUT YOU.	36	FRANCESCA	4
AND ALL THE ANGELS SAT ABOUT	45	FROM HEINE: 4	3
COMPLAIN ABOUT THE AWFUL NOISE	45	FROM HEINE: 5	3
THAT ROUND KING HARRY ABOUT	48	FROM HEINE: 7	30
HER HAIR WAS SPREAD ABOUT, A SHEAF OF WINGS,	49	OF SPLENDOUR	7
WHERE TIME BURNS BACK ABOUT TH' ETERNAL EMBERS.	50	THE FLAME	21
WHO CALL'ST ABOUT MY GATES FOR SOME LOST ME;	51	THE FLAME	35
FLOWED IN, AND THROUGH THEE AND ABOUT THY HEELS?	60	TOMB AKR CAAR	23
LONDON HAS SWEPT ABOUT YOU THIS SCORE YEARS.	61	PORTRAIT FEMME	2
GOLDEN ABOUT THEE.	68	APPARUIT	8
FADED ABOUT THEE.	68	APPARUIT	16
STRANDS OF LIGHT INWOVEN ABOUT IT, LOVELIEST	68	APPARUIT	18
DO NOT SET ABOUT TO PROCURE ME AN AUDIENCE.	81	TENZONE	9
WHO WANDERS ABOUT ANNOUNCING HIS SEX	82	THE CONDOLENCE	15
AND ROUND ABOUT THERE IS A RABBLE	83	THE GARDEN	5
HERE THEY ARE WITH NOTHING ARCHAIC ABOUT THEM,	85	SALUTATION 2ND	8
A BROWN ROBE, WITH THREADS OF GOLD WOVEN IN PATTERNS, HAST THOU GATHERED ABOUT THEE,	91	DANCE FIGURE	17
THEIR MUSIC ABOUT THEE!	91	DANCE FIGURE	22

PAGE 1

ABOUT -- ABOVE

	PAGE	TITLE	LINE
ABOUT (CONTINUED)			
LET US EXPRESS OUR ENVY OF THE MAN WITH A STEADY JOB AND NO WORRY ABOUT THE FUTURE.	94	INSTRUCTIONS	2
YOU STAND ABOUT IN THE STREETS,	94	INSTRUCTIONS	5
I ALMOST SEE YOU ABOUT ME,	94	INSTRUCTIONS	13
LEAPT ABOUT, SNATCHING AT THE BRIGHT FISH	97	AESTHETICS	13
WHO USED TO WALK ABOUT AMONGST US	102	LADIES	10
FAINT, ALMOST, AS THE LINES OF CRUELTY ABOUT YOUR CHIN,	103	LADIES	19
GATHER ABOUT ME, O MUSES!	104	ANCORA	9
ABOUT AMONG MY FLOWERS.	109	THE FAUN	2
AND WHAT, PRAY, DO YOU KNOW ABOUT	109	THE FAUN	3
THE NIGHT ABOUT US IS RESTLESS.	110	COITUS	9
WHY SHOULD ONE ALWAYS LIE ABOUT SUCH MATTERS?	113	TAME CAT	2
AND THE GLOW OF YOUTH THAT SHE SPREAD ABOUT US	116	THE TEA SHOP	6
WILL BE SPREAD ABOUT US NO LONGER.	116	THE TEA SHOP	8
AND MIST CLOTTED ABOUT THE TREES IN THE VALLEY,	119	THE GYPSY	8
BLUE, BLUE IS THE GRASS ABOUT THE RIVER	128	BEAU TOILET	1
I PLAYED ABOUT THE FRONT GATE, PULLING FLOWERS.	130	RIVER-MER WIFE	2
YOU WALKED ABOUT MY SEAT, PLAYING WITH BLUE PLUMS.	130	RIVER-MER WIFE	4
AND THE PRINCES STILL STAND IN ROWS, ABOUT THE THRONE,	131	AT TEN-SHIN	10
TO THE DYNASTIC TEMPLE, WITH WATER ABOUT IT CLEAR AS BLUE JADE,	135	EXILE'S LETTER	50
AND THE VERMILIONED GIRLS GETTING DRUNK ABOUT SUNSET,	136	EXILE'S LETTER	55
FOR YOU WILL HAVE NO FRIENDS ABOUT YOU	137	OF DEPARTURE	EPI
WHITE RIVER WINDING ABOUT THEM;	137	TAKING LEAVE	2
FEEL YOUR HATES WRIGGLING ABOUT MY FEET	145	SALUTATION 3RD	28
HOW WOULD YOU LIVE, WITH NEIGHBOURS SET ABOUT YOU--	152	NEAR PERIGORD	28
AND ALL MY HEART IS BOUND ABOUT WITH LOVE.	153	NEAR PERIGORD	73
UP AND ABOUT AND IN AND OUT THE LAND,	153	NEAR PERIGORD	84
ABOUT HIS CASTLE, CATTLE DRIVEN OUT!	155	NEAR PERIGORD	125
OR SLITHERS ABOUT BETWEEN THE DISHONEST WAITERS--	162	CABARET DANCER	23
LIKE THE BRANCH THAT TURNS ABOUT	173	LANGUE D'OC: 2	12
OR TURN ME INSIDE OUT, AND ABOUT.	175	LANGUE D'OC: 3	47
IS AN INFANT, AGED ABOUT 14 MONTHS,	180	MOEURS CON: 5	11
AND HE TALKED ABOUT "THE GREAT MARY,"	181	MOEURS CON: 7	10
A YOUNG MUSE WITH YOUNG LOVES CLUSTERED ABOUT HER	207	SEXTUS PROP: 1	13
AND THERE IS NO HURRY ABOUT IT;	207	SEXTUS PROP: 1	22
"WHO HAS ORDERED A BOOK ABOUT HEROES?	210	SEXTUS PROP: 2	18
"ABOUT ACQUIRING THAT SORT OF A REPUTATION.	210	SEXTUS PROP: 2	20
WHAT IS TO BE DONE ABOUT IT?	212	SEXTUS PROP: 3	6
AS GOLD THAT RAINS ABOUT SOME BURIED KING.	236	MIDDLE-AGED	2
WITH RED CLOTHS ABOUT THEIR BUTTOCKS,	237	ABU SALAMMAMM	13
WHO WROUGHT ABOUT HIS "SOUL" THEIR STALE INFECTION.	241	MOYEN SENSUEL	81
I RUSHED ABOUT IN THE MOST AGITATED WAY	247	PIERROTS	5
I CAN WALK ABOUT WITHOUT FIDGETING WHEN PEOPLE PASS,	247	PIERROTS	20
THEY HAVE TO STAND ABOUT IN MUD	266	ALF'S ELEVENTH	13
AND THINKS ABOUT A ROWTON 'OUSE	270	OF 600 M.P.'S	15
ABOUT THE PRIV'LEGE OF LIBERTY.	271	OLE KATE	8
STARTIN' IN ABOUT 6 A. M.	271	OLE KATE	11
ABOVE			
THAT WHIRRED IN THE AIR ABOVE US.	3	THRENOS	6
AND WE THAT ARE GROWN FORMLESS, RISE ABOVE--	32	PARACELSUS	9
YE MIGHT LET ONE REMAIN ABOVE WITH US.	38	LADY'S LIFE	4
YE MIGHT LET ONE REMAIN ABOVE WITH US.	38	LADY'S LIFE	14
ABOVE THE BONES AND MIRE,	41	HER MONUMENT	4
HER GOLD IS SPREAD, ABOVE, AROUND, INWOVEN;	49	OF SPLENDOUR	4
YOU ARE VIOLETS WITH WIND ABOVE THEM.	62	A GIRL	8
MUST BIDE ABOVE BRINE.	64	THE SEAFARER	31
BUT, ABOVE ALL, GO TO PRACTICAL PEOPLE--	86	SALUTATION 2ND	34
THE WIND MOVES ABOVE THE WHEAT--	95	OF THE DEGREES	3
I HAVE SEEN IT MELTING ABOVE ME.	95	OF THE DEGREES	7
AND ABOVE MY FINGERS	109	HEATHER	2
WITH MINDS STILL HOVERING ABOVE THEIR TESTICLES	148	FRATRES MINORE	1
AIMLESSLY WATCHING A HAWK ABOVE THE VALLEYS,	154	NEAR PERIGORD	108
AND GREAT WINGS BEAT ABOVE US IN THE TWILIGHT,	157	NEAR PERIGORD	176
SILK, STIFF AND LARGE ABOVE THE LACERTUS,	180	MOEURS CON: 5	4
OF LESBIA, KNOWN ABOVE HELEN;	230	SEXTUS PROP:12	69
AND SPATS ABOVE MY SHOES,	266	ALF'S ELEVENTH	10

PAGE 2

	PAGE	TITLE	LINE

A-BRISTLE
A-BRISTLE WITH ANTENNAE TO FEEL ROADS, ... 153 NEAR PERIGORD 62
ABROAD
WAS GOT ABROAD, WHAT BETTER LUCK DO YOU WISH 'EM, 240 MOYEN SENSUEL 60
AND MAKE THE TOUR ABROAD FOR THEIR WILD TILLAGE-- 245 MOYEN SENSUEL 208
ABSENT
THE COMIC DETAIL WILL BE ABSENT. .... 146 MONUMENTUM AER 5
THE PERFUMED CLOTHS SHALL BE ABSENT. .... 219 SEXTUS PROP: 6 17
ABSOLUTE
THE ABSOLUTE UNIMPORTANT. .... 52 AU SALON 27
ABSTRUSE
WERE MUCH TOO ABSTRUSE FOR HIS COMPREHENSION, ... 181 MOEURS CON: 7 9
ABU
ABU SALAMMAMM--A SONG OF EMPIRE .... 237 ABU SALAMMAMM T
ABUNDANT
HOW MANY WORDS TALKED OUT WITH ABUNDANT CANDLES; 220 SEXTUS PROP: 7 3
ABUSED
AND ROSSETTI STILL ABUSED. .... 192 YEUX GLAUQUES 4
ACCELERATED
OF ITS ACCELERATED GRIMACE, ... 188 HUGH SELWYN: 2 2
WHAT IF YOUR FATES ARE ACCELERATED, ... 222 SEXTUS PROP: 8 27
ACCENTS
HERE'S TO YOU, OLD HIPPETY-HOP O' THE ACCENTS, ... 13 MESMERISM 17
ACCEPT
WILL PEOPLE ACCEPT THEM? .... 81 TENZONE 1
ACCEPT OPINION. THE "NINETIES" TRIED YOUR GAME .... 194 MR. NIXON 23
ACCEPTABLE
TO WRITE THE ACCEPTABLE WORD. ... . 18 DE AEGYPTO 11
ACCESS
THOU A SLIGHT THING, THOU IN ACCESS OF CUNNING .... 68 APPARUIT 23
ACCLAIMED
MY TALENT ACCLAIMED IN THEIR BANQUETS, ... 229 SEXTUS PROP:12 56
ACCOMPANIMENT
THE TWISTED RHOMBS CEASED THEIR CLAMOUR OF
   ACCOMPANIMENT; .... 223 SEXTUS PROP: 9 1
ACCOMPLISHED
BUT HE ACCOMPLISHED THIS FEAT AT SOME COST; .... 100 TEMPERAMENTS 7
ACCORD
HATH AS FAINT LUTE-STRINGS IN ITS DIM ACCORD ...... 43 SATIEMUS 15
ACCOST
AND ACCOST THE PROCESSION OF MAIDENS. .... 108 CH'U YUAN 10
ACCOSTED
ACCOSTED, THAT'S THE WORD, ACCOSTED HIM, ... 242 MOYEN SENSUEL 121
ACCOSTED, THAT'S THE WORD, ACCOSTED HIM, ... 242 MOYEN SENSUEL 121
ACCOUNT
AND ON THIS ACCOUNT THE LITTLE AURELIA, ... 111 SOCIETY 2
YET YOU ASK ON WHAT ACCOUNT I WRITE SO MANY
   LOVE-LYRICS .... 217 SEXTUS PROP: 5 23
ACCOUTREMENTS
LICE SWARM LIKE ANTS OVER OUR ACCOUTREMENTS. ...... 139 SOUTH-FOLK 8
ACCUSTOMED
SOME CERTAIN ACCUSTOMED FORMS, ... 52 AU SALON 26
ACHAIA
AND ALL THE FAIR FROM TROY AND ALL FROM ACHAIA, ... 38 LADY'S LIFE 7
TO FORGE ACHAIA. .... 198 MAUBERLEY: 1 16
IOPE, AND TYRO, AND PASIPHAE, AND THE FORMAL GIRLS
   OF ACHAIA, ... 223 SEXTUS PROP: 9 16
ACHE
NOR FEEL MY ACHE--GREAT AS IT IS, ... 174 LANGUE D'OC: 3 21
ACHELOUS
AND YOU WRITE OF ACHELOUS, WHO CONTENDED WITH
   HERCULES, ... 228 SEXTUS PROP:12 18
ACHENOR
YOU WRITE OF ADRASTUS' HORSES AND THE FUNERAL RITES
   OF ACHENOR, ... 228 SEXTUS PROP:12 19
ACHERON
MOVING NAKED OVER ACHERON .... 218 SEXTUS PROP: 6 2
ONE RAFT ON THE VEILED FLOOD OF ACHERON. .... 219 SEXTUS PROP: 6 11
ACHILLES
OR OF ACHILLES WITHSTAYING WATERS BY SIMOIS .... 208 SEXTUS PROP: 1 28

PAGE 3

ACHILLES -- ADOLESCENT

	PAGE	TITLE	LINE
ACHILLES (CONTINUED)			
WITHOUT AN INFERNO, WITHOUT ACHILLES ATTENDED OF GODS,	218	SEXTUS PROP: 5	51
ACHIN'			
UPON THE NATIONAL BRAINS AND SET 'EM ACHIN'.	245	MOYEN SENSUEL	216
ACORN			
BENT RESOLUTELY ON WRINGING LILIES FROM THE ACORN;	187	E. P. ODE	7
ACQUAINTANCE			
HATH SET ACQUAINTANCE WHERE MIGHT BE AFFECTIONS,	63	AN OBJECT	2
ACQUAINTANCES			
SUNSET LIKE THE PARTING OF OLD ACQUAINTANCES	137	TAKING LEAVE	6
ACQUIRE			
AND ACQUIRE A ROMAN RELIGION;	219	SEXTUS PROP: 6	10
ACQUIRING			
"ABOUT ACQUIRING THAT SORT OF A REPUTATION.	210	SEXTUS PROP: 2	20
ACRE			
OVER THE WHALE'S ACRE, WOULD WANDER WIDE.	65	THE SEAFARER	61
ACROSS			
THAT STRIVETH TO OURS ACROSS THE PAIN.	11	OF THE GIBBET	24
WHILE MY HAIR WAS STILL CUT STRAIGHT ACROSS MY FOREHEAD	130	RIVER-MER WIFE	1
TO BE LOOKING OUT ACROSS THE BRIGHT SEA,	164	QUINTUS SEPTIM	5
LEVEL ACROSS THE FACE	193	BRENNBAUM	7
ACT			
THEREFORE LET US ACT AS IF WE WERE	43	MR. HOUSMAN	4
THE MERE WILL TO ACT IS SUFFICIENT."	216	SEXTUS PROP: 5	6
ACTAEON			
THE COMING OF WAR: ACTAEON	107	COMING OF WAR	T
"THIS IS ACTAEON."	107	COMING OF WAR	14
ACTAEON OF GOLDEN GREAVES!	107	COMING OF WAR	15
ACTIAN			
UPON THE ACTIAN MARSHES VIRGIL IS PHOEBUS' CHIEF OF POLICE,	228	SEXTUS PROP:12	31
ACTIVE			
OR WHAT HIS ACTIVE VIRTU IS, OR WHAT HIS FORCE;	248	DONNA MI PREGA	14
ACTIVITIES			
THE MIDNIGHT ACTIVITIES OF WHATS-HIS-NAME,	264	ALF'S NINTH	2
ACTOR			
WHO HAS THE PHRASE "AS IGNORANT AS AN ACTOR."	246	MOYEN SENSUEL	222
ACTS			
HERE IN THE EVERY-DAY WHERE OUR ACTS	52	AU SALON	4
THE HARSH ACTS OF YOUR LEVITY!	226	SEXTUS PROP:11	1
HID HEALTH STATISTICS, DODGED THE LABOUR ACTS.	260	ALF'S FIFTH	8
AD.			
YET SAW AN "AD." "TO-NIGHT, THE HUDSON SAIL,	242	MOYEN SENSUEL	111
I HAVE MISLAID THE "AD.," BUT NOTE THE TOUCH,	242	MOYEN SENSUEL	115
WITH A LIVELY WOOD-PULP "AD."	268	ALF'S TWELFTH	19
ADAPTATIONS			
TRANSLATIONS AND ADAPTATIONS FROM HEINE	44	FROM HEINE	T
ADDRESS			
AND BADE HER BE OUT WITH ILL ADDRESS	11	OF THE GIBBET	11
ADDRESSED			
OF HOW YOU HAVE ADDRESSED ME.	44	FROM HEINE: 1	4
ADEST			
HESPER ADEST. HESPER ADEST.	231	CANTUS PLANUS	6
HESPER ADEST. HESPER ADEST.	231	CANTUS PLANUS	6
HESPER ADEST.	231	CANTUS PLANUS	7
ADJUNCT			
NO ADJUNCT TO THE MUSES' DIADEM.	187	E. P. ODE	20
ADMIRABLE			
WITH ALL THE ADMIRABLE CONCEPTS THAT MOVED FROM IT	42	HER MONUMENT	39
ADMIRED			
SOMEONE ADMIRED YOUR WORKS,	159	PSYCHOLOG HOUR	32
ADMIT			
SEEN, WE ADMIT, AMID AMBROSIAL CIRCUMSTANCES	202	AGE DEMANDED	34
ADMONISHETH			
ALL THIS ADMONISHETH MAN EAGER OF MOOD,	65	THE SEAFARER	51
ADO			
DARING ADO, . . .	66	THE SEAFARER	77
ADOLESCENT			
GO TO THE ADOLESCENT WHO ARE SMOTHERED IN FAMILY--	89	COMMISSION	28

ADONIS -- AERE

	PAGE	TITLE	LINE
ADONIS			
SINCE ADONIS WAS GORED IN IDALIA, AND THE CYTHAREAN	219	SEXTUS PROP: 6	33
ADOPTED			
"DO YOU THINK I HAVE ADOPTED YOUR HABITS?"	225	SEXTUS PROP:10	35
ADORATION			
BEHOLD MINE ADORATION	49	OF SPLENDOUR	18
ADORED			
I HAVE ADORED YOU FOR THREE FULL YEARS;	102	LADIES	6
ADORN			
HOW HIS COAT AND PANTS ADORN HIM!	46	FROM HEINE: 6	5
ADORNED			
IT IS ADORNED WITH YOUNG GODS RIDING UPON DOLPHINS	237	ABU SALAMMAMM	20
ADORNING			
YET HIS TIES ARE MORE ADORNING,	46	FROM HEINE: 6	6
ADORNMENT			
STANDS GENIUS A DEATHLESS ADORNMENT,	209	SEXTUS PROP: 1	72
LEISURE'S ADORNMENT PUTS HE THEN NEVER ON,	249	DONNA MI PREGA	51
ADRASTUS'			
YOU WRITE OF ADRASTUS' HORSES AND THE FUNERAL RITES OF ACHENOR,	228	SEXTUS PROP:12	19
ADS			
FROM DRESS GOODS ADS, AND SPORTS.	266	ALF'S ELEVENTH	20
ADS.			
OF 25 PER CENT. ON THEIR ADS., AND THE WOODS	262	ALF'S SEVENTH	12
ADULTERERS			
PAINTERS AND ADULTERERS.	192	YEUX GLAUQUES	8
ADULTERIES			
NINE ADULTERIES, 12 LIAISONS, 64 FORNICATIONS AND SOMETHING APPROACHING A RAPE	100	TEMPERAMENTS	1
HER CHILDREN HAVE NEVER DISCOVERED HER ADULTERIES.	103	THE PATTERNS	2
ADULTERIES.	192	YEUX GLAUQUES	24
ADULTEROUS			
A TROJAN AND ADULTEROUS PERSON CAME TO MENELAUS UNDER THE RITES OF HOSPITIUM,	227	SEXTUS PROP:12	6
ADULTERY			
"THOUGH SPIRITS ARE CELEBRATED FOR ADULTERY.	225	SEXTUS PROP:10	40
ADVANCE			
MR. NIXON ADVISED ME KINDLY, TO ADVANCE WITH FEWER	194	MR. NIXON	2
"ADVANCE ON ROYALTIES, FIFTY AT FIRST," SAID MR. NIXON,	194	MR. NIXON	7
ADVENTURE			
SOME FOR ADVENTURE,	190	HUGH SELWYN: 4	5
ADVERTISING			
THAT'S WHAT YOU MEAN YOU ADVERTISING SPADE,	162	CABARET DANCER	34
ADVISED			
MR. NIXON ADVISED ME KINDLY, TO ADVANCE WITH FEWER	194	MR. NIXON	2
LIKEWISE A FRIEND OF BLOUGHRAM'S ONCE ADVISED ME:	194	MR. NIXON	21
AEGIS-DAY			
GLORY TO ZEUS' AEGIS-DAY,	7	CINO	43
AEGRUM			
THAN HEAR THE WHOLE AEGRUM VULGUS	52	AU SALON	21
AEGYPTO			
DE AEGYPTO	18	DE AEGYPTO	T
AELIS			
SAIL OF CLAUSTRA, AELIS, AZALAIS,	75	THE ALCHEMIST	1
SAIL OF CLAUSTRA, AELIS, AZALAIS,	75	THE ALCHEMIST	5
I ASK OF MIDONS AELIS (OF MONTFORT)	105	DOMPNA POIS	28
THINKING OF AELIS, WHOM HE LOVED HEART AND SOUL	154	NEAR PERIGORD	110
AEMELIS			
ANHES OF ROCACOART, ARDENCA, AEMELIS,	75	THE ALCHEMIST	29
AEMILIA			
"OF" ROYAL AEMILIA, DRAWN ON THE MEMORIAL RAFT,	210	SEXTUS PROP: 2	10
AENEAS			
HE SHAKES THE TROJAN WEAPONS OF AENEAS,	228	SEXTUS PROP:12	34
AEONIUM			
"NOR MARS SHOUT YOU IN THE WOOD AT AEONIUM,	211	SEXTUS PROP: 2	44
AERA			
"VACUOS EXERCET AERA MORSUS."	198	MAUBERLEY 1920	EPI
AERE			
MONUMENTUM AERE, ETC.	146	MONUMENTUM AER	T

PAGE 5

		PAGE	TITLE	LINE
AERIAL				
	(AMID AERIAL FLOWERS) ... TIME FOR ARRANGEMENTS--	199	MAUBERLEY: 2	13
AERY				
	BY AERY APOSTLES OF TERRENE DELIGHT, ...	39	BLANDULA	8
AESCHYLUS				
	AND YOU WILL NOT LEAVE OFF IMITATING AESCHYLUS. ...	228	SEXTUS PROP:12	20
AESTHETIC				
	THE INVITATION HAD NO NEED OF FINE AESTHETIC, ...	242	MOYEN SENSUEL	127
AESTHETICS				
	THE STUDY IN AESTHETICS	96	AESTHETICS	T
	AND I AM SLICED WITH LOYAL AESTHETICS.	247	PIERROTS	13
AESTUS				
	"VOCAT AESTUS IN UMBRAM"	186	HUGH SELWYN	EPI
AETHER				
	DARKLY HAST THOU DARED AND THE DREADED AETHER	68	APPARUIT	11
	AND LEFT ME CLOAKED AS WITH A GAUZE OF AETHER;	71	A VIRGINAL	5
	LAPPED IN THE GOLD-COLOURED FLAME I DESCEND THROUGH THE AETHER.	169	PHANOPOEIA	5
	ASCENDS WITH ME INTO THE AETHER, ...	207	SEXTUS PROP: 1	14
AETNA				
	TURN TO YOUR DRIPPING HORSES, BECAUSE OF A TUNE, UNDER AETNA?	208	SEXTUS PROP: 1	47
AFAR				
	THAT I FARE FORTH, THAT I AFAR HENCE	65	THE SEAFARER	38
	THOU AFAR, MOVING IN THE GLAMOROUS SUN, ...	68	APPARUIT	6
	AND I CAN NOT SEE CHOAN AFAR	138	CITY OF CHOAN	12
AFFAIR				
	WHO CAN UNDERSTAND ANY AFFAIR OF THEIRS. YET	97	THE BELLAIRES	10
	BEHIND THEM? WHAT'S THERE? HER SOUL'S AN AFFAIR FOR OCULISTS.	247	PIERROTS	12
AFFAIRS				
	DO NOT UNDERSTAND THE CONDUCT OF THIS WORLD'S AFFAIRS.	97	THE BELLAIRES	2
	MET TO DISCUSS THEIR AFFAIRS;	97	THE BELLAIRES	7
	BUT THE GOOD BELLAIRES HAVE SO LITTLE UNDERSTOOD THEIR AFFAIRS	97	THE BELLAIRES	8
	MET TO DISCUSS THEIR AFFAIRS, ...	98	THE BELLAIRES	29
	THERE IS NO EASE IN ROYAL AFFAIRS, WE HAVE NO COMFORT.	127	BOWMEN OF SHU	11
	AND I SHALL FOLLOW THE CAMP, I SHALL BE DULY CELEBRATED FOR SINGING THE AFFAIRS OF YOUR CAVALRY.	216	SEXTUS PROP: 5	21
	I SHOULD REMEMBER CAESAR'S AFFAIRS	218	SEXTUS PROP: 5	47
AFFECT				
	AND WEIGHED, REVEALED HIS GREAT AFFECT, ...	200	MAUBERLEY: 2	31
	OF AN AFFECT THAT COMES OFTEN AND IS FELL	248	DONNA MI PREGA	2
AFFECTION				
	THEY TRY TO STIR NEW AFFECTION, ...	142	UNMOVING CLOUD	19
AFFECTIONS				
	HATH SET ACQUAINTANCE WHERE MIGHT BE AFFECTIONS,	63	AN OBJECT	2
AFFLICTED				
	WHILE SHE TOSSED CLOSE TO CLIFFS. COLDLY AFFLICTED,	64	THE SEAFARER	8
AFFORD				
	THE HIGH TRACKS OF HERMES WOULD NOT AFFORD YOU SHELTER.	226	SEXTUS PROP:11	10
AFFRAY				
	YOU SHOULD HAVE SEEN ME AFTER THE AFFRAY, ...	247	PIERROTS	4
AFFRONTS				
	ULTIMATE AFFRONTS TO	202	AGE DEMANDED	56
AFIELD				
	TO LEAD EMATHIAN HORSES AFIELD, ...	216	SEXTUS PROP: 5	2
AFLAME				
	AND THY LIGHT LIMBS, WHEREWTHROUGH I LEAPT AFLAME,	60	TOMB AKR CAAR	4
AFLASH				
	HALF THE GRAVEN SHOULDER, THE THROAT AFLASH WITH	68	APPARUIT	17
AFOOT				
	FOR THEM THERE IS SOMETHING AFOOT.	158	PSYCHOLOG HOUR	18
AFORESAID				
	A PALE GOLD, IN THE AFORESAID PATTERN, ...	202	AGE DEMANDED	41

AFORETIME -- AGAINST

	PAGE	TITLE	LINE
AFORETIME			
SUCH DERELICTIONS HAVE DESTROYED OTHER YOUNG LADIES AFORETIME,	221	SEXTUS PROP: 8	7
AFORE-TIME			
KNOW THEN THAT I LOVED YOU FROM AFORE-TIME,	96	DUM CAPITOLIUM	7
AFRAID			
AND IS ALMOST AFRAID THAT I	83	THE GARDEN	11
THE GOD PAN IS AFRAID TO ASK YOU,	110	TEMPORA	7
AFRAID TO SAY THAT THEY HATE YOU;	146	SALUTATION 3RD	32
AND I AM AFRAID OF NUMERICAL ESTIMATE,	224	SEXTUS PROP:10	6
AFTER			
I AM HOMESICK AFTER MINE OWN KIND,	20	IN DURANCE	1
BUT I AM HOMESICK AFTER MINE OWN KIND.	20	IN DURANCE	3
FOR I AM HOMESICK AFTER MINE OWN KIND	20	IN DURANCE	12
AFTER MINE OWN KIND THAT KNOW, AND FEEL	20	IN DURANCE	15
BUT FOR ALL THAT, I AM HOMESICK AFTER MINE OWN KIND	20	IN DURANCE	23
NO WORD, DAY AFTER DAY.	60	TOMB AKR CAAR	28
AND FOR THIS, EVERY EARL WHATEVER, FOR THOSE SPEAKING AFTER--	66	THE SEAFARER	73
SO THAT ALL MEN SHALL HONOUR HIM AFTER	66	THE SEAFARER	78
HOW MANY WILL COME AFTER ME	96	DUM CAPITOLIUM	1
BUT THREE YEARS AFTER THIS	96	AESTHETICS	6
TO ONE, ON RETURNING CERTAIN YEARS AFTER.	101	AMITIES	ST
AFTER CH'U YUAN	108	CH'U YUAN	T
AND TEN YEARS AFTER, OR TWENTY, AS YOU WILL,	155	NEAR PERIGORD	127
NIGHT AFTER NIGHT,	163	CABARET DANCER	84
FOR AFTER DEATH THERE COMES NO OTHER CALAMITY.	164	QUINTUS SEPTIM	11
CRYING AFTER THE FOLLIES GONE BY ME,	168	OF AROUET	30
AND TO FOLLOW AFTER FRIENDSHIP, AS THEY CALL IT,	168	OF AROUET	33
YOU ENTER AND PASS HALL AFTER HALL,	180	MOEURS CON: 5	18
AFTER YEARS OF CONTINENCE	181	MOEURS CON: 6	1
IN ROME, AFTER THE OPERA,	182	MOEURS CON: 7	18
DEFECTS--AFTER SAMOTHRACE;	189	HUGH SELWYN: 3	14
I SHALL HAVE, DOUBTLESS, A BOOM AFTER MY FUNERAL,	207	SEXTUS PROP: 1	23
AFTER TWELVE MONTHS OF DISCOMFORT?	215	SEXTUS PROP: 4	42
AFTER WE CROSS THE INFERNAL RIPPLES,	228	SEXTUS PROP:12	28
YOU SHOULD HAVE SEEN ME AFTER THE AFFRAY,	247	PIERROTS	4
AFTER MY WORK IS DONE	268	ANOTHER BIT	10
AFTERMATH			
NO COIN, NO WILL TO SNATCH THE AFTERMATH	14	FAMAM CANO	31
AGAIN			
. . . I HOPE SHE WILL NOT COME AGAIN.	5	LA FRAISNE	44
OH, TILL THOU COME AGAIN.	9	NA AUDIART	37
AIE! THE LEAN BARE TREE IS WIDOWED AGAIN	12	OF THE GIBBET	33
HELL GRANT SOON WE HEAR AGAIN THE SWORDS CLASH!	28	ALTAFORTE	13
HELL GRANT SOON WE HEAR AGAIN THE SWORDS CLASH!	29	ALTAFORTE	38
AH! CABARET! AH CABARET, THY HILLS AGAIN!	32	PIERE VIDAL	65
SO THAT I MIGHT FIND YOU AGAIN,	36	FRANCESCA	11
TIME HAS SEEN THIS, AND WILL NOT TURN AGAIN;	59	SILET	12
SPEAK ONCE AGAIN FOR ITS SOLE STIMULATION,	63	PHASELLUS ILLE	10
THE CORN HAS AGAIN ITS MOTHER AND SHE, LEUCONOE,	90	SURGIT FAMA	5
I WILL NEVER AGAIN GATHER	105	DOMPNA POIS	6
TILL I AGAIN FIND YOU READY.	105	DOMPNA POIS	20
AND IS NOT AGAIN TO BE MET WITH.	136	EXILE'S LETTER	64
AND ONCE AGAIN, LATER, WE MET AT THE SOUTH BRIDGEHEAD.	136	EXILE'S LETTER	70
MAENT, MAENT, AND YET AGAIN MAENT,	154	NEAR PERIGORD	92
"BUT THEY PROMISED AGAIN:	159	PSYCHOLOG HOUR	37
"MY PRETTY BOY, MAKE WE OUR PLAY AGAIN	177	LANGUE D'OC: 4	16
I NEVER SAW HER AGAIN.	182	MOEURS CON: 8	15
AND YET AGAIN, AND NEWLY RUMOUR STRIKES ON MY EARS.	226	SEXTUS PROP:11	17
TILL UP AGAIN, RIGHT UP, WE REACH THE PRESIDENT,	239	MOYEN SENSUEL	16
AND LET THE BLIGHTERS START IT ALL OVER AGAIN.	265	ALF'S NINTH	30
THEY'LL TRICK YOU AGAIN AND AGAIN, AS YOU SLEEP;	265	ALF'S NINTH	31
THEY'LL TRICK YOU AGAIN AND AGAIN, AS YOU SLEEP;	265	ALF'S NINTH	31
TO OWN HIS COIN AGAIN.	269	SAFE AND SOUND	28
AGAINST			
A SORT OF CURSE AGAINST ITS GUZZLING	14	FAMAM CANO	25
AGAINST THE DEATH OF THE YOUNG ENGLISH KING.	36	THE YOUNG KING	5
BRIGHT NOTES AGAINST THE EAR,	45	FROM HEINE: 5	6
WHAT IF THE WIND HAVE TURNED AGAINST THE RAIN?	59	SILET	10

PAGE 7

AGAINST -- AGE-LASTING

	PAGE	TITLE	LINE
AGAINST (CONTINUED)			
AND I AM TORN AGAINST THE JAGGED DARK,	60	TOMB AKR CAAR	26
BUT AGE FARES AGAINST HIM, HIS FACE PALETH,	66	THE SEAFARER	93
THAT BEARS US UP, SHALL TURN AGAINST THE POLE.	69	THE NEEDLE	7
LIKE A SKEIN OF LOOSE SILK BLOWN AGAINST A WALL	83	THE GARDEN	1
SPEAK AGAINST UNCONSCIOUS OPPRESSION,	88	COMMISSION	6
SPEAK AGAINST THE TYRANNY OF THE UNIMAGINATIVE,	88	COMMISSION	7
SPEAK AGAINST BONDS.	88	COMMISSION	8
GO WITH YOUR EDGE AGAINST THIS,	88	COMMISSION	19
BE AGAINST ALL FORMS OF OPPRESSION.	89	COMMISSION	25
GO AGAINST THIS VEGETABLE BONDAGE OF THE BLOOD.	89	COMMISSION	34
BE AGAINST ALL SORTS OF MORTMAIN.	89	COMMISSION	35
ARTISTS BROKEN AGAINST HER,	92	THE REST	3
HELPLESS AGAINST THE CONTROL;	92	THE REST	8
BROKEN AGAINST FALSE KNOWLEDGE,	93	THE REST	14
LET US TAKE ARMS AGAINST THIS SEA OF STUPIDITIES--	99	SALVATIONISTS	12
AND AGAINST THIS SEA OF VULGARITIES--	99	SALVATIONISTS	14
AND AGAINST THIS SEA OF IMBECILES--	99	SALVATIONISTS	16
FOR A MOMENT SHE RESTED AGAINST ME	112	SHOP GIRL	1
THE AUGUST HAS WORN AGAINST HER.	116	THE TEA SHOP	3
STOLE HER AWAY FOR HIMSELF, KEPT HER AGAINST ARMED	123	PROVINC DESERT	75
THEIR CORDS TANGLE IN MIST, AGAINST THE BROCADE-LIKE PALACE.	129	THE RIVER SONG	26
WITH HEAD GEAR GLITTERING AGAINST THE CLOUD AND SUN,	131	AT TEN-SHIN	13
THE DAI HORSE NEIGHS AGAINST THE BLEAK WIND OF ETSU,	139	SOUTH-FOLK	1
AGAINST HER; GIVE HER PRIDE IN THEM?	153	NEAR PERIGORD	78
DON'T KICK AGAINST THE PRICKS,	194	MR. NIXON	22
CAME AGAINST HIS GAZE,	201	AGE DEMANDED	10
AGAINST UTTER CONSTERNATION,	202	AGE DEMANDED	32
STRENGTHENED HIM AGAINST	202	AGE DEMANDED	35
BUT AGAINST THIS?	209	SEXTUS PROP: 1	65
CAESAR PLOTS AGAINST INDIA,	219	SEXTUS PROP: 6	6
NOW WITH BARED BREASTS SHE WRESTLED AGAINST ME,	220	SEXTUS PROP: 7	5
THE DRY EARTH PANTS AGAINST THE CANICULAR HEAT,	221	SEXTUS PROP: 8	4
"NO INCUBUS HAS CRUSHED HIS BODY AGAINST ME,	225	SEXTUS PROP:10	39
YOU DO NOTHING, YOU PLOT INANE SCHEMES AGAINST ME,	226	SEXTUS PROP:11	14
'AGALMA			
NUKTIS 'AGALMA	199	MAUBERLEY: 2	7
AGATE			
LET THEM ASSUME THE MILK-WHITE BODIES OF AGATE.	76	THE ALCHEMIST	52
AGATHAS			
AGATHAS	102	LADIES	ST
FOUR AND FORTY LOVERS HAD AGATHAS IN THE OLD DAYS,	102	LADIES	1
AGATHON			
TO SIFT TO AGATHON FROM THE CHAFF	199	MAUBERLEY: 2	17
AGDE			
RESIDES NOW AT AGDE AND BIAUCAIRE.	98	THE BELLAIRES	35
AGE			
THAT OLD AGE WEARETH FOR A CLOAK.	4	LA FRAISNE	4
SUCH AGE	15	FAMAM CANO	45
O AGE GONE LAX! O STUNTED FOLLOWERS,	32	PIERE VIDAL	60
BUT AGE FARES AGAINST HIM, HIS FACE PALETH,	66	THE SEAFARER	93
GO TO THOSE WHO ARE THICKENED WITH MIDDLE AGE,	89	COMMISSION	26
O MOST UNFORTUNATE AGE!	113	FORMIANUS LADY	10
WHY DOES THE HORSE-FACED LADY OF JUST THE UNMENTIONABLE AGE	114	SIMULACRA	1
UNDETERRED BY THE MANIFEST AGE OF MY TRAPPINGS?	114	SIMULACRA	6
THAT AGE IS GONE;	123	PROVINC DESERT	78
CAN YOU EVEN TELL THE AGE OF A TURTLE?	140	SENNIN POEM	16
AT THE AGE OF 28,	178	MOEURS CON: 1	4
HE BEING AT THAT AGE A VIRGIN,	178	MOEURS CON: 1	5
AT THE AGE OF 27	179	MOEURS CON: 4	1
THE AGE DEMANDED AN IMAGE	188	HUGH SELWYN: 2	1
THE "AGE DEMANDED" CHIEFLY A MOULD IN PLASTER,	188	HUGH SELWYN: 2	9
"THE AGE DEMANDED"	201	AGE DEMANDED	T
AGED			
FROM THE SUNDERED REALMS, OF THEBES AND OF AGED PRIAMUS;	38	LADY'S LIFE	8
IS AN INFANT, AGED ABOUT 14 MONTHS,	180	MOEURS CON: 5	11
AGE-LASTING			
AND ITS AGE-LASTING WALLOW FOR RED GREED	14	FAMAM CANO	26

PAGE 8

AGENT -- AID

	PAGE	TITLE	LINE
AGENT			
I KNEW A TOURIST AGENT, ONE WHOSE ART IS	245	MOYEN SENSUEL	209
AGE-OLD			
THAN ALL THE AGE-OLD KNOWLEDGE OF THY BOOKS:	35	THE EYES	17
USURY AGE-OLD AND AGE-THICK	190	HUGH SELWYN: 4	18
AGES			
MIGHT, IN NEW AGES, GAIN HER WORSHIPPERS,	197	ENVOI (1919)	22
THE PRIMITIVE AGES SANG VENUS,	216	SEXTUS PROP: 5	7
AGETH			
EARTHLY GLORY AGETH AND SEARETH.	66	THE SEAFARER	91
AGE-THICK			
USURY AGE-OLD AND AGE-THICK	190	HUGH SELWYN: 4	18
AGGLUTINOUS			
"LIKE TO LIKE NATURE": THESE AGGLUTINOUS YELLOWS!	114	BEFORE A SHOP	2
AGGRESSION			
IRRESPONSE TO HUMAN AGGRESSION,	202	AGE DEMANDED	51
AGILITY			
FOR THIS AGILITY CHANCE FOUND	201	AGE DEMANDED	1
AGITATED			
I RUSHED ABOUT IN THE MOST AGITATED WAY	247	PIERROTS	5
A-GLEAMING			
THE IMPERIAL GUARDS COME FORTH FROM THE GOLDEN HOUSE WITH THEIR ARMOUR A-GLEAMING	129	THE RIVER SONG	34
AGNES'			
THE VOICE AT MONTFORT, LADY AGNES' HAIR,	151	NEAR PERIGORD	7
AGO			
THAT WAS VERY LONG AGO.	5	LA FRAISNE	47
--EVEN THE RIVER MANY DAYS AGO,	60	TOMB AKR CAAR	16
OF THINGS THAT HAPPENED VERY LONG AGO,	265	ALF'S NINTH	27
AGRADIVA			
AGRADIVA, ANHES, ARDENCA,	75	THE ALCHEMIST	16
AGUE			
AN AGUE HATH MY HAM.	116	ANCIENT MUSIC	7
AH			
"AH YES, PASSED ONCE OUR WAY,	6	CINO	27
BUT AH! WHEN I SEE THE STANDARDS GOLD, VAIR, PURPLE, OPPOSING	28	ALTAFORTE	4
AND CONQUERED! AH GOD! CONQUERED!	31	PIERE VIDAL	31
AH GOD, THE LOBA! AND MY ONLY MATE!	31	PIERE VIDAL	44
AH! CABARET! AH CABARET, THY HILLS AGAIN!	32	PIERE VIDAL	65
AH! CABARET! AH CABARET, THY HILLS AGAIN!	32	PIERE VIDAL	65
AH, I COVERED HIS EARS WITH THEM	48	FROM HEINE: 7	31
DRIPS FROM MY DEATHLESS PEN--AH, WELL-AWAY!	59	SILET	2
MY CITY, MY BELOVED, MY WHITE! AH, SLENDER,	62	N. Y.	1
OF ALL THINGS, FRAIL ALABASTER, AH ME!	68	APPARUIT	19
AH! BOW YOUR HEADS, YE MAIDENS ALL,	72	PAN IS DEAD	2
SEE, THEY RETURN; AH, SEE THE TENTATIVE	74	THE RETURN	1
AH YES, MY SONGS, LET US RESURRECT	99	SALVATIONISTS	3
AH, BELS SENHER, MAENT, AT LAST	106	DOMPNA POIS	61
AH, LADY, WHY HAVE YOU CAST	107	DOMPNA POIS	69
AH, HOW SHALL YOU KNOW THE DREARY SORROW AT THE NORTH GATE,	133	FRONTIER GUARD	22
"YOUR SON, AH, SINCE HE DIED	152	NEAR PERIGORD	44
THERE IS A THROAT; AH, THERE ARE TWO WHITE HANDS;	153	NEAR PERIGORD	71
AND LIKE A SWINGING LAMP THAT SAYS, "AH ME!	156	NEAR PERIGORD	166
GONE--AH, GONE UNTOUCHED, UNREACHABLE!	157	NEAR PERIGORD	188
AH GOD! HOW SWIFT THE NIGHT	177	LANGUE D'OC: 4	19
AH GOD! HOW SWIFT THE NIGHT.	177	LANGUE D'OC: 4	24
"AH, POOR JENNY'S CASE" . . .	192	YEUX GLAUQUES	20
AHEAD			
JUST GOES AHEAD AND SUCKS A TEAT	272	THE BABY	11
AH-EH			
"AH-EH! THE STRANGE RARE NAME . . .	15	FAMAM CANO	42
AH-EH! HE MUST BE RARE IF EVEN I HAVE NOT . . ."	15	FAMAM CANO	43
AHI			
GUARDA! AHI, GUARDA! OH' E BE'A!	96	AESTHETICS	5
A-HUNTING			
"'TIS THE WHITE STAG, FAME, WE'RE A-HUNTING,	25	THE WHITE STAG	6
AID			
GIVE MY GOOD-FELLOW AID IN FOOLS' DESPITE	172	LANGUE D'OC: 1	3
GODS' AID, LET NOT MY BONES LIE IN A PUBLIC LOCATION	213	SEXTUS PROP: 3	32

AID -- ALAS

	PAGE	TITLE	LINE
AID (CONTINUED)			
AND HIS POCKETS BY MA'S AID, THAT NIGHT WITH CASH FULL,	242	MOYEN SENSUEL	126
AIE			
AIE! THE LEAN BARE TREE IS WIDOWED AGAIN	12	OF THE GIBBET	33
AIE-E			
AIE-E! 'TIS TRUE THAT I AM GAY	5	LA FRAISNE	37
AILES			
LEURS AILES	160	DANS OMNIBUS	26
AIMLESSLY			
AND HEARD THE FIVE-SCORE NIGHTINGALES AIMLESSLY SINGING.	129	THE RIVER SONG	22
AIMLESSLY WATCHING A HAWK ABOVE THE VALLEYS,	154	NEAR PERIGORD	108
AINT			
"I COULDN'T," SHE SEZ, "AN' I AINT TRIED,	270	OF 600 M.P.'S	21
AIN'T			
AIN'T ALWAYS A PLEASURE,	259	ALF'S FOURTH	4
AIN'T IT ALWAYS BEEN SO?	259	ALF'S FOURTH	11
AIN'T YEH GOT PRECEDENT?	259	ALF'S THIRD	17
WHAT AIN'T GOT WORK NO MORE	269	SAFE AND SOUND	10
AIR			
THAT WHIRRED IN THE AIR ABOVE US.	3	THRENOS	6
YEA, I FILL ALL THE AIR WITH MY MUSIC.	29	ALTAFORTE	30
NOR HELD ME SAVE AS AIR THAT BRUSHETH BY ONE	39	FOR PSYCHE	3
AND CLOSER ME THAN AIR,	39	FOR PSYCHE	7
DRINKST IN LIFE OF EARTH, OF THE AIR, THE TISSUE	68	APPARUIT	7
FOR MY SURROUNDING AIR HATH A NEW LIGHTNESS;	71	A VIRGINAL	3
SNIFFING THE TRACE OF AIR!	74	THE RETURN	14
OUT OF EREBUS, OUT OF THE FLAT WASTE OF AIR, LYING BENEATH THE WORLD;	76	THE ALCHEMIST	46
IN THE AIR SHE SEVERED,	92	GENTILDONNA	3
OR TAKES THE SEA AIR	98	THE BELLAIRES	38
YOU HAD THE SAME OLD AIR OF CONDESCENSION	101	AMITIES	3
ARE THRUSTING AT THE SPRING AIR.	110	COITUS	2
HAS SUCH A CARESSING AIR	115	SOCIAL ORDER	3
TO THE PERFUMED AIR AND GIRLS DANCING,	132	AT TEN-SHIN	21
LET US GO OUT IN THE AIR A BIT.	145	SALUTATION 3RD	16
OF DRY AIR, AS CLEAR AS METAL.	146	CANTILATIONS	12
THE AIR IS ALIVE WITH THAT FACT.	158	PSYCHOLOG HOUR	13
HAS HELD IN THE AIR BEFORE YOU.	169	PHANOPOEIA	15
THE SEA-CLEAR SAPPHIRE OF AIR, THE SEA-DARK CLARITY, STRETCHES BOTH SEA-CLIFF AND OCEAN.	170	PHANOPOEIA	24
WHEN THE SWEET AIR GOES BITTER,	174	LANGUE D'OC: 3	1
SUCH TREASURE IN THE AIR,	197	ENVOI (1919)	9
MOUTHS BITING EMPTY AIR,	200	MAUBERLEY: 2	34
THE TIME IS COME, THE AIR HEAVES IN TORRIDITY,	221	SEXTUS PROP: 8	3
THOUGH YOU HEAVE INTO THE AIR UPON THE GILDED PEGASEAN BACK,	226	SEXTUS PROP:11	7
TO LIFT YOU UP THROUGH SPLIT AIR,	226	SEXTUS PROP:11	9
DRIFTS THROUGH THE AIR, AND THE SARCOPHAGUS	236	MIDDLE-AGED	10
WITH COWED AND CROUCHING AIR	257	BREAD BRIGADE	25
FROM PROFITS ON HOT AIR.	266	ALF'S ELEVENTH	16
I LEND YOU ENGLISHMEN HOT AIR	269	SAFE AND SOUND	3
I LEND YOU ENGLISHMEN HOT AIR	269	SAFE AND SOUND	5
A-JUMBLING			
A-JUMBLING O' FIGURES FOR MAITRE JACQUES POLIN,	22	MARVOIL	4
AKR			
THE TOMB AT AKR CAAR	60	TOMB AKR CAAR	T
AL			
SCRATCHED AND ERASED WITH AL AND OCHAISOS.	154	NEAR PERIGORD	100
NOW IN VENICE, 'STORANTE AL GIARDINO, I WENT EARLY,	163	CABARET DANCER	79
ALABASTER			
OF ALL THINGS, FRAIL ALABASTER, AH ME!	68	APPARUIT	19
WITH THEIR PERFUMES IN LITTLE ALABASTER BOXES?	165	QUINTUS SEPTIM	15
A PROSE KINEMA, NOT, NOT ASSUREDLY, ALABASTER	188	HUGH SELWYN: 2	11
ALAIS			
TO CARCASSONNE, PUI, AND ALAIS	98	THE BELLAIRES	36
ALAS			
ALAS, HE DIED OF ALCOHOL.	117	EPITAPHS	2
ALAS! WHO'ER IT PLEASE OR PAIN,	175	LANGUE D'OC: 3	58
ALAS, EHEU, ONE QUESTION THAT SORELY VEXES	244	MOYEN SENSUEL	161

ALBA -- ALL

	PAGE	TITLE	LINE
ALBA			
ALBA	109	ALBA	T
ALBA	171	LANGUE D'OC	SUB
ALBA, YOUR KINGS, AND THE REALM YOUR FOLK	210	SEXTUS PROP: 2	3
ALBAS			
COMPOSING OUR ALBAS,	104	ANCORA	4
ALBATRE			
ALBATRE	87	ALBATRE	T
ALBION			
THUS ROSE IN ALBION, AND TICKLED THE STATE	264	ALF'S NINTH	11
ALBIRAR			
"ET ALBIRAR AB LOR BORDON--"	153	NEAR PERIGORD	90
ALCHEMIST			
THE ALCHEMIST	75	THE ALCHEMIST	T
ALCMENA			
ELAIN, TIREIS, ALCMENA	75	THE ALCHEMIST	14
ELAIN, TIREIS, ALCMENA,	76	THE ALCHEMIST	49
ALCYON, PHAETONA, ALCMENA,	76	THE ALCHEMIST	57
ALCOHOL			
ALAS, HE DIED OF ALCOHOL.	117	EPITAPHS	2
BUT SHOWED NO TRACE OF ALCOHOL	193	SIENA MI FE	9
ALCYON			
ALCYON, PHAETONA, ALCMENA,	76	THE ALCHEMIST	57
ALDER			
WHEN TALL STAGS FLED ME THROUGH THE ALDER BRAKES,	30	PIERE VIDAL	9
ALE			
TRY PHOTOGRAPHS, WOLF DOWN THEIR ALE AND CAKES	236	MIDDLE-AGED	6
ALEMBIC			
GUARD THIS ALEMBIC.	76	THE ALCHEMIST	60
ALERT			
SO EAGER AND ALERT,	105	DOMPNA POIS	13
A-LEVEL			
LOW, PANEL-SHAPED, A-LEVEL WITH HER KNEES,	49	OF SPLENDOUR	11
CHALAIS IS HIGH, A-LEVEL WITH THE POPLARS.	152	NEAR PERIGORD	54
ALEXIS			
CORYDON TEMPTED ALEXIS,	229	SEXTUS PROP:12	47
ALFONSO			
ALFONSO THE HALF-BALD, TOOK TO HANGING	22	MARVOIL	9
ALFONSO, QUATTRO, POKE-NOSE.	22	MARVOIL	22
ALF'S			
ALF'S SECOND BIT	258	ALF'S SECOND	T
ALF'S THIRD BIT	258	ALF'S THIRD	T
ALF'S FOURTH BIT	259	ALF'S FOURTH	T
ALF'S FIFTH BIT	260	ALF'S FIFTH	T
ALF'S SIXTH BIT	261	ALF'S SIXTH	T
ALF'S SEVENTH BIT	262	ALF'S SEVENTH	T
ALF'S EIGHTH BIT	263	ALF'S EIGHTH	T
ALF'S NINTH BIT	264	ALF'S NINTH	T
ALF'S TENTH BIT	265	ALF'S TENTH	T
ALF'S ELEVENTH BIT	266	ALF'S ELEVENTH	T
ALF'S TWELFTH BIT	267	ALF'S TWELFTH	T
ALGAE			
ALGAE REACH UP AND OUT, BENEATH	69	SUB MARE	6
BRING CONFIDENCE UPON THE ALGAE AND THE TENTACLES OF THE SOUL.	88	COMMISSION	21
ALI			
CAID ALI	199	MAUBERLEY: 2	EPI
ALIEN			
ALIEN PEOPLE!	70	THE PLUNGE	20
ALIKE			
TO BE SO MUCH ALIKE THAT EVERY DOG THAT SMELLS 'EM,	244	MOYEN SENSUEL	172
LEST IT SHOULD FAIL TO TREAT ALL MEN ALIKE.	244	MOYEN SENSUEL	178
ALIVE			
FROM THE WHITE, ALIVE IN THE SEED,	76	THE ALCHEMIST	31
THIS BOARD IS ALIVE WITH LIGHT;	120	GAME OF CHESS	6
THE AIR IS ALIVE WITH THAT FACT.	158	PSYCHOLOG HOUR	13
ALL			
BEING IN ALL THINGS WISE, AND VERY OLD.	4	LA FRAISNE	2
AND I? I HAVE PUT ASIDE ALL FOLLY AND ALL GRIEF.	4	LA FRAISNE	24
AND I? I HAVE PUT ASIDE ALL FOLLY AND ALL GRIEF.	4	LA FRAISNE	24
ALL FOLLY FROM ME, PUTTING IT ASIDE	4	LA FRAISNE	28

ALL

ALL (CONTINUED)

	PAGE	TITLE	LINE
THOUGH ALL MEN SAY THAT I AM MAD	5	LA FRAISNE	32
BUT IT IS ALL THE SAME;	6	CINO	2
(OH THEY ARE ALL ONE THESE VAGABONDS),	6	CINO	29
AND ALL I KNEW WERE OUT, MY LORD, YOU	7	CINO	34
BUT IT IS ALL ONE.	7	CINO	38
BUT IT IS ALL ONE, I WILL SING OF THE SUN.	7	CINO	41
BUT IT IS ALL ONE.	7	CINO	53
BROAD AS ALL OCEAN AND LEANIN' MAN-KIN'ARDS.	13	MESMERISM	12
SOUND IN YOUR WIND PAST ALL SIGNS O' CORRUPTION.	13	MESMERISM	16
PIERCED OF THE POINT THAT TOUCHETH LASTLY ALL,	19	FOR E. MCC	24
BEHOLD THE SHIELD! HE SHALL NOT TAKE THEE ALL.	19	FOR E. MCC	26
BUT REACH ME NOT AND ALL MY LIFE'S BECOME	20	IN DURANCE	6
BUT FOR ALL THAT, I AM HOMESICK AFTER MINE OWN KIND	20	IN DURANCE	23
"ALL THEY THAT WITH STRANGE SADNESS"	20	IN DURANCE	26
HAVE THE EARTH IN MOCKERY, AND ARE KIND TO ALL,	20	IN DURANCE	27
OF SUN AND SPRAY ALL SHATTERED AT THE BOWS;	21	IN DURANCE	37
YEA THOU, AND THOU, AND THOU, AND ALL MY KIN	21	IN DURANCE	42
TIBORS ALL TONGUE AND TEMPER AT MONT-AUSIER,	22	MARVOIL	18
ALL FOR ONE HALF-BALD, KNOCK-KNEE'D KING OF THE ARAGONESE,	22	MARVOIL	21
TO ALL MEN EXCEPT THE KING OF ARAGON,	23	MARVOIL	31
SHALL ALL MEN SCATTER ROSE LEAVES	24	THUS NINEVEH	17
ALL THE BLIND EARTH KNOWS NOT TH' EMPRISE	25	GUIDO INVITES	5
LIFE, ALL OF IT, MY SEA, AND ALL MEN'S STREAMS	25	GUIDO INVITES	9
LIFE, ALL OF IT, MY SEA, AND ALL MEN'S STREAMS	25	GUIDO INVITES	9
DAMN IT ALL! ALL THIS OUR SOUTH STINKS PEACE.	28	ALTAFORTE	1
DAMN IT ALL! ALL THIS OUR SOUTH STINKS PEACE.	28	ALTAFORTE	1
AND THROUGH ALL THE RIVEN SKIES GOD'S SWORDS CLASH.	28	ALTAFORTE	12
AND IT FILLS ALL MY HEART WITH REJOICING	29	ALTAFORTE	21
HIS LONE MIGHT 'GAINST ALL DARKNESS OPPOSING.	29	ALTAFORTE	24
YEA, I FILL ALL THE AIR WITH MY MUSIC.	29	ALTAFORTE	30
MAY GOD DAMN FOR EVER ALL WHO CRY "PEACE!"	29	ALTAFORTE	36
OF SOME THIN SILK STUFF THAT'S SCARCE STUFF AT ALL,	31	PIERE VIDAL	29
IT FAINTS IN TAKING AND IN GIVING ALL.	31	PIERE VIDAL	36
HA' WE LOST THE GOODLIEST FERE O' ALL	33	GOODLY FERE	1
"YE SHALL SEE ONE THING TO MASTER ALL:	34	GOODLY FERE	31
THAN ALL THE AGE-OLD KNOWLEDGE OF THY BOOKS:	35	THE EYES	17
IF ALL THE GRIEF AND WOE AND BITTERNESS,	36	THE YOUNG KING	1
ALL DOLOUR, ILL AND EVERY EVIL CHANCE	36	THE YOUNG KING	2
VOID OF ALL JOY AND FULL OF IRE AND SADNESS.	36	THE YOUNG KING	8
THAT WAS MOST VALIANT 'MID ALL WORTHIEST MEN!	37	THE YOUNG KING	30
AND ALL THE FAIR FROM TROY AND ALL FROM ACHAIA,	38	LADY'S LIFE	7
AND ALL THE FAIR FROM TROY AND ALL FROM ACHAIA,	38	LADY'S LIFE	7
AND ALL THE MAIDENS OF ROME, AS MANY AS THEY WERE,	38	LADY'S LIFE	9
ALL NIGHT, AND AS THE WIND LIETH AMONG	39	FOR PSYCHE	1
SHE IS TIME'S PREY AND TIME CONSUMETH ALL.	40	ROME	8
THAT YE WERE ONCE! OF ALL THE GRACE YE HAD	41	HER MONUMENT	18
ALL, ALL OUR LIFE'S ETERNAL MYSTERY!	41	HER MONUMENT	25
ALL, ALL OUR LIFE'S ETERNAL MYSTERY!	41	HER MONUMENT	25
ALL THIS ANGELIC ASPECT CAN RETURN	42	HER MONUMENT	37
WITH ALL THE ADMIRABLE CONCEPTS THAT MOVED FROM IT	42	HER MONUMENT	39
FRAIL AND SO VILE IN ALL.	42	HER MONUMENT	51
AND ALL THE TIME THOU SAYEST THEM O'ER I SAID,	43	SATIEMUS	4
THROUGH ALL THE WORLD WILL I COMPLAIN	44	FROM HEINE: 1	3
THAT THERE'S NO THING MORE SWEET OR FALSE AT ALL.	44	FROM HEINE: 2	8
AND ALL THE ANGELS SAT ABOUT	45	FROM HEINE: 4	3
ALL THE FLAMES ARE DEAD AND SPED NOW	45	FROM HEINE: 3	5
AND ALL THE LADIES SWIM THROUGH TEARS	45	FROM HEINE: 5	11
ALL GOOD THINGS GO VANISHING.	46	FROM HEINE: 6	20
IN ALL THEIR SPLENDID GEAR.	47	FROM HEINE: 7	24
AND RED THE SUNLIGHT WAS, BEHIND IT ALL.	49	OF SPLENDOUR	8
AND ALL HER ROBE WAS WOVEN OF PALE GOLD.	49	OF SPLENDOUR	12
THERE ARE THERE MANY ROOMS AND ALL OF GOLD,	49	OF SPLENDOUR	13
AND ALL THE TALES OF OISIN SAY BUT THIS:	50	THE FLAME	9
THESE, AND THE REST, AND ALL THE REST WE KNEW.	50	THE FLAME	15
WE ARE NOT SHUT FROM ALL THE THOUSAND HEAVENS:	50	THE FLAME	22
THROUGH ALL THY VARIOUS MOOD I KNOW THEE MINE;	50	THE FLAME	31
IF THOU HAST SEEN THAT MIRROR OF ALL MOMENTS,	51	THE FLAME	40
THAT GLASS TO ALL THINGS THAT O'ERSHADOW IT,	51	THE FLAME	41
AND IT'LL ALL COME RIGHT,	53	AU JARDIN	21

PAGE 12

ALL

		PAGE	TITLE	LINE
ALL	(CONTINUED)			
	"TIME'S BITTER FLOOD"! OH, THAT'S ALL VERY WELL,	59	EXIT' CUIUSDAM	1
	WHY SHOULD WE STOP AT ALL FOR WHAT I THINK?	59	SILET	3
	AND THERE IS NO NEW THING IN ALL THIS PLACE.	60	TOMB AKR CAAR	11
	AND ALL THY ROBES I HAVE KEPT SMOOTH ON THEE.	60	TOMB AKR CAAR	14
	AND ALL THEIR CRAFTY WORK UPON THE DOOR,	60	TOMB AKR CAAR	30
	IDEAS, OLD GOSSIP, ODDMENTS OF ALL THINGS,	61	PORTRAIT FEMME	4
	FOR ALL THIS SEA-HOARD OF DECIDUOUS THINGS,	61	PORTRAIT FEMME	25
	NO! THERE IS NOTHING! IN THE WHOLE AND ALL,	61	PORTRAIT FEMME	28
	AND ALL THIS IS FOLLY TO THE WORLD.	62	A GIRL	10
	NAY, SHOULD THE DEATHLESS VOICE OF ALL THE WORLD	63	PHASELLUS ILLE	9
	THE MEWS' SINGING ALL MY MEAD-DRINK.	64	THE SEAFARER	22
	ALL THIS ADMONISHETH MAN EAGER OF MOOD,	65	THE SEAFARER	51
	SO THAT ALL MEN SHALL HONOUR HIM AFTER	66	THE SEAFARER	78
	AND ALL ARROGANCE OF EARTHEN RICHES,	66	THE SEAFARER	83
	DREAR ALL THIS EXCELLENCE, DELIGHTS UNDURABLE!	66	THE SEAFARER	88
	NO MAN AT ALL GOING THE EARTH'S GAIT,	66	THE SEAFARER	92
	OF ALL THINGS, FRAIL ALABASTER, AH ME!	68	APPARUIT	19
	THIS THAT IS ALL I WANTED	70	THE PLUNGE	7
	DO I NOT LOATHE ALL WALLS, STREETS, STONES,	70	THE PLUNGE	11
	ALL MIRE, MIST, ALL FOG,	70	THE PLUNGE	12
	ALL MIRE, MIST, ALL FOG,	70	THE PLUNGE	12.
	ALL WAYS OF TRAFFIC?	70	THE PLUNGE	13
	AH! BOW YOUR HEADS, YE MAIDENS ALL,	72	PAN IS DEAD	2
	READY ARE ALL FOLKS TO REWARD HER.	72	DIEU! QU'IL	4
	BUT, ABOVE ALL, GO TO PRACTICAL PEOPLE--	86	SALUTATION 2ND	34
	BE AGAINST ALL FORMS OF OPPRESSION.	89	COMMISSION	25
	BE AGAINST ALL SORTS OF MORTMAIN.	89	COMMISSION	35
	YOU DO NEXT TO NOTHING AT ALL.	94	INSTRUCTIONS	7
	THAT NOW THERE IS NO ONE AT ALL	97	THE BELLAIRES	9
	AND FOR ALL THIS I HAVE CONSIDERABLE REGRET,	98	THE BELLAIRES	41
	LET US APPLY IT IN ALL ITS OPPROBRIUM	99	SALVATIONISTS	5
	ALL THE BULMENIAN LITERATI.	99	SALVATIONISTS	17
	YOU TOOK NO PLEASURE AT ALL IN MY TRIUMPHS,	101	AMITIES	2
	ALL OF WHOM SHE REFUSED;	102	LADIES	2
	I SHALL HAVE MISSED NOTHING AT ALL,	105	DOMPNA POIS	26
	ALL THE WHILE THEY WERE TALKING THE NEW MORALITY	110	THE ENCOUNTER	1
	ALL HAIL! YOUNG LADY WITH A NOSE	113	FORMIANUS LADY	1
	WHERE ONE NEEDS ONE'S BRAINS ALL THE TIME.	117	THE LAKE ISLE	16
	A YELLOW STORK FOR A CHARGER, AND ALL OUR SEAMEN	128	THE RIVER SONG	7
	AND WE ALL SPOKE OUT OUR HEARTS AND MINDS, AND			
	WITHOUT REGRET.	134	EXILE'S LETTER	11
	THROUGH ALL THE THIRTY-SIX FOLDS OF THE TURNING AND			
	TWISTING WATERS,	134	EXILE'S LETTER	18
	AND MY SPIRIT SO HIGH IT WAS ALL OVER THE HEAVENS,	135	EXILE'S LETTER	32
	AND ALL THIS COMES TO AN END.	136	EXILE'S LETTER	63
	HOW SHALL WE KNOW ALL THE FRIENDS	141	IDEA OF CHOAN	01
	ARE ALL FOLDED INTO ONE DARKNESS,	142	UNMOVING CLOUD	4
	I WISH YOU JOY, I PROFFER YOU ALL MY ASSISTANCE.	145	SALUTATION 3RD	19
	AND LAUGHTER IS THE END OF ALL THINGS.	147	POST MORTEM	5
	SET ALL TOGETHER, ARE NOT WORTHY OF YOU. . . ."	151	NEAR PERIGORD	9
	AND ALL THE WHILE YOU SING OUT THAT CANZONE,	151	NEAR PERIGORD	10
	HIS BROTHER-IN-LAW WAS ALL THERE WAS OF POWER	151	NEAR PERIGORD	17
	GOBBLED ALL THE LAND, AND HELD IT LATER FOR SOME			
	HUNDRED YEARS.	151	NEAR PERIGORD	19
	AND ALL HIS NET-LIKE THOUGHT OF NEW ALLIANCE?	152	NEAR PERIGORD	53
	ALL OF HIS FLANK--HOW COULD HE DO WITHOUT HER?	153	NEAR PERIGORD	66
	AND ALL THE ROAD TO CAHORS, TO TOULOUSE?	153	NEAR PERIGORD	67
	AND ALL MY HEART IS BOUND ABOUT WITH LOVE.	153	NEAR PERIGORD	73
	OR CARRY HIM FORWARD. "GO THROUGH ALL THE COURTS,	154	NEAR PERIGORD	115
	ROSE OVER US; AND WE KNEW ALL THAT STREAM,	157	NEAR PERIGORD	172
	AND ALL THE REST OF HER A SHIFTING CHANGE,	157	NEAR PERIGORD	191
	SAY "FORGET TO-MORROW," BEING OF ALL MEN	161	CABARET DANCER	7
	GOOD HEDGETHORN, THEY ALL HAVE FUTURES,	163	CABARET DANCER	60
	ALL THESE PEOPLE.	163	CABARET DANCER	61
	LUST HAS TAKEN YOUR ALL	165	QUINTUS SEPTIM	18
	THE PARKS WITH THE SWARDS ALL OVER DEW,	167	OF AROUET	19
	QUIET TALKING IS ALL THAT IS LEFT US--	168	OF AROUET	31
	LORD POWERFUL, ENGIRDLED ALL WITH MIGHT,	172	LANGUE D'OC: 1	2
	MY HEART ALL WAKES AND GRIEVES;	173	LANGUE D'OC: 2	8
	IF ALL THE WORLD BE IN DESPITE	174	LANGUE D'OC: 3	14

PAGE 13

ALL -- ALLIANCE

	PAGE	TITLE	LINE
ALL (CONTINUED)			
FOR IN HER IS ALL MY DELIGHT	174	LANGUE D'OC: 3	26
AND ALL THAT CAN SAVE ME.	174	LANGUE D'OC: 3	27
ALL VILE, OR ALL GENTLE,	175	LANGUE D'OC: 3	52
ALL VILE, OR ALL GENTLE,	175	LANGUE D'OC: 3	52
I LOSE ALL WIT AND SENSE.	176	LANGUE D'OC: 3	69
AND STICKING OUT ALL THE WAY ROUND;	181	MOEURS CON: 7	5
ALL THINGS ARE A FLOWING,	189	HUGH SELWYN: 3	9
ALL MEN, IN LAW, ARE EQUALS.	189	HUGH SELWYN: 3	21
RED OVERWROUGHT WITH ORANGE AND ALL MADE	197	ENVOI (1919)	14
ALL THINGS SAVE BEAUTY ALONE.	197	ENVOI (1919)	26
ALL PASSES, ANANGKE PREVAILS,	199	MAUBERLEY: 2	3
HIM OF ALL MEN, UNFIT	201	AGE DEMANDED	2
SEEING THAT LONG STANDING INCREASES ALL THINGS	207	SEXTUS PROP: 1	24
AND THEY ALL GO TO RACK RUIN BENEATH THE THUD OF THE YEARS.	209	SEXTUS PROP: 1	71
I HAD SUNG OF ALL THESE	210	SEXTUS PROP: 2	13
THUS ALL ROADS ARE PERFECTLY SAFE	212	SEXTUS PROP: 3	24
OUT WITH IT, TELL IT TO ME, ALL OF IT, FROM THE BEGINNING,	214	SEXTUS PROP: 4	11
SHE DID NOT RESPECT ALL THE GODS;	221	SEXTUS PROP: 8	6
THOUGH YOU GIVE ALL YOUR KISSES	221	SEXTUS PROP: 7	33
AND AMID ALL THE GLORIED AND STORIED BEAUTIES OF MAEONIA	222	SEXTUS PROP: 8	34
"ALL LOVELY WOMEN HAVE KNOWN THIS,"	226	SEXTUS PROP:11	22
ALL THINGS ARE FORGIVEN FOR ONE NIGHT OF YOUR GAMES.	227	SEXTUS PROP:11	39
OF ALL THESE YOUNG WOMEN	228	SEXTUS PROP:12	24
HAD TRIED ALL WAYS;	235	TO WHISTLER	2
AN ART! YOU ALL RESPECT THE ARTS, FROM THAT INFANT TICK	239	MOYEN SENSUEL	13
ALL ONE CAN SAY OF THIS REFINING MEDIUM	239	MOYEN SENSUEL	35
DESPITE IT ALL, DESPITE YOUR RED BLOODS, FEBRILE CONCUPISCENCE	240	MOYEN SENSUEL	67
DESPITE IT ALL, YOUR COMPOUND PREDILECTION	240	MOYEN SENSUEL	69
THE SOCIAL ITCH, THE ALMOST, ALL BUT, NOT QUITE, FASCINATING,	241	MOYEN SENSUEL	83
THREE THOUSAND CHORUS GIRLS AND ALL UNKISSED,	241	MOYEN SENSUEL	87
THE SELECT COMPANY: BEAUTIES YOU ALL WOULD KNOW	242	MOYEN SENSUEL	113
DE GOURMONT SAYS THAT FIFTY GRUNTS ARE ALL THAT WILL BE PRIZED.	244	MOYEN SENSUEL	165
LEST IT SHOULD FAIL TO TREAT ALL MEN ALIKE.	244	MOYEN SENSUEL	178
"ALL THE SAME STYLE, SAME CUT, WITH PERFECT LOATHING."	244	MOYEN SENSUEL	184
HAVING NO HOPE AT ALL	248	DONNA MI PREGA	6
IT TWISTS ITSELF FROM OUT ALL NATURAL MEASURE;	249	DONNA MI PREGA	50
LOVE DOTH NOT MOVE, BUT DRAWETH ALL TO HIM;	250	DONNA MI PREGA	64
BEYOND ALL FALSITY, WORTHY OF FAITH, ALONE	250	DONNA MI PREGA	86
STORMED AT BY PRESS AND ALL,	257	BREAD BRIGADE	21
HOW SHALL WE DRESS 'EM ALL?	257	BREAD BRIGADE	22
SEE HOW THEY TAKE IT ALL,	259	ALF'S THIRD	12
ALL DREW THEIR PAY, AND AS THE PAY GREW LESS,	260	ALF'S FIFTH	9
THE UNSAFE SAFE, WHEREIN ALL ROTS, AND NO MAN CAN SAY HOW	261	ALF'S FIFTH	19
LIKE ALL HIS CLASS WAS TOLD TO HOLD IT IN THOSE DAYS,	263	ALF'S EIGHTH	26
ON SEA AND LAND, WITH ALL CONVENIENCE FOUND	264	ALF'S NINTH	19
NEVER AT ALL WILL THEY DO	265	ALF'S TENTH	3
ONE THING AMONG ALL THINGS YOU WILL NOT	265	ALF'S TENTH	11
BURY IT ALL, BURY IT ALL WELL DEEP,	265	ALF'S NINTH	29
BURY IT ALL, BURY IT ALL WELL DEEP,	265	ALF'S NINTH	29
AND LET THE BLIGHTERS START IT ALL OVER AGAIN.	265	ALF'S NINTH	30
MY SALES BEAT ALL THE OTHER TEN,	266	ALF'S ELEVENTH	3
AND I GET ALL THE BEEF	269	SAFE AND SOUND	6
ALLAIT			
M. POM-POM ALLAIT EN GUERRE	273	M. POM-POM	1
ALL-CONQUERING			
ALL-CONQUERING, NOW CONQUERED, BECAUSE	40	ROME	7
ALLEYS			
FILLED THE BACK ALLEYS AND THE BACK TO BACK HOUSES.	260	ALF'S FIFTH	14
ALLIANCE			
AND ALL HIS NET-LIKE THOUGHT OF NEW ALLIANCE?	152	NEAR PERIGORD	53

PAGE 14

ALLODETTA -- ALREADY

	PAGE	TITLE	LINE
ALLODETTA			
ELAIN, TIREIS, ALLODETTA	76	THE ALCHEMIST	61
ALLOTTED			
THUS MUCH THE FATES HAVE ALLOTTED ME, AND IF, MAECENAS,	217	SEXTUS PROP: 5	37
ALLUREMENT			
RAVENS, NIGHTS, ALLUREMENT:	6	CINO	7
ALMOND			
WHITE AS AN ALMOND ARE THY SHOULDERS;	91	DANCE FIGURE	12
ALMONDS			
AS NEW ALMONDS STRIPPED FROM THE HUSK.	91	DANCE FIGURE	13
ALMOST			
AND IS ALMOST AFRAID THAT I	83	THE GARDEN	11
I ALMOST SEE YOU ABOUT ME,	94	INSTRUCTIONS	13
FAINT, ALMOST, AS THE LINES OF CRUELTY ABOUT YOUR CHIN,	103	LADIES	19
ASSAILS ME, AND CONCERNS ME ALMOST AS LITTLE.	103	LADIES	20
I HAD ALMOST TURNED DOWN THE PAGES.	158	PSYCHOLOG HOUR	3
AND CABINETS AND CHESTS FROM MARTIN (ALMOST LACQUER),	167	OF AROUET	11
AND YOU, O POLYPHEMUS? DID HARSH GALATEA ALMOST	208	SEXTUS PROP: 1	46
THE SOCIAL ITCH, THE ALMOST, ALL BUT, NOT QUITE, FASCINATING,	241	MOYEN SENSUEL	83
THE DESTINIES OF ENGLAND WERE ALMOST SOLD	264	ALF'S NINTH	6
ALODETTA			
VANNA, MANDETTA, VIERA, ALODETTA, PICARDA, MANUELA	76	THE ALCHEMIST	38
ALOFT			
FIVE CLOUDS HANG ALOFT, BRIGHT ON THE PURPLE SKY,	129	THE RIVER SONG	33
ALONE			
QUITE GAY, FOR I HAVE HER ALONE HERE	5	LA FRAISNE	38
FOR WE ARE QUITE ALONE	5	LA FRAISNE	51
LO, I WOULD SAIL THE SEAS WITH THEE ALONE!	25	GUIDO INVITES	2
IN US ALONE THE ELEMENT OF CALM."	32	PARACELSUS	13
ALONE IN THE TOWN?" SAYS HE.	33	GOODLY FERE	12
ALONE.	36	FRANCESCA	12
ROME'S NAME ALONE WITHIN THESE WALLS KEEPS HOME.	40	ROME	4
ROME THAT ALONE HAST CONQUERED ROME THE TOWN,	40	ROME	10
TIBER ALONE, TRANSIENT AND SEAWARD BENT,	40	ROME	11
THE SALT-WAVY TUMULT TRAVERSE ALONE.	65	THE SEAFARER	36
OUT, AND ALONE, AMONG SOME	70	THE PLUNGE	19
MOVE AMONG THE LOVERS OF PERFECTION ALONE.	95	ITE	2
AND LEAVES HER TOO MUCH ALONE.	128	BEAU TOILET	9
WHO DEPARTED ALONE WITH HIS MISTRESS,	132	AT TEN-SHIN	32
THE PHOENIX ARE GONE, THE RIVER FLOWS ON ALONE.	138	CITY OF CHOAN	2
TO FIND HER HALF ALONE, MONTFORT AWAY,	154	NEAR PERIGORD	111
ALL THINGS SAVE BEAUTY ALONE.	197	ENVOI (1919)	26
"WHERE A GIRL WAITS ALONE FOR HER LOVER;	210	SEXTUS PROP: 2	23
"DOES HE LIKE ME TO SLEEP HERE ALONE,	213	SEXTUS PROP: 4	38
AND IT WAS MORNING, AND I WANTED TO SEE IF SHE WAS ALONE, AND RESTING,	225	SEXTUS PROP:10	27
AND CYNTHIA WAS ALONE IN HER BED.	225	SEXTUS PROP:10	28
BUT IN ONE BED, IN ONE BED ALONE, MY DEAR LYNCEUS	228	SEXTUS PROP:12	15
BEYOND ALL FALSITY, WORTHY OF FAITH, ALONE	250	DONNA MI PREGA	86
I SIT ALONE IN THE TWILIGHT	268	ANOTHER BIT	9
ALONG			
TRAILING ALONG THE WIND.	18	DE AEGYPTO	6
WITH SIX GREAT SAPPHIRES HUNG ALONG THE WALL,	49	OF SPLENDOUR	10
WERE SEEN LYING ALONG THE UPPER SEATS	93	LES MILLWIN	3
"SHOVE ALONG THERE, SHOVE ALONG!"	224	SEXTUS PROP:10	15
"SHOVE ALONG THERE, SHOVE ALONG!"	224	SEXTUS PROP:10	15
GET ALONG NOW!"	225	SEXTUS PROP:10	24
A-LOOSE			
A-LOOSE THE CLOAK OF THE BODY, CAMEST	68	APPARUIT	14
ALORS			
ET ALORS JE VIS BIEN DES CHOSES	160	DANS OMNIBUS	6
ALREADY			
DEAD ALREADY.	43	MR. HOUSMAN	5
ALREADY THEY FLEE, HOWLING IN TERROR.	91	TENZONE	5
HE STROKED THOSE WHICH WERE ALREADY ARRANGED,	97	AESTHETICS	18
THE PAIRED BUTTERFLIES ARE ALREADY YELLOW WITH AUGUST	131	RIVER-MER WIFE	23
THE JEWELLED STEPS ARE ALREADY QUITE WHITE WITH DEW,	132	JEWEL STAIRS'	1
MEN'S FATES ARE ALREADY SET,	138	NEAR SHOKU	10

PAGE 15

ALREADY -- AMBER

	PAGE	TITLE	LINE
ALREADY (CONTINUED)			
WITH WHICH I AM ALREADY FAMILIAR,	226	SEXTUS PROP:11	16
ALSO			
WE ALSO SHALL BE DEAD PRETTY SOON	43	MR. HOUSMAN	3
BUT HE DIES ALSO, PRESENTLY.	43	MR. HOUSMAN	7
GO ALSO TO THE NERVE-WRACKED, GO TO THE ENSLAVED-BY-CONVENTION,	88	COMMISSION	2
FOR TWELVE HORSES AND ALSO FOR TWELVE BOARHOUNDS	98	THE BELLAIRES	19
TE VOILA, MON BOURRIENNE, YOU ALSO SHALL BE IMMORTAL.	101	AMITIES	6
AND WE SAY GOOD-BYE TO YOU ALSO,	101	AMITIES	7
AND HER HAIR ALSO IS TURNING.	102	LADIES	4
LALAGE IS ALSO A MODEL PARENT,	103	THE PATTERNS	3
YOU ALSO ARE LAID ASIDE.	108	FAN-PIECE	3
YES, SHE ALSO WILL TURN MIDDLE-AGED,	116	THE TEA SHOP	5
SHE ALSO WILL TURN MIDDLE-AGED.	116	THE TEA SHOP	9
AND LI PO ALSO DIED DRUNK.	117	EPITAPHS	3
AND THERE CAME ALSO THE "TRUE MAN" OF SHI-YO TO MEET ME,	134	EXILE'S LETTER	24
SO SHALL YOU BE ALSO,	145	SALUTATION 3RD	9
AND THERE ARE ALSO THE INANE EXPENSES OF THE FUNERAL;	164	QUINTUS SEPTIM	9
ALSO, IN THE CASE OF REVOLUTION,	196	HUGH SELWIN:12	19
AND I ALSO AMONG THE LATER NEPHEWS OF THIS CITY	208	SEXTUS PROP: 1	35
AND I ALSO WILL SING WAR WHEN THIS MATTER OF A GIRL IS EXHAUSTED.	216	SEXTUS PROP: 5	9
AND BELIEVE IT, AND SHE ALSO WILL BELIEVE IT,	222	SEXTUS PROP: 8	32
AND UNTO ME ALSO PAY DEBT:	224	SEXTUS PROP: 9	27
AND YOU ALSO FOLLOW HIM "NEATH PHRYGIAN PINE SHADE:	229	SEXTUS PROP:12	41
YOU ALSO, OUR FIRST GREAT,	235	TO WHISTLER	1
ALSO, HE'D READ OF CHRISTIAN VIRTUES IN	241	MOYEN SENSUEL	97
ALTAFORT			
AND OUR EN BERTRANS WAS IN ALTAFORT,	151	NEAR PERIGORD	20
ALTAFORTE			
SESTINA: ALTAFORTE	28	ALTAFORTE	T
ALTAR			
ARE FUSED IN IT AS FLAMES OF AN ALTAR FIRE!	25	GUIDO INVITES	10
THE ALTAR	51	THE ALTAR	T
"ONCE MORE IN DELOS, ONCE MORE IS THE ALTAR A-QUIVER.	90	SURGIT FAMA	16
ALTER			
TO ALTER THEM TO HIS PURPOSE;	90	SURGIT FAMA	14
ALTERED			
ARLES GREATLY ALTERED,	122	PROVINC DESERT	60
ALTHOUGH			
ALTHOUGH CALLIMACHUS DID WITHOUT THEM,	218	SEXTUS PROP: 5	49
ALTITUDE			
FOR THE NOBLENESS OF THE POPULACE BROOKS NOTHING BELOW ITS OWN ALTITUDE.	230	SEXTUS PROP:12	64
ALWAY			
HELL BLOT BLACK FOR ALWAY THE THOUGHT "PEACE"!	29	ALTAFORTE	39
DEAD MEN STAY ALWAY DEAD MEN,	47	FROM HEINE: 7	17
MOANETH ALWAY MY MIND'S LUST	65	THE SEAFARER	37
WHEN SPELLS ARE ALWAY RENEWED ON HER?	72	DIEU! QU'IL	6
ALWAYS			
AND SMITE ALWAYS AT THEIR FAIBLENESS?	12	OF THE GIBBET	40
YOU HAVE BEEN SECOND ALWAYS. TRAGICAL?	61	PORTRAIT FEMME	7
WHY SHOULD ONE ALWAYS LIE ABOUT SUCH MATTERS?	113	TAME CAT	2
'WHY DO YOU LOVE ME? WILL YOU ALWAYS LOVE ME?'	157	NEAR PERIGORD	181
YOU WERE NOT ALWAYS SURE, NOT ALWAYS SET	235	TO WHISTLER	14
YOU WERE NOT ALWAYS SURE, NOT ALWAYS SET	235	TO WHISTLER	14
AIN'T ALWAYS A PLEASURE,	259	ALF'S FOURTH	4
AIN'T IT ALWAYS BEEN SO?	259	ALF'S FOURTH	11
AM (68)			
AMAVI			
"QUIA PAUPER AMAVI."	206	SEXTUS PROP	EPI
AMBASSADOR			
"HE WAS YOUR AMBASSADOR HERE?"	182	MOEURS CON: 8	3
AMBASSADORS			
WHO SHOWS HIS TASTE IN HIS AMBASSADORS:	239	MOYEN SENSUEL	17
AMBER			
FROM AMBER LATTICES UPON THE COBALT NIGHT,	53	AU JARDIN	3
FROM THE POPLARS WEEPING THEIR AMBER,	75	THE ALCHEMIST	22

	PAGE	TITLE	LINE
AMBER (CONTINUED)			
MIDONZ, WITH THE GOLD OF THE SUN, THE LEAF OF THE POPLAR, BY THE LIGHT OF THE AMBER,	75	THE ALCHEMIST	25
MIDONZ, DAUGHTER OF THE SUN, SHAFT OF THE TREE, SILVER OF THE LEAF, LIGHT OF THE YELLOW OF THE AMBER,	75	THE ALCHEMIST	26
MIDONZ, GIFT OF THE GOD, GIFT OF THE LIGHT, GIFT OF THE AMBER OF THE SUN,	75	THE ALCHEMIST	27
O FILAMENTS OF AMBER, TWO-FACED IRIDESCENCE!	95	OF THE DEGREES	15
THE GEW-GAWS OF FALSE AMBER AND FALSE TURQUOISE ATTRACT THEM.	114	BEFORE A SHOP	1
AS ROSES MIGHT, IN MAGIC AMBER LAID,	197	ENVOI (1919)	13
FROM METAL, OR INTRACTABLE AMBER;	204	MEDALLION	12
AMBERGRIS			
IDOLS AND AMBERGRIS AND RARE INLAYS,	61	PORTRAIT FEMME	23
AMBITION			
HER AMBITION IS VAGUE AND INDEFINITE,	179	MOEURS CON: 2	10
AMBROSIA			
HE DRANK AMBROSIA,	199	MAUBERLEY: 2	2
AMBROSIAL			
PHALLIC AND AMBROSIAL	189	HUGH SELWYN: 3	6
SEEN, WE ADMIT, AMID AMBROSIAL CIRCUMSTANCES	202	AGE DEMANDED	34
A-MEAOWLING			
A-MEAOWLING OUR PRAISES.	52	AU SALON	23
A-MEN			
A-A-A-A--A-MEN.	101	AMITIES	20
AMERICA			
THE THOUGHT OF WHAT AMERICA WOULD BE LIKE	183	CANTICO SOLE	1
THE THOUGHT OF WHAT AMERICA,	183	CANTICO SOLE	4
THE THOUGHT OF WHAT AMERICA,	183	CANTICO SOLE	5
THE THOUGHT OF WHAT AMERICA WOULD BE LIKE	183	CANTICO SOLE	6
THE THOUGHT OF WHAT AMERICA,	183	CANTICO SOLE	12
THE THOUGHT OF WHAT AMERICA,	183	CANTICO SOLE	13
THE THOUGHT OF WHAT AMERICA WOULD BE LIKE	183	CANTICO SOLE	14
WHO BEAR THE BRUNT OF OUR AMERICA	235	TO WHISTLER	12
AMERICAN			
THE YOUNG AMERICAN PILGRIM	179	MOEURS CON: 3	5
TO WHISTLER, AMERICAN	235	TO WHISTLER	T
AMERICA'S			
THAT AMERICA'S STURDY SONS	268	ANOTHER BIT	2
AMIABLE			
GRINS UP AN AMIABLE GRIN,	163	CABARET DANCER	58
AMIABLE AND HARMONIOUS PEOPLE ARE PUSHED INCONTINENT INTO DUELS,	227	SEXTUS PROP:12	5
AMIC			
BUT YOU, BOS AMIC, WE KEEP ON,	101	AMITIES	13
AMID			
I STOOD STILL AND WAS A TREE AMID THE WOOD,	3	THE TREE	1
THAT GREW ELM-OAK AMID THE WOLD	3	THE TREE	5
NATHLESS I HAVE BEEN A TREE AMID THE WOOD	3	THE TREE	10
I WHO HAVE SEEN YOU AMID THE PRIMAL THINGS	36	FRANCESCA	5
I AM BELOW AMID THE PINE TREES,	53	AU JARDIN	4
AMID THE LITTLE PINE TREES, HEAR ME!	53	AU JARDIN	5
SHE, WHO MOVED HERE AMID THE CYCLAMEN,	87	THE SPRING	12
HE HAD MOVED AMID HER PHANTASMAGORIA,	199	MAUBERLEY: 2	5
AMID HER GALAXIES,	199	MAUBERLEY: 2	6
(AMID AERIAL FLOWERS) . . . TIME FOR ARRANGEMENTS--	199	MAUBERLEY: 2	13
MILDNESS, AMID THE NEO-NIETZSCHEAN CLATTER,	201	AGE DEMANDED	21
QUITE OUT OF PLACE AMID	201	AGE DEMANDED	23
SEEN, WE ADMIT, AMID AMBROSIAL CIRCUMSTANCES	202	AGE DEMANDED	34
AMID THE PRECIPITATION, DOWN-FLOAT	202	AGE DEMANDED	52
AND AMID ALL THE GLORIED AND STORIED BEAUTIES OF MAEONIA	222	SEXTUS PROP: 8	34
HEAD FARMERS DO LIKEWISE, AND LYING WEARY AMID THEIR OATS	229	SEXTUS PROP:12	48
AMITIES			
AMITIES	101	AMITIES	T
AMONG			
ONCE WHEN I WAS AMONG THE YOUNG MEN . . .	5	LA FRAISNE	40
AND THEY SAID I WAS QUITE STRONG, AMONG THE YOUNG MEN.	5	LA FRAISNE	41

AMONG -- ANCIENT

	PAGE	TITLE	LINE
AMONG (CONTINUED)			
OR HIDES AMONG THE ASHES THERE FOR THEE.	20	IN DURANCE	9
THE LIGHT BECAME HER GRACE AND DWELT AMONG	38	BALLATETTA	1
ALL NIGHT, AND AS THE WIND LIETH AMONG	39	FOR PSYCHE	1
WHISPERING AMONG THEM, "THE FAIR DEAD	43	SATIEMUS	10
OUT, AND ALONE, AMONG SOME	70	THE PLUNGE	19
AS YOU MOVE AMONG THE BRIGHT TREES;	75	THE ALCHEMIST	2
THERE IS A TRUCE AMONG THE GODS,	90	SURGIT FAMA	1
THERE IS NONE LIKE THEE AMONG THE DANCERS,	91	DANCE FIGURE	4
AMONG THE WOMEN WITH PITCHERS.	91	DANCE FIGURE	9
AS A RILLET AMONG THE SEDGE ARE THY HANDS UPON ME;	91	DANCE FIGURE	19
THERE IS NONE LIKE THEE AMONG THE DANCERS;	91	DANCE FIGURE	23
MOVING AMONG THE TREES, AND CLINGING	92	GENTILDONNA	2
MOVE AMONG THE LOVERS OF PERFECTION ALONE.	95	ITE	2
WILL YOU FIND YOUR LOST DEAD AMONG THEM?	103	CODA	3
ABOUT AMONG MY FLOWERS.	109	THE FAUN	2
"IT RESTS ME TO BE AMONG BEAUTIFUL WOMEN.	113	TAME CAT	1
WHO AMONG THEM IS A MAN LIKE HAN-REI	132	AT TEN-SHIN	31
AND OF THE BEST, AMONG THEM,	191	HUGH SELWYN: 5	2
AMONG THE PICKLED FOETUSES AND BOTTLED BONES,	193	SIENA MI FE	1
AND I ALSO AMONG THE LATER NEPHEWS OF THIS CITY	208	SEXTUS PROP: 1	35
AND ONE AMONG THEM LOOKED AT ME WITH FACE OFFENDED,	211	SEXTUS PROP: 2	38
AND NO GOOD RUMOUR AMONG THEM.	226	SEXTUS PROP:11	19
I SHALL TRIUMPH AMONG YOUNG LADIES OF INDETERMINATE CHARACTER,	229	SEXTUS PROP:12	55
AND NOW PROPERTIUS OF CYNTHIA, TAKING HIS STAND AMONG THESE.	230	SEXTUS PROP:12	75
SOME FORCES AMONG THOSE WHICH "FORMED" HIS YOUTH:	241	MOYEN SENSUEL	78
ONE THING AMONG ALL THINGS YOU WILL NOT	265	ALF'S TENTH	11
AMONGST			
EVEN THAT SEMBLANCE THAT APPEARS AMONGST US	41	HER MONUMENT	23
WHO USED TO WALK ABOUT AMONGST US	102	LADIES	10
AMOR			
AMOR STANDS UPON YOU, LOVE DRIVES UPON LOVERS,	226	SEXTUS PROP:11	11
AMOROUS			
GONE IS HIS BODY FINE AND AMOROUS,	37	THE YOUNG KING	31
PHYLLIDULA IS SCRAWNY BUT AMOROUS,	103	PHYLLIDULA	1
THE AMOROUS NERVES WILL GIVE WAY TO DIGESTIVE;	163	CABARET DANCER	68
THEREON THE AMOROUS CALOR SLIGHTLY FROSTED HIM.	242	MOYEN SENSUEL	122
AMPHIBIOUS			
LURKING, SERPENTINE, AMPHIBIOUS AND INSIDIOUS	244	MOYEN SENSUEL	170
AN (89)			
AN'			
'TWAS AS A BUSINESS ASSET PURE AN' SIMPLE	246	MOYEN SENSUEL	239
AN' 'E LOOKS LIKE A TOFF.	260	ALF'S FOURTH	15
AN' BE THANKFUL FOR OCCASIONAL HOLIDAYS.	263	ALF'S EIGHTH	28
AN' KEEP THE BANK IN POWER.	270	OF 600 M.P.'S	4
AN' EVERY YEAR WE MEET TO LET	270	OF 600 M.P.'S	11
AN' THEM SPRAWLING ON THE BENCHES	270	OF 600 M.P.'S	14
"I COULDN'T," SHE SEZ, "AN' I AINT TRIED,	270	OF 600 M.P.'S	21
ANADYOMENE			
AS ANADYOMENE IN THE OPENING	204	MEDALLION	7
ANAEMIA			
OF A SORT OF EMOTIONAL ANAEMIA.	83	THE GARDEN	4
ANAEMIC			
WITH THEIR LARGE AND ANAEMIC EYES THEY LOOKED OUT UPON THIS CONFIGURATION.	93	LES MILLWIN	12
ANAETHESIS			
WHICH ANAETHESIS, NOTED A YEAR LATE,	200	MAUBERLEY: 2	30
ANAGRAM			
AND THAT WAS AN ANAGRAM FOR VITTORIO	182	MOEURS CON: 7	20
ANALYSES			
HE ANALYSES FORM AND THOUGHT TO SEE	15	FAMAM CANO	47
ANANGKE			
ALL PASSES, ANANGKE PREVAILS,	199	MAUBERLEY: 2	3
ANCESTRAL			
BEARING ANCESTRAL LARES AND IMAGES;	219	SEXTUS PROP: 6	14
ANCIENNES			
JE VIS LES COLONNES ANCIENNES EN "TOC"	160	DANS OMNIBUS	12
ANCIENT			
BROKEN OF ANCIENT PRIDE,	9	NA AUDIART	49

ANCIENT -- ANOTHER

	PAGE	TITLE	LINE
ANCIENT (CONTINUED)			
THIS IS ANOTHER OF OUR ANCIENT LOVES.	63	QUIES	1
HOSTS OF AN ANCIENT PEOPLE,	107	COMING OF WAR	19
ANCIENT MUSIC	116	ANCIENT MUSIC	T
ANCIENT WISDOM, RATHER COSMIC	118	ANCIENT WISDOM	T
TO SO-KIN OF RAKUYO, ANCIENT FRIEND, CHANCELLOR OF GEN.	134	EXILE'S LETTER	1
NOR OF THEBES IN ITS ANCIENT RESPECTABILITY,	217	SEXTUS PROP: 5	42
GO ON, TO ASCRAEUS' PRESCRIPTION, THE ANCIENT,	229	SEXTUS PROP:12	50
ANCORA			
ANCORA	104	ANCORA	T
AND (1421)			
ANDAR			
PORQUE POR ANDAR CONMIGO	82	THE CONDOLENCE	EPI
ANDRA			
TIN' ANDRA, TIN' HEROA, TINA THEON,	189	HUGH SELWYN: 3	26
ANDROMEDA			
ANDROMEDA WAS OFFERED TO A SEA-SERPENT	222	SEXTUS PROP: 8	22
AND RELEASED THE MAIDEN ANDROMEDA.	237	ABU SALAMMAMM	9
ANEAR			
COME NOT ANEAR THE DARK-BROWED SOPHIST	263	ALF'S EIGHTH	8
ANECDOTES			
AND TELL ANECDOTES OF CYBELE!	86	SALUTATION 2ND	29
ANGELIC			
ALL THIS ANGELIC ASPECT CAN RETURN	42	HER MONUMENT	37
ANGELS			
AND ALL THE ANGELS SAT ABOUT	45	FROM HEINE: 4	3
ANGER			
WHO HAS BROUGHT THE FLAMING IMPERIAL ANGER?	133	FRONTIER GUARD	11
ANGLE			
AND ANGLE AND TERGIVERSATE	265	ALF'S TENTH	10
ANGLES			
REACHING AND STRIKING IN ANGLES,	120	GAME OF CHESS	4
ANGLICIZE			
GOOD "HEDGETHORN," FOR WE'LL ANGLICIZE YOUR NAME	161	CABARET DANCER	1
ANGRY			
WAS ANGRY WHEN THEY SPOKE YOUR NAME	36	FRANCESCA	6
ANGUISH			
SITH NO THING IS BUT TURNETH UNTO ANGUISH	37	THE YOUNG KING	27
ANGULAR			
MARSH-CRANBERRIES, THE RIBBED AND ANGULAR PODS	162	CABARET DANCER	19
ANHES			
AGRADIVA, ANHES, ARDENCA,	75	THE ALCHEMIST	16
ANHES OF ROCACOART, ARDENCA, AEMELIS,	75	THE ALCHEMIST	29
SWIFT-FOOT TO MY LADY ANHES,	106	DOMPNA POIS	36
GO FORTHRIGHT SINGING--ANHES, CEMBELINS.	153	NEAR PERIGORD	70
ANIENAN			
"ANIENAN SPRING WATER FALLS INTO FLAT-SPREAD POOLS."	212	SEXTUS PROP: 3	5
ANIMAL			
THAT MAN IS THE SUPERIOR ANIMAL.	102	MEDITATIO	3
SUCH ANIMAL INVIGORATING CARRIAGE	245	MOYEN SENSUEL	191
ANIMAM			
MANUS ANIMAM PINXIT,	18	DE AEGYPTO	9
ANKLES			
SPEAK OF THEIR KNEES AND ANKLES.	86	SALUTATION 2ND	33
AND KEEP MAD DOGS OFF HIS ANKLES.	212	SEXTUS PROP: 3	23
ANNALISTS			
ANNALISTS WILL CONTINUE TO RECORD ROMAN REPUTATIONS,	207	SEXTUS PROP: 1	16
ANNOUNCING			
WHO WANDERS ABOUT ANNOUNCING HIS SEX	82	THE CONDOLENCE	15
ANNUBIS			
THE GODS OF THE UNDERWORLD ATTEND ME, O ANNUBIS,	147	BEFORE SLEEP	6
ANOMALY			
('TIS AN ANOMALY IN OUR LARGE LAND OF FREEDOM,	245	MOYEN SENSUEL	217
ANOTHER			
IN ANOTHER FASHION THAT MORE SUITETH ME.	4	LA FRAISNE	8
THIS IS ANOTHER OF OUR ANCIENT LOVES.	63	QUIES	1
TO ANOTHER.	101	AMITIES	ST
ASK OF YOU THAN HOLD ANOTHER,	107	DOMPNA POIS	67
ONE BIRD CASTS ITS GLEAM ON ANOTHER,	139	SENNIN POEM	3
BEFORE IT ANOTHER HOUSE WHICH I DO NOT KNOW.	141	IDEA OF CHOAN	30

PAGE 19

ANOTHER -- ANY

	PAGE	TITLE	LINE
ANOTHER (CONTINUED)			
ONE AT CHALAIS, ANOTHER AT MALEMORT	151	NEAR PERIGORD	12
TO SING ONE THING WHEN YOUR SONG MEANS ANOTHER,	153	NEAR PERIGORD	89
ONLY ANOTHER MAN'S NOTE:	159	PSYCHOLOG HOUR	42
AND YOUR PAINTED GRIN ANOTHER,	162	CABARET DANCER	42
HAVE DRIVEN HIS WIFE FROM ONE RELIGIOUS EXCESS TO ANOTHER.	178	MOEURS CON: 1	8
"LET ANOTHER OAR CHURN THE WATER,	210	SEXTUS PROP: 2	26
"ANOTHER WHEEL, THE ARENA; MID-CROWD IS AS BAD AS MID-SEA."	210	SEXTUS PROP: 2	27
AND ANOTHER SAID "GET HIM PLUMB IN THE MIDDLE!	224	SEXTUS PROP:10	14
AND ANOTHER BROKE IN UPON THIS:	224	SEXTUS PROP:10	16
AND THEY GAVE ANOTHER YANK TO MY CLOAK,	225	SEXTUS PROP:10	26
GAINS YET ANOTHER CRUST	236	MIDDLE-AGED	11
THESE AND ANOTHER GODLET OF THAT DAY, YOUR DAY	240	MOYEN SENSUEL	47
AND YET ANOTHER, A "CHARMING MAN," "SWEET NATURE," BUT WAS GILDER,	240	MOYEN SENSUEL	57
ANOTHER BIT--AND AN OFFER	268	ANOTHER BIT	T
ANSWER			
BUT HIS ANSWER COMETH, AS WINDS AND AS LUTANY,	16	PRAISE YSOLT	5
WHAT ANSWER? O YE MYRIAD	35	HIS OWN FACE	4
MOVED NOT, NOR EVER ANSWER MY DESIRE,	60	TOMB AKR CAAR	3
AND ANSWER THEIR PRAYERS.	258	ALF'S SECOND	4
ANTEDATES			
AND ANTEDATES THE PHILADELPHIA CENTENNIAL.	239	MOYEN SENSUEL	26
ANTENNAE			
THE PURRING OF THE INVISIBLE ANTENNAE	113	TAME CAT	6
A-BRISTLE WITH ANTENNAE TO FEEL ROADS,	153	NEAR PERIGORD	62
MY SOUL'S ANTENNAE ARE PREY TO SUCH PERTURBATIONS,	247	PIERROTS	7
ANTHONY			
SHE'D FIND A MODEL FOR ST. ANTHONY	63	PHASELLUS ILLE	13
ANTIMACHUS			
THOUGH YOU MAKE A HASH OF ANTIMACHUS,	228	SEXTUS PROP:12	21
ANTIQUITY			
AN HOMELY, TRANSIENT ANTIQUITY.	114	EPILOGUE	8
ANTS			
LICE SWARM LIKE ANTS OVER OUR ACCOUTREMENTS.	139	SOUTH-FOLK	8
ANXIOUS			
THERE CANST THOU FIND ME, O THOU ANXIOUS THOU,	51	THE FLAME	34
AN ANXIOUS SENTIMENT WAS HIS EMPLOYMENT,	245	MOYEN SENSUEL	194
ANY			
I DO NOT LIKE TO REMEMBER THINGS ANY MORE.	5	LA FRAISNE	48
OR MORE SWEET IN TONE THAN ANY, BUT THAT I	24	THUS NINEVEH	21
THAT ANY FOLK E'ER HAD, HAST FROM US TAKEN;	37	THE YOUNG KING	19
SOUL, IF SHE MEET US THERE, WILL ANY RUMOUR	39	BLANDULA	13
MAY NOT MAKE BOAST OF ANY BETTER THING	40	ERAT HORA	6
NOBLE IN ANY PART	42	HER MONUMENT	54
OF ANY ONE WHO EVER KISSED YOU?	44	FROM HEINE: 1	8
BURN NOT WITH ME NOR ANY SAFFRON THING.	60	TOMB AKR CAAR	5
NEITHER COULD I PLAY UPON ANY REED IF I HAD ONE.	62	N. Y.	7
NOT ANY PROTECTOR	64	THE SEAFARER	26
NOR ANY WHIT ELSE SAVE THE WAVE'S SLASH,	65	THE SEAFARER	47
THAT ANY EARTH-WEAL ETERNAL STANDETH	66	THE SEAFARER	68
DAME NOR DAMSEL THERE'S NOT ANY	72	DIEU! QU'IL	10
WHO CAN UNDERSTAND ANY AFFAIR OF THEIRS. YET	97	THE BELLAIRES	10
I'LL HAVE NO OTHER LOVE AT ANY COST.	105	DOMPNA POIS	10
OR INSTALL ME IN ANY PROFESSION	117	THE LAKE ISLE	14
"HAVE YOU SEEN ANY OTHERS, ANY OF OUR LOT,	119	THE GYPSY	2
"HAVE YOU SEEN ANY OTHERS, ANY OF OUR LOT,	119	THE GYPSY	2
AND HE SAID, "HAVE YOU SEEN ANY OF OUR LOT?"	119	THE GYPSY	11
ANY BUT "MAJESTIES" AND ITALIAN NOBLES.	163	CABARET DANCER	66
GOD GRANT I DIE NOT BY ANY MAN'S STROKE	173	LANGUE D'OC: 2	21
OR ANY MORE CHILDREN.	179	MOEURS CON: 2	9
NOT, AT ANY RATE, AN ATTIC GRACE;	188	HUGH SELWYN: 2	4
THESE FOUGHT IN ANY CASE,	190	HUGH SELWYN: 4	1
PRO DOMO, IN ANY CASE . . .	190	HUGH SELWYN: 4	3
IF ANY MAN WOULD BE A LOVER	212	SEXTUS PROP: 3	17
AND AT ANY HOUR;	212	SEXTUS PROP: 3	25
AT ANY RATE I SHALL NOT HAVE MY EPITAPH IN A HIGH ROAD.	213	SEXTUS PROP: 3	38
IF ANY LAND SHRINK INTO A DISTANT SEACOAST,	216	SEXTUS PROP: 5	19

ANY -- APPLY

	PAGE	TITLE	LINE
ANY (CONTINUED)			
NOR AT MY FUNERAL EITHER WILL THERE BY ANY LONG TRAIL,	219	SEXTUS PROP: 6	13
THERE COMES, IT SEEMS, AND AT ANY RATE	222	SEXTUS PROP: 8	16
THERE WILL BE, IN ANY CASE, A STIR ON OLYMPUS.	222	SEXTUS PROP: 8	42
NOR WHETHER THERE BE ANY PATCH LEFT OF US	228	SEXTUS PROP:12	27
I DON'T QUITE SEE THE JOKE ANY MORE,	264	ALF'S EIGHTH	29
ANYHOW			
O'ER TRACKS OF OCEAN; SEEING THAT ANYHOW	65	THE SEAFARER	65
ANYONE			
WHEN ANYONE SAYS "RETURN," THE OTHERS ARE FULL OF SORROW.	127	BOWMEN OF SHU	6
NOR IS THERE ANYONE TO WHOM LOVERS ARE NOT SACRED AT MIDNIGHT	212	SEXTUS PROP: 3	15
ANYTHING			
BESPEAK THYSELF FOR ANYTHING.	8	NA AUDIART	19
WELL DO THIS AS ANYTHING ELSE.	100	ARIDES	5
HE WAS UNCERTAIN WHY HE SHOULD TRY TO FEEL LIKE ANYTHING ELSE,	118	ANCIENT WISDOM	3
NOR ANYTHING ELSE OF IMPORTANCE.	228	SEXTUS PROP:12	30
AOI			
AOI!	170	PHANOPOEIA	21
APART			
AND DREW ME APART	92	APRIL	2
SPLITS THE TWO STREAMS APART.	138	CITY OF CHOAN	10
BORE US TOGETHER . . . SURGING . . AND APART . . .	157	NEAR PERIGORD	178
THERE, BEYOND COLOUR, ESSENCE, SET APART,	250	DONNA MI PREGA	84
APATHEIN			
BECAME AN OLYMPIAN APATHEIN	202	AGE DEMANDED	39
A'PAYIN'			
A'PAYIN' US THE TAXES.	270	OF 600 M.P.'S	8
APE			
WITH CARAVANS, BUT NEVER AN APE OR A BEAR.	119	THE GYPSY	16
APELIOTA			
"COME, AUSTER, COME APELIOTA,	109	THE FAUN	5
APES			
"WITH APES OR BEARS?"	119	THE GYPSY	3
APHRODITE			
FLAWLESS AS APHRODITE,	103	LADIES	15
APOCRYPHAL			
"IN SACRED ODOUR"--(THAT'S APOCRYPHAL!)	156	NEAR PERIGORD	161
APOLLO			
O BRIGHT APOLLO,	189	HUGH SELWYN: 3	25
OUT-WEARIERS OF APOLLO WILL, AS WE KNOW, CONTINUE THEIR MARTIAN GENERALITIES,	207	SEXTUS PROP: 1	10
BACCHUS AND APOLLO IN FAVOUR OF IT,	208	SEXTUS PROP: 1	49
NEITHER CALLIOPE NOR APOLLO SUNG THESE THINGS INTO MY EAR,	217	SEXTUS PROP: 5	25
APOLOGIZES			
"THE EUPHRATES DENIES ITS PROTECTION TO THE PARTHIAN AND APOLOGIZES FOR CRASSUS,"	216	SEXTUS PROP: 5	16
APOSTLES			
BY AERY APOSTLES OF TERRENE DELIGHT,	39	BLANDULA	8
APPAREL			
YOU, MASTER BOB BROWNING, SPITE YOUR APPAREL	13	MESMERISM	7
APPARITION			
THE APPARITION OF THESE FACES IN THE CROWD;	109	IN THE METRO	1
APPARUIT			
APPARUIT	68	APPARUIT	T
APPEARS			
EVEN THAT SEMBLANCE THAT APPEARS AMONGST US	41	HER MONUMENT	23
APPLES			
WITH HIS BLOUSE FULL OF APPLES	181	MOEURS CON: 7	1
HAPPY SELLING POOR LOVES FOR CHEAP APPLES.	229	SEXTUS PROP:12	45
APPLICATION			
HE MADE NO IMMEDIATE APPLICATION	201	AGE DEMANDED	13
APPLIES			
TO THOSE TO WHOM IT APPLIES.	99	SALVATIONISTS	6
APPLY			
LET US APPLY IT IN ALL ITS OPPROBRIUM	99	SALVATIONISTS	5

PAGE 21

APPROACH -- 'ARFT

	PAGE	TITLE	LINE
APPROACH			
WHY DOES THE REALLY HANDSOME YOUNG WOMAN APPROACH ME IN SACKVILLE STREET	114	SIMULACRA	5
APPROACHES			
AND NO BOAT, NO CARRIAGE, APPROACHES.	142	UNMOVING CLOUD	16
APPROACHING			
NINE ADULTERIES, 12 LIAISONS, 64 FORNICATIONS AND SOMETHING APPROACHING A RAPE	100	TEMPERAMENTS	1
APPROBATION			
OF WELL-GOWNED APPROBATION	196	HUGH SELWIN:12	10
APPROVED			
THOUGH SOME APPROVED OF THEM, AND SOME DEPLORED 'EM.	242	MOYEN SENSUEL	108
APRICOT			
PEACH BOUGHS AND APRICOT BOUGHS HANG OVER A THOUSAND GATES,	131	AT TEN-SHIN	2
APRIL			
GREEN COME THE SHOOTS, AYE APRIL IN THE BRANCHES,	71	A VIRGINAL	11
APRIL	92	APRIL	T
APULEIUS			
SPEECH FOR PSYCHE IN THE GOLDEN BOOK OF APULEIUS	39	FOR PSYCHE	T
AQUEOUS			
LET THE MANES PUT OFF THEIR TERROR, LET THEM PUT OFF THEIR AQUEOUS BODIES WITH FIRE.	76	THE ALCHEMIST	51
A-QUIVER			
"ONCE MORE IN DELOS, ONCE MORE IS THE ALTAR A-QUIVER.	90	SURGIT FAMA	16
ARABIA			
AND SO FORTH, AUGUSTUS. "VIRGIN ARABIA SHAKES IN HER INMOST DWELLING."	216	SEXTUS PROP: 5	18
ARABIAN			
AND WITH MORE THAN ARABIAN ODOURS,	225	SEXTUS PROP:10	20
ARAB'S			
A SORT OF ARAB'S DREAM IN THE NIGHT.	262	ALF'S SEVENTH	16
ARAGON			
VERS AND CANZONE, TILL THAT DAMN'D SON OF ARAGON,	22	MARVOIL	8
ARAGON CURSING IN ARAGON, BEZIERS BUSY AT BEZIERS--	22	MARVOIL	16
ARAGON CURSING IN ARAGON, BEZIERS BUSY AT BEZIERS--	22	MARVOIL	16
TO ALL MEN EXCEPT THE KING OF ARAGON,	23	MARVOIL	31
ARAGONESE			
AND ONE LEAN ARAGONESE CURSING THE SENESCHAL	22	MARVOIL	14
ALL FOR ONE HALF-BALD, KNOCK-KNEE'D KING OF THE ARAGONESE,	22	MARVOIL	21
ARBOUR			
IS A PLEACHED ARBOUR;	121	PROVINC DESERT	10
ARBOURS			
A NET-WORK OF ARBOURS AND PASSAGES AND COVERED WAYS,	141	IDEA OF CHOAN	22
ARCADIA			
CAME END, AT LAST, TO THAT ARCADIA.	199	MAUBERLEY: 2	4
ARCADIAN			
WANDERED THROUGH THE ARCADIAN PRAIRIES	222	SEXTUS PROP: 8	25
ARCANE			
THE ARCANE SPIRIT OF THE WHOLE MANKIND	42	HER MONUMENT	44
ARCHAIC			
HERE THEY ARE WITH NOTHING ARCHAIC ABOUT THEM.	85	SALUTATION 2ND	8
ARCHES			
ARCHES WORN OLD AND PALACES MADE COMMON,	40	ROME	3
ARCHITECT			
AND AN ARCHITECT.	179	MOEURS CON: 4	7
ARDENCA			
AGRADIVA, ANHES, ARDENCA,	75	THE ALCHEMIST	16
ANHES OF ROCACOART, ARDENCA, AEMELIS,	75	THE ALCHEMIST	29
ARDOUR			
NOT TO DELIGHT, BUT IN AN ARDOUR OF THOUGHT	249	DONNA MI PREGA	31
ARE (214)			
ARENA			
"ANOTHER WHEEL, THE ARENA; MID-CROWD IS AS BAD AS MID-SEA;"	210	SEXTUS PROP: 2	27
'ARF			
DID I 'EAR IT 'ARF IN A DOZE:	262	ALF'S SEVENTH	1
OLE KATE WOULD GIT HER 'ARF A PINT	271	OLE KATE	3
'ARFT			
FER 'ARFT A PINT O' BITTER?"	270	OF 600 M.P.'S	20

ARGO -- ARRANGE

	PAGE	TITLE	LINE
ARGO			
WITHOUT IXION, AND WITHOUT THE SONS OF MENOETIUS AND THE ARGO AND WITHOUT JOVE'S GRAVE AND THE TITANS.	218	SEXTUS PROP: 5	52
ARIDES			
ARIDES	100	ARIDES	T
THE BASHFUL ARIDES	100	ARIDES	1
ARIEL			
CALIBAN CASTS OUT ARIEL.	189	HUGH SELWYN: 3	8
ARIGHT			
"HI! HARRY, HEAR ME, FOR I SING ARIGHT	172	LANGUE D'OC: 1	10
AND SAVE THEY KNOW'T ARIGHT FROM NATURE'S SOURCE	248	DONNA MI PREGA	10
'ARK			
YOU 'ARK TO THE SARGENT,	260	ALF'S FOURTH	16
ARLES			
GRAY ARLES AND BIAUCAIRE,	119	THE GYPSY	10
ARLES GREATLY ALTERED,	122	PROVINC DESERT	60
ARM			
THAT IS, THE UPPER ARM,	180	MOEURS CON: 5	5
SOME QUICK TO ARM,	190	HUGH SELWYN: 4	4
ARMED			
STOLE HER AWAY FOR HIMSELF, KEPT HER AGAINST ARMED	123	PROVINC DESERT	75
ARMOUR			
THE IMPERIAL GUARDS COME FORTH FROM THE GOLDEN HOUSE WITH THEIR ARMOUR A-GLEAMING.	129	THE RIVER SONG	34
YIELDED AN ARMOUR	202	AGE DEMANDED	31
I WERE ABLE TO LEAD HEROES INTO ARMOUR, I WOULD NOT,	217	SEXTUS PROP: 5	38
ARMOURED			
THEIR HORSES' ARMOURED FEET	111	IMAGE ORLEANS	6
ARMOURER'S			
STRAY GLEAMS ON HANGING MAIL, AN ARMOURER'S TORCH-FLARE	155	NEAR PERIGORD	134
ARMOURESS			
TYBALDE AND THAT ARMOURESS	11	OF THE GIBBET	7
ARMS			
TO WHOM MY BREAST AND ARMS ARE EVER WARM,	21	IN DURANCE	43
CLOSE IN MY ARMS HERE.	23	MARVOIL	43
THOU WILT IN MY WHITE ARMS THERE,	47	FROM HEINE: 7	9
YET SHALL MY WHITE ARMS HOLD THEE,	48	FROM HEINE: 7	9
THE SAP HAS ASCENDED MY ARMS,	62	A GIRL	2
THE BRANCHES GROW OUT OF ME, LIKE ARMS.	62	A GIRL	5
SLIGHT ARE HER ARMS, YET THEY HAVE BOUND ME STRAITLY	71	A VIRGINAL	4
THINE ARMS ARE AS A YOUNG SAPLING UNDER THE BARK;	91	DANCE FIGURE	10
WITH ARMS EXALTED, WITH FORE-ARMS	93	LES MILLWIN	8
LET US TAKE ARMS AGAINST THIS SEA OF STUPIDITIES--	99	SALVATIONISTS	12
SAD GARMENT DRAPED ON HER SLENDER ARMS.	214	SEXTUS PROP: 4	20
IN HOW MANY VARIED EMBRACES, OUR CHANGING ARMS,	220	SEXTUS PROP: 7	10
HE THRILLS TO ILIAN ARMS,	228	SEXTUS PROP:12	33
ARMY			
WHO HAS BROUGHT THE ARMY WITH DRUMS AND WITH KETTLE-DRUMS?	133	FRONTIER GUARD	12
FOR HIS ARMY IS LEGION,	237	ABU SALAMMAMM	11
HIS ARMY IS A THOUSAND AND FORTY-EIGHT SOLDIERS	237	ABU SALAMMAMM	12
ARNAUT			
A POOR CLERK I, "ARNAUT THE LESS" THEY CALL ME,	22	MARVOIL	1
THEY'LL KNOW MORE OF ARNAUT OF MARVOIL	22	MARVOIL	25
GLAD TO HEAR ARNAUT,	121	PROVINC DESERT	26
ARNAUT AND RICHARD LODGE BENEATH CHALUS:	155	NEAR PERIGORD	128
AND ARNAUT PARRIES: "DID HE LOVE YOUR SISTER?"	155	NEAR PERIGORD	146
ENDS OUR DISCUSSION. ARNAUT ENDS	156	NEAR PERIGORD	160
OF ARNAUT DE MAREUIL, I THOUGHT, "QU'IEU GUI AVINEN,	166	FISH & SHADOW	19
AROSE			
AND WHEN I AROSE TO GO	110	THE ENCOUNTER	3
AROSE TOWARD NEWMAN AS THE WHISKEY WARMED.	193	SIENA MI FE	12
AROUET			
IMPRESSIONS OF FRANCOIS-MARIE AROUET (DE VOLTAIRE)	167	OF AROUET	T
AROUND			
HER GOLD IS SPREAD, ABOVE, AROUND, INWOVEN;	49	OF SPLENDOUR	4
NOT TIED TO THE RING AROUND,	261	ALF'S SIXTH	19
AND BASIL WAS THE GREEK THAT RODE AROUND	264	ALF'S NINTH	18
ARRANGE			
AND WHEN THEY WOULD NOT LET HIM ARRANGE	97	AESTHETICS	16

PAGE 23

ARRANGED -- AS

	PAGE	TITLE	LINE
ARRANGED			
HE STROKED THOSE WHICH WERE ALREADY ARRANGED, ...	97	AESTHETICS	18
ARRANGEMENTS			
(AMID AERIAL FLOWERS) . . . TIME FOR ARRANGEMENTS--	199	MAUBERLEY: 2	13
ARRIMON			
NO ONE HEARS SAVE ARRIMON LUC D'ESPARO--	154	NEAR PERIGORD	119
SIR ARRIMON COUNTS ON HIS FINGERS, MONTFORT, ...	155	NEAR PERIGORD	121
ARRIVED			
AND I SAID: "THAT WAS BEFORE I ARRIVED."	182	MOEURS CON: 8	4
ARROGANCE			
AND ALL ARROGANCE OF EARTHEN RICHES, ...	66	THE SEAFARER	83
ARROWS			
THE HORSES ARE WELL TRAINED, THE GENERALS HAVE IVORY			
ARROWS AND QUIVERS ORNAMENTED WITH FISH-SKIN. ..	127	BOWMEN OF SHU	19
AND OTHERS HELD ONTO ARROWS, ...	224	SEXTUS PROP:10	8
ARS			
BEFORE THE "ARS POETICA" OF HIRAM MAXIM.	239	MOYEN SENSUEL	34
ARSENIC			
GREEN ARSENIC SMEARED ON AN EGG-WHITE CLOTH, ...	113	L'ART, 1910	1
ART			
WHILE IN HIS HEART ART THOU?	17	PRAISE YSOLT	58
'THOUT MASK OR GAUNTLET, AND ART LAID	19	FOR E. MCC	16
SO ART THOU WITH US, BEING GOOD TO KEEP	19	FOR E. MCC	21
FOR EVEN AS THOU ART HOLLOW BEFORE I FILL THEE WITH			
THIS PARCHMENT, ...	23	MARVOIL	37
ROME THAT ART ROME'S ONE SOLE LAST MONUMENT, ...	40	ROME	9
WHO ART NOW	41	HER MONUMENT	2
O GLANCE, WHEN THOU WAST STILL AS THOU ART NOW, ...	41	HER MONUMENT	10
IF THOU ART	42	HER MONUMENT	50
YET IF THOU ART	42	HER MONUMENT	53
TOWARD SUCH A WORK OF ART.	45	FROM HEINE: 5	12
THOU ART A MAID WITH NO BREASTS, ...	62	N. Y.	9
THOU ART SLENDER AS A SILVER REED.	62	N. Y.	10
THE TURBULENT AND UNDISCIPLINED HOST OF ART			
STUDENTS--	93	LES MILLWIN	5
CROSSED IN GREAT FUTURISTIC X'S, THE ART STUDENTS	93	LES MILLWIN	9
NOR WITH SUCH ART	105	DOMPNA POIS	14
"SST! MY GOOD FELLOW, ART AWAKE OR SLEEPING?	172	LANGUE D'OC: 1	6
"LOVELY THOU ART, TO HOLD ME CLOSE AND KISST, ...	177	LANGUE D'OC: 4	11
HE STROVE TO RESUSCITATE THE DEAD ART	187	E. P. ODE	2
HIS ART, BUT AN ART	198	MAUBERLEY: 1	11
HIS ART, BUT AN ART	198	MAUBERLEY: 1	11
AND TRY TO WRENCH HER IMPULSE INTO ART.	235	TO WHISTLER	13
AN ART! YOU ALL RESPECT THE ARTS, FROM THAT INFANT			
TICK	239	MOYEN SENSUEL	13
I KNEW A TOURIST AGENT, ONE WHOSE ART IS	245	MOYEN SENSUEL	209
THOU ART SO FAIR ATTIRED THAT EVERY MAN AND EACH	250	DONNA MI PREGA	89
ARTEMIS			
WE WHO HAVE SEEN EVEN ARTEMIS A-BINDING HER SANDALS,	104	ANCORA	6
ARTICULATE			
I WOULD ARTICULATE YOUR PERDAMNATION.	238	MOYEN SENSUEL	8
ARTIST			
"I AM AN ARTIST, YOU HAVE TRIED BOTH METIERS."	156	NEAR PERIGORD	152
ARTISTS			
ARTISTS BROKEN AGAINST HER, ...	92	THE REST	3
ARTIST'S			
DESTROYING, CERTAINLY, THE ARTIST'S URGE, ...	202	AGE DEMANDED	43
ARTS			
AND HAVE SOME BREATH FOR BEAUTY AND THE ARTS.	20	IN DURANCE	16
SPANISH AND PARIS, LOVE OF THE ARTS PART OF YOUR			
GEISHA-CULTURE!	163	CABARET DANCER	52
AN ART! YOU ALL RESPECT THE ARTS, FROM THAT INFANT			
TICK	239	MOYEN SENSUEL	13
ART'S			
PHILISTIA'S POMP AND ART'S POMPOSITIES!	46	TRANSLATOR	4
AS			
DREAMS, WORDS, AND THEY ARE AS JEWELS, ...	6	CINO	5
WERE LACK-LAND CINO, E'EN AS I AM, ...	7	CINO	35
AS IVY FINGERS CLUTCHING THROUGH	8	NA AUDIART	4
FINDS THE EARTH AS BITTER	9	NA AUDIART	44
AS NOW SEEMS IT SWEET, ...	9	NA AUDIART	45

PAGE 24

AS

		PAGE	TITLE	LINE
AS	(CONTINUED)			
	AS THEN ONLY IN DREAMS,	9	NA AUDIART	47
	(SUCH AS I DRINK TO MINE FASHION)	10	FOR THIS YULE	15
	I SKOAL TO THE EYES AS GREY-BLOWN MERE	10	FOR THIS YULE	22
	AS A FOOL THAT MOCKETH HIS DRUE'S DISDEIGN.	11	OF THE GIBBET	12
	AS LIPS SHRINK BACK WHEN WE FEEL THE STRAIN	11	OF THE GIBBET	20
	JUMP TO YOUR SENSE AND GIVE PRAISE AS WE'D LIEF DO.	13	MESMERISM	8
	YOU WHEEZE AS A HEAD-COLD LONG-TONSILLED CALLIOPE,	13	MESMERISM	9
	MAD AS A HATTER BUT SURELY NO MYOPE,	13	MESMERISM	11
	BROAD AS ALL OCEAN AND LEANIN' MAN-KIN'ARDS.	13	MESMERISM	12
	HEART THAT WAS BIG AS THE BOWELS OF VESUVIUS,	13	MESMERISM	13
	WORDS THAT WERE WING'D AS HER SPARKS IN ERUPTION,	13	MESMERISM	14
	EAGLED AND THUNDERED AS JUPITER PLUVIUS,	13	MESMERISM	15
	SUCH AS ARE UP AND WIDE,	14	FAMAM CANO	10
	AS WE HAD SEEN HIM YESTERDAY.	14	FAMAM CANO	22
	SUCH AN ONE AS THE WORLD FEELS	14	FAMAM CANO	24
	SUCH AN ONE AS WOMEN DRAW AWAY FROM	15	FAMAM CANO	33
	AS HIS PARDONS THE HABIT,	15	FAMAM CANO	46
	BUT HIS ANSWER COMETH, AS WINDS AND AS LUTANY,	16	PRAISE YSOLT	5
	BUT HIS ANSWER COMETH, AS WINDS AND AS LUTANY,	16	PRAISE YSOLT	5
	AS A VAGUE CRYING UPON THE NIGHT	16	PRAISE YSOLT	6
	AS DARK RED CIRCLES FILLED WITH DUST.	16	PRAISE YSOLT	13
	THE WORDS ARE AS LEAVES, OLD BROWN LEAVES IN THE SPRING TIME	16	PRAISE YSOLT	19
	WHITE WORDS AS SNOW FLAKES BUT THEY ARE COLD,	16	PRAISE YSOLT	21
	AS MOONLIGHT CALLING,	16	PRAISE YSOLT	28
	AS THE MOON CALLETH THE TIDES,	16	PRAISE YSOLT	29
	AS THE MOON DOTH FROM THE SEA,	17	PRAISE YSOLT	32
	A WOMAN AS FIRE UPON THE PINE WOODS	17	PRAISE YSOLT	00
	AS THE FLAME CRIETH UNTO THE SAP.	17	PRAISE YSOLT	41
	AS FLAME LEAVETH THE EMBERS SO WENT SHE UNTO NEW FORESTS	17	PRAISE YSOLT	43
	TILL MY SOUL SENT A WOMAN AS THE SUN:	17	PRAISE YSOLT	47
	YEA AS THE SUN CALLETH TO THE SEED,	17	PRAISE YSOLT	48
	AS THE SPRING UPON THE BOUGH	17	PRAISE YSOLT	49
	GONE AS A GUST OF BREATH	19	FOR E. MCC	10
	AS MEMORABLE BROKEN BLADES THAT BE	19	FOR E. MCC	17
	KEPT AS BOLD TROPHIES OF OLD PAGEANTRY.	19	FOR E. MCC	18
	AS OLD TOLEDOS PAST THEIR DAYS OF WAR	19	FOR E. MCC	19
	AND WOULD MEET KINDRED EVEN AS I AM,	20	IN DURANCE	24
	AS I HIDE MOST THE WHILE	21	IN DURANCE	30
	FOR THAT I LOVE YE AS THE WIND THE TREES	21	IN DURANCE	44
	THAT 'THOUT HIM, SAVE THE ASPEN, WERE AS DUMB	21	IN DURANCE	47
	AS FOR WILL AND TESTAMENT I LEAVE NONE,	22	MARVOIL	27
	AS NE'ER HAD I OTHER, AND WHEN THE WIND BLOWS,	23	MARVOIL	35
	FOR EVEN AS THOU ART HOLLOW BEFORE I FILL THEE WITH THIS PARCHMENT,	23	MARVOIL	37
	EVEN AS THOU SHALT SOON HAVE THIS PARCHMENT.	23	MARVOIL	44
	EVEN AS I KEEP HER IMAGE IN MY HEART HERE.	23	MARVOIL	48
	AS LESSER MEN DRINK WINE."	24	THUS NINEVEH	23
	YET THEIR EYES ARE AS THE EYES OF A MAID TO HER LOVER,	25	THE WHITE STAG	3
	ARE FUSED IN IT AS FLAMES OF AN ALTAR FIRE!	25	GUIDO INVITES	10
	EVEN AS ARE THY STARS	27	NIGHT LITANY	45
	SWIFT AS THE KING WOLF WAS I AND AS STRONG	30	PIERE VIDAL	8
	SWIFT AS THE KING WOLF WAS I AND AS STRONG	30	PIERE VIDAL	8
	AS DID FIRST SCORN, THEN LIPS OF THE PENAUTIER!	30	PIERE VIDAL	17
	SWIFT CAME THE LOBA, AS A BRANCH THAT'S CAUGHT,	31	PIERE VIDAL	26
	SILENT MY MATE CAME AS THE NIGHT WAS STILL.	31	PIERE VIDAL	32
	SILENT AS FATE IS, AND AS STRONG UNTIL	31	PIERE VIDAL	35
	SILENT AS FATE IS, AND AS STRONG UNTIL	01	PIERE VIDAL	35
	GOD! SHE WAS WHITE THEN, SPLENDID AS SOME TOMB	31	PIERE VIDAL	30
	BEHOLD ME SHRIVELLED AS AN OLD OAK'S TRUNK	31	PIERE VIDAL	52
	SO SIMPLY ELEMENT AS WHAT I AM.	32	PARACELSUS	5
	WE SEEM AS STATUES ROUND WHOSE HIGH-RISEN BASE	32	PARACELSUS	11
	NO MAN HATH DARED AND WON HIS DARE AS I:	32	PIERE VIDAL	55
	THEY WHINED AS HE WALKED OUT CALM BETWEEN,	34	GOODLY FERE	43
	AND THAT THE WORLD SHOULD DRY AS A DEAD LEAF,	36	FRANCESCA	9
	OR AS A DANDELION SEED-POD AND BE SWEPT AWAY,	36	FRANCESCA	10
	HIM DO WE PRAY AS TO A LORD MOST RIGHTEOUS	37	THE YOUNG KING	36
	HE PLEASE TO PARDON, AS TRUE PARDON IS,	37	THE YOUNG KING	38

PAGE 25

AS

	PAGE	TITLE	LINE
AS (CONTINUED)			
BLIND EYES AND SHADOWS THAT ARE FORMED AS MEN;	38	BALLATETTA	2
SO DELICATE AS SHE IS, WHEN THE SUN	38	BALLATETTA	8
AND ALL THE MAIDENS OF ROME, AS MANY AS THEY WERE,	38	LADY'S LIFE	9
AND ALL THE MAIDENS OF ROME, AS MANY AS THEY WERE,	38	LADY'S LIFE	9
ALL NIGHT, AND AS THE WIND LIETH AMONG	39	FOR PSYCHE	1
NOR HELD ME SAVE AS AIR THAT BRUSHETH BY ONE	39	FOR PSYCHE	3
CLOSE, AND AS THE PETALS OF FLOWERS IN FALLING	39	FOR PSYCHE	4
SEEMED OVER ME TO HOVER LIGHT AS LEAVES :..........	39	FOR PSYCHE	6
AND, AS THE RAY OF SUN ON HANGING FLOWERS	40	ERAT HORA	2
THAN TO HAVE WATCHED THAT HOUR AS IT PASSED.	40	ERAT HORA	7
O GLANCE, WHEN THOU WAST STILL AS THOU ART NOW. ...	41	HER MONUMENT	10
THEREFORE LET US ACT AS IF WE WERE	43	MR. HOUSMAN	4
SIGHING AS THOU DOST THROUGH THE GOLDEN SPEECH."	43	SATIEMUS	6
OR, AS OUR LAUGHTERS MINGLE EACH WITH EACH, ...	43	SATIEMUS	7
AS CRUSHED LIPS TAKE THEIR RESPITE FITFULLY, ...	43	SATIEMUS	8
HATH AS FAINT LUTE-STRINGS IN ITS DIM ACCORD	43	SATIEMUS	15
WITH TIMES TOLD OVER AS WE TELL BY ROTE;	43	SATIEMUS	17
AS THEY WERE HIS AND MINE.	47	FROM HEINE: 7	14
THIS THING THAT MOVES AS MAN IS NO MORE MORTAL. ...	51	THE FLAME	38
THOU ART SLENDER AS A SILVER REED.	62	N. Y.	10
BE IN ME AS THE ETERNAL MOODS	67	DORIA	1
AS TRANSIENT THINGS ARE--	67	DORIA	3
AS I? WILL THE NEW ROSES MISS THEE?	67	THE CLOAK	6
GONE AS WIND! THE CLOTH OF THE MAGICAL HANDS!	68	APPARUIT	22
AND ONE GROPES IN THESE THINGS AS DELICATE	69	SUB MARE	5
AND LEFT ME CLOAKED AS WITH A GAUZE OF AETHER;	71	A VIRGINAL	5
AS WITH SWEET LEAVES; AS WITH SUBTLE CLEARNESS. ...	71	A VIRGINAL	6
AS WITH SWEET LEAVES; AS WITH SUBTLE CLEARNESS. ...	71	A VIRGINAL	6
SOFT AS SPRING WIND THAT'S COME FROM BIRCHEN BOWERS.	71	A VIRGINAL	10
AS WINTER'S WOUND WITH HER SLEIGHT HAND SHE STAUNCHES, ...	71	A VIRGINAL	12
AS WHITE THEIR BARK, SO WHITE THIS LADY'S HOURS. ..	71	A VIRGINAL	14
WITH FEAR, AS HALF-AWAKENED;	74	THE RETURN	6
AS IF THE SNOW SHOULD HESITATE	74	THE RETURN	7
AS YOU MOVE AMONG THE BRIGHT TREES;	75	THE ALCHEMIST	2
AS YOUR VOICES, UNDER THE LARCHES OF PARADISE	75	THE ALCHEMIST	3
AS A TIMOROUS WENCH FROM A CENTAUR	81	TENZONE	3
AS IF HE HAD JUST DISCOVERED IT.	82	THE CONDOLENCE	16
SHE IS BEAUTIFUL AS THE SUNLIGHT, AND AS FLUID. ...	84	ORTUS	5
SHE IS BEAUTIFUL AS THE SUNLIGHT, AND AS FLUID. ...	84	ORTUS	5
AS SHE SITS IN THE GREAT CHAIR	87	ALBATRE	6
GO AS A GREAT WAVE OF COOL WATER, ...	88	COMMISSION	4
I COME TO YOU AS A GROWN CHILD	89	A PACT	3
THINE ARMS ARE AS A YOUNG SAPLING UNDER THE BARK; .	91	DANCE FIGURE	10
THY FACE AS A RIVER WITH LIGHTS.	91	DANCE FIGURE	11
WHITE AS AN ALMOND ARE THY SHOULDERS;	91	DANCE FIGURE	12
AS NEW ALMONDS STRIPPED FROM THE HUSK.	91	DANCE FIGURE	13
AS A RILLET AMONG THE SEDGE ARE THY HANDS UPON ME;	91	DANCE FIGURE	19
SINGING AS WELL AS I SING, NONE BETTER;	96	DUM CAPITOLIUM	2
SINGING AS WELL AS I SING, NONE BETTER;	96	DUM CAPITOLIUM	2
STOPPED IN THEIR PLAY AS SHE PASSED THEM	96	AESTHETICS	3
AS I HAVE TAUGHT THEM TO TELL IT;	96	DUM CAPITOLIUM	4
AS A BATHTUB LINED WITH WHITE PORCELAIN, ...	100	THE BATH TUB	1
INDIFFERENT AND DISCOURAGED HE THOUGHT HE MIGHT AS WELL DO THIS AS ANYTHING ELSE.	100	ARIDES	4
WELL DO THIS AS ANYTHING ELSE.	100	ARIDES	5
I WHO AM AS MUCH EMBITTERED	102	TO DIVES	2
AS YOU ARE WITH USELESS RICHES?	102	TO DIVES	4
FLAWLESS AS APHRODITE, ...	103	LADIES	15
FAINT, ALMOST, AS THE LINES OF CRUELTY ABOUT YOUR CHIN, ...	103	LADIES	19
ASSAILS ME, AND CONCERNS ME ALMOST AS LITTLE.	103	LADIES	20
FOR, AS TO COLOUR AND EYES	105	DOMPNA POIS	25
AS I'VE FOR YOU, SUCH FLAME-LAP.	107	DOMPNA POIS	65
CLEAR AS FROST ON THE GRASS-BLADE, ...	108	FAN-PIECE	1
AS COOL AS THE PALE WET LEAVES	109	ALBA	1
AS COOL AS THE PALE WET LEAVES	109	ALBA	1
IS NOT SO BEAUTIFUL AS SHE WAS, ...	116	THE TEA SHOP	2
AS SHE BROUGHT US OUR MUFFINS	116	THE TEA SHOP	7
I HAVE SEEN THE FIELDS, PALE, CLEAR AS AN EMERALD,	122	PROVINC DESERT	54
AS FAR AS CHO-FU-SA.	131	RIVER-MER WIFE	29

PAGE 26

AS

		PAGE	TITLE	LINE
AS	(CONTINUED)			
	AS FAR AS CHO-FU-SA.	131	RIVER-MER WIFE	29
	HAUGHTY THEIR STEPS AS THEY GO IN TO GREAT BANQUETS,	132	AT TEN-SHIN	19
	AND YOUR FATHER, WHO WAS BRAVE AS A LEOPARD,	135	EXILE'S LETTER	36
	TO THE DYNASTIC TEMPLE, WITH WATER ABOUT IT CLEAR AS BLUE JADE,	135	EXILE'S LETTER	50
	AS WE ARE DEPARTING.	137	TAKING LEAVE	9
	SHEER AS THE MOUNTAINS.	138	NEAR SHOKU	2
	AS BUTEI OF KAN HAD MADE THE HIGH GOLDEN LOTUS	141	IDEA OF CHOAN	28
	AS A PLEASANT TICKLE,	145	SALUTATION 3RD	29
	AS FOR YOU, YOU WILL ROT IN THE EARTH,	146	MONUMENTUM AER	6
	OF DRY AIR, AS CLEAR AS METAL.	146	CANTILATIONS	12
	OF DRY AIR, AS CLEAR AS METAL.	146	CANTILATIONS	12
	YOU WERE GONE UP AS A ROCKET,	147	BEFORE SLEEP	14
	AS CAUGHT BY DANTE IN THE LAST WALLOW OF HELL--	151	NEAR PERIGORD	22
	(ST. LEIDER HAD DONE AS MUCH AS POLHONAC,	153	NEAR PERIGORD	86
	(ST. LEIDER HAD DONE AS MUCH AS POLHONAC,	153	NEAR PERIGORD	86
	SINGING A DIFFERENT STAVE, AS CLOSELY HIDDEN.)	153	NEAR PERIGORD	87
	AND TEN YEARS AFTER, OR TWENTY, AS YOU WILL,	155	NEAR PERIGORD	127
	DISPRAISES HIS OWN SKILL?--THAT'S AS YOU WILL.	155	NEAR PERIGORD	143
	AS FOR ME;	158	PSYCHOLOG HOUR	19
	HERE'S PEPITA, TALL AND SLIM AS AN EGYPTIAN MUMMY,	162	CABARET DANCER	18
	AS LIGHT AS THE SHADOW OF THE FISH	166	FISH & SHADOW	5
	AS LIGHT AS THE SHADOW OF THE FISH	166	FISH & SHADOW	5
	LIGHT AS THE SHADOW OF THE FISH	166	FISH & SHADOW	20
	AND TO FOLLOW AFTER FRIENDSHIP, AS THEY CALL IT,	168	OF AROUET	33
	AS I DESIROUS,	174	LANGUE D'OC: 3	10
	NOR FEEL MY ACHE--GREAT AS IT IS,	174	LANGUE D'OC: 3	21
	AS SHE DESIRE,	175	LANGUE D'OC: 3	54
	'GAINST HER I PRIZE NOT AS A GLOVE	176	LANGUE D'OC: 3	71
	DESPITE THE CUCKOLD, DO THOU AS THOU LIST,	177	LANGUE D'OC: 4	13
	HER MIND IS, AS EVER, UNCULTIVATED,	179	MOEURS CON: 2	6
	NOW, QUENCHED AS THE BRAND OF MELEAGAR,	181	MOEURS CON: 6	3
	"OH! ABELARD!" AS IF THE TOPIC	181	MOEURS CON: 7	8
	DARING AS NEVER BEFORE, WASTAGE AS NEVER BEFORE.	190	HUGH SELWYN: 4	20
	DARING AS NEVER BEFORE, WASTAGE AS NEVER BEFORE.	190	HUGH SELWYN: 4	20
	FORTITUDE AS NEVER BEFORE	190	HUGH SELWYN: 4	23
	FRANKNESS AS NEVER BEFORE,	190	HUGH SELWYN: 4	24
	DISILLUSIONS AS NEVER TOLD IN THE OLD DAYS,	190	HUGH SELWYN: 4	25
	AROSE TOWARD NEWMAN AS THE WHISKEY WARMED.	193	SIENA MI FE	12
	"I WAS AS POOR AS YOU ARE;	194	MR. NIXON	5
	"I WAS AS POOR AS YOU ARE;	194	MR. NIXON	5
	"THE TIP'S A GOOD ONE, AS FOR LITERATURE	194	MR. NIXON	16
	AS THOU HAST SUBJECTS KNOWN,	197	ENVOI (1919)	4
	AS ROSES MIGHT, IN MAGIC AMBER LAID,	197	ENVOI (1919)	13
	MAY BE AS FAIR AS HERS,	197	ENVOI (1919)	21
	MAY BE AS FAIR AS HERS,	197	ENVOI (1919)	21
	LEFT HIM AS EPILOGUES.	200	MAUBERLEY: 2	37
	AS THE RED-BEAKED STEEDS OF	201	AGE DEMANDED	3
	TEMPERED AS IF	201	AGE DEMANDED	11
	LEADING, AS HE WELL KNEW,	202	AGE DEMANDED	59
	AS ANADYOMENE IN THE OPENING	204	MEDALLION	7
	A BASKET-WORK OF BRAIDS WHICH SEEM AS IF THEY WERE	204	MEDALLION	10
	BRIGHT IN ITS SUAVE BOUNDING-LINE, AS,	204	MEDALLION	14
	OUT-WEARIERS OF APOLLO WILL, AS WE KNOW, CONTINUE THEIR MARTIAN GENERALITIES,	207	SEXTUS PROP: 1	10
	AS THE FORESTS OF PHAEACIA.	209	SEXTUS PROP: 1	54
	"ANOTHER WHEEL, THE ARENA; MID-CROWD IS AS BAD AS MID-SEA."	210	SEXTUS PROP: 2	27
	"ANOTHER WHEEL, THE ARENA; MID-CROWD IS AS BAD AS MID-SEA."	210	SEXTUS PROP: 2	27
	NINE GIRLS, FROM AS MANY COUNTRYSIDES	211	SEXTUS PROP: 2	33
	WHO SO INDECOROUS AS TO SHED THE PURE GORE OF A SUITOR?!	212	SEXTUS PROP: 3	26
	OF SOME AS YET UNCATALOGUED SAND;	213	SEXTUS PROP: 3	37
	MUCH CONVERSATION IS AS GOOD AS HAVING A HOME.	214	SEXTUS PROP: 4	10
	MUCH CONVERSATION IS AS GOOD AS HAVING A HOME.	214	SEXTUS PROP: 4	10
	CALLISTO, DISGUISED AS A BEAR,	222	SEXTUS PROP: 8	24
	OR JOVE, HARSH AS HE IS, MAY TURN ASIDE YOUR ULTIMATE DAY.	222	SEXTUS PROP: 8	38
	PERFECT AS DURER!	235	TO WHISTLER	7

PAGE 27

AS -- ASIDE

		PAGE	TITLE	LINE
AS	(CONTINUED)			
	AS GOLD THAT RAINS ABOUT SOME BURIED KING.	236	MIDDLE-AGED	2
	AS THE FINE FLAKES,	236	MIDDLE-AGED	3
	AS THE FINE DUST, IN THE HID CELL	236	MIDDLE-AGED	8
	COULD I BUT SPEAK AS 'TWERE IN THE "RESTORATION"	238	MOYEN SENSUEL	7
	THAN IF I TREAT THE NATION AS A WHOLE.	239	MOYEN SENSUEL	43
	AS HELD BEFORE HIM IN THAT UNSULLIED MIRROR	241	MOYEN SENSUEL	93
	AS HE INHALED THE STILL FUMES OF RICE-POWDER.	243	MOYEN SENSUEL	132
	AS THE EDITOR OF THE CENTURY SAYS IN PRINT,	243	MOYEN SENSUEL	137
	STILL WE WILL BRING OUR "FICTION AS NEAR TO FACT" AS	243	MOYEN SENSUEL	139
	STILL WE WILL BRING OUR "FICTION AS NEAR TO FACT" AS	243	MOYEN SENSUEL	139
	MUST THINK TRUTH LOOKS AS THEY DO IN WOOL PYJAMAS.	243	MOYEN SENSUEL	148
	AS TO HOW AND WHY AND WHEREBY THEY GOT IN	244	MOYEN SENSUEL	159
	WITH SIGNS AS MANY, THAT SHALL REPRESENT 'EM	244	MOYEN SENSUEL	167
	"AS FREE OF MOBS AS KINGS"? I'D HAVE MEN FREE OF THAT INVIDIOUS,	244	MOYEN SENSUEL	169
	"AS FREE OF MOBS AS KINGS"? I'D HAVE MEN FREE OF THAT INVIDIOUS,	244	MOYEN SENSUEL	169
	AS NOTHING CAN RESTRAIN OR MUCH DISPARAGE.	245	MOYEN SENSUEL	192
	WAS NEVER ONE OF WHOM ONE SPEAKS AS "BRAZEN'D."	245	MOYEN SENSUEL	206
	SOME MEN WILL LIVE AS PRUDES IN THEIR OWN VILLAGE	245	MOYEN SENSUEL	207
	RADWAY WAS IGNORANT AS AN EDITOR,	246	MOYEN SENSUEL	219
	WHO HAS THE PHRASE "AS IGNORANT AS AN ACTOR."	246	MOYEN SENSUEL	222
	WHO HAS THE PHRASE "AS IGNORANT AS AN ACTOR."	246	MOYEN SENSUEL	222
	FOR AS BEN FRANKLIN SAID, WITH SUCH URBANITY:	246	MOYEN SENSUEL	235
	'TWAS AS A BUSINESS ASSET PURE AN' SIMPLE	246	MOYEN SENSUEL	239
	IS, AT BOTTOM, DISTINGUISHED AND FRESH AS A MARCH HERB.	247	PIERROTS	18
	FORMED THERE IN MANNER AS A MIST OF LIGHT	248	DONNA MI PREGA	20
	AS IN A SUBJECT READY--	249	DONNA MI PREGA	26
	NOT YET WILD-CRUEL AS DARTS,	250	DONNA MI PREGA	74
	SUCH AS THE FASCISTS WEAR,	258	ALF'S THIRD	4
	ALL DREW THEIR PAY, AND AS THE PAY GREW LESS,	260	ALF'S FIFTH	9
	CONSIDERING SOMETHING THAT WOULD, AS YOU	262	ALF'S SEVENTH	7
	THEY'LL TRICK YOU AGAIN AND AGAIN, AS YOU SLEEP;	265	ALF'S NINTH	31
	WAS I STARTED WRONG AS A KIDDIE,	268	ANOTHER BIT	13
	"AS FOOTLIN' A LOT AS WAS EVER SPAWNED	270	OF 600 M.P.'S	23
	"AS FOOTLIN' A LOT AS WAS EVER SPAWNED	270	OF 600 M.P.'S	23
	NEVER GOT PROPERLY TANKED AS I SAW,	271	OLE KATE	15
	AS TENNYSON HAS WRITTEN,	272	THE BABY	10
ASCENDED				
	THE SAP HAS ASCENDED MY ARMS,	62	A GIRL	2
ASCENDS				
	ASCENDS WITH ME INTO THE AETHER,	207	SEXTUS PROP: 1	14
ASCRAEUS'				
	GO ON, TO ASCRAEUS' PRESCRIPTION, THE ANCIENT,	229	SEXTUS PROP:12	50
ASCRIPTION				
	WITH PERPETUAL ASCRIPTION OF GRACES?	222	SEXTUS PROP: 8	15
A-SEARCHING				
	I WILL GO OUT A-SEARCHING,	105	DOMPNA POIS	17
ASH				
	I HAVE CURLED 'MID THE BOLES OF THE ASH WOOD,	4	LA FRAISNE	9
	IN THE ASH TREES HERE:	5	LA FRAISNE	50
	HERE 'MID THE ASH TREES.	5	LA FRAISNE	52
	THAT BURNT ME TO THIS ASH.	32	PIERE VIDAL	64
ASHES				
	FOR THE TOBACCO ASHES SCATTERED ON HIS COAT	15	FAMAM CANO	34
	OR HIDES AMONG THE ASHES THERE FOR THEE.	20	IN DURANCE	9
	BEHOLD THIS BOOK, THE URN OF ASHES,	45	FROM HEINE: 3	7
ASHORE				
	I WITH MY BEAK HAULED ASHORE WOULD PROCEED IN A MORE STATELY MANNER,	216	SEXTUS PROP: 5	10
ASIDE				
	BUT I HAVE PUT ASIDE THIS FOLLY AND THE COLD	4	LA FRAISNE	3
	BUT I HAVE PUT ASIDE THIS FOLLY, BEING GAY	4	LA FRAISNE	7
	OF THE OLD WAYS OF MEN HAVE I CAST ASIDE.	4	LA FRAISNE	12
	AND I? I HAVE PUT ASIDE ALL FOLLY AND ALL GRIEF.	4	LA FRAISNE	24
	ALL FOLLY FROM ME, PUTTING IT ASIDE	4	LA FRAISNE	28
	WILL TURN ASIDE TO SNEER AT	14	FAMAM CANO	29
	FADES WHEN THE WIND HATH LIFTED THEM ASIDE,	40	ERAT HORA	3
	UNTIL THIS COURSE TURNETH ASIDE.	69	THE NEEDLE	15

PAGE 28

ASIDE -- ASSISTANT

	PAGE	TITLE	LINE
ASIDE (CONTINUED)			
BREAKS NOT NOR TURNS ASIDE.	106	DOMPNA POIS	46
NO CHANGE NOR TURNING ASIDE.	106	DOMPNA POIS	60
YOU ALSO ARE LAID ASIDE.	108	FAN-PIECE	3
"MY WIT AND WORTH ARE COBWEBS BRUSHED ASIDE	152	NEAR PERIGORD	45
WE, IN OUR NARROW BED, TURNING ASIDE FROM BATTLES:	218	SEXTUS PROP: 5	57
OR JOVE, HARSH AS HE IS, MAY TURN ASIDE YOUR ULTIMATE DAY.	222	SEXTUS PROP: 8	38
ASK			
ASK YE WHAT GHOSTS I DREAM UPON?	10	FOR THIS YULE	9
PRINCE: ASK ME NOT WHAT I HAVE DONE	10	FOR THIS YULE	25
BUT YE ASK FIRST WHERE THE WINDS ARE GONE	10	FOR THIS YULE	27
IN THESE HE DAILY COMES TO ASK ME:	46	FROM HEINE: 6	7
I ASK OF MIDONS AELIS (OF MONTFORT)	105	DOMPNA POIS	28
I ASK, AND THE FINE COURTESY	106	DOMPNA POIS	52
I ASK NAUGHT FROM YOU,	106	DOMPNA POIS	62
ASK OF YOU THAN HOLD ANOTHER,	107	DOMPNA POIS	67
THE GOD PAN IS AFRAID TO ASK YOU,	110	TEMPORA	7
AND IF YOU ASK HOW I REGRET THAT PARTING:	136	EXILE'S LETTER	72
WHO KNOW NOT HOW TO ASK HER;	175	LANGUE D'OC: 3	32
"'I ASK YOU, DO I	182	MOEURS CON: 8	10
I ASK A WREATH WHICH WILL NOT CRUSH MY HEAD.	207	SEXTUS PROP: 1	21
YET YOU ASK ON WHAT ACCOUNT I WRITE SO MANY LOVE-LYRICS	217	SEXTUS PROP: 5	23
I WOULD ASK A LIKE BOON OF JOVE.	228	SEXTUS PROP:12	17
AND ASK INCONVENIENT QUEERIES.	273	NATIONAL SONG	16
ASKED			
THEY HAVE ASKED THE SENATE TO GUESS	268	ANOTHER BIT	6
OR ASKED US IF THE COW	272	THE BABY	4
ASKING			
THERE IS NO NEED OF ASKING DIVINERS.	138	NEAR SHOKU	11
ASKING TIME TO BE RID OF . . .	199	MAUBERLEY: 2	9
WITH HER HUSBAND ASKING A REMISSION OF SENTENCE,	230	SEXTUS PROP:12	61
ASKS			
BECAUSE A LADY ASKS ME, I WOULD TELL	248	DONNA MI PREGA	1
ASLEEP			
BY THE TROUT ASLEEP IN THE GRAY-GREEN OF WATER;	76	THE ALCHEMIST	37
BUT DEAD, OR ASLEEP, SHE PLEASES.	165	QUINTUS SEPTIM	21
A-SLOSHIN'			
AN A-SLOSHIN' ROUND WITH 'ER MOP,	271	OLE KATE	10
ASPECT			
ALL THIS ANGELIC ASPECT CAN RETURN	42	HER MONUMENT	37
PERILOUS ASPECT;	107	COMING OF WAR	12
SUCH ASPECT WAS PRESENTED TO ME, ME RECENTLY EMERGED FROM MY VISIONS,	225	SEXTUS PROP:10	32
ASPEN			
THAT 'THOUT HIM, SAVE THE ASPEN, WERE AS DUMB	21	IN DURANCE	47
ASPIRATIONS			
IN SPIRITUAL ASPIRATIONS, BUT HE FOUND IT PROFITABLE,	246	MOYEN SENSUEL	334
ASQUITH			
WHEN FEEBLE MR. ASQUITH, GETTING OLD,	264	ALF'S NINTH	5
ASS			
LET SOME NEW LYING ASS,	261	ALF'S SIXTH	1
ASSAILANT			
I SHALL BE PREY TO LAMENTATIONS WORSE THAN A NOCTURNAL ASSAILANT.	212	SEXTUS PROP: 3	11
ASSAILS			
ASSAILS ME, AND CONCERNS ME ALMOST AS LITTLE.	103	LADIES	20
ASSES			
A LOT OF ASSES PRAISE YOU BECAUSE YOU ARE "VIRILE,"	82	THE CONDOLENCE	2
ASSET			
'TWAS AS A BUSINESS ASSET PURE AN' SIMPLE	246	MOYEN SENSUEL	239
ASSIDUOUS			
WITH CROWDS TOO ASSIDUOUS IN THEIR CROSSING OF IT;	213	SEXTUS PROP: 3	33
ASSISTANCE			
I WISH YOU JOY, I PROFFER YOU ALL MY ASSISTANCE.	145	SALUTATION 3RD	19
ASSISTANT			
THE EYES OF THE VERY LEARNED BRITISH MUSEUM ASSISTANT.	161	PAGANI'S NOV 8	3

PAGE 29

ASSOCIATED -- ATTHIS

	PAGE	TITLE	LINE
ASSOCIATED			
THOUGH MY HOUSE IS NOT PROPPED UP BY TAENARIAN COLUMNS FROM LACONIA (ASSOCIATED WITH NEPTUNE AND CERBERUS),	208	SEXTUS PROP: 1	51
ASSUME			
DAR'DST TO ASSUME THIS?	68	APPARUIT	24
LET THEM ASSUME THE MILK-WHITE BODIES OF AGATE.	76	THE ALCHEMIST	52
ASSUMPTION			
THAT I STRUT IN THE ROBES OF ASSUMPTION.	146	MONUMENTUM AER	2
ASSUREDLY			
A PROSE KINEMA, NOT, NOT ASSUREDLY, ALABASTER	188	HUGH SELWYN: 2	11
ASTHETICS			
DOES NOT BELIEVE IN ASTHETICS.	178	MOEURS CON: 1	14
A-STRAY			
A-STRAY, LOST IN THE VILLAGES,	92	THE REST	4
ASTRIDE			
CUPID, ASTRIDE A PHALLUS WITH TWO WINGS,	162	CABARET DANCER	36
A-SUDDEN			
FELT HANDS TURN ICE A-SUDDEN, TOUCHING YE,	41	HER MONUMENT	17
AT (156)			
ATALIC			
NOR SHALL IT BE ON AN ATALIC BED;	219	SEXTUS PROP: 6	16
ATE			
WHO ATE THE PROFITS, AND WHO LOCKED 'EM IN	260	ALF'S FIFTH	18
ATHEIST			
WHO WAS "SO OLD THAT SHE WAS AN ATHEIST,"	115	SOCIAL ORDER	6
ATLANTIC			
WHO'S NOW THE EDITOR OF THE ATLANTIC,	239	MOYEN SENSUEL	14
A'TOP			
BROUGHT FROM GT. BRITAIN AND DUMPED DOWN A'TOP OF US,	240	MOYEN SENSUEL	64
A-TREMBLE			
A-TREMBLE IN MEN'S VEINS; O LIP CURVED HIGH	41	HER MONUMENT	12
'ATS			
I SEE THEIR 'IGH 'ATS ON THE SEATS	270	OF 600 M.P.'S	13
ATTACK			
WHOM CAN THESE DUDS ATTACK?	258	ALF'S THIRD	1
ATTAINDER			
BUT THESE MAY NOT SUFFER ATTAINDER,	98	THE BELLAIRES	13
A "FREEDOM FROM ATTAINDER"	98	THE BELLAIRES	18
ATTAINED			
AND WHATS-HIS-NAME ATTAINED NOBILITY.	264	ALF'S NINTH	8
ATTEMPT			
IF I HAVE NOT THE FACULTY, "THE BARE ATTEMPT WOULD BE PRAISE-WORTHY."	216	SEXTUS PROP: 5	4
ATTEND			
DELICATELY UPON THE REED, ATTEND ME!	62	N. Y.	3
LISTEN TO ME, ATTEND ME!	62	N. Y.	11
THE LITTLE MILLWINS ATTEND THE RUSSIAN BALLET.	93	LES MILLWIN	1
THE GODS OF THE UNDERWORLD ATTEND ME, O ANNUBIS,	147	BEFORE SLEEP	6
WITH A PATHETIC SOLICITUDE THEY ATTEND ME;	147	BEFORE SLEEP	8
THE GODS OF DRUGGED SLEEP ATTEND ME,	147	BEFORE SLEEP	17
ATTENDANCE			
I DEPRECATE YOUR ATTENDANCE;	228	SEXTUS PROP:12	16
ATTENDANT			
CYDONIAN SPRING WITH HER ATTENDANT TRAIN,	87	THE SPRING	1
ATTENDANTS			
SADNESS HUNG OVER THE HOUSE, AND THE DESOLATED FEMALE ATTENDANTS	214	SEXTUS PROP: 4	22
ATTENDED			
WITHOUT AN INFERNO, WITHOUT ACHILLES ATTENDED OF GODS,	218	SEXTUS PROP: 5	51
HE HAD ATTENDED COUNTRY CHRISTIAN ENDEAVOUR CONVENTIONS,	242	MOYEN SENSUEL	102
ATTENTION			
WILL PAY NO ATTENTION TO THIS,	98	THE BELLAIRES	25
A HOOK TO CATCH THE LADY JANE'S ATTENTION,	196	HUGH SELWIN:12	17
OR WHY WE SHOULD STAND TO ATTENTION	264	ALF'S EIGHTH	30
ATTHIS			
ATTHIS.	112	HIMERRO	3
O ATTHIS,	112	HIMERRO	4

ATTIC -- AULTAFORTE

	PAGE	TITLE	LINE
ATTIC			
NOT, AT ANY RATE, AN ATTIC GRACE;	188	HUGH SELWYN: 2	4
ATTIRE			
PRETEND HUMANITY OR DON THE FRAIL ATTIRE?	32	PARACELSUS	2
IN ATTIRE, NOR SO GAY	105	DOMPNA POIS	15
ATTIRED			
THOU ART SO FAIR ATTIRED THAT EVERY MAN AND EACH	250	DONNA MI PREGA	89
ATTITUDES			
WIT, NOR GOOD SPIRITS, NOR THE PLEASING ATTITUDES	101	AMITIES	11
ATTRACT			
THE GEW-GAWS OF FALSE AMBER AND FALSE TURQUOISE ATTRACT THEM.	114	BEFORE A SHOP	1
AND EVEN THIS INFAMY WOULD NOT ATTRACT NUMEROUS READERS	230	SEXTUS PROP:12	62
ATTRACTION			
AUGUST ATTRACTION OR CONCENTRATION.	202	AGE DEMANDED	49
AU			
AU SALON	52	AU SALON	T
AU JARDIN	53	AU JARDIN	T
AU DEDANS DE MA MEMOIRE	160	DANS OMNIBUS	7
M. POM-POM EST AU SENAT	273	M. POM-POM	6
AUBETERRE			
AUBETERRE IS EASTWARD, ...	121	PROVINC DESERT	19
DODGING HIS WAY PAST AUBETERRE, SINGING AT CHALAIS	154	NEAR PERIGORD	105
AUCTION			
BETWEEN AUCTION AND PLAIN BRIDGE, ...	258	ALF'S SECOND	10
AUDIARDA			
MIRALS, CEMBELINS, AUDIARDA.	75	THE ALCHEMIST	12
AUDIART			
NA AUDIART	8	NA AUDIART	T
AUDIART, AUDIART, ...	8	NA AUDIART	2
AUDIART, AUDIART, ...	8	NA AUDIART	2
AUDIART, AUDIART, ...	8	NA AUDIART	6
AUDIART, AUDIART, ...	8	NA AUDIART	6
AUDIART, AUDIART, ...	8	NA AUDIART	9
AUDIART, AUDIART, ...	8	NA AUDIART	9
"AUDIART, AUDIART"	9	NA AUDIART	29
"AUDIART, AUDIART"	9	NA AUDIART	29
AUDIART, AUDIART.	9	NA AUDIART	34
AUDIART, AUDIART.	9	NA AUDIART	34
AUDIART, ...	9	NA AUDIART	36
AUDIART, AUDIART	9	NA AUDIART	53
AUDIART, AUDIART	9	NA AUDIART	53
AUDIART, ...	9	NA AUDIART	55
AUDIART	9	NA AUDIART	56
OF AUDIART AT MALEMORT, ...	106	DOMPNA POIS	40
AUDIBLE			
BUT THE BLACK OMINOUS OWL HOOT WAS AUDIBLE, ...	223	SEXTUS PROP: 9	4
AUDIENCE			
BEHOLD MINE AUDIENCE, ...	14	FAMAM CANO	21
DO NOT SET ABOUT TO PROCURE ME AN AUDIENCE.	81	TENZONE	9
SO YOU FOUND AN AUDIENCE READY.	85	SALUTATION 2ND	4
AUDITION			
AUDITION OF THE PHANTASMAL SEA-SURGE.	202	AGE DEMANDED	45
AUGHT			
NOR FIND AUGHT NOVEL IN THY MERRIMENT?	43	SATIEMUS	19
AM SOLVED AND BOUND IN, THROUGH AUGHT HERE, ON EARTH,	51	THE FLAME	33
NOR HAS LIFE IN IT AUGHT BETTER	83	THE GARRET	9
NO ONE HEARS AUGHT SAVE THE GRACIOUS SOUND OF COMPLIMENTS.	154	NEAR PERIGORD	120
AUGHT OF THE SLIGHTEST USE.	206	ALF'S TENTH	4
AUGUST			
THE AUGUST HAS WORN AGAINST HER.	116	THE TEA SHOP	3
THE PAIRED BUTTERFLIES ARE ALREADY YELLOW WITH AUGUST	131	RIVER-MER WIFE	23
AUGUST ATTRACTION OR CONCENTRATION.	202	AGE DEMANDED	49
OH AUGUST PIERIDES! NOW FOR A LARGE-MOUTHED PRODUCT.	216	SEXTUS PROP: 5	14
AUGUSTUS			
AND SO FORTH AUGUSTUS. "VIRGIN ARABIA SHAKES IN HER INMOST DWELLING.	216	SEXTUS PROP: 5	18
AULTAFORTE			
BERTRANS OF AULTAFORTE THY PRAISE	0	NA AUDIART	31

PAGE 31

AUPRES -- AVERAGE

	PAGE	TITLE	LINE
AUPRES			
AUPRES D'UN PETIT ENFANT GAI, BOSSU.	160	DANS OMNIBUS	11
AUREATE			
OF BLISSFUL KINGDOMS AND THE AUREATE SPHERES;	42	HER MONUMENT	34
SET TO SOME WEAVING, COMES THE AUREATE LIGHT.	49	OF SPLENDOUR	16
AURELIA			
AND ON THIS ACCOUNT THE LITTLE AURELIA,	111	SOCIETY	2
AUS			
AUS MEINEN GROSSEN SCHMERZEN	97	THE BELLAIRES	EPI
AUSTER			
"COME, AUSTER, COME APELIOTA,	109	THE FAUN	5
AUSTERE			
"THE WOUNDING OF AUSTERE MEN BY CHICANE."	211	SEXTUS PROP: 2	51
AUSTORS			
"THE CASTLE TO AUSTORS!"	123	PROVINC DESERT	71
AUSTRALIAN			
AND GIVES YOU AUSTRALIAN ICED RABBITS' MEAT	263	ALF'S EIGHTH	18
AUTEM			
EGO AUTEM JOVIALIS	101	AMITIES	21
AUTHOR			
SO SPOKE THE AUTHOR OF "THE DORIAN MOOD,"	193	SIENA MI FE	16
THERE ARE NEW JOBS FOR THE AUTHOR;	217	SEXTUS PROP: 5	32
AUTHORS			
MAKE WAY, YE ROMAN AUTHORS,	229	SEXTUS PROP:12	36
AUTOMOBILES			
THERE IS BLOKES IN AUTOMOBILES	269	SAFE AND SOUND	13
AUTOPSY			
AT THE AUTOPSY, PRIVATELY PERFORMED--	193	SIENA MI FE	10
AUTRES			
"EST-CE QUE VOUS AVEZ VU DES AUTRES--DES CAMARADES--AVEC DES SINGES OU DES OURS?"	119	THE GYPSY	EPI
DONT TOUS LES AUTRES TRAITS ETAIENT BANALS,	160	DANS OMNIBUS	4
AUTUMN			
THE FLAME, THE AUTUMN, AND THE GREEN ROSE OF LOVE	51	THE ALTAR	2
WHEN IT IS AUTUMN DO WE GET SPRING WEATHER,	59	SILET	7
THIS FABRICATION BUILT OF AUTUMN ROSES,	69	SUB MARE	3
BRING THE LIGHT OF THE BIRCH TREE IN AUTUMN	75	THE ALCHEMIST	11
FROM THE COPPER OF THE LEAF IN AUTUMN,	76	THE ALCHEMIST	33
THE LEAVES FALL EARLY THIS AUTUMN, IN WIND.	131	RIVER-MER WIFE	22
AND WATCH THE MOON THROUGH THE CLEAR AUTUMN.	132	JEWEL STAIRS'	4
TREES FALL, THE GRASS GOES YELLOW WITH AUTUMN.	133	FRONTIER GUARD	3
A GRACIOUS SPRING, TURNED TO BLOOD-RAVENOUS AUTUMN,	133	FRONTIER GUARD	14
AUTUMNS			
AND THEY THINK IT WILL LAST A THOUSAND AUTUMNS,	132	AT TEN-SHIN	26
UNWEARYING AUTUMNS.	132	AT TEN-SHIN	27
AUVERGNAT			
SOME LITTLE PRIZED PLACE IN AUVERGNAT:	122	PROVINC DESERT	65
AUVERGNE			
AUVERGNE ROSE TO THE SONG;	122	PROVINC DESERT	69
AUVEZERE			
BEWILDERING SPRING, AND BY THE AUVEZERE	157	NEAR PERIGORD	170
AUX			
AUX TOISONS COULEUR DE LIN,	160	DANS OMNIBUS	16
AVAIL			
TO MAKE THESE AVAIL	106	DOMPNA POIS	58
AVAILETH			
WHOSE SMILE MORE AVAILETH	35	THE EYES	16
AVARICIOUS			
I SEARCH THE FEATURES, THE AVARICIOUS FEATURES	162	CABARET DANCER	28
'AVE			
I SAYS! 'AVE YOU SEEN 'EM?	258	ALF'S SECOND	13
I WOULDN'T 'AVE THE NEEDLE	269	SAFE AND SOUND	23
'AVE YOU SEEN YER LARST SWEET LITTER?	270	OF 600 M.P.'S	18
AVEC			
"EST-CE QUE VOUS AVEZ VU DES AUTRES--DES CAMARADES--AVEC DES SINGES OU DES OURS?"	119	THE GYPSY	EPI
EN COMPARAISON AVEC LAQUELLE LA ROSE	199	MAUBERLEY: 2	EPI
AVENUE			
THE FLOOD OF LIMBS UPON EIGHTH AVENUE	245	MOYEN SENSUEL	189
AVERAGE			
ONE AVERAGE MIND--WITH ONE THOUGHT LESS, EACH YEAR.	61	PORTRAIT FEMME	10

AVERNUS -- AYE

	PAGE	TITLE	LINE
AVERNUS			
SO MANY THOUSAND BEAUTIES ARE GONE DOWN TO AVERNUS,	38	LADY'S LIFE	3
SO MANY THOUSAND FAIR ARE GONE DOWN TO AVERNUS, ...	38	LADY'S LIFE	13
GO BEFORE HER INTO AVERNUS;	115	SOCIAL ORDER	12
ON THE VEILED LAKE TOWARD AVERNUS	223	SEXTUS PROP: 9	6
AVERNUS LUSTS FOR THE LOT OF THEM, ...	223	SEXTUS PROP: 9	19
AVERTED			
IO MOOED THE FIRST YEARS WITH AVERTED HEAD, ...	222	SEXTUS PROP: 8	19
AVEZ			
"EST-CE QUE VOUS AVEZ VU DES AUTRES--DES CAMARADES--AVEC DES SINGES OU DES OURS?"	119	THE GYPSY	EPI
AVIGNON			
ME! IN THIS DAMN'D INN OF AVIGNON, ...	22	MARVOIL	19
AVINEN			
QU'IEU SUI AVINEN, ...	166	FISH & SHADOW	16
OF ARNAUT DE MAREUIL, I THOUGHT, "QU'IEU SUI AVINEN."	166	FISH & SHADOW	19
AVIONS			
OU NOUS AVIONS LOUE DES CHAISES	160	DANS OMNIBUS	22
AVOID			
EASTWARD AVOID THE HOUR OF ITS DECLINE, ...	69	THE NEEDLE	2
AVRIL			
AVRIL	173	LANGUE D'OC: 2	SUB
AWAIT			
BUT I AWAIT WITH PATIENCE, ...	111	BLACK SLIPPERS	9
I AWAIT THE LADY VALENTINE'S COMMANDS, ...	196	HUGH SELWIN:12	4
AWAITING			
AND I HAVE MOPED IN THE EMPEROR'S GARDEN, AWAITING AN ORDER-TO-WRITE!	129	THE RIVER SONG	19
A GLITTER OF GOLDEN SADDLES, AWAITING THE PRINCESS;	141	IDEA OF CHOAN	7
AWAKE			
"SST! MY GOOD FELLOW, ART AWAKE OR SLEEPING?	172	LANGUE D'OC: 1	6
FROM LOVE, AWAKE AND IN SWEVYN, ...	175	LANGUE D'OC: 3	29
AWARDED			
THUS HAVE THE GODS AWARDED HER, ...	103	PHYLLIDULA	2
AWAY			
THAT PLAGUE AND BURN AND DRIVE ONE AWAY.	5	LA FRAISNE	36
BID THY 'FULGENCE BEAR AWAY CARE.	7	CINO	48
SUCH AN ONE AS WOMEN DRAW AWAY FROM	15	FAMAM CANO	33
OR AS A DANDELION SEED-POD AND BE SWEPT AWAY, ...	36	FRANCESCA	10
O YOU AWAY HIGH THERE, ...	53	AU JARDIN	1
AND TAKES STRANGE GAIN AWAY:	61	PORTRAIT FEMME	15
COME, OR THE STELLAR TIDE WILL SLIP AWAY.	69	THE NEEDLE	1
THE WAVES BORE IN, SOON WILL THEY BEAR AWAY.	69	THE NEEDLE	10
THAT HE HAS TAKEN OUR LORD AWAY	72	PAN IS DEAD	12
AND HERE DESIRE, NOT TO BE KISSED AWAY.	73	THE PICTURE	3
WHY AM I WARNED? WHY AM I SENT AWAY?	95	OF THE DEGREES	12
AND SINCE YOU HAVE SHUT ME AWAY FROM YOU	105	DOMPNA POIS	2
STOLE HER AWAY FOR HIMSELF, KEPT HER AGAINST ARMED	123	PROVINC DESERT	75
TOO DEEP TO CLEAR THEM AWAY!	131	RIVER-MER WIFE	21
I HAD TO BE OFF TO SO, FAR AWAY OVER THE WATERS,	135	EXILE'S LETTER	34
TO DO AWAY WITH GOOD WRITERS, ...	145	SALUTATION 3RD	21
TO FIND HER HALF ALONE, MONTFORT AWAY, ...	154	NEAR PERIGORD	111
WHEN WE SET STRIFE AWAY, ...	173	LANGUE D'OC: 2	18
REFT ME AWAY;	176	LANGUE D'OC: 3	63
STRUGGLES WHEN THE LIGHTS WERE TAKEN AWAY;	220	SEXTUS PROP: 7	4
WIND AND WAVE SCATTERED AWAY.	221	SEXTUS PROP: 8	9
MOST TIDILY AWAY	269	SAFE AND SOUND	18
TO KEEP THE WOLF AWAY	269	SAFE AND SOUND	20
A-WEARY			
REST MASTER, FOR WE BE A-WEARY, WEARY	35	THE EYES	1
AWFUL			
THAT YOU CAN SAY SUCH AWFUL THINGS	44	FROM HEINE: 1	7
COMPLAIN ABOUT THE AWFUL NOISE	45	FROM HEINE: 5	3
AWHILE			
YOUTH WOULD AWHILE FORGET	158	PSYCHOLOG HOUR	29
AXES			
TOD GRIND THE SAME OLD AXES	270	OF 600 M.P.'S	6
AYE			
AYE! WHERE ARE THE GLANCES FEAT AND CLEAR	10	FOR THIS YULE	20
AYE YOU'RE A MAN THAT! YE OLD MESMERIZER	13	MESMERISM	1
AYE, I AM WISTFUL FOR MY KIN OF THE SPIRIT	20	IN DURANCE	17

PAGE 33

AYE -- BACKGROUND

	PAGE	TITLE	LINE
AYE (CONTINUED)			
MY FELLOWS, AYE I KNOW THE GLORY	20	IN DURANCE	28
"AYE! I AM A POET AND UPON MY TOMB	24	THUS NINEVEH	1
AYE YE ARE FOOLS, IF YE THINK TIME CAN BLOT	30	PIERE VIDAL	18
AYE LOVER HE WAS OF BRAWNY MEN,	33	GOODLY FERE	3
AYE HE SENT US OUT THROUGH THE CROSSED HIGH SPEARS BUT AYE LOVED THE OPEN SEA.	33	GOODLY FERE	9
	33	GOODLY FERE	24
THIS HE LITTLE BELIEVES, WHO AYE IN WINSOME LIFE	64	THE SEAFARER	28
AYE, FOR EVER, A LASTING LIFE'S-BLAST,	66	THE SEAFARER	80
GREEN COME THE SHOOTS, AYE APRIL IN THE BRANCHES,	71	A VIRGINAL	11
AZALAIS			
SAIL OF CLAUSTRA, AELIS, AZALAIS,	75	THE ALCHEMIST	1
SAIL OF CLAUSTRA, AELIS, AZALAIS,	75	THE ALCHEMIST	5
AZURE			
AZURE AND FLAKING SILVER OF WATER,	76	THE ALCHEMIST	56
AZURES			
ON TRIUNE AZURES, THE IMPALPABLE	39	BLANDULA	11
B.			
OLD FRIENDS THE MOST.--W. B. Y.	101	AMITIES	EPI
SKETCH 48 B. 2	179	MOEURS CON: 4	SUB
BABE			
A BROWN, FAT BABE SITTING IN THE LOTUS,	147	POST MORTEM	1
BABY			
SAW THE PERFORMERS COME: HIM, HER, THE BABY,	163	CABARET DANCER	80
THE BABY	272	THE BABY	T
THE BABY NEW TO EARTH AND SKY	272	THE BABY	1
"THE BABY NEW TO EARTH AND SKY,"	272	THE BABY	9
BACCHO			
EVOE, EVOE, EVOE BACCHO, O	231	CANTUS PLANUS	3
BACCHUS			
WITH RAPTURES FOR BACCHUS, TERPSICHORE AND THE CHURCH.	193	SIENA MI FE	15
BACCHUS AND APOLLO IN FAVOUR OF IT,	208	SEXTUS PROP: 1	49
BACK			
HOW THE STAYS PLY BACK FROM IT;	8	NA AUDIART	15
LIPS SHRUNK BACK FOR THE WIND'S CARESS	11	OF THE GIBBET	19
AS LIPS SHRINK BACK WHEN WE FEEL THE STRAIN	11	OF THE GIBBET	20
THAT PLUNDERED ST. HUBERT BACK O' THE FANE:	12	OF THE GIBBET	32
WHERE TIME BURNS BACK ABOUT TH' ETERNAL EMBERS.	50	THE FLAME	21
SWEEP BACK UPON ME AND ENGULF MY MIND!	51	HORAE BEATAE	2
I SAY MY SOUL FLOWED BACK, BECAME TRANSLUCENT.	51	THE FLAME	36
AND HALF TURN BACK;	74	THE RETURN	9
THOUGH EVERY BRANCH HAVE BACK WHAT LAST YEAR LOST,	87	THE SPRING	11
I HAVE LOOKED BACK OVER THE STREAM	121	PROVINC DESERT	33
AND SAYING: WHEN SHALL WE GET BACK TO OUR COUNTRY?	127	BOWMEN OF SHU	2
WE SAY: WILL WE BE LET TO GO BACK IN OCTOBER?	127	BOWMEN OF SHU	10
WE COME BACK IN THE SNOW,	127	BOWMEN OF SHU	22
CALLED TO, A THOUSAND TIMES, I NEVER LOOKED BACK.	130	RIVER-MER WIFE	10
YOU BACK TO YOUR RIVER-BRIDGE.	135	EXILE'S LETTER	35
AND THE GIRLS SINGING BACK AT EACH OTHER,	136	EXILE'S LETTER	59
AND WENT BACK TO THE EAST MOUNTAINS	136	EXILE'S LETTER	68
HE CLAPS HIS HAND ON THE BACK OF THE GREAT WATER SENNIN.	140	SENNIN POEM	14
DRINKS IN AND CASTS BACK THE SUN	141	IDEA OF CHOAN	10
BUT ONE HUGE BACK HALF-COVERED UP WITH PINE,	152	NEAR PERIGORD	33
GIVE ME BACK THE TIME OF THE THING.	167	OF AROUET	16
TO BRING THEE SAFE BACK, MY COMPANION.	172	LANGUE D'OC: 1	20
IN VAIN, YOU CALL BACK THE SHADE,	219	SEXTUS PROP: 6	35
GO BACK TO GREAT DIAN'S DANCES BEARING SUITABLE GIFTS,	224	SEXTUS PROP: 9	24
THOUGH YOU HEAVE INTO THE AIR UPON THE GILDED PEGASEAN BACK,	226	SEXTUS PROP:11	7
AND SHE WAS LED BACK, LIVING, HOME;	227	SEXTUS PROP:11	26
FILLED THE BACK ALLEYS AND THE BACK TO BACK HOUSES.	260	ALF'S FIFTH	14
FILLED THE BACK ALLEYS AND THE BACK TO BACK HOUSES.	260	ALF'S FIFTH	14
FILLED THE BACK ALLEYS AND THE BACK TO BACK HOUSES.	260	ALF'S FIFTH	14
BACKED			
THE DAUPHIN BACKED HIM.	122	PROVINC DESERT	70
BACKGROUND			
FOR A BACKGROUND,	218	SEXTUS PROP: 5	48

BACKLESS -- BANKER'S

	PAGE	TITLE	LINE
BACKLESS			
BACKLESS COPY FROM THE STALL,	15	FAMAM CANO	39
BACK-SWIRLING			
AND ON THE BACK-SWIRLING EDDIES,	131	AT TEN-SHIN	6
BACKWASH			
STIFFENED OUR FACE WITH THE BACKWASH OF PHILETAS THE COAN.	211	SEXTUS PROP: 2	54
BAD			
THE VICOMTE OF BEZIERS'S NOT SUCH A BAD LOT.	22	MARVOIL	6
I FEAR YOU WILL COME TO A BAD END.	94	INSTRUCTIONS	4
YOU WILL COME TO A VERY BAD END.	94	INSTRUCTIONS	9
"ANOTHER WHEEL, THE ARENA; MID-CROWD IS AS BAD AS MID-SEA."	210	SEXTUS PROP: 2	27
TO CHEER THE BAD AND SAD,	268	ALF'S TWELFTH	20
BADE			
THAT BADE MY HEART HIS VALOUR DON?	10	FOR THIS YULE	21
AND BADE HER BE OUT WITH ILL ADDRESS	11	OF THE GIBBET	11
STILL SHADE, AND BADE NO WHISPER SPEAK THE BIRDS OF HOW	21	IN DURANCE	48
THAT BADE US HIS BROTHERS BE.	34	GOODLY FERE	34
BADEST			
BADEST ME TO SEE THAT A GOOD WATCH WAS DONE,	172	LANGUE D'OC: 1	23
BADLY			
IN FACT THEY UNDERSTOOD THEM SO BADLY	97	THE BELLAIRES	3
BAH			
BAH! I HAVE SUNG WOMEN IN THREE CITIES,	6	CINO	1
BAH! THERE'S NO WINE LIKE THE BLOOD'S CRIMSON!	28	ALTAFORTE	18
BAIL			
ENTER THAT MUCH FOR HIS BAIL.	225	SEXTUS PROP:10	23
BAIT			
CAPANEUS; TROUT FOR FACTITIOUS BAIT;	187	E. P. ODE	8
ENDYMION'S NAKED BODY, BRIGHT BAIT FOR DIANA,"	220	SEXTUS PROP: 7	15
BALANCE			
THE BALANCE FOR THIS LOSS IN IRE AND SADNESS!	37	THE YOUNG KING	16
BALDWIN			
MY COUSIN'S NAMED BALDWIN	260	ALF'S FOURTH	14
BALFOUR			
HE USED TO LUNCH WITH BALFOUR IN THOSE DAYS	265	ALF'S NINTH	22
BALL			
THE SILVER BALL FORMS IN MY HAND,	169	PHANOPOEIA	6
BALLAD			
A VILLONAUD: BALLAD OF THE GIBBET	11	OF THE GIBBET	T
BALLAD OF THE GOODLY FERE	33	GOODLY FERE	T
A BALLAD OF THE MULBERRY ROAD	140	MULBERRY ROAD	T
BALLAD FOR THE TIMES' SPECIAL SILVER NUMBER	267	ALF'S TWELFTH	SUB
BALLATETTA			
BALLATETTA	38	BALLATETTA	T
BALLET			
THE LITTLE MILLWINS ATTEND THE RUSSIAN BALLET.	93	LES MILLWIN	1
BALM			
SO 'GAINST THE WINTER'S BALM.	116	ANCIENT MUSIC	11
BAMBOO			
YOU CAME BY ON BAMBOO STILTS, PLAYING HORSE,	130	RIVER-MER WIFE	3
BANALS			
DONT TOUS LES AUTRES TRAITS ETAIENT BANALS,	160	DANS OMNIBUS	4
BAND			
I LIKE ONE LITTLE BAND OF WINDS THAT BLOW	5	LA FRAISNE	49
BANDS			
CLASH, LEAPING OF BANDS, STRAIGHT STRIPS OF HARD COLOUR,	120	GAME OF CHESS	14
THE WIRE-LIKE BANDS OF COLOUR INVOLUTE MOUNT FROM MY FINGERS;	170	PHANOPOEIA	17
BANISHED			
IS "ZUT! CINQUE LETTRES!" A BANISHED GALLIC IDIOM,	239	MOYEN SENSUEL	36
BANK			
AN' KEEP THE BANK IN POWER.	270	OF 600 M.P.'S	4
HAVE BANK SHARKS TO BLEED 'EM	272	NATIONAL SONG	12
BANK-CLERKLY			
WITH THE MOST BANK-CLERKLY OF ENGLISHMEN?	105	HUGH SELWIN:11	4
BANKER'S			
VEX NOT THOU THE BANKER'S MIND	263	ALF'S EIGHTH	1

PAGE 35

BANKER'S -- BASER

	PAGE	TITLE	LINE
BANKER'S (CONTINUED)			
IN HIS EYE THERE IS DEATH,--I MEAN THE BANKER'S,--	263	ALF'S EIGHTH	15
BANKERS'			
TER LICK TH' BANKERS' DIRTY BOOTS	270	OF 600 M.P.'S	3
BANKS			
WHERE BANKS RISE DAY BY DAY,	272	NATIONAL SONG	2
THERE ARE NO BANKS LIKE ENGLISH BANKS	272	NATIONAL SONG	3
THERE ARE NO BANKS LIKE ENGLISH BANKS	272	NATIONAL SONG	3
BANNER			
THE LAZY LEOPARDS ON THE LARGEST BANNER,	155	NEAR PERIGORD	133
BANNERETS			
THE CRACKLING OF SMALL FIRES, THE BANNERETS,	155	NEAR PERIGORD	132
BANNERS			
MIND AND SPIRIT DRIVE ON THE FEATHERY BANNERS.	139	SOUTH-FOLK	9
BANQUETS			
HAUGHTY THEIR STEPS AS THEY GO IN TO GREAT BANQUETS,	132	AT TEN-SHIN	19
MY TALENT ACCLAIMED IN THEIR BANQUETS,	229	SEXTUS PROP:12	56
BAPTIST			
THAT RADWAY JOINED THE BAPTIST BROADWAY TEMPLE.	246	MOYEN SENSUEL	240
BARBARIAN			
WAS GOVERNOR IN HEI SHU, AND PUT DOWN THE BARBARIAN RABBLE.	135	EXILE'S LETTER	37
FLYING SNOW BEWILDERS THE BARBARIAN HEAVEN.	139	SOUTH-FOLK	7
BARBARISM			
NO BARBARISM WOULD GO TO THE EXTENT OF DOING HIM HARM,	212	SEXTUS PROP: 3	19
BARBAROUS			
TO WATCH OUT THE BARBAROUS LAND:	133	FRONTIER GUARD	5
BARBAROUS KINGS.	133	FRONTIER GUARD	13
"NOR WHERE THE RHINE FLOWS WITH BARBAROUS BLOOD,	211	SEXTUS PROP: 2	46
BARBECUES			
AND YOUR BARBECUES OF GREAT OXEN,	165	QUINTUS SEPTIM	13
BARBITOS			
SAPPHO'S BARBITOS.	189	HUGH SELWYN: 3	4
BARE			
AIE! THE LEAN BARE TREE IS WIDOWED AGAIN	12	OF THE GIBBET	33
IF I HAVE NOT THE FACULTY, "THE BARE ATTEMPT WOULD BE PRAISE-WORTHY."	216	SEXTUS PROP: 5	4
YOU WILL FOLLOW THE BARE SCARIFIED BREAST	219	SEXTUS PROP: 6	22
BARED			
NOW WITH BARED BREASTS SHE WRESTLED AGAINST ME,	220	SEXTUS PROP: 7	5
BAREFOOT			
COME BEAUTY BAREFOOT FROM THE CYCLADES,	63	PHASELLUS ILLE	12
BARGE			
BUT I DRAW PEN ON THIS BARGE	128	THE RIVER SONG	13
BARK			
AS WHITE THEIR BARK, SO WHITE THIS LADY'S HOURS.	71	A VIRGINAL	14
THINE ARMS ARE AS A YOUNG SAPLING UNDER THE BARK;	91	DANCE FIGURE	10
"DAPHNE WITH HER THIGHS IN BARK	196	HUGH SELWIN:12	1
BARLEY			
EARTH SHALL BRING WHEAT FROM BARLEY,	220	SEXTUS PROP: 7	24
BARONS			
THEY EDDY BEFORE THE GATE OF THE BARONS.	141	IDEA OF CHOAN	8
BARREN			
TO LEAVE THE OLD BARREN WAYS OF MEN,	4	LA FRAISNE	29
IS NOW BUT BARREN HILL,	128	THE RIVER SONG	12
SO MUCH BARREN REGRET,	158	PSYCHOLOG HOUR	8
BARS			
NOT WITH BARS OF COPPER.	91	DANCE FIGURE	15
BARTER			
'TIS NOT A GAME OF BARTER, LANDS AND HOUSES,	50	THE FLAME	3
'TIS NOT A GAME OF BARTER, LANDS AND HOUSES,	50	THE FLAME	17
BASE			
WE SEEM AS STATUES ROUND WHOSE HIGH-RISEN BASE	32	PARACELSUS	11
OR TO SUCH BASE OCCASION LIT AND QUENCHED?	42	HER MONUMENT	57
ARE NOW THE BASE OF OLD HILLS.	138	CITY OF CHOAN	7
THOUGH I KNOW ONE, A VERY BASE DETRACTOR,	246	MOYEN SENSUEL	221
THAT MAN WHO IS BASE IN HEART	248	DONNA MI PREGA	7
THAT THE BASE LIKENESS OF IT KINDLETH NOT.	249	DONNA MI PREGA	32
BASER			
COME, MY SONGS, LET US EXPRESS OUR BASER PASSIONS,	94	INSTRUCTIONS	1

BASHFUL -- BEAMS

	PAGE	TITLE	LINE
BASHFUL			
THE BASHFUL ARIDES	100	ARIDES	1
I NEVER LAUGHED, BEING BASHFUL.	130	RIVER-MER WIFE	8
I'VE TOLD HIS TRAINING, HE WAS NEVER BASHFUL,	242	MOYEN SENSUEL	125
BASIL			
WILL DINE NEXT WEEK WITH MRS. BASIL,	163	CABARET DANCER	63
AND BASIL WAS THE GREEK THAT RODE AROUND	264	ALF'S NINTH	18
BASKET			
WITH GREEN STRINGS SHE MAKES THE WARP OF HER BASKET,	140	MULBERRY ROAD	8
SHE MAKES THE SHOULDER-STRAPS OF HER BASKET	140	MULBERRY ROAD	9
AND BY HER LEFT FOOT, IN A BASKET,	180	MOEURS CON: 5	10
THE BASKET IS LINED WITH SATIN,	180	MOEURS CON: 5	14
BASKETS			
THEIR STALKS ARE WOVEN IN BASKETS,	221	SEXTUS PROP: 7	30
BASKET-WORK			
A BASKET-WORK OF BRAIDS WHICH SEEM AS IF THEY WERE	204	MEDALLION	10
BASTAN			
MI BASTAN MIS PENSAMIENTOS.	82	THE CONDOLENCE	EPI
BASTIDIDES			
BASTIDIDES, ON THE CONTRARY, WHO BOTH TALKS AND WRITES OF NOTHING SAVE COPULATION,	100	TEMPERAMENTS	5
BATH			
THE BATH TUB	100	THE BATH TUB	T
BATHE			
I WOULD BATHE MYSELF IN STRANGENESS:	70	THE PLUNGE	1
SHE WILL NOT BATHE TOO OFTEN, BUT HER JEWELS	161	CABARET DANCER	13
BATH-ROBE			
THIS LADY IN THE WHITE BATH-ROBE WHICH SHE CALLS A PEIGNOIR,	87	ALBATRE	1
BATHTUB			
AS A BATHTUB LINED WITH WHITE PORCELAIN,	100	THE BATH TUB	1
BATTERED			
FOR A FEW THOUSAND BATTERED BOOKS.	191	HUGH SELWYN: 5	8
BATTERS			
THAT WHICH STANDS FIRM IN THEE TIME BATTERS DOWN,	40	ROME	13
BATTLE			
AND THE SHRILL NEIGHS OF DESTRIERS IN BATTLE REJOICING,	28	ALTAFORTE	14
"OF" THE VICTORIOUS DELAY OF FABIUS, AND THE LEFT-HANDED BATTLE AT CANNAE,	210	SEXTUS PROP: 2	11
"NOR WILL THE NOISE OF HIGH HORSES LEAD YOU EVER TO BATTLE;	211	SEXTUS PROP: 2	41
BATTLE-GUERDON			
SUCH BATTLE GUERDON WITH HIS "PROWESSE HIGH"?	32	PIERE VIDAL	59
BATTLES			
WE HAVE NO REST, THREE BATTLES A MONTH.	127	BOWMEN OF SHU	16
WE, IN OUR NARROW BED, TURNING ASIDE FROM BATTLES:	218	SEXTUS PROP. 5	57
BATTLE'S			
NO CRY LIKE THE BATTLE'S REJOICING	29	ALTAFORTE	33
BAUDELAIRE			
AND THE HARLOTS OF BAUDELAIRE.	112	SHOP GIRL	5
BAWDS			
WITH FAT DOARDS, BAWDS, WINE AND FRAIL MUSIC!	28	ALTAFORTE	17
BAWDY			
IF I SET FORTH A BAWDY PLOT LIKE BYRON	239	MOYEN SENSUEL	42
BUT THE BAWDY LITTLE BRITONS	272	NATIONAL SONG	11
BAY			
TO BAY LIKE SIR ROGER DE COVERLEY'S	52	AU SALON	15
BE (130)			
BE'A			
GUARDA! AHI, GUARDA! CH' E BE'A!	96	AESTHETICS	5
CH' E DE'A	97	AESTHETICS	21
BEACH			
THE UNFORECASTED BEACH;	203	MAUBERLEY: 4	19
BEACHES			
AND CASTS STONES ON LAVINIAN BEACHES.	228	SEXTUS PROP:12	35
BEAK			
I WITH MY BEAK HAULED ASHORE WOULD PROCEED IN A MORE STATELY MANNER,	216	SEXTUS PROP: 5	10
BEAMS			
THE INFANT BEAMS AT THE PARENT,	180	MOEURS CON: 5	12

PAGE 37

BEAMS -- BEAUTIFUL

	PAGE	TITLE	LINE
BEAMS (CONTINUED)			
THOUGH IT IS NOT STRETCHED UPON GILDED BEAMS;	208	SEXTUS PROP: 1	52
BEAR			
BID THY 'FULGENCE BEAR AWAY CARE.	7	CINO	48
THE WAVES BORE IN, SOON WILL THEY BEAR AWAY.	69	THE NEEDLE	10
BEAR TO THEM MY CONTEMPT FOR THEIR OPPRESSORS.	88	COMMISSION	3
BEAR MY CONTEMPT OF OPPRESSORS.	88	COMMISSION	5
WITH CARAVANS, BUT NEVER AN APE OR A BEAR.	119	THE GYPSY	16
CALLISTO, DISGUISED AS A BEAR,	222	SEXTUS PROP: 8	24
NOW YOU MAY BEAR FATE'S STROKE UNPERTURBED.	222	SEXTUS PROP: 8	37
WHO BEAR THE BRUNT OF OUR AMERICA	235	TO WHISTLER	12
CAN BEAR HIS PART OF WIT	248	DONNA MI PREGA	8
BEARD			
AND THREE DAYS' BEARD;	15	FAMAM CANO	37
WITH A RED STRAGGLING BEARD?	154	NEAR PERIGORD	102
BEARETH			
THE BROKEN SUNLIGHT FOR A HEALM SHE BEARETH	38	BALLATETTA	4
BEARING			
THEY THAT COME MEWARDS, BEARING OLD MAGIC.	20	IN DURANCE	22
FLESH-SHROUDED BEARING THE SECRET.	20	IN DURANCE	25
BEARING HER OFFERINGS IN THEIR UNHARDENED HANDS,	211	SEXTUS PROP: 2	34
BEARING ANCESTRAL LARES AND IMAGES;	219	SEXTUS PROP: 6	14
GO BACK TO GREAT DIAN'S DANCES BEARING SUITABLE GIFTS,	224	SEXTUS PROP: 9	24
BEARS			
THAT BEARS US UP, SHALL TURN AGAINST THE POLE.	69	THE NEEDLE	7
NOW BEARS THE PALSIED CONTACT OF PHIDIPPUS.	111	SOCIETY	4
"WITH APES OR BEARS?"	119	THE GYPSY	3
GOES ON THAT HEADLESS TRUNK, THAT BEARS FOR LIGHT	156	NEAR PERIGORD	164
THE WATER-JET OF GOLD LIGHT BEARS US UP THROUGH THE CEILINGS;	169	PHANOPOEIA	4
AND ONE RAFT BEARS OUR FATES	223	SEXTUS PROP: 9	5
BEASTS			
INSOLENT LITTLE BEASTS, SHAMELESS, DEVOID OF CLOTHING!	94	INSTRUCTIONS	14
FOR ORPHEUS TAMED THE WILD BEASTS--	208	SEXTUS PROP: 1	42
BEAT			
AND I FLOWED IN UPON THEE, BEAT THEM OFF;	60	TOMB AKR CAAR	20
AND GREAT WINGS BEAT ABOVE US IN THE TWILIGHT,	157	NEAR PERIGORD	176
WHAT FOOT BEAT OUT YOUR TIME-BAR,	207	SEXTUS PROP: 1	8
TO BEAT PRAGUE, BUDAPESTH, VIENNA OR MOSCOW,	245	MOYEN SENSUEL	190
MY SALES BEAT ALL THE OTHER TEN,	266	ALF'S ELEVENTH	3
BEATAE			
HORAE BEATAE INSCRIPTIO	51	HORAE BEATAE	T
BEATEN			
OF BEATEN WORK; AND THROUGH THE CLARET STONE,	49	OF SPLENDOUR	15
STORMS, ON THE· STONE-CLIFFS BEATEN, FELL ON THE STERN	64	THE SEAFARER	23
I HAVE BEATEN OUT MY EXILE.	93	THE REST	19
BEATEN AT LAST,	152	NEAR PERIGORD	42
BEATS			
AND NO LIGHT BEATS UPON ME, AND YOU SAY	60	TOMB AKR CAAR	27
BEATS OUT THE BREATH FROM DOOM-GRIPPED BODY.	66	THE SEAFARER	72
BEAU			
MON BEAU GRAND FRERE	273	M. POM-POM	3
BEAUTIES			
SO MANY THOUSAND BEAUTIES ARE GONE DOWN TO AVERNUS,	38	LADY'S LIFE	3
AND AMID ALL THE GLORIED AND STORIED BEAUTIES OF MAEONIA	222	SEXTUS PROP: 8	34
THE SELECT COMPANY: BEAUTIES YOU ALL WOULD KNOW	242	MOYEN SENSUEL	113
BEAUTIFUL			
OTHERS ARE BEAUTIFUL, NONE MORE, SOME LESS.	52	AU SALON	EPI
SHE IS BEAUTIFUL AS THE SUNLIGHT, AND AS FLUID.	84	ORTUS	5
THOROUGHLY BEAUTIFUL,	103	LADIES	16
"IT RESTS ME TO BE AMONG BEAUTIFUL WOMEN.	113	TAME CAT	3
IT RESTS ME TO CONVERSE WITH BEAUTIFUL WOMEN	113	TAME CAT	4
AND THEY CALL YOU BEAUTIFUL IN THE PROVINCE,	113	FORMIANUS LADY	8
IS NOT SO BEAUTIFUL AS SHE WAS,	116	THE TEA SHOP	2
THE BEAUTIFUL TOILET	128	BEAU TOILET	T
LET COME BEAUTIFUL PEOPLE	146	CANTILATIONS	6
SUDDENLY DISCOVERING IN THE EYES OF THE VERY BEAUTIFUL	161	PAGANI'S NOV 8	1

PAGE 38

BEAUTIFUL -- BECOME

	PAGE	TITLE	LINE
BEAUTIFUL (CONTINUED)			
THE OLD MEN WITH BEAUTIFUL MANNERS.	181	MOEURS CON: 7	2
OLD MEN WITH BEAUTIFUL MANNERS,	182	MOEURS CON: 7	23
QUITE ENOUGH BEAUTIFUL WOMEN,	223	SEXTUS PROP: 9	15
I HAD NEVER SEEN HER LOOKING SO BEAUTIFUL,	225	SEXTUS PROP:10	30
BEAUTY			
AND HAVE SOME BREATH FOR BEAUTY AND THE ARTS.	20	IN DURANCE	16
"QUASI KALOUN." S. T. SAYS BEAUTY IS MOST THAT, A "CALLING TO THE SOUL."	20	IN DURANCE	20
FOR LOVE, OR HOPE, OR BEAUTY OR FOR POWER,	21	IN DURANCE	32
MY WAVE-WORN BEAUTY WITH HIS WIND OF FLOWERS,	24	THUS NINEVEH	15
AND THE BEAUTY OF THIS THY VENICE	26	NIGHT LITANY	5
OF THY BEAUTY HATH WALKED	26	NIGHT LITANY	26
STANDETH THIS IMAGE OF THE BEAUTY SPED.	41	HER MONUMENT	9
OF SENSE UNTELLABLE, BEAUTY	41	HER MONUMENT	28
HOW WILL THIS BEAUTY, WHEN I AM FAR HENCE,	51	HORAE BEATAE	1
COME BEAUTY BAREFOOT FROM THE CYCLADES,	63	PHASELLUS ILLE	12
BOSQUE TAKETH BLOSSOM, COMETH BEAUTY OF BERRIES,	65	THE SEAFARER	49
LOVERS OF BEAUTY, STARVED,	92	THE REST	6
BEAUTY IS SO RARE A THING.	158	PSYCHOLOG HOUR	6
BEAUTY IS SO RARE A THING	158	PSYCHOLOG HOUR	21
BEAUTY WOULD DRINK OF MY MIND.	158	PSYCHOLOG HOUR	28
FORGETTING EVEN HER BEAUTY.	168	OF AROUET	42
FOR HER GREAT BEAUTY, MANY MEN LOOK ON HER,	177	LANGUE D'OC: 4	27
EVEN THE CHRISTIAN BEAUTY	189	HUGH SELWYN: 3	13
ALL THINGS SAVE BEAUTY ALONE.	197	ENVOI (1919)	26
BECAUSE THIS BEAUTY HAD BEEN.	201	AGE DEMANDED	16
THE SONGS SHALL BE A FINE TOMB-STONE OVER THEIR BEAUTY.	209	SEXTUS PROP: 1	64
BEAUTY IS NOT ETERNAL, NO MAN HAS PERENNIAL FORTUNE,	223	SEXTUS PROP: 9	20
"BEAUTY IS SLANDER'S COCK-SHY.	226	SEXTUS PROP:11	21
BEAUTY SO NEAR,	250	DONNA MI PREGA	73
BEAVERBROOK			
WHILE MILORD BEAVERBROOK	257	BREAD BRIGADE	28
BECAME			
THE LIGHT BECAME HER GRACE AND DWELT AMONG	38	BALLATETTA	1
I SAY MY SOUL FLOWED BACK, BECAME TRANSLUCENT.	51	THE FLAME	36
BECAME A PASTIME FOR	192	YEUX GLAUQUES	7
BECAME AN OLYMPIAN APATHEIN	202	AGE DEMANDED	39
BECAUSE			
AND NOW MEN CALL ME MAD BECAUSE I HAVE THROWN	4	LA FRAISNE	27
BECAUSE MY BRIDE	5	LA FRAISNE	30
AND BECAUSE I HAVE SMALL MIND TO SIT	22	MARVOIL	2
SET DEEP IN CRYSTAL; AND BECAUSE MY SLEEP	30	PIERE VIDAL	22
ALL-CONQUERING, NOW CONQUERED, BECAUSE	40	ROME	7
A LOT OF ASSES PRAISE YOU BECAUSE YOU ARE "VIRILE."	82	THE CONDOLENCE	2
BECAUSE I HAD JUET COME FROM THE COUNTRY;	85	SALUTATION 2ND	2
AND NOW YOU GRUMBLE BECAUSE YOUR DRESS DOES NOT FIT	102	LADIES	7
AND BECAUSE I HAPPEN TO SAY SO.	102	LADIES	8
HERE WE ARE BECAUSE WE HAVE THE KEN-NIN FOR OUR FOEMEN,	127	BOWMEN OF SHU	3
WE HAVE NO COMFORT BECAUSE OF THESE MONGOLS.	127	BOWMEN OF SHU	4
BECAUSE HIS LONG SLEEVES WOULDN'T KEEP STILL	135	EXILE'S LETTER	29
BECAUSE THEY CAN'T FIND A SOFT SEAT.	142	UNMOVING CLOUD	21
BECAUSE ONE HAS JUST, AT LAST, FOUND THEM?	158	PSYCHOLOG HOUR	25
BECAUSE OF THESE REVERIES.	193	SIENA MI FE	20
BECAUSE THIS BEAUTY HAD BEEN.	201	AGE DEMANDED	16
TURN TO YOUR DRIPPING HORSES, BECAUSE OF A TUNE, UNDER AETNA?	208	SEXTUS PROP: 1	47
BECAUSE OF THIS RESPECTABLE TERROR,	212	SEXTUS PROP: 3	10
WERE DESOLATED BECAUSE SHE HAD TOLD THEM HER DREAMS.	214	SEXTUS PROP: 4	23
BECAUSE HELEN'S CONDUCT IS "UNSUITABLE."	218	SEXTUS PROP: 5	63
BECAUSE A LADY ASKS ME, I WOULD TELL	248	DONNA MI PREGA	1
BECAUSE I PRINT MOST LIES.	266	ALF'S ELEVENTH	4
BECOME			
HAVING BECOME THE SOULS OF SONG.	6	CINO	9
BUT REACH ME NOT AND ALL MY LIFE'S BECOME	20	IN DURANCE	6
UNTIL IS ITS LOVELINESS BECOME UNTO ME,	26	NIGHT LITANY	7
BECOME SILENT WITHIN ME.	27	NIGHT LITANY	48
WAS GROWN SO FREE AN ESSENCE OR BECOME	32	PARACELSUS	4
HAS BECOME THE FATHER OF TWINS,	100	TEMPERAMENTS	6

BED -- BEFORE

	PAGE	TITLE	LINE
BED			
"I AM JUST FROM BED. THE SLEEP IS STILL IN MY EYES.	166	FISH & SHADOW	9
"COME NOW! OLD SWENKIN! RISE UP FROM THY BED, ...	172	LANGUE D'OC: 1	14
SAW HER STRETCHED ON HER BED,--	214	SEXTUS PROP: 4	17
"BLACK SPIDERS SPIN IN HER BED!	215	SEXTUS PROP: 4	35
WE, IN OUR NARROW BED, TURNING ASIDE FROM BATTLES:	218	SEXTUS PROP: 5	57
NOR SHALL IT BE ON AN ATALIC BED;	219	SEXTUS PROP: 6	16
PARIS TOOK HELEN NAKED COMING FROM THE BED OF MENELAUS, ...	220	SEXTUS PROP: 7	14
AND CYNTHIA WAS ALONE IN HER BED.	225	SEXTUS PROP:10	28
THERE WERE UPON THE BED NO SIGNS OF A VOLUPTUOUS ENCOUNTER, ...	225	SEXTUS PROP:10	36
BUT IN ONE BED, IN ONE BED ALONE, MY DEAR LYNCEUS	228	SEXTUS PROP:12	15
BUT IN ONE BED, IN ONE BED ALONE, MY DEAR LYNCEUS	228	SEXTUS PROP:12	15
BED-FEET			
HER ESCRITOIRES LAY SHUT BY THE BED-FEET.	214	SEXTUS PROP: 4	21
BED-POSTS			
MOUNTS FROM THE FOUR HORNS OF MY BED-POSTS, ...	169	PHANOPOEIA	3
BEDROOM			
"HE STOMPED INTO MY BEDROOM.	182	MOEURS CON: 8	6
"... STOMPED INTO MY BEDROOM.	182	MOEURS CON: 8	8
BEE			
AND HAVING DREAMED THAT HE WAS A BIRD, A BEE, AND A BUTTERFLY, ...	118	ANCIENT WISDOM	2
BEEF			
IN PLACE OF THE ROAST BEEF OF BRITAIN, ...	263	ALF'S EIGHTH	19
AND I GET ALL THE BEEF	269	SAFE AND SOUND	6
BEEF-BONES			
HE FEEDS ME WITH BEEF-BONES AND WINE.	237	ABU SALAMMAMM	3
BEEFY			
WE ARE SIX HUNDRED BEEFY MEN	270	OF 600 M.P.'S	9
BEEN (23)			
BEERY			
SPLITTING ITS BEERY JOWL	52	AU SALON	22
BEFALL			
BEHOLD HOW PRIDE AND RUIN CAN BEFALL	40	ROME	5
BEFORE			
KNOWING THE TRUTH OF THINGS UNSEEN BEFORE;	3	THE TREE	2
THAT WAS RANK FOLLY TO MY HEAD BEFORE.	3	THE TREE	12
FOR EVEN AS THOU ART HOLLOW BEFORE I FILL THEE WITH THIS PARCHMENT, ...	23	MARVOIL	37
BEFORE THE TIME OF ITS COMING?	26	NIGHT LITANY	18
AND BEFORE THE HOLINESS	26	NIGHT LITANY	29
AND DECLAIMS BEFORE THE LADIES	46	FROM HEINE: 6	15
YOU'VE GOT THE WHOLE NIGHT BEFORE YOU, ...	48	FROM HEINE: 8	5
PARTED BEFORE THEE.	68	APPARUIT	12
COME NOW, BEFORE THIS POWER	69	THE NEEDLE	6
WAS BEFORE THEM.	93	LES MILLWIN	7
WOMEN BEFORE A SHOP	114	BEFORE A SHOP	T
GO BEFORE HER INTO AVERNUS;	115	SOCIAL ORDER	12
AND BEFORE THE END OF THE DAY WE WERE SCATTERED LIKE STARS, OR RAIN.	135	EXILE'S LETTER	33
BEFORE THE ROYAL LODGE:	141	IDEA OF CHOAN	6
THEY EDDY BEFORE THE GATE OF THE BARONS.	141	IDEA OF CHOAN	8
BEFORE IT ANOTHER HOUSE WHICH I DO NOT KNOW:	141	IDEA OF CHOAN	30
BEFORE SLEEP	147	BEFORE SLEEP	T
BEFORE THE HARD OLD KING:	152	NEAR PERIGORD	43
SPOILING HIS VISIT, WITH A YEAR BEFORE THE NEXT ONE.	154	NEAR PERIGORD	113
SURELY I SAW, AND STILL BEFORE MY EYES	156	NEAR PERIGORD	163
FLARES ON THE CROWDED STAGE BEFORE OUR TABLES	162	CABARET DANCER	22
HAS HELD IN THE AIR BEFORE YOU.	169	PHANOPOEIA	15
AND I SAID: "THAT WAS BEFORE I ARRIVED."	182	MOEURS CON: 8	4
DARING AS NEVER BEFORE, WASTAGE AS NEVER BEFORE.	190	HUGH SELWYN: 4	20
DARING AS NEVER BEFORE, WASTAGE AS NEVER BEFORE.	190	HUGH SELWYN: 4	20
FORTITUDE AS NEVER BEFORE	190	HUGH SELWYN: 4	23
FRANKNESS AS NEVER BEFORE, ...	190	HUGH SELWYN: 4	24
"WHEREFROM FATHER ENNIUS, SITTING BEFORE I CAME, HATH DRUNK."	210	SEXTUS PROP: 2	7
CUPID WILL CARRY LIGHTED TORCHES BEFORE HIM	212	SEXTUS PROP: 3	22
OR SHE WILL SIT BEFORE YOUR FEET IN A VEIL, ...	223	SEXTUS PROP: 9	11
BEFORE THE "ARS POETICA" OF HIRAM MAXIM.	239	MOYEN SENSUEL	34

PAGE 40

BEFORE -- BEING

	PAGE	TITLE	LINE
BEFORE (CONTINUED)			
AS HELD BEFORE HIM IN THAT UNSULLIED MIRROR	241	MOYEN SENSUEL	93
DO, THAT IS: THINK, BEFORE IT'S TOO LATE.	265	ALF'S TENTH	12
BEFOREHAND			
PLEASE LET ME KNOW BEFOREHAND,	131	RIVER-MER WIFE	27
BEFRIENDED			
IN THE YOUNG DAYS WHEN THE DEEP SKY BEFRIENDED.	157	NEAR PERIGORD	175
BEG			
I BEG YOU, MY FRIENDLY CRITICS,	81	TENZONE	8
BEGAN			
"WHEN I BEGAN I GOT, OF COURSE,	194	MR. NIXON	6
AND THEN RADWAY BEGAN TO GO THE PACES:	243	MOYEN SENSUEL	144
BEGIN			
WHEN I BEGIN TO SING	45	FROM HEINE: 5	2
BEGINNING			
BEGINNING WITH MUMPODORUS;	99	SALVATIONISTS	13
BEGINNING WITH NIMMIM;	99	SALVATIONISTS	15
LONELY FROM THE BEGINNING OF TIME UNTIL NOW!	133	FRONTIER GUARD	2
OUT WITH IT, TELL IT TO ME, ALL OF IT, FROM THE BEGINNING,	214	SEXTUS PROP: 4	11
BEGOT			
HEW MY HEART ROUND AND HUNGER BEGOT	64	THE SEAFARER	11
BEHAVIOUR			
IN THIS THING'S SURE DECORUM AND BEHAVIOUR.	63	PHASELLUS ILLE	14
BEHELD			
I HAVE BEHELD THE LADY OF LIFE,	18	DE AEGYPTO	3
AND HERE IN NINEVEH HAVE I BEHELD	24	THUS NINEVEH	8
EXULTED, THEY BEHELD THE SPLENDOURS OF CLEOPATRA.	93	LES MILLWIN	10
AND THE LITTLE MILLWINS BEHELD THESE THINGS;	93	LES MILLWIN	11
BEHIND			
"LAPPO I LEAVE BEHIND AND DANTE TOO,	25	GUIDO INVITES	1
AND RED THE SUNLIGHT WAS, BEHIND IT ALL.	49	OF SPLENDOUR	8
WHAT YOU HAVE KEPT AND WHAT YOU'VE LEFT BEHIND:	59	EXIT' CUIUSDAM	5
I WAS TWENTY YEARS BEHIND THE TIMES	85	SALUTATION 2ND	3
HE MOVES BEHIND ME	90	SURGIT FAMA	9
AND I'D THE LONG WAYS BEHIND ME,	119	THE GYPSY	9
OR HUGGED TWO GIRLS AT ONCE BEHIND A CHAPEL.)	242	MOYEN SENSUEL	106
BEHIND THEM? WHAT'S THERE? HER SOUL'S AN AFFAIR FOR OCULISTS.	247	PIERROTS	12
BEHOLD			
BEHOLD MINE AUDIENCE,	14	FAMAM CANO	21
BEHOLD THE SHIELD! HE SHALL NOT TAKE THEE ALL.	19	FOR E. MCC	26
BEHOLD ME, VIDAL, THAT WAS FOOL OF FOOLS!	30	PIERE VIDAL	7
BEHOLD HERE VIDAL, THAT WAS HUNTED, FLAYED,	31	PIERE VIDAL	47
BEHOLD ME SHRIVELLED AS AN OLD OAK'S TRUNK	31	PIERE VIDAL	52
BEHOLD! THE WORLD OF FORMS IS SWEPT BENEATH--	32	PARACELSUS	7
BEHOLD ME SHRIVELLED, AND YOUR MOCK OF MOCKS:	32	PIERE VIDAL	62
BEHOLD HOW PRIDE AND RUIN CAN BEFALL	40	ROME	5
BEHOLD THIS BOOK, THE URN OF ASHES,	45	FROM HEINE: 3	7
BEHOLD MINE ADORATION	49	OF SPLENDOUR	18
WHEN I BEHOLD HOW BLACK, IMMORTAL INK	59	SILET	1
AND BEHOLD ME, SMALL FORTUNE LEFT IN MY HOUSE.	229	SEXTUS PROP:12	53
BEHOLDING			
KEEP SMALL WITH REVERENCE, BEHOLDING HER IMAGE.	164	QUINTUS SEPTIM	7
BEING			
BEING IN ALL THINGS WISE, AND VERY OLD,	4	LA FRAISNE	2
BUT I HAVE PUT ASIDE THIS FOLLY, BEING GAY	4	LA FRAISNE	7
BEING UPON THE ROAD ONCE MORE,	6	CINO	11
AND BEING BENT AND WRINKLED, IN A FORM	9	NA AUDIART	38
BEING SO YOUNG AND FAIR	9	NA AUDIART	46
BEING THEN YOUNG AND WRY'D,	9	NA AUDIART	48
SO ART THOU WITH US, BEING GOOD TO KEEP	19	FOR E. MCC	21
"BEING NO LONGER HUMAN, WHY SHOULD I	32	PARACELSUS	1
TO GIVE HER A NAME AND HER BEING!	84	ORTUS	8
NO PORTION, BUT A BEING.	84	ORTUS	16
IS, FOR THE TIME BEING, THE MISTRESS OF MY FRIEND,	87	ALBATRE	2
BEING SMITTEN WITH AN UNUSUAL WISDOM,	96	AESTHETICS	2
BEING FREE OF MEDIAEVAL SCHOLARSHIP	98	THE BELLAIRES	24
I NEVER LAUGHED, BEING BASHFUL.	100	RIVER-MER WIFE	8
SAY "FORGET TO-MORROW," BEING OF ALL MEN	161	CABARET DANCER	7
TWO DEATHS--AND TO STOP LOVING AND BEING LOVABLE,	168	OF AROUET	27

BEING -- BELS

	PAGE	TITLE	LINE
BEING (CONTINUED)			
HE BEING AT THAT AGE A VIRGIN,	178	MOEURS CON: 1	5
THE TERM "VIRGO" BEING MADE MALE IN MEDIAEVAL LATINITY;	178	MOEURS CON: 1	6
BEING BUT THIS OVERBLOTTED	203	MAUBERLEY: 4	15
BEING EXPERT FROM EXPERIENCE,	222	SEXTUS PROP: 8	33
POOR IN DISCERNMENT, BEING THUS WEAKNESS' FRIEND,	249	DONNA MI PREGA	38
BEING A PHYSICIST	261	ALF'S SIXTH	21
INSTEAD OF BEING A CARTER?	268	ANOTHER BIT	16
BEL			
BEL MIRAL'S STATURE, THE VISCOUNTESS' THROAT,	151	NEAR PERIGORD	8
BELAUD			
CELEBRITIES FROM THE TRANS-CAUCASUS WILL BELAUD ROMAN CELEBRITIES	207	SEXTUS PROP: 1	17
BELIEVE			
TELL US THIS THING RATHER, THEN WE'LL BELIEVE YOU,	13	MESMERISM	6
WHO CAN LOOK ON THAT BLUE AND NOT BELIEVE?	50	THE FLAME	28
ON LOAN AND ON LAND, I BELIEVE NOT	65	THE SEAFARER	67
DOES NOT BELIEVE IN ASTHETICS.	178	MOEURS CON: 1	14
TO THINGS WHICH YOU THINK I WOULD LIKE TO BELIEVE.	214	SEXTUS PROP: 4	7
AND YOU EXPECT ME TO BELIEVE THIS	215	SEXTUS PROP: 4	41
AND BELIEVE IT, AND SHE ALSO WILL BELIEVE IT,	222	SEXTUS PROP: 8	32
AND BELIEVE IT, AND SHE ALSO WILL BELIEVE IT,	222	SEXTUS PROP: 8	32
"YOU SHOULD NOT BELIEVE HOSTILE TONGUES.	226	SEXTUS PROP:11	20
THAT FIRST MADE HIM BELIEVE IN IMMORAL SUASION.	245	MOYEN SENSUEL	198
BELIEVES			
THIS HE LITTLE BELIEVES, WHO AYE IN WINSOME LIFE	64	THE SEAFARER	28
BELIEVING			
BELIEVING WE SHOULD MEET WITH LIPS AND HANDS,	157	NEAR PERIGORD	179
AND SOME BELIEVING,	190	HUGH SELWYN: 4	2
BELIEVING IN OLD MEN'S LIES, THEN UNBELIEVING	190	HUGH SELWYN: 4	14
BELL			
DOLE THE BELL! BELL THE DOLE!	258	ALF'S THIRD	SUB
DOLE THE BELL! BELL THE DOLE!	258	ALF'S THIRD	SUB
BELLAIRE			
THE GOOD SQUIRE BELLAIRE;	97	THE BELLAIRES	12
FOR THEY MAY NOT BELONG TO THE GOOD SQUIRE BELLAIRE	98	THE BELLAIRES	14
WHEREFORE THE GOOD SQUIRE BELLAIRE	98	THE BELLAIRES	34
BELLAIRES			
THE BELLAIRES	97	THE BELLAIRES	T
THE GOOD BELLAIRES	97	THE BELLAIRES	1
TOGETHER WITH THE RESPECTIVE WIVES, HUSBANDS, SISTERS AND HETEROGENEOUS CONNECTIONS OF THE GOOD BELLAIRES,	97	THE BELLAIRES	6
BUT THE GOOD BELLAIRES HAVE SO LITTLE UNDERSTOOD THEIR AFFAIRS	97	THE BELLAIRES	8
FOR THE GOOD BELLAIRES	98	THE BELLAIRES	42
BELLEROPHON'S			
THE WATER DRIPPING FROM BELLEROPHON'S HORSE,	210	SEXTUS PROP: 2	2
BELLIES			
LAUGHTER OUT OF DEAD BELLIES.	190	HUGH SELWYN: 4	27
BELLOTTI			
BLACK SLIPPERS: BELLOTTI	111	BLACK SLIPPERS	T
BELLS			
HERE ARE YOUR BELLS AND CONFETTI.	86	SALUTATION 2ND	23
BELONG			
AND THE SPHERES THEY BELONG IN,	52	AU SALON	3
FOR THEY MAY NOT BELONG TO THE GOOD SQUIRE BELLAIRE	98	THE BELLAIRES	14
ON THE CONTRARY, IF THEY DO NOT BELONG TO HIS WIFE,	98	THE BELLAIRES	16
BELOVED			
MY CITY, MY BELOVED, MY WHITE! AH, SLENDER,	62	N. Y.	1
MY CITY, MY BELOVED,	62	N. Y.	8
NOR TAKE MY BELOVED FROM MY SIGHT,	177	LANGUE D'OC: 4	7
BELOW			
IF MY HEART STAY BELOW THERE,	47	FROM HEINE: 7	21
I AM BELOW AMID THE PINE TREES,	53	AU JARDIN	4
FOR THE NOBLENESS OF THE POPULACE BROOKS NOTHING BELOW ITS OWN ALTITUDE.	230	SEXTUS PROP:12	64
BELS			
BELS CEMBELINS, I TAKE OF YOU YOUR COLOUR,	105	DOMPNA POIS	21
OF BELS MIRALS, THE REST,	106	DOMPNA POIS	56

PAGE 42

BELS -- BERNARD

	PAGE	TITLE	LINE
BELS (CONTINUED)			
AH, BELS SENHER, MAENT, AT LAST	106	DOMPNA POIS	61
BE-M			
QUE BE-M VOLS MAL.	9	NA AUDIART	57
BEN			
FOR AS BEN FRANKLIN SAID, WITH SUCH URBANITY:	246	MOYEN SENSUEL	235
BENACUS			
SAPPHIRE BENACUS, IN THY MISTS AND THEE	50	THE FLAME	26
BENCH			
"TIME FOR THAT QUESTION!" FRONT BENCH INTERPOSES.	260	ALF'S FIFTH	16
AND LEAVES YOU A PARK BENCH TO SIT ON	263	ALF'S EIGHTH	20
BENCHES			
AN' THEM SPRAWLING ON THE BENCHES	270	OF 600 M.P.'S	14
BEND			
CRIMSON, FROSTY WITH DEW, THE ROSES BEND WHERE	68	APPARUIT	5
BEND OVER WITH HEAVY HEADS.	112	IONE, DEAD	4
THEY BEND IN VAIN.	112	IONE, DEAD	5
BENDED			
DRIVES THE CLEAR EMERALDS FROM THE BENDED GRASSES	38	BALLATETTA	9
BENDING			
BENDING YOUR PASSAGES FROM RIGHT TO LEFT AND FROM LEFT TO RIGHT	147	BEFORE SLEEP	15
BENDS			
SOUTHWARD TOWARD MONTAIGNAC, AND HE BENDS AT A TABLE	154	NEAR PERIGORD	97
BENDS INTO THE TURN OF THE WIND,	170	PHANOPOEIA	20
BENEATH			
THAT TRAMP OLD WAYS BENEATH THE SUN-LIGHT,	6	CINO	21
AND THE BROAD FIELDS BENEATH THEM TURN CRIMSON,	28	ALTAFORTE	5
BEHOLD! THE WORLD OF FORMS IS SWEPT BENEATH--	32	PARACELSUS	7
TURMOIL GROWN VISIBLE BENEATH OUR PEACE,	32	PARACELSUS	8
AND COOLNESS BENEATH THE TREES.	35	THE EYES	10
ALGAE REACH UP AND OUT, BENEATH	69	SUB MARE	6
BREATH THAT IS STRETCHED OUT BENEATH THE WORLD:	76	THE ALCHEMIST	45
OUT OF EREBUS, OUT OF THE FLAT WASTE OF AIR, LYING BENEATH THE WORLD;	76	THE ALCHEMIST	46
STEPPING BENEATH A BOISTEROUS WIND FROM THRACE,	87	THE SPRING	3
GREY OLIVE LEAVES BENEATH A RAIN-COLD SKY.	92	GENTILDONNA	5
PALE CARNAGE BENEATH BRIGHT MIST.	92	APRIL	5
AND BENEATH THEM	107	COMING OF WAR	6
AND SHE THE REJOICER OF THE HEART IS BENEATH THEM:	108	LIU CH'E	5
CRAWL IN THE VERY BLACK GUTTER BENEATH THE GRAPE STAND?	114	SIMULACRA	4
MALEMORT, GUESSES BENEATH, SENDS WORD TO COEUR-DE-LION:	155	NEAR PERIGORD	123
ARNAUT AND RICHARD LODGE BENEATH CHALUS:	155	NEAR PERIGORD	128
IS WOVEN AND GROWS SOLID BENEATH US;	170	PHANOPOEIA	23
"AND THOU OUT HERE BENEATH THE PORCH OF STONE	172	LANGUE D'OC: 1	22
BENEATH THE SAGGING ROOF	196	HUGH SELWYN: 10	1
PLACID BENEATH WARM SUNS,	203	MAUBERLEY: 4	7
THE FACE-OVAL BENEATH THE GLAZE,	204	MEDALLION	13
BENEATH HALF-WATT RAYS,	204	MEDALLION	15
AND THEY ALL GO TO RACK RUIN BENEATH THE THUD OF THE YEARS.	209	SEXTUS PROP: 1	71
OR MAY I INTER BENEATH THE HUMMOCK	213	SEXTUS PROP: 3	36
BENEATH THEIR TRANSITORY STEP AND MERRIMENT,	236	MIDDLE-AGED	9
THE SHUDDER OF VAE SOLI GURGLES BENEATH MY RIBS.	247	PIERROTS	3
BENNETT			
READ BENNETT OR SOME OTHER FLACCID FLATTERER.	240	MOYEN SENSUEL	66
BENT			
AND BEING BENT AND WRINKLED, IN A FORM	9	NA AUDIART	38
TIBER ALONE, TRANSIENT AND SEAWARD BENT,	40	ROME	11
"LO, ONE THERE WAS WHO BENT HER FAIR BRIGHT HEAD,	43	SATIEMUS	5
O LIGHT BOUND AND BENT IN, O SOUL OF THE CAPTIVE,	95	OF THE DEGREES	11
BENT RESOLUTELY ON WRINGING LILIES FROM THE ACORN;	187	E. P. ODE	7
BENUMBED			
MY FEET WERE BY FROST BENUMBED.	64	THE SEAFARER	9
BERANGERE			
RAIMONA, TIBORS, BERANGERE,	75	THE ALCHEMIST	6
BERNARD			
NOR WILL THE HORRID THREATS OF BERNARD SHAW	63	PHASELLUS ILLE	7

	PAGE	TITLE	LINE
BERRIES			
BOSQUE TAKETH BLOSSOM, COMETH BEAUTY OF BERRIES,	65	THE SEAFARER	49
BERTRANS			
BERTRANS, MASTER OF HIS LAYS,	9	NA AUDIART	30
BERTRANS OF AULTAFORTE THY PRAISE	9	NA AUDIART	31
BERTRANS, EN BERTRANS, LEFT A FINE CANZONE:	151	NEAR PERIGORD	5
BERTRANS, EN BERTRANS, LEFT A FINE CANZONE:	151	NEAR PERIGORD	5
AND OUR EN BERTRANS WAS IN ALTAFORT,	151	NEAR PERIGORD	20
EN BERTRANS, A TOWER-ROOM AT HAUTEFORT,	154	NEAR PERIGORD	95
MY MAGNET," BERTRANS HAD SAID.	154	NEAR PERIGORD	116
OR NO ONE SEES IT, AND EN BERTRANS PROSPERED?	155	NEAR PERIGORD	126
OR TAKE EN BERTRANS?	156	NEAR PERIGORD	169
BERTRAN'S			
WALKED OVER EN BERTRAN'S OLD LAYOUT,	122	PROVINC DESERT	39
BERTRANS'			
FOIX' COUNT KNEW THAT. WHAT IS SIR BERTRANS' SINGING?	153	NEAR PERIGORD	91
BERYL			
BULWARKS OF BERYL AND OF CHRYSOPHRASE.	50	THE FLAME	25
BESEECH			
I BESEECH YOU ENTER YOUR LIFE.	84	ORTUS	12
I BESEECH YOU LEARN TO SAY "I,"	84	ORTUS	13
GIVE ME IN DUE TIME, I BESEECH YOU, A LITTLE TOBACCO-SHOP,	117	THE LAKE ISLE	2
BESIDE			
SHE LAY BESIDE ME IN THE DAWN.	109	ALBA	3
THE OTHER IS LITTLE BESIDE IT.	168	OF AROUET	29
BESIDE THIS THOROUGHFARE	196	HUGH SELWIN:12	25
BESIDES			
AND BESIDES, LYNCEUS,	228	SEXTUS PROP:12	8
BESPEAK			
BESPEAK THYSELF FOR ANYTHING.	8	NA AUDIART	19
BE-SPECTACLED			
SCRAWNY, BE-SPECTACLED, OUT AT HEELS,	14	FAMAM CANO	23
BEST			
WELL MAYST THOU BOAST THAT THOU THE BEST CHEVALIER	37	THE YOUNG KING	18
"NO! HIS FIRST WORK WAS THE BEST."	85	SALUTATION 2ND	14
BUT WE LIKE THIS FELLOW THE BEST,	142	UNMOVING CLOUD	25
AND THE "BEST CRAFTSMAN" SINGS OUT HIS FRIEND'S SONG,	155	NEAR PERIGORD	141
AND OF THE BEST, AMONG THEM,	191	HUGH SELWYN: 5	2
DESPITE SUCH REINS AND CHECKS I'LL DO MY BEST,	238	MOYEN SENSUEL	12
ARE NOT THE BEST OF PULSE FOR INFANT NATIONS.	239	MOYEN SENSUEL	30
"TENT PREACHIN' IS THE KIND THAT PAYS THE BEST."	246	MOYEN SENSUEL	238
BETIDE			
SHE KNOWETH WELL, BETIDE	106	DOMPNA POIS	59
BETTER			
BETTER ONE HOUR'S STOUR THAN A YEAR'S PEACE	28	ALTAFORTE	16
AND BETTER WERE IT, SHOULD GOD GRANT HIS PLEASURE,	37	THE YOUNG KING	22
MAY NOT MAKE BOAST OF ANY BETTER THING	40	ERAT HORA	6
I KNOW NOT IF THE LOVE OR IF THE LAY WERE BETTER STUFF,	44	FROM HEINE: 2	7
COME, LET US PITY THOSE WHO ARE BETTER OFF THAN WE ARE.	83	THE GARRET	1
NOR HAS LIFE IN IT AUGHT BETTER	83	THE GARRET	9
SINGING AS WELL AS I SING, NONE BETTER;	96	DUM CAPITOLIUM	2
BUT YOU, SIR, HAD BETTER TAKE WINE ERE YOUR DEPARTURE,	137	OF DEPARTURE	EPI
BETTER MENDACITIES	188	HUGH SELWYN: 2	7
EMENDATION, CONSERVATION OF THE "BETTER TRADITION,"	202	AGE DEMANDED	47
THERE SHALL BE NONE IN A BETTER SEAT, NOT	222	SEXTUS PROP: 8	35
WAS GOT ABROAD, WHAT BETTER LUCK DO YOU WISH 'EM,	240	MOYEN SENSUEL	60
YOUR OWN MA' WARN'T NO BETTER	260	ALF'S FOURTH	12
C.3, C.4, 'TWERE BETTER TO FORGET	260	ALF'S FIFTH	12
HOW THEY BETTER START TAKIN' CARE,	262	ALF'S SEVENTH	4
BETTERS			
NON-ESTEEM OF SELF-STYLED "HIS BETTERS"	202	AGE DEMANDED	58
BETWEEN			
OH YE, MY FELLOWS: WITH THE SEAS BETWEEN US SOME BE,	21	IN DURANCE	35
THEY WHINED AS HE WALKED OUT CALM BETWEEN,	34	GOODLY FERE	43
THE SPUR-CLINKS SOUND BETWEEN,	47	FROM HEINE: 7	26
BETWEEN THE TWO INDOLENT CANDLES.	87	ALBATRE	7
LET THERE BE COMMERCE BETWEEN US.	89	A PACT	9

BETWEEN -- BIDDING

	PAGE	TITLE	LINE
BETWEEN (CONTINUED)			
BETWEEN MARSEILLES	98	THE BELLAIRES	39
FLASH BETWEEN THE ORCHIDS AND CLOVER,	139	SENNIN POEM	2
RIGHT ENOUGH? THEN READ BETWEEN THE LINES OF UC ST. CIRC,	151	NEAR PERIGORD	3
AND HE WHO SET THE STRIFE BETWEEN BROTHER AND BROTHER	151	NEAR PERIGORD	25
NOT A NEAT LEDGE, NOT FOIX BETWEEN ITS STREAMS, ...	152	NEAR PERIGORD	32
SCRIBBLING, SWEARING BETWEEN HIS TEETH; BY HIS LEFT HAND	154	NEAR PERIGORD	98
"BETWEEN THE NIGHT AND MORNING?"	158	PSYCHOLOG HOUR	27
IT JUTS LIKE A SHELF BETWEEN THE JOWL AND CORSET.	161	CABARET DANCER	16
OR SLITHERS ABOUT BETWEEN THE DISHONEST WAITERS--	162	CABARET DANCER	23
WHO HAVE COME BETWEEN ME AND MY CHARMER,	173	LANGUE D'OC: 2	24
OR SHAKING BETWEEN,	175	LANGUE D'OC: 3	53
IDA HAS LAIN WITH A SHEPHERD, SHE HAS SLEPT BETWEEN SHEEP.	227	SEXTUS PROP:11	36
BETWEEN AUCTION AND PLAIN BRIDGE,	258	ALF'S SECOND	10
AN IDEA BETWEEN 'EM	258	ALF'S SECOND	12
BEWILDER			
SO DOTH BEWILDER ME	176	LANGUE D'OC: 3	64
BEWILDERED			
O BEWILDERED HEART,	87	THE SPRING	10
BEWILDERED THAT A WORLD	192	YEUX GLAUQUES	21
BEWILDERING			
BEWILDERING SPRING, AND BY THE AUVEZERE	157	NEAR PERIGORD	170
BEWILDERMENT			
OF HIS BEWILDERMENT; TO DESIGNATE	199	MAUBERLEY: 2	10
BEWILDERS			
FLYING SNOW BEWILDERS THE BARBARIAN HEAVEN.	139	SOUTH-FOLK	7
BEWRAYED			
BEWRAYED	249	DONNA MI PREGA	42
BEYOND			
ONE FLAME, THAT REACHES NOT BEYOND	20	IN DURANCE	7
"BEYOND, BEYOND, BEYOND, THERE LIES . . ."	21	IN DURANCE	49
"BEYOND, BEYOND, BEYOND, THERE LIES . . ."	21	IN DURANCE	49
"BEYOND, BEYOND, BEYOND, THERE LIES . . ."	21	IN DURANCE	49
LURE US BEYOND THE CLOUDY PEAK OF RIVA?	39	BLANDULA	15
BUT OUT SOMEWHERE BEYOND THE WORLDLY WAYS	49	OF SPLENDOUR	3
WE WHO ARE WISE BEYOND YOUR DREAM OF WISDOM,	50	THE FLAME	5
WE HAVE GONE FORTH BEYOND YOUR BONDS AND BORDERS,	50	THE FLAME	7
OVER BEYOND THE MOON THERE,	53	AU JARDIN	16
AND HIS LAUD BEYOND THEM REMAIN 'MID THE ENGLISH,	66	THE SEAFARER	79
AT THE TABLE BEYOND US	111	BLACK SLIPPERS	1
BEYOND SALVATION, HOLDETH ITS JUDGING FORCE,	249	DONNA MI PREGA	36
THERE, BEYOND COLOUR, ESSENCE SET APART,	250	DONNA MI PREGA	84
BEYOND ALL FALSITY, WORTHY OF FAITH, ALONE	250	DONNA MI PREGA	86
BEZIERS			
HIS HELMET AT BEZIERS.	22	MARVOIL	10
BEZIERS OFF AT MONT-AUSIER, I AND HIS LADY	22	MARVOIL	12
SINGING THE STARS IN THE TURRETS OF BEZIERS,	22	MARVOIL	13
ARAGON CURSING IN ARAGON, BEZIERS BUSY AT BEZIERS--	22	MARVOIL	16
ARAGON CURSING IN ARAGON, BEZIERS BUSY AT BEZIERS--	22	MARVOIL	16
SAVE THIS: "VERS AND CANZONE TO THE COUNTESS OF BEZIERS	22	MARVOIL	28
AND MAY I COME SPEEDILY TO BEZIERS	23	MARVOIL	32
SING THOU THE GRACE OF THE LADY OF BEZIERS,	23	MARVOIL	36
THAT I HAVE NOT THE COUNTESS OF BEZIERS	23	MARVOIL	42
AND BEZIERS.	98	THE BELLAIRES	40
BEZIERS'S			
THE VICOMTE OF BEZIERS'S NOT SUCH A BAD LOT.	22	MARVOIL	6
BIAUCAIRE			
RESIDES NOW AT AGDE AND BIAUCAIRE.	98	THE BELLAIRES	35
GRAY ARLES AND BIAUCAIRE,	119	THE GYPSY	10
BID			
BID THY 'FULGENCE BEAR AWAY CARE.	7	CINO	48
BID THE WORLD'S HOUNDS COME TO HORN!"	25	THE WHITE STAG	7
AND BID GO IN WITH HONOURED COMPANIONS	37	THE YOUNG KING	39
OR SET ME QUIET, OR BID ME CHATTER.	175	LANGUE D'OC: 3	45
I WOULD BID THEM LIVE	197	ENVOI (1919)	12
BIDDING			
BIDDING ME PRAISE	4	LA FRAISNE	18

PAGE 45

BIDDING -- BIT

	PAGE	TITLE	LINE
BIDDING (CONTINUED)			
TIGRIS AND EUPHRATES SHALL, FROM NOW ON, FLOW AT HIS BIDDING,	219	SEXTUS PROP: 6	7
BIDE			
MUST BIDE ABOVE BRINE.	64	THE SEAFARER	31
BIEN			
ET ALORS JE VIS BIEN DES CHOSES	160	DANS OMNIBUS	6
BIG			
HEART THAT WAS BIG AS THE BOWELS OF VESUVIUS,	13	MESMERISM	13
THE SMALL DOGS LOOK AT THE BIG DOGS;	104	THE SEEING EYE	1
BIG TALK AND LITTLE USE.	173	LANGUE D'OC: 2	26
LOOKING SO BIG AND BURLY.	266	ALF'S ELEVENTH	8
BIG-BELLIES			
LET US SPIT UPON THOSE WHO PAT THE BIG-BELLIES FOR PROFIT,	145	SALUTATION 3RD	15
BIGGEST			
THE KING WAS ONCE THE BIGGEST THING	267	ALF'S ELEVENTH	21
BILIOUS			
TESTING HIS LIST OF RHYMES, A LEAN MAN? BILIOUS?	154	NEAR PERIGORD	101
BILLS			
BUT THE SOLE RESULT WAS BILLS	98	THE BELLAIRES	30
BINDS			
"SHE BINDS ME WITH RAVVLES OF SHROUDS.	215	SEXTUS PROP: 4	34
BIRCH			
BRING THE LIGHT OF THE BIRCH TREE IN AUTUMN	75	THE ALCHEMIST	11
BIRCHEN			
SOFT AS SPRING WIND THAT'S COME FROM BIRCHEN BOWERS.	71	A VIRGINAL	10
BIRD			
THE BIRD SITS ON THE HAWTHORN TREE	43	MR. HOUSMAN	6
AND HAVING DREAMED THAT HE WAS A BIRD, A BEE, AND A BUTTERFLY,	118	ANCIENT WISDOM	2
ONE BIRD CASTS ITS GLEAM ON ANOTHER.	139	SENNIN POEM	3
SLEEP NOT THOU NOW, I HEAR THE BIRD IN FLIGHT	172	LANGUE D'OC: 1	11
OH HOW THE BIRD FLEW FROM TROJAN RAFTERS,	227	SEXTUS PROP:11	35
BIRDS			
I WILL SING OF THE WHITE BIRDS	7	CINO	54
STILL SHADE, AND BADE NO WHISPER SPEAK THE BIRDS OF HOW	21	IN DURANCE	48
AND HIGH OVER THE WILLOWS, THE FINE BIRDS SING TO EACH OTHER, AND LISTEN,	129	THE RIVER SONG	28
THE BIRDS OF ETSU HAVE NO LOVE FOR EN, IN THE NORTH,	139	SOUTH-FOLK	2
NIGHT BIRDS, AND NIGHT WOMEN,	141	IDEA OF CHOAN	15
BIRDS WITH FLOWERY WING, HOVERING BUTTERFLIES	141	IDEA OF CHOAN	17
THE BIRDS FLUTTER TO REST IN MY TREE,	142	UNMOVING CLOUD	22
BIRDS SINGING LATE IN THE YEAR!	168	OF AROUET	38
AND THE BIRDS REPEAT	173	LANGUE D'OC: 2	2
AND THE COLD BIRDS TWITTER	174	LANGUE D'OC: 3	2
NOW CRY THE BIRDS OUT, IN THE MEADOW MIST,	177	LANGUE D'OC: 4	12
HERE IN THE ORCHARD WHERE THE BIRDS COMPLAIN,	177	LANGUE D'OC: 4	17
THE SMALL BIRDS OF THE CYTHAREAN MOTHER,	211	SEXTUS PROP: 2	31
BIRTH			
TO BRING HER SOUL TO BIRTH,	84	ORTUS	3
HAD NOT ONE STYLE FROM BIRTH, BUT TRIED AND PRIED	235	TO WHISTLER	16
BIRTHDAY			
HIS MOTHER'S BIRTHDAY GIFT. (HOW PITIFUL	242	MOYEN SENSUEL	117
BISHOPS			
RED KNIGHTS, BROWN BISHOPS, BRIGHT QUEENS,	120	GAME OF CHESS	1
BISTRE			
"CARMEN EST MAIGRE, UN TRAIT DE BISTRE	162	CABARET DANCER	24
BIT			
FOR A FLIP WORD, AND TO TIDY THEIR HAIR A BIT.	117	THE LAKE ISLE	11
LET US GO OUT IN THE AIR A BIT.	145	SALUTATION 3RD	16
THE CYTHERAEAN FOR A CHAIN BIT.	201	AGE DEMANDED	4
ALF'S SECOND BIT	258	ALF'S SECOND	T
ALF'S THIRD BIT	258	ALF'S THIRD	T
ALF'S FOURTH BIT	259	ALF'S FOURTH	T
ALF'S FIFTH BIT	260	ALF'S FIFTH	T
ALF'S SIXTH BIT	261	ALF'S SIXTH	T
ALF'S SEVENTH BIT	262	ALF'S SEVENTH	T
ALF'S EIGHTH BIT	263	ALF'S EIGHTH	T
ALF'S NINTH BIT	264	ALF'S NINTH	T

BIT -- BLEAK

	PAGE	TITLE	LINE
BIT (CONTINUED)			
ALF'S TENTH BIT	265	ALF'S TENTH	T
ALF'S ELEVENTH BIT	266	ALF'S ELEVENTH	T
ALF'S TWELFTH BIT	267	ALF'S TWELFTH	T
ANOTHER BIT--AND AN OFFER	268	ANOTHER BIT	T
BITCH			
FOR AN OLD BITCH GONE IN THE TEETH,	191	HUGH SELWYN: 5	3
BITES			
HE BITES THROUGH THE FLOWER PISTIL	139	SENNIN POEM	9
BITING			
MOUTHS BITING EMPTY AIR,	200	MAUBERLEY: 2	34
BITTER			
FINDS THE EARTH AS BITTER	9	NA AUDIART	44
"TIME'S BITTER FLOOD"! OH, THAT'S ALL VERY WELL,	59	EXIT' CUIUSDAM	1
BITTER BREAST-CARES HAVE I ABIDED,	64	THE SEAFARER	4
THE BITTER HEART'S BLOOD. BURGHER KNOWS NOT--	65	THE SEAFARER	56
OUR SORROW IS BITTER, BUT WE WOULD NOT RETURN TO OUR COUNTRY.	127	BOWMEN OF SHU	12
WHEN THE SWEET AIR GOES BITTER,	174	LANGUE D'OC: 3	1
FER 'ARFT A PINT O' BITTER?"	270	OF 600 M.P.'S	20
BITTERNESS			
FOR I KNOW THAT THE WAILING AND BITTERNESS ARE A FOLLY.	4	LA FRAISNE	23
IF ALL THE GRIEF AND WOE AND BITTERNESS,	36	THE YOUNG KING	1
GRIEVING AND SAD AND FULL OF BITTERNESS	36	THE YOUNG KING	9
O SKILLFUL DEATH AND FULL OF BITTERNESS,	37	THE YOUNG KING	17
FROM THIS FAINT WORLD, HOW FULL OF BITTERNESS	37	THE YOUNG KING	25
HIM, WHOM IT PLEASED FOR OUR GREAT BITTERNESS	37	THE YOUNG KING	33
BLACK			
BLACK IS THE PITCH O' THEIR WEDDING DRESS,	11	OF THE GIBBET	18
AND THE LIGHTNINGS FROM BLACK HEAV'N FLASH CRIMSON,	28	ALTAFORTE	9
HELL BLOT BLACK FOR ALWAY THE THOUGHT "PEACE"!	29	ALTAFORTE	39
OF UGLY PRINT MARKS, BLACK	35	THE EYES	13
WHEN I BEHOLD HOW BLACK, IMMORTAL INK	59	SILET	1
FALLS LIKE BLACK LIGHTNING.	87	THE SPRING	9
THE BLACK PANTHER TREADS AT MY SIDE,	109	HEATHER	1
PETALS ON A WET, BLACK BOUGH.	109	IN THE METRO	2
BLACK SLIPPERS: BELLOTTI	111	BLACK SLIPPERS	T
AND WITH EYES THAT ARE NOT BLACK,	113	FORMIANUS LADY	4
CRAWL IN THE VERY BLACK GUTTER BENEATH THE GRAPE STAND?	114	SIMULACRA	4
A LITTLE BLACK BOX CONTAINS THEM.	145	SALUTATION 3RD	8
SUNK IN A FROWSY COLLAR--AN UNBRUSHED BLACK.	161	CABARET DANCER	12
WITH A BLACK TINT STAINING YOUR CUTICLE,	162	CABARET DANCER	49
"BLACK SPIDERS SPIN IN HER BED!	215	SEXTUS PROP: 4	35
FOR THE SUN SHALL DRIVE WITH BLACK HORSES,	220	SEXTUS PROP: 7	23
WHILE A BLACK VEIL WAS OVER HER STARS,	222	SEXTUS PROP: 8	26
BUT THE BLACK OMINOUS OWL HOOT WAS AUDIBLE.	223	SEXTUS PROP: 9	4
THE BLACK PANTHER LIES UNDER HIS ROSE TREE	231	CANTUS PLANUS	1
THE BLACK PANTHER LIES UNDER HIS ROSE TREE.	231	CANTUS PLANUS	5
BLACKING			
LICK OFF THE BLACKING.	146	SALUTATION 3RD	36
BLADE			
STRUCK OF THE BLADE THAT NO MAN PARRIETH;	19	FOR E. MCC	4
THOU TRUSTED'ST IN THYSELF AND MET THE BLADE	19	FOR E. MCC	15
STRUCK OF THE BLADE THAT NO MAN PARRIETH	19	FOR E. MCC	23
JUST THEN SHE WOKE AND MOCKED THE LESS KEEN BLADE.	31	PIERE VIDAL	43
TOMB HIDETH TROUBLE. THE BLADE IS LAYED LOW.	66	THE SEAFARER	90
BLADES			
AS MEMORABLE BROKEN BLADES THAT BE	19	FOR E. MCC	17
YOU HAVE PERCEIVED THE BLADES OF THE FLAME	169	PHANOPOEIA	12
BLAGUEUR			
BLAGUEUR! "CON GLI OCCHI ONESTI E TARDI,"	181	MOEURS CON: 7	6
BLAME			
AND BLAME THE SUN HIS GLADNESS;	30	PIERE VIDAL	4
BLANDULA			
"BLANDULA, TENULLA, VAGULA"	39	BLANDULA	T
BLANKNESS			
UNABLE IN THE SUPERVENING BLANKNESS	100	MAUBERLEY: 2	16
BLEAK			
OF THE BLEAK WIND, AND NOT	67	DORIA	2

BLEAK -- BLOSSOMS

	PAGE	TITLE	LINE
BLEAK (CONTINUED)			
THE DAI HORSE NEIGHS AGAINST THE BLEAK WIND OF ETSU,	139	SOUTH-FOLK	1
BLEARY			
WHEN OUR MINDS ARE VERY BLEARY,	267	ALF'S TWELFTH	5
BLEED			
HAVE BANK SHARKS TO BLEED 'EM	272	NATIONAL SONG	12
BLEMISH			
WITHOUT BLEMISH, FOR HER LOVE	106	DOMPNA POIS	45
BLENDING			
THE EDGE, UNCERTAIN, BUT A MEANS OF BLENDING	196	HUGH SELWIN:12	14
BLESS			
CULDOU LACKING A COAT TO BLESS	12	OF THE GIBBET	30
BLESSED			
IF SHE DOES NOT COUNT THIS BLESSED	103	PHYLLIDULA	4
BLIGHT			
GO LIKE A BLIGHT UPON THE DULNESS OF THE WORLD;	88	COMMISSION	18
BLIGHTERS			
AND LET THE BLIGHTERS START IT ALL OVER AGAIN.	265	ALF'S NINTH	30
BLIND			
ALL THE BLIND EARTH KNOWS NOT TH' EMPRISE	25	GUIDO INVITES	5
"YE HA' SEEN ME HEAL THE LAME AND BLIND,	34	GOODLY FERE	29
BLIND EYES AND SHADOWS THAT ARE FORMED AS MEN;	38	BALLATETTA	2
DIM TALES THAT BLIND ME, RUNNING ONE BY ONE	43	SATIEMUS	16
WILL GIVE, SAVE TO THE BLIND.	263	ALF'S EIGHTH	7
BLINDED			
"TURN NOT VENUS INTO A BLINDED MOTION,	220	SEXTUS PROP: 7	12
BLINK			
YOU EITHER DRIVE THEM MAD, OR ELSE YOU BLINK AT THEIR SUICIDES,	145	SALUTATION 3RD	22
BLISSFUL			
OF BLISSFUL KINGDOMS AND THE AUREATE SPHERES;	42	HER MONUMENT	34
BLOCKED			
BLOCKED LIGHTS WORKING IN. ESCAPES. RENEWAL OF CONTEST.	120	GAME OF CHESS	15
BLOKE			
TO LICK THE BOOTS OF THE BLOKE	259	ALF'S FOURTH	6
BLOKES			
ONWARD TH' 'UNGRY BLOKES,	257	BREAD BRIGADE	5
THERE IS BLOKES IN AUTOMOBILES	269	SAFE AND SOUND	13
BLOOD			
MY WORDS FOR STOUR, HATH NO BLOOD OF CRIMSON	29	ALTAFORTE	26
GOD! HOW THE SWIFTEST HIND'S BLOOD SPURTED HOT	30	PIERE VIDAL	14
HOT WAS THAT HIND'S BLOOD YET IT SCORCHED ME NOT	30	PIERE VIDAL	16
AND THE BLOOD GUSHED HOT AND FREE,	34	GOODLY FERE	38
THE BITTER HEART'S BLOOD. BURGHER KNOWS NOT--	65	THE SEAFARER	56
THESE WERE THE SOULS OF BLOOD.	74	THE RETURN	18
GO AGAINST THIS VEGETABLE BONDAGE OF THE BLOOD.	89	COMMISSION	34
YOUNG BLOOD AND HIGH BLOOD,	190	HUGH SELWYN: 4	21
YOUNG BLOOD AND HIGH BLOOD,	190	HUGH SELWYN: 4	21
"NOR WHERE THE RHINE FLOWS WITH BARBAROUS BLOOD,	211	SEXTUS PROP: 2	46
RECORD "ODD'S BLOOD! OUCH! OUCH!" A PRAYER, HIS SWIFT REPENTANCE.	243	MOYEN SENSUEL	130
BLOOD ON EACH TIRED FANG	261	ALF'S SIXTH	11
BLOOD-CRIMSON			
AND I LOVE TO SEE THE SUN RISE BLOOD-CRIMSON.	29	ALTAFORTE	19
BLOODLESS			
THAT HE PASSES FOR BOTH BLOODLESS AND SEXLESS.	100	TEMPERAMENTS	4
BLOOD-RAVENOUS			
A GRACIOUS SPRING, TURNED TO BLOOD-RAVENOUS AUTUMN,	133	FRONTIER GUARD	14
BLOODS			
WE, YOU, I! WE ARE "RED BLOODS"!	82	THE CONDOLENCE	3
DESPITE IT ALL, DESPITE YOUR RED BLOODS, FEBRILE CONCUPISCENCE	240	MOYEN SENSUEL	67
BLOOD'S			
BAH! THERE'S NO WINE LIKE THE BLOOD'S CRIMSON!	28	ALTAFORTE	18
BLOSSOM			
BOSQUE TAKETH BLOSSOM, COMETH BEAUTY OF BERRIES,	65	THE SEAFARER	49
WHAT FLOWER HAS COME INTO BLOSSOM?	127	BOWMEN OF SHU	13
BLOSSOMS			
THAT HOLDS THEIR BLOSSOMS AND THEIR LEAVES IN CURE	21	IN DURANCE	45

BLOT -- BOAST

	PAGE	TITLE	LINE
BLOT			
HELL BLOT BLACK FOR ALWAY THE THOUGHT "PEACE"!	29	ALTAFORTE	39
AYE YE ARE FOOLS, IF YE THINK TIME CAN BLOT	30	PIERE VIDAL	18
BLOTS			
HIS LONE SAIL BLOTS THE FAR SKY.	137	ON RIVER KIANG	3
BLOUGHRAM'S			
LIKEWISE A FRIEND OF BLOUGHRAM'S ONCE ADVISED ME:	194	MR. NIXON	21
BLOUSE			
WITH HIS BLOUSE FULL OF APPLES	181	MOEURS CON: 7	4
BLOW			
I LIKE ONE LITTLE BAND OF WINDS THAT BLOW	5	LA FRAISNE	49
THE DARK DWARFS BLOW AND BOW THERE	47	FROM HEINE: 7	27
OVER THE DYING HALF-WITS BLOW, ...	265	ALF'S TENTH	5
BLOWING			
BLOWING THEY KNOW NOT WHITHER, SEEKING A SONG.	16	PRAISE YSOLT	20
BLOWN			
LIKE A SKEIN OF LOOSE SILK BLOWN AGAINST A WALL ...	83	THE GARDEN	1
LIKE A SWALLOW HALF BLOWN TO THE WALL, ...	112	SHOP GIRL	2
IS ONE DAY BLOWN UP LARGE, THE NEXT, SUCKED IN? ...	261	ALF'S FIFTH	21
BLOWS			
AS NE'ER HAD I OTHER, AND WHEN THE WIND BLOWS, ...	23	MARVOIL	35
WHEN THE WIND BLOWS SIGH THOU FOR MY SORROW	23	MARVOIL	41
BY THE NORTH GATE, THE WIND BLOWS FULL OF SAND, ...	133	FRONTIER GUARD	1
"OUT OF THE WIND THAT BLOWS FROM HER, ...	177	LANGUE D'OC: 4	21
BLUBBERING			
WHOSE BLUBBERING YOWLS YOU TAKE FOR PASSION'S			
ESSENCE;	240	MOYEN SENSUEL	68
BLUE			
IN THE BLUE WATERS OF HEAVEN, ...	7	CINO	55
WITH HER BLUE SWORD.	24	THUS NINEVEH	19
FROM PIERE VIDAL'S REMEMBRANCE THAT BLUE NIGHT. ...	30	PIERE VIDAL	19
WHO CAN LOOK ON THAT BLUE AND NOT BELIEVE?	50	THE FLAME	28
BY THE SILVER BLUE FLOOD	108	CH'U YUAN	3
BLUE, BLUE IS THE GRASS ABOUT THE RIVER	128	BEAU TOILET	1
BLUE, BLUE IS THE GRASS ABOUT THE RIVER	128	BEAU TOILET	1
LIKE THE JOY OF BLUE ISLANDS.	129	THE RIVER SONG	16
YOU WALKED ABOUT MY SEAT, PLAYING WITH BLUE PLUMS.	130	RIVER-MER WIFE	4
RED JADE CUPS, FOOD WELL SET ON A BLUE JEWELLED			
TABLE, ...	135	EXILE'S LETTER	47
TO THE DYNASTIC TEMPLE, WITH WATER ABOUT IT CLEAR AS			
BLUE JADE, ...	135	EXILE'S LETTER	50
BLUE MOUNTAINS TO THE NORTH OF THE WALLS, ...	137	TAKING LEAVE	1
A "BLUE" AND A CLIMBER OF MOUNTAINS, HAS MARRIED	178	MOEURS CON: 1	3
AND THE BLUE SATIN RIBBON, ...	180	MOEURS CON: 5	23
BLUE-GRAY			
SKIRTING THE BLUE-GRAY SEA	90	SURGIT FAMA	3
BLUER			
SOUTH OF THE POND THE WILLOW-TIPS ARE HALF-BLUE AND			
BLUER, ...	129	THE RIVER SONG	25
BLUISH			
THE WIND BUNDLES ITSELF INTO A BLUISH CLOUD AND			
WANDERS OFF.	129	THE RIVER SONG	30
BLUNDER'D			
MONTY HAS BLUNDER'D.	257	BREAD BRIGADE	12
BLURB			
THAT'S HOW THE PRESS BLURB RAN.--	261	ALF'S SIXTH	14
BLURRED			
THE SMOKE-FLOWERS ARE BLURRED OVER THE RIVER.	137	ON RIVER KIANG	2
BLUSH			
DANCE AND MAKE PEOPLE BLUSH, ...	86	SALUTATION 2ND	27
BOARD			
STRIKING THE BOARD, FALLING IN STRONG L'S OF	120	GAME OF CHESS	2
THIS BOARD IS ALIVE WITH LIGHT;	120	GAME OF CHESS	6
BOARDS			
WITH FAT BOARDS, BAWDS, WINE AND FRAIL MUSIC!	28	ALTAFORTE	17
BOARHOUNDS			
FOR TWELVE HORSES AND ALSO FOR TWELVE BOARHOUNDS ..	98	THE BELLAIRES	19
BOAS			
LIKE SO MANY UNUSED BOAS.	93	LES MILLWIN	4
BOAST			
WELL MAYST THOU BOAST THAT THOU THE BEST CHEVALIER	37	THE YOUNG KING	18

PAGE 49

BOAST -- BONNY

	PAGE	TITLE	LINE
BOAST (CONTINUED)			
MAY NOT MAKE BOAST OF ANY BETTER THING	40	ERAT HORA	6
BOASTETH			
LAUD OF THE LIVING, BOASTETH SOME LAST WORD, ...	66	THE SEAFARER	74
BOAT			
THIS BOAT IS OF SHATO-WOOD, AND ITS GUNWALES ARE CUT MAGNOLIA, ...	128	THE RIVER SONG	1
AND NO BOAT, NO CARRIAGE, APPROACHES.	142	UNMOVING CLOUD	16
BOATS			
WITH BOATS FLOATING, AND THE SOUND OF MOUTH-ORGANS AND DRUMS, ...	135	EXILE'S LETTER	51
BOB			
YOU, MASTER BOB BROWNING, SPITE YOUR APPAREL	13	MESMERISM	7
BODETH			
HE SINGETH SUMMERWARD, BODETH SORROW, ...	65	THE SEAFARER	55
BODICE			
WHERE THY BODICE LACES START	8	NA AUDIART	3
BODIES			
HIS BORN BROTHERS, THEIR BURIED BODIES	66	THE SEAFARER	100
LET THE MANES PUT OFF THEIR TERROR, LET THEM PUT OFF THEIR AQUEOUS BODIES WITH FIRE.	76	THE ALCHEMIST	51
LET THEM ASSUME THE MILK-WHITE BODIES OF AGATE. ...	76	THE ALCHEMIST	52
FAIR CHEEKS, AND FINE BODIES;	190	HUGH SELWYN: 4	22
BODY			
THROUGH THE SKY, AND THE WIND THEREOF IS MY BODY.	18	DE AEGYPTO	2
THROUGH THE SKY, AND THE WIND THEREOF IS MY BODY.	18	DE AEGYPTO	8
THROUGH THE SKY, AND THE WIND THEREOF IS MY BODY.	18	DE AEGYPTO	16
THROUGH THE SKY, AND THE WIND THEREOF IS MY BODY.	18	DE AEGYPTO	24
ONE NIGHT, ONE BODY AND ONE WELDING FLAME!	32	PIERE VIDAL	56
GONE IS HIS BODY FINE AND AMOROUS, ...	37	THE YOUNG KING	31
BEATS OUT THE BREATH FROM DOOM-GRIPPED BODY.	66	THE SEAFARER	72
A-LOOSE THE CLOAK OF THE BODY, CAMEST	68	APPARUIT	14
HER STRAIGHT FRESH BODY, ...	106	DOMPNA POIS	48
ENDYMION'S NAKED BODY, BRIGHT BAIT FOR DIANA,"	220	SEXTUS PROP: 7	15
"NO INCUBUS HAS CRUSHED HIS BODY AGAINST ME, ...	225	SEXTUS PROP:10	39
BODYKINS			
TO CATCH YOU AT WORM TURNING. HOLY ODD'S BODYKINS!	13	MESMERISM	4
BOIL			
AND IT WILL SURELY BOIL THE POT, ...	267	ALF'S TWELFTH	14
BOISTEROUS			
STEPPING BENEATH A BOISTEROUS WIND FROM THRACE, ...	87	THE SPRING	3
BOLD			
KEPT AS BOLD TROPHIES OF OLD PAGEANTRY.	19	FOR E. MCC	18
WHERE BOLD HANDS MAY DO VIOLENCE TO MY PERSON?	212	SEXTUS PROP: 3	8
LET ME RETURN TO THIS BOLD THEME OF MINE, ...	246	MOYEN SENSUEL	226
BOLES			
I HAVE CURLED 'MID THE BOLES OF THE ASH WOOD, ...	4	LA FRAISNE	9
BOMBS			
DESTROYERS, BOMBS AND SPITTING MITRAILLEUSES.	265	ALF'S NINTH	21
BONDAGE			
GO AGAINST THIS VEGETABLE BONDAGE OF THE BLOOD. ...	89	COMMISSION	34
BONDS			
WE HAVE GONE FORTH BEYOND YOUR BONDS AND BORDERS,	50	THE FLAME	7
SPEAK AGAINST BONDS.	88	COMMISSION	8
BONE			
HE SUCKS HIS CHOP BONE, ...	163	CABARET DANCER	56
BONES			
ABOVE THE BONES AND MIRE, ...	41	HER MONUMENT	4
LET THEM DRAW TOGETHER THE BONES OF THE METAL.	76	THE ALCHEMIST	53
BONES WHITE WITH A THOUSAND FROSTS, ...	133	FRONTIER GUARD	8
AMONG THE PICKLED FOETUSES AND BOTTLED BONES, ...	193	SIENA MI FE	1
GODS' AID, LET NOT MY BONES LIE IN A PUBLIC LOCATION	213	SEXTUS PROP: 3	32
"SHE STEWS PUFFED FROGS, SNAKE'S BONES, THE MOULTED FEATHERS OF SCREECH OWLS, ...	215	SEXTUS PROP: 4	33
SMALL TALK COMES FROM SMALL BONES.	219	SEXTUS PROP: 6	37
BONITA			
"-ITA, BONITA, CHIQUITA,"	162	CABARET DANCER	33
BONNY			
HOW SHE IS SO FAIR AND BONNY;	72	DIEU! QU'IL	2
HOW SHE IS SO FAIR AND BONNY.	72	DIEU! QU'IL	8

PAGE 50

BOOK -- BORN

		PAGE	TITLE	LINE
BOOK				
	A BOOK IS KNOWN BY THEM THAT READ	14	FAMAM CANO	18
	THEY'LL NO' GET HIM A' IN A BOOK I THINK	33	GOODLY FERE	21
	SPEECH FOR PSYCHE IN THE GOLDEN BOOK OF APULEIUS	39	FOR PSYCHE	T
	BEHOLD THIS BOOK, THE URN OF ASHES, ...	45	FROM HEINE: 3	7
	GO, DUMB-BORN BOOK,	197	ENVOI (1919)	1
	"WHO HAS ORDERED A BOOK ABOUT HEROES?	210	SEXTUS PROP: 2	18
	AND WHENCE THIS SOFT BOOK COMES INTO MY MOUTH.	217	SEXTUS PROP: 5	24
BOOKS				
	THAN ALL THE AGE-OLD KNOWLEDGE OF THY BOOKS:	35	THE EYES	17
	YOU WERE PRAISED, MY BOOKS, ...	85	SALUTATION 2ND	1
	I HAD LAID OUT JUST THE RIGHT BOOKS.	158	PSYCHOLOG HOUR	4
	AND THE NEAT PILES OF UNOPENED, UNOPENING BOOKS,	180	MOEURS CON: 5	25
	FOR A FEW THOUSAND BATTERED BOOKS.	191	HUGH SELWYN: 5	8
	WILL KEEP THEIR COLLECTIVE NOSE IN MY BOOKS, ...	209	SEXTUS PROP: 1	61
	THERE WILL BE THREE BOOKS AT MY OBSEQUIES	219	SEXTUS PROP: 6	20
	THESE AND A TASTE IN BOOKS THAT'S GROWN PERENNIAL	239	MOYEN SENSUEL	25
	"KNOW WHAT THEY THINK, AND JUST WHAT BOOKS THEY'VE READ, ...	244	MOYEN SENSUEL	182
	ESPECIALLY ON BOOKS, LEST KNOWLEDGE BREAK IN	245	MOYEN SENSUEL	215
	YOU CAN NOT GET CHEAP BOOKS, EVEN IF YOU NEED 'EM).	246	MOYEN SENSUEL	218
	AND DON'T READ NO BOOKS;	260	ALF'S FOURTH	17
BOOK-STALL				
	(NEAR Q. H. FLACCUS' BOOK-STALL).	210	SEXTUS PROP: 2	9
BOOM				
	I SHALL HAVE, DOUBTLESS, A BOOM AFTER MY FUNERAL,	207	SEXTUS PROP: 1	23
BOON				
	I WOULD ASK A LIKE BOON OF JOVE.	228	SEXTUS PROP.12	17
BOOT				
	THE TASTE OF MY BOOT?	146	SALUTATION 3RD	33
	HERE IS THE TASTE OF MY BOOT, ...	146	SALUTATION 3RD	34
BOOTS				
	TO LICK THE BOOTS OF THE BLOKE	259	ALF'S FOURTH	6
	TER LICK TH' BANKERS' DIRTY BOOTS	270	OF 600 M.P.'S	3
BOOZY				
	BOOZY, UNCERTAIN.	259	ALF'S THIRD	11
BORD				
	JE VIS DES CANARDS SUR LE BORD D'UN LAC MINUSCULE,	160	DANS OMNIBUS	10
BORDER				
	FROM HERE TO THERE TO THE SEA'S BORDER, ...	72	DIEU! QU'IL	9
	INTELLIGENT MEN CAME DRIFTING IN FROM THE SEA AND FROM THE WEST BORDER, ...	134	EXILE'S LETTER	6
	BORDER THE NET-WORK OF WAYS:	141	IDEA OF CHOAN	24
	POETRY, HER BORDER OF IDEAS, ...	196	HUGH SELWYN:12	13
BORDERED				
	THE TRAPPINGS ARE BORDERED WITH MIST.	141	IDEA OF CHOAN	12
BORDERS				
	WE HAVE GONE FORTH BEYOND YOUR BONDS AND BORDERS,	50	THE FLAME	7
	WHO COULD PART HIM FROM HER BORDERS	72	DIEU! QU'IL	5
	THE LORDS GO FORTH FROM THE COURT, AND INTO FAR BORDERS.	132	AT TEN-SHIN	14
BORDON				
	"ET ALBIRAR AB LOR BORDON--"	153	NEAR PERIGORD	90
BORE				
	ARE KEPT MNEMONIC OF THE STROKES THEY BORE, ...	19	FOR E. MCC	20
	THE WAVES BORE IN, SOON WILL THEY BEAR AWAY.	69	THE NEEDLE	10
	BORE US TOGETHER . . . SURGING . . . AND APART . . .	157	NEAR PERIGORD	178
BOREAL				
	BUT YOU STUFFED COATS WHO'RE NEITHER TEPID NOR DISTINCTLY BOREAL, ...	238	MOYEN SENSUEL	5
BORED				
	BORED TO AN INCH OF EXTINCTION, ...	22	MARVOIL	17
	WE WERE IN ESPECIAL BORED WITH MALE STUPIDITY. ...	82	THE CONDOLENCE	8
	HE WAS BORED WITH HIS MANNER OF LIFE, ...	100	ARIDES	3
BOREDOM				
	HER BOREDOM IS EXQUISITE AND EXCESSIVE.	83	THE GARDEN	9
	SUCH PRACTICES DILUTED RURAL BOREDOM	242	MOYEN SENSUEL	107
BORGNE				
	FOR MICHAULT LE BORGNE THAT WOULD CONFESS	12	OF THE GIBBET	34
BORN				
	PEOPLE ARE BORN AND DIE, ...	43	MR. HOUSMAN	2

PAGE 51

BORN -- BOUND

	PAGE	TITLE	LINE
BORN (CONTINUED)			
HIS BORN BROTHERS, THEIR BURIED BODIES	66	THE SEAFARER	100
EMOTION IS BORN OUT OF HABIT.	139	SOUTH-FOLK	3
WORKED FOR AND SNATCHED FROM THE STRING-PURSE OF BORN--	152	NEAR PERIGORD	34
WHILE BORN, HIS OWN CLOSE PURSE, HIS RABBIT WARREN,	153	NEAR PERIGORD	60
BORN OF A JONGLEUR'S TONGUE, FREELY TO PASS	153	NEAR PERIGORD	83
THE COMPACT, DE BORN SMOKED OUT, TREES FELLED	155	NEAR PERIGORD	124
THEY PROBE OLD SCANDALS, SAY DE BORN IS DEAD;	155	NEAR PERIGORD	137
"YOU WERE BORN NEAR HIM."	156	NEAR PERIGORD	153
NO, HARDLY, BUT SEEING HE HAD BEEN BORN	187	E. P. ODE	5
THAT IN HIM SOLELY IS COMPASSION BORN.	250	DONNA MI PREGA	87
AND THOSE BORN WITH A SILVER SPOON,	266	ALF'S TENTH	14
BORROWED			
TO MAKE ME A BORROWED LADY	105	DOMPNA POIS	19
BOS			
BUT YOU, BOS AMIC, WE KEEP ON,	101	AMITIES	13
BOSQUE			
BOSQUE TAKETH BLOSSOM, COMETH BEAUTY OF BERRIES,	65	THE SEAFARER	49
BOSS			
HATH FOR BOSS THY LUSTRE GAY!	7	CINO	45
BOSSU			
AUPRES D'UN PETIT ENFANT GAI, BOSSU.	160	DANS OMNIBUS	11
BOSTON			
IN BOSTON, TO HENRY JAMES, THE GREATEST WHOM WE'VE SEEN LIVING.	240	MOYEN SENSUEL	62
BOTCHED			
FOR A BOTCHED CIVILIZATION,	191	HUGH SELWYN: 5	4
BOTH			
BUT I KNOW NOW, THEY BOTH WERE GOOD ENOUGH.	44	FROM HEINE: 2	8
AND GETTING IN BOTH OF THEIR WAYS;	97	AESTHETICS	14
THAT HE PASSES FOR BOTH BLOODLESS AND SEXLESS.	100	TEMPERAMENTS	4
BASTIDIDES, ON THE CONTRARY, WHO BOTH TALKS AND WRITES OF NOTHING SAVE COPULATION,	100	TEMPERAMENTS	5
IS BOTH STIMULATING AND DELIGHTFUL."	113	TAME CAT	7
"I AM AN ARTIST, YOU HAVE TRIED BOTH METIERS."	156	NEAR PERIGORD	152
SPREAD ON BOTH HANDS AND ON THE UP-PUSHED-BOSOM--	161	CABARET DANCER	15
THE SEA-CLEAR SAPPHIRE OF AIR, THE SEA-DARK CLARITY, STRETCHES BOTH SEA-CLIFF AND OCEAN.	170	PHANOPOEIA	24
BOTTICELLIAN			
AND BOTTICELLIAN SPRAYS IMPLIED	200	MAUBERLEY: 2	28
BOTTLED			
AMONG THE PICKLED FOETUSES AND BOTTLED BONES,	193	SIENA MI FE	1
BOTTOM			
IS, AT BOTTOM, DISTINGUISHED AND FRESH AS A MARCH HERB.	247	PIERROTS	18
BOTTS			
THAT ARE THE NATION'S BOTTS, COLLICKS AND GLANDERS.	241	MOYEN SENSUEL	74
BOUGH			
AS THE SPRING UPON THE BOUGH	17	PRAISE YSOLT	49
FROM THE BRONZE OF THE MAPLE, FROM THE SAP IN THE BOUGH;	76	THE ALCHEMIST	34
PETALS ON A WET, BLACK BOUGH.	109	IN THE METRO	2
'TILL THE SUN COME, AND THE GREEN LEAF ON THE BOUGH.	173	LANGUE D'OC: 2	16
BOUGHS			
AND CALLS THE UTMOST SINGING FROM THE BOUGHS	21	IN DURANCE	46
TO WHERE THE OLIVE BOUGHS	92	APRIL	3
PEACH BOUGHS AND APRICOT BOUGHS HANG OVER A THOUSAND GATES,	131	AT TEN-SHIN	2
PEACH BOUGHS AND APRICOT BOUGHS HANG OVER A THOUSAND GATES,	131	AT TEN-SHIN	2
FROM THE BOUGHS OF KATSURA,	140	MULBERRY ROAD	10
BOUGHT			
GO TO THE BOUGHT WIFE,	88	COMMISSION	14
AND MAY THE BOUGHT YOKE OF A MISTRESS LIE WITH	214	SEXTUS PROP: 4	3
BOUGHT-CHEAP			
TALK ME NO LOVE TALK, NO BOUGHT-CHEAP FIDDL'RY,	25	GUIDO INVITES	3
BOUND			
LO, I HAVE SEEN THEE BOUND ABOUT WITH DREAMS,	25	GUIDO INVITES	7
THAT BOUND KING HARRY ABOUT.	48	FROM HEINE: 7	30
AM SOLVED AND BOUND IN, THROUGH AUGHT HERE ON EARTH,	51	THE FLAME	33

PAGE 52

BOUND -- BRAKE

	PAGE	TITLE	LINE
BOUND (CONTINUED)			
SLIGHT ARE HER ARMS, YET THEY HAVE BOUND ME STRAITLY	71	A VIRGINAL	4
SURELY YOU ARE BOUND AND ENTWINED,	84	ORTUS	9
O LIGHT BOUND AND BENT IN, O SOUL OF THE CAPTIVE,	95	OF THE DEGREES	11
AND ALL MY HEART IS BOUND ABOUT WITH LOVE.	153	NEAR PERIGORD	73
SUCH MY COHORT AND SETTING. AND SHE BOUND IVY TO HIS THYRSOS;	211	SEXTUS PROP: 2	35
BOUNDING-LINE			
BRIGHT IN ITS SUAVE BOUNDING-LINE, AS,	204	MEDALLION	14
BOUNTIFUL			
NOR WITH GIFT SO BOUNTIFUL AND SO TRUE,	105	DOMPNA POIS	16
BOURGEOIS			
HER BOURGEOIS DULNESS IS DEFERRED.	163	CABARET DANCER	76
BOURGEOISE			
GO TO THE BOURGEOISE WHO IS DYING OF HER ENNUIS,	88	COMMISSION	9
BOURRIENNE			
TE VOILA, MON BOURRIENNE, YOU ALSO SHALL BE IMMORTAL.	101	AMITIES	6
BOW			
OF DAPHNE AND THE LAUREL BOW	3	THE TREE	3
TO TEACH MY HEART TO BOW;	16	PRAISE YSOLT	2
TO TEACH MY SOUL TO BOW,	16	PRAISE YSOLT	24
TO TEACH MY SOUL TO BOW.	17	PRAISE YSOLT	56
THE DARK DWARFS BLOW AND BOW THERE	47	FROM HEINE: 7	27
AH! BOW YOUR HEADS, YE MAIDENS ALL,	72	PAN IS DEAD	2
WHO BOW OVER THEIR CLASPED HANDS AT A DISTANCE.	137	TAKING LEAVE	7
I BOW MY HEAD AND STAND STILL.	142	UNMOVING CLOUD	9
THERE IS A SATIN-LIKE BOW ON THE HARP	180	MOEURS CON: 5	15
THERE IS A SATIN-LIKE BOW ON AN HARP.	180	MOEURS CON: 5	17
BOWED			
SHAMED AND YET BOWED NOT AND THAT WON AT LAST.	31	PIERE VIDAL	48
BOWELS			
HEART THAT WAS BIG AS THE BOWELS OF VESUVIUS,	13	MESMERISM	13
BOWER			
IN BOWER,	171	LANGUE D'OC	EPI
BOWERS			
SOFT AS SPRING WIND THAT'S COME FROM BIRCHEN BOWERS.	71	A VIRGINAL	10
BOWETH			
WHAT SOUL BOWETH	17	PRAISE YSOLT	57
BOWMAN			
PARDONS THE BOWMAN, DIES,	156	NEAR PERIGORD	159
BOWMEN			
SONG OF THE BOWMEN OF SHU	127	BOWMEN OF SHU	T
BOWS			
OF SUN AND SPRAY ALL SHATTERED AT THE BOWS;	21	IN DURANCE	37
BOX			
A LITTLE BLACK BOX CONTAINS THEM.	145	SALUTATION 3RD	8
BOXES			
WERE PACKING THEM IN THE GREAT WOODEN BOXES	96	AESTHETICS	11
THE FISH IN THE BOXES	97	AESTHETICS	17
WITH THE LITTLE BRIGHT BOXES	117	THE LAKE ISLE	3
WITH THEIR PERFUMES IN LITTLE ALABASTER BOXES?	165	QUINTUS SEPTIM	15
BOY			
I CALL IN THE BOY,	136	EXILE'S LETTER	77
"MY PRETTY BOY, MAKE WE OUR PLAY AGAIN	177	LANGUE D'OC: 4	16
"AND GIVE UP VERSE, MY BOY,	194	MR. NIXON	19
PREFERABLE, MY DEAR BOY, MY DEAR LYNCEUS,	228	SEXTUS PROP:12	13
BOYS			
THE MUTILATED CHOIR BOYS	45	FROM HEINE: 5	1
AND A MINUTE CROWD OF SMALL BOYS CAME FROM OPPOSITE,	224	SEXTUS PROP:10	4
I DO NOT KNOW WHAT BOYS,	224	SEXTUS PROP:10	5
BRAIDS			
A BASKET-WORK OF BRAIDS WHICH SEEM AS IF THEY WERE	204	MEDALLION	10
BRAINLESS			
BRAINLESS,	103	LADIES	17
BRAINS			
WHERE ONE NEEDS ONE'S BRAINS ALL THE TIME.	117	THE LAKE ISLE	16
UPON THE NATIONAL BRAINS AND SET 'EM ACHIN'.	245	MOYEN SENSUEL	216
COULD YEH SWAP TH' BRAINS OF ORL THIS LOT	270	OF 600 M.P.'S	19
BRAKE			
I THAT HAVE KNOWN STRATH, GARTH, DRAKE, DALE,	31	PIERE VIDAL	50

PAGE 53

BRAKES -- BREATHE

	PAGE	TITLE	LINE
BRAKES			
WHEN TALL STAGS FLED ME THROUGH THE ALDER BRAKES,	30	PIERE VIDAL	9
BRANCH			
SWIFT CAME THE LOBA, AS A BRANCH THAT'S CAUGHT, ...	31	PIERE VIDAL	26
THOUGH EVERY BRANCH HAVE BACK WHAT LAST YEAR LOST,	87	THE SPRING	11
LIKE THE BRANCH THAT TURNS ABOUT	173	LANGUE D'OC: 2	12
BRANCHES			
THE BRANCHES GROW OUT OF ME, LIKE ARMS.	62	A GIRL	5
GREEN COME THE SHOOTS, AYE APRIL IN THE BRANCHES,	71	A VIRGINAL	11
AND WITH SOME BRANCHES ROTTED AND FALLING.	89	COMMISSION	32
BRAND			
NOW, QUENCHED AS THE BRAND OF MELEAGAR,	181	MOEURS CON: 6	3
BRANDED			
THEY TELL ME THAT BRANDED GOODS	262	ALF'S SEVENTH	10
BRAVE			
'TIS HOW A BRAVE MAN DIES ON THE TREE."	34	GOODLY FERE	32
AND YOUR FATHER, WHO WAS BRAVE AS A LEOPARD,	135	EXILE'S LETTER	36
BRAVING			
BRAVING TIME.	197	ENVOI (1919)	16
BRAWNY			
AYE LOVER HE WAS OF BRAWNY MEN,	33	GOODLY FERE	3
BRAZEN'D			
WAS NEVER ONE OF WHOM ONE SPEAKS AS "BRAZEN'D." ...	245	MOYEN SENSUEL	206
BREAD			
THE CHARGE OF THE BREAD BRIGADE	257	BREAD BRIGADE	T
BREADTH			
OUT OF EREBUS, THE FLAT-LYING BREADTH,	76	THE ALCHEMIST	44
BREAK			
BREAK DOWN THE FOUR-SQUARE WALLS OF STANDING TIME.	49	OF SPLENDOUR	21
THEIR MOVES BREAK AND REFORM THE PATTERN:	120	GAME OF CHESS	8
THOUGH DAY BREAK."	172	LANGUE D'OC: 1	30
ESPECIALLY ON BOOKS, LEST KNOWLEDGE BREAK IN	245	MOYEN SENSUEL	215
BREAKETH			
THAT BREAKETH INTO FLAME.	250	DONNA MI PREGA	61
BREAKS			
WHEN THE WHITE HART BREAKS HIS COVER	25	THE WHITE STAG	4
AND THE WHITE WIND BREAKS THE MORN.	25	THE WHITE STAG	5
BREAKS NOT NOR TURNS ASIDE.	106	DOMPNA POIS	46
BREAST			
TO WHOM MY BREAST AND ARMS ARE EVER WARM,	21	IN DURANCE	43
KEEP YET MY SECRET IN THY BREAST HERE;	23	MARVOIL	47
SPIKED BREAST TO SPIKED BREAST OPPOSING!	28	ALTAFORTE	15
SPIKED BREAST TO SPIKED BREAST OPPOSING!	28	ALTAFORTE	15
NAY, ON MY BREAST THOU MUST	47	FROM HEINE: 7	10
THE TREE HAS GROWN IN MY BREAST--	62	A GIRL	3
YOU WILL FOLLOW THE BARE SCARIFIED BREAST	219	SEXTUS PROP: 6	22
BREAST-CARES			
BITTER BREAST-CARES HAVE I ABIDED,	64	THE SEAFARER	4
BREASTLOCK			
SO THAT BUT NOW MY HEART BURST FROM MY BREASTLOCK,	65	THE SEAFARER	59
BREASTS			
THOU ART A MAID WITH NO BREASTS,	62	N. Y.	9
I LONG FOR THY NARROW BREASTS,	112	HIMERRO	6
NOW WITH BARED BREASTS SHE WRESTLED AGAINST ME, ...	220	SEXTUS PROP: 7	5
BREATH			
GONE AS A GUST OF BREATH	19	FOR E. MCC	10
AND HAVE SOME BREATH FOR BEAUTY AND THE ARTS.	20	IN DURANCE	16
HIGH WROUGHT OF MARBLE, AND THE PANTING BREATH	31	PIERE VIDAL	39
BEATS OUT THE BREATH FROM DOOM-GRIPPED BODY.	66	THE SEAFARER	72
GREEN THE WAYS, THE BREATH OF THE FIELDS IS THINE THERE,	68	APPARUIT	9
BREATH THAT IS STRETCHED OUT BENEATH THE WORLD: ...	76	THE ALCHEMIST	45
TWO FRIENDS: A BREATH OF THE FOREST . . .	158	PSYCHOLOG HOUR	23
TO-DAY WE TAKE THE GREAT BREATH OF LOVERS,	221	SEXTUS PROP: 7	31
BREATHE			
I BREATHE NO HOPE	8	NA AUDIART	16
LISTEN! LISTEN TO ME, AND I WILL BREATHE INTO THEE A SOUL.	62	N. Y.	2
AND I WILL BREATHE INTO THEE A SOUL,	62	N. Y.	12
"BREATHE NOT THE WORD TO-MORROW IN HER EARS"	161	CABARET DANCER	EPI

PAGE 54

BREATHLESS -- BRIGHTNESS

	PAGE	TITLE	LINE
BREATHLESS			
WITH JOY BREATHLESS AT HEART.	47	FROM HEINE: 7	20
BREEDING			
IN HER IS THE END OF BREEDING.	83	THE GARDEN	8
BRENN			
THAT HELL BRENN NOT HER O'ER CRUELLY.	11	OF THE GIBBET	16
BRENNBAUM			
BRENNBAUM	193	BRENNBAUM	T
OF BRENNBAUM "THE IMPECCABLE."	193	BRENNBAUM	8
BRESCIA			
FOR THE MARKET IN BRESCIA, AND HE	97	AESTHETICS	12
BRIBE			
KIDS FOR A BRIBE AND PRESSED UDDERS,	229	SEXTUS PROP:12	44
THEY CAN'T QUITE BRIBE HIM.	261	ALF'S SIXTH	22
BRICKS			
AND THEY HAVE RED FACES LIKE BRICKS.	237	ABU SALAMMAMM	14
BRIDE			
HAVE I FOUND ME A BRIDE	4	LA FRAISNE	14
BECAUSE MY BRIDE	5	LA FRAISNE	30
VERY GLAD, FOR MY BRIDE HATH TOWARD ME A GREAT LOVE	5	LA FRAISNE	34
BRIDEGHEAD			
AND ONCE AGAIN, LATER, WE MET AT THE SOUTH BRIDEGHEAD.	136	EXILE'S LETTER	70
BRIDGE			
POEM BY THE BRIDGE AT TEN-SHIN	131	AT TEN-SHIN	T
MARCH HAE COME TO THE BRIDGE HEAD,	131	AT TEN-SHIN	1
BY THE SOUTH SIDE OF THE BRIDGE AT TEN-SHIN.	134	EXILE'S LETTER	3
BETWEEN AUCTION AND PLAIN BRIDGE,	258	ALF'S SECOND	10
BRIDGERAIL			
THOUGH THEY HANG IN THE SAME WAY OVER THE BRIDGERAIL.	131	AT TEN-SHIN	8
BRIDLE			
AT HIS HORSE'S BRIDLE.	138	NEAR SHOKU	5
BRIEF			
NOTHING, IN BRIEF, BUT MAUDLIN CONFESSION,	202	AGE DEMANDED	50
IN BRIEF, VIOLET IS THE GROUND TONE OF MY PHONETICS.	247	PIERROTS	15
BRIGADE			
THE CHARGE OF THE BREAD BRIGADE	257	BREAD BRIGADE	T
THERE GOES THE NIGHT BRIGADE,	257	BREAD BRIGADE	9
BRIGHT			
"LO, ONE THERE WAS WHO BENT HER FAIR BRIGHT HEAD,	43	SATIEMUS	5
IN THE BRIGHT GLAD DAYS!"	43	SATIEMUS	13
BRIGHT NOTES AGAINST THE EAR,	45	FROM HEINE: 5	6
AND BRIGHT SHIPS LEFT YOU THIS OR THAT IN FEE:	61	PORTRAIT FEMME	3
AS YOU MOVE AMONG THE BRIGHT TREES;	75	THE ALCHEMIST	2
BY THE BRIGHT FLAME OF THE FISHING TORCH	75	THE ALCHEMIST	23
SPREADS THE BRIGHT TIPS,	87	THE SPRING	5
PALE CARNAGE BENEATH BRIGHT MIST.	92	APRIL	5
LEAPT ABOUT, SNATCHING AT THE BRIGHT FISH	97	AESTHETICS	13
IN THE BRIGHT NEW SEASON	111	IMAGE ORLEANS	2
IN THE BRIGHT NEW SEASON.	111	IMAGE ORLEANS	8
WITH THE LITTLE BRIGHT BOXES	117	THE LAKE ISLE	3
AND THE BRIGHT VIRGINIA	117	THE LAKE ISLE	7
LOOSE UNDER THE BRIGHT GLASS CASES,	117	THE LAKE ISLE	8
RED KNIGHTS, BROWN BISHOPS, BRIGHT QUEENS,	120	GAME OF CHESS	1
FIVE CLOUDS HANG ALOFT, BRIGHT ON THE PURPLE SKY,	129	THE RIVER SONG	33
INTO A VALLEY OF THE THOUSAND BRIGHT FLOWERS,	134	EXILE'S LETTER	19
THE BRIGHT CLOTHS AND BRIGHT CAPS OF SHIN	138	CITY OF CHOAN	6
THE BRIGHT CLOTHS AND BRIGHT CAPS OF SHIN	138	CITY OF CHOAN	6
TO BE LOOKING OUT ACROSS THE BRIGHT SEA,	161	QUINTUS SEPTIM	5
THE SALMON MOVES IN THE SUN-SHOT, BRIGHT SHALLOW SEA.	166	FISH & SHADOW	4
O BRIGHT APOLLO,	189	HUGH SELWYN: 3	25
BRIGHT IN ITS SUAVE BOUNDING-LINE, AS,	204	MEDALLION	14
"BRIGHT TIPS REACH UP FROM TWIN TOWERS,	212	SEXTUS PROP: 3	4
ENDYMION'S NAKED BODY, BRIGHT BAIT FOR DIANA,"	220	SEXTUS PROP: 7	15
THUS HE ESCHEWED THE BRIGHT RED-WALLED CAFES AND	245	MOYEN SENSUEL	205
BRIGHTER			
STRANGE WOODS HALF SODDEN, AND NEW BRIGHTER STUFF:	61	PORTRAIT FEMME	26
BRIGHTNESS			
I WILL NOT SPOIL MY SHEATH WITH LESSER BRIGHTNESS,	71	A VIRGINAL	2
THE FOLDING AND LAPPING BRIGHTNESS	169	PHANOPOEIA	14

BRIGHTNESS -- BROCADE

	PAGE	TITLE	LINE
BRIGHTNESS (CONTINUED)			
ME HAPPY, NIGHT, NIGHT FULL OF BRIGHTNESS;	220	SEXTUS PROP: 7	1
TO SEE THE BRIGHTNESS OF."	236	MIDDLE-AGED	23
BRILLIANCIES			
CLAD IN NEW BRILLIANCIES.	87	THE SPRING	7
BRINE			
MUST BIDE ABOVE BRINE.	64	THE SEAFARER	31
BRING			
AND BRING THEIR SOULS TO HIS "HAULTE CITEE."	12	OF THE GIBBET	43
DO THOU, PLUTO, BRING HERE NO GREATER HARSHNESS.	38	LADY'S LIFE	2
DO THOU, PLUTO, BRING HERE NO GREATER HARSHNESS.	38	LADY'S LIFE	12
TO FIND HIM SUCH, WHEN THE DAYS BRING	46	FROM HEINE: 6	18
BRING THE SAFFRON-COLOURED SHELL,	75	THE ALCHEMIST	9
BRING THE RED GOLD OF THE MAPLE,	75	THE ALCHEMIST	10
BRING THE LIGHT OF THE BIRCH TREE IN AUTUMN	75	THE ALCHEMIST	11
BRING THE BURNISHED NATURE OF FIRE;	75	THE ALCHEMIST	19
BRING THE IMPERCEPTIBLE COOL.	76	THE ALCHEMIST	48
TO BRING HER SOUL TO BIRTH,	84	ORTUS	3
HOW HAVE I LABOURED TO BRING HER SOUL INTO SEPARATION;	84	ORTUS	7
BRING CONFIDENCE UPON THE ALGAE AND THE TENTACLES OF THE SOUL.	88	COMMISSION	21
YET TO OUR FEASTS YOU BRING NEITHER	101	AMITIES	10
TO BRING THEE SAFE BACK, MY COMPANION.	172	LANGUE D'OC: 1	20
SHE WOULD BRING FRANKINCENSE AND WREATHS TO MY TOMB,	213	SEXTUS PROP: 3	30
EARTH SHALL BRING WHEAT FROM BARLEY,	220	SEXTUS PROP: 7	24
STILL WE WILL BRING OUR "FICTION AS NEAR TO FACT" AS	243	MOYEN SENSUEL	139
BRINGING			
BRINGING THE GRECIAN ORGIES INTO ITALY,	207	SEXTUS PROP: 1	4
BRINGS			
THE EASTERN WIND BRINGS THE GREEN COLOUR INTO THE ISLAND GRASSES AT YEI-SHU,	129	THE RIVER SONG	23
AND BRINGS UP A FINE FOUNTAIN.	139	SENNIN POEM	10
THE SUNDAY SCHOOL BRINGS VIRTUES INTO PRACTICE.	243	MOYEN SENSUEL	140
BRINK			
WHEN WE SAT UPON THE GRANITE BRINK IN HELICON	104	ANCORA	10
BRISEIS			
BRISEIS, LIANOR, LOICA,	75	THE ALCHEMIST	20
BRISKER			
FIELDS TO FAIRNESS, LAND FARES BRISKER,	65	THE SEAFARER	50
BRISTLE			
NOR BRISTLE WITH WINE JARS,	209	SEXTUS PROP: 1	58
BRITAIN			
BROUGHT FROM GT. BRITAIN AND DUMPED DOWN A'TOP OF US,	240	MOYEN SENSUEL	64
IN PLACE OF THE ROAST BEEF OF BRITAIN,	263	ALF'S EIGHTH	19
"O BRITAIN, MUVVER OF PARLIAMENTS,	270	OF 600 M.P.'S	17
LIKE TO-DAY'S GREAT MEN IN BRITAIN.	272	THE BABY	12
BRITANNIA			
GOD SAVE BRITANNIA!	259	ALF'S THIRD	20
BRITISH			
TO A BRITISH HOUSEHOLDER.	103	LADIES	13
THE EYES OF THE VERY LEARNED BRITISH MUSEUM ASSISTANT.	161	PAGANI'S NOV 8	3
BRITONS			
THE SIMPLE BRITONS NEVER KNEW HE WAS,	265	ALF'S NINTH	24
NOT THAT NICE BRITONS READ 'EM,	272	NATIONAL SONG	10
BUT THE BAWDY LITTLE BRITONS	272	NATIONAL SONG	11
BRIVE			
HARD OVER BRIVE--FOR EVERY LADY A CASTLE,	151	NEAR PERIGORD	13
POICTIERS AND BRIVE, UNTAKEN ROCHECOUART,	152	NEAR PERIGORD	29
AND MALEMORT KEEPS ITS CLOSE HOLD ON BRIVE,	153	NEAR PERIGORD	59
BROAD			
BROAD AS ALL OCEAN AND LEANIN' MAN-KIN'ARDS.	13	MESMERISM	12
AND THE BROAD FIELDS BENEATH THEM TURN CRIMSON,	28	ALTAFORTE	5
BROADWAY			
THAT RADWAY JOINED THE BAPTIST BROADWAY TEMPLE.	246	MOYEN SENSUEL	240
BROCADE			
AND I, WRAPPED IN BROCADE, WENT TO SLEEP WITH MY HEAD ON HIS LAP,	135	EXILE'S LETTER	31
DANCING IN TRANSPARENT BROCADE,	136	EXILE'S LETTER	60

	PAGE	TITLE	LINE
BROCADE-LIKE			
THEIR CORDS TANGLE IN MIST, AGAINST THE BROCADE-LIKE PALACE.	129	THE RIVER SONG	26
BROKE			
IT WAS YOU THAT BROKE THE NEW WOOD, ...	89	A PACT	6
AND THEN THE CROWD BROKE UP, YOU WENT NORTH TO SAN PALACE, ...	136	EXILE'S LETTER	71
AND ANOTHER BROKE IN UPON THIS:	224	SEXTUS PROP:10	16
BROKEN			
BROKEN OF ANCIENT PRIDE, ...	9	NA AUDIART	49
AS MEMORABLE BROKEN BLADES THAT BE	19	FOR E. MCC	17
THE BROKEN SUNLIGHT FOR A HEALM SHE BEARETH	38	BALLATETTA	4
IN THE BROKEN DARKNESS.	91	DANCE FIGURE	7
ARTISTS BROKEN AGAINST HER, ...	92	THE REST	3
BROKEN AGAINST FALSE KNOWLEDGE, ...	93	THE REST	14
AND WHAT WITH BROKEN WHEELS AND SO ON, I WON'T SAY IT WASN'T HARD GOING, ...	135	EXILE'S LETTER	40
OR WAR AND BROKEN HEAUMES AND POLITICS?	154	NEAR PERIGORD	93
A BROKEN BUNDLE OF MIRRORS . . . !	157	NEAR PERIGORD	192
FOR TWO GROSS OF BROKEN STATUES, ...	191	HUGH SELWYN: 5	7
TILL CHANGE HATH BROKEN DOWN	197	ENVOI (1919)	25
WHEN THE SYRIAN ONYX IS BROKEN.	219	SEXTUS PROP: 6	25
BRONZE			
FROM THE BRONZE OF THE MAPLE, FROM THE SAP IN THE BOUGH;	76	THE ALCHEMIST	34
BROODS			
MANY INSTRUMENTS, LIKE THE SOUND OF YOUNG PHOENIX BROODS.	135	EXILE'S LETTER	27
BROOKS			
LIKE THE SEA THAT BROOKS NO VOYAGING	34	GOODLY FERE	45
FOR THE NOBLENESS OF THE POPULACE BROOKS NOTHING BELOW ITS OWN ALTITUDE.	230	SEXTUS PROP:12	64
BROOK-WATER			
THIN LIKE BROOK-WATER, ...	192	YEUX GLAUQUES	13
BROTHER			
REST BROTHER, FOR LO! THE DAWN IS WITHOUT!	35	THE EYES	5
AND HE WHO SET THE STRIFE BETWEEN BROTHER AND BROTHER	151	NEAR PERIGORD	25
AND HE WHO SET THE STRIFE BETWEEN BROTHER AND BROTHER	151	NEAR PERIGORD	25
HIS BROTHER HAS TAKEN TO GIPSIES, ...	178	MOEURS CON: 1	15
BROTHER-IN-LAW			
HIS BROTHER-IN-LAW WAS ALL THERE WAS OF POWER	151	NEAR PERIGORD	17
BROTHERS			
"WHICH OF HIS BROTHERS HAD HE SLAIN?"	12	OF THE GIBBET	36
THAT BADE US HIS BROTHERS BE.	34	GOODLY FERE	34
HIS BORN BROTHERS, THEIR BURIED BODIES	66	THE SEAFARER	100
THE FOUR ROUND TOWERS, FOUR BROTHERS--MOSTLY FOOLS:	152	NEAR PERIGORD	35
I HAD REHEARSED THE CURIAN BROTHERS, AND MADE REMARKS ON THE HORATIAN JAVELIN	210	SEXTUS PROP: 2	8
BROUGHT			
KINDLY ENTREATED, AND BEEN BROUGHT WITHIN	3	THE TREE	7
(THUS FAR HATH MODERNITY BROUGHT US)	52	AU SALON	9
WHICH BROUGHT THE HAIR-CLOTH CHAIR TO SUCH PERFECTION, ...	63	PHASELLUS ILLE	6
AS SHE BROUGHT US OUR MUFFINS	116	THE TEA SHOP	7
WHO BROUGHT THIS TO PASS?	133	FRONTIER GUARD	10
WHO HAS BROUGHT THE FLAMING IMPERIAL ANGER?	133	FRONTIER GUARD	11
WHO HAS BROUGHT THE ARMY WITH DRUMS AND WITH KETTLE-DRUMS?	133	FRONTIER GUARD	12
BROUGHT NO REFORMING SENSE	201	AGE DEMANDED	6
FOR A FEW PAGES BROUGHT DOWN FROM THE FORKED HILL UNSULLIED?	207	SEXTUS PROP: 1	20
THE GODS HAVE BROUGHT SHAME ON THEIR RELATIVES; ...	227	SEXTUS PROP:12	3
A FOREIGN LOVER BROUGHT DOWN HELEN'S KINGDOM	227	SEXTUS PROP:11	25
THE CYTHAREAN BROUGHT LOW BY MARS' LECHERY	227	SEXTUS PROP:11	27
BROUGHT FROM GT. BRITAIN AND DUMPED DOWN A'TOP OF US,	240	MOYEN SENSUEL	64
BROWN			
LITTLE BROWN LEAF WORDS CRYING "A SONG,"	16	PRAISE YSOLT	17
THE WORDS ARE AS LEAVES, OLD BROWN LEAVES IN THE SPRING TIME	16	PRAISE YSOLT	19
BUT STILL CAME THE LEAF WORDS, LITTLE BROWN ELF WORDS	17	PRAISE YSOLT	33
OUT OF THE BROWN LEAF-BROWN COLOURLESS	76	THE ALCHEMIST	47

PAGE 57

BROWN -- BURIED

	PAGE	TITLE	LINE
BROWN (CONTINUED)			
A BROWN ROBE, WITH THREADS OF GOLD WOVEN IN			
PATTERNS, HAST THOU GATHERED ABOUT THEE,	91	DANCE FIGURE	17
--A BROWN UPSTANDING FELLOW	119	THE GYPSY	4
RED KNIGHTS, BROWN BISHOPS, BRIGHT QUEENS,	120	GAME OF CHESS	1
A BROWN, FAT BABE SITTING IN THE LOTUS,	147	POST MORTEM	1
AND A BROWN, PLACID, HATED WOMAN VISITING HER,	154	NEAR PERIGORD	112
BROWNING			
"AND A CAT'S IN THE WATER-BUTT."--ROBERT BROWNING	13	MESMERISM	EPI
YOU, MASTER BOB BROWNING, SPITE YOUR APPAREL	13	MESMERISM	7
(BY THAT TIME SHE HAD GOT ON TO BROWNING.)	182	MOEURS CON: 8	7
BROWNISH			
A FADED, PALE BROWNISH PHOTOGRAPH,	180	MOEURS CON: 5	2
BRUNT			
WHO BEAR THE BRUNT OF OUR AMERICA	235	TO WHISTLER	12
BRUSHED			
"MY WIT AND WORTH ARE COBWEBS BRUSHED ASIDE	152	NEAR PERIGORD	45
BRUSHETH			
NOR HELD ME SAVE AS AIR THAT BRUSHETH BY ONE	39	FOR PSYCHE	3
BRUTE			
STILL HE WAS NOT GIVEN UP TO BRUTE ENJOYMENT,	245	MOYEN SENSUEL	193
BUCHANAN			
FOETID BUCHANAN LIFTED UP HIS VOICE	192	YEUX GLAUQUES	5
BUD			
FROM THE HEAT OF THE BUD,	76	THE ALCHEMIST	32
BUDAPESTH			
TO BEAT PRAGUE, BUDAPESTH, VIENNA OR MOSCOW,	245	MOYEN SENSUEL	190
BUFFO			
IN A FEW YEARS NO ONE WILL REMEMBER THE BUFFO,	146	MONUMENTUM AER	3
BUG			
AND DON'T KNOW WHAT BUG IS A-BITIN'	269	SAFE AND SOUND	11
BUILD			
LET US BUILD HERE AN EXQUISITE FRIENDSHIP,	51	THE ALTAR	1
AND BUILD HER GLORIES THEIR LONGEVITY.	197	ENVOI (1919)	7
BUILDER			
DE MORTUIS VERUM, TRULY THE MASTER BUILDER?	240	MOYEN SENSUEL	58
BUILDING			
AND SEEN THE HIGH BUILDING,	121	PROVINC DESERT	34
BUILT			
THIS FABRICATION BUILT OF AUTUMN ROSES,	69	SUB MARE	3
NOW I REMEMBER THAT YOU BUILT ME A SPECIAL TAVERN	134	EXILE'S LETTER	2
"SANSO, KING OF SHOKU, BUILT ROADS"	138	NEAR SHOKU	EPI
THE VERY SPUR'S END, BUILT ON SHEEREST CLIFF,	153	NEAR PERIGORD	58
BULMENIAN			
ALL THE BULMENIAN LITERATI.	99	SALVATIONISTS	17
BULWARK			
AND DANCED THEM INTO A BULWARK AT HIS PLEASURE,	208	SEXTUS PROP: 1	45
BULWARKS			
BULWARKS OF BERYL AND OF CHRYSOPHRASE.	50	THE FLAME	25
BUNCH			
LET US DUMP OUR HATREDS INTO ONE BUNCH AND BE DONE			
WITH THEM,	146	CANTILATIONS	2
"THIS IS A DARN'D CLEVER BUNCH!"	179	MOEURS CON: 3	7
BUNDLE			
WI' A BUNDLE O' CORDS SWUNG FREE,	33	GOODLY FERE	18
A BROKEN BUNDLE OF MIRRORS . . .	157	NEAR PERIGORD	192
AND YOUR BUNDLE OF MUNDANE COMPLICATIONS.	247	PIERROTS	9
BUNDLES			
THE WIND BUNDLES ITSELF INTO A BLUISH CLOUD AND			
WANDERS OFF.	129	THE RIVER SONG	30
BURDENS			
THEY SET DOWN THEIR BURDENS,	140	MULBERRY ROAD	16
BURGHER			
THE BITTER HEART'S BLOOD. BURGHER KNOWS NOT--	65	THE SEAFARER	56
BURGHERS			
ABIDES 'MID BURGHERS SOME HEAVY BUSINESS,	64	THE SEAFARER	29
BURIED			
BUT BURIED DUST AND RUSTED SKELETON.	41	HER MONUMENT	3
HIS BORN BROTHERS, THEIR BURIED BODIES	66	THE SEAFARER	100
AS GOLD THAT RAINS ABOUT SOME BURIED KING.	236	MIDDLE-AGED	2

BURLATZ -- BUTTERFLIES

	PAGE	TITLE	LINE
BURLATZ			
STRINGING LONG VERSE FOR THE BURLATZ;	22	MARVOIL	20
BURLY			
LOOKING SO BIG AND BURLY.	266	ALF'S ELEVENTH	8
BURN			
NO MORE DO I BURN.	3	THRENOS	4
THAT PLAGUE AND BURN AND DRIVE ONE AWAY.	5	LA FRAISNE	36
BURN NOT WITH ME NOR ANY SAFFRON THING.	60	TOMB AKR CAAR	5
I BURN, I SCALD SO FOR THE NEW,	70	THE PLUNGE	3
I SHAKE AND BURN AND QUIVER	175	LANGUE D'OC: 3	28
(I BURN, I FREEZE, I SWEAT, SAID THE FAIR GREEK,	242	MOYEN SENSUEL	123
BURNE-JONES			
THE BURNE-JONES CARTONS	192	YEUX GLAUQUES	9
BURNISHED			
BRING THE BURNISHED NATURE OF FIRE;	75	THE ALCHEMIST	19
BY THE MIRROR OF BURNISHED COPPER,	76	THE ALCHEMIST	42
WE SPEAK OF BURNISHED LAKES,	146	CANTILATIONS	11
BURNS			
WHERE TIME BURNS BACK ABOUT TH' ETERNAL EMBERS.	50	THE FLAME	21
FLAME BURNS, RAIN SINKS INTO THE CRACKS	209	SEXTUS PROP: 1	70
BURNT			
THAT BURNT ME TO THIS ASH.	32	PIERE VIDAL	64
BURST			
SHALL BURST TO LILTING AT THE PRAISE	9	NA AUDIART	28
AND BURST FORTH TO THE WINDOWS ONLY WHILES OR WHILES	21	IN DURANCE	31
SO THAT BUT NOW MY HEART BURST FROM MY BREASTLOCK,	65	THE SEAFARER	50
THEIR TRUNKS BURST THROUGH THE PAVING.	138	NEAR SHOKU	7
BURST IN UPON THE PORCELAIN REVERY:	201	AGE DEMANDED	18
BURSTING			
AND FRESHETS ARE BURSTING THEIR ICE	138	NEAR SHOKU	8
ARE BURSTING OUT WITH NEW TWIGS,	142	UNMOVING CLOUD	18
BURY			
STILL I'D RESPECT YOU MORE IF YOU COULD BURY	239	MOYEN SENSUEL	27
BURY IT ALL, BURY IT ALL WELL DEEP,	265	ALF'S NINTH	29
BURY IT ALL, BURY IT ALL WELL DEEP,	265	ALF'S NINTH	29
BUS			
SKIDDETH BUS AND SLOPPETH US,	116	ANCIENT MUSIC	6
BUSINESS			
PULLING ON THEIR SHOES FOR THE DAY'S BUSINESS,	14	FAMAM CANO	12
SERIOUS CHILD BUSINESS THAT THE WORLD	14	FAMAM CANO	13
ABIDES 'MID BURGHERS SOME HEAVY BUSINESS,	64	THE SEAFARER	29
'TWAS AS A BUSINESS ASSET PURE AN' SIMPLE	246	MOYEN SENSUEL	239
BUSSES			
THE RAIN, THE WANDERING BUSSES.	158	PSYCHOLOG HOUR	11
BUS-STOPS			
YOU LOITER AT THE CORNERS AND BUS-STOPS.	94	INSTRUCTIONS	6
BUST			
AND THE OTHER WAS RATHER LIKE MY BUST BY GAUDIER,	181	MOEURS CON: 7	13
BUSY			
ARAGON CURSING IN ARAGON, BEZIERS BUSY AT BEZIERS--	22	MARVOIL	16
BUT (163)			
BUTCHERY			
THE POMPS OF BUTCHERY, FINANCIAL POWER,	260	ALF'S FIFTH	1
BUTEI			
AS BUTEI OF KAN HAD MADE THE HIGH GOLDEN LOTUS	141	IDEA OF CHOAN	28
BUTLERS			
THAT THE RICH HAVE BUTLERS AND NO FRIENDS,	83	THE GARRET	3
AND WE HAVE FRIENDS AND NO BUTLERS.	83	THE GARRET	4
BUT-NOT-ALTOGETHER-SATISFACTORY			
O MY MUCH PRAISED BUT-NOT-ALTOGETHER-SATISFACTORY LADY.	100	THE BATH TUB	4
BUTT			
"CAT'S I' THE WATER BUTT!" THOUGHT'S IN YOUR VERSE-BARREL,	13	MESMERISM	5
BUTTER			
"BUTTER REVIEWERS. FROM FIFTY TO THREE HUNDRED	194	MR. NIXON	10
BUTTERFLIES			
THE PAIRED BUTTERFLIES ARE ALREADY YELLOW WITH AUGUST	131	RIVER-MER WIFE	23
BIRDS WITH FLOWERY WING, HOVERING BUTTERFLIES	141	IDEA OF CHOAN	17

	PAGE	TITLE	LINE
BUTTERFLY			
AND HAVING DREAMED THAT HE WAS A BIRD, A BEE, AND A BUTTERFLY,	118	ANCIENT WISDOM	2
BUTTOCKS			
WITH RED CLOTHS ABOUT THEIR BUTTOCKS,	237	ABU SALAMMAMM	13
BUXOM			
WOT OH! MY BUXOM HEARTIES,	269	SAFE AND SOUND	9
BUY			
WHAT DO YE OWN, YE NIGGARDS! THAT CAN BUY	32	PIERE VIDAL	57
THEIRS BUT TO BUY THE PIE,	257	BREAD BRIGADE	14
BUYER			
OR A BUYER OF SPACE IN THE PAPERS.	264	ALF'S EIGHTH	34
BUYS			
IT IS HE WHO BUYS GOLD-BRAID FOR THE SWANKERS	263	ALF'S EIGHTH	17
BY (108)			
BYRON			
--GEORGE GORDON, LORD BYRON.	238	MOYEN SENSUEL	EPI
IF I SET FORTH A BAWDY PLOT LIKE BYRON	239	MOYEN SENSUEL	42
C.			
NATIONAL SONG (E. C.)	272	NATIONAL SONG	T
CAAR			
THE TOMB AT AKR CAAR	60	TOMB AKR CAAR	T
CABARET			
AH! CABARET! AH CABARET, THY HILLS AGAIN!	32	PIERE VIDAL	65
AH! CABARET! AH CABARET, THY HILLS AGAIN!	32	PIERE VIDAL	65
TO A FRIEND WRITING ON CABARET DANCERS	161	CABARET DANCER	T
MY GOOD FELLOW, YOU, ON A CABARET SILENCE	161	CABARET DANCER	5
CABARETS			
HAVE YOU, OR I, SEEN MOST OF CABARETS, GOOD HEDGETHORN?	161	CABARET DANCER	17
CABIN			
IN THE CREAM GILDED CABIN OF HIS STEAM YACHT	194	MR. NIXON	1
CABINETS			
AND CABINETS AND CHESTS FROM MARTIN (ALMOST LACQUER),	167	OF AROUET	11
CAESAR			
CAESAR PLOTS AGAINST INDIA,	219	SEXTUS PROP: 6	6
CAESARIAL			
AND MY VENTRICLES DO NOT PALPITATE TO CAESARIAL ORE ROTUNDOS,	218	SEXTUS PROP: 5	53
CAESARS			
HAVE TEA, DAMN THE CAESARS,	52	AU SALON	11
THERE COME NOW NO KINGS NOR CAESARS	66	THE SEAFARER	84
CAESAR'S			
I SHOULD REMEMBER CAESAR'S AFFAIRS . . .	218	SEXTUS PROP: 5	47
HE CAN TABULATE CAESAR'S GREAT SHIPS.	228	SEXTUS PROP:12	32
CAFES			
THUS HE ESCHEWED THE BRIGHT RED-WALLED CAFES AND	245	MOYEN SENSUEL	205
CAHORS			
HAVE SEEN NARBONNE, AND CAHORS AND CHALUS,	122	PROVINC DESERT	40
AND ALL THE ROAD TO CAHORS, TO TOULOUSE?	153	NEAR PERIGORD	67
CAID			
CAID ALI	199	MAUBERLEY: 2	EPI
CAKE			
THE NEW CAKE OF SOAP	99	CAKE OF SOAP	T
CAKES			
TRY PHOTOGRAPHS, WOLF DOWN THEIR ALE AND CAKES	236	MIDDLE-AGED	6
CAL			
"DOMPNA POIS DE ME NO'US CAL"	105	DOMPNA POIS	T
CALAMITOUS			
SAVE THERE BE SOMEWHAT CALAMITOUS	66	THE SEAFARER	69
CALAMITY			
FOR AFTER DEATH THERE COMES NO OTHER CALAMITY.	164	QUINTUS SEPTIM	11
CALASH			
A HOOP-SKIRT, A CALASH,	114	EPILOGUE	7
CALIBAN			
CALIBAN CASTS OUT ARIEL.	189	HUGH SELWYN: 3	8
CALL			
AND NOW MEN CALL ME MAD BECAUSE I HAVE THROWN	4	LA FRAISNE	27
THAT SOME CALL CHILDREN,	14	FAMAM CANO	9
THAT CALL EVER UNTO ME,	17	PRAISE YSOLT	53
GONE WHERE THE GREY WINDS CALL TO YOU,	19	FOR E. MCC	2

CALL -- CAME

	PAGE	TITLE	LINE
CALL (CONTINUED)			
WELL THEN, SO CALL THEY, THE SWIRLERS OUT OF THE MIST OF MY SOUL,	20	IN DURANCE	21
A POOR CLERK I, "ARNAUT THE LESS" THEY CALL ME,	22	MARVOIL	1
WHERETO THOU CALLEDST AND WHERETO I CALL.	25	GUIDO INVITES	6
AND FIND'ST IN ROME NO THING THOU CANST CALL ROMAN;	40	ROME	2
AND CALL MY VOICE TOO THICK A THING.	45	FROM HEINE: 5	4
CALL NOT THAT MIRROR ME, FOR I HAVE SLIPPED	51	THE FLAME	42
AND THEY CALL YOU BEAUTIFUL IN THE PROVINCE,	113	FORMIANUS LADY	8
I CALL IN THE BOY,	136	EXILE'S LETTER	77
AND TO FOLLOW AFTER FRIENDSHIP, AS THEY CALL IT,	168	OF AROUET	33
IN VAIN, YOU CALL BACK THE SHADE,	219	SEXTUS PROP: 6	35
IN VAIN, CYNTHIA. VAIN CALL TO UNANSWERING SHADOW,	219	SEXTUS PROP: 6	36
I FOR THE NONCE TO THEM THAT KNOW IT CALL,	248	DONNA MI PREGA	5
CALL HIM "PROFESSOR."	261	ALF'S SIXTH	6
CALLED			
SHE HATH CALLED ME FROM MINE OLD WAYS	4	LA FRAISNE	16
CALLED TO, A THOUSAND TIMES, I NEVER LOOKED BACK.	130	RIVER-MER WIFE	10
"THERE WAS ONCE A MAN CALLED VOLTAIRE."	181	MOEURS CON: 7	16
THAT CANTING RAG CALLED EVERYBODY'S MAGAZINE,	241	MOYEN SENSUEL	98
CALLEDST			
WHERETO THOU CALLEDST AND WHERETO I CALL.	25	GUIDO INVITES	6
CALLETH			
AS THE MOON CALLETH THE TIDES,	16	PRAISE YSOLT	29
YEA AS THE SUN CALLETH TO THE SEED,	17	PRAISE YSOLT	48
CUCKOO CALLETH WITH GLOOMY CRYING	65	THE SEAFARER	54
CALLIMACHUS			
SHADES OF CALLIMACHUS, COAN GHOSTS OF PHILETAS	207	SEXTUS PROP: 1	1
ALTHOUGH CALLIMACHUS DID WITHOUT THEM,	218	SEXTUS PROP: 5	49
CALLING			
AS MOONLIGHT CALLING,	16	PRAISE YSOLT	28
"QUASI KALOUN." S. T. SAYS BEAUTY IS MOST THAT, A "CALLING TO THE SOUL."	20	IN DURANCE	20
NOR WILL YOU BE WEARY OF CALLING MY NAME, NOR TOO WEARY	219	SEXTUS PROP: 6	23
CALLIOPE			
YOU WHEEZE AS A HEAD-COLD LONG-TONSILLED CALLIOPE,	13	MESMERISM	9
CALLIOPE:	211	SEXTUS PROP: 2	39
THUS MISTRESS CALLIOPE,	211	SEXTUS PROP: 2	52
NEITHER CALLIOPE NOR APOLLO SUNG THESE THINGS INTO MY EAR,	217	SEXTUS PROP: 5	25
CALLISTO			
CALLISTO, DISGUISED AS A BEAR,	222	SEXTUS PROP: 8	24
CALLS			
AND CALLS THE UTMOST SINGING FROM THE BOUGHS	21	IN DURANCE	16
GO! AND MAKE CAT CALLS!	86	SALUTATION 2ND	26
THIS LADY IN THE WHITE BATH-ROBE WHICH SHE CALLS A PEIGNOIR,	87	ALBATRE	1
TO RUN SUCH TOURS, HE CALLS 'EM. . . . HOUSE PARTIES.	245	MOYEN SENSUEL	210
CALL'ST			
WHO CALL'ST ABOUT MY GATES FOR SOME LOST ME;	51	THE FLAME	35
CALM			
IN US ALONE THE ELEMENT OF CALM."	32	PARACELSUS	13
THEY WHINED AS HE WALKED OUT CALM BETWEEN,	34	GOODLY FERE	43
FLAT CALM ENGULPHS MY JIBS,	247	PIERROTS	2
CALOR			
THEREON THE AMOROUS CALOR SLIGHTLY FROSTED HIM.	242	MOYEN SENSUEL	122
CALVES			
AN HOUR LATER: A SHOW OF CALVES AND SPANGLES,	163	CABARET DANCER	82
CALVUS			
AND IN THE DYED PAGES OF CALVUS,	230	SEXTUS PROP:12	70
CALVUS MOURNING QUINTILIA,	230	SEXTUS PROP:12	71
CAMARADES			
"EST-CE QUE VOUS AVEZ VU DES AUTRES--DES CAMARADES--AVEC DES SINGES OU DES OURS?"	119	THE GYPSY	EPI
CAMBRIDGE			
DOWN THERE IN CAMBRIDGE	258	ALF'S SECOND	9
THE FLOWER OF CAMBRIDGE,	258	ALF'S SECOND	14
CAME			
FOR IN THE HORN OF MY YEARS THERE CAME A WOMAN	16	PRAISE YSOLT	27
BUT STILL CAME THE LEAF WORDS, LITTLE BROWN ELF WORDS	17	PRAISE YSOLT	33

PAGE 61

CAME -- CANNONI

	PAGE	TITLE	LINE
CAME (CONTINUED)			
THEN CAME WHAT MIGHT COME, TO WIT: THREE MEN AND ONE WOMAN,	22	MARVOIL	11
--RARE VISITOR--CAME NOT,--THE SAINTS I GUERDON ...	30	PIERE VIDAL	23
SWIFT CAME THE LOBA, AS A BRANCH THAT'S CAUGHT, ...	31	PIERE VIDAL	26
SILENT MY MATE CAME AS THE NIGHT WAS STILL.	31	PIERE VIDAL	32
WHEN THEY CAME WI' A HOST TO TAKE OUR MAN	33	GOODLY FERE	5
YOU CAME IN OUT OF THE NIGHT	36	FRANCESCA	1
THAT EVER CAME UPON THIS GRIEVING WORLD	36	THE YOUNG KING	3
IT IS ENOUGH THAT WE ONCE CAME TOGETHER;	59	SILET	5
IT IS ENOUGH THAT WE ONCE CAME TOGETHER;	59	SILET	9
IT IS ENOUGH THAT WE ONCE CAME TOGETHER;	59	SILET	11
AND THREE SOULS CAME UPON THEE--	60	TOMB AKR CAAR	18
AND I CAME.	60	TOMB AKR CAAR	19
HOW 'CAME I IN'? WAS I NOT THEE AND THEE?	60	TOMB AKR CAAR	24
THREE SPIRITS CAME TO ME	92	APRIL	1
WHEN YOU CAME OUT IN THE MAGAZINES	114	EPILOGUE	3
THE WIND CAME, AND THE RAIN,	119	THE GYPSY	7
YOU CAME BY ON BAMBOO STILTS, PLAYING HORSE,	130	RIVER-MER WIFE	3
INTELLIGENT MEN CAME DRIFTING IN FROM THE SEA AND FROM THE WEST BORDER,	134	EXILE'S LETTER	6
OUT CAME THE EAST OF KAN FOREMAN AND HIS COMPANY.	134	EXILE'S LETTER	23
AND THERE CAME ALSO THE "TRUE MAN" OF SHI-YO TO MEET ME,	134	EXILE'S LETTER	24
WE CAME TO VENTADOUR	154	NEAR PERIGORD	117
SHE CAME INTO THE LARGE ROOM BY THE STAIR,	166	FISH & SHADOW	7
YAWNING A LITTLE SHE CAME WITH THE SLEEP STILL UPON HER.	166	FISH & SHADOW	8
I CAME INTO HER SWAY.	175	LANGUE D'OC: 3	39
CAME HOME, HOME TO A LIE,	190	HUGH SELWYN: 4	15
CAME END, AT LAST, TO THAT ARCADIA.	199	MAUBERLEY: 2	4
CAME AGAINST HIS GAZE,	201	AGE DEMANDED	10
"WHEREFROM FATHER ENNIUS, SITTING BEFORE I CAME, HATH DRUNK."	210	SEXTUS PROP: 2	7
AND A MINUTE CROWD OF SMALL BOYS CAME FROM OPPOSITE,	224	SEXTUS PROP:10	4
A TROJAN AND ADULTEROUS PERSON CAME TO MENELAUS UNDER THE RITES OF HOSPITIUM,	227	SEXTUS PROP:12	6
THEN THERE CAME OTHER NIGHTS, CAME SLOW BUT CERTAIN	243	MOYEN SENSUEL	133
THEN THERE CAME OTHER NIGHTS, CAME SLOW BUT CERTAIN	243	MOYEN SENSUEL	133
CAMEST			
A-LOOSE THE CLOAK OF THE BODY, CAMEST	68	APPARUIT	14
CAMP			
AND TO NAME OVER THE CENSUS OF MY CHIEFS IN THE ROMAN CAMP.	216	SEXTUS PROP: 5	3
AND I SHALL FOLLOW THE CAMP, I SHALL BE DULY CELEBRATED FOR SINGING THE AFFAIRS OF YOUR CAVALRY.	216	SEXTUS PROP: 5	21
CAMPANIA			
AND OUT OF TROAD, AND FROM THE CAMPANIA,	223	SEXTUS PROP: 9	17
CAN (52)			
CANARDS			
JE VIS DES CANARDS SUR LE BORD D'UN LAC MINUSCULE,	160	DANS OMNIBUS	10
CANDIDIA			
CANDIDIA HAS TAKEN A NEW LOVER	118	THREE POETS	1
AND THE THIRD WRITES AN EPIGRAM TO CANDIDIA.	118	THREE POETS	7
CANDLE			
THE MOON WILL CARRY HIS CANDLE,	212	SEXTUS PROP: 3	20
CANDLES			
BETWEEN THE TWO INDOLENT CANDLES.	87	ALBATRE	7
BY SIX CANDLES AND A CRUCIFIX,	115	SOCIAL ORDER	8
HOW MANY WORDS TALKED OUT WITH ABUNDANT CANDLES;	220	SEXTUS PROP: 7	3
CANICULAR			
THE DRY EARTH PANTS AGAINST THE CANICULAR HEAT, ...	221	SEXTUS PROP: 8	4
CANNAE			
"OF" THE VICTORIOUS DELAY OF FABIUS, AND THE LEFT-HANDED BATTLE AT CANNAE.	210	SEXTUS PROP: 2	11
CANNONI			
PER VENDERE CANNONI	273	M. POM-POM	2
PER VENDERE CANNONI.	273	M. POM-POM	5
PER VENDERE CANNONI	273	M. POM-POM	7

PAGE 62

CANO -- CARE

	PAGE	TITLE	LINE
CANO			
FAMAM LIBROSQUE CANO	14	FAMAM CANO	T
CANON			
A FEW MORE CANON.	273	M. POM-POM	11
CANONS			
POUR VENDRE DES CANONS	273	M. POM-POM	8
POUR VENDRE DES CANONS	273	M. POM-POM	9
CANOPY			
THE CANOPY EMBROIDERED WITH DRAGONS	141	IDEA OF CHOAN	9
CANST			
AND FIND'ST IN ROME NO THING THOU CANST CALL ROMAN;	40	ROME	2
HOW CANST THOU REACH SO HIGH WITH THY POOR SENSE;	42	HER MONUMENT	52
THERE CANST THOU FIND ME, O THOU ANXIOUS THOU,	51	THE FLAME	34
CAN'T (7)			
CANTICO			
CANTICO DEL SOLE	183	CANTICO SOLE	T
CANTILATION			
UP, UP MY SOUL, FROM YOUR LOWLY CANTILATION,	216	SEXTUS PROP 5	12
CANTILATIONS			
COME MY CANTILATIONS	146	CANTILATIONS	T
COME MY CANTILATIONS,	146	CANTILATIONS	1
CANTING			
THAT CANTING RAG CALLED EVERYBODY'S MAGAZINE,	241	MOYEN SENSUEL	98
CANTUS			
CANTUS PLANUS	231	CANTUS PLANUS	T
CANZON			
IN THE MID LOVE COURT, HE SINGS OUT THE CANZON,	134	NEAR PERIGORD	118
SAFE MAY'ST THOU GO MY CANZON WHITHER THEE PLEASETH	250	DONNA MI PREGA	88
CANZONE			
VERS AND CANZONE, TILL THAT DAMN'D SON OF ARAGON,	22	MARVOIL	8
SAVE THIS: "VERS AND CANZONE TO THE COUNTESS OF BEZIERS	22	MARVOIL	28
BERTRANS, EN BERTRANS, LEFT A FINE CANZONE:	151	NEAR PERIGORD	5
AND ALL THE WHILE YOU SING OUT THAT CANZONE,	151	NEAR PERIGORD	10
CANZONETTI			
O CANZONETTI!	104	ANCORA	2
CANZONI			
THAN HALF HIS CANZONI SAY OF HIM.	22	MARVOIL	26
CAP			
AND IN A NEW SIDONIAN NIGHT CAP,	225	SEXTUS PROP:10	19
CAPANEUS			
CAPANEUS; TROUT FOR FACTITIOUS BAIT;	187	E. P. ODE	8
CAPERS			
AND YEARNED TO IMITATE THE WALDORF CAPERS	241	MOYEN SENSUEL	92
I'M GETTING TOO OLD FOR SUCH CAPERS.	264	ALF'S EIGHTH	35
CAPITOLIUM			
DUM CAPITOLIUM SCANDET	96	DUM CAPITOLIUM	T
CAPON			
NO CAPON PRIEST WAS THE GOODLY FERE	33	GOODLY FERE	15
CAPPED			
'TIS TIME THAT IT WAS CAPPED WITH SOMETHING QUOTABLE.	239	MOYEN SENSUEL	38
CAPRIPED			
HORTICULTURE, YOU CAPRIPED?	109	THE FAUN	4
CAPS			
THE BRIGHT CLOTHS AND BRIGHT CAPS OF SHIN	138	CITY OF CHOAN	6
CAPSIZE			
AND IN HIS DAILY WALKS DULY CAPSIZE HIM.	245	MOYEN SENSUEL	204
CAPTIVATING			
PIQUANTE, DELICIOUS, LUSCIOUS, CAPTIVATING:	241	MOYEN SENSUEL	84
CAPTIVE			
O LIGHT BOUND AND BENT IN, O SOUL OF THE CAPTIVE,	95	OF THE DEGREES	11
CAR			
THE EMPEROR IN HIS JEWELLED CAR GOES OUT TO INSPECT HIS FLOWERS,	129	THE RIVER SONG	35
CARAVANS			
WITH CARAVANS, BUT NEVER AN APE OR A BEAR.	119	THE GYPSY	16
CARCASSONNE			
TO CARCASSONNE, PUI, AND ALAIS	98	THE BELLAIRES	36
CARE			
BID THY 'FULGENCE BEAR AWAY CARE.	7	CINO	48
LADY, SINCE YOU CARE NOTHING FOR ME,	105	DOMPNA POIS	1

PAGE 63

CARE -- CASE

	PAGE	TITLE	LINE
CARE (CONTINUED)			
WITH MIDDLE-AGEING CARE	158	PSYCHOLOG HOUR	3
I CARE NOT FOR THEIR CLAMOUR	173	LANGUE D'OC: 2	23
I CARE NOT A GLOVE.	174	LANGUE D'OC: 3	15
"'CARE TOO MUCH FOR SOCIETY DINNERS?'	182	MOEURS CON: 8	11
THIS CARE FOR PAST MEN,	219	SEXTUS PROP: 6	32
HOW THEY BETTER START TAKIN' CARE,	262	ALF'S SEVENTH	4
CARED			
AND THINKING HOW LITTLE YOU CARED FOR THE COST,	135	EXILE'S LETTER	44
CAREFUL			
THE ENEMY IS SWIFT, WE MUST BE CAREFUL.	127	BOWMEN OF SHU	20
AND TRUTH SHOULD HERE BE CAREFUL OF HER THIN DRESS--	243	MOYEN SENSUEL	146
CAREFULLY			
WHEN I CAREFULLY CONSIDER THE CURIOUS HABITS OF DOGS	102	MEDITATIO	1
CAREFULLY KEPT FROM THE FLOOR BY A NAPKIN,	111	BLACK SLIPPERS	4
HAVE SEEN EXCIDEUIL, CAREFULLY FASHIONED.	122	PROVINC DESERT	41
"CAREFULLY THE REVIEWER.	194	MR. NIXON	4
CARE'S			
KNOWN ON MY KEEL MANY A CARE'S HOLD,	64	THE SEAFARER	5
CARESS			
LIPS SHRUNK BACK FOR THE WIND'S CARESS	11	OF THE GIBBET	19
CARESS IT,	146	SALUTATION 3RD	35
THE LATERAL VIBRATIONS CARESS ME,	147	BEFORE SLEEP	1
THEY LEAP AND CARESS ME,	147	BEFORE SLEEP	2
CARESSES			
UP AND OUT OF THEIR CARESSES.	147	BEFORE SLEEP	13
WITH A DISTASTE FOR CARESSES.	179	MOEURS CON: 2	2
CARESSING			
HAS SUCH A CARESSING AIR	115	SOCIAL ORDER	3
CARE-WRETCHED			
LIST HOW I, CARE-WRETCHED, ON ICE-COLD SEA,	64	THE SEAFARER	14
CARI			
CARI LARESQUE, PENATES,	52	AU SALON	25
CARING			
AND YOU CARING ENOUGH TO PAY IT.	135	EXILE'S LETTER	45
CARMEN			
"CARMEN EST MAIGRE, UN TRAIT DE BISTRE	162	CABARET DANCER	24
CARNAGE			
PALE CARNAGE BENEATH BRIGHT MIST.	92	APRIL	5
CARPETS			
AND CARPETS FROM SAVONNIER, AND FROM PERSIA,	167	OF AROUET	8
CARRIAGE			
AND NO BOAT, NO CARRIAGE, APPROACHES.	142	UNMOVING CLOUD	16
SUCH ANIMAL INVIGORATING CARRIAGE	245	MOYEN SENSUEL	191
CARRIES			
AND FLOOD CARRIES WOUNDED SUEVI.	211	SEXTUS PROP: 2	47
CARRY			
WE CARRY SINGING GIRLS, DRIFT WITH THE DRIFTING WATER,	128	THE RIVER SONG	5
OR CARRY HIM FORWARD. "GO THROUGH ALL THE COURTS,	154	NEAR PERIGORD	115
THE MOON WILL CARRY HIS CANDLE,	212	SEXTUS PROP: 3	20
CUPID WILL CARRY LIGHTED TORCHES BEFORE HIM	212	SEXTUS PROP: 3	22
CARS			
MOVE OTHERS WITH IVORY CARS.	108	CH'U YUAN	4
FOR THERE ARE LEOPARDS DRAWING THE CARS.	108	CH'U YUAN	7
CARTER			
INSTEAD OF BEING A CARTER?	268	ANOTHER BIT	16
CARTHAGINIAN			
NOR OF DIGNIFIED CARTHAGINIAN CHARACTERS,	217	SEXTUS PROP: 5	45
CARTONS			
THE BURNE-JONES CARTONS	192	YEUX GLAUQUES	9
CARVED			
VINE-STRINGS A HUNDRED FEET LONG HANG DOWN FROM CARVED RAILINGS.	129	THE RIVER SONG	27
CARVEN			
THEE, A MARVEL, CARVEN IN SUBTLE STUFF, A	68	APPARUIT	2
CARVING			
NOW IS A TIME FOR CARVING.	89	A PACT	7
CASE			
DE SON EAGE; THE CASE PRESENTS	187	E. P. ODE	19
THESE FOUGHT IN ANY CASE,	190	HUGH SELWYN: 4	1

CASE -- CATCH

	PAGE	TITLE	LINE
CASE (CONTINUED)			
PRO DOMO, IN ANY CASE ...	190	HUGH SELWYN: 4	3
"AH, POOR JENNY'S CASE" ...	192	YEUX GLAUQUES	20
ALSO, IN THE CASE OF REVOLUTION,	196	HUGH SELWIN:12	19
IF HOMER HAD NOT STATED YOUR CASE!	208	SEXTUS PROP: 1	34
THERE WILL BE, IN ANY CASE, A STIR ON OLYMPUS.	222	SEXTUS PROP: 8	42
AND THERE WAS A CASE IN COLCHIS, JASON AND THAT WOMAN IN COLCHIS;	228	SEXTUS PROP:12	7
RAINS DOWN AND SO ENRICHES SOME STIFF CASE,	236	MIDDLE-AGED	17
CASEMENT			
SCORNING A NEW, WRY'D CASEMENT,	9	NA AUDIART	42
CASES			
LOOSE UNDER THE BRIGHT GLASS CASES,	117	THE LAKE ISLE	8
CASH			
AND HIS POCKETS BY MA'S AID, THAT NIGHT WITH CASH FULL,	242	MOYEN SENSUEL	126
WAS FOUND IN HIS EMPLOYER'S CASH. HE LEARNED THE LAY OF CHEAPER PLACES,	243	MOYEN SENSUEL	143
CASK			
I PAT MY NEW CASK OF WINE.	142	UNMOVING CLOUD	7
CAST			
OF THE OLD WAYS OF MEN HAVE I CAST ASIDE.	4	LA FRAISNE	12
THAT SEEMS TO BE SOME QUIVERING SPLENDOUR CAST	41	HER MONUMENT	29
HAD WE EVER SUCH AN EPITHET CAST UPON US!!	104	ANCORA	16
AH, LADY, WHY HAVE YOU CAST	107	DOMPNA POIS	69
SAW WHAT THE CITY OFFERED, CAST AN EYE	245	MOYEN SENSUEL	187
FOR MEMORY OF THE FIRST WARM NIGHT STILL CAST A HAZE O'ER	245	MOYEN SENSUEL	195
CASTALIAN			
THE LUCID CASTALIAN SPRAY,	104	ANCORA	15
AND PHOEBUS LOOKING UPON ME FROM THE CASTALIAN TREE,	210	SEXTUS PROP: 2	16
CASTE			
OR THAT THERE IS NO CASTE IN THIS FAMILY.	94	INSTRUCTIONS	22
CASTING			
SWIFT AT COURAGE THOU IN THE SHELL OF GOLD, CASTING	68	APPARUIT	13
CASTLE			
COME WITH ME TO THAT CASTLE	47	FROM HEINE: 7	3
TWO MEN TOSSING A COIN, ONE KEEPING A CASTLE, ...	122	PROVINC DESERT	66
"THE CASTLE TO AUSTORS!"	123	PROVINC DESERT	71
DESOLATE CASTLE, THE SKY, THE WIDE DESERT.	133	FRONTIER GUARD	6
AND YOU WOULD WALK OUT WITH ME TO THE WESTERN CORNER OF THE CASTLE,	135	EXILE'S LETTER	49
HARD OVER BRIVE--FOR EVERY LADY A CASTLE,	151	NEAR PERIGORD	13
HE LOVED THIS LADY IN CASTLE MONTAIGNAC?	152	NEAR PERIGORD	48
THE CASTLE FLANKED HIM--HE HAD NEED OF IT.	152	NEAR PERIGORD	49
THE TEN GOOD MILES FROM THERE TO MAENT'S CASTLE,	153	NEAR PERIGORD	65
ABOUT HIS CASTLE, CATTLE DRIVEN OUT!	155	NEAR PERIGORD	125
THERE SHUT UP IN HIS CASTLE, TAIRIRAN'S,	157	NEAR PERIGORD	186
CASTLES			
SHARP PEAKS, HIGH SPURS, DISTANT CASTLES.	122	PROVINC DESERT	55
"PAWN YOUR CASTLES, LORDS!	152	NEAR PERIGORD	38
"SAY THAT HE SAW THE CASTLES, SAY THAT HE LOVED MAENT!"	156	NEAR PERIGORD	155
THERE IS NO SUCH LAND OF CASTLES	272	NATIONAL SONG	5
CASTS			
ONE BIRD CASTS ITS GLEAM ON ANOTHER.	139	SENNIN POEM	3
DRINKS IN AND CASTS BACK THE SUN.	141	IDEA OF CHOAN	10
CALIBAN CASTS OUT ARIEL.	189	HUGH SELWYN: 3	8
AND CASTS STORES ON LAVINIAN BEACHES.	228	SEXTUS PROP:12	35
CAT			
GO! AND MAKE CAT CALLS!	86	SALUTATION 2ND	20
TAME CAT	113	TAME CAT	1
THE WHICH, NO CAT HAS EYES ENOUGH	236	MIDDLE-AGED	23
AND KISSIN' HER CAT FER DIVERSION,	371	OLE KATE	19
CATALOGUE			
ENGAGED IN PERFECTING THE CATALOGUE,	193	SIENA MI FE	2
CATALOGUING			
TOO CHEAP FOR CATALOGUING,	15	FAMAM CANO	40
CATCH			
TO CATCH YOU AT WORM TURNING. HOLY ODD'S BODYKINS!	13	MESMERISM	4
EAGER TO CATCH MY WORDS,	90	SURGIT FAMA	10

PAGE 66

CATCH -- CEASED

	PAGE	TITLE	LINE
CATCH (CONTINUED)			
AND THERE HAD BEEN A GREAT CATCH OF SARDINES, ...	96	AESTHETICS	9
HE WROTE THE CATCH TO PIT THEIR JEALOUSIES	153	NEAR PERIGORD	77
A HOOK TO CATCH THE LADY JANE'S ATTENTION, ...	196	HUGH SELWIN:12	17
CAT-O'-NINE-TAILS			
SWINGING A CAT-O'-NINE-TAILS.	162	CABARET DANCER	37
CATS			
HER TWO CATS	115	SOCIAL ORDER	11
CAT'S			
"AND A CAT'S IN THE WATER-BUTT."--ROBERT BROWNING	13	MESMERISM	EPI
"CAT'S I' THE WATER BUTT!" THOUGHT'S IN YOUR			
VERSE-BARREL, ...	13	MESMERISM	5
CAT'S-EYE			
AND THE GREEN CAT'S-EYE LIFTS TOWARD MONTAIGNAC.	154	NEAR PERIGORD	103
CATTLE			
ABOUT HIS CASTLE, CATTLE DRIVEN OUT!	155	NEAR PERIGORD	125
CATULLI			
FOR THERE ARE, IN SIRMIONE, TWENTY-EIGHT YOUNG			
DANTES AND THIRTY-FOUR CATULLI;	96	AESTHETICS	8
CATULLUS			
THERE IS SONG IN THE PARCHMENT; CATULLUS THE HIGHLY			
INDECOROUS, ...	230	SEXTUS PROP:12	68
CAUGHT			
SWIFT CAME THE LOBA, AS A BRANCH THAT'S CAUGHT, ...	31	PIERE VIDAL	26
CAUGHT AT THE WONDER.	68	APPARUIT	4
AS CAUGHT BY DANTE IN THE LAST WALLOW OF HELL--	151	NEAR PERIGORD	22
AND YOU ARE CAUGHT UP TO THE SKIES, ...	169	PHANOPOEIA	9
CAUGHT IN THE UNSTOPPED EAR;	187	E. P. ODE	10
CAUGHT IN METAMORPHOSIS, WERE	200	MAUBERLEY: 2	36
"SHE HAS CAUGHT ME WITH HERBACEOUS POISON, ...	215	SEXTUS PROP: 4	31
HE, CAUGHT, FALLETH	250	DONNA MI PREGA	80
CAUSA			
CAUSA	88	CAUSA	T
CAUSE			
THAT WAS CAUSE OF HATE!	132	AT TEN-SHIN	30
THEN WERE THERE CAUSE IN THEE THAT SHOULD CONDONE	197	ENVOI (1919)	5
NOT ONE HAS ENQUIRED THE CAUSE OF THE WORLD, ...	228	SEXTUS PROP:12	25
MIGHT CAUSE THOUGHT AND BE THEREFORE	262	ALF'S SEVENTH	19
'CAUSE			
'CAUSE NEVER A FLAW WAS THERE	8	NA AUDIART	23
'CAUSE HE HATH	14	FAMAM CANO	30
CAUSELESSLY			
CAUSELESSLY, ...	105	DOMPNA POIS	3
CAUSEWAYS			
NOR OF CAUSEWAYS OVER PELION, ...	217	SEXTUS PROP: 5	41
CAUSING			
CAUSING THEIR STEEDS TO LEAP.	111	IMAGE ORLEANS	4
CAUSING THE FIVE PEAKS TO TREMBLE, ...	128	THE RIVER SONG	14
CAVALRY			
AND I SHALL FOLLOW THE CAMP, I SHALL BE DULY			
CELEBRATED FOR SINGING THE AFFAIRS OF YOUR			
CAVALRY.	216	SEXTUS PROP: 5	21
CAVENDISH			
AND THE LOOSE FRAGRANT CAVENDISH	117	THE LAKE ISLE	5
CAVERNS			
NOR ARE MY CAVERNS STUFFED STIFF WITH A MARCIAN			
VINTAGE, ...	209	SEXTUS PROP: 1	56
BY DEW-SPREAD CAVERNS, ...	227	SEXTUS PROP:11	30
CE			
"QU'EST CE QU'ILS SAVENT DE L'AMOUR, ET	199	MAUBERLEY: 2	EPI
QU'EST CE QU'ILS PEUVENT COMPRENDRE?	199	MAUBERLEY: 2	EPI
S'ILS NE SENTENT PAS LA MUSIQUE, QU'EST CE	199	MAUBERLEY: 2	EPI
CEASE			
LET US THEREFORE CEASE FROM PITYING THE DEAD	164	QUINTUS SEPTIM	10
NO, NOW WHILE IT MAY BE, LET NOT THE FRUIT OF LIFE			
CEASE.	220	SEXTUS PROP: 7	28
CEASED			
CEASED UTTERLY. WELL, THEN I WAITED, DREW, ...	31	PIERE VIDAL	40
THE TWISTED RHOMBS CEASED THEIR CLAMOUR OF			
ACCOMPANIMENT;	223	SEXTUS PROP: 9	1

CEASETH -- CERTAIN

	PAGE	TITLE	LINE
CEASETH			
NOR MAY HE THEN THE FLESH-COVER, WHOSE LIFE CEASETH,	66	THE SEAFARER	96
CEASING			
UNSTILL, NEVER CEASING;	107	COMING OF WAR	9
CEILINGS			
THE WATER-JET OF GOLD LIGHT BEARS US UP THROUGH THE CEILINGS;	169	PHANOPOEIA	4
CELEBRATED			
AND I SHALL FOLLOW THE CAMP, I SHALL BE DULY CELEBRATED FOR SINGING THE AFFAIRS OF YOUR CAVALRY.	216	SEXTUS PROP: 5	21
"THOUGH SPIRITS ARE CELEBRATED FOR ADULTERY.	225	SEXTUS PROP:10	40
CELEBRITIES			
CELEBRITIES FROM THE TRANS-CAUCASUS WILL BELAUD ROMAN CELEBRITIES	207	SEXTUS PROP: 1	17
CELEBRITIES FROM THE TRANS-CAUCASUS WILL BELAUD ROMAN CELEBRITIES	207	SEXTUS PROP: 1	17
CELEBRITY			
AT SIXTEEN SHE WAS A POTENTIAL CELEBRITY	179	MOEURS CON: 2	1
CELESTIAL			
O PLASMATOUR AND TRUE CELESTIAL LIGHT,	172	LANGUE D'OC: 1	1
CELESTINE			
TO SEE HOW CELESTINE WILL RE-ENTER HER SLIPPERS.	111	BLACK SLIPPERS	10
CELL			
AS THE FINE DUST, IN THE HID CELL	236	MIDDLE-AGED	8
CELLAR			
MY CELLAR DOES NOT DATE FROM NUMA POMPILIUS,	209	SEXTUS PROP: 1	57
CEMBELINS			
MIRALS, CEMBELINS, AUDIARDA,	75	THE ALCHEMIST	12
BELS CEMBELINS, I TAKE OF YOU YOUR COLOUR,	105	DOMPNA POIS	21
GO FORTHRIGHT SINGING--ANHES, CEMBELINS.	153	NEAR PERIGORD	70
CENSURE			
SOME FROM FEAR OF CENSURE,	190	HUGH SELWYN: 4	7
CENSUS			
AND TO NAME OVER THE CENSUS OF MY CHIEFS IN THE ROMAN CAMP.	216	SEXTUS PROP: 5	3
CENT			
OF 25 PER CENT. ON THEIR ADS., AND THE WOODS	262	ALF'S SEVENTH	12
CENTAUR			
AS A TIMOROUS WENCH FROM A CENTAUR	81	TENZONE	3
CENTENNIAL			
AND ANTEDATES THE PHILADELPHIA CENTENNIAL.	239	MOYEN SENSUEL	26
MAY WE REPEAT; THE CENTENNIAL EXPOSITION	240	MOYEN SENSUEL	54
CENTRE			
TO GIVE THESE ELEMENTS A NAME AND A CENTRE!	84	ORTUS	1
CENTRIPETAL			
WHIRL! CENTRIPETAL! MATE! KING DOWN IN THE VORTEX,	120	GAME OF CHESS	13
CENTS			
YOU GRABBED AT THE GOLD SURE; HAD NO NEED TO PACK CENTS	13	MESMERISM	19
THE DAILY PRESS, AND MONTHLIES NINE CENTS DEARER.	241	MOYEN SENSUEL	94
CENTURION			
(OR A CENTURION),	81	TENZONE	4
CENTURY			
AS THE EDITOR OF THE CENTURY SAYS IN PRINT,	243	MOYEN SENSUEL	137
HE READ THE CENTURY AND THOUGHT IT NICE	245	MOYEN SENSUEL	201
CERBERUS			
THOUGH MY HOUSE IS NOT PROPPED UP BY TAENARIAN COLUMNS FROM LACONIA (ASSOCIATED WITH NEPTUNE AND CERBERUS),	208	SEXTUS PROP: 1	51
CERCLAMON			
DESCANT ON A THEME BY CERCLAMON	174	LANGUE D'OC: 3	SUB
I, CERCLAMON, SORRY AND GLAD,	175	LANGUE D'OC: 3	55
CERNE			
CERNE SON OEIL DE GITANA"	162	CABARET DANCER	25
CERTAIN			
SOME CERTAIN PECULIAR THINGS,	52	AU SALON	24
SOME CERTAIN ACCUSTOMED FORMS	52	AU SALON	26
TO ONE, ON RETURNING CERTAIN YEARS AFTER.	101	AMITIES	ST
REPLIES WITH A CERTAIN HAUTEUR, '	111	BLACK SLIPPERS	8
FOR IT IS CERTAIN THAT SHE HAS LEFT ON THIS EARTH	115	SOCIAL ORDER	17

PAGE 67

CERTAIN -- CHANCES

	PAGE	TITLE	LINE
CERTAIN (CONTINUED)			
CERTAIN POETS HERE AND IN FRANCE	148	FRATRES MINORE	2
TO BE CERTAIN . . . CERTAIN . . .	199	MAUBERLEY: 2	12
TO BE CERTAIN . . . CERTAIN . . .	199	MAUBERLEY: 2	12
THEN THERE CAME OTHER NIGHTS, CAME SLOW BUT CERTAIN	243	MOYEN SENSUEL	133
"COMPEL A CERTAIN SILENCE AND RESTRAINT."	243	MOYEN SENSUEL	138
DELIGHT MAKETH CERTAIN IN SEEMING	250	DONNA MI PREGA	71
CERTAINLY			
FOR CERTAINLY	105	DOMPNA POIS	5
NOT, NOT CERTAINLY, THE OBSCURE REVERIES	188	HUGH SELWYN: 2	5
DESTROYING, CERTAINLY, THE ARTIST'S URGE,	202	AGE DEMANDED	43
CERULEAN			
SAILS SPREAD ON CERULEAN WATERS, I WOULD SHED TEARS FOR TWO;	223	SEXTUS PROP: 9	7
CETTE			
QU'ILS PEUVENT COMPRENDRE DE CETTE PASSION	199	MAUBERLEY: 2	EPI
CH			
THAN E'ER WERE HEARD OF BY OUR LORD CH.... J....	241	MOYEN SENSUEL	100
CH'			
GUARDA! AHI, GUARDA! CH' E BE'A!	96	AESTHETICS	5
CH' E BE'A.	97	AESTHETICS	21
CHAFF			
TO SIFT TO AGATHON FROM THE CHAFF	199	MAUBERLEY: 2	17
CHAFING			
CHILL ITS CHAINS ARE; CHAFING SIGHS	64	THE SEAFARER	10
CHAIN			
THE CYTHERAEAN FOR A CHAIN BIT.	201	AGE DEMANDED	4
HE WILL UNDOUBTEDLY CHAIN SOMEONE ELSE TO THIS FOUNTAIN,	238	ABU SALAMMAMM	31
CHAINED			
FOR HE HAS CHAINED ME TO THIS FOUNTAIN;	237	ABU SALAMMAMM	2
FOR HE HAS CHAINED ME TO THIS FOUNTAIN;	237	ABU SALAMMAMM	16
CHAINS			
CHILL ITS CHAINS ARE; CHAFING SIGHS	64	THE SEAFARER	10
LET THE GODS LAY CHAINS UPON US	220	SEXTUS PROP: 7	20
AND THE REST LAID THEIR CHAINS UPON ME,	224	SEXTUS PROP:10	9
CHAIR			
WHICH BROUGHT THE HAIR-CLOTH CHAIR TO SUCH PERFECTION,	63	PHASELLUS ILLE	6
AS SHE SITS IN THE GREAT CHAIR	87	ALBATRE	6
THE JEWELLED CHAIR IS HELD UP AT THE CROSSWAY,	141	IDEA OF CHOAN	5
"YOUR PAMPHLETS WILL BE THROWN, THROWN OFTEN INTO A CHAIR	210	SEXTUS PROP: 2	22
CHAISES			
OU NOUS AVIONS LOUE DES CHAISES	160	DANS OMNIBUS	22
CHALAIS			
AT CHALAIS OF THE VISCOUNTESS, I WOULD	106	DOMPNA POIS	31
AT CHALAIS	121	PROVINC DESERT	9
ONE AT CHALAIS, ANOTHER AT MALEMORT	151	NEAR PERIGORD	12
CHALAIS IS HIGH, A-LEVEL WITH THE POPLARS.	152	NEAR PERIGORD	54
DODGING HIS WAY PAST AUBETERRE, SINGING AT CHALAIS	154	NEAR PERIGORD	105
ROCHECOUART, CHALAIS, THE REST, THE TACTIC,	155	NEAR PERIGORD	122
CHALLENGE			
JEST, CHALLENGE, COUNTERLIE!	35	HIS OWN FACE	6
CHALUS			
HAVE SEEN NARBONNE, AND CAHORS AND CHALUS,	122	PROVINC DESERT	40
ARNAUT AND RICHARD LODGE BENEATH CHALUS:	155	NEAR PERIGORD	128
CHAMBER			
HIS SUBTERRANEAN CHAMBER WITH A DOZEN DOORS,	153	NEAR PERIGORD	61
CHANCE			
ALL DOLOUR, ILL AND EVERY EVIL CHANCE	36	THE YOUNG KING	2
THERE IS ENOUGH IN WHAT I CHANCE TO SAY.	59	SILET	4
FOR THIS AGILITY CHANCE FOUND	201	AGE DEMANDED	1
SHOW US THERE'S CHANCE AT LEAST OF WINNING THROUGH.	235	TO WHISTLER	19
NOR CAN MAN SAY HE HATH HIS LIFE BY CHANCE	249	DONNA MI PREGA	46
CHANCELLOR			
TO SO-KIN OF RAKUYO, ANCIENT FRIEND, CHANCELLOR OF GEN.	134	EXILE'S LETTER	1
CHANCES			
THE DISCOURAGING DOCTRINE OF CHANCES,	202	AGE DEMANDED	36
WHERE ONE GETS MORE CHANCES	242	MOYEN SENSUEL	103

PAGE 68

CHANCES -- CHASE

	PAGE	TITLE	LINE
CHANCES (CONTINUED)			
IN WRITING FICTION ON UNCERTAIN CHANCES	243	MOYEN SENSUEL	135
CHANGE			
MIRRORS UNSTILL OF THE ETERNAL CHANGE?	39	BLANDULA	12
TO SET UPON THEM HIS CHANGE	90	SURGIT FAMA	12
LET HER CHANGE HER RELIGION.	103	PHYLLIDULA	5
NO CHANGE NOR TURNING ASIDE.	106	DOMPNA POIS	60
AND ALL THE REST OF HER A SHIFTING CHANGE,	157	NEAR PERIGORD	191
SIX PENCE THE OBJECT FOR A CHANGE OF PASSION.	162	CABARET DANCER	30
NO CHANGE, NO CHANGE OF PROGRAM, "CHE!	163	CABARET DANCER	85
NO CHANGE, NO CHANGE OF PROGRAM, "CHE!	163	CABARET DANCER	85
TILL CHANGE HATH BROKEN DOWN	197	ENVOI (1919)	25
CHANGED			
NOR HATH IT EVER SINCE CHANGED THAT CONCOCTION.	63	PHASELLUS ILLE	4
NOT THAT HE'D CHANGED HIS TASTES, NOR YET HIS HABITS,	246	MOYEN SENSUEL	231
CHANGES			
(SUCH CHANGES DON'T OCCUR IN MEN, OR RABBITS).	246	MOYEN SENSUEL	232
CHANGING			
IN HOW MANY VARIED EMBRACES, OUR CHANGING ARMS,	220	SEXTUS PROP: 7	10
NEVER THEREAFTER, BUT MOVES CHANGING STATE,	249	DONNA MI PREGA	52
MOVES CHANGING COLOUR, OR TO LAUGH OR WEEP	250	DONNA MI PREGA	53
CHANNEL			
THAT THEY HAVE HAD TO CROSS THE CHANNEL.	97	THE BELLAIRES	4
CHANSONS			
O CHANSONS FOREGOING	114	EPILOGUE	1
CHANT			
MY MOUTH TO CHANT THE PURE SINGING!	18	DE AEGYPTO	12
ONCE MORE IS THE CHANT HEARD.	90	SURGIT FAMA	17
CHAP			
I AM NOT "THAT CHAP THERE" NOR YET "THE SUPERB"	247	PIERROTS	16
CHAPEL			
OR HUGGED TWO GIRLS AT ONCE BEHIND A CHAPEL.)	242	MOYEN SENSUEL	106
CHARACTER			
IF THOU HAST SEEN MY SHADE SANS CHARACTER,	51	THE FLAME	39
I SHALL TRIUMPH AMONG YOUNG LADIES OF INDETERMINATE CHARACTER,	229	SEXTUS PROP:12	55
CHARACTERS			
NOR OF DIGNIFIED CARTHAGINIAN CHARACTERS,	217	SEXTUS PROP: 5	45
CHARGE			
THE CHARGE OF THE BREAD BRIGADE	257	BREAD BRIGADE	T
CHARGER			
A YELLOW STORK FOR A CHARGER, AND ALL OUR SEAMEN	128	THE RIVER SONG	7
CHARGES			
AND OUR CHARGES 'GAINST "THE LEOPARD'S" RUSH CLASH.	29	ALTAFORTE	35
CHARIOT			
WHOSE CHARIOT? THE GENERAL'S.	127	BOWMEN OF SHU	14
A NEW-FANGLED CHARIOT FOLLOWS THE FLOWER-HUNG HORSES;	207	SEXTUS PROP· 1	13
CHARITY			
IT IS CHARITY	121	PROVINC DESERT	13
CHARLES			
FROM CHARLES THE FOURTH;	98	THE BELLAIRES	20
CHARM			
MY WIT, CHARM, DEFINITIONS,	46	FROM HEINE: 6	10
CHARM, SMILING AT THE GOOD MOUTH,	191	HUGH SELWYN: 5	5
HENRY VAN DYKE, WHO THINKS TO CHARM THE MUSE YOU PACK HER IN	239	MOYEN SENSUEL	21
CHARMER			
WHO HAVE COME BETWEEN ME AND MY CHARMER,	173	LANGUE D'OC: 2	24
CHARMING			
ARE VERY CHARMING PEOPLE.	98	THE BELLAIRES	43
SEEING YOUR WIFE IS CHARMING AND YOUR CHILD	161	CABARET DANCER	3
AND YET ANOTHER, A "CHARMING MAN," "SWEET NATURE," BUT WAS GILDER.	240	MOYEN SENSUEL	57
"OH, WHAT A CHARMING MAN,"--	261	ALF'S SIXTH	13
CHARMINGLY			
CHARMINGLY IDENTICAL, WITH SEMELE'S,	222	SEXTUS PROP: 8	31
CHARMS			
FOR THE GREAT CHARMS THAT ARE UPON HER	72	DIEU! QU'IL	3
HATH OF PERFECT CHARMS SO MANY.	72	DIEU! QU'IL	11
CHASE			
TO THE MAD CHASE THROUGH THE GARDENS.	132	AT TEN-SHIN	24

CHASTE -- CHILD

	PAGE	TITLE	LINE
CHASTE			
TO "CHLORIS CHASTE AND COLD," HIS "ONLY CHLORIS."	118	THREE POETS	4
CHATELET			
TO MADAME DU CHATELET	167	OF AROUET	ST
CHATTER			
OR SET ME QUIET, OR BID ME CHATTER.	175	LANGUE D'OC: 3	45
LEST THEY SHOULD OVERHEAR THE DISTRESSING CHATTER	272	NATIONAL SONG	14
CHE			
NO CHANGE, NO CHANGE OF PROGRAM, "CHE!	163	CABARET DANCER	85
CH'E			
LIU CH'E	108	LIU CH'E	T
CHEAP			
TOO CHEAP FOR CATALOGUING,	15	FAMAM CANO	40
AND DINE IN A SOGGY, CHEAP RESTAURANT?	167	OF AROUET	4
HAPPY SELLING POOR LOVES FOR CHEAP APPLES.	229	SEXTUS PROP:12	45
YOU CAN NOT GET CHEAP BOOKS, EVEN IF YOU NEED 'EM).	246	MOYEN SENSUEL	218
CHEAPER			
DOWSON FOUND HARLOTS CHEAPER THAN HOTELS;	193	SIENA MI FE	13
WAS FOUND IN HIS EMPLOYER'S CASH. HE LEARNED THE LAY OF CHEAPER PLACES,	243	MOYEN SENSUEL	143
CHEAPNESS			
BUT A TAWDRY CHEAPNESS	189	HUGH SELWYN: 3	11
CHECKS			
DESPITE SUCH REINS AND CHECKS I'LL DO MY BEST,	238	MOYEN SENSUEL	12
CHEEK			
MAY HER EYES AND HER CHEEK BE FAIR	23	MARVOIL	30
LIKE THE CHEEK OF A CHESTERTON.	99	CAKE OF SOAP	2
CHEEK-BONE			
OF EYE-LID AND CHEEK-BONE	200	MAUBERLEY: 2	22
CHEEKS			
OF CHEEKS GROWN SUNKEN AND GLAD HAIR GONE GRAY;	50	THE FLAME	19
FAIR CHEEKS, AND FINE BODIES;	190	HUGH SELWYN: 4	22
CHEER			
THEN MAKYTH MY HEART HIS YULE-TIDE CHEER	10	FOR THIS YULE	6
AND SLAY THE MEMORIES THAT ME CHEER	10	FOR THIS YULE	14
NOR WHAT GOD HATH THAT CAN ME CHEER	10	FOR THIS YULE	26
AND HE SAID THEY USED TO CHEER VERDI,	182	MOEURS CON: 7	17
TO CHEER THE BAD AND SAD,	268	ALF'S TWELFTH	20
CHEERED			
THEREFORE THE SAILORS ARE CHEERED, AND THE WAVES	164	QUINTUS SEPTIM	6
CHEERFUL			
WAS OTHER, OR THAT THIS CHEERFUL GIVER	263	ALF'S EIGHTH	6
CHEERFULLY			
WILL CHEERFULLY TELL YOU A FIST IS NO FIST,	263	ALF'S EIGHTH	10
CHELSEA			
WALKING ON THE CHELSEA EMBANKMENT.	182	MOEURS CON: 7	25
CHESS			
THE GAME OF CHESS	120	GAME OF CHESS	T
WHAT COULD HE DO BUT PLAY THE DESPERATE CHESS,	152	NEAR PERIGORD	36
CHESTERTON			
LIKE THE CHEEK OF A CHESTERTON.	99	CAKE OF SOAP	2
CHESTS			
AND CABINETS AND CHESTS FROM MARTIN (ALMOST LACQUER),	167	OF AROUET	11
CHEVALIER			
WELL MAYST THOU BOAST THAT THOU THE BEST CHEVALIER	37	THE YOUNG KING	18
CHICAGO			
YOU CREATED CONSIDERABLE STIR IN CHICAGO,	114	EPILOGUE	4
CHICANE			
"THE WOUNDING OF AUSTERE MEN BY CHICANE."	211	SEXTUS PROP: 2	51
CHIEF			
UPON THE ACTIAN MARSHES VIRGIL IS PHOEBUS' CHIEF OF POLICE,	228	SEXTUS PROP:12	31
CHIEFLY			
THE "AGE DEMANDED" CHIEFLY A MOULD IN PLASTER,	188	HUGH-SELWYN: 2	9
CHIEFS			
AND TO NAME OVER THE CENSUS OF MY CHIEFS IN THE ROMAN CAMP.	216	SEXTUS PROP: 5	3
CHI'H			
TS'AI CHI'H	108	TS'AI CHI'H	T
CHILD			
SERIOUS CHILD BUSINESS THAT THE WORLD	14	FAMAM CANO	13

PAGE 70

CHILD -- CHORUS

	PAGE	TITLE	LINE
CHILD (CONTINUED)			
A CHILD--SO HIGH--YOU ARE,	62	A GIRL	9
I COME TO YOU AS A GROWN CHILD	89	A PACT	3
WHY DOES THE SMALL CHILD IN THE SOILED-WHITE IMITATION FUR COAT	114	SIMULACRA	3
SEEING YOUR WIFE IS CHARMING AND YOUR CHILD	161	CABARET DANCER	3
LIKE A WOMAN HEAVY WITH CHILD.	237	ABU SALAMMAMM	25
CHILDREN			
THAT SOME CALL CHILDREN,	14	FAMAM CANO	9
THE VERY SMALL CHILDREN IN PATCHED CLOTHING,	96	AESTHETICS	1
O MY UNNAMEABLE CHILDREN.	96	DUM CAPITOLIUM	6
HER CHILDREN HAVE NEVER DISCOVERED HER ADULTERIES.	103	THE PATTERNS	2
AND NO CHILDREN OF WARFARE UPON THEM,	133	FRONTIER GUARD	20
SHE DOES NOT DESIRE HER CHILDREN,	179	MOEURS CON: 2	8
OR ANY MORE CHILDREN.	179	MOEURS CON: 2	9
LISTEN, MY CHILDREN, AND YOU SHALL HEAR	264	ALF'S NINTH	1
LISTEN, MY CHILDREN, AND YOU SHALL HEAR	265	ALF'S NINTH	26
CHILL			
DRINK OF THE WINDS THEIR CHILL SMALL-BEER	10	FOR THIS YULE	4
CHILL ITS CHAINS ARE; CHAFING SIGHS	64	THE SEAFARER	10
CHIN			
FAINT, ALMOST, AS THE LINES OF CRUELTY ABOUT YOUR CHIN,	103	LADIES	19
CHINA			
I WILL GET YOU A GREEN COAT OUT OF CHINA	94	INSTRUCTIONS	17
CHINESE			
REST ME WITH CHINESE COLOURS,	95	OF THE DEGREES	1
FIND PRETTY IRISH GIRLS IN CHINESE LAUNDRIES,	244	MOYEN SENSUEL	157
CHIPS			
YES, I HAVE RUBBED SHOULDERS AND KNOCKED OFF MY CHIPS	247	PIERROTS	22
CHIQUITA			
"-ITA, BONITA, CHIQUITA,"	162	CABARET DANCER	33
CHIVALROUS			
SO IS THE SLOW COOLING OF OUR CHIVALROUS PASSION,	100	THE BATH TUB	3
CHLORIS			
THE FIRST HAS WRITTEN A LONG ELEGY TO "CHLORIS,"	118	THREE POETS	3
TO "CHLORIS CHASTE AND COLD," HIS "ONLY CHLORIS."	118	THREE POETS	4
TO "CHLORIS CHASTE AND COLD," HIS "ONLY CHLORIS."	118	THREE POETS	4
CHLOROFORMED			
A SORT OF CHLOROFORMED SUTTEE,	115	SOCIAL ORDER	13
CHOAN			
THE CITY OF CHOAN	138	CITY OF CHOAN	T
AND I CAN NOT SEE CHOAN AFAR	138	CITY OF CHOAN	12
OLD IDEA OF CHOAN BY ROSORIU	141	IDEA OF CHOAN	T
THE NARROW STREETS CUT INTO THE WIDE HIGHWAY AT CHOAN,	141	IDEA OF CHOAN	1
CHO-FU-SA			
AS FAR AS CHO-FU-SA,	131	RIVER-MER WIFE	29
CHOICE			
"IN THE STUDIO" AND THESE TWO PORTRAITS, IF I HAD MY CHOICE!	235	TO WHISTLER	8
TILL YOU MAY TAKE YOUR CHOICE: TO FEEL THE EDGE OF SATIRE OR	240	MOYEN SENSUEL	65
CHOIR			
THE MUTILATED CHOIR BOYS	45	FROM HEINE: 5	1
CHOKAN			
AND WE WENT ON LIVING IN THE VILLAGE OF CHOKAN:	130	RIVER-MER WIFE	5
CHOOSE			
WE CHOOSE A KNAVE OR AN EUNUCH	189	HUGH SELWYN: 3	23
I DO WHATEVER I CHOOSE.	266	ALF'S ELEVENTH	12
CHOP			
HE SUCKS HIS CHOP BONE,	163	CABARET DANCER	56
CHOP-HOUSE			
YOU ONCE DISCOVERED A MODERATE CHOP-HOUSE.	101	AMITIES	16
CHOPPED			
THE CHOPPED SEAS HELD HIM, THEREFORE, THAT YEAR.	187	E. P. ODE	12
CHORTLES			
DULNESS HERSELF, THAT ABJECT SPIRIT, CHORTLES	239	MOYEN SENSUEL	31
CHORUS			
THREE THOUSAND CHORUS GIRLS AND ALL UNKISSED,	241	MOYEN SENSUEL	87

PAGE 71

CHOSES -- CIRCULATION

	PAGE	TITLE	LINE
CHOSES			
ET ALORS JE VIS BIEN DES CHOSES	160	DANS OMNIBUS	6
CHOYO			
TRIED LAYU'S LUCK, OFFERED THE CHOYO SONG, ...	136	EXILE'S LETTER	66
CHRIST			
(CHRIST MAKE THE SHEPHERDS' HOMAGE DEAR!)	10	FOR THIS YULE	2
FROM THE STATUE OF THE INFANT CHRIST IN SANTA MARIA			
NOVELLA, ...	94	INSTRUCTIONS	20
CHRIST FOLLOWS DIONYSUS, ...	189	HUGH SELWYN: 3	5
CHRISTIAN			
EVEN THE CHRISTIAN BEAUTY	189	HUGH SELWYN: 3	13
ALSO, HE'D READ OF CHRISTIAN VIRTUES IN	241	MOYEN SENSUEL	97
HE HAD ATTENDED COUNTRY CHRISTIAN ENDEAVOUR			
CONVENTIONS, ...	242	MOYEN SENSUEL	102
CHRISTIANITY			
"NOTHING WILL PAY THEE, FRIEND, LIKE CHRISTIANITY."	246	MOYEN SENSUEL	236
CHRISTIANUS			
HOMAGE TO QUINTUS SEPTIMIUS FLORENTIS CHRISTIANUS	164	QUINTUS SEPTIM	T
CHRYSOPHRASE			
BULWARKS OF BERYL AND OF CHRYSOPHRASE.	50	THE FLAME	25
CHU			
THE FOREMAN OF KAN CHU, DRUNK, DANCED	135	EXILE'S LETTER	28
CH'U			
AFTER CH'U YUAN	108	CH'U YUAN	T
CHURCH			
PAINTING THE FRONT OF THAT CHURCH;	121	PROVINC DESERT	31
WITH RAPTURES FOR BACCHUS, TERPSICHORE AND THE			
CHURCH.	193	SIENA MI FE	15
CHURL			
DEATH WAS EVER A CHURL.	72	PAN IS DEAD	9
CHURLISH			
CHURLISH AT SEEMED MISPLACEMENT, ...	9	NA AUDIART	43
CHURN			
"LET ANOTHER OAR CHURN THE WATER, ...	210	SEXTUS PROP: 2	26
CICERONE			
CYPRIS IS HIS CICERONE.	212	SEXTUS PROP: 3	27
CIGARETTES			
OBJECTS TO PERFUMED CIGARETTES.	178	MOEURS CON: 1	17
CINO			
CINO	6	CINO	T
SIGHING, SAY, "WOULD CINO, ...	6	CINO	16
PASSIONATE CINO, OF THE WRINKLING EYES, ...	6	CINO	17
GAY CINO, OF QUICK LAUGHTER, ...	6	CINO	18
CINO, OF THE DARE, THE JIBE, ...	6	CINO	19
FRAIL CINO, STRONGEST OF HIS TRIBE	6	CINO	20
WOULD CINO OF THE LUTH WERE HERE!"	6	CINO	22
"CINO?" "OH, EH, CINO POLNESI	6	CINO	25
"CINO?" "OH, EH, CINO POLNESI	6	CINO	25
WERE LACK-LAND CINO, E'EN AS I AM, ...	7	CINO	35
AND TELL THEIR SECRETS, MESSIRE CINO, ...	151	NEAR PERIGORD	2
CINQUE			
IS "ZUT! CINQUE LETTRES!" A BANISHED GALLIC IDIOM,	239	MOYEN SENSUEL	36
CIRC			
RIGHT ENOUGH? THEN READ BETWEEN THE LINES OF UC ST.			
CIRC, ...	151	NEAR PERIGORD	3
CIRCE'S			
OBSERVED THE ELEGANCE OF CIRCE'S HAIR	187	E. P. ODE	15
CIRCLE			
SOME CIRCLE OF NOT MORE THAN THREE	52	AU SALON	18
I KNOW YOUR CIRCLE AND CAN FAIRLY TELL	59	EXIT' CUIUSDAM	4
I KNOW MY CIRCLE AND KNOW VERY WELL	59	EXIT' CUIUSDAM	6
"THUS THINGS PROCEED IN THEIR CIRCLE";	178	MOEURS CON: 1	19
CIRCLES			
AS DARK RED CIRCLES FILLED WITH DUST.	16	PRAISE YSOLT	13
CIRCULAR			
THE CIRCULAR INFANT'S FACE, ...	193	BRENNBAUM	2
CIRCULATION			
IF THE CLASSICS HAD A WIDE CIRCULATION	183	CANTICO SOLE	2
IF THE CLASSICS HAD A WIDE CIRCULATION	183	CANTICO SOLE	7
IF THE CLASSICS HAD A WIDE CIRCULATION	183	CANTICO SOLE	15

CIRCUMCISION -- CLASPED

	PAGE	TITLE	LINE
CIRCUMCISION			
FRANCHISE FOR CIRCUMCISION.	189	HUGH SELWYN: 3	20
CIRCUMSPECTION			
THIS YEAR PERFORCE I MUST WITH CIRCUMSPECTION-- ...	238	MOYEN SENSUEL	9
CIRCUMSPECTIOUS			
YET RADWAY WENT. A CIRCUMSPECTIOUS PRIG!	242	MOYEN SENSUEL	119
CIRCUMSTANCES			
SEEN, WE ADMIT, AMID AMBROSIAL CIRCUMSTANCES	202	AGE DEMANDED	34
BUT FOR SOMETHING TO READ IN NORMAL CIRCUMSTANCES?	207	SEXTUS PROP: 1	19
OF PUBLICATION; "CIRCUMSTANCES,"	243	MOYEN SENSUEL	136
CITEE			
AND BRING THEIR SOULS TO HIS "HAULTE CITEE."	12	OF THE GIBBET	43
CITHARAON			
AND CITHARAON SHOOK UP THE ROCKS BY THEBES	208	SEXTUS PROP: 1	44
CITIES			
BAH! I HAVE SUNG WOMEN IN THREE CITIES,	6	CINO	1
I HAVE SUNG WOMEN IN THREE CITIES.	7	CINO	37
I HAVE SUNG WOMEN IN THREE CITIES	7	CINO	52
CITY			
BUT YOU, MY LORD, HOW WITH YOUR CITY?"	6	CINO	32
MY CITY, MY BELOVED, MY WHITE! AH, SLENDER,	62	N. Y.	1
MY CITY, MY BELOVED,	62	N. Y.	8
THE CITY OF CHOAN	138	CITY OF CHOAN	T
IN THE MIDST OF SHOKU, A PROUD CITY.	138	NEAR SHOKU	9
IN THEIR PARTS OF THE CITY	158	PSYCHOLOG HOUR	14
WHITHER, O CITY, ARE YOUR PROFITS AND YOUR GILDED SHRINES,	165	QUINTUS SEPTIM	12
AND I ALSO AMONG THE LATER NEPHEWS OF THIS CITY ...	208	SEXTUS PROP: 1	35
IT IS OUR EYES YOU FLEE, NOT THE CITY,	226	SEXTUS PROP:11	13
RUMOURS OF YOU THROUGHOUT THE CITY,	226	SEXTUS PROP:11	18
SAW WHAT THE CITY OFFERED, CAST AN EYE	245	MOYEN SENSUEL	187
CIVILIZATION			
FOR A BOTCHED CIVILIZATION,	191	HUGH SELWYN: 5	4
CLAD			
CLAD IN NEW BRILLIANCIES.	87	THE SPRING	7
CLAMOUR			
DID FOR MY GAMES THE GANNET'S CLAMOUR,	64	THE SEAFARER	20
I CARE NOT FOR THEIR CLAMOUR	173	LANGUE D'OC: 2	23
AND A CLAMOUR LOUD	176	LANGUE D'OC: 3	77
THE TWISTED RHOMBS CEASED THEIR CLAMOUR OF ACCOMPANIMENT;	223	SEXTUS PROP: 9	1
CLANKING			
CLANKING THE DOOR SHUT,	167	OF AROUET	6
CLAP			
OF RADWAY. O CLAP HAND YE MORALISTS!	246	MOYEN SENSUEL	227
CLAPS			
HE CLAPS HIS HAND ON THE BACK OF THE GREAT WATER SENNIN.	140	SENNIN POEM	14
CLARA			
CLARA	179	MOEURS CON: 2	SUB
CLARET			
OF BEATEN WORK; AND THROUGH THE CLARET STONE,	49	OF SPLENDOUR	15
CLARITY			
WITH MY WAVES' CLARITY	47	FROM HEINE: 7	6
THE SEA-CLEAR SAPPHIRE OF AIR, THE SEA-DARK CLARITY, STRETCHES BOTH SEA-CLIFF AND OCEAN.	170	PHANOPOEIA	24
CLASH			
I HAVE NO LIFE SAVE WHEN THE SWORDS CLASH.	28	ALTAFORTE	3
AND THROUGH ALL THE RIVEN SKIES GOD'S SWORDS CLASH.	28	ALTAFORTE	12
HELL GRANT SOON WE HEAR AGAIN THE SWORDS CLASH! ...	28	ALTAFORTE	13
AND I WATCH HIS SPEARS THROUGH THE DARK CLASH	29	ALTAFORTE	20
FAR FROM WHERE WORTH'S WON AND THE SWORDS CLASH ...	29	ALTAFORTE	28
AND OUR CHARGES 'GAINST "THE LEOPARD'S" RUSH CLASH.	29	ALTAFORTE	35
HELL GRANT SOON WE HEAR AGAIN THE SWORDS CLASH! ...	29	ALTAFORTE	38
CLAGH, LEAPING OF BANDS, STRAIGHT STRIPS OF HARD COLOUR,	120	GAME OF CHESS	14
CLASHING			
CLASHING WITH Y'S OF QUEENS,	120	GAME OF CHESS	10
CLASPED			
WHO BOW OVER THEIR CLASPED HANDS, AT A DISTANCE. ...	137	TAKING LEAVE	7

PAGE 73

CLASS -- CLERMONT

	PAGE	TITLE	LINE
CLASS			
LIKE ALL HIS CLASS WAS TOLD TO HOLD IT IN THOSE DAYS,	263	ALF'S EIGHTH	26
CLASSIC			
A GLAMOUR OF CLASSIC YOUTH IN THEIR DEPORTMENT. ...	163	CABARET DANCER	74
IN THEIR CLASSIC HORNS,	211	SEXTUS PROP: 2	43
CLASSICS			
IF THE CLASSICS HAD A WIDE CIRCULATION	183	CANTICO SOLE	2
IF THE CLASSICS HAD A WIDE CIRCULATION	183	CANTICO SOLE	7
IF THE CLASSICS HAD A WIDE CIRCULATION ...	183	CANTICO SOLE	15
THAN THE CLASSICS IN PARAPHRASE!	188	HUGH SELWYN: 2	8
CLATTER			
MILDNESS, AMID THE NEO-NIETZSCHEAN CLATTER,	201	AGE DEMANDED	21
CLAUSTRA			
SAIL OF CLAUSTRA, AELIS, AZALAIS,	75	THE ALCHEMIST	1
SAIL OF CLAUSTRA, AELIS, AZALAIS,	75	THE ALCHEMIST	5
CLEAN			
MAKE CLEAN OUR HEARTS WITHIN US,	27	NIGHT LITANY	37
CLEANSE			
NOW IF EVER IT IS TIME TO CLEANSE HELICON;	216	SEXTUS PROP: 5	1
CLEAR			
(SKOAL! WITH THE DREGS IF THE CLEAR BE GONE!)	10	FOR THIS YULE	7
AYE! WHERE ARE THE GLANCES FEAT AND CLEAR	10	FOR THIS YULE	20
CLEAR SIGHT'S ELECTOR!	13	MESMERISM	21
CLEAR, DEEP, TRANSLUCENT, SO THE STARS ME SEEMED	30	PIERE VIDAL	21
DRIVES THE CLEAR EMERALDS FROM THE BENDED GRASSES	38	BALLATETTA	9
GET US TO SOME CLEAR PLACE WHEREIN THE SUN	39	BLANDULA	3
CLEAR SAPPHIRE, COBALT, CYANINE,	39	BLANDULA	10
RING DELICATE AND CLEAR.	45	FROM HEINE: 5	8
MY CRYSTAL HALLS RING CLEAR	47	FROM HEINE: 7	22
MAKETH ME CLEAR, AND THERE ARE POWERS IN THIS	49	OF SPLENDOUR	19
THERE IS THE SUBTLER MUSIC, THE CLEAR LIGHT	50	THE FLAME	20
MAKE A CLEAR SOUND,	75	THE ALCHEMIST	4
THAN THIS HOUR OF CLEAR COOLNESS,	83	THE GARRET	10
THE HALL OF CLEAR COLOURS.	95	OF THE DEGREES	9
CLEAR SPEAKERS, NAKED IN THE SUN, UNTRAMMELLED. ...	96	DUM CAPITOLIUM	8
CLEAR AS FROST ON THE GRASS-BLADE,	108	FAN-PIECE	2
I HAVE SEEN THE FIELDS, PALE, CLEAR AS AN EMERALD,	122	PROVINC DESERT	54
TOO DEEP TO CLEAR THEM AWAY!	131	RIVER-MER WIFE	21
AND WATCH THE MOON THROUGH THE CLEAR AUTUMN.	132	JEWEL STAIRS'	4
TO CLEAR FLUTES AND CLEAR SINGING;	132	AT TEN-SHIN	22
TO CLEAR FLUTES AND CLEAR SINGING;	132	AT TEN-SHIN	22
TO THE DYNASTIC TEMPLE, WITH WATER ABOUT IT CLEAR AS BLUE JADE,	135	EXILE'S LETTER	50
HE PURRS AND PATS THE CLEAR STRINGS.	139	SENNIN POEM	7
HOT SUN, CLEAR WATER, FRESH WIND,	146	CANTILATIONS	3
OF DRY AIR, AS CLEAR AS METAL.	146	CANTILATIONS	12
THE THIN, CLEAR GAZE, THE SAME	192	YEUX GLAUQUES	17
PROTEST WITH HER CLEAR SOPRANO.	204	MEDALLION	4
I WHO COME FIRST FROM THE CLEAR FONT	207	SEXTUS PROP: 1	3
CLEAR THE STREET, O YE GREEKS,	229	SEXTUS PROP:12	37
CLEAR THE STREETS, O YE GREEKS!	229	SEXTUS PROP:12	40
CLEARNESS			
AS WITH SWEET LEAVES; AS WITH SUBTLE CLEARNESS. ...	71	A VIRGINAL	6
CLEAVES			
MY GREAT PRESS CLEAVES THE GUTS OF MEN,	266	ALF'S ELEVENTH	1
CLEAVING			
"Y" PAWNS, CLEAVING, EMBANKING!	120	GAME OF CHESS	12
CLEMENCY			
HERE LET THY CLEMENCY, PERSEPHONE, HOLD FIRM,	38	LADY'S LIFE	1
HERE LET THY CLEMENCY, PERSEPHONE, HOLD FIRM,	38	LADY'S LIFE	11
CLEOPATRA			
EXULTED, THEY BEHELD THE SPLENDOURS OF CLEOPATRA.	93	LES MILLWIN	10
CLERGY			
AND HEARD A CLERGY THAT TRIES ON MORE WHEEZES	241	MOYEN SENSUEL	99
CLERK			
A POOR CLERK I, "ARNAUT THE LESS" THEY CALL ME, ...	22	MARVOIL	1
CLERKENWALL			
DOWN THERE IN CLERKENWALL	259	ALF'S THIRD	13
CLERMONT			
UP ON THE WET ROAD NEAR CLERMONT.	119	THE GYPSY	6

CLEVER -- CLOTHING

```
                                                    PAGE      TITLE          LINE
CLEVER
    "THIS IS A DARN'D CLEVER BUNCH!"         ..........    179     MOEURS CON: 3      7
    ZEUS' CLEVER RAPES, IN THE OLD DAYS,     .........    227     SEXTUS PROP:11    33
CLIFF
    THE VERY SPUR'S END, BUILT ON SHEEREST CLIFF,  .....  153     NEAR PERIGORD     58
CLIFFS
    WHILE SHE TOSSED CLOSE TO CLIFFS. COLDLY AFFLICTED,    64     THE SEAFARER       8
    OF SUNLESS CLIFFS                 ....................... 67  DORIA              6
    GRAY CLIFFS,                      .....................  107  COMING OF WAR      5
CLIMATES
    IT MAY LAST WELL IN THESE DARK NORTHERN CLIMATES,     163     CABARET DANCER    71
CLIMB
    WHY SHOULD I CLIMB THE LOOK OUT?         .............   130   RIVER-MER WIFE   14
    I CLIMB THE TOWERS AND TOWERS           ..............  133   FRONTIER GUARD     4
CLIMBED
    I HAVE CLIMBED RICKETY STAIRS, HEARD TALK OF CROY,    122     PROVINC DESERT    38
CLIMBER
    A "BLUE" AND A CLIMBER OF MOUNTAINS, HAS MARRIED      178     MOEURS CON: 1      3
CLINGING
    MOVES ONLY NOW A CLINGING TENUOUS GHOST.      .........  87   THE SPRING        13
    MOVING AMONG THE TREES, AND CLINGING      ............   92   GENTILDONNA        2
    THE MUSES CLINGING TO THE MOSSY RIDGES;   ...........   227   SEXTUS PROP:11    31
CLINGS
    THEIR OCHRE CLINGS TO THE STONE.       ................  108  TS'AI CHI'H        3
    A WET LEAF THAT CLINGS TO THE THRESHOLD  ...........    108   LIU CH'E           6
    AND CLINGS TO THE WALLS AND THE GATE-TOP.  .........    131   AT TEN-SHIN       12
    CLINGS TO THE SKIRT IN STRICT (VIDE: "VOGUE")
      PROPRIETY.                     .........................  241  MOYEN SENSUEL  86
CLOAK
    THAT OLD AGE WEARETH FOR A CLOAK.        ................   4  LA FRAISNE         4
    THE CLOAK                        .........................  67  THE CLOAK        T
    PREFER MY CLOAK UNTO THE CLOAK OF DUST     ............   67  THE CLOAK          7
    PREFER MY CLOAK UNTO THE CLOAK OF DUST     ............   67  THE CLOAK          7
    A-LOOSE THE CLOAK OF THE BODY, CAMEST      ............   68  APPARUIT          14
    'TILL I HAVE MY HAND 'NEATH HER CLOAK.     ............  173  LANGUE D'OC: 2    22
    AND THEY GAVE ANOTHER YANK TO MY CLOAK,    ...........   225  SEXTUS PROP:10    26
CLOAKED
    AND LEFT ME CLOAKED AS WITH A GAUZE OF AETHER;   ....     71  A VIRGINAL         5
CLOSE
    CLOSE IN MY ARMS HERE.          .........................   23  MARVOIL         43
    GREEN WAS HER MANTLE, CLOSE, AND WROUGHT    ..........     31  PIERE VIDAL      28
    CLOSE, AND AS THE PETALS OF FLOWERS IN FALLING  ....       39  FOR PSYCHE        4
    WHILE SHE TOSSED CLOSE TO CLIFFS. COLDLY AFFLICTED,        64  THE SEAFARER      8
    MAYHAP, RIGHT CLOSE AND KISSED.   ....................    107  DOMPNA POIS      68
    AND THE WILLOWS HAVE OVERFILLED THE CLOSE GARDEN.        128   BEAU TOILET       2
    AND MALEMORT KEEPS ITS CLOSE HOLD ON BRIVE,   .......    133  NEAR PERIGORD    59
    WHILE BORN, HIS OWN CLOSE PURSE, HIS RABBIT WARREN,      153  NEAR PERIGORD    00
    "LOVELY THOU ART, TO HOLD ME CLOSE AND KISST,   .....    177  LANGUE D'OC: 4   11
    RUNNING SO CLOSE TO "HELL" IT SENDS A SHIVER    ......   246  MOYEN SENSUEL   224
CLOSED
    THEN SMOULDER, WITH THE LIDS HALF CLOSED   ..........    21   IN DURANCE        33
CLOSELY
    SINGING A DIFFERENT STAVE, AS CLOSELY HIDDEN.)   ....   153   NEAR PERIGORD     87
CLOSER
    AND CLOSER ME THAN AIR,          .......................   39  FOR PSYCHE        7
    "WHERE THE GREAT HALLS WERE CLOSER TOGETHER."   .....   122   PROVINC DESERT    58
CLOSES
    WHEN , WHEN, AND WHENEVER DEATH CLOSES OUR EYELIDS,    218    SEXTUS PROP: 6     1
CLOSING
    HONEY-RED, CLOSING THE FACE-OVAL,  ..................    204   MEDALLION         9
CLOTH
    GONE AS WIND! THE CLOTH OF THE MAGICAL HANDS!   .....    68   APPARUIT         22
    GREEN ARSENIC SMEARED ON AN EGG-WHITE CLOTH,   ......   113   L'ART, 1910       1
CLOTHED
    CLOTHED IN GOLDISH WEFT, DELICATELY PERFECT,   ......    68   APPARUIT         21
    CLOTHED IN THE TATTERED SUNLIGHT,   .................   104   ANCORA           11
CLOTHES
    AND THE TALL WOMEN WALKING YOUR STREETS, IN OIL
      CLOTHES,                      ........................  165  QUINTUS SEPTIM  14
CLOTHING
    AND DO NOT EVEN OWN CLOTHING.      ....................   85   SALUTATION       10
```

PAGE 75

CLOTHING -- COAT

	PAGE	TITLE	LINE
CLOTHING (CONTINUED)			
INSOLENT LITTLE BEASTS, SHAMELESS, DEVOID OF CLOTHING!	94	INSTRUCTIONS	14
THE VERY SMALL CHILDREN IN PATCHED CLOTHING,	96	AESTHETICS	1
YOU WORE THE SAME QUITE CORRECT CLOTHING,	101	AMITIES	1
GLAD TO LEND ONE DRY CLOTHING.	121	PROVINC DESERT	27
"TILL I HAVE VIEWED STRAW HATS AND THEIR HABITUAL CLOTHING	244	MOYEN SENSUEL	183
CLOTHS			
THE BRIGHT CLOTHS AND BRIGHT CAPS OF SHIN	138	CITY OF CHOAN	6
THE PERFUMED CLOTHS SHALL BE ABSENT.	219	SEXTUS PROP: 6	17
WITH RED CLOTHS ABOUT THEIR BUTTOCKS,	237	ABU SALAMMAMM	13
CLOTTED			
AND MIST CLOTTED ABOUT THE TREES IN THE VALLEY,	119	THE GYPSY	8
CLOUD			
CLOUD AND RAIN-TEARS PASS THEY FLEET!	7	CINO	49
FU I LOVED THE HIGH CLOUD AND THE HILL,	117	EPITAPHS	1
THE WIND BUNDLES ITSELF INTO A BLUISH CLOUD AND WANDERS OFF.	129	THE RIVER SONG	30
WITH HEAD GEAR GLITTERING AGAINST THE CLOUD AND SUN.	131	AT TEN-SHIN	13
MIND LIKE A FLOATING WIDE CLOUD,	137	TAKING LEAVE	5
TO-EM-MEI'S "THE UNMOVING CLOUD"	142	UNMOVING CLOUD	T
AND GO DARK WITH CLOUD,	176	LANGUE D'OC: 3	74
CLOUDS			
THE CLOUDS THAT ARE SPRAY TO ITS SEA.	7	CINO	56
I HA' SEEN THEM 'MID THE CLOUDS ON THE HEATHER.	25	THE WHITE STAG	1
AND THE WINDS SHRIEK THROUGH THE CLOUDS MAD, OPPOSING,	28	ALTAFORTE	11
FIVE CLOUDS HANG ALOFT, BRIGHT ON THE PURPLE SKY,	129	THE RIVER SONG	33
TOSSING IT UP UNDER THE CLOUDS.	136	EXILE'S LETTER	62
CLOUDS GROW OUT OF THE HILL	138	NEAR SHOKU	4
NOW THE HIGH CLOUDS COVER THE SUN	138	CITY OF CHOAN	11
THE CLOUDS HAVE GATHERED, AND GATHERED,	142	UNMOVING CLOUD	1
RAIN, RAIN, AND THE CLOUDS HAVE GATHERED,	142	UNMOVING CLOUD	10
CLOUDY			
LURE US BEYOND THE CLOUDY PEAK OF RIVA?	39	BLANDULA	15
CLOVER			
FLASH BETWEEN THE ORCHIDS AND CLOVER,	139	SENNIN POEM	2
CLUB			
OF DOWSON; OF THE RHYMERS' CLUB;	193	SIENA MI FE	6
"I SEE THEM SITTING IN THE HARVARD CLUB,	244	MOYEN SENSUEL	180
CLUS			
TALKING OF TROBAR CLUS WITH DANIEL.	155	NEAR PERIGORD	140
CLUSTERED			
A YOUNG MUSE WITH YOUNG LOVES CLUSTERED ABOUT HER	207	SEXTUS PROP: 1	13
CLUSTERS			
HANG IN YELLOW-WHITE AND DARK CLUSTERS READY FOR PRESSING.	167	OF AROUET	22
CLUTCHING			
AS IVY FINGERS CLUTCHING THROUGH	8	NA AUDIART	4
COACHES			
DRAG ON THE SEVEN COACHES WITH OUTRIDERS.	141	IDEA OF CHOAN	3
THE COACHES ARE PERFUMED WOOD,	141	IDEA OF CHOAN	4
COAL			
AND TOTIN' UP SCUTTLES OF COAL,	271	OLE KATE	18
COALS			
SHE'D COME A SWEATIN' UP WITH THE COALS	271	OLE KATE	9
COAN			
SHADES OF CALLIMACHUS, COAN GHOSTS OF PHILETAS	207	SEXTUS PROP: 1	1
STIFFENED OUR FACE WITH THE BACKWASH OF PHILETAS THE COAN.	211	SEXTUS PROP: 2	54
COAST			
HE MAY WALK ON THE SCYTHIAN COAST,	212	SEXTUS PROP: 3	18
COAT			
CULDOU LACKING A COAT TO DRESS	12	OF THE GIBBET	30
FOR THE TOBACCO ASHES SCATTERED ON HIS COAT	15	FANAM GANO	34
HOW HIS COAT AND PANTS ADORN HIM!	46	FROM HEINE: 6	5
I WILL GET YOU A GREEN COAT OUT OF CHINA	94	INSTRUCTIONS	17
WHY DOES THE SMALL CHILD IN THE SOILED-WHITE IMITATION FUR COAT	114	SIMULACRA	3
KNOWING MY COAT HAS NEVER BEEN	196	HUGH SELWIN:12	5

PAGE 76

COAT -- COLLECTION

	PAGE	TITLE	LINE
COAT (CONTINUED)			
I WEAR A FINE FUR COAT AND GLOVES, ...	266	ALF'S ELEVENTH	9
COATS			
BUT YOU STUFFED COATS WHO'RE NEITHER TEPID NOR DISTINCTLY BOREAL, ...	238	MOYEN SENSUEL	5
COBALT			
CLEAR SAPPHIRE, COBALT, CYANINE, ...	39	BLANDULA	10
FROM AMBER LATTICES UPON THE COBALT NIGHT, ...	53	AU JARDIN	3
WASHED IN THE COBALT OF OBLIVIONS;	203	MAUBERLEY: 4	9
COBBLED			
STRIKE SPARKS FROM THE COBBLED STREET	111	IMAGE ORLEANS	7
COBBLES			
AND CRIED UP FROM THEIR COBBLES:	96	AESTHETICS	4
COBWEBS			
"MY WIT AND WORTH ARE COBWEBS BRUSHED ASIDE	152	NEAR PERIGORD	45
COCK-SHY			
"BEAUTY IS SLANDER'S COCK-SHY.	226	SEXTUS PROP:11	21
COCOANUT			
SHE RUSHED OUT INTO THE SUNLIGHT AND SWARMED UP A COCOANUT PALM TREE, ...	118	CONTEMPORARIES	3
COCOTTE			
NORMANDE COCOTTE	161	PAGANI'S NOV 8	2
CODA			
CODA	103	CODA	T
CODE			
THIS THING, THAT HATH A CODE AND NOT A CORE, ...	63	AN OBJECT	1
COEUR-DE-LION			
"HERE COEUR-DE-LION WAS SLAIN.	122	PROVINC DESERT	44
MALEMORT, GUESSES BENEATH, SENDS WORD TO COEUR-DE-LION:	155	NEAR PERIGORD	123
COEURS			
O DIEU, PURIFIEZ NOS COEURS!	26	NIGHT LITANY	1
PURIFIEZ NOS COEURS!	26	NIGHT LITANY	2
PURIFIEZ NOS COEURS, ...	26	NIGHT LITANY	20
PURIFIEZ NOS COEURS, ...	26	NIGHT LITANY	21
PURIFIEZ NOS COEURS, ...	27	NIGHT LITANY	34
PURIFIEZ NOS COEURS, ...	27	NIGHT LITANY	35
PURIFIEZ NOS COEURS	27	NIGHT LITANY	49
PURIFIEZ NOS COEURS	27	NIGHT LITANY	51
COHORT			
SUCH MY COHORT AND SETTING, AND SHE BOUND IVY TO HIS THYRSOS;	211	SEXTUS PROP: 2	35
COIN			
NO COIN, NO WILL TO SNATCH THE AFTERMATH	14	FAMAM CANO	31
TWO MEN TOSSING A COIN, ONE KEEPING A CASTLE, ...	122	PROVINC DESERT	66
TO OWN HIS COIN AGAIN.	269	SAFE AND SOUND	28
COITUS			
COITUS	110	COITUS	T
COLCHIS			
AND THERE WAS A CASE IN COLCHIS, JASON AND THAT WOMAN IN COLCHIS;	228	SEXTUS PROP:12	7
AND THERE WAS A CASE IN COLCHIS, JASON AND THAT WOMAN IN COLCHIS;	228	SEXTUS PROP:12	7
COLD			
BUT I HAVE PUT ASIDE THIS FOLLY AND THE COLD	4	LA FRAISNE	3
YOUTH DEW IS COLD	9	NA AUDIART	40
WHITE WORDS AS SNOW FLAKES BUT THEY ARE COLD, ...	16	PRAISE YSOLT	21
AND MY HEART IS COLD AND SERE;	45	FROM HEINE: 3	6
TO "CHLORIS CHAETE AND COLD, HIS "ONLY CHLORIS."	118	THREE POETS	4
SOUTH-FOLK IN COLD COUNTRY	139	SOUTH-FOLK	T
AND THE COLD BIRDS TWITTER	174	LANGUE D'OC: 3	2
AND COLD FIT FOR DESPAIR, ...	266	ALF'S ELEVENTH	14
COLDEST			
CORN OF THE COLDEST. NATHLESS THERE KNOCKETH NOW	64	THE SEAFARER	34
COLDLY			
WHILE SHE TOSSED CLOSE TO CLIFFS. COLDLY AFFLICTED,	64	THE SEAFARER	8
COLLAR			
SUNK IN A FROWSY COLLAR--AN UNBRUSHED BLACK, ...	161	CABARET DANCER	11
THE STIFFNESS FROM SPATS TO COLLAR	193	BRENNBAUM	3
COLLECTION			
THESE ARE THE HIGH-BROWS, AND TO THIS COLLECTION	241	MOYEN SENSUEL	82

COLLECTIVE -- COME

	PAGE	TITLE	LINE
COLLECTIVE			
WILL KEEP THEIR COLLECTIVE NOSE IN MY BOOKS,	209	SEXTUS PROP: 1	61
COLLICKS			
THAT ARE THE NATION'S BOTTS, COLLICKS AND GLANDERS.	241	MOYEN SENSUEL	74
COLONEL			
OR LIKE A REAL TEXAS COLONEL,	181	MOEURS CON: 7	14
COLONNES			
JE VIS LES COLONNES ANCIENNES EN "TOC"	160	DANS OMNIBUS	12
COLOUR			
THEN THERE'S A GOLDISH COLOUR, DIFFERENT.	69	SUB MARE	4
BELS CEMBELINS, I TAKE OF YOU YOUR COLOUR,	105	DOMPNA POIS	21
FOR, AS TO COLOUR AND EYES	105	DOMPNA POIS	25
COLOUR.	120	GAME OF CHESS	3
HOLDING LINES IN ONE COLOUR.	120	GAME OF CHESS	5
CLASH, LEAPING OF BANDS, STRAIGHT STRIPS OF HARD COLOUR,	120	GAME OF CHESS	14
THE EASTERN WIND BRINGS THE GREEN COLOUR INTO THE ISLAND GRASSES AT YEI-SHU,	129	THE RIVER SONG	23
THE SEA'S COLOUR MOVES AT THE DAWN	131	AT TEN-SHIN	9
WITH GLITTER OF COLOUR	141	IDEA OF CHOAN	27
WEARING RAW SILK OF GOOD COLOUR,	146	CANTILATIONS	7
THE WIRE-LIKE BANDS OF COLOUR INVOLUTE MOUNT FROM MY FINGERS;	170	PHANOPOEIA	17
ONE SUBSTANCE AND ONE COLOUR	197	ENVOI (1919)	15
THUS, IF HER COLOUR	201	AGE DEMANDED	9
MOVES CHANGING COLOUR, OR TO LAUGH OR WEEP	250	DONNA MI PREGA	53
THERE, BEYOND COLOUR, ESSENCE SET APART,	250	DONNA MI PREGA	84
COLOURLESS			
OUT OF THE BROWN LEAF-BROWN COLOURLESS	76	THE ALCHEMIST	47
COLOURLESS	198	MAUBERLEY: 1	13
COLOURS			
FREE US, FOR WITHOUT BE GOODLY COLOURS,	35	THE EYES	8
GREEN OF THE WOOD-MOSS AND FLOWER COLOURS,	35	THE EYES	9
MINE EYES UPON NEW COLOURS.	39	FOR PSYCHE	9
REST ME WITH CHINESE COLOURS,	95	OF THE DEGREES	1
THE HALL OF CLEAR COLOURS.	95	OF THE DEGREES	9
O GLASS SUBTLY EVIL, O CONFUSION OF COLOURS!	95	OF THE DEGREES	10
COLUMN			
"FOLLOW ME, AND TAKE A COLUMN,	194	MR. NIXON	8
COLUMNS			
THOUGH MY HOUSE IS NOT PROPPED UP BY TAENARIAN COLUMNS FROM LACONIA (ASSOCIATED WITH NEPTUNE AND CERBERUS),	208	SEXTUS PROP: 1	51
COMBAT			
UPON A TALE, TO COMBAT OTHER TRACTS,	241	MOYEN SENSUEL	72
COMBINATION			
FROM THEIR VAULTS AND COMBINATION	269	SAFE AND SOUND	21
COMBUSTED			
COMBUSTED SEMELE'S, OF IO STRAYED.	227	SEXTUS PROP:11	34
COME			
... I HOPE SHE WILL NOT COME AGAIN.	5	LA FRAISNE	44
OH, TILL THOU COME AGAIN.	9	NA AUDIART	37
WHEN COME THEY, SURGING OF POWER, "DAEMON,"	20	IN DURANCE	19
THEY THAT COME MEWARDS, BEARING OLD MAGIC.	20	IN DURANCE	22
THEN CAME WHAT MIGHT COME, TO WIT: THREE MEN AND ONE WOMAN,	22	MARVOIL	11
AND MAY I COME SPEEDILY TO BEZIERS	23	MARVOIL	32
BID THE WORLD'S HOUNDS COME TO HORN!"	25	THE WHITE STAG	7
YOU WHORESON DOG, PAPIOLS, COME! LET'S TO MUSIC!	28	ALTAFORTE	2
NOW YOU WILL COME OUT OF A CONFUSION OF PEOPLE,	36	FRANCESCA	3
TO COME TO EARTH TO DRAW US FROM MISVENTURE,	37	THE YOUNG KING	34
COME WITH ME TO THAT CASTLE	47	FROM HEINE: 7	3
AND ARE YOU NOT READY WHEN EVENING'S COME?	48	FROM HEINE: 8	3
HERE AM I COME PERFORCE MY LOVE OF HER,	49	OF SPLENDOUR	17
TURNED IN THEIR SAPPHIRE TIDE, COME FLOODING O'ER US!	51	HORAE BEATAE	4
BUT THERE'LL COME SORROW OF IT.	53	AU JARDIN	14
AND IT'LL ALL COME RIGHT,	53	AU JARDIN	21
COME BEAUTY BAREFOOT FROM THE CYCLADES,	63	PHASELLUS ILLE	12
THERE COME NOW NO KINGS NOR CAESARS	66	THE SEAFARER	84
COME, OR THE STELLAR TIDE WILL SLIP AWAY.	69	THE NEEDLE	1
SINCE YOU HAVE COME THIS PLACE HAS HOVERED ROUND ME,	69	SUB MARE	2

PAGE 78

COME -- COMES

	PAGE	TITLE	LINE
COME (CONTINUED)			
COME NOW, BEFORE THIS POWER	69	THE NEEDLE	6
O LOVE, COME NOW, THIS LAND TURNS EVIL SLOWLY.	69	THE NEEDLE	9
SOFT AS SPRING WIND THAT'S COME FROM BIRCHEN BOWERS.	71	A VIRGINAL	10
GREEN COME THE SHOOTS, AYE APRIL IN THE BRANCHES,	71	A VIRGINAL	11
COME, LET US PITY THOSE WHO ARE BETTER OFF THAN WE ARE.	83	THE GARRET	1
COME, MY FRIEND, AND REMEMBER	83	THE GARRET	2
COME, LET US PITY THE MARRIED AND THE UNMARRIED.	83	THE GARRET	5
BECAUSE I HAD JUST COME FROM THE COUNTRY;	85	SALUTATION 2ND	2
I COME TO YOU AS A GROWN CHILD	89	A PACT	3
COME, MY SONGS, LET US EXPRESS OUR BASER PASSIONS,	94	INSTRUCTIONS	1
I FEAR YOU WILL COME TO A BAD END.	94	INSTRUCTIONS	4
YOU WILL COME TO A VERY BAD END.	94	INSTRUCTIONS	9
HOW MANY WILL COME AFTER ME	96	DUM CAPITOLIUM	1
COME, MY SONGS, LET US SPEAK OF PERFECTION--	99	SALVATIONISTS	1
COME, MY SONGS,	99	SALVATIONISTS	11
THERE COME FORTH MANY MAIDENS	108	CH'U YUAN	4
I WILL COME OUT FROM THE NEW THICKET	108	CH'U YUAN	9
"COME, AUSTER, COME APELIOTA,	109	THE FAUN	5
"COME, AUSTER, COME APELIOTA,	109	THE FAUN	5
CRUSHED STRAWBERRIES! COME, LET US FEAST OUR EYES.	113	L'ART, 1910	2
HAVE SEEN THE COPPER COME DOWN	122	PROVINC DESERT	52
WHAT FLOWER HAS COME INTO BLOSSOM?	127	BOWMEN OF SHU	13
WE COME BACK IN THE SNOW,	127	BOWMEN OF SHU	22
THE IMPERIAL GUARDS COME FORTH FROM THE GOLDEN HOUSE WITH THEIR ARMOUR A-GLEAMING.	129	THE RIVER SONG	34
MARCH HAS COME TO THE BRIDGE HEAD,	131	AT TEN-SHIN	1
AND I WILL COME OUT TO MEET YOU	131	RIVER-MER WIFE	28
AND THEN, WHEN SEPARATION HAD COME TO ITS WORST,	134	EXILE'S LETTER	16
WHEN YOU COME TO THE GATES OF GO.	137	OF DEPARTURE	EPI
COME, LET US ON WITH THE NEW DEAL,	145	SALUTATION 3RD	13
COME MY CANTILATIONS	146	CANTILATIONS	T
COME MY CANTILATIONS,	146	CANTILATIONS	1
LET COME BEAUTIFUL PEOPLE	146	CANTILATIONS	6
LET COME THE GRACEFUL SPEAKERS,	146	CANTILATIONS	8
LET COME THE READY OF WIT,	146	CANTILATIONS	9
LET COME THE GAY OF MANNER, THE INSOLENT AND THE EXULTING.	146	CANTILATIONS	10
WHERE AM I COME WITH COMPOUND FLATTERIES--	153	NEAR PERIGORD	74
TWICE THEY PROMISED TO COME.	158	PSYCHOLOG HOUR	26
COME NOW, MY DEAR PEPITA,	162	CABARET DANCER	32
COME, COME TO-MORROW,	162	CABARET DANCER	45
COME, COME TO-MORROW,	162	CABARET DANCER	45
SAW THE PERFORMERS COME: HIM, HER, THE BABY,	163	CABARET DANCER	80
"COME, I HAVE HAD A LONG DREAM,"	166	FISH & SHADOW	10
"COME NOW! OLD SWENKIN! RISE UP FROM THY BED,	172	LANGUE D'OC: 1	14
IF THOU COME NOT, THE COST BE ON THY HEAD.	172	LANGUE D'OC: 1	16
'TILL THE SUN COME, AND THE GREEN LEAF ON THE BOUGH.	173	LANGUE D'OC: 2	16
WHO HAVE COME BETWEEN ME AND MY CHARMER,	173	LANGUE D'OC: 2	24
SHE WILL NEITHER STAY IN, NOR COME OUT.	179	MOEURS CON: 2	11
THEY WILL COME NO MORE,	181	MOEURS CON: 7	1
I WHO COME FIRST FROM THE CLEAR FONT	207	SEXTUS PROP: 1	3
TELLING ME TO COME TO TIBUR:	212	SEXTUS PROP: 3	2
NO MESSENGER SHOULD COME WHOLLY EMPTY.	214	SEXTUS PROP: 4	8
"DEATH WHY TARDILY COME?"	219	SEXTUS PROP: 6	29
THE TIME IS COME, THE AIR HEAVES IN TORRIDITY,	221	SEXTUS PROP: 8	3
AND THE FAWNS COME TO SNIFF AT HIS SIDES.	231	CANTUS PLANUS	2
UPON A DUSK THAT IS COME FROM MARS AND STAYS.	248	DONNA MI PREGA	21
COME NOT ANEAR THE DARK-BROWED SOPHIST	263	ALF'S EIGHTH	8
COME NOT HERE	263	ALF'S EIGHTH	11
ELECTION WILL NOT COME VERY SOON,	265	ALF'S TENTH	13
SHE'D COME A SWEATIN' UP WITH THE COALS	271	OLE KATE	9
COMER			
O THOU NEW COMER WHO SEEK'ST ROME IN ROME	40	ROME	1
COMES			
"THANK YOU, WHATEVER COMES." AND THEN SHE TURNED	40	ERAT HORA	1
WENT SWIFTLY FROM ME, NAY WHATEVER COMES	40	ERAT HORA	4
IN THESE HE DAILY COMES TO ASK ME:	46	FROM HEINE: 6	7
SET TO SOME WEAVING, COMES THE AUREATE LIGHT.	49	OF SPLENDOUR	16
I SUPPOSE, WHEN POETRY COMES DOWN TO FACTS,	52	AU SALON	1

PAGE 79

COMES -- COMME

	PAGE	TITLE	LINE
COMES (CONTINUED)			
AND NO SUN COMES TO REST ME IN THIS PLACE, ...	60	TOMB AKR CAAR	25
YOU ARE A PERSON OF SOME INTEREST, ONE COMES TO YOU	61	PORTRAIT FEMME	14
YET LONGING COMES UPON HIM TO FARE FORTH ON THE			
WATER.	65	THE SEAFARER	48
AND ALL THIS COMES TO AN END.	136	EXILE'S LETTER	63
EVENING COMES.	141	IDEA OF CHOAN	11
FOR AFTER DEATH THERE COMES NO OTHER CALAMITY.	164	QUINTUS SEPTIM	11
AND DAY COMES ON.	172	LANGUE D'OC: 1	5
AND DAY COMES ON!	172	LANGUE D'OC: 1	9
AND DAY COMES ON!	172	LANGUE D'OC: 1	13
AND DAY COMES ON!	172	LANGUE D'OC: 1	17
AND DAY COMES ON.	172	LANGUE D'OC: 1	21
OUR LOVE COMES OUT	173	LANGUE D'OC: 2	11
AND DAY COMES ON.	177	LANGUE D'OC: 4	5
AND DAY COMES ON.	177	LANGUE D'OC: 4	10
AND DAY COMES ON.	177	LANGUE D'OC: 4	15
AND DAY COMES ON."	177	LANGUE D'OC: 4	20
AND DAY COMES ON."	177	LANGUE D'OC: 4	25
AND DAY COMES ON.	177	LANGUE D'OC: 4	30
MIDNIGHT, AND A LETTER COMES TO ME FROM OUR MISTRESS:	212	SEXTUS PROP: 3	1
AND WHENCE THIS SOFT BOOK COMES INTO MY MOUTH.	217	SEXTUS PROP: 5	24
SMALL TALK COMES FROM SMALL BONES.	219	SEXTUS PROP: 6	37
FOR LONG NIGHT COMES UPON YOU	220	SEXTUS PROP: 7	18
THERE COMES, IT SEEMS, AND AT ANY RATE	222	SEXTUS PROP: 8	16
AND WHEN HE COMES INTO POWER	238	ABU SALAMMAMM	30
OF AN AFFECT THAT COMES OFTEN AND IS FELL	248	DONNA MI PREGA	2
HE COMES TO BE AND IS WHEN WILL'S SO GREAT	249	DONNA MI PREGA	49
HERE COMES THE HIRED GANG	261	ALF'S SIXTH	10
COMETH			
BUT HIS ANSWER COMETH, AS WINDS AND AS LUTANY, ...	16	PRAISE YSOLT	5
SO IS SHE THAT COMETH, THE MOTHER OF SONGS, ...	17	PRAISE YSOLT	50
"THEE"? OH, "THEE" IS WHO COMETH FIRST	20	IN DURANCE	10
COMETH UNTO US, ...	26	NIGHT LITANY	16
BOSQUE TAKETH BLOSSOM, COMETH BEAUTY OF BERRIES,	65	THE SEAFARER	49
ON EARTH'S SHELTER COMETH OFT TO ME, ...	65	THE SEAFARER	62
COMFORT			
O WHAT COMFORT IS IT FOR ME	46	FROM HEINE: 6	17
NO COMFORT, AT MY TIME OF LIFE WHEN	46	FROM HEINE: 6	19
WE HAVE NO COMFORT BECAUSE OF THESE MONGOLS.	127	BOWMEN OF SHU	4
THERE IS NO EASE IN ROYAL AFFAIRS, WE HAVE NO			
COMFORT.	127	BOWMEN OF SHU	11
COMFORTER			
A POSSIBLE FRIEND AND COMFORTER.	196	HUGH SELWIN:12	20
COMFORTS			
THESE COMFORTS HEAPED UPON ME, SMOTHER ME!	70	THE PLUNGE	2
COMIC			
THE COMIC DETAIL WILL BE ABSENT.	146	MONUMENTUM AER	5
FOR THE FRENCH HAVE COMIC PAPERS--	272	NATIONAL SONG	9
COMING			
BEFORE THE TIME OF ITS COMING?	26	NIGHT LITANY	18
THE COMING OF WAR: ACTAEON	107	COMING OF WAR	T
COMING DOWN FROM THE FAIR	119	THE GYPSY	14
IF YOU ARE COMING DOWN THROUGH THE NARROWS OF THE			
RIVER KIANG, ...	131	RIVER-MER WIFE	26
PLEASURE LASTING, WITH COURTEZANS, GOING AND COMING			
WITHOUT HINDRANCE, ...	136	EXILE'S LETTER	53
MY VOTE COMING FROM THE TEMPLE OF PHOEBUS IN LYCIA,			
AT PATARA, ...	208	SEXTUS PROP: 1	38
PARIS TOOK HELEN NAKED COMING FROM THE BED OF			
MENELAUS, ...	220	SEXTUS PROP: 7	14
WE WERE COMING NEAR TO THE HOUSE, ...	225	SEXTUS PROP:10	25
COMMAND			
I WOULD MAKE VERSE IN YOUR FASHION, IF SHE SHOULD			
COMMAND IT, ...	229	SEXTUS PROP:12	60
COMMANDED			
AND IN VAIN THEY COMMANDED HIM TO STA FERMO!	97	AESTHETICS	15
COMMANDS			
I AWAIT THE LADY VALENTINE'S COMMANDS, ...	196	HUGH SELWIN:12	4
COMME			
COMME DES POULARDES.	160	DANS OMNIBUS	19

PAGE 80

COMME -- COMPOSING

	PAGE	TITLE	LINE
COMME (CONTINUED)			
IL ETAIT COMME UN TOUT PETIT GARCON	181	MOEURS CON: 7	3
COMMERCE			
LET THERE BE COMMERCE BETWEEN US.	89	A PACT	9
COMMISSION			
COMMISSION	88	COMMISSION	T
COMMIT			
WILL COMMIT THAT INDISCRETION.	83	THE GARDEN	12
COMMON			
ARCHES WORN OLD AND PALACES MADE COMMON,	40	ROME	3
TILL WE HAD NOTHING BUT THOUGHTS AND MEMORIES IN COMMON.	134	EXILE'S LETTER	15
COMPACT			
THE COMPACT, DE BORN SMOKED OUT, TREES FELLED	155	NEAR PERIGORD	124
COMPANION			
OR THE SONG OF THE SIXTH COMPANION	11	OF THE GIBBET	SUB
TO BRING THEE SAFE BACK, MY COMPANION.	172	LANGUE D'OC: 1	20
COMPANIONS			
AND BID GO IN WITH HONOURED COMPANIONS	37	THE YOUNG KING	39
GREY-HAIRED HE GROANETH, KNOWS GONE COMPANIONS,	66	THE SEAFARER	94
YET THE COMPANIONS OF THE MUSES	209	SEXTUS PROP: 1	60
COMPANY			
WHEN WE LAST MADE COMPANY,	33	GOODLY FERE	14
O RIBALD COMPANY, O SAINTLY HOST,	35	HIS OWN FACE	2
IN EVENING COMPANY HE SETS HIS FACE	46	FROM HEINE: 6	13
OUT CAME THE FAST OF KAN FOREMAN AND HIS COMPANY.	134	EXILE'S LETTER	23
THESE ARE THEY OF THY COMPANY.	147	BEFORE SLEEP	7
THE TEN NIGHTS OF YOUR COMPANY YOU HAVE	224	SEXTUS PROP: 9	28
THE SELECT COMPANY: BEAUTIES YOU ALL WOULD KNOW	242	MOYEN SENSUEL	113
COMPARABLE			
WAS VENUS EXACERBATED BY THE EXISTENCE OF A COMPARABLE EQUAL?	221	SEXTUS PROP: 8	10
COMPARAISON			
EN COMPARAISON AVEC LAQUELLE LA ROSE	199	MAUBERLEY: 2	EPI
COMPARED			
WE ARE COMPARED TO THAT SORT OF PERSON	82	THE CONDOLENCE	14
AND YOU ARE EVEN COMPARED TO LESBIA.	113	FORMIANUS LADY	9
AND WHAT ARE THEY COMPARED TO THE LADY RIOKUSHU,	132	AT TEN-SHIN	29
COMPASSION			
THAT IN HIM SOLELY IS COMPASSION BORN.	250	DONNA MI PREGA	87
COMPEL			
"COMPEL A CERTAIN SILENCE AND RESTRAINT."	243	MOYEN SENSUEL	138
COMPELLED			
I AM COMPELLED TO CONCLUDE	102	MEDITATIO	2
COMPELS			
POWER THAT COMPELS 'EM	244	MOYEN SENSUEL	171
COMPILATION			
FURNISH MORE DATE FOR A COMPILATION	243	MOYEN SENSUEL	153
COMPLAIN			
THROUGH ALL THE WORLD WILL I COMPLAIN	44	FROM HEINE: 1	3
COMPLAIN ABOUT THE AWFUL NOISE	45	FROM HEINE: 5	3
THEY HOWL, THEY COMPLAIN IN DELICATE AND EXHAUSTED METRES	148	FRATRES MINORE	5
HERE IN THE ORCHARD WHERE THE BIRDS COMPLAIN,	177	LANGUE D'OC: 4	17
COMPLETE			
ARE A COMPLETE ELUCIDATION OF DEATH.	209	SEXTUS PROP: 1	69
COMPLETELY			
THEE, AND HELD THY HEART COMPLETELY.	46	FROM HEINE: 3	4
COMPLEYNT			
COMPLEYNT OF A GENTLEMAN WHO HAS BEEN WAITING OUTSIDE FOR SOME TIME	172	LANGUE D'OC: 1	SUB
COMPLICATIONS			
AND YOUR BUNDLE OF MUNDANE COMPLICATIONS.	247	PIERROTS	9
COMPLIMENT			
WHAT DOORS ARE OPEN TO FINE COMPLIMENT?"	153	NEAR PERIGORD	75
COMPLIMENTS			
NO ONE HEARS AUGHT SAVE THE GRACIOUS SOUND OF COMPLIMENTS.	161	NEAR PERIGORD	120
COMPOSING			
COMPOSING OUR ALBAS,	104	ANCORA	4

COMPOSITION -- CONFER

	PAGE	TITLE	LINE
COMPOSITION			
INCAPABLE OF THE LEAST UTTERANCE OR COMPOSITION,	202	AGE DEMANDED	46
COMPOSITIONS			
MY GOD-LIKE COMPOSITIONS.	46	FROM HEINE: 6	16
COMPOUND			
WHERE AM I COME WITH COMPOUND FLATTERIES--	153	NEAR PERIGORD	74
DESPITE IT ALL, YOUR COMPOUND PREDILECTION	240	MOYEN SENSUEL	69
COMPREHENSION			
WERE MUCH TOO ABSTRUSE FOR HIS COMPREHENSION,	181	MOEURS CON: 7	9
COMPRENDRE			
QU'EST CE QU'ILS PEUVENT COMPRENDRE?	199	MAUBERLEY: 2	EPI
QU'ILS PEUVENT COMPRENDRE DE CETTE PASSION	199	MAUBERLEY: 2	EPI
COMPRENNENT			
S'ILS NE COMPRENNENT PAS LA POESIE,	199	MAUBERLEY: 2	EPI
COMRADE			
COMRADE, COMRADE OF MY LIFE, OF MY PURSE, OF MY PERSON;	228	SEXTUS PROP:12	14
COMRADE, COMRADE OF MY LIFE, OF MY PURSE, OF MY PERSON;	228	SEXTUS PROP:12	14
COMRADES			
DRINK WE THE COMRADES MERRILY	11	OF THE GIBBET	3
COMSTOCK'S			
FROM COMSTOCK'S SELF, DOWN TO THE MEANEST RESIDENT,	239	MOYEN SENSUEL	15
CON			
BLAGUEUR! "CON GLI OCCHI ONESTI E TARDI,"	181	MOEURS CON: 7	6
CONCAVA			
CONCAVA VALLIS	170	PHANOPOEIA	ST
CONCEALED			
GO TO THEM WHOSE FAILURE IS CONCEALED,	88	COMMISSION	12
CONCEITED			
PIMPING, CONCEITED, PLACID, EDITORIAL,	238	MOYEN SENSUEL	6
CONCENTRATION			
AUGUST ATTRACTION OR CONCENTRATION.	202	AGE DEMANDED	49
CONCEPTS			
WITH ALL THE ADMIRABLE CONCEPTS THAT MOVED FROM IT	42	HER MONUMENT	39
CONCERNING			
SAILOR, OF WINDS; A PLOWMAN, CONCERNING HIS OXEN;	218	SEXTUS PROP: 5	55
CONCERNS			
AND RETURN TO THAT WHICH CONCERNS US.	82	THE CONDOLENCE	18
ASSAILS ME, AND CONCERNS ME ALMOST AS LITTLE.	103	LADIES	20
CONCESSIONS			
THESE NEW CONCESSIONS	248	PIERROTS	27
CONCLUDE			
I AM COMPELLED TO CONCLUDE	102	MEDITATIO	2
CONCOCTION			
NOR HATH IT EVER SINCE CHANGED THAT CONCOCTION.	63	PHASELLUS ILLE	4
CONCORD			
AND THE WISE CONCORD, WHENCE THROUGH DELICIOUS SEAS	42	HER MONUMENT	43
CONCUPISCENCE			
DESPITE IT ALL, DESPITE YOUR RED BLOODS, FEBRILE CONCUPISCENCE	240	MOYEN SENSUEL	67
CONDEMN			
WHO AM I TO CONDEMN YOU, O DIVES,	102	TO DIVES	1
CONDESCENSION			
YOU HAD THE SAME OLD AIR OF CONDESCENSION	101	AMITIES	3
CONDITION			
THEY SET THEIR MIND (IT'S STILL IN THAT CONDITION)--	240	MOYEN SENSUEL	53
CONDOLENCE			
THE CONDOLENCE	82	THE CONDOLENCE	T
CONDONE			
OR ELSE YOU CONDONE THEIR DRUGS,	145	SALUTATION 3RD	23
THEN WERE THERE CAUSE IN THEE THAT SHOULD CONDONE	197	ENVOI (1919)	5
CONDUCT			
SPEAK OF THE INDECOROUS CONDUCT OF THE GODS!	86	SALUTATION 2ND	30
DO NOT UNDERSTAND THE CONDUCT OF THIS WORLD'S AFFAIRS.	97	THE BELLAIRES	2
CONDUCT, ON THE OTHER HAND, THE SOUL	196	HUGH SELWIN:12	21
BECAUSE HELEN'S CONDUCT IS "UNSUITABLE."	218	SEXTUS PROP: 5	63
CONFER			
IF SHE CONFER SUCH NIGHTS UPON ME,	221	SEXTUS PROP: 7	37

PAGE 82

CONFESS -- CONSPECTU

	PAGE	TITLE	LINE
CONFESS			
FOR MICHAULT LE BORGNE THAT WOULD CONFESS	12	OF THE GIBBET	34
I CONFESS, MY FRIEND, I AM PUZZLED.	102	MEDITATIO	5
HID MORE STATISTICS, MORE FEARED TO CONFESS	260	ALF'S FIFTH	11
CONFESSION			
NOTHING, IN BRIEF, BUT MAUDLIN CONFESSION,	202	AGE DEMANDED	50
CONFESSIONS			
HYSTERIAS, TRENCH CONFESSIONS,	190	HUGH SELWYN: 4	26
SOOTHINGS, CONFESSIONS;	248	PIERROTS	26
CONFETTI			
HERE ARE YOUR BELLS AND CONFETTI.	86	SALUTATION 2ND	23
CONFIDENCE			
BRING CONFIDENCE UPON THE ALGAE AND THE TENTACLES OF THE SOUL.	88	COMMISSION	21
CONFIGURATION			
WITH THEIR LARGE AND ANAEMIC EYES THEY LOOKED OUT UPON THIS CONFIGURATION.	93	LES MILLWIN	12
CONFUSED			
CONFUSED, WHIRLED IN A TANGLE.	136	EXILE'S LETTER	74
CONFUSION			
NOW YOU WILL COME OUT OF A CONFUSION OF PEOPLE,	36	FRANCESCA	3
O GLASS SUBTLY EVIL, O CONFUSION OF COLOURS!	95	OF THE DEGREES	10
AND THERE WILL BE ONLY THE MORE CONFUSION,	98	THE BELLAIRES	26
CONMIGO			
PORQUE POR ANDAR CONMIGO	82	THE CONDOLENCE	EP 1
CONNAISSEZ-VOUS			
"CONNAISSEZ-VOUS OSTENDE?"	111	BLACK SLIPPERS	6
CONNECTION			
FOR MENCKEN STATES SOMEWHERE, IN THIS CONNECTION:	238	MOYEN SENSUEL	10
CONNECTIONS			
TOGETHER WITH THE RESPECTIVE WIVES, HUSBANDS, SISTERS AND HETEROGENEOUS CONNECTIONS OF THE GOOD BELLAIRES,	97	THE BELLAIRES	4
SAVE A SQUABBLE OF FEMALE CONNECTIONS.	115	SOCIAL ORDER	15
CONQUERED			
AND CONQUERED! AH GOD! CONQUERED!	31	PIERE VIDAL	3
AND CONQUERED! AH GOD! CONQUERED!	31	PIERE VIDAL	3
ALL-CONQUERING, NOW CONQUERED, BECAUSE	40	ROME	
ROME THAT ALONE HAST CONQUERED ROME THE TOWN,	40	ROME	1
UPON THE ONE RAFT, VICTOR AND CONQUERED TOGETHER,	218	SEXTUS PROP: 6	
CONQUESTS			
AND MEDITATE UPON THE LORD'S CONQUESTS.	246	MOYEN SENSUEL	22
CONSCIOUSNESS			
A CONSCIOUSNESS DISJUNCT,	203	MAUBERLEY: 4	1
OF MY STILL CONSCIOUSNESS	236	MIDDLE-AGED	2
CONSECRATED			
WILL WE NOT FIND SOME HEADLAND CONSECRATED	39	BLANDULA	
CONSERVATION			
EMENDATION, CONSERVATION OF THE "BETTER TRADITION,"	202	AGE DEMANDED	4
CONSERVATORY			
CONSERVATORY FOLLOWS CONSERVATORY,	180	MOEURS CON: 5	1
CONSERVATORY FOLLOWS CONSERVATORY,	180	MOEURS CON: 5	1
CONSERVATRIX			
"CONSERVATRIX OF MILESIEN"	195	HUGH SELWIN:11	
CONSIDER			
FOR WE SHALL CONSIDER THEM AND THEIR STATE	99	SALVATIONISTS	
WHEN I CAREFULLY CONSIDER THE CURIOUS HABITS OF DOGS	102	MEDITATIO	
WHEN I CONSIDER THE CURIOUS HABITS OF MAN	102	MEDITATIO	
THEY CONSIDER THE ELDERLY MIND	104	THE SEEING EYE	
DANGERS OF DELAY. "CONSIDER	194	MR. NIXON	
CONSIDERABLE			
AND FOR ALL THIS I HAVE CONSIDERABLE REGRET,	98	THE BELLAIRES	4
YOU CREATED CONSIDERABLE STIR IN CHICAGO,	114	EPILOGUE	
CONSIDERING			
CONSIDERING SOMETHING THAT WOULD, AS YOU	262	ALF'S SEVENTH	
CONSIGNED			
"THAT INCENSED FEMALE HAS CONSIGNED HIM TO OUR PLEASURE."	224	SEXTUS PROP:10	1
CONSPECTU			
POST MORTEM CONSPECTU	147	POST MORTEM	

PAGE 83

	PAGE	TITLE	LINE
CONSTANT			
BY CONSTANT ELIMINATION	202	AGE DEMANDED	29
TELL ME THE TRUTHS WHICH YOU HEAR OF OUR CONSTANT			
YOUNG LADY,	214	SEXTUS PROP: 4	1
CONSTERNATION			
AGAINST UTTER CONSTERNATION,	202	AGE DEMANDED	32
CONSTITUTION			
THE CONSTITUTION OF OUR LAND, O SOCRATES,	239	MOYEN SENSUEL	23
CONSTRUCT			
WE SHALL CONSTRUCT MANY ILIADS.	217	SEXTUS PROP: 5	34
CONSTRUCTED			
HAVE CONSTRUCTED WITH SUCH INDUSTRY	210	SEXTUS PROP: 2	4
CONSTRUCTION			
FOR A MUCH LARGER ILIAD IS IN THE COURSE OF			
CONSTRUCTION	229	SEXTUS PROP:12	38
CONSUMERS			
THE EXAMPLE OF THESE CONSUMERS IN COOPERATION	262	ALF'S SEVENTH	18
CONSUMES			
THEY DIED AND THE GREED OF YOUR FLAME CONSUMES THEM.	38	LADY'S LIFE	10
CONSUMETH			
SHE IS TIME'S PREY AND TIME CONSUMETH ALL.	40	ROME	8
CONSUMMATE			
SET LOOSE THE WHOLE CONSUMMATE PACK	52	AU SALON	14
WOMAN? OH, WOMAN IS A CONSUMMATE RAGE,	165	QUINTUS SEPTIM	20
CONTACT			
NOW BEARS THE PALSIED CONTACT OF PHIDIPPUS.	111	SOCIETY	4
CONTAINS			
A LITTLE BLACK BOX CONTAINS THEM.	145	SALUTATION 3RD	8
CONTEMPORAINES			
MOEURS CONTEMPORAINES	178	MOEURS CONTEMP	T
CONTEMPORARIES			
OUR CONTEMPORARIES	118	CONTEMPORARIES	T
DETACHED FROM HIS CONTEMPORARIES,	193	SIENA MI FE	18
CONTEMPT			
BEAR TO THEM MY CONTEMPT FOR THEIR OPPRESSORS.	88	COMMISSION	3
BEAR MY CONTEMPT OF OPPRESSORS.	88	COMMISSION	5
CONTEMPTED			
HAVE YOU CONTEMPTED JUNO'S PELASGIAN TEMPLES,	221	SEXTUS PROP: 8	12
CONTEMPTIBLE			
WITH NO STONE UPON MY CONTEMPTIBLE SEPULCHRE;	208	SEXTUS PROP: 1	37
CONTENDED			
AND YOU WRITE OF ACHELOUS, WHO CONTENDED WITH			
HERCULES,	228	SEXTUS PROP:12	18
CONTENT			
"CONTENT EVER TO MOVE WITH WHITE SWANS!	211	SEXTUS PROP: 2	4
CONTENTIONS			
THE HAVEN FROM SOPHISTICATIONS AND CONTENTIONS	195	HUGH SELWIN:10	9
CONTENTMENT			
HENCE HIS CONTENTMENT.	118	ANCIENT WISDOM	4
CONTEST			
BLOCKED LIGHTS WORKING IN. ESCAPES. RENEWAL OF			
CONTEST.	120	GAME OF CHESS	15
CONTINENCE			
AFTER YEARS OF CONTINENCE	181	MOEURS CON: 6	
CONTINUE			
OUT-WEARIERS OF APOLLO WILL, AS WE KNOW, CONTINUE			
THEIR MARTIAN GENERALITIES,	207	SEXTUS PROP: 1	1
ANNALISTS WILL CONTINUE TO RECORD ROMAN REPUTATIONS,	207	SEXTUS PROP: 1	1
I SHALL LIVE, IF SHE CONTINUE IN LIFE,	223	SEXTUS PROP: 9	
CONTINUED			
SHE CONTINUED:	225	SEXTUS PROP:10	3
CONTINUOUS			
YOU FUNGUS, YOU CONTINUOUS GANGRENE.	145	SALUTATION 3RD	1
CONTRA-BASS'			
MY NERVES STILL REGISTER THE SOUNDS OF CONTRA-BASS',	247	PIERROTS	1
CONTRADICTIONS			
I SPEAK IN CONTRADICTIONS, SO TO SPEAK.)	242	MOYEN SENSUEL	12
CONTRARY			
ON THE CONTRARY, IF THEY DO NOT BELONG TO HIS WIFE,	98	THE BELLAIRES	1
BASTIDIDES, ON THE CONTRARY, WHO BOTH TALKS AND			
WRITES OF NOTHING SAVE COPULATION,	100	TEMPERAMENTS	

CONTRASTS -- CORDS

	PAGE	TITLE	LINE
CONTRASTS			
NOR WOULD GAUTIER HIMSELF HAVE DESPISED THEIR			
CONTRASTS IN WHITENESS	87	ALBATRE	5
CONTROL			
HELPLESS AGAINST THE CONTROL;	92	THE REST	8
CONTUBERNALIS			
GAUDERO CONTUBERNALIS	101	AMITIES	22
CONVENIENCE			
ON SEA AND LAND, WITH ALL CONVENIENCE FOUND	264	ALF'S NINTH	19
CONVENT			
SHE NOW WRITES TO ME FROM A CONVENT;	179	MOEURS CON: 2	3
CONVENTIONS			
HE HAD ATTENDED COUNTRY CHRISTIAN ENDEAVOUR			
CONVENTIONS,	242	MOYEN SENSUEL	102
CONVERSATION			
MUCH CONVERSATION IS AS GOOD AS HAVING A HOME.	214	SEXTUS PROP: 4	10
CONVERSE			
IT RESTS ME TO CONVERSE WITH BEAUTIFUL WOMEN	113	TAME CAT	4
CONVERSES			
SHE CONVERSES:	111	BLACK SLIPPERS	5
CONVEY			
THIS URGE TO CONVEY THE RELATION	200	MAUBERLEY: 2	21
CONVICTIONS			
SHAKE UP THE STAGNANT POOL OF ITS CONVICTIONS;	63	PHASELLUS ILLE	8
COOKING			
HE OFFERS SUCCULENT COOKING;	195	HUGH SELWIN:10	11
COOL			
COOL TO MY FINGERS THE FLOWING WATERS.	18	DE AEGYPTO	22
I WOULD THAT THE COOL WAVES MIGHT FLOW OVER MY MIND,	36	FRANCESCA	8
BRING THE IMPERCEPTIBLE COOL.	76	THE ALCHEMIST	48
IN THE COOL LIGHT,	81	TENZONE	13
GO AS A GREAT WAVE OF COOL WATER,	88	COMMISSION	4
OVER THE COOL FACE OF THAT FIELD,	107	COMING OF WAR	17
AS COOL AS THE PALE WET LEAVES	109	ALBA	1
COOLING			
SO IS THE SLOW COOLING OF OUR CHIVALROUS PASSION,	100	THE BATH TUB	3
COOLNESS			
AND COOLNESS BENEATH THE TREES.	35	THE EYES	10
THAN THIS HOUR OF CLEAR COOLNESS,	83	THE GARRET	10
COOPED			
DAY LONG, LONG DAY COOPED ON A STOOL	22	MARVOIL	3
COOPERATION			
THE EXAMPLE OF THESE CONSUMERS IN COOPERATION	262	ALF'S SEVENTH	18
CO-OPERATION			
IS NOT SUITED TO CO-OPERATION--	262	ALF'S SEVENTH	15
CO-OPS			
THE CO-OPS WAS A GOIN' SOMEWHERE,	262	ALF'S SEVENTH	2
TO THE CO-OPS, A ECHO OR SOMETHIN'?	262	ALF'S SEVENTH	9
IS WHERE THE CO-OPS ARE GOIN' TO,	262	ALF'S SEVENTH	13
COPHETUA			
COPHETUA TO RHAPSODIZE;	192	YEUX GLAUQUES	12
COPPER			
FROM THE COPPER OF THE LEAF IN AUTUMN,	76	THE ALCHEMIST	33
FROM THE RED GLEAM OF COPPER,	76	THE ALCHEMIST	39
BY THE MIRROR OF BURNISHED COPPER,	76	THE ALCHEMIST	42
NOT WITH BARS OF COPPER.	91	DANCE FIGURE	15
HAVE SEEN THE COPPER COME DOWN	122	PROVINCE DESERT	52
COPULATION			
BASTIDIDES, ON THE CONTRARY, WHO BOTH TALKS AND			
WRITES OF NOTHING SAVE COPULATION,	100	TEMPERAMENTS	5
COPY			
BACKLESS COPY FROM THE STALL,	15	FAMAM CANO	39
AND THE COPY OF "HATHA YOGA"	180	MOEURS CON: 5	24
COR			
"SE IL COR TI MANCA," BUT IT FAILED THEE NOT!	19	FOR E. MCC	12
CORACLE			
CORACLE OF PACIFIC VOYAGES,	203	MAUBERLEY: 4	18
CORAL			
THE CORAL ISLE, THE LION-COLOURED SAND	201	AGE DEMANDED	17
CORDS			
WI' A BUNDLE O' CORDS SWUNG FREE,	33	GOODLY FERE	18

PAGE 85

CORDS -- COULD

	PAGE	TITLE	LINE
CORDS (CONTINUED)			
STRENGTHEN THE SUBTLE CORDS, ...	88	COMMISSION	20
THEIR CORDS TANGLE IN MIST, AGAINST THE BROCADE-LIKE PALACE.	129	THE RIVER SONG	26
THE HUNDRED CORDS OF MIST ARE SPREAD THROUGH	141	IDEA OF CHOAN	13
CORE			
THIS THING, THAT HATH A CODE AND NOT A CORE, ...	63	AN OBJECT	1
CORMORANT			
MY NAME IS NUNTY CORMORANT	269	SAFE AND SOUND	1
CORN			
WHERE TIME IS SHRIVELLED DOWN TO TIME'S SEED CORN	50	THE FLAME	11
CORN OF THE COLDEST. NATHLESS THERE KNOCKETH NOW	64	THE SEAFARER	34
THE CORN HAS AGAIN ITS MOTHER AND SHE, LEUCONOE,	90	SURGIT FAMA	5
CORNER			
THAT NEVER FITS A CORNER OR SHOWS USE, ...	61	PORTRAIT FEMME	20
AND YOU WOULD WALK OUT WITH ME TO THE WESTERN CORNER OF THE CASTLE, ...	135	EXILE'S LETTER	49
THE SUN RISES IN SOUTH EAST CORNER OF THINGS	140	MULBERRY ROAD	1
CORNERS			
YOU LOITER AT THE CORNERS AND BUS-STOPS, ...	94	INSTRUCTIONS	6
CORONAL			
AND WEAVE YE HIM HIS CORONAL."	72	PAN IS DEAD	3
HOW SHALL WE WEAVE A CORONAL, ...	72	PAN IS DEAD	6
CORRECT			
YOU WORE THE SAME QUITE CORRECT CLOTHING, ...	101	AMITIES	1
CORRELATIONS			
AND OBSERVE ITS INEXPLICABLE CORRELATIONS.	104	THE SEEING EYE	7
CORRUPT			
AND HOW TEN SINS CAN CORRUPT YOUNG MAIDENS;	229	SEXTUS PROP:12	43
CORRUPTION			
SOUND IN YOUR WIND PAST ALL SIGNS O' CORRUPTION.	13	MESMERISM	16
CORSET			
IT JUTS LIKE A SHELF BETWEEN THE JOWL AND CORSET.	161	CABARET DANCER	16
CORTEGE			
THE SILENT CORTEGE.	107	COMING OF WAR	20
CORYDON			
CORYDON TEMPTED ALEXIS, ...	229	SEXTUS PROP:12	47
COS			
SUPPLANTS THE MOUSSELINE OF COS.	189	HUGH SELWYN: 3	2
IF SHE GOES IN A GLEAM OF COS, IN A SLITHER OF DYED STUFF, ...	217	SEXTUS PROP: 5	30
COSIER			
TO MAKE 'EM COSIER.	269	SAFE AND SOUND	16
COSMETICS			
YOU ARE THE FRIEND OF FORMIANUS, THE VENDOR OF COSMETICS, ...	113	FORMIANUS LADY	7
COSMIC			
ANCIENT WISDOM, RATHER COSMIC	118	ANCIENT WISDOM	T
COSMOS			
"THEIR LITTLE COSMOS IS SHAKEN"--	158	PSYCHOLOG HOUR	12
COST			
BUT HE ACCOMPLISHED THIS FEAT AT SOME COST;	100	TEMPERAMENTS	7
I'LL HAVE NO OTHER LOVE AT ANY COST.	105	DOMPNA POIS	10
AND THINKING HOW LITTLE YOU CARED FOR THE COST, ...	135	EXILE'S LETTER	44
IF THOU COME NOT, THE COST BE ON THY HEAD.	172	LANGUE D'OC: 1	16
COUCH			
OH COUCH MADE HAPPY BY MY LONG DELECTATIONS;	220	SEXTUS PROP: 7	2
COULD			
OH! I COULD GET ME OUT, DESPITE THE MARKS	60	TOMB AKR CAAR	29
NEITHER COULD I PLAY UPON ANY REED IF I HAD ONE.	62	N. Y.	7
WHO COULD PART HIM FROM HER BORDERS	72	DIEU! QU'IL	5
NO MAN COULD PAINT SUCH THINGS WHO DID NOT KNOW.	73	JACOPO SELLAIO	2
AND SINCE I COULD NOT FIND A PEER TO YOU, ...	105	DOMPNA POIS	11
(IF GLORY COULD LAST FOREVER	129	THE RIVER SONG	17
IF ONLY THEY COULD BE OF THAT FELLOWSHIP, ...	134	EXILE'S LETTER	10
WHAT COULD HE DO BUT PLAY THE DESPERATE CHESS, ...	152	NEAR PERIGORD	36
ALL OF HIS FLANK--HOW COULD HE DO WITHOUT HER?	153	NEAR PERIGORD	66
SHE WHO COULD NEVER LIVE SAVE THROUGH ONE PERSON,	157	NEAR PERIGORD	189
SHE WHO COULD NEVER SPEAK SAVE TO ONE PERSON, ...	157	NEAR PERIGORD	190
WHEN YOU COULD GO OUT IN A HIRED HANSOM	167	OF AROUET	2
AND TIBULLUS COULD SAY OF HIS DEATH, IN HIS LATIN:	168	OF AROUET	39

PAGE 86

COULD -- COURSE

	PAGE	TITLE	LINE
COULD (CONTINUED)			
SHE COULD SCARCELY KEEP HER EYES OPEN	225	SEXTUS PROP:10	22
COULD YOU ENDURE SUCH PROMISCUITY?	228	SEXTUS PROP:12	10
COULD I BUT SPEAK AS 'TWERE IN THE "RESTORATION"	238	MOYEN SENSUEL	7
STILL I'D RESPECT YOU MORE IF YOU COULD BURY	239	MOYEN SENSUEL	27
COULD FREUD OR JUNG UNFATHOM SUCH A SINK?	241	MOYEN SENSUEL	76
AND WOULD NOT THINK A THING THAT COULD UPSET HER. . . .	242	MOYEN SENSUEL	110
SOON OUR HERO COULD MANAGE ONCE A WEEK,	243	MOYEN SENSUEL	141
FOR FIRES AND ODD RISKS, COULD IN THIS SECTOR	243	MOYEN SENSUEL	152
COULD YEH SWAP TH' BRAINS OF ORL THIS LOT	270	OF 600 M.P.'S	19
COULDN'T			
AND THE GUARDS COULDN'T STOP THEM,	182	MOEURS CON: 7	19
AND THE GUARDS COULDN'T STOP THEM.	182	MOEURS CON: 7	22
"I COULDN'T," SHE SEZ, "AN' I AINT TRIED,	270	OF 600 M.P.'S	21
COULEUR			
AUX TOISONS COULEUR DE LIN,	160	DANS OMNIBUS	16
TEINTEES DE COULEUR SANG-DE-DRAGON,	160	DANS OMNIBUS	27
COUNCIL			
SHE HATH HUSHED MY RANCOUR OF COUNCIL,	4	LA FRAISNE	17
COUNCILLOR			
FOR I WAS A GAUNT, GRAVE COUNCILLOR	4	LA FRAISNE	1
COUNSELS			
NINE LAWYERS, FOUR COUNSELS, FIVE JUDGES AND THREE PROCTORS OF THE KING,	97	THE BELLAIRES	5
NINE LAWYERS, FOUR COUNSELS, ETC.,	98	THE BELLAIRES	28
COUNT			
IF SHE DOES NOT COUNT THIS BLESSED	103	PHYLLIDULA	4
FOIX' COUNT KNEW THAT. WHAT IS SIR BERTRANS' SINGING?	153	NEAR PERIGORD	91
WOULD COUNT ON THE PRICE OF A GUN.	268	ANOTHER BIT	12
COUNTERLIE			
JEST, CHALLENGE, COUNTERLIE!	35	HIS OWN FACE	6
COUNTERPART			
YE SEE HERE SEVERED, MY LIFE'S COUNTERPART."	156	NEAR PERIGORD	168
COUNTERPASS			
VICED IN SUCH TORTURE FOR THE "COUNTERPASS."	151	NEAR PERIGORD	27
COUNTERTHRUST			
HIGH, HIGH AND SURE . . . AND THEN THE COUNTERTHRUST:	157	NEAR PERIGORD	180
COUNTESS			
SAVE THIS: "VERS AND CANZONE TO THE COUNTESS OF BEZIERS	22	MARVOIL	28
THAT I HAVE NOT THE COUNTESS OF BEZIERS	23	MARVOIL	42
COUNTRY			
BECAUSE I HAD JUST COME FROM THE COUNTRY;	85	SALUTATION 2ND	2
O HELPLESS FEW IN MY COUNTRY,	92	THE REST	1
AND SAYING: WHEN SHALL WE GET BACK TO OUR COUNTRY?	127	BOWMEN OF SHU	2
OUR SORROW IS BITTER, BUT WE WOULD NOT RETURN TO OUR COUNTRY.	127	BOWMEN OF SHU	12
SOUTH-FOLK IN COLD COUNTRY	139	SOUTH-FOLK	T
IN A HALF SAVAGE COUNTRY, OUT OF DATE;	187	E. P. ODE	6
'TIS OF MY COUNTRY THAT I WOULD ENDITE,	238	MOYEN SENSUEL	1
MY COUNTRY? I LOVE IT WELL, AND THOSE GOOD FELLOWS	238	MOYEN SENSUEL	3
HE HAD ATTENDED COUNTRY CHRISTIAN ENDEAVOUR CONVENTIONS,	242	MOYEN SENSUEL	102
(MY COUNTRY, I'VE SAID YOUR MORALS AND YOUR THOUGHTS ARE STALE ONES,	243	MOYEN SENSUEL	149
COUNTRYSIDES			
NINE GIRLS, FROM AS MANY COUNTRYSIDES	211	SEXTUS PROP: 2	33
COUNTS			
SIR ARRIMON COUNTS ON HIS FINGERS, MONTFORT,	155	NEAR PERIGORD	121
WHAT COUNTS IS THE LOOKS.	260	ALF'S FOURTH	19
COUPLE			
AND THAT GOD-FEASTING COUPLE OLD	3	THE TREE	4
COUPLES			
TO THE DANCE OF THE SEVENTY COUPLES;	132	AT TEN-SHIN	23
COURAGE			
SWIFT AT COURAGE THOU IN THE SHELL OF GOLD, CASTING	68	APPARUIT	12
COURSE			
UNTIL THIS COURSE TURNETH ASIDE.	69	THE NEEDLE	15
GOD GIVE ME LIFE, AND LET MY COURSE RUN	174	LANGUE D'OC: 3	17
"WHEN I BEGAN I GOT, OF COURSE,	194	MR. NIXON	6

COURSE -- CRACKLING

	PAGE	TITLE	LINE
COURSE (CONTINUED)			
"WHY WRENCH YOUR PAGE OUT OF ITS COURSE?	210	SEXTUS PROP: 2	24
FOR A MUCH LARGER ILIAD IS IN THE COURSE OF CONSTRUCTION	229	SEXTUS PROP:12	38
THOUGH IT WILL, OF COURSE, PASS OFF WITH SOCIAL SCIENCE	244	MOYEN SENSUEL	163
I HAVE NO WILL TO PROVE LOVE'S COURSE	248	DONNA MI PREGA	11
OR FROM TRUE COURSE	249	DONNA MI PREGA	41
GOLD, OF COURSE, IS SOLID TOO,	267	ALF'S TWELFTH	16
COURSES			
HAVE SEEN THIS THING, OUT OF THEIR FAR COURSES	27	NIGHT LITANY	42
THEIR REALM IS THE LATERAL COURSES.	147	BEFORE SLEEP	10
COURT			
THE LORDS GO FORTH FROM THE COURT, AND INTO FAR BORDERS.	132	AT TEN-SHIN	14
I WENT UP TO THE COURT FOR EXAMINATION,	136	EXILE'S LETTER	65
IN THE MID LOVE COURT, HE SINGS OUT THE CANZON,	154	NEAR PERIGORD	118
COURTEOUS			
ARE LEFT IN TEEN THE LIEGEMEN COURTEOUS,	36	THE YOUNG KING	10
COURTESY			
I ASK, AND THE FINE COURTESY	106	DOMPNA POIS	52
COURTEZAN			
AND SHE WAS A COURTEZAN IN THE OLD DAYS,	128	BEAU TOILET	6
COURTEZANS			
PLEASURE LASTING, WITH COURTEZANS, GOING AND COMING WITHOUT HINDRANCE,	136	EXILE'S LETTER	53
COURTS			
OF HAVENS MORE HIGH AND COURTS DESIRABLE	39	BLANDULA	14
OR CARRY HIM FORWARD. "GO THROUGH ALL THE COURTS,	154	NEAR PERIGORD	115
COURT-YARD			
DUST DRIFTS OVER THE COURT-YARD,	108	LIU CH'E	2
THE DRYAD STANDS IN MY COURT-YARD	110	TEMPORA	2
COUSIN'S			
MY COUSIN'S NAMED BALDWIN	260	ALF'S FOURTH	14
COVER			
WHEN THE WHITE HART BREAKS HIS COVER	25	THE WHITE STAG	4
THY HEAD WILL I COVER OVER	47	FROM HEINE: 7	5
COVER OVER THE DARK PATH	138	CITY OF CHOAN	4
NOW THE HIGH CLOUDS COVER THE SUN	138	CITY OF CHOAN	11
MAY A WOODY AND SEQUESTERED PLACE COVER ME WITH ITS FOLIAGE	213	SEXTUS PROP: 3	35
COVERED			
AH, I COVERED HIS EARS WITH THEM	48	FROM HEINE: 7	31
HIGH HEAPS, COVERED WITH TREES AND GRASS;	133	FRONTIER GUARD	9
A NET-WORK OF ARBOURS AND PASSAGES AND COVERED WAYS,	141	IDEA OF CHOAN	22
LIE LITTLE STRIPS OF PARCHMENT COVERED OVER,	154	NEAR PERIGORD	99
COVERED WITH LIP-STICK.	261	ALF'S SIXTH	12
COVERLEY'S			
TO BAY LIKE SIR ROGER DE COVERLEY'S	52	AU SALON	15
COVERT			
NOR CAN IN COVERT COWER,	250	DONNA MI PREGA	72
COVETOUS			
WHO MADE THE FREEST HAND SEEM COVETOUS.	37	THE YOUNG KING	14
COW			
I HA' SEEN HIM COW A THOUSAND MEN.	34	GOODLY FERE	35
I HA' SEEN HIM COW A THOUSAND MEN	34	GOODLY FERE	41
OR ASKED US IF THE COW	272	THE BABY	4
OR IF THE COW REFRAINS FROM FOOD	272	THE BABY	7
COWED			
LIKE THE SEA THAT HE COWED AT GENSERET	34	GOODLY FERE	47
WITH COWED AND CROUCHING AIR	257	BREAD BRIGADE	25
COWER			
NOR CAN IN COVERT COWER,	250	DONNA MI PREGA	72
CRACK			
"THE HARDEST NUT I HAD TO CRACK	194	MR. NIXON	12
CRACKED			
I HAVE GONE HALF CRACKED,	94	INSTRUCTIONS	11
CRACKIN'			
CRACKIN' THEIR SMUTTY JOKES!	257	BREAD BRIGADE	6
CRACKLING			
THE CRACKLING OF SMALL FIRES, THE BANNERETS,	155	NEAR PERIGORD	132

CRACKS -- CROPPED

	PAGE	TITLE	LINE
CRACKS			
FLAME BURNS, RAIN SINKS INTO THE CRACKS	209	SEXTUS PROP: 1	70
AND HOLDS HER SIDES WHERE SWELLING LAUGHTER CRACKS			
'EM	239	MOYEN SENSUEL	33
CRAFT			
SO HATH MAN CRAFT FROM FEAR	250	DONNA MI PREGA	75
CRAFTILY			
MORE CRAFTILY, MORE SUBTLE-SOULED THAN I;	24	THUS NINEVEH	13
CRAFTSMAN			
MARK HIM A CRAFTSMAN AND A STRATEGIST?	153	NEAR PERIGORD	85
AND THE "BEST CRAFTSMAN" SINGS OUT HIS FRIEND'S SONG,	155	NEAR PERIGORD	141
CRAFTY			
TRUE TO THE TRUTH'S SAKE AND CRAFTY DISSECTOR, ...	13	MESMERISM	18
AND ALL THEIR CRAFTY WORK UPON THE DOOR, ...	60	TOMB AKR CAAR	30
CRAFTY AND SUBTLE;	90	SURGIT FAMA	13
CRAGS			
I MATE WITH MY FREE KIND UPON THE CRAGS;	81	TENZONE	10
CRAMP			
"MAY THE GOUT CRAMP UP HER FEET!	215	SEXTUS PROP: 4	37
CRASHING			
WITH A SILVER CRASHING, ...	95	OF THE DEGREES	4
CRASSUS			
"THE EUPHRATES DENIES ITS PROTECTION TO THE PARTHIAN			
AND APOLOGIZES FOR CRASSUS,"	216	SEXTUS PROP: 5	16
CRAWL			
CRAWL IN THE VERY BLACK GUTTER BENEATH THE GRAPE			
STAND?	114	SIMULACRA	4
CREAKING			
THE DOOR HAS A CREAKING LATCH.	195	HUGH SELWIN:10	12
CREAM			
IN THE CREAM GILDED CABIN OF HIS STEAM YACHT	194	MR. NIXON	1
CREATED			
YOU CREATED CONSIDERABLE STIR IN CHICAGO, ...	114	EPILOGUE	4
LOVE IS CREATED, HATH A SENSATE NAME, ...	248	DONNA MI PREGA	22
CREPT			
I HAVE CREPT OVER OLD RAFTERS, ...	121	PROVINC DESERT	14
CREPUSCULAR			
OUT INTO THE CREPUSCULAR HALF-LIGHT, NOW AND THEN;	244	MOYEN SENSUEL	186
CRESCIT			
SIC CRESCIT GLORIA MUNDI:	52	AU SALON	17
CREVICES			
ITS CREVICES, ...	8	NA AUDIART	5
CRIED			
AND IN VAIN I CRIED UNTO THEM "I HAVE NO SONG	17	PRAISE YSOLT	36
HE CRIED NO CRY WHEN THEY DRAVE THE NAILS	34	GOODLY FERE	37
BUT NEVER A CRY CRIED HE.	34	GOODLY FERE	40
AND CRIED UP FROM THEIR COBBLES;	96	AESTHETICS	4
CRIERS			
"NOR WILL THE PUBLIC CRIERS EVER HAVE YOUR NAME ...	211	SEXTUS PROP: 2	42
CRIES			
AND ICE-COLD WAVE, AT WHILES THE SWAN CRIES, ...	64	THE SEAFARER	19
MY GREAT NOISE DROWNS THEIR CRIES, ...	266	ALF'S ELEVENTH	2
CRIETH			
AS THE FLAME CRIETH UNTO THE SAP.	17	PRAISE YSOLT	41
CRIMSON			
AND THE BROAD FIELDS BENEATH THEM TURN CRIMSON, ...	28	ALTAFORTE	5
AND THE LIGHTNINGS FROM BLACK HEAV'N FLASH CRIMSON,	28	ALTAFORTE	9
BAH! THERE'S NO WINE LIKE THE BLOOD'S CRIMSON!	28	ALTAFORTE	18
MY WORDS FOR STOUR, HATH NO BLOOD OF CRIMSON	29	ALTAFORTE	26
WHEN OUR ELBOWS AND SWORDS DRIP THE CRIMSON	29	ALTAFORTE	34
AND LET THE MUSIC OF THE SWORDS MAKE THEM CRIMSON!	29	ALTAFORTE	37
THE HOUNDS OF THE CRIMSON SKY GAVE TONGUE	34	GOODLY FERE	39
CRIMSON, FROSTY WITH DEW, THE ROSES BEND WHERE	68	APPARUIT	5
THE PURPLE HOUSE AND THE CRIMSON ARE FULL OF SPRING			
SOFTNESS.	129	THE RIVER SONG	24
CRITICS			
I BEG YOU, MY FRIENDLY CRITICS, ...	81	TENZONE	8
CROCUSES			
THE GILDED PHALOI OF THE CROCUSES	110	COITUS	1
CROPPED			
WHILE THAT CROPPED FOOL, ...	162	CABARET DANCER	43

	PAGE	TITLE	LINE
CROSS			
THAT THEY HAVE HAD TO CROSS THE CHANNEL.	97	THE BELLAIRES	4
THERE WAS NOTHING AT CROSS PURPOSE,	134	EXILE'S LETTER	8
AFTER WE CROSS THE INFERNAL RIPPLES,	228	SEXTUS PROP:12	28
CROSSED			
AYE HE SENT US OUT THROUGH THE CROSSED HIGH SPEARS	33	GOODLY FERE	9
CROSSED IN GREAT FUTURISTIC X'S, THE ART STUDENTS	93	LES MILLWIN	9
CROSSING			
WITH CROWDS TOO ASSIDUOUS IN THEIR CROSSING OF IT;	213	SEXTUS PROP: 3	33
CROSS-LIGHT			
SUNSET, THE RIBBON-LIKE ROAD LIES, IN RED CROSS-LIGHT,	154	NEAR PERIGORD	96
CROSSWAY			
THE JEWELLED CHAIR IS HELD UP AT THE CROSSWAY,	141	IDEA OF CHOAN	5
CROUCHING			
WITH COWED AND CROUCHING AIR	257	BREAD BRIGADE	25
CROWD			
THE APPARITION OF THESE FACES IN THE CROWD;	109	IN THE METRO	1
AND THEN THE CROWD BROKE UP, YOU WENT NORTH TO SAN PALACE,	136	EXILE'S LETTER	71
BUT YOU, YOU DAM'D CROWD OF GNATS,	140	SENNIN POEM	15
CROWD OVER THE THOUSAND GATES,	141	IDEA OF CHOAN	18
THERE WILL BE A CROWD OF YOUNG WOMEN DOING HOMAGE TO MY PALAVER,	208	SEXTUS PROP: 1	50
AND A MINUTE CROWD OF SMALL BOYS CAME FROM OPPOSITE,	224	SEXTUS PROP:10	4
CROWDED			
FLARES ON THE CROWDED STAGE BEFORE OUR TABLES	162	CABARET DANCER	22
CROWDS			
WITH CROWDS TOO ASSIDUOUS IN THEIR CROSSING OF IT;	213	SEXTUS PROP: 3	33
CROWNED			
"OBVIOUSLY CROWNED LOVERS AT UNKNOWN DOORS,	211	SEXTUS PROP: 2	48
CROY			
I HAVE CLIMBED RICKETY STAIRS, HEARD TALK OF CROY,	122	PROVINC DESERT	38
CRUCIFIX			
BY SIX CANDLES AND A CRUCIFIX,	115	SOCIAL ORDER	8
CRUELLY			
THAT HELL BRENN NOT HER O'ER CRUELLY.	11	OF THE GIBBET	16
CRUELTY			
FAINT, ALMOST, AS THE LINES OF CRUELTY ABOUT YOUR CHIN,	103	LADIES	19
CRUSADERS			
CRUSADERS, LECTURERS AND SECRET LECHERS,	241	MOYEN SENSUEL	80
CRUSH			
I ASK A WREATH WHICH WILL NOT CRUSH MY HEAD.	207	SEXTUS PROP: 1	21
CRUSHED			
AS CRUSHED LIPS TAKE THEIR RESPITE FITFULLY,	43	SATIEMUS	8
CRUSHED STRAWBERRIES! COME, LET US FEAST OUR EYES.	113	L'ART, 1910	2
"NO INCUBUS HAS CRUSHED HIS BODY AGAINST ME,	225	SEXTUS PROP:10	39
CRUST			
I HAVE SEEN THROUGH THE CRUST.	162	CABARET DANCER	39
GAINS YET ANOTHER CRUST	236	MIDDLE-AGED	11
CRY			
NO CRY LIKE THE BATTLE'S REJOICING	29	ALTAFORTE	33
MAY GOD DAMN FOR EVER ALL WHO CRY "PEACE!"	29	ALTAFORTE	36
HE CRIED NO CRY WHEN THEY DRAVE THE NAILS	34	GOODLY FERE	37
BUT NEVER A CRY CRIED HE.	34	GOODLY FERE	40
CRY:	171	LANGUE D'OC	EPI
TILL THE TRAIST MAN CRY OUT TO WARN	177	LANGUE D'OC: 4	3
NOW CRY THE BIRDS OUT, IN THE MEADOW MIST,	177	LANGUE D'OC: 4	12
CRYING			
AS A VAGUE CRYING UPON THE NIGHT	16	PRAISE YSOLT	6
AND LITTLE RED ELF WORDS CRYING "A SONG,"	16	PRAISE YSOLT	15
LITTLE GREY ELF WORDS CRYING FOR A SONG,	16	PRAISE YSOLT	16
LITTLE BROWN LEAF WORDS CRYING "A SONG,"	16	PRAISE YSOLT	17
LITTLE GREEN LEAF WORDS CRYING FOR A SONG.	16	PRAISE YSOLT	18
CRYING "SONG, A SONG."	17	PRAISE YSOLT	40
CRYING EVER "SONG, A SONG."	17	PRAISE YSOLT	45
CUCKOO CALLETH WITH GLOOMY CRYING,	65	THE SEAFARER	54
EAGER AND READY, THE CRYING LONE-FLYER,	65	THE SEAFARER	63
WITH PLAINTIVE, QUERULOUS CRYING,	110	TEMPORA	3
OH, NO, SHE IS NOT CRYING: "TAMUZ."	110	TEMPORA	5

CRYING -- CURIOUS

	PAGE	TITLE	LINE
CRYING (CONTINUED)			
CRYING--"KWAN, KUAN," FOR THE EARLY WIND, AND THE			
FEEL OF IT.	129	THE RIVER SONG	29
CRYING AFTER THE FOLLIES GONE BY ME, ...	168	OF AROUET	30
RAN CRYING WITH OUT-SPREAD HAIR, ...	219	SEXTUS PROP: 6	34
CRYING: MY GOD, MY GOD, WHAT WILL SHE SAY?!	247	PIERROTS	6
CRYSTAL			
SET DEEP IN CRYSTAL; AND BECAUSE MY SLEEP	30	PIERE VIDAL	22
THROUGH TRILLS AND RUNS LIKE CRYSTAL, ...	45	FROM HEINE: 5	7
MY CRYSTAL HALLS RING CLEAR	47	FROM HEINE: 7	22
AND I LET DOWN THE CRYSTAL CURTAIN	132	JEWEL STAIRS'	3
CUBE			
HIS PALACE IS LIKE A CUBE CUT IN THIRDS, ...	237	ABU SALAMMAMM	7
CUCKOLD			
HE HAD TO BE FOUR TIMES CUCKOLD.	100	TEMPERAMENTS	8
FOR YAMMER OF THE CUCKOLD, ...	172	LANGUE D'OC: 1	29
DESPITE THE CUCKOLD, DO THOU AS THOU LIST, ...	177	LANGUE D'OC: 4	13
CUCKOO			
CUCKOO CALLETH WITH GLOOMY CRYING, ...	65	THE SEAFARER	54
CUIUSDAM			
IN EXITUM CUIUSDAM	59	EXIT' CUIUSDAM	T
CULDOU			
CULDOU LACKING A COAT TO BLESS	12	OF THE GIBBET	30
CULL			
OR FROM THE FEATS OF SUMNER CULL IT? THINK, ...	241	MOYEN SENSUEL	75
CULLING			
CULLING FROM EACH A FAIR TRAIT	105	DOMPNA POIS	18
CULT			
WILL NOT OUR CULT BE FOUNDED ON THE WAVES, ...	39	BLANDULA	9
OF A MODERN AND ETHICAL CULT, ...	178	MOEURS CON: 1	12
CULTIVATION			
LONG SINCE SUPERSEDED THE CULTIVATION	196	HUGH SELWIN:12	27
CULTURES			
"WHICH THE HIGHEST CULTURES HAVE NOURISHED"	196	HUGH SELWIN:12	22
CUM			
CUM JOCUNDA FEMINA.	101	AMITIES	23
CUNNING			
THOU A SLIGHT THING, THOU IN ACCESS OF CUNNING	68	APPARUIT	23
O GLASS SUBTLE AND CUNNING, O POWDERY GOLD!	95	OF THE DEGREES	14
THAT MY PHANTOM LACK NOT IN CUNNING.	105	DOMPNA POIS	30
CUNNINGLY			
THOUGH THEY WRITE IT CUNNINGLY;	33	GOODLY FERE	22
SO CUNNINGLY, ...	106	DOMPNA POIS	44
CUPBOARD			
AND WHAT THEY SWORE IN THE CUPBOARD	221	SEXTUS PROP: 8	8
CUPID			
CUPID, ASTRIDE A PHALLUS WITH TWO WINGS, ...	162	CABARET DANCER	36
CUPID WILL CARRY LIGHTED TORCHES BEFORE HIM	213	SEXTUS PROP. 3	22
CUPIDINESQUE			
LUGETE, VENERES! LUGETE, CUPIDINESQUE!	103	LADIES	14
CUPS			
IS RICH FOR A THOUSAND CUPS.	128	THE RIVER SONG	4
RED JADE CUPS, FOOD WELL SET ON A BLUE JEWELLED			
TABLE, ...	135	EXILE'S LETTER	47
LILIES LIFT THEIR WHITE SYMBOLICAL CUPS, ...	180	MOEURS CON: 5	20
CURE			
THAT HOLDS THEIR BLOSSOMS AND THEIR LEAVES IN CURE	21	IN DURANCE	45
I DO NOT LIVE, NOR CURE ME, ...	174	LANGUE D'OC: 3	20
CURIAN			
I HAD REHEARSED THE CURIAN BROTHERS, AND MADE			
REMARKS ON THE HORATIAN JAVELIN	210	SEXTUS PROP: 2	8
CURIOUS			
TROPHIES FISHED UP; SOME CURIOUS SUGGESTION;	61	PORTRAIT FEMME	16
WHY IS YOUR GLITTER FULL OF CURIOUS MISTRUST?	95	OF THE DEGREES	13
MINGLED WITH A CURIOUS FEAR	101	AMITIES	4
WHEN I CAREFULLY CONSIDER THE CURIOUS HABITS OF DOGS	102	MEDITATIO	1
WHEN I CONSIDER THE CURIOUS HABITS OF MAN	102	MEDITATIO	4
AND CURIOUS IMPERFECTIONS OF ODOR, ...	104	THE SEEING EYE	8
TO HIGH HALLS AND CURIOUS FOOD, ...	132	AT TEN-SHIN	20
OF CURIOUS HEADS IN MEDALLION--	200	MAUBERLEY: 2	25

PAGE 91

CURIOUSLY -- CYPRIAN'S

	PAGE	TITLE	LINE
CURIOUSLY			
WHY DO YOU LOOK SO EAGERLY AND SO CURIOUSLY INTO PEOPLE'S FACES,	103	CODA	2
CURLED			
I HAVE CURLED 'MID THE BOLES OF THE ASH WOOD,	4	LA FRAISNE	9
CURRENT			
RESISTANCE TO CURRENT EXACERBATIONS,	201	AGE DEMANDED	24
CURSE			
A SORT OF CURSE AGAINST ITS GUZZLING	14	FAMAM CANO	25
LO! I DO CURSE MY STRENGTH	30	PIERE VIDAL	3
GOD CURSE THE YEARS THAT TURN SUCH WOMEN GREY!	31	PIERE VIDAL	46
AND YET I CURSE THE SUN FOR HIS RED GLADNESS,	31	PIERE VIDAL	49
CURSES			
O HARRY HEINE, CURSES BE,	46	TRANSLATOR	1
CURSING			
AND ONE LEAN ARAGONESE CURSING THE SENESCHAL	22	MARVOIL	14
ARAGON CURSING IN ARAGON, BEZIERS BUSY AT BEZIERS--	22	MARVOIL	16
CURTAIN			
AND I LET DOWN THE CRYSTAL CURTAIN	132	JEWEL STAIRS'	3
AND WERE SUCH NIGHTS THAT WE SHOULD "DRAW THE CURTAIN"	243	MOYEN SENSUEL	134
CURVED			
A-TREMBLE IN MEN'S VEINS; O LIP CURVED HIGH	41	HER MONUMENT	12
CUSHIONED			
I HAD SEEN IN THE SHADE, RECUMBENT ON CUSHIONED HELICON,	210	SEXTUS PROP: 2	1
CUSTOM			
FOR THE CUSTOM IS FULL OLD,	24	THUS NINEVEH	7
FOR IT IS A CUSTOM:	219	SEXTUS PROP: 6	31
CUT			
HER MONUMENT, THE IMAGE CUT THEREON	41	HER MONUMENT	T
THIS BOAT IS OF SHATO-WOOD, AND ITS GUNWALES ARE CUT MAGNOLIA,	128	THE RIVER SONG	1
WHILE MY HAIR WAS STILL CUT STRAIGHT ACROSS MY FOREHEAD	130	RIVER-MER WIFE	1
AT MORNING THERE ARE FLOWERS TO CUT THE HEART,	131	AT TEN-SHIN	3
THE NARROW STREETS CUT INTO THE WIDE HIGHWAY AT CHOAN,	141	IDEA OF CHOAN	1
HIS PALACE IS LIKE A CUBE CUT IN THIRDS,	237	ABU SALAMMAMM	7
"ALL THE SAME STYLE, SAME CUT, WITH PERFECT LOATHING."	244	MOYEN SENSUEL	184
THEN CUT THEIR SAVING TO THE HALF OR LOWER;	260	ALF'S FIFTH	3
CUTICLE			
WITH A BLACK TINT STAINING YOUR CUTICLE,	162	CABARET DANCER	49
CUTTING			
IN THE CUTTING WIND FROM THE NORTH,	135	EXILE'S LETTER	43
CYANINE			
CLEAR SAPPHIRE, COBALT, CYANINE,	39	BLANDULA	10
CYBELE			
AND TELL ANECDOTES OF CYBELE!	86	SALUTATION 2ND	29
CYCLADES			
COME BEAUTY BAREFOOT FROM THE CYCLADES,	63	PHASELLUS ILLE	12
CYCLAMEN			
SHE, WHO MOVED HERE AMID THE CYCLAMEN,	87	THE SPRING	12
CYDONIAN			
CYDONIAN SPRING WITH HER ATTENDANT TRAIN,	87	THE SPRING	1
CYGNES			
JE VIS LES CYGNES NOIRS,	160	DANS OMNIBUS	24
CYNTHIA			
IN VAIN, CYNTHIA. VAIN CALL TO UNANSWERING SHADOW,	219	SEXTUS PROP: 6	36
AND CYNTHIA WAS ALONE IN HER BED.	225	SEXTUS PROP:10	28
AND NOW PROPERTIUS OF CYNTHIA, TAKING HIS STAND AMONG THESE.	230	SEXTUS PROP:12	75
CYPRESS			
THE CYPRESS TREES, HE LAY,	39	FOR PSYCHE	2
O QUEEN OF CYPRESS,	76	THE ALCHEMIST	43
CYPRIAN			
AND NOW SHE'S GONE, WHO WAS HIS CYPRIAN,	73	JACOPO SELLAIO	3
CYPRIAN'S			
THIS PLACE IS THE CYPRIAN'S FOR SHE HAS EVER THE FANCY	164	QUINTUS SEPTIM	4

CYPRIS -- DANCE

	PAGE	TITLE	LINE
CYPRIS			
CYPRIS IS HIS CICERONE.	212	SEXTUS PROP: 3	27
CYTHAREAN			
THE SMALL BIRDS OF THE CYTHAREAN MOTHER,	211	SEXTUS PROP: 2	31
SINCE ADONIS WAS GORED IN IDALIA, AND THE CYTHAREAN	219	SEXTUS PROP: 6	33
THE CYTHAREAN BROUGHT LOW BY MARS' LECHERY	227	SEXTUS PROP:11	27
CYTHERAEAN			
THE CYTHERAEAN FOR A CHAIN BIT.	201	AGE DEMANDED	4
C.3			
C.3, C.4, 'TWERE BETTER TO FORGET	260	ALF'S FIFTH	12
C.4			
C.3, C.4, 'TWERE BETTER TO FORGET	260	ALF'S FIFTH	12
D.			
A STRAY GIPSY--A. D. 1912	119	THE GYPSY	EPI
D'			
EMANUELE RE D' ITALIA,	182	MOEURS CON: 7	21
DABBLING			
DABBLING HER HANDS IN THE FOUNT, THUS SHE	211	SEXTUS PROP: 2	53
DAEMON			
WHEN COME THEY, SURGING OF POWER, "DAEMON,"	20	IN DURANCE	19
DAGGER			
DREW FULL THIS DAGGER THAT DOTH TREMBLE HERE.	31	PIERE VIDAL	42
DAI			
THE DAI HORSE NEIGHS AGAINST THE BLEAK WIND OF ETSU,	139	SOUTH-FOLK	1
DAILY			
IN THESE HE DAILY COMES TO ASK ME:	46	FROM HEINE: 6	7
THE DAILY PRESS, AND MONTHLIES NINE CENTS DEARER.	241	MOYEN SENSUEL	94
AND IN HIS DAILY WALKS DULY CAPSIZE HIM.	245	MOYEN SENSUEL	204
DALE			
I THAT HAVE KNOWN STRATH, GARTH, BRAKE, DALE,	31	PIERE VIDAL	50
D'ALLMAIN			
MATURIN, GUILLAUME, JACQUES D'ALLMAIN,	12	OF THE GIBBET	29
DAM'D			
BUT YOU, YOU DAM'D CROWD OF GNATS,	140	SENNIN POEM	15
DAME			
DAME NOR DAMSEL THERE'S NOT ANY	72	DIEU! QU'IL	10
DAMM			
DAMM YOU, SING: GODDAMM.	116	ANCIENT MUSIC	9
SING GODDAMM, DAMM, SING GODDAMM,	116	ANCIENT MUSIC	12
SING GODDAMM, SING GODDAMM, DAMM.	116	ANCIENT MUSIC	13
DAMN			
GOD DAMN HIS HELL OUT SPEEDILY	12	OF THE GIBBET	42
DAMN IT ALL! ALL THIS OUR SOUTH STINKS PEACE.	28	ALTAFORTE	1
MAY GOD DAMN FOR EVER ALL WHO CRY "PEACE!"	29	ALTAFORTE	36
"TEA" (DAMN YOU!)	52	AU SALON	10
HAVE TEA, DAMN THE CAESARS,	52	AU SALON	11
DAMN THE TEN MILLION!	257	BREAD BRIGADE	8
DAMN THE TEN MILLION.	257	BREAD BRIGADE	20
AND WOULDN'T GIV' A DAMN HOOT.	271	OLE KATE	4
DAMN'D			
VERS AND CANZONE, TILL THAT DAMN'D SON OF ARAGON,	22	MARVOIL	8
ME! IN THIS DAMN'D INN OF AVIGNON,	22	MARVOIL	19
SAVE THIS DAMN'D PROFESSION OF WRITING,	117	THE LAKE ISLE	15
TO SELL THE GOD DAMN'D FROGS	273	M. POM-POM	10
DAMNED			
"OR I'LL SEE YE DAMNED," SAYS HE.	33	GOODLY FERE	8
DAMP			
HAVE DAMP AND PLAIN TO BE OUR SHUTTING IN.	21	IN DURANCE	40
DAMP WOOLLY HANDKERCHIEFS WERE STUFFED INTO HER UNDRYABLE EYES,	214	SEXTUS PROP: 4	25
DAMSEL			
DAME NOR DAMSEL THERE'S NOT ANY	72	DIEU! QU'IL	10
DANCE			
TO THE DANCE OF LORDS AND LADIES	47	FROM HEINE: 7	23
GO AND DANCE SHAMELESSLY!	86	SALUTATION 2ND	19
DANCE AND MAKE PEOPLE BLUSH,	86	SALUTATION 2ND	27
DANCE THE DANCE OF THE PHALLUS	86	SALUTATION 2ND	18
DANCE THE DANCE OF THE PHALLUS	86	SALUTATION 2ND	28
DANCE FIGURE	91	DANCE FIGURE	T
TO THE DANCE OF THE SEVENTY COUPLES;	132	AT TEN-SHIN	23
AND THE DANCE INTO ITALY.	207	SEXTUS PROP: 1	5

PAGE 93

DANCE -- DARK

	PAGE	TITLE	LINE
DANCE (CONTINUED)			
AND WEARY WITH HISTORICAL DATA, THEY WILL TURN TO MY DANCE TUNE.	209	SEXTUS PROP: 1	62
DANCED			
BUT SHE DANCED LIKE A PINK MOTH IN THE SHRUBBERY.	53	AU JARDIN	19
THE FOREMAN OF KAN CHU, DRUNK, DANCED	135	EXILE'S LETTER	28
("SPEAK UP! YOU HAVE DANCED SO STIFFLY?	159	PSYCHOLOG HOUR	31
AND DANCED THEM INTO A BULWARK AT HIS PLEASURE,	208	SEXTUS PROP: 1	45
NO, NO, THEY DANCED. THE MUSIC GREW MUCH LOUDER	243	MOYEN SENSUEL	131
DANCERS			
THERE IS NONE LIKE THEE AMONG THE DANCERS,	91	DANCE FIGURE	4
THERE IS NONE LIKE THEE AMONG THE DANCERS;	91	DANCE FIGURE	23
TO A FRIEND WRITING ON CABARET DANCERS	161	CABARET DANCER	T
VIR QUIDEM, ON DANCERS	161	CABARET DANCER	EPI
AND THE DANCERS, YOU WRITE A SONNET;	161	CABARET DANCER	6
DANCES			
GO BACK TO GREAT DIAN'S DANCES BEARING SUITABLE GIFTS,	224	SEXTUS PROP: 9	24
DANCING			
TO THE PERFUMED AIR AND GIRLS DANCING,	132	AT TEN-SHIN	21
DANCING IN TRANSPARENT BROCADE,	136	EXILE'S LETTER	60
THAT DANCING AND GENTLE IS AND THEREBY PLEASANTER,	177	LANGUE D'OC: 4	22
DANDELION			
OR AS A DANDELION SEED-POD AND BE SWEPT AWAY,	36	FRANCESCA	10
DANGER			
YOU WILL SAY THAT YOU SUCCUMBED TO A DANGER IDENTICAL,	222	SEXTUS PROP: 8	30
DANGERS			
DANGERS OF DELAY. "CONSIDER	194	MR. NIXON	3
DANIEL			
TALKING OF TROBAR CLUS WITH DANIEL.	155	NEAR PERIGORD	140
DANS			
DANS UN OMNIBUS DE LONDRES	160	DANS OMNIBUS	T
ENCHASSES DANS UN VISAGE STUPIDE	160	DANS OMNIBUS	3
DANTE			
"LAPPO I LEAVE BEHIND AND DANTE TOO,	25	GUIDO INVITES	1
I HEARD THE YOUNG DANTE, WHOSE LAST NAME I DO NOT KNOW--	96	AESTHETICS	7
AS CAUGHT BY DANTE IN THE LAST WALLOW OF HELL--	151	NEAR PERIGORD	22
AND WE CAN LEAVE THE TALK TILL DANTE WRITES:	156	NEAR PERIGORD	162
DANTES			
FOR THERE ARE, IN SIRMIONE, TWENTY-EIGHT YOUNG DANTES AND THIRTY-FOUR CATULLI;	96	AESTHETICS	8
DAPHNE			
OF DAPHNE AND THE LAUREL BOW	3	THE TREE	3
"DAPHNE WITH HER THIGHS IN BARK	196	HUGH SELWIN:12	1
DAPHNIS			
THYRSIS AND DAPHNIS UPON WHITTLED REEDS,	229	SEXTUS PROP:12	42
DAR'DST			
DAR'DST TO ASSUME THIS?	68	APPARUIT	24
DARE			
CINO, OF THE DARE, THE JIBE,	6	CINO	19
NO MAN HATH DARED AND WON HIS DARE AS I:	32	PIERE VIDAL	55
DARED			
NO MAN HATH DARED AND WON HIS DARE AS I:	32	PIERE VIDAL	55
DARKLY HAST THOU DARED AND THE DREADED AETHER	68	APPARUIT	11
DARING			
NOR HIS DEED TO THE DARING, NOR HIS KING TO THE FAITHFUL	65	THE SEAFARER	42
DARING ADO, . . .	66	THE SEAFARER	77
VIERNA, JOCELYNN, DARING OF SPIRITS,	76	THE ALCHEMIST	41
DARING AS NEVER BEFORE, WASTAGE AS NEVER BEFORE.	190	HUGH SELWYN: 4	20
DARK			
AS DARK RED CIRCLES FILLED WITH DUST.	16	PRAISE YSOLT	13
SLAYS DAY WITH HER DARK SWORD.	24	THUS NINEVEH	4
AND I WATCH HIS SPEARS THROUGH THE DARK CLASH	29	ALTAFORTE	20
THE DARK DWARFS BLOW AND BOW THERE	47	FROM HEINE: 7	27
O THOU DARK SECRET WITH A SHIMMERING FLOOR,	50	THE FLAME	30
AND I AM TORN AGAINST THE JAGGED DARK,	60	TOMB AKR CAAR	26
THINK'ST THOU THAT THE DARK HOUSE	67	THE CLOAK	4
'NEATH THE DARK GLEAM OF THE SKY;	75	THE ALCHEMIST	7

DARK -- DAY

	PAGE	TITLE	LINE
DARK (CONTINUED)			
DARK EYED,	91	DANCE FIGURE	1
HEARD, UNDER THE DARK, WHIRLING LAUGHTER.	121	PROVINC DESERT	32
COVER OVER THE DARK PATH	138	CITY OF CHOAN	4
DARK OXEN, WHITE HORSES,	141	IDEA OF CHOAN	2
IT MAY LAST WELL IN THESE DARK NORTHERN CLIMATES,	163	CABARET DANCER	71
HANG IN YELLOW-WHITE AND DARK CLUSTERS READY FOR PRESSING.	167	OF AROUET	22
AND GO DARK WITH CLOUD,	176	LANGUE D'OC: 3	74
DARK-BROWED			
COME NOT ANEAR THE DARK-BROWED SOPHIST	263	ALF'S EIGHTH	8
DARKLING			
O SMOKE AND SHADOW OF A DARKLING WORLD,	50	THE FLAME	14
DARKLY			
DARKLY HAST THOU DARED AND THE DREADED AETHER	68	APPARUIT	11
DARKNESS			
HIS LONE MIGHT 'GAINST ALL DARKNESS OPPOSING.	29	ALTAFORTE	24
IN THE DARKNESS.	81	TENZONE	14
IN THE BROKEN DARKNESS.	91	DANCE FIGURE	7
ARE ALL FOLDED INTO ONE DARKNESS,	142	UNMOVING CLOUD	4
THE EIGHT PLY OF THE HEAVENS ARE DARKNESS,	142	UNMOVING CLOUD	11
IN MIDST OF DARKNESS LIGHT LIGHT GIVETH FORTH	250	DONNA MI PREGA	85
D'ARMENONVILLE			
D'ARMENONVILLE.	160	DANS OMNIBUS	29
DARN'D			
"THIS IS A DARN'D CLEVER BUNCH!"	179	MOEURS CON: 3	7
DART			
EDGE, THAT IS, AND POINT TO THE DART,	250	DONNA MI PREGA	78
DARTS			
STILL DARTS OUT FAUN-LIKE FROM THE HALF-RUIN'D FACE,	192	YEUX GLAUQUES	18
NOT YET WILD-CRUEL AS DARTS,	250	DONNA MI PREGA	74
DASHING			
THE DASHING RUPERT OF THE PULPING TRADE,	264	ALF'S NINTH	9
DASTARD			
THAT HE SHOULD LIVE THAN MANY A LIVING DASTARD	37	THE YOUNG KING	23
DATA			
AND WEARY WITH HISTORICAL DATA, THEY WILL TURN TO MY DANCE TUNE.	209	SEXTUS PROP: 1	62
DATE			
IN A HALF SAVAGE COUNTRY, OUT OF DATE;	187	E. P. ODE	6
MY CELLAR DOES NOT DATE FROM NUMA POMPILIUS,	209	SEXTUS PROP: 1	57
FURNISH MORE DATE FOR A COMPILATION	243	MOYEN SENSUEL	153
DAUGHTER			
MIDONZ, DAUGHTER OF THE SUN, SHAFT OF THE TREE, SILVER OF THE LEAF, LIGHT OF THE YELLOW OF THE AMBER	75	THE ALCHEMIST	26
FOR THEY HAVE A DAUGHTER NAMED RAFU,	140	MULBERRY ROAD	3
AND THAT THE FRIEND OF THE SECOND DAUGHTER WAS UNDERGOING A NOVEL,	179	MOEURS CON: 3	4
DAUPHIN			
THE DAUPHIN BACKED HIM.	122	PROVINC DESERT	70
DAVE			
DAVE WAS THE MAN TO SELL THE SHOT AND SHELL,	264	ALF'S NINTH	17
DAVID			
"FIND US A HARPIST!! DAVID IS THE MAN!!"	264	ALF'S NINTH	16
DAVID'S			
AND DAVID'S HARP LET OUT HEART-RENDING SQUEALE;	264	ALF'S NINTH	15
DAWN			
SHRINKETH THE KISS OF THE DAWN	14	FAMAM CANO	5
REST BROTHER, FOR LO! THE DAWN IS WITHOUT!	35	THE EYES	5
DAWN ENTERS WITH LITTLE FEET	83	THE GARRET	6
SHE LAY BESIDE ME IN THE DAWN.	109	ALBA	3
THE SEA'S COLOUR MOVES AT THE DAWN	131	AT TEN-SHIN	9
WILL YOU GIVE ME DAWN LIGHT AT EVENING?	167	OF AROUET	17
THAT HATH THE DAWN IN KEEPING,	172	LANGUE D'OC: 1	8
DAWN-MIST			
OR THROUGH DAWN-MIST	203	MAUBERLEY: 4	10
DAY			
DAY LONG, LONG DAY COOPED ON A STOOL,	22	MARVOIL	3
DAY LONG, LONG DAY COOPED ON A STOOL	22	MARVOIL	3
SLAYS DAY WITH HER DARK SWORD.	24	THUS NINEVEH	4

PAGE 95

DAY -- DAYS

	PAGE	TITLE	LINE
DAY (CONTINUED)			
NOT ONCE BUT MANY A DAY	41	HER MONUMENT	16
NO WORD, DAY AFTER DAY.	60	TOMB AKR CAAR	28
NO WORD, DAY AFTER DAY.	60	TOMB AKR CAAR	28
PASS AND BE SILENT, RULLUS, FOR THE DAY	63	QUIES	2
HERE WE HAVE HAD OUR DAY, YOUR DAY AND MINE.	69	THE NEEDLE	5
HERE WE HAVE HAD OUR DAY, YOUR DAY AND MINE.	69	THE NEEDLE	5
HE FARETH FROM DAY TO DAY,	98	THE BELLAIRES	37
HE FARETH FROM DAY TO DAY,	98	THE BELLAIRES	37
NIGHT AND DAY ARE GIVEN OVER TO PLEASURE	132	AT TEN-SHIN	25
AND BEFORE THE END OF THE DAY WE WERE SCATTERED LIKE STARS, OR RAIN.	135	EXILE'S LETTER	33
END THE DISCUSSION, RICHARD GOES OUT NEXT DAY	156	NEAR PERIGORD	157
NOW THE THIRD DAY IS HERE--	159	PSYCHOLOG HOUR	39
AND DAY COMES ON.	172	LANGUE D'OC: 1	5
AND DAY COMES ON!	172	LANGUE D'OC: 1	9
AND DAY COMES ON!	172	LANGUE D'OC: 1	13
AND DAY COMES ON!	172	LANGUE D'OC: 1	17
AND DAY COMES ON.	172	LANGUE D'OC: 1	21
THOUGH DAY BREAK."	172	LANGUE D'OC: 1	30
I REMEMBER THE YOUNG DAY	173	LANGUE D'OC: 2	17
WOULD I HAD DIED THAT DAY	175	LANGUE D'OC: 3	38
AND DAY COMES ON.	177	LANGUE D'OC: 4	5
AND DAY COMES ON.	177	LANGUE D'OC: 4	10
AND DAY COMES ON.	177	LANGUE D'OC: 4	15
AND DAY COMES ON."	177	LANGUE D'OC: 4	20
AND DAY COMES ON."	177	LANGUE D'OC: 4	25
AND DAY COMES ON.	177	LANGUE D'OC: 4	30
NOT KNOWING, DAY TO DAY,	203	MAUBERLEY: 4	2
NOT KNOWING, DAY TO DAY,	203	MAUBERLEY: 4	2
SHALL HAVE MY DOG'S DAY,	208	SEXTUS PROP: 1	36
MAY THE FATES WATCH OVER MY DAY.	216	SEXTUS PROP: 5	22
EACH MAN WHERE HE CAN, WEARING OUT THE DAY IN HIS MANNER.	218	SEXTUS PROP: 5	58
AND A DAY WHEN NO DAY RETURNS.	220	SEXTUS PROP: 7	19
AND A DAY WHEN NO DAY RETURNS.	220	SEXTUS PROP: 7	19
SO THAT NO DAY SHALL UNBIND THEM.	220	SEXTUS PROP: 7	21
THE GENTLER HOUR OF AN ULTIMATE DAY.	222	SEXTUS PROP: 8	18
OR JOVE, HARSH AS HE IS, MAY TURN ASIDE YOUR ULTIMATE DAY.	222	SEXTUS PROP: 8	38
SINCE THAT DAY I HAVE HAD NO PLEASANT NIGHTS.	225	SEXTUS PROP:10	43
THESE AND ANOTHER GODLET OF THAT DAY, YOUR DAY	240	MOYEN SENSUEL	47
THESE AND ANOTHER GODLET OF THAT DAY, YOUR DAY	240	MOYEN SENSUEL	47
STILL WE LOOK TOWARD THE DAY WHEN MAN, WITH UNCTION,	244	MOYEN SENSUEL	175
A TEMPERATE MAN, A THIN POTATIONIST, EACH DAY	245	MOYEN SENSUEL	199
AND IN OUR DAY THUS SAITH THE EVANGELIST:	246	MOYEN SENSUEL	237
IS ONE DAY BLOWN UP LARGE, THE NEXT, SUCKED IN?	261	ALF'S FIFTH	21
CAN TELL YOU OF THAT FAMOUS DAY AND YEAR.	264	ALF'S NINTH	4
WHERE BANKS RISE DAY BY DAY,	272	NATIONAL SONG	2
WHERE BANKS RISE DAY BY DAY,	272	NATIONAL SONG	2
DAYLIGHT			
NOR I, NOR TOWER-MAN, LOOK ON DAYLIGHT,	177	LANGUE D'OC: 4	8
SHOWED ONLY WHEN THE DAYLIGHT FELL	193	BRENNBAUM	6
DAY-LONG			
SINGS DAY-LONG AND NIGHT LATE	171	LANGUE D'OC	EPI
DAYS			
AS OLD TOLEDOS PAST THEIR DAYS OF WAR	19	FOR E. MCC	19
WHEN I BUT THINK UPON THE GREAT DEAD DAYS	30	PIERE VIDAL	1
NO MAN HATH HEARD THE GLORY OF MY DAYS:	32	PIERE VIDAL	54
IN THE BRIGHT GLAD DAYS!"	43	SATIEMUS	13
TO FIND HIM SUCH, WHEN THE DAYS BRING	46	FROM HEINE: 6	18
THAT MAN DOTH PASS THE NET OF DAYS AND HOURS.	50	THE FLAME	10
'TIS NOT "OF DAYS AND NIGHTS" AND TROUBLING YEARS,	50	THE FLAME	18
BUT YOU NEVER STRING TWO DAYS UPON ONE WIRE	53	AU JARDIN	13
--EVEN THE RIVER MANY DAYS AGO,	60	TOMB AKR CAAR	16
OR FINDS ITS HOUR UPON THE LOOM OF DAYS:	61	PORTRAIT FEMME	21
JOURNEY'S JARGON, HOW I IN HARSH DAYS	64	THE SEAFARER	2
DAYS LITTLE DURABLE,	66	THE SEAFARER	82
IN DAYS HEREAFTER,	67	DORIA	9
FOUR AND FORTY LOVERS HAD AGATHAS IN THE OLD DAYS,	102	LADIES	1
THINKING OF OLD DAYS.	121	PROVINC DESERT	8

DAYS -- DEAD

	PAGE	TITLE	LINE
DAYS (CONTINUED)			
AND SHE WAS A COURTEZAN IN THE OLD DAYS,	128	BEAU TOILET	6
BUT TO-DAY'S MEN ARE NOT THE MEN OF THE OLD DAYS,	131	AT TEN-SHIN	7
IN THE YOUNG DAYS WHEN THE DEEP SKY BEFRIENDED.	157	NEAR PERIGORD	175
WHERE, LADY, ARE THE DAYS	167	OF AROUET	1
SHALL OUTLAST OUR DAYS.	189	HUGH SELWYN: 3	12
DISILLUSIONS AS NEVER TOLD IN THE OLD DAYS,	190	HUGH SELWYN: 4	25
IN THOSE DAYS.	192	YEUX GLAUQUES	16
INO IN HER YOUNG DAYS FLED PELLMELL OUT OF THEBES,	222	SEXTUS PROP: 8	21
ZEUS' CLEVER RAPES, IN THE OLD DAYS,	227	SEXTUS PROP:11	33
WHY PAINT THESE DAYS? AN INSURANCE INSPECTOR	243	MOYEN SENSUEL	151
LIKE ALL HIS CLASS WAS TOLD TO HOLD IT IN THOSE DAYS,	263	ALF'S EIGHTH	26
HE USED TO LUNCH WITH BALFOUR IN THOSE DAYS	265	ALF'S NINTH	22
DAY'S			
PULLING ON THEIR SHOES FOR THE DAY'S BUSINESS,	14	FAMAM CANO	12
POPPIES AND DAY'S EYES IN THE GREEN EMAIL	157	NEAR PERIGORD	171
THE FIRST DAY'S END, IN THE NEXT NOON;	203	MAUBERLEY: 4	3
AND WONDER IF MY DAY'S THREE AND EIGHT-PENCE	268	ANOTHER BIT	11
DAYS'			
AND THREE DAYS' BEARD;	15	FAMAM CANO	37
YOU WERE A SEVEN DAYS' WONDER.	114	EPILOGUE	2
DE			
FOR JEHAN AND RAOUL DE VALLERIE	12	OF THE GIBBET	27
DE AEGYPTO	18	DE AEGYPTO	T
TO BAY LIKE SIR ROGER DE COVERLEY'S	52	AU SALON	15
DE MIS SOLEDADES VENGO,	82	THE CONDOLENCE	EPI
LOPE DE VEGA.	82	THE CONDOLENCE	EPI
EN ROBE DE PARADE.	83	THE GARDEN	EPI
"DOMPNA POIS DE ME NO'US CAL"	105	DOMPNA POIS	T
PIEIRE DE MAENSAC IS GONE.	123	PROVINC DESERT	79
THE COMPACT, DE BORN SMOKED OUT, TREES FELLED	155	NEAR PERIGORD	124
THEY PROBE OLD SCANDALS, SAY DE BORN IS DEAD;	155	NEAR PERIGORD	137
DANS UN OMNIBUS DE LONDRES	160	DANS OMNIBUS	T
AU DEDANS DE MA MEMOIRE	160	DANS OMNIBUS	7
AUX TOISONS COULEUR DE LIN,	160	DANS OMNIBUS	16
TEINTEES DE COULEUR SANG-DE-DRAGON,	160	DANS OMNIBUS	27
"CARMEN EST MAIGRE, UN TRAIT DE BISTRE	162	CABARET DANCER	24
CERNE SON OEIL DE GITANA"	162	CABARET DANCER	25
OF ARNAUT DE MAREUIL, I THOUGHT, "QU'IEU SUI AVINEN."	166	FISH & SHADOW	19
IMPRESSIONS OF FRANCOIS-MARIE AROUET (DE VOLTAIRE)	167	OF AROUET	T
E. P. ODE POUR L'ELECTION DE SON SEPULCHRE	187	E. P. ODE	T
DE SON EAGE; THE CASE PRESENTS	187	E. P. ODE	19
QU'ILS PEUVENT COMPRENDRE DE CETTE PASSION	199	MAUBERLEY: 2	EPI
"QU'EST CE QU'ILS SAVENT DE L'AMOUR, ET	199	MAUBERLEY: 2	EPI
DE MORTUIS VERUM, TRULY THE MASTER BUILDER?	210	MOYEN SENSUEL	58
DE GOURMONT SAYS THAT FIFTY GRUNTS ARE ALL THAT WILL BE PRIZED.	244	MOYEN SENSUEL	165
DEAD			
LO THE FAIR DEAD!	3	THRENOS	3
LO THE FAIR DEAD!	3	THRENOS	7
LO THE FAIR DEAD!	3	THRENOS	11
LO THE FAIR DEAD!	3	THRENOS	14
(LO THE FAIR DEAD!)	3	THRENOS	17
THE GHOSTS OF DEAD LOVES EVERYONE	10	FOR THIS YULE	11
AND IF WHEN I AM DEAD	22	MARVOIL	23
WHEN I BUT THINK UPON THE GREAT DEAD DAYS	30	PIERE VIDAL	1
FOR THAT THE ONE IS DEAD	30	PIERE VIDAL	5
AND WAKE THE DEAD," SAYS HE,	34	GOODLY FERE	30
AND THAT THE WORLD SHOULD DRY AS A DEAD LEAF,	36	FRANCESCA	9
WE ALSO SHALL BE DEAD PRETTY SOON	43	MR. HOUSMAN	3
DEAD ALREADY.	43	MR. HOUSMAN	5
WHISPERING AMONG THEM, "THE FAIR DEAD	43	SATIEMUS	10
ALL THE FLAMES ARE DEAD AND SPED NOW	45	FROM HEINE: 3	5
AND HE IS DEAD LANG SYNE.	47	FROM HEINE: 7	16
DEAD MEN STAY ALWAY DEAD MEN,	47	FROM HEINE: 7	17
DEAD MEN STAY ALWAY DEAD MEN,	47	FROM HEINE: 7	17
THESE FIVE MILLENIA, AND THY DEAD EYES	60	TOMB AKR CAAR	1
MY LORD DEEMS TO ME THIS DEAD LIFE	65	THE SEAFARER	66
PAN IS DEAD	72	PAN IS DEAD	T
"PAN IS DEAD. GREAT PAN IS DEAD.	72	PAN IS DEAD	1
"PAN IS DEAD. GREAT PAN IS DEAD.	72	PAN IS DEAD	1

DEAD -- DEATH

	PAGE	TITLE	LINE
DEAD (CONTINUED)			
THE EYES OF THIS DEAD LADY SPEAK TO ME,	73	THE PICTURE	1
THE EYES OF THIS DEAD LADY SPEAK TO ME.	73	THE PICTURE	4
THE EYES OF THIS DEAD LADY SPEAK TO ME.	73	JACOPO SELLAIO	6
WILL YOU FIND YOUR LOST DEAD AMONG THEM?	103	CODA	3
HERE IS THERE NAUGHT OF DEAD GODS	110	COITUS	3
"IONE, DEAD THE LONG YEAR"	112	IONE, DEAD	T
AND GO OUT THROUGH A THOUSAND MILES OF DEAD GRASS.	137	TAKING LEAVE	4
THEY PROBE OLD SCANDALS, SAY DE BORN IS DEAD;	155	NEAR PERIGORD	137
AND THEY DISCUSS THE DEAD MAN,	155	NEAR PERIGORD	144
ITS OWN HEAD SWINGING, GRIPPED BY THE DEAD HAIR,	156	NEAR PERIGORD	165
LET US THEREFORE CEASE FROM PITYING THE DEAD	164	QUINTUS SEPTIM	10
BUT DEAD, OR ASLEEP, SHE PLEASES.	165	QUINTUS SEPTIM	21
HE SAID: "WHY FLAY DEAD HORSES?	181	MOEURS CON: 7	15
HE STROVE TO RESUSCITATE THE DEAD ART	187	E. P. ODE	2
LAUGHTER OUT OF DEAD BELLIES.	190	HUGH SELWYN: 4	27
HERS WILL I BE DEAD,	221	SEXTUS PROP: 7	36
LIE DEAD WITHIN FOUR WALLS	236	MIDDLE-AGED	15
DEADLY			
O'ER MUCH HATH TA'EN SIR DEATH THAT DEADLY WARRIOR	37	THE YOUNG KING	12
DEAL			
GET A GOOD DEAL OF KISSING DONE.	48	FROM HEINE: 8	8
COME, LET US ON WITH THE NEW DEAL,	145	SALUTATION 3RD	13
YOU SAY THAT I TAKE A GOOD DEAL UPON MYSELF;	146	MONUMENTUM AER	1
DEAL-WOOD			
PULLED DOWN BY A DEAL-WOOD HORSE;	208	SEXTUS PROP: 1	27
DEAR			
(CHRIST MAKE THE SHEPHERDS' HOMAGE DEAR!)	10	FOR THIS YULE	2
HOW IF THE LOW DEAR SOUND WITHIN THY THROAT	43	SATIEMUS	14
"POOR DEAR! HE HAS LOST HIS ILLUSIONS."	85	SALUTATION 2ND	15
"DEAR POUND, I AM LEAVING ENGLAND."	159	PSYCHOLOG HOUR	43
COME NOW, MY DEAR PEPITA,	162	CABARET DANCER	32
PREFERABLE, MY DEAR BOY, MY DEAR LYNCEUS,	228	SEXTUS PROP:12	13
PREFERABLE, MY DEAR BOY, MY DEAR LYNCEUS,	228	SEXTUS PROP:12	13
BUT IN ONE BED, IN ONE BED ALONE, MY DEAR LYNCEUS	228	SEXTUS PROP:12	15
DEARER			
THE DAILY PRESS, AND MONTHLIES NINE CENTS DEARER.	241	MOYEN SENSUEL	94
DEATH			
BY THAT HIGH FENCER, EVEN DEATH,	19	FOR E. MCC	3
'GAINST THAT GREY FENCER, EVEN DEATH.	19	FOR E. MCC	9
'GAINST THAT GREY FENCER, EVEN DEATH,	19	FOR E. MCC	25
FOR THE DEATH OF SUCH SLUTS I GO REJOICING;	29	ALTAFORTE	29
STARK, KEEN, TRIUMPHANT, TILL IT PLAYS AT DEATH.	31	PIERE VIDAL	37
AGAINST THE DEATH OF THE YOUNG ENGLISH KING.	36	THE YOUNG KING	5
O'ER MUCH HATH TA'EN SIR DEATH THAT DEADLY WARRIOR	37	THE YOUNG KING	12
O SKILLFUL DEATH AND FULL OF BITTERNESS,	37	THE YOUNG KING	17
WHO DRANK OF DEATH FOR OUR SALVACIOUN,	37	THE YOUNG KING	35
THINK'ST THOU THAT DEATH WILL KISS THEE?	67	THE CLOAK	3
DEATH WAS EVER A CHURL.	72	PAN IS DEAD	9
I WILL NOT FLATTER YOU WITH AN EARLY DEATH,	145	SALUTATION 3RD	26
THEODORUS WILL BE PLEASED AT MY DEATH,	164	QUINTUS SEPTIM	1
AND SOMEONE ELSE WILL BE PLEASED AT THE DEATH OF THEODORUS,	164	QUINTUS SEPTIM	2
AND YET EVERYONE SPEAKS EVIL OF DEATH.	164	QUINTUS SEPTIM	3
A SAD AND GREAT EVIL IS THE EXPECTATION OF DEATH--	164	QUINTUS SEPTIM	8
FOR AFTER DEATH THERE COMES NO OTHER CALAMITY.	164	QUINTUS SEPTIM	11
THAT IS THE REAL DEATH,	168	OF AROUET	28
AND TIBULLUS COULD SAY OF HIS DEATH, IN HIS LATIN:	168	OF AROUET	39
IF SHE WON'T HAVE ME NOW, DEATH IS MY PORTION,	175	LANGUE D'OC: 3	37
ARE A COMPLETE ELUCIDATION OF DEATH.	209	SEXTUS PROP: 1	69
SUCH A DEATH IS WORTH DYING.	213	SEXTUS PROP: 3	29
WHEN , WHEN, AND WHENEVER DEATH CLOSES OUR EYELIDS,	218	SEXTUS PROP: 6	1
"DEATH WHY TARDILY COME?"	219	SEXTUS PROP: 6	29
OR AN ORNAMENTAL DEATH WILL BE HELD TO YOUR DEBIT,	221	SEXTUS PROP: 8	2
DEATH HAS HIS TOOTH IN THE LOT,	223	SEXTUS PROP: 9	18
SLOW FOOT, OR SWIFT FOOT, DEATH DELAYS BUT FOR A SEASON.	223	SEXTUS PROP: 9	21
OFTEN HIS POWER MEETETH WITH DEATH IN THE END	249	DONNA MI PREGA	39
IN HIS EYE THERE IS DEATH,--I MEAN THE BANKER'S,--	263	ALF'S EIGHTH	15
WILL BE THE DEATH OF ME."	271	OLE KATE	6

PAGE 98

DEATHLESS -- DEFEAT

	PAGE	TITLE	LINE
DEATHLESS			
DRIPS FROM MY DEATHLESS PEN--AH, WELL-AWAY!	59	SILET	2
NAY, SHOULD THE DEATHLESS VOICE OF ALL THE WORLD	63	PHASELLUS ILLE	9
YOU KNOW THE DEATHLESS VERSES.	162	CABARET DANCER	27
STANDS GENIUS A DEATHLESS ADORNMENT,	209	SEXTUS PROP: 1	72
DEATHS			
TWO DEATHS--AND TO STOP LOVING AND BEING LOVABLE,	168	OF AROUET	27
DEBIT			
OR AN ORNAMENTAL DEATH WILL BE HELD TO YOUR DEBIT,	221	SEXTUS PROP: 8	2
DEBT			
FOR TO YOU WE OWE A REAL DEBT:	101	AMITIES	14
AND UNTO ME ALSO PAY DEBT:	224	SEXTUS PROP: 9	27
DECADE			
M. VEROG, OUT OF STEP WITH THE DECADE,	193	SIENA MI FE	17
FOR MORE THAN A DECADE.	262	ALF'S SIXTH	30
DECEIT			
IN HIS PURSE THERE IS DECEIT,	263	ALF'S EIGHTH	16
DECEITFUL			
LOVE TAKES HIS WAY AND HOLDS HIS JOY DECEITFUL,	37	THE YOUNG KING	26
DECEITS			
HOME TO MANY DECEITS,	190	HUGH SELWYN: 4	16
DECEIVED			
AND DECEIVED BY YOUR REFERENCE	214	SEXTUS PROP: 4	6
DECIDED			
HEARD THAT HE HAD DECIDED,	118	CONTEMPORARIES	2
DECIDUOUS			
FOR ALL THIS SEA-HOARD OF DECIDUOUS THINGS,	61	PORTRAIT FEMME	25
DECLAIMS			
AND DECLAIMS BEFORE THE LADIES	46	FROM HEINE: 6	15
DECLINE			
EASTWARD AVOID THE HOUR OF ITS DECLINE,	69	THE NEEDLE	2
AND YOU MAY DECLINE TO MAKE THEM IMMORTAL,	99	SALVATIONISTS	7
DECLINED			
THE MOON STILL DECLINED TO DESCEND OUT OF HEAVEN,	223	SEXTUS PROP: 9	3
DECOLLETE			
AND DECOLLETE.	180	MOEURS CON: 5	6
DECOR			
NON "DULCE" NON "ET DECOR"	190	HUGH SELWYN: 4	12
DECORATIONS			
EXPLAINS THE DECORATIONS.	163	CABARET DANCER	59
DECOROUS			
THE MOST PRUDENT, ORDERLY, AND DECOROUS!	161	CABARET DANCER	8
DECORUM			
IN THIS THING'S SURE DECORUM AND BEHAVIOUR.	63	PHASELLUS ILLE	14
DECREED			
DECREED IN THE MARKET PLACE.	189	HUGH SELWYN: 3	16
DEDANS			
AU DEDANS DE MA MEMOIRE	160	DANS OMNIBUS	7
DEED			
NOR HIS DEED TO THE DARING, NOR HIS KING TO THE FAITHFUL	65	THE SEAFARER	42
DEEMS			
MY LORD DEEMS TO ME THIS DEAD LIFE	65	THE SEAFARER	66
DEEP			
GOD! BUT THE PURPLE OF THE SKY WAS DEEP!	30	PIERE VIDAL	20
CLEAR, DEEP, TRANSLUCENT, GO THE STARS ME SEEMED	30	PIERE VIDAL	21
SET DEEP IN CRYSTAL; AND BECAUSE MY SLEEP	30	PIERE VIDAL	22
OF WOVEN WALLS DEEP PATTERNED, OF EMAIL,	49	OF SPLENDOUR	14
IN THE SLOW FLOAT OF DIFFERING LIGHT AND DEEP,	61	PORTRAIT FEMME	27
TOO DEEP TO CLEAR THEM AWAY!	131	RIVER-MER WIFE	21
AND THE WATER, A HUNDRED FEET DEEP, REFLECTING GREEN EYEBROWS	136	EXILE'S LETTER	56
IN THE YOUNG DAYS WHEN THE DEEP SKY BEFRIENDED.	157	NEAR PERIGORD	175
BURY IT ALL, BURY IT ALL WELL DEEP,	265	ALF'S NINTH	29
DEEPEST			
WHENCE HAVE WE GRIEF, DISCORD AND DEEPEST SADNESS	37	THE YOUNG KING	32
DEER			
AND THE HOUNDS FLED AND THE DEER FLED	30	PIERE VIDAL	11
DEFEAT			
DEFEAT	173	LANGUE D'OC: 2	9

PAGE 99

DEFECTS -- DELIGHT

```
                                                            PAGE    TITLE              LINE
DEFECTS
    DEFECTS--AFTER SAMOTHRACE;       .......................  189   HUGH SELWYN: 3      14
DEFENCE
    OUR DEFENCE IS NOT YET MADE SURE, NO ONE CAN LET HIS
        FRIEND RETURN.           ..................................  127   BOWMEN OF SHU       8
    NO LONGER THE MEN FOR OFFENCE AND DEFENCE.         ........  133   FRONTIER GUARD     21
DEFEND
    TO DEFEND DEMOCRACY."        ...........................  270   OF 600 M.P.'S      24
DEFERRED
    HER BOURGEOIS DULNESS IS DEFERRED.          ................  163   CABARET DANCER     76
DEFILING
    PERHAPS YOU WILL HAVE THE PLEASURE OF DEFILING MY
        PAUPER'S GRAVE;        ...............................  145   SALUTATION 3RD     18
DEFINITIONS
    MY WIT, CHARM, DEFINITIONS,            .......................   46   FROM HEINE: 6      10
DEFY
    WHEN I SEE HIM SO SCORN AND DEFY PEACE,         ............   29   ALTAFORTE          23
    GO OUT AND DEFY OPINION,          ..........................   89   COMMISSION         33
DEGREE
    THEY ARE FOOLS TO THE LAST DEGREE.           ................   33   GOODLY FERE        26
DEGREES
    A SONG OF THE DEGREES             ...........................   95   OF THE DEGREES      T
DEIPHOIBOS
    OR OF POLYDMANTUS, BY SCAMANDER, OR HELENUS AND
        DEIPHOIBOS?         .................................  208   SEXTUS PROP: 1     30
DEITY
    STRANGE SPELLS OF OLD DEITY,             ......................    6   CINO                6
DEL
    OF JACOPO DEL SELLAIO              ...........................   73   JACOPO SELLAIO      T
    A PERIGORD, PRES DEL MURALH                .....................  151   NEAR PERIGORD     EPI
    CANTICO DEL SOLE             .................................  183   CANTICO SOLE        T
DELAY
    DANGERS OF DELAY. "CONSIDER                .......................  194   MR. NIXON           3
    "OF" THE VICTORIOUS DELAY OF FABIUS, AND THE
        LEFT-HANDED BATTLE AT CANNAE,             .................  210   SEXTUS PROP: 2     11
    TUNIC SPREAD IN DELAY;             .........................  220   SEXTUS PROP: 7      6
DELAYS
    SLOW FOOT, OR SWIFT FOOT, DEATH DELAYS BUT FOR A
        SEASON.        .......................................  223   SEXTUS PROP: 9     21
DELECTABLE
    O MUSES WITH DELECTABLE KNEE-JOINTS,            ..............  104   ANCORA             13
DELECTATIONS
    OH COUCH MADE HAPPY BY MY LONG DELECTATIONS;              ......  220   SEXTUS PROP: 7      2
DELIA
    "DELIA, I WOULD LOOK ON YOU, DYING."             ..............  168   OF AROUET          40
    AND DELIA HERSELF FADING OUT,            .....................  168   OF AROUET          41
DELICATE
    SO DELICATE AS SHE IS, WHEN THE SUN                 ...............   38   BALLATETTA          8
    RING DELICATE AND CLEAR.            ........................   45   FROM HEINE: 5       8
    AND ONE GROPES IN THESE THINGS AS DELICATE                ........   69   SUB MARE            5
    WE WENT FORTH GATHERING DELICATE THOUGHTS,               ........   82   THE CONDOLENCE      9
    AND THE DELICATE WHITE FEET OF HER LITTLE WHITE DOG
        ARE NOT MORE DELICATE THAN SHE IS,             ................   87   ALBATRE             3
                                                                    87   ALBATRE             4
    GO TO THOSE WHO HAVE DELICATE LUST,              ...............   88   COMMISSION         16
    GO TO THOSE WHOSE DELICATE DESIRES ARE THWARTED,                  .   88   COMMISSION         17
    IN DELICATE          .......................................   99   SALVATIONISTS       9
    REST NIGHTLY UPON THE SOUL OF OUR DELICATE FRIEND
        FLORIALIS,         ....................................  100   TEMPERAMENTS        2
    O MUSES WITH DELICATE SHINS,             .....................  104   ANCORA             12
    GROWN DELICATE WITH SATIETIES,             ....................  112   HIMERRO             2
    THEY HOWL. THEY COMPLAIN IN DELICATE AND EXHAUSTED
        METRES         ........................................  148   FRATRES MINORE      5
DELICATELY
    DELICATELY UPON THE REED, ATTEND ME!             ..............   62   N. Y.               3
    CLOTHED IN GOLDISH WEFT, DELICATELY PERFECT,              ......   68   APPARUIT           21
DELICIOUS
    AND THE WISE CONCORD, WHENCE THROUGH DELICIOUS SEAS                42   HER MONUMENT       43
    PIQUANTE, DELICIOUS, LUSCIOUS, CAPTIVATING:               .......  241   MOYEN SENSUEL      84
DELIGHT
    BY AERY APOSTLES OF TERRENE DELIGHT,              ..............   39   BLANDULA            8
    TO MIND ME OF SOME URN OF FULL DELIGHT,            ............   41   HER MONUMENT       13
```

DELIGHT -- DEPRIVED

	PAGE	TITLE	LINE
DELIGHT (CONTINUED)			
NOR WINSOMENESS TO WIFE, NOR WORLD'S DELIGHT	65	THE SEAFARER	46
DELIGHT 'MID THE DOUGHTY.	66	THE SEAFARER	81
"DELIGHT THY SOUL IN FATNESS," SAITH THE PREACHER.	163	CABARET DANCER	69
FOR IN HER IS ALL MY DELIGHT	174	LANGUE D'OC: 3	26
'TIS BUT A VAGUE, INVARIOUS DELIGHT	236	MIDDLE-AGED	1
NOT TO DELIGHT, BUT IN AN ARDOUR OF THOUGHT	249	DONNA MI PREGA	31
TO FIND DELIGHT	250	DONNA MI PREGA	67
DELIGHT MAKETH CERTAIN IN SEEMING	250	DONNA MI PREGA	71
DELIGHTED			
OUR "FANTASTIKON" DELIGHTED TO SERVE US.	82	THE CONDOLENCE	10
LEFT HIM DELIGHTED WITH THE IMAGINARY	202	AGE DEMANDED	44
DELIGHTFUL			
THIS DELIGHTFUL YOUNG MAN	46	FROM HF---'E: 6	1
IS BOTH STIMULATING AND DELIGHTFUL."	113	TAME CAT	7
DELIGHTS			
DREAR ALL THIS EXCELLENCE, DELIGHTS UNDURABLE!	66	THE SEAFARER	88
DELIVER			
SUCH FEAR I HAVE SHE DELIVER	175	LANGUE D'OC: 3	30
DELOS			
"ONCE MORE IN DELOS, ONCE MORE IS THE ALTAR A-QUIVER.	90	SURGIT FAMA	16
DEMAND			
I OF MIELS-DE-BEN DEMAND	106	DOMPNA POIS	47
DEMANDED			
THE AGE DEMANDED AN IMAGE	188	HUGH SELWYN: 2	1
THE "AGE DEMANDED" CHIEFLY A MOULD IN PLASTER,	188	HUGH SELWYN: 2	9
"THE AGE DEMANDED"	201	AGE DEMANDED	T
DEMEANOUR			
AND YET THE MAN IS SO QUIET AND RESERVED IN DEMEANOUR	100	TEMPERAMENTS	3
DEMOCRACY			
TO DEFEND DEMOCRACY."	270	OF 600 M.P.'S	24
DEMOLISH			
WHO CAN DEMOLISH AT SUCH POLISHED EASE	46	TRANSLATOR	3
DENIED			
EVEN IN MY DREAMS YOU HAVE DENIED YOURSELF TO ME	96	TO KALON	1
HAVE YOU DENIED PALLAS GOOD EYES?	221	SEXTUS PROP: 8	13
DENIERS			
E'EN ITS DENIERS CAN NOW HEAR THE TRUTH.	248	DONNA MI PREGA	4
DENIES			
"THE EUPHRATES DENIES ITS PROTECTION TO THE PARTHIAN			
AND APOLOGIZES FOR CRASSUS,"	216	SEXTUS PROP: 5	16
DENYING			
ONE DENYING YOUR PRESTIGE,	222	SEXTUS PROP: 8	36
DEO			
DEO LAUS, QUOD EST SEPULTUS,	101	AMITIES	18
DEPART			
DEPART IN PEACE.	183	CANTICO SOLE	11
DEPARTED			
AT SIXTEEN YOU DEPARTED,	130	RIVER-MER WIFE	15
WHO DEPARTED ALONE WITH HIS MISTRESS,	132	AT TEN-SHIN	32
DEPARTING			
ON FLOOD-WAYS TO BE FAR DEPARTING.	65	THE SEAFARER	53
SWIFT IN DEPARTING.	68	APPARUIT	20
AS WE ARE DEPARTING.	137	TAKING LEAVE	9
DEPARTURE			
SWEPT FROM THE MIND WITH IT IN ITS DEPARTURE	42	HER MONUMENT	40
FOUR POEMS OF DEPARTURE	137	OF DEPARTURE	T
BUT YOU, SIR, HAD BETTER TAKE WINE ERE YOUR			
DEPARTURE.	137	OF DEPARTURE	EPI
DEPLETED			
YOU'RE A VERY DEPLETED FASHION,	114	EPILOGUE	6
DEPLORED			
THOUGH SOME APPROVED OF THEM, AND SOME DEPLORED 'EM.	242	MOYEN SENSUEL	108
DEPLORES			
ENVIES ITS VIGOUR . . . AND DEPLORES THE TECHNIQUE,	155	NEAR PERIGORD	142
DEPORTMENT			
A GLAMOUR OF CLASSIC YOUTH IN THEIR DEPORTMENT.	163	CABARET DANCER	T1
DEPRECATE			
I DEPRECATE YOUR ATTENDANCE;	228	SEXTUS PROP:12	16
DEPRIVED			
DEPRIVED OF MY KINSMEN;	64	THE SEAFARER	16

PAGE 101

	PAGE	TITLE	LINE
DEPUTATION			
THE RIGOROUS DEPUTATION FROM "SLADE"--	93	LES MILLWIN	6
DERELICTIONS			
SUCH DERELICTIONS HAVE DESTROYED OTHER YOUNG LADIES AFORETIME,	221	SEXTUS PROP: 8	7
DERIDE			
LET US DERIDE THE SMUGNESS OF "THE TIMES":	145	SALUTATION 3RD	1
DERISION			
TO BE OBSERVED WITH DERISION,	145	SALUTATION 3RD	30
DES			
"EST-CE QUE VOUS AVEZ VU DES AUTRES--DES CAMARADES--AVEC DES SINGES OU DES OURS?"	119	THE GYPSY	EPI
"EST-CE QUE VOUS AVEZ VU DES AUTRES--DES CAMARADES--AVEC DES SINGES OU DES OURS?"	119	THE GYPSY	EPI
"EST-CE QUE VOUS AVEZ VU DES AUTRES--DES CAMARADES--AVEC DES SINGES OU DES OURS?"	119	THE GYPSY	EPI
"EST-CE QUE VOUS AVEZ VU DES AUTRES--DES CAMARADES--AVEC DES SINGES OU DES OURS?"	119	THE GYPSY	EPI
ET ALORS JE VIS BIEN DES CHOSES	160	DANS OMNIBUS	6
JE VIS DES CANARDS SUR LE BORD D'UN LAC MINUSCULE,	160	DANS OMNIBUS	10
DES PATRICIENNES,	160	DANS OMNIBUS	15
ET DES PIGEONNES	160	DANS OMNIBUS	17
COMME DES POULARDES.	160	DANS OMNIBUS	19
OU NOUS AVIONS LOUE DES CHAISES	160	DANS OMNIBUS	22
EST GROSSIERE ET LE PARFUM DES VIOLETTES UN	199	MAUBERLEY: 2	EPI
POUR VENDRE DES CANONS	273	M. POM-POM	8
POUR VENDRE DES CANONS	273	M. POM-POM	9
DESCANT			
DESCANT ON A THEME BY CERCLAMON	174	LANGUE D'OC: 3	SUB
DESCEND			
LAPPED IN THE GOLD-COLOURED FLAME I DESCEND THROUGH THE AETHER.	169	PHANOPOEIA	5
THE MOON STILL DECLINED TO DESCEND OUT OF HEAVEN,	223	SEXTUS PROP: 9	3
DESECRATED			
FOR THUS ARE TOMBS OF LOVERS MOST DESECRATED.	213	SEXTUS PROP: 3	34
DESERT			
DESOLATE CASTLE, THE SKY, THE WIDE DESERT.	133	FRONTIER GUARD	6
SURPRISED. DESERT TURMOIL. SEA SUN.	139	SOUTH-FOLK	6
DESERTA			
PROVINCIA DESERTA	121	PROVINC DESERT	T
DESIGNATE			
OF HIS BEWILDERMENT; TO DESIGNATE	199	MAUBERLEY: 2	10
DESIRABLE			
OF HAVENS MORE HIGH AND COURTS DESIRABLE	39	BLANDULA	14
DESIRE			
NO MORE DESIRE FLAYETH ME,	3	THRENOS	8
WHITHER MY DESIRE AND MY DREAM HAVE PRECEDED ME.	23	MARVOIL	33
LO, I HAVE KNOWN THY HEART AND ITS DESIRE;	25	GUIDO INVITES	8
THAT MASK AT PASSIONS AND DESIRE DESIRES,	32	PIERE VIDAL	61
O THROAT GIRT ROUND OF OLD WITH SWIFT DESIRE,	41	HER MONUMENT	14
MOVED NOT, NOR EVER ANSWER MY DESIRE,	60	TOMB AKR CAAR	3
AND HERE DESIRE, NOT TO BE KISSED AWAY.	73	THE PICTURE	3
AND I AM NEAR MY DESIRE.	83	THE GARRET	8
AND WILD DESIRE	87	THE SPRING	8
TO MY DESIRE, WORTH YOURS WHOM I HAVE LOST,	105	DOMPNA POIS	9
AS SHE DESIRE,	175	LANGUE D'OC: 3	54
NOR MY DESIRE,	176	LANGUE D'OC: 3	66
SHE DOES NOT DESIRE HER CHILDREN,	179	MOEURS CON: 2	8
AND HIS DESIRE FOR SURVIVAL,	202	AGE DEMANDED	37
DESIRE WILL FOLLOW YOU THITHER,	226	SEXTUS PROP:11	6
IN SUCH HIS DESIRE	250	DONNA MI PREGA	76
HAST THOU NO DESIRE.	250	DONNA MI PREGA	93
DESIRED			
INFINITE THINGS DESIRED, LOFTY VISIONS	42	HER MONUMENT	41
LOVE, YOU THE MUCH, THE MORE DESIRED!	70	THE PLUNGE	10
I DESIRED MY DUST TO BE MINGLED WITH YOURS	130	RIVER-MER WIFE	12
DESIRES			
THAT MASK AT PASSIONS AND DESIRE DESIRES,	32	PIERE VIDAL	61
GO TO THOSE WHOSE DELICATE DESIRES ARE THWARTED,	88	COMMISSION	17
DESIROUS			
'GOT ON DESIROUS THOUGHT BY NATURAL VIRTUE,	42	HER MONUMENT	42

DESIROUS -- DEVOID

	PAGE	TITLE	LINE
DESIROUS (CONTINUED)			
THEY SING OF LOVE THAT'S GROWN DESIROUS,	45	FROM HEINE: 5	9
AS I DESIROUS,	174	LANGUE D'OC: 3	10
DESOLATE			
DESOLATE CASTLE, THE SKY, THE WIDE DESERT.	133	FRONTIER GUARD	6
DESOLATE, DESOLATE FIELDS,	133	FRONTIER GUARD	19
DESOLATE, DESOLATE FIELDS,	133	FRONTIER GUARD	19
DESOLATED			
SADNESS HUNG OVER THE HOUSE, AND THE DESOLATED FEMALE ATTENDANTS	214	SEXTUS PROP: 4	22
WERE DESOLATED BECAUSE SHE HAD TOLD THEM HER DREAMS.	214	SEXTUS PROP: 4	23
DESPAIR			
AND COLD FIT FOR DESPAIR,	266	ALF'S ELEVENTH	14
D'ESPARO			
NO ONE HEARS SAVE ARRIMON LUC D'ESPARO--	154	NEAR PERIGORD	119
DESPERATE			
WHAT COULD HE DO BUT PLAY THE DESPERATE CHESS,	152	NEAR PERIGORD	36
DESPISED			
NOR WOULD GAUTIER HIMSELF HAVE DESPISED THEIR CONTRASTS IN WHITENESS	87	ALBATRE	5
DESPITE			
OH! I COULD GET ME OUT, DESPITE THE MARKS	60	TOMB AKR CAAR	29
DESPITE THE LONG DISTANCE.	135	EXILE'S LETTER	39
NELL GWYNN'S STILL HERE, DESPITE THE REFORMATION,	163	CABARET DANCER	72
GIVE MY GOOD-FELLOW AID IN FOOLS' DESPITE	172	LANGUE D'OC: 1	3
SUFFERS DESPITE	173	LANGUE D'OC: 2	15
IF ALL THE WORLD BE IN DESPITE	174	LANGUE D'OC: 3	14
DESPITE THE CUCKOLD, DO THOU AS THOU LIST,	177	LANGUE D'OC: 4	13
DESPITE SUCH REINS AND CHECKS I'LL DO MY BEST,	238	MOYEN SENSUEL	12
DESPITE IT ALL, DESPITE YOUR RED BLOODS, FEBRILE CONCUPISCENCE	240	MOYEN SENSUEL	67
DESPITE IT ALL, DESPITE YOUR RED BLOODS, FEBRILE CONCUPISCENCE	240	MOYEN SENSUEL	67
DESPITE IT ALL, YOUR COMPOUND PREDILECTION	240	MOYEN SENSUEL	69
DESTINIES			
THE DESTINIES OF ENGLAND WERE ALMOST SOLD	264	ALF'S NINTH	6
DESTRIERS			
AND THE SHRILL NEIGHS OF DESTRIERS IN BATTLE REJOICING,	28	ALTAFORTE	14
DESTROYED			
SUCH DERELICTIONS HAVE DESTROYED OTHER YOUNG LADIES AFORETIME,	221	SEXTUS PROP: 8	7
DESTROYERS			
DESTROYERS, BOMBS AND SPITTING MITRAILLEUSES.	265	ALF'S NINTH	21
DESTROYING			
DESTROYING, CERTAINLY, THE ARTIST'S URGE,	202	AGE DEMANDED	43
DETACHED			
DETACHED FROM HIS CONTEMPORARIES,	193	SIENA MI FE	18
DETAIL			
THE COMIC DETAIL WILL BE ABSENT.	146	MONUMENTUM AER	5
DETAILED			
IS DETAILED IN HIS PROVISIONS.	46	FROM HEINE: 6	12
DETERDING			
THERE IS SIR HEN. DETERDING	267	ALF'S TWELFTH	7
DETEST			
DO YOU, TRULY, SO DETEST ME?	44	FROM HEINE: 1	2
GARBLE A NAME WE DETEST, AND FOR PREJUDICE?	52	AU SALON	13
DETESTED			
I HAVE DETESTED YOU LONG ENOUGH.	89	A PACT	2
DETRACTOR			
THOUGH I KNOW ONE, A VERY BASE DETRACTOR,	246	MOYEN SENSUEL	221
DEUX			
ET DEUX PETITES FILLES GRACILES,	160	DANS OMNIBUS	14
DEVICES			
HERE THEY STAND WITHOUT QUAINT DEVICES,	85	SALUTATION 2ND	7
DEVIRGINATED			
AND THE DEVIRGINATED YOUNG LADIES WILL ENJOY THEM	208	SEXTUS PROP: 1	40
DEVOID			
INSOLENT LITTLE BEASTS, SHAMELESS, DEVOID OF CLOTHING!	94	INSTRUCTIONS	14

DEW

	PAGE	TITLE	LINE
YOUTH DEW IS COLD	9	NA AUDIART	40
CRIMSON, FROSTY WITH DEW, THE ROSES BEND WHERE	68	APPARUIT	5
BY THESE, FROM THE MALEVOLENCE OF THE DEW	76	THE ALCHEMIST	59
WE WHO SHOOK OFF OUR DEW WITH THE RABBITS,	104	ANCORA	5
THE DEW IS UPON THE LEAF.	110	COITUS	8
THE JEWELLED STEPS ARE ALREADY QUITE WHITE WITH DEW,	132	JEWEL STAIRS'	1
IT IS SO LATE THAT THE DEW SOAKS MY GAUZE STOCKINGS,	132	JEWEL STAIRS'	2
THE PARKS WITH THE SWARDS ALL OVER DEW,	167	OF AROUET	19

DEWS

TO GATHER HIS DEWS,	141	IDEA OF CHOAN	29

DEW-SPREAD

BY DEW-SPREAD CAVERNS,	227	SEXTUS PROP:11	30

DIABOLUS

FOR THREE YEARS, DIABOLUS IN THE SCALE,	199	MAUBERLEY: 2	1

DIADEM

NO ADJUNCT TO THE MUSES' DIADEM.	187	E. P. ODE	20

DIAMONDS

AND THE LUSTRE OF DIAMONDS,	167	OF AROUET	13

DIAN

TO DIAN GODDESS OF VIRGINS,	224	SEXTUS PROP: 9	26

DIANA

ENDYMION'S NAKED BODY, BRIGHT BAIT FOR DIANA,"	220	SEXTUS PROP: 7	15

DIAN'S

GO BACK TO GREAT DIAN'S DANCES BEARING SUITABLE GIFTS,	224	SEXTUS PROP: 9	24

DIASTASIS

IN THEIR DIASTASIS;	200	MAUBERLEY: 2	29

DID

	PAGE	TITLE	LINE
AND SO WERE MY MIND HOLLOW, DID SHE NOT FILL UTTERLY MY THOUGHT.	23	MARVOIL	39
AS DID FIRST SCORN, THEN LIPS OF THE PENAUTIER!	30	PIERE VIDAL	17
WHOM THOU ONCE DID SING SO SWEETLY,	45	FROM HEINE: 3	2
DID HE SO?	53	AU JARDIN	7
DID HE SO?	53	AU JARDIN	24
DID FOR MY GAMES THE GANNET'S CLAMOUR,	64	THE SEAFARER	20
NO MAN COULD PAINT SUCH THINGS WHO DID NOT KNOW.	73	JACOPO SELLAIO	2
IS IT A LOVE POEM? DID HE SING OF WAR?	153	NEAR PERIGORD	81
PLANTAGENET PUTS THE RIDDLE: "DID HE LOVE HER?"	155	NEAR PERIGORD	145
AND ARNAUT PARRIES: "DID HE LOVE YOUR SISTER?	155	NEAR PERIGORD	146
"DID YOU TALK LIKE A FOOL,	159	PSYCHOLOG HOUR	34
AND YOU, O POLYPHEMUS? DID HARSH GALATEA ALMOST	208	SEXTUS PROP: 1	46
ALTHOUGH CALLIMACHUS DID WITHOUT THEM,	218	SEXTUS PROP: 5	49
SHE DID NOT RESPECT ALL THE GODS;	221	SEXTUS PROP: 8	6
NOR DID DISGUST PROVE SUCH A STRONG EMETIC	242	MOYEN SENSUEL	128
DID I 'EAR IT 'ARF IN A DOZE:	262	ALF'S SEVENTH	1
DID I 'EAR IT WHILE PICKIN' 'OPS;	262	ALF'S SEVENTH	3

DIDN'T

"AND I WOULDN'T SAY THAT HE DIDN'T.	182	MOEURS CON: 8	12
AND DIDN'T SEEM NEVER TO STOP.	271	OLE KATE	12

DIE

PEOPLE ARE BORN AND DIE,	43	MR. HOUSMAN	2
SONG FROM "DIE HARZREISE"	47	FROM HEINE: 7	SUB
MACH' ICH DIE KLEINEN LIEDER	97	THE BELLAIRES	EPI
OR PERHAPS I WILL DIE AT THIRTY?	145	SALUTATION 3RD	17
RICHARD SHALL DIE TO-MORROW--LEAVE HIM THERE	155	NEAR PERIGORD	139
GOD GRANT I DIE NOT BY ANY MAN'S STROKE	173	LANGUE D'OC: 2	21
IT IS NOBLE TO DIE OF LOVE, AND HONOURABLE TO REMAIN	218	SEXTUS PROP: 5	59
TOLD 'EM TO DIE IN WAR, AND THEN TO SAVE,	260	ALF'S FIFTH	2

DIED

THEY DIED AND THE GREED OF YOUR FLAME CONSUMES THEM.	38	LADY'S LIFE	10
PORTENT. LIFE DIED DOWN IN THE LAMP AND FLICKERED,	68	APPARUIT	3
ALAS, HE DIED OF ALCOHOL.	117	EPITAPHS	2
AND LI PO ALSO DIED DRUNK.	117	EPITAPHS	3
"YOUR SON, AH, SINCE HE DIED	152	NEAR PERIGORD	44
BUT I REMEMBERED THE NAME OF HIS FEVER MEDICINE AND DIED.	165	QUINTUS SEPTIM	24
WOULD I HAD DIED THAT DAY	175	LANGUE D'OC: 3	38
DIED SOME, PRO PATRIA,	190	HUGH SELWYN: 4	11
THERE DIED A MYRIAD,	191	HUGH SELWYN: 5	1
TOLD ME HOW JOHNSON (LIONEL) DIED	193	SIENA MI FE	7

DIED -- DISCLOSES

	PAGE	TITLE	LINE
DIED (CONTINUED)			
AND DIED, THERE'S NOTHING IN IT.	194	MR. NIXON	24
SHE DIED ON THE JOB THEY TELLS ME,	271	OLE KATE	13
DIES			
'TIS HOW A BRAVE MAN DIES ON THE TREE."	34	GOODLY FERE	32
BUT HE DIES ALSO, PRESENTLY.	43	MR. HOUSMAN	7
PARDONS THE BOWMAN, DIES,	156	NEAR PERIGORD	159
IF SHE DIES, I SHALL GO WITH HER.	223	SEXTUS PROP: 9	9
DIEU			
O DIEU, PURIFIEZ NOS COEURS!	26	NIGHT LITANY	1
DIEU! QU'IL LA FAIT	72	DIEU! QU'IL	T
DIFFERENCE			
DIFFERENCE OF OPINION WITH LYGDAMUS	214	SEXTUS PROP: 4	SUB
DIFFERENT			
THEN THERE'S A GOLDISH COLOUR, DIFFERENT.	69	SUB MARE	4
BY THE GATE NOW, THE MOSS IS GROWN, THE DIFFERENT			
MOSSES,	131	RIVER-MER WIFE	20
SINGING A DIFFERENT STAVE, AS CLOSELY HIDDEN.)	153	NEAR PERIGORD	87
DIFFERING			
IN THE SLOW FLOAT OF DIFFERING LIGHT AND DEEP,	61	PORTRAIT FEMME	27
DIGESTIVE			
THE AMOROUS NERVES WILL GIVE WAY TO DIGESTIVE;	163	CABARET DANCER	68
DIGNIFIED			
NOR OF DIGNIFIED CARTHAGINIAN CHARACTERS,	217	SEXTUS PROP: 5	45
DILIGENT			
AND IS DILIGENT TO SERVE ME,	46	FROM HEINE: 6	11
DILIQUESCENT			
A SORT OF STINKING DILIQUESCENT SACCHARINE.	239	MOYEN SENSUEL	22
DILUTED			
SUCH PRACTICES DILUTED RURAL BOREDOM	242	MOYEN SENSUEL	107
DIM			
IN THOSE DIM HALLS WHERE NO MAN TROUBLETH	24	THUS NINEVEH	10
HATH AS FAINT LUTE-STRINGS IN ITS DIM ACCORD	43	SATIEMUS	15
DIM TALES THAT BLIND ME, RUNNING ONE BY ONE	43	SATIEMUS	16
IN THEIR DIM HALLS WAS HEARD	262	ALF'S SIXTH	29
DIMENSIONS			
THEY OBSERVE UNWIELDLY DIMENSIONS	104	THE SEEING EYE	2
DIMITTIS			
NUNC DIMITTIS, NOW LETTEST THOU THY SERVANT,	183	CANTICO SOLE	9
DIMMED			
STRANGE SPARS OF KNOWLEDGE AND DIMMED WARES OF PRICE.	61	PORTRAIT FEMME	5
DINE			
WILL DINE NEXT WEEK WITH MRS. BASIL,	163	CABARET DANCER	63
AND DINE IN A SOGGY, CHEAP RESTAURANT?	167	OF AROUET	4
DINNER			
AND YOUR NEW SERVICE AT DINNER,	167	OF AROUET	9
DINNERS			
"'CARE TOO MUCH FOR SOCIETY DINNERS?'	182	MOEURS CON: 8	11
DIONE			
DIONE, YOUR NIGHTS ARE UPON US.	110	COITUS	7
DIONYSUS			
CHRIST FOLLOWS DIONYSUS,	189	HUGH SELWYN: 3	5
DIRE			
AND DIRE SEA-SURGE, AND THERE I OFT SPENT	64	THE SEAFARER	6
DIRT			
AND LICK THE DIRT OFF THE FLOOR	264	ALF'S EIGHTH	31
DIRTY			
THEY HAVE TO DO THE DIRTY WORK,	266	ALF'S ELEVENTH	11
TER LICK TH' BANKERS' DIRTY BOOTS	270	OF 600 M.P.'S	3
DIS			
PERSEPHONE AND DIS, DIS, HAVE MERCY UPON HER,	223	SEXTUS PROP: 9	13
PERSEPHONE AND DIS, DIS, HAVE MERCY UPON HER,	223	SEXTUS PROP: 9	13
DISC			
I HAVE KNOWN THE GOLDEN DISC,	95	OF THE DEGREES	6
DISCERNMENT			
POOR IN DISCERNMENT, BEING THUS WEAKNESS' FRIEND,	249	DONNA MI PREGA	38
DISCIPLESHIP			
OF DISCIPLESHIP.	101	AMITIES	12
DISCLOSES			
"THE MEDICAL REPORT THIS WEEK DISCLOSES . . ."	260	ALF'S FIFTH	15

DISCOMFORT -- DISTANCE

	PAGE	TITLE	LINE
DISCOMFORT			
AFTER TWELVE MONTHS OF DISCOMFORT?	215	SEXTUS PROP: 4	42
DISCONTINUED			
THE RUSTLING OF THE SILK IS DISCONTINUED, ...	108	LIU CH'E	1
DISCORD			
WHENCE HAVE WE GRIEF, DISCORD AND DEEPEST SADNESS.	37	THE YOUNG KING	32
DISCOUNT			
DON'T GET A DISCOUNT LIKE MR. SELFRIDGE	262	ALF'S SEVENTH	11
DISCOURAGED			
INDIFFERENT AND DISCOURAGED HE THOUGHT HE MIGHT AS	100	ARIDES	4
DISCOURAGING			
THE DISCOURAGING DOCTRINE OF CHANCES, ...	202	AGE DEMANDED	36
DISCOVERED			
AS IF HE HAD JUST DISCOVERED IT.	82	THE CONDOLENCE	16
FOR YOU SEEM NEVER TO HAVE DISCOVERED	101	AMITIES	8
YOU ONCE DISCOVERED A MODERATE CHOP-HOUSE.	101	AMITIES	16
HER CHILDREN HAVE NEVER DISCOVERED HER ADULTERIES.	103	THE PATTERNS	2
DISCOVERING			
SUDDENLY DISCOVERING IN THE EYES OF THE VERY BEAUTIFUL	161	PAGANI'S NOV 8	1
DISCUSS			
MET TO DISCUSS THEIR AFFAIRS;	97	THE BELLAIRES	7
MET TO DISCUSS THEIR AFFAIRS, ...	98	THE BELLAIRES	29
AND THEY DISCUSS THE DEAD MAN, ...	155	NEAR PERIGORD	144
DISCUSSED			
LONG SINCE FULLY DISCUSSED BY OVID.	148	FRATRES MINORE	4
DISCUSSION			
END THE DISCUSSION, RICHARD GOES OUT NEXT DAY	156	NEAR PERIGORD	157
ENDS OUR DISCUSSION. ARNAUT ENDS	156	NEAR PERIGORD	160
DISDEIGN			
AS A FOOL THAT MOCKETH HIS DRUE'S DISDEIGN.	11	OF THE GIBBET	12
OF LOVE THAT LOVETH IN HELL'S DISDEIGN, ...	11	OF THE GIBBET	21
DISEASE			
DISEASE OR OLDNESS OR SWORD-HATE ....;..	66	THE SEAFARER	71
DISEMBOWELED			
UNTIL THE LAST SLUT'S HANGED AND THE LAST PIG DISEMBOWELED, ...	161	CABARET DANCER	2
DISFECEMI			
"SIENA MI FE'; DISFECEMI MAREMMA"	193	SIENA MI FE	T
DISGUISED			
CALLISTO, DISGUISED AS A BEAR, ...	222	SEXTUS PROP: 8	24
DISGUST			
NOR DID DISGUST PROVE SUCH A STRONG EMETIC	242	MOYEN SENSUEL	128
DISGUST WITH HOKUM.	259	ALF'S THIRD	7
DISHONEST			
OR SLITHERS ABOUT BETWEEN THE DISHONEST WAITERS--	162	CABARET DANCER	23
DISH-WASH			
LIFE'S A SORT OF SUGARED DISH-WASH!"	241	MOYEN SENSUEL	90
DISILLUSIONS			
DISILLUSIONS AS NEVER TOLD IN THE OLD DAYS, ...	190	HUGH SELWYN: 4	25
DISJECTA			
NYMPHARUM MEMBRA DISJECTA	92	APRIL	EPI
DISJUNCT			
A CONSCIOUSNESS DISJUNCT, ...	203	MAUBERLEY: 4	14
DISLIKE			
TWO SMALL PEOPLE, WITHOUT DISLIKE OR SUSPICION. ...	130	RIVER-MER WIFE	6
DISLIKED			
WE SHALL GET OURSELVES RATHER DISLIKED.	99	SALVATIONISTS	2
DISOWN			
I DO NOT DISOWN YOU, ...	85	SALUTATION 2ND	5
DO NOT YOU DISOWN YOUR PROGENY.	85	SALUTATION 2ND	6
DISPARAGE			
AS NOTHING CAN RESTRAIN OR MUCH DISPARAGE. ...	245	MOYEN SENSUEL	192
DISPRAISES			
DISPRAISES HIS OWN SKILL?--THAT'S AS YOU WILL.	155	NEAR PERIGORD	143
DISSECTOR			
TRUE TO THE TRUTH'S SAKE AND CRAFTY DISSECTOR, ...	13	MESMERISM	18
DISTANCE			
DESPITE THE LONG DISTANCE.	135	EXILE'S LETTER	39
WHO BOW OVER THEIR CLASPED HANDS AT A DISTANCE. ...	137	TAKING LEAVE	7

DISTANT -- DO

	PAGE	TITLE	LINE
DISTANT			
SHARP PEAKS, HIGH SPURS, DISTANT CASTLES.	122	PROVINC DESERT	55
MY FRIENDS ARE ESTRANGED, OR FAR DISTANT,	142	UNMOVING CLOUD	8
IF ANY LAND SHRINK INTO A DISTANT SEACOAST,	216	SEXTUS PROP: 5	19
THAN I CAN FROM THIS DISTANT LAND AND STATION,	243	MOYEN SENSUEL	154
DISTASTE			
WITH A DISTASTE FOR CARESSES.	179	MOEURS CON: 2	2
DISTENTIONS			
AND EXPOUND THE DISTENTIONS OF EMPIRE,	207	SEXTUS PROP: 1	18
DISTINCTLY			
BUT YOU STUFFED COATS WHO'RE NEITHER TEPID NOR			
DISTINCTLY BOREAL,	238	MOYEN SENSUEL	5
DISTINGUISHED			
IS, AT BOTTOM, DISTINGUISHED AND FRESH AS A MARCH			
HERB.	247	PIERROTS	18
DISTRESS			
'GAINST OUR LIPS FOR THE SOUL'S DISTRESS	11	OF THE GIBBET	23
AND THE SOIL MEETS HIS DISTRESS.	195	HUGH SELWIN:10	8
DISTRESSED			
HATH IT NEVER ONCE DISTRESSED YOU,	44	FROM HEINE: 1	6
DISTRESSING			
LEST THEY SHOULD OVERHEAR THE DISTRESSING CHATTER	272	NATIONAL SONG	14
DISTURB			
BUT MY SOUL, THE SORT WHICH HARSH SOUNDS DISTURB,	247	PIERROTS	17
DISTURBETH			
DISTURBETH HIS REFLECTIONS.	63	AN OBJECT	4
DITCH			
SHE WILL BE DRUNK IN THE DITCH, BUT YOU, PEPITA,	162	CABARET DANCER	47
DIVERGENT			
HURL ME INTO SUCH A MASS OF DIVERGENT IMPRESSIONS.	248	PIERROTS	28
DIVERS			
ET TOUS LES GAZONS DIVERS	160	DANS OMNIBUS	21
DIVERSE			
THEY ARE PLAYED ON BY DIVERSE FORCES.	158	PSYCHOLOG HOUR	15
DIVERSION			
AND KISSIN' HER CAT FER DIVERSION,	271	OLE KATE	19
DIVES			
TO DIVES	102	TO DIVES	T
WHO AM I TO CONDEMN YOU, O DIVES,	102	TO DIVES	1
DIVINE			
I THOUGHT: YES, DIVINE, THESE EYES, BUT WHAT EXISTS	247	PIERROTS	11
DIVINERS			
THERE IS NO NEED OF ASKING DIVINERS.	138	NEAR SHOKU	11
DIVORCE			
HER SECOND HUSBAND WILL NOT DIVORCE HER;	179	MOEURS CON: 2	5
DO			
NO MORE DO I BURN.	3	THRENOS	4
THAT THEY MIGHT DO THIS WONDER THING;	3	THE TREE	9
. . . I DO NOT REMEMBER	5	LA FRAISNE	45
I DO NOT LIKE TO REMEMBER THINGS ANY MORE.	5	LA FRAISNE	48
JUMP TO YOUR SENSE AND GIVE PRAISE AS WE'D LIEF DO.	13	MESMERISM	8
LO! I DO CURSE MY STRENGTH	30	PIERE VIDAL	3
WHAT DO YE OWN, YE NIGGARDS! THAT CAN BUY	32	PIERE VIDAL	57
HIM DO WE PRAY AS TO A LORD MOST RIGHTEOUS	37	THE YOUNG KING	36
DO THOU, PLUTO, BRING HERE NO GREATER HARSHNESS.	38	LADY'S LIFE	2
DO THOU, PLUTO, BRING HERE NO GREATER HARSHNESS.	38	LADY'S LIFE	12
DO YOU, TRULY, SO DETEST ME?	44	FROM HEINE. 1	2
WHEN IT IS AUTUMN DO WE GET SPRING WEATHER,	59	SILET	7
I DO NOT GO."	60	TOMB AKR CAAR	33
NOW DO I KNOW THAT I AM MAD,	62	N. Y.	4
DO I NOT LOATHE ALL WALLS, STREETS, STONES,	70	THE PLUNGE	11
DO NOT SET ABOUT TO PROCURE ME AN AUDIENCE.	81	TENZONE	9
I DO NOT DISOWN YOU,	85	SALUTATION 2ND	5
DO NOT YOU DISOWN YOUR PROGENY.	85	SALUTATION 2ND	6
AND DO NOT EVEN OWN CLOTHING.	85	SALUTATION	10
SAY THAT YOU DO NO WORK	86	SALUTATION 2ND	36
YOU DO NOT KNOW THESE FOUR PEOPLE.	88	CAUSA	4
BUT DO THOU SPEAK TRUE, EVEN TO THE LETTER:	90	SURGIT FAMA	15
YOU DO NEXT TO NOTHING AT ALL.	94	INSTRUCTIONS	7
YOU DO NOT EVEN EXPRESS OUR INNER NOBILITIES,	94	INSTRUCTIONS	8

PAGE 107

DO -- DOES

	PAGE	TITLE	LINE
DO (CONTINUED)			
I HEARD THE YOUNG DANTE, WHOSE LAST NAME I DO NOT KNOW--	96	AESTHETICS	7
DO NOT UNDERSTAND THE CONDUCT OF THIS WORLD'S AFFAIRS.	97	THE BELLAIRES	2
ON THE CONTRARY, IF THEY DO NOT BELONG TO HIS WIFE,	98	THE BELLAIRES	16
WELL DO THIS AS ANYTHING ELSE.	100	ARIDES	5
WHY DO YOU LOOK SO EAGERLY AND SO CURIOUSLY INTO PEOPLE'S FACES,	103	CODA	2
A PROUD THING I DO HERE,	105	DOMPNA POIS	24
SUCH GRACE OF LOCKS, I DO YE TO WIT,	106	DOMPNA POIS	38
HER ROBES CAN' BUT DO HER WRONG.	106	DOMPNA POIS	50
AND WHAT, PRAY, DO YOU KNOW ABOUT	109	THE FAUN	3
BEFORE IT ANOTHER HOUSE WHICH I DO NOT KNOW:	141	IDEA OF CHOAN	30
TO DO AWAY WITH GOOD WRITERS,	145	SALUTATION 3RD	21
WHAT COULD HE DO BUT PLAY THE DESPERATE CHESS,	152	NEAR PERIGORD	36
"IN THE FULL FLARE OF GRIEF. DO WHAT, YOU WILL."	152	NEAR PERIGORD	46
ALL OF HIS FLANK--HOW COULD HE DO WITHOUT HER?	153	NEAR PERIGORD	66
WHAT WOULD HE DO WITHOUT HER?	153	NEAR PERIGORD	68
"DO WE KNOW OUR FRIENDS?"	156	NEAR PERIGORD	154
'WHY DO YOU LOVE ME? WILL YOU ALWAYS LOVE ME?	157	NEAR PERIGORD	181
HOW DO I KNOW?	158	PSYCHOLOG HOUR	16
I DO NOT LIVE, NOR CURE ME,	174	LANGUE D'OC: 3	20
NOR DO I KNOW WHEN I TURN LEFT OR RIGHT	174	LANGUE D'OC: 3	24
DESPITE THE CUCKOLD, DO THOU AS THOU LIST,	177	LANGUE D'OC: 4	13
"AND SAID: 'DO I,	182	MOEURS CON: 8	9
"'I ASK YOU, DO I	182	MOEURS CON: 8	10
MY ORCHARDS DO NOT LIE LEVEL AND WIDE	209	SEXTUS PROP: 1	53
WHERE BOLD HANDS MAY DO VIOLENCE TO MY PERSON?	212	SEXTUS PROP: 3	8
AND MY VENTRICLES DO NOT PALPITATE TO CAESARIAL ORE ROTUNDOS,	218	SEXTUS PROP: 5	53
I DO NOT KNOW WHAT BOYS,	224	SEXTUS PROP:10	5
"DO YOU THINK I HAVE ADOPTED YOUR HABITS?"	225	SEXTUS PROP:10	35
YOU DO NOTHING, YOU PLOT INANE SCHEMES AGAINST ME,	226	SEXTUS PROP:11	14
YOU THINK YOU ARE GOING TO DO HOMER.	228	SEXTUS PROP:12	22
HEAD FARMERS DO LIKEWISE, AND LYING WEARY AMID THEIR OATS	229	SEXTUS PROP:12	48
DESPITE SUCH REINS AND CHECKS I'LL DO MY BEST,	238	MOYEN SENSUEL	12
WAS GOT ABROAD, WHAT BETTER LUCK DO YOU WISH 'EM,	240	MOYEN SENSUEL	60
MUST THINK TRUTH LOOKS AS THEY DO IN WOOL PYJAMAS.	243	MOYEN SENSUEL	148
NEVER AT ALL WILL THEY DO	265	ALF'S TENTH	3
DO, THAT IS: THINK, BEFORE IT'S TOO LATE.	265	ALF'S TENTH	12
THEY HAVE TO DO THE DIRTY WORK,	266	ALF'S ELEVENTH	11
I DO WHATEVER I CHOOSE.	266	ALF'S ELEVENTH	12
MIGHT DO, TOO. MONTAGUE!	267	ALF'S TWELFTH	18
SOME OTHER FELLER DO IT.	270	OF 600 M.P.'S	12
TILL SHE FINDS WORK TO DO.	272	THE BABY	8
D'OC			
LANGUE D'OC	171	LANGUE D'OC	T
DOCTOR			
NICHARCUS UPON PHIDON HIS DOCTOR	165	QUINTUS SEPTIM	ST
DOCTRINE			
THE DISCOURAGING DOCTRINE OF CHANCES,	202	AGE DEMANDED	36
DODDERING			
THEIR DODDERING IGNORANCE IS WAXED SO NOTABLE	239	MOYEN SENSUEL	37
DODGED			
HID HEALTH STATISTICS, DODGED THE LABOUR ACTS.	260	ALF'S FIFTH	8
DODGERS			
THESE HEAVY WEIGHTS, THESE DODGERS AND THESE PREACHERS,	241	MOYEN SENSUEL	79
DODGING			
DODGING HIS WAY PAST AUBETERRE, SINGING AT CHALAIS	154	NEAR PERIGORD	105
DOES			
AND NOW YOU GRUMBLE BECAUSE YOUR DRESS DOES NOT FIT	102	LADIES	7
IF SHE DOES NOT COUNT THIS BLESSED	103	PHYLLIDULA	4
WALKED ONCE, AND NOW DOES NOT WALK	112	IONE, DEAD	8
WHY DOES THE HORSE-FACED LADY OF JUST THE UNMENTIONABLE AGE	114	SIMULACRA	1
WHY DOES THE SMALL CHILD IN THE SOILED-WHITE IMITATION FUR COAT	114	SIMULACRA	3

PAGE 108

DOES -- DONNA

	PAGE	TITLE	LINE
DOES (CONTINUED)			
WHY DOES THE REALLY HANDSOME YOUNG WOMAN APPROACH ME IN SACKVILLE STREET	114	SIMULACRA	5
SHE DOES NOT GET UP THE STAIRS SO EAGERLY;	116	THE TEA SHOP	4
"SAY THAT HE LOVED HER, DOES IT SOLVE THE RIDDLE?"	156	NEAR PERIGORD	156
DOES NOT BELIEVE IN ASTHETICS.	178	MOEURS CON: 1	14
SHE DOES NOT DESIRE HER CHILDREN,	179	MOEURS CON: 2	8
MY CELLAR DOES NOT DATE FROM NUMA POMPILIUS,	209	SEXTUS PROP: 1	57
"DOES HE LIKE ME TO SLEEP HERE ALONE,	215	SEXTUS PROP: 4	38
AND WHATEVER SHE DOES OR SAYS	217	SEXTUS PROP: 5	35
DOG			
YOU WHORESON DOG, PAPIOLS, COME! LET'S TO MUSIC!	28	ALTAFORTE	2
AND THE DELICATE WHITE FEET OF HER LITTLE WHITE DOG	87	ALBATRE	3
TO BE SO MUCH ALIKE THAT EVERY DOG THAT SMELLS 'EM,	244	MOYEN SENSUEL	172
DOGS			
WHEN I CAREFULLY CONSIDER THE CURIOUS HABITS OF DOGS	102	MEDITATIO	1
THE SMALL DOGS LOOK AT THE BIG DOGS;	104	THE SEEING EYE	1
THE SMALL DOGS LOOK AT THE BIG DOGS;	104	THE SEEING EYE	1
IT IS ONLY IN SMALL DOGS AND THE YOUNG	104	THE SEEING EYE	9
FOR THEM THE YELLOW DOGS HOWL PORTENTS IN VAIN,	132	AT TEN-SHIN	28
THE STILL STONE DOGS,	200	MAUBERLEY: 2	35
"NIGHT DOGS, THE MARKS OF A DRUNKEN SCURRY,	211	SEXTUS PROP: 2	49
AND KEEP MAD DOGS OFF HIS ANKLES.	212	SEXTUS PROP: 3	23
DOG'S			
SHALL HAVE MY DOG'S DAY,	208	SEXTUS PROP: 1	36
DOG-WOOD			
THAT WAS A DOG-WOOD TREE SOME SYNE.	4	LA FRAISNE	15
DOGWOODS			
ON HOW WHITE DOGWOODS MURMURED OVERHEAD	43	SATIEMUS	12
DOING			
THERE WILL BE A CROWD OF YOUNG WOMEN DOING HOMAGE TO MY PALAVER,	208	SEXTUS PROP: 1	50
SAID THEN "YOU IDIOT! WHAT ARE YOU DOING WITH THAT WATER:	210	SEXTUS PROP: 2	17
NO BARBARISM WOULD GO TO THE EXTENT OF DOING HIM HARM,	212	SEXTUS PROP: 3	19
DOLE			
DOLE THE BELL! BELL THE DOLE!	258	ALF'S THIRD	SUB
DOLE THE BELL! BELL THE DOLE!	258	ALF'S THIRD	SUB
DOLOROUS			
WORTH LIETH RIVEN AND YOUTH DOLOROUS,	36	THE YOUNG KING	6
DOLOUR			
ALL DOLOUR, ILL AND EVERY EVIL CHANCE	36	THE YOUNG KING	2
DOLPHINS			
IT IS ADORNED WITH YOUNG GODS RIDING UPON DOLPHINS	237	ABU SALAMMAMM	20
DOLTS			
YOU AND ABE LINCOLN FROM THAT MASS OF DOLTS	235	TO WHISTLER	18
DOMINATION			
IT IS A MERE POSTPONEMENT OF YOUR DOMINATION.	216	SEXTUS PROP: 5	20
DOMO			
PRO DOMO, IN ANY CASE . . .	190	HUGH SELWYN: 4	3
DOMPNA			
"DOMPNA POIS DE ME NO'US CAL"	105	DOMPNA POIS	T
DON			
THAT BADE MY HEART HIS VALOUR DON?	10	FOR THIS YULE	21
PRETEND HUMANITY OR DON THE FRAIL ATTIRE?	32	PARACELSUS	2
DONE			
PRINCE: ASK ME NOT WHAT I HAVE DONE	10	FOR THIS YULE	25
HAVE WE DONE IN TIMES PAST	26	NIGHT LITANY	10
GET A GOOD DEAL OF KISSING DONE.	48	FROM HEINE: 8	8
YOU ARE NOT OLD ENOUGH TO HAVE DONE MUCH MISCHIEF,	94	INSTRUCTIONS	16
LET US BE DONE WITH PANDARS AND JOBBERY,	145	SALUTATION 3RD	14
LET US DUMP OUR HATREDS INTO ONE BUNCH AND BE DONE WITH THEM,	146	CANTILATIONS	2
(ST. LEIDER HAD DONE AS MUCH AS POLHONAC,	153	NEAR PERIGORD	86
BADEST ME TO SEE THAT A GOOD WATCH WAS DONE,	172	LANGUE D'OC: 1	23
WHAT IS TO BE DONE ABOUT IT?	211	SEXTUS PROP: 2	C
TEN MORE AND NOTHING DONE,	259	ALF'S THIRD	19
AFTER MY WORK IS DONE	268	ANOTHER BIT	10
DONNA			
"LA DONNA E MOBILE."	163	CABARET DANCER	86

DONNA -- DOUBTFUL

```
                                                         PAGE      TITLE              LINE
DONNA  (CONTINUED)
     DONNA MI PREGA   ..................................  248    DONNA MI PREGA       T
DONT
     DONT TOUS LES AUTRES TRAITS ETAIENT BANALS,  .......  160    DANS OMNIBUS         4
DON'T
     I DON'T KNOW WHAT YOU LOOK LIKE   .................   162    CABARET DANCER      40
     DON'T KICK AGAINST THE PRICKS,    .................   194    MR. NIXON           22
     (SUCH CHANGES DON'T OCCUR IN MEN, OR RABBITS).  ...   246    MOYEN SENSUEL      232
     DON'T TELL WHAT YOU KNOW,  ........................   259    ALF'S FOURTH         9
     AND DON'T READ NO BOOKS;  .........................   260    ALF'S FOURTH        17
     DON'T GET A DISCOUNT LIKE MR. SELFRIDGE  ..........   262    ALF'S SEVENTH       11
     I DON'T QUITE SEE THE JOKE ANY MORE,  .............   264    ALF'S EIGHTH        29
     AND DON'T KNOW WHAT BUG IS A-BITIN'  ..............   269    SAFE AND SOUND      11
DOODLEDE
     SING: TOODLE DOODLEDE OOT!   ......................   271    OLE KATE             2
DOOM
     HE WENT TO HIS DOOM.   ............................   100    ARIDES               8
DOOM-GRIPPED
     BEATS OUT THE BREATH FROM DOOM-GRIPPED BODY.  .....    66    THE SEAFARER        72
DOOR
     AND ALL THEIR CRAFTY WORK UPON THE DOOR,  .........    60    TOMB AKR CAAR       30
     WHITE, WHITE OF FACE, HESITATES, PASSING THE DOOR.    128    BEAU TOILET          4
     CLANKING THE DOOR SHUT,  ..........................   167    OF AROUET            6
     THE DOOR HAS A CREAKING LATCH.  ...................   195    HUGH SELWIN:10      12
DOOR-BELLS
     GO! JANGLE THEIR DOOR-BELLS!   ....................    86    SALUTATION 2ND      35
DOORS
     OVER A THOUSAND GATES, OVER A THOUSAND DOORS ARE THE
          SOUNDS OF SPRING SINGING,  ...................   129    THE RIVER SONG      31
     HIS SUBTERRANEAN CHAMBER WITH A DOZEN DOORS,  .....   153    NEAR PERIGORD       61
     WHAT DOORS ARE OPEN TO FINE COMPLIMENT?"  .........   153    NEAR PERIGORD       75
     "OBVIOUSLY CROWNED LOVERS AT UNKNOWN DOORS,  ......   211    SEXTUS PROP: 2      48
DOOR-YARDS
     THEIR DOOR-YARDS WOULD SCARCELY KNOW THEM, OR PARIS.  208    SEXTUS PROP: 1      31
DOPE
     SYRUP AND SOOTHING DOPE,  .........................   259    ALF'S THIRD         15
DORATA
     I HAVE SEEN THE RUINED "DORATA."  .................   122    PROVINC DESERT      61
DORIA
     DORIA   ...........................................    67    DORIA                T
DORIAN
     SO SPOKE THE AUTHOR OF "THE DORIAN MOOD," ........    193    SIENA MI FE         16
D'ORLEANS
     IMAGE FROM D'ORLEANS  .............................   111    IMAGE ORLEANS        T
DOST
     THOUGH THOU WELL DOST WISH ME ILL  ................     8    NA AUDIART           1
     SIGHING AS THOU DOST THROUGH THE GOLDEN SPEECH."       43    SATIEMUS             6
DOTH
     AS THE MOON DOTH FROM THE SEA,  ...................    17    PRAISE YSOLT        32
     AND MANY A ONE NOW DOTH SURPASS  ..................    24    THUS NINEVEH        14
     AM HERE A POET, THAT DOTH DRINK OF LIFE  ..........    24    THUS NINEVEH        22
     DREW FULL THIS DAGGER THAT DOTH TREMBLE HERE. .....    31    PIERE VIDAL         42
     THAT DOTH BUT WOUND THE GOOD WITH IRE AND SADNESS.     37    THE YOUNG KING      24
     LO, HOW THE LIGHT DOTH MELT US INTO SONG:  ........    38    BALLATETTA           3
     AND THAT WHICH FLEETETH DOTH OUTRUN SWIFT TIME. ...    40    ROME                14
     THAT MAN DOTH PASS THE NET OF DAYS AND HOURS. .....    50    THE FLAME           10
     AND HOW THE WIND DOTH RAMM!  ......................   116    ANCIENT MUSIC        4
     MY ILL DOTH SHE TURN SWEET.  ......................   175    LANGUE D'OC: 3      48
     SO DOTH BEWILDER ME  ..............................   176    LANGUE D'OC: 3      64
     FROM FORM SEEN DOTH HE START, THAT, UNDERSTOOD, ...   249    DONNA MI PREGA      24
     LOVE DOTH NOT MOVE, BUT DRAWETH ALL TO HIM;  ......   250    DONNA MI PREGA      64
     NOR DOTH HE TURN  .................................   250    DONNA MI PREGA      65
DOTING
     OLD 'ERB WAS DOTING, SO THE RUMOUR RAN, ..........    264    ALF'S NINTH         13
DOUBLE
     AND DOUBLE THE TREES,  ............................   141    IDEA OF CHOAN       14
     DOUBLE TOWERS, WINGED ROOFS,  .....................   141    IDEA OF CHOAN       23
DOUBTFUL
     AND IT IS DOUBTFUL IF EVEN YOUR MANURE WILL BE RICH
          ENOUGH   ......................................   146    MONUMENTUM AER      7
     DOUBTFUL, SOMEWHAT, OF THE VALUE  .................   196    HUGH SELWIN:12       9
```

PAGE 110

	PAGE	TITLE	LINE
DOUBTLESS			
I SHALL HAVE, DOUBTLESS, A BOOM AFTER MY FUNERAL,	207	SEXTUS PROP: 1	23
DOUGHTY			
DELIGHT 'MID THE DOUGHTY.	66	THE SEAFARER	81
DOUGTH			
DOUGTH OF THE SHIRES,	258	ALF'S SECOND	2
DOUTH			
SAVE YOUR DOUTH AND YOUR STORY.	165	QUINTUS SEPTIM	19
DOWN			
SO MANY THOUSAND BEAUTIES ARE GONE DOWN TO AVERNUS,	38	LADY'S LIFE	3
SO MANY THOUSAND FAIR ARE GONE DOWN TO AVERNUS, ...	38	LADY'S LIFE	13
THAT WHICH STANDS FIRM IN THEE TIME BATTERS DOWN,	40	ROME	13
BREAK DOWN THE FOUR-SQUARE WALLS OF STANDING TIME.	49	OF SPLENDOUR	21
WHERE TIME IS SHRIVELLED DOWN TO TIME'S SEED CORN	50	THE FLAME	11
I SUPPOSE, WHEN POETRY COMES DOWN TO FACTS,	52	AU SALON	1
PORTENT. LIFE DIED DOWN IN THE LAMP AND FLICKERED,	68	APPARUIT	3
WALK DOWN LONGACRE RECITING SWINBURNE TO HERSELF, INAUDIBLY?	114	SIMULACRA	2
COMING DOWN FROM THE FAIR	119	THE GYPSY	14
WHIRL! CENTRIPETAL! MATE! KING DOWN IN THE VORTEX,	120	GAME OF CHESS	13
PEERING DOWN	121	PROVINC DESERT	15
HAVE SEEN THE COPPER COME DOWN	122	PROVINC DESERT	52
VINE-STRINGS A HUNDRED FEET LONG HANG DOWN FROM CARVED RAILINGS,	129	THE RIVER SONG	27
IF YOU ARE COMING DOWN THROUGH THE NARROWS OF THE RIVER KIANG,	131	RIVER-MER WIFE	26
AND I LET DOWN THE CRYSTAL CURTAIN	132	JEWEL STAIRS'	3
WAS GOVERNOR IN HEI SHU, AND PUT DOWN THE BARBARIAN RABBLE.	135	EXILE'S LETTER	37
THEY SET DOWN THEIR BURDENS,	140	MULBERRY ROAD	16
I HAD ALMOST TURNED DOWN THE PAGES.	158	PSYCHOLOG HOUR	5
"AND HERE I AM SINCE GOING DOWN OF SUN,	172	LANGUE D'OC: 1	18
TILL CHANGE HATH BROKEN DOWN	197	ENVOI (1919)	25
FOR A FEW PAGES DROUGHT DOWN FROM THE FORKED HILL UNSULLIED?	207	SEXTUS PROP: 1	20
PULLED DOWN BY A DEAL-WOOD HORSE;	208	SEXTUS PROP: 1	27
A FOREIGN LOVER BROUGHT DOWN HELEN'S KINGDOM	227	SEXTUS PROP:11	25
TRY PHOTOGRAPHS, WOLF DOWN THEIR ALE AND CAKES	236	MIDDLE-AGED	6
RAINS DOWN AND SO ENRICHES SOME STIFF CASE,	236	MIDDLE-AGED	17
FROM COMSTOCK'S SELF, DOWN TO THE MEANEST RESIDENT,	239	MOYEN SENSUEL	15
BROUGHT FROM GT. BRITAIN AND DUMPED DOWN A'TOP OF US,	240	MOYEN SENSUEL	64
DOWN RODYHEAVER'S PROPHYLACTIC SPINE,	246	MOYEN SENSUEL	225
SPREADING ITS RAYS, IT TENDETH NEVER DOWN	249	DONNA MI PREGA	29
DOWN THROUGH THE VALE OF GLOOM	257	BREAD BRIGADE	3
DOWN THERE IN CAMBRIDGE	258	ALF'S SECOND	9
DOWN THERE IN CLERKENWALL	259	ALF'S THIRD	13
WHEN WILL THIS SYSTEM LIE DOWN IN ITS GRAVE?	260	ALF'S FIFTH	4
I PUMP THE MARKET UP AND DOWN	266	ALF'S ELEVENTH	17
DOWN-FLOAT			
AMID THE PRECIPITATION, DOWN-FLOAT	202	AGE DEMANDED	52
DOWNWARD			
DOWNWARD,	62	A GIRL	4
DOWSON			
OF DOWSON; OF THE RHYMERS' CLUB;	193	SIENA MI FE	6
DOWSON FOUND HARLOTS CHEAPER THAN HOTELS;	193	SIENA MI FE	13
DOZE			
DID I 'EAR IT 'ARF IN A DOZE:	262	ALF'S SEVENTH	1
DOZEN			
I SUPPOSE THERE ARE A FEW DOZEN VERITIES	52	AU SALON	6
HIS SUBTERRANEAN CHAMBER WITH A DOZEN DOORS,	153	NEAR PERIGORD	61
DR.			
"WAS DR. DUNDAS.	194	MR. NIXON	13
DR. JOHNSON FLOURISHED;	196	HUGH SELWIN:12	24
THESE, AND YET GOD, AND DR. PARKHURST'S GOD, THE N. Y. JOURNAL	240	MOYEN·SENSUEL	45
STILL DR. B——'S	261	ALF'S SIXTH	18
DRAG			
DRAG ON THE SEVEN COACHES WITH OUTRIDERS.	141	IDEA OF CHOAN	3
DRAGGED			
YOU DRAGGED YOUR FEET WHEN YOU WENT OUT.	131	RIVER-MER WIFE	19

	PAGE	TITLE	LINE
DRAGON			
IT IS HE WHO HAS SLAIN THE DRAGON	237	ABU SALAMMAMM	8
DRAGON-LIKE			
THEY RIDE UPON DRAGON-LIKE HORSES, ...	132	AT TEN-SHIN	15
DRAGON-PEN			
TO-DAY FROM THE DRAGON-PEN.	139	SOUTH-FOLK	5
DRAGON-POND			
I LOOKED AT THE DRAGON-POND, WITH ITS WILLOW-COLOURED WATER	129	THE RIVER SONG	20
DRAGONS			
WITH DRAGONS WORKED UPON IT, ...	94	INSTRUCTIONS	18
THE CANOPY EMBROIDERED WITH DRAGONS	141	IDEA OF CHOAN	9
DRAGON-SCALES			
WITH RIPPLES LIKE DRAGON-SCALES, GOING GRASS GREEN ON THE WATER, ...	136	EXILE'S LETTER	52
DRANK			
WHO DRANK OF DEATH FOR OUR SALVACIOUN, ...	37	THE YOUNG KING	35
HE DRANK AMBROSIA, ...	199	MAUBERLEY: 2	2
DRAPED			
SAD GARMENT DRAPED ON HER SLENDER ARMS.	214	SEXTUS PROP: 4	20
DRAUGHT			
HAVE I DRUNK A DRAUGHT, SWEETER THAN SCENT OF MYRRH.	177	LANGUE D'OC: 4	23
DRAVE			
HE CRIED NO CRY WHEN THEY DRAVE THE NAILS	34	GOODLY FERE	37
DRAW			
SUCH AN ONE AS WOMEN DRAW AWAY FROM	15	FAMAM CANO	33
TO COME TO EARTH TO DRAW US FROM MISVENTURE, ...	37	THE YOUNG KING	34
LET THEM DRAW TOGETHER THE BONES OF THE METAL.	76	THE ALCHEMIST	53
BUT I DRAW PEN ON THIS BARGE	128	THE RIVER SONG	13
AND WERE SUCH NIGHTS THAT WE SHOULD "DRAW THE CURTAIN"	243	MOYEN SENSUEL	134
DRAWETH			
WHERE WANDERING THEM WIDEST DRAWETH.	65	THE SEAFARER	58
LOVE DOTH NOT MOVE, BUT DRAWETH ALL TO HIM;	250	DONNA MI PREGA	64
DRAWING			
FOR THERE ARE LEOPARDS DRAWING THE CARS.	108	CH'U YUAN	7
DRAWINGROOM			
SUBJECTIVELY. IN THE STUFFED-SATIN DRAWINGROOM	196	HUGH SELWIN:12	3
DRAWN			
SHE HATH DRAWN ME FROM MINE OLD WAYS, ...	4	LA FRAISNE	20
(SATURN AND MARS TO ZEUS DRAWN NEAR!)	10	FOR THIS YULE	18
WAVER AND SEEM NOT DRAWN TO EARTH, SO HE	39	FOR PSYCHE	5
THE TENTS TIGHT DRAWN, HORSES AT TETHER	155	NEAR PERIGORD	130
"OF" ROYAL AEMILIA, DRAWN ON THE MEMORIAL RAFT, ...	210	SEXTUS PROP: 2	10
LOOK DRAWN FROM LIKE, ...	250	DONNA MI PREGA	70
DREADED			
DARKLY HAST THOU DARED AND THE DREADED AETHER	68	APPARUIT	11
DREAM			
THEY DREAM US-TOWARD AND	6	CINO	15
ASK YE WHAT GHOSTS I DREAM UPON?	10	FOR THIS YULE	9
WHITHER MY DESIRE AND MY DREAM HAVE PRECEDED ME. ..	23	MARVOIL	33
FORGET AND REST AND DREAM THERE	47	FROM HEINE: 7	11
WE WHO ARE WISE BEYOND YOUR DREAM OF WISDOM, ...	50	THE FLAME	5
"COME. I HAVE HAD A LONG DREAM."	166	FISH & SHADOW	10
A SORT OF ARAB'S DREAM IN THE NIGHT.	262	ALF'S SEVENTH	16
DREAMED			
SO-SHU DREAMED, ...	118	ANCIENT WISDOM	1
AND HAVING DREAMED THAT HE WAS A BIRD, A BEE, AND A BUTTERFLY, ...	118	ANCIENT WISDOM	2
DREAMS			
DREAMS, WORDS, AND THEY ARE AS JEWELS, ...	6	CINO	5
EYES, DREAMS, LIPS, AND THE NIGHT GOES.	6	CINO	10
AS THEN ONLY IN DREAMS, ...	9	NA AUDIART	47
LO, I HAVE SEEN THEE BOUND ABOUT WITH DREAMS, ...	25	GUIDO INVITES	7
O WOMAN OF MY DREAMS, ...	91	DANCE FIGURE	2
EVEN IN MY DREAMS YOU HAVE DENIED YOURSELF TO ME	96	TO KALON	1
WERE DESOLATED BECAUSE SHE HAD TOLD THEM HER DREAMS.	214	SEXTUS PROP: 4	23
SO I, THE FIRES THAT LIT ONCE DREAMS	236	MIDDLE-AGED	13
DREAM'S			
THOUGHTS OF HER ARE OF DREAM'S ORDER:	72	DIEU! QU'IL	12

DREAMT -- DRIPS

	PAGE	TITLE	LINE
DREAMT			
I DREAMT THAT I WAS GOD HIMSELF	45	FROM HEINE: 4	1
DREAR			
DREAR ALL THIS EXCELLENCE, DELIGHTS UNDURABLE!	66	THE SEAFARER	88
DREARY			
AH, HOW SHALL YOU KNOW THE DREARY SORROW AT THE NORTH GATE,	133	FRONTIER GUARD	22
DREGS			
(SKOAL! WITH THE DREGS IF THE CLEAR BE GONE!)	10	FOR THIS YULE	7
DRESS			
BLACK IS THE PITCH O' THEIR WEDDING DRESS,	11	OF THE GIBBET	18
AND NOW YOU GRUMBLE BECAUSE YOUR DRESS DOES NOT FIT	102	LADIES	7
AND TRUTH SHOULD HERE BE CAREFUL OF HER THIN DRESS--	243	MOYEN SENSUEL	146
HOW SHALL WE DPESS 'EM ALL?	257	BREAD BRIGADE	22
FROM DRESS GOODS ADS, AND SPORTS.	266	ALF'S ELEVENTH	20
DREW			
DREW YOU YOUR SWORD MOST GALLANTLY	19	FOR E. MCC	7
CEASED UTTERLY. WELL, THEN I WAITED, DREW,	31	PIERE VIDAL	40
DREW FULL THIS DAGGER THAT DOTH TREMBLE HERE.	31	PIERE VIDAL	42
AND DREW ME APART	92	APRIL	2
ALL DREW THEIR PAY, AND AS THE PAY GREW LESS,	260	ALF'S FIFTH	9
DRIFT			
LETS DRIFT IN ON US THROUGH THE OLIVE LEAVES	39	BLANDULA	4
WE CARRY SINGING GIRLS, DRIFT WITH THE DRIFTING WATER,	128	THE RIVER SONG	5
DRIFTED			
DRIFTED . . . DRIFTED PRECIPITATE,	199	MAUBERLEY: 2	8
DRIFTED . . . DRIFTED PRECIPITATE,	199	MAUBERLEY: 2	8
DRIFTED ON	199	MAUBERLEY: 2	14
HERE DRIFTED	203	MAUBERLEY: 4	24
DRIFTING			
WE CARRY SINGING GIRLS, DRIFT WITH THE DRIFTING WATER,	128	THE RIVER SONG	5
INTELLIGENT MEN CAME DRIFTING IN FROM THE SEA AND FROM THE WEST BORDER,	134	EXILE'S LETTER	6
DRIFTS			
DUST DRIFTS OVER THE COURT-YARD,	108	LIU CH'E	2
THE SALMON-TROUT DRIFTS IN THE STREAM,	166	FISH & SHADOW	1
DRIFTS THROUGH THE AIR, AND THE SARCOPHAGUS	236	MIDDLE-AGED	10
DRINK			
DRINK OF THE WINDS THEIR CHILL SMALL-BEER	10	FOR THIS YULE	4
(SUCH AS I DRINK TO MINE FASHION)	10	FOR THIS YULE	15
DRINK YE A SKOAL FOR THE GALLOWS TREE!	11	OF THE GIBBET	1
DRINK WE THE COMRADES MERRILY	11	OF THE GIBBET	3
DRINK WE A SKOAL FOR THE GALLOWS TREE!	11	OF THE GIBBET	13
DRINK WE TO MARIENNE YDOLE,	11	OF THE GIBBET	15
DRINK WE THE LUSTY ROBBERS TWAIN,	11	OF THE GIBBET	17
DRINK WE SKOAL TO THE GALLOWS TREE!	12	OF THE GIBBET	25
BUT DRINK WE SKOAL TO THE GALLOWS TREE!	12	OF THE GIBBET	37
AM HERE A POET, THAT DOTH DRINK OF LIFE	24	THUS NINEVEH	22
AS LESSER MEN DRINK WINE.."	24	THUS NINEVEH	23
DRINK OUR IMMORTAL MOMENTS; WE "PASS THROUGH."	50	THE FLAME	6
I DRINK BY MY EASTERN WINDOW.	142	UNMOVING CLOUD	14
SO FEW DRINK OF MY FOUNTAIN.	158	PSYCHOLOG HOUR	7
SO FEW DRINK OF MY FOUNTAIN.	158	PSYCHOLOG HOUR	22
BEAUTY WOULD DRINK OF MY MIND.	158	PSYCHOLOG HOUR	28
DRINKS			
DRINKS IN AND CASTS BACK THE SUN.	141	IDEA OF CHOAN	10
AND NOW DRINKS NILE WATER LIKE A GOD,	222	SEXTUS PROP: 8	20
HE PROVIDES ME WITH WOMEN AND DRINKS.	237	ABU SALAMMAMM	17
DRINKST			
DRINKST IN LIFE OF EARTH, OF THE AIR, THE TISSUE	68	APPARUIT	7
DRIP			
WHEN OUR ELBOWS AND SWORDS DRIP THE CRIMSON	20	ALTAFORTE	34
DRIPPING			
TURN TO YOUR DRIPPING HORSES, BECAUSE OF A TUNE, UNDER AETNA?	208	SEXTUS PROP: 1	47
THE WATER DRIPPING FROM BELLEROPHON'S HORSE,	210	SEXTUS PROP. 2	1
DRIPS			
DRIPS FROM MY DEATHLESS PEN--AH, WELL-AWAY!	50	SILET	2

PAGE 113

DRIVE -- DRY

	PAGE	TITLE	LINE
DRIVE			
THAT PLAGUE AND BURN AND DRIVE ONE AWAY.	5	LA FRAISNE	36
I HA' SEEN HIM DRIVE A HUNDRED MEN	33	GOODLY FERE	17
MIND AND SPIRIT DRIVE ON THE FEATHERY BANNERS.	139	SOUTH-FOLK	9
YOU EITHER DRIVE THEM MAD, OR ELSE YOU BLINK AT THEIR SUICIDES,	145	SALUTATION 3RD	22
IF SHE WITH IVORY FINGERS DRIVE A TUNE THROUGH THE LYRE,	217	SEXTUS PROP: 5	27
FOR THE SUN SHALL DRIVE WITH BLACK HORSES,	220	SEXTUS PROP: 7	23
DRIVEN			
ABOUT HIS CASTLE, CATTLE DRIVEN OUT!	155	NEAR PERIGORD	125
TIME HAS DRIVEN ME OUT FROM THE FINE PLAISAUNCES,	167	OF AROUET	18
HAVE DRIVEN HIS WIFE FROM ONE RELIGIOUS EXCESS TO ANOTHER.	178	MOEURS CON: 1	8
DRIVES			
DRIVES THE CLEAR EMERALDS FROM THE BENDED GRASSES	38	BALLATETTA	9
AND EVENING DRIVES THEM ON THE EASTWARD-FLOWING WATERS.	131	AT TEN-SHIN	4
AMOR STANDS UPON YOU, LOVE DRIVES UPON LOVERS,	226	SEXTUS PROP: 11	11
DRONNE			
OVER THE DRONNE,	121	PROVINC DESERT	16
WHERE THE LOW DRONNE IS FILLED WITH WATER-LILIES.	152	NEAR PERIGORD	56
DROOPING			
WHEN WE SET OUT, THE WILLOWS WERE DROOPING WITH SPRING,	127	BOWMEN OF SHU	21
DROP			
RAINETH DROP AND STAINETH SLOP,	116	ANCIENT MUSIC	3
DRY WREATHS DROP THEIR PETALS,	221	SEXTUS PROP: 7	29
JUST DROP IT IN THE SLOT	267	ALF'S TWELFTH	13
DROPPING			
AND THE WHORES DROPPING IN FOR A WORD OR TWO IN PASSING,	117	THE LAKE ISLE	10
DROWNED			
FOR HERE WAS LOVE, WAS NOT TO BE DROWNED OUT.	73	THE PICTURE	2
DROWNS			
MY GREAT NOISE DROWNS THEIR CRIES,	266	ALF'S ELEVENTH	2
DRUE'S			
AS A FOOL THAT MOCKETH HIS DRUE'S DISDEIGN.	11	OF THE GIBBET	12
DRUGGED			
THE GODS OF DRUGGED SLEEP ATTEND ME,	147	BEFORE SLEEP	17
DRUGS			
OR ELSE YOU CONDONE THEIR DRUGS,	145	SALUTATION 3RD	23
DRUMS			
WHO HAS BROUGHT THE ARMY WITH DRUMS AND WITH KETTLE-DRUMS?	133	FRONTIER GUARD	12
WITH BOATS FLOATING, AND THE SOUND OF MOUTH-ORGANS AND DRUMS,	135	EXILE'S LETTER	51
DRUNK			
OH WE DRUNK HIS "HALE" IN THE GOOD RED WINE	33	GOODLY FERE	13
AND LI PO ALSO DIED DRUNK.	117	EPITAPHS	3
AND WE WERE DRUNK FOR MONTH ON MONTH, FORGETTING THE KINGS AND PRINCES.	134	EXILE'S LETTER	5
THE FOREMAN OF KAN CHU, DRUNK, DANCED	135	EXILE'S LETTER	28
AND I WAS DRUNK, AND HAD NO THOUGHT OF RETURNING.	135	EXILE'S LETTER	48
AND THE VERMILIONED GIRLS GETTING DRUNK ABOUT SUNSET,	136	EXILE'S LETTER	55
SHE WILL BE DRUNK IN THE DITCH, BUT YOU, PEPITA,	162	CABARET DANCER	47
HAVE I DRUNK A DRAUGHT, SWEETER THAN SCENT OF MYRRH.	177	LANGUE D'OC: 4	23
"WHEREFROM FATHER ENNIUS, SITTING BEFORE I CAME, HATH DRUNK."	210	SEXTUS PROP: 2	7
YOU WERE DRUNK.	228	SEXTUS PROP: 12	9
DRUNKEN			
"NIGHT DOGS, THE MARKS OF A DRUNKEN SCURRY,	211	SEXTUS PROP: 2	49
DRUNKENLY			
WHO NOW GOES DRUNKENLY OUT	128	BEAU TOILET	8
DRY			
AND THAT THE WORLD SHOULD DRY AS A DEAD LEAF,	36	FRANCESCA	9
THAT HE ON DRY LAND LOVELIEST LIVETH,	64	THE SEAFARER	13
GLAD TO LEND ONE DRY CLOTHING.	121	PROVINC DESERT	27
OF DRY AIR, AS CLEAR AS METAL.	146	CANTILATIONS	12
THE FISH SHALL SWIM IN DRY STREAMS.	220	SEXTUS PROP: 7	27
THE DRY EARTH PANTS AGAINST THE CANICULAR HEAT,	221	SEXTUS PROP: 8	4

DRY -- DUO

	PAGE	TITLE	LINE
DRY (CONTINUED)			
DRY WREATHS DROP THEIR PETALS,	221	SEXTUS PROP: 7	29
DRYAD			
THE DRYAD STANDS IN MY COURT-YARD	110	TEMPORA	2
DU			
DU PARC MONCEAU,	160	DANS OMNIBUS	13
TO MADAME DU CHATELET	167	OF AROUET	ST
DUCHESS			
WILL MEET A DUCHESS AND AN EX-DIPLOMAT'S WIDOW	163	CABARET DANCER	64
THAN THE DUCHESS OF KAUGH.	260	ALF'S FOURTH	13
DUCTILE			
FOR THE FEMALE IS DUCTILE.	82	THE CONDOLENCE	12
DUD			
RUDYARD THE DUD YARD,	259	ALF'S FOURTH	1
DUDS			
WHOM CAN THESE DUDS ATTACK?	258	ALF'S THIRD	1
DUE			
GIVE ME IN DUE TIME, I BESEECH YOU, A LITTLE TOBACCO-SHOP,	117	THE LAKE ISLE	2
ED ERAN DUE IN UNO, ED UNO IN DUE;	157	NEAR PERIGORD	EPI
ED ERAN DUE IN UNO, ED UNO IN DUE;	157	NEAR PERIGORD	EPI
DUELS			
AMIABLE AND HARMONIOUS PEOPLE ARE PUSHED INCONTINENT INTO DUELS,	227	SEXTUS PROP:12	5
DULCE			
NON "DULCE" NON "ET DECOR" . . .	190	HUGH SELWYN: 4	12
DULL			
ONE DULL MAN, DULLING AND UXORIOUS,	61	PORTRAIT FEMME	9
THE DULL ROUND TOWERS ENCROACHING ON THE FIELD,	155	NEAR PERIGORD	129
ONE TO BE DULL IN;	168	OF AROUET	26
DULLARDS			
DUNDERING DULLARDS!	257	BREAD BRIGADE	26
DULLING			
ONE DULL MAN, DULLING AND UXORIOUS,	61	PORTRAIT FEMME	9
DULNESS			
GO LIKE A BLIGHT UPON THE DULNESS OF THE WORLD;	88	COMMISSION	18
HER BOURGEOIS DULNESS IS DEFERRED.	163	CABARET DANCER	76
HER PRESENT DULNESS . . .	163	CABARET DANCER	77
OH WELL, HER PRESENT DULNESS . . .	163	CABARET DANCER	78
DULNESS HERSELF, THAT ABJECT SPIRIT, CHORTLES	239	MOYEN SENSUEL	31
DULY			
AND I SHALL FOLLOW THE CAMP, I SHALL BE DULY CELEBRATED FOR SINGING THE AFFAIRS OF YOUR CAVALRY.	216	SEXTUS PROP: 5	21
AND IN HIS DAILY WALKS DULY CAPSIZE HIM.	245	MOYEN SENSUEL	204
DUM			
DUM CAPITOLIUM SCANDET	96	DUM CAPITOLIUM	T
DUMB			
THAT 'THOUT HIM, SAVE THE ASPEN, WERE AS DUMB	21	IN DURANCE	47
DUMB-BORN			
GO, DUMB-BORN BOOK,	197	ENVOI (1919)	1
DUMP			
LET US DUMP OUR HATREDS INTO ONE BUNCH AND BE DONE WITH THEM,	146	CANTILATIONS	2
DUMPED			
BROUGHT FROM GT. BRITAIN AND DUMPED DOWN A'TOP OF US,	240	MOYEN SENSUEL	64
DUMPY			
"I HATE A DUMPY WOMAN"	238	MOYEN SENSUEL	EPI
D'UN			
JE VIS DES CANARDS SUR LE BORD D'UN LAC MINUSCULE,	160	DANS OMNIBUS	10
AUPRES D'UN PETIT ENFANT GAI, BOSSU.	160	DANS OMNIBUS	11
DUNDAS			
"WAS DR. DUNDAS.	194	MR. NIXON	13
DUNDERING			
DUNDERING DULLARDS!	257	BREAD BRIGADE	26
D'UNE			
PORTRAIT D'UNE FEMME	61	PORTRAIT FEMME	T
LES YEUX D'UNE MORTE	160	DANS OMNIBUS	1
LES YEUX D'UNE MORTE	160	DANS OMNIBUS	30
DUO			
"UN E DUO FANNO TRE,,"	163	CABARET DANCER	83

DUPONT -- EACH

	PAGE	TITLE	LINE
DUPONT			
WHETHER MR. DUPONT AND THE GUN-SHARKS	268	ANOTHER BIT	7
DURABLE			
DAYS LITTLE DURABLE,	66	THE SEAFARER	82
A DURABLE PASSION;	196	HUGH SELWIN:12	8
DURANCE			
IN DURANCE	20	IN DURANCE	T
DURER			
PERFECT AS DURER!	235	TO WHISTLER	7
DUSK			
UPON A DUSK THAT IS COME FROM MARS AND STAYS.	248	DONNA MI PREGA	21
DUST			
AS DARK RED CIRCLES FILLED WITH DUST.	16	PRAISE YSOLT	13
BUT BURIED DUST AND RUSTED SKELETON.	41	HER MONUMENT	3
PREFER MY CLOAK UNTO THE CLOAK OF DUST	67	THE CLOAK	7
DUST DRIFTS OVER THE COURT-YARD,	108	LIU CH'E	2
I DESIRED MY DUST TO BE MINGLED WITH YOURS	130	RIVER-MER WIFE	12
LIGHT RAIN IS ON THE LIGHT DUST	137	OF DEPARTURE	EPI
YOU'D HAVE MEN'S HEARTS UP FROM THE DUST	151	NEAR PERIGORD	1
"HE WHO IS NOW VACANT DUST	219	SEXTUS PROP: 6	26
AS THE FINE DUST, IN THE HID CELL	236	MIDDLE-AGED	8
DUSTS			
WHEN OUR TWO DUSTS WITH WALLER'S SHALL BE LAID,	197	ENVOI (1919)	23
DWARFS			
THE DARK DWARFS BLOW AND BOW THERE	47	FROM HEINE: 7	27
DWELL			
FIT FOR YOUR SPIRIT TO DWELL IN.	110	COITUS	6
DWELLING			
AND SO FORTH, AUGUSTUS. "VIRGIN ARABIA SHAKES IN HER INMOST DWELLING."	216	SEXTUS PROP: 5	14
DWELT			
THE LIGHT BECAME HER GRACE AND DWELT AMONG	38	BALLATETTA	1
DYED			
HER OVERSKIRT IS THE SAME SILK DYED IN PURPLE,	140	MULBERRY ROAD	14
THEIR PUNIC FACES DYED IN THE GORGON'S LAKE;	211	SEXTUS PROP: 2	31
IF SHE GOES IN A GLEAM OF COS, IN A SLITHER OF DYED STUFF,	217	SEXTUS PROP: 5	36
AND IN THE DYED PAGES OF CALVUS,	230	SEXTUS PROP:12	74
DYES			
FROM THE MOLTEN DYES OF THE WATER	75	THE ALCHEMIST	14
DYING			
AND SHE IS DYING PIECE-MEAL	83	THE GARDEN	
GO TO THE BOURGEOISE WHO IS DYING OF HER ENNUIS,	88	COMMISSION	
"DELIA, I WOULD LOOK ON YOU, DYING."	168	OF AROUET	4
SUCH A DEATH IS WORTH DYING.	213	SEXTUS PROP: 3	2
OVER THE DYING HALF-WITS BLOW,	265	ALF'S TENTH	
DYKE			
HENRY VAN DYKE, WHO THINKS TO CHARM THE MUSE YOU PACK HER IN	239	MOYEN SENSUEL	2
DYNASTIC			
TO THE DYNASTIC TEMPLE, WITH WATER ABOUT IT CLEAR AS BLUE JADE,	135	EXILE'S LETTER	5
WHERE LAY THE DYNASTIC HOUSE OF THE GO.	138	CITY OF CHOAN	
E			
GUARDA! AHI, GUARDA! CH' E BE'A!	96	AESTHETICS	
CH' E BE'A.	97	AESTHETICS	2
"UN E DUO FANNO TRE,"	163	CABARET DANCER	8
"LA DONNA E MOBILE."	163	CABARET DANCER	8
BLAGUEUR! "CON GLI OCCHI ONESTI E TARDI,"	181	MOEURS CON: 7	
E.			
FOR E. MCC	19	FOR E. MCC	
(I. E. THESE SONGS).	81	TENZONE	
E. P. ODE POUR L'ELECTION DE SON SEPULCHRE	187	E. P. ODE	
NATIONAL SONG (E. C.)	272	NATIONAL SONG	
'E			
AN' 'E LOOKS LIKE A TOFF.	260	ALF'S FOURTH	1
EACH			
WILL LAUGH YOUR VERSES TO EACH OTHER,	14	FAMAM CANO	2
THEIR ECHOES PLAY UPON EACH OTHER IN THE TWILIGHT	16	PRAISE YSOLT	2
AND EACH TO-DAY 'VAILS LESS THAN YESTERE'EN,	37	THE YOUNG KING	2
LET EACH MAN VISAGE THIS YOUNG ENGLISH KING	37	THE YOUNG KING	2

PAGE 116

EACH -- EARTH

	PAGE	TITLE	LINE
EACH (CONTINUED)			
OR, AS OUR LAUGHTERS MINGLE EACH WITH EACH,	43	SATIEMUS	7
OR, AS OUR LAUGHTERS MINGLE EACH WITH EACH,	43	SATIEMUS	7
ONE AVERAGE MIND--WITH ONE THOUGHT LESS, EACH YEAR.	61	PORTRAIT FEMME	10
CULLING FROM EACH A FAIR TRAIT	105	DOMPNA POIS	18
AND HIGH OVER THE WILLOWS, THE FINE BIRDS SING TO EACH OTHER, AND LISTEN,	129	THE RIVER SONG	28
AND THE GIRLS SINGING BACK AT EACH OTHER,	136	EXILE'S LETTER	59
OUR HORSES NEIGH TO EACH OTHER	137	TAKING LEAVE	8
EACH PLACE STRONG.	151	NEAR PERIGORD	14
EACH MAN WHERE HE CAN, WEARING OUT THE DAY IN HIS MANNER.	218	SEXTUS PROP: 5	58
EACH MAN WANTS THE POMEGRANATE FOR HIMSELF;	227	SEXTUS PROP:12	4
A TEMPERATE MAN, A THIN POTATIONIST, EACH DAY	245	MOYEN SENSUEL	199
THOU ART SO FAIR ATTIRED THAT EVERY MAN AND EACH	250	DONNA MI PREGA	89
BLOOD ON EACH TIRED FANG	261	ALF'S SIXTH	11
EAGE			
DE SON EAGE; THE CASE PRESENTS	187	E. P. ODE	19
EAGER			
ALL THIS ADMONISHETH MAN EAGER OF MOOD,	65	THE SEAFARER	51
EAGER AND READY, THE CRYING LONE-FLYER,	65	THE SEAFARER	63
BE EAGER TO FIND NEW EVILS AND NEW GOOD,	89	COMMISSION	24
EAGER TO CATCH MY WORDS,	90	SURGIT FAMA	10
EAGER TO SPREAD THEM WITH RUMOUR;	90	SURGIT FAMA	11
SO EAGER AND ALERT,	105	DOMPNA POIS	13
MY MUSE IS EAGER TO INSTRUCT ME IN A NEW GAMUT, OR GAMBETTO,	216	SEXTUS PROP: 5	11
EAGERLY			
WHY DO YOU LOOK SO EAGERLY AND SO CURIOUSLY INTO PEOPLE'S FACES,	103	CODA	2
SHE DOES NOT GET UP THE STAIRS SO EAGERLY;	116	THE TEA SHOP	4
EAGLE			
IN ICY FEATHERS; FULL OFT THE EAGLE SCREAMED	64	THE SEAFARER	24
EAGLED			
EAGLED AND THUNDERED AS JUPITER PLUVIUS,	13	MESMERISM	15
EALING			
POSSIBLY, BUT IN EALING	195	HUGH SELWIN:11	3
EAR			
BRIGHT NOTES AGAINST THE EAR,	45	FROM HEINE: 5	6
CAUGHT IN THE UNSTOPPED EAR;	187	E. P. ODE	10
NEITHER CALLIOPE NOR APOLLO SUNG THESE THINGS INTO MY EAR,	217	SEXTUS PROP: 5	25
EAR			
DID I 'EAR IT 'ARF IN A DOZE:	262	ALF'S SEVENTH	1
DID I 'EAR IT WHILE PICKIN' 'OPS;	262	ALF'S SEVENTH	3
EARL			
AND FOR THIS, EVERY EARL WHATEVER, FOR THOSE SPEAKING AFTER--	66	THE SEAFARER	73
EARLY			
ONE MUST OF NEEDS BE A HANG'D EARLY RISER	13	MESMERISM	3
CRYING--"KWAN, KUAN," FOR THE EARLY WIND, AND THE FEEL OF IT.	129	THE RIVER SONG	29
THE LEAVES FALL EARLY THIS AUTUMN, IN WIND.	131	RIVER-MER WIFE	22
I WILL NOT FLATTER YOU WITH AN EARLY DEATH,	145	SALUTATION 3RD	26
THERE IS A TRELLIS FULL OF EARLY ROSES,	153	NEAR PERIGORD	72
NOW IN VENICE, 'STORANTE AL GIARDINO, I WENT EARLY,	163	CABARET DANCER	79
"YOU ARE A VERY EARLY INSPECTOR OF MISTRESSES.	225	SEXTUS PROP:10	34
TO SELL THE PAPERS EARLY,	200	ALF'S ELEVENTH	6
EARN			
THAT TOM-BOY WHO CAN'T EARN HER LIVING,	162	CABARET DANCER	44
EARRINGS			
HER EARRINGS ARE MADE OF PEARL,	140	MULBERRY ROAD	12
EARS			
AH, I COVERED HIS EARS WITH THEM	48	FROM HEINE: 7	31
SHE WHO HAD NOR EARS NOR TONGUE SAVE IN HER HANDS,	157	NEAR PERIGORD	187
"BREATHE NOT THE WORD TO-MORROW IN HER EARS"	161	CABARET DANCER	EPI
IN MY EARS	176	LANGUE D'OC: 3	78
I GUZZLE WITH OUTSTRETCHED EARS.	214	SEXTUS PROP: 4	12
AND YET AGAIN, AND NEWLY RUMOUR STRIKES ON MY EARS.	226	SEXTUS PROP:11	17
EARTH			
FINDS THE EARTH AS BITTER	9	NA AUDIART	44

PAGE 117

EARTH -- EAT

	PAGE	TITLE	LINE
EARTH (CONTINUED)			
HAVE THE EARTH IN MOCKERY, AND ARE KIND TO ALL, ...	20	IN DURANCE	27
ALL THE BLIND EARTH KNOWS NOT TH' EMPRISE	25	GUIDO INVITES	5
SUCH GLORY OF THE EARTH? OR WHO WILL WIN	32	PIERE VIDAL	58
TO COME TO EARTH TO DRAW US FROM MISVENTURE, ...	37	THE YOUNG KING	34
WAVER AND SEEM NOT DRAWN TO EARTH, SO HE	39	FOR PSYCHE	5
AM SOLVED AND BOUND IN, THROUGH AUGHT HERE ON EARTH,	51	THE FLAME	33
FROST FROZE THE LAND, HAIL FELL ON EARTH THEN, ...	64	THE SEAFARER	33
FRAME ON THE FAIR EARTH 'GAINST FOES HIS MALICE,	66	THE SEAFARER	76
LORDLY MEN, ARE TO EARTH O'ERGIVEN, ...	66	THE SEAFARER	95
DRINKST IN LIFE OF EARTH, OF THE AIR, THE TISSUE	68	APPARUIT	7
FROM THE WIDE EARTH AND THE OLIVE, ...	75	THE ALCHEMIST	21
THEY SHALL INHERIT THE EARTH.	83	THE GARDEN	7
FAILS NOT THE EARTH NOW.	90	SURGIT FAMA	7
FOR IT IS CERTAIN THAT SHE HAS LEFT ON THIS EARTH	115	SOCIAL ORDER	17
AS FOR YOU, YOU WILL ROT IN THE EARTH, ...	146	MONUMENTUM AER	6
EARTH SHALL BRING WHEAT FROM BARLEY, ...	220	SEXTUS PROP: 7	24
THE DRY EARTH PANTS AGAINST THE CANICULAR HEAT, ...	221	SEXTUS PROP: 8	4
THE BABY NEW TO EARTH AND SKY	272	THE BABY	1
"THE BABY NEW TO EARTH AND SKY,"	272	THE BABY	9
EAR-THE-LESS			
THOMAS LARRON "EAR-THE-LESS,"	11	OF THE GIBBET	6
EARTHEN			
AND ALL ARROGANCE OF EARTHEN RICHES, ...	66	THE SEAFARER	83
EARTHERN			
ORGIES OF VINTAGES, AN EARTHERN IMAGE OF SILENUS	211	SEXTUS PROP: 2	29
EARTHLY			
EARTHLY GLORY AGETH AND SEARETH.	66	THE SEAFARER	91
AND FOR WHAT EARTHLY REASON THEY REMAIN.	244	MOYEN SENSUEL	160
EARTH'S			
WHEN THE TEMPESTS KILL THE EARTH'S FOUL PEACE, ...	28	ALTAFORTE	8
FOR THIS THERE'S NO MOOD-LOFTY MAN OVER EARTH'S MIDST, ...	65	THE SEAFARER	40
ON EARTH'S SHELTER COMETH OFT TO ME, ...	65	THE SEAFARER	62
NO MAN AT ALL GOING THE EARTH'S GAIT, ...	66	THE SEAFARER	92
QUICK EYES GONE UNDER EARTH'S LID, ...	191	HUGH SELWYN: 5	6
EARTH-WEAL			
THAT ANY EARTH-WEAL ETERNAL STANDETH	66	THE SEAFARER	68
EASE			
WHO CAN DEMOLISH AT SUCH POLISHED EASE	46	TRANSLATOR	3
THERE IS NO EASE IN ROYAL AFFAIRS, WE HAVE NO COMFORT.	127	BOWMEN OF SHU	11
EAST			
THE LITTLE HILLS TO EAST OF US, THOUGH HERE WE	21	IN DURANCE	39
OUT CAME THE EAST OF KAN FOREMAN AND HIS COMPANY.	134	EXILE'S LETTER	23
AND WENT BACK TO THE EAST MOUNTAINS	136	EXILE'S LETTER	68
THE SUN RISES IN SOUTH EAST CORNER OF THINGS	140	MULBERRY ROAD	1
I STOP IN MY ROOM TOWARD THE EAST, QUIET, QUIET,	142	UNMOVING CLOUD	6
NOR HOUSES MODELLED UPON THAT OF JOVE IN EAST ELIS,	209	SEXTUS PROP: 1	67
EASTERN			
THE EASTERN WIND BRINGS THE GREEN COLOUR INTO THE ISLAND GRASSES AT YEI-SHU, ...	129	THE RIVER SONG	23
I DRINK BY MY EASTERN WINDOW.	142	UNMOVING CLOUD	14
EAST-LOOKING			
THE TREES IN MY EAST-LOOKING GARDEN	142	UNMOVING CLOUD	17
EASTWARD			
EASTWARD AVOID THE HOUR OF ITS DECLINE, ...	69	THE NEEDLE	2
EASTWARD THE ROAD LIES, ...	121	PROVINC DESERT	18
AUBETERRE IS EASTWARD, ...	121	PROVINC DESERT	19
EASTWARD-FLOWING			
AND EVENING DRIVES THEM ON THE EASTWARD-FLOWING WATERS.	131	AT TEN-SHIN	
EASY			
OH, IS IT EASY ENOUGH?	151	NEAR PERIGORD	1
HOW EASY THE MOVING FINGERS; IF HAIR IS MUSSED ON HER FOREHEAD, ...	217	SEXTUS PROP: 5	29
EAT			
I HA' SEEN HIM EAT O' THE HONEY-COMB	34	GOODLY FERE	5
NOR EAT THE SWEET NOR FEEL THE SORRY, ...	66	THE SEAFARER	9
FOURTEEN HUNTERS STILL EAT IN THE STABLES OF	97	THE BELLAIRES	1
IF I HAD MORE GRUB TO EAT.	269	SAFE AND SOUND	2

PAGE 118

EATABLE -- EGYPTIAN

	PAGE	TITLE	LINE
EATABLE			
THE STERILE EGG THAT IS STILL EATABLE:	240	MOYEN SENSUEL	49
EAU-FORTE			
TURNED FROM THE "EAU-FORTE	198	MAUBERLEY: 1	1
EC.			
NEMESIANUS, EC. 4.	186	HUGH SELWYN	EPI
ECHO			
HAVE HEARD THE ECHO OF MY HEELS,	81	TENZONE	12
TO THE CO-OPS, A ECHO OR SOMETHIN'?	262	ALF'S SEVENTH	9
ECHOES			
THEIR ECHOES PLAY UPON EACH OTHER IN THE TWILIGHT	16	PRAISE YSOLT	9
AND ARE UNTOUCHED BY ECHOES OF THE WORLD.	21	IN DURANCE	34
ECLIPSES			
NOR THE MODUS OF LUNAR ECLIPSES	228	SEXTUS PROP:12	26
ECONOMICAL			
OF THE NEW ECONOMICAL THEORIES	273	NATIONAL SONG	15
ECONOMICS			
TALK ECONOMICS,	261	ALF'S SIXTH	3
ED			
ED ERAN DUE IN UNO, ED UNO IN DUE;	157	NEAR PERIGORD	EPI
ED ERAN DUE IN UNO, ED UNO IN DUE;	157	NEAR PERIGORD	EPI
EDDIES			
YOU WENT INTO FAR KU-TO-YEN, BY THE RIVER OF SWIRLING EDDIES,	130	RIVER-MER WIFE	16
AND ON THE BACK-SWIRLING EDDIES,	131	AT TEN-SHIN	6
EDDY			
THEY EDDY BEFORE THE GATE OF THE BARONS.	141	IDEA OF CHOAN	8
EDGE			
THEY REACH ME NOT, TOUCH ME SOME EDGE OR THAT,	20	IN DURANCE	5
GO WITH YOUR EDGE AGAINST THIS,	88	COMMISSION	19
THE EDGE, UNCERTAIN, BUT A MEANS OF BLENDING	196	HUGH SELWIN:12	14
TILL YOU MAY TAKE YOUR CHOICE: TO FEEL THE EDGE OF SATIRE OR	240	MOYEN SENSUEL	65
EDGE, THAT IS, AND POINT TO THE DART,	250	DONNA MI PREGA	78
YOUR GRANDAD GOT THE ROUGH EDGE.	259	ALF'S FOURTH	10
EDITOR			
WHO'S NOW THE EDITOR OF THE ATLANTIC,	239	MOYEN SENSUEL	14
AS THE EDITOR OF THE CENTURY SAYS IN PRINT,	243	MOYEN SENSUEL	137
RADWAY WAS IGNORANT AS AN EDITOR,	246	MOYEN SENSUEL	219
EDITORIAL			
PIMPING, CONCEITED, PLACID, EDITORIAL,	238	MOYEN SENSUEL	6
EDITORS			
SAITH 'TWAS THE WORTHIEST OF EDITORS.	63	PHASELLUS ILLE	2
FROM THESE HE (RADWAY) LEARNT, FROM PROVOSTS AND FROM EDITORS UNYIELDING	240	MOYEN SENSUEL	51
EDWARD'S			
AND EDWARD'S MISTRESSES STILL LIGHT THE STAGE,	103	CABARET DANCER	73
E'EN			
WERE LACK-LAND CINO, E'EN AS I AM,	7	CINO	35
E'EN ITS DENIERS CAN NOW HEAR THE TRUTH,	248	DONNA MI PREGA	4
E'EN THOUGH HE MEET NOT WITH HATE	249	DONNA MI PREGA	43
OR LOSETH POWER, E'EN LOST TO MEMORY.	249	DONNA MI PREGA	48
E'ER			
SEEKING E'ER THE NEW-LAID RAST-WAY	7	CINO	50
THAT ANY FOLK E'ER HAD, HAST FROM US TAKEN;	37	THE YOUNG KING	19
THAN E'ER WERE HEARD OF BY OUR LORD CH.... J....	241	MOYEN SENSUEL	100
EFFECT			
BY QUALITY, BUT IS ITS OWN EFFECT UNENDINGLY	249	DONNA MI PREGA	30
EFFIGIES			
NOR THE MONUMENTAL EFFIGIES OF MAUSOLUS,	209	SEXTUS PROP: 1	68
EFFORT			
OF LITERARY EFFORT,	196	HUGH SELWIN:12	11
EGG			
THE STERILE EGG THAT IS STILL EATABLE:	240	MOYEN SENSUEL	49
EGG-WHITE			
GREEN ARSENIC SMEARED ON AN EGG-WHITE CLOTH,	113	L'ART, 1910	1
EGO			
EGO AUTEM JOVIALIS	101	AMITIES	21
EGYPTIAN			
HERE'S PEPITA, TALL AND SLIM AS AN EGYPTIAN MUMMY,	162	CABARET DANCER	18

EH -- ELSE

	PAGE	TITLE	LINE
EH			
"CINO?" "OH, EH, CINO POLNESI	6	CINO	25
. . . EH? . . . THEY MOSTLY HAD GREY EYES, ...	7	CINO	40
EH, MAKE IT UP?	248	PIERROTS	25
EHEU			
ALAS, EHEU, ONE QUESTION THAT SORELY VEXES	244	MOYEN SENSUEL	161
EIGHT			
THE EIGHT PLY OF THE HEAVENS	142	UNMOVING CLOUD	3
THE EIGHT PLY OF THE HEAVENS ARE DARKNESS, ...	142	UNMOVING CLOUD	11
EIGHTEEN			
WHO HAD LAUGHED ON EIGHTEEN SUMMERS, ...	111	SOCIETY	3
"I ROSE IN EIGHTEEN MONTHS;	194	MR. NIXON	11
EIGHTH			
THE FLOOD OF LIMBS UPON EIGHTH AVENUE	245	MOYEN SENSUEL	189
ALF'S EIGHTH BIT	263	ALF'S EIGHTH	T
EIGHT-PENCE			
AND WONDER IF MY DAY'S THREE AND EIGHT-PENCE	268	ANOTHER BIT	11
EIGHTY			
YOU'LL WONDER THAT AN OLD MAN OF EIGHTY	168	OF AROUET	35
EITHER (3)			
EIUS			
VERMES HABENT EIUS VULTUM	101	AMITIES	19
EKE			
AND HUMBLE EKE, THAT THE YOUNG ENGLISH KING	37	THE YOUNG KING	37
ELAIN			
ELAIN, TIREIS, ALCMENA	75	THE ALCHEMIST	14
ELAIN, TIREIS, ALCMENA, ...	76	THE ALCHEMIST	49
ELAIN, TIREIS, ALLODETTA	76	THE ALCHEMIST	61
ELBOWS			
WHEN OUR ELBOWS AND SWORDS DRIP THE CRIMSON	29	ALTAFORTE	34
ELDERLY			
THEY CONSIDER THE ELDERLY MIND	104	THE SEEING EYE	6
ELDERS			
AND HIS ELDERS	96	AESTHETICS	10
ELECTION			
ELECTION WILL NOT COME VERY SOON, ...	265	ALF'S TENTH	13
ELECTOR			
CLEAR SIGHT'S ELECTOR!	13	MESMERISM	21
ELEGANCE			
OBSERVED THE ELEGANCE OF CIRCE'S HAIR	187	E. P. ODE	15
ELEGANT			
AND WITH A TONGUE BY NO MEANS TOO ELEGANT, ...	113	FORMIANUS LADY	6
ELEGY			
THE FIRST HAS WRITTEN A LONG ELEGY TO "CHLORIS,"	118	THREE POETS	3
ELEMENT			
SO SIMPLY ELEMENT AS WHAT I AM.	32	PARACELSUS	5
IN US ALONE THE ELEMENT OF CALM."	32	PARACELSUS	13
ELEMENTS			
TO GIVE THESE ELEMENTS A NAME AND A CENTRE!	84	ORTUS	4
YOU ARE MINGLED WITH THE ELEMENTS UNBORN;	84	ORTUS	10
ELEVENTH			
ALF'S ELEVENTH BIT	266	ALF'S ELEVENTH	T
ELF			
AND LITTLE RED ELF WORDS CRYING "A SONG,"	16	PRAISE YSOLT	15
LITTLE GREY ELF WORDS CRYING FOR A SONG, ...	16	PRAISE YSOLT	16
BUT STILL CAME THE LEAF WORDS, LITTLE BROWN ELF WORDS	17	PRAISE YSOLT	33
THE WORDS, LITTLE ELF WORDS	17	PRAISE YSOLT	52
ELIMINATION			
BY CONSTANT ELIMINATION	202	AGE DEMANDED	29
REFINEMENT OF MEDIUM, ELIMINATION OF SUPERFLUITIES,	202	AGE DEMANDED	48
ELIS			
NOR HOUSES MODELLED UPON THAT OF JOVE IN EAST ELIS,	209	SEXTUS PROP: 1	67
ELLUM			
I WRAPPED MY TEARS IN AN ELLUM LEAF	4	LA FRAISNE	25
ELM-OAK			
THAT GREW ELM-OAK AMID THE WOLD.	3	THE TREE	5
ELSE			
GREAT MINDS HAVE SOUGHT YOU--LACKING SOMEONE ELSE.	61	PORTRAIT FEMME	6
PREGNANT WITH MANDRAKES, OR WITH SOMETHING ELSE ...	61	PORTRAIT FEMME	18
NOR ANY WHIT ELSE SAVE THE WAVE'S SLASH, ...	65	THE SEAFARER	47
WELL DO THIS AS ANYTHING ELSE.	100	ARIDES	5

ELSE -- EMBANKMENT

	PAGE	TITLE	LINE
ELSE (CONTINUED)			
HE WAS UNCERTAIN WHY HE SHOULD TRY TO FEEL LIKE ANYTHING ELSE,	118	ANCIENT WISDOM	3
YOU EITHER DRIVE THEM MAD, OR ELSE YOU BLINK AT THEIR SUICIDES,	145	SALUTATION 3RD	22
OR ELSE YOU CONDONE THEIR DRUGS,	145	SALUTATION 3RD	23
THAT SOME ONE ELSE HAS PAID FOR,	163	CABARET DANCER	57
AND SOMEONE ELSE WILL BE PLEASED AT THE DEATH OF THEODORUS,	164	QUINTUS SEPTIM	2
THERE IS A PLACE--BUT NO ONE ELSE KNOWS IT--	166	FISH & SHADOW	14
WEEPING THAT WE CAN FOLLOW NAUGHT ELSE.	168	OF AROUET	34
RECKING NAUGHT ELSE BUT THAT HER GRACES GIVE	197	ENVOI (1919)	10
NOR ANYTHING ELSE OF IMPORTANCE.	228	SEXTUS PROP:12	30
HE WILL UNDOUBTEDLY CHAIN SOMEONE ELSE TO THIS FOUNTAIN,	238	ABU SALAMMAMM	31
ELUCIDATION			
ARE A COMPLETE ELUCIDATION OF DEATH.	209	SEXTUS PROP: 1	69
ELUDED			
YOUR GRASP, I HAVE ELUDED.	51	THE FLAME	43
ELUSIVE			
WE CAN'T PRESERVE THE ELUSIVE "MICA SALIS,"	163	CABARET DANCER	70
'EM			
AND HOLDE HER SIDES WHERE SWELLING LAUGHTER CRACKS 'EM	239	MOYEN SENSUEL	33
WAS GOT ABROAD, WHAT BETTER LUCK DO YOU WISH 'EM,	240	MOYEN SENSUEL	60
THOUGH SOME APPROVED OF THEM, AND SOME DEPLORED 'EM,	242	MOYEN SENSUEL	108
WITH SIGNS AS MANY, THAT SHALL REPRESENT 'EM	244	MOYEN SENSUEL	167
WHEN THOROUGHLY SOCIALIZED PRINTERS WANT TO PRINT 'EM.	244	MOYEN SENSUEL	168
POWER THAT COMPELS 'EM	244	MOYEN SENSUEL	171
TO BE SO MUCH ALIKE THAT EVERY DOG THAT SMELLS 'EM,	244	MOYEN SENSUEL	172
"AND RATE 'EM UP AT JUST SO MUCH PER HEAD,	244	MOYEN SENSUEL	181
TO RUN SUCH TOURS. HE CALLS 'EM. . . . HOUSE PARTIES.	245	MOYEN SENSUEL	210
UPON THE NATIONAL BRAINS AND SET 'EM ACHIN'.	245	MOYEN SENSUEL	216
YOU CAN NOT GET CHEAP BOOKS, EVEN IF YOU NEED 'EM).	246	MOYEN SENSUEL	218
WE'LL SEND 'EM MOUCHIN' 'OME,	257	BREAD BRIGADE	7
PLENTY TO RIGHT OF 'EM,	257	BREAD BRIGADE	17
PLENTY TO LEFT OF 'EM,	257	BREAD BRIGADE	18
YES, WOT IS LEFT OF 'EM,	257	BREAD BRIGADE	19
HOW SHALL WE DRESS 'EM ALL?	257	BREAD BRIGADE	22
SEE 'EM GO SLOUCHING THERE,	257	BREAD BRIGADE	24
FED 'EM WITH HOGWASH!	257	BREAD BRIGADE	29
WANT RUSSIA TO SAVE 'EM	258	ALF'S SECOND	3
WANT RUSSIA TO SAVE 'EM,	258	ALF'S SECOND	5
LENIN TO SAVE 'EM, TROTSKY TO SAVE 'EM	258	ALF'S SECOND	6
LENIN TO SAVE 'EM, TROTSKY TO SAVE 'EM	258	ALF'S SECOND	6
(AND VALETS TO SHAVE 'EM)	258	ALF'S SECOND	7
AN IDEA BETWEEN 'EM	258	ALF'S SECOND	12
I SAYS! 'AVE YOU SEEN 'EM?	258	ALF'S SECOND	13
TOLD 'EM THAT GLORY	259	ALF'S FOURTH	3
PLENTY TO RIGHT OF 'EM,	259	ALF'S THIRD	8
PLENTY TO LEFT OF 'EM,	259	ALF'S THIRD	9
YEH! WHAT IS LEFT OF 'EM,	259	ALF'S THIRD	10
TOLD 'EM TO DIE IN WAR, AND THEN TO SAVE,	260	ALF'S FIFTH	2
WHO ATE THE PROFITS, AND WHO LOCKED 'EM IN	260	ALF'S FIFTH	18
TO MAKE 'EM COOIER.	269	SAFE AND SOUND	16
NOT THAT NICE BRITONS READ 'EM,	272	NATIONAL SONG	10
HAVE BANK SHARKS TO BLEED 'EM	272	NATIONAL SONG	12
EMAIL			
OF WOVEN WALLS DEEP PATTERNED, OF EMAIL,	49	OF SPLENDOUR	14
POPPIES AND DAY'S EYES IN THE GREEN EMAIL	157	NEAR PERIGORD	171
EMANATION			
FOLLOWING HIS OWN EMANATION.	250	DONNA MI PREGA	83
EMANUELE			
EMANUELE RE D' ITALIA,	182	MOEURS CON: 7	21
EMATHIAN			
TO LEAD EMATHIAN HORSES AFIELD,	210	SEXTUS PROP: 5	2
EMBANKING			
"Y" PAWNS, CLEAVING, EMBANKING!	120	GAME OF CHESS	12
EMBANKMENT			
WALKING ON THE CHELSEA EMBANKMENT.	182	MOEURS CON: 7	25

PAGE 121

EMBANKMENT -- EN

```
                                                          PAGE     TITLE              LINE
EMBANKMENT (CONTINUED)
    IF YOU GIT OFF THE EMBANKMENT. .....................  263     ALF'S EIGHTH         21
EMBERS
    AS FLAME LEAVETH THE EMBERS SO WENT SHE UNTO NEW
       FORESTS ........................................    17     PRAISE YSOLT         43
    WHERE TIME BURNS BACK ABOUT TH' ETERNAL EMBERS.  ...   50     THE FLAME            21
EMBITTERED
    I WHO AM AS MUCH EMBITTERED  ......................   102     TO DIVES              2
EMBRACE
    HE TRIED TO EMBRACE A MOON  .......................   117     EPITAPHS              4
EMBRACED
    TO HOLD EMBRACED, AND WILL NOT HER FORSAKE  .......   172     LANGUE D'OC: 1       28
EMBRACES
    IN HOW MANY VARIED EMBRACES, OUR CHANGING ARMS,  ...  220     SEXTUS PROP: 7       10
EMBROIDERED
    THE CANOPY EMBROIDERED WITH DRAGONS  ..............   141     IDEA OF CHOAN         9
EMENDATION
    EMENDATION, CONSERVATION OF THE "BETTER TRADITION,"   202     AGE DEMANDED         47
EMERALD
    I HAVE SEEN THE FIELDS, PALE, CLEAR AS AN EMERALD,    122     PROVINC DESERT       54
EMERALDS
    DRIVES THE CLEAR EMERALDS FROM THE BENDED GRASSES      38     BALLATETTA            9
EMERGED
    SUCH ASPECT WAS PRESENTED TO ME, ME RECENTLY EMERGED
       FROM MY VISIONS, .............................    225     SEXTUS PROP:10       32
EMERGES
    THE SLEEK HEAD EMERGES  ..........................    204     MEDALLION             5
EMETIC
    NOR DID DISGUST PROVE SUCH A STRONG EMETIC  .......   242     MOYEN SENSUEL       128
EMOTION
    "WHERE IS THE VERTIGO OF EMOTION?"  ...............    85     SALUTATION 2ND       13
    ONLY EMOTION REMAINS. ............................    114     EPILOGUE              9
    EMOTION IS BORN OUT OF HABIT. ....................    139     SOUTH-FOLK            3
EMOTIONAL
    OF A SORT OF EMOTIONAL ANAEMIA. ..................     83     THE GARDEN            4
EMOTIONS
    YOUR EMOTIONS? ...................................    114     EPILOGUE             10
EMPEROR
    AND THE EMPEROR IS AT KO. ........................    129     THE RIVER SONG       32
    THE EMPEROR IN HIS JEWELLED CAR GOES OUT TO INSPECT
       HIS FLOWERS, .................................    129     THE RIVER SONG       35
EMPEROR'S
    AND I HAVE MOPED IN THE EMPEROR'S GARDEN, AWAITING
       AN ORDER-TO-WRITE! ...........................    129     THE RIVER SONG       19
EMPIRE
    AND THUS THE EMPIRE IS MAINTAINED. ...............    178     MOEURS CON: 1        20
    AND EXPOUND THE DISTENTIONS OF EMPIRE, ...........    207     SEXTUS PROP: 1       18
    ABU SALAMMAMM--A SONG OF EMPIRE  .................    237     ABU SALAMMAMM         T
EMPLOYER
    FROM A GREAT EMPLOYER LIKE SELFRIDGE  ............    264     ALF'S EIGHTH         33
EMPLOYER'S
    WAS FOUND IN HIS EMPLOYER'S CASH. HE LEARNED THE LAY
       OF CHEAPER PLACES, ..........................     243     MOYEN SENSUEL       143
EMPLOYMENT
    AN ANXIOUS SENTIMENT WAS HIS EMPLOYMENT, .........    245     MOYEN SENSUEL       194
EMPRISE
    ALL THE BLIND EARTH KNOWS NOT TH' EMPRISE  .......     25     GUIDO INVITES         5
EMPTINESS
    NO TRUMPETS FILLED WITH MY EMPTINESS, ............    219     SEXTUS PROP: 6       15
EMPTY
    EMPTY ARE THE WAYS, .............................     112     IONE, DEAD            1
    EMPTY ARE THE WAYS OF THIS LAND  ................     112     IONE, DEAD            2
    EMPTY ARE THE WAYS OF THIS LAND  ................     112     IONE, DEAD            6
    MOUTHS BITING EMPTY AIR, ........................     200     MAUBERLEY: 2         34
    NO MESSENGER SHOULD COME WHOLLY EMPTY, ..........,    214     SEXTUS PROP: 4        8
EMPTY-HEADED
    OVER THE EMPTY-HEADED, AND THE SLOW  ............     265     ALF'S TENTH           6
EN
    EN ROBE DE PARADE. ..............................      83     THE GARDEN          EPI
    WALKED OVER EN BERTRAN'S OLD LAYOUT,. ...........     122     PROVINC DESERT       39
    THE BIRDS OF ETSU HAVE NO LOVE FOR EN, IN THE NORTH,  139     SOUTH-FOLK            2
```

PAGE 122

EN -- ENGLAND

	PAGE	TITLE	LINE
EN (CONTINUED)			
BERTRANS, EN BERTRANS, LEFT A FINE CANZONE:	151	NEAR PERIGORD	5
AND OUR EN BERTRANS WAS IN ALTAFORT, ...	151	NEAR PERIGORD	20
EN BERTRANS, A TOWER-ROOM AT HAUTEFORT, ...	154	NEAR PERIGORD	95
OR NO ONE SEES IT, AND EN BERTRANS PROSPERED?	155	NEAR PERIGORD	126
OR TAKE EN BERTRANS?	156	NEAR PERIGORD	169
JE VIS LES COLONNES ANCIENNES EN "TOC"	160	DANS OMNIBUS	12
EN COMPARAISON AVEC LAQUELLE LA ROSE	199	MAUBERLEY: 2	EPI
M. POM-POM ALLAIT EN GUERRE	273	M. POM-POM	1
ENCHASSES			
ENCHASSES DANS UN VISAGE STUPIDE	160	DANS OMNIBUS	3
ENCOUNTER			
THE ENCOUNTER	110	THE ENCOUNTER	T
THERE WERE UPON THE BED NO SIGNS OF A VOLUPTUOUS ENCOUNTER, ...	225	SEXTUS PROP:10	36
ENCROACHING			
THE DULL ROUND TOWERS ENCROACHING ON THE FIELD, ...	155	NEAR PERIGORD	129
ENCRUSTED			
THE PUG-DOG'S FEATURES ENCRUSTED WITH TALLOW	161	CABARET DANCER	11
END			
TO THE END THAT YOU SEE, FRIENDS:	22	MARVOIL	15
IN HER IS THE END OF BREEDING.	83	THE GARDEN	8
I FEAR YOU WILL COME TO A BAD END.	94	INSTRUCTIONS	4
YOU WILL COME TO A VERY BAD END.	94	INSTRUCTIONS	9
AND BEFORE THE END OF THE DAY WE WERE SCATTERED LIKE STARS, OR RAIN.	135	EXILE'S LETTER	33
AND ALL THIS COMES TO AN END.	136	EXILE'S LETTER	63
IT IS LIKE THE FLOWERS FALLING AT SPRING'S END	136	EXILE'S LETTER	73
WHAT IS THE USE OF TALKING, AND THERE IS NO END OF TALKING, ...	136	EXILE'S LETTER	75
THERE IS NO END OF THINGS IN THE HEART.	136	EXILE'S LETTER	76
AND LAUGHTER IS THE END OF ALL THINGS.	147	POST MORTEM	5
THE VERY SPUR'S END, BUILT ON SHEEREST CLIFF, ...	153	NEAR PERIGORD	58
END FACT. TRY FICTION. LET US SAY WE SEE	154	NEAR PERIGORD	94
END THE DISCUSSION, RICHARD GOES OUT NEXT DAY	156	NEAR PERIGORD	157
O PLASMATOUR, THAT THOU END NOT THE NIGHT, ...	177	LANGUE D'OC: 4	6
CAME AT LAST, TO THAT ARCADIA.	199	MAUBERLEY: 2	4
THE FIRST DAY'S END, IN THE NEXT NOON;	203	MAUBERLEY: 4	3
BE AT AN END.	238	ABU SALAMMAMM	33
OFTEN HIS POWER MEETETH WITH DEATH IN THE END	249	DONNA MI PREGA	39
ENDEAVOUR			
HE HAD ATTENDED COUNTRY CHRISTIAN ENDEAVOUR CONVENTIONS, ...	242	MOYEN SENSUEL	102
ENDING			
WHERE THE LOWER AND HIGHER HAVE ENDING;	196	HUGH SELWYN:12	16
ENDITE			
'TIS OF MY COUNTRY THAT I WOULD ENDITE, ...	238	MOYEN SENSUEL	1
ENDS			
ENDS WITH A WILLINGNESS-TO-OBLIGE.	99	EPITAPH	2
SO ENDS THAT STORY.	123	PROVINC DESERT	77
ENDS OUR DISCUSSION. ARNAUT ENDS	156	NEAR PERIGORD	160
ENDS OUR DISCUSSION. ARNAUT ENDS	156	NEAR PERIGORD	160
ENDURE			
COULD YOU ENDURE SUCH PROMISCUITY?	228	SEXTUS PROP:12	10
ENDURED			
HARDSHIP ENDURED OFT.	64	THE SEAFARER	3
ENDURES			
FANNING THE GRASS SHE WALKED ON THEN, ENDURES:	92	GENTILDONNA	4
ENDYMION'S			
ENDYMION'S NAKED BODY, BRIGHT BAIT FOR DIANA,"	220	SEXTUS PROP: 7	15
ENEMY			
THE ENEMY IS SWIFT, WE MUST BE CAREFUL.	127	BOWMEN OF SHU	20
ENFANT			
AUPRES D'UN PETIT ENFANT GAI, BOSSU.	160	DANS OMNIBUS	11
ENGAGED			
ENGAGED IN PERFECTING THE CATALOGUE, ...	193	SIENA MI FE	2
ENGIRDLED			
LORD POWERFUL, ENGIRDLED ALL WITH MIGHT, ...	172	LANGUE D'OC: 1	2
ENGLAND			
"DEAR POUND, I AM LEAVING ENGLAND."	159	PSYCHOLOG HOUR	43

ENGLAND -- ENOUGH

	PAGE	TITLE	LINE
ENGLAND (CONTINUED)			
GREAT IS THE KING OF ENGLAND AND GREATLY TO BE FEARED,	237	ABU SALAMMAMM	15
MANHOOD OF ENGLAND,	258	ALF'S SECOND	1
THE DESTINIES OF ENGLAND WERE ALMOST SOLD	264	ALF'S NINTH	6
IN ENGLAND? I'LL SAY YES!	267	ALF'S ELEVENTH	22
THERE IS NO LAND LIKE ENGLAND	272	NATIONAL SONG	1
ENGLISH			
PLANH FOR THE YOUNG ENGLISH KING	36	THE YOUNG KING	T
AGAINST THE DEATH OF THE YOUNG ENGLISH KING.	36	THE YOUNG KING	5
IN TAKING FROM THEM THE YOUNG ENGLISH KING,	37	THE YOUNG KING	13
BUT HAD ITS LIFE IN THE YOUNG ENGLISH KING	37	THE YOUNG KING	21
LET EACH MAN VISAGE THIS YOUNG ENGLISH KING	37	THE YOUNG KING	29
AND HUMBLE EKE, THAT THE YOUNG ENGLISH KING	37	THE YOUNG KING	37
AND HIS LAUD BEYOND THEM REMAIN 'MID THE ENGLISH,	66	THE SEAFARER	79
AND HAD HIS WAY WITH THE OLD ENGLISH KING,	151	NEAR PERIGORD	26
THE ENGLISH RUBAIYAT WAS STILL-BORN	192	YEUX GLAUQUES	15
THERE ARE NO BANKS LIKE ENGLISH BANKS	272	NATIONAL SONG	3
ENGLISHMAN			
WHERE AN ENGLISHMAN IS FREE	272	NATIONAL SONG	6
ENGLISHMEN			
WITH THE MOST BANK-CLERKLY OF ENGLISHMEN?	195	HUGH SELWIN:11	4
I LEND YOU ENGLISHMEN HOT AIR	269	SAFE AND SOUND	3
I LEND YOU ENGLISHMEN HOT AIR	269	SAFE AND SOUND	5
ENGLOBED			
YOU ARE ENGLOBED IN MY SAPPHIRE.	169	PHANOPOEIA	10
ENGRAVER'S			
THE ENGRAVER'S.	198	MAUBERLEY: 1	8
ENGULF			
SWEEP BACK UPON ME AND ENGULF MY MIND!	51	HORAE BEATAE	2
ENGULPHS			
FLAT CALM ENGULPHS MY JIBS,	247	PIERROTS	2
ENI			
HIDMEN GAR TOI PANTH', HOS' ENI TROIEI	187	E. P. ODE	9
ENJOY			
AND THE DEVIRGINATED YOUNG LADIES WILL ENJOY THEM	208	SEXTUS PROP: 1	40
ENJOYED			
THAT I, MYSELF, MIGHT HAVE ENJOYED THEM.	101	AMITIES	5
ENJOYMENT			
STILL HE WAS NOT GIVEN UP TO BRUTE ENJOYMENT,	245	MOYEN SENSUEL	193
ENNIUS			
"WHEREFROM FATHER ENNIUS, SITTING BEFORE I CAME, HATH DRUNK."	210	SEXTUS PROP: 2	7
ENNUIS			
GO TO THE BOURGEOISE WHO IS DYING OF HER ENNUIS,	88	COMMISSION	9
ENOUGH			
BUT I KNOW NOW, THEY BOTH WERE GOOD ENOUGH.	44	FROM HEINE: 2	8
THERE IS ENOUGH IN WHAT I CHANCE TO SAY.	59	SILET	4
IT IS ENOUGH THAT WE ONCE CAME TOGETHER;	59	SILET	5
IT IS ENOUGH THAT WE ONCE CAME TOGETHER;	59	SILET	9
IT IS ENOUGH THAT WE ONCE CAME TOGETHER;	59	SILET	11
IT IS, AND IS NOT, I AM SANE ENOUGH,	69	SUB MARE	1
OH, SUN ENOUGH!	70	THE PLUNGE	18
I HAVE DETESTED YOU LONG ENOUGH.	89	A PACT	2
I AM OLD ENOUGH NOW TO MAKE FRIENDS.	89	A PACT	5
YOU ARE NOT OLD ENOUGH TO HAVE DONE MUCH MISCHIEF,	94	INSTRUCTIONS	16
AND YOU CARING ENOUGH TO PAY IT.	135	EXILE'S LETTER	45
AND IT IS DOUBTFUL IF EVEN YOUR MANURE WILL BE RICH ENOUGH	146	MONUMENTUM AER	7
RIGHT ENOUGH? THEN READ BETWEEN THE LINES OF UC ST. CIRC,	151	NEAR PERIGORD	3
OH, IS IT EASY ENOUGH?	151	NEAR PERIGORD	15
LITTLE ENOUGH?	154	NEAR PERIGORD	114
OH, I KNOW WELL ENOUGH.	158	PSYCHOLOG HOUR	17
ENOUGH, ENOUGH AND IN PLENTY	219	SEXTUS PROP: 6	19
ENOUGH, ENOUGH AND IN PLENTY	219	SEXTUS PROP: 6	19
THERE ARE ENOUGH WOMEN IN HELL,	223	SEXTUS PROP: 9	14
QUITE ENOUGH BEAUTIFUL WOMEN,	223	SEXTUS PROP: 9	15
OH, OH, AND ENOUGH OF THIS,	227	SEXTUS PROP:11	29
THE WHICH, NO CAT HAS EYES ENOUGH	236	MIDDLE-AGED	22

ENQUIRED -- EQUALS

	PAGE	TITLE	LINE
ENQUIRED			
NOT ONE HAS ENQUIRED THE CAUSE OF THE WORLD, ...	228	SEXTUS PROP:12	25
ENRICHES			
RAINS DOWN AND SO ENRICHES SOME STIFF CASE, ...	236	MIDDLE-AGED	17
ENSHROUDED			
WHEN THE FAIRY FLAMES ENSHROUDED	45	FROM HEINE: 3	3
ENSLAVED			
O REMNANT ENSLAVED!	92	THE REST	2
ENSLAVED-BY-CONVENTION			
GO ALSO TO THE NERVE-WRACKED, GO TO THE ENSLAVED-BY-CONVENTION, ...	88	COMMISSION	2
ENTAILED			
GO TO THE WOMAN ENTAILED.	88	COMMISSION	15
ENTANGLED			
SHALL I ENTRUST MYSELF TO ENTANGLED SHADOWS, ...	212	SEXTUS PROP: 3	7
ENTER			
I BESEECH YOU ENTER YOUR LIFE.	84	ORTUS	12
YOU ENTER AND PASS HALL AFTER HALL, ...	180	MOEURS CON: 5	18
ENTER THAT MUCH FOR HIS BAIL.	225	SEXTUS PROP:10	23
ENTERED			
THE TREE HAS ENTERED MY HANDS, ...	62	A GIRL	1
ENTERS			
DAWN ENTERS WITH LITTLE FEET	83	THE GARRET	6
ENTICED			
AND THE OTHER WOMAN "HAS NOT ENTICED ME	215	SEXTUS PROP: 4	29
ENTREATED			
KINDLY ENTREATED, AND BEEN BROUGHT WITHIN	3	THE TREE	7
ENTRUST			
SHALL I ENTRUST MYSELF TO ENTANGLED SHADOWS, ...	212	SEXTUS PROP: 3	7
WHO, WILL BE THE NEXT MAN TO ENTRUST HIS GIRL TO A FRIEND?	227	SEXTUS PROP:12	1
ENTWINED			
SURELY YOU ARE BOUND AND ENTWINED, ...	84	ORTUS	9
ENUMERATION			
SOLDIER, THE ENUMERATION OF WOUNDS; THE SHEEP-FEEDER, OF EWES;	218	SEXTUS PROP: 5	56
ENVIES			
ENVIES ITS VIGOUR . . . AND DEPLORES THE TECHNIQUE,	155	NEAR PERIGORD	142
ENVOI			
ENVOI	19	FOR E. MCC	ST
ENVOI (1919)	197	ENVOI (1919)	T
ENVY			
LET US EXPRESS OUR ENVY OF THE MAN WITH A STEADY JOB AND NO WORRY ABOUT THE FUTURE.	94	INSTRUCTIONS	2
ENVY HAS TAKEN YOUR ALL, ...	165	QUINTUS SEPTIM	18
IS THE ORNAMENTAL GODDESS FULL OF ENVY?	221	SEXTUS PROP: 8	11
EOS			
NOT THE HYRCANIAN SEABOARD, NOT IN SEEKING THE SHORE OF EOS.	227	SEXTUS PROP:11	38
EPIGRAM			
AND THE THIRD WRITES AN EPIGRAM TO CANDIDIA.	118	THREE POETS	7
EPILOGUE			
EPILOGUE	114	EPILOGUE	T
EPILOGUES			
LEFT HIM AS EPILOGUES.	200	MAUBERLEY: 2	37
EPITAPH			
EPITAPH	99	EPITAPH	T
AT ANY RATE I SHALL NOT HAVE MY EPITAPH IN A HIGH ROAD.	213	SEXTUS PROP: 3	38
EPITAPHS			
EPITAPHS	117	EPITAPHS	T
EPITHET			
HAD WE EVER SUCH AN EPITHET CAST UPON US!!	104	ANCORA	16
EQUAL			
TO SAY MANY THINGS IS EQUAL TO HAVING A HOME.	215	SEXTUS PROP: 4	28
WAS VENUS EXACERBATED BY THE EXISTENCE OF A COMPARABLE EQUAL?	221	SEXTUS PROP: 8	10
SMEARED O'ER THE LOT IN EQUAL QUANTITIES.	244	MOYEN SENSUEL	174
EQUALS			
ALL MEN, IN LAW, ARE EQUALS, ...	189	HUGH SELWYN: 3	21

EQUIPMENTS -- ESSENCE

	PAGE	TITLE	LINE
EQUIPMENTS			
WITHOUT FOOTMEN AND EQUIPMENTS?	167	OF AROUET	3
EQUIPPED			
NOR IS IT EQUIPPED WITH A FRIGIDAIRE PATENT;	209	SEXTUS PROP: 1	59
EQUITABLE			
EQUITABLE WEIGHT ON YOUR SHOULDERS;	214	SEXTUS PROP: 4	4
'ER			
AN A-SLOSHIN' ROUND WITH 'ER MOP, ...	271	OLE KATE	10
ERAN			
ED ERAN DUE IN UNO, ED UNO IN DUE;	157	NEAR PERIGORD	EPI
ERASED			
SCRATCHED AND ERASED WITH AL AND OCHAISOS.	154	NEAR PERIGORD	100
ERASERS			
WE HAVE KEPT OUR ERASERS IN ORDER.	207	SEXTUS PROP: 1	11
ERAT			
ERAT HORA	40	ERAT HORA	T
'ERB			
OLD 'ERB WAS DOTING, SO THE RUMOUR RAN, ...	264	ALF'S NINTH	13
ERE			
AND MEN MYRTLES, ERE THE NIGHT	24	THUS NINEVEH	3
ERE THE NIGHT SLAY LIGHT	24	THUS NINEVEH	18
THAT, ERE A MAN'S TIDE GO, TURN IT TO TWAIN.	66	THE SEAFARER	70
THAT HE WILL WORK ERE HE PASS ONWARD, ...	66	THE SEAFARER	75
BUT YOU, SIR, HAD BETTER TAKE WINE ERE YOUR DEPARTURE, ...	137	OF DEPARTURE	EPI
ERE LOVE KNOW MODERATIONS, ...	220	SEXTUS PROP: 7	26
'ERE			
"WE ARE 'ERE MET TOGETHER	270	OF 600 M.P.'S	1
WE ARE 'ERE MET TOGETHER	270	OF 600 M.P.'S	5
EREBUS			
OUT OF EREBUS, THE FLAT-LYING BREADTH, ...	76	THE ALCHEMIST	44
OUT OF EREBUS, OUT OF THE FLAT WASTE OF AIR, LYING BENEATH THE WORLD;	76	THE ALCHEMIST	46
ERI			
ERI MEN HAI TE KUDONIAI--IBYCUS.	87	THE SPRING	EPI
ERINNA			
ERINNA IS A MODEL PARENT, ...	103	THE PATTERNS	1
EROS			
OF EROS, A RETROSPECT.	200	MAUBERLEY: 2	33
ERUDITE			
WERE THERE AN ERUDITE OR VIOLENT PASSION, ...	230	SEXTUS PROP:12	63
ERUPTION			
WORDS THAT WERE WING'D AS HER SPARKS IN ERUPTION,	13	MESMERISM	14
ESCAPE			
ESCAPE! THERE IS, O IDIOT, NO ESCAPE, ...	226	SEXTUS PROP:11	4
ESCAPE! THERE IS, O IDIOT, NO ESCAPE, ...	226	SEXTUS PROP:11	4
EVEN THERE, NO ESCAPE \	227	SEXTUS PROP:11	37
WHO, SINCE THEIR WIT'S UNKNOWN, ESCAPE THE GALLOWS.	238	MOYEN SENSUEL	4
ESCAPED			
YOU ARE ESCAPED FROM GREAT PERIL, ...	224	SEXTUS PROP: 9	23
ESCAPES			
BLOCKED LIGHTS WORKING IN. ESCAPES. RENEWAL OF CONTEST.	120	GAME OF CHESS	15
ESCHEWED			
THUS HE ESCHEWED THE BRIGHT RED-WALLED CAFES AND	245	MOYEN SENSUEL	205
ESCRITOIRES			
HER ESCRITOIRES LAY SHUT BY THE BED-FEET.	214	SEXTUS PROP: 4	21
ESPAVIN			
REPLEVIN, ESTOPPEL, ESPAVIN AND WHAT NOT.	98	THE BELLAIRES	27
ESPECIAL			
WE WERE IN ESPECIAL BORED WITH MALE STUPIDITY, ...	82	THE CONDOLENCE	8
ESPECIALLY			
AND WITH THEM, AND WITH YOU ESPECIALLY	134	EXILE'S LETTER	7
ESPECIALLY ON BOOKS, LEST KNOWLEDGE BREAK IN	245	MOYEN SENSUEL	215
ESSENCE			
WAS GROWN SO FREE AN ESSENCE, OR BECOME	32	PARACELSUS	4
WHOSE BLUBBERING YOWLS YOU TAKE FOR PASSION'S ESSENCE;	240	MOYEN SENSUEL	68
NAY, NOR HIS VERY ESSENCE OR HIS MODE;	248	DONNA MI PREGA	15
THERE, BEYOND COLOUR, ESSENCE SET APART, ...	250	DONNA MI PREGA	84

PAGE 126

EST -- EUPHRATES

```
                                                          PAGE     TITLE             LINE
EST
    DEO LAUS, QUOD EST SEPULTUS,         .................  101     AMITIES             18
    "CARMEN EST MAIGRE, UN TRAIT DE BISTRE   ...........   162     CABARET DANCER      24
    EST GROSSIERE ET LE PARFUM DES VIOLETTES UN   .......  199     MAUBERLEY: 2       EPI
    M. POM-POM EST AU SENAT          ........................  273     M. POM-POM           6
ESTABLISHED
    STILL SIGH OVER ESTABLISHED AND NATURAL FACT    ......  148     FRATRES MINORE      3
ESTATE
    MR. HECATOMB STYRAX, THE OWNER OF A LARGE ESTATE        178     MOEURS CON: 1       1
EST-CE
    "EST-CE QUE VOUS AVEZ VU DES AUTRES--DES
       CAMARADES--AVEC DES SINGES OU DES OURS?"    .......  119     THE GYPSY          EPI
ESTIMATE
    AND I AM AFRAID OF NUMERICAL ESTIMATE,       ............ 224     SEXTUS PROP:10      6
ESTOPPEL
    REPLEVIN, ESTOPPEL, ESPAVIN AND WHAT NOT.       .........   98     THE BELLAIRES      27
ESTRANGED
    MY FRIENDS ARE ESTRANGED, OR FAR DISTANT,       .........  142     UNMOVING CLOUD      8
ESTRANGEMENT
    SO TO THIS LAST ESTRANGEMENT, TAIRIRAN!     ............  157     NEAR PERIGORD     185
    TO THE FINAL ESTRANGEMENT;        .......................  199     MAUBERLEY: 2       15
ET
    "ET ALDIRAR AB LOR BORDON--"     ..................... 153     NEAR PERIGORD      90
    ET ALORS JE VIS BIEN DES CHOSES         ................. 160     DANS OMNIBUS        0
    ET DEUX PETITES FILLES GRACILES,        .................. 160     DANS OMNIBUS       14
    ET DES PIGEONNES         .................................. 160     DANS OMNIBUS       17
    ET TOUS LES GAZONS DIVERS        ......................... 160     DANS OMNIBUS       21
    ET TOUTES LES FLEURS        .............................. 160     DANS OMNIBUS       28
    NON "DULCE" NON "ET DECOR"      . . . ..............    190     HUGH SELWYN: 4     12
    "QU'EST CE QU'ILS SAVENT DE L'AMOUR, ET    ............  199     MAUBERLEY: 2       EPI
    EST GROSSIERE ET LE PARFUM DES VIOLETTES UN    ....... 199     MAUBERLEY: 2       EPI
ETAIENT
    DONT TOUS LES AUTRES TRAITS ETAIENT BANALS,    .......  160     DANS OMNIBUS        4
ETAIT
    IL ETAIT COMME UN TOUT PETIT GARCON        .............. 181     MOEURS CON: 7       3
ETC.
    NINE LAWYERS, FOUR COUNSELS, ETC.,       .................   98     THE BELLAIRES      28
    MONUMENTUM AERE, ETC.        ............................. 146     MONUMENTUM AER      T
    THE TEA-ROSE TEA-GOWN, ETC.          ..................... 189     HUGH SELWYN: 3      1
ETCETERA
    WOE! WOE, ETCETERA. . . .       ....................    43     MR. HOUSMAN         10
    OH, WOE, WOE, WOE, ETCETERA. . . .       ..............    44     MR. HOUSMAN         15
    ETCETERA, ETCETERA, AND ETCETERA?       ................. 167     OF AROUET          14
    ETCETERA, ETCETERA, AND ETCETERA?       ,................ 167     OF AROUET          14
    ETCETERA, ETCETERA, AND ETCETERA?       ................. 167     OF AROUET          14
ETERNAL
    MIRRORS UNSTILL OF THE ETERNAL CHANGE?      ..............   39     BLANDULA           12
    ALL, ALL OUR LIFE'S ETERNAL MYSTERY!     ...............   41     HER MONUMENT       25
    WHERE TIME BURNS BACK ABOUT TH' ETERNAL EMBERS.    ...   50     THE FLAME          21
    THOU HOODED OPAL, THOU ETERNAL PEARL,     ..............   50     THE FLAME          29
    THAT ANY EARTH-WEAL ETERNAL STANDETH       .............   66     THE SEAFARER       68
    BE IN ME AS THE ETERNAL MOODS          ...................   67     DORIA               1
    BEAUTY IS NOT ETERNAL, NO MAN HAS PERENNIAL FORTUNE,    223     SEXTUS PROP: 9     20
ETERNALLY
    THEY ARE FOOLS ETERNALLY.           .......................   34     GOODLY FERE        52
ETHICAL
    OF A MODERN AND ETHICAL CULT,         ....................  178     MOEURS CON: 1      12
ETSU
    THE DAI HORSE NEIGHS AGAINST THE BLEAK WIND OF ETSU,    139     SOUTH-FOLK          1
    THE BIRDS OF ETSU HAVE NO LOVE FOR EN, IN THE NORTH,    139     SOUTH-FOLK          2
EUHENIA
    EUHENIA, IN SHORT SKIRTS, SLAPS HER WIDE STOMACH,       163     CABARET DANCER     53
    EUHENIA WILL HAVE A FONDA IN ORBAJOSA.      ............ 163     CABARET DANCER     67
EUNUCH
    WE CHOOSE A KNAVE OR AN EUNUCH         ...................  189     HUGH SELWYN: 3     23
EUNUCHS
    THEY GUARD THEE NOT WITH EUNUCHS;        .................   91     DANCE FIGURE       14
EUPHRATES
    "THE EUPHRATES DENIES ITS PROTECTION TO THE PARTHIAN
        AND APOLOGIZES FOR CRASSUS,"       ....................  216     SEXTUS PROP: 5     16
```

EUPHRATES -- EVER

	PAGE	TITLE	LINE
EUPHRATES (CONTINUED)			
TIGRIS AND EUPHRATES SHALL, FROM NOW ON, FLOW AT HIS BIDDING,	219	SEXTUS PROP: 6	7
EUROPA			
WITH YOU IS EUROPA AND THE SHAMELESS PASIPHAE,	38	LADY'S LIFE	6
EVANGELIST			
AND IN OUR DAY THUS SAITH THE EVANGELIST:	246	MOYEN SENSUEL	237
EVANOE'S			
'TIS EVANOE'S,	49	OF SPLENDOUR	1
EVEN			
AH-EH! HE MUST BE RARE IF EVEN I HAVE NOT ..."	15	FAMAM CANO	43
I EVEN I, AM HE WHO KNOWETH THE ROADS	18	DE AEGYPTO	1
I, EVEN I, WHO FLY WITH THE SWALLOWS.	18	DE AEGYPTO	4
I, EVEN I, AM HE WHO KNOWETH THE ROADS	18	DE AEGYPTO	7
I, EVEN I, AM HE WHO KNOWETH THE ROADS	18	DE AEGYPTO	15
I, EVEN I, WHO FLY WITH THE SWALLOWS.	18	DE AEGYPTO	18
I, EVEN I, AM HE WHO KNOWETH THE ROADS	18	DE AEGYPTO	23
BY THAT HIGH FENCER, EVEN DEATH,	19	FOR E. MCC	3
'GAINST THAT GREY FENCER, EVEN DEATH.	19	FOR E. MCC	9
'GAINST THAT GREY FENCER, EVEN DEATH,	19	FOR E. MCC	25
AND WOULD MEET KINDRED EVEN AS I AM,	20	IN DURANCE	24
FOR EVEN AS THOU ART HOLLOW BEFORE I FILL THEE WITH THIS PARCHMENT,	23	MARVOIL	37
EVEN AS THOU SHALT SOON HAVE THIS PARCHMENT.	23	MARVOIL	44
EVEN AS I KEEP HER IMAGE IN MY HEART HERE.	23	MARVOIL	48
EVEN AS ARE THY STARS	27	NIGHT LITANY	45
EVEN SO IS MINE HEART	27	NIGHT LITANY	47
EVEN THE GREY PACK KNEW ME AND KNEW FEAR.	30	PIERE VIDAL	13
EVEN THAT SEMBLANCE THAT APPEARS AMONGST US	41	HER MONUMENT	23
--EVEN THE RIVER MANY DAYS AGO,	60	TOMB AKR CAAR	16
AND DO NOT EVEN OWN CLOTHING.	85	SALUTATION	10
REJUVENATE EVEN "THE SPECTATOR."	86	SALUTATION 2ND	25
BUT DO THOU SPEAK TRUE, EVEN TO THE LETTER:	90	SURGIT FAMA	15
YOU DO NOT EVEN EXPRESS OUR INNER NOBILITIES,	94	INSTRUCTIONS	8
EVEN IN MY DREAMS YOU HAVE DENIED YOURSELF TO ME	96	TO KALON	1
AND EVEN THE LAWYERS	98	THE BELLAIRES	32
WE WHO HAVE SEEN EVEN ARTEMIS A-BINDING HER SANDALS,	104	ANCORA	6
EVEN THOUGH WE TALK NOTHING BUT NONSENSE,	113	TAME CAT	5
AND YOU ARE EVEN COMPARED TO LESBIA.	113	FORMIANUS LADY	9
HORSES, HIS HORSES EVEN, ARE TIRED. THEY WERE STRONG.	127	BOWMEN OF SHU	15
CAN YOU EVEN TELL THE AGE OF A TURTLE?	140	SENNIN POEM	16
AND IT IS DOUBTFUL IF EVEN YOUR MANURE WILL BE RICH ENOUGH	146	MONUMENTUM AER	7
FORGETTING EVEN HER BEAUTY.	168	OF AROUET	42
AND EVEN NOW MR. STYRAX	178	MOEURS CON: 1	13
EVEN THE CHRISTIAN BEAUTY	189	HUGH SELWYN: 3	13
"EVEN IF YOU HAVE TO WORK FREE.	194	MR. NIXON	9
EVEN MY FAULTS THAT HEAVY UPON ME LIE,	197	ENVOI (1919)	6
EVEN THERE, NO ESCAPE	227	SEXTUS PROP:11	37
AND EVEN THIS INFAMY WOULD NOT ATTRACT NUMEROUS READERS	230	SEXTUS PROP:12	62
AND EVEN ZEUS' WILD LIGHTNING FEAR TO STRIKE	244	MOYEN SENSUEL	177
YOU CAN NOT GET CHEAP BOOKS, EVEN IF YOU NEED 'EM).	246	MOYEN SENSUEL	218
EVENING			
IN EVENING COMPANY HE SETS HIS FACE	46	FROM HEINE: 6	13
AND EVENING DRIVES THEM ON THE EASTWARD-FLOWING WATERS.	131	AT TEN-SHIN	4
EVENING COMES.	141	IDEA OF CHOAN	11
WAITING HIS TURN IN THE MID-SUMMER EVENING,	154	NEAR PERIGORD	109
THE SECOND EVENING?"	159	PSYCHOLOG HOUR	36
WILL YOU GIVE ME DAWN LIGHT AT EVENING?	167	OF AROUET	17
RADWAY HAD READ THE VARIOUS EVENING PAPERS	241	MOYEN SENSUEL	91
EVENING'S			
AND ARE YOU NOT READY WHEN EVENING'S COME?	48	FROM HEINE: 8	3
EVENT			
I HAD OVER-PREPARED THE EVENT,	158	PSYCHOLOG HOUR	1
I HAD OVER-PREPARED THE EVENT--	158	PSYCHOLOG HOUR	20
EVENTS			
UNAFFECTED BY "THE MARCH OF EVENTS,"	187	E. P. ODE	17
EVER			
THAT LEAVETH ME NO REST, SAYING EVER,	16	PRAISE YSOLT	7

EVER -- EVILS

```
                                                         PAGE    TITLE              LINE
EVER  (CONTINUED)
    SEEKING EVER A SONG. ...............................   16    PRAISE YSOLT         10
    CRYING EVER "SONG, A SONG." .......................    17    PRAISE YSOLT         45
    THAT CALL EVER UNTO ME, ...........................    17    PRAISE YSOLT         53
    TO WHOM MY BREAST AND ARMS ARE EVER WARM, .........    21    IN DURANCE           43
    MAY GOD DAMN FOR EVER ALL WHO CRY "PEACE!" ........    29    ALTAFORTE            36
    WAS THERE SUCH FLESH MADE EVER AND UNMADE! ........    31    PIERE VIDAL          45
    THAT EVER CAME UPON THIS GRIEVING WORLD ...........    36    THE YOUNG KING        3
    OF ANY ONE WHO EVER KISSED YOU? ...................    44    FROM HEINE: 1         8
    MOVED NOT, NOR EVER ANSWER MY DESIRE, .............    60    TOMB AKR CAAR         3
    AND THOU SHALT LIVE FOR EVER. .....................    62    N. Y.                13
    NOR HATH IT EVER SINCE CHANGED THAT CONCOCTION. ...    63    PHASELLUS ILLE        4
    AYE, FOR EVER, A LASTING LIFE'S-BLAST, ............    66    THE SEAFARER         80
    DEATH WAS EVER A CHURL. ...........................    72    PAN IS DEAD           9
    SEEK EVER TO STAND IN THE HARD SOPHOCLEAN LIGHT ...    95    ITE                   3
    HAVE WE EVER HEARD THE LIKE? ......................   104    ANCORA                7
    HAD WE EVER SUCH AN EPITHET CAST UPON US!! ........   104    ANCORA               16
    JOY SO RICH, AND IF I FIND NOT EVER ...............   105    DOMPNA POIS           7
    UNSTILL, EVER MOVING ..............................   107    COMING OF WAR        18
    EVER SINCE RHODEZ, ................................   119    THE GYPSY            13
    THIS PLACE IS THE CYPRIAN'S FOR SHE HAS EVER THE
        FANCY .........................................   164    QUINTUS SEPTIM        4
    AND HAS EVER; .....................................   175    LANGUE D'OC: 3       57
    HER MIND IS, AS EVER, UNCULTIVATED, ...............   179    MOEURS CON: 3         6
    "CONTENT EVER TO MOVE WITH WHITE SWANS! ...........   211    SEXTUS PROP: 2       40
    "NOR WILL THE NOISE OF HIGH HORSES LEAD YOU EVER TO
        BATTLE; .......................................   211    SEXTUS PROP: 2       41
    "NOR WILL THE PUBLIC CRIERS EVER HAVE YOUR NAME ...   211    SEXTUS PROP: 2       42
    NOW IF EVER IT IS TIME TO CLEANSE HELICON; ........   216    SEXTUS PROP: 5        1
    YET IN THAT PLACE IT EVER IS UNSTILL, .............   249    DONNA MI PREGA       28
    THE PIMPS OF WHITEHALL EVER MORE IN FEAR, .........   260    ALF'S FIFTH           7
    ON THE SUPPOSITION THAT IT EVER ...................   263    ALF'S EIGHTH          5
    "AS FOOTLIN' A LOT AS WAS EVER SPAWNED ............   270    OF 600 M.P.'S        23
ER-FLOWING
    IN THIS EVER-FLOWING MONOTONY .....................    35    THE EYES             12
VER-LIVING
    WE OF THE EVER-LIVING, IN THAT LIGHT ..............    50    THE FLAME            12
EVERY
    AND EVERY JONGLEUR KNEW ME IN HIS SONG, ...........    30    PIERE VIDAL          10
    AND EVERY RUN-AWAY OF THE WOOD THROUGH THAT GREAT
        MADNESS, ......................................    31    PIERE VIDAL          51
    ALL DOLOUR, ILL AND EVERY EVIL CHANCE .............    36    THE YOUNG KING        2
    AND FOR THIS, EVERY EARL WHATEVER, FOR THOSE
        SPEAKING AFTER-- ..............................    66    THE SEAFARER         73
    AND EVERY VINE-STOCK IS ...........................    87    THE SPRING            6
    THOUGH EVERY BRANCH HAVE BACK WHAT LAST YEAR LOST,    87    THE SPRING            11
    HARD OVER BRIVE--FOR EVERY LADY A CASTLE, .........   151    NEAR PERIGORD        13
    AND EVERY ONE HALF JEALOUS OF MAENT? ..............   153    NEAR PERIGORD        76
    TO BE SO MUCH ALIKE THAT EVERY DOG THAT SMELLS 'EM,   244    MOYEN SENSUEL       172
    THOU ART SO FAIR ATTIRED THAT EVERY MAN AND EACH      250    DONNA MI PREGA       89
    AN' EVERY YEAR WE MEET TO LET .....................   270    OF 600 M.P.'S        11
EVERYBODY'S
    THAT CANTING RAG CALLED EVERYBODY'S MAGAZINE, .....   241    MOYEN SENSUEL        98
EVERYCHONE
    THEN WHEN THE GREY WOLVES EVERYCHONE ..............    10    FOR THIS YULE         3
EVERY-DAY
    HERE IN THE EVERY-DAY WHERE OUR ACTS ..............    52    AU SALON              4
EVERYONE
    THE GHOSTS OF DEAD LOVES EVERYONE .................    10    FOR THIS YULE        11
    AND YET EVERYONE SPEAKS EVIL OF DEATH. ............   164    QUINTUS SEPTIM        3
EVIL
    ALL DOLOUR, ILL AND EVERY EVIL CHANCE .............    36    THE YOUNG KING        2
    O LOVE, COME NOW, THIS LAND TURNS EVIL SLOWLY. ....    69    THE NEEDLE            9
    FOR I THINK THE GLASS IS EVIL. ....................    95    OF THE DEGREES        2
    O GLASS SUBTLY EVIL, O CONFUSION OF COLOURS! ......    95    OF THE DEGREES       10
    AND YET EVERYONE SPEAKS EVIL OF DEATH .............   164    QUINTUS SEPTIM        3
    A SAD AND GREAT EVIL IS THE EXPECTATION OF DEATH--   164    QUINTUS SEPTIM        8
    THERE IS NOT MUCH BUT ITS EVIL LEFT US. ...........   168    OF AROUET            24
EVILS
    BE EAGER TO FIND NEW EVILS AND NEW GOOD. ..........    89    COMMISSION           24
```

	PAGE	TITLE	LINE
EVOE			
EVOE, EVOE, EVOE BACCHO, O	231	CANTUS PLANUS	3
EVOE, EVOE, EVOE BACCHO, O	231	CANTUS PLANUS	3
EVOE, EVOE, EVOE BACCHO, O	231	CANTUS PLANUS	3
EWES			
SOLDIER, THE ENUMERATION OF WOUNDS; THE SHEEP-FEEDER, OF EWES;	218	SEXTUS PROP: 5	56
EXACERBATED			
WAS VENUS EXACERBATED BY THE EXISTENCE OF A COMPARABLE EQUAL?	221	SEXTUS PROP: 8	10
EXACERBATIONS			
RESISTANCE TO CURRENT EXACERBATIONS,	201	AGE DEMANDED	24
EXAGGERATION			
NO, "MILESIAN" IS AN EXAGGERATION.	195	HUGH SELWIN:11	5
EXALTED			
WITH ARMS EXALTED, WITH FORE-ARMS	93	LES MILLWIN	8
EXAMINATION			
I WENT UP TO THE COURT FOR EXAMINATION,	136	EXILE'S LETTER	65
UNDER A MORE TOLERANT, PERHAPS, EXAMINATION.	201	AGE DEMANDED	28
EXAMPLE			
THE EXAMPLE OF THESE CONSUMERS IN COOPERATION	262	ALF'S SEVENTH	18
EXASPERATED			
WE WERE NOT EXASPERATED WITH WOMEN,	82	THE CONDOLENCE	11
EXCEEDING			
LIGHT, LIGHT OF MY EYES, AT AN EXCEEDING LATE HOUR I WAS WANDERING,	224	SEXTUS PROP:10	1
EXCELLENCE			
DREAR ALL THIS EXCELLENCE, DELIGHTS UNDURABLE!	66	THE SEAFARER	88
EXCELLENT			
THE VERY EXCELLENT TERM RUSTICUS.	99	SALVATIONISTS	4
TAKE HER. SHE HAS TWO EXCELLENT SEASONS.	165	QUINTUS SEPTIM	22
EXCELSIS			
PARACELSUS IN EXCELSIS	32	PARACELSUS	T
EXCEPT			
TO ALL MEN EXCEPT THE KING OF ARAGON,	23	MARVOIL	31
EXCERPTED			
WHENCE THEIR SYMBOLICAL POLLEN HAS BEEN EXCERPTED,	180	MOEURS CON: 5	21
EXCESS			
HAVE DRIVEN HIS WIFE FROM ONE RELIGIOUS EXCESS TO ANOTHER.	178	MOEURS CON: 1	8
EXCESSIVE			
HER BOREDOM IS EXQUISITE AND EXCESSIVE.	83	THE GARDEN	9
EXCIDEUIL			
HAVE SEEN EXCIDEUIL, CAREFULLY FASHIONED.	122	PROVINC DESERT	41
EXCLAIMED			
EXCLAIMED:	179	MOEURS CON: 3	6
EXCLUSION			
EXCLUSION FROM THE WORLD OF LETTERS.	202	AGE DEMANDED	61
EXCUSE			
THE GOVERNMENT'S EXCUSE,	265	ALF'S TENTH	2
EX-DIPLOMAT'S			
WILL MEET A DUCHESS AND AN EX-DIPLOMAT'S WIDOW	163	CABARET DANCER	64
EXERCET			
"VACUOS EXERCET AERA MORSUS."	198	MAUBERLEY 1920	EPI
EXERCISES			
HE EXERCISES HIS TALENTS	195	HUGH SELWIN:10	7
EXHAUSTED			
THEY HOWL. THEY COMPLAIN IN DELICATE AND EXHAUSTED METRES	148	FRATRES MINORE	5
AND I ALSO WILL SING WAR WHEN THIS MATTER OF A GIRL IS EXHAUSTED.	216	SEXTUS PROP: 5	9
EXILE			
I HAVE BEATEN OUT MY EXILE.	93	THE REST	19
EXILE'S			
EXILE'S LETTER	134	EXILE'S LETTER	T
EXIST			
AND I NO MORE EXIST;	203	MAUBERLEY: 4	23
EXISTENCE			
WAS VENUS EXACERBATED BY THE EXISTENCE OF A COMPARABLE EQUAL?	221	SEXTUS PROP: 8	10

EXISTS -- EYELIDS

	PAGE	TITLE	LINE
EXISTS			
I THOUGHT: YES, DIVINE, THESE EYES, BUT WHAT EXISTS	247	PIERROTS	11
EXITUM			
IN EXITUM CUIUSDAM	59	EXIT' CUIUSDAM	T
EXPECT			
THAT WE EXPECT OF POETS?"	85	SALUTATION 2ND	11
AND YOU EXPECT ME TO BELIEVE THIS	215	SEXTUS PROP: 4	41
EXPECTATION			
A SAD AND GREAT EVIL IS THE EXPECTATION OF DEATH--	164	QUINTUS SEPTIM	8
EXPEDITION			
VARRO SANG JASON'S EXPEDITION,	230	SEXTUS PROP:12	66
EXPENSES			
AND THERE ARE ALSO THE INANE EXPENSES OF THE FUNERAL;	164	QUINTUS SEPTIM	9
EXPENSIVE			
NEITHER EXPENSIVE PYRAMIDS SCRAPING THE STARS IN THEIR ROUTE,	209	SEXTUS PROP: 1	66
EXPERIENCE			
BEING EXPERT FROM EXPERIENCE,	222	SEXTUS PROP: 8	33
EXPERT			
BEING EXPERT FROM EXPERIENCE,	222	SEXTUS PROP: 8	33
EXPLAIN			
LOYALTY IS HARD TO EXPLAIN.	139	SOUTH-FOLK	11
EXPLAINS			
EXPLAINS THE DECORATIONS.	163	CABARET DANCER	59
EXPLORED			
HER EYES EXPLORED ME.	110	THE ENCOUNTER	2
EXPOSITION			
MAY WE REPEAT; THE CENTENNIAL EXPOSITION	240	MOYEN SENSUEL	54
EXPOUND			
AND EXPOUND THE DISTENTIONS OF EMPIRE,	207	SEXTUS PROP: 1	18
EXPRESS			
COME, MY SONGS, LET US EXPRESS OUR BASER PASSIONS,	94	INSTRUCTIONS	1
LET US EXPRESS OUR ENVY OF THE MAN WITH A STEADY JOB AND NO WORRY ABOUT THE FUTURE.	94	INSTRUCTIONS	2
YOU DO NOT EVEN EXPRESS OUR INNER NOBILITIES,	94	INSTRUCTIONS	8
EXQUISITE			
LET US BUILD HERE AN EXQUISITE FRIENDSHIP,	51	THE ALTAR	1
HER BOREDOM IS EXQUISITE AND EXCESSIVE.	83	THE GARDEN	9
EXTENDED			
HE SPEAKS OF MY EXTENDED FAME,	46	FROM HEINE: 6	9
EXTENT			
NO BARBARISM WOULD GO TO THE EXTENT OF DOING HIM HARM,	212	SEXTUS PROP: 3	19
EXTINCTION			
DORED TO AN INCH OF EXTINCTION,	22	MARVOIL	17
EXULTED			
EXULTED, THEY BEHELD THE SPLENDOURS OF CLEOPATRA.	93	LES MILLWIN	10
EXULTING			
LET COME THE GAY OF MANNER, THE INSOLENT AND THE EXULTING.	146	CANTILATIONS	10
EYE			
THE SEEING EYE	104	THE SEEING EYE	T
SAW WHAT THE CITY OFFERED, CAST AN EYE	245	MOYEN SENSUEL	187
IN HIS EYE THERE IS DEATH,--I MEAN THE BANKER'S,--	263	ALF'S EIGHTH	15
TO A WELSH SHIFTER WITH AN OGLING EYE,	264	ALF'S NINTH	7
AND TO KEEP AN EYE ON THEIR READIN' MATTER	272	NATIONAL SONG	13
EYEBROWS			
AND THE WATER, A HUNDRED FEET DEEP, REFLECTING GREEN EYEBROWS	136	EXILE'S LETTER	56
--EYEBROWS PAINTED GREEN ARE A FINE SIGHT IN YOUNG MOONLIGHT,	136	EXILE'S LETTER	57
EYED			
DARK EYED,	91	DANCE FIGURE	1
EYE-DEEP			
WALKED EYE-DEEP IN HELL	190	HUGH SELWYN: 4	13
EYE-LID			
OF EYE-LID AND CHEEK-BONE	200	MAUBERLEY: 2	22
EYELIDS			
THERE IS A VOLUME IN THE MATTER; IF HER EYELIDS SINK INTO SLEEP,	217	SEXTUS PROP: 5	31
WHEN , WHEN, AND WHENEVER DEATH CLOSES OUR EYELIDS,	218	SEXTUS PROP: 6	1

PAGE 131

EYELIDS -- FACE

	PAGE	TITLE	LINE
EYELIDS (CONTINUED)			
AND SHE THEN OPENING MY EYELIDS FALLEN IN SLEEP,	220	SEXTUS PROP: 7	7
EYES			
EYES, DREAMS, LIPS, AND THE NIGHT GOES.	6	CINO	10
PASSIONATE CINO, OF THE WRINKLING EYES,	6	CINO	17
. . . EH? . . . THEY MOSTLY HAD GREY EYES,	7	CINO	40
I SKOAL TO THE EYES AS GREY-BLOWN MERE	10	FOR THIS YULE	22
AND THE WANDERING OF MANY ROADS HATH MADE MY EYES	16	PRAISE YSOLT	12
SHE THAT HOLDETH THE WONDER WORDS WITHIN HER EYES	17	PRAISE YSOLT	51
MAY HER EYES AND HER CHEEK BE FAIR	23	MARVOIL	30
SO IS MY HEART HOLLOW WHEN SHE FILLETH NOT MINE EYES,	23	MARVOIL	38
YET THEIR EYES ARE AS THE EYES OF A MAID TO HER LOVER,	25	THE WHITE STAG	3
YET THEIR EYES ARE AS THE EYES OF A MAID TO HER LOVER,	25	THE WHITE STAG	3
HAVE I HIDDEN MINE EYES,	27	NIGHT LITANY	31
WI' HIS EYES LIKE THE GREY O' THE SEA,	34	GOODLY FERE	44
THE EYES	35	THE EYES	T
BLIND EYES AND SHADOWS THAT ARE FORMED AS MEN;	38	BALLATETTA	2
MINE EYES UPON NEW COLOURS.	39	FOR PSYCHE	9
THESE FIVE MILLENIA, AND THY DEAD EYES	60	TOMB AKR CAAR	2
TIME THAN MY EYES.	67	THE CLOAK	10
THE EYES OF THIS DEAD LADY SPEAK TO ME,	73	THE PICTURE	1
THE EYES OF THIS DEAD LADY SPEAK TO ME.	73	THE PICTURE	4
THE EYES OF THIS DEAD LADY SPEAK TO ME.	73	JACOPO SELLAIO	6
WITH THEIR LARGE AND ANAEMIC EYES THEY LOOKED OUT UPON THIS CONFIGURATION.	93	LES MILLWIN	12
FOR, AS TO COLOUR AND EYES	105	DOMPNA POIS	25
HER EYES EXPLORED ME.	110	THE ENCOUNTER	2
CRUSHED STRAWBERRIES! COME, LET US FEAST OUR EYES.	113	L'ART, 1910	2
AND WITH EYES THAT ARE NOT BLACK,	113	FORMIANUS LADY	4
SURELY I SAW, AND STILL BEFORE MY EYES	156	NEAR PERIGORD	163
POPPIES AND DAY'S EYES IN THE GREEN EMAIL	157	NEAR PERIGORD	171
SUDDENLY DISCOVERING IN THE EYES OF THE VERY BEAUTIFUL	161	PAGANI'S NOV 8	1
THE EYES OF THE VERY LEARNED BRITISH MUSEUM ASSISTANT.	161	PAGANI'S NOV 8	3
"I AM JUST FROM BED. THE SLEEP IS STILL IN MY EYES."	166	FISH & SHADOW	9
QUICK EYES GONE UNDER EARTH'S LID,	191	HUGH SELWYN: 5	6
HAVE PRESERVED HER EYES;	192	YEUX GLAUQUES	10
THE SKY-LIKE LIMPID EYES,	193	BRENNBAUM	1
THE EYES TURN TOPAZ.	204	MEDALLION	16
VAST WATERS FLOWED FROM HER EYES?	214	SEXTUS PROP: 4	15
DAMP WOOLLY HANDKERCHIEFS WERE STUFFED INTO HER UNDRYABLE EYES,	214	SEXTUS PROP: 4	25
EYES ARE THE GUIDES OF LOVE,	220	SEXTUS PROP: 7	13
WHILE OUR FATES TWINE TOGETHER, SATE WE OUR EYES WITH LOVE;	220	SEXTUS PROP: 7	17
HAVE YOU DENIED PALLAS GOOD EYES?	221	SEXTUS PROP: 8	13
LIGHT, LIGHT OF MY EYES, AT AN EXCEEDING LATE HOUR I WAS WANDERING,	224	SEXTUS PROP:10	1
MY LIGHT, LIGHT OF MY EYES,	224	SEXTUS PROP: 9	22
SHE COULD SCARCELY KEEP HER EYES OPEN	225	SEXTUS PROP:10	22
IT IS OUR EYES YOU FLEE, NOT THE CITY,	226	SEXTUS PROP:11	13
THE WHICH, NO CAT HAS EYES ENOUGH	236	MIDDLE-AGED	22
YOUR EYES! SINCE I LOST THEIR INCANDESCENCE	247	PIERROTS	1
YOUR EYES PUT ME UP TO IT.	247	PIERROTS	10
I THOUGHT: YES, DIVINE, THESE EYES, BUT WHAT EXISTS	247	PIERROTS	11
OUTSIDE YOUR SET BUT, HAVING KEPT FAITH IN YOUR EYES,	247	PIERROTS	23
FABIUS			
"OF" THE VICTORIOUS DELAY OF FABIUS, AND THE LEFT-HANDED BATTLE AT CANNAE,	210	SEXTUS PROP: 2	11
FABRICATION			
THIS FABRICATION BUILT OF AUTUMN ROSES,	69	SUB MARE	3
FACE			
I HAVE HIDDEN MY FACE WHERE THE OAK	4	LA FRAISNE	10
ON HIS OWN FACE IN A GLASS	35	HIS OWN FACE	T
O STRANGE FACE THERE IN THE GLASS!	35	HIS OWN FACE	1
IN EVENING COMPANY HE SETS HIS FACE	46	FROM HEINE: 6	13
BUT AGE FARES AGAINST HIM, HIS FACE PALETH,	66	THE SEAFARER	93
THY FACE AS A RIVER WITH LIGHTS.	91	DANCE FIGURE	11

PAGE 132

FACE -- FAINT

	PAGE	TITLE	LINE
FACE (CONTINUED)			
OVER THE COOL FACE OF THAT FIELD,	107	COMING OF WAR	17
WHITE, WHITE OF FACE, HESITATES, PASSING THE DOOR.	128	BEAU TOILET	4
THE WALLS RISE IN A MAN'S FACE,	138	NEAR SHOKU	3
STILL DARTS OUT FAUN-LIKE FROM THE HALF-RUIN'D FACE,	192	YEUX GLAUQUES	18
THE CIRCULAR INFANT'S FACE,	193	BRENNBAUM	2
LEVEL ACROSS THE FACE	193	BRENNBAUM	7
AND ONE AMONG THEM LOOKED AT ME WITH FACE OFFENDED,	211	SEXTUS PROP: 2	38
STIFFENED OUR FACE WITH THE BACKWASH OF PHILETAS THE COAN.	211	SEXTUS PROP: 2	54
OR WRIES THE FACE WITH FEAR AND LITTLE STAYS,	250	DONNA MI PREGA	54
THOUGH FROM HER FACE INDISCERNIBLE;	250	DONNA MI PREGA	79
FACED			
SO HE "FACED LIFE" WITH RATHER MIXED INTENTIONS,	242	MOYEN SENSUEL	101
FACE-OVAL			
HONEY-RED, CLOSING THE FACE-OVAL,	204	MEDALLION	9
THE FACE-OVAL BENEATH THE GLAZE,	204	MEDALLION	13
FACES			
OH I KNOW THAT THERE ARE FOLK ABOUT ME, FRIENDLY FACES,	20	IN DURANCE	2
HOW MANY FACES I'D HAVE OUT OF MIND.	59	EXIT' CUIUSDAM	7
NEW FRIENDS, NEW FACES,	70	THE PLUNGE	4
WHY DO YOU LOOK SO EAGERLY AND SO CURIOUSLY INTO PEOPLE'S FACES,	103	CODA	3
THE APPARITION OF THESE FACES IN THE CROWD;	109	IN THE METRO	1
THEIR PUNIC FACES DYED IN THE GORGON'S LAKE;	211	SEXTUS PROP: 2	32
AND THEY HAVE RED FACES LIKE BRICKS.	237	ABU SALAMMAMM	14
FACT			
FACT THAT LEADS NOWHERE; AND A TALE OR TWO,	61	PORTRAIT FEMME	17
LET US THEREFORE MENTION THE FACT,	93	LES MILLWIN	13
IN FACT THEY UNDERSTOOD THEM SO BADLY	97	THE BELLAIRES	3
STILL SIGH OVER ESTABLISHED AND NATURAL FACT	148	FRATRES MINORE	3
END FACT. TRY FICTION. LET US SAY WE SEE	154	NEAR PERIGORD	94
THE AIR IS ALIVE WITH THAT FACT.	158	PSYCHOLOG HOUR	13
STILL WE WILL BRING OUR "FICTION AS NEAR TO FACT" AS	243	MOYEN SENSUEL	139
FACTITIOUS			
CAPANEUS; TROUT FOR FACTITIOUS BAIT;	187	E. P. ODE	8
FACTS			
I SUPPOSE, WHEN POETRY COMES DOWN TO FACTS,	52	AU SALON	1
(VIDE THE TARIFF), I WILL HANG SIMPLE FACTS	241	MOYEN SENSUEL	71
HID TRUTH AND LIED, AND LIED AND HID THE FACTS.	260	ALF'S FIFTH	6
FACULTY			
IF I HAVE NOT THE FACULTY, "THE BARE ATTEMPT WOULD BE PRAISE-WORTHY."	216	SEXTUS PROP: 5	4
FADED			
FADED ABOUT THEE.	68	APPARUIT	16
A FADED, PALE BROWNISH PHOTOGRAPH,	180	MOEURS CON: 5	2
FADES			
FADES WHEN THE WIND HATH LIFTED THEM ASIDE,	40	ERAT HORA	3
FADING			
AND DELIA HERSELF FADING OUT,	168	OF AROUET	41
FAIBLENESS			
AND SMITE ALWAYS AT THEIR FAIBLENESS?	12	OF THE GIBBET	40
FAIDITA			
HER WHITE TEETH, OF THE LADY FAIDITA	106	DOMPNA POIS	51
FAIL			
LEST IT SHOULD FAIL TO TREAT ALL MEN ALIKE.	244	MOYEN SENSUEL	178
FAILED			
"SE IL COR TI MANCA," BUT IT FAILED THEE NOT!	19	FOR E. MCC	12
THAT FAILED NEVER WOMEN,	90	SURGIT FAMA	6
AND MAENT FAILED HIM? OR SAW THROUGH THE SCHEME?	152	NEAR PERIGORD	52
FAILS			
FAILS NOT THE EARTH NOW.	90	SURGIT FAMA	7
SAVE THAT PERFECTION FAILS, BE IT BUT A LITTLE;	249	DONNA MI PREGA	45
FAILURE			
GO TO THEM WHOSE FAILURE IS CONCEALED;	88	COMMISSION	12
FAIN			
PINNING THE GUISE THAT HAD BEEN FAIN	11	OF THE GIBBET	9
FAINT			
FROM THIS FAINT WORLD, HOW FULL OF BITTERNESS	37	THE YOUNG KING	25
HATH AS FAINT LUTE-STRINGS IN ITS DIM ACCORD	43	SATIEMUS	15

FAINT -- FALLING

	PAGE	TITLE	LINE
FAINT (CONTINUED)			
THE FAINT ODOUR OF YOUR PATCHOULI,	103	LADIES	18
FAINT, ALMOST, AS THE LINES OF CRUELTY ABOUT YOUR CHIN,	103	LADIES	19
FULL OF FAINT LIGHT	107	COMING OF WAR	3
FAINT IN THE MOST STRENUOUS MOODS,	202	AGE DEMANDED	38
LIFTING THE FAINT SUSURRUS	202	AGE DEMANDED	54
FAINTS			
IT FAINTS IN TAKING AND IN GIVING ALL.	31	PIERE VIDAL	36
FAIR			
LO THE FAIR DEAD!	3	THRENOS	3
LO THE FAIR DEAD!	3	THRENOS	7
LO THE FAIR DEAD!	3	THRENOS	11
LO THE FAIR DEAD!	3	THRENOS	14
(LO THE FAIR DEAD!)	3	THRENOS	17
BEING SO YOUNG AND FAIR	9	NA AUDIART	46
MAY HER EYES AND HER CHEEK BE FAIR	23	MARVOIL	30
AND ALL THE FAIR FROM TROY AND ALL FROM ACHAIA,	38	LADY'S LIFE	7
SO MANY THOUSAND FAIR ARE GONE DOWN TO AVERNUS,	38	LADY'S LIFE	13
"LO, ONE THERE WAS WHO BENT HER FAIR BRIGHT HEAD,	43	SATIEMUS	5
WHISPERING AMONG THEM, "THE FAIR DEAD	43	SATIEMUS	10
AND I AM FAIR AND GOLDEN	47	FROM HEINE: 7	19
FRAME ON THE FAIR EARTH 'GAINST FOES HIS MALICE,	66	THE SEAFARER	76
HOW SHE IS SO FAIR AND BONNY;	72	DIEU! QU'IL	2
HOW SHE IS SO FAIR AND BONNY.	72	DIEU! QU'IL	8
NEITHER ONE SO FAIR, NOR OF SUCH HEART,	105	DOMPNA POIS	12
CULLING FROM EACH A FAIR TRAIT	105	DOMPNA POIS	18
OVER FAIR MEADOWS,	107	COMING OF WAR	16
COMING DOWN FROM THE FAIR	119	THE GYPSY	14
"A FAIR MAN AND A PLEASANT."	123	PROVINC DESERT	73
FAIR CHEEKS, AND FINE BODIES;	190	HUGH SELWYN: 4	22
MAY BE AS FAIR AS HERS,	197	ENVOI (1919)	21
FAIR, FAIREST LYCORIS--	230	SEXTUS PROP:12	73
(I BURN, I FREEZE, I SWEAT, SAID THE FAIR GREEK,	242	MOYEN SENSUEL	123
THOU ART SO FAIR ATTIRED THAT EVERY MAN AND EACH	250	DONNA MI PREGA	89
FAIREST			
FAIR, FAIREST LYCORIS--	230	SEXTUS PROP:12	73
THE VERY FAIREST FLOWER OF THEIR GYNOCRACY.	239	MOYEN SENSUEL	40
FAIRLY			
I KNOW YOUR CIRCLE AND CAN FAIRLY TELL	59	EXIT' CUIUSDAM	4
FAIRNESS			
FOR WHOSE FAIRNESS ONE FORGAVE	9	NA AUDIART	54
FIELDS TO FAIRNESS, LAND FARES BRISKER,	65	THE SEAFARER	50
FAIRY			
WHEN THE FAIRY FLAMES ENSHROUDED	45	FROM HEINE: 3	3
FAIT			
DIEU! QU'IL LA FAIT	72	DIEU! QU'IL	T
FAITH			
IN "FAITH AND TROTH" TO A TRAITORESS,	12	OF THE GIBBET	35
FAITH! NO MAN TARRIETH,	19	FOR E. MCC	11
OUTSIDE YOUR SET BUT, HAVING KEPT FAITH IN YOUR EYES,	247	PIERROTS	23
BEYOND ALL FALSITY, WORTHY OF FAITH, ALONE	250	DONNA MI PREGA	86
FAITHFUL			
NOR HIS DEED TO THE DARING, NOR HIS KING TO THE FAITHFUL	65	THE SEAFARER	42
FALL			
THE PETALS FALL IN THE FOUNTAIN,	108	TS'AI CHI'H	1
THE LEAVES FALL EARLY THIS AUTUMN, IN WIND.	131	RIVER-MER WIFE	22
TREES FALL, THE GRASS GOES YELLOW WITH AUTUMN.	133	FRONTIER GUARD	3
THE THREE MOUNTAINS FALL THROUGH THE FAR HEAVEN,	138	CITY OF CHOAN	8
NOR IF THE THUNDER FALL FROM PREDESTINATION;	228	SEXTUS PROP:12	29
FALLEN			
BUT WHERE'S THE OLD FRIEND HASN'T FALLEN OFF,	59	EXIT' CUIUSDAM	2
AND SHE THEN OPENING MY EYELIDS FALLEN IN SLEEP,	220	SEXTUS PROP: 7	7
FALLETH			
HE, CAUGHT, FALLETH	250	DONNA MI PREGA	80
FALLING			
CLOSE, AND AS THE PETALS OF FLOWERS IN FALLING	39	FOR PSYCHE	4
AND WITH SOME BRANCHES ROTTED AND FALLING.	89	COMMISSION	32
STRIKING THE BOARD, FALLING IN STRONG L'S OF	120	GAME OF CHESS	2
WITH THE WILLOW FLAKES FALLING LIKE SNOW,	136	EXILE'S LETTER	54

FALLING -- FANTASTIKON

	PAGE	TITLE	LINE
FALLING (CONTINUED)			
IT IS LIKE THE FLOWERS FALLING AT SPRING'S END	136	EXILE'S LETTER	73
BY FALLING FROM A HIGH STOOL IN A PUB	193	SIENA MI FE	8
FALLOW			
IN WILD-WOOD NEVER FAWN NOR FALLOW FARETH	38	BALLATETTA	6
FALLS			
FALLS LIKE BLACK LIGHTNING.	87	THE SPRING	9
AND THE MOON FALLS OVER THE PORTALS OF SEI-GO-YO,	131	AT TEN-SHIN	11
AND THE RAIN FALLS AND FALLS, ...	142	UNMOVING CLOUD	2
AND THE RAIN FALLS AND FALLS, ...	142	UNMOVING CLOUD	2
THAT FALLS THROUGH THE WATER, ...	166	FISH & SHADOW	6
THAT FALLS THROUGH THE PALE GREEN WATER.	166	FISH & SHADOW	21
IT FALLS AND ROLLS TO YOUR FEET.	169	PHANOPOEIA	7
WHERE THE LEAF FALLS FROM THE TWIG, ...	174	LANGUE D'OC: 3	3
"ANIENAN SPRING WATER FALLS INTO FLAT-SPREAD POOLS."	212	SEXTUS PROP: 3	5
FALSE			
THY LITTLE HEART, SO SWEET AND FALSE AND SMALL	44	FROM HEINE: 2	3
THAT THERE'S NO THING MORE SWEET OR FALSE AT ALL.	44	FROM HEINE: 2	4
BROKEN AGAINST FALSE KNOWLEDGE, ...	93	THE REST	14
THE GEW-GAWS OF FALSE AMBER AND FALSE TURQUOISE			
ATTRACT THEM.	114	BEFORE A SHOP	1
THE GEW-GAWS OF FALSE AMBER AND FALSE TURQUOISE			
ATTRACT THEM.	114	BEFORE A SHOP	1
RUDYARD THE FALSE MEASURE, ...	259	ALF'S FOURTH	2
FALSITY			
BEYOND ALL FALSITY, WORTHY OF FAITH, ALONE	250	DONNA MI PREGA	86
FAMA			
SURGIT FAMA	90	SURGIT FAMA	T
FAMAM			
FAMAM LIBROSQUE CANO	14	FAMAM CANO	T
FAME			
"'TIS THE WHITE STAG, FAME, WE'RE A-HUNTING, ...	25	THE WHITE STAG	6
HE SPEAKS OF MY EXTENDED FAME, ...	46	FROM HEINE: 6	9
OR SLACKED HIS HAND-GRIP WHEN YOU FIRST GRIPPED FAME?	59	EXIT' CUIUSDAM	3
THROUGH SHE'D THE FAR FAME FOR IT.	106	DOMPNA POIS	39
SCARCELY A GENERAL NOW KNOWN TO FAME	264	ALF'S NINTH	3
FAMILIAR			
WITH WHICH I AM ALREADY FAMILIAR, ...	226	SEXTUS PROP:11	16
FAMILIARS			
THESE THINGS THAT ARE FAMILIARS OF THE GOD.	69	SUB MARE	9
FAMILIES			
I HAVE SEEN THEM WITH UNTIDY FAMILIES, ...	85	SALUTATION	4
SENATORIAL FAMILIES OF STRASBOURG, MONSIEUR VEROG.	193	SIENA MI FE	4
FAMILY			
GO TO THE ADOLESCENT WHO ARE SMOTHERED IN FAMILY--	89	COMMISSION	28
OR THAT THERE IS NO CASTE IN THIS FAMILY.	94	INSTRUCTIONS	22
THE FAMILY POSITION WAS WANING, ...	111	SOCIETY	1
NOR OF XERXES' TWO-BARRELED KINGDOM, NOR OF REMUS			
AND HIS ROYAL FAMILY, ...	217	SEXTUS PROP: 5	44
FAMOUS			
CAN TELL YOU OF THAT FAMOUS DAY AND YEAR.	264	ALF'S NINTH	4
FAN			
O FAN OF WHITE SILK, ...	108	FAN-PIECE	1
THOUGH YOU WALK IN THE VIA SACRA, WITH A PEACOCK'S			
TAIL FOR A FAN.	227	SEXTUS PROP:11	40
FANCY			
THIS PLACE IS THE CYPRIAN'S FOR SHE HAS EVER THE			
FANCY	164	QUINTUS SEPTIM	4
FANE			
THAT PLUNDERED ST. HUBERT BACK O' THE FANE:	12	OF THE GIBBET	32
FANG			
BLOOD ON EACH TIRED FANG	261	ALF'S SIXTH	11
FANNING			
FANNING THE GRASS SHE WALKED ON THEN, ENDURES:	92	GENTILDONNA	4
FANNO			
"UN E DUO FANNO TRE, ...	163	CABARET DANCER	83
FAN-PIECE			
FAN-PIECE, FOR HER IMPERIAL LORD	108	FAN-PIECE	T
FANTASTIKON			
OUR "FANTASTIKON" DELIGHTED TO SERVE US.	82	THE CONDOLENCE	10

FAR -- FATE

	PAGE	TITLE	LINE
FAR			
HAVE SEEN THIS THING, OUT OF THEIR FAR COURSES	27	NIGHT LITANY	42
FAR FROM WHERE WORTH'S WON AND THE SWORDS CLASH ...	29	ALTAFORTE	28
HOW WILL THIS BEAUTY, WHEN I AM FAR HENCE, ...	51	HORAE BEATAE	1
(THUS FAR HATH MODERNITY BROUGHT US)	52	AU SALON	9
ON FLOOD-WAYS TO BE FAR DEPARTING.	65	THE SEAFARER	53
OH, BUT FAR OUT OF THIS!	70	THE PLUNGE	15
THROUGH SHE'D THE FAR FAME FOR IT.	106	DOMPNA POIS	39
YOU WENT INTO FAR KU-TO-YEN, BY THE RIVER OF SWIRLING EDDIES, ...	130	RIVER-MER WIFE	16
AS FAR AS CHO-FU-SA.	131	RIVER-MER WIFE	29
THE LORDS GO FORTH FROM THE COURT, AND INTO FAR BORDERS.	132	AT TEN-SHIN	14
I HAD TO BE OFF TO SO, FAR AWAY OVER THE WATERS,	135	EXILE'S LETTER	34
HIS LONE SAIL BLOTS THE FAR SKY.	137	ON RIVER KIANG	3
THE THREE MOUNTAINS FALL THROUGH THE FAR HEAVEN,	138	CITY OF CHOAN	8
MY FRIENDS ARE ESTRANGED, OR FAR 'DISTANT, ...	142	UNMOVING CLOUD	8
"NOT SO FAR, NO, NOT SO FAR NOW, ...	166	FISH & SHADOW	13
"NOT SO FAR, NO, NOT SO FAR NOW, ...	166	FISH & SHADOW	13
FAR-COURSING			
SILENT UNTO US IN THEIR FAR-COURSING, ...	27	NIGHT LITANY	46
FARE			
IN ILSENSTEIN I FARE, ...	47	FROM HEINE: 7	2
THAT I FARE FORTH, THAT I AFAR HENCE	65	THE SEAFARER	38
YET LONGING COMES UPON HIM TO FARE FORTH ON THE WATER.	65	THE SEAFARER	48
FARES			
FIELDS TO FAIRNESS, LAND FARES BRISKER, ...	65	THE SEAFARER	50
BUT AGE FARES AGAINST HIM, HIS FACE PALETH, ...	66	THE SEAFARER	93
FARETH			
IN WILD-WOOD NEVER FAWN NOR FALLOW FARETH	38	BALLATETTA	6
HE FARETH FROM DAY TO DAY, ...	98	THE BELLAIRES	37
FARING			
MAY MAKE MERRY MAN FARING NEEDY.	64	THE SEAFARER	27
FARMERS			
HEAD FARMERS DO LIKEWISE, AND LYING WEARY AMID THEIR OATS	229	SEXTUS PROP:12	48
FASCINATING			
THE SOCIAL ITCH, THE ALMOST, ALL BUT, NOT QUITE, FASCINATING, ...	241	MOYEN SENSUEL	83
FASCISTS			
SUCH AS THE FASCISTS WEAR, ...	258	ALF'S THIRD	4
FASHION			
IN ANOTHER FASHION THAT MORE SUITETH ME.	4	LA FRAISNE	8
PRAISES MEET UNTO THY FASHION?	8	NA AUDIART	10
(SUCH AS I DRINK TO MINE FASHION)	10	FOR THIS YULE	15
FOLK OF UNEARTHLY FASHION, PLACES SPLENDID, ...	50	THE FLAME	24
YOU'RE A VERY DEPLETED FASHION, ...	114	EPILOGUE	6
OF PRECISELY THE FASHION	196	HUGH SELWIN:12	6
I WOULD MAKE VERSE IN YOUR FASHION, IF SHE SHOULD COMMAND IT, ...	229	SEXTUS PROP:12	60
FASHIONED			
STRANGE WAYS AND WALLS ARE FASHIONED OUT OF IT. ...	49	OF SPLENDOUR	5
HAVE SEEN EXCIDEUIL, CAREFULLY FASHIONED.	122	PROVINC DESERT	41
FASHIONS			
TESTED AND PRIED AND WORKED IN MANY FASHIONS, ...	235	TO WHISTLER	3
FAST			
AND PRIES WIDE MY MOUTH WITH FAST MUSIC	29	ALTAFORTE	22
THE TREASURE IS OURS, MAKE WE FAST LAND WITH IT.	69	THE NEEDLE	11
ME OUT, KNOWING YOU HOLD ME SO FAST!	107	DOMPNA POIS	70
FASTNESS			
SEEK OUT A FOREIGN FASTNESS.	65	THE SEAFARER	39
FAT			
FAT PIERRE WITH THE HOOK GAUCHE-MAIN, ...	11	OF-THE GIBBET	5
WITH FAT BOARDS, BAWDS, WINE AND FRAIL MUSIC!	28	ALTAFORTE	17
HER OFFSPRING ARE FAT AND HAPPY.	103	THE PATTERNS	4
A BROWN, FAT BABE SITTING IN THE LOTUS, ...	147	POST MORTEM	1
OR TAKE THE INTAGLIO, MY FAT GREAT-UNCLE'S HEIRLOOM:	162	CABARET DANCER	35
PULLS UP A ROLL OF FAT FOR THE PIANIST, ...	163	CABARET DANCER	54
FATE			
SILENT AS FATE IS, AND AS STRONG UNTIL	31	PIERE VIDAL	35

FATE -- FEAR

	PAGE	TITLE	LINE
FATE (CONTINUED)			
AND STILL WHEN FATE RECALLETH,	41	HER MONUMENT	22
TO-MORROW FATE SHUTS US IN.	221	SEXTUS PROP: 7	32
FATES			
AND BY SURHUMAN FATES	42	HER MONUMENT	31
MEN'S FATES ARE ALREADY SET,	138	NEAR SHOKU	10
MAY THE FATES WATCH OVER MY DAY.	216	SEXTUS PROP: 5	22
THUS MUCH THE FATES HAVE ALLOTTED ME, AND IF, MAECENAS,	217	SEXTUS PROP: 5	37
WHILE OUR FATES TWINE TOGETHER, SATE WE OUR EYES WITH LOVE;	220	SEXTUS PROP: 7	17
WHAT IF YOUR FATES ARE ACCELERATED,	222	SEXTUS PROP: 8	27
AND ONE RAFT BEARS OUR FATES	223	SEXTUS PROP: 9	5
FATE'S			
TIME'S TOOTH IS INTO THE LOT, AND WAR'S AND FATE'S TOO.	165	QUINTUS SEPTIM	17
NOW YOU MAY BEAR FATE'S STROKE UNPERTURBED,	222	SEXTUS PROP: 8	37
FATHER			
WHO HAS HAD A PIG-HEADED FATHER;	89	A PACT	4
HAS BECOME THE FATHER OF TWINS,	100	TEMPERAMENTS	6
AND YOUR FATHER, WHO WAS BRAVE AS A LEOPARD,	135	EXILE'S LETTER	36
AND THAT THE FATHER WROTE VERSES,	179	MOEURS CON: 3	2
"WHEREFROM FATHER ENNIUS, SITTING BEFORE I CAME, HATH DRUNK."	210	SEXTUS PROP: 2	7
FATHERS			
NOR TO THE TUNE OF THE PHRYGIAN FATHERS.	218	SEXTUS PROP: 5	54
FATNESS			
"DELIGHT THY SOUL IN FATNESS," SAITH THE PREACHER.	163	CABARET DANCER	69
FAUGH			
SPEECH? WORDS? FAUGH! WHO TALKS OF WORDS AND LOVE?!	31	PIERE VIDAL	33
FAULTS			
EVEN MY FAULTS THAT HEAVY UPON ME LIE,	197	ENVOI (1919)	6
FAUN			
THE FAUN	109	THE FAUN	T
AND SEE THE FAUN IN OUR GARDEN.	109	THE FAUN	6
FAUN-LIKE			
STILL DARTS OUT FAUN-LIKE FROM THE HALF-RUIN'D FACE,	192	YEUX GLAUQUES	18
FAUN'S			
FAUN'S FLESH IS NOT TO US,	189	HUGH SELWYN: 3	17
WHEN THAT FAUN'S HEAD OF HERS	192	YEUX GLAUQUES	6
FAVOUR			
MOVE WE AND TAKE THE TIDE, WITH ITS NEXT FAVOUR,	69	THE NEEDLE	12
THEY WORK PATHETICALLY IN MY FAVOUR,	147	BEFORE SLEEP	3
THE FAVOUR OF YOUR PARTY; HAD BEEN WELL RECEIVED."	155	NEAR PERIGORD	149
BACCHUS AND APOLLO IN FAVOUR OF IT,	208	SEXTUS PROP: 1	49
FAWN			
IN WILD-WOOD NEVER FAWN NOR FALLOW FARETH	38	BALLATETTA	6
FAWNS			
AND THE FAWNS COME TO SNIFF AT HIS SIDES:	231	CANTUS PLANUS	2
FE'			
"SIENA MI FE'; DISFECEMI MAREMMA"	193	SIENA MI FE	T
FEAR			
THAT MAKE THE STARK WINDS REEK WITH FEAR	10	FOR THIS YULE	12
EVEN THE GREY PACK KNEW ME AND KNEW FEAR.	30	PIERE VIDAL	13
WITH FEAR, AS HALF-AWAKENED;	74	THE RETURN	6
I FEAR YOU WILL COME TO A BAD END.	94	INSTRUCTIONS	4
MINGLED WITH A CURIOUS FEAR	101	AMITIES	4
SUCH FEAR I HAVE SHE DELIVER	175	LANGUE D'OC: 3	30
AND THOUGH I FEAR TO SPEAK OUT,	175	LANGUE D'OC: 3	35
SOME FROM FEAR OF WEAKNESS,	190	HUGH SELWYN: 4	6
SOME FROM FEAR OF CENSURE,	190	HUGH SELWYN: 4	7
SOME IN FEAR, LEARNING LOVE OF SLAUGHTER;	190	HUGH SELWYN: 4	10
AND A SLAVE SHOULD FEAR PLAUSIBILITIES;	214	SEXTUS PROP: 1	9
THOUGH MALES OF SEVENTY, WHO FEAR TRUTHS NAKED HARM US,	243	MOYEN SENSUEL	147
AND EVEN ZEUS' WILD LIGHTNING FEAR TO STRIKE	244	MOYEN SENSUEL	177
OR WRIES THE FACE WITH FEAR AND LITTLE STAYS,	250	DONNA MI PREGA	54
SO HATH MAN CRAFT FROM FEAR	250	DONNA MI PREGA	75
THE PIMPS OF WHITEHALL EVER MORE IN FEAR,	260	ALF'S FIFTH	7

PAGE 137

FEARED -- FEELS

	PAGE	TITLE	LINE
FEARED			
GREAT IS THE KING OF ENGLAND AND GREATLY TO BE FEARED,	237	ABU SALAMMAMM	15
HID MORE STATISTICS, MORE FEARED TO CONFESS	260	ALF'S FIFTH	11
FEARS			
THE MAN WHO FEARS WAR AND SQUATS OPPOSING	29	ALTAFORTE	25
FEAST			
"I'LL GO TO THE FEAST," QUO' OUR GOODLY FERE,	33	GOODLY FERE	27
CRUSHED STRAWBERRIES! COME, LET US FEAST OUR EYES.	113	L'ART, 1910	2
FEASTS			
YET TO OUR FEASTS YOU BRING NEITHER	101	AMITIES	10
FEAT			
AYE! WHERE ARE THE GLANCES FEAT AND CLEAR	10	FOR THIS YULE	20
BUT HE ACCOMPLISHED THIS FEAT AT SOME COST;	100	TEMPERAMENTS	7
FEATHERS			
IN ICY FEATHERS; FULL OFT THE EAGLE SCREAMED	64	THE SEAFARER	24
"SHE STEWS PUFFED FROGS, SNAKE'S BONES, THE MOULTED FEATHERS OF SCREECH OWLS,	215	SEXTUS PROP: 4	33
FEATHERY			
MIND AND SPIRIT DRIVE ON THE FEATHERY BANNERS.	139	SOUTH-FOLK	9
THOUGH YOU HAD THE FEATHERY SANDALS OF PERSEUS	226	SEXTUS PROP:11	8
FEATS			
OR FROM THE FEATS OF SUMNER CULL IT? THINK,	241	MOYEN SENSUEL	75
FEATURE			
THAT'S SENT TO HOLLAND, A MOST PARTICULAR FEATURE,	239	MOYEN SENSUEL	20
FEATURES			
THE PUG-DOG'S FEATURES ENCRUSTED WITH TALLOW	161	CABARET DANCER	11
I SEARCH THE FEATURES, THE AVARICIOUS FEATURES	162	CABARET DANCER	28
I SEARCH THE FEATURES, THE AVARICIOUS FEATURES	162	CABARET DANCER	28
WILL BE QUITE RICH, QUITE PLUMP, WITH PUG-BITCH FEATURES,	162	CABARET DANCER	48
FEBRILE			
DESPITE IT ALL, DESPITE YOUR RED BLOODS, FEBRILE CONCUPISCENCE	240	MOYEN SENSUEL	67
FED			
I HAVE FED YOUR LAR WITH POPPIES,	102	LADIES	5
AND WE GUARDSMEN FED TO THE TIGERS.	133	FRONTIER GUARD	24
THAT FED HIS SPIRIT; WERE HIS MENTAL MEALS.	241	MOYEN SENSUEL	96
FED 'EM WITH HOGWASH!	257	BREAD BRIGADE	29
FEE			
WHOSE FRAMES HAVE THE NIGHT AND ITS WINDS IN FEE.	12	OF THE GIBBET	28
AND BRIGHT SHIPS LEFT YOU THIS OR THAT IN FEE:	61	PORTRAIT FEMME	3
FEEBLE			
WHEN FEEBLE MR. ASQUITH, GETTING OLD,	264	ALF'S NINTH	5
FEED			
(YOU FEED A HEN ON GREASE, PERHAPS SHE'LL LAY	240	MOYEN SENSUEL	48
FEEDS			
FOR SHE FEEDS MULBERRIES TO SILKWORMS.	140	MULBERRY ROAD	6
HE FEEDS ME WITH BEEF-BONES AND WINE.	237	ABU SALAMMAMM	3
FEEL			
AS LIPS SHRINK BACK WHEN WE FEEL THE STRAIN	11	OF THE GIBBET	20
AFTER MINE OWN KIND THAT KNOW, AND FEEL	20	IN DURANCE	15
AND WOULD FEEL THE FINGERS OF THE WIND	35	THE EYES	2
NOR EAT THE SWEET NOR FEEL THE SORRY,	66	THE SEAFARER	97
HE WAS UNCERTAIN WHY HE SHOULD TRY TO FEEL LIKE ANYTHING ELSE,	118	ANCIENT WISDOM	3
CRYING--"KWAN, KUAN," FOR THE EARLY WIND, AND THE FEEL OF IT.	129	THE RIVER SONG	29
FEEL YOUR HATES WRIGGLING ABOUT MY FEET	145	SALUTATION 3RD	28
A-BRISTLE WITH ANTENNAE TO FEEL ROADS,	153	NEAR PERIGORD	62
NOR FEEL MY ACHE--GREAT AS IT IS,	174	LANGUE D'OC: 3	21
TILL YOU MAY TAKE YOUR CHOICE: TO FEEL THE EDGE OF SATIRE OR	240	MOYEN SENSUEL	65
FEELING			
"ARE YOU FEELING WELL THIS MORNING?"	46	FROM HEINE: 6	8
HABITS OF MIND AND FEELING,	195	HUGH SELWIN:11	2
FEELIN'S			
TO KEEP YOUR FEELIN'S SORE,	269	SAFE AND SOUND	12
FEELS			
SUCH AN ONE AS THE WORLD FEELS	14	FAMAM CANO	24

FEET -- FENCER

```
                                                        PAGE    TITLE             LINE
FEET
   MY FEET WERE BY FROST BENUMBED. ....................   64    THE SEAFARER        9
   MOVEMENTS, AND THE SLOW FEET, .....................    74    THE RETURN          2
   DAWN ENTERS WITH LITTLE FEET ......................    83    THE GARRET          6
   (OR WITH TWO LIGHT FEET, IF IT PLEASE YOU!) .......    86    SALUTATION 2ND     18
   AND THE DELICATE WHITE FEET OF HER LITTLE WHITE DOG    87    ALBATRE             3
   NONE WITH SWIFT FEET. .............................    91    DANCE FIGURE        5
   NONE WITH SWIFT FEET. .............................    91    DANCE FIGURE       24
   WITH HER WHITE-STOCKING'D FEET ....................   111    BLACK SLIPPERS      3
   THEIR HORSES' ARMOURED FEET .......................   111    IMAGE ORLEANS       6
   VINE-STRINGS A HUNDRED FEET LONG HANG DOWN FROM
      CARVED RAILINGS, ...............................   129    THE RIVER SONG     27
   YOU DRAGGED YOUR FEET WHEN YOU WENT OUT. ..........   131    RIVER-MER WIFE     19
   AND THE WATER, A HUNDRED FEET DEEP, REFLECTING GREEN
      EYEBROWS .......................................   136    EXILE'S LETTER     56
   FEEL YOUR HATES WRIGGLING ABOUT MY FEET ...........   145    SALUTATION 3RD     28
   IT FALLS AND ROLLS TO YOUR FEET. ..................   169    PHANOPOEIA          7
   "MAY THE GOUT CRAMP UP HER FEET! ..................   215    SEXTUS PROP: 4     37
   OR SHE WILL SIT BEFORE YOUR FEET IN A VEIL, .......   223    SEXTUS PROP: 9     11
FELICITOUS
   A PLACE OF FELICITOUS MEETING. ....................   141    IDEA OF CHOAN      25
FELL
   STORMS, ON THE STONE-CLIFFS BEATEN, FELL ON THE STERN  64    THE SEAFARER       23
   FROST FROZE THE LAND, HAIL FELL ON EARTH THEN, ....    64    THE SEAFARER       33
   SHOWED ONLY WHEN THE DAYLIGHT FELL ................   193    BRENNBAUM           6
   OF AN AFFECT THAT COMES OFTEN AND IS FELL .........   248    DONNA MI PREGA      2
   FELL PLUMP INTO HER PAIL. .........................   271    OLE KATE           14
FELLED
   THE COMPACT, DE BORN SMOKED OUT, TREES FELLED .....   155    NEAR PERIGORD     124
FELLER
   SOME OTHER FELLER DO IT. ..........................   270    OF 600 M.P.'S      12
FELLERS
   I READ THESE FELLERS PUTS IT ......................   269    SAFE AND SOUND     17
FELLOW
   A SAUCY FELLOW, BUT . . . ..........................    6    CINO               28
   O MY FELLOW SUFFERERS, SONGS OF MY YOUTH, .........    82    THE CONDOLENCE      1
   IMAGINE IT, MY FELLOW SUFFERERS-- .................    82    THE CONDOLENCE      4
   O MY FELLOW SUFFERERS, WE WENT OUT UNDER THE TREES,    82    THE CONDOLENCE      7
   --A BROWN UPSTANDING FELLOW .......................   119    THE GYPSY           4
   BUT WE LIKE THIS FELLOW THE BEST, .................   142    UNMOVING CLOUD     25
   MY GOOD FELLOW, YOU, ON A CABARET SILENCE .........   161    CABARET DANCER      5
   "SST! MY GOOD FELLOW, ART AWAKE OR SLEEPING? ......   172    LANGUE D'OC: 1      6
   "WAIT, MY GOOD FELLOW. FOR SUCH JOY I TAKE ........   172    LANGUE D'OC: 1     26
   MY SUFFERIN' FELLOW MEN, ..........................   269    SAFE AND SOUND     26
FELLOWS
   MY FELLOWS, AYE I KNOW THE GLORY ..................    20    IN DURANCE         28
   OH YE, MY FELLOWS: WITH THE SEAS BETWEEN US SOME BE,   21    IN DURANCE         35
   MY COUNTRY? I LOVE IT WELL, AND THOSE GOOD FELLOWS    238    MOYEN SENSUEL       3
FELLOWSHIP
   IF ONLY THEY COULD BE OF THAT FELLOWSHIP, .........   134    EXILE'S LETTER     10
FELT
   FELT HANDS TURN ICE A-SUDDEN, TOUCHING YE, ........    41    HER MONUMENT       17
   NOT BY THE REASON, BUT 'TIS FELT, I SAY, ..........   249    DONNA MI PREGA     35
FEMALE
   FOR THE FEMALE IS DUCTILE. ........................    82    THE CONDOLENCE     12
   GAVE A SQUADDLE OF FEMALE CONNECTIONS .............   115    SOCIAL ORDER       19
   SADNESS HUNG OVER THE HOUSE, AND THE DESOLATED
      FEMALE ATTENDANTS ..............................   214    SEXTUS PROP: 4     22
   "THAT INCENSED FEMALE HAS CONSIGNED HIM TO OUR
      PLEASURE." ....................................    224    SEXTUS PROP:10     12
FEMINA
   CUM JOCUNDA FEMINA. ...............................   101    AMITIES            23
FEMME
   PORTRAIT D'UNE FEMME ..............................    61    PORTRAIT FEMME      T
   "PAUNVRE FEMME MAIGRE!" SHE SAYS. .................   163    CABARET DANCER     55
FENCE
   SUCH IS YOUR FENCE, ONE SAITH, ....................    19    FOR E. MCC          5
FENCER
   BY THAT HIGH FENCER, EVEN DEATH, ..................    19    FOR E. MCC          3
   'GAINST THAT GREY FENCER, EVEN DEATH. .............    19    FOR E. MCC          9
   'GAINST THAT GREY FENCER, EVEN DEATH, .............    19    FOR E. MCC         25
```

FER -- FIELDING

	PAGE	TITLE	LINE
FER			
FER 'ARFT A PINT O' BITTER?"	270	OF 600 M.P.'S	20
AND KISSIN' HER CAT FER DIVERSION,	271	OLE KATE	19
FERE			
BALLAD OF THE GOODLY FERE	33	GOODLY FERE	T
HA' WE LOST THE GOODLIEST FERE O' ALL	33	GOODLY FERE	1
"FIRST LET THESE GO!" QUO' OUR GOODLY FERE,	33	GOODLY FERE	7
NO CAPON PRIEST WAS THE GOODLY FERE	33	GOODLY FERE	15
NO MOUSE OF THE SCROLLS WAS THE GOODLY FERE	33	GOODLY FERE	23
IF THEY THINK THEY HA' SNARED OUR GOODLY FERE	33	GOODLY FERE	25
"I'LL GO TO THE FEAST," QUO' OUR GOODLY FERE,	33	GOODLY FERE	27
A SON OF GOD WAS THE GOODLY FERE	34	GOODLY FERE	33
A MASTER OF MEN WAS THE GOODLY FERE,	34	GOODLY FERE	49
IF THEY THINK THEY HA' SLAIN OUR GOODLY FERE	34	GOODLY FERE	51
FERMO			
AND IN VAIN THEY COMMANDED HIM TO STA FERMO!	97	AESTHETICS	15
FERN-SHOOTS			
HERE WE ARE, PICKING THE FIRST FERN-SHOOTS	127	BOWMEN OF SHU	1
WE GRUB THE SOFT FERN-SHOOTS,	127	BOWMEN OF SHU	5
FERN-STALKS			
WE GRUB THE OLD FERN-STALKS.	127	BOWMEN OF SHU	9
FESTER			
FESTER AND ROT, FESTER AND ROT,	265	ALF'S TENTH	9
FESTER AND ROT, FESTER AND ROT,	265	ALF'S TENTH	9
FESTERING			
THE POMPS OF FLEET ST., FESTERING YEAR ON YEAR,	260	ALF'S FIFTH	5
FESTIVAL			
BUT A PROCESSION OF FESTIVAL,	110	COITUS	4
FEVER			
BUT I REMEMBERED THE NAME OF HIS FEVER MEDICINE AND DIED.	165	QUINTUS SEPTIM	24
FEW			
I SUPPOSE THERE ARE A FEW DOZEN VERITIES	52	AU SALON	6
SOME FEW WHOM WE'D RATHER PLEASE	52	AU SALON	20
O HELPLESS FEW IN MY COUNTRY,	92	THE REST	1
IN A FEW YEARS NO ONE WILL REMEMBER THE BUFFO,	146	MONUMENTUM AER	3
SO FEW DRINK OF MY FOUNTAIN.	158	PSYCHOLOG HOUR	7
SO FEW DRINK OF MY FOUNTAIN.	158	PSYCHOLOG HOUR	22
FOR A FEW THOUSAND BATTERED BOOKS.	191	HUGH SELWYN: 5	8
FOR A FEW PAGES BROUGHT DOWN FROM THE FORKED HILL UNSULLIED?	207	SEXTUS PROP: 1	20
YOU GIVE BUT FEW.	221	SEXTUS PROP: 7	34
AND MUCH OF LITTLE MOMENT, AND SOME FEW	235	TO WHISTLER	6
A FEW MORE CANON.	273	M. POM-POM	11
FEWER			
MR. NIXON ADVISED ME KINDLY, TO ADVANCE WITH FEWER	194	MR. NIXON	2
FICTION			
THE TALLEYRANDS, HAVE HELD THE PLACE; IT WAS NO TRANSIENT FICTION.	152	NEAR PERIGORD	51
END FACT. TRY FICTION. LET US SAY WE SEE	154	NEAR PERIGORD	94
IN WRITING FICTION ON UNCERTAIN CHANCES	243	MOYEN SENSUEL	135
STILL WE WILL BRING OUR "FICTION AS NEAR TO FACT" AS	243	MOYEN SENSUEL	139
FIDAR			
"NON TI FIDAR," IT IS THE SWORD THAT SPEAKS	19	FOR E. MCC	13
FIDDL'RY			
TALK ME NO LOVE TALK, NO BOUGHT-CHEAP FIDDL'RY,	25	GUIDO INVITES	3
FIDELITIES			
LOVE INTERFERES WITH FIDELITIES;	227	SEXTUS PROP:12	2
FIDELITY			
SHE WAS NOT RENOWNED FOR FIDELITY;	228	SEXTUS PROP:12	11
FIDGETING			
I CAN WALK ABOUT WITHOUT FIDGETING WHEN PEOPLE PASS,	247	PIERROTS	20
FIELD			
OVER THE COOL FACE OF THAT FIELD,	107	COMING OF WAR	17
THE DULL ROUND TOWERS ENCROACHING ON THE FIELD,	155	NEAR PERIGORD	129
A FIELD IN A VALLEY . . .	166	FISH & SHADOW	15
"A FLAT FIELD FOR RUSHES, GRAPES GROW ON THE SLOPE."	229	SEXTUS PROP:12	52
FIELDING			
AND INNOCENT OF STENDHAL, FLAUBERT, MAUPASSANT AND FIELDING.	240	MOYEN SENSUEL	52

PAGE 140

FIELDS -- FIND

```
                                                              PAGE    TITLE             LINE
FIELDS
    AND THE BROAD FIELDS BENEATH THEM TURN CRIMSON,    ...     28    ALTAFORTE            5
    OUT THROUGH THE GLASS-GREEN FIELDS. . . .                  60    TOMB AKR CAAR       31
    FIELDS TO FAIRNESS, LAND FARES BRISKER, . . . . . . . . .  65    THE SEAFARER        50
    GREEN THE WAYS, THE BREATH OF THE FIELDS IS THINE
        THERE, . . . . . . . . . . . . . . . . . . . . . . . . 68    APPARUIT             9
    GRASS, AND LOW FIELDS, AND HILLS, . . . . . . . . . . . .  70    THE PLUNGE          16
    AND THE FIELDS . . . . . . . . . . . . . . . . . . . . . 107    COMING OF WAR        2
    I HAVE SEEN THE FIELDS, PALE, CLEAR AS AN EMERALD,        122    PROVINC DESERT      54
    DESOLATE, DESOLATE FIELDS, . . . . . . . . . . . . . . . 133    FRONTIER GUARD      19
    "SOFT FIELDS MUST BE WORN BY SMALL WHEELS, . . . . . . . 210    SEXTUS PROP: 2      21
FIERCE
    AND THE FIERCE THUNDERS ROAR ME THEIR MUSIC . . . . . .    28    ALTAFORTE           10
FIFTEEN
    AT FIFTEEN I STOPPED SCOWLING, . . . . . . . . . . . . . 130    RIVER-MER WIFE      11
FIFTH
    GREAT IS KING GEORGE THE FIFTH, . . . . . . . . . . . . 237    ABU SALAMMAMM        1
    GREAT IS KING GEORGE THE FIFTH-- . . . . . . . . . . . . 237    ABU SALAMMAMM        4
    GREAT IS KING GEORGE THE FIFTH; . . . . . . . . . . . . 237    ABU SALAMMAMM       10
    GREAT IS KING GEORGE THE FIFTH . . . . . . . . . . . . . 237    ABU SALAMMAMM       18
    ALF'S FIFTH BIT . . . . . . . . . . . . . . . . . . . . 260    ALF'S FIFTH          T
FIFTY
    "ADVANCE ON ROYALTIES, FIFTY AT FIRST," SAID MR.
        NIXON, . . . . . . . . . . . . . . . . . . . . . . . 194    MR. NIXON            7
    "BUTTER REVIEWERS. FROM FIFTY TO THREE HUNDRED    . . . . 194    MR. NIXON           10
    DE GOURMONT SAYS THAT FIFTY GRUNTS ARE ALL THAT WILL
        BE PRIZED. . . . . . . . . . . . . . . . . . . . . . 244    MOYEN SENSUEL      165
FIGHT
    HARD FIGHT GETS NO REWARD. . . . . . . . . . . . . . . . 139    SOUTH-FOLK          10
FIGURE
    DANCE FIGURE . . . . . . . . . . . . . . . . . . . . . .  91    DANCE FIGURE         T
FIGURES
    A-JUMBLING O' FIGURES FOR MAITRE JACQUES POLIN,    ...     22    MARVOIL              4
FILAMENTS
    O FILAMENTS OF AMBER, TWO-FACED IRIDESCENCE! . . . . . .   95    OF THE DEGREES      15
FILL
    FOR EVEN AS THOU ART HOLLOW BEFORE I FILL THEE WITH
        THIS PARCHMENT. . . . . . . . . . . . . . . . . . . . 23    MARVOIL             37
    AND SO WERE MY MIND HOLLOW, DID SHE NOT FILL UTTERLY
        MY THOUGHT. . . . . . . . . . . . . . . . . . . . . . 23    MARVOIL             39
    YEA, I FILL ALL THE AIR WITH MY MUSIC. . . . . . . . . .   29    ALTAFORTE           30
    FILL FULL THE SIDES IN ROWS, AND OUR WINE . . . . . . . 128    THE RIVER SONG       3
    OR LUCK, I MUST HAVE MY FILL. . . . . . . . . . . . . . 173    LANGUE D'OC: 2      10
FILLED
    AS DARK RED CIRCLES FILLED WITH DUST. . . . . . . . . . .  16    PRAISE YSOLT        13
    WHERE THE LOW DRONNE IS FILLED WITH WATER LILIES, . . . 152    NEAR PERIGORD       56
    NO TRUMPETS FILLED WITH MY EMPTINESS, . . . . . . . . . 219    SEXTUS PROP: 6      15
    FILLED THE BACK ALLEYS AND THE BACK TO BACK HOUSES. . . 260    ALF'S FIFTH         14
FILLES
    ET DEUX PETITES FILLES GRACILES, . . . . . . . . . . . . 160    DANS OMNIBUS        14
FILLETH
    SO IS MY HEART HOLLOW WHEN SHE FILLETH NOT MINE EYES,     23    MARVOIL             38
FILLS
    WHAT TIMES THE SWALLOW FILLS . . . . . . . . . . . . . .  14    FAMAM CANO           7
    AND IT FILLS ALL MY HEART WITH REJOICING . . . . . . . .  29    ALTAFORTE           21
FILTHY
    OF THE FILTHY, STURDY, UNKILLABLE INFANTS OF THE
        VERY POOR. . . . . . . . . . . . . . . . . . . . . . . 83   THE GARDEN           6
FIN
    BY THE STIR OF THE FIN, . . . . . . . . . . . . . . . . . 76   THE ALCHEMIST       36
FINAL
    TO THE FINAL ESTRANGEMENT; . . . . . . . . . . . . . . . 199    MAUBERLEY: 2        15
    TO HIS FINAL . . . . . . . . . . . . . . . . . . . . . . 202    AGE DEMANDED        60
FINANCE
    AND MY FINANCE IS SOUND, . . . . . . . . . . . . . . . . 269    SAFE AND SOUND       2
FINANCIAL
    THEY SEEK MY FINANCIAL GOOD. . . . . . . . . . . . . . . 147    BEFORE SLEEP         4
    THE POMPS OF BUTCHERY, FINANCIAL POWER, . . . . . . . . 260    ALF'S FIFTH          1
FIND
    SO THAT I MIGHT FIND YOU AGAIN, . . . . . . . . . . . . . 36   FRANCESCA           11
    WILL WE NOT FIND SOME HEADLAND CONSECRATED . . . . . . .  39    BLANDULA             7
```

FIND -- FIRE

	PAGE	TITLE	LINE
FIND (CONTINUED)			
NOR FIND AUGHT NOVEL IN THY MERRIMENT?	43	SATIEMUS	19
TO FIND HIM SUCH, WHEN THE DAYS BRING	46	FROM HEINE: 6	18
THERE CANST THOU FIND ME, O THOU ANXIOUS THOU,	51	THE FLAME	34
SHE'D FIND A MODEL FOR ST. ANTHONY	63	PHASELLUS ILLE	13
WILL FIND THEE SUCH A LOVER	67	THE CLOAK	5
BE EAGER TO FIND NEW EVILS AND NEW GOOD,	89	COMMISSION	24
WILL YOU FIND YOUR LOST DEAD AMONG THEM?	103	CODA	3
THAT WE FIND MINUTE OBSERVATION.	104	THE SEEING EYE	10
JOY SO RICH, AND IF I FIND NOT EVER	105	DOMPNA POIS	7
AND SINCE I COULD NOT FIND A PEER TO YOU,	105	DOMPNA POIS	11
TILL I AGAIN FIND YOU READY.	105	DOMPNA POIS	20
BECAUSE THEY CAN'T FIND A SOFT SEAT.	142	UNMOVING CLOUD	21
TO FIND HER HALF ALONE, MONTFORT AWAY,	154	NEAR PERIGORD	111
YOU MAY FIND INTERMENT PLEASING,	222	SEXTUS PROP: 8	29
FIND PRETTY IRISH GIRLS IN CHINESE LAUNDRIES,	244	MOYEN SENSUEL	157
I FIND NO MORAL FOR A PERORATION, '	246	MOYEN SENSUEL	241
TO FIND DELIGHT	250	DONNA MI PREGA	67
"FIND US A HARPIST!! DAVID IS THE MAN!!"	264	ALF'S NINTH	16
FINDS			
FINDS THE EARTH AS BITTER	9	NA AUDIART	44
FINDS 'NEATH THIS ROCK FIT MOULD, FIT RESTING PLACE!	41	HER MONUMENT	21
OR FINDS ITS HOUR UPON THE LOOM OF DAYS:	61	PORTRAIT FEMME	21
TILL SHE FINDS WORK TO DO.	272	THE BABY	8
FIND'ST			
AND FIND'ST IN ROME NO THING THOU CANST CALL ROMAN;	40	ROME	2
FINE			
GONE IS HIS BODY FINE AND AMOROUS,	37	THE YOUNG KING	31
I ASK, AND THE FINE COURTESY	106	DOMPNA POIS	52
AND HIGH OVER THE WILLOWS, THE FINE BIRDS SING TO EACH OTHER, AND LISTEN,	129	THE RIVER SONG	28
--EYEBROWS PAINTED GREEN ARE A FINE SIGHT IN YOUNG MOONLIGHT,	136	EXILE'S LETTER	57
AND BRINGS UP A FINE FOUNTAIN.	139	SENNIN POEM	10
BERTRANS, EN BERTRANS, LEFT A FINE CANZONE:	151	NEAR PERIGORD	5
WHAT DOORS ARE OPEN TO FINE COMPLIMENT?"	153	NEAR PERIGORD	75
TIME HAS DRIVEN ME OUT FROM THE FINE PLAISAUNCES,	167	OF AROUET	18
FAIR CHEEKS, AND FINE BODIES;	190	HUGH SELWYN: 4	22
THE SONGS SHALL BE A FINE TOMB-STONE OVER THEIR BEAUTY.	209	SEXTUS PROP: 1	64
AS THE FINE FLAKES,	236	MIDDLE-AGED	3
AS THE FINE DUST, IN THE HID CELL	236	MIDDLE-AGED	8
THE INVITATION HAD NO NEED OF FINE AESTHETIC,	242	MOYEN SENSUEL	127
I WEAR A FINE FUR COAT AND GLOVES,	266	ALF'S ELEVENTH	9
FINER			
YOU OF THE FINER SENSE,	93	THE REST	13
FINGERS			
AS IVY FINGERS CLUTCHING THROUGH	8	NA AUDIART	4
COOL TO MY FINGERS THE FLOWING WATERS.	18	DE AEGYPTO	22
AND WOULD FEEL THE FINGERS OF THE WIND	35	THE EYES	2
THY FINGERS A FROSTED STREAM.	91	DANCE FIGURE	20
AND ABOVE MY FINGERS	109	HEATHER	2
HER FINGERS WERE LIKE THE TISSUE	110	THE ENCOUNTER	4
WITH FINGERS THAT ARE NOT LONG, AND WITH A MOUTH UNDRY,	113	FORMIANUS LADY	5
SIR ARRIMON COUNTS ON HIS FINGERS, MONTFORT,	155	NEAR PERIGORD	121
THE WIRE-LIKE BANDS OF COLOUR INVOLUTE MOUNT FROM MY FINGERS;	170	PHANOPOEIA	17
IF SHE WITH IVORY FINGERS DRIVE A TUNE THROUGH THE LYRE,	217	SEXTUS PROP: 5	27
HOW EASY THE MOVING FINGERS; IF HAIR IS MUSSED ON HER FOREHEAD,	217	SEXTUS PROP: 5	29
FINGER-TIPS			
HAVE I NOT TOUCHED THY PALMS AND FINGER-TIPS,	60	TOMB-AKR CAAR	22
SPREAD LIKE THE FINGER-TIPS OF ONE FRAIL HAND;	152	NEAR PERIGORD	30
FIRE			
A WOMAN AS FIRE UPON THE PINE WOODS	17	PRAISE YSOLT	39
ARE FUSED IN IT AS FLAMES OF AN ALTAR FIRE!	25	GUIDO INVITES	10
HOW HAST THOU SET THE FIRE	41	HER MONUMENT	11
REMEMBER THIS FIRE.	75	THE ALCHEMIST	13
BRING THE BURNISHED NATURE OF FIRE;	75	THE ALCHEMIST	19

FIRE -- FIT

	PAGE	TITLE	LINE
FIRE (CONTINUED)			
REMEMBER THIS FIRE.	75	THE ALCHEMIST	24
LET THE MANES PUT OFF THEIR TERROR, LET THEM PUT OFF THEIR AQUEOUS BODIES WITH FIRE.	76	THE ALCHEMIST	51
SO HE HAVE SENSE OR GLOW WITH REASON'S FIRE,	250	DONNA MI PREGA	91
NOW THEY CAN'T FIRE HIM.	261	ALF'S SIXTH	16
FIRE-DUST			
THE SCORCHED LAUREL LAY IN THE FIRE-DUST;	223	SEXTUS PROP: 9	2
FIRES			
AND YET I MOCK YOU BY THE MIGHTY FIRES	32	PIERE VIDAL	63
THE CRACKLING OF SMALL FIRES, THE BANNERETS,	155	NEAR PERIGORD	132
SO I, THE FIRES THAT LIT ONCE DREAMS	236	MIDDLE-AGED	13
FOR FIRES AND ODD RISKS, COULD IN THIS SECTOR	243	MOYEN SENSUEL	152
FIRM			
HERE LET THY CLEMENCY, PERSEPHONE, HOLD FIRM,	38	LADY'S LIFE	1
HERE LET THY CLEMENCY, PERSEPHONE, HOLD FIRM,	38	LADY'S LIFE	11
THAT WHICH STANDS FIRM IN THEE TIME BATTERS DOWN,	40	ROME	13
FIRM-FACED			
ONE OF THOSE FIRM-FACED INSPECTING WOMEN, WHO	243	MOYEN SENSUEL	156
FIRMNESS			
FIRMNESS,	198	MAUBERLEY: 1	9
FIRST			
BUT YE ASK FIRST WHERE THE WINDS ARE GONE,	10	FOR THIS YULE	27
"THEE"? OH, "THEE" IS WHO COMETH FIRST	20	IN DURANCE	10
IN RETURN FOR THE FIRST KISS SHE GAVE ME."	23	MARVOIL	29
AS DID FIRST SCORN, THEN LIPS OF THE PENAUTIER!	30	PIERE VIDAL	17
"FIRST LET THESE GO!" QUO' OUR GOODLY FERE,	33	GOODLY FERE	7
OR SLACKED HIS HAND-GRIP WHEN YOU FIRST GRIPPED FAME?	59	EXIT' CUIUSDAM	3
"NO! HIS FIRST WORK WAS THE BEST."	85	SALUTATION 2ND	14
YOU WHO CAN KNOW AT FIRST HAND,	93	THE REST	15
THE FIRST HAS WRITTEN A LONG ELEGY TO "CHLORIS,"	118	THREE POETS	3
HERE WE ARE, PICKING THE FIRST FERN-SHOOTS	127	BOWMEN OF SHU	1
THAT WAS THE FIRST VALLEY;	134	EXILE'S LETTER	20
AND STILL THE KNOT, THE FIRST KNOT, OF MAENT?	153	NEAR PERIGORD	80
THE FIRST NIGHT?	159	PSYCHOLOG HOUR	35
GENTLE TALKING, NOT LIKE THE FIRST TALKING, LESS LIVELY;	168	OF AROUET	32
"ADVANCE ON ROYALTIES, FIFTY AT FIRST," SAID MR. NIXON,	194	MR. NIXON	7
THE FIRST DAY'S END, IN THE NEXT NOON;	203	MAUBERLEY: 4	3
I WHO CAME FIRST FROM THE CLEAR FONT	207	SEXTUS PROP: 1	3
IO MOOED THE FIRST YEARS WITH AVERTED HEAD,	222	SEXTUS PROP: 8	19
YOU ALSO, OUR FIRST GREAT,	235	TO WHISTLER	1
FOR MEMORY OF THE FIRST WARM NIGHT STILL CAST A HAZE O'ER	245	MOYEN SENSUEL	195
THAT FIRST MADE HIM BELIEVE IN IMMORAL SUASION.	245	MOYEN SENSUEL	198
BUT TURN TO RADWAY: THE FIRST NIGHT ON THE RIVER,	246	MOYEN SENSUEL	223
FISH			
AND THE FISH SWIM IN THE LAKE	85	SALUTATION	9
LEAPT ABOUT, SNATCHING AT THE BRIGHT FISH	97	AESTHETICS	13
THE FISH IN THE BOXES	97	AESTHETICS	17
FISH AND THE SHADOW	166	FISH & SHADOW	T
AS LIGHT AS THE SHADOW OF THE FISH	166	FISH & SHADOW	5
LIGHT AS THE SHADOW OF THE FISH	166	FISH & SHADOW	20
THE FISH SHALL SWIM IN DRY STREAMS.	220	SEXTUS PROP: 7	27
FISHED			
TROPHIES FISHED UP; SOME CURIOUS SUGGESTION;	61	PORTRAIT FEMME	16
HE FISHED BY OBSTINATE ISLES;	187	E. P. ODE	14
FISHERMEN			
I HAVE SEEN FISHERMEN PICNICKING IN THE SUN,	85	SALUTATION	3
FISHING			
BY THE BRIGHT FLAME OF THE FISHING TORCH	75	THE ALCHEMIST	23
FISH-SKIN			
THE HORSES ARE WELL TRAINED, THE GENERALS HAVE IVORY ARROWS AND QUIVERS ORNAMENTED WITH FISH-SKIN.	127	BOWMEN OF SHU	19
FIST			
WILL CHEERFULLY TELL YOU A FIST IS NO FIST,	263	ALF'S EIGHTH	10
WILL CHEERFULLY TELL YOU A FIST IS NO FIST,	263	ALF'S EIGHTH	10
FIT			
BUT IS FIT ONLY TO ROT IN WOMANISH PEACE	29	ALTAFORTE	27
FINDS 'NEATH THIS ROCK FIT MOULD, FIT RESTING PLACE!	41	HER MONUMENT	21

FIT -- FLARE

```
                                                          PAGE    TITLE           LINE
FIT (CONTINUED)
    FINDS 'NEATH THIS ROCK FIT MOULD, FIT RESTING PLACE!   41    HER MONUMENT       21
    AND NOW YOU GRUMBLE BECAUSE YOUR DRESS DOES NOT FIT   102    LADIES              7
    FIT FOR YOUR SPIRIT TO DWELL IN. ................    110    COITUS              6
    AND IF NOW WE CAN'T FIT WITH OUR TIME OF LIFE .....   168    OF AROUET          23
    TOLD HER WOULD FIT HER STATION. ..................    195    HUGH SELWIN:11      8
    AND COLD FIT FOR DESPAIR, ........................    266    ALF'S ELEVENTH     14
FITFULLY
    AS CRUSHED LIPS TAKE THEIR RESPITE FITFULLY, ......    43    SATIEMUS            8
FITS
    THAT NEVER FITS A CORNER OR SHOWS USE, ............    61    PORTRAIT FEMME     20
FITTED
    FITTED SONG TO THE STRINGS; ......................    211    SEXTUS PROP: 2     36
FIVE
    THESE FIVE MILLENIA,. AND THY DEAD EYES ...........    60    TOMB AKR CAAR       2
    NINE LAWYERS, FOUR COUNSELS, FIVE JUDGES AND THREE
        PROCTORS OF THE KING, ........................     97    THE BELLAIRES       5
    CAUSING THE FIVE PEAKS TO TREMBLE, ...............    128    THE RIVER SONG     14
    FIVE CLOUDS HANG ALOFT, BRIGHT ON THE PURPLE SKY,    129    THE RIVER SONG     33
    AND YOU HAVE BEEN GONE FIVE MONTHS. ..............    130    RIVER-MER WIFE     17
FIVE-SCORE
    AND HEARD THE FIVE-SCORE NIGHTINGALES AIMLESSLY
        SINGING. ....................................    129    THE RIVER SONG     22
FLACCID
    READ BENNETT OR SOME OTHER FLACCID FLATTERER. ....    240    MOYEN SENSUEL      66
FLACCUS'
    (NEAR Q. H. FLACCUS' BOOK-STALL). ................    210    SEXTUS PROP: 2      9
FLAKES
    WHITE WORDS AS SNOW FLAKES BUT THEY ARE COLD, ....     16    PRAISE YSOLT       21
    RAIN FLAKES OF GOLD ON THE WATER .................     76    THE ALCHEMIST      55
    WITH THE WILLOW FLAKES FALLING LIKE SNOW, ........    136    EXILE'S LETTER     54
    AS THE FINE FLAKES, .............................    233    MIDDLE-AGED         3
FLAKING
    AZURE AND FLAKING SILVER OF WATER, ...............     76    THE ALCHEMIST      56
FLAME
    AS THE FLAME CRIETH UNTO THE SAP. ................     17    PRAISE YSOLT       41
    AS FLAME LEAVETH THE EMBERS SO WENT SHE UNTO NEW
        FORESTS, ...................................     17    PRAISE YSOLT       43
    I AM FLAME THAT RISETH IN THE SUN, ...............     18    DE AEGYPTO         17
    ONE FLAME, THAT REACHES NOT BEYOND ...............     20    IN DURANCE          7
    ONE NIGHT, ONE BODY AND ONE WELDING FLAME! .......     32    PIERE VIDAL        56
    THE YELLOW FLAME PALETH ..........................     35    THE EYES            6
    THEY DIED AND THE GREED OF YOUR FLAME CONSUMES THEM.   38    LADY'S LIFE        10
    THE FLAME ........................................     50    THE FLAME           T
    THE FLAME, THE AUTUMN, AND THE GREEN ROSE OF LOVE     51    THE ALTAR           2
    BY THE BRIGHT FLAME OF THE FISHING TORCH .........     75    THE ALCHEMIST      23
    LAPPED IN THE GOLD-COLOURED FLAME I DESCEND THROUGH
        THE AETHER. ................................    169    PHANOPOEIA          5
    YOU HAVE PERCEIVED THE BLADES OF THE FLAME .......    169    PHANOPOEIA         12
    YOU HAVE PERCEIVED THE LEAVES OF THE FLAME. ......    169    PHANOPOEIA         16
    FLAME BURNS, RAIN SINKS INTO THE CRACKS ..........    209    SEXTUS PROP: 1     70
    THAT BREAKETH INTO FLAME. .......................    250    DONNA MI PREGA     61
FLAME-LAP
    AS I'VE FOR YOU, SUCH FLAME-LAP, .................    107    DOMPNA POIS        65
FLAMES
    ARE FUSED IN IT AS FLAMES OF AN ALTAR FIRE! ......     25    GUIDO INVITES      10
    WHEN THE FAIRY FLAMES ENSHROUDED .................     45    FROM HEINE: 3       3
    ALL THE FLAMES ARE DEAD AND SPED NOW .............     45    FROM HEINE: 3       5
    THERE FLOAT THE PETAL-LIKE FLAMES. ...............    109    HEATHER             3
FLAMING
    WHO HAS BROUGHT THE FLAMING IMPERIAL ANGER? .....    133    FRONTIER GUARD     12
FLAMINGOES
    FLAMINGOES; ....................................    203    MAUBERLEY: 4       12
FLAMME
    AND "REND LA FLAMME", .........................    162    CABARET DANCER     20
FLANK
    ALL OF HIS FLANK--HOW COULD HE DO WITHOUT HER? ..    153    NEAR PERIGORD      66
FLANKED
    THE CASTLE FLANKED HIM--HE HAD NEED OF IT. ......    152    NEAR PERIGORD      40
FLARE
    "IN THE FULL FLARE OF GRIEF. DO WHAT YOU WILL." ..    152    NEAR PERIGORD       4
```

PAGE 144

FLARE -- FLESH-SHROUDED

	PAGE	TITLE	LINE
FLARE (CONTINUED)			
FLARE UP WITH SCARLET ORANGE ON STIFF STALKS	162	CABARET DANCER	20
FLARES			
FLARES ON THE CROWDED STAGE BEFORE OUR TABLES	162	CABARET DANCER	22
FLASH			
AND THE LIGHTNINGS FROM BLACK HEAV'N FLASH CRIMSON,	28	ALTAFORTE	9
FLASH BETWEEN THE ORCHIDS AND CLOVER, ...	139	SENNIN POEM	2
FLAT			
OUT OF EREBUS, OUT OF THE FLAT WASTE OF AIR, LYING BENEATH THE WORLD;	76	THE ALCHEMIST	46
AND THE WIDE, FLAT ROAD STRETCHES OUT.	142	UNMOVING CLOUD	5
THE FLAT LAND IS TURNED INTO RIVER.	142	UNMOVING CLOUD	12
IN THE FLAT PROJECTION OF A SPIRAL.	147	BEFORE SLEEP	16
"A FLAT FIELD FOR RUSHES, GRAPES GROW ON THE SLOPE."	229	SEXTUS PROP:12	52
FLAT CALM ENGULPHS MY JIBS, ...	247	PIERROTS	2
FLAT-LYING			
OUT OF EREBUS, THE FLAT-LYING BREADTH, ...	76	THE ALCHEMIST	44
FLAT-SPREAD			
"ANIENAN SPRING WATER FALLS INTO FLAT-SPREAD POOLS."	212	SEXTUS PROP: 3	5
FLATTER			
I WILL NOT FLATTER YOU WITH AN EARLY DEATH, ...	145	SALUTATION 3RD	26
FLATTERER			
READ BENNETT OR SOME OTHER FLACCID FLATTERER.	240	MOYEN SENSUEL	66
FLATTERIES			
WHERE AM I COME WITH COMPOUND FLATTERIES--	153	NEAR PERIGORD	74
FLAUBERT			
HIS TRUE PENELOPE WAS FLAUBERT, ...	187	E. P. ODE	13
WAS FLAUBERT,"	198	MAUBERLEY: 1	6
AND INNOCENT OF STENDHAL, FLAUBERT, MAUPASSANT AND FIELDING.	240	MOYEN SENSUEL	52
FLAVOUR			
NO, NO! GO FROM ME. I HAVE STILL THE FLAVOUR, ...	71	A VIRGINAL	9
FLAW			
'CAUSE NEVER A FLAW WAS THERE	8	NA AUDIART	23
FLAWLESS			
FLAWLESS AS APHRODITE, ...	103	LADIES	15
FLAWS			
IN SPITE OF YOUR OBVIOUS FLAWS, ...	101	AMITIES	15
FLAY			
HE SAID: "WHY FLAY DEAD HORSES?	181	MOEURS CON: 7	15
FLAYED			
BEHOLD HERE VIDAL, THAT WAS HUNTED, FLAYED, ...	31	PIERE VIDAL	47
FLAYETH			
NO MORE DESIRE FLAYETH ME, ...	3	THRENOS	8
FLED			
WHEN TALL STAGS FLED ME THROUGH THE ALDER BRAKES,	30	PIERE VIDAL	9
AND THE HOUNDS FLED AND THE DEER FLED	30	PIERE VIDAL	11
AND THE HOUNDS FLED AND THE DEER FLED	30	PIERE VIDAL	11
AND NONE FLED OVER LONG.	30	PIERE VIDAL	12
INO IN HER YOUNG DAYS FLED PELLMELL OUT OF THEBES,	222	SEXTUS PROP: 8	21
FLEE			
ALREADY THEY FLEE, HOWLING IN TERROR.	81	TENZONE	5
FLEE IF YOU LIKE INTO RANAUS, ...	226	SEXTUS PROP:11	5
IT IS OUR EYES YOU FLEE, NOT THE CITY, ...	226	SEXTUS PROP:11	13
FLEEING			
OF LARES FLEEING THE "ROMAN SEAT"	210	SEXTUS PROP: 2	12
FLEET			
CLOUD AND RAIN-TEARS PASS THEY FLEET!	7	CINO	49
TO FLEET ST. WHERE	196	HUGH SELWIN:12	23
THE POMPS OF FLEET ST., FESTERING YEAR ON YEAR, ...	260	ALF'S FIFTH	5
IN THESE QUARTERS OR FLEET ST.?	263	ALF'S EIGHTH	14
FLEETETH			
AND THAT WHICH FLEETETH DOTH OUTRUN SWIFT TIME, ...	40	ROME	14
FLESH			
WAS THERE SUCH FLESH MADE EVER AND UNMADE!	31	PIERE VIDAL	45
FAUN'S FLESH IS NOT TO US, ...	189	HUGH SELWYN: 3	17
FLESH-COVER			
NOR MAY HE THEN THE FLESH-COVER, WHOSE LIFE CEASETH,	66	THE SEAFARER	96
FLESH-SHROUDED			
FLESH-SHROUDED BEARING THE SECRET.	20	IN DURANCE	25

PAGE 145

FLEURS -- FLOWER

	PAGE	TITLE	LINE
FLEURS			
ET TOUTES LES FLEURS	160	DANS OMNIBUS	28
FLEW			
HUNG WITH HARD ICE-FLAKES, WHERE HAIL-SCUR FLEW,	64	THE SEAFARER	17
OH HOW THE BIRD FLEW FROM TROJAN RAFTERS,	227	SEXTUS PROP:11	35
FLICKERED			
PORTENT. LIFE DIED DOWN IN THE LAMP AND FLICKERED,	68	APPARUIT	3
FLIES			
FLIES."	171	LANGUE D'OC	EPI
FLIGHT			
MUTE MIRROR OF THE FLIGHT OF SPEEDING YEARS,	41	HER MONUMENT	6
SLEEP NOT THOU NOW, I HEAR THE BIRD IN FLIGHT	172	LANGUE D'OC: 1	11
FLIP			
FOR A FLIP WORD, AND TO TIDY THEIR HAIR A BIT.	117	THE LAKE ISLE	11
FLOAT			
IN THE SLOW FLOAT OF DIFFERING LIGHT AND DEEP,	61	PORTRAIT FEMME	27
THERE FLOAT THE PETAL-LIKE FLAMES.	109	HEATHER	3
FLOATED			
HOURS, WHERE SOMETHING MIGHT HAVE FLOATED UP.	61	PORTRAIT FEMME	12
FLOATING			
FLOATING UPON THE WATERS,	27	NIGHT LITANY	40
WITH BOATS FLOATING, AND THE SOUND OF MOUTH-ORGANS AND DRUMS,	135	EXILE'S LETTER	51
MIND LIKE A FLOATING WIDE CLOUD,	137	TAKING LEAVE	5
HE TAKES "FLOATING HILL" BY THE SLEEVE,	140	SENNIN POEM	13
FLOATS			
THE SOUL OF THE SALMON-TROUT FLOATS OVER THE STREAM	166	FISH & SHADOW	2
FLOOD			
"TIME'S BITTER FLOOD"! OH, THAT'S ALL VERY WELL,	59	EXIT' CUIUSDAM	1
MOCK NOT THE FLOOD OF STARS, THE THING'S TO BE.	69	THE NEEDLE	8
BY THE SILVER BLUE FLOOD	108	CH'U YUAN	3
AND FLOOD CARRIES WOUNDED SUEVI.	211	SEXTUS PROP: 2	47
ONE RAFT ON THE VEILED FLOOD OF ACHERON,	219	SEXTUS PROP: 6	11
THE FLOOD SHALL MOVE TOWARD THE FOUNTAIN	220	SEXTUS PROP: 7	25
THE FLOOD OF LIMBS UPON EIGHTH AVENUE	245	MOYEN SENSUEL	189
FLOODED			
KNEW THE LOW FLOODED LANDS SQUARED OUT WITH POPLARS,	157	NEAR PERIGORD	174
FLOODING			
TURNED IN THEIR SAPPHIRE TIDE, COME FLOODING O'ER US!	51	HORAE BEATAE	4
FLOOD-WAYS			
ON FLOOD-WAYS TO BE FAR DEPARTING.	65	THE SEAFARER	53
FLOOR			
O THOU DARK SECRET WITH A SHIMMERING FLOOR,	50	THE FLAME	30
CAREFULLY KEPT FROM THE FLOOR BY A NAPKIN,	111	BLACK SLIPPERS	4
UP STAIRS, THE THIRD FLOOR UP, AND HAVE SUCH QUANDARIES	244	MOYEN SENSUEL	158
AND LICK THE DIRT OFF THE FLOOR	264	ALF'S EIGHTH	3
FLORAL			
OR GATHER FLORAL PLEDGES?"	72	PAN IS DEAD	7
FLORENTIS			
HOMAGE TO QUINTUS SEPTIMIUS FLORENTIS CHRISTIANUS	164	QUINTUS SEPTIM	1
FLORIALIS			
REST NIGHTLY UPON THE SOUL OF OUR DELICATE FRIEND FLORIALIS,	100	TEMPERAMENTS	5
FLOURISHED			
DR. JOHNSON FLOURISHED;	196	HUGH SELWIN:12	2
FLOUT			
GOOD IS IT TO ME IF SHE FLOUT	175	LANGUE D'OC: 3	4
FLOW			
I WOULD THAT THE COOL WAVES MIGHT FLOW OVER MY MIND.	36	FRANCESCA	4
YOU, I WOULD HAVE FLOW OVER ME LIKE WATER,	70	THE PLUNGE	1
THEN THE WATERS OF HAN WOULD FLOW NORTHWARD.)	129	THE RIVER SONG	1
TIGRIS AND EUPHRATES SHALL, FROM NOW ON, FLOW AT HIS BIDDING,	219	SEXTUS PROP: 6	
FLOWED			
I SAY MY SOUL FLOWED BACK, BECAME TRANSLUCENT.	51	THE FLAME	3
AND I FLOWED IN UPON THEE, BEAT THEM OFF;	60	TOMB AKR CAAR	2
FLOWED IN, AND THROUGH THEE AND ABOUT THY HEELS?	60	TOMB AKR CAAR	2
VAST WATERS FLOWED FROM HER EYES?	214	SEXTUS PROP: 4	1
FLOWER			
GREEN OF THE WOOD-MOSS AND FLOWER COLOURS,	35	THE EYES	

PAGE 146

FLOWER -- FOISON

	PAGE	TITLE	LINE
FLOWER (CONTINUED)			
WHAT FLOWER HAS COME INTO BLOSSOM?	127	BOWMEN OF SHU	13
HE BITES THROUGH THE FLOWER PISTIL	139	SENNIN POEM	9
IN FLOWER,	171	LANGUE D'OC	EPI
THE VERY FAIREST FLOWER OF THEIR GYNOCRACY.	239	MOYEN SENSUEL	40
THE FLOWER OF CAMBRIDGE,	258	ALF'S SECOND	14
FLOWER-HUNG			
A NEW-FANGLED CHARIOT FOLLOWS THE FLOWER-HUNG HORSES;	207	SEXTUS PROP: 1	12
FLOWERS			
MY WAVE-WORN BEAUTY WITH HIS WIND OF FLOWERS,	24	THUS NINEVEH	15
AND THERE WERE FLOWERS IN YOUR HANDS,	36	FRANCESCA	2
CLOSE, AND AS THE PETALS OF FLOWERS IN FALLING	39	FOR PSYCHE	4
AND, AS THE RAY OF SUN ON HANGING FLOWERS	40	ERAT HORA	2
GAIETY OF FLOWERS.	67	DORIA	4
THE SHADOWY FLOWERS OF ORCUS	67	DORIA	10
ABOUT AMONG MY FLOWERS.	109	THE FAUN	2
AND THE FLOWERS	112	IONE, DEAD	3
THE EMPEROR IN HIS JEWELLED CAR GOES OUT TO INSPECT HIS FLOWERS,	129	THE RIVER SONG	35
I PLAYED ABOUT THE FRONT GATE, PULLING FLOWERS.	130	RIVER-MER WIFE	2
AT MORNING THERE ARE FLOWERS TO CUT THE HEART,	131	AT TEN-SHIN	3
INTO A VALLEY OF THE THOUSAND BRIGHT FLOWERS,	134	EXILE'S LETTER	19
IT IS LIKE THE FLOWERS FALLING AT SPRING'S END	136	EXILE'S LETTER	73
FLOWERS AND GRASS	138	CITY OF CHOAN	3
(AMID AERIAL FLOWERS) . . . TIME FOR ARRANGEMENTS--	199	MAUBERLEY: 2	13
FLOWERY			
BIRDS WITH FLOWERY WING, HOVERING BUTTERFLIES	141	IDEA OF CHOAN	17
FLOWING			
COOL TO MY FINGERS THE FLOWING WATERS.	18	DE AEGYPTO	22
AND MUSIC FLOWING THROUGH ME SEEMED TO OPEN	39	FOR PSYCHE	8
ALL THINGS ARE A FLOWING,	189	HUGH SELWYN: 3	9
FLOWS			
THE PHOENIX ARE GONE, THE RIVER FLOWS ON ALONE.	138	CITY OF CHOAN	2
"NOR WHERE THE RHINE FLOWS WITH BARBAROUS BLOOD,	211	SEXTUS PROP: 2	46
FLUID			
SHE IS BEAUTIFUL AS THE SUNLIGHT, AND AS FLUID.	84	ORTUS	5
FLUIDS			
FLUIDS INTANGIBLE THAT HAVE BEEN MEN,	32	PARACELSUS	10
FLUTE			
THEIR SOUND IS MIXED IN THIS FLUTE,	130	THE RIVER SONG	39
FLUTES			
MUSICIANS WITH JEWELLED FLUTES AND WITH PIPES OF GOLD	128	THE RIVER SONG	2
TO CLEAR FLUTES AND CLEAR SINGING;	132	AT TEN-SHIN	22
FLUTTER			
THE BIRDS FLUTTER TO REST IN MY TREE,	142	UNMOVING CLOUD	22
THE FLUTTER OF SHARP-EDGED SANDALS.	169	PHANOPOEIA	13
FLUTTERING			
NO MORE FOR US THE FLUTTERING OF WINGS	3	THRENOS	5
FLUTTERS			
NAUGHT BUT THE WIND THAT FLUTTERS IN THE LEAVES.	4	LA FRAISNE	19
FLY			
I, EVEN I, WHO FLY WITH THE SWALLOWS.	18	DE AEGYPTO	4
I, EVEN I, WHO FLY WITH THE SWALLOWS.	18	DE AEGYPTO	18
FLYING			
FLYING SNOW BEWILDERS THE BARBARIAN HEAVEN.	139	SOUTH-FOLK	7
FOE			
YOU SWORN FOE TO FREE SPEECH AND GOOD LETTERS,	145	SALUTATION 3RD	11
FOEMEN			
HERE WE ARE BECAUSE WE HAVE THE KEN-NIN FOR OUR FOEMEN,	127	BOWMEN OF SHU	3
FOES			
FRAME ON THE FAIR EARTH 'GAINST FOES HIS MALICE,	66	THE SEAFARER	76
FOETID			
FOETID BUCHANAN LIFTED UP HIS VOICE	192	YEUX GLAUQUES	5
FOETUSES			
AMONG THE PICKLED FOETUSES AND BOTTLED BONES,	193	SIENA MI FE	1
FOG			
ALL MIRE, MIST, ALL FOG,	70	THE PLUNGE	12
FOISON			
LEST LOVE RETURN WITH THE FOISON SUN	10	FOR THIS YULE	10

PAGE 147

FOIX -- FONT

	PAGE	TITLE	LINE
FOIX			
I HAVE SEEN FOIX ON ITS ROCK, SEEN TOULOUSE, AND	122	PROVINC DESERT	59
NOT A NEAT LEDGE, NOT FOIX BETWEEN ITS STREAMS, ...	152	NEAR PERIGORD	32
FOIX'			
FOIX' COUNT KNEW THAT. WHAT IS SIR BERTRANS' SINGING?	153	NEAR PERIGORD	91
FOLDED			
ARE ALL FOLDED INTO ONE DARKNESS, ...	142	UNMOVING CLOUD	4
FOLDING			
THE FOLDING AND LAPPING BRIGHTNESS	169	PHANOPOEIA	14
FOLDS			
THROUGH ALL THE THIRTY-SIX FOLDS OF THE TURNING AND TWISTING WATERS, ...	134	EXILE'S LETTER	18
FOLIAGE			
THICK FOLIAGE	203	MAUBERLEY: 4	6
MAY A WOODY AND SEQUESTERED PLACE COVER ME WITH ITS FOLIAGE	213	SEXTUS PROP: 3	35
FOLK			
HER NOTE, THE LITTLE RABBIT FOLK	14	FAMAM CANO	8
OH I KNOW THAT THERE ARE FOLK ABOUT ME, FRIENDLY FACES, ...	20	IN DURANCE	2
THAT ANY FOLK E'ER HAD, HAST FROM US TAKEN;	37	THE YOUNG KING	19
FOLK OF UNEARTHLY FASHION, PLACES SPLENDID, ...	50	THE FLAME	24
OH, I KNOW YOU WOMEN FROM THE "OTHER FOLK,"	53	AU JARDIN	20
ALBA, YOUR KINGS, AND THE REALM YOUR FOLK	210	SEXTUS PROP: 2	3
THE SERIOUS SOCIAL FOLK IS "JUST WHAT SEX IS."	244	MOYEN SENSUEL	162
WHERE FOLK OF WORTH BE HOST.	250	DONNA MI PREGA	57
FOLKS			
READY ARE ALL FOLKS TO REWARD HER.	72	DIEU! QU'IL	4
FOLLIES			
CRYING AFTER THE FOLLIES GONE BY ME, ...	168	OF AROUET	3
FOLLOW			
WATCHES TO FOLLOW OUR TRACE.	109	HEATHER	7
WOULD FOLLOW THE WHITE GULLS OR RIDE THEM.	128	THE RIVER SONG	8
I AM UP TO FOLLOW THEE, PALLAS.	147	BEFORE SLEEP	12
I AM UP TO FOLLOW THEE, PALLAS.	147	BEFORE SLEEP	15
AND TO FOLLOW AFTER FRIENDSHIP, AS THEY CALL IT,	168	OF AROUET	3
WEEPING THAT WE CAN FOLLOW NAUGHT ELSE.	168	OF AROUET	3
"FOLLOW ME, AND TAKE A COLUMN, ...	194	MR. NIXON	
WHAT IF UNDERTAKERS FOLLOW MY TRACK, ...	213	SEXTUS PROP: 3	2
AND I SHALL FOLLOW THE CAMP, I SHALL BE DULY CELEBRATED FOR SINGING THE AFFAIRS OF YOUR CAVALRY.	216	SEXTUS PROP: 5	2
YOU WILL FOLLOW THE BARE SCARIFIED BREAST	219	SEXTUS PROP: 6	2
DESIRE WILL FOLLOW YOU THITHER, ...	226	SEXTUS PROP:11	
AND YOU ALSO FOLLOW HIM "NEATH PHRYGIAN PINE SHADE:	229	SEXTUS PROP:12	4
TO FOLLOW A NOBLE SPIRIT, ...	250	DONNA MI PREGA	7
FOLLOWERS			
O AGE GONE LAX! O STUNTED FOLLOWERS, ...	32	PIERE VIDAL	6
FOLLOWING			
FOLLOWING HIS OWN EMANATION.	250	DONNA MI PREGA	8
FOLLOWS			
THE SWIRL OF LIGHT FOLLOWS ME THROUGH THE SQUARE,	169	PHANOPOEIA	
CONSERVATORY FOLLOWS CONSERVATORY, ...	180	MOEURS CON: 5	1
CHRIST FOLLOWS DIONYSUS, ...	189	HUGH SELWYN: 3	
A NEW-FANGLED CHARIOT FOLLOWS THE FLOWER-HUNG HORSES;	207	SEXTUS PROP: 1	1
FOLLY			
THAT WAS RANK FOLLY TO MY HEAD BEFORE.	3	THE TREE	1
BUT I HAVE PUT ASIDE THIS FOLLY AND THE COLD	4	LA FRAISNE	
BUT I HAVE PUT ASIDE THIS FOLLY, BEING GAY	4	LA FRAISNE	
FOR I KNOW THAT THE WAILING AND BITTERNESS ARE A FOLLY.	4	LA FRAISNE	2
AND I? I HAVE PUT ASIDE ALL FOLLY AND ALL GRIEF.	4	LA FRAISNE	2
ALL FOLLY FROM ME, PUTTING IT ASIDE	4	LA FRAISNE	2
AND ALL THIS IS FOLLY TO THE WORLD.	62	A GIRL	
FOND			
UPON FOND NATURE'S MORBID GRACE.	44	MR. HOUSMAN	
FONDA			
EUHENIA WILL HAVE A FONDA IN ORBAJOSA.	163	CABARET DANCER	
FONT			
I WHO COME FIRST FROM THE CLEAR FONT	207	SEXTUS PROP: 1	

FOOD -- FOREIGN

	PAGE	TITLE	LINE
FOOD			
TO HIGH HALLS AND CURIOUS FOOD,	132	AT TEN-SHIN	20
RED JADE CUPS, FOOD WELL SET ON A BLUE JEWELLED TABLE,	135	EXILE'S LETTER	47
OR IF THE COW REFRAINS FROM FOOD	272	THE BABY	7
FOOD'S			
AND LAP O' THE SNOWS FOOD'S GUEREDON	10	FOR THIS YULE	5
FOOL			
AS A FOOL THAT MOCKETH HIS DRUE'S DISDEIGN.	11	OF THE GIBBET	12
BEHOLD ME, VIDAL, THAT WAS FOOL OF FOOLS!	30	PIERE VIDAL	7
O SORROW-SWEPT MY FOOL,	35	HIS OWN FACE	3
"DID YOU TALK LIKE A FOOL,	159	PSYCHOLOG HOUR	34
WHILE THAT CROPPED FOOL,	162	CABARET DANCER	43
FOOL WHO WOULD SET A TERM TO LOVE'S MADNESS,	220	SEXTUS PROP: 7	22
FOOLISH			
FOR THE YOUNG PRINCE IS FOOLISH AND HEADSTRONG;	237	ABU SALAMMAMM	28
FOOLS			
BEHOLD ME, VIDAL, THAT WAS FOOL OF FOOLS!	30	PIERE VIDAL	7
AYE YE ARE FOOLS, IF YE THINK TIME CAN BLOT	30	PIERE VIDAL	18
THEY ARE FOOLS TO THE LAST DEGREE.	33	GOODLY FERE	26
THEY ARE FOOLS ETERNALLY.	34	GOODLY FERE	52
THE FOUR ROUND TOWERS, FOUR BROTHERS--MOSTLY FOOLS:	152	NEAR PERIGORD	35
FOOL'S			
ONE MORE FOOL'S VIGIL WITH THE HOLLYHOCKS.	31	PIERE VIDAL	25
FOOLS'			
GIVE MY GOOD-FELLOW AID IN FOOLS' DESPITE	172	LANGUE D'OC: 1	3
FOOT			
GO WITH A LIGHT FOOT!	85	SALUTATION 2ND	17
WITH A FOOT UNBEAUTIFUL,	113	FORMIANUS LADY	3
AND BY HER LEFT FOOT, IN A BASKET,	180	MOEURS CON: 5	10
WHAT FOOT BEAT OUT YOUR TIME-BAR,	207	SEXTUS PROP: 1	8
SLOW FOOT, OR SWIFT FOOT, DEATH DELAYS BUT FOR A SEASON.	223	SEXTUS PROP: 9	21
SLOW FOOT, OR SWIFT FOOT, DEATH DELAYS BUT FOR A SEASON.	223	SEXTUS PROP: 9	21
AND WHERE HE ONCE SET FOOT, RIGHT THERE HE STAYED.	264	ALF'S NINTH	12
FOOT-FALL			
THERE IS NO SOUND OF FOOT-FALL, AND THE LEAVES	108	LIU CH'E	3
FOOTLIN'			
"AS FOOTLIN' A LOT AS WAS EVER SPAWNED	270	OF 600 M.P.'S	23
FOOTMAN			
PHYLLIDULA NOW, WITH YOUR POWDERED SWISS FOOTMAN	167	OF AROUET	5
FOOTMEN			
WITHOUT FOOTMEN AND EQUIPMENTS?	167	OF AROUET	3
FOR (302)			
FOR'ARDER			
MARCHERS, NOT GETTING FOR'ARDER,	265	ALF'S TENTH	7
FORCE			
UNDER SOME NEUTRAL FORCE	69	THE NEEDLE	14
FORCE:	123	PROVINC DESERT	76
OR WHAT HIS ACTIVE VIRTU IS, OR WHAT HIS FORCE;	248	DONNA MI PREGA	14
BEYOND SALVATION, HOLDETH ITS JUDGING FORCE,	249	DONNA MI PREGA	36
FORCES			
THEY ARE PLAYED ON BY DIVERSE FORCES.	158	PSYCHOLOG HOUR	15
RADWAY GREW UP. THESE FORCES SHAPED HIS SOUL;	239	MOYEN SENSUEL	44
SOME FORCES AMONG THOSE WHICH "FORMED" HIS YOUTH:	241	MOYEN SENSUEL	78
FORE			
'FORE GOD, HOW SWIFT THE NIGHT,	177	LANGUE D'OC: 4	9
FORE-ARMS			
WITH ARMS EXALTED, WITH FORE-ARMS	93	LES MILLWIN	8
FOREGOING			
O CHANSONS FOREGOING	114	EPILOGUE	1
FOREHEAD			
THE MOON IS UPON MY FOREHEAD,	18	DE AEGYPTO	19
WHILE MY HAIR WAS STILL CUT STRAIGHT ACROSS MY FOREHEAD	130	RIVER-MER WIFE	1
HOW EASY THE MOVING FINGERS; IF HAIR IS MUSSED ON HER FOREHEAD,	217	SEXTUS PROP: 5	29
FOREIGN			
SEEK OUT A FOREIGN FASTNESS.	65	THE SEAFARER	39
A FOREIGN LOVER BROUGHT DOWN HELEN'S KINGDOM	227	SEXTUS PROP:11	25

PAGE 149

	PAGE	TITLE	LINE
FOREMAN			
OUT CAME THE EAST OF KAN FOREMAN AND HIS COMPANY.	134	EXILE'S LETTER	23
THE FOREMAN OF KAN CHU, DRUNK, DANCED	135	EXILE'S LETTER	28
FORESEEN			
WHO'D HAVE FORESEEN IT?	82	THE CONDOLENCE	6
FORE-SHORES			
TAWN FORE-SHORES	203	MAUBERLEY: 4	8
FOREST			
GREEN VINES HANG THROUGH THE HIGH FOREST,	139	SENNIN POEM	4
TWO FRIENDS: A BREATH OF THE FOREST ...	158	PSYCHOLOG HOUR	23
FORESTS			
AS FLAME LEAVETH THE EMBERS SO WENT SHE UNTO NEW FORESTS	17	PRAISE YSOLT	43
AS THE FORESTS OF PHAECIA,	209	SEXTUS PROP: 1	54
ROUGH FROM THE VIRGIN FORESTS INVIOLATE,	264	ALF'S NINTH	10
FOREVER			
AND THAT YOU WILL LIVE FOREVER.	86	SALUTATION 2ND	37
(IF GLORY COULD LAST FOREVER	129	THE RIVER SONG	17
FOREVER AND FOREVER AND FOREVER.	130	RIVER-MER WIFE	13
FOREVER AND FOREVER AND FOREVER.	130	RIVER-MER WIFE	13
FOREVER AND FOREVER AND FOREVER.	130	RIVER-MER WIFE	13
OH MAY THE KING LIVE FOREVER!	237	ABU SALAMMAMM	26
FORGAVE			
FOR WHOSE FAIRNESS ONE FORGAVE	9	NA AUDIART	54
FORGE			
TO FORGE ACHAIA.	198	MAUBERLEY: 1	16
FORGET			
... BUT I FORGET ... SHE WAS ..	5	LA FRAISNE	43
TILL THOU FORGET THY SORROW,	47	FROM HEINE: 7	7
FORGET AND REST AND DREAM THERE	47	FROM HEINE: 7	11
O THOU UNMINDFUL! HOW SHOULD I FORGET!	60	TOMB AKR CAAR	15
YOUTH WOULD AWHILE FORGET	158	PSYCHOLOG HOUR	29
SAY "FORGET TO-MORROW," BEING OF ALL MEN	161	CABARET DANCER	7
C.3, C.4, 'TWERE BETTER TO FORGET	260	ALF'S FIFTH	12
FORGETFUL			
FORGETFUL IN THEIR TOWERS OF OUR TUNEING	6	CINO	13
FORGETTING			
AND WE WERE DRUNK FOR MONTH ON MONTH, FORGETTING THE KINGS AND PRINCES.	134	EXILE'S LETTER	5
FORGETTING EVEN HER BEAUTY.	168	OF AROUET	42
FORGIVEN			
ALL THINGS ARE FORGIVEN FOR ONE NIGHT OF YOUR GAMES. ...	227	SEXTUS PROP:11	39
WHEN WRITING WELL HAS NOT YET BEEN FORGIVEN	240	MOYEN SENSUEL	61
FORGOTTEN			
AND FORGOTTEN IT,	26	NIGHT LITANY	11
SO THOU HAST FORGOTTEN FULLY	44	FROM HEINE: 2	1
LOVE AND LAY THOU HAST FORGOTTEN FULLY,	44	FROM HEINE: 2	5
WITH RIHOKU'S NAME FORGOTTEN,	133	FRONTIER GUARD	23
FORK			
FORK OUT TO SOUTH AND NORTH,	121	PROVINC DESERT	5
FORKED			
FOR A FEW PAGES BROUGHT DOWN FROM THE FORKED HILL UNSULLIED?	207	SEXTUS PROP: 1	26
FORM			
AND BEING BENT AND WRINKLED, IN A FORM	9	NA AUDIART	38
HE ANALYSES FORM AND THOUGHT TO SEE	15	FAMAM CANO	47
BUT LIKE A MIST WHERETHROUGH HER WHITE FORM FOUGHT,	31	PIERE VIDAL	36
I'D HAVE HER FORM THAT'S LACED	106	DOMPNA POIS	43
THESE PIECES ARE LIVING IN FORM,	120	GAME OF CHESS	
YOU WILL OBSERVE THAT PURE FORM HAS ITS VALUE. ...	225	SEXTUS PROP:10	33
FROM FORM SEEN DOTH HE START, THAT, UNDERSTOOD, ...	249	DONNA MI PREGA	2
WHO WELL PROCEEDETH, FORM NOT SEETH,	250	DONNA MI PREGA	83
FORMAL			
HERE IS A FORMAL MALE GROUP:	104	THE SEEING EYE	
IOPE, AND TYRO, AND PASIPHAE, AND THE FORMAL GIRLS OF ACHAIA,	223	SEXTUS PROP: 9	1
FORMED			
BLIND EYES AND SHADOWS THAT ARE FORMED AS MEN;	38	BALLATETTA	
SOME FORCES AMONG THOSE WHICH "FORMED" HIS YOUTH:	241	MOYEN SENSUEL	7
FORMED THERE IN MANNER AS A MIST OF LIGHT	248	DONNA MI PREGA	2

FORMIANUS -- FOUND

	PAGE	TITLE	LINE
FORMIANUS			
YOU ARE THE FRIEND OF FORMIANUS, THE VENDOR OF COSMETICS,	113	FORMIANUS LADY	7
FORMIANUS'			
TO FORMIANUS' YOUNG LADY FRIEND	113	FORMIANUS LADY	T
FORMLESS			
AND WE THAT ARE GROWN FORMLESS, RISE ABOVE--	32	PARACELSUS	9
FORMS			
BEHOLD! THE WORLD OF FORMS IS SWEPT BENEATH--	32	PARACELSUS	7
SOME CERTAIN ACCUSTOMED FORMS,	52	AU SALON	26
BE AGAINST ALL FORMS OF OPPRESSION.	89	COMMISSION	25
HIGH FORMS	107	COMING OF WAR	10
THE SILVER BALL FORMS IN MY HAND,	169	PHANOPOEIA	6
FORNICATIONS			
NINE ADULTERIES, 12 LIAISONS, 64 FORNICATIONS AND SOMETHING APPROACHING A RAPE	100	TEMPERAMENTS	1
FORSAKE			
TO HOLD EMBRACED, AND WILL NOT HER FORSAKE	172	LANGUE D'OC: 1	28
FORTH			
SETS FORTH, AND THOUGH THOU HATE ME WELL,	9	NA AUDIART	32
AND BURST FORTH TO THE WINDOWS ONLY WHILES OR WHILES	21	IN DURANCE	31
WE HAVE GONE FORTH BEYOND YOUR BONDS AND BORDERS,	50	THE FLAME	7
THAT I FARE FORTH THAT I AFAR HENCE	65	THE SEAFARER	38
YET LONGING COMES UPON HIM TO FARE FORTH ON THE WATER.	65	THE SEAFARER	48
WE WENT FORTH GATHERING DELICATE THOUGHTS,	82	THE CONDOLENCE	9
THERE COME FORTH MANY MAIDENS	108	CH'U YUAN	5
SLENDER, SHE PUTS FORTH A SLENDER HAND;	128	BEAU TOILET	5
THE IMPERIAL GUARDS COME FORTH FROM THE GOLDEN HOUSE WITH THEIR ARMOUR A-GLEAMING.	129	THE RIVER SONG	34
THE LORDS GO FORTH FROM THE COURT, AND INTO FAR BORDERS.	132	AT TEN-SHIN	14
WHO STIRS NOT FORTH THIS NIGHT,	172	LANGUE D'OC: 1	4
AND SO FORTH, AUGUSTUS. "VIRGIN ARABIA SHAKES IN HER INMOST DWELLING."	216	SEXTUS PROP: 5	18
IF I SET FORTH A BAWDY PLOT LIKE BYRON	239	MOYEN SENSUEL	42
IN MIDST OF DARKNESS LIGHT LIGHT GIVETH FORTH	250	DONNA MI PREGA	85
FORTHRIGHT			
GO FORTHRIGHT SINGING--ANHES, CEMBELINS.	153	NEAR PERIGORD	70
FORTITUDE			
FORTITUDE AS NEVER BEFORE	190	HUGH SELWYN: 4	23
FORTUNE			
BEAUTY IS NOT ETERNAL, NO MAN HAS PERENNIAL FORTUNE,	223	SEXTUS PROP: 9	20
AND BEHOLD ME, SMALL FORTUNE LEFT IN MY HOUSE.	229	SEXTUS PROP:12	53
FORTY			
FOUR AND FORTY LOVERS HAD AGATHAE IN THE OLD DAYS,	102	LADIES	1
THE HEAVY MEMORIES OF HOREB, SINAI AND THE FORTY YEARS,	193	BRENNBAUM	5
TO SEE YOUR FORTY SELF-BAPTIZED IMMORTALS,	239	MOYEN SENSUEL	32
WITH FORTY QUEENS, AND MUSIC TO REGALE	242	MOYEN SENSUEL	112
FORTY-EIGHT			
HIS ARMY IS A THOUSAND AND FORTY-EIGHT SOLDIERS	237	ABU SALAMMAMM	12
FORWARD			
OR CARRY HIM FORWARD. "GO THROUGH ALL THE COURTS,	154	NEAR PERIGORD	115
YOUR QUIET HOUR PUT FORWARD,	222	SEXTUS PROP: 8	28
FOUGHT			
BUT LIKE A MIST WHERETHROUGH HER WHITE FORM FOUGHT,	31	PIERE VIDAL	20
FOUGHT OUT THEIR STRIFE HERE, 'TIS A PLACE OF WONDER;	51	THE ALTAR	3
THESE FOUGHT IN ANY CASE,	190	HUGH SELWYN: 4	1
FOUL			
WHEN THE TEMPESTS KILL THE EARTH'S FOUL PEACE,	28	ALTAFORTE	8
FOUND			
HAVE I FOUND ME A BRIDE	4	LA FRAISNE	14
SO YOU FOUND AN AUDIENCE READY.	85	SALUTATION 2ND	4
I HAVE NOT FOUND THEE IN THE TENTS,	91	DANCE FIGURE	6
I HAVE NOT FOUND THEE AT THE WELL-HEAD	91	DANCE FIGURE	8
BECAUSE ONE HAS JUST, AT LAST, FOUND THEM?	158	PSYCHOLOG HOUR	85
I FOUND THE LAST SCION OF THE	193	SIENA MI FE	3
DOWSON FOUND HARLOTS CHEAPER THAN HOTELS,	193	SIENA MI FE	13
HIS NEW FOUND ORCHID.	199	MAUBERLEY: 2	11
UNTIL HE FOUND HIS SIEVE	199	MAUBERLEY: 2	18

FOUND -- FRANCESCA

	PAGE	TITLE	LINE
FOUND (CONTINUED)			
FOR THIS AGILITY CHANCE FOUND	201	AGE DEMANDED	1
WAS FOUND IN HIS EMPLOYER'S CASH. HE LEARNED THE LAY			
OF CHEAPER PLACES,	243	MOYEN SENSUEL	143
THE MIND OF RADWAY, WHENE'ER HE FOUND A PAIR OF			
PURPLE STAYS OR	245	MOYEN SENSUEL	196
IN SPIRITUAL ASPIRATIONS, BUT HE FOUND IT PROFITABLE,	246	MOYEN SENSUEL	234
YET IS FOUND THE MOST	250	DONNA MI PREGA	56
ON SEA AND LAND, WITH ALL CONVENIENCE FOUND	264	ALF'S NINTH	19
FOUNDED			
WILL NOT OUR CULT BE FOUNDED ON THE WAVES,	39	BLANDULA	9
FOR MINDS SO WHOLLY FOUNDED UPON QUOTATIONS	239	MOYEN SENSUEL	29
FOUNT			
MOUNTS, FROM OUR MIGHTY THOUGHTS AND FROM THE FOUNT	41	HER MONUMENT	27
DABBLING HER HANDS IN THE FOUNT, THUS SHE	211	SEXTUS PROP: 2	53
FOUNTAIN			
THE PETALS FALL IN THE FOUNTAIN,	108	TS'AI CHI'H	1
AND BRINGS UP A FINE FOUNTAIN.	139	SENNIN POEM	10
SO FEW DRINK OF MY FOUNTAIN.	158	PSYCHOLOG HOUR	7
SO FEW DRINK OF MY FOUNTAIN.	158	PSYCHOLOG HOUR	22
THE FLOOD SHALL MOVE TOWARD THE FOUNTAIN	220	SEXTUS PROP: 7	25
FOR HE HAS CHAINED ME TO THIS FOUNTAIN;	237	ABU SALAMMAMM	2
FOR HE HAS CHAINED ME TO THIS FOUNTAIN;	237	ABU SALAMMAMM	16
AND VERY RESPLENDENT IS THIS FOUNTAIN.	237	ABU SALAMMAMM	19
GREAT AND LOFTY IS THIS FOUNTAIN;	237	ABU SALAMMAMM	22
HE WILL UNDOUBTEDLY CHAIN SOMEONE ELSE TO THIS			
FOUNTAIN,	238	ABU SALAMMAMM	31
FOUNTAINS			
MY LITTLE MOUTH SHALL GOBBLE IN SUCH GREAT FOUNTAINS,	210	SEXTUS PROP: 2	6
FOUR			
I JOIN THESE WORDS FOR FOUR PEOPLE,	88	CAUSA	1
YOU DO NOT KNOW THESE FOUR PEOPLE.	88	CAUSA	4
NINE LAWYERS, FOUR COUNSELS, FIVE JUDGES AND THREE			
PROCTORS OF THE KING,	97	THE BELLAIRES	5
NINE LAWYERS, FOUR COUNSELS, ETC.,	98	THE BELLAIRES	28
HE HAD TO BE FOUR TIMES CUCKOLD.	100	TEMPERAMENTS	8
FOUR AND FORTY LOVERS HAD AGATHAS IN THE OLD DAYS,	102	LADIES	1
WE WHO WENT OUT INTO THE FOUR A. M. OF THE WORLD	104	ANCORA	3
FOUR POEMS OF DEPARTURE	137	OF DEPARTURE	T
THE FOUR ROUND TOWERS, FOUR BROTHERS--MOSTLY FOOLS:	152	NEAR PERIGORD	35
THE FOUR ROUND TOWERS, FOUR BROTHERS--MOSTLY FOOLS:	152	NEAR PERIGORD	35
MOUNTS FROM THE FOUR HORNS OF MY BED-POSTS,	169	PHANOPOEIA	3
LIE DEAD WITHIN FOUR WALLS	236	MIDDLE-AGED	15
FOUR-SQUARE			
BREAK DOWN THE FOUR-SQUARE WALLS OF STANDING TIME.	49	OF SPLENDOUR	21
FOURTEEN			
FOURTEEN HUNTERS STILL EAT IN THE STABLES OF	97	THE BELLAIRES	11
AT FOURTEEN I MARRIED MY LORD YOU.	130	RIVER-MER WIFE	7
FOURTH			
FROM CHARLES THE FOURTH;	98	THE BELLAIRES	20
OF HORSES, FROM HENRY THE FOURTH.	98	THE BELLAIRES	22
ALF'S FOURTH BIT	259	ALF'S FOURTH	T
FRAGRANT			
AND THE LOOSE FRAGRANT CAVENDISH	117	THE LAKE ISLE	5
FRAIL			
FRAIL CINO, STRONGEST OF HIS TRIBE	6	CINO	20
WITH FAT BOARDS, BAWDS, WINE AND FRAIL MUSIC!	28	ALTAFORTE	17
PRETEND HUMANITY OR DON THE FRAIL ATTIRE?	32	PARACELSUS	2
FRAIL AND SO VILE IN ALL,	42	HER MONUMENT	51
OF ALL THINGS, FRAIL ALABASTER, AH ME!	68	APPARUIT	19
SPREAD LIKE THE FINGER-TIPS OF ONE FRAIL HAND;	152	NEAR PERIGORD	30
FRAISNE			
LA FRAISNE	4	LA FRAISNE	T
FRAME			
FRAME ON THE FAIR EARTH 'GAINST FOES HIS MALICE,	66	THE SEAFARER	76
FRAMES			
WHOSE FRAMES HAVE THE NIGHT AND ITS WINDS IN FEE.	12	OF THE GIBBET	28
FRANCE			
CERTAIN POETS HERE AND IN FRANCE	148	FRATRES MINORE	2
FRANCESCA			
FRANCESCA	36	FRANCESCA	T

FRANCESCA -- FRESH

	PAGE	TITLE	LINE
FRANCESCA (CONTINUED)			
PIER FRANCESCA, ...	198	MAUBERLEY: 1	14
FRANCHISE			
FRANCHISE FOR CIRCUMCISION.	189	HUGH SELWYN: 3	20
FRANCOIS			
FRANCOIS AND MARGOT AND THEE AND ME, ...	11	OF THE GIBBET	2
FRANCOIS AND MARGOT AND THEE AND ME, ...	11	OF THE GIBBET	14
FRANCOIS AND MARGOT AND THEE AND ME, ...	12	OF THE GIBBET	26
FRANCOIS AND MARGOT AND THEE AND ME:	12	OF THE GIBBET	38
FRANCOIS-MARIE			
IMPRESSIONS OF FRANCOIS-MARIE AROUET (DE VOLTAIRE)	167	OF AROUET	T
FRANKINCENSE			
SHE WOULD BRING FRANKINCENSE AND WREATHS TO MY TOMB,	213	SEXTUS PROP: 3	30
FRANKLIN			
FOR AS BEN FRANKLIN SAID, WITH SUCH URBANITY:	246	MOYEN SENSUEL	235
FRANKLY			
AND SAID SO FRANKLY.	159	PSYCHOLOG HOUR	33
FRANKNESS			
FRANKNESS AS NEVER BEFORE, ...	190	HUGH SELWYN: 4	24
FRATRES			
FRATRES MINORES	148	FRATRES MINORE	T
FREE			
WAS GROWN SO FREE AN ESSENCE, OR BECOME	32	PARACELSUS	4
AND THE SCORN OF HIS LAUGH RANG FREE, ...	00	GOODLY FERE	10
WI' A BUNDLE O' CORDS SWUNG FREE, ...	33	GOODLY FERE	18
AND THE BLOOD GUSHED HOT AND FREE, ...	34	GOODLY FERE	38
WITH THE WINDS UNLEASHED AND FREE, ...	34	GOODLY FERE	46
FREE US, FOR WITHOUT BE GOODLY COLOURS, ...	35	THE EYES	8
FREE US, FOR WE PERISH	35	THE EYES	11
FREE US, FOR THERE IS ONE	35	THE EYES	15
I MATE WITH MY FREE KIND UPON THE CRAGS;	81	TENZONE	10
BEING FREE OF MEDIAEVAL SCHOLARSHIP, ...	98	THE BELLAIRES	24
YOU SWORN FOE TO FREE SPEECH AND GOOD LETTERS, ...	145	SALUTATION 3RD	11
LET ME BE FREE OF PAVEMENTS, ...	146	CANTILATIONS	4
LET ME BE FREE OF THE PRINTERS.	146	CANTILATIONS	5
FREE OF PISISTRATUS, ...	189	HUGH SELWYN: 3	22
"EVEN IF YOU HAVE TO WORK FREE.	194	MR. NIXON	9
A HEAVY MASS ON FREE NECKS.	226	SEXTUS PROP:11	12
"AS FREE OF MOBS AS KINGS"? I'D HAVE MEN FREE OF			
THAT INVIDIOUS, ...	244	MOYEN SENSUEL	169
"AS FREE OF MOBS AS KINGS"? I'D HAVE MEN FREE OF			
THAT INVIDIOUS, ...	244	MOYEN SENSUEL	169
WHERE AN ENGLISHMAN IS FREE	272	NATIONAL SONG	6
FREEDOM			
A "FREEDOM FROM ATTAINDER"	98	THE BELLAIRES	18
AND A FURTHER FREEDOM FOR THE REMAINDER	98	THE BELLAIRES	21
('TIS AN ANOMALY IN OUR LARGE LAND OF FREEDOM, ...	245	MOYEN SENSUEL	217
WHILE YOU STALWART SHEEP OF FREEDOM	269	SAFE AND SOUND	7
FREEDOM'S			
WILL WE NOT RATHER, WHEN OUR FREEDOM'S WON, ...	39	BLANDULA	2
FREELY			
BORN OF A JONGLEUR'S TONGUE, FREELY TO PASS	153	NEAR PERIGORD	83
FREE-RUNNING			
HER STRAIGHT SPEECH FREE-RUNNING, ...	106	DOMPNA POIS	29
FREEST			
WHO MADE THE FREEST HAND SEEM COVETOUS ,.........	37	THE YOUNG KING	14
FREEZE			
(I BURN, I FREEZE, I SWEAT, SAID THE FAIR GREEK,	242	MOYEN SENSUEL	123
FREEZETH			
FREEZETH RIVER, TURNETH LIVER, ...	116	ANCIENT MUSIC	8
FRENCH			
FOR THE FRENCH HAVE COMIC PAPERS--	272	NATIONAL SONG	9
FRENETICS			
HATE TREMOLOS AND NATIONAL FRENETICS.	247	PIERROTS	14
FRERE			
MON BEAU GRAND FRERE	273	M. POM-POM	3
FRESH			
HER STRAIGHT FRESH BODY, ...	106	DOMPNA POIS	48
HOT SUN, CLEAR WATER, FRESH WIND, ...	146	CANTILATIONS	3
IS, AT BOTTOM, DISTINGUISHED AND FRESH AS A MARCH			
HERB.	247	PIERROTS	18

PAGE 153

	PAGE	TITLE	LINE
FRESHETS			
AND FRESHETS ARE BURSTING THEIR ICE	138	NEAR SHOKU	8
FREUD			
COULD FREUD OR JUNG UNFATHOM SUCH A SINK?	241	MOYEN SENSUEL	76
FRIEND			
BUT WHERE'S THE OLD FRIEND HASN'T FALLEN OFF,	59	EXIT' CUIUSDAM	2
COME, MY FRIEND, AND REMEMBER	83	THE GARRET	2
IS, FOR THE TIME BEING, THE MISTRESS OF MY FRIEND,	87	ALBATRE	2
REST NIGHTLY UPON THE SOUL OF OUR DELICATE FRIEND FLORIALIS,	100	TEMPERAMENTS	2
I CONFESS, MY FRIEND, I AM PUZZLED.	102	MEDITATIO	5
TO GATHER GRAPES FOR THE LEOPARDS, MY FRIEND,	108	CH'U YUAN	6
TO FORMIANUS' YOUNG LADY FRIEND	113	FORMIANUS LADY	T
YOU ARE THE FRIEND OF FORMIANUS, THE VENDOR OF COSMETICS,	113	FORMIANUS LADY	7
OUR DEFENCE IS NOT YET MADE SURE, NO ONE CAN LET HIS FRIEND RETURN.	127	BOWMEN OF SHU	8
TO SO-KIN OF RAKUYO, ANCIENT FRIEND, CHANCELLOR OF GEN.	134	EXILE'S LETTER	1
TAKING LEAVE OF A FRIEND	137	TAKING LEAVE	T
TO A FRIEND WRITING ON CABARET DANCERS	161	CABARET DANCER	T
AND THAT THE FRIEND OF THE SECOND DAUGHTER WAS UNDERGOING A NOVEL,	179	MOEURS CON: 3	4
AT A FRIEND OF MY WIFE'S THERE IS A PHOTOGRAPH,	180	MOEURS CON: 5	1
LIKEWISE A FRIEND OF BLOUGHRAM'S ONCE ADVISED ME:	194	MR. NIXON	21
A POSSIBLE FRIEND AND COMFORTER.	196	HUGH SELWIN:12	20
YOU, SOMETIMES, WILL LAMENT A LOST FRIEND,	219	SEXTUS PROP: 6	30
WHO, WHO WILL BE THE NEXT MAN TO ENTRUST HIS GIRL TO A FRIEND?	227	SEXTUS PROP:12	1
"NOTHING WILL PAY THEE, FRIEND, LIKE CHRISTIANITY."	246	MOYEN SENSUEL	236
POOR IN DISCERNMENT, BEING THUS WEAKNESS' FRIEND,	249	DONNA MI PREGA	38
FRIENDLY			
OH I KNOW THAT THERE ARE FOLK ABOUT ME, FRIENDLY FACES,	20	IN DURANCE	2
I BEG YOU, MY FRIENDLY CRITICS,	81	TENZONE	8
GO IN A FRIENDLY MANNER,	89	COMMISSION	22
FRIENDS			
TO THE END THAT YOU SEE, FRIENDS:	22	MARVOIL	15
THIS PAPIER-MACHE, WHICH YOU SEE, MY FRIENDS,	63	PHASELLUS ILLE	1
NEW FRIENDS, NEW FACES,	70	THE PLUNGE	4
THAT THE RICH HAVE BUTLERS AND NO FRIENDS,	83	THE GARRET	3
AND WE HAVE FRIENDS AND NO BUTLERS.	83	THE GARRET	4
I AM OLD ENOUGH NOW TO MAKE FRIENDS.	89	A PACT	5
OLD FRIENDS THE MOST.--W. B. Y.	101	AMITIES	EPI
FOR YOU WILL HAVE NO FRIENDS ABOUT YOU	137	OF DEPARTURE	EPI
HOW SHALL WE KNOW ALL THE FRIENDS	141	IDEA OF CHOAN	31
MY FRIENDS ARE ESTRANGED, OR FAR DISTANT,	142	UNMOVING CLOUD	8
"DO WE KNOW OUR FRIENDS?"	156	NEAR PERIGORD	154
TWO FRIENDS: A BREATH OF THE FOREST . . .	158	PSYCHOLOG HOUR	23
FRIENDS? ARE PEOPLE LESS FRIENDS	158	PSYCHOLOG HOUR	24
FRIENDS? ARE PEOPLE LESS FRIENDS	158	PSYCHOLOG HOUR	24
FRIEND'S			
AND THE "BEST CRAFTSMAN" SINGS OUT HIS FRIEND'S SONG,	155	NEAR PERIGORD	141
FRIENDSHIP			
LET US BUILD HERE AN EXQUISITE FRIENDSHIP,	51	THE ALTAR	1
AND TO FOLLOW AFTER FRIENDSHIP, AS THEY CALL IT,	168	OF AROUET	33
FRIGIDAIRE			
NOR IS IT EQUIPPED WITH A FRIGIDAIRE PATENT;	209	SEXTUS PROP: 1	59
FROCK			
FROM THE GOLD-YELLOW FROCK	204	MEDALLION	6
FROGS			
"SHE STEWS PUFFED FROGS, SNAKE'S BONES, THE MOULTED FEATHERS OF SCREECH OWLS,	215	SEXTUS PROP: 4	33
TO SELL THE GOD DAMN'D FROGS	273	M. POM-POM	10
FROLIC			
GO WITH AN IMPERTINENT FROLIC!	86	SALUTATION 2ND	20
FROLICKING			
WHEN TOURISTS FROLICKING	236	MIDDLE-AGED	4
FROM (200)			
FRONT			
PAINTING THE FRONT OF THAT CHURCH;	121	PROVINC DESERT	31

FRONT -- FULL

	PAGE	TITLE	LINE
FRONT (CONTINUED)			
I PLAYED ABOUT THE FRONT GATE, PULLING FLOWERS. ...	130	RIVER-MER WIFE	2
"TIME FOR THAT QUESTION!" FRONT BENCH INTERPOSES.	260	ALF'S FIFTH	16
FRONTIER			
LAMENT OF THE FRONTIER GUARD	133	FRONTIER GUARD	T
FROST			
MY FEET WERE BY FROST BENUMBED.	64	THE SEAFARER	9
FROST FROZE THE LAND, HAIL FELL ON EARTH THEN, ...	64	THE SEAFARER	33
CLEAR AS FROST ON THE GRASS-BLADE, ...	108	FAN-PIECE	2
WITH FROST AND HAIL AT NIGHT	173	LANGUE D'OC: 2	14
FROSTED			
THY FINGERS A FROSTED STREAM.	91	DANCE FIGURE	20
THEREON THE AMOROUS CALOR SLIGHTLY FROSTED HIM. ...	242	MOYEN SENSUEL	122
FROSTS			
BONES WHITE WITH A THOUSAND FROSTS, ...	133	FRONTIER GUARD	8
FROSTY			
CRIMSON, FROSTY WITH DEW, THE ROSES BEND WHERE	68	APPARUIT	5
FROWSY			
SUNK IN A FROWSY COLLAR--AN UNBRUSHED BLACK.	161	CABARET DANCER	12
FROZE			
FROST FROZE THE LAND, HAIL FELL ON EARTH THEN, ...	64	THE SEAFARER	33
FRUIT			
FRUIT OF MY SEED, ... ,,,...............	96	DUM CAPITOLIUM	5
NO, NOW WHILE IT MAY BE, LET NOT THE FRUIT OF LIFE			
CEASE. .... ,,,.......................	220	SEXTUS PROP: 7	28
HERE RADWAY GREW, THE FRUIT OF PANTOSOCRACY, ...	239	MOYEN SENSUEL	39
FU			
FU I	117	EPITAPHS	ST
FU I LOVED THE HIGH CLOUD AND THE HILL, ...	117	EPITAPHS	1
FUIT			
ISTE FUIT VIR INCULTUS, ...	101	AMITIES	17
'FULGENCE			
BID THY 'FULGENCE BEAR AWAY CARE.	7	CINO	48
FULL			
AND YET; FULL SPEED	14	FAMAM CANO	27
FOR THE CUSTOM IS FULL OLD, ...	24	THUS NINEVEH	7
DREW FULL THIS DAGGER THAT DOTH TREMBLE HERE.	31	PIERE VIDAL	42
VOID OF ALL JOY AND FULL OF IRE AND SADNESS.	36	THE YOUNG KING	8
GRIEVING AND SAD AND FULL OF BITTERNESS	36	THE YOUNG KING	9
O SKILLFUL DEATH AND FULL OF BITTERNESS, ...	37	THE YOUNG KING	17
FROM THIS FAINT WORLD, HOW FULL OF BITTERNESS	37	THE YOUNG KING	25
TO MIND ME OF SOME URN OF FULL DELIGHT, ...	41	HER MONUMENT	13
IN ICY FEATHERS; FULL OFT THE EAGLE SCREAMED	64	THE SEAFARER	24
I HAVE SEEN THEIR SMILES FULL OF TEETH	85	SALUTATION	5
FULL OF GOSSIP AND OLD TALES."	90	SURGIT FAMA	19
WHY IS YOUR GLITTER FULL OF CURIOUS MISTRUST?	95	OF THE DEGREES	13
I HAVE ADORED YOU FOR THREE FULL YEARS;	102	LADIES	6
THOUGH SHE WITH A FULL HEART	106	DOMPNA POIS	41
FULL OF FAINT LIGHT	107	COMING OF WAR	3
AND THREE VALLEYS, FULL OF WINDING ROADS, ...	121	PROVINC DESERT	4
OVER A STREAM FULL OF LILIES.	121	PROVINC DESERT	17
WHEN ANYONE SAYS "RETURN," THE OTHERS ARE FULL OF			
SORROW. .... ,,,....	127	BOWMEN OF SHU	6
OUR MIND IS FULL OF SORROW, WHO WILL KNOW OF OUR			
GRIEF? ,,,....................................	127	BOWMEN OF SHU	24
FILL FULL THE SIDES IN ROWS, AND OUR WINE ,........	128	THE RIVER SONG	3
THE PURPLE HOUSE AND THE CRIMSON ARE FULL OF SPRING			
SOFTNESS.	129	THE RIVER SONG	24
FOR THE GARDENS AT JO-RUN ARE FULL OF NEW			
NIGHTINGALES, ...	130	THE RIVER SONG	38
BY THE NORTH GATE, THE WIND BLOWS FULL OF SAND, ...	133	FRONTIER GUARD	1
AND INTO TEN THOUSAND VALLEYS FULL OF VOICES AND			
PINE-WINDS.	134	EXILE'S LETTER	21
"IN THE FULL FLARE OF GRIEF. DO WHAT YOU WILL." ...	152	NEAR PERIGORD	40
THERE IS A TRELLIS FULL OF EARLY ROSES, ...	153	NEAR PERIGORD	72
WITH HIS BLOUSE FULL OF APPLES ,,,,.... ,,,,,,,..	181	MOEURS CON: 7	4
NOT THE FULL SMILE, ...	198	MAUBERLEY: 1	10
HE HAD PASSED, INCONSCIENT, FULL GAZE, ...	200	MAUBERLEY: 2	26
TIBET SHALL BE FULL OF ROMAN POLICEMEN, ...	219	SEXTUS PROP: 6	8
ME HAPPY, NIGHT, NIGHT FULL OF BRIGHTNESS;	220	SEXTUS PROP: 7	1
IS THE ORNAMENTAL GODDESS FULL OF ENVY?	221	SEXTUS PROP: 8	11

FULL -- 'GAINST

	PAGE	TITLE	LINE
FULL (CONTINUED)			
IS FULL OF GILDED SNOW,	236	MIDDLE-AGED	21
AND HIS POCKETS BY MA'S AID, THAT NIGHT WITH CASH FULL,	242	MOYEN SENSUEL	126
FULLY			
SO THOU HAST FORGOTTEN FULLY	44	FROM HEINE: 2	1
LOVE AND LAY THOU HAST FORGOTTEN FULLY,	44	FROM HEINE: 2	5
LONG SINCE FULLY DISCUSSED BY OVID.	148	FRATRES MINORE	4
FUMES			
AS HE INHALED THE STILL FUMES OF RICE-POWDER.	243	MOYEN SENSUEL	132
FUNCTION			
WILL LONG ONLY TO BE A SOCIAL FUNCTION,	244	MOYEN SENSUEL	176
FUNDAMENTAL			
--GIVEN THAT IS HIS "FUNDAMENTAL PASSION,"	200	MAUBERLEY: 2	20
FUNERAL			
AND THERE ARE ALSO THE INANE EXPENSES OF THE FUNERAL;	164	QUINTUS SEPTIM	9
I SHALL HAVE, DOUBTLESS, A BOOM AFTER MY FUNERAL,	207	SEXTUS PROP: 1	23
"WILL HE SAY NASTY THINGS AT MY FUNERAL?"	215	SEXTUS PROP: 4	40
NOR AT MY FUNERAL EITHER WILL THERE BY ANY LONG TRAIL,	219	SEXTUS PROP: 6	13
YOU WRITE OF ADRASTUS' HORSES AND THE FUNERAL RITES OF ACHENOR,	228	SEXTUS PROP:12	19
FUNGUS			
YOU FUNGUS, YOU CONTINUOUS GANGRENE.	145	SALUTATION 3RD	12
WILL BE A STUFFY, OPULENT SORT OF FUNGUS	161	CABARET DANCER	14
FUR			
WHY DOES THE SMALL CHILD IN THE SOILED-WHITE IMITATION FUR COAT	114	SIMULACRA	3
I WEAR A FINE FUR COAT AND GLOVES,	266	ALF'S ELEVENTH	9
AND THEIR NECKS SUNK INTO FUR	269	SAFE AND SOUND	14
FURNISH			
FURNISH MORE DATE FOR A COMPILATION	243	MOYEN SENSUEL	153
FURTHER			
FURTHER INSTRUCTIONS	94	INSTRUCTIONS	7
AND A FURTHER FREEDOM FOR THE REMAINDER	98	THE BELLAIRES	2
FURTHER AND OUT OF REACH, THE PURPLE NIGHT,	155	NEAR PERIGORD	13
AND START TO INSPECT SOME FURTHER PYRAMID;	236	MIDDLE-AGED	
FUSED			
ARE FUSED IN IT AS FLAMES OF AN ALTAR FIRE!	25	GUIDO INVITES	1
FUSS			
OH WHAT A FUSS THEY MADE	262	ALF'S SIXTH	2
FUTURE			
LET US EXPRESS OUR ENVY OF THE MAN WITH A STEADY JOB AND NO WORRY ABOUT THE FUTURE.	94	INSTRUCTIONS	
THE PRUDENT WHORE IS NOT WITHOUT HER FUTURE,	163	CABARET DANCER	7
FUTURES			
GOOD HEDGETHORN, THEY ALL HAVE FUTURES,	163	CABARET DANCER	6
FUTURISTIC			
CROSSED IN GREAT FUTURISTIC X'S, THE ART STUDENTS	93	LES MILLWIN	
GAG			
THEY SUPPORTED THE GAG AND THE RING:	145	SALUTATION 3RD	
GAGGED			
SO MUCH FOR THE GAGGED REVIEWERS,	145	SALUTATION 3RD	
GAI			
AUPRES D'UN PETIT ENFANT GAI, BOSSU.	160	DANS OMNIBUS	
GAIETY			
GAIETY OF FLOWERS.	67	DORIA	
TALL STATURE AND GAIETY,	106	DOMPNA POIS	
GAIN			
AND TAKES STRANGE GAIN AWAY:	61	PORTRAIT FEMME	
MIGHT, IN NEW AGES, GAIN HER WORSHIPPERS,	197	ENVOI (1919)	
GAINS			
GAINS YET ANOTHER CRUST	236	MIDDLE-AGED	
'GAINST			
'GAINST OUR LIPS FOR THE SOUL'S DISTRESS	11	OF THE GIBBET	
'GAINST THAT GREY FENCER, EVEN DEATH.	19	FOR E. MCC	
'GAINST THAT GREY FENCER, EVEN DEATH.	19	FOR E. MCC	
HIS LONE MIGHT 'GAINST ALL DARKNESS OPPOSING.	29	ALTAFORTE	
AND OUR CHARGES 'GAINST "THE LEOPARD'S" RUSH CLASH.	29	ALTAFORTE	
FRAME ON THE FAIR EARTH 'GAINST FOES HIS MALICE,	66	THE SEAFARER	
SO 'GAINST THE WINTER'S BALM.	116	ANCIENT MUSIC	

PAGE 156

'GAINST -- GARDEN

	PAGE	TITLE	LINE
'GAINST (CONTINUED)			
'GAINST HER I PRIZE NOT AS A GLOVE	176	LANGUE D'OC: 3	71
GAIT			
NO MAN AT ALL GOING THE EARTH'S GAIT,	66	THE SEAFARER	92
GALATEA			
AND YOU, O POLYPHEMUS? DID HARSH GALATEA ALMOST	208	SEXTUS PROP: 1	46
GALAXIES			
AMID HER GALAXIES,	199	MAUBERLEY: 2	6
GALILEE			
ON THE HILLS O' GALILEE,	34	GOODLY FERE	42
GALLANTLY			
DREW YOU YOUR SWORD MOST GALLANTLY	19	FOR E. MCC	7
GALLIC			
IS "ZUT! CINQUE LETTRES!" A BANISHED GALLIC IDIOM,	239	MOYEN SENSUEL	36
GALLIFET			
FOR TWO HOURS HE TALKED OF GALLIFET;	193	SIENA MI FE	5
GALLOWS			
DRINK YE A SKOAL FOR THE GALLOWS TREE!	11	OF THE GIBBET	1
THAT SAID US, "TILL THEN" FOR THE GALLOWS TREE!	11	OF THE GIBBET	4
DRINK WE A SKOAL FOR THE GALLOWS TREE!	11	OF THE GIBBET	13
DRINK WE SKOAL TO THE GALLOWS TREE!	12	OF THE GIBBET	25
BUT DRINK WE SKOAL TO THE GALLOWS TREE!	12	OF THE GIBBET	37
SKOAL!! TO THE GALLOWS! AND THEN PRAY WE:	12	OF THE GIBBET	41
FOR THE PRIESTS AND THE GALLOWS TREE?	33	GOODLY FERE	2
"THOUGH I GO TO THE GALLOWS TREE."	33	GOODLY FERE	28
WHO, SINCE THEIR WIT'S UNKNOWN, ESCAPE THE GALLOWS.	238	MOYEN SENSUEL	4
GALLUS			
AND BUT NOW GALLUS HAD SUNG OF LYCORIS.	230	SEXTUS PROP:12	72
GAMBETTO			
MY MUSE IS EAGER TO INSTRUCT ME IN A NEW GAMUT, OR GAMBETTO,	216	SEXTUS PROP: 5	11
GAME			
'TIS NOT A GAME THAT PLAYS AT MATES AND MATING,	50	THE FLAME	1
'TIS NOT A GAME OF BARTER, LANDS AND HOUSES,	50	THE FLAME	3
'TIS NOT A GAME THAT PLAYS AT MATES AND MATING,	50	THE FLAME	16
'TIS NOT A GAME OF BARTER, LANDS AND HOUSES,	50	THE FLAME	17
THE GAME OF CHESS	120	GAME OF CHESS	T
ACCEPT OPINION. THE "NINETIES" TRIED YOUR GAME	194	MR. NIXON	23
AND THIS MUCH GIVES ME HEART TO PLAY THE GAME.	235	TO WHISTLER	4
GAMES			
DID FOR MY GAMES THE GANNET'S CLAMOUR,	64	THE SEAFARER	20
ALL THINGS ARE FORGIVEN FOR ONE NIGHT OF YOUR GAMES.	227	SEXTUS PROP:11	39
GAMUT			
MY MUSE IS EAGER TO INSTRUCT ME IN A NEW GAMUT, OR GAMBETTO,	216	SEXTUS PROP: 5	11
GANG			
HERE COMES THE HIRED GANG	261	ALF'S SIXTH	10
GANGRENE			
YOU FUNGUS, YOU CONTINUOUS GANGRENE.	145	SALUTATION 3RD	12
GANNET'S			
DID FOR MY GAMES THE GANNET'S CLAMOUR,	64	THE SEAFARER	20
GAR			
HIDMEN GAR TOI PANTH', HOS' ENI TROIEI	187	E. P. ODE	9
GARBLE			
GARBLE A NAME WE DETEST, AND FOR PREJUDICE?	52	AU SALON	13
GARCIA			
"MESSAGE TO GARCIA," MOSHER'S PROPAGANDAS	241	MOYEN SENSUEL	73
GARCON			
IL ETAIT COMME UN TOUT PETIT GARCON	181	MOEURS CON: 7	3
GARDEN			
"THE JESTER WALKED IN THE GARDEN."	53	AU JARDIN	6
"THE JESTER WALKED IN THE GARDEN."	53	AU JARDIN	23
THE GARDEN	83	THE GARDEN	T
AND SEE THE FAUN IN OUR GARDEN.	109	THE FAUN	6
AND THE WILLOWS HAVE OVERFILLED THE CLOSE GARDEN	128	BEAU TOILET	2
AND I HAVE MOPED IN THE EMPEROR'S GARDEN, AWAITING AN ORDER-TO-WRITE!	129	THE RIVER SONG	19
OVER THE GRASS IN THE WEST GARDEN,	131	RIVER-MER WIFE	24
"WET SPRINGTIME," SAYS TO-EM-MEI, "WET SPRING IN THE GARDEN."	142	UNMOVING CLOUD	EPI

GARDEN -- GAUNTLET

	PAGE	TITLE	LINE
GARDEN (CONTINUED)			
THE TREES IN MY EAST-LOOKING GARDEN	142	UNMOVING CLOUD	17
GARDENS			
TO THE GARDENS OF THE SUN . . .	7	CINO	51
SHE WALKS BY THE RAILING OF A PATH IN KENSINGTON GARDENS,	83	THE GARDEN	2
ONCE MORE ARE THE NEVER ABANDONED GARDENS	90	SURGIT FAMA	18
FOR THE GARDENS AT JO-RUN ARE FULL OF NEW NIGHTINGALES,	130	THE RIVER SONG	38
TO THE MAD CHASE THROUGH THE GARDENS.	132	AT TEN-SHIN	24
SPREAD OUT THEIR SOUNDS THROUGH THE GARDENS.	141	IDEA OF CHOAN	16
GARLANDED			
WHERE THE GODS WALK GARLANDED IN WISTARIA,	108	CH'U YUAN	2
GARMENT			
SAD GARMENT DRAPED ON HER SLENDER ARMS.	214	SEXTUS PROP: 4	20
GARRET			
THE GARRET	83	THE GARRET	T
GARRULOUS			
WITH A GARRULOUS OLD MAN AT THE INN.	121	PROVINC DESERT	20
GARTH			
I THAT HAVE KNOWN STRATH, GARTH, BRAKE, DALE,	31	PIERE VIDAL	50
GAS			
(BUT MOSTLY GAS AND SUET)	270	OF 600 M.P.'S	10
GATE			
I PLAYED ABOUT THE FRONT GATE, PULLING FLOWERS.	130	RIVER-MER WIFE	2
BY THE GATE NOW, THE MOSS IS GROWN, THE DIFFERENT MOSSES,	131	RIVER-MER WIFE	20
BY THE NORTH GATE, THE WIND BLOWS FULL OF SAND,	133	FRONTIER GUARD	1
AH, HOW SHALL YOU KNOW THE DREARY SORROW AT THE NORTH GATE,	133	FRONTIER GUARD	22
YESTERDAY WE WENT OUT OF THE WILD-GOOSE GATE,	139	SOUTH-FOLK	4
THEY EDDY BEFORE THE GATE OF THE BARONS.	141	IDEA OF CHOAN	8
GATES			
WHO CALL'ST ABOUT MY GATES FOR SOME LOST ME;	51	THE FLAME	35
OVER A THOUSAND GATES, OVER A THOUSAND DOORS ARE THE SOUNDS OF SPRING SINGING,	129	THE RIVER SONG	31
PEACH BOUGHS AND APRICOT BOUGHS HANG OVER A THOUSAND GATES,	131	AT TEN-SHIN	2
WHEN YOU COME TO THE GATES OF GO.	137	OF DEPARTURE	EPI
CROWD OVER THE THOUSAND GATES,	141	IDEA OF CHOAN	18
GATE-TOP			
AND CLINGS TO THE WALLS AND THE GATE-TOP.	131	AT TEN-SHIN	12
GATHER			
OR GATHER MAY OF HARSH NORTHWINDISH TIME?	59	SILET	8
OR GATHER FLORAL PLEDGES?"	72	PAN IS DEAD	7
GATHER ABOUT ME, O MUSES!	104	ANCORA	9
I WILL NEVER AGAIN GATHER	105	DOMPNA POIS	6
TO GATHER GRAPES FOR THE LEOPARDS, MY FRIEND,	108	CH'U YUAN	6
TO GATHER HIS DEWS,	141	IDEA OF CHOAN	29
GATHERED			
TO SEE THREE GENERATIONS OF ONE HOUSE GATHERED TOGETHER!	89	COMMISSION	30
A BROWN ROBE, WITH THREADS OF GOLD WOVEN IN PATTERNS, HAST THOU GATHERED ABOUT THEE,	91	DANCE FIGURE	17
THE CLOUDS HAVE GATHERED, AND GATHERED,	142	UNMOVING CLOUD	1
THE CLOUDS HAVE GATHERED, AND GATHERED,	142	UNMOVING CLOUD	1
RAIN, RAIN, AND THE CLOUDS HAVE GATHERED,	142	UNMOVING CLOUD	10
GATHERING			
WE WENT FORTH GATHERING DELICATE THOUGHTS,	82	THE CONDOLENCE	9
GAUCHE-MAIN			
FAT PIERRE WITH THE HOOK GAUCHE-MAIN,	11	OF THE GIBBET	5
GAUDERO			
GAUDERO CONTUBERNALIS	101	AMITIES	22
GAUDIER			
AND THE OTHER WAS RATHER LIKE MY BUST BY GAUDIER,	181	MOEURS CON: 7	13
GAUDY			
THE TARNISHED, GAUDY, WONDERFUL OLD WORK;	61	PORTRAIT FEMME	23
GAUNT			
FOR I WAS A GAUNT, GRAVE COUNCILLOR	4	LA FRAISNE	
GAUNTLET			
'THOUT MASK OR GAUNTLET, AND ART LAID	19	FOR E. MCC	16

GAUTIER -- GENIUS

	PAGE	TITLE	LINE
GAUTIER			
NOR WOULD GAUTIER HIMSELF HAVE DESPISED THEIR CONTRASTS IN WHITENESS	87	ALBATRE	5
GAUZE			
AND LEFT ME CLOAKED AS WITH A GAUZE OF AETHER;	71	A VIRGINAL	5
IT IS SO LATE THAT THE DEW SOAKS MY GAUZE STOCKINGS,	132	JEWEL STAIRS'	2
SHE MADE THE NAME FOR HERSELF: "GAUZE VEIL,"	140	MULBERRY ROAD	5
GAVE			
WHO GAVE THIS POIGNARD ITS PREMIER STAIN	11	OF THE GIBBET	8
IN RETURN FOR THE FIRST KISS SHE GAVE ME."	23	MARVOIL	29
THE HOUNDS OF THE CRIMSON SKY GAVE TONGUE	34	GOODLY FERE	39
IN THE STORIED HOUSES OF SAN-KO THEY GAVE US MORE SENNIN MUSIC,	135	EXILE'S LETTER	26
AND SHE GAVE ME SUCH GESNING,	173	LANGUE D'OC: 2	19
AND THEY GAVE ANOTHER YANK TO MY CLOAK,	225	SEXTUS PROP:10	26
GAWDS			
NO GAWDS ON HER SNOWY HANDS, NO ORFEVRERIE,	214	SEXTUS PROP: 4	19
GAY			
BUT I HAVE PUT ASIDE THIS FOLLY, BEING GAY	4	LA FRAISNE	7
AIE-E! 'TIS TRUE THAT I AM GAY	5	LA FRAISNE	37
QUITE GAY, FOR I HAVE HER ALONE HERE	5	LA FRAISNE	38
GAY CINO, OF QUICK LAUGHTER,	6	CINO	18
HATH FOR BOSS THY LUSTRE GAY!	7	CINO	45
TO SAY THAT LIFE IS, SOME WAY, A GAY THING,	53	AU JARDIN	12
IN ATTIRE, NOR SO GAY	105	DOMPNA POIS	15
LET COME THE GAY OF MANNER, THE INSOLENT AND THE EXULTING.	146	CANTILATIONS	10
GAZE			
OF THE INWARD GAZE;	188	HUGH SELWYN: 2	6
WITH A VACANT GAZE.	192	YEUX GLAUQUES	14
THE THIN, CLEAR GAZE, THE SAME	192	YEUX GLAUQUES	17
HE HAD PASSED, INCONSCIENT, FULL GAZE,	200	MAUBERLEY: 2	26
CAME AGAINST HIS GAZE,	201	AGE DEMANDED	10
GAZONS			
ET TOUS LES GAZONS DIVERS	160	DANS OMNIBUS	21
GEAR			
(WHAT OF THE MAGIANS' SCENTED GEAR?)	10	FOR THIS YULE	10
IN ALL THEIR SPLENDID GEAR.	47	FROM HEINE: 7	24
WITH HEAD GEAR GLITTERING AGAINST THE CLOUD AND SUN,	131	AT TEN-SHIN	13
GEESE			
AND OF JOVE PROTECTED BY GEESE.	210	SEXTUS PROP: 2	15
GEISHA-CULTURE			
SPANISH AND PARIS, LOVE OF THE ARTS PART OF YOUR GEISHA-CULTURE!	163	CABARET DANCER	52
GEN			
TO SO-KIN OF RAKUYO, ANCIENT FRIEND, CHANCELLOR OF GEN.	134	EXILE'S LETTER	1
GENDER			
ITS PARENT OF THE OPPOSITE GENDER.	179	MOEURS CON: 4	4
GENERAL			
OBSERVE THE IRRITATION IN GENERAL:	85	SALUTATION 2ND	9
WHO WILL BE SORRY FOR GENERAL RISHOGU,	139	SOUTH-FOLK	12
ME, WHO HAD NO GENERAL FOR A GRANDFATHER!	229	SEXTUS PROP:12	54
SCARCELY A GENERAL NOW KNOWN TO FAME	264	ALF'S NINTH	3
GENERALITIES			
OUT-WEARIERS OF APOLLO WILL, AS WE KNOW, CONTINUE THEIR MARTIAN GENERALITIES,	207	SEXTUS PROP. 1	10
GENERALS			
THE GENERALS ARE ON THEM, THE SOLDIERS ARE BY THEM.	127	BOWMEN OF SHU	18
THE HORSES ARE WELL TRAINED, THE GENERALS HAVE IVORY ARROWS AND QUIVERS ORNAMENTED WITH FISH-SKIN.	127	BOWMEN OF SHU	19
GENERAL'S			
WHOSE CHARIOT? THE GENERAL'S.	127	BOWMEN OF SHU	14
GENERATION			
O GENERATION OF THE THOROUGHLY SMUG	85	SALUTATION	1
GENERATIONS			
TO SEE THREE GENERATIONS OF ONE HOUSE GATHERED TOGETHER!	89	COMMISSION	30
GENIUS			
AND TALK OF INSANITY AND GENIUS,	145	SALUTATION 3RD	24
STANDS GENIUS A DEATHLESS ADORNMENT,	209	SEXTUS PROP: 1	72

PAGE 159

GENIUS -- GETTIN'

	PAGE	TITLE	LINE
GENIUS (CONTINUED)			
"NO KEEL WILL SINK WITH YOUR GENIUS	210	SEXTUS PROP: 2	25
MY GENIUS IS NO MORE THAN A GIRL.	217	SEXTUS PROP: 5	26
GENSERET			
LIKE THE SEA THAT HE COWED AT GENSERET	34	GOODLY FERE	47
GENTILDONNA			
GENTILDONNA	92	GENTILDONNA	T
GENTLE			
AND WITH A PLAINTIVE, GENTLE MEWING,	115	SOCIAL ORDER	16
GENTLE TALKING, NOT LIKE THE FIRST TALKING, LESS LIVELY;	168	OF AROUET	32
ALL VILE, OR ALL GENTLE,	175	LANGUE D'OC: 3	52
THAT DANCING AND GENTLE IS AND THEREBY PLEASANTER,	177	LANGUE D'OC: 4	22
GENTLEMAN			
COMPLEYNT OF A GENTLEMAN WHO HAS BEEN WAITING OUTSIDE FOR SOME TIME	172	LANGUE D'OC: 1	SUB
AND A GENTLEMAN,	179	MOEURS CON: 4	6
GENTLER			
THE GENTLER HOUR OF AN ULTIMATE DAY.	222	SEXTUS PROP: 8	18
GEORGE			
GREAT IS KING GEORGE THE FIFTH,	237	ABU SALAMMAMM	1
GREAT IS KING GEORGE THE FIFTH--	237	ABU SALAMMAMM	4
GREAT IS KING GEORGE THE FIFTH;	237	ABU SALAMMAMM	10
GREAT IS KING GEORGE THE FIFTH	237	ABU SALAMMAMM	18
--GEORGE GORDON, LORD BYRON.	238	MOYEN SENSUEL	EPI
MABIE, AND LYMAN ABBOT AND GEORGE WOODBERRY,	239	MOYEN SENSUEL	28
GERMAIN			
AND PLATES FROM GERMAIN,	167	OF AROUET	10
GERMAN			
NOR WHERE ROME RUINS GERMAN RICHES,	211	SEXTUS PROP: 2	45
UNTIL A NARSTY GERMAN TOLD THEM SO.	265	ALF'S NINTH	25
GESNING			
AND SHE GAVE ME SUCH GESNING,	173	LANGUE D'OC: 2	19
GET			
THEY'LL NO' GET HIM A' IN A BOOK I THINK	33	GOODLY FERE	21
GET US TO SOME CLEAR PLACE WHEREIN THE SUN	39	BLANDULA	3
SOME LADS GET HUNG, AND SOME GET SHOT.	43	MR. HOUSMAN	8
SOME LADS GET HUNG, AND SOME GET SHOT.	43	MR. HOUSMAN	8
GET A GOOD DEAL OF KISSING DONE.	48	FROM HEINE: 8	8
WHEN IT IS AUTUMN DO WE GET SPRING WEATHER,	59	SILET	7
OH! I COULD GET ME OUT, DESPITE THE MARKS	60	TOMB AKR CAAR	29
I WILL GET YOU A GREEN COAT OUT OF CHINA	94	INSTRUCTIONS	17
I WILL GET YOU THE SCARLET SILK TROUSERS	94	INSTRUCTIONS	19
WE SHALL GET OURSELVES RATHER DISLIKED.	99	SALVATIONISTS	2
I WILL GET ME TO THE WOOD	108	CH'U YUAN	1
SHE DOES NOT GET UP THE STAIRS SO EAGERLY;	116	THE TEA SHOP	4
AND SAYING: WHEN SHALL WE GET BACK TO OUR COUNTRY?	127	BOWMEN OF SHU	2
NO MESSAGE I GET;	173	LANGUE D'OC: 2	7
NO MAN CAN GET OR HAS GOT.	174	LANGUE D'OC: 3	12
FOR WHICH THINGS YOU WILL GET A REWARD FROM ME, LYGDAMUS?	215	SEXTUS PROP: 4	27
THE PARTHIANS SHALL GET USED TO OUR STATUARY	219	SEXTUS PROP: 6	9
OLD LECHER, LET NOT JUNO GET WIND OF THE MATTER,	222	SEXTUS PROP: 8	39
AND ANOTHER SAID "GET HIM PLUMB IN THE MIDDLE!	224	SEXTUS PROP:10	14
GET ALONG NOW!"	225	SEXTUS PROP:10	24
THEY GET PRAISE FROM TOLERANT HAMADRYADS."	229	SEXTUS PROP:12	49
YOU CAN NOT GET CHEAP BOOKS, EVEN IF YOU NEED 'EM).	246	MOYEN SENSUEL	218
GET THE KID NICE NEW TOYS,	261	ALF'S SIXTH	5
DON'T GET A DISCOUNT LIKE MR. SELFRIDGE	262	ALF'S SEVENTH	11
I GET THE KIDS OUT ON THE STREET	266	ALF'S ELEVENTH	5
AND GET MY PICKINGS ON THE SIDE	266	ALF'S ELEVENTH	19
AND I GET ALL THE BEEF	269	SAFE AND SOUND	6
GETS			
HARD FIGHT GETS NO REWARD.	139	SOUTH-FOLK	10
SHE GETS THEM BY THE SOUTH WALL OF THE TOWN.	140	MULBERRY ROAD	7
AND GETS A QUARREL-BOLT SHOT THROUGH HIS VIZARD,	156	NEAR PERIGORD	158
WHERE ONE GETS MORE CHANCES	242	MOYEN SENSUEL	103
UNTIL THE MIND OF THE OLD NATION GETS A LITTLE STRONGER.	266	ALF'S TENTH	16
GETTIN'			
THAT THE PAPERS WERE GETTIN' TOGETHER	262	ALF'S SEVENTH	5

PAGE 160

GETTIN' -- GIRL

	PAGE	TITLE	LINE
GETTIN' (CONTINUED)			
THAT KEEP ON GETTIN' USURY	269	SAFE AND SOUND	15
GETTING			
THOUGH IT SHOULD RUN FOR ITS OWN GETTING,	14	FAMAM CANO	28
AND GETTING IN BOTH OF THEIR WAYS;	97	AESTHETICS	14
AND THE VERMILIONED GIRLS GETTING DRUNK ABOUT SUNSET,	136	EXILE'S LETTER	55
WHEN FEEBLE MR. ASQUITH, GETTING OLD,	264	ALF'S NINTH	5
I'M GETTING TOO OLD FOR SUCH CAPERS.	264	ALF'S EIGHTH	35
MARCHERS, NOT GETTING FOR'ARDER,	265	ALF'S TENTH	7
GEW-GAWS			
THE GEW-GAWS OF FALSE AMBER AND FALSE TURQUOISE ATTRACT THEM.	114	BEFORE A SHOP	1
GHOST			
MOVES ONLY NOW A CLINGING TENUOUS GHOST.	87	THE SPRING	13
GHOSTS			
WINING THE GHOSTS OF YESTER-YEAR.	10	FOR THIS YULE	8
ASK YE WHAT GHOSTS I DREAM UPON?	10	FOR THIS YULE	9
THE GHOSTS OF DEAD LOVES EVERYONE	10	FOR THIS YULE	11
WINING THE GHOSTS OF YESTER-YEAR.	10	FOR THIS YULE	16
WINING THE GHOSTS OF YESTER-YEAR.	10	FOR THIS YULE	24
WINING THE GHOSTS OF YESTER-YEAR.	10	FOR THIS YULE	28
SHADES OF CALLIMACHUS, COAN GHOSTS OF PHILETAS	207	SEXTUS PROP: 1	1
GIARDINO			
NOW IN VENICE, 'STORANTE AL GIARDINO, I WENT EARLY,	160	CABARET DANCER	79
GIBBET			
A VILLONAUD: BALLAD OF THE GIBBET	11	OF THE GIBBET	T
GIFT			
MIDONZ, GIFT OF THE GOD, GIFT OF THE LIGHT, GIFT OF THE AMBER OF THE SUN,	75	THE ALCHEMIST	27
MIDONZ, GIFT OF THE GOD, GIFT OF THE LIGHT, GIFT OF THE AMBER OF THE SUN,	75	THE ALCHEMIST	27
MIDONZ, GIFT OF THE GOD, GIFT OF THE LIGHT, GIFT OF THE AMBER OF THE SUN,	75	THE ALCHEMIST	27
NOR WITH GIFT SO BOUNTIFUL AND SO TRUE,	105	DOMPNA POIS	16
WHICH I TAKE, MY NOT UNWORTHY GIFT, TO PERSEPHONE.	219	SEXTUS PROP: 6	21
HIS MOTHER'S BIRTHDAY GIFT. (HOW PITIFUL	242	MOYEN SENSUEL	117
GIFTS			
GO BACK TO GREAT DIAN'S DANCES BEARING SUITABLE GIFTS.	224	SEXTUS PROP: 9	24
GILDED			
LIKE A GILDED PAVLOVA,	83	THE GARRET	7
IN GILDED AND RUSSET MANTLE.	90	SURGIT FAMA	4
THE GILDED PHALOI OF THE CROCUSES	110	COITUS	1
WHITHER, O CITY, ARE YOUR PROFITS AND YOUR GILDED SHRINES,	166	QUINTUS SEPTIM	12
IN THE CREAM GILDED CABIN OF HIS STEAM YACHT	194	MR. NIXON	1
THOUGH IT IS NOT STRETCHED UPON GILDED BEAMS;	208	SEXTUS PROP: 1	52
THOUGH YOU HEAVE INTO THE AIR UPON THE GILDED PEGASEAN BACK,	226	SEXTUS PROP:11	7
IS FULL OF GILDED SNOW,	236	MIDDLE-AGED	21
GILDER			
AND YET ANOTHER, A "CHARMING MAN," "SWEET NATURE," BUT WAS GILDER,	240	MOYEN SENSUEL	57
GILT			
GILT TURQUOISE AND SILVER ARE IN THE PLACE OF THY REST.	91	DANCE FIGURE	16
AND THE TALL WOMEN WALKING YOUR STREETS, IN GILT CLOTHES.	165	QUINTUS SEPTIM	14
GIMME			
"GIMME A KISSY-CUDDLE"	271	OLE KATE	21
GIPSIES			
HIS BROTHER HAS TAKEN TO GIPSIES,	178	MOEURS CON: 1	15
GIPSY			
A STRAY GIPSY--A. D. 1912	119	THE GYPSY	EPI
GIRDLE'S			
HAVING PRAISED THY GIRDLE'S SCOPE	8	NA AUDIART	14
GIRL,			
JUST A WORD IN THY PRAISE, GIRL,	8	NA AUDIART	20
A GIRL	62	A GIRL	T
SHOP GIRL	112	SHOP GIRL	T
THE GIRL IN THE TEA SHOP	116	THE TEA SHOP	1

PAGE 161

GIRL -- GIVEN

	PAGE	TITLE	LINE
GIRL (CONTINUED)			
(PRETTY GIRL)	140	MULBERRY ROAD	4
"WHERE A GIRL WAITS ALONE FOR HER LOVER;	210	SEXTUS PROP: 2	23
AND I ALSO WILL SING WAR WHEN THIS MATTER OF A GIRL IS EXHAUSTED.	216	SEXTUS PROP: 5	9
MY GENIUS IS NO MORE THAN A GIRL.	217	SEXTUS PROP: 5	26
WHO, WHO WILL BE THE NEXT MAN TO ENTRUST HIS GIRL TO A FRIEND?	227	SEXTUS PROP:12	1
AND STILL A GIRL SCORNS THE GODS,	228	SEXTUS PROP:12	23
GIRLS			
THE MILK-WHITE GIRLS	109	HEATHER	4
WE CARRY SINGING GIRLS, DRIFT WITH THE DRIFTING WATER,	128	THE RIVER SONG	5
TO THE PERFUMED AIR AND GIRLS DANCING,	132	AT TEN-SHIN	21
AND THE VERMILIONED GIRLS GETTING DRUNK ABOUT SUNSET,	136	EXILE'S LETTER	55
AND THE GIRLS SINGING BACK AT EACH OTHER,	136	EXILE'S LETTER	59
THE NOBLEST GIRLS MEN LOVE	176	LANGUE D'OC: 3	70
NINE GIRLS, FROM AS MANY COUNTRYSIDES	211	SEXTUS PROP: 2	33
IOPE, AND TYRO, AND PASIPHAE, AND THE FORMAL GIRLS OF ACHAIA,	223	SEXTUS PROP: 9	16
THREE THOUSAND CHORUS GIRLS AND ALL UNKISSED,	241	MOYEN SENSUEL	87
OR HUGGED TWO GIRLS AT ONCE BEHIND A CHAPEL.)	242	MOYEN SENSUEL	106
FIND PRETTY IRISH GIRLS IN CHINESE LAUNDRIES,	244	MOYEN SENSUEL	157
GIRT			
O THROAT GIRT ROUND OF OLD WITH SWIFT DESIRE,	41	HER MONUMENT	14
GIT			
IF YOU GIT OFF THE EMBANKMENT.	263	ALF'S EIGHTH	21
OLE KATE WOULD GIT HER 'ARF A PINT	271	OLE KATE	3
GITANA			
CERNE SON OEIL DE GITANA"	162	CABARET DANCER	25
GITAR			
TAN QUE I PUOSCH' OM GITAR AB MALH.	151	NEAR PERIGORD	EPI
GIULIO			
A PROCESSION, O GIULIO ROMANO,	110	COITUS	5
GIV'			
AND WOULDN'T GIV' A DAMN HOOT.	271	OLE KATE	4
GIVE			
JUMP TO YOUR SENSE AND GIVE PRAISE AS WE'D LIEF DO.	13	MESMERISM	8
TALK OF THE LATEST SUCCESS, GIVE WING TO SOME SCANDAL,	52	AU SALON	12
FOR I'VE NOTHING BUT SONGS TO GIVE YOU.	53	AU JARDIN	10
GIVE LIGHT TO THE METAL.	75	THE ALCHEMIST	28
TO GIVE THESE ELEMENTS A NAME AND A CENTRE!	84	ORTUS	4
TO GIVE HER A NAME AND HER BEING!	84	ORTUS	8
THAT IN PLEASURE SHE RECEIVES MORE THAN SHE CAN GIVE;	103	PHYLLIDULA	3
THAT SHE GIVE ME OUTRIGHT	106	DOMPNA POIS	32
GIVE ME IN DUE TIME, I BESEECH YOU, A LITTLE TOBACCO-SHOP,	117	THE LAKE ISLE	2
AGAINST HER; GIVE HER PRIDE IN THEM?	153	NEAR PERIGORD	78
THE AMOROUS NERVES WILL GIVE WAY TO DIGESTIVE;	163	CABARET DANCER	68
GIVE ME BACK THE TIME OF THE THING.	167	OF AROUET	16
WILL YOU GIVE ME DAWN LIGHT AT EVENING?	167	OF AROUET	17
GIVE MY GOOD-FELLOW AID IN FOOLS' DESPITE	172	LANGUE D'OC: 1	3
GOD GIVE ME LIFE, AND LET MY COURSE RUN	174	LANGUE D'OC: 3	17
FOR LOVE WILL GIVE	174	LANGUE D'OC: 3	22
"AND GIVE UP VERSE, MY BOY,	194	MR. NIXON	19
RECKING NAUGHT ELSE BUT THAT HER GRACES GIVE	197	ENVOI (1919)	10
GIVE THAT MUCH INSCRIPTION	219	SEXTUS PROP: 6	28
THOUGH YOU GIVE ALL YOUR KISSES	221	SEXTUS PROP: 7	33
YOU GIVE BUT FEW.	221	SEXTUS PROP: 7	34
IF SHE GIVE ME MANY,	221	SEXTUS PROP: 7	39
GIVE T'OLD ONES A NEWER TWIST	261	ALF'S SIXTH	8
WILL GIVE, SAVE TO THE BLIND.	263	ALF'S EIGHTH	7
GIVEN			
GIVEN TO MORTAL STATE	42	HER MONUMENT	32
NOT THOUGH HE BE GIVEN HIS GOOD, BUT WILL HAVE IN HIS YOUTH GREED;	65	THE SEAFARER	41
NIGHT AND DAY ARE GIVEN OVER TO PLEASURE	132	AT TEN-SHIN	25
--GIVEN THAT IS HIS "FUNDAMENTAL PASSION,"	200	MAUBERLEY: 2	20
AND ONE OF THE LOT WAS GIVEN TO LUST.	224	SEXTUS PROP:10	11
STILL HE WAS NOT GIVEN UP TO BRUTE ENJOYMENT,	245	MOYEN SENSUEL	193

GIVER -- GLEAM

	PAGE	TITLE	LINE
GIVER			
WAS OTHER, OR THAT THIS CHEERFUL GIVER	263	ALF'S EIGHTH	6
GIVES			
WHEN THE HOT WATER GIVES OUT OR GOES TEPID,	100	THE BATH TUB	2
LIFE GIVES US TWO MINUTES, TWO SEASONS--	168	OF AROUET	25
"IT GIVES NO MAN A SINECURE.	194	MR. NIXON	17
AND "IT IS, I THINK, INDIA WHICH NOW GIVES NECKS TO YOUR TRIUMPH,"	216	SEXTUS PROP: 5	17
AND THIS MUCH GIVES ME HEART TO PLAY THE GAME.	235	TO WHISTLER	4
AND GIVES YOU AUSTRALIAN ICED RABBITS' MEAT	263	ALF'S EIGHTH	18
GIVEST			
THAT THOU GIVEST THIS WONDER UNTO US,	26	NIGHT LITANY	12
GIVETH			
IN MIDST OF DARKNESS LIGHT LIGHT GIVETH FORTH	250	DONNA MI PREGA	85
GIVING			
IT FAINTS IN TAKING AND IN GIVING ALL.	31	PIERE VIDAL	36
GIVING THE ROCKS SMALL LEE-WAY	187	E. P. ODE	11
GLAD			
BUT I HAVE SEEN THE SORROW OF MEN, AND AM GLAD,	4	LA FRAISNE	22
IT IS ONLY THAT I AM GLAD,	5	LA FRAISNE	33
VERY GLAD, FOR MY BRIDE HATH TOWARD ME A GREAT LOVE	5	LA FRAISNE	34
IN THE BRIGHT GLAD DAYS!"	43	SATIEMUS	13
OF CHEEKS GROWN SUNKEN AND GLAD HAIR GONE GRAY;	50	THE FLAME	19
GLAD TO HEAR ARNAUT,	121	PROVINC DESERT	20
GLAD TO LEND ONE DRY CLOTHING.	121	PROVINC DESERT	27
AND YOU WERE GLAD AND LAUGHING	147	POST MORTEM	2
I, CERCLAMON, SORRY AND GLAD,	175	LANGUE D'OC: 3	55
GLADE			
I WILL WALK IN THE GLADE,	108	CH'U YUAN	8
GLADLY			
AND TAKE YOUR WOUNDS FROM IT GLADLY.	95	ITE	4
GLADNESS			
AND BLAME THE SUN HIS GLADNESS;	30	PIERE VIDAL	4
AND YET I CURSE THE SUN FOR HIS RED GLADNESS,	31	PIERE VIDAL	49
GLADSTONE			
GLADSTONE WAS STILL RESPECTED,	192	YEUX GLAUQUES	1
GLAMOROUS			
THOU AFAR, MOVING IN THE GLAMOROUS SUN,	68	APPARUIT	6
GLAMOUR			
A GLAMOUR OF CLASSIC YOUTH IN THEIR DEPORTMENT.	163	CABARET DANCER	74
GLANCE			
O GLANCE, WHEN THOU WAST STILL AS THOU ART NOW,	41	HER MONUMENT	10
FOR IT'S YOUR OWN, AND YOUR GLANCE	105	DOMPNA POIS	22
GLANCES			
AYE! WHERE ARE THE GLANCES FEAT AND CLEAR	10	FOR THIS YULE	20
GLANDERS			
THAT ARE THE NATION'S BOTTS, COLLICKS AND GLANDERS.	241	MOYEN SENSUEL	74
GLASS			
ON HIS OWN FACE IN A GLASS	35	HIS OWN FACE	T
O STRANGE FACE THERE IN THE GLASS!	35	HIS OWN FACE	1
THAT GLASS TO ALL THINGS THAT O'ERSHADOW IT,	51	THE FLAME	41
FOR I THINK THE GLASS IS EVIL.	95	OF THE DEGREES	2
O GLASS SUBTLY EVIL, O CONFUSION OF COLOURS!	95	OF THE DEGREES	10
O GLASS SUBTLE AND CUNNING, O POWDERY GOLD!	95	OF THE DEGREES	11
LOOSE UNDER THE BRIGHT GLASS CASES,	117	THE LAKE ISLE	8
GLASS-GREEN			
OUT THROUGH THE GLASS-GREEN FIELDS.	60	TOMB AKR CAAR	31
GLASSY			
AND GRASS GOING GLASSY WITH THE LIGHT ON IT,	167	OF AROUET	20
GLAUQUES			
YEUX GLAUQUES	192	YEUX GLAUQUES	T
GLAZE			
IT WERE THROUGH A PERFECT GLAZE	201	AGE DEMANDED	12
THE FACE-OVAL BENEATH THE GLAZE,	204	MEDALLION	13
GLAZING			
STAMP ON HIS ROOF OR IN THE GLAZING LIGHT	236	MIDDLE-AGED	5
GLEAM			
'NEATH THE DARK GLEAM OF THE SKY;	75	THE ALCHEMIST	7
FROM THE RED GLEAM OF COPPER,	76	THE ALCHEMIST	39
ONE BIRD CASTS ITS GLEAM ON ANOTHER.	139	SENNIN POEM	3

	PAGE	TITLE	LINE
GLEAM (CONTINUED)			
IF SHE GOES IN A GLEAM OF COS, IN A SLITHER OF DYED STUFF,	217	SEXTUS PROP: 5	30
GLEAMS			
LO, HOW IT GLEAMS AND GLISTENS IN THE SUN	99	CAKE OF SOAP	1
STRAY GLEAMS ON HANGING MAIL, AN ARMOURER'S TORCH-FLARE	155	NEAR PERIGORD	134
GLI			
BLAGUEUR! "CON GLI OCCHI ONESTI E TARDI,"	181	MOEURS CON: 7	6
GLIMPSE			
IT WAS NO GLIMPSE IN A MIRROR;	214	SEXTUS PROP: 4	18
GLISTENS			
LO, HOW IT GLEAMS AND GLISTENS IN THE SUN	99	CAKE OF SOAP	1
GLITTER			
WHY IS YOUR GLITTER FULL OF CURIOUS MISTRUST?	95	OF THE DEGREES	13
A GLITTER OF GOLDEN SADDLES, AWAITING THE PRINCESS;	141	IDEA OF CHOAN	7
TREES THAT GLITTER LIKE JADE,	141	IDEA OF CHOAN	19
WITH GLITTER OF COLOUR	141	IDEA OF CHOAN	27
WHERE MY LOVE IS, THERE IS A GLITTER OF SUN;	174	LANGUE D'OC: 3	16
GLITTERING			
WITH HEAD GEAR GLITTERING AGAINST THE CLOUD AND SUN,	131	AT TEN-SHIN	13
GLOOM			
DOWN THROUGH THE VALE OF GLOOM	257	BREAD BRIGADE	3
GLOOMING			
GLOOMING AND MOUCHING!	257	BREAD BRIGADE	23
GLOOMY			
CUCKOO CALLETH WITH GLOOMY CRYING,	65	THE SEAFARER	54
GLORIA			
SIC CRESCIT GLORIA MUNDI:	52	AU SALON	17
GLORIED			
AND AMID ALL THE GLORIED AND STORIED BEAUTIES OF MAEONIA	222	SEXTUS PROP: 8	34
GLORIES			
AND BUILD HER GLORIES THEIR LONGEVITY.	197	ENVOI (1919)	7
GLORIOUS			
BUT SAID IT WUZ GLORIOUS NEVERTHELESS	259	ALF'S FOURTH	5
GLORY			
GLORY TO ZEUS' AEGIS-DAY,	7	CINO	43
MY FELLOWS, AYE I KNOW THE GLORY	20	IN DURANCE	28
THE GLORY OF THE SHADOW OF THE	26	NIGHT LITANY	23
YEA, THE GLORY OF THE SHADOW	26	NIGHT LITANY	25
NO MAN HATH HEARD THE GLORY OF MY DAYS:	32	PIERE VIDAL	54
SUCH GLORY OF THE EARTH? OR WHO WILL WIN	32	PIERE VIDAL	58
A LIQUID GLORY? IF AT SIRMIO,	39	BLANDULA	5
EARTHLY GLORY AGETH AND SEARETH.	66	THE SEAFARER	91
(IF GLORY COULD LAST FOREVER	129	THE RIVER SONG	17
"YOUR GLORY IS NOT OUTBLOTTED BY VENOM,"	226	SEXTUS PROP:11	23
AND MY GLORY WILL	238	ABU SALAMMAMM	32
TOLD 'EM THAT GLORY	259	ALF'S FOURTH	3
GLOVE			
I CARE NOT A GLOVE.	174	LANGUE D'OC: 3	15
'GAINST HER I PRIZE NOT AS A GLOVE	176	LANGUE D'OC: 3	71
GLOVES			
I WEAR A FINE FUR COAT AND GLOVES,	266	ALF'S ELEVENTH	9
GLOW			
AND THE GLOW OF YOUTH THAT SHE SPREAD ABOUT US	116	THE TEA SHOP	6
THE GLOW OF PORCELAIN	201	AGE DEMANDED	5
SO HE HAVE SENSE OR GLOW WITH REASON'S FIRE,	250	DONNA MI PREGA	91
GNATS			
BUT YOU, YOU DAM'D CROWD OF GNATS,	140	SENNIN POEM	15
GO			
FOR THE DEATH OF SUCH SLUTS I GO REJOICING;	29	ALTAFORTE	29
"FIRST LET THESE GO!" QUO' OUR GOODLY FERE,	33	GOODLY FERE	7
"I'LL GO TO THE FEAST," QUO' OUR GOODLY FERE,	33	GOODLY FERE	27
"THOUGH I GO TO THE GALLOWS TREE."	33	GOODLY FERE	28
AND BID GO IN WITH HONOURED COMPANIONS	37	THE YOUNG KING	39
ALL GOOD THINGS GO VANISHING.	46	FROM HEINE: 6	20
THE SILKEN TRAINS GO RUSTLING,	47	FROM HEINE: 7	25
SEARCH NOT MY LIPS, O LOVE, LET GO MY HANDS,	51	THE FLAME	37
I DO NOT GO."	60	TOMB AKR CAAR	33
THAT, ERE A MAN'S TIDE GO, TURN IT TO TWAIN.	66	THE SEAFARER	70

GO

	PAGE	TITLE	LINE
GO (CONTINUED)			
NO, NO! GO FROM ME. I HAVE LEFT HER LATELY.	71	A VIRGINAL	1
NO, NO! GO FROM ME. I HAVE STILL THE FLAVOUR,	71	A VIRGINAL	9
GO, LITTLE NAKED AND IMPUDENT SONGS,	85	SALUTATION 2ND	16
GO WITH A LIGHT FOOT!	85	SALUTATION 2ND	17
GO AND DANCE SHAMELESSLY!	86	SALUTATION 2ND	19
GO WITH AN IMPERTINENT FROLIC!	86	SALUTATION 2ND	20
GO! REJUVENATE THINGS!	86	SALUTATION 2ND	24
GO! AND MAKE CAT CALLS!	86	SALUTATION 2ND	26
BUT, ABOVE ALL, GO TO PRACTICAL PEOPLE--	86	SALUTATION 2ND	34
GO! JANGLE THEIR DOOR-BELLS!	86	SALUTATION 2ND	35
GO, MY SONGS, TO THE LONELY AND THE UNSATISFIED,	88	COMMISSION	1
GO ALSO TO THE NERVE-WRACKED, GO TO THE ENSLAVED-BY-CONVENTION,	88	COMMISSION	2
GO ALSO TO THE NERVE-WRACKED, GO TO THE ENSLAVED-BY-CONVENTION,	88	COMMISSION	2
GO AS A GREAT WAVE OF COOL WATER,	88	COMMISSION	4
GO TO THE BOURGEOISE WHO IS DYING OF HER ENNUIS,	88	COMMISSION	9
GO TO THE WOMEN IN SUBURBS.	88	COMMISSION	10
GO TO THE HIDEOUSLY WEDDED,	88	COMMISSION	11
GO TO THEM WHOSE FAILURE IS CONCEALED,	88	COMMISSION	12
GO TO THE UNLUCKILY MATED,	88	COMMISSION	13
GO TO THE BOUGHT WIFE,	88	COMMISSION	14
GO TO THE WOMAN ENTAILED.	88	COMMISSION	15
GO TO THOSE WHO HAVE DELICATE LUST,	88	COMMISSION	16
GO TO THOSE WHOSE DELICATE DESIRES ARE THWARTED,	88	COMMISSION	17
GO LIKE A BLIGHT UPON THE DULNESS OF THE WORLD;	88	COMMISSION	18
GO WITH YOUR EDGE AGAINST THIS,	88	COMMISSION	19
GO IN A FRIENDLY MANNER,	89	COMMISSION	22
GO WITH AN OPEN SPEECH.	89	COMMISSION	23
GO TO THOSE WHO ARE THICKENED WITH MIDDLE AGE,	89	COMMISSION	26
GO TO THE ADOLESCENT WHO ARE SMOTHERED IN FAMILY--	89	COMMISSION	28
GO OUT AND DEFY OPINION,	89	COMMISSION	33
GO AGAINST THIS VEGETABLE BONDAGE OF THE BLOOD.	89	COMMISSION	34
GO, MY SONGS, SEEK YOUR PRAISE FROM THE YOUNG AND FROM THE INTOLERANT,	95	ITE	1
I KNOW NOT WHERE TO GO SEEKING.	105	DOMPNA POIS	4
I WILL GO OUT A-SEARCHING,	105	DOMPNA POIS	17
AND WHEN I AROSE TO GO	110	THE ENCOUNTER	3
GO BEFORE HER INTO AVERNUS;	115	SOCIAL ORDER	12
WE SAY: WILL WE BE LET TO GO BACK IN OCTOBER?	127	BOWMEN OF SHU	10
WE GO SLOWLY, WE ARE HUNGRY AND THIRSTY,	127	BOWMEN OF SHU	23
THE LORDS GO FORTH FROM THE COURT, AND INTO FAR BORDERS.	132	AT TEN-SHIN	14
HAUGHTY THEIR STEPS AS THEY GO IN TO GREAT BANQUETS,	132	AT TEN-SHIN	19
SORROW TO GO, AND SORROW, SORROW RETURNING.	133	FRONTIER GUARD	10
WHEN YOU COME TO THE GATES OF GO.	137	OF DEPARTURE	EPI
AND GO OUT THROUGH A THOUSAND MILES OF DEAD GRASS.	137	TAKING LEAVE	4
WHERE LAY THE DYNASTIC HOUSE OF THE GO.	138	CITY OF CHOAN	5
LET US GO OUT IN THE AIR A BIT.	145	SALUTATION 3RD	16
BUT I WILL NOT GO MAD TO PLEASE YOU,	145	SALUTATION 3RD	25
GO FORTHRIGHT SINGING--ANHES, CEMBELINS.	153	NEAR PERIGORD	70
OR CARRY HIM FORWARD. "GO THROUGH ALL THE COURTS,	154	NEAR PERIGORD	115
WHEN YOU COULD GO OUT IN A HIRED HANSOM	167	OF AROUET	2
IF YOU'D HAVE ME GO ON LOVING YOU	167	OF AROUET	15
CAN GO ON WRITING YOUR VERSES.	168	OF AROUET	36
A MAN GO WHERE HE WILL.	173	LANGUE D'OC: 2	5
NOR WHEN I GO OUT.	174	LANGUE D'OC: 3	25
AND GO DARK WITH CLOUD,	176	LANGUE D'OC: 3	74
GO, DUMB-BORN BOOK,	197	ENVOI (1919)	1
AND THEY ALL GO TO RACK RUIN BENEATH THE THUD OF THE YEARS.	209	SEXTUS PROP: 1	71
NO BARBARISM WOULD GO TO THE EXTENT OF DOING HIM HARM,	212	SEXTUS PROP: 3	19
OR PERHAPS JUNO HERSELF WILL GO UNDER,	222	SEXTUS PROP: 8	40
IF SHE DIES, I SHALL GO WITH HER.	223	SEXTUS PROP: 9	9
GO BACK TO GREAT DIAN'S DANCES BEARING SUITABLE GIFTS,	224	SEXTUS PROP: 9	24
GO ON, TO ASCRAEUS' PRESCRIPTION, THE ANCIENT,	229	SEXTUS PROP:12	50
AND THEN RADWAY BEGAN TO GO THE PACES:	243	MOYEN SENSUEL	144
SAFE MAY'ST THOU GO MY CANZON WHITHER THEE PLEASETH	250	DONNA MI PREGA	88

PAGE 165

GO -- GODDAMM

	PAGE	TITLE	LINE
GO (CONTINUED)			
SEE 'EM GO SLOUCHING THERE,	257	BREAD BRIGADE	24
GO TO GOD LIKE A SOJER;	260	ALF'S FOURTH	18
AT ONE O'CLOCK I GO TO LUNCH,	266	ALF'S ELEVENTH	7
GOBBLE			
MY LITTLE MOUTH SHALL GOBBLE IN SUCH GREAT FOUNTAINS,	210	SEXTUS PROP: 2	6
GOBBLED			
GOBBLED ALL THE LAND, AND HELD IT LATER FOR SOME HUNDRED YEARS.	151	NEAR PERIGORD	19
GOD			
NOR WHAT GOD HATH THAT CAN ME CHEER	10	FOR THIS YULE	26
THESE THAT WE LOVED SHALL GOD LOVE LESS	12	OF THE GIBBET	39
GOD DAMN HIS HELL OUT SPEEDILY	12	OF THE GIBBET	42
BUT GOD! WHAT A SIGHT YOU HA' GOT O' OUR IN'ARDS,	13	MESMERISM	10
O GOD, WHAT GREAT KINDNESS	26	NIGHT LITANY	9
O GOD OF WATERS?	26	NIGHT LITANY	13
O GOD OF THE NIGHT,	26	NIGHT LITANY	14
O GOD OF SILENCE,	26	NIGHT LITANY	19
O GOD OF WATERS.	27	NIGHT LITANY	32
O GOD OF SILENCE,	27	NIGHT LITANY	33
O GOD OF WATERS,	27	NIGHT LITANY	36
O GOD OF WATERS,	27	NIGHT LITANY	44
O GOD OF THE SILENCE,	27	NIGHT LITANY	50
O GOD OF WATERS.	27	NIGHT LITANY	52
MAY GOD DAMN FOR EVER ALL WHO CRY "PEACE!"	29	ALTAFORTE	36
GOD! HOW THE SWIFTEST HIND'S BLOOD SPURTED HOT	30	PIERE VIDAL	14
GOD! BUT THE PURPLE OF THE SKY WAS DEEP!	30	PIERE VIDAL	20
AND CONQUERED! AH GOD! CONQUERED!	31	PIERE VIDAL	31
GOD! SHE WAS WHITE THEN, SPLENDID AS SOME TOMB	31	PIERE VIDAL	38
AH GOD, THE LOBA! AND MY ONLY MATE!	31	PIERE VIDAL	44
GOD CURSE THE YEARS THAT TURN SUCH WOMEN GREY!	31	PIERE VIDAL	46
A SON OF GOD WAS THE GOODLY FERE	34	GOODLY FERE	33
AND BETTER WERE IT, SHOULD GOD GRANT HIS PLEASURE,	37	THE YOUNG KING	22
I DREAMT THAT I WAS GOD HIMSELF	45	FROM HEINE: 4	1
THESE THINGS THAT ARE FAMILIARS OF THE GOD.	69	SUB MARE	9
GOD! THAT MAD'ST HER WELL REGARD HER,	72	DIEU! QU'IL	1
GOD! THAT MAD'ST HER WELL REGARD HER,	72	DIEU! QU'IL	7
GOD! THAT MAD'ST HER WELL REGARD HER.	72	DIEU! QU'IL	13
MIDONZ, GIFT OF THE GOD, GIFT OF THE LIGHT, GIFT OF THE AMBER OF THE SUN,	75	THE ALCHEMIST	27
GOOD GOD! THEY SAY YOU ARE RISQUE,	104	ANCORA	1
THE GOD PAN IS AFRAID TO ASK YOU,	110	TEMPORA	7
O GOD, O VENUS, O MERCURY, PATRON OF THIEVES,	117	THE LAKE ISLE	1
O GOD, O VENUS, O MERCURY, PATRON OF THIEVES,	117	THE LAKE ISLE	12
THE RED-PINE-TREE GOD LOOKS AT HIM AND WONDERS.	139	SENNIN POEM	11
AND PRAY TO GOD THAT IS ST. MARY'S SON,	172	LANGUE D'OC: 1	19
GOD GRANT I DIE NOT BY ANY MAN'S STROKE	173	LANGUE D'OC: 2	21
GOD GIVE ME LIFE, AND LET MY COURSE RUN	174	LANGUE D'OC: 3	17
GOD! HOW SOFTLY THIS KILLS!	175	LANGUE D'OC: 3	40
THEM. GOD HOW SWIFT THE NIGHT,	177	LANGUE D'OC: 4	4
'FORE GOD, HOW SWIFT THE NIGHT,	177	LANGUE D'OC: 4	9
AH GOD! HOW SWIFT THE NIGHT	177	LANGUE D'OC: 4	19
AH GOD! HOW SWIFT THE NIGHT.	177	LANGUE D'OC: 4	24
BY GOD, HOW SWIFT THE NIGHT.	177	LANGUE D'OC: 4	29
WHAT GOD, MAN, OR HERO	189	HUGH SELWYN: 3	27
GOD AM I FOR THE TIME.	221	SEXTUS PROP: 7	40
AND NOW DRINKS NILE WATER LIKE A GOD,	222	SEXTUS PROP: 8	20
GOD KNOWS WHERE HE HAS BEEN.	225	SEXTUS PROP:10	21
AND THE GOD STRIKES TO THE MARROW.	229	SEXTUS PROP:12	58
THESE, AND YET GOD, AND DR. PARKHURST'S GOD, THE N.Y. JOURNAL	240	MOYEN SENSUEL	45
THESE, AND YET GOD, AND DR. PARKHURST'S GOD, THE N.Y. JOURNAL	240	MOYEN SENSUEL	45
CRYING: MY GOD, MY GOD, WHAT WILL SHE SAY?!	247	PIERROTS	6
CRYING: MY GOD, MY GOD, WHAT WILL SHE SAY?!	247	PIERROTS	6
GOD SAVE BRITANNIA!	259	ALF'S THIRD	20
GO TO GOD LIKE A SOJER;	260	ALF'S FOURTH	18
GOD REST HER SLOSHIN' SOUL.	271	OLE KATE	20
TO SELL THE GOD DAMN'D FROGS	273	M. POM-POM	10
GODDAMM			
LHUDE SING GODDAMM,	116	ANCIENT MUSIC	2

GODDAMM -- GOES

	PAGE	TITLE	LINE
GODDAMM (CONTINUED)			
SING: GODDAMM.	116	ANCIENT MUSIC	5
DAMM YOU, SING: GODDAMM.	116	ANCIENT MUSIC	9
GODDAMM, GODDAMM, 'TIS WHY I AM, GODDAMM,	116	ANCIENT MUSIC	10
GODDAMM, GODDAMM, 'TIS WHY I AM, GODDAMM,	116	ANCIENT MUSIC	10
GODDAMM, GODDAMM, 'TIS WHY I AM, GODDAMM,	116	ANCIENT MUSIC	10
SING GODDAMM, DAMM, SING GODDAMM,	116	ANCIENT MUSIC	12
SING GODDAMM, DAMM, SING GODDAMM,	116	ANCIENT MUSIC	12
SING GODDAMM, SING GODDAMM, DAMM.	116	ANCIENT MUSIC	13
SING GODDAMM, SING GODDAMM, DAMM.	116	ANCIENT MUSIC	13
GODDESS			
IS THE ORNAMENTAL GODDESS FULL OF ENVY?	221	SEXTUS PROP: 8	11
TO DIAN GODDESS OF VIRGINS,	224	SEXTUS PROP: 9	26
GOD-FEASTING			
AND THAT GOD-FEASTING COUPLE OLD	3	THE TREE	4
GODLET			
THESE AND ANOTHER GODLET OF THAT DAY, YOUR DAY	240	MOYEN SENSUEL	47
GOD-LIKE			
MY GOD-LIKE COMPOSITIONS.	46	FROM HEINE: 6	16
GODS			
'TWAS NOT UNTIL THE GODS HAD BEEN	3	THE TREE	6
ONE HOUR WAS GUNLIT AND THE MOST HIGH GODS	40	ERAT HORA	5
LO, THERE ARE MANY GODS WHOM WE HAVE SEEN,	50	THE FLAME	23
WHEN OUR SOULS ARE RETURNED TO THE GODS	52	AU SALON	2
LET THE GODS SPEAK SOFTLY OF US	67	DORIA	8
GODS OF THE WINGED SHOE!	74	THE RETURN	12
SPEAK OF THE INDECOROUS CONDUCT OF THE GODS!	86	SALUTATION 2ND	30
THERE IS A TRUCE AMONG THE GODS,	90	SURGIT FAMA	1
THUS HAVE THE GODS AWARDED HER,	103	PHYLLIDULA	2
WITH THE MOVEMENT OF GODS,	107	COMING OF WAR	11
WHERE THE GODS WALK GARLANDED IN WISTARIA,	108	CH'U YUAN	2
HERE IS THERE NAUGHT OF DEAD GODS	110	COITUS	3
THE GODS OF THE UNDERWORLD ATTEND ME, O ANNUBIS,	147	BEFORE SLEEP	6
THE GODS OF DRUGGED SLEEP ATTEND ME,	147	BEFORE SLEEP	17
TWICE TAKEN BY OETIAN GODS,	208,	SEXTUS PROP: 1	33
WITHOUT AN INFERNO, WITHOUT ACHILLES ATTENDED OF GODS,	218	SEXTUS PROP: 5	51
LET THE GODS LAY CHAINS UPON US	220	SEXTUS PROP: 7	20
SHE DID NOT RESPECT ALL THE GODS;	221	SEXTUS PROP: 8	6
"HE THINKS THAT WE ARE NOT GODS."	224	SEXTUS PROP:10	17
THE GODS HAVE BROUGHT SHAME ON THEIR RELATIVES;	227	SEXTUS PROP:12	3
AND STILL A GIRL SCORNS THE GODS,	228	SEXTUS PROP:12	23
IT IS ADORNED WITH YOUNG GODS RIDING UPON DOLPHINS	237	ABU SALAMMAMM	20
AND HEAVENLY, HOLY GODS! I CAN'T SAY MORE,	246	MOYEN SENSUEL	220
GOD'S			
BUT YOU "MY LORD," GOD'S PITY!	7	CINO	00
AND THROUGH ALL THE RIVEN SKIES GOD'S SWORDS CLASH.	28	ALTAFORTE	12
GODS'			
GODS' AID, LET NOT MY BONES LIE IN A PUBLIC LOCATION	213	SEXTUS PROP: 3	32
GOES			
EYES, DREAMS, LIPS, AND THE NIGHT GOES.	6	CINO	10
THE MIST GOES FROM THE MIRROR AND I SEE.	32	PARACELSUS	6
WHEN THE HOT WATER GIVES OUT OR GOES TEPID,	100	THE BATH TUB	2
WHO NOW GOES DRUNKENLY OUT	128	BEAU TOILET	8
THE EMPEROR IN HIS JEWELLED CAR GOES OUT TO INSPECT HIS FLOWERS,	129	THE RIVER SONG	35
HE GOES OUT TO HORI, TO LOOK AT THE WING-FLAPPING STORKS,	130	THE RIVER SONG	36
TREES FALL, THE GRASS GOES YELLOW WITH AUTUMN.	133	FRONTIER GUARD	3
KO-JIN GOES WEST FROM KO-KAKU-RO,	137	ON RIVER KIANG	1
END THE DISCUSSION, RICHARD GOES OUT NEXT DAY	156	NEAR PERIGORD	157
GOES ON THAT HEADLESS TRUNK, THAT BEARS FOR LIGHT	156	NEAR PERIGORD	164
WHEN THE SWEET AIR GOES BITTER,	174	LANGUE D'OC: 3	1
THAT LOVE GOES OUT	174	LANGUE D'OC: 3	5
SO SWIFTLY GOES THE NIGHT	177	LANGUE D'OC: 4	14
TELL HER THAT GOES	197	ENVOI (1919)	17
IF SHE GOES IN A GLEAM OF COS, IN A SLITHER OF DYED STUFF,	217	SEXTUS PROP: 5	30
THERE GOES THE NIGHT BRIGADE,	257	BREAD BRIGADE	9
JUST GOES AHEAD AND SUCKS A TEAT	272	THE BABY	11

GOIN' -- GOLDISH

	PAGE	TITLE	LINE
GOIN'			
THE CO-OPS WAS A GOIN' SOMEWHERE,	262	ALF'S SEVENTH	2
IS WHERE THE CO-OPS ARE GOIN' TO,	262	ALF'S SEVENTH	13
GOING			
NO MAN AT ALL GOING THE EARTH'S GAIT,	66	THE SEAFARER	92
OPEN LIES THE LAND, YET THE STEELY GOING	68	APPARUIT	10
PETALS ARE ON THE GONE WATERS AND ON THE GOING, ...	131	AT TEN-SHIN	5
AND WHAT WITH BROKEN WHEELS AND SO ON, I WON'T SAY IT WASN'T HARD GOING,	135	EXILE'S LETTER	40
AND I WAS STILL GOING, LATE IN THE YEAR,	135	EXILE'S LETTER	42
WITH RIPPLES LIKE DRAGON-SCALES, GOING GRASS GREEN ON THE WATER,	136	EXILE'S LETTER	52
PLEASURE LASTING, WITH COURTEZANS, GOING AND COMING WITHOUT HINDRANCE,	136	EXILE'S LETTER	53
WILL BE GOING GREENER AND GREENER,	137	OF DEPARTURE	EPI
AND WHEN MEN GOING BY LOOK ON RAFU	140	MULBERRY ROAD	15
AND GRASS GOING GLASSY WITH THE LIGHT ON IT,	167	OF AROUET	20
THAT PLAINETH OF THE GOING OF THE NIGHT,	172	LANGUE D'OC: 1	12
"AND HERE I AM SINCE GOING DOWN OF SUN,	172	LANGUE D'OC: 1	18
"AND I AM GOING TO THE TEMPLE OF VESTA ... "	225	SEXTUS PROP:10	41
YOU THINK YOU ARE GOING TO DO HOMER.	228	SEXTUS PROP:12	22
GOLD			
IN ROSE AND GOLD.	9	NA AUDIART	26
YOU GRABBED AT THE GOLD SURE; HAD NO NEED TO PACK CENTS	13	MESMERISM	19
BUT AH! WHEN I SEE THE STANDARDS GOLD, VAIR, PURPLE, OPPOSING	28	ALTAFORTE	4
HER GOLD IS SPREAD, ABOVE, AROUND, INWOVEN;	49	OF SPLENDOUR	4
AND ALL HER ROBE WAS WOVEN OF PALE GOLD.	49	OF SPLENDOUR	12
THERE ARE THERE MANY ROOMS AND ALL OF GOLD,	49	OF SPLENDOUR	13
I HAVE READ OUT THE GOLD UPON THE WALL,	60	TOMB AKR CAAR	9
AND THOUGH HE STREW THE GRAVE WITH GOLD,	66	THE SEAFARER	99
SWIFT AT COURAGE THOU IN THE SHELL OF GOLD, CASTING	68	APPARUIT	13
BRING THE RED GOLD OF THE MAPLE,	75	THE ALCHEMIST	10
MIDONZ, WITH THE GOLD OF THE SUN, THE LEAF OF THE POPLAR, BY THE LIGHT OF THE AMBER,	75	THE ALCHEMIST	25
RAIN FLAKES OF GOLD ON THE WATER	76	THE ALCHEMIST	55
A BROWN ROBE, WITH THREADS OF GOLD WOVEN IN PATTERNS, HAST THOU GATHERED ABOUT THEE,	91	DANCE FIGURE	17
O GLASS SUBTLE AND CUNNING, O POWDERY GOLD!	95	OF THE DEGREES	14
MUSICIANS WITH JEWELLED FLUTES AND WITH PIPES OF GOLD WITH YELLOW GOLD AND WHITE JEWELS, WE PAID FOR SONGS AND LAUGHTER	128	THE RIVER SONG	2
AND WITH SILVER HARNESS AND REINS OF GOLD,	134	EXILE'S LETTER	4
THE WATER-JET OF GOLD LIGHT BEARS US UP THROUGH THE CEILINGS;	134	EXILE'S LETTER	22
A PALE GOLD, IN THE AFORESAID PATTERN,	169	PHANOPOEIA	4
AS GOLD THAT RAINS ABOUT SOME BURIED KING.	202	AGE DEMANDED	41
GOLD, OF COURSE, IS SOLID TOO,	236	MIDDLE-AGED	2
	267	ALF'S TWELFTH	16
GOLD-BRAID			
IT IS HE WHO BUYS GOLD-BRAID FOR THE SWANKERS	263	ALF'S EIGHTH	17
GOLD-COLOURED			
LAPPED IN THE GOLD-COLOURED FLAME I DESCEND THROUGH THE AETHER.	169	PHANOPOEIA	8
GOLDEN			
SPEECH FOR PSYCHE IN THE GOLDEN BOOK OF APULEIUS	39	FOR PSYCHE	
SIGHING AS THOU DOST THROUGH THE GOLDEN SPEECH."	43	SATIEMUS	6
AND I AM FAIR AND GOLDEN	47	FROM HEINE: 7	15
GOLDEN ROSE THE HOUSE, IN THE PORTAL I SAW	68	APPARUIT	
GOLDEN ABOUT THEE.	68	APPARUIT	
I HAVE KNOWN THE GOLDEN DISC,	95	OF THE DEGREES	6
BUT GOLDEN,	107	COMING OF WAR	
ACTAEON OF GOLDEN GREAVES!	107	COMING OF WAR	1
THE IMPERIAL GUARDS COME FORTH FROM THE GOLDEN HOUSE WITH THEIR ARMOUR A-GLEAMING.	129	THE RIVER SONG	3
A GLITTER OF GOLDEN SADDLES, AWAITING THE PRINCESS;	141	IDEA OF CHOAN	
AS BUTEI OF KAN HAD MADE THE HIGH GOLDEN LOTUS	141	IDEA OF CHOAN	2
GOLD-GIVING			
NOR GOLD-GIVING LORDS LIKE THOSE GONE.	66	THE SEAFARER	8
GOLDISH			
CLOTHED IN GOLDISH WEFT, DELICATELY PERFECT,	68	APPARUIT	2

GOLDISH -- GOOD

	PAGE	TITLE	LINE
GOLDISH (CONTINUED)			
THEN THERE'S A GOLDISH COLOUR, DIFFERENT.	69	SUB MARE	4
GOLD-YELLOW			
FROM THE GOLD-YELLOW FROCK	204	MEDALLION	6
GONE			
(SKOAL! WITH THE DREGS IF THE CLEAR BE GONE!)	10	FOR THIS YULE	7
BUT YE ASK FIRST WHERE THE WINDS ARE GONE	10	FOR THIS YULE	27
FOR SHE I SANG OF HATH GONE FROM ME."	17	PRAISE YSOLT	37
GONE WHILE YOUR TASTES WERE KEEN TO YOU, ...	19	FOR E. MCC	1
GONE WHERE THE GREY WINDS CALL TO YOU, ...	19	FOR E. MCC	2
GONE AS A GUST OF BREATH	19	FOR E. MCC	10
O AGE GONE LAX! O STUNTED FOLLOWERS, ...	32	PIERE VIDAL	60
GONE IS HIS BODY FINE AND AMOROUS, ...	37	THE YOUNG KING	31
SO MANY THOUSAND BEAUTIES ARE GONE DOWN TO AVERNUS,	38	LADY'S LIFE	3
SO MANY THOUSAND FAIR ARE GONE DOWN TO AVERNUS, ...	38	LADY'S LIFE	13
WE HAVE GONE FORTH BEYOND YOUR BONDS AND BORDERS,	50	THE FLAME	7
OF CHEEKS GROWN SUNKEN AND GLAD HAIR GONE GRAY; ...	50	THE FLAME	19
NOR GOLD-GIVING LORDS LIKE THOSE GONE.	66	THE SEAFARER	85
GREY-HAIRED HE GROANETH, KNOWS GONE COMPANIONS, ...	66	THE SEAFARER	94
GONE AS WIND! THE CLOTH OF THE MAGICAL HANDS!	68	APPARUIT	22
AND NOW SHE'S GONE, WHO WAS HIS CYPRIAN, ...	73	JACOPO SELLAIO	3
I HAVE GONE HALF CRACKED, ...	94	INSTRUCTIONS	11
BUT SEEMS LIKE A PERSON JUST GONE.	112	IONE, DEAD	9
AND THREE POETS ARE GONE INTO MOURNING.	118	THREE POETS	2
I HAVE GONE IN RIBEYRAC	122	PROVINC DESERT	36
"MEN HAVE GONE BY SUCH AND SUCH VALLEYS	122	PROVINC DESERT	57
THAT AGE IS GONE;	123	PROVINC DESERT	78
PIEIRE DE MAENSAC IS GONE.	123	PROVINC DESERT	79
AND YOU HAVE BEEN GONE FIVE MONTHS.	130	RIVER-MER WIFE	17
PETALS ARE ON THE GONE WATERS AND ON THE GOING, ...	131	AT TEN-SHIN	5
THE PHOENIX ARE GONE, THE RIVER FLOWS ON ALONE. ...	138	CITY OF CHOAN	2
YOU WERE GONE UP AS A ROCKET, ...	147	BEFORE SLEEP	14
GONE--AH, GONE--UNTOUCHED, UNREACHABLE!	157	NEAR PERIGORD	188
GONE--AH, GONE--UNTOUCHED, UNREACHABLE!	157	NEAR PERIGORD	188
MY YOUTH IS GONE FROM ME.	158	PSYCHOLOG HOUR	30
CRYING AFTER THE FOLLIES GONE BY ME, ...	168	OF AROUET	30
I AM GONE FROM ONE JOY, ...	176	LANGUE D'OC: 3	60
FOR AN OLD BITCH GONE IN THE TEETH, ...	191	HUGH SELWYN: 5	3
QUICK EYES GONE UNDER EARTH'S LID, ...	191	HUGH SELWYN: 5	6
HERE IS A PART THAT'S SLIGHT, AND PART GONE WRONG,	235	TO WHISTLER	5
TEN YEARS AND TWELVE YEARS GONE, ...	259	ALF'S THIRD	18
GONGULA			
GONGULA	112	PAPYRUS	3
GOOD			
SO ART THOU WITH US, BEING GOOD TO KEEP	19	FOR E. MCC	21
HIS SMILE WAS GOOD TO SEE, ...	33	GOODLY FERE	6
OH WE DRUNK HIS "HALE" IN THE GOOD RED WINE	33	GOODLY FERE	13
THAT DOTH BUT WOUND THE GOOD WITH IRE AND SADNESS.	37	THE YOUNG KING	24
BUT I KNOW NOW, THEY BOTH WERE GOOD ENOUGH.	44	FROM HEINE: 2	8
ALL GOOD THINGS GO VANISHING.	46	FROM HEINE: 6	20
HIS? WHY THE GOOD KING HARRY'S, ...	47	FROM HEINE: 7	15
GET A GOOD DEAL OF KISSING DONE.	48	FROM HEINE: 8	8
NOT THOUGH HE BE GIVEN HIS GOOD, BUT WILL HAVE IN			
HIS YOUTH GREED;	65	THE SEAFARER	41
HERE HAVE WE HAD OUR VANTAGE, THE GOOD HOUR.	69	THE NEEDLE	4
BE EAGER TO FIND NEW EVILS AND NEW GOOD, ...	89	COMMISSION	24
THE GOOD BELLAIRES	97	THE BELLAIRES	1
TOGETHER WITH THE RESPECTIVE WIVES, HUSBANDS,			
SISTERS AND HETEROGENEOUS CONNECTIONS OF THE GOOD			
BELLAIRES, ...	97	THE BELLAIRES	6
BUT THE GOOD BELLAIRES HAVE SO LITTLE UNDERSTOOD			
THEIR AFFAIRS	97	THE BELLAIRES	8
THE GOOD SQUIRE BELLAIRE;	97	THE BELLAIRES	12
FOR THEY MAY NOT BELONG TO THE GOOD SQUIRE BELLAIRE	98	THE BELLAIRES	14
WHEREFORE THE GOOD SQUIRE BELLAIRE	98	THE BELLAIRES	34
FOR THE GOOD BELLAIRES	98	THE BELLAIRES	42
WIT, NOR GOOD SPIRITS, NOR THE PLEASING ATTITUDES	101	AMITIES	11
GOOD GOD! THEY SAY YOU ARE RISQUE, ...	104	ANCORA	1
"HERE WAS GOOD SINGING.	122	PROVINC DESERT	45
YOU SWORN FOE TO FREE SPEECH AND GOOD LETTERS, ...	145	SALUTATION 3RD	11
TO DO AWAY WITH GOOD WRITERS, ...	145	SALUTATION 3RD	21

PAGE 169

GOOD -- GOT

	PAGE	TITLE	LINE
GOOD (CONTINUED)			
YOU SAY THAT I TAKE A GOOD DEAL UPON MYSELF;	146	MONUMENTUM AER	1
WEARING RAW SILK OF GOOD COLOUR,	146	CANTILATIONS	7
THEY SEEK MY FINANCIAL GOOD.	147	BEFORE SLEEP	4
IT IS GOOD TO SPLASH IN THE WATER	147	POST MORTEM	4
IN PERIGORD, AND THIS GOOD UNION	151	NEAR PERIGORD	18
THE TEN GOOD MILES FROM THERE TO MAENT'S CASTLE,	153	NEAR PERIGORD	65
GOOD "HEDGETHORN," FOR WE'LL ANGLICIZE YOUR NAME	161	CABARET DANCER	1
MY GOOD FELLOW, YOU, ON A CABARET SILENCE	161	CABARET DANCER	5
HAVE YOU, OR I, SEEN MOST OF CABARETS, GOOD HEDGETHORN?	161	CABARET DANCER	17
GOOD HEDGETHORN, THEY ALL HAVE FUTURES,	163	CABARET DANCER	60
"SST! MY GOOD FELLOW, ART AWAKE OR SLEEPING?	172	LANGUE D'OC: 1	6
BADEST ME TO SEE THAT A GOOD WATCH WAS DONE,	172	LANGUE D'OC: 1	23
"WAIT, MY GOOD FELLOW. FOR SUCH JOY I TAKE	172	LANGUE D'OC: 1	26
GOOD IS IT TO ME IF SHE FLOUT	175	LANGUE D'OC: 3	46
CHARM, SMILING AT THE GOOD MOUTH,	191	HUGH SELWYN: 5	5
"THE TIP'S A GOOD ONE, AS FOR LITERATURE	194	MR. NIXON	16
MUCH CONVERSATION IS AS GOOD AS HAVING A HOME.	214	SEXTUS PROP: 4	10
HAVE YOU DENIED PALLAS GOOD EYES?	221	SEXTUS PROP: 8	13
AND NO GOOD RUMOUR AMONG THEM.	226	SEXTUS PROP:11	19
AND THIS IS GOOD TO KNOW--FOR US, I MEAN,	235	TO WHISTLER	11
MY COUNTRY? I LOVE IT WELL, AND THOSE GOOD FELLOWS	238	MOYEN SENSUEL	3
GOOD-BYE			
AND WE SAY GOOD-BYE TO YOU ALSO,	101	AMITIES	7
GOOD-FELLOW			
GIVE MY GOOD-FELLOW AID IN FOOLS' DESPITE	172	LANGUE D'OC: 1	3
GOODLIEST			
HA' WE LOST THE GOODLIEST FERE O' ALL	33	GOODLY FERE	1
GOODLY			
BALLAD OF THE GOODLY FERE	33	GOODLY FERE	T
"FIRST LET THESE GO!" QUO' OUR GOODLY FERE,	33	GOODLY FERE	7
NO CAPON PRIEST WAS THE GOODLY FERE	33	GOODLY FERE	15
NO MOUSE OF THE SCROLLS WAS THE GOODLY FERE	33	GOODLY FERE	23
IF THEY THINK THEY HA' SNARED OUR GOODLY FERE	33	GOODLY FERE	25
"I'LL GO TO THE FEAST," QUO' OUR GOODLY FERE,	33	GOODLY FERE	27
A SON OF GOD WAS THE GOODLY FERE	34	GOODLY FERE	33
A MASTER OF MEN WAS THE GOODLY FERE,	34	GOODLY FERE	49
IF THEY THINK THEY HA' SLAIN OUR GOODLY FERE	34	GOODLY FERE	51
FREE US, FOR WITHOUT BE GOODLY COLOURS,	35	THE EYES	8
GOODS			
THEY TELL ME THAT BRANDED GOODS	262	ALF'S SEVENTH	10
FROM DRESS GOODS ADS, AND SPORTS.	266	ALF'S ELEVENTH	20
GOOSE			
ONE MUST HAVE RESONANCE, RESONANCE AND SONORITY . . LIKE A GOOSE.	230	SEXTUS PROP:12	65
GORDAM			
"THEM STAIRS! THEM STAIRS, THEM GORDAM STAIRS	271	OLE KATE	5
GORDON			
--GEORGE GORDON, LORD BYRON.	238	MOYEN SENSUEL	EPI
GORE			
WHO SO INDECOROUS AS TO SHED THE PURE GORE OF A SUITOR?!	212	SEXTUS PROP: 3	26
GORED			
SINCE ADONIS WAS GORED IN IDALIA, AND THE CYTHAREAN	219	SEXTUS PROP: 6	33
GORGEOUS			
UPON MANHATTAN'S GORGEOUS PANOPLY,	245	MOYEN SENSUEL	188
GORGON'S			
THEIR PUNIC FACES DYED IN THE GORGON'S LAKE;	211	SEXTUS PROP: 2	32
GOSSAMER			
SO SILENT LIGHT; NO GOSSAMER IS SPUN	38	BALLATETTA	7
GOSSIP			
IDEAS, OLD GOSSIP, ODDMENTS OF ALL THINGS,	61	PORTRAIT FEMME	4
FULL OF GOSSIP AND OLD TALES."	90	SURGIT FAMA	15
AND WE'VE THE GOSSIP (SKIPPED SIX HUNDRED YEARS).	155	NEAR PERIGORD	138
GOT			
BUT GOD! WHAT A SIGHT YOU HA' GOT O' OUR IN'ARDS,	13	MESMERISM	16
YOU'VE GOT THE WHOLE NIGHT BEFORE YOU,	48	FROM HEINE: 8	
AND GOT NO PROMOTION,	136	EXILE'S LETTER	65
NO MAN CAN GET OR HAS GOT.	174	LANGUE D'OC: 3	1
(BY THAT TIME SHE HAD GOT ON TO BROWNING.)	182	MOEURS CON: 8	

PAGE 170

	PAGE	TITLE	LINE

GOT (CONTINUED)
- "WHEN I BEGAN I GOT, OF COURSE, ... 194   MR. NIXON   6
- WHEN THEY HAVE GOT OVER THE STRANGENESS, ... 208   SEXTUS PROP: 1   41
- WAS GOT ABROAD, WHAT BETTER LUCK DO YOU WISH 'EM, 240   MOYEN SENSUEL   60
- SUCH WAS HE WHEN HE GOT HIS MOTHER'S LETTER 242   MOYEN SENSUEL   109
- AS TO HOW AND WHY AND WHEREBY THEY GOT IN 244   MOYEN SENSUEL   159
- THEY GOT NO STEADY TRADE, ... 257   BREAD BRIGADE   10
- YOUR GRANAD GOT THE ROUGH EDGE. 259   ALF'S FOURTH   10
- AIN'T YEH GOT PRECEDENT? 259   ALF'S THIRD   17
- MY OLD MAN GOT NO INDEMNITY 263   ALF'S EIGHTH   24
- WHAT AIN'T GOT WORK NO MORE 269   SAFE AND SOUND   10
- NEVER GOT PROPERLY TANKED AS I SAW, ... 271   OLE KATE   15
- AND NEVER GOT TOOK TO JAIL, ... 271   OLE KATE   16

'GOT
- 'GOT ON DESIROUS THOUGHT BY NATURAL VIRTUE, ... 42   HER MONUMENT   42

GOURMONT
- DE GOURMONT SAYS THAT FIFTY GRUNTS ARE ALL THAT WILL
  BE PRIZED. 244   MOYEN SENSUEL   165

GOUT
- "MAY THE GOUT CRAMP UP HER FEET! 215   SEXTUS PROP: 4   37

GOUVERNET
- PHYLLIDULA AND THE SPOILS OF GOUVERNET 167   OF AROUET   ST

GOVERNMENT
- THIS GOVERNMENT OFFICIAL 115   SOCIAL ORDER   1

GOVERNMENT'S
- THE GOVERNMENT'S EXCUSE, ... 265   ALF'S TENTH   2

GOVERNOR
- WAS GOVERNOR IN HEI SHU, AND PUT DOWN THE BARBARIAN
  RABBLE. 135   EXILE'S LETTER   37

GRABBED
- YOU GRABBED AT THE GOLD SURE; HAD NO NEED TO PACK
  CENTS 13   MESMERISM   19

GRACE
- SING THOU THE GRACE OF THE LADY OF BEZIERS, ... 23   MARVOIL   36
- THE LIGHT BECAME HER GRACE AND DWELT AMONG 38   BALLATETTA   1
- THAT YE WERE ONCE! OF ALL THE GRACE YE HAD 41   HER MONUMENT   18
- UPON FOND NATURE'S MORBID GRACE. 44   MR. HOUSMAN   14
- SUCH GRACE OF LOCKS, I DO YE TO WIT, ... 106   DOMPNA POIS   38
- NOT, AT ANY RATE, AN ATTIC GRACE; 188   HUGH SELWYN: 2   4
- NEVER RELAXING INTO GRACE; 193   BRENNBAUM   4

GRACEFUL
- LET COME THE GRACEFUL SPEAKERS, ... 146   CANTILATIONS   8

GRACEFULLY
- GRACEFULLY PAINTED-- 136   EXILE'S LETTER   58

GRACES
- RECKING NAUGHT ELSE BUT THAT HER GRACES GIVE 197   ENVOI (1919)   10
- WITH PERPETUAL ASCRIPTION OF GRACES? 222   SEXTUS PROP: 8   15

GRACILES
- ET DEUX PETITES FILLES GRACILES, ... 160   DANS OMNIBUS   14

GRACIOUS
- WITH SUCH GRACIOUS UNCERTAINITY, ... 103   LADIES   11
- A GRACIOUS SPRING, TURNED TO BLOOD-RAVENOUS AUTUMN, 133   FRONTIER GUARD   14
- NO ONE HEARS AUGHT SAVE THE GRACIOUS SOUND OF
  COMPLIMENTS. 154   NEAR PERIGORD   120

GRADUALLY
- GRADUALLY LED HIM TO THE ISOLATION 201   AGE DEMANDED   26

GRADUATIONS
- HIS SENSE OF GRADUATIONS, ... 201   AGE DEMANDED   22

GRAND
- LEUCIS, WHO INTENDED A GRAND PASSION, ... 99   EPITAPH   1
- THE GRAND PIANO 204   MEDALLION   2
- KEEP UP THE GRAND SYSTEM 259   ALF'S FOURTH   8
- MON BEAU GRAND FRERE 273   M. POM-POM   3

GRANDAD
- YOUR GRANDAD GOT THE ROUGH EDGE 259   ALF'S FOURTH   10

GRANDFATHER
- ME, WHO HAD NO GENERAL FOR A GRANDFATHER! 229   SEXTUS PROP:12   54

GRANDMOTHER
- OLDER THAN THOSE HER GRANDMOTHER 195   HUGH SELWIN:11   7

GRANITE
- WHEN WE SAT UPON THE GRANITE BRINK IN HELICON 104   ANCORA   10

PAGE 171

GRANITE -- GREASE

	PAGE	TITLE	LINE
GRANITE (CONTINUED)			
HARSHER THAN GRANITE,	107	COMING OF WAR	8
GRANT			
HELL GRANT SOON WE HEAR AGAIN THE SWORDS CLASH! ...	28	ALTAFORTE	13
HELL GRANT SOON WE HEAR AGAIN THE SWORDS CLASH! ...	29	ALTAFORTE	38
AND BETTER WERE IT, SHOULD GOD GRANT HIS PLEASURE,	37	THE YOUNG KING	22
GOD GRANT I DIE NOT BY ANY MAN'S STROKE	173	LANGUE D'OC: 2	21
GRAPE			
CRAWL IN THE VERY BLACK GUTTER BENEATH THE GRAPE STAND?	114	SIMULACRA	4
GRAPES			
TO GATHER GRAPES FOR THE LEOPARDS, MY FRIEND,	108	CH'U YUAN	6
THE GREEN STRETCHES WHERE LOVE IS AND THE GRAPES	167	OF AROUET	21
"A FLAT FIELD FOR RUSHES, GRAPES GROW ON THE SLOPE."	229	SEXTUS PROP:12	52
GRAPPLE			
(LET HIM REBUKE WHO NE'ER HAS KNOWN THE PURE PLATONIC GRAPPLE,	242	MOYEN SENSUEL	105
GRASP			
YOUR GRASP, I HAVE ELUDED.	51	THE FLAME	43
GRASS			
MUST KNOW SUCH MOMENTS, THINKING ON THE GRASS;	43	SATIEMUS	11
SEE, THE LIGHT GRASS SPRANG UP TO PILLOW THEE, ...	60	TOMB AKR CAAR	6
GRASS, AND LOW FIELDS, AND HILLS,	70	THE PLUNGE	16
FROM THE POWER OF GRASS,	75	THE ALCHEMIST	30
FANNING THE GRASS SHE WALKED ON THEN, ENDURES:	92	GENTILDONNA	4
BLUE, BLUE IS THE GRASS ABOUT THE RIVER	128	BEAU TOILET	1
OVER THE GRASS IN THE WEST GARDEN;	131	RIVER-MER WIFE	24
TREES FALL, THE GRASS GOES YELLOW WITH AUTUMN.	133	FRONTIER GUARD	3
HIGH HEAPS, COVERED WITH TREES AND GRASS;	133	FRONTIER GUARD	9
WITH RIPPLES LIKE DRAGON-SCALES, GOING GRASS GREEN ON THE WATER,	136	EXILE'S LETTER	52
AND GO OUT THROUGH A THOUSAND MILES OF DEAD GRASS.	137	TAKING LEAVE	4
FLOWERS AND GRASS	138	CITY OF CHOAN	3
TO KEEP GRASS	146	MONUMENTUM AER	8
BUT I AM LIKE THE GRASS, I CAN NOT LOVE YOU.'	157	NEAR PERIGORD	182
AND GRASS GOING GLASSY WITH THE LIGHT ON IT,	167	OF AROUET	20
GRASS SHOWING UNDER THE SNOW,	168	OF AROUET	37
GRASS-BLADE			
CLEAR AS FROST ON THE GRASS-BLADE,	108	FAN-PIECE	2
GRASSES			
DRIVES THE CLEAR EMERALDS FROM THE BENDED GRASSES	38	BALLATETTA	9
THE EASTERN WIND BRINGS THE GREEN COLOUR INTO THE ISLAND GRASSES AT YEI-SHU,	129	THE RIVER SONG	23
GRASSES	160	DANS OMNIBUS	18
GRASSY			
AND KISSED THEE WITH A MYRIAD GRASSY TONGUES;	60	TOMB AKR CAAR	7
GRAVE			
FOR I WAS A GAUNT, GRAVE COUNCILLOR	4	LA FRAISNE	1
HER GRAVE, SWEET HAUGHTINESS	52	AU SALON	EPI
AND THOUGH HE STREW THE GRAVE WITH GOLD,	66	THE SEAFARER	99
GREET THE GRAVE AND THE STODGY,	86	SALUTATION 2ND	21
PERHAPS YOU WILL HAVE THE PLEASURE OF DEFILING MY PAUPER'S GRAVE;	145	SALUTATION 3RD	18
OVER YOUR GRAVE.	146	MONUMENTUM AER	9
WITHOUT IXION, AND WITHOUT THE SONS OF MENOETIUS AND THE ARGO AND WITHOUT JOVE'S GRAVE AND THE TITANS.	218	SEXTUS PROP: 5	52
WHEN WILL THIS SYSTEM LIE DOWN IN ITS GRAVE?	260	ALF'S FIFTH	4
GRAVEN			
HALF THE GRAVEN SHOULDER, THE THROAT AFLASH WITH	68	APPARUIT	17
GRAY			
GREEN AND GRAY IS HER RAIMENT,	18	DE AEGYPTO	5
OF CHEEKS GROWN SUNKEN AND GLAD HAIR GONE GRAY; ...	50	THE FLAME	19
HOW WILL THESE HOURS, WHEN WE TWAIN ARE GRAY,	51	HORAE BEATAE	3
GRAY CLIFFS,	107	COMING OF WAR	5
GRAY ARLES AND BIAUCAIRE,	119	THE GYPSY	10
THERE IS A PLACE OF TREES . . . GRAY WITH LICHEN.	121	PROVINC DESERT	6
GRAY-GREEN			
BY THE TROUT ASLEEP IN THE GRAY-GREEN OF WATER; ...	76	THE ALCHEMIST	37
GREASE			
(YOU FEED A HEN ON GREASE, PERHAPS SHE'LL LAY	240	MOYEN SENSUEL	48

PAGE 172

GREASY -- GREATLY

	PAGE	TITLE	LINE
GREASY			
AND A PAIR OF SCALES NOT TOO GREASY,	117	THE LAKE ISLE	9
GREAT			
VERY GLAD, FOR MY BRIDE HATH TOWARD ME A GREAT LOVE	5	LA FRAISNE	34
THE MOON IS A GREAT PEARL IN THE WATERS OF SAPPHIRE,	18	DE AEGYPTO	21
O GOD, WHAT GREAT KINDNESS	26	NIGHT LITANY	9
WHAT GREAT SORROW	26	NIGHT LITANY	15
IN HOT SUMMER HAVE I GREAT REJOICING	28	ALTAFORTE	7
WHEN I BUT THINK UPON THE GREAT DEAD DAYS	30	PIERE VIDAL	1
AND EVERY RUN-AWAY OF THE WOOD THROUGH THAT GREAT MADNESS,	31	PIERE VIDAL	51
HIM, WHOM IT PLEASED FOR OUR GREAT BITTERNESS	37	THE YOUNG KING	33
WITH SIX GREAT SAPPHIRES HUNG ALONG THE WALL,	49	OF SPLENDOUR	10
GREAT MINDS HAVE SOUGHT YOU--LACKING SOMEONE ELSE.	61	PORTRAIT FEMME	6
THESE ARE YOUR RICHES, YOUR GREAT STORE; AND YET	61	PORTRAIT FEMME	24
"PAN IS DEAD. GREAT PAN IS DEAD.	72	PAN IS DEAD	1
FOR THE GREAT CHARMS THAT ARE UPON HER	72	DIEU! QU'IL	3
AS SHE SITS IN THE GREAT CHAIR	87	ALBATRE	6
GO AS A GREAT WAVE OF COOL WATER,	88	COMMISSION	4
CROSSED IN GREAT FUTURISTIC X'S, THE ART STUDENTS	93	LES MILLWIN	9
AND THERE HAD BEEN A GREAT CATCH OF SARDINES,	96	AESTHETICS	9
WERE PACKING THEM IN THE GREAT WOODEN BOXES	96	AESTHETICS	11
"WHERE THE GREAT HALLS WERE CLOSER TOGETHER."	122	PROVINC DESERT	58
HAUGHTY THEIR STEPS AS THEY GO IN TO GREAT BANQUETS,	132	AT TEN-SHIN	19
HE CLAPS HIS HAND ON THE BACK OF THE GREAT WATER SENNIN.	140	SENNIN POEM	14
AND YOU ON THAT GREAT MOUNTAIN OF A PALM--	152	NEAR PERIGORD	31
AND THE GREAT SCENE--	152	NEAR PERIGORD	40
AND GREAT WINGS BEAT ABOVE US IN THE TWILIGHT,	157	NEAR PERIGORD	176
AND THE GREAT WHEELS IN HEAVEN	157	NEAR PERIGORD	177
A SAD AND GREAT EVIL IS THE EXPECTATION OF DEATH--	164	QUINTUS SEPTIM	8
AND YOUR BARBECUES OF GREAT OXEN,	165	QUINTUS SEPTIM	13
NOR FEEL MY ACHE--GREAT AS IT IS,	174	LANGUE D'OC: 3	21
FOR HER GREAT BEAUTY, MANY MEN LOOK ON HER,	177	LANGUE D'OC: 4	27
AND HE TALKED ABOUT "THE GREAT MARY,"	181	MOEURS CON: 7	10
AND WEIGHED, REVEALED HIS GREAT AFFECT,	200	MAUBERLEY: 2	31
MY LITTLE MOUTH SHALL GOBBLE IN SUCH GREAT FOUNTAINS,	210	SEXTUS PROP: 2	6
TO-DAY WE TAKE THE GREAT BREATH OF LOVERS,	221	SEXTUS PROP: 7	31
GREAT ZEUS, SAVE THE WOMAN,	223	SEXTUS PROP: 9	10
YOU ARE ESCAPED FROM GREAT PERIL,	224	SEXTUS PROP: 9	23
GO BACK TO GREAT DIAN'S DANCES BEARING SUITABLE GIFTS,	224	SEXTUS PROP: 9	24
HE CAN TABULATE CAESAR'S GREAT SHIPS.	228	SEXTUS PROP:12	32
VARRO, OF HIS GREAT PASSION LEUCADIA,	230	SEXTUS PROP:12	67
YOU ALSO, OUR FIRST GREAT,	235	TO WHISTLER	1
GREAT IS KING GEORGE THE FIFTH,	237	ABU SALAMMAMM	1
GREAT IS KING GEORGE THE FIFTH--	237	ABU SALAMMAMM	4
GREAT IS KING GEORGE THE FIFTH;	237	ABU SALAMMAMM	10
GREAT IS THE KING OF ENGLAND AND GREATLY TO BE FEARED,	237	ABU SALAMMAMM	15
GREAT IS KING GEORGE THE FIFTH	237	ABU SALAMMAMM	18
GREAT AND LOFTY IS THIS FOUNTAIN;	237	ABU SALAMMAMM	22
THE MOTHER OF THE GREAT KING, IN A HOOP-SKIRT,	237	ABU SALAMMAMM	24
A SILENT HUNTER OFF THE GREAT WHITE WAY,	245	MOYEN SENSUEL	200
HE COMES TO BE AND IS WHEN WILL'S SO GREAT	249	DONNA MI PREGA	49
GREAT KNOWLEDGE OR SLIGHT.	250	DONNA MI PREGA	69
FROM A GREAT EMPLOYER LIKE SELFRIDGE	264	ALF'S EIGHTH	33
MY GREAT PRESS CLEAVES THE GUTS OF MEN,	266	ALF'S ELEVENTH	1
MY GREAT NOISE DROWNS THEIR CRIES,	266	ALF'S ELEVENTH	2
LIKE TO-DAY'S GREAT MEN IN BRITAIN.	272	THE BABY	12
GREATER			
"THERE BE MANY SINGERS GREATER THAN THOU."	16	PRAISE YSOLT	4
"THERE BE GREATER SOULS THAN THOU."	16	PRAISE YSOLT	26
DO THOU, PLUTO, BRING HERE NO GREATER HARSHNESS.	38	LADY'S LIFE	2
DO THOU, PLUTO, BRING HERE NO GREATER HARSHNESS.	38	LADY'S LIFE	12
GREATEST			
IN BOSTON, TO HENRY JAMES, THE GREATEST WHOM WE'VE SEEN LIVING.	240	MOYEN SENSUEL	62
GREATLY			
ARLES GREATLY ALTERED,	122	PROVINC DESERT	60

PAGE 173

GREATLY -- GREY

	PAGE	TITLE	LINE
GREATLY (CONTINUED)			
GREAT IS THE KING OF ENGLAND AND GREATLY TO BE FEARED,	237	ABU SALAMMAMM	15
GREAT-UNCLE'S			
OR TAKE THE INTAGLIO, MY FAT GREAT-UNCLE'S HEIRLOOM:	162	CABARET DANCER	35
GREAVES			
ACTAEON OF GOLDEN GREAVES!	107	COMING OF WAR	15
GRECIAN			
BRINGING THE GRECIAN ORGIES INTO ITALY,	207	SEXTUS PROP: 1	4
GREECE			
AND THEN THESE SKETCHES IN THE MOOD OF GREECE?	235	TO WHISTLER	9
GREED			
AND ITS AGE-LASTING WALLOW FOR RED GREED	14	FAMAM CANO	26
THEY DIED AND THE GREED OF YOUR FLAME CONSUMES THEM.	38	LADY'S LIFE	10
NOT THOUGH HE BE GIVEN HIS GOOD, BUT WILL HAVE IN HIS YOUTH GREED;	65	THE SEAFARER	41
GREEK			
(I BURN, I FREEZE, I SWEAT, SAID THE FAIR GREEK,	242	MOYEN SENSUEL	123
AND BASIL WAS THE GREEK THAT RODE AROUND	264	ALF'S NINTH	18
GREEKS			
CLEAR THE STREET, O YE GREEKS,	229	SEXTUS PROP:12	37
CLEAR THE STREETS, O YE GREEKS!	229	SEXTUS PROP:12	40
GREEN			
LITTLE GREEN LEAF WORDS CRYING FOR A SONG.	16	PRAISE YSOLT	18
GREEN AND GRAY IS HER RAIMENT,	18	DE AEGYPTO	5
TORN, GREEN AND SILENT IN THE SWOLLEN RHONE,	31	PIERE VIDAL	27
GREEN WAS HER MANTLE, CLOSE, AND WROUGHT	31	PIERE VIDAL	28
GREEN OF THE WOOD-MOSS AND FLOWER COLOURS,	35	THE EYES	9
THE FLAME, THE AUTUMN, AND THE GREEN ROSE OF LOVE	51	THE ALTAR	2
GREEN THE WAYS, THE BREATH OF THE FIELDS IS THINE THERE,	68	APPARUIT	9
PALE SLOW GREEN SURGINGS OF THE UNDERWAVE,	69	SUB MARE	7
GREEN COME THE SHOOTS, AYE APRIL IN THE BRANCHES,	71	A VIRGINAL	11
I WILL GET YOU A GREEN COAT OUT OF CHINA	94	INSTRUCTIONS	17
GREEN ARSENIC SMEARED ON AN EGG-WHITE CLOTH,	113	L'ART, 1910	1
LUMINOUS GREEN FROM THE ROOKS,	120	GAME OF CHESS	9
THE EASTERN WIND BRINGS THE GREEN COLOUR INTO THE ISLAND GRASSES AT YEI-SHU,	129	THE RIVER SONG	23
WITH RIPPLES LIKE DRAGON-SCALES, GOING GRASS GREEN ON THE WATER,	136	EXILE'S LETTER	52
AND THE WATER, A HUNDRED FEET DEEP, REFLECTING GREEN EYEBROWS	136	EXILE'S LETTER	56
--EYEBROWS PAINTED GREEN ARE A FINE SIGHT IN YOUNG MOONLIGHT,	136	EXILE'S LETTER	57
THE RED AND GREEN KINGFISHERS	139	SENNIN POEM	1
GREEN VINES HANG THROUGH THE HIGH FOREST,	139	SENNIN POEM	4
WITH GREEN STRINGS SHE MAKES THE WARP OF HER BASKET,	140	MULBERRY ROAD	8
HER UNDERSKIRT IS OF GREEN PATTERN-SILK,	140	MULBERRY ROAD	13
AND THE GREEN CAT'S-EYE LIFTS TOWARD MONTAIGNAC.	154	NEAR PERIGORD	103
POPPIES AND DAY'S EYES IN THE GREEN EMAIL	157	NEAR PERIGORD	171
THAT FALLS THROUGH THE PALE GREEN WATER.	166	FISH & SHADOW	21
THE GREEN STRETCHES WHERE LOVE IS AND THE GRAPES	167	OF AROUET	21
'TILL THE SUN COME, AND THE GREEN LEAF ON THE BOUGH.	173	LANGUE D'OC: 2	16
GREENER			
WILL BE GOING GREENER AND GREENER,	137	OF DEPARTURE	EPI
WILL BE GOING GREENER AND GREENER,	137	OF DEPARTURE	EPI
GREENISH			
THE MAUVE AND GREENISH SOULS OF THE LITTLE MILLWINS	93	LES MILLWIN	2
GREET			
GREET THE GRAVE AND THE STODGY,	86	SALUTATION 2ND	21
GREW			
THAT GREW ELM-OAK AMID THE WOLD.	3	THE TREE	5
HERE RADWAY GREW, THE FRUIT OF PANTOSOCRACY,	239	MOYEN SENSUEL	39
RADWAY GREW UP. THESE FORCES SHAPED HIS SOUL;	239	MOYEN SENSUEL	44
NO, NO, THEY DANCED. THE MUSIC GREW MUCH LOUDER	243	MOYEN SENSUEL	131
ALL DREW THEIR PAY, AND AS THE PAY GREW LESS,	260	ALF'S FIFTH	9
GREY			
. . . EH? . . . THEY MOSTLY HAD GREY EYES,	7	CINO	40
THEN WHEN THE GREY WOLVES EVERYCHONE	10	FOR THIS YULE	3
LITTLE GREY ELF WORDS CRYING FOR A SONG,	16	PRAISE YSOLT	16
GONE WHERE THE GREY WINDS CALL TO YOU,	19	FOR E. MCC	2

PAGE 174

GREY -- GROW

	PAGE	TITLE	LINE
GREY (CONTINUED)			
'GAINST THAT GREY FENCER, EVEN DEATH.	19	FOR E. MCC	9
'GAINST THAT GREY FENCER, EVEN DEATH, ...	19	FOR E. MCC	25
EVEN THE GREY PACK KNEW ME AND KNEW FEAR.	30	PIERE VIDAL	13
GOD CURSE THE YEARS THAT TURN SUCH WOMEN GREY!	31	PIERE VIDAL	46
WI' HIS EYES LIKE THE GREY O' THE SEA, ...	34	GOODLY FERE	44
AND OF GREY WATERS.	67	DORIA	7
GREY OLIVE LEAVES BENEATH A RAIN-COLD SKY.	92	GENTILDONNA	5
THE GREY AND ROSE	203	MAUBERLEY: 4	11
GREY-BLOWN			
I SKOAL TO THE EYES AS GREY-BLOWN MERE	10	FOR THIS YULE	22
GREY-HAIRED			
GREY-HAIRED HE GROANETH, KNOWS GONE COMPANIONS, ...	66	THE SEAFARER	94
GRIEF			
AND I? I HAVE PUT ASIDE ALL FOLLY AND ALL GRIEF.	4	LA FRAISNE	24
IF ALL THE GRIEF AND WOE AND BITTERNESS, ...	36	THE YOUNG KING	1
WHENCE HAVE WE GRIEF, DISCORD AND DEEPEST SADNESS.	37	THE YOUNG KING	32
THERE WHERE THERE IS NO GRIEF, NOR SHALL BE SADNESS.	37	THE YOUNG KING	40
SOLE GUARD OF GRIEF	41	HER MONUMENT	7
OUR MIND IS FULL OF SORROW, WHO WILL KNOW OF OUR GRIEF?	127	BOWMEN OF SHU	24
"IN THE FULL FLARE OF GRIEF, DO WHAT YOU WILL." ...	152	NEAR PERIGORD	46
GRIEVANCE			
THE JEWEL STAIRS' GRIEVANCE	132	JEWEL STAIRS'	T
GRIEVES			
MY HEART ALL WAKES AND GRIEVES;	173	LANGUE D'OC: 2	8
GRIEVING			
THAT EVER CAME UPON THIS GRIEVING WORLD	36	THE YOUNG KING	3
GRIEVING AND SAD AND FULL OF BITTERNESS	36	THE YOUNG KING	9
GRIEVOUS			
AND NOTHING IS GRIEVOUS	174	LANGUE D'OC: 3	9
GRIMACE			
OF ITS ACCELERATED GRIMACE, ...	188	HUGH SELWYN: 2	2
GRIN			
AND YOUR PAINTED GRIN ANOTHER, ...	162	CABARET DANCER	42
GRINS UP AN AMIABLE GRIN, ...	163	CABARET DANCER	58
GRIND			
TER GRIND THE SAME OLD AXES	270	OF 600 M.P.'S	6
GRINS			
GRINS UP AN AMIABLE GRIN, ...	163	CABARET DANCER	58
GRIPPED			
OR SLACKED HIS HAND-GRIP WHEN YOU FIRST GRIPPED FAME?	59	EXIT' CUIUSDAM	3
ITS OWN HEAD SWINGING, GRIPPED BY THE DEAD HAIR, .	156	NEAR PERIGORD	165
GROAN			
SHE RE-ENTERS THEM WITH A GROAN, .,,,,,,,,,,,,,,,,	111	BLACK SLIPPERS	11
GROANETH			
GREY-HAIRED HE GROANETH, KNOWS GONE COMPANIONS, ...	66	THE SEAFARER	94
GROPES			
AND ONE GROPES IN THESE THINGS AS DELICATE	69	SUB MARE	5
GROSS			
FOR TWO GROSS OF BROKEN STATUES, ...	191	HUGH SELWYN: 5	7
GROSSEN			
AUS MEINEN GROSSEN SCHMERZEN	97	THE BELLAIRES	EPI
GROSSIERE			
EST GROSSIERE ET LE PARFUM DES VIOLETTES UN	199	MAUBERLEY: 2	EPI
GROUND			
WHERE THESE HAVE BEEN, MEET 'TIS, THE GROUND IS HOLY.	51	THE ALTAR	4
LAY STRIPPED UPON THE GROUND:	92	APRIL	4
IN BRIEF, VIOLET IS THE GROUND TONE OF MY PHONETICS.	247	PIERROTS	15
WHO ON THE SO WELL-PAID GROUND	263	ALF'S EIGHTH	9
GROUP			
HERE IS A FORMAL MALE GROUP:	104	THE SEEING EYE	4
GROVE			
IT IS IN YOUR GROVE I WOULD WALK, ...	207	SEXTUS PROP: 1	2
GROVES			
SMOTHERED IN LAUREL GROVES, ...	124	EXILE'S LETTER	13
GROW			
THE BRANCHES GROW OUT OF ME, LIKE ARMS.	62	A GIRL	5
THEY HURT ME. I GROW OLDER.	131	RIVER-MER WIFE	25
CLOUDS GROW OUT OF THE HILL	138	NEAR SHOKU	4
"A FLAT FIELD FOR RUSHES, GRAPES GROW ON THE SLOPE."	229	SEXTUS PROP:12	52

PAGE 175

GROWN -- GUISCARDA

	PAGE	TITLE	LINE
GROWN			
WAS GROWN SO FREE AN ESSENCE, OR BECOME	32	PARACELSUS	4
TURMOIL GROWN VISIBLE BENEATH OUR PEACE,	32	PARACELSUS	8
AND WE THAT ARE GROWN FORMLESS, RISE ABOVE--	32	PARACELSUS	9
THEY SING OF LOVE THAT'S GROWN DESIROUS,	45	FROM HEINE: 5	9
OF CHEEKS GROWN SUNKEN AND GLAD HAIR GONE GRAY;	50	THE FLAME	19
THE TREE HAS GROWN IN MY BREAST--	62	A GIRL	3
I COME TO YOU AS A GROWN CHILD	89	A PACT	3
GROWN DELICATE WITH SATIETIES,	112	HIMERRO	2
BY THE GATE NOW, THE MOSS IS GROWN, THE DIFFERENT MOSSES,	131	RIVER-MER WIFE	20
THESE AND A TASTE IN BOOKS THAT'S GROWN PERENNIAL	239	MOYEN SENSUEL	25
GROWS			
LAUGHS AT, AND GROWS STALE;	14	FAMAM CANO	14
IS WOVEN AND GROWS SOLID BENEATH US;	170	PHANOPOEIA	23
GROWTH			
FOR IGNORANCE, ITS GROWTH AND ITS PROTECTION	241	MOYEN SENSUEL	70
GRUB			
WE GRUB THE SOFT FERN-SHOOTS,	127	BOWMEN OF SHU	5
WE GRUB THE OLD FERN-STALKS.	127	BOWMEN OF SHU	9
IF I HAD MORE GRUB TO EAT.	269	SAFE AND SOUND	24
GRUDGES			
AND STIR OLD GRUDGES?	152	NEAR PERIGORD	37
GRUMBLE			
AND NOW YOU GRUMBLE BECAUSE YOUR DRESS DOES NOT FIT	102	LADIES	7
GRUNTS			
DE GOURMONT SAYS THAT FIFTY GRUNTS ARE ALL THAT WILL BE PRIZED.	244	MOYEN SENSUEL	165
GT.			
BROUGHT FROM GT. BRITAIN AND DUMPED DOWN A'TOP OF US,	240	MOYEN SENSUEL	64
GUARD			
SOLE GUARD OF GRIEF	41	HER MONUMENT	7
SOLE GUARD OF MEMORY	41	HER MONUMENT	8
GUARD THIS ALEMBIC.	76	THE ALCHEMIST	60
THEY GUARD THEE NOT WITH EUNUCHS;	91	DANCE FIGURE	14
LAMENT OF THE FRONTIER GUARD	133	FRONTIER GUARD	T
GUARDA			
GUARDA! AHI, GUARDA! CH' E BE'A!	96	AESTHETICS	5
GUARDA! AHI, GUARDA! CH' E BE'A!	96	AESTHETICS	5
GUARDS			
THE IMPERIAL GUARDS COME FORTH FROM THE GOLDEN HOUSE WITH THEIR ARMOUR A-GLEAMING.	129	THE RIVER SONG	34
AND THE GUARDS COULDN'T STOP THEM,	182	MOEURS CON: 7	19
AND THE GUARDS COULDN'T STOP THEM.	182	MOEURS CON: 7	22
GUARDSMEN			
AND WE GUARDSMEN FED TO THE TIGERS.	133	FRONTIER GUARD	24
GUERDON			
--RARE VISITOR--CAME NOT,--THE SAINTS I GUERDON	30	PIERE VIDAL	23
GUEREDON			
AND LAP O' THE SNOWS FOOD'S GUEREDON	10	FOR THIS YULE	5
GUERRE			
M. POM-POM ALLAIT EN GUERRE	273	M. POM-POM	1
GUESS			
THEY HAVE ASKED THE SENATE TO GUESS	268	ANOTHER BIT	6
GUESSES			
MALEMORT, GUESSES BENEATH, SENDS WORD TO COEUR-DE-LION:	155	NEAR PERIGORD	123
GUFFAW			
GUFFAW!	145	SALUTATION 3RD	2
GUIDES			
EYES ARE THE GUIDES OF LOVE,	220	SEXTUS PROP: 7	13
GUIDO			
GUIDO INVITES YOU THUS	25	GUIDO INVITES	T
AND THE SHEPHERDESS MEETING WITH GUIDO.	112	SHOP GIRL	4
"RIQUIER! GUIDO."	122	PROVINC DESERT	63
GUILLAUME			
MATURIN, GUILLAUME, JACQUES D'ALLMAIN,	12	OF THE GIBBET	29
GUINEA-PIG			
AND THEN THAT WOMAN LIKE A GUINEA-PIG	242	MOYEN SENSUEL	120
GUISCARDA			
SELVAGGIA, GUISCARDA, MANDETTA,	76	THE ALCHEMIST	54

GUISE -- HABITUAL

		PAGE	TITLE	LINE
GUISE				
	PINNING THE GUISE THAT HAD BEEN FAIN	11	OF THE GIBBET	9
GULLS				
	WOULD FOLLOW THE WHITE GULLS OR RIDE THEM.	128	THE RIVER SONG	8
GUN				
	WOULD COUNT ON THE PRICE OF A GUN.	268	ANOTHER BIT	12
GUNS				
	OF THE MAKING OF GUNS.	268	ANOTHER BIT	4
GUN-SHARKS				
	WHETHER MR. DUPONT AND THE GUN-SHARKS	268	ANOTHER BIT	7
GUNWALES				
	THIS BOAT IS OF SHATO-WOOD, AND ITS GUNWALES ARE CUT MAGNOLIA,	128	THE RIVER SONG	1
GURGLES				
	THE SHUDDER OF VAE SOLI GURGLES BENEATH MY RIBS.	247	PIERROTS	3
GURGLING				
	THE GURGLING ITALIAN LADY ON THE OTHER SIDE OF THE RESTAURANT	111	BLACK SLIPPERS	7
GUSHED				
	AND THE BLOOD GUSHED HOT AND FREE.	34	GOODLY FERE	38
GUST				
	GONE AS A GUST OF BREATH	19	FOR E. MCC	10
GUTS				
	OVER ROADS TWISTED LIKE SHEEP'S GUTS.	106	EXILE'S LETTER	41
	MY GREAT PRESS CLEAVES THE GUTS OF MEN,	266	ALF'S ELEVENTH	1
GUTTER				
	CRAWL IN THE VERY BLACK GUTTER BENEATH THE GRAPE STAND?	114	SIMULACRA	4
GUZZLE				
	I GUZZLE WITH OUTSTRETCHED EARS.	214	SEXTUS PROP: 4	12
GUZZLING				
	A SORT OF CURSE AGAINST ITS GUZZLING	14	FAMAM CANO	25
GWYNN'S				
	NELL GWYNN'S STILL HERE, DESPITE THE REFORMATION,	163	CABARET DANCER	72
GYNOCRACY				
	THE VERY FAIREST FLOWER OF THEIR GYNOCRACY.	239	MOYEN SENSUEL	40
GYPSY				
	THE GYPSY	119	THE GYPSY	T
H.				
	BUT THE SON-IN-LAW OF MR. H. STYRAX	178	MOEURS CON: 1	16
	(NEAR Q. H. FLACCUS' BOOK-STALL).	210	SEXTUS PROP: 2	9
HA				
	HA! THIS SCENT IS HOT!	32	PIERE VIDAL	67
	HA! SIR, I HAVE SEEN YOU SNIFFING AND SNOOZLING	109	THE FAUN	1
HA'				
	BUT GOD! WHAT A SIGHT YOU HA' GOT O' OUR IN'ARDS.	13	MESMERISM	10
	I HA' TAKEN TO RAMBLING THE SOUTH HERE.	22	MARVOIL	6
	HA' SEEN THEM 'MID THE CLOUDS ON THE HEATHER.	25	THE WHITE STAG	1
	HA' WE LOST THE GOODLIEST FERE O' ALL	33	GOODLY FERE	1
	I HA' SEEN HIM DRIVE A HUNDRED MEN	33	GOODLY FERE	17
	IF THEY THINK THEY HA' SNARED OUR GOODLY FERE	33	GOODLY FERE	25
	"YE HA' SEEN ME HEAL THE LAME AND BLIND,	34	GOODLY FERE	29
	I HA' SEEN HIM COW A THOUSAND MEN.	34	GOODLY FERE	35
	I HA' SEEN HIM COW A THOUSAND MEN	34	GOODLY FERE	41
	IF THEY THINK THEY HA' SLAIN OUR GOODLY FERE	34	GOODLY FERE	51
	I HA' SEEN HIM EAT O' THE HONEY-COMB	34	GOODLY FERE	53
HABENT				
	VERMES HABENT EIUS VULTUM	101	AMITIES	19
HABIT				
	AS HIS PARDONS THE HABIT,	15	FAMAM CANO	46
	EMOTION IS BORN OUT OF HABIT.	139	SOUTH-FOLK	3
	IT HAS BEEN YOUR HABIT FOR LONG	145	SALUTATION 3RD	20
HABITS				
	WHEN I CAREFULLY CONSIDER THE CURIOUS HABITS OF DOGS	102	MEDITATIO	1
	WHEN I CONSIDER THE CURIOUS HABITS OF MAN	102	MEDITATIO	4
	HABITS OF MIND AND FEELING,	195	HUGH SELWIN:11	2
	"DO YOU THINK I HAVE ADOPTED YOUR HABITS?"	225	SEXTUS PROP:10	25
	NOT THAT HE'D CHANGED HIS TASTES, NOR YET HIS HABITS,	246	MOYEN SENSUEL	231
HABITUAL				
	"TILL I HAVE VIEWED STRAW HATS AND THEIR HABITUAL CLOTHING	244	MOYEN SENSUEL	183

PAGE 177

HAD -- HALF-COVERED

	PAGE	TITLE	LINE
HAD (79)			
HADST			
HADST THOU BUT SONG	197	ENVOI (1919)	3
HAI			
ERI MEN HAI TE KUDONIAI--IBYCUS.	87	THE SPRING	EPI
HAIE			
HAIE! HAIE!	74	THE RETURN	15
HAIE! HAIE!	74	THE RETURN	15
HAIL			
FROST FROZE THE LAND, HAIL FELL ON EARTH THEN, ...	64	THE SEAFARER	33
ALL HAIL! YOUNG LADY WITH A NOSE	113	FORMIANUS LADY	1
WITH FROST AND HAIL AT NIGHT	173	LANGUE D'OC: 2	14
HAIL-SCUR			
HUNG WITH HARD ICE-FLAKES, WHERE HAIL-SCUR FLEW,	64	THE SEAFARER	17
HAIR			
HER HAIR WAS SPREAD ABOUT, A SHEAF OF WINGS,	49	OF SPLENDOUR	7
OF CHEEKS GROWN SUNKEN AND GLAD HAIR GONE GRAY; ...	50	THE FLAME	19
AND HER HAIR ALSO IS TURNING.	102	LADIES	4
FOR A FLIP WORD, AND TO TIDY THEIR HAIR A BIT.	117	THE LAKE ISLE	11
WHILE MY HAIR WAS STILL CUT STRAIGHT ACROSS MY FOREHEAD	130	RIVER-MER WIFE	1
WITH HER HAIR UNBOUND, AND HE HIS OWN SKIFFSMAN!	132	AT TEN-SHIN	33
AND SHE PILES HER HAIR UP ON THE LEFT SIDE OF HER HEAD-PIECE.	140	MULBERRY ROAD	11
THE VOICE AT MONTFORT, LADY AGNES' HAIR,	151	NEAR PERIGORD	7
ITS OWN HEAD SWINGING, GRIPPED BY THE DEAD HAIR,	156	NEAR PERIGORD	165
OBSERVED THE ELEGANCE OF CIRCE'S HAIR	187	E. P. ODE	15
THUS? SHE WEPT INTO UNCOMBED HAIR,	214	SEXTUS PROP: 4	13
HOW EASY THE MOVING FINGERS; IF HAIR IS MUSSED ON HER FOREHEAD,	217	SEXTUS PROP: 5	29
RAN CRYING WITH OUT-SPREAD HAIR,	219	SEXTUS PROP: 6	34
HAIR-CLOTH			
WHICH BROUGHT THE HAIR-CLOTH CHAIR TO SUCH PERFECTION,	63	PHASELLUS ILLE	6
HALE			
OH WE DRUNK HIS "HALE" IN THE GOOD RED WINE	33	GOODLY FERE	13
HALF			
OR WHEN THE MINSTREL, TALE HALF TOLD,	9	NA AUDIART	27
THEN SMOULDER, WITH THE LIDS HALF CLOSED	21	IN DURANCE	33
THAN HALF HIS CANZONI SAY OF HIM.	22	MARVOIL	26
STRANGE WOODS HALF SODDEN, AND NEW BRIGHTER STUFF:	61	PORTRAIT FEMME	26
HALF THE GRAVEN SHOULDER, THE THROAT AFLASH WITH	68	APPARUIT	17
TO SHEATHE ME HALF IN HALF THE THINGS THAT SHEATHE HER.	71	A VIRGINAL	8
TO SHEATHE ME HALF IN HALF THE THINGS THAT SHEATHE HER.	71	A VIRGINAL	8
AND HALF TURN BACK;	74	THE RETURN	9
I HAVE GONE HALF CRACKED,	94	INSTRUCTIONS	11
LIKE A SWALLOW HALF BLOWN TO THE WALL,	112	SHOP GIRL	2
AND EVERY ONE HALF JEALOUS OF MAENT?	153	NEAR PERIGORD	76
TO FIND HER HALF ALONE, MONTFORT AWAY,	154	NEAR PERIGORD	111
IN A HALF SAVAGE COUNTRY, OUT OF DATE;	187	E. P. ODE	6
HE IS THE PROTOTYPE OF HALF THE NATION.	246	MOYEN SENSUEL	242
HALF A LOAF, HALF A LOAF,	257	BREAD BRIGADE	1
HALF A LOAF, HALF A LOAF,	257	BREAD BRIGADE	1
HALF A LOAF? UM-HUM?	257	BREAD BRIGADE	2
THEN CUT THEIR SAVING TO THE HALF OR LOWER;	260	ALF'S FIFTH	3
HALF-AWAKENED			
WITH FEAR, AS HALF-AWAKENED;	74	THE RETURN	6
HALF-BALD			
ALFONSO THE HALF-BALD, TOOK TO HANGING	22	MARVOIL	9
ALL FOR ONE HALF-BALD, KNOCK-KNEE'D KING OF THE ARAGONESE,	22	MARVOIL	21
HALF-BLUE			
SOUTH OF THE POND THE WILLOW-TIPS ARE HALF-BLUE AND BLUER,	129	THE RIVER SONG	25
HALF-CASTES			
NOT LIKE THE HALF-CASTES,	119	THE GYPSY	5
HALF-COVERED			
BUT ONE HUGE BACK HALF-COVERED UP WITH PINE,	152	NEAR PERIGORD	33

PAGE 178

	PAGE	TITLE	LINE
HALF-HOSE			
THE SALE OF HALF-HOSE HAS	196	HUGH SELWIN:12	26
HALF-LIGHT			
OUT INTO THE CREPUSCULAR HALF-LIGHT, NOW AND THEN;	244	MOYEN SENSUEL	186
HALF-RUIN'D			
STILL DARTS OUT FAUN-LIKE FROM THE HALF-RUIN'D FACE,	192	YEUX GLAUQUES	18
HALF-SHEATHED			
HALF-SHEATHED, THEN NAKED FROM ITS SAFFRON SHEATH	31	PIERE VIDAL	41
HALF-WATT			
BENEATH HALF-WATT RAYS,	204	MEDALLION	15
HALF-WITS			
OVER THE DYING HALF-WITS BLOW,	265	ALF'S TENTH	5
HALL			
THE HALL OF CLEAR COLOURS.	95	OF THE DEGREES	9
TAIRIRAN HELD HALL IN MONTAIGNAC,	151	NEAR PERIGORD	16
IN THE VAULTED HALL,	154	NEAR PERIGORD	106
YOU ENTER AND PASS HALL AFTER HALL,	180	MOEURS CON: 5	18
YOU ENTER AND PASS HALL AFTER HALL,	180	MOEURS CON: 5	18
SPUN IN KING MINOS' HALL	204	MEDALLION	11
IN WHAT HALL HAVE YOU HEARD IT;	207	SEXTUS PROP: 1	7
HALLS			
IN THOSE DIM HALLS WHERE NO MAN TROUBLETH	24	THUS NINEVEH	10
MY CRYSTAL HALLS RING CLEAR	47	FROM HEINE: 7	22
"WHERE THE GREAT HALLS WERE CLOSER TOGETHER."	122	PROVINC DESERT	58
TO HIGH HALLS AND CURIOUS FOOD,	132	AT TEN-SHIN	30
IN THEIR DIM HALLS WAS HEARD	262	ALF'S SIXTH	29
HAM			
AN AGUE HATH MY HAM.	116	ANCIENT MUSIC	7
HAMADRYADS			
THEY GET PRAISE FROM TOLERANT HAMADRYADS."	229	SEXTUS PROP:12	49
HAN			
THEN THE WATERS OF HAN WOULD FLOW NORTHWARD.)	129	THE RIVER SONG	18
HAND			
MY PEN IS IN MY HAND	18	DE AEGYPTO	10
WHO MADE THE FREEST HAND SEEM COVETOUS.	37	THE YOUNG KING	14
NOR STIR HAND NOR THINK IN MID HEART,	66	THE SEAFARER	98
AS WINTER'S WOUND WITH HER SLEIGHT HAND SHE STAUNCHES,	71	A VIRGINAL	12
YOU WHO CAN KNOW AT FIRST HAND,	93	THE REST	15
SLENDER, SHE PUTS FORTH A SLENDER HAND;	128	BEAU TOILET	5
HE CLAPS HIS HAND ON THE BACK OF THE GREAT WATER SENNIN.	140	SENNIN POEM	14
SPREAD LIKE THE FINGER-TIPS OF ONE FRAIL HAND;	152	NEAR PERIGORD	30
SCRIBBLING, SWEARING BETWEEN HIS TEETH; BY HIS LEFT HAND	154	NEAR PERIGORD	98
THE SILVER BALL FORMS IN MY HAND,	169	PHANOPOEIA	6
'TILL I HAVE MY HAND 'NEATH HER CLOAK.	170	LANGUE D'OC: 2	22
CONDUCT, ON THE OTHER HAND, THE SOUL	196	HUGH SELWIN:12	21
OF RADWAY. O CLAP HAND YE MORALISTS!	246	MOYEN SENSUEL	227
HAND-GRIP			
OR SLACKED HIS HAND-GRIP WHEN YOU FIRST GRIPPED FAME?	59	EXIT' CUIUSDAM	3
HANDKERCHIEFS			
DAMP WOOLLY HANDKERCHIEFS WERE STUFFED INTO HER UNDRYABLE EYES,	214	SEXTUS PROP: 4	25
HANDMAID			
LIKENESS OF THINE HANDMAID	26	NIGHT LITANY	24
OF THE SHADOW OF THY HANDMAID	27	NIGHT LITANY	30
HANDMAIDS			
AND SENT ME ONLY YOUR HANDMAIDS.	96	TO KALON	2
HANDS			
AT THE MEETING OF HANDS.	3	THRENOS	10
UPON THY HANDS, AND THY OLD SOUL	9	NA AUDIART	41
TAKE YOUR HANDS OFF ME!	32	PIERE VIDAL	66
AND THERE WERE FLOWERS IN YOUR HANDS,	36	FRANCESCA	2
FELT HANDS TURN ICE A-SUDDEN, TOUCHING YE,	41	HER MONUMENT	17
A HOUSE NOT MADE WITH HANDS,	49	OF SPLENDOUR	2
SEARCH NOT MY LIPS, O LOVE, LET GO MY HANDS,	51	THE FLAME	37
THE TREE HAS ENTERED MY HANDS,	62	A GIRL	1
GONE AS WIND! THE CLOTH OF THE MAGICAL HANDS!	68	APPARUIT	22
AS A RILLET AMONG THE SEDGE ARE THY HANDS UPON ME;	91	DANCE FIGURE	19
HER TWO HANDS AND HER THROAT,	106	DOMPNA POIS	33

HANDS -- HARD

	PAGE	TITLE	LINE
HANDS (CONTINUED)			
WHEN HE SHAKES HANDS WITH YOUNG LADIES.	115	SOCIAL ORDER	4
WHO BOW OVER THEIR CLASPED HANDS AT A DISTANCE. ...	137	TAKING LEAVE	7
THERE IS A THROAT; AH, THERE ARE TWO WHITE HANDS;	153	NEAR PERIGORD	71
BELIEVING WE SHOULD MEET WITH LIPS AND HANDS, ...	157	NEAR PERIGORD	179
AND HATE YOUR MIND, NOT YOU, YOUR SOUL, YOUR HANDS.'	157	NEAR PERIGORD	184
SHE WHO HAD NOR EARS NOR TONGUE SAVE IN HER HANDS,	157	NEAR PERIGORD	187
PEPITA HAS SUCH TO-MORROWS: WITH THE HANDS PUFFED OUT, ...	161	CABARET DANCER	10
SPREAD ON BOTH HANDS AND ON THE UP-PUSHED-BOSOM--	161	CABARET DANCER	15
STRETCHES TOWARD ME HER LEAFY HANDS,"--	196	HUGH SELWIN:12	2
BEARING HER OFFERINGS IN THEIR UNHARDENED HANDS,	211	SEXTUS PROP: 2	34
ROSES TWINED IN HER HANDS.	211	SEXTUS PROP: 2	37
DABBLING HER HANDS IN THE FOUNT, THUS SHE	211	SEXTUS PROP: 2	53
WHERE BOLD HANDS MAY DO VIOLENCE TO MY PERSON?	212	SEXTUS PROP: 3	
FOR HER HANDS HAVE NO KINDNESS ME-WARD, ...	212	SEXTUS PROP: 3	1
NO GAWDS ON HER SNOWY HANDS, NO ORFEVRERIE, ...	214	SEXTUS PROP: 4	1
"PHOEBUS OUR WITNESS, YOUR HANDS ARE UNSPOTTED."	226	SEXTUS PROP:11	2
HANDSOME			
WHY DOES THE REALLY HANDSOME YOUNG WOMAN APPROACH ME IN SACKVILLE STREET	114	SIMULACRA	
HANG			
VINE-STRINGS A HUNDRED FEET LONG HANG DOWN FROM CARVED RAILINGS, ...	129	THE RIVER SONG	2
FIVE CLOUDS HANG ALOFT, BRIGHT ON THE PURPLE SKY,	129	THE RIVER SONG	3
PEACH BOUGHS AND APRICOT BOUGHS HANG OVER A THOUSAND GATES, ...	131	AT TEN-SHIN	
THOUGH THEY HANG IN THE SAME WAY OVER THE BRIDGERAIL.	131	AT TEN-SHIN	
GREEN VINES HANG THROUGH THE HIGH FOREST, ...	139	SENNIN POEM	
HANG IN YELLOW-WHITE AND DARK CLUSTERS READY FOR PRESSING.	167	OF AROUET	
(VIDE THE TARIFF), I WILL HANG SIMPLE FACTS	241	MOYEN SENSUEL	
HANG'D			
ONE MUST OF NEEDS BE A HANG'D EARLY RISER	13	MESMERISM	
HANGED			
UNTIL THE LAST SLUT'S HANGED AND THE LAST PIG DISEMBOWELED, ...	161	CABARET DANCER	
HANGING			
ALFONSO THE HALF-BALD, TOOK TO HANGING	22	MARVOIL	
AND, AS THE RAY OF SUN ON HANGING FLOWERS	40	ERAT HORA	
STRAY GLEAMS ON HANGING MAIL, AN ARMOURER'S TORCH-FLARE	155	NEAR PERIGORD	1
HANGS			
HANGS WITH THE SUN AND MOON.	128	THE RIVER SONG	
HANNIBAL			
AND OF HANNIBAL, ...	210	SEXTUS PROP: 2	
HAN-REI			
WHO AMONG THEM IS A MAN LIKE HAN-REI	132	AT TEN-SHIN	
HANSOM			
WHEN YOU COULD GO OUT IN A HIRED HANSOM	167	OF AROUET	
HAPPEN			
AND BECAUSE I HAPPEN TO SAY SO.	102	LADIES	
HAPPENED			
(THAT, MAYBE, NEVER HAPPENED!)	152	NEAR PERIGORD	
OF THINGS THAT HAPPENED VERY LONG AGO, ...	265	ALF'S NINTH	
HAPPIER			
AND I AM HAPPIER THAN YOU ARE, ...	85	SALUTATION	
AND THEY WERE HAPPIER THAN I AM;	85	SALUTATION	
HAPPY			
AND WE'LL BE HAPPY THERE.	47	FROM HEINE: 7	
HER OFFSPRING ARE FAT AND HAPPY.	103	THE PATTERNS	
HAPPY WHO ARE MENTIONED IN MY PAMPHLETS, ...	209	SEXTUS PROP: 1	
ME HAPPY, NIGHT, NIGHT FULL OF BRIGHTNESS;	220	SEXTUS PROP: 7	
OH COUCH MADE HAPPY BY MY LONG DELECTATIONS, ...	220	SEXTUS PROP: 7	
HAPPY SELLING POOR LOVES FOR CHEAP APPLES.	229	SEXTUS PROP:12	
HARD			
HUNG WITH HARD ICE-FLAKES, WHERE HAIL-SCUR FLEW,	64	THE SEAFARER	
SEEK EVER TO STAND IN THE HARD SOPHOCLEAN LIGHT ...	95	ITE	
CLASH, LEAPING OF BANDS, STRAIGHT STRIPS OF HARD COLOUR, ...	120	GAME OF CHESS	

PAGE 180

HARD -- HASH

	PAGE	TITLE	LINE
HARD (CONTINUED)			
AND WHAT WITH BROKEN WHEELS AND SO ON, I WON'T SAY IT WASN'T HARD GOING,	135	EXILE'S LETTER	40
HARD FIGHT GETS NO REWARD.	139	SOUTH-FOLK	10
LOYALTY IS HARD TO EXPLAIN.	139	SOUTH-FOLK	11
HARD OVER BRIVE--FOR EVERY LADY A CASTLE,	151	NEAR PERIGORD	13
BEFORE THE HARD OLD KING:	152	NEAR PERIGORD	43
AND THAT HARD PHALANX, THAT UNBROKEN LINE,	153	NEAR PERIGORD	64
HARDER			
HARDER TO UNTIE.	261	ALF'S SIXTH	9
HARDEST			
"THE HARDEST NUT I HAD TO CRACK	194	MR. NIXON	12
ARDLY			
NO, HARDLY, BUT SEEING HE HAD BEEN BORN	187	E. P. ODE	5
ARDSHIP			
HARDSHIP ENDURED OFT.	64	THE SEAFARER	3
HARDY			
TURNS HARDY PILOT . . . AND IF ONE WRONG NOTE	42	HER MONUMENT	45
ARLOTS			
AND THE HARLOTS OF BAUDELAIRE.	112	SHOP GIRL	5
DOWSON FOUND HARLOTS CHEAPER THAN HOTELS;	193	SIENA MI FE	13
ARM			
NO BARBARISM WOULD GO TO THE EXTENT OF DOING HIM HARM,	212	SEXTUS PROP: 3	19
THOUGH MALES OF SEVENTY, WHO FEAR TRUTHS NAKED HARM US,	243	MOYEN SENSUEL	147
ARMONIOUS			
AMIABLE AND HARMONIOUS PEOPLE ARE PUSHED INCONTINENT INTO DUELS,	227	SEXTUS PROP:12	5
ARNESS			
AND WITH SILVER HARNESS AND REINS OF GOLD,	134	EXILE'S LETTER	22
ARP			
SHE SITS AT A HARP,	180	MOEURS CON: 5	8
THERE IS A SATIN-LIKE BOW ON THE HARP.	180	MOEURS CON: 5	15
THERE IS A SATIN-LIKE BOW ON AN HARP.	180	MOEURS CON: 5	17
NEAR THEM I NOTICED AN HARP	180	MOEURS CON: 5	22
AND DAVID'S HARP LET OUT HEART-RENDING SQUEALS:	264	ALF'S NINTH	15
ARPING			
HE HATH NOT HEART FOR HARPING, NOR IN RING-HAVING	65	THE SEAFARER	45
ARPIST			
"FIND US A HARPIST!! DAVID IS THE MAN!!"	264	ALF'S NINTH	16
ARRY			
O HARRY HEINE, CURSES BE,	46	TRANSLATOR	1
THAT DOUND KING HARRY ABOUT,	48	FROM HEINE: 7	30
THESE WERE THE SWIFT TO HARRY;	74	THE RETURN	16
"HI! HARRY, HEAR ME, FOR I SING ARIGHT	172	LANGUE D'OC. 1	10
RY'S			
HIS? WHY THE GOOD KING HARRY'S,	47	FROM HEINE: 7	15
SH			
OR GATHER MAY OF HARSH NORTHWINDISH TIME?	59	SILET	8
JOURNEY'S JARGON, HOW I IN HARSH DAYS	64	THE SEAFARER	2
THERE I HEARD NAUGHT SAVE THE HARSH SEA	64	THE SEAFARER	18
AND YOU, O POLYPHEMUS? DID HARSH GALATEA ALMOST	208	SEXTUS PROP: 1	46
OR JOVE, HARSH AS HE IS, MAY TURN ASIDE YOUR ULTIMATE DAY.	222	SEXTUS PROP. 8	38
THE HARSH ACTS OF YOUR LEVITY!	226	SEXTUS PROP:11	1
BUT MY SOUL, THE SORT WHICH HARSH SOUNDS DISTURB,	247	PIERROTS	17
SHER			
HARSHER THAN GRANITE,	107	COMING OF WAR	8
SHNESS			
DO THOU, PLUTO, BRING HERE NO GREATER HARSHNESS.	38	LADY'S LIFE	2
DO THOU, PLUTO, BRING HERE NO GREATER HARSHNESS.	38	LADY'S LIFE	12
T			
WHEN THE WHITE HART BREAKS HIS COVER	25	THE WHITE STAG	4
ARD			
"I SEE THEM SITTING IN THE HARVARD CLUB,	244	MOYEN SENSUEL	180
REISE			
SONG FROM "DIE HARZREISE"	47	FROM HEINE: 7	SUB
(79)			
THOUGH YOU MAKE A HASH OF ANTIMACHUS,	228	SEXTUS PROP:12	21

	PAGE	TITLE	LINE
HASN'T (1)			
HAST			
LO, THOU HAST VOYAGED NOT! THE SHIP IS MINE."	25	GUIDO INVITES	11
YEA THE LINES HAST THOU LAID UNTO ME	26	NIGHT LITANY	3
HAST THOU SHOWN UNTO ME	26	NIGHT LITANY	6
THAT ANY FOLK E'ER HAD, HAST FROM US TAKEN;	37	THE YOUNG KING	19
WHAT HAST THOU, O MY SOUL, WITH PARADISE?	39	BLANDULA	1
ROME THAT ALONE HAST CONQUERED ROME THE TOWN, ...	40	ROME	10
HOW HAST THOU SET THE FIRE	41	HER MONUMENT	11
SO THOU HAST FORGOTTEN FULLY	44	FROM HEINE: 2	1
LOVE AND LAY THOU HAST FORGOTTEN FULLY, ...	44	FROM HEINE: 2	5
IF THOU HAST SEEN MY SHADE SANS CHARACTER, ...	51	THE FLAME	39
IF THOU HAST SEEN THAT MIRROR OF ALL MOMENTS, ...	51	THE FLAME	40
DARKLY HAST THOU DARED AND THE DREADED AETHER	68	APPARUIT	11
A BROWN ROBE, WITH THREADS OF GOLD WOVEN IN PATTERNS, HAST THOU GATHERED ABOUT THEE, ...	91	DANCE FIGURE	17
AS THOU HAST SUBJECTS KNOWN, ...	197	ENVOI (1919)	4
HAST THOU NO DESIRE.	250	DONNA MI PREGA	93
HASTE			
THERE WAS NO PARTICULAR HASTE, ...	48	FROM HEINE: 8	2
THERE'S NO PARTICULAR HASTE.	48	FROM HEINE: 8	4
HASTENED			
"HERE ONE MAN HASTENED HIS STEP.	122	PROVINC DESERT	40
HATE			
THOUGH THOU HATE ME, READ IT SET	8	NA AUDIART	2
SETS FORTH, AND THOUGH THOU HATE ME WELL, ...	9	NA AUDIART	3
IS YOUR HATE, THEN, OF SUCH MEASURE?	44	FROM HEINE: 1	
THAT WAS CAUSE OF HATE!	132	AT TEN-SHIN	3
AFRAID TO SAY THAT THEY HATE YOU;	146	SALUTATION 3RD	3
AND HATE YOUR MIND, NOT YOU, YOUR SOUL, YOUR HANDS.'	157	NEAR PERIGORD	18
"I HATE A DUMPY WOMAN"	238	MOYEN SENSUEL	EP
HATE TREMOLOS AND NATIONAL FRENETICS.	247	PIERROTS	1
E'EN THOUGH HE MEET NOT WITH HATE	249	DONNA MI PREGA	4
HATED			
HATED, SHUT IN, MISTRUSTED:	93	THE REST	1
AND A BROWN, PLACID, HATED WOMAN VISITING HER, ...	154	NEAR PERIGORD	11
HATES			
FEEL YOUR HATES WRIGGLING ABOUT MY FEET	145	SALUTATION 3RD	2
HATH			
SHE HATH CALLED ME FROM MINE OLD WAYS	4	LA FRAISNE	1
SHE HATH HUSHED MY RANCOUR OF COUNCIL, ...	4	LA FRAISNE	
SHE HATH DRAWN ME FROM MINE OLD WAYS, ...	4	LA FRAISNE	2
VERY GLAD, FOR MY BRIDE HATH TOWARD ME A GREAT LOVE	5	LA FRAISNE	3
HATH FOR BOSS THY LUSTRE GAY!	7	CINO	4
THAT HATH NO PERFECT LIMNING, WHEN THE WARM	9	NA AUDIART	
NOR WHAT GOD HATH THAT CAN ME CHEER	10	FOR THIS YULE	
'CAUSE HE HATH ....\...............	14	FAMAM CANO	
AND THE WANDERING OF MANY ROADS HATH MADE MY EYES	16	PRAISE YSOLT	
FOR SHE I SANG OF HATH GONE FROM ME."	17	PRAISE YSOLT	
WHO HATH THE MOUTH TO RECEIVE IT, ...	18	DE AEGYPTO	
ONE THAT HATH KNOWN YOU.	19	FOR E. MCC	
AND MANY A ONE HATH SUNG HIS SONGS	24	THUS NINEVEH	
OF THY BEAUTY HATH WALKED	26	NIGHT LITANY	
MY WORDS FOR STOUR, HATH NO BLOOD OF CRIMSON	29	ALTAFORTE	
NO MAN HATH HEARD THE GLORY OF MY DAYS:	32	PIERE VIDAL	
NO MAN HATH DARED AND WON HIS DARE AS I:	32	PIERE VIDAL	
O'ER MUCH HATH TA'EN SIR DEATH THAT DEADLY WARRIOR	37	THE YOUNG KING	
WHO HATH MY HEART IN JURISDICTION.	38	BALLATETTA	
FADES WHEN THE WIND HATH LIFTED THEM ASIDE, ...	40	ERAT HORA	
ONE WHO HATH SET THE WHOLE WORLD 'NEATH HER LAWS,	40	ROME	
HATH AS FAINT LUTE-STRINGS IN ITS DIM ACCORD	43	SATIEMUS	
HATH IT NEVER ONCE DISTRESSED YOU, ...	44	FROM HEINE: 1	
(THUS FAR HATH MODERNITY BROUGHT US)	52	AU SALON	
THIS THING, THAT HATH A CODE AND NOT A CORE, ...	63	AN OBJECT	
HATH SET ACQUAINTANCE WHERE MIGHT BE AFFECTIONS,	63	AN OBJECT	
HATH LACKED A SOMETHING SINCE THIS LADY PASSED; ...	63	QUIES	
NOR HATH IT EVER SINCE CHANGED THAT CONCOCTION. ...	63	PHASELLUS ILLE	
HATH LACKED A SOMETHING. 'TWAS BUT MARGINAL.	63	QUIES	
HE HATH NOT HEART FOR HARPING, NOR IN RING-HAVING	65	THE SEAFARER	
FOR MY SURROUNDING AIR HATH A NEW LIGHTNESS;	71	A VIRGINAL	
HATH OF THE TREES A LIKENESS OF THE SAVOUR:	71	A VIRGINAL	

PAGE 182

HATH -- HE

	PAGE	TITLE	LINE
HATH (CONTINUED)			
HATH OF PERFECT CHARMS SO MANY.	72	DIEU! QU'IL	11
SHE HATH TO WELCOME ONE,	106	DOMPNA POIS	53
AN AGUE HATH MY HAM.	116	ANCIENT MUSIC	7
THAT HATH THE DAWN IN KEEPING,	172	LANGUE D'OC: 1	8
TILL CHANGE HATH BROKEN DOWN	197	ENVOI (1919)	25
WHO HATH TAUGHT YOU SO SUBTLE A MEASURE,	207	SEXTUS PROP: 1	6
"WHEREFROM FATHER ENNIUS, SITTING BEFORE I CAME, HATH DRUNK."	210	SEXTUS PROP: 2	7
LOVE IS CREATED, HATH A SENSATE NAME,	248	DONNA MI PREGA	22
NOR CAN MAN SAY HE HATH HIS LIFE BY CHANCE	249	DONNA MI PREGA	46
OR THAT HE HATH NOT STABLISHED SEIGNIORY	249	DONNA MI PREGA	47
SO HATH MAN CRAFT FROM FEAR	250	DONNA MI PREGA	75
HATHA			
AND THE COPY OF "HATHA YOGA"	180	MOEURS CON: 5	24
HATREDS			
LET US DUMP OUR HATREDS INTO ONE BUNCH AND BE DONE WITH THEM,	146	CANTILATIONS	2
HATS			
"TILL I HAVE VIEWED STRAW HATS AND THEIR HABITUAL CLOTHING	244	MOYEN SENSUEL	183
HATTER			
MAD AS A HATTER BUT SURELY NO MYOPE,	13	MESMERISM	11
HAUGHTINESS			
HER GRAVE, SWEET HAUGHTINESS	52	AU SALON	EPI
HAUGHTY			
HAUGHTY THEIR PASSING,	132	AT TEN-SHIN	18
HAUGHTY THEIR STEPS AS THEY GO IN TO GREAT BANQUETS,	132	AT TEN-SHIN	19
HAULED			
I WITH MY BEAK HAULED ASHORE WOULD PROCEED IN A MORE STATELY MANNER,	216	SEXTUS PROP: 5	10
HAULTE			
TO MAKE HIM A MATE OF THE "HAULTE NOBLESSE"	11	OF THE GIBBET	10
AND BRING THEIR SOULS TO HIS "HAULTE CITEE."	12	OF THE GIBBET	43
HAUNTS			
TO BE NOT TOO WELL KNOWN IN HAUNTS OF VICE--	245	MOYEN SENSUEL	202
THE PROMINENT HAUNTS, WHERE ONE MIGHT RECOGNIZE HIM,	245	MOYEN SENSUEL	203
HAUTEFORT			
I HAVE LOOKED SOUTH FROM HAUTEFORT,	122	PROVINC DESERT	48
EN BERTRANS, A TOWER-ROOM AT HAUTEFORT,	154	NEAR PERIGORD	95
HAUTEUR			
REPLIES WITH A CERTAIN HAUTEUR,	111	BLACK SLIPPERS	8
HAVE (258)			
HAVEN			
THE HAVEN FROM SOPHISTICATIONS AND CONTENTIONS	195	HUGH SELWIN:10	9
HAVENS			
OF HAVENS MORE HIGH AND COURTS DESIRABLE	39	BLANDULA	14
HAVING			
HAVING BECOME THE SOULS OF SONG.	6	CINO	9
HAVING PRAISED THY GIRDLE'S SCOPE	8	NA AUDIART	14
HAVING YOURS..	105	DOMPNA POIS	27
AND HAVING DREAMED THAT HE WAS A BIRD, A BEE, AND A BUTTERFLY,	118	ANCIENT WISDOM	2
MUCH CONVERSATION IS AS GOOD AS HAVING A HOME.	214	SEXTUS PROP: 4	10
TO SAY MANY THINGS IS EQUAL TO HAVING A HOME.	215	SEXTUS PROP: 4	28
OUTSIDE YOUR SET BUT, HAVING KEPT FAITH IN YOUR EYES,	247	PIERROTS	23
HAVING NO HOPE AT ALL	248	DONNA MI PREGA	6
HAWK			
AIMLESSLY WATCHING A HAWK ABOVE THE VALLEYS,	154	NEAR PERIGORD	108
HAWTHORN			
THE BIRD SITS ON THE HAWTHORN TREE	43	MR. HOUSMAN	6
HAWTHORNE			
ON THE TOP OF THE HAWTHORNE,	173	LANGUE D'OC: 2	13
IN ORCHARD UNDER THE HAWTHORNE	177	LANGUE D'OC: 4	1
HAY			
MAKES HAY WITH THE THINGS IN HER HOUSE	115	SOCIAL ORDER	10
HAZE			
FOR MEMORY OF THE FIRST WARM NIGHT STILL CAST A HAZE O'ER	245	MOYEN SENSUEL	195
HE (187)			

HEAD -- HEAR

	PAGE	TITLE	LINE
HEAD			
THAT WAS RANK FOLLY TO MY HEAD BEFORE.	3	THE TREE	12
"LO, ONE THERE WAS WHO BENT HER FAIR BRIGHT HEAD,	43	SATIEMUS	5
THY HEAD WILL I COVER OVER	47	FROM HEINE: 7	5
NARROW NIGHTWATCH NIGH THE SHIP'S HEAD	64	THE SEAFARER	7
LOWERING MY HEAD, I LOOKED AT THE WALL.	130	RIVER-MER WIFE	9
MARCH HAS COME TO THE BRIDGE HEAD, ...	131	AT TEN-SHIN	1
WITH HEAD GEAR GLITTERING AGAINST THE CLOUD AND SUN,	131	AT TEN-SHIN	13
AND I, WRAPPED IN BROCADE, WENT TO SLEEP WITH MY HEAD ON HIS LAP, ...	135	EXILE'S LETTER	31
WHOSE WHITE HEAD IS LOST FOR THIS PROVINCE?	139	SOUTH-FOLK	14
I BOW MY HEAD AND STAND STILL.	142	UNMOVING CLOUD	9
THE HEADLESS TRUNK "THAT MADE ITS HEAD A LAMP," ...	151	NEAR PERIGORD	23
ITS OWN HEAD SWINGING, GRIPPED BY THE DEAD HAIR,	156	NEAR PERIGORD	165
I SEVERED MEN, MY HEAD AND HEART	156	NEAR PERIGORD	167
IF THOU COME NOT, THE COST BE ON THY HEAD.	172	LANGUE D'OC: 1	16
WHEN THAT FAUN'S HEAD OF HERS	192	YEUX GLAUQUES	6
TO THE STRAIT HEAD	198	MAUBERLEY: 1	3
THE SLEEK HEAD EMERGES	204	MEDALLION	5
I ASK A WREATH WHICH WILL NOT CRUSH MY HEAD.	207	SEXTUS PROP: 1	21
IO MOOED THE FIRST YEARS WITH AVERTED HEAD, ...	222	SEXTUS PROP: 8	19
HEAD FARMERS DO LIKEWISE, AND LYING WEARY AMID THEIR OATS	229	SEXTUS PROP:12	48
"AND RATE 'EM UP AT JUST SO MUCH PER HEAD, ...	244	MOYEN SENSUEL	181
HEAD-COLD			
YOU WHEEZE AS A HEAD-COLD LONG-TONSILLED CALLIOPE,	13	MESMERISM	9
HEADLAM			
HEADLAM FOR UPLIFT; IMAGE IMPARTIALLY IMBUED	193	SIENA MI FE	14
HEADLAND			
WILL WE NOT FIND SOME HEADLAND CONSECRATED	39	BLANDULA	7
HEADLESS			
THE HEADLESS TRUNK "THAT MADE ITS HEAD A LAMP," ...	151	NEAR PERIGORD	23
GOES ON THAT HEADLESS TRUNK, THAT BEARS FOR LIGHT	156	NEAR PERIGORD	164
HEAD-PIECE			
AND SHE PILES HER HAIR UP ON THE LEFT SIDE OF HER HEAD-PIECE.	140	MULBERRY ROAD	11
HEADS			
AH! BOW YOUR HEADS, YE MAIDENS ALL, ...	72	PAN IS DEAD	2
BEND OVER WITH HEAVY HEADS.	112	IONE, DEAD	4
OF CURIOUS HEADS IN MEDALLION--	200	MAUBERLEY: 2	25
HEADSTRONG			
FOR THE YOUNG PRINCE IS FOOLISH AND HEADSTRONG; ...	237	ABU SALAMMAMM	28
HEAD-TRAPPINGS			
UPON HORSES WITH HEAD-TRAPPINGS OF YELLOW METAL,	132	AT TEN-SHIN	16
HEAL			
"YE HA' SEEN ME HEAL THE LAME AND BLIND, ...	34	GOODLY FERE	29
HEALM			
THE BROKEN SUNLIGHT FOR A HEALM SHE BEARETH	38	BALLATETTA	4
HEALTH			
HID HEALTH STATISTICS, DODGED THE LABOUR ACTS.	260	ALF'S FIFTH	8
HEAPED			
THESE COMFORTS HEAPED UPON ME, SMOTHER ME!	70	THE PLUNGE	2
HEAPS			
SCURRY INTO HEAPS AND LIE STILL, ...	108	LIU CH'E	4
HIGH HEAPS, COVERED WITH TREES AND GRASS;	133	FRONTIER GUARD	9
HEAR			
HELL GRANT SOON WE HEAR AGAIN THE SWORDS CLASH! ...	28	ALTAFORTE	13
HELL GRANT SOON WE HEAR AGAIN THE SWORDS CLASH! ...	29	ALTAFORTE	38
THAN HEAR THE WHOLE AEGRUM VULGUS	52	AU SALON	21
AMID THE LITTLE PINE TREES, HEAR ME!	53	AU JARDIN	
AND NOW YOU HEAR WHAT IS SAID TO US:	82	THE CONDOLENCE	1
GLAD TO HEAR ARNAUT, ...	121	PROVINC DESERT	20
HE RETURNS BY WAY OF SEI ROCK, TO HEAR THE NEW NIGHTINGALES, ...	130	THE RIVER SONG	3
"HI! HARRY, HEAR ME, FOR I SING ARIGHT	172	LANGUE D'OC: 1	16
SLEEP NOT THOU NOW, I HEAR THE BIRD IN FLIGHT	172	LANGUE D'OC: 1	1
TELL ME THE TRUTHS WHICH YOU HEAR OF OUR CONSTANT YOUNG LADY, ...	214	SEXTUS PROP: 4	
AND I CAN HEAR AN OLD MAN SAYING: "OH, THE RUB! ...	244	MOYEN SENSUEL	17
E'EN ITS DENIERS CAN NOW HEAR THE TRUTH, ...	248	DONNA MI PREGA	
LISTEN, MY CHILDREN, AND YOU SHALL HEAR	264	ALF'S NINTH	

HEAR -- HEART

	PAGE	TITLE	LINE
HEAR (CONTINUED)			
LISTEN, MY CHILDREN, AND YOU SHALL HEAR	265	ALF'S NINTH	26
AND SCARCELY HEED ONE WORD OF WHAT YOU HEAR.	265	ALF'S NINTH	28
HEARD			
NO MAN HATH HEARD THE GLORY OF MY DAYS:	32	PIERE VIDAL	54
THERE I HEARD NAUGHT SAVE THE HARSH SEA	64	THE SEAFARER	18
HAVE HEARD THE ECHO OF MY HEELS,	81	TENZONE	12
AND HEARD UNGAINLY LAUGHTER.	85	SALUTATION	6
ONCE MORE IS THE CHANT HEARD.	90	SURGIT FAMA	17
I HEARD THE YOUNG DANTE, WHOSE LAST NAME I DO NOT KNOW--	96	AESTHETICS	7
HAVE WE EVER HEARD THE LIKE?	104	ANCORA	7
HEARD THAT HE HAD DECIDED,	118	CONTEMPORARIES	2
HEARD, UNDER THE DARK, WHIRLING LAUGHTER.	121	PROVINC DESERT	32
I HAVE CLIMBED RICKETY STAIRS, HEARD TALK OF CROY,	122	PROVINC DESERT	38
AND HEARD THE FIVE-SCORE NIGHTINGALES AIMLESSLY SINGING.	129	THE RIVER SONG	22
AND I THINK I HAVE HEARD THEM SAYING,	142	UNMOVING CLOUD	23
IN WHAT HALL HAVE YOU HEARD IT;	207	SEXTUS PROP: 1	7
AND HEARD A CLERGY THAT TRIES ON MORE WHEEZES	241	MOYEN SENSUEL	99
THAN E'ER WERE HEARD OF BY OUR LORD CH.... J....	241	MOYEN SENSUEL	100
IN THEIR DIM HALLS WAS HEARD	262	ALF'S SIXTH	29
HEARS			
NO ONE HEARS SAVE ARRIMON LUC D'ESPARO--	154	NEAR PERIGORD	119
NO ONE HEARS AUGHT SAVE THE GRACIOUS SOUND OF COMPLIMENTS.	154	NEAR PERIGORD	120
HEART			
THEN MAKYTH MY HEART HIS YULE-TIDE CHEER	10	FOR THIS YULE	6
WHERE ARE THE JOYS MY HEART HAD WON?	10	FOR THIS YULE	17
THAT BADE MY HEART HIS VALOUR DON?	10	FOR THIS YULE	21
HEART THAT WAS BIG AS THE BOWELS OF VESUVIUS,	13	MESMERISM	13
TO TEACH MY HEART TO BOW;	16	PRAISE YSOLT	2
WHILE IN HIS HEART ART THOU?	17	PRAISE YSOLT	58
SO IS MY HEART HOLLOW WHEN SHE FILLETH NOT MINE EYES,	23	MARVOIL	38
EVEN AS I KEEP HER IMAGE IN MY HEART HERE.	23	MARVOIL	48
LO, I HAVE KNOWN THY HEART AND ITS DESIRE;	25	GUIDO INVITES	8
EVEN SO IS MINE HEART	27	NIGHT LITANY	47
THEN HOWL I MY HEART NIGH MAD WITH REJOICING.	28	ALTAFORTE	6
AND IT FILLS ALL MY HEART WITH REJOICING	29	ALTAFORTE	21
WHO HATH MY HEART IN JURISDICTION.	38	BALLATETTA	5
THAT I SO LONG HELD THY HEART WHOLLY,	44	FROM HEINE: 2	2
THY LITTLE HEART, SO SWEET AND FALSE AND SMALL	44	FROM HEINE: 2	3
AND MY HEART WORKED AT THEM UNDULY.	44	FROM HEINE: 2	6
THEE, AND HELD THY HEART COMPLETELY.	45	FROM HEINE: 3	4
AND MY HEART IS COLD AND SERE;	45	FROM HEINE: 3	6
MY LIPS AND MY HEART ARE THINE THERE	47	FROM HEINE: 7	13
WITH JOY BREATHLESS AT HEART.	47	FROM HEINE: 7	20
IF MY HEART STAY BELOW THERE,	47	FROM HEINE: 7	21
HEW MY HEART ROUND AND HUNGER BEGOT	64	THE SEAFARER	11
HE HATH NOT HEART FOR HARPING, NOR IN RING-HAVING	65	THE SEAFARER	45
THE HEART TURNS TO TRAVEL SO THAT HE THEN THINKS	65	THE SEAFARER	52
SO THAT BUT NOW MY HEART BURST FROM MY BREASTLOCK,	65	THE SEAFARER	59
WHETS FOR THE WHALE-PATH THE HEART IRRESISTIBLY,	65	THE SEAFARER	64
NOR STIR HAND NOR THINK IN MID HEART,	66	THE SEAFARER	98
O BEWILDERED HEART,	87	THE SPRING	10
TELLING THE HEART OF THEIR TRUTH	96	DUM CAPITOLIUM	3
SAYING WITHIN HIS HEART, "I AM NO USE TO MYSELF,	100	ARIDES	6
NEITHER ONE SO FAIR, NOR OF SUCH HEART,	105	DOMPNA POIS	12
THOUGH SHE WITH A FULL HEART	106	DOMPNA POIS	41
AND SHE THE REJOICER OF THE HEART IS BENEATH THEM:	108	LIU CH'E	5
AT MORNING THERE ARE FLOWERS TO CUT THE HEART,	131	AT TEN-SHIN	3
THERE IS NO END OF THINGS IN THE HEART.	136	EXILE'S LETTER	76
HE THROWS HIS HEART UP THROUGH THE SKY,	139	SENNIN POEM	8
AND ALL MY HEART IS BOUND ABOUT WITH LOVE.	153	NEAR PERIGORD	73
THINKING OF AELIS, WHOM HE LOVED HEART AND SOUL ...	154	NEAR PERIGORD	110
I SEVERED MEN MY HEAD AND HEART	156	NEAR PERIGORD	167
BUT FROM WHERE MY HEART IS SET	170	LANGUE D'OC: 2	6
MY HEART ALL WAKES AND GRIEVES;	173	LANGUE D'OC: 2	8
OUT OF MY LOVE WILL HER HEART NOT STIR.	177	LANGUE D'OC: 4	28
AND THIS MUCH GIVES ME HEART TO PLAY THE GAME.	235	TO WHISTLER	4
THAT MAN WHO IS BASE IN HEART	248	DONNA MI PREGA	7

PAGE 185

HEART -- HECATOMB

	PAGE	TITLE	LINE
HEART (CONTINUED)			
HIS MODUS TAKES FROM SOUL, FROM HEART HIS WILL; ...	249	DONNA MI PREGA	23
HEARTH			
UNTO THE HEARTH OF THEIR HEART'S HOME	3	THE TREE	8
MY HEART'S OWN HEARTH, ...	20	IN DURANCE	8
HEARTIES			
WOT OH! MY BUXOM HEARTIES, ...	269	SAFE AND SOUND	9
HEART-RENDING			
AND DAVID'S HARP LET OUT HEART-RENDING SQUEALS: ...	264	ALF'S NINTH	15
HEARTS			
MAKE CLEAN OUR HEARTS WITHIN US, ...	27	NIGHT LITANY	37
AND WE ALL SPOKE OUT OUR HEARTS AND MINDS, AND WITHOUT REGRET.	134	EXILE'S LETTER	11
YOU'D HAVE MEN'S HEARTS UP FROM THE DUST	151	NEAR PERIGORD	1
HEART'S			
UNTO THE HEARTH OF THEIR HEART'S HOME	3	THE TREE	8
IN OUR HEART'S SWORD-RACK, THOUGH THY SWORD-ARM SLEEP.	19	FOR E. MCC	22
MY HEART'S OWN HEARTH, ...	20	IN DURANCE	8
* THE HEART'S THOUGHT THAT I ON HIGH STREAMS	65	THE SEAFARER	35
THE BITTER HEART'S BLOOD. BURGHER KNOWS NOT--	65	THE SEAFARER	56
HEART'S-ALL-BELOVED-MY-OWN			
HEART'S-ALL-BELOVED-MY-OWN;	48	FROM HEINE: 8	6
HEAT			
FROM THE HEAT OF THE BUD, ...	76	THE ALCHEMIST	32
THE DRY EARTH PANTS AGAINST THE CANICULAR HEAT, ...	221	SEXTUS PROP: 8	4
BUT THIS HEAT IS NOT THE ROOT OF THE MATTER:	221	SEXTUS PROP: 8	5
HEATHER			
I HA' SEEN THEM 'MID THE CLOUDS ON THE HEATHER. ...	25	THE WHITE STAG	1
HEATHER	109	HEATHER	T
HEAUMES			
OR WAR AND BROKEN HEAUMES AND POLITICS?	154	NEAR PERIGORD	93
HEAVE			
THOUGH YOU HEAVE INTO THE AIR UPON THE GILDED PEGASEAN BACK, ...	226	SEXTUS PROP:11	7
HEAVEN			
SHIELD O' STEEL-BLUE, TH' HEAVEN O'ER US	7	CINO	44
IN THE BLUE WATERS OF HEAVEN, ...	7	CINO	55
BY HEAVEN, HIS HORSES ARE TIRED.	127	BOWMEN OF SHU	17
THE LONG KIANG, REACHING HEAVEN.	137	ON RIVER KIANG	5
THE THREE MOUNTAINS FALL THROUGH THE FAR HEAVEN,	138	CITY OF CHOAN	8
FLYING SNOW BEWILDERS THE BARBARIAN HEAVEN.	139	SOUTH-FOLK	7
AND THE GREAT WHEELS IN HEAVEN	157	NEAR PERIGORD	177
THE MOON STILL DECLINED TO DESCEND OUT OF HEAVEN,	223	SEXTUS PROP: 9	3
HEAVENLY			
WHOM HEAVENLY JOY IMMERSES, ...	45	FROM HEINE: 4	2
AND, HEAVENLY, HOLY GODS! I CAN'T SAY MORE, ...	246	MOYEN SENSUEL	220
HEAVENS			
WE ARE NOT SHUT FROM ALL THE THOUSAND HEAVENS:	50	THE FLAME	22
AND MY SPIRIT SO HIGH IT WAS ALL OVER THE HEAVENS,	135	EXILE'S LETTER	32
THE EIGHT PLY OF THE HEAVENS	142	UNMOVING CLOUD	3
THE EIGHT PLY OF THE HEAVENS ARE DARKNESS, ...	142	UNMOVING CLOUD	11
REIGNS IN RESPECTABLE HEAVENS, ...	227	SEXTUS PROP:11	28
HEAVEN'S			
IS LIKE TO HEAVEN'S MOST 'LIVE IMAGINING.	41	HER MONUMENT	24
HEAVES			
THE TIME IS COME, THE AIR HEAVES IN TORRIDITY, ...	221	SEXTUS PROP: 8	3
HEAV'N			
AND THE LIGHTNINGS FROM BLACK HEAV'N FLASH CRIMSON,	28	ALTAFORTE	9
HEAVY			
ABIDES 'MID BURGHERS SOME HEAVY BUSINESS, ...	64	THE SEAFARER	29
BEND OVER WITH HEAVY HEADS.	112	IONE, DEAD	4
THE HEAVY MEMORIES OF HOREB, SINAI AND THE FORTY YEARS, ...	193	BRENNBAUM	3
EVEN MY FAULTS THAT HEAVY UPON ME LIE, ...	197	ENVOI (1919)	3
A HEAVY MASS ON FREE NECKS.	226	SEXTUS PROP:11	1
LIKE A WOMAN HEAVY WITH CHILD.	237	ABU SALAMMAMM	2
THESE HEAVY WEIGHTS, THESE DODGERS AND THESE PREACHERS, ...	241	MOYEN SENSUEL	7
HECATOMB			
MR. HECATOMB STYRAX, THE OWNER OF A LARGE ESTATE	178	MOEURS CON: 1	

HECTOR -- HELLAS

	PAGE	TITLE	LINE
HECTOR			
OR OF HECTOR SPATTERING WHEEL-RIMS, ...	208	SEXTUS PROP: 1	29
HE'D (2)			
HEDGETHORN			
GOOD "HEDGETHORN," FOR WE'LL ANGLICIZE YOUR NAME HAVE YOU, OR I, SEEN MOST OF CABARETS, GOOD	161	CABARET DANCER	1
HEDGETHORN?	161	CABARET DANCER	17
GOOD HEDGETHORN, THEY ALL HAVE FUTURES, ...	163	CABARET DANCER	60
HEDONIST			
AN HEDONIST."	203	MAUBERLEY: 4	25
HEED			
AND SCARCELY HEED ONE WORD OF WHAT YOU HEAR.	265	ALF'S NINTH	28
HEELS			
SCRAWNY, BE-SPECTACLED, OUT AT HEELS, ...	14	FAMAM CANO	23
FLOWED IN, AND THROUGH THEE AND ABOUT THY HEELS?	60	TOMB AKR CAAR	23
HAVE HEARD THE ECHO OF MY HEELS, ...	81	TENZONE	12
HEERD			
I NEVER HEERD HER SAY NOTHIN'	271	OLE KATE	7
HEI			
WAS GOVERNOR IN HEI SHU, AND PUT DOWN THE BARBARIAN RABBLE.	135	EXILE'S LETTER	37
HEINE			
TRANSLATIONS AND ADAPTATIONS FROM HEINE	44	FROM HEINE	T
O HARRY HEINE, CURSES BE, ...	46	TRANSLATOR	1
HEIRLOOM			
OR TAKE THE INTAGLIO, MY FAT GREAT-UNCLE'S HEIRLOOM:	162	CABARET DANCER	85
HELD			
NOR HELD ME SAVE AS AIR THAT BRUSHETH BY ONE	39	FOR PSYCHE	3
THAT I SO LONG HELD THY HEART WHOLLY, ...	44	FROM HEINE: 2	2
THEE, AND HELD THY HEART COMPLETELY.	45	FROM HEINE: 3	4
THE JEWELLED CHAIR IS HELD UP AT THE CROSSWAY, ...	141	IDEA OF CHOAN	5
TAIRIRAN HELD HALL IN MONTAIGNAC, ...	151	NEAR PERIGORD	16
GOBBLED ALL THE LAND, AND HELD IT LATER FOR SOME HUNDRED YEARS.	151	NEAR PERIGORD	19
THE TALLEYRANDS, HAVE HELD THE PLACE; IT WAS NO TRANSIENT FICTION.	152	NEAR PERIGORD	51
HAS HELD IN THE AIR BEFORE YOU.	169	PHANOPOEIA	15
THE CHOPPED SEAS HELD HIM, THEREFORE, THAT YEAR.	187	E. P. ODE	12
AND HELD UP THE THREICIAN RIVER;	208	SEXTUS PROP: 1	43
OR AN ORNAMENTAL DEATH WILL BE HELD TO YOUR DEBIT,	221	SEXTUS PROP: 8	2
AND OTHERS HELD ONTO ARROWS, ...	224	SEXTUS PROP:10	8
AS HELD BEFORE HIM IN THAT UNSULLIED MIRROR	241	MOYEN SENSUEL	93
THEY HELD THE VERY MARROW OF THE IDEALS	241	MOYEN SENSUEL	95
HELEN			
PARIS TOOK HELEN NAKED COMING FROM THE BED OF MENELAUS, ...	220	SEXTUS PROP: 7	14
OF LESBIA, KNOWN ABOVE HELEN;	230	SEXTUS PROP:12	69
HELEN'S			
BECAUSE HELEN'S CONDUCT IS "UNSUITABLE."	218	SEXTUS PROP: 5	63
A FOREIGN LOVER BROUGHT DOWN HELEN'S KINGDOM	227	SEXTUS PROP:11	25
HELENUS			
OR OF POLYDMANTUS, BY SCAMANDER, OR HELENUS AND DEIPHOIBOS?	208	SEXTUS PROP: 1	30
HELICON			
WHEN WE SAT UPON THE GRANITE BRINK IN HELICON ,....	104	ANCORA	10
I HAD OGEN IN THE SHADE, RECUMBENT ON CUSHIONED HELICON, ...	210	SEXTUS PROP: 2	1
NOW IF EVER IT IS TIME TO CLEANSE HELICON;	216	SEXTUS PROP: 5	1
HELL			
THAT HELL BRENN NOT HER O'ER CRUELLY.	11	OF THE GIBBET	16
GOD DAMN HIS HELL OUT SPEEDILY	12	OF THE GIBBET	42
HELL GRANT SOON WE HEAR AGAIN THE SWORDS CLASH! ...	28	ALTAFORTE	13
HELL GRANT SOON WE HEAR AGAIN THE SWORDS CLASH! ...	29	ALTAFORTE	38
HELL BLOT BLACK FOR ALWAY THE THOUGHT "PEACE"! ...	29	ALTAFORTE	39
AS CAUGHT BY DANTE IN THE LAST WALLOW OF HELL-- ...	151	NEAR PERIGORD	22
WALKED EYE DEEP IN HELL	190	HUGH SELWYN: 4	13
THERE ARE ENOUGH WOMEN IN HELL, ...	223	SEXTUS PROP: 9	14
RUNNING SO CLOSE TO "HELL" IT SENDS A SHIVER	246	MOYEN SENSUEL	224
HELLAS			
O MOUNTAINS OF HELLAS!!	104	ANCORA	8

HELL'S -- HERE

	PAGE	TITLE	LINE
HELL'S			
OF LOVE THAT LOVETH IN HELL'S DISDEIGN,	11	OF THE GIBBET	21
HELMET			
HIS HELMET AT BEZIERS.	22	MARVOIL	10
HELPLESS			
O HELPLESS FEW IN MY COUNTRY,	92	THE REST	1
HELPLESS AGAINST THE CONTROL;	92	THE REST	8
HEN			
(YOU FEED A HEN ON GREASE, PERHAPS SHE'LL LAY	240	MOYEN SENSUEL	48
HEN.			
THERE IS SIR HEN. DETERDING	267	ALF'S TWELFTH	7
HENCE			
IS LISTED. WELL! SOME SCORE YEARS HENCE	14	FAMAM CANO	20
HOW WILL THIS BEAUTY, WHEN I AM FAR HENCE,	51	HORAE BEATAE	1
THAT I FARE FORTH, THAT I AFAR HENCE	65	THE SEAFARER	38
HENCE HIS CONTENTMENT.	118	ANCIENT WISDOM	4
HENRY			
OF HORSES, FROM HENRY THE FOURTH.	98	THE BELLAIRES	22
HENRY VAN DYKE, WHO THINKS TO CHARM THE MUSE YOU PACK HER IN	239	MOYEN SENSUEL	21
IN BOSTON, TO HENRY JAMES, THE GREATEST WHOM WE'VE SEEN LIVING.	240	MOYEN SENSUEL	62
HER (218)			
HERACLEITUS			
SAGE HERACLEITUS SAYS;	189	HUGH SELWYN: 3	10
HERB			
IS, AT BOTTOM, DISTINGUISHED AND FRESH AS A MARCH HERB.	247	PIERROTS	18
HERBACEOUS			
"SHE HAS CAUGHT ME WITH HERBACEOUS POISON,	215	SEXTUS PROP: 4	31
HERCULES			
AND YOU WRITE OF ACHELOUS, WHO CONTENDED WITH HERCULES,	228	SEXTUS PROP:12	18
HERE			
QUITE GAY, FOR I HAVE HER ALONE HERE	5	LA FRAISNE	38
IN THE ASH TREES HERE:	5	LA FRAISNE	50
HERE 'MID THE ASH TREES.	5	LA FRAISNE	52
WOULD CINO OF THE LUTH WERE HERE!"	6	CINO	22
HERE A WORD KISS!	8	NA AUDIART	11
THY LOVELINESS IS HERE WRIT TILL,	9	NA AUDIART	35
THE LITTLE HILLS TO EAST OF US, THOUGH HERE WE	21	IN DURANCE	39
I HA' TAKEN TO RAMBLING THE SOUTH HERE.	22	MARVOIL	5
THEY TAKE THE TROUBLE TO TEAR OUT THIS WALL HERE,	22	MARVOIL	24
O HOLE IN THE WALL HERE! BE THOU MY JONGLEUR	23	MARVOIL	34
WHEREFORE, O HOLE IN THE WALL HERE,	23	MARVOIL	40
CLOSE IN MY ARMS HERE.	23	MARVOIL	43
O HOLE IN THE WALL HERE, BE THOU MY JONGLEUR,	23	MARVOIL	45
KEEP YET MY SECRET IN THY BREAST HERE;	23	MARVOIL	47
EVEN AS I KEEP HER IMAGE IN MY HEART HERE.	23	MARVOIL	48
AND HERE IN NINEVEH HAVE I BEHELD	24	THUS NINEVEH	8
AM HERE A POET, THAT DOTH DRINK OF LIFE	24	THUS NINEVEH	22
DREW FULL THIS DAGGER THAT DOTH TREMBLE HERE.	31	PIERE VIDAL	42
BEHOLD HERE VIDAL, THAT WAS HUNTED, FLAYED,	31	PIERE VIDAL	47
HERE LET THY CLEMENCY, PERSEPHONE, HOLD FIRM,	38	LADY'S LIFE	1
DO THOU, PLUTO, BRING HERE NO GREATER HARSHNESS.	38	LADY'S LIFE	2
HERE LET THY CLEMENCY, PERSEPHONE, HOLD FIRM,	38	LADY'S LIFE	11
DO THOU, PLUTO, BRING HERE NO GREATER HARSHNESS.	38	LADY'S LIFE	12
HERE AM I COME PERFORCE MY LOVE OF HER,	49	OF SPLENDOUR	17
LET US BUILD HERE AN EXQUISITE FRIENDSHIP,	51	THE ALTAR	1
FOUGHT OUT THEIR STRIFE HERE, 'TIS A PLACE OF WONDER;	51	THE ALTAR	3
AM SOLVED AND BOUND IN, THROUGH AUGHT HERE ON EARTH,	51	THE FLAME	33
HERE IN THE EVERY-DAY WHERE OUR ACTS	52	AU SALON	4
YET IT IS QUIET HERE:	60	TOMB AKR CAAR	32
FOR HERE ARE A MILLION PEOPLE SURLY WITH TRAFFIC;	62	N. Y.	5
HERE HAVE WE HAD OUR VANTAGE, THE GOOD HOUR.	69	THE NEEDLE	4
HERE WE HAVE HAD OUR DAY, YOUR DAY AND MINE.	69	THE NEEDLE	5
FROM HERE TO THERE TO THE SEA'S BORDER,	72	DIEU! QU'IL	9
FOR HERE WAS LOVE, WAS NOT TO BE DROWNED OUT.	73	THE PICTURE	2
AND HERE DESIRE, NOT TO BE KISSED AWAY.	73	THE PICTURE	3
AND YOU ARE HERE, WHO ARE "THE ISLES" TO ME.	73	JACOPO SELLAIO	4
HERE THEY STAND WITHOUT QUAINT DEVICES,	85	SALUTATION 2ND	7

PAGE 188

HERE -- HERSELF

	PAGE	TITLE	LINE
HERE (CONTINUED)			
HERE THEY ARE WITH NOTHING ARCHAIC ABOUT THEM.	85	SALUTATION 2ND	8
HERE ARE YOUR BELLS AND CONFETTI.	86	SALUTATION 2ND	23
SHE, WHO MOVED HERE AMID THE CYCLAMEN,	87	THE SPRING	12
THE TRICKSOME HERMES IS HERE;	90	SURGIT FAMA	8
HERE IS A FORMAL MALE GROUP:	104	THE SEEING EYE	4
A PROUD THING I DO HERE,	105	DOMPNA POIS	24
HERE IS THERE NAUGHT OF DEAD GODS	110	COITUS	3
"HERE SUCH A ONE WALKED.	122	PROVINC DESERT	43
"HERE COEUR-DE-LION WAS SLAIN.	122	PROVINC DESERT	44
"HERE WAS GOOD SINGING.	122	PROVINC DESERT	45
"HERE ONE MAN HASTENED HIS STEP.	122	PROVINC DESERT	46
"HERE ONE LAY PANTING."	122	PROVINC DESERT	47
I HAVE SAID: "THE OLD ROADS HAVE LAIN HERE.	122	PROVINC DESERT	56
HERE WE ARE, PICKING THE FIRST FERN-SHOOTS	127	BOWMEN OF SHU	1
HERE WE ARE BECAUSE WE HAVE THE KEN-NIN FOR OUR FOEMEN,	127	BOWMEN OF SHU	3
THEIR VOICE IS IN THE TWELVE PIPES HERE.	130	THE RIVER SONG	40
HAVE HIM SIT ON HIS KNEES HERE	136	EXILE'S LETTER	78
HERE WE MUST MAKE SEPARATION	137	TAKING LEAVE	3
"WINE, WINE, HERE IS WINE!"	142	UNMOVING CLOUD	13
HERE ARE THEIR TOMB-STONES.	145	SALUTATION 3RD	6
HERE IS THE TASTE OF MY BOOT,	146	SALUTATION 3RD	34
CERTAIN POETS HERE AND IN FRANCE.	148	FRATRES MINORE	2
YE GEE HERE SEVERED, MY LIFE'S COUNTERPART."	156	NEAR PERIGORD	168
NOW THE THIRD DAY IS HERE--	159	PSYCHOLOG HOUR	39
NELL GWYNN'S STILL HERE, DESPITE THE REFORMATION,	163	CABARET DANCER	72
"AND HERE I AM SINCE GOING DOWN OF SUN,	172	LANGUE D'OC: 1	18
"AND THOU OUT HERE BENEATH THE PORCH OF STONE	172	LANGUE D'OC: 1	22
HERE IN THE ORCHARD WHERE THE BIRDS COMPLAIN,	177	LANGUE D'OC: 4	17
"HE WAS YOUR AMBASSADOR HERE?"	182	MOEURS CON: 8	3
HERE DRIFTED	203	MAUBERLEY: 4	24
"DOES HE LIKE ME TO SLEEP HERE ALONE,	215	SEXTUS PROP: 4	38
I AM HUNG HERE, A SCARE-CROW FOR LOVERS.	226	SEXTUS PROP:11	3
HERE IS A PART THAT'S SLIGHT, AND PART GONE WRONG,	235	TO WHISTLER	5
HERE RADWAY GREW, THE FRUIT OF PANTOSOCRACY,	239	MOYEN SENSUEL	39
AND TRUTH SHOULD HERE BE CAREFUL OF HER THIN DRESS--	243	MOYEN SENSUEL	146
HERE COMES THE HIRED GANG	261	ALF'S SIXTH	10
COME NOT HERE	263	ALF'S EIGHTH	11
OF THIS HERE PROLETARIAT.	271	OLE KATE	24
HEREAFTER			
IN DAYS HEREAFTER,	67	DORIA	9
HERE'S			
HERE'S TO YOU, OLD HIPPETY-HOP O' THE ACCENTS,	13	MESMERISM	17
AND HERE'S THE THING THAT LASTS THE WHOLE THING OUT:	73	JACOPO SELLAIO	5
HERE'S PEPITA, TALL AND SLIM AS AN EGYPTIAN MUMMY,	162	CABARET DANCER	18
HERMES			
THE TRICKSOME HERMES IS HERE;	90	SURGIT FAMA	8
THE HIGH TRACKS OF HERMES WOULD NOT AFFORD YOU SHELTER.	226	SEXTUS PROP:11	10
HERO			
WHAT GOD, MAN, OR HERO	189	HUGH SELWYN: 3	27
RADWAY? MY HERO, FOR IT WILL BE MORE INSPIRING	239	MOYEN SENSUEL	41
MY HERO, RADWAY, I HAVE NAMED, IN TRUTH,	241	MOYEN SENSUEL	77
SOON OUR HERO COULD MANAGE ONCE A WEEK,	243	MOYEN SENSUEL	141
HEROA			
TIN' ANDRA, TIN' HEROA, TINA THEON,	189	HUGH SELWYN: 3	26
HEROES			
"WHO HAS ORDERED A BOOK ABOUT HEROES?	210	SEXTUS PROP: 2	18
I WERE ABLE TO LEAD HEROES INTO ARMOUR, I WOULD NOT,	217	SEXTUS PROP: 5	38
HERON			
THE ISLE OF WHITE HERON	138	CITY OF CHOAN	9
HERS (3)			
HERSELF			
WALK DOWN LONGACRE RECITING SWINBURNE TO HERSELF, INAUDIBLY?	114	SIMULACRA	2
SHE MADE THE NAME FOR HERSELF: "GAULE VEIL,"	140	MULBERRY ROAD	5
AND DELIA HERSELF FADING OUT,	168	OF AROUET	41
OR PERHAPS JUNO HERSELF WILL GO UNDER,	222	SEXTUS PROP: 8	40
DULNESS HERSELF, THAT ABJECT SPIRIT, CHORTLES	239	MOYEN SENSUEL	31

	PAGE	TITLE	LINE
HERSELF'S			
NATURE HERSELF'S TURNED METAPHYSICAL,	50	THE FLAME	27
HESITATE			
AS IF THE SNOW SHOULD HESITATE	74	THE RETURN	7
HESITATES			
WHITE, WHITE OF FACE, HESITATES, PASSING THE DOOR.	128	BEAU TOILET	4
HESPER			
HESPER ADEST. HESPER ADEST.	231	CANTUS PLANUS	6
HESPER ADEST. HESPER ADEST.	231	CANTUS PLANUS	6
HESPER ADEST.	231	CANTUS PLANUS	7
HETEROGENEOUS			
TOGETHER WITH THE RESPECTIVE WIVES, HUSBANDS, SISTERS AND HETEROGENEOUS CONNECTIONS OF THE GOOD BELLAIRES,	97	THE BELLAIRES	6
HEW			
HEW MY HEART ROUND AND HUNGER BEGOT	64	THE SEAFARER	11
HI			
"HI! HARRY, HEAR ME, FOR I SING ARIGHT	172	LANGUE D'OC: 1	10
HID			
AS THE FINE DUST, IN THE HID CELL	236	MIDDLE-AGED	8
HID TRUTH AND LIED, AND LIED AND HID THE FACTS.	260	ALF'S FIFTH	6
HID TRUTH AND LIED, AND LIED AND HID THE FACTS.	260	ALF'S FIFTH	6
HID HEALTH STATISTICS, DODGED THE LABOUR ACTS.	260	ALF'S FIFTH	8
HID MORE STATISTICS, MORE FEARED TO CONFESS	260	ALF'S FIFTH	11
HIDDEN			
I HAVE HIDDEN MY FACE WHERE THE OAK	4	LA FRAISNE	10
HAVE I HIDDEN MINE EYES,	27	NIGHT LITANY	31
THE HIDDEN RECESSES	81	TENZONE	11
SINGING A DIFFERENT STAVE, AS CLOSELY HIDDEN.)	153	NEAR PERIGORD	87
HIDE			
OF TH' UNBOUNDED ONES, BUT YE, THAT HIDE	21	IN DURANCE	29
AS I HIDE MOST THE WHILE	21	IN DURANCE	30
HIDEOUS			
OH HOW HIDEOUS IT IS	89	COMMISSION	29
HIDEOUSLY			
GO TO THE HIDEOUSLY WEDDED,	88	COMMISSION	11
HIDES			
OR HIDES AMONG THE ASHES THERE FOR THEE.	20	IN DURANCE	9
HIDETH			
TOMB HIDETH TROUBLE. THE BLADE IS LAYED LOW.	66	THE SEAFARER	90
HIDING			
TO HIDING NIGHT OR TUNING "SYMPHONIES";	235	TO WHISTLER	15
HIDMEN			
HIDMEN GAR TOI PANTH', HOS' ENI TROIEI	187	E. P. ODE	9
HIGH			
BY THAT HIGH FENCER, EVEN DEATH,	19	FOR E. MCC	3
HIGH WROUGHT OF MARBLE, AND THE PANTING BREATH	31	PIERE VIDAL	39
SUCH BATTLE-GUERDON WITH HIS "PROWESSE HIGH"?	32	PIERE VIDAL	59
AYE HE SENT US OUT THROUGH THE CROSSED HIGH SPEARS	33	GOODLY FERE	9
THAT THEY TOOK THE HIGH AND HOLY HOUSE	33	GOODLY FERE	19
OF HAVENS MORE HIGH AND COURTS DESIRABLE	39	BLANDULA	14
ONE HOUR WAS SUNLIT AND THE MOST HIGH GODS	40	ERAT HORA	5
A-TREMBLE IN MEN'S VEINS; O LIP CURVED HIGH	41	HER MONUMENT	12
TO-DAY, ON HIGH	41	HER MONUMENT	26
HOW CANST THOU REACH SO HIGH WITH THY POOR SENSE;	42	HER MONUMENT	52
O YOU AWAY HIGH THERE,	53	AU JARDIN	1
A CHILD--SO HIGH--YOU ARE,	62	A GIRL	9
THE HEART'S THOUGHT THAT I ON HIGH STREAMS	65	THE SEAFARER	35
HIGH FORMS	107	COMING OF WAR	10
FU I LOVED THE HIGH CLOUD AND THE HILL,	117	EPITAPHS	1
AND SEEN THE HIGH BUILDING,	121	PROVINC DESERT	34
SHARP PEAKS, HIGH SPURS, DISTANT CASTLES.	122	PROVINC DESERT	55
AND HIGH OVER THE WILLOWS, THE FINE BIRDS SING TO EACH OTHER, AND LISTEN,	129	THE RIVER SONG	28
TO HIGH HALLS AND CURIOUS FOOD,	132	AT TEN-SHIN	20
HIGH HEAPS, COVERED WITH TREES AND GRASS;	133	FRONTIER GUARD	9
AND MY SPIRIT SO HIGH IT WAS ALL OVER THE HEAVENS,	135	EXILE'S LETTER	32
NOW THE HIGH CLOUDS COVER THE SUN	138	CITY OF CHOAN	11
GREEN VINES HANG THROUGH THE HIGH FOREST,	139	SENNIN POEM	4
AS BUTEI OF KAN HAD MADE THE HIGH GOLDEN LOTUS	141	IDEA OF CHOAN	28
CHALAIS IS HIGH, A-LEVEL WITH THE POPLARS.	152	NEAR PERIGORD	54

HIGH -- HIPPETY-HOP

	PAGE	TITLE	LINE
HIGH (CONTINUED)			
HIGH, HIGH AND SURE . . . AND THEN THE COUNTERTHRUST:	157	NEAR PERIGORD	180
HIGH, HIGH AND SURE . . . AND THEN THE COUNTERTHRUST:	157	NEAR PERIGORD	180
YOUNG BLOOD AND HIGH BLOOD,	190	HUGH SELWYN: 4	21
BY FALLING FROM A HIGH STOOL IN A PUB . . .	193	SIENA MI FE	8
"NOR WILL THE NOISE OF HIGH HORSES LEAD YOU EVER TO BATTLE;	211	SEXTUS PROP: 2	41
AT ANY RATE I SHALL NOT HAVE MY EPITAPH IN A HIGH ROAD.	213	SEXTUS PROP: 3	38
THE HIGH TRACKS OF HERMES WOULD NOT AFFORD YOU SHELTER.	226	SEXTUS PROP:11	10
HIGH-BROWS			
THESE ARE THE HIGH-BROWS, AND TO THIS COLLECTION	241	MOYEN SENSUEL	82
HIGHER			
WHERE THE LOWER AND HIGHER HAVE ENDING;	196	HUGH SELWIN:12	16
IS HIGHER IN THE MENTAL SCALE	272	THE BABY	5
HIGHEST			
"IT IS NOT, RAANA, THAT MY SONG RINGS HIGHEST	24	THUS NINEV:	20
"WHICH THE HIGHEST CULTURES HAVE NOURISHED"	196	HUGH SELWIN:12	22
HIGH-LEAPING			
I HAVE SEEN THE TORCH-FLAMES, HIGH-LEAPING,	121	PROVINC DESERT	30
HIGHLY			
THERE IS SONG IN THE PARCHMENT; CATULLUS THE HIGHLY INDECOROUS,	230	SEXTUS PROP:12	68
HIGH-PRIESTESS			
SHE IS NOW THE HIGH-PRIESTESS	178	MOEURS CON: 1	11
HIGH-RISEN			
WE SEEM AS STATUES ROUND WHOSE HIGH-RISEN BASE	32	PARACELSUS	11
HIGH-ROAD			
AND THERE IS NO HIGH-ROAD TO THE MUSES.	207	SEXTUS PROP: 1	15
HIGHWAY			
ONE SET ON THE HIGHWAY TO SING.	122	PROVINC DESERT	67
THE NARROW STREETS CUT INTO THE WIDE HIGHWAY AT CHOAN,	141	IDEA OF CHOAN	1
HILL			
FU I LOVED THE HIGH CLOUD AND THE HILL,	117	EPITAPHS	1
IS NOW BUT BARREN HILL,	128	THE RIVER SONG	12
CLOUDS GROW OUT OF THE HILL	138	NEAR SHOKU	4
HE TAKES "FLOATING HILL" BY THE SLEEVE,	140	SENNIN POEM	13
FOR A FEW PAGES BROUGHT DOWN FROM THE FORKED HILL UNSULLIED?	207	SEXTUS PROP: 1	20
HILLS			
AND SOME THE HILLS HOLD OFF,	21	IN DURANCE	38
THE LITTLE HILLS TO EAST OF US, THOUGH HERE WE	21	IN DURANCE	39
AH! CABARET! AH CABARET, THY HILLS AGAIN!	32	PIERE VIDAL	65
ON THE HILLS O' GALILEE,	64	GOODLY FERE	42
GRASS, AND LOW FIELDS, AND HILLS,	70	THE PLUNGE	16
WHERE THE HILLS PART	121	PROVINC DESERT	2
ARE NOW THE BASE OF OLD HILLS.	138	CITY OF CHOAN	7
HIM (67)			
HIMERRO			
HIMERRO	112	HIMERRO	T
HIMSELF			
I DREAMT THAT I WAS GOD HIMSELF	45	FROM HEINE: 4	1
NOR WOULD GAUTIER HIMSELF HAVE DESPISED THEIR CONTRASTS IN WHITENESS	87	ALBATRE	5
STOLE HER AWAY FOR HIMSELF, KEPT HER AGAINST ARMED	123	PROVINC DESERT	75
HE HURLED HIMSELF INTO A SEA OF SIX WOMEN.	181	MOEURS CON: 6	2
EACH MAN WANTS THE POMEGRANATE FOR HIMSELF;	227	SEXTUS PROP:12	4
UNTO HIMSELF THE QUESTION PUT	272	THE BABY	3
HINDER			
NOR THINE TO HINDER,	24	THUS NINEVEH	6
HINDRANCE			
PLEASURE LASTING, WITH COURTEZANS, GOING AND COMING WITHOUT HINDRANCE,	136	EXILE'S LETTER	53
HINDS			
GOD! HOW THE SWIFTEST HIND'S BLOOD SPURTED HOT	30	PIERE VIDAL	14
HOT WAS THAT HIND'S BLOOD YET IT SCORCHED ME NOT	30	PIERE VIDAL	16
HIPPETY-HOP			
HERE'S TO YOU, OLD HIPPETY-HOP O' THE ACCENTS,	13	MESMERISM	17

HIRAM -- HOMAGE

	PAGE	TITLE	LINE
HIRAM			
BEFORE THE "ARS POETICA" OF HIRAM MAXIM.	239	MOYEN SENSUEL	34
HIRE			
NO! THEY WON'T HIRE HIM.	261	ALF'S SIXTH	17
HIRED			
WHEN YOU COULD GO OUT IN A HIRED HANSOM	167	OF AROUET	2
HERE COMES THE HIRED GANG	261	ALF'S SIXTH	10
HIS (224)			
HISTORICAL			
AND WEARY WITH HISTORICAL DATA, THEY WILL TURN TO MY DANCE TUNE.	209	SEXTUS PROP: 1	62
HOARD			
BE AN UNLIKELY TREASURE HOARD.	66	THE SEAFARER	101
HOGWASH			
FED 'EM WITH HOGWASH!	257	BREAD BRIGADE	29
HOKUM			
DISGUST WITH HOKUM.	259	ALF'S THIRD	7
HOLD			
AND SOME THE HILLS HOLD OFF,	21	IN DURANCE	38
HERE LET THY CLEMENCY, PERSEPHONE, HOLD FIRM,	38	LADY'S LIFE	1
HERE LET THY CLEMENCY, PERSEPHONE, HOLD FIRM,	38	LADY'S LIFE	11
YET SHALL MY WHITE ARMS HOLD THEE,	48	FROM HEINE: 7	29
KNOWN ON MY KEEL MANY A CARE'S HOLD,	64	THE SEAFARER	5
ASK OF YOU THAN HOLD ANOTHER,	107	DOMPNA POIS	67
ME OUT, KNOWING YOU HOLD ME SO FAST!	107	DOMPNA POIS	70
AND MALEMORT KEEPS ITS CLOSE HOLD ON BRIVE,	153	NEAR PERIGORD	59
TO HOLD EMBRACED, AND WILL NOT HER FORSAKE	172	LANGUE D'OC: 1	28
LEAVING ME NO POWER TO HOLD HIM.	174	LANGUE D'OC: 3	6
"LOVELY THOU ART, TO HOLD ME CLOSE AND KISST,	177	LANGUE D'OC: 4	11
LIKE ALL HIS CLASS WAS TOLD TO HOLD IT IN THOSE DAYS,	263	ALF'S EIGHTH	26
HOLDETH			
SHE THAT HOLDETH THE WONDER WORDS WITHIN HER EYES	17	PRAISE YSOLT	51
WANETH THE WATCH, BUT THE WORLD HOLDETH.	66	THE SEAFARER	89
BEYOND SALVATION, HOLDETH ITS JUDGING FORCE,	249	DONNA MI PREGA	36
HOLDING			
HOLDING LINES IN ONE COLOUR.	120	GAME OF CHESS	5
HOLDS			
THAT HOLDS THEIR BLOSSOMS AND THEIR LEAVES IN CURE	21	IN DURANCE	45
LOVE TAKES HIS WAY AND HOLDS HIS JOY DECEITFUL,	37	THE YOUNG KING	26
AND HOLDS HER SIDES WHERE SWELLING LAUGHTER CRACKS 'EM	239	MOYEN SENSUEL	33
HOLE			
O HOLE IN THE WALL HERE! BE THOU MY JONGLEUR	23	MARVOIL	34
WHEREFORE, O HOLE IN THE WALL HERE,	23	MARVOIL	40
O HOLE IN THE WALL HERE, BE THOU MY JONGLEUR,	23	MARVOIL	45
HOLIDAYS			
AN' BE THANKFUL FOR OCCASIONAL HOLIDAYS.	263	ALF'S EIGHTH	28
HOLINESS			
AND BEFORE THE HOLINESS	26	NIGHT LITANY	29
HOLLAND			
THAT'S SENT TO HOLLAND, A MOST PARTICULAR FEATURE,	239	MOYEN SENSUEL	20
HOLLOW			
FOR EVEN AS THOU ART HOLLOW BEFORE I FILL THEE WITH THIS PARCHMENT,	23	MARVOIL	37
SO IS MY HEART HOLLOW WHEN SHE FILLETH NOT MINE EYES,	23	MARVOIL	38
AND SO WERE MY MIND HOLLOW, DID SHE NOT FILL UTTERLY MY THOUGHT.	23	MARVOIL	39
UPON SUCH HOLLOW SEASON?"	72	PAN IS DEAD	13
HOLLYHOCKS			
ONE MORE FOOL'S VIGIL WITH THE HOLLYHOCKS.	31	PIERE VIDAL	25
HOLLY-TREES			
UNBEND FROM THE HOLLY-TREES,	109	HEATHER	5
HOLY			
TO CATCH YOU AT WORM TURNING. HOLY ODD'S BODYKINS!	13	MESMERISM	4
THAT THEY TOOK THE HIGH AND HOLY HOUSE	33	GOODLY FERE	19
WHERE THESE HAVE BEEN, MEET 'TIS, THE GROUND IS HOLY.	51	THE ALTAR	4
AND, HEAVENLY, HOLY GODS! I CAN'T SAY MORE,	246	MOYEN SENSUEL	220
HOMAGE			
(CHRIST MAKE THE SHEPHERDS' HOMAGE DEAR!)	10	FOR THIS YULE	2
HOMAGE TO QUINTUS SEPTIMIUS FLORENTIS CHRISTIANUS	164	QUINTUS SEPTIM	T
HOMAGE TO SEXTUS PROPERTIUS	205	SEXTUS PROP	T

HOMAGE -- HOPE

	PAGE	TITLE	LINE
HOMAGE (CONTINUED)			
THERE WILL BE A CROWD OF YOUNG WOMEN DOING HOMAGE TO MY PALAVER,	208	SEXTUS PROP: 1	50
HOME			
UNTO THE HEARTH OF THEIR HEART'S HOME	3	THE TREE	8
ROME'S NAME ALONE WITHIN THESE WALLS KEEPS HOME.	40	ROME	4
ITS HOME MAIL IS STILL OPENED BY ITS MATERNAL PARENT	179	MOEURS CON: 4	2
AND IN THE HOME OF THE NOVELIST	180	MOEURS CON: 5	16
CAME HOME, HOME TO A LIE,	190	HUGH SELWYN: 4	15
CAME HOME, HOME TO A LIE,	190	HUGH SELWYN: 4	15
HOME TO MANY DECEITS,	190	HUGH SELWYN: 4	16
HOME TO OLD LIES AND NEW INFAMY;	190	HUGH SELWYN: 4	17
MUCH CONVERSATION IS AS GOOD AS HAVING A HOME.	214	SEXTUS PROP: 4	10
TO SAY MANY THINGS IS EQUAL TO HAVING A HOME.	215	SEXTUS PROP: 4	28
AND SHE WAS LED BACK, LIVING, HOME;	227	SEXTUS PROP:11	26
HOME-BORN			
WHERE IS THE WORK OF YOUR HOME-BORN SCULPTORS?	165	QUINTUS SEPTIM	16
HOME-GROWN			
O STATE SANS SONG, SANS HOME-GROWN WINE, SANS REALIST!	241	MOYEN SENSUEL	88
HOME-INDUSTRIOUS			
A HOME-INDUSTRIOUS WORKER TO PERFECTION,	245	MOYEN SENSUEL	213
HOMELY			
AN HOMELY, TRANSIENT ANTIQUITY.	114	EPILOGUE	8
HOMER			
IF HOMER HAD NOT STATED YOUR CASE!	208	SEXTUS PROP: 1	34
AND WILL NOT PRAISE HOMER	218	SEXTUS PROP: 5	62
YOU THINK YOU ARE GOING TO DO HOMER.	228	SEXTUS PROP:12	22
HOMER'S			
NOR OF HOMER'S REPUTATION IN PERGAMUS,	217	SEXTUS PROP: 5	43
MESICK			
I AM HOMESICK AFTER MINE OWN KIND,	20	IN DURANCE	1
BUT I AM HOMESICK AFTER MINE OWN KIND.	20	IN DURANCE	3
FOR I AM HOMESICK AFTER MINE OWN KIND	20	IN DURANCE	12
AND I AM HOMESICK	20	IN DURANCE	14
BUT FOR ALL THAT, I AM HOMESICK AFTER MINE OWN KIND	20	IN DURANCE	23
HONEST			
NEVER AN HONEST WORD	262	ALF'S SIXTH	28
HONEY-COMB			
I HA' SEEN HIM EAT O' THE HONEY-COMB	34	GOODLY FERE	53
HONEY-RED			
HONEY-RED, CLOSING THE FACE-OVAL,	204	MEDALLION	9
HONOUR			
SO THAT ALL MEN SHALL HONOUR HIM AFTER	66	THE SEAFARER	78
HONOURABLE			
IT IS NOBLE TO DIE OF LOVE, AND HONOURABLE TO REMAIN	218	SEXTUS PROP: 5	59
IN THE HOPE OF HONOURABLE MENTION	264	ALF'S EIGHTH	32
HONOURED			
AND BID GO IN WITH HONOURED COMPANIONS	37	THE YOUNG KING	39
I SHALL BE HONOURED WITH YESTERDAY'S WREATHS.	229	SEXTUS PROP:12	57
HONOURERS			
SHOULD NOT LACK FOR HONOURERS,	46	FROM HEINE: 6	2
HOODED			
THOU HOODED OPAL, THOU ETERNAL PEARL,	50	THE FLAME	29
HOOK			
FAT PIERRE WITH THE HOOK GAUCHE-MAIN,	11	OF THE GIBBET	5
A HOOK TO CATCH THE LADY JANE'S ATTENTION,	196	HUGH SELWIN:12	17
HOOP-SKIRT			
A HOOP-SKIRT, A CALASH,	114	EPILOGUE	7
THE MOTHER OF THE GREAT KING, IN A HOOP-SKIRT,	237	ABU SALAMMAMM	24
HOOT			
BUT THE BLACK OMINOUS OWL HOOT WAS AUDIBLE.	223	SEXTUS PROP: 9	4
AND WOULDN'T GIV' A DAMN HOOT.	271	OLE KATE	1
HOPE			
. . . I HOPE SHE WILL NOT COME AGAIN.	5	LA FRAISNE	44
I BREATHE NO HOPE	8	NA AUDIART	16
FOR LOVE, OR HOPE, OR BEAUTY OR FOR POWER,	21	IN DURANCE	32
TO BE A SIGN AND AN HOPE MADE SECURE	42	HER MONUMENT	33
IN HOPE TO SET SOME MISCONCEPTIONS RIGHT.	238	MOYEN SENSUEL	2
HAVING NO HOPE AT ALL	248	DONNA MI PREGA	6
SURE, THEY CAN LIVE ON HOPE,	259	ALF'S THIRD	16

PAGE 193

HOPE -- HOSPITIUM

	PAGE	TITLE	LINE
HOPE (CONTINUED)			
IN THE HOPE OF HONOURABLE MENTION	264	ALF'S EIGHTH	32
HOPED			
AND IT IS TO BE HOPED THAT THEIR SPIRITS WILL WALK	115	SOCIAL ORDER	14
HORA			
ERAT HORA	40	ERAT HORA	T
HORAE			
HORAE BEATAE INSCRIPTIO	51	HORAE BEATAE	T
HORATIAN			
I HAD REHEARSED THE CURIAN BROTHERS, AND MADE REMARKS ON THE HORATIAN JAVELIN	210	SEXTUS PROP: 2	8
HOREB			
THE HEAVY MEMORIES OF HOREB, SINAI AND THE FORTY YEARS,	193	BRENNBAUM	5
HORI			
HE GOES OUT TO HORI, TO LOOK AT THE WING-FLAPPING STORKS,	130	THE RIVER SONG	36
HORN			
BID THE WORLD'S HOUNDS COME TO HORN!"	25	THE WHITE STAG	7
SMALL HORN AND VIOLIN.	47	FROM HEINE: 7	28
HORNS			
MOUNTS FROM THE FOUR HORNS OF MY BED-POSTS,	169	PHANOPOEIA	3
IN THEIR CLASSIC HORNS,	211	SEXTUS PROP: 2	43
HORRID			
NOR WILL THE HORRID THREATS OF BERNARD SHAW	63	PHASELLUS ILLE	7
HORSE			
YOU CAME BY ON BAMBOO STILTS, PLAYING HORSE,	130	RIVER-MER WIFE	3
THE DAI HORSE NEIGHS AGAINST THE BLEAK WIND OF ETSU,	139	SOUTH-FOLK	1
PULLED DOWN BY A DEAL-WOOD HORSE;	208	SEXTUS PROP: 1	27
THE WATER DRIPPING FROM BELLEROPHON'S HORSE,	210	SEXTUS PROP: 2	2
HORSE-FACED			
WHY DOES THE HORSE-FACED LADY OF JUST THE UNMENTIONABLE AGE	114	SIMULACRA	1
HORSES			
FOR TWELVE HORSES AND ALSO FOR TWELVE BOARHOUNDS	98	THE BELLAIRES	19
OF HORSES, FROM HENRY THE FOURTH.	98	THE BELLAIRES	22
HORSES, HIS HORSES EVEN, ARE TIRED. THEY WERE STRONG.	127	BOWMEN OF SHU	15
HORSES, HIS HORSES EVEN, ARE TIRED. THEY WERE STRONG.	127	BOWMEN OF SHU	15
BY HEAVEN, HIS HORSES ARE TIRED.	127	BOWMEN OF SHU	17
THE HORSES ARE WELL TRAINED, THE GENERALS HAVE IVORY ARROWS AND QUIVERS ORNAMENTED WITH FISH-SKIN.	127	BOWMEN OF SHU	19
THEY RIDE UPON DRAGON-LIKE HORSES,	132	AT TEN-SHIN	15
UPON HORSES WITH HEAD-TRAPPINGS OF YELLOW METAL,	132	AT TEN-SHIN	16
OUR HORSES NEIGH TO EACH OTHER	137	TAKING LEAVE	8
DARK OXEN, WHITE HORSES,	141	IDEA OF CHOAN	2
THE TENTS TIGHT DRAWN, HORSES AT TETHER	155	NEAR PERIGORD	130
AND OUR TWO HORSES HAD TRACED OUT THE VALLEYS;	157	NEAR PERIGORD	173
HE SAID: "WHY FLAY DEAD HORSES?	181	MOEURS CON: 7	15
A NEW-FANGLED CHARIOT FOLLOWS THE FLOWER-HUNG HORSES;	207	SEXTUS PROP: 1	12
TURN TO YOUR DRIPPING HORSES, BECAUSE OF A TUNE, UNDER AETNA?	208	SEXTUS PROP: 1	47
"NOR WILL THE NOISE OF HIGH HORSES LEAD YOU EVER TO BATTLE;	211	SEXTUS PROP: 2	41
TO LEAD EMATHIAN HORSES AFIELD,	216	SEXTUS PROP: 5	2
FOR THE SUN SHALL DRIVE WITH BLACK HORSES,	220	SEXTUS PROP: 7	23
YOU WRITE OF ADRASTUS' HORSES AND THE FUNERAL RITES OF ACHENOR,	228	SEXTUS PROP:12	19
HORSE'S			
AT HIS HORSE'S BRIDLE.	138	NEAR SHOKU	5
HORSES'			
THEIR HORSES' ARMOURED FEET	111	IMAGE ORLEANS	6
HORTICULTURE			
HORTICULTURE, YOU CAPRIPED?	109	THE FAUN	4
HOS'			
HIDMEN GAR TOI PANTH', HOS' ENI TROIEI	187	E. P. ODE	9
HOSANNAH			
OF HIS SUBJECTIVE HOSANNAH.	202	AGE DEMANDED	55
HOSPITIUM			
A TROJAN AND ADULTEROUS PERSON CAME TO MENELAUS UNDER THE RITES OF HOSPITIUM,	227	SEXTUS PROP:12	6

HOST -- HOUSE

	PAGE	TITLE	LINE
HOST			
WHEN THEY CAME WI' A HOST TO TAKE OUR MAN	33	GOODLY FERE	5
O RIBALD COMPANY, O SAINTLY HOST,	35	HIS OWN FACE	2
THE TURBULENT AND UNDISCIPLINED HOST OF ART STUDENTS--	93	LES MILLWIN	5
WHERE FOLK OF WORTH BE HOST.	250	DONNA MI PREGA	57
HOSTILE			
"YOU SHOULD NOT BELIEVE HOSTILE TONGUES.	226	SEXTUS PROP:11	20
HOSTS			
HOSTS OF AN ANCIENT PEOPLE,	107	COMING OF WAR	19
HOT			
IN HOT SUMMER HAVE I GREAT REJOICING	28	ALTAFORTE	7
GOD! HOW THE SWIFTEST HIND'S BLOOD SPURTED HOT	30	PIERE VIDAL	14
HOT WAS THAT HIND'S BLOOD YET IT SCORCHED ME NOT	30	PIERE VIDAL	16
HOT IS SUCH LOVE AND SILENT,	81	PIERE VIDAL	34
HA! THIS SCENT IS HOT!	32	PIERE VIDAL	67
AND THE BLOOD GUSHED HOT AND FREE,	34	GOODLY FERE	38
WHEN THE HOT WATER GIVES OUT OR GOES TEPID,	100	THE BATH TUB	2
HOT SUN, CLEAR WATER, FRESH WIND,	146	CANTILATIONS	3
FROM PROFITS ON HOT AIR.	266	ALF'S ELEVENTH	16
I LEND YOU ENGLISHMEN HOT AIR	269	SAFE AND SOUND	3
I LEND YOU ENGLISHMEN HOT AIR	269	SAFE AND SOUND	5
HOTELS			
DOWSON FOUND HARLOTS CHEAPER THAN HOTELS;	193	SIENA MI FE	13
HOUNDS			
BID THE WORLD'S HOUNDS COME TO HORN!"	25	THE WHITE STAG	7
AND THE HOUNDS FLED AND THE DEER FLED	30	PIERE VIDAL	11
THE HOUNDS OF THE CRIMSON SKY GAVE TONGUE	34	GOODLY FERE	39
WITH THEM THE SILVER HOUNDS,	74	THE RETURN	13
HOUR			
ONE HOUR WAS SUNLIT AND THE MOST HIGH GODS	40	ERAT HORA	5
THAN TO HAVE WATCHED THAT HOUR AS IT PASSED.	40	ERAT HORA	7
OR FINDS ITS HOUR UPON THE LOOM OF DAYS:	61	PORTRAIT FEMME	21
EASTWARD AVOID THE HOUR OF ITS DECLINE,	69	THE NEEDLE	2
HERE HAVE WE HAD OUR VANTAGE, THE GOOD HOUR.	69	THE NEEDLE	4
THAN THIS HOUR OF CLEAR COOLNESS,	83	THE GARRET	10
THE HOUR OF WAKING TOGETHER.	83	THE GARRET	11
VILLANELLE: THE PSYCHOLOGICAL HOUR	158	PSYCHOLOG HOUR	T
AN HOUR LATER: A SHOW OF CALVES AND SPANGLES,	163	CABARET DANCER	82
AND AT ANY HOUR;	212	SEXTUS PROP: 3	25
THE GENTLER HOUR OF AN ULTIMATE DAY.	222	SEXTUS PROP: 8	18
YOUR QUIET HOUR PUT FORWARD,	222	SEXTUS PROP: 8	28
LIGHT, LIGHT OF MY EYES, AT AN EXCEEDING LATE HOUR I WAS WANDERING,	224	SEXTUS PROP:10	1
HOURS			
THAT MAN DOTH PASS THE NET OF DAYS AND HOURS.	50	THE FLAME	10
HOW WILL THESE HOURS, WHEN WE TWAIN ARE GRAY,	51	HORAE BEATAE	3
HOURS, WHERE SOMETHING MIGHT HAVE FLOATED UP.	61	PORTRAIT FEMME	12
AS WHITE THEIR BARK, SO WHITE THIS LADY'S HOURS.	71	A VIRGINAL	14
SO MANY HOURS WASTED!	158	PSYCHOLOG HOUR	9
FOR TWO HOURS HE TALKED OF GALLIFET;	193	SIENA MI FE	5
HOUR'S			
BETTER ONE HOUR'S STOUR THAN A YEAR'S PEACE	28	ALTAFORTE	16
HOUSE			
THAT THEY TOOK THE HIGH AND HOLY HOUSE	33	GOODLY FERE	19
THE HOUSE OF SPLENDOUR	49	OF SPLENDOUR	T
A HOUSE NOT MADE WITH HANDS,	49	OF SPLENDOUR	2
AND I HAVE SEEN HER THERE WITHIN HER HOUSE,	49	OF SPLENDOUR	9
THINK'ST THOU THAT THE DARK HOUSE	67	THE CLOAK	4
GOLDEN ROSE THE HOUSE, IN THE PORTAL I SAW	68	APPARUIT	1
TO SEE THREE GENERATIONS OF ONE HOUSE GATHERED TOGETHER!	89	COMMISSION	30
MAKES HAY WITH THE THINGS IN HER HOUSE.	115	SOCIAL ORDER	10
THE PURPLE HOUSE AND THE CRIMSON ARE FULL OF SPRING SOFTNESS.	129	THE RIVER SONG	24
THE IMPERIAL GUARDS COME FORTH FROM THE GOLDEN HOUSE WITH THEIR ARMOUR A-GLEAMING.	129	THE RIVER SONG	34
WHERE LAY THE DYNASTIC HOUSE OF THE GO,	138	CITY OF CHOAN	5
TO LOOK ON THE TALL HOUSE OF THE SHIN	140	MULBERRY ROAD	2
RIU'S HOUSE STANDS OUT ON THE SKY,	141	IDEA OF CHOAN	26
BEFORE IT ANOTHER HOUSE WHICH I DO NOT KNOW:	141	IDEA OF CHOAN	30

PAGE 195

	PAGE	TITLE	LINE
HOUSE (CONTINUED)			
"SHELLEY USED TO LIVE IN THIS HOUSE."	182	MOEURS CON: 8	13
THOUGH MY HOUSE IS NOT PROPPED UP BY TAENARIAN COLUMNS FROM LACONIA (ASSOCIATED WITH NEPTUNE AND CERBERUS),	208	SEXTUS PROP: 1	51
SADNESS HUNG OVER THE HOUSE, AND THE DESOLATED FEMALE ATTENDANTS	214	SEXTUS PROP: 4	22
WE WERE COMING NEAR TO THE HOUSE,	225	SEXTUS PROP:10	25
AND BEHOLD ME, SMALL FORTUNE LEFT IN MY HOUSE.	229	SEXTUS PROP:12	53
TO RUN SUCH TOURS. HE CALLS 'EM. . . . HOUSE PARTIES.	245	MOYEN SENSUEL	210
HOUSEHOLDER			
TO A BRITISH HOUSEHOLDER.	103	LADIES	13
HOUSES			
'TIS NOT A GAME OF BARTER, LANDS AND HOUSES,	50	THE FLAME	3
'TIS NOT A GAME OF BARTER, LANDS AND HOUSES,	50	THE FLAME	17
IN THE STORIED HOUSES OF SAN-KO THEY GAVE US MORE SENNIN MUSIC,	135	EXILE'S LETTER	26
NOR HOUSES MODELLED UPON THAT OF JOVE IN EAST ELIS,	209	SEXTUS PROP: 1	67
FILLED THE BACK ALLEYS AND THE BACK TO BACK HOUSES.	260	ALF'S FIFTH	14
HOUSMAN'S			
MR. HOUSMAN'S MESSAGE	43	MR. HOUSMAN	T
HOVER			
SEEMED OVER ME TO HOVER LIGHT AS LEAVES	39	FOR PSYCHE	6
HOVERED			
SINCE YOU HAVE COME THIS PLACE HAS HOVERED ROUND ME,	69	SUB MARE	2
HOVERING			
BIRDS WITH FLOWERY WING, HOVERING BUTTERFLIES	141	IDEA OF CHOAN	17
WITH MINDS STILL HOVERING ABOVE THEIR TESTICLES	148	FRATRES MINORE	1
HOW			
BUT YOU, MY LORD, HOW WITH YOUR CITY?"	6	CINO	32
HOW THE STAYS PLY BACK FROM IT;	8	NA AUDIART	15
KNOWING, I KNOW NOT HOW,	9	NA AUDIART	51
HOW I 'SCAPED IMMORTALITY.	15	FAMAM CANO	48
STILL SHADE, AND BADE NO WHISPER SPEAK THE BIRDS OF HOW	21	IN DURANCE	48
GOD! HOW THE SWIFTEST HIND'S BLOOD SPURTED HOT	30	PIERE VIDAL	14
'TIS HOW A BRAVE MAN DIES ON THE TREE."	34	GOODLY FERE	32
FROM THIS FAINT WORLD, HOW FULL OF BITTERNESS	37	THE YOUNG KING	25
LO, HOW THE LIGHT DOTH MELT US INTO SONG:	38	BALLATETTA	3
BEHOLD HOW PRIDE AND RUIN CAN BEFALL	40	ROME	5
HOW HAST THOU SET THE FIRE	41	HER MONUMENT	11
HOW CANST THOU REACH SO HIGH WITH THY POOR SENSE;	42	HER MONUMENT	52
HOW IS THE NOBLEST OF THY SPEECH AND THOUGHT	42	HER MONUMENT	55
ON HOW WHITE DOGWOODS MURMURED OVERHEAD	43	SATIEMUS	12
HOW IF THE LOW DEAR SOUND WITHIN THY THROAT	43	SATIEMUS	14
OF HOW YOU HAVE ADDRESSED ME.	44	FROM HEINE: 1	4
HOW HIS COAT AND PANTS ADORN HIM!	46	FROM HEINE: 6	5
HOW WILL THIS BEAUTY, WHEN I AM FAR HENCE,	51	HORAE BEATAE	1
HOW WILL THESE HOURS, WHEN WE TWAIN ARE GRAY,	51	HORAE BEATAE	3
WHEN I BEHOLD HOW BLACK, IMMORTAL INK	59	SILET	1
HOW MANY FACES I'D HAVE OUT OF MIND.	59	EXIT' CUIUSDAM	7
O THOU UNMINDFUL! HOW SHOULD I FORGET!	60	TOMB AKR CAAR	15
HOW 'CAME I IN'? WAS I NOT THEE AND THEE?	60	TOMB AKR CAAR	24
JOURNEY'S JARGON, HOW I IN HARSH DAYS	64	THE SEAFARER	2
LIST HOW I, CARE-WRETCHED, ON ICE-COLD SEA,	64	THE SEAFARER	14
WEALTHY AND WINE-FLUSHED, HOW I WEARY OFT	64	THE SEAFARER	30
HOW SHE IS SO FAIR AND BONNY;	72	DIEU! QU'IL	2
HOW SHALL WE WEAVE A CORONAL,	72	PAN IS DEAD	6
HOW SHE IS SO FAIR AND BONNY.	72	DIEU! QU'IL	8
HOW SHOULD HE SHOW A REASON,	72	PAN IS DEAD	11
HOW HAVE I LABOURED?	84	ORTUS	1
HOW HAVE I NOT LABOURED	84	ORTUS	2
HOW HAVE I LABOURED TO BRING HER SOUL INTO SEPARATION;	84	ORTUS	7
OH HOW HIDEOUS IT IS	89	COMMISSION	25
HOW MANY WILL COME AFTER ME	96	DUM CAPITOLIUM	
LO, HOW IT GLEAMS AND GLISTENS IN THE SUN	99	CAKE OF SOAP	
TO SEE HOW CELESTINE WILL RE-ENTER HER SLIPPERS.	111	BLACK SLIPPERS	10
AND HOW THE WIND DOTH RAMM!	116	ANCIENT MUSIC	
AH, HOW SHALL YOU KNOW THE DREARY SORROW AT THE NORTH GATE,	133	FRONTIER GUARD	2

PAGE 196

HOW -- HUMANITY

	PAGE	TITLE	LINE
HOW (CONTINUED)			
AND THINKING HOW LITTLE YOU CARED FOR THE COST, ...	135	EXILE'S LETTER	44
AND IF YOU ASK HOW I REGRET THAT PARTING:	136	EXILE'S LETTER	72
HOW SHALL WE KNOW ALL THE FRIENDS	141	IDEA OF CHOAN	31
HOW WOULD YOU LIVE, WITH NEIGHBOURS SET ABOUT YOU--	152	NEAR PERIGORD	28
YOU READ TO-DAY, HOW LONG THE OVERLORDS OF PERIGORD,	152	NEAR PERIGORD	50
ALL OF HIS FLANK--HOW COULD HE DO WITHOUT HER?	153	NEAR PERIGORD	66
HOW DO I KNOW?	158	PSYCHOLOG HOUR	16
FOR I KNOW HOW WORDS RUN LOOSE, ...	173	LANGUE D'OC: 2	25
WHO KNOW NOT HOW TO ASK HER;	175	LANGUE D'OC: 3	32
GOD! HOW SOFTLY THIS KILLS!	175	LANGUE D'OC: 3	40
KILLED ME SHE HAS, I KNOW NOT HOW IT WAS, ...	175	LANGUE D'OC: 3	42
HOW SWIFT IT IS.	175	LANGUE D'OC: 3	49
THEM. GOD HOW SWIFT THE NIGHT, ...	177	LANGUE D'OC: 4	4
'FORE GOD, HOW SWIFT THE NIGHT, ...	177	LANGUE D'OC: 4	9
AH GOD! HOW SWIFT THE NIGHT	177	LANGUE D'OC: 4	19
AH GOD! HOW SWIFT THE NIGHT.	177	LANGUE D'OC: 4	24
BY GOD, HOW SWIFT THE NIGHT.	177	LANGUE D'OC: 4	29
TOLD ME HOW JOHNSON (LIONEL) DIED	193	SIENA MI FE	7
HOW EASY THE MOVING FINGERS; IF HAIR IS MUSSED ON HER FOREHEAD, ...	217	SEXTUS PROP: 5	29
HOW MANY WORDS TALKED OUT WITH ABUNDANT CANDLES;	220	SEXTUS PROP: 7	3
IN HOW MANY VARIED EMBRACES, OUR CHANGING ARMS ...	220	SEXTUS PROP: 7	10
HER KISSES, HOW MANY, LINGERING ON MY LIPS.	220	SEXTUS PROP: 7	11
OH HOW THE BIRD FLEW FROM TROJAN RAFTERS, ...	227	SEXTUS PROP:11	35
AND HOW TEN SINS CAN CORRUPT YOUNG MAIDENS;	229	SEXTUS PROP:12	43
HIS MOTHER'S BIRTHDAY GIFT. (HOW PITIFUL	242	MOYEN SENSUEL	117
AS TO HOW AND WHY AND WHEREBY THEY GOT IN	244	MOYEN SENSUEL	159
HOW SHALL WE DRESS 'EM ALL?	257	BREAD BRIGADE	22
HOW THE WHOLE NATION SHOOK	257	BREAD BRIGADE	27
SEE HOW THEY TAKE IT ALL, ...	259	ALF'S THIRD	12
HOW MANY WEAK OF MIND, HOW MUCH TUBERCULOSIS	260	ALF'S FIFTH	13
HOW MANY WEAK OF MIND, HOW MUCH TUBERCULOSIS	260	ALF'S FIFTH	13
THAT'S HOW THE PRESS BLURB RAN,--	261	ALF'S SIXTH	14
THE UNSAFE SAFE, WHEREIN ALL ROTS, AND NO MAN CAN SAY HOW	261	ALF'S FIFTH	19
HOW THEY BETTER START TAKIN' CARE, ...	262	ALF'S SEVENTH	4
HOWE'ER			
HOWE'ER IN MIRTH MOST MAGNIFIED, ...	66	THE SEAFARER	86
HOWER			
IN THIS MOMENTOUS HOWER, ...	270	OF 600 M.P.'S	2
HOWEVER			
BUT HOWEVER WE LONG TO SPEAK	142	UNMOVING CLOUD	26
HOWL			
THEN HOWL I MY HEART NIGH MAD WITH REJOICING.	28	ALTAFORTE	6
FOR THEM THE YELLOW DOGS HOWL PORTENTS IN VAIN, ...	132	AT TEN EHIN	28
THEY HOWL. THEY COMPLAIN IN DELICATE AND EXHAUSTED METRES	148	FRATRES MINORE	5
HOWLING			
ALREADY THEY FLEE, HOWLING IN TERROR.	81	TENZONE	5
HUB			
HUB OF THE WHEEL, THE STIRRER-UP OF STRIFE, ...	151	NEAR PERIGORD	21
HUBERT			
THAT PLUNDERED ST. HUBERT BACK O' THE FANE:	12	OF THE GIBBET	32
HUDSON			
YET SAW AN "AD." "TO-NIGHT, THE HUDSON SAIL, ...	242	MOYEN SENSUEL	111
HUES			
THE SEED OF A MYRIAD HUES, ...	141	IDEA OF CHOAN	21
HUGE			
BUT ONE HUGE BACK HALF-COVERED UP WITH PINE, ...	152	NEAR PERIGORD	33
HUGGED			
OR HUGGED TWO GIRLS AT ONCE BEHIND A CHAPEL.)	242	MOYEN SENSUEL	106
HUGH			
HUGH SELWIN MAUBERLEY	185	HUGH SELWYN	T
HUMAN			
"BEING NO LONGER HUMAN, WHY SHOULD I	22	PARACELSUS	1
WOEFUL IS THIS HUMAN LOT.	43	MR. HOUSMAN	9
IRRESPONSE TO HUMAN AGGRESSION.	202	AGE DEMANDED	51
HUMAN REDUNDANCIES;	202	AGE DEMANDED	57
HUMANITY			
PRETEND HUMANITY OR DON THE FRAIL ATTIRE?	32	PARACELSUS	2

PAGE 197

HUMBLE -- I'

	PAGE	TITLE	LINE
HUMBLE			
AND HUMBLE EKE, THAT THE YOUNG ENGLISH KING	37	THE YOUNG KING	37
HUMMOCK			
OR MAY I INTER BENEATH THE HUMMOCK	213	SEXTUS PROP: 3	36
HUNDRED			
I HA' SEEN HIM DRIVE A HUNDRED MEN	33	GOODLY FERE	17
VINE-STRINGS A HUNDRED FEET LONG HANG DOWN FROM CARVED RAILINGS, ...	129	THE RIVER SONG	27
THREE HUNDRED AND SIXTY THOUSAND, ...	133	FRONTIER GUARD	16
AND THE WATER, A HUNDRED FEET DEEP, REFLECTING GREEN EYEBROWS	136	EXILE'S LETTER	56
THE HUNDRED CORDS OF MIST ARE SPREAD THROUGH	141	IDEA OF CHOAN	13
GOBBLED ALL THE LAND, AND HELD IT LATER FOR SOME HUNDRED YEARS.	151	NEAR PERIGORD	19
AND WE'VE THE GOSSIP (SKIPPED SIX HUNDRED YEARS)...	155	NEAR PERIGORD	138
"BUTTER REVIEWERS, FROM FIFTY TO THREE HUNDRED	194	MR. NIXON	10
SONG OF SIX HUNDRED M. P.'S	270	OF 600 M.P.'S	T
WE ARE SIX HUNDRED BEEFY MEN	270	OF 600 M.P.'S	9
HUNG			
SOME LADS GET HUNG, AND SOME GET SHOT.	43	MR. HOUSMAN	8
WITH SIX GREAT SAPPHIRES HUNG ALONG THE WALL, ...	49	OF SPLENDOUR	10
HUNG WITH HARD ICE-FLAKES, WHERE HAIL-SCUR FLEW,	64	THE SEAFARER	17
SADNESS HUNG OVER THE HOUSE, AND THE DESOLATED FEMALE ATTENDANTS	214	SEXTUS PROP: 4	22
I AM HUNG HERE, A SCARE-CROW FOR LOVERS.	226	SEXTUS PROP:11	3
HUNGER			
HEW MY HEART ROUND AND HUNGER BEGOT	64	THE SEAFARER	11
SAVE THAT I HAVE SUCH HUNGER FOR	106	DOMPNA POIS	63
HUNGRY			
SORROWFUL MINDS, SORROW IS STRONG, WE ARE HUNGRY AND THIRSTY.	127	BOWMEN OF SHU	7
WE GO SLOWLY, WE ARE HUNGRY AND THIRSTY, ...	127	BOWMEN OF SHU	23
HUNTED			
BEHOLD HERE VIDAL, THAT WAS HUNTED, FLAYED, ...	31	PIERE VIDAL	47
HUNTER			
A SILENT HUNTER OFF THE GREAT WHITE WAY, ...	245	MOYEN SENSUEL	200
HUNTERS			
FOURTEEN HUNTERS STILL EAT IN THE STABLES OF	97	THE BELLAIRES	11
HURL			
HURL ME INTO SUCH A MASS OF DIVERGENT IMPRESSIONS.	248	PIERROTS	28
HURLED			
THAT PARADISE IS HURLED TO NOTHINGNESS.	42	HER MONUMENT	48
HE HURLED HIMSELF INTO A SEA OF SIX WOMEN.	181	MOEURS CON: 6	2
HURRY			
AND THERE IS NO HURRY ABOUT IT;	207	SEXTUS PROP: 1	22
HURT			
I THINK SHE HURT ME ONCE, BUT	5	LA FRAISNE	46
THEY HURT ME. I GROW OLDER.	131	RIVER-MER WIFE	25
HUSBAND			
HER SECOND HUSBAND WILL NOT DIVORCE HER;	179	MOEURS CON: 2	5
WITH HER HUSBAND ASKING A REMISSION OF SENTENCE, .	230	SEXTUS PROP:12	61
HUSBANDS			
TOGETHER WITH THE RESPECTIVE WIVES, HUSBANDS, SISTERS AND HETEROGENEOUS CONNECTIONS OF THE GOOD BELLAIRES, ...	97	THE BELLAIRES	6
HUSHED			
SHE HATH HUSHED MY RANCOUR OF COUNCIL, ...	4	LA FRAISNE	17
HUSK			
AS NEW ALMONDS STRIPPED FROM THE HUSK.	91	DANCE FIGURE	13
HYRCANIAN			
NOT THE HYRCANIAN SEABOARD, NOT IN SEEKING THE SHORE OF EOS.	227	SEXTUS PROP:11	38
HYSTERIAS			
HYSTERIAS, TRENCH CONFESSIONS, ...	190	HUGH SELWYN: 4	26
I (610)			
I.			
(I. E. THESE SONGS).	81	TENZONE	2
I'			
"CAT'S I' THE WATER BUTT!" THOUGHT'S IN YOUR VERSE-BARREL, ...	13	MESMERISM	5

IBYCUS -- IF

	PAGE	TITLE	LINE
IBYCUS			
ERI MEN HAI TE KUDONIAI--IBYCUS.	87	THE SPRING	EPI
ICE			
FELT HANDS TURN ICE A-SUDDEN, TOUCHING YE,	41	HER MONUMENT	17
AND FRESHETS ARE BURSTING THEIR ICE	138	NEAR SHOKU	8
ICE-COLD			
LIST HOW I, CARE-WRETCHED, ON ICE-COLD SEA,	64	THE SEAFARER	14
AND ICE-COLD WAVE, AT WHILES THE SWAN CRIES,	64	THE SEAFARER	19
ICED			
AND GIVES YOU AUSTRALIAN ICED RABBITS' MEAT	263	ALF'S EIGHTH	18
ICE-FLAKES			
HUNG WITH HARD ICE-FLAKES, WHERE HAIL-SCUR FLEW,	64	THE SEAFARER	17
ICH			
MACH' ICH DIE KLEINEN LIEDER	97	THE BELLAIRES	EPI
ICUMMEN			
WINTER IS ICUMMEN IN,	116	ANCIENT MUSIC	1
ICY			
IN ICY FEATHERS; FULL OFT THE EAGLE SCREAMED	64	THE SEAFARER	24
I'D (7)			
IDA			
IDA HAS LAIN WITH A SHEPHERD, SHE HAS SLEPT BETWEEN SHEEP.	227	SEXTUS PROP:11	36
IDALIA			
SINCE ADONIS WAS GORED IN IDALIA, AND THE CYTHAREAN	219	SEXTUS PROP: 6	33
IDEA			
OLD IDEA OF CHOAN BY ROSORIU	141	IDEA OF CHOAN	T
AN IDEA BETWEEN 'EM	258	ALF'S SECOND	12
IDEALS			
THEY HELD THE VERY MARROW OF THE IDEALS	241	MOYEN SENSUEL	95
IDEAS			
IDEAS, OLD GOSSIP, ODDMENTS OF ALL THINGS,	61	PORTRAIT FEMME	4
POETRY, HER BORDER OF IDEAS,	196	HUGH SELWIN:12	13
·IDENTICAL			
THIS IDENTICAL PHRASE:	97	AESTHETICS	20
YOU WILL SAY THAT YOU SUCCUMBED TO A DANGER IDENTICAL,	222	SEXTUS PROP: 8	30
CHARMINGLY IDENTICAL, WITH SEMELE'S,	222	SEXTUS PROP: 8	31
IDENTITY			
THINKS ONE IDENTITY IS	244	MOYEN SENSUEL	173
IDIOM			
IS "ZUT! CINQUE LETTRES!" A BANISHED GALLIC IDIOM,	239	MOYEN SENSUEL	36
IDIOT			
SAID THEN "YOU IDIOT! WHAT ARE YOU DOING WITH THAT WATER:	210	SEXTUS PROP: 2	17
ESCAPE! THERE IS, O IDIOT, NO ESCAPE,	226	SEXTUS PROP:11	4
IDLE			
YOU ARE VERY IDLE, MY SONGS.	94	INSTRUCTIONS	3
IDOLS			
IDOLS AND AMBERGRIS AND RARE INLAYS,	61	PORTRAIT FEMME	23
IEU			
IEU LO SAI."	166	FISH & SHADOW	17
IF			
(SKOAL! WITH THE DREGS IF THE CLEAR BE GONE!)	10	FOR THIS YULE	7
AH-EH! HE MUST BE RARE IF EVEN I HAVE NOT . . ."	15	FAMAM CANO	43
AND IF WHEN I AM DEAD	22	MARVOIL	23
AYE, YE, ARE FOOLS, IF YE THINK TIME CAN BLOT	30	PIERE VIDAL	18
IF THEY THINK THEY HA' SNARED OUR GOODLY FERE	33	GOODLY FERE	25
IF THEY THINK THEY HA' SLAIN OUR GOODLY FERE	34	GOODLY FERE	51
IF ALL THE GRIEF AND WOE AND BITTERNESS,	36	THE YOUNG KING	1
A LIQUID GLORY? IF AT SIRMIO,	39	BLANDULA	5
SOUL, IF SHE MEET US THERE, WILL ANY RUMOUR	39	BLANDULA	13
TURNS HARDY PILOT . . . AND IF ONE WRONG NOTE	42	HER MONUMENT	45
IF THOU ART	42	HER MONUMENT	50
YET IF THOU ART	42	HER MONUMENT	53
WHAT IF I KNOW THY SPEECHES WORD BY WORD?	43	SATIEMUS	1
AND IF THOU KNEW'ST I KNEW THEM WOULDST THOU SPEAK?	43	SATIEMUS	2
WHAT IF I KNOW THY SPEECHES WORD BY WORD,	43	SATIEMUS	3
THEREFORE LET US ACT AS IF WE WERE	43	MR. HOUSMAN	4
WHAT IF MY THOUGHTS WERE TURNED IN THEIR MID REACH	43	SATIEMUS	9
HOW IF THE LOW DEAR SOUND WITHIN THY THROAT	43	SATIEMUS	14
WHAT IF I KNOW THY LAUGHTER WORD BY WORD	43	SATIEMUS	18

PAGE 199

IF

	PAGE	TITLE	LINE
IF (CONTINUED)			
I KNOW NOT IF THE LOVE OR IF THE LAY WERE BETTER STUFF,	44	FROM HEINE: 2	7
I KNOW NOT IF THE LOVE OR IF THE LAY WERE BETTER STUFF,	44	FROM HEINE: 2	7
IF MY HEART STAY BELOW THERE,	47	FROM HEINE: 7	21
IF I HAVE MERGED MY SOUL, OR UTTERLY	51	THE FLAME	32
IF THOU HAST SEEN MY SHADE SANS CHARACTER,	51	THE FLAME	39
IF THOU HAST SEEN THAT MIRROR OF ALL MOMENTS,	51	THE FLAME	40
WHAT IF THE WIND HAVE TURNED AGAINST THE RAIN?	59	SILET	10
NEITHER COULD I PLAY UPON ANY REED IF I HAD ONE.	62	N. Y.	7
AS IF THE SNOW SHOULD HESITATE	74	THE RETURN	7
AS IF HE HAD JUST DISCOVERED IT.	82	THE CONDOLENCE	16
(OR WITH TWO LIGHT FEET, IF IT PLEASE YOU!)	86	SALUTATION 2ND	18
ON THE CONTRARY, IF THEY DO NOT BELONG TO HIS WIFE,	98	THE BELLAIRES	16
"LET HER, IF SHE WANTS ME, TAKE ME."	100	ARIDES	7
IF SHE DOES NOT COUNT THIS BLESSED	103	PHYLLIDULA	4
JOY SO RICH, AND IF I FIND NOT EVER	105	DOMPNA POIS	7
BUT IF YOU MOVE OR SPEAK	109	THE FAUN	7
(IF GLORY COULD LAST FOREVER	129	THE RIVER SONG	17
IF YOU ARE COMING DOWN THROUGH THE NARROWS OF THE RIVER KIANG,	131	RIVER-MER WIFE	26
IF ONLY THEY COULD BE OF THAT FELLOWSHIP,	134	EXILE'S LETTER	10
AND IF YOU ASK HOW I REGRET THAT PARTING:	136	EXILE'S LETTER	72
AND IT IS DOUBTFUL IF EVEN YOUR MANURE WILL BE RICH ENOUGH	146	MONUMENTUM AER	7
IF YOU'D HAVE ME GO ON LOVING YOU	167	OF AROUET	15
AND IF NOW WE CAN'T FIT WITH OUR TIME OF LIFE	168	OF AROUET	23
IF THOU COME NOT, THE COST BE ON THY HEAD.	172	LANGUE D'OC: 1	16
IF ALL THE WORLD BE IN DESPITE	174	LANGUE D'OC: 3	14
IF SHE WON'T HAVE ME NOW, DEATH IS MY PORTION,	175	LANGUE D'OC: 3	37
JOY I HAVE NONE, IF SHE MAKE ME NOT MAD	175	LANGUE D'OC: 3	44
GOOD IS IT TO ME IF SHE FLOUT	175	LANGUE D'OC: 3	46
"OH! ABELARD!" AS IF THE TOPIC	181	MOEURS CON: 7	8
IF THE CLASSICS HAD A WIDE CIRCULATION	183	CANTICO SOLE	2
IF THE CLASSICS HAD A WIDE CIRCULATION	183	CANTICO SOLE	7
IF THE CLASSICS HAD A WIDE CIRCULATION . . .	183	CANTICO SOLE	15
"EVEN IF YOU HAVE TO WORK FREE.	194	MR. NIXON	9
THUS, IF HER COLOUR	201	AGE DEMANDED	9
TEMPERED AS IF	201	AGE DEMANDED	11
A BASKET-WORK OF BRAIDS WHICH SEEM AS IF THEY WERE	204	MEDALLION	10
IF HOMER HAD NOT STATED YOUR CASE!	208	SEXTUS PROP: 1	34
YET IF I POSTPONE MY OBEDIENCE	212	SEXTUS PROP: 3	9
IF ANY MAN WOULD BE A LOVER	212	SEXTUS PROP: 3	17
WHAT IF UNDERTAKERS FOLLOW MY TRACK,	213	SEXTUS PROP: 3	28
NOW IF EVER IT IS TIME TO CLEANSE HELICON;	216	SEXTUS PROP: 5	1
IF I HAVE NOT THE FACULTY, "THE BARE ATTEMPT WOULD BE PRAISE-WORTHY."	216	SEXTUS PROP: 5	4
IF ANY LAND SHRINK INTO A DISTANT SEACOAST,	216	SEXTUS PROP: 5	19
IF SHE WITH IVORY FINGERS DRIVE A TUNE THROUGH THE LYRE,	217	SEXTUS PROP: 5	27
HOW EASY THE MOVING FINGERS; IF HAIR IS MUSSED ON HER FOREHEAD,	217	SEXTUS PROP: 5	29
IF SHE GOES IN A GLEAM OF COS, IN A SLITHER OF DYED STUFF,	217	SEXTUS PROP: 5	30
THERE IS A VOLUME IN THE MATTER; IF HER EYELIDS SINK INTO SLEEP,	217	SEXTUS PROP: 5	31
AND IF SHE PLAYS WITH ME WITH HER SHIRT OFF,	217	SEXTUS PROP: 5	33
THUS MUCH THE FATES HAVE ALLOTTED ME, AND IF, MAECENAS,	217	SEXTUS PROP: 5	37
IF SHE CONFER SUCH NIGHTS UPON ME,	221	SEXTUS PROP: 7	37
IF SHE GIVE ME MANY,	221	SEXTUS PROP: 7	39
WHAT IF YOUR FATES ARE ACCELERATED,	222	SEXTUS PROP: 8	27
IF THE YOUNG LADY IS TAKEN?	222	SEXTUS PROP: 8	41
I SHALL LIVE, IF SHE CONTINUE IN LIFE,	223	SEXTUS PROP: 9	8
IF SHE DIES, I SHALL GO WITH HER.	223	SEXTUS PROP: 9	9
AND IT WAS MORNING, AND I WANTED TO SEE IF SHE WAS ALONE, AND RESTING,	225	SEXTUS PROP:10	27
FLEE IF YOU LIKE INTO RANAUS,	226	SEXTUS PROP:11	5
NOR IF THE THUNDER FALL FROM PREDESTINATION;	228	SEXTUS PROP:12	29

IF -- IMAGE

	PAGE	TITLE	LINE
IF (CONTINUED)			
I WOULD MAKE VERSE IN YOUR FASHION, IF SHE SHOULD COMMAND IT,	229	SEXTUS PROP:12	60
"IN THE STUDIO" AND THESE TWO PORTRAITS, IF I HAD MY CHOICE!	235	TO WHISTLER	8
STILL I'D RESPECT YOU MORE IF YOU COULD BURY	239	MOYEN SENSUEL	27
IF I SET FORTH A BAWDY PLOT LIKE BYRON	239	MOYEN SENSUEL	42
THAN IF I TREAT THE NATION AS A WHOLE.	239	MOYEN SENSUEL	43
BY NAME, IF NAMED." SO IT WAS PHRASED, OR RATHER SOMEWHAT SO	242	MOYEN SENSUEL	114
YOU CAN NOT GET CHEAP BOOKS, EVEN IF YOU NEED 'EM).	246	MOYEN SENSUEL	218
OR IF A MAN HAVE MIGHT	248	DONNA MI PREGA	17
IF YOU GIT OFF THE EMBANKMENT.	263	ALF'S EIGHTH	21
AND IF THE PAPERS SELDOM SANG HIS PRAISE,	265	ALF'S NINTH	23
AND WONDER IF MY DAY'S THREE AND EIGHT-PENCE	268	ANOTHER BIT	11
IF I HAD MORE GRUB TO EAT.	269	SAFE AND SOUND	24
OR ASKED US IF THE COW	272	THE BABY	4
OR IF THE COW REFRAINS FROM FOOD	272	THE BABY	7
'IGH			
I SEE THEIR 'IGH 'ATS ON THE SEATS	270	OF 600 M.P.'S	13
IGNORANCE			
THEIR DODDERING IGNORANCE IS WAXED SO NOTABLE	239	MOYEN SENSUEL	37
FOR IGNORANCE, ITS GROWTH AND ITS PROTECTION	241	MOYEN SENSUEL	70
IGNORANT			
RADWAY WAS IGNORANT AS AN EDITOR,	246	MOYEN SENSUEL	219
WHO HAS THE PHRASE "AS IGNORANT AS AN ACTOR."	246	MOYEN SENSUEL	222
IL			
"SE IL COR TI MANCA," BUT IT FAILED THEE NOT!	19	FOR E. MCC	12
IL ETAIT COMME UN TOUT PETIT GARCON	181	MOEURS CON: 7	3
ILIAD			
FOR A MUCH LARGER ILIAD IS IN THE COURSE OF CONSTRUCTION	229	SEXTUS PROP:12	38
ILIADS			
WE SHALL CONSTRUCT MANY ILIADS.	217	SEXTUS PROP: 5	34
ILIAN			
HE THRILLS TO ILIAN ARMS,	228	SEXTUS PROP:12	33
ILION			
SMALL TALK O ILION, AND O TROAD	208	SEXTUS PROP: 1	32
ILL			
THOUGH THOU WELL DOST WISH ME ILL	8	NA AUDIART	1
YEA THOUGH THOU WISH ME ILL,	9	NA AUDIART	33
AND BADE HER BE OUT WITH ILL ADDRESS	11	OF THE GIBBET	11
ALL DOLOUR, ILL AND EVERY EVIL CHANCE	36	THE YOUNG KING	2
WISH ME ILL,	106	DOMPNA POIS	42
MY ILL DOTH SHE TURN SWEET.	175	LANGUE D'OC: 3	10
AND SHE SPEAKS ILL OF LIGHT WOMEN,	218	SEXTUS PROP: 5	61
I'LL			
"OR I'LL SEE YE DAMNED," SAYS HE.	33	GOODLY FERE	8
"I'LL GO TO THE FEAST," QUO' OUR GOODLY FERE,	33	GOODLY FERE	27
I'LL HAVE NO OTHER LOVE AT ANY COST.	105	DOMPNA POIS	10
DESPITE SUCH REINS AND CHECKS I'LL DO MY BEST,	238	MOYEN SENSUEL	12
IN ENGLAND? I'LL SAY YES!	267	ALF'S ELEVENTH	22
ILLA			
LESBIA ILLA	102	LADIES	ST
ILLE			
"PHASELLUS ILLE"	63	PHASELLUS ILLE	T
ILLUSIONS			
"POOR DEAR! HE HAS LOST HIS ILLUSIONS."	85	SALUTATION 2ND	15
ILS			
ILS M'ONT SALUE	160	DANS OMNIBUS	5
ILSENSTEIN			
IN ILSENSTEIN I FARE,	47	FROM HEINE: 7	2
ILZA			
I AM THE PRINCESS ILZA	47	FROM HEINE: 7	1
I'M (1)			
IMAGE			
EVEN AS I KEEP HER IMAGE IN MY HEART HERE.	23	MARVOIL	48
HER MONUMENT, THE IMAGE CUT THEREON	41	HER MONUMENT	T
STANDETH THIS IMAGE OF THE BEAUTY SPED.	41	HER MONUMENT	9
AN IMAGE OF LETHE,	107	COMING OF WAR	1
IMAGE FROM D'ORLEANS	111	IMAGE ORLEANS	T

PAGE 201

IMAGE -- IMPORTANCE

	PAGE	TITLE	LINE
IMAGE (CONTINUED)			
KEEP SMALL WITH REVERENCE, BEHOLDING HER IMAGE. ...	164	QUINTUS SEPTIM	7
THE AGE DEMANDED AN IMAGE	188	HUGH SELWYN: 2	1
HEADLAM FOR UPLIFT; IMAGE IMPARTIALLY IMBUED	193	SIENA MI FE	14
ORGIES OF VINTAGES, AN EARTHERN IMAGE OF SILENUS	211	SEXTUS PROP: 2	29
IMAGERY			
OF HIS IMAGERY.	201	AGE DEMANDED	20
IMAGES			
"THESE ARE YOUR IMAGES, AND FROM YOU THE SORCERIZING			
OF SHUT-IN YOUNG LADIES, ...	211	SEXTUS PROP: 2	50
BEARING ANCESTRAL LARES AND IMAGES;	219	SEXTUS PROP: 6	14
IMAGINARY			
LEFT HIM DELIGHTED WITH THE IMAGINARY	202	AGE DEMANDED	44
IMAGINATION			
SOME FOR LOVE OF SLAUGHTER, IN IMAGINATION, ...	190	HUGH SELWYN: 4	8
IMAGINE			
IMAGINE IT, MY FELLOW SUFFERERS--	82	THE CONDOLENCE	4
NONE CAN IMAGINE LOVE	250	DONNA MI PREGA	62
IMAGINING			
IS LIKE TO HEAVEN'S MOST 'LIVE IMAGINING.	41	HER MONUMENT	24
IMBECILES			
AND AGAINST THIS SEA OF IMBECILES--	99	SALVATIONISTS	16
IMBUED			
HEADLAM FOR UPLIFT; IMAGE IMPARTIALLY IMBUED	193	SIENA MI FE	14
IMITATE			
AND YEARNED TO IMITATE THE WALDORF CAPERS	241	MOYEN SENSUEL	92
IMITATING			
AND YOU WILL NOT LEAVE OFF IMITATING AESCHYLUS. ...	228	SEXTUS PROP:12	20
IMITATION			
WHY DOES THE SMALL CHILD IN THE SOILED-WHITE			
IMITATION FUR COAT	114	SIMULACRA	3
IMMEDIATE			
HE MADE NO IMMEDIATE APPLICATION	201	AGE DEMANDED	13
IMMERSES			
WHOM HEAVENLY JOY IMMERSES, ...	45	FROM HEINE: 4	2
IMMORAL			
THAT FIRST MADE HIM BELIEVE IN IMMORAL SUASION. ...	245	MOYEN SENSUEL	198
IMMORTAL			
BY THE IMMORTAL NATURE ON THIS QUICKSAND, ...	41	HER MONUMENT	30
DRINK OUR IMMORTAL MOMENTS; WE "PASS THROUGH."	50	THE FLAME	6
WHEN I BEHOLD HOW BLACK, IMMORTAL INK	59	SILET	1
AND YOU MAY DECLINE TO MAKE THEM IMMORTAL, ...	99	SALVATIONISTS	7
TE VOILA, MON BOURRIENNE, YOU ALSO SHALL BE IMMORTAL.	101	AMITIES	6
IMMORTALITY			
HOW I 'SCAPED IMMORTALITY.	15	FAMAM CANO	48
IMMORTALS			
TO SEE YOUR FORTY SELF-BAPTIZED IMMORTALS, ...	239	MOYEN SENSUEL	32
IMPALPABLE			
ON TRIUNE AZURES, THE IMPALPABLE	39	BLANDULA	11
IMPARTIALLY			
HEADLAM FOR UPLIFT; IMAGE IMPARTIALLY IMBUED	193	SIENA MI FE	14
IMPECCABLE			
OF BRENNBAUM "THE IMPECCABLE."	193	BRENNBAUM	8
IMPERCEPTIBLE			
BRING THE IMPERCEPTIBLE COOL.	76	THE ALCHEMIST	48
IMPERFECTIONS			
AND CURIOUS IMPERFECTIONS OF ODOR.	104	THE SEEING EYE	3
IMPERIAL			
FAN-PIECE, FOR HER IMPERIAL LORD	108	FAN-PIECE	T
THE IMPERIAL GUARDS COME FORTH FROM THE GOLDEN HOUSE			
WITH THEIR ARMOUR A-GLEAMING.	129	THE RIVER SONG	34
WHO HAS BROUGHT THE FLAMING IMPERIAL ANGER?	133	FRONTIER GUARD	11
(AND TO IMPERIAL ORDER)	229	SEXTUS PROP:12	39
IMPERTINENT			
GO WITH AN IMPERTINENT FROLIC!	86	SALUTATION 2ND	20
IMPETUOUS			
IMPETUOUS TROUBLING	201	AGE DEMANDED	19
IMPLIED			
AND BOTTICELLIAN SPRAYS IMPLIED	200	MAUBERLEY: 2	28
IMPORTANCE			
NOR ANYTHING ELSE OF IMPORTANCE.	228	SEXTUS PROP:12	30

IMPRESSIONS -- INDIFFERENT

	PAGE	TITLE	LINE
IMPRESSIONS			
IMPRESSIONS OF FRANCOIS-MARIE AROUET (DE VOLTAIRE)	167	OF AROUET	T
HURL ME INTO SUCH A MASS OF DIVERGENT IMPRESSIONS.	248	PIERROTS	28
IMPUDENT			
GO, LITTLE NAKED AND IMPUDENT SONGS,	85	SALUTATION 2ND	16
IMPULSE			
AND TRY TO WRENCH HER IMPULSE INTO ART.	235	TO WHISTLER	13
IN (651)			
INANE			
AND THERE ARE ALSO THE INANE EXPENSES OF THE FUNERAL;	164	QUINTUS SEPTIM	9
FOR I AM SWELLED UP WITH INANE PLEASURABILITIES ...	214	SEXTUS PROP: 4	5
YOU DO NOTHING, YOU PLOT INANE SCHEMES AGAINST ME,	226	SEXTUS PROP:11	14
IN'ARDS			
BUT GOD! WHAT A SIGHT YOU HA' GOT O' OUR IN'ARDS,	13	MESMERISM	10
INAUDIBLY			
WALK DOWN LONGACRE RECITING SWINBURNE TO HERSELF, INAUDIBLY?	114	SIMULACRA	2
INCANDESCENCE			
YOUR EYES! SINCE I LOST THEIR INCANDESCENCE	247	PIERROTS	1
INCAPABLE			
IS INCAPABLE OF PRODUCING A LASTING NIRVANA.	148	FRATRES MINORE	7
INCAPABLE OF THE LEAST UTTERANCE OR COMPOSITION,	202	AGE DEMANDED	46
INCENSE			
THE SMOKE OF INCENSE	169	PHANOPOEIA	2
INCENSED			
"THAT INCENSED FEMALE HAS CONSIGNED HIM TO OUR PLEASURE."	224	SEXTUS PROP:10	12
INCH			
BORED TO AN INCH OF EXTINCTION,	22	MARVOIL	17
INCONSCIENT			
HE HAD PASSED, INCONSCIENT, FULL GAZE,	200	MAUBERLEY: 2	26
INCONSEQUENCE			
OF THE SOCIAL INCONSEQUENCE.	201	AGE DEMANDED	8
INCONTINENT			
AMIABLE AND HARMONIOUS PEOPLE ARE PUSHED INCONTINENT INTO DUELS,	227	SEXTUS PROP:12	5
INCONVENIENT			
AND ASK INCONVENIENT QUEERIES.	273	NATIONAL SONG	16
INCREASES			
SEEING THAT LONG STANDING INCREASES ALL THINGS	207	SEXTUS PROP: 1	24
INCUBATE			
WAS MADE TO INCUBATE SUCH MEDIOCRITIES,	239	MOYEN SENSUEL	24
INCUBUS			
"NO INCUBUS HAS CRUSHED HIS BODY AGAINST ME,	225	SEXTUS PROP:10	39
INCULTUS			
ISTE FUIT VIR INCULTUS,	101	AMITIES	17
INCUMBENT			
NO SIGNS OF A SECOND INCUMBENT.	225	SEXTUS PROP:10	37
INDEBTED			
FROM LAWYERS TO WHOM NO ONE WAS INDEBTED,	98	THE BELLAIRES	31
WERE UNCERTAIN WHO WAS SUPPOSED TO BE INDEBTED TO THEM.	98	THE BELLAIRES	33
INDECOROUS			
SPEAK OF THE INDECOROUS CONDUCT OF THE GODS!	86	SALUTATION 2ND	30
WHO SO INDECOROUS AS TO SHED THE PURE GORE OF A SUITOR?!	212	SEXTUS PROP: 3	26
THERE IS SONG IN THE PARCHMENT; CATULLUS THE HIGHLY INDECOROUS,	230	SEXTUS PROP:12	68
INDEFINITE			
HER AMBITION IS VAGUE AND INDEFINITE,	179	MOEURS CON: 2	10
INDEMNITY			
MY OLD MAN GOT NO INDEMNITY	263	ALF'S EIGHTH	24
INDETERMINATE			
I SHALL TRIUMPH AMONG YOUNG LADIES OF INDETERMINATE CHARACTER,	229	SEXTUS PROP:12	55
INDIA			
AND IT IS, I THINK, INDIA WHICH NOW GIVES NECKS TO YOUR TRIUMPH,"	216	SEXTUS PROP: 5	17
CAESAR PLOTS AGAINST INDIA,	219	SEXTUS PROP: 6	6
INDIFFERENT			
INDIFFERENT AND DISCOURAGED HE THOUGHT HE MIGHT AS	100	ARIDES	4

INDIRECTNESS -- INNOCENT

	PAGE	TITLE	LINE
INDIRECTNESS			
WOUNDED BY YOUR INDIRECTNESS IN THESE SITUATIONS	247	PIERROTS	8
INDISCERNIBLE			
THOUGH FROM HER FACE INDISCERNIBLE;	250	DONNA MI PREGA	79
INDISCRETION			
WILL COMMIT THAT INDISCRETION.	83	THE GARDEN	12
INDIVIDUAL			
TO THE INDIVIDUAL, THE MONTH WAS MORE TEMPERATE ...	201	AGE DEMANDED	15
INDOLENT			
BETWEEN THE TWO INDOLENT CANDLES.	87	ALBATRE	7
INDUSTRY			
HAVE CONSTRUCTED WITH SUCH INDUSTRY	210	SEXTUS PROP: 2	4
SHALL BE YAWNED OUT ON MY LYRE--WITH SUCH INDUSTRY.	210	SEXTUS PROP: 2	5
INEPTITUDES			
HIS INEPTITUDES	178	MOEURS CON: 1	7
INEXPLICABLE			
AND OBSERVE ITS INEXPLICABLE CORRELATIONS.	104	THE SEEING EYE	7
INFAMY			
HOME TO OLD LIES AND NEW INFAMY;	190	HUGH SELWYN: 4	17
AND EVEN THIS INFAMY WOULD NOT ATTRACT NUMEROUS READERS	230	SEXTUS PROP:12	62
INFANT			
FROM THE STATUE OF THE INFANT CHRIST IN SANTA MARIA NOVELLA,	94	INSTRUCTIONS	20
IS AN INFANT, AGED ABOUT 14 MONTHS,	180	MOEURS CON: 5	11
THE INFANT BEAMS AT THE PARENT,	180	MOEURS CON: 5	12
AN ART! YOU ALL RESPECT THE ARTS, FROM THAT INFANT TICK	239	MOYEN SENSUEL	13
ARE NOT THE BEST OF PULSE FOR INFANT NATIONS.	239	MOYEN SENSUEL	30
INFANTS			
OF THE FILTHY, STURDY, UNKILLABLE INFANTS OF THE VERY POOR.	83	THE GARDEN	6
INFANT'S			
THE CIRCULAR INFANT'S FACE,	193	BRENNBAUM	2
INFECTION			
WHO WROUGHT ABOUT HIS "SOUL" THEIR STALE INFECTION.	241	MOYEN SENSUEL	81
INFERNAL			
AFTER WE CROSS THE INFERNAL RIPPLES,	228	SEXTUS PROP:12	28
INFERNO			
INFERNO, 28, 125	157	NEAR PERIGORD	EPI
WITHOUT AN INFERNO, WITHOUT ACHILLES ATTENDED OF GODS,	218	SEXTUS PROP: 5	51
INFEST			
"IT IS A MORAL NATION WE INFEST."	238	MOYEN SENSUEL	11
INFINITE			
INFINITE THINGS DESIRED, LOFTY VISIONS	42	HER MONUMENT	41
INFLUENCE			
HAVE INFLUENCE WITH THE PRESS.	268	ANOTHER BIT	8
INGRESS			
A ROSY PATH, A SORT OF VERNAL INGRESS,	243	MOYEN SENSUEL	145
INHALED			
AS HE INHALED THE STILL FUMES OF RICE-POWDER.	243	MOYEN SENSUEL	132
INHERIT			
THEY SHALL INHERIT THE EARTH.	83	THE GARDEN	7
INK			
WHEN I BEHOLD HOW BLACK, IMMORTAL INK	59	SILET	1
INLAYS			
IDOLS AND AMBERGRIS AND RARE INLAYS,	61	PORTRAIT FEMME	23
INMOST			
OF LOVE, AND JOY THAT IS LOVE'S INMOST PART,	45	FROM HEINE: 5	10
AND SO FORTH, AUGUSTUS. "VIRGIN ARABIA SHAKES IN HER INMOST DWELLING."	216	SEXTUS PROP: 5	18
INN			
ME! IN THIS DAMN'D INN OF AVIGNON,	22	MARVOIL	19
WITH A GARRULOUS OLD MAN AT THE INN.	121	PROVINC DESERT	20
INNER			
YOU DO NOT EVEN EXPRESS OUR INNER NOBILITIES,	94	INSTRUCTIONS	
INNOCENT			
AND INNOCENT OF STENDHAL, FLAUBERT, MAUPASSANT AND FIELDING.	240	MOYEN SENSUEL	5

PAGE 204

INNOCUOUS -- INTENTIONS

	PAGE	TITLE	LINE
INNOCUOUS			
AND TIMOROUS LOVE OF THE INNOCUOUS	240	MOYEN SENSUEL	63
INN-YARD			
THE WILLOWS OF THE INN-YARD	137	OF DEPARTURE	EPI
INO			
INO IN HER YOUNG DAYS FLED PELLMELL OUT OF THEBES,	222	SEXTUS PROP: 8	21
INSANITY			
AND TALK OF INSANITY AND GENIUS,	145	SALUTATION 3RD	24
INSCRIPTIO			
HORAE BEATAE INSCRIPTIO	51	HORAE BEATAE	T
INSCRIPTION			
GIVE THAT MUCH INSCRIPTION	219	SEXTUS PROP: 6	28
INSIDE			
OR TURN ME INSIDE OUT, AND ABOUT.	175	LANGUE D'OC: 3	47
NEVER THE MAN INSIDE	258	ALF'S THIRD	5
INSIDIOUS			
LURKING, SERPENTINE, AMPHIBIOUS AND INSIDIOUS	244	MOYEN SENSUEL	170
INSOLENT			
INSOLENT LITTLE BEASTS, SHAMELESS, DEVOID OF CLOTHING!	94	INSTRUCTIONS	14
LET COME THE GAY OF MANNER, THE INSOLENT AND THE EXULTING.	146	CANTILATIONS	10
INSPECT			
THE EMPEROR IN HIS JEWELLED CAR GOES OUT TO INSPECT HIS FLOWERS,	129	THE RIVER SONG	35
AND START TO INSPECT SOME FURTHER PYRAMID;	236	MIDDLE-AGED	7
INSPECTING			
ONE OF THOSE FIRM-FACED INSPECTING WOMEN, WHO	243	MOYEN SENSUEL	156
INSPECTOR			
"YOU ARE A VERY EARLY INSPECTOR OF MISTRESSES.	225	SEXTUS PROP:10	34
WHY PAINT THESE DAYS? AN INSURANCE INSPECTOR	243	MOYEN SENSUEL	151
INSPIRING			
RADWAY? MY HERO, FOR IT WILL BE MORE INSPIRING	239	MOYEN SENSUEL	41
INSTALL			
OR INSTALL ME IN ANY PROFESSION	117	THE LAKE ISLE	14
INSTANTLY			
INSTANTLY	42	HER MONUMENT	47
INSTEAD			
INSTEAD OF BEING A CARTER?	268	ANOTHER BIT	16
INSTINCT			
NO INSTINCT HAS SURVIVED IN HER	195	HUGH SELWIN:11	6
INSTRUCT			
MY MUSE IS EAGER TO INSTRUCT ME IN A NEW GAMUT, OR GAMBETTO,	216	SEXTUS PROP: 5	11
INSTRUCTIONS			
FURTHER INSTRUCTIONS	94	INSTRUCTIONS	T
INSTRUMENTS			
MANY INSTRUMENTS, LIKE THE SOUND OF YOUNG PHOENIX BROODS.	135	EXILE'S LETTER	27
INSUBSTANTIAL			
OF INSUBSTANTIAL MANNA,	202	AGE DEMANDED	53
INSURANCE			
WHY PAINT THESE DAYS? AN INSURANCE INSPECTOR	243	MOYEN SENSUEL	151
INTAGLIO			
OR TAKE THE INTAGLIO, MY FAT GREAT-UNCLE'S HEIRLOOM;	162	CABARET DANCER	35
INTANGIBLE			
FLUIDS INTANGIBLE THAT HAVE BEEN MEN,	32	PARACELSUS	10
INTELLECT			
TAKETH IN LATENT INTELLECT--	249	DONNA MI PREGA	25
INTELLIGENT			
INTELLIGENT MEN CAME DRIFTING IN FROM THE SEA AND FROM THE WEST BORDER,	134	EXILE'S LETTER	6
INTENDED			
LEUCIS, WHO INTENDED A GRAND PASSION,	99	EPITAPH	1
INTENT			
AND WHO ARE WE, WHO KNOW THAT LAST INTENT,	59	SILET	12
INTENTION			
MAINTAINS INTENTION REASON'S PEER AND MATE;	249	DONNA MI PREGA	37
INTENTIONS			
SO HE "FACED LIFE" WITH RATHER MIXED INTENTIONS,	242	MOYEN SENSUEL	101

INTER -- IONE

	PAGE	TITLE	LINE
INTER			
OR MAY I INTER BENEATH THE HUMMOCK	213	SEXTUS PROP: 3	36
INTEREST			
YOU ARE A PERSON OF SOME INTEREST, ONE COMES TO YOU	61	PORTRAIT FEMME	14
TO THOSE WHO HAVE LOST THEIR INTEREST.	89	COMMISSION	27
INTERFERES			
LOVE INTERFERES WITH FIDELITIES;	227	SEXTUS PROP:12	2
INTERLARDING			
HIS PHRASES INTERLARDING, ...	267	ALF'S TWELFTH	8
INTERMENT			
YOU MAY FIND INTERMENT PLEASING, ...	222	SEXTUS PROP: 8	29
INTERMITTENCES			
OF INTERMITTENCES;	203	MAUBERLEY: 4	17
INTERPOSES			
"TIME FOR THAT QUESTION!" FRONT BENCH INTERPOSES.	260	ALF'S FIFTH	16
INTERRUPTING			
AND THE WIND LIFTING THE SONG, AND INTERRUPTING IT,	136	EXILE'S LETTER	61
INTIMATE			
I HAVE BEEN INTIMATE WITH THEE, KNOWN THY WAYS. ...	60	TOMB AKR CAAR	21
INTO (64)			
INTOLERANT			
GO, MY SONGS, SEEK YOUR PRAISE FROM THE YOUNG AND			
FROM THE INTOLERANT, ...	95	ITE	1
INTOXICATED			
AND INTOXICATED, ...	224	SEXTUS PROP:10	2
INTRACTABLE			
FROM METAL, OR INTRACTABLE AMBER;	204	MEDALLION	12
INTRIGUE			
IS IT AN INTRIGUE TO RUN SUBTLY OUT, ...	153	NEAR PERIGORD	82
INVARIOUS			
'TIS BUT A VAGUE, INVARIOUS DELIGHT	236	MIDDLE-AGED	1
INVESTIGATION			
HAVE STARTED A INVESTIGATION	268	ANOTHER BIT	3
INVIDIOUS			
"AS FREE OF MOBS AS KINGS"? I'D HAVE MEN FREE OF			
THAT INVIDIOUS, ...	244	MOYEN SENSUEL	169
INVIGORATING			
SUCH ANIMAL INVIGORATING CARRIAGE	245	MOYEN SENSUEL	191
INVIOLABLE			
INVIOLABLE.	74	THE RETURN	11
INVIOLATE			
ROUGH FROM THE VIRGIN FORESTS INVIOLATE, ...	264	ALF'S NINTH	10
INVISIBLE			
THE PURRING OF THE INVISIBLE ANTENNAE	113	TAME CAT	6
INVITATION			
INVITATION, MERE INVITATION TO PERCEPTIVITY	201	AGE DEMANDED	25
INVITATION, MERE INVITATION TO PERCEPTIVITY	201	AGE DEMANDED	25
THE INVITATION HAD NO NEED OF FINE AESTHETIC, ...	242	MOYEN SENSUEL	127
INVITES			
GUIDO INVITES YOU THUS	25	GUIDO INVITES	1
INVOLUTE			
THE WIRE-LIKE BANDS OF COLOUR INVOLUTE MOUNT FROM MY			
FINGERS;	170	PHANOPOEIA	17
INWARD			
OF THE INWARD GAZE;	188	HUGH SELWYN: 2	6
INWOVEN			
HER GOLD IS SPREAD, ABOVE, AROUND, INWOVEN;	49	OF SPLENDOUR	
STRANDS OF LIGHT INWOVEN ABOUT IT, LOVELIEST	68	APPARUIT	1
IO			
IO! IO! TAMUZ!	110	TEMPORA	
IO! IO! TAMUZ!	110	TEMPORA	
(TAMUZ. IO! TAMUZ!)	110	TEMPORA	
IO! IO!	169	PHANOPOEIA	1
IO! IO!	169	PHANOPOEIA	1
IO MOOED THE FIRST YEARS WITH AVERTED HEAD, ...	222	SEXTUS PROP: 8	1
COMBUSTED SEMELE'S, OF IO STRAYED.	227	SEXTUS PROP:11	3
IOANNA			
LIANOR, IOANNA, LOICA, ...	76	THE ALCHEMIST	3
IONE			
"IONE, DEAD THE LONG YEAR"	112	IONE, DEAD	
WHERE IONE	112	IONE, DEAD	

IONIAN -- ITSELF

	PAGE	TITLE	LINE
IONIAN			
THE LUXURIOUS AND IONIAN,	209	SEXTUS PROP: 1	55
IOPE			
WITH YOU IS IOPE, WITH YOU THE WHITE-GLEAMING TYRO,	38	LADY'S LIFE	5
IOPE, AND TYRO, AND PASIPHAE, AND THE FORMAL GIRLS OF ACHAIA,	223	SEXTUS PROP: 9	16
IRE			
VOID OF ALL JOY AND FULL OF IRE AND SADNESS.	36	THE YOUNG KING	8
THE BALANCE FOR THIS LOSS IN IRE AND SADNESS!	37	THE YOUNG KING	16
THAT DOTH BUT WOUND THE GOOD WITH IRE AND SADNESS.	37	THE YOUNG KING	24
IRIDES			
THE WIDE-BANDED IRIDES	200	MAUBERLEY: 2	27
IRIDESCENCE			
O FILAMENTS OF AMBER, TWO-FACED IRIDESCENCE!	95	OF THE DEGREES	15
IRISH			
FIND PRETTY IRISH GIRLS IN CHINESE LAUNDRIES,	244	MOYEN SENSUEL	157
IRONIES			
HER QUIET IRONIES.	52	AU SALON	EP1
IRRESISTIBLY			
WHETS FOR THE WHALE-PATH THE HEART IRRESISTIBLY,	65	THE SEAFARER	64
IRRESPONSE			
IRRESPONSE TO HUMAN AGGRESSION,	202	AGE DEMANDED	51
IRRITATION			
OBSERVE THE IRRITATION IN GENERAL:	85	SALUTATION 2ND	9
IS (393)			
ISEUTZ			
SEEING THAT TRISTAN'S LADY ISEUTZ HAD NEVER	106	DOMPNA POIS	37
ISLAND			
BUT HE RETURNED TO THIS ISLAND	118	CONTEMPORARIES	4
THE EASTERN WIND BRINGS THE GREEN COLOUR INTO THE ISLAND GRASSES AT YEI-SHU,	129	THE RIVER SONG	23
ISLANDS			
LIKE THE JOY OF BLUE ISLANDS.	129	THE RIVER SONG	16
ISLE			
THE LAKE ISLE	117	THE LAKE ISLE	T
THE ISLE OF WHITE HERON	138	CITY OF CHOAN	9
THE CORAL ISLE, THE LION-COLOURED SAND	201	AGE DEMANDED	17
ISLES			
AND YOU ARE HERE, WHO ARE "THE ISLES" TO ME.	73	JACOPO SELLAIO	4
HE FISHED BY OBSTINATE ISLES;	187	E. P. ODE	14
ISOLATION			
GRADUALLY LED HIM TO THE ISOLATION	201	AGE DEMANDED	26
ISSUE			
AND NO ISSUE PRESENTS ITSELF.	179	MOEURS CON: 2	7
IS'T			
THE SINGER IS'T YOU MEAN?"	6	CINO	26
ISTE			
ISTE FUIT VIR INCULTUS,	101	AMITIES	17
T (203)			
ITA			
"-ITA, BONITA, CHIQUITA,"	162	CABARET DANCER	33
TALIA			
EMANUELE RE D' ITALIA,	182	MOEURS CON; 7	21
TALIAN			
THE GURGLING ITALIAN LADY ON THE OTHER SIDE OF THE RESTAURANT	111	BLACK SLIPPERS	7
ANY BUT "MAJESTIES" AND ITALIAN NOBLES.	163	CABARET DANCER	66
TALY			
BRINGING THE GRECIAN ORGIES INTO ITALY,	207	SEXTUS PROP: 1	4
AND THE DANCE INTO ITALY.	207	SEXTUS PROP: 1	5
TCH			
THE SOCIAL ITCH, THE ALMOST, ALL BUT, NOT QUITE, FASCINATING,	241	MOYEN SENSUEL	83
TE			
ITE	95	ITE	T
T'LL			
AND IT'LL ALL COME RIGHT,	53	AU JARDIN	21
'S (62)			
'S (3)			
SELF			
AND SCARE ITSELF TO SPASMS."	109	THE FAUN	9

PAGE 207

ITSELF -- JAVELIN

	PAGE	TITLE	LINE
ITSELF (CONTINUED)			
THE WIND BUNDLES ITSELF INTO A BLUISH CLOUD AND WANDERS OFF.	129	THE RIVER SONG	30
AND NO ISSUE PRESENTS ITSELF.	179	MOEURS CON: 2	7
IT TWISTS ITSELF FROM OUT ALL NATURAL MEASURE;	249	DONNA MI PREGA	50
I'VE (4)			
IVORY			
IVORY SANDALED,	91	DANCE FIGURE	3
MOVE OTHERS WITH IVORY CARS.	108	CH'U YUAN	4
THE HORSES ARE WELL TRAINED, THE GENERALS HAVE IVORY ARROWS AND QUIVERS ORNAMENTED WITH FISH-SKIN.	127	BOWMEN OF SHU	19
IF SHE WITH IVORY FINGERS DRIVE A TUNE THROUGH THE LYRE,	217	SEXTUS PROP: 5	27
IVY			
AS IVY FINGERS CLUTCHING THROUGH	8	NA AUDIART	4
SUCH MY COHORT AND SETTING. AND SHE BOUND IVY TO HIS THYRSOS;	211	SEXTUS PROP: 2	35
IXION			
WITHOUT IXION, AND WITHOUT THE SONS OF MENOETIUS AND THE ARGO AND WITHOUT JOVE'S GRAVE AND THE TITANS.	218	SEXTUS PROP: 5	52
J			
THAN E'ER WERE HEARD OF BY OUR LORD CH.... J....	241	MOYEN SENSUEL	100
JAB			
BUT TO JAB A KNIFE IN MY VITALS, TO HAVE PASSED ON A SWIG OF POISON,	228	SEXTUS PROP:12	12
JACOPO			
OF JACOPO DEL SELLAIO	73	JACOPO SELLAIO	T
JACQUES			
MATURIN, GUILLAUME, JACQUES D'ALLMAIN,	12	OF THE GIBBET	29
A-JUMBLING O' FIGURES FOR MAITRE JACQUES POLIN,	22	MARVOIL	4
JADE			
RED JADE CUPS, FOOD WELL SET ON A BLUE JEWELLED TABLE,	135	EXILE'S LETTER	47
TO THE DYNASTIC TEMPLE, WITH WATER ABOUT IT CLEAR AS BLUE JADE,	135	EXILE'S LETTER	50
TREES THAT GLITTER LIKE JADE,	141	IDEA OF CHOAN	19
JAGGED			
AND I AM TORN AGAINST THE JAGGED DARK,	60	TOMB AKR CAAR	26
JAIL			
AND NEVER GOT TOOK TO JAIL,	271	OLE KATE	16
JAMES			
IN BOSTON, TO HENRY JAMES, THE GREATEST WHOM WE'VE SEEN LIVING.	240	MOYEN SENSUEL	62
JANE'S			
A HOOK TO CATCH THE LADY JANE'S ATTENTION,	196	HUGH SELWIN:12	17
JANGLE			
GO! JANGLE THEIR DOOR-BELLS!	86	SALUTATION 2ND	35
JAPAN			
AND YOUR WHITE VASES FROM JAPAN,	167	OF AROUET	12
JAPANESE			
OF A JAPANESE PAPER NAPKIN.	110	THE ENCOUNTER	5
JAPONAIS			
JAPONAIS,	160	DANS OMNIBUS	25
JAQUEMART			
PAR JAQUEMART"	198	MAUBERLEY: 1	2
JARDIN			
AU JARDIN	53	AU JARDIN	1
JARGON			
JOURNEY'S JARGON, HOW I IN HARSH DAYS	64	THE SEAFARER	2
JARS			
I HAVE BEEN KIND. SEE, I HAVE LEFT THE JARS SEALED,	60	TOMB AKR CAAR	1
NOR BRISTLE WITH WINE JARS,	209	SEXTUS PROP: 1	54
JASON			
AND THERE WAS A CASE IN COLCHIS, JASON AND THAT WOMAN IN COLCHIS;	228	SEXTUS PROP:12	1
JASON'S			
VARRO SANG JASON'S EXPEDITION,	230	SEXTUS PROP:12	6
JAVELIN			
I HAD REHEARSED THE CURIAN BROTHERS, AND MADE REMARKS ON THE HORATIAN JAVELIN	210	SEXTUS PROP: 2	

JE -- JOKE

	PAGE	TITLE	LINE
JE			
ET ALORS JE VIS BIEN DES CHOSES	160	DANS OMNIBUS	6
JE VIS DES CANARDS SUR LE BORD D'UN LAC MINUSCULE,	160	DANS OMNIBUS	10
JE VIS LES COLONNES ANCIENNES EN "TOC"	160	DANS OMNIBUS	12
JE VIS LE PARC,	160	DANS OMNIBUS	20
JE VIS LES CYGNES NOIRS,	160	DANS OMNIBUS	24
JEALOUS			
AND EVERY ONE HALF JEALOUS OF MAENT?	153	NEAR PERIGORD	76
JEALOUSIES			
HE WROTE THE CATCH TO PIT THEIR JEALOUSIES	153	NEAR PERIGORD	77
JEHAN			
FOR JEHAN AND RAOUL DE VALLERIE	12	OF THE GIBBET	27
JENNY'S			
"AH, POOR JENNY'S CASE" . . .	192	YEUX GLAUQUES	20
JEST			
JEST, CHALLENGE, COUNTERLIE!	35	HIS OWN FACE	6
JESTER			
"THE JESTER WALKED IN THE GARDEN."	53	AU JARDIN	6
"THE JESTER WALKED IN THE GARDEN."	53	AU JARDIN	23
JEWEL			
THE JEWEL STAIRS' GRIEVANCE	132	JEWEL STAIRS'	T
JEWELLED			
MUSICIANS WITH JEWELLED FLUTES AND WITH PIPES OF GOLD	128	THE RIVER SONG	2
THE EMPEROR IN HIS JEWELLED CAR GOES OUT TO INSPECT HIS FLOWERS,	129	THE RIVER SONG	35
THE JEWELLED STEPS ARE ALREADY QUITE WHITE WITH DEW.	132	JEWEL STAIRS'	1
PLAYING ON A JEWELLED MOUTH-ORGAN.	135	EXILE'S LETTER	25
RED JADE CUPS, FOOD WELL SET ON A BLUE JEWELLED TABLE,	135	EXILE'S LETTER	47
THE JEWELLED CHAIR IS HELD UP AT THE CROSSWAY,	141	IDEA OF CHOAN	5
JEWELS			
DREAMS, WORDS, AND THEY ARE AS JEWELS,	6	CINO	5
WITH YELLOW GOLD AND WHITE JEWELS, WE PAID FOR SONGS AND LAUGHTER	134	EXILE'S LETTER	4
SHE WILL NOT BATHE TOO OFTEN, BUT HER JEWELS	161	CABARET DANCER	13
JEWS			
LET THE JEWS PAY."	152	NEAR PERIGORD	39
JIBE			
CINO, OF THE DARE, THE JIBE,	6	CINO	19
JIBES			
HE PLAGUES ME WITH JIBES AND STICKS,	237	ABU SALAMMAMM	29
JIBS			
FLAT CALM ENGULPHS MY JIBS,	247	PIERROTS	2
JOB			
LET US EXPRESS OUR ENVY OF THE MAN WITH A STEADY JOB AND NO WORRY ABOUT THE FUTURE.	94	INSTRUCTIONS	2
SHE DIED ON THE JOB THEY TELLS ME,	271	OLE KATE	13
JOBBER			
A SENATORIAL JOBBER FOR PROTECTION,	245	MOYEN SENSUEL	214
JOBBERY			
LET US BE DONE WITH PANDARS AND JOBBERY,	145	SALUTATION 3RD	14
JOBS			
THERE ARE NEW JOBS FOR THE AUTHOR;	217	SEXTUS PROP: 5	32
JOCELYNN			
VIERNA, JOCELYNN, DARING OF SPIRITS,	76	THE ALCHEMIST	41
JOCUNDA			
CUM JOCUNDA FEMINA.	101	AMITIES	23
JOGLARS			
THE JOGLARS SUPPLE AND THE TROUBADOURS.	36	THE YOUNG KING	11
JOHN			
OF ST. JOHN,	119	THE GYPSY	15
WHEN JOHN RUSKIN PRODUCED	192	YEUX GLAUQUES	2
JOHNSON			
TOLD ME HOW JOHNSON (LIONEL) DIED	193	SIENA MI FE	7
DR. JOHNSON FLOURISHED;	196	HUGH SELWIN:12	24
JOIN			
I JOIN THESE WORDS FOR FOUR PEOPLE,	88	CAUSA	1
JOINED			
THAT RADWAY JOINED THE BAPTIST BROADWAY TEMPLE.	246	MOYEN SENSUEL	210
JOKE			
I DON'T QUITE SEE THE JOKE ANY MORE,	264	ALF'S EIGHTH	29

JOKES -- JUPITER

	PAGE	TITLE	LINE
JOKES			
CRACKIN' THEIR SMUTTY JOKES!	257	BREAD BRIGADE	6
JONGLEUR			
O HOLE IN THE WALL HERE! BE THOU MY JONGLEUR	23	MARVOIL	34
O HOLE IN THE WALL HERE, BE THOU MY JONGLEUR,	23	MARVOIL	45
AND EVERY JONGLEUR KNEW ME IN HIS SONG,	30	PIERE VIDAL	10
JONGLEUR'S			
BORN OF A JONGLEUR'S TONGUE, FREELY TO PASS	153	NEAR PERIGORD	83
JO-RUN			
FOR THE GARDENS AT JO-RUN ARE FULL OF NEW NIGHTINGALES,	130	THE RIVER SONG	38
JOT			
'TWOULD NOT MOVE IT ONE JOT FROM LEFT TO RIGHT	63	PHASELLUS ILLE	11
JOURNAL			
THESE, AND YET GOD, AND DR. PARKHURST'S GOD, THE N. Y. JOURNAL	240	MOYEN SENSUEL	45
JOURNEY'S			
JOURNEY'S JARGON, HOW I IN HARSH DAYS	64	THE SEAFARER	2
JOVE			
NOR HOUSES MODELLED UPON THAT OF JOVE IN EAST ELIS,	209	SEXTUS PROP: 1	67
AND OF JOVE PROTECTED BY GEESE.	210	SEXTUS PROP: 2	15
JOVE, BE MERCIFUL TO THAT UNFORTUNATE WOMAN	221	SEXTUS PROP: 8	1
OR JOVE, HARSH AS HE IS, MAY TURN ASIDE YOUR ULTIMATE DAY.	222	SEXTUS PROP: 8	38
I WOULD ASK A LIKE BOON OF JOVE.	228	SEXTUS PROP:12	17
JOVE'S			
WITHOUT IXION, AND WITHOUT THE SONS OF MENOETIUS AND THE ARGO AND WITHOUT JOVE'S GRAVE AND THE TITANS.	218	SEXTUS PROP: 5	52
JOVIALIS			
EGO AUTEM JOVIALIS	101	AMITIES	21
JOWL			
SPLITTING ITS BEERY JOWL	52	AU SALON	22
IT JUTS LIKE A SHELF BETWEEN THE JOWL AND CORSET.	161	CABARET DANCER	16
JOY			
VOID OF ALL JOY AND FULL OF IRE AND SADNESS.	36	THE YOUNG KING	
LOVE TAKES HIS WAY AND HOLDS HIS JOY DECEITFUL,	37	THE YOUNG KING	2
WHOM HEAVENLY JOY IMMERSES,	45	FROM HEINE: 4	
OF LOVE, AND JOY THAT IS LOVE'S INMOST PART,	45	FROM HEINE: 5	1
WITH JOY BREATHLESS AT HEART.	47	FROM HEINE: 7	2
JOY SO RICH, AND IF I FIND NOT EVER	105	DOMPNA POIS	
AND I HAVE JOY IN THESE WORDS	129	THE RIVER SONG	1
LIKE THE JOY OF BLUE ISLANDS.	129	THE RIVER SONG	1
I WISH YOU JOY, I PROFFER YOU ALL MY ASSISTANCE.	145	SALUTATION 3RD	1
"WAIT, MY GOOD FELLOW. FOR SUCH JOY I TAKE	172	LANGUE D'OC: 1	2
JOY I HAVE NONE, IF SHE MAKE ME NOT MAD	175	LANGUE D'OC: 3	4
I AM GONE FROM ONE JOY,	176	LANGUE D'OC: 3	6
JOYS			
WHERE ARE THE JOYS MY HEART HAD WON?	10	FOR THIS YULE	1
JUDGE			
RISE UP AND JUDGE US;	52	AU SALON	
JUDGES			
NINE LAWYERS, FOUR COUNSELS, FIVE JUDGES AND THREE PROCTORS OF THE KING,	97	THE BELLAIRES	
BUT THE JUDGES,	98	THE BELLAIRES	2
JUDGING			
BEYOND SALVATION, HOLDETH ITS JUDGING FORCE,	249	DONNA MI PREGA	
JUGURTHA			
MARIUS AND JUGURTHA TOGETHER,	218	SEXTUS PROP: 6	
MARIUS AND JUGURTHA TOGETHER.	219	SEXTUS PROP: 6	
JUMP			
JUMP TO YOUR SENSE AND GIVE PRAISE AS WE'D LIEF DO.	13	MESMERISM	
JUNG			
COULD FREUD OR JUNG UNFATHOM SUCH A SINK?	241	MOYEN SENSUEL	
JUNO			
OLD LECHER, LET NOT JUNO GET WIND OF THE MATTER,	222	SEXTUS PROP: 8	
OR PERHAPS JUNO HERSELF WILL GO UNDER,	222	SEXTUS PROP: 8	
JUNO'S			
HAVE YOU CONTEMPTED JUNO'S PELASGIAN TEMPLES,	221	SEXTUS PROP: 8	
JUPITER			
EAGLED AND THUNDERED AS JUPITER PLUVIUS,	13	MESMERISM	

JURIDICAL -- KEEP

	PAGE	TITLE	LINE
JURIDICAL			
OF THE JURIDICAL	203	MAUBERLEY: 4	12
JURISDICTION			
WHO HATH MY HEART IN JURISDICTION.	38	BALLATETTA	5
JUST			
JUST A WORD IN THY PRAISE, GIRL,	8	NA AUDIART	20
JUST FOR THE SWIRL	8	NA AUDIART	21
JUST THEN SHE WOKE AND MOCKED THE LESS KEEN BLADE.	31	PIERE VIDAL	43
AS IF HE HAD JUST DISCOVERED IT.	82	THE CONDOLENCE	16
BECAUSE I HAD JUST COME FROM THE COUNTRY;	85	SALUTATION 2ND	2
BUT SEEMS LIKE A PERSON JUST GONE.	112	IONE, DEAD	9
WHY DOES THE HORSE-FACED LADY OF JUST THE UNMENTIONABLE AGE	114	SIMULACRA	1
JUST REFLECTING THE SKY'S TINGE,	129	THE RIVER SONG	21
ITS LOWEST STONES JUST MEET THE VALLEY TIPS	152	NEAR PERIGORD	55
I HAD LAID OUT JUST THE RIGHT BOOKS.	158	PSYCHOLOG HOUR	4
BECAUSE ONE HAS JUST, AT LAST, FOUND THEM?	158	PSYCHOLOG HOUR	25
"I AM JUST FROM BED. THE SLEEP IS STILL IN MY EYES.	166	FISH & SHADOW	9
THE SERIOUS SOCIAL FOLK IS "JUST WHAT SEX IS."	244	MOYEN SENSUEL	162
"AND RATE 'EM UP AT JUST SO MUCH PER HEAD,	244	MOYEN SENSUEL	181
"KNOW WHAT THEY THINK, AND JUST WHAT BOOKS THEY'VE READ,	244	MOYEN SENSUEL	182
JUST DROP IT IN THE SLOT	267	ALF'S TWELFTH	13
JUST WENT ON A SLOSHIN'	271	OLE KATE	17
JUST GOES AHEAD AND SUCKS A TEAT	272	THE BABY	11
JUTS			
IT JUTS LIKE A SHELF BETWEEN THE JOWL AND CORSET.	161	CABARET DANCER	16
KAKUHAKU			
SENNIN POEM BY KAKUHAKU	139	SENNIN POEM	T
KALON			
TO KALON	96	TO KALON	T
WE SEE TO KALON	189	HUGH SELWYN: 3	15
KALOUN			
"QUASI KALOUN." S. T. SAYS BEAUTY IS MOST THAT, A "CALLING TO THE SOUL."	20	IN DURANCE	20
KAN			
OUT CAME THE EAST OF KAN FOREMAN AND HIS COMPANY.	134	EXILE'S LETTER	23
THE FOREMAN OF KAN CHU, DRUNK, DANCED	135	EXILE'S LETTER	28
AS BUTEI OF KAN HAD MADE THE HIGH GOLDEN LOTUS	141	IDEA OF CHOAN	28
KATE			
OLE KATE	271	OLE KATE	T
OLE KATE WOULD GIT HER 'ARF A PINT	271	OLE KATE	3
KATSURA			
FROM THE BOUGHS OF KATSURA,	140	MULBERRY ROAD	10
KAUGH			
THAN THE DUCHESS OF KAUGH.	260	ALF'S FOURTH	13
KEEL			
KNOWN ON MY KEEL MANY A CARE'S HOLD,	64	THE SEAFARER	5
"NO KEEL WILL SINK WITH YOUR GENIUS	210	SEXTUS PROP: 2	25
KEEN			
GONE WHILE YOUR TASTES WERE KEEN TO YOU,	19	FOR E. MCC	1
STARK, KEEN, TRIUMPHANT, TILL IT PLAYS AT DEATH.	31	PIERE VIDAL	37
JUST THEN SHE WOKE AND MOCKED THE LESS KEEN BLADE.	31	PIERE VIDAL	43
KEEN-SCENTED			
THESE THE KEEN-SCENTED;	74	THE RETURN	17
KEEP			
SO ART THOU WITH US, BEING GOOD TO KEEP	19	FOR E. MCC	21
KEEP YET MY SECRET IN THY BREAST HERE;	23	MARVOIL	47
EVEN AS I KEEP HER IMAGE IN MY HEART HERE.	23	MARVOIL	48
FOR THAT RESTLESSNESS--PIERE SET TO KEEP	30	PIERE VIDAL	24
BUT YOU, BOS AMIC, WE KEEP ON,	101	AMITIES	13
AND AT THE PACE THEY KEEP	111	IMAGE ORLEANS	5
BECAUSE HIS LONG SLEEVES WOULDN'T KEEP STILL	135	EXILE'S LETTER	29
AND MEN SAY THE SUN AND MOON KEEP ON MOVING	142	UNMOVING CLOUD	20
TO KEEP GRASS	146	MONUMENTUM AER	8
KEEP SMALL WITH REVERENCE, BEHOLDING HER IMAGE.	164	QUINTUS SEPTIM	7
MY LOVE AND I KEEP STATE	171	LANGUE D'OC	EPI
WILL KEEP THEIR COLLECTIVE NOSE IN MY BOOKS,	209	SEXTUS PROP: 1	61
AND KEEP MAD DOGS OFF HIS ANKLES.	212	SEXTUS PROP: 3	23
SHE COULD SCARCELY KEEP HER EYES OPEN	225	SEXTUS PROP:10	22
KEEP UP THE GRAND SYSTEM	259	ALF'S FOURTH	8

PAGE 211

KEEP -- KIND

	PAGE	TITLE	LINE
KEEP (CONTINUED)			
WILL KEEP IT A LITTLE LONGER,	266	ALF'S TENTH	15
TO KEEP YOUR FEELIN'S SORE,	269	SAFE AND SOUND	12
THAT KEEP ON GETTIN' USURY	269	SAFE AND SOUND	15
TO KEEP THE WOLF AWAY	269	SAFE AND SOUND	20
AN' KEEP THE BANK IN POWER.	270	OF 600 M.P.'S	4
AND KEEP THE PEOPLE IN ITS PLACE	270	OF 600 M.P.'S	7
AND TO KEEP AN EYE ON THEIR READIN' MATTER	272	NATIONAL SONG	13
KEEPING			
TWO MEN TOSSING A COIN, ONE KEEPING A CASTLE,	122	PROVINC DESERT	66
THAT HATH THE DAWN IN KEEPING,	172	LANGUE D'OC: 1	8
KEEPS			
ROME'S NAME ALONE WITHIN THESE WALLS KEEPS HOME.	40	ROME	4
THERE ARE THREE KEEPS NEAR MAREUIL,	121	PROVINC DESERT	24
AND MALEMORT KEEPS ITS CLOSE HOLD ON BRIVE,	153	NEAR PERIGORD	59
KEEP'ST			
THOU KEEP'ST THY ROSE-LEAF	67	THE CLOAK	1
KEN-NIN			
HERE WE ARE BECAUSE WE HAVE THE KEN-NIN FOR OUR FOEMEN,	127	BOWMEN OF SHU	3
KENSINGTON			
SHE WALKS BY THE RAILING OF A PATH IN KENSINGTON GARDENS,	83	THE GARDEN	2
KEPT			
KEPT AS BOLD TROPHIES OF OLD PAGEANTRY.	19	FOR E. MCC	18
ARE KEPT MNEMONIC OF THE STROKES THEY BORE,	19	FOR E. MCC	20
WHAT YOU HAVE KEPT AND WHAT YOU'VE LEFT BEHIND:	59	EXIT' CUIUSDAM	5
AND ALL THY ROBES I HAVE KEPT SMOOTH ON THEE.	60	TOMB AKR CAAR	14
CAREFULLY KEPT FROM THE FLOOR BY A NAPKIN,	111	BLACK SLIPPERS	4
"PIEIRE KEPT THE SINGING--	123	PROVINC DESERT	72
STOLE HER AWAY FOR HIMSELF, KEPT HER AGAINST ARMED	123	PROVINC DESERT	75
WE HAVE KEPT OUR ERASERS IN ORDER.	207	SEXTUS PROP: 1	11
OUTSIDE YOUR SET BUT, HAVING KEPT FAITH IN YOUR EYES,	247	PIERROTS	23
KETTLE-DRUMS			
WHO HAS BROUGHT THE ARMY WITH DRUMS AND WITH KETTLE-DRUMS?	133	FRONTIER GUARD	12
KEY			
FOR THREE YEARS, OUT OF KEY WITH HIS TIME,	187	E. P. ODE	1
KIANG			
IF YOU ARE COMING DOWN THROUGH THE NARROWS OF THE RIVER KIANG,	131	RIVER-MER WIFE	2
SEPARATION ON THE RIVER KIANG	137	ON RIVER KIANG	1
THE LONG KIANG, REACHING HEAVEN.	137	ON RIVER KIANG	4
KICK			
DON'T KICK AGAINST THE PRICKS,	194	MR. NIXON	2
KID			
GET THE KID NICE NEW TOYS,	261	ALF'S SIXTH	1
KIDDIE			
WAS I STARTED WRONG AS A KIDDIE,	268	ANOTHER BIT	1
KIDS			
KIDS FOR A BRIBE AND PRESSED UDDERS,	229	SEXTUS PROP:12	4
I GET THE KIDS OUT ON THE STREET	266	ALF'S ELEVENTH	1
KILL			
WHEN THE TEMPESTS KILL THE EARTH'S FOUL PEACE,	28	ALTAFORTE	1
KILLED			
KILLED ME SHE HAS, I KNOW NOT HOW IT WAS,	175	LANGUE D'OC: 3	4
KILLS			
THAT LOVES AND KILLS,	14	FAMAM CANO	1
GOD! HOW SOFTLY THIS KILLS!	175	LANGUE D'OC: 3	1
KIN			
AYE, I AM WISTFUL FOR MY KIN OF THE SPIRIT	20	IN DURANCE	1
YEA THOU, AND THOU, AND THOU, AND ALL MY KIN	21	IN DURANCE	1
WHAT WAS THE NATION'S, NOW BY NORMAN'S KIN	261	ALF'S FIFTH	1
KIND			
I AM HOMESICK AFTER MINE OWN KIND,	20	IN DURANCE	1
BUT I AM HOMESICK AFTER MINE OWN KIND.	20	IN DURANCE	1
FOR I AM HOMESICK AFTER MINE OWN KIND	20	IN DURANCE	1
AFTER MINE OWN KIND THAT KNOW, AND FEEL	20	IN DURANCE	1
BUT FOR ALL THAT, I AM HOMESICK AFTER MINE OWN KIND	20	IN DURANCE	1
HAVE THE EARTH IN MOCKERY, AND ARE KIND TO ALL,	20	IN DURANCE	1
I HAVE BEEN KIND. SEE, I HAVE LEFT THE JARS SEALED,	60	TOMB AKR CAAR	1

KIND -- KING'S

	PAGE	TITLE	LINE
KIND (CONTINUED)			
I MATE WITH MY FREE KIND UPON THE CRAGS;	81	TENZONE	10
"TENT PREACHIN' IS THE KIND THAT PAYS THE BEST."	246	MOYEN SENSUEL	238
THIS IS THE KIND OF TONE AND SOLEMNITY	263	ALF'S EIGHTH	22
KINDLETH			
THAT THE BASE LIKENESS OF IT KINDLETH NOT.	249	DONNA MI PREGA	32
KINDLY			
KINDLY ENTREATED, AND BEEN BROUGHT WITHIN	3	THE TREE	7
MR. NIXON ADVISED ME KINDLY, TO ADVANCE WITH FEWER	194	MR. NIXON	2
KINDNESS			
O GOD, WHAT GREAT KINDNESS	26	NIGHT LITANY	9
FOR HER HANDS HAVE NO KINDNESS ME-WARD,	212	SEXTUS PROP: 3	14
KINDRED			
AND WOULD MEET KINDRED EVEN AS I AM,	20	IN DURANCE	24
KINEMA			
A PROSE KINEMA, NOT, NOT ASSUREDLY, ALABASTER	188	HUGH SELWYN: 2	11
KING			
ALL FOR ONE HALF-BALD, KNOCK-KNEE'D KING OF THE ARAGONESE,	22	MARVOIL	21
TO ALL MEN EXCEPT THE KING OF ARAGON,	23	MARVOIL	31
SWIFT AS THE KING WOLF WAS I AND AS STRONG	30	PIERE VIDAL	8
PLANH FOR THE YOUNG ENGLISH KING	36	THE YOUNG KING	T
AGAINST THE DEATH OF THE YOUNG ENGLISH KING.	36	THE YOUNG KING	5
IN TAKING FROM THEM THE YOUNG ENGLISH KING.	37	THE YOUNG KING	13
BUT HAD ITS LIFE IN THE YOUNG ENGLISH KING	37	THE YOUNG KING	21
LET EACH MAN VISAGE THIS YOUNG ENGLISH KING	37	THE YOUNG KING	29
AND HUMBLE EKE, THAT THE YOUNG ENGLISH KING	37	THE YOUNG KING	37
HIS? WHY THE GOOD KING HARRY'S,	47	FROM HEINE: 7	15
THAT BOUND KING HARRY ABOUT.	48	FROM HEINE: 7	30
NOR HIS DEED TO THE DARING, NOR HIS KING TO THE FAITHFUL	65	THE SEAFARER	42
NINE LAWYERS, FOUR COUNSELS, FIVE JUDGES AND THREE PROCTORS OF THE KING,	97	THE BELLAIRES	5
WHIRL! CENTRIPETAL! MATE! KING DOWN IN THE VORTEX,	120	GAME OF CHESS	13
KING SO'S TERRACED PALACE	128	THE RIVER SONG	11
"SANSO, KING OF SHOKU, BUILT ROADS"	138	NEAR SHOKU	EPI
AND HAD HIS WAY WITH THE OLD ENGLISH KING,	151	NEAR PERIGORD	26
BEFORE THE HARD OLD KING:	152	NEAR PERIGORD	43
SPUN IN KING MINOS' HALL	204	MEDALLION	11
AS GOLD THAT RAINS ABOUT SOME BURIED KING.	236	MIDDLE-AGED	2
GREAT IS KING GEORGE THE FIFTH,	237	ABU SALAMMAMM	1
GREAT IS KING GEORGE THE FIFTH--	237	ABU SALAMMAMM	4
GREAT IS KING GEORGE THE FIFTH;	237	ABU SALAMMAMM	10
GREAT IS THE KING OF ENGLAND AND GREATLY TO BE FEARED,	237	ABU SALAMMAMM	15
GREAT IS KING GEORGE THE FIFTH	237	ABU SALAMMAMM	18
THE MOTHER OF THE GREAT KING, IN A HOOP-SKIRT,	237	ABU SALAMMAMM	24
OH MAY THE KING LIVE FOREVER!	237	ABU SALAMMAMM	26
OH MAY THE KING LIVE FOR A THOUSAND YEARS!	237	ABU SALAMMAMM	27
THE KING WAS ONCE THE BIGGEST THING	267	ALF'S ELEVENTH	21
TILL THE KING SHALL TAKE THE NOTION	269	SAFE AND SOUND	27
INGDOM			
A TURMOIL OF WARS-MEN, SPREAD OVER THE MIDDLE KINGDOM,	133	FRONTIER GUARD	15
NOR OF XERXES' TWO-BARRELED KINGDOM, NOR OF REMUS AND HIS ROYAL FAMILY,	217	SEXTUS PROP: 5	44
A FOREIGN LOVER BROUGHT DOWN HELEN'S KINGDOM	227	SEXTUS PROP:11	20
INGDOMS			
OF BLISSFUL KINGDOMS AND THE AUREATE SPHERES;	42	HER MONUMENT	34
INGFISHERS			
THE RED AND GREEN KINGFISHERS	139	SENNIN POEM	1
NGS			
THERE COME NOW NO KINGS NOR CAESARS	66	THE SEAFARER	84
BARBAROUS KINGS.	133	FRONTIER GUARD	13
AND WE WERE DRUNK FOR MONTH ON MONTH, FORGETTING THE KINGS AND PRINCES.	134	EXILE'S LETTER	5
ALBA YOUR KINGS, AND THE REALM YOUR FOLK	210	OBITUS F T. E	8
"AS FREE OF MOBS AS KINGS"? I'D HAVE MEN FREE OF THAT INVIDIOUS,	244	MOYEN SENSUEL	169
NG'S			
"KING'S TREASURIES"; SWINBURNE	192	YEUX GLAUQUES	3

PAGE 213

KINSMEN -- KNOCKETH

	PAGE	TITLE	LINE
KINSMEN			
DEPRIVED OF MY KINSMEN;	64	THE SEAFARER	16
KISS			
HERE A WORD KISS!	8	NA AUDIART	11
SHRINKETH THE KISS OF THE DAWN	14	FAMAM CANO	5
IN RETURN FOR THE FIRST KISS SHE GAVE ME."	23	MARVOIL	29
THINK'ST THOU THAT DEATH WILL KISS THEE?	67	THE CLOAK	3
TO PLACE THE LAST KISS ON MY LIPS	219	SEXTUS PROP: 6	24
KISSED			
OF ANY ONE WHO EVER KISSED YOU?	44	FROM HEINE: 1	8
AND HAVE YOU THOROUGHLY KISSED MY LIPS?	48	FROM HEINE: 8	1
AND KISSED THEE WITH A MYRIAD GRASSY TONGUES;	60	TOMB AKR CAAR	7
AND HERE DESIRE, NOT TO BE KISSED AWAY.	73	THE PICTURE	3
MAYHAP, RIGHT CLOSE AND KISSED.	107	DOMPNA POIS	68
KISSES			
HER KISSES, HOW MANY, LINGERING ON MY LIPS.	220	SEXTUS PROP: 7	11
THOUGH YOU GIVE ALL YOUR KISSES	221	SEXTUS PROP: 7	33
KISSIN'			
AND KISSIN' HER CAT FER DIVERSION,	271	OLE KATE	19
KISSING			
GET A GOOD DEAL OF KISSING DONE.	48	FROM HEINE: 8	8
KISST			
"LOVELY THOU ART, TO HOLD ME CLOSE AND KISST,	177	LANGUE D'OC: 4	11
KISSY-CUDDLE			
"GIMME A KISSY-CUDDLE"	271	OLE KATE	21
KLEINEN			
MACH' ICH DIE KLEINEN LIEDER	97	THE BELLAIRES	EPI
KNAVE			
WE CHOOSE A KNAVE OR AN EUNUCH	189	HUGH SELWYN: 3	23
KNEE			
PUFFED SATIN, AND SILK STOCKINGS, WHERE THE KNEE	241	MOYEN SENSUEL	85
KNEE-JOINTS			
O MUSES WITH DELECTABLE KNEE-JOINTS,	104	ANCORA	13
KNEES			
LOW, PANEL-SHAPED, A-LEVEL WITH HER KNEES,	49	OF SPLENDOUR	11
SPEAK OF THEIR KNEES AND ANKLES.	86	SALUTATION 2ND	33
HAVE HIM SIT ON HIS KNEES HERE	136	EXILE'S LETTER	78
KNEW			
AND ALL I KNEW WERE OUT, MY LORD, YOU	7	CINO	34
AND EVERY JONGLEUR KNEW ME IN HIS SONG,	30	PIERE VIDAL	10
EVEN THE GREY PACK KNEW ME AND KNEW FEAR.	30	PIERE VIDAL	13
EVEN THE GREY PACK KNEW ME AND KNEW FEAR.	30	PIERE VIDAL	13
AND IF THOU KNEW'ST I KNEW THEM WOULDST THOU SPEAK?	43	SATIEMUS	2
PROVENCE KNEW;	50	THE FLAME	2
PROVENCE KNEW.	50	THE FLAME	4
PROVENCE KNEW;	50	THE FLAME	8
THESE, AND THE REST, AND ALL THE REST WE KNEW.	50	THE FLAME	11
THIS MAN KNEW OUT THE SECRET WAYS OF LOVE,	73	JACOPO SELLAIO	
FOIX' COUNT KNEW THAT. WHAT IS SIR BERTRANS' SINGING?	153	NEAR PERIGORD	9
"YOU KNEW THE MAN."	155	NEAR PERIGORD	15
"YOU KNEW THE MAN."	155	NEAR PERIGORD	15
ROSE OVER US; AND WE KNEW ALL THAT STREAM,	157	NEAR PERIGORD	17
KNEW THE LOW FLOODED LANDS SQUARED OUT WITH POPLARS,	157	NEAR PERIGORD	17
LEADING, AS HE WELL KNEW,	202	AGE DEMANDED	5
WHAT IT KNEW THEN, IT KNOWS, AND THERE IT STICKS.	240	MOYEN SENSUEL	5
I KNEW A TOURIST AGENT, ONE WHOSE ART IS	245	MOYEN SENSUEL	20
THE SIMPLE BRITONS NEVER KNEW HE WAS,	265	ALF'S NINTH	2
KNEW'ST			
AND IF THOU KNEW'ST I KNEW THEM WOULDST THOU SPEAK?	43	SATIEMUS	
KNIFE			
BUT TO JAB A KNIFE IN MY VITALS, TO HAVE PASSED ON A SWIG OF POISON,	228	SEXTUS PROP:12	
KNIGHT-LEAPS			
LOOPED WITH THE KNIGHT-LEAPS.	120	GAME OF CHESS	
KNIGHTS			
RED KNIGHTS, BROWN BISHOPS, BRIGHT QUEENS,	120	GAME OF CHESS	
BUT KNIGHTS AND LORDS TO-DAY RESPECT	267	ALF'S ELEVENTH	
KNOCKED			
YES, I HAVE RUBBED SHOULDERS AND KNOCKED OFF MY CHIPS	247	PIERROTS	
KNOCKETH			
CORN OF THE COLDEST. NATHLESS THERE KNOCKETH NOW	64	THE SEAFARER	

PAGE 214

KNOCK-KNEE'D -- KNOW

	PAGE	TITLE	LINE
KNOCK-KNEE'D			
ALL FOR ONE HALF-BALD, KNOCK-KNEE'D KING OF THE ARAGONESE,	22	MARVOIL	21
KNOT			
AND STILL THE KNOT, THE FIRST KNOT, OF MAENT?	153	NEAR PERIGORD	80
AND STILL THE KNOT, THE FIRST KNOT, OF MAENT?	153	NEAR PERIGORD	80
KNOW			
FOR I KNOW THAT THE WAILING AND BITTERNESS ARE A FOLLY.	4	LA FRAISNE	23
KNOWING, I KNOW NOT HOW,	9	NA AUDIART	51
BLOWING THEY KNOW NOT WHITHER, SEEKING A SONG.	16	PRAISE YSOLT	20
OH I KNOW THAT THERE ARE FOLK ABOUT ME, FRIENDLY FACES,	20	IN DURANCE	2
AFTER MINE OWN KIND THAT KNOW, AND FEEL	20	IN DURANCE	15
MY FELLOWS, AYE I KNOW THE GLORY	20	IN DURANCE	28
THEY'LL KNOW MORE OF ARNAUT OF MARVOIL	22	MARVOIL	25
WHAT IF I KNOW THY SPEECHES WORD BY WORD?	43	SATIEMUS	1
WHAT IF I KNOW THY SPEECHES WORD BY WORD,	43	SATIEMUS	3
MUST KNOW SUCH MOMENTS, THINKING ON THE GRASS;	43	SATIEMUS	11
WHAT IF I KNOW THY LAUGHTER WORD BY WORD	43	SATIEMUS	18
I KNOW NOT IF THE LOVE OR IF THE LAY WERE BETTER STUFF,	44	FROM HEINE: 2	7
BUT I KNOW NOW, THEY BOTH WERE GOOD ENOUGH.	44	FROM HEINE: 2	8
THROUGH ALL THY VARIOUS MOOD I KNOW THEE MIND;	50	THE FLAME	31
OH, I KNOW YOU WOMEN FROM THE "OTHER FOLK,"	53	AU JARDIN,	20
I KNOW YOUR CIRCLE AND CAN FAIRLY TELL	59	EXIT' CUIUSDAM	4
I KNOW MY CIRCLE AND KNOW VERY WELL	59	EXIT' CUIUSDAM	6
I KNOW MY CIRCLE AND KNOW VERY WELL	59	EXIT' CUIUSDAM	6
AND WHO ARE WE, WHO KNOW THAT LAST INTENT,	59	SILET	13
NOW DO I KNOW THAT I AM MAD,	62	N. Y.	4
MERE-WEARY MOOD. LEST MAN KNOW NOT	64	THE SEAFARER	12
NO MAN COULD PAINT SUCH THINGS WHO DID NOT KNOW.	73	JACOPO SELLAIO	2
YOU DO NOT KNOW THESE FOUR PEOPLE.	88	CAUSA	4
YOU WHO CAN KNOW AT FIRST HAND,	93	THE REST	15
KNOW THEN THAT I LOVED YOU FROM AFORE-TIME,	96	DUM CAPITOLIUM	7
I HEARD THE YOUNG DANTE, WHOSE LAST NAME I DO NOT KNOW--	96	AESTHETICS	7
I KNOW NOT WHERE TO GO SEEKING,	105	DOMPNA POIS	4
AND WHAT, PRAY, DO YOU KNOW ABOUT	109	THE FAUN	3
I KNOW THE ROADS IN THAT PLACE:	121	PROVINC DESERT	21
OUR MIND IS FULL OF SORROW, WHO WILL KNOW OF OUR GRIEF?	127	BOWMEN OF SHU	24
PLEASE LET ME KNOW BEFOREHAND,	131	RIVER-MER WIFE	27
AH, HOW SHALL YOU KNOW THE DREARY SORROW AT THE NORTH GATE,	133	FRONTIER GUARD	22
BEFORE IT ANOTHER HOUSE WHICH I DO NOT KNOW:	141	IDEA OF CHOAN	30
HOW SHALL WE KNOW ALL THE FRIENDS	141	IDEA OF CHOAN	31
HE CAN NOT KNOW OF OUR SORROW."	142	UNMOVING CLOUD	27
SOLVE ME THE RIDDLE, FOR YOU KNOW THE TALE.	151	NEAR PERIGORD	4
"DO WE KNOW OUR FRIENDS?"	156	NEAR PERIGORD	154
HOW DO I KNOW?	158	PSYCHOLOG HOUR	16
OH, I KNOW WELL ENOUGH.	158	PSYCHOLOG HOUR	17
YOU KNOW THE DEATHLESS VERSES.	162	CABARET DANCER	27
I DON'T KNOW WHAT YOU LOOK LIKE	162	CABARET DANCER	40
FOR I KNOW HOW WORDS RUN LOOSE,	173	LANGUE D'OC: 2	25
NOR DO I KNOW WHEN I TURN LEFT OR RIGHT	174	LANGUE D'OC: 3	24
WHO KNOW NOT HOW TO ASK HER;	175	LANGUE D'OC: 3	32
STILL SHE MUST KNOW IT.	175	LANGUE D'OC: 3	36
KILLED ME SHE HAS, I KNOW NOT HOW IT WAS,	175	LANGUE D'OC: 3	42
OUT-WEARIERS OF APOLLO WILL, AS WE KNOW, CONTINUE THEIR MARTIAN GENERALITIES,	207	SEXTUS PROP: 1	10
THEIR DOOR-YARDS WOULD SCARCELY KNOW THEM, OR PARIS.	208	SEXTUS PROP: 1	31
ERE LOVE KNOW MODERATIONS,	220	SEXTUS PROP: 7	26
I DO NOT KNOW WHAT BOYS,	224	SEXTUS PROP:10	5
AND THIS IS GOOD TO KNOW--FOR US, I MEAN,	235	TO WHISTLER	11
THE SELECT COMPANY: BEAUTIES YOU ALL WOULD KNOW	242	MOYEN SENSUEL	113
"KNOW WHAT THEY THINK, AND JUST WHAT BOOKS THEY'VE READ,	244	MOYEN SENSUEL	182
THOUGH I KNOW ONE, A VERY DAGO DETRACTOR,	246	MOYEN SENSUEL	221
I FOR THE NONCE TO THEM THAT KNOW IT CALL,	248	DONNA MI PREGA	5
SEVERAL OLD SO'JERS KNOW	257	BREAD BRIGADE	11

PAGE 215

KNOW -- KORE

	PAGE	TITLE	LINE
KNOW (CONTINUED)			
DON'T TELL WHAT YOU KNOW,	259	ALF'S FOURTH	9
BUT YOU SHALL KNOW THAT THESE WERE THE MEN.	265	ALF'S NINTH	32
AND DON'T KNOW WHAT BUG IS A-BITIN'	269	SAFE AND SOUND	11
KNOWEST			
KNOWEST THOU NOT THE TRUTH IS NEVER IN SEASON	263	ALF'S EIGHTH	13
KNOWETH			
I EVEN I, AM HE WHO KNOWETH THE ROADS	18	DE AEGYPTO	1
I, EVEN I, AM HE WHO KNOWETH THE ROADS	18	DE AEGYPTO	7
I, EVEN I, AM HE WHO KNOWETH THE ROADS	18	DE AEGYPTO	15
I, EVEN I, AM HE WHO KNOWETH THE ROADS	18	DE AEGYPTO	23
SHE KNOWETH WELL, BETIDE	106	DOMPNA POIS	59
KNOWING			
KNOWING THE TRUTH OF THINGS UNSEEN BEFORE;	3	THE TREE	2
KNOWING, I KNOW NOT HOW,	9	NA AUDIART	51
ME OUT, KNOWING YOU HOLD ME SO FAST!	107	DOMPNA POIS	70
KNOWING MY COAT HAS NEVER BEEN	196	HUGH SELWIN:12	5
NOT KNOWING, DAY TO DAY,	203	MAUBERLEY: 4	2
KNOWLEDGE			
NO MORE FOR US THE KNOWLEDGE.	3	THRENOS	13
THAN ALL THE AGE-OLD KNOWLEDGE OF THY BOOKS:	35	THE EYES	17
STRANGE SPARS OF KNOWLEDGE AND DIMMED WARES OF PRICE.	61	PORTRAIT FEMME	5
BROKEN AGAINST FALSE KNOWLEDGE,	93	THE REST	14
ESPECIALLY ON BOOKS, LEST KNOWLEDGE BREAK IN	245	MOYEN SENSUEL	215
GREAT KNOWLEDGE OR SLIGHT.	250	DONNA MI PREGA	69
KNOWN			
A BOOK IS KNOWN BY THEM THAT READ	14	FAMAM CANO	18
ONE THAT HATH KNOWN YOU.	19	FOR E. MCC	6
LO, I HAVE KNOWN THY HEART AND ITS DESIRE;	25	GUIDO INVITES	8
I THAT HAVE KNOWN STRATH, GARTH, BRAKE, DALE,	31	PIERE VIDAL	50
MEN HAVE I KNOWN AND MEN, BUT NEVER ONE	32	PARACELSUS	3
I HAVE BEEN INTIMATE WITH THEE, KNOWN THY WAYS.	60	TOMB AKR CAAR	21
KNOWN ON MY KEEL MANY A CARE'S HOLD,	64	THE SEAFARER	5
I HAVE KNOWN THE GOLDEN DISC,	95	OF THE DEGREES	6
I HAVE KNOWN THE STONE-BRIGHT PLACE,	95	OF THE DEGREES	8
FROM WEEHAWKEN--WHO HAS NEVER KNOWN	163	CABARET DANCER	65
AS THOU HAST SUBJECTS KNOWN,	197	ENVOI (1919)	4
AND WHO WOULD HAVE KNOWN THE TOWERS	208	SEXTUS PROP: 1	26
"ALL LOVELY WOMEN HAVE KNOWN THIS,"	226	SEXTUS PROP:11	22
OF LESBIA, KNOWN ABOVE HELEN;	230	SEXTUS PROP:12	69
(LET HIM REBUKE WHO NE'ER HAS KNOWN THE PURE PLATONIC GRAPPLE,	242	MOYEN SENSUEL	105
TO BE NOT TOO WELL KNOWN IN HAUNTS OF VICE--	245	MOYEN SENSUEL	202
SCARCELY A GENERAL NOW KNOWN TO FAME	264	ALF'S NINTH	3
KNOWS			
(WHO KNOWS WHOSE WAS THAT PARAGON?)	10	FOR THIS YULE	23
ALL THE BLIND EARTH KNOWS NOT TH' EMPRISE	25	GUIDO INVITES	5
THE BITTER HEART'S BLOOD. BURGHER KNOWS NOT--	65	THE SEAFARER	56
GREY-HAIRED HE GROANETH, KNOWS GONE COMPANIONS,	66	THE SEAFARER	94
THERE IS A PLACE--BUT NO ONE ELSE KNOWS IT--	166	FISH & SHADOW	14
"AND NO ONE KNOWS, AT SIGHT, A MASTERPIECE.	194	MR. NIXON	18
BUT SINGS NOT OUT THE SONG, NOR KNOWS	197	ENVOI (1919)	19
GOD KNOWS WHERE HE HAS BEEN.	225	SEXTUS PROP:10	21
WHAT IT KNEW THEN, IT KNOWS, AND THERE IT STICKS.	240	MOYEN SENSUEL	56
THAT KNOWS NOT LOVE;	250	DONNA MI PREGA	63
WHO KNOWS NOT WHAT IS OR WAS,	261	ALF'S SIXTH	2
KNOW'T			
AND SAVE THEY KNOW'T ARIGHT FROM NATURE'S SOURCE	248	DONNA MI PREGA	10
KO			
AND THE EMPEROR IS AT KO.	129	THE RIVER SONG	32
KODAK			
SINGS IN THE OPEN MEADOW--AT LEAST THE KODAK SAYS SO--	161	CABARET DANCER	4
KOHL			
PULLED BY THE KOHL AND ROUGE OUT OF RESEMBLANCE--	162	CABARET DANCER	29
KO-JIN			
KO-JIN GOES WEST FROM KO-KAKU-RO,	137	ON RIVER KIANG	1
KO-KAKU-RO			
KO-JIN GOES WEST FROM KO-KAKU-RO,	137	ON RIVER KIANG	1
KORE			
KORE IS SEEN IN THE NORTH	90	SURGIT FAMA	2

K---S -- LADIES

	PAGE	TITLE	LINE
K---S			
"PROFESSOR K---S IS."	261	ALF'S SIXTH	15
KUAN			
CRYING--"KWAN, KUAN," FOR THE EARLY WIND, AND THE FEEL OF IT.	129	THE RIVER SONG	29
KUDONIAI			
ERI MEN HAI TE KUDONIAI--IBYCUS.	87	THE SPRING	EPI
KUMI			
THE SONG OF THE LOTUS OF KUMI?	18	DE AEGYPTO	14
KU-TO-YEN			
YOU WENT INTO FAR KU-TO-YEN, BY THE RIVER OF SWIRLING EDDIES,	130	RIVER-MER WIFE	16
KUTSU'S			
KUTSU'S PROSE SONG	128	THE RIVER SONG	9
KWAN			
CRYING--"KWAN, KUAN," FOR THE EARLY WIND, AND THE FEEL OF IT.	129	THE RIVER SONG	29
LA			
LA FRAISNE	4	LA FRAISNE	T
DIEU! QU'IL LA FAIT	72	DIEU! QU'IL	T
LA TOUR,	121	PROVINC DESERT	23
AND "REND LA FLAMME",	162	CABARET DANCER	26
"LA DONNA E MOBILE."	163	CABARET DANCER	86
O'ILS NO CONTENT PAS LA MUSIQUE, QU'EST CE	199	MAUBERLEY: 2	EPI
EN COMPARAISON AVEC LAQUELLE LA ROSE	199	MAUBERLEY: 2	EPI
S'ILS NE COMPRENNENT PAS LA POESIE,	199	MAUBERLEY: 2	EPI
LABOUR			
HID HEALTH STATISTICS, DODGED THE LABOUR ACTS.	260	ALF'S FIFTH	8
LABOURED			
HOW HAVE I LABOURED?	84	ORTUS	1
HOW HAVE I NOT LABOURED	84	ORTUS	2
HOW HAVE I LABOURED TO BRING HER SOUL INTO SEPARATION;	84	ORTUS	7
LAC			
JE VIS DES CANARDS SUR LE BORD D'UN LAC MINUSCULE,	160	DANS OMNIBUS	10
LACED			
I'D HAVE HER FORM THAT'S LACED	106	DOMPNA POIS	43
LACERTUS			
SILK, STIFF AND LARGE ABOVE THE LACERTUS,	180	MOEURS CON: 5	4
LACES			
WHERE THY BODICE LACES START	8	NA AUDIART	3
LACK			
SHOULD NOT LACK FOR HONOURERS,	46	FROM HEINE: 6	2
THAT MY PHANTOM LACK NOT IN CUNNING.	105	DOMPNA POIS	30
LACKED			
HATH LACKED A SOMETHING SINCE THIS LADY PASSED;	63	QUIES	3
HATH LACKED A SOMETHING. 'TWAS BUT MARGINAL.	63	QUIES	4
LACKING			
CULDOU LACKING A COAT TO BLESS	12	OF THE GIBBET	30
GREAT MINDS HAVE SOUGHT YOU--LACKING SOMEONE ELSE.	61	PORTRAIT FEMME	6
LEST THEY SAY WE ARE LACKING IN TASTE,	94	INSTRUCTIONS	21
FOR HE WAS LACKING IN VEHEMENCE;	178	MOEURS CON: 1	10
PISANELLO LACKING THE SKILL	198	MAUBERLEY: 1	15
LACK LAND			
WERE LACK-LAND CINO, E'EN AS I AM,	7	CINO	35
LACONIA			
THOUGH MY HOUSE IS NOT PROPPED UP BY TAENARIAN COLUMNS FROM LACONIA (ASSOCIATED WITH NEPTUNE AND CERBERUS),	208	SEXTUS PROP: 1	51
LACQUER			
AND CABINETS AND CHESTS FROM MARTIN (ALMOST LACQUER),	167	OF AROUET	11
LADIES			
AND ALL THE LADIES SWIM THROUGH TEARS	45	FROM HEINE: 5	11
AND DECLAIMS BEFORE THE LADIES	46	FROM HEINE: 6	15
TO THE DANCE OF LORDS AND LADIES	47	FROM HEINE: 7	23
"THAT I MAY NOT SAY, LADIES.	72	PAN IS DEAD	8
THAT I MAY NOT SAY, LADIES.	72	PAN IS DEAD	10
LADIES	102	LADIES	T
WHEN HE SHAKES HANDS WITH YOUNG LADIES.	115	SOCIAL ORDER	4
AND THE DEVIRGINATED YOUNG LADIES WILL ENJOY THEM	208	SEXTUS PROP: 1	40

PAGE 217

	PAGE	TITLE	LINE
LADIES (CONTINUED)			
"THESE ARE YOUR IMAGES, AND FROM YOU THE SORCERIZING OF SHUT-IN YOUNG LADIES,	211	SEXTUS PROP: 2	50
SUCH DERELICTIONS HAVE DESTROYED OTHER YOUNG LADIES AFORETIME,	221	SEXTUS PROP: 8	7
I SHALL TRIUMPH AMONG YOUNG LADIES OF INDETERMINATE CHARACTER,	229	SEXTUS PROP:12	55
THAN SPANISH LADIES HAD IN OLD ROMANCES.	242	MOYEN SENSUEL	104
LADS			
SOME LADS GET HUNG, AND SOME GET SHOT.	43	MR. HOUSMAN	8
LADY			
UNTO LADY "MIELS-DE-BEN,"	8	NA AUDIART	13
I HAVE BEHELD THE LADY OF LIFE,	18	DE AEGYPTO	3
I MADE RIMES TO HIS LADY THIS THREE YEAR:	22	MARVOIL	7
BEZIERS OFF AT MONT-AUSIER, I AND HIS LADY	22	MARVOIL	12
SING THOU THE GRACE OF THE LADY OF BEZIERS,	23	MARVOIL	36
AND I HAVE SEEN MY LADY IN THE SUN,	49	OF SPLENDOUR	6
THAT WAY, LADY;	53	AU JARDIN	9
HATH LACKED A SOMETHING SINCE THIS LADY PASSED;	63	QUIES	3
THE EYES OF THIS DEAD LADY SPEAK TO ME,	73	THE PICTURE	1
THE EYES OF THIS DEAD LADY SPEAK TO ME.	73	THE PICTURE	4
THE EYES OF THIS DEAD LADY SPEAK TO ME.	73	JACOPO SELLAIO	6
THIS LADY IN THE WHITE BATH-ROBE WHICH SHE CALLS A PEIGNOIR,	87	ALBATRE	1
O MY MUCH PRAISED BUT-NOT-ALTOGETHER-SATISFACTORY LADY.	100	THE BATH TUB	4
YOUNG LADY	102	LADIES	ST
MEMNON, MEMNON, THAT LADY	102	LADIES	9
LADY, SINCE YOU CARE NOTHING FOR ME,	105	DOMPNA POIS	1
A LADY WITH LOOK SO SPEAKING	105	DOMPNA POIS	8
TO MAKE ME A BORROWED LADY	105	DOMPNA POIS	19
SWIFT-FOOT TO MY LADY ANHES,	106	DOMPNA POIS	36
SEEING THAT TRISTAN'S LADY ISEUTZ HAD NEVER	106	DOMPNA POIS	37
HER WHITE TEETH, OF THE LADY FAIDITA	106	DOMPNA POIS	51
AH, LADY, WHY HAVE YOU CAST	107	DOMPNA POIS	69
THE GURGLING ITALIAN LADY ON THE OTHER SIDE OF THE RESTAURANT	111	BLACK SLIPPERS	7
TO FORMIANUS' YOUNG LADY FRIEND	113	FORMIANUS LADY	T
ALL HAIL! YOUNG LADY WITH A NOSE	113	FORMIANUS LADY	1
WHY DOES THE HORSE-FACED LADY OF JUST THE UNMENTIONABLE AGE	114	SIMULACRA	1
THIS OLD LADY,	115	SOCIAL ORDER	5
HE WON THE LADY,	123	PROVINC DESERT	74
AND WHAT ARE THEY COMPARED TO THE LADY RIOKUSHU,	132	AT TEN-SHIN	29
THE VOICE AT MONTFORT, LADY AGNES' HAIR,	151	NEAR PERIGORD	7
HARD OVER BRIVE--FOR EVERY LADY A CASTLE,	151	NEAR PERIGORD	13
HE LOVED THIS LADY IN CASTLE MONTAIGNAC?	152	NEAR PERIGORD	48
WHERE, LADY, ARE THE DAYS	167	OF AROUET	1
VENUST THE LADY, AND NONE LOVELIER,	177	LANGUE D'OC: 4	26
IT IS A LADY,	180	MOEURS CON: 5	7
SHE WAS A VERY OLD LADY,	182	MOEURS CON: 8	14
I AWAIT THE LADY VALENTINE'S COMMANDS,	196	HUGH SELWIN:12	4
BUT NEVER OF THE LADY VALENTINE'S VOCATION:	196	HUGH SELWIN:12	12
A HOOK TO CATCH THE LADY JANE'S ATTENTION,	196	HUGH SELWIN:12	17
TELL ME THE TRUTHS WHICH YOU HEAR OF OUR CONSTANT YOUNG LADY,	214	SEXTUS PROP: 4	1
IF THE YOUNG LADY IS TAKEN?	222	SEXTUS PROP: 8	41
BECAUSE A LADY ASKS ME, I WOULD TELL	248	DONNA MI PREGA	1
LADY'S			
PRAYER FOR HIS LADY'S LIFE	38	LADY'S LIFE	T
AS WHITE THEIR BARK, SO WHITE THIS LADY'S HOURS.	71	A VIRGINAL	14
LAID			
'THOUT MASK OR GAUNTLET, AND ART LAID	19	FOR E. MCC	16
YEA THE LINES HAST THOU LAID UNTO ME	26	NIGHT LITANY	3
YOU ALSO ARE LAID ASIDE.	108	FAN-PIECE	3
I HAD LAID OUT JUST THE RIGHT BOOKS.	158	PSYCHOLOG HOUR	4
AS ROSES MIGHT, IN MAGIC AMBER LAID,	197	ENVOI (1919)	13
WHEN OUR TWO DUSTS WITH WALLER'S SHALL BE LAID,	197	ENVOI (1919)	23
AND THE REST LAID THEIR CHAINS UPON ME,	224	SEXTUS PROP:10	9
LAIN			
I HAVE LAIN IN ROCAFIXADA,	122	PROVINC DESERT	50

	PAGE	TITLE	LINE
LAIN (CONTINUED)			
I HAVE SAID: "THE OLD ROADS HAVE LAIN HERE.	122	PROVINC DESERT	56
IDA HAS LAIN WITH A SHEPHERD, SHE HAS SLEPT BETWEEN SHEEP.	227	SEXTUS PROP:11	36
LAKE			
FROM THE PLUM-COLOURED LAKE, IN STILLNESS, ...	75	THE ALCHEMIST	17
AND THE FISH SWIM IN THE LAKE	85	SALUTATION	9
THE LAKE ISLE	117	THE LAKE ISLE	T
THEIR PUNIC FACES DYED IN THE GORGON'S LAKE;	211	SEXTUS PROP: 2	32
ON THE VEILED LAKE TOWARD AVERNUS	223	SEXTUS PROP: 9	6
LAKES			
WE SPEAK OF BURNISHED LAKES, ...	146	CANTILATIONS	11
LALAGE			
LALAGE IS ALSO A MODEL PARENT, ...	103	THE PATTERNS	3
LAME			
"YE HA' SEEN ME HEAL THE LAME AND BLIND, ...	34	GOODLY FERE	29
LAMENT			
LAMENT OF THE FRONTIER GUARD	133	FRONTIER GUARD	T
YOU, SOMETIMES, WILL LAMENT A LOST FRIEND, ...	219	SEXTUS PROP: 6	30
LAMENTATIONS			
I SHALL BE PREY TO LAMENTATIONS WORSE THAN A NOCTURNAL ASSAILANT.	212	SEXTUS PROP: 3	11
L'AMOUR			
"QU'EST CE QU'ILS SAVENT DE L'AMOUR, ET	199	MAUBERLEY: 2	EPI
LAMP			
PORTENT, LIFE DIED DOWN IN THE LAMP AND FLICKERED,	68	APPARUIT	3
THE HEADLESS TRUNK "THAT MADE ITS HEAD A LAMP," ...	151	NEAR PERIGORD	23
AND LIKE A SWINGING LAMP THAT SAYS, "AH ME!	156	NEAR PERIGORD	166
L'AN			
HE PASSED FROM MEN'S MEMORY IN L'AN TRENTIESME	187	E. P. ODE	18
LAND			
THAT HE ON DRY LAND LOVELIEST LIVETH, ...	64	THE SEAFARER	13
FROST FROZE THE LAND, HAIL FELL ON EARTH THEN, ...	64	THE SEAFARER	33
FIELDS TO FAIRNESS, LAND FARES BRISKER, ...	65	THE SEAFARER	50
ON LOAN AND ON LAND, I BELIEVE NOT	65	THE SEAFARER	67
OPEN LIES THE LAND, YET THE STEELY GOING	68	APPARUIT	10
O LOVE, COME NOW, THIS LAND TURNS EVIL SLOWLY.	69	THE NEEDLE	9
THE TREASURE IS OURS, MAKE WE FAST LAND WITH IT. ..	69	THE NEEDLE	11
EMPTY ARE THE WAYS OF THIS LAND	112	IONE, DEAD	2
EMPTY ARE THE WAYS OF THIS LAND	112	IONE, DEAD	6
TO WATCH OUT THE BARBAROUS LAND:	133	FRONTIER GUARD	5
THE FLAT LAND IS TURNED INTO RIVER.	142	UNMOVING CLOUD	12
GOBBLED ALL THE LAND, AND HELD IT LATER FOR SOME HUNDRED YEARS.	151	NEAR PERIGORD	19
UP AND ABOUT AND IN AND OUT THE LAND, ...	153	NEAR PERIGORD	84
IF ANY LAND SHRINK INTO A DISTANT SEACOAST, ...	216	SEXTUS PROP: 5	19
THE CONSTITUTION OF OUR LAND, O SOCRATES	239	MOYEN SENSUEL	23
THAN I CAN FROM THIS DISTANT LAND AND STATION, ...	243	MOYEN SENSUEL	154
('TIS AN ANOMALY IN OUR LARGE LAND OF FREEDOM, ...	245	MOYEN SENSUEL	217
ON SEA AND LAND, WITH ALL CONVENIENCE FOUND	264	ALF'S NINTH	19
THERE IS NO LAND LIKE ENGLAND	272	NATIONAL SONG	1
THERE IS NO SUCH LAND OF CASTLES	272	NATIONAL SONG	5
LANDS			
'TIS NOT A GAME OF BARTER, LANDS AND HOUSES, ...	50	THE FLAME	3
'TIS NOT A GAME OF BARTER, LANDS AND HOUSES, ...	50	THE FLAME	17
KNEW THE LOW FLOODED LANDS SQUARED OUT WITH POPLARS,	157	NEAR PERIGORD	174
LANG			
AND HE IS DEAD LANG SYNE.	47	FROM HEINE. 7	16
LANGUAGE			
OF LANGUAGE, BY MEN WHOLLY SOCIALIZED, ...	244	MOYEN SENSUEL	166
LANGUE			
LANGUE D'OC	171	LANGUE D'OC	T
LANGUIDLY			
LANGUIDLY YOU STRETCH OUT THE SNARE	226	SEXTUS PROP:11	15
LAP			
AND LAP O' THE SNOWS FOOD'S GUEREDON	10	FOR THIS YULE	5
AND I, WRAPPED IN BROCADE, WENT TO SLEEP WITH MY HEAD ON HIS LAP, ...	135	EXILE'S LETTER	51
LAPPED			
LAPPED IN THE GOLD-COLOURED FLAME I DESCEND THROUGH THE AETHER.	169	PHANOPOEIA	5

LAPPING -- LAST

	PAGE	TITLE	LINE
LAPPING			
THE FOLDING AND LAPPING BRIGHTNESS	169	PHANOPOEIA	14
LAPPO			
"LAPPO I LEAVE BEHIND AND DANTE TOO, ...	25	GUIDO INVITES	1
LAQUELLE			
EN COMPARAISON AVEC LAQUELLE LA ROSE	199	MAUBERLEY: 2	EPI
LAR			
I HAVE FED YOUR LAR WITH POPPIES, ...	102	LADIES	5
LARCHES			
AS YOUR VOICES, UNDER THE LARCHES OF PARADISE	75	THE ALCHEMIST	3
LARES			
OF LARES FLEEING THE "ROMAN SEAT"	210	SEXTUS PROP: 2	12
BEARING ANCESTRAL LARES AND IMAGES;	219	SEXTUS PROP: 6	14
LARESQUE			
CARI LARESQUE, PENATES, ...	52	AU SALON	25
LARGE			
WITH THEIR LARGE AND ANAEMIC EYES THEY LOOKED OUT UPON THIS CONFIGURATION.	93	LES MILLWIN	12
SHE CAME INTO THE LARGE ROOM BY THE STAIR, ...	166	FISH & SHADOW	7
MR. HECATOMB STYRAX, THE OWNER OF A LARGE ESTATE	178	MOEURS CON: 1	1
AND OF LARGE MUSCLES, ...	178	MOEURS CON: 1	2
OF THE TIMES WHEN THE SLEEVES WERE LARGE, ...	180	MOEURS CON: 5	3
SILK, STIFF AND LARGE ABOVE THE LACERTUS, ...	180	MOEURS CON: 5	4
('TIS AN ANOMALY IN OUR LARGE LAND OF FREEDOM, ...	245	MOYEN SENSUEL	217
IS ONE DAY BLOWN UP LARGE, THE NEXT, SUCKED IN? ...	261	ALF'S FIFTH	21
LARGE-MOUTHED			
OH AUGUST PIERIDES! NOW FOR A LARGE-MOUTHED PRODUCT.	216	SEXTUS PROP: 5	14
LARGER			
FOR A MUCH LARGER ILIAD IS IN THE COURSE OF CONSTRUCTION	229	SEXTUS PROP:12	38
AND THE LARGER STORES WERE LIKEWISE	262	ALF'S SEVENTH	6
LARGEST			
THE LAZY LEOPARDS ON THE LARGEST BANNER, ...	155	NEAR PERIGORD	133
LARRON			
THOMAS LARRON "EAR-THE-LESS,"	11	OF THE GIBBET	6
LARST			
'AVE YOU SEEN YER LARST SWEET LITTER?	270	OF 600 M.P.'S	18
L'ART			
L'ART, 1910	113	L'ART, 1910	7
'LAS			
'LAS! NEVER WAS NOR WILL BE IN THIS WORLD	37	THE YOUNG KING	15
LAST			
SHAMED AND YET BOWED NOT AND THAT WON AT LAST.	31	PIERE VIDAL	4
WHEN WE LAST MADE COMPANY, ...	33	GOODLY FERE	1
THEY ARE FOOLS TO THE LAST DEGREE.	33	GOODLY FERE	2
ROME THAT ART ROME'S ONE SOLE LAST MONUMENT, ...	40	ROME	
AND WHO ARE WE, WHO KNOW THAT LAST INTENT, ...	59	SILET	1
LAUD OF THE LIVING, BOASTETH SOME LAST WORD, ...	66	THE SEAFARER	7
'NEATH WHICH THE LAST YEAR LIES, ...	67	THE CLOAK	
THOUGH EVERY BRANCH HAVE BACK WHAT LAST YEAR LOST,	87	THE SPRING	1
I HEARD THE YOUNG DANTE, WHOSE LAST NAME I DO NOT KNOW--	96	AESTHETICS	
AH, BELS SENHER, MAENT, AT LAST	106	DOMPNA POIS	6
(IF GLORY COULD LAST FOREVER	129	THE RIVER SONG	
AND THEY THINK IT WILL LAST A THOUSAND AUTUMNS, ...	132	AT TEN-SHIN	2
AS CAUGHT BY DANTE IN THE LAST WALLOW OF HELL-- ...	151	NEAR PERIGORD	2
BEATEN AT LAST, ...	152	NEAR PERIGORD	4
SO TO THIS LAST ESTRANGEMENT, TAIRIRAN!	157	NEAR PERIGORD	15
BECAUSE ONE HAS JUST, AT LAST, FOUND THEM?	158	PSYCHOLOG HOUR	
UNTIL THE LAST SLUT'S HANGED AND THE LAST PIG DISEMBOWELED, ...	161	CABARET DANCER	
UNTIL THE LAST SLUT'S HANGED AND THE LAST PIG DISEMBOWELED, ...	161	CABARET DANCER	
IT MAY LAST WELL IN THESE DARK NORTHERN CLIMATES,	163	CABARET DANCER	
AT HER LAST MAQUERO'S	192	YEUX GLAUQUES	
I FOUND THE LAST SCION OF THE	193	SIENA MI FE	
AT LAST FROM THE WORLD'S WELTER	195	HUGH SELWIN:10	
CAME END, AT LAST, TO THAT ARCADIA.	199	MAUBERLEY: 2	
AND IT WILL LAST A TWELVE MONTH, ...	212	SEXTUS PROP: 3	
THE LAST SINGS OF A TUMULT, ...	216	SEXTUS PROP: 5	
TO PLACE THE LAST KISS ON MY LIPS	219	SEXTUS PROP: 6	

```
                                                     PAGE    TITLE         LINE
LAST  (CONTINUED)
    WHEN LAST I MET HIM, HE WAS A PILLAR IN    .........  246   MOYEN SENSUEL   229
LASTING
    AYE, FOR EVER, A LASTING LIFE'S-BLAST,  ............   66   THE SEAFARER     80
    PLEASURE LASTING, WITH COURTEZANS, GOING AND COMING
        WITHOUT HINDRANCE,  ............................  136   EXILE'S LETTER   53
    IS INCAPABLE OF PRODUCING A LASTING NIRVANA.  ......  148   FRATRES MINORE    7
LASTLY
    PIERCED OF THE POINT THAT TOUCHETH LASTLY ALL,  ....   19   FOR E. MCC       24
LASTS
    AND HERE'S THE THING THAT LASTS THE WHOLE THING OUT:   73   JACOPO SELLAIO    5
LATCH
    THE DOOR HAS A CREAKING LATCH.  ....................  195   HUGH SELWIN:10   12
LATE
    I LIVE TOO LATE TO SUP WITH THEE!  .................   46   TRANSLATOR        2
    IT IS SO LATE THAT THE DEW SOAKS MY GAUZE STOCKINGS,  132   JEWEL STAIRS'     2
    AND I WAS STILL GOING, LATE IN THE YEAR,  ..........  135   EXILE'S LETTER   42
    BIRDS SINGING LATE IN THE YEAR!  ...................  168   OF AROUET        38
    SINGS DAY-LONG AND NIGHT LATE  .....................  171   LANGUE D'OC     EPI
    WHICH ANAETHESIS, NOTED A YEAR LATE,  ..............  200   MAUBERLEY: 2     30
    LIGHT, LIGHT OF MY EYES, AT AN EXCEEDING LATE HOUR I
        WAS WANDERING,  ................................  224   SEXTUS PROP:10    1
    AND SEATED UPON IT IS THE LATE QUEEN, VICTORIA,  ...  237   ABU SALAMMAMM    23
    DO, THAT IS: THINK, BEFORE IT'S TOO LATE.  .........  266   ALF'S TENTH      12
LATELY
    NO, NO! GO FROM ME. I HAVE LEFT HER LATELY.  ......   71   A VIRGINAL        1
LATENT
    TAKETH IN LATENT INTELLECT--  .....................  249   DONNA MI PREGA   25
LATER
    AND ONCE AGAIN, LATER, WE MET AT THE SOUTH
        BRIDEGHEAD.  ...................................  136   EXILE'S LETTER   70
    GOBBLED ALL THE LAND, AND HELD IT LATER FOR SOME
        HUNDRED YEARS.  ................................  151   NEAR PERIGORD    19
    AN HOUR LATER: A SHOW OF CALVES AND SPANGLES,  ....  163   CABARET DANCER   82
    LEARNING LATER . . .  ..............................  190   HUGH SELWYN: 4    9
    AND I ALSO AMONG THE LATER NEPHEWS OF THIS CITY  ...  208   SEXTUS PROP: 1   35
LATERAL
    THE LATERAL VIBRATIONS CARESS ME,  .................  147   BEFORE SLEEP      1
    THEIR REALM IS THE LATERAL COURSES.  ...............  147   BEFORE SLEEP     10
LATEST
    TALK OF THE LATEST SUCCESS, GIVE WING TO SOME
        SCANDAL,  ......................................   52   AU SALON         12
    TO-MORROW IN TEN YEARS AT THE LATEST,  .............  162   CABARET DANCER   46
LATIN
    AND TIBULLUS COULD SAY OF HIS DEATH, IN HIS LATIN:   168   OF AROUET        99
LATINITY
    THE TERM "VIRGO" BEING MADE MALE IN MEDIAEVAL
        LATINITY;  .....................................  178   MOEURS CON: 1     6
LATONA
    PALLOR OF SILVER, PALE LUSTRE OF LATONA,  .........   76   THE ALCHEMIST    58
LATTICES
    FROM AMBER LATTICES UPON THE COBALT NIGHT,  .......   53   AU JARDIN         3
LAUD
    LAUD OF THE LIVING, BOASTETH SOME LAST WORD,  .....   66   THE SEAFARER     74
    AND HIS LAUD BEYOND THEM REMAIN 'MID THE ENGLISH,     66   THE SEAFARER     79
LAUGH
    MAKE THY LAUGH OUR WANDER-LIED;  ..................    7   CINO             47
    WILL LAUGH YOUR VERSES TO EACH OTHER,  ............   14   FAMAM CANO       11
    AND THE SCORN OF HIS LAUGH RANG FREE,  ............   33   GOODLY FERE      10
    MOVES CHANGING COLOUR, OR TO LAUGH OR WEEP  .......  250   DONNA MI PREGA   53
LAUGHED
    WHO HAD LAUGHED ON EIGHTEEN SUMMERS,  .............  111   SOCIETY           3
    I NEVER LAUGHED, BEING BASHFUL.  ..................  130   RIVER-MER WIFE    8
LAUGHING
    AND YOU WERE GLAD AND LAUGHING  ...................  147   POST MORTEM       2
LAUGHS
    LAUGHS AT, AND GROWS STALE;  ......................   14   FAMAM CANO       14
LAUGHTER
    GAY CINO, OF QUICK LAUGHTER,  .....................    6   CINO             18
    WHAT IF I KNOW THY LAUGHTER WORD BY WORD  .........   43   SATIEMUS         18
    SEA-FOWLS' LOUDNESS WAS FOR ME LAUGHTER,  .........   64   THE SEAFARER     21
```

LAUGHTER -- LE

	PAGE	TITLE	LINE
LAUGHTER (CONTINUED)			
AND HEARD UNGAINLY LAUGHTER.	85	SALUTATION	6
HEARD, UNDER THE DARK, WHIRLING LAUGHTER.	121	PROVINC DESERT	32
WITH YELLOW GOLD AND WHITE JEWELS, WE PAID FOR SONGS AND LAUGHTER	134	EXILE'S LETTER	4
WITH A LAUGHTER NOT OF THIS WORLD.	147	POST MORTEM	3
AND LAUGHTER IS THE END OF ALL THINGS.	147	POST MORTEM	5
LAUGHTER OUT OF DEAD BELLIES.	190	HUGH SELWYN: 4	27
AND HOLDS HER SIDES WHERE SWELLING LAUGHTER CRACKS 'EM	239	MOYEN SENSUEL	33
LAUGHTERS			
OR, AS OUR LAUGHTERS MINGLE EACH WITH EACH,	43	SATIEMUS	7
LAUNCELOT			
SIR LAUNCELOT HAS A NEWSPAPER NOW	266	ALF'S ELEVENTH	SUB
LAUNDRIES			
FIND PRETTY IRISH GIRLS IN CHINESE LAUNDRIES,	244	MOYEN SENSUEL	157
LAUREL			
OF DAPHNE AND THE LAUREL BOW	3	THE TREE	3
SMOTHERED IN LAUREL GROVES,	134	EXILE'S LETTER	13
THE SCORCHED LAUREL LAY IN THE FIRE-DUST;	223	SEXTUS PROP: 9	2
LAUS			
DEO LAUS, QUOD EST SEPULTUS,	101	AMITIES	18
LAVINIAN			
AND CASTS STORES ON LAVINIAN BEACHES.	228	SEXTUS PROP:12	35
LAVISHES			
AND SUCH REPLIES SHE LAVISHES	106	DOMPNA POIS	54
LAW			
ALL MEN, IN LAW, ARE EQUALS.	189	HUGH SELWYN: 3	21
LAWES			
TELL HER THAT SANG ME ONCE THAT SONG OF LAWES:	197	ENVOI (1919)	2
LAWS			
ONE WHO HATH SET THE WHOLE WORLD 'NEATH HER LAWS,	40	ROME	6
LAWYERS			
NINE LAWYERS, FOUR COUNSELS, FIVE JUDGES AND THREE PROCTORS OF THE KING,	97	THE BELLAIRES	5
NINE LAWYERS, FOUR COUNSELS, ETC.,	98	THE BELLAIRES	28
FROM LAWYERS TO WHOM NO ONE WAS INDEBTED,	98	THE BELLAIRES	31
AND EVEN THE LAWYERS	98	THE BELLAIRES	32
LAX			
O AGE GONE LAX! O STUNTED FOLLOWERS,	32	PIERE VIDAL	60
LAY			
WHERE ARE THE LIPS MINE LAY UPON,	10	FOR THIS YULE	19
THE CYPRESS TREES, HE LAY,	39	FOR PSYCHE	2
LOVE AND LAY THOU HAST FORGOTTEN FULLY,	44	FROM HEINE: 2	5
I KNOW NOT IF THE LOVE OR IF THE LAY WERE BETTER STUFF,	44	FROM HEINE: 2	7
LAY STRIPPED UPON THE GROUND:	92	APRIL	4
SHE LAY BESIDE ME IN THE DAWN.	109	ALBA	3
"HERE ONE LAY PANTING."	122	PROVINC DESERT	47
WHERE LAY THE DYNASTIC HOUSE OF THE GO.	138	CITY OF CHOAN	5
HER ESCRITOIRES LAY SHUT BY THE BED-FEET.	214	SEXTUS PROP: 4	21
LET THE GODS LAY CHAINS UPON US	220	SEXTUS PROP: 7	20
THE SCORCHED LAUREL LAY IN THE FIRE-DUST;	223	SEXTUS PROP: 9	2
(YOU FEED A HEN ON GREASE, PERHAPS SHE'LL LAY	240	MOYEN SENSUEL	48
WAS FOUND IN HIS EMPLOYER'S CASH. HE LEARNED THE LAY OF CHEAPER PLACES,	243	MOYEN SENSUEL	143
LAYED			
TOMB HIDETH TROUBLE. THE BLADE IS LAYED LOW.	66	THE SEAFARER	90
LAYOUT			
WALKED OVER EN BERTRAN'S OLD LAYOUT,	122	PROVINC DESERT	39
LAYS			
BERTRANS, MASTER OF HIS LAYS,	9	NA AUDIART	30
LAYU'S			
TRIED LAYU'S LUCK, OFFERED THE CHOYO SONG,	136	EXILE'S LETTER	66
LAZY			
THE LAZY LEOPARDS ON THE LARGEST BANNER,	155	NEAR PERIGORD	133
LE			
FOR MICHAULT LE BORGNE THAT WOULD CONFESS	12	OF THE GIBBET	34
JE VIS DES CANARDS SUR LE BORD D'UN LAC MINUSCULE,	160	DANS OMNIBUS	1
JE VIS LE PARC,	160	DANS OMNIBUS	2
EST GROSSIERE ET LE PARFUM DES VIOLETTES UN	199	MAUBERLEY: 2	EP

PAGE 222

LEAD -- LEASH

	PAGE	TITLE	LINE
LEAD			
"NOR WILL THE NOISE OF HIGH HORSES LEAD YOU EVER TO BATTLE;	211	SEXTUS PROP: 2	41
TO LEAD EMATHIAN HORSES AFIELD,	216	SEXTUS PROP: 5	2
I WERE ABLE TO LEAD HEROES INTO ARMOUR, I WOULD NOT,	217	SEXTUS PROP: 5	38
LEAD-HEAVY			
SODDEN AND LEAD-HEAVY.	35	THE EYES	4
LEADING			
LEADING, AS HE WELL KNEW,	202	AGE DEMANDED	59
AND NO SERVANT WAS LEADING ME,	224	SEXTUS PROP:10	3
LEADS			
FACT THAT LEADS NOWHERE; AND A TALE OR TWO,	61	PORTRAIT FEMME	17
LEAF			
I WRAPPED MY TEARS IN AN ELLUM LEAF	4	LA FRAISNE	25
LITTLE BROWN LEAF WORDS CRYING "A SONG,"	16	PRAISE YSOLT	17
LITTLE GREEN LEAF WORDS CRYING FOR A SONG.	16	PRAISE YSOLT	18
BUT STILL CAME THE LEAF WORDS, LITTLE BROWN ELF WORDS	17	PRAISE YSOLT	33
AND THAT THE WORLD SHOULD DRY AS A DEAD LEAF,	36	FRANCESCA	9
MIDONZ, WITH THE GOLD OF THE SUN, THE LEAF OF THE POPLAR, BY THE LIGHT OF THE AMBER,	75	THE ALCHEMIST	25
MIDONZ, DAUGHTER OF THE SUN, SHAFT OF THE TREE, SILVER OF THE LEAF, LIGHT OF THE YELLOW OF THE AMBER,	75	THE ALCHEMIST	26
FROM THE COPPER OF THE LEAF IN AUTUMN,	76	THE ALCHEMIST	33
A WET LEAF THAT CLINGS TO THE THRESHOLD.	108	LIU CH'E	6
THE DEW IS UPON THE LEAF.	110	COITUS	8
'TILL THE SUN COME, AND THE GREEN LEAF ON THE BOUGH.	173	LANGUE D'OC: 2	16
WHERE THE LEAF FALLS FROM THE TWIG,	174	LANGUE D'OC: 3	3
LEAF-BROWN			
OUT OF THE BROWN LEAF-BROWN COLOURLESS	76	THE ALCHEMIST	47
LEAFY			
STRETCHES TOWARD ME HER LEAFY HANDS,"--	196	HUGH SELWIN:12	2
LEAK			
NOT THAT HIS PAY HAD RISEN, AND NO LEAK	243	MOYEN SENSUEL	142
LEAKS			
LEAKS THROUGH ITS THATCH;	195	HUGH SELWIN:10	10
LEAN			
ONE LEAN MOIETY OF HIS NAKEDNESS	12	OF THE GIBBET	31
AIE! THE LEAN BARE TREE IS WIDOWED AGAIN	12	OF THE GIBBET	33
AND ONE LEAN ARAGONESE CURSING THE SENESCHAL	22	MARVOIL	14
YOU THAT LEAN	53	AU JARDIN	2
TESTING HIS LIST OF RHYMES, A LEAN MAN? BILIOUS?	154	NEAR PERIGORD	101
LEANIN'			
BROAD AS ALL OCEAN AND LEANIN' MAN-KIN'ARDS.	13	MESMERISM	12
LEAP			
CAUSING THEIR STEEDS TO LEAP.	111	IMAGE ORLEANS	4
THEY LEAP AND CARESS ME,	147	BEFORE SLEEP	2
LEAPING			
CLASH, LEAPING OF BANDS, STRAIGHT STRIPS OF HARD COLOUR,	120	GAME OF CHESS	14
LEAPT			
AND THY LIGHT LIMBS, WHERETHROUGH I LEAPT AFLAME,	60	TOMB AKR CAAR	4
LEAPT ABOUT, SNATCHING AT THE BRIGHT FISH	97	AESTHETICS	13
LEARN			
I BESEECH YOU LEARN TO SAY "I,"	84	ORTUS	13
LEARNED			
THE EYES OF THE VERY LEARNED BRITISH MUSEUM ASSISTANT,	161	PAGANI'S NOV 8	3
WAS FOUND IN HIS EMPLOYER'S CASH. HE LEARNED THE LAY OF CHEAPER PLACES,	243	MOYEN SENSUEL	143
LEARNING			
UPON LEARNING THAT THE MOTHER WROTE VERSES,	179	MOEURS CON: 3	1
LEARNING LATER . . .	190	HUGH SELWYN: 4	9
SOME IN FEAR, LEARNING LOVE OF SLAUGHTER;	190	HUGH SELWYN: 4	10
LEARNT			
FROM THESE HE (BADLY) LEARNT. FROM PROVOSTS AND FROM EDITORS UNYIELDING	240	MOYEN SENSUEL	51
FROM THESE HE LEARNT. POE, WHITMAN, WHISTLER, MEN, THEIR RECOGNITION	240	MOYEN SENSUEL	50
LEASH			
SLOW ON THE LEASH,	74	THE RETURN	19

LEASH-MEN -- LEFT

	PAGE	TITLE	LINE
LEASH-MEN			
PALLID THE LEASH-MEN!	74	THE RETURN	20
LEAST			
I WAS QUITE STRONG--AT LEAST THEY SAID SO--	4	LA FRAISNE	5
SINGS IN THE OPEN MEADOW--AT LEAST THE KODAK SAYS SO--	161	CABARET DANCER	4
INCAPABLE OF THE LEAST UTTERANCE OR COMPOSITION,	202	AGE DEMANDED	46
--SUCH AT LEAST IS THE STORY.	220	SEXTUS PROP: 7	16
SHOW US THERE'S CHANCE AT LEAST OF WINNING THROUGH.	235	TO WHISTLER	19
LEAVE			
TO LEAVE THE OLD BARREN WAYS OF MEN,	4	LA FRAISNE	29
AS FOR WILL AND TESTAMENT I LEAVE NONE,	22	MARVOIL	27
"LAPPO I LEAVE BEHIND AND DANTE TOO,	25	GUIDO INVITES	1
LET US LEAVE THIS MATTER, MY SONGS,	82	THE CONDOLENCE	17
TAKING LEAVE OF A FRIEND	137	TAKING LEAVE	T
RICHARD SHALL DIE TO-MORROW--LEAVE HIM THERE	155	NEAR PERIGORD	139
AND WE CAN LEAVE THE TALK TILL DANTE WRITES:	156	NEAR PERIGORD	162
AND YOU WILL NOT LEAVE OFF IMITATING AESCHYLUS.	228	SEXTUS PROP:12	20
LEAVES			
SPREAD HIS LEAVES OVER ME, AND THE YOKE	4	LA FRAISNE	11
NAUGHT BUT THE WIND THAT FLUTTERS IN THE LEAVES.	4	LA FRAISNE	19
THE WORDS ARE AS LEAVES, OLD BROWN LEAVES IN THE SPRING TIME	16	PRAISE YSOLT	19
THE WORDS ARE AS LEAVES, OLD BROWN LEAVES IN THE SPRING TIME	16	PRAISE YSOLT	19
THAT HOLDS THEIR BLOSSOMS AND THEIR LEAVES IN CURE	21	IN DURANCE	45
SHALL MAIDENS SCATTER ROSE LEAVES	24	THUS NINEVEH	2
SHALL ALL MEN SCATTER ROSE LEAVES	24	THUS NINEVEH	17
LETS DRIFT IN ON US THROUGH THE OLIVE LEAVES	39	BLANDULA	4
SEEMED OVER ME TO HOVER LIGHT AS LEAVES	39	FOR PSYCHE	6
AS WITH SWEET LEAVES; AS WITH SUBTLE CLEARNESS.	71	A VIRGINAL	6
"THERE IS NO SUMMER IN THE LEAVES,	72	PAN IS DEAD	4
YSAUT, YDONE, SLIGHT RUSTLING OF LEAVES,	76	THE ALCHEMIST	40
GREY OLIVE LEAVES BENEATH A RAIN-COLD SKY.	92	GENTILDONNA	5
THERE IS NO SOUND OF FOOT-FALL, AND THE LEAVES	108	LIU CH'E	3
AS COOL AS THE PALE WET LEAVES	109	ALBA	1
AND LEAVES HER TOO MUCH ALONE.	128	BEAU TOILET	9
THE LEAVES FALL EARLY THIS AUTUMN, IN WIND.	131	RIVER-MER WIFE	22
YOU HAVE PERCEIVED THE LEAVES OF THE FLAME.	169	PHANOPOEIA	16
THEIR NEW SONG IN THE LEAVES.	173	LANGUE D'OC: 2	3
AND LEAVES YOU A PARK BENCH TO SIT ON	263	ALF'S EIGHTH	20
LEAVE-TAKING			
LEAVE-TAKING NEAR SHOKU	138	NEAR SHOKU	T
LEAVETH			
THAT LEAVETH ME NO REST, SAYING EVER,	16	PRAISE YSOLT	7
AS FLAME LEAVETH THE EMBERS SO WENT SHE UNTO NEW FORESTS	17	PRAISE YSOLT	43
LEAVING			
"DEAR POUND, I AM LEAVING ENGLAND."	159	PSYCHOLOG HOUR	43
LEAVING ME NO POWER TO HOLD HIM.	174	LANGUE D'OC: 3	6
LECHER			
OLD LECHER, LET NOT JUNO GET WIND OF THE MATTER,	222	SEXTUS PROP: 8	39
LECHERS			
CRUSADERS, LECTURERS AND SECRET LECHERS,	241	MOYEN SENSUEL	80
LECHERY			
THE CYTHAREAN BROUGHT LOW BY MARS' LECHERY	227	SEXTUS PROP:11	27
LECTURERS			
CRUSADERS, LECTURERS AND SECRET LECHERS,	241	MOYEN SENSUEL	80
LED			
GRADUALLY LED HIM TO THE ISOLATION	201	AGE DEMANDED	26
AND SHE WAS LED BACK, LIVING, HOME;	227	SEXTUS PROP:11	26
LEDGE			
NOT A NEAT LEDGE, NOT FOIX BETWEEN ITS STREAMS,	152	NEAR PERIGORD	32
TO THE LEDGE OF THE ROCKS;	227	SEXTUS PROP:11	32
LEE-WAY			
GIVING THE ROCKS SMALL LEE-WAY	187	E. P. ODE	11
LEFT			
AND LEFT THEM UNDER A STONE	4	LA FRAISNE	26
ARE LEFT IN TEEN THE LIEGEMEN COURTEOUS,	36	THE YOUNG KING	16
WHAT YOU HAVE KEPT AND WHAT YOU'VE LEFT BEHIND:	59	EXIT' CUIUSDAM	5
I HAVE BEEN KIND. SEE, I HAVE LEFT THE JARS SEALED,	60	TOMB AKR CAAR	13

LEFT -- LES

	PAGE	TITLE	LINE
LEFT (CONTINUED)			
AND BRIGHT SHIPS LEFT YOU THIS OR THAT IN FEE:	61	PORTRAIT FEMME	3
'TWOULD NOT MOVE IT ONE JOT FROM LEFT TO RIGHT. ...	63	PHASELLUS ILLE	11
NO, NO! GO FROM ME. I HAVE LEFT HER LATELY.	71	A VIRGINAL	1
AND LEFT ME CLOAKED AS WITH A GAUZE OF AETHER;	71	A VIRGINAL	5
SHE PASSED AND LEFT NO QUIVER IN THE VEINS, WHO NOW	92	GENTILDONNA	1
FOR IT IS CERTAIN THAT SHE HAS LEFT ON THIS EARTH	115	SOCIAL ORDER	17
THERE IS NO WALL LEFT TO THIS VILLAGE.	133	FRONTIER GUARD	7
AND SHE PILES HER HAIR UP ON THE LEFT SIDE OF HER HEAD-PIECE.	140	MULBERRY ROAD	11
BENDING YOUR PASSAGES FROM RIGHT TO LEFT AND FROM LEFT TO RIGHT	147	BEFORE SLEEP	15
BENDING YOUR PASSAGES FROM RIGHT TO LEFT AND FROM LEFT TO RIGHT	147	BEFORE SLEEP	15
BERTRANS, EN BERTRANS, LEFT A FINE CANZONE:	151	NEAR PERIGORD	5
SCRIBBLING, SWEARING BETWEEN HIS TEETH; BY HIS LEFT HAND	154	NEAR PERIGORD	98
THERE IS NOT MUCH BUT ITS EVIL LEFT US.	168	OF AROUET	24
QUIET TALKING IS ALL THAT IS LEFT US--	168	OF AROUET	31
NOR DO I KNOW WHEN I TURN LEFT OR RIGHT	174	LANGUE D'OC: 3	24
AND BY HER LEFT FOOT, IN A BASKET, ...	180	MOEURS CON: 5	10
LEFT HIM AS EPILOGUES.	200	MAUBERLEY: 2	37
LEFT HIM DELIGHTED WITH THE IMAGINARY	202	AGE DEMANDED	44
NOR WHETHER THERE BE ANY PATCH LEFT OF US	228	SEXTUS PROP:12	27
AND BEHOLD ME, SMALL FORTUNE LEFT IN MY HOUSE.	229	SEXTUS PROP:12	53
PLENTY TO LEFT OF 'EM, ...	257	BREAD BRIGADE	18
YES, WOT IS LEFT OF 'EM, ...	257	BREAD BRIGADE	19
PLENTY TO LEFT OF 'EM, ...	259	ALF'S THIRD	9
YEH! WHAT IS LEFT OF 'EM, ...	259	ALF'S THIRD	10
LEFT-HANDED			
"OF" THE VICTORIOUS DELAY OF FABIUS, AND THE LEFT-HANDED BATTLE AT CANNAE, ...	210	SEXTUS PROP: 2	11
LEGAL			
OH, THERE IS PRECEDENT, LEGAL TRADITION, ...	153	NEAR PERIGORD	88
LEGEND-LUST			
FOR THINE OLD LEGEND-LUST.	47	FROM HEINE: 7	12
LEGION			
FOR HIS ARMY IS LEGION, ...	237	ABU SALAMMAMM	11
LEIDER			
(ST. LEIDER HAD DONE AS MUCH AS POLHONAC, ...	153	NEAR PERIGORD	86
LEISURE'S			
LEISURE'S ADORNMENT PUTS HE THEN NEVER ON, ...	249	DONNA MI PREGA	51
L'ELECTION			
E. P. ODE POUR L'ELECTION DE SON SEPULCHRE	187	E. P. ODE	T
LEND			
LEND ME A LITTLE TOBACCO SHOP, ...	117	THE LAKE ISLE	13
GLAD TO LEND ONE DRY CLOTHING.	121	PROVINC DESERT	27
I LEND YOU ENGLISHMEN HOT AIR	269	SAFE AND SOUND	3
I LEND YOU ENGLISHMEN HOT AIR	269	SAFE AND SOUND	5
LENDS			
AND THEN LENDS OUT THEIR PRINTED SLIPS	269	SAFE AND SOUND	19
LENIN			
LENIN TO SAVE 'EM, TROTSKY TO SAVE 'EM	258	ALF'S SECOND	6
LEOPARD			
AND THEIR SNOW-WHITE LEOPARD	109	HEATHER	6
AND YOUR FATHER, WHO WAS BRAVE AS A LEOPARD	135	EXILE'S LETTER	36
LEOPARDS			
TO GATHER GRAPES FOR THE LEOPARDS, MY FRIEND, ...	108	CH'U YUAN	6
FOR THERE ARE LEOPARDS DRAWING THE CARS.	108	CH'U YUAN	7
THE LAZY LEOPARDS ON THE LARGEST BANNER, ...	155	NEAR PERIGORD	133
LEOPARD'S			
AND OUR CHARGES 'GAINST "THE LEOPARD'S" RUSH CLASH.	29	ALTAFORTE	35
LES			
LES MILLWIN	93	LES MILLWIN	T
LES YEUX D'UNE MORTE	160	DANS OMNIBUS	1
DONT TOUS LES AUTRES TRAITS ETAIENT PANES,	160	DANS OMNIBUS	4
JE VIS LES COLONNES ANCIENNES EN "TOC"	160	DANS OMNIBUS	12
ET TOUS LES GAZONS DIVERS	160	DANS OMNIBUS	21
JE VIS LES CYGNES NOIRS, ...	160	DANS OMNIBUS	24
ET TOUTES LES FLEURS	160	DANS OMNIBUS	28
LES YEUX D'UNE MORTE	160	DANS OMNIBUS	30

LESBIA -- LET

	PAGE	TITLE	LINE
LESBIA			
LESBIA ILLA	102	LADIES	ST
AND YOU ARE EVEN COMPARED TO LESBIA.	113	FORMIANUS LADY	9
OF LESBIA, KNOWN ABOVE HELEN;	230	SEXTUS PROP:12	69
LESS			
THESE THAT WE LOVED SHALL GOD LOVE LESS	12	OF THE GIBBET	39
A POOR CLERK I, "ARNAUT THE LESS" THEY CALL ME,	22	MARVOIL	1
JUST THEN SHE WOKE AND MOCKED THE LESS KEEN BLADE.	31	PIERE VIDAL	43
AND EACH TO-DAY 'VAILS LESS THAN YESTERE'EN,	37	THE YOUNG KING	28
OTHERS ARE BEAUTIFUL, NONE MORE, SOME LESS.	52	AU SALON	EPI
ONE AVERAGE MIND--WITH ONE THOUGHT LESS, EACH YEAR.	61	PORTRAIT FEMME	10
FRIENDS? ARE PEOPLE LESS FRIENDS	158	PSYCHOLOG HOUR	24
GENTLE TALKING, NOT LIKE THE FIRST TALKING, LESS LIVELY;	168	OF AROUET	32
ALL DREW THEIR PAY, AND AS THE PAY GREW LESS,	260	ALF'S FIFTH	9
LESSER			
AS LESSER MEN DRINK WINE."	24	THUS NINEVEH	23
I WILL NOT SPOIL MY SHEATH WITH LESSER BRIGHTNESS,	71	A VIRGINAL	2
LEST			
LEST LOVE RETURN WITH THE FOISON SUN	10	FOR THIS YULE	13
LEST THEY SHOULD PARCH TOO SWIFTLY, WHERE SHE PASSES.	38	BALLATETTA	10
LEST THOU SHOULDST WAKE AND WHIMPER FOR THY WINE.	60	TOMB AKR CAAR	13
MERE-WEARY MOOD. LEST MAN KNOW NOT	64	THE SEAFARER	12
LEST THEY SAY WE ARE LACKING IN TASTE,	94	INSTRUCTIONS	21
LEST IT SHOULD FAIL TO TREAT ALL MEN ALIKE.	244	MOYEN SENSUEL	178
ESPECIALLY ON BOOKS, LEST KNOWLEDGE BREAK IN	245	MOYEN SENSUEL	215
LEST THEY SHOULD OVERHEAR THE DISTRESSING CHATTER	272	NATIONAL SONG	14
LET			
AND LET THE MUSIC OF THE SWORDS MAKE THEM CRIMSON!	29	ALTAFORTE	37
"FIRST LET THESE GO!" QUO' OUR GOODLY FERE,	33	GOODLY FERE	7
LET EACH MAN VISAGE THIS YOUNG ENGLISH KING	37	THE YOUNG KING	29
HERE LET THY CLEMENCY, PERSEPHONE, HOLD FIRM,	38	LADY'S LIFE	1
YE MIGHT LET ONE REMAIN ABOVE WITH US.	38	LADY'S LIFE	4
HERE LET THY CLEMENCY, PERSEPHONE, HOLD FIRM,	38	LADY'S LIFE	11
YE MIGHT LET ONE REMAIN ABOVE WITH US.	38	LADY'S LIFE	14
THEREFORE LET US ACT AS IF WE WERE	43	MR. HOUSMAN	4
THEN LET US SMILE A LITTLE SPACE	44	MR. HOUSMAN	13
LET US BUILD HERE AN EXQUISITE FRIENDSHIP,	51	THE ALTAR	1
SEARCH NOT MY LIPS, O LOVE, LET GO MY HANDS,	51	THE FLAME	37
LET THE GODS SPEAK SOFTLY OF US	67	DORIA	8
LET THE MANES PUT OFF THEIR TERROR, LET THEM PUT OFF THEIR AQUEOUS BODIES WITH FIRE.	76	THE ALCHEMIST	51
LET THE MANES PUT OFF THEIR TERROR, LET THEM PUT OFF THEIR AQUEOUS BODIES WITH FIRE.	76	THE ALCHEMIST	51
LET THEM ASSUME THE MILK-WHITE BODIES OF AGATE.	76	THE ALCHEMIST	52
LET THEM DRAW TOGETHER THE BONES OF THE METAL.	76	THE ALCHEMIST	53
LET US LEAVE THIS MATTER, MY SONGS,	82	THE CONDOLENCE	17
COME, LET US PITY THOSE WHO ARE BETTER OFF THAN WE ARE.	83	THE GARRET	1
COME, LET US PITY THE MARRIED AND THE UNMARRIED.	83	THE GARRET	5
LET THERE BE COMMERCE BETWEEN US.	89	A PACT	9
LET US THEREFORE MENTION THE FACT,	93	LES MILLWIN	13
COME, MY SONGS, LET US EXPRESS OUR BASER PASSIONS,	94	INSTRUCTIONS	1
LET US EXPRESS OUR ENVY OF THE MAN WITH A STEADY JOB AND NO WORRY ABOUT THE FUTURE.	94	INSTRUCTIONS	2
AND WHEN THEY WOULD NOT LET HIM ARRANGE	97	AESTHETICS	16
COME, MY SONGS, LET US SPEAK OF PERFECTION--	99	SALVATIONISTS	1
AH YES, MY SONGS, LET US RESURRECT	99	SALVATIONISTS	3
LET US APPLY IT IN ALL ITS OPPROBRIUM	99	SALVATIONISTS	5
LET US TAKE ARMS AGAINST THIS SEA OF STUPIDITIES--	99	SALVATIONISTS	12
"LET HER, IF SHE WANTS ME, TAKE ME."	100	ARIDES	7
LET HER CHANGE HER RELIGION.	103	PHYLLIDULA	5
CRUSHED STRAWBERRIES! COME, LET US FEAST OUR EYES.	113	L'ART, 1910	2
OUR DEFENCE IS NOT YET MADE SURE, NO ONE CAN LET HIS FRIEND RETURN.	127	BOWMEN OF SHU	8
WE SAY: WILL WE BE LET TO GO BACK IN OCTOBER?	127	BOWMEN OF SHU	10
PLEASE LET ME KNOW BEFOREHAND,	131	RIVER-MER WIFE	27
AND I LET DOWN THE CRYSTAL CURTAIN	132	JEWEL STAIRS'	3
LET US DERIDE THE SMUGNESS OF "THE TIMES":	145	SALUTATION 3RD	1
COME, LET US ON WITH THE NEW DEAL,	145	SALUTATION 3RD	13
LET US BE DONE WITH PANDARS AND JOBBERY,	145	SALUTATION 3RD	14

PAGE 226

LET -- LHUDE

	PAGE	TITLE	LINE

LET (CONTINUED)
LET US SPIT UPON THOSE WHO PAT THE BIG-BELLIES FOR
   PROFIT, ... 145 SALUTATION 3RD 15
LET US GO OUT IN THE AIR A BIT. .... 145 SALUTATION 3RD 16
LET US DUMP OUR HATREDS INTO ONE BUNCH AND BE DONE
   WITH THEM, ... 146 CANTILATIONS 2
LET ME BE FREE OF PAVEMENTS, ... 146 CANTILATIONS 4
LET ME BE FREE OF THE PRINTERS. .... 146 CANTILATIONS 5
LET COME BEAUTIFUL PEOPLE .... 146 CANTILATIONS 6
LET COME THE GRACEFUL SPEAKERS, ... 146 CANTILATIONS 8
LET COME THE READY OF WIT, ... 146 CANTILATIONS 9
LET COME THE GAY OF MANNER, THE INSOLENT AND THE
   EXULTING. .... 146 CANTILATIONS 10
LET THE JEWS PAY." .... 152 NEAR PERIGORD 39
END FACT. TRY FICTION. LET US SAY WE SEE .... 154 NEAR PERIGORD 94
LET US THEREFORE CEASE FROM PITYING THE DEAD .... 164 QUINTUS SEPTIM 10
GOD GIVE ME LIFE, AND LET MY COURSE ·RUN .... 174 LANGUE D'OC: 3 17
"LET ANOTHER OAR CHURN THE WATER, ... 210 SEXTUS PROP: 2 26
GODS' AID, LET NOT MY BONES LIE IN A PUBLIC LOCATION 213 SEXTUS PROP: 3 32
"LET HER LOVERS SNORE AT HER IN THE MORNING! .... 215 SEXTUS PROP: 4 36
LET THE GODS LAY CHAINS UPON US .... 220 SEXTUS PROP: 7 20
NO, NOW WHILE IT MAY BE, LET NOT THE FRUIT OF LIFE
   CEASE. .... 220 SEXTUS PROP: 7 28
OLD LECHER, LET NOT JUNO GET WIND OF THE MATTER, 222 SEXTUS PROP: 8 39
(LET HIM REBUKE WHO NE'ER HAS KNOWN THE PURE
   PLATONIC GRAPPLE, ... 242 MOYEN SENSUEL 105
LET ME RETURN TO THIS BOLD THEME OF MINE, ... 246 MOYEN SENSUEL 226
LET SOME NEW LYING ASS, ... 261 ALF'S SIXTH 1
"WE HAVE PLENTY, SO LET IT BE." .... 262 ALF'S SEVENTH 17
AND DAVID'S HARP LET OUT HEART-RENDING SQUEALS: . 264 ALF'S NINTH 15
AND LET THE BLIGHTERS START IT ALL OVER AGAIN. .. 265 ALF'S NINTH 30
AN' EVERY YEAR WE MEET TO LET .... 270 OF 600 M.P.'S 11
LETHE
   AN IMAGE OF LETHE, ... 107 COMING OF WAR 1
LETS
   LETS DRIFT IN ON US THROUGH THE OLIVE LEAVES ... 39 BLANDULA 4
LET'S
   YOU WHORESON DOG, PAPIOLS, COME! LET'S TO MUSIC! 28 ALTAFORTE 2
LETTER
   BUT DO THOU SPEAK TRUE, EVEN TO THE LETTER: .... 90 SURGIT FAMA 15
   THE RIVER-MERCHANT'S WIFE: A LETTER .... 130 RIVER-MER WIFE T
   EXILE'S LETTER .... 134 EXILE'S LETTER T
   MIDNIGHT, AND A LETTER COMES TO ME FROM OUR MISTRESS: 212 SEXTUS PROP: 3 1
   SUCH WAS HE WHEN HE GOT HIS MOTHER'S LETTER .... 242 MOYEN SENSUEL 109
LETTERS
   YOU SWORN FOE TO FREE SPEECH AND GOOD LETTERS, . 116 SALUTATION 3RD 11
   EXCLUSION FROM THE WORLD OF LETTERS. .... 202 AGE DEMANDED 61
LETTEST
   NUNC DIMITTIS, NOW LETTEST THOU THY SERVANT, ... 183 CANTICO SOLE 9
   NOW LETTEST THOU THY SERVANT .... 183 CANTICO SOLE 10
LETTRES
   IS "ZUT! CINQUE LETTRES!" A BANISHED GALLIC IDIOM, 239 MOYEN SENSUEL 36
LEUCADIA
   VARRO, OF HIS GREAT PASSION LEUCADIA, ... 230 SEXTUS PROP:12 67
LEUCIS
   LEUCIS, WHO INTENDED A GRAND PASSION, ... 99 EPITAPH 1
LEUCONOE
   THE CORN HAS AGAIN ITS MOTHER AND SHE, LEUCONOE, 90 SURGIT FAMA 5
LEURS
   LEURS AILES .... 160 DANS OMNIBUS 26
LEVEL
   LEVEL WITH SUNSET, ... 122 PROVINC DESERT 51
   LEVEL ACROSS THE FACE .... 193 BRENNBAUM 7
   MY ORCHARDS DO NOT LIE LEVEL AND WIDE .... 209 SEXTUS PROP: 1 53
LEVITY
   AND SAID: "MR. POUND IS SHOCKED AT MY LEVITY." . 181 MOEURS CON: 7 11
   THE HARSH ACTS OF YOUR LEVITY! .... 226 SEXTUS PROP:11 1
L'HOMME
   L'HOMME MOYEN SENSUEL .... 238 MOYEN SENSUEL T
LHUDE
   LHUDE SING GODDAMM, ... 116 ANCIENT MUSIC 2

LI -- LIETH

LI	PAGE	TITLE	LINE
LI PO	117	EPITAPHS	ST
AND LI PO ALSO DIED DRUNK.	117	EPITAPHS	3
LIAISONS			
NINE ADULTERIES, 12 LIAISONS, 64 FORNICATIONS AND SOMETHING APPROACHING A RAPE	100	TEMPERAMENTS	1
LIANOR			
BRISEIS, LIANOR, LOICA,	75	THE ALCHEMIST	20
LIANOR, IOANNA, LOICA,	76	THE ALCHEMIST	35
LIAR			
I AM TRUE, OR A LIAR,	175	LANGUE D'OC: 3	51
LIARS			
AND LIARS IN PUBLIC PLACES.	190	HUGH SELWYN: 4	19
LIBERTY			
ABOUT THE PRIV'LEGE OF LIBERTY.	271	OLE KATE	8
LIBROSQUE			
FAMAM LIBROSQUE CANO	14	FAMAM CANO	T
LICE			
LICE SWARM LIKE ANTS OVER OUR ACCOUTREMENTS.	139	SOUTH-FOLK	8
LICHEN			
THERE IS A PLACE OF TREES . . . GRAY WITH LICHEN.	121	PROVINC DESERT	6
LICHENED			
OR, BY A LICHENED TREE AT ROCHECOUART	154	NEAR PERIGORD	107
LICK			
LICK OFF THE BLACKING.	146	SALUTATION 3RD	36
TO LICK THE BOOTS OF THE BLOKE	259	ALF'S FOURTH	6
AND LICK THE DIRT OFF THE FLOOR	264	ALF'S EIGHTH	31
TER LICK TH' BANKERS' DIRTY BOOTS	270	OF 600 M.P.'S	3
LID			
QUICK EYES GONE UNDER EARTH'S LID,	191	HUGH SELWYN: 5	6
LIDS			
THEN SMOULDER, WITH THE LIDS HALF CLOSED	21	IN DURANCE	33
UPON THESE LIDS THAT LIE OVER US	35	THE EYES	3
LIE			
UPON THESE LIDS THAT LIE OVER US	35	THE EYES	3
SCURRY INTO HEAPS AND LIE STILL,	108	LIU CH'E	4
WHY SHOULD ONE ALWAYS LIE ABOUT SUCH MATTERS?	113	TAME CAT	2
LIE LITTLE STRIPS OF PARCHMENT COVERED OVER,	154	NEAR PERIGORD	99
TO LIE WITH AND PROVE.	174	LANGUE D'OC: 3	19
CAME HOME, HOME TO A LIE,	190	HUGH SELWYN: 4	15
EVEN MY FAULTS THAT HEAVY UPON ME LIE,	197	ENVOI (1919)	6
MY ORCHARDS DO NOT LIE LEVEL AND WIDE	209	SEXTUS PROP: 1	53
GODS' AID, LET NOT MY BONES LIE IN A PUBLIC LOCATION	213	SEXTUS PROP: 3	32
AND MAY THE BOUGHT YOKE OF A MISTRESS LIE WITH	214	SEXTUS PROP: 4	3
LIE DEAD WITHIN FOUR WALLS	236	MIDDLE-AGED	15
WHEN WILL THIS SYSTEM LIE DOWN IN ITS GRAVE?	260	ALF'S FIFTH	4
LIED			
HID TRUTH AND LIED, AND LIED AND HID THE FACTS.	260	ALF'S FIFTH	6
HID TRUTH AND LIED, AND LIED AND HID THE FACTS.	260	ALF'S FIFTH	6
LIEDER			
MACH' ICH DIE KLEINEN LIEDER	97	THE BELLAIRES	EPI
LIEF			
JUMP TO YOUR SENSE AND GIVE PRAISE AS WE'D LIEF DO.	13	MESMERISM	8
LIEGEMEN			
ARE LEFT IN TEEN THE LIEGEMEN COURTEOUS,	36	THE YOUNG KING	10
LIES			
"BEYOND, BEYOND, BEYOND, THERE LIES . . ."	21	IN DURANCE	49
'NEATH WHICH THE LAST YEAR LIES,	67	THE CLOAK	8
OPEN LIES THE LAND, YET THE STEELY GOING	68	APPARUIT	10
EASTWARD THE ROAD LIES,	121	PROVINC DESERT	18
SUNSET, THE RIBBON-LIKE ROAD LIES, IN RED CROSS-LIGHT,	154	NEAR PERIGORD	96
HE LIES BY THE POLUPHLOIBOIOUS SEA-COAST.	181	MOEURS CON: 6	4
BELIEVING IN OLD MEN'S LIES, THEN UNBELIEVING	190	HUGH SELWYN: 4	14
HOME TO OLD LIES AND NEW INFAMY;	190	HUGH SELWYN: 4	17
THE BLACK PANTHER LIES UNDER HIS ROSE TREE	231	CANTUS PLANUS	1
THE BLACK PANTHER LIES UNDER HIS ROSE TREE.	231	CANTUS PLANUS	5
LIES FROM THE SPECIALIST	261	ALF'S SIXTH	7
BECAUSE I PRINT MOST LIES.	266	ALF'S ELEVENTH	4
LIETH			
WORTH LIETH RIVEN AND YOUTH DOLOROUS,	36	THE YOUNG KING	6

PAGE 228

LIETH -- LIGHT

	PAGE	TITLE	LINE
LIETH (CONTINUED)			
ALL NIGHT, AND AS THE WIND LIETH AMONG	39	FOR PSYCHE	1
LIFE			
I HAVE BEHELD THE LADY OF LIFE, ...	18	DE AEGYPTO	3
AM HERE A POET, THAT DOTH DRINK OF LIFE	24	THUS NINEVEH	22
LIFE, ALL OF IT, MY SEA, AND ALL MEN'S STREAMS	25	GUIDO INVITES	9
I HAVE NO LIFE SAVE WHEN THE SWORDS CLASH.	28	ALTAFORTE	3
BUT HAD ITS LIFE IN THE YOUNG ENGLISH KING	37	THE YOUNG KING	21
PRAYER FOR HIS LADY'S LIFE	38	LADY'S LIFE	T
NO COMFORT, AT MY TIME OF LIFE WHEN	46	FROM HEINE: 6	19
LIFE IS THE LIVE MAN'S PART, ...	47	FROM HEINE: 7	18
TO SAY THAT LIFE IS, SOME WAY, A GAY THING, ...	53	AU JARDIN	12
THIS HE LITTLE BELIEVES, WHO AYE IN WINSOME LIFE	64	THE SEAFARER	28
MY LORD DEEMS TO ME THIS DEAD LIFE	65	THE SEAFARER	66
WHOE'ER LIVED IN LIFE MOST LORDLIEST, ...	66	THE SEAFARER	87
NOR MAY HE THEN THE FLESH-COVER, WHOSE LIFE CEASETH,	66	THE SEAFARER	96
PORTENT. LIFE DIED DOWN IN THE LAMP AND FLICKERED,	68	APPARUIT	3
DRINKST IN LIFE OF EARTH, OF THE AIR, THE TISSUE	68	APPARUIT	7
NOR HAS LIFE IN IT AUGHT BETTER	83	THE GARRET	9
I BESEECH YOU ENTER YOUR LIFE.	84	ORTUS	12
HE WAS BORED WITH HIS MANNER OF LIFE, ...	100	ARIDES	3
AND IF NOW WE CAN'T FIT WITH OUR TIME OF LIFE	168	OF AROUET	23
LIFE GIVES US TWO MINUTES, TWO SEASONS--	168	OF AROUET	26
GOD GIVE ME LIFE, AND LET MY COURSE RUN	174	LANGUE D'OC: 3	17
HER LIFE IS OBSCURE AND TROUBLED;	179	MOEURS CON: 2	4
LIFE TO THE MOMENT, ...	197	ENVOI (1919)	11
NO, NOW WHILE IT MAY BE, LET NOT THE FRUIT OF LIFE CEASE.	220	SEXTUS PROP: 7	28
LONG IS MY LIFE, LONG IN YEARS, ...	221	SEXTUS PROP: 7	38
THROUGH PERILS, (SO MANY) AND OF A VEXED LIFE, ...	222	SEXTUS PROP: 8	17
I SHALL LIVE, IF SHE CONTINUE IN LIFE, ...	223	SEXTUS PROP: 9	8
COMRADE, COMRADE OF MY LIFE, OF MY PURSE, OF MY PERSON;	228	SEXTUS PROP:12	14
SO HE "FACED LIFE" WITH RATHER MIXED INTENTIONS,	242	MOYEN SENSUEL	101
NOR CAN MAN SAY HE HATH HIS LIFE BY CHANCE	249	DONNA MI PREGA	46
LIFE'S			
BUT REACH ME NOT AND ALL MY LIFE'S BECOME	20	IN DURANCE	6
MY SOUL, I MEET THEE, WHEN THIS LIFE'S OUTRUN, ...	39	BLANDULA	6
ALL, ALL OUR LIFE'S ETERNAL MYSTERY!	41	HER MONUMENT	25
YE SEE HERE SEVERED, MY LIFE'S COUNTERPART."	156	NEAR PERIGORD	168
LIFE'S A SORT OF SUGARED DISH-WASH!"	241	MOYEN SENSUEL	90
LIFE'S-BLAST			
AYE, FOR EVER, A LASTING LIFE'S-BLAST, ...	66	THE SEAFARER	80
LIFT			
WHEN LIGHT THEIR VOICES LIFT THEM UP, ...	45	FROM HEINE: 5	5
LILIES LIFT THEIR WHITE SYMBOLICAL CUPS, ...	180	MOEURS CON: 5	20
TO LIFT YOU UP THROUGH SPLIT AIR, ...	226	SEXTUS PROP:11	9
LIFTED			
FADES WHEN THE WIND HATH LIFTED THEM ASIDE, ...	40	ERAT HORA	3
FOETID BUCHANAN LIFTED UP HIS VOICE	192	YEUX GLAUQUES	5
LIFTING			
AND THE WIND LIFTING THE SONG, AND INTERRUPTING IT,	136	EXILE'S LETTER	61
LIFTING THE FAINT SUSURRUS	202	AGE DEMANDED	54
LIFTS			
OUR MALENESS LIFTS US OUT OF THE RUCK, ...	82	THE CONDOLENCE	5
AND THE GREEN CAT'S-EYE LIFTS TOWARD MONTAIGNAC.	154	NEAR PERIGORD	103
LIGHT			
ERE THE NIGHT SLAY LIGHT	24	THUS NINEVEH	18
WERE SET TOGETHER THEY WOULD SEEM BUT LIGHT	36	THE YOUNG KING	4
THE LIGHT BECAME HER GRACE AND DWELT AMONG	38	BALLATETTA	1
LO, HOW THE LIGHT DOTH MELT US INTO SONG:	38	BALLATETTA	3
SO SILENT LIGHT; NO GOSSAMER IS SPUN	38	BALLATETTA	7
SEEMED OVER ME TO HOVER LIGHT AS LEAVES	39	FOR PSYCHE	6
WHEN LIGHT THEIR VOICES LIFT THEM UP, ...	45	FROM HEINE: 5	5
SET TO SOME WEAVING, COMES THE AUREATE LIGHT.	49	OF SPLENDOUR	16
WE OF THE EVER-LIVING, IN THAT LIGHT	50	THE FLAME	12
THERE IS THE SUBTLER MUSIC, THE CLEAR LIGHT	50	THE FLAME	20
AND THY LIGHT LIMBS, WHERETHROUGH I LEAPT AFLAME,	60	TOMB AKR CAAR	4
SEE, THE LIGHT GRASS SPRANG UP TO PILLOW THEE, ...	60	TOMB AKR CAAR	6
AND NO LIGHT BEATS UPON ME, AND YOU SAY	60	TOMB AKR CAAR	27
IN THE SLOW FLOAT OF DIFFERING LIGHT AND DEEP, ...	61	PORTRAIT FEMME	27

PAGE 229

LIGHT -- LIKE

	PAGE	TITLE	LINE
LIGHT (CONTINUED)			
STRAIGHT, THEN SHONE THINE ORIEL AND THE STUNNED LIGHT	68	APPARUIT	15
STRANDS OF LIGHT INWOVEN ABOUT IT, LOVELIEST	68	APPARUIT	18
BRING THE LIGHT OF THE BIRCH TREE IN AUTUMN	75	THE ALCHEMIST	11
MIDONZ, WITH THE GOLD OF THE SUN, THE LEAF OF THE POPLAR, BY THE LIGHT OF THE AMBER,	75	THE ALCHEMIST	25
MIDONZ, DAUGHTER OF THE SUN, SHAFT OF THE TREE, SILVER OF THE LEAF, LIGHT OF THE YELLOW OF THE AMBER,	75	THE ALCHEMIST	26
MIDONZ, GIFT OF THE GOD, GIFT OF THE LIGHT, GIFT OF THE AMBER OF THE SUN,	75	THE ALCHEMIST	27
GIVE LIGHT TO THE METAL.	75	THE ALCHEMIST	28
IN THE COOL LIGHT,	81	TENZONE	13
GO WITH A LIGHT FOOT!	85	SALUTATION 2ND	17
(OR WITH TWO LIGHT FEET, IF IT PLEASE YOU!)	86	SALUTATION 2ND	18
SEEK EVER TO STAND IN THE HARD SOPHOCLEAN LIGHT	95	ITE	3
O LIGHT BOUND AND BENT IN, O SOUL OF THE CAPTIVE,	95	OF THE DEGREES	11
FULL OF FAINT LIGHT	107	COMING OF WAR	3
THIS BOARD IS ALIVE WITH LIGHT;	120	GAME OF CHESS	6
LIGHT RAIN IS ON THE LIGHT DUST	137	OF DEPARTURE	EPI
LIGHT RAIN IS ON THE LIGHT DUST	137	OF DEPARTURE	EPI
LIGHT!	147	BEFORE SLEEP	11
GOES ON THAT HEADLESS TRUNK, THAT BEARS FOR LIGHT	156	NEAR PERIGORD	164
AND EDWARD'S MISTRESSES STILL LIGHT THE STAGE,	163	CABARET DANCER	73
LIKE A LITTLE WAFER OF LIGHT.	166	FISH & SHADOW	3
AS LIGHT AS THE SHADOW OF THE FISH	166	FISH & SHADOW	5
LIGHT AS THE SHADOW OF THE FISH	166	FISH & SHADOW	20
WILL YOU GIVE ME DAWN LIGHT AT EVENING?	167	OF AROUET	17
AND GRASS GOING GLASSY WITH THE LIGHT ON IT,	167	OF AROUET	20
THE SWIRL OF LIGHT FOLLOWS ME THROUGH THE SQUARE,	169	PHANOPOEIA	1
THE WATER-JET OF GOLD LIGHT BEARS US UP THROUGH THE CEILINGS;	169	PHANOPOEIA	4
THE WHIRLING TISSUE OF LIGHT	170	PHANOPOEIA	22
LIGHT	171	LANGUE D'OC	EPI
O PLASMATOUR AND TRUE CELESTIAL LIGHT,	172	LANGUE D'OC: 1	1
LIGHT IS	176	LANGUE D'OC: 3	75
AND SHE SPEAKS ILL OF LIGHT WOMEN,	218	SEXTUS PROP: 5	61
LIGHT, LIGHT OF MY EYES, AT AN EXCEEDING LATE HOUR I WAS WANDERING,	224	SEXTUS PROP:10	1
LIGHT, LIGHT OF MY EYES, AT AN EXCEEDING LATE HOUR I WAS WANDERING,	224	SEXTUS PROP:10	1
MY LIGHT, LIGHT OF MY EYES,	224	SEXTUS PROP: 9	22
MY LIGHT, LIGHT OF MY EYES,	224	SEXTUS PROP: 9	22
STAMP ON HIS ROOF OR IN THE GLAZING LIGHT	236	MIDDLE-AGED	5
INTO THE LIGHT OF IT,	248	DONNA MI PREGA	9
FORMED THERE IN MANNER AS A MIST OF LIGHT	248	DONNA MI PREGA	20
IN MIDST OF DARKNESS LIGHT LIGHT GIVETH FORTH	250	DONNA MI PREGA	85
IN MIDST OF DARKNESS LIGHT LIGHT GIVETH FORTH	250	DONNA MI PREGA	85
LIGHTED			
CUPID WILL CARRY LIGHTED TORCHES BEFORE HIM	212	SEXTUS PROP: 3	22
LIGHTLY			
SO LIGHTLY WROUGHT	42	HER MONUMENT	56
LIGHTNESS			
FOR MY SURROUNDING AIR HATH A NEW LIGHTNESS;	71	A VIRGINAL	3
LIGHTNING			
FALLS LIKE BLACK LIGHTNING.	87	THE SPRING	9
AND EVEN ZEUS' WILD LIGHTNING FEAR TO STRIKE	244	MOYEN SENSUEL	177
LIGHTNINGS			
AND THE LIGHTNINGS FROM BLACK HEAV'N FLASH CRIMSON,	28	ALTAFORTE	9
LIGHTS			
THY FACE AS A RIVER WITH LIGHTS.	91	DANCE FIGURE	11
BLOCKED LIGHTS WORKING IN. ESCAPES. RENEWAL OF CONTEST.	120	GAME OF CHESS	15
STRUGGLES WHEN THE LIGHTS WERE TAKEN AWAY;	220	SEXTUS PROP: 7	4
LIGHTSOME			
AND ON THE MORROW, BY SOME LIGHTSOME TWIST,	42	HER MONUMENT	35
LIKE			
I DO NOT LIKE TO REMEMBER THINGS ANY MORE.	5	LA FRAISNE	48
I LIKE ONE LITTLE BAND OF WINDS THAT BLOW	5	LA FRAISNE	49
BAH! THERE'S NO WINE LIKE THE BLOOD'S CRIMSON!	28	ALTAFORTE	18

PAGE 230

LIKE

	PAGE	TITLE	LINE
LIKE (CONTINUED)			
THERE'S NO SOUND LIKE TO SWORDS SWORDS OPPOSING,	29	ALTAFORTE	32
NO CRY LIKE THE BATTLE'S REJOICING	29	ALTAFORTE	33
BUT LIKE A MIST WHERETHROUGH HER WHITE FORM FOUGHT,	31	PIERE VIDAL	30
WI' HIS EYES LIKE THE GREY O' THE SEA, ...	34	GOODLY FERE	44
LIKE THE SEA THAT BROOKS NO VOYAGING	34	GOODLY FERE	45
LIKE THE SEA THAT HE COWED AT GENSERET	34	GOODLY FERE	47
IS LIKE TO HEAVEN'S MOST 'LIVE IMAGINING.	41	HER MONUMENT	24
THROUGH TRILLS AND RUNS LIKE CRYSTAL, ...	45	FROM HEINE: 5	7
PLEASETH ME, AND IN LIKE WISE	52	AU SALON	EPI
TO BAY LIKE SIR ROGER DE COVERLEY'S	52	AU SALON	15
BUT SHE DANCED LIKE A PINK MOTH IN THE SHRUBBERY.	53	AU JARDIN	19
THE BRANCHES GROW OUT OF ME, LIKE ARMS.	62	A GIRL	5
NOR GOLD-GIVING LORDS LIKE THOSE GONE.	66	THE SEAFARER	85
YOU, I WOULD HAVE FLOW OVER ME LIKE WATER, ...	70	THE PLUNGE	14
LIKE A SKEIN OF LOOSE SILK BLOWN AGAINST A WALL ...	83	THE GARDEN	1
LIKE A GILDED PAVLOVA, ...	83	THE GARRET	7
SHE WOULD LIKE SOME ONE TO SPEAK TO HER, ...	83	THE GARDEN	10
FALLS LIKE BLACK LIGHTNING.	87	THE SPRING	9
GO LIKE A BLIGHT UPON THE DULNESS OF THE WORLD; ...	88	COMMISSION	18
IT IS LIKE AN OLD TREE WITH SHOOTS, ...	89	COMMISSION	31
THERE IS NONE LIKE THEE AMONG THE DANCERS, ...	91	DANCE FIGURE	4
THY MAIDENS ARE WHITE LIKE PEBBLES;	91	DANCE FIGURE	21
THERE IS NONE LIKE THEE AMONG THE DANCERS;	91	DANCE FIGURE	23
LIKE SO MANY UNUSED BOAS.	93	LES MILLWIN	4
LIKE THE CHEEK OF A CHESTERTON.	99	CAKE OF SOAP	2
HAVE WE EVER HEARD THE LIKE?	104	ANCORA	7
HER FINGERS WERE LIKE THE TISSUE	110	THE ENCOUNTER	4
LIKE A SWALLOW HALF BLOWN TO THE WALL, ...	112	SHOP GIRL	2
BUT SEEMS LIKE A PERSON JUST GONE.	112	IONE, DEAD	9
"LIKE TO LIKE NATURE": THESE AGGLUTINOUS YELLOWS!	114	BEFORE A SHOP	2
"LIKE TO LIKE NATURE": THESE AGGLUTINOUS YELLOWS!	114	BEFORE A SHOP	2
HE WAS UNCERTAIN WHY HE SHOULD TRY TO FEEL LIKE ANYTHING ELSE, ...	118	ANCIENT WISDOM	3
NOT LIKE THE HALF-CASTES, ...	119	THE GYPSY	5
LIKE THE JOY OF BLUE ISLANDS.	129	THE RIVER SONG	16
WHO AMONG THEM IS A MAN LIKE HAN-REI	132	AT TEN-SHIN	31
AND SORROW, SORROW LIKE RAIN.	133	FRONTIER GUARD	17
MANY INSTRUMENTS, LIKE THE SOUND OF YOUNG PHOENIX BROODS.	135	EXILE'S LETTER	27
AND BEFORE THE END OF THE DAY WE WERE SCATTERED LIKE STARS, OR RAIN.	135	EXILE'S LETTER	33
OVER ROADS TWISTED LIKE SHEEP'S GUTS.	135	EXILE'S LETTER	41
WITH RIPPLES LIKE DRAGON-SCALES, GOING GRASS GREEN ON THE WATER, ...	136	EXILE'S LETTER	52
WITH THE WILLOW FLAKES FALLING LIKE SNOW, ...	136	EXILE'S LETTER	54
IT IS LIKE THE FLOWERS FALLING AT SPRING'S END	136	EXILE'S LETTER	73
MIND LIKE A FLOATING WIDE CLOUD, ...	137	TAKING LEAVE	5
SUNSET LIKE THE PARTING OF OLD ACQUAINTANCES	137	TAKING LEAVE	6
LICE SWARM LIKE ANTS OVER OUR ACCOUTREMENTS.	139	SOUTH-FOLK	8
TREES THAT GLITTER LIKE JADE, ...	141	IDEA OF CHOAN	19
BUT WE LIKE THIS FELLOW THE BEST, ...	142	UNMOVING CLOUD	25
SPREAD LIKE THE FINGER-TIPS OF ONE FRAIL HAND;	152	NEAR PERIGORD	30
AND LIKE A SWINGING LAMP THAT SAYS, "AH ME!	156	NEAR PERIGORD	166
BUT I AM LIKE THE GRASS, I CAN NOT LOVE YOU.'	157	NEAR PERIGORD	182
"DID YOU TALK LIKE A FOOL, ...	159	PSYCHOLOG HOUR	34
IT JUTS LIKE A SHELF BETWEEN THE JOWL AND CORSET.	161	CABARET DANCER	16
I DON'T KNOW WHAT YOU LOOK LIKE	162	CABARET DANCER	40
LIKE A LITTLE WAFER OF LIGHT.	166	FISH & SHADOW	3
GENTLE TALKING, NOT LIKE THE FIRST TALKING, LESS LIVELY;	168	OF AROUET	32
LIKE THE BRANCH THAT TURNS ABOUT	173	LANGUE D'OC: 2	12
AND THE OTHER WAS RATHER LIKE MY BUST BY GAUDIER,	181	MOEURS CON: 7	13
OR LIKE A REAL TEXAS COLONEL, ...	181	MOEURS CON: 7	14
THE THOUGHT OF WHAT AMERICA WOULD BE LIKE	183	CANTICO SOLE	1
THE THOUGHT OF WHAT AMERICA WOULD BE LIKE	183	CANTICO SOLE	6
THE THOUGHT OF WHAT AMERICA WOULD BE LIKE	183	CANTICO SOLE	14
THIN LIKE BROOK-WATER, ...	192	YEUX GLAUQUES	13
SHE WOULD SIT LIKE AN ORNAMENT ON MY PYRE.	213	SEXTUS PROP: 3	31
TO THINGS WHICH YOU THINK I WOULD LIKE TO BELIEVE.	214	SEXTUS PROP: 4	7
"DOES HE LIKE ME TO SLEEP HERE ALONE, ...	215	SEXTUS PROP: 4	38

LIKE -- LINING

```
                                                          PAGE     TITLE            LINE
LIKE (CONTINUED)
     AND NOW DRINKS NILE WATER LIKE A GOD, ..............  222     SEXTUS PROP: 8    20
     FLEE IF YOU LIKE INTO RANAUS, .....................   226     SEXTUS PROP:11     5
     I WOULD ASK A LIKE BOON OF JOVE. ..................   228     SEXTUS PROP:12    17
     LIKE A TRAINED AND PERFORMING TORTOISE, ...........   229     SEXTUS PROP:12    59
     ONE MUST HAVE RESONANCE, RESONANCE AND SONORITY ..
       LIKE A GOOSE. ...................................   230     SEXTUS PROP:12    65
     HIS PALACE IS WHITE LIKE MARBLE, ..................   237     ABU SALAMMAMM      5
     HIS PALACE IS LIKE A CUBE CUT IN THIRDS, ..........   237     ABU SALAMMAMM      7
     AND THEY HAVE RED FACES LIKE BRICKS. ..............   237     ABU SALAMMAMM     14
     AND ITS WATERS ARE WHITE LIKE SILK. ...............   237     ABU SALAMMAMM     21
     LIKE A WOMAN HEAVY WITH CHILD. ....................   237     ABU SALAMMAMM     25
     IF I SET FORTH A BAWDY PLOT LIKE BYRON ............   239     MOYEN SENSUEL     42
     AND THEN THAT WOMAN LIKE A GUINEA-PIG .............   242     MOYEN SENSUEL    120
     SO RADWAY WALKED, QUITE LIKE THE OTHER MEN, .......   244     MOYEN SENSUEL    185
     "NOTHING WILL PAY THEE, FRIEND, LIKE CHRISTIANITY."   246     MOYEN SENSUEL    236
     LOOK DRAWN FROM LIKE, .............................   250     DONNA MI PREGA    70
     AN' 'E LOOKS LIKE A TOFF. .........................   260     ALF'S FOURTH      15
     GO TO GOD LIKE A SOJER; ...........................   260     ALF'S FOURTH      18
     DON'T GET A DISCOUNT LIKE MR. SELFRIDGE ...........   262     ALF'S SEVENTH     11
     LIKE ALL HIS CLASS WAS TOLD TO HOLD IT IN THOSE DAYS, 263     ALF'S EIGHTH      26
     FROM A GREAT EMPLOYER LIKE SELFRIDGE ..............   264     ALF'S EIGHTH      33
     THERE IS NO LAND LIKE ENGLAND .....................   272     NATIONAL SONG      1
     THERE ARE NO BANKS LIKE ENGLISH BANKS .............   272     NATIONAL SONG      3
     THAN MEN LIKE ME AND YOU, .........................   272     THE BABY           6
     LIKE TO-DAY'S GREAT MEN IN BRITAIN. ...............   272     THE BABY          12
LIKENESS
     LIKENESS OF THINE HANDMAID, .......................    26     NIGHT LITANY      24
     HATH OF THE TREES A LIKENESS OF THE SAVOUR: .......    71     A VIRGINAL        13
     THAT THE BASE LIKENESS OF IT KINDLETH NOT. ........   249     DONNA MI PREGA    32
LIKEWISE
     LIKEWISE A FRIEND OF BLOUGHRAM'S ONCE ADVISED ME:     194     MR. NIXON         21
     HEAD FARMERS DO LIKEWISE, AND LYING WEARY AMID THEIR
       OATS ............................................   229     SEXTUS PROP:12    48
     AND THE LARGER STORES WERE LIKEWISE ...............   262     ALF'S SEVENTH      6
LILIES
     OVER A STREAM FULL OF LILIES. .....................   121     PROVINC DESERT    17
     LILIES LIFT THEIR WHITE SYMBOLICAL CUPS. ..........   180     MOEURS CON: 5     20
     BENT RESOLUTELY ON WRINGING LILIES FROM THE ACORN;    187     E. P. ODE          7
LILTING
     SHALL BURST TO LILTING AT THE PRAISE ..............     9     NA AUDIART        28
LILY-OF-THE-VALLEY
     OF LILY-OF-THE-VALLEY .............................   109     ALBA               2
LIMBS
     WHERE THY TORSE AND LIMBS ARE MET .................     8     NA AUDIART        24
     AND THY LIGHT LIMBS, WHERETHROUGH I LEAPT AFLAME,      60     TOMB AKR CAAR      4
     THE FLOOD OF LIMBS UPON EIGHTH AVENUE .............   245     MOYEN SENSUEL    189
LIMNING
     THAT HATH NO PERFECT LIMNING, WHEN THE WARM .......     9     NA AUDIART        39
LIMPID
     THE SKY-LIKE LIMPID EYES, .........................   193     BRENNBAUM          1
LIN
     AUX TOISONS COULEUR DE LIN, .......................   160     DANS OMNIBUS      16
LINCOLN
     YOU AND ABE LINCOLN FROM THAT MASS OF DOLTS .......   235     TO WHISTLER       18
LINE
     AND THAT HARD PHALANX, THAT UNBROKEN LINE, ........   153     NEAR PERIGORD     64
LINED
     AS A BATHTUB LINED WITH WHITE PORCELAIN, ..........   100     THE BATH TUB       1
     THE BASKET IS LINED WITH SATIN, ...................   180     MOEURS CON: 5     14
LINES
     YEA THE LINES HAST THOU LAID UNTO ME ..............    26     NIGHT LITANY
     FAINT, ALMOST, AS THE LINES OF CRUELTY ABOUT YOUR
       CHIN, ...........................................   103     LADIES            15
     HOLDING LINES IN ONE COLOUR. ......................   120     GAME OF CHESS
     RIGHT ENOUGH? THEN READ BETWEEN THE LINES OF UC ST.
       CIRC, ...........................................   151     NEAR PERIGORD
LINGERING
     HER KISSES, HOW MANY, LINGERING ON MY LIPS. .......   220     SEXTUS PROP: 7     1
LINING
     SEZ THE TIMES A SILVER LINING .....................   267     ALF'S TWELFTH
```

PAGE 232

LION-COLOURED -- LITTLE

	PAGE	TITLE	LINE
LION-COLOURED			
THE CORAL ISLE, THE LION-COLOURED SAND	201	AGE DEMANDED	17
LIONEL			
TOLD ME HOW JOHNSON (LIONEL) DIED	193	SIENA MI FE	7
LIP			
MOSS WORDS, LIP WORDS, WORDS OF SLOW STREAMS.	16	PRAISE YSOLT	22
A-TREMBLE IN MEN'S VEINS; O LIP CURVED HIGH	41	HER MONUMENT	12
LIPS			
NO MORE FOR US THE WINE OF THE LIPS,	3	THRENOS	12
LIPS, WORDS, AND YOU SNARE THEM,	6	CINO	4
EYES, DREAMS, LIPS, AND THE NIGHT GOES.	6	CINO	10
WHERE ARE THE LIPS MINE LAY UPON,	10	FOR THIS YULE	19
LIPS SHRUNK BACK FOR THE WIND'S CARESS	11	OF THE GIBBET	19
AS LIPS SHRINK BACK WHEN WE FEEL THE STRAIN	11	OF THE GIBBET	20
AND SENSE THE TEETH THROUGH THE LIPS THAT PRESS	11	OF THE GIBBET	22
'GAINST OUR LIPS FOR THE SOUL'S DISTRESS	11	OF THE GIBBET	23
THE WINDS ARE UNDER MY LIPS.	18	DE AEGYPTO	20
OVER THE SHARPENED TEETH AND PURPLING LIPS!	30	PIERE VIDAL	15
AS DID FIRST SCORN, THEN LIPS OF THE PENAUTIER!	30	PIERE VIDAL	17
AS CRUSHED LIPS TAKE THEIR RESPITE FITFULLY,	43	SATIEMUS	8
O YE LIPS THAT ARE UNGRATEFUL,	44	FROM HEINE: 1	5
MY LIPS AND MY HEART ARE THINE THERE	47	FROM HEINE: 7	13
AND HAVE YOU THOROUGHLY KISSED MY LIPS?	48	FROM HEINE: 8	1
SEARCH NOT MY LIPS, O LOVE, LET GO MY HANDS,	51	THE FLAME	37
I LONG FOR THY LIPS.	112	HIMERRO	5
BELIEVING WE SHOULD MEET WITH LIPS AND HANDS,	157	NEAR PERIGORD	179
WITH SONG UPON HER LIPS	197	ENVOI (1919)	18
TO PLACE THE LAST KISS ON MY LIPS	219	SEXTUS PROP: 6	24
HER LIPS UPON THEM; AND IT WAS HER MOUTH SAYING:	220	SEXTUS PROP: 7	8
HER KISSES, HOW MANY, LINGERING ON MY LIPS.	220	SEXTUS PROP: 7	11
LIP-STICK			
COVERED WITH LIP-STICK.	261	ALF'S SIXTH	12
LIQUEURS			
WITH RHINE WINE AND LIQUEURS.	46	FROM HEINE: 6	4
LIQUID			
A LIQUID GLORY? IF AT SIRMIO,	39	BLANDULA	5
LIST			
LIST HOW I, CARE-WRETCHED, ON ICE-COLD SEA,	64	THE SEAFARER	14
TESTING HIS LIST OF RHYMES, A LEAN MAN? BILIOUS?	154	NEAR PERIGORD	101
DESPITE THE CUCKOLD, DO THOU AS THOU LIST,	177	LANGUE D'OC: 4	13
AND TELL OUT THE LONG LIST OF HER TROUBLES.	223	SEXTUS PROP: 9	12
LISTED			
IS LISTED. WELL! SOME SCORE YEARS HENCE	14	FAMAM CANO	20
LISTEN			
LISTEN! LISTEN TO ME, AND I WILL BREATHE INTO THEE A SOUL.	62	N. Y.	2
LISTEN! LISTEN TO ME, AND I WILL BREATHE INTO THEE A SOUL.	62	N. Y.	2
LISTEN TO ME, ATTEND ME!	62	N. Y.	11
AND HIGH OVER THE WILLOWS, THE FINE BIRDS SING TO EACH OTHER, AND LISTEN,	129	THE RIVER SONG	28
LISTEN, MY CHILDREN, AND YOU SHALL HEAR	264	ALF'S NINTH	1
LISTEN, MY CHILDREN, AND YOU SHALL HEAR	265	ALF'S NINTH	26
LIT			
OR TO SUCH BASE OCCASION LIT AND QUENCHED?	42	HER MONUMENT	57
GO I, THE FIRES THAT LIT ONCE DREAMS	236	MIDDLE-AGED	13
LITANY			
NIGHT LITANY	26	NIGHT LITANY	T
LITERARY			
OF LITERARY EFFORT,	196	HUGH SELWIN:12	11
LITERATI			
ALL THE BULMENIAN LITERATI.	99	SALVATIONISTS	17
LITERATURE			
"THE TIP'S A GOOD ONE, AS FOR LITERATURE	194	MR. NIXON	16
TO READ HIS SMUTTY LITERATURE	272	NATIONAL SONG	7
LITER			
'AVE YOU SEEN YER LARST SWEET LITTER?	270	OF 600 M.P.'S	18
LITTLE			
NO MORE FOR US THE LITTLE SIGHING.	3	THRENOS	1
I LIKE ONE LITTLE BAND OF WINDS THAT BLOW	5	LA FRAISNE	49
OH! THE LITTLE MOTHERS	14	FAMAM CANO	2

PAGE 233

LITTLE -- LIVE

	PAGE	TITLE	LINE
LITTLE (CONTINUED)			
HER NOTE, THE LITTLE RABBIT FOLK	14	FAMAM CANO	8
AND LITTLE RED ELF WORDS CRYING "A SONG,"	16	PRAISE YSOLT	15
LITTLE GREY ELF WORDS CRYING FOR A SONG, ...	16	PRAISE YSOLT	16
LITTLE BROWN LEAF WORDS CRYING "A SONG,"	16	PRAISE YSOLT	17
LITTLE GREEN LEAF WORDS CRYING FOR A SONG.	16	PRAISE YSOLT	18
BUT STILL CAME THE LEAF WORDS, LITTLE BROWN ELF WORDS	17	PRAISE YSOLT	33
THE WORDS, LITTLE ELF WORDS	17	PRAISE YSOLT	52
THE LITTLE HILLS TO EAST OF US, THOUGH HERE WE	21	IN DURANCE	39
THY LITTLE HEART, SO SWEET AND FALSE AND SMALL	44	FROM HEINE: 2	3
THEN LET US SMILE A LITTLE SPACE	44	MR. HOUSMAN	13
AMID THE LITTLE PINE TREES, HEAR ME!	53	AU JARDIN	5
THIS HE LITTLE BELIEVES, WHO AYE IN WINSOME LIFE .	64	THE SEAFARER	28
DAYS LITTLE DURABLE, ...	66	THE SEAFARER	82
DAWN ENTERS WITH LITTLE FEET	83	THE GARRET	6
GO, LITTLE NAKED AND IMPUDENT SONGS, ...	85	SALUTATION 2ND	16
AND THE DELICATE WHITE FEET OF HER LITTLE WHITE DOG	87	ALBATRE	3
THE LITTLE MILLWINS ATTEND THE RUSSIAN BALLET.	93	LES MILLWIN	1
THE MAUVE AND GREENISH SOULS OF THE LITTLE MILLWINS	93	LES MILLWIN	2
AND THE LITTLE MILLWINS BEHELD THESE THINGS;	93	LES MILLWIN	11
INSOLENT LITTLE BEASTS, SHAMELESS, DEVOID OF CLOTHING!	94	INSTRUCTIONS	14
BUT THE GOOD BELLAIRES HAVE SO LITTLE UNDERSTOOD THEIR AFFAIRS	97	THE BELLAIRES	8
ASSAILS ME, AND CONCERNS ME ALMOST AS LITTLE.	103	LADIES	20
WITH HER LITTLE SUEDE SLIPPERS OFF, ...	111	BLACK SLIPPERS	2
AND ON THIS ACCOUNT THE LITTLE AURELIA, ...	111	SOCIETY	2
GIVE ME IN DUE TIME, I BESEECH YOU, A LITTLE TOBACCO-SHOP, ...	117	THE LAKE ISLE	2
WITH THE LITTLE BRIGHT BOXES	117	THE LAKE ISLE	3
LEND ME A LITTLE TOBACCO-SHOP, ...	117	THE LAKE ISLE	13
SOME LITTLE PRIZED PLACE IN AUVERGNAT:	122	PROVINC DESERT	65
AND THINKING HOW LITTLE YOU CARED FOR THE COST, ...	135	EXILE'S LETTER	44
A LITTLE BLACK BOX CONTAINS THEM.	145	SALUTATION 3RD	8
LIE LITTLE STRIPS OF PARCHMENT COVERED OVER, ...	154	NEAR PERIGORD	99
LITTLE ENOUGH?	154	NEAR PERIGORD	114
"THEIR LITTLE COSMOS IS SHAKEN"--	158	PSYCHOLOG HOUR	12
WITH THEIR PERFUMES IN LITTLE ALABASTER BOXES?	165	QUINTUS SEPTIM	15
LIKE A LITTLE WAFER OF LIGHT.	166	FISH & SHADOW	3
YAWNING A LITTLE SHE CAME WITH THE SLEEP STILL UPON HER.	166	FISH & SHADOW	8
THE OTHER IS LITTLE BESIDE IT.	168	OF AROUET	29
BIG TALK AND LITTLE USE.	173	LANGUE D'OC: 2	26
MY LITTLE MOUTH SHALL GOBBLE IN SUCH GREAT FOUNTAINS,	210	SEXTUS PROP: 2	
AND SOME OF THEM SHOOK LITTLE TORCHES, ...	224	SEXTUS PROP:10	
AND MUCH OF LITTLE MOMENT, AND SOME FEW	235	TO WHISTLER	
SAVE THAT PERFECTION FAILS, BE IT BUT A LITTLE; ...	249	DONNA MI PREGA	4
OR WRIES THE FACE WITH FEAR AND LITTLE STAYS, ...	250	DONNA MI PREGA	5
YEA, RESTETH LITTLE	250	DONNA MI PREGA	5
WILL KEEP IT A LITTLE LONGER, ...	266	ALF'S TENTH	1
UNTIL THE MIND OF THE OLD NATION GETS A LITTLE STRONGER.	266	ALF'S TENTH	1
BUT THE BAWDY LITTLE BRITONS	272	NATIONAL SONG	1
LIU			
LIU CH'E	108	LIU CH'E	
LIVE			
THAT HE SHOULD LIVE THAN MANY A LIVING DASTARD	37	THE YOUNG KING	2
I LIVE TOO LATE TO SUP WITH THEE!	46	TRANSLATOR	
LIFE IS THE LIVE MAN'S PART, ...	47	FROM HEINE: 7	
AND THOU SHALT LIVE FOR EVER.	62	N. Y.	
AND THAT YOU WILL LIVE FOREVER.	86	SALUTATION 2ND	
HOW WOULD YOU LIVE, WITH NEIGHBOURS SET ABOUT YOU--	152	NEAR PERIGORD	
SHE WHO COULD NEVER LIVE SAVE THROUGH ONE PERSON, .	157	NEAR PERIGORD	1
I DO NOT LIVE, NOR CURE ME, ...	174	LANGUE D'OC: 3	
"SHELLEY USED TO LIVE IN THIS HOUSE."	182	MOEURS CON: 8	
I WOULD BID THEM LIVE	197	ENVOI (1919)	
I SHALL LIVE, IF SHE CONTINUE IN LIFE, ...	223	SEXTUS PROP: 9	
OH MAY THE KING LIVE FOREVER!	237	ABU SALAMMAMM	
OH MAY THE KING LIVE FOR A THOUSAND YEARS!	237	ABU SALAMMAMM	
SOME MEN WILL LIVE AS PRUDES IN THEIR OWN VILLAGE .	245	MOYEN SENSUEL	2
SURE, THEY CAN LIVE ON HOPE, ...	259	ALF'S THIRD	

PAGE 234

'LIVE -- LODGE

	PAGE	TITLE	LINE
'LIVE			
IS LIKE TO HEAVEN'S MOST 'LIVE IMAGINING.	41	HER MONUMENT	24
LIVED			
WHOE'ER LIVED IN LIFE MOST LORDLIEST, ...	66	THE SEAFARER	87
THINK YOU THAT MAENT LIVED AT MONTAIGNAC, ...	151	NEAR PERIGORD	11
LIVELY			
GENTLE TALKING, NOT LIKE THE FIRST TALKING, LESS LIVELY;	168	OF AROUET	32
WITH A LIVELY WOOD-PULP "AD."	268	ALF'S TWELFTH	19
LIVER			
FREEZETH RIVER, TURNETH LIVER, ...	116	ANCIENT MUSIC	8
LIVETH			
THAT HE ON DRY LAND LOVELIEST LIVETH, ...	64	THE SEAFARER	13
LIVING			
THAT HE SHOULD LIVE THAN MANY A LIVING DASTARD	37	THE YOUNG KING	23
LAUD OF THE LIVING, BOASTETH SOME LAST WORD, ...	66	THE SEAFARER	74
THESE PIECES ARE LIVING IN FORM, ...	120	GAME OF CHESS	7
I HAVE THOUGHT OF THEM LIVING.	123	PROVINC DESERT	81
AND WE WENT ON LIVING IN THE VILLAGE OF CHOKAN: ...	130	RIVER-MER WIFE	5
THAT TOM-BOY WHO CAN'T EARN HER LIVING, ...	162	CABARET DANCER	44
AND SHE WAS LED BACK, LIVING, HOME;	227	SEXTUS PROP:11	26
IN BOSTON, TO HENRY JAMES, THE GREATEST WHOM WE'VE SEEN LIVING.	240	MOYEN SENSUEL	63
LO			
LO THE FAIR DEAD!	3	THRENOS	3
LO THE FAIR DEAD!	3	THRENOS	7
LO THE FAIR DEAD!	3	THRENOS	11
LO THE FAIR DEAD!	3	THRENOS	14
(LO THE FAIR DEAD!)	3	THRENOS	17
LO, I AM WORN WITH TRAVAIL	16	PRAISE YSOLT	11
"LO! THIS THING IS NOT MINE	24	THUS NINEVEH	5
LO, I WOULD SAIL THE SEAS WITH THEE ALONE!	25	GUIDO INVITES	2
LO! THEY PAUSE NOT FOR LOVE NOR FOR SORROW, ...	25	THE WHITE STAG	2
LO, I HAVE SEEN THEE BOUND ABOUT WITH DREAMS, ...	25	GUIDO INVITES	7
LO, I HAVE KNOWN THY HEART AND ITS DESIRE;	25	GUIDO INVITES	8
LO, THOU HAST VOYAGED NOT! THE SHIP IS MINE."	25	GUIDO INVITES	11
LO! I DO CURSE MY STRENGTH	30	PIERE VIDAL	3
REST BROTHER, FOR LO! THE DAWN IS WITHOUT!	35	THE EYES	5
LO, HOW THE LIGHT DOTH MELT US INTO SONG:	38	BALLATETTA	3
"LO, ONE THERE WAS WHO BENT HER FAIR BRIGHT HEAD, .	43	SATIEMUS	5
LO, THERE ARE MANY GODS WHOM WE HAVE SEEN, ...	50	THE FLAME	23
LO, HOW IT GLEAMS AND GLISTENS IN THE SUN	99	CAKE OF SOAP	1
IEU LO SAI."	166	FISH & SHADOW	17
LOAF			
HALF A LOAF, HALF A LOAF, ...	257	BREAD BRIGADE	1
HALF A LOAF, HALF A LOAF, ...	257	BREAD BRIGADE	1
HALF A LOAF? UM-HUM?	257	BREAD BRIGADE	2
LOAN			
ON LOAN AND ON LAND, I BELIEVE NOT	65	THE SEAFARER	67
LOATHE			
DO I NOT LOATHE ALL WALLS, STREETS, STONES, ...	70	THE PLUNGE	11
LOATHING			
"ALL THE SAME STYLE, SAME CUT, WITH PERFECT LOATHING."	244	MOYEN SENSUEL	184
LOBA			
SWIFT CAME THE LOBA, AS A BRANCH THAT'S CAUGHT, ...	31	PIERE VIDAL	26
AH GOD, THE LOBA! AND MY ONLY MATE!	31	PIERE VIDAL	44
LOCALITY			
WAS PURER IN ITS LOVE OF ONE LOCALITY, ...	245	MOYEN SENSUEL	212
LOCATION			
GODS' AID, LET NOT MY BONES LIE IN A PUBLIC LOCATION	213	SEXTUS PROP: 3	32
LOCKED			
WHO ATE THE PROFITS, AND WHO LOCKED 'EM IN	260	ALF'S FIFTH	18
LOCKS			
SUCH GRACE OF LOCKS, I DO YE TO WIT, ...	106	DOMPNA POIS	38
LOCUS			
IN MEMORY'S LOCUS TAKETH HE HIS STATE	248	DONNA MI PREGA	19
LODGE			
BEFORE THE ROYAL LODGE:	141	IDEA OF CHOAN	6
ARNAUT AND RICHARD LODGE BENEATH CHALUS:	155	NEAR PERIGORD	128

LOFTY -- LONGER

	PAGE	TITLE	LINE
LOFTY			
INFINITE THINGS DESIRED, LOFTY VISIONS	42	HER MONUMENT	41
GREAT AND LOFTY IS THIS FOUNTAIN;	237	ABU SALAMMAMM	22
LOICA			
BRISEIS, LIANOR, LOICA,	75	THE ALCHEMIST	20
LIANOR, IOANNA, LOICA,	76	THE ALCHEMIST	35
LOITER			
YOU LOITER AT THE CORNERS AND BUS-STOPS,	94	INSTRUCTIONS	6
LONDON			
LONDON IS A WOEFUL PLACE,	44	MR. HOUSMAN	11
LONDON HAS SWEPT ABOUT YOU THIS SCORE YEARS	61	PORTRAIT FEMME	2
LONDRES			
DANS UN OMNIBUS DE LONDRES	160	DANS OMNIBUS	T
LONE			
HIS LONE MIGHT 'GAINST ALL DARKNESS OPPOSING.	29	ALTAFORTE	24
HIS LONE SAIL BLOTS THE FAR SKY.	137	ON RIVER KIANG	3
THE LONE MAN SITS WITH SHUT SPEECH,	139	SENNIN POEM	6
LONE-FLYER			
EAGER AND READY, THE CRYING LONE-FLYER,	65	THE SEAFARER	63
LONELINESS			
HAVE ME IN THE STRONG LONELINESS	67	DORIA	5
LONELY			
GO, MY SONGS, TO THE LONELY AND THE UNSATISFIED,	88	COMMISSION	1
LONELY FROM THE BEGINNING OF TIME UNTIL NOW!	133	FRONTIER GUARD	2
LONG			
THAT WAS VERY LONG AGO.	5	LA FRAISNE	47
DAY LONG, LONG DAY COOPED ON A STOOL	22	MARVOIL	3
DAY LONG, LONG DAY COOPED ON A STOOL	22	MARVOIL	3
STRINGING LONG VERSE FOR THE BURLATZ;	22	MARVOIL	20
AND NONE FLED OVER LONG.	30	PIERE VIDAL	12
THAT I SO LONG HELD THY HEART WHOLLY,	44	FROM HEINE: 2	2
I HAVE DETESTED YOU LONG ENOUGH.	89	A PACT	2
"IONE, DEAD THE LONG YEAR"	112	IONE, DEAD	T
TOO LONG	112	PAPYRUS	2
I LONG FOR THY LIPS.	112	HIMERRO	5
I LONG FOR THY NARROW BREASTS,	112	HIMERRO	6
WITH FINGERS THAT ARE NOT LONG, AND WITH A MOUTH UNDRY,	113	FORMIANUS LADY	5
THE FIRST HAS WRITTEN A LONG ELEGY TO "CHLORIS,"	118	THREE POETS	3
AND I'D THE LONG WAYS BEHIND ME,	119	THE GYPSY	9
SEEN THE LONG MINARETS, THE WHITE SHAFTS.	122	PROVINC DESERT	35
VINE-STRINGS A HUNDRED FEET LONG HANG DOWN FROM CARVED RAILINGS,	129	THE RIVER SONG	27
BECAUSE HIS LONG SLEEVES WOULDN'T KEEP STILL	135	EXILE'S LETTER	29
DESPITE THE LONG DISTANCE.	135	EXILE'S LETTER	39
THE LONG KIANG, REACHING HEAVEN.	137	ON RIVER KIANG	5
BUT HOWEVER WE LONG TO SPEAK	142	UNMOVING CLOUD	26
IT HAS BEEN YOUR HABIT FOR LONG	145	SALUTATION 3RD	20
LONG SINCE FULLY DISCUSSED BY OVID.	148	FRATRES MINORE	4
YOU READ TO-DAY, HOW LONG THE OVERLORDS OF PERIGORD,	152	NEAR PERIGORD	50
"COME. I HAVE HAD A LONG DREAM."	166	FISH & SHADOW	10
LONG SINCE SUPERSEDED THE CULTIVATION	196	HUGH SELWIN:12	27
SEEING THAT LONG STANDING INCREASES ALL THINGS	207	SEXTUS PROP: 1	24
WE SHALL SPIN LONG YARNS OUT OF NOTHING.	217	SEXTUS PROP: 5	36
NOR AT MY FUNERAL EITHER WILL THERE BY ANY LONG TRAIL,	219	SEXTUS PROP: 6	13
OH COUCH MADE HAPPY BY MY LONG DELECTATIONS;	220	SEXTUS PROP: 7	2
FOR LONG NIGHT COMES UPON YOU	220	SEXTUS PROP: 7	18
LONG IS MY LIFE, LONG IN YEARS,	221	SEXTUS PROP: 7	38
LONG IS MY LIFE, LONG IN YEARS,	221	SEXTUS PROP: 7	38
AND TELL OUT THE LONG LIST OF HER TROUBLES.	223	SEXTUS PROP: 9	12
WILL LONG ONLY TO BE A SOCIAL FUNCTION,	244	MOYEN SENSUEL	176
OF THINGS THAT HAPPENED VERY LONG AGO,	265	ALF'S NINTH	27
LONGACRE			
WALK DOWN LONGACRE RECITING SWINBURNE TO HERSELF, INAUDIBLY?	114	SIMULACRA	2
LONGER			
"BEING NO LONGER HUMAN, WHY SHOULD I	32	PARACELSUS	1
WILL BE SPREAD ABOUT US NO LONGER.	116	THE TEA SHOP	8
NO LONGER THE MEN FOR OFFENCE AND DEFENCE.	133	FRONTIER GUARD	21
WILL KEEP IT A LITTLE LONGER,	266	ALF'S TENTH	15

LONGEVITY -- LORD

	PAGE	TITLE	LINE
LONGEVITY			
AND BUILD HER GLORIES THEIR LONGEVITY.	197	ENVOI (1919)	7
LONGING			
YET LONGING COMES UPON HIM TO FARE FORTH ON THE WATER.	65	THE SEAFARER	48
LONG-TONSILLED			
YOU WHEEZE AS A HEAD-COLD LONG-TONSILLED CALLIOPE,	13	MESMERISM	9
LOOK			
AND WE WOULD LOOK THEREON.	35	THE EYES	18
WHO CAN LOOK ON THAT BLUE AND NOT BELIEVE?	50	THE FLAME	28
WHY DO YOU LOOK SO EAGERLY AND SO CURIOUSLY INTO PEOPLE'S FACES,	103	CODA	2
THE SMALL DOGS LOOK AT THE BIG DOGS;	104	THE SEEING EYE	1
THE YOUNG MEN LOOK UPON THEIR SENIORS,	104	THE SEEING EYE	5
A LADY WITH LOOK SO SPEAKING	105	DOMPNA POIS	8
WHY SHOULD I CLIMB THE LOOK OUT?	130	RIVER-MER WIFE	14
HE GOES OUT TO HORI, TO LOOK AT THE WING-FLAPPING STORKS,	130	THE RIVER SONG	36
TO LOOK ON THE TALL HOUSE OF THE SHIN	140	MULBERRY ROAD	2
AND WHEN MEN GOING BY LOOK ON RAFU	140	MULBERRY ROAD	15
I DON'T KNOW WHAT YOU LOOK LIKE	162	CABARET DANCER	40
"DELIA, I WOULD LOOK ON YOU, DYING."	168	OF AROUET	40
WHEN HER LOVE LOOK STEALS ON ME.	175	LANGUE D'OC: 3	41
FOR I WOULD NOT LOOK ON A WOMAN.	175	LANGUE D'OC: 3	43
NOR I, NOR TOWER-MAN, LOOK ON DAYLIGHT,	177	LANGUE D'OC: 4	8
FOR HER GREAT BEAUTY, MANY MEN LOOK ON HER,	177	LANGUE D'OC: 4	27
WE MUST LOOK INTO THE MATTER.	208	SEXTUS PROP: 1	48
WE LOOK AT THE PROCESS.	217	SEXTUS PROP: 5	28
STILL WE LOOK TOWARD THE DAY WHEN MAN, WITH UNCTION,	244	MOYEN SENSUEL	175
AND WILLS MAN LOOK INTO UNFORMED SPACE	250	DONNA MI PREGA	59
LOOK DRAWN FROM LIKE,	250	DONNA MI PREGA	70
LOOKED			
WITH THEIR LARGE AND ANAEMIC EYES THEY LOOKED OUT UPON THIS CONFIGURATION.	93	LES MILLWIN	12
I HAVE LOOKED BACK OVER THE STREAM	121	PROVINC DESERT	33
I HAVE LOOKED SOUTH FROM HAUTEFORT,	122	PROVINC DESERT	48
I LOOKED AT THE DRAGON-POND, WITH ITS WILLOW-COLOURED WATER	129	THE RIVER SONG	20
LOWERING MY HEAD, I LOOKED AT THE WALL.	130	RIVER-MER WIFE	9
CALLED TO, A THOUSAND TIMES, I NEVER LOOKED BACK.	130	RIVER-MER WIFE	10
AND ONE AMONG THEM LOOKED AT ME WITH FACE OFFENDED,	211	SEXTUS PROP: 2	38
LOOKING			
TO BE LOOKING OUT ACROSS THE BRIGHT SEA,	164	QUINTUS SEPTIM	5
AND PHOEBUS LOOKING UPON ME FROM THE CASTALIAN TREE,	210	SEXTUS PROP: 2	16
I HAD NEVER SEEN HER LOOKING SO BEAUTIFUL,	225	SEXTUS PROP:10	30
LOOKING SO BIG AND BURLY.	266	ALF'S ELEVENTH	8
LOOKS			
THE RED-PINE-TREE GOD LOOKS AT HIM AND WONDERS.	139	SENNIN POEM	11
AND WHEN SHE LOOKS ON ME	176	LANGUE D'OC: 3	67
MUST THINK TRUTH LOOKS AS THEY DO IN WOOL PYJAMAS.	243	MOYEN SENSUEL	148
AN' 'E LOOKS LIKE A TOFF.	260	ALF'S FOURTH	15
WHAT COUNTS IS THE LOOKS.	260	ALF'S FOURTH	19
LOOM			
OR FINDS ITS HOUR UPON THE LOOM OF DAYS:	61	PORTRAIT FEMME	21
LOOPED			
LOOPED WITH THE KNIGHT-LEAPS.	120	GAME OF CHESS	11
LOOSE			
SET LOOSE THE WHOLE CONSUMMATE PACK	52	AU SALON	14
LIKE A SKEIN OF LOOSE SILK BLOWN AGAINST A WALL	83	THE GARDEN	1
AND THE LOOSE FRAGRANT CAVENDISH	117	THE LAKE ISLE	5
LOOSE UNDER THE BRIGHT GLASS CASES,	117	THE LAKE ISLE	8
FOR I KNOW HOW WORDS RUN LOOSE,	173	LANGUE D'OC: 2	25
FOR I AM TRAIST AND LOOSE,	175	LANGUE D'OC: 3	50
LOPE			
LOPE DE VEGA	82	THE CONDOLENCE	EPI
LOQUITUR			
LOQUITUR,	15	FAMAM CANO	41
LOR			
"ET ALBIRAR AB LOR BORDON--"	153	NEAR PERIGORD	90
LORD			
BUT YOU, MY LORD, HOW WITH YOUR CITY?"	6	CINO	32

PAGE 237

	PAGE	TITLE	LINE
LORD (CONTINUED)			
BUT YOU "MY LORD," GOD'S PITY!	7	CINO	33
AND ALL I KNEW WERE OUT, MY LORD, YOU	7	CINO	34
HIM DO WE PRAY AS TO A LORD MOST RIGHTEOUS	37	THE YOUNG KING	36
WHATEVER HIS LORD WILL.	65	THE SEAFARER	44
MY LORD DEEMS TO ME THIS DEAD LIFE	65	THE SEAFARER	66
THAT HE HAS TAKEN OUR LORD AWAY	72	PAN IS DEAD	12
FAN-PIECE, FOR HER IMPERIAL LORD	108	FAN-PIECE	T
AT FOURTEEN I MARRIED MY LORD YOU.	130	RIVER-MER WIFE	7
LORD POWERFUL, ENGIRDLED ALL WITH MIGHT,	172	LANGUE D'OC: 1	2
--GEORGE GORDON, LORD BYRON.	238	MOYEN SENSUEL	EPI
THAN E'ER WERE HEARD OF BY OUR LORD CH.... J....	241	MOYEN SENSUEL	100
LORDLIEST			
WHOE'ER LIVED IN LIFE MOST LORDLIEST,	66	THE SEAFARER	87
LORDLY			
LORDLY MEN, ARE TO EARTH O'ERGIVEN,	66	THE SEAFARER	95
LORDS			
TO THE DANCE OF LORDS AND LADIES	47	FROM HEINE: 7	23
NOR GOLD-GIVING LORDS LIKE THOSE GONE.	66	THE SEAFARER	85
THE LORDS GO FORTH FROM THE COURT, AND INTO FAR BORDERS.	132	AT TEN-SHIN	14
"PAWN YOUR CASTLES, LORDS!	152	NEAR PERIGORD	38
BUT KNIGHTS AND LORDS TO-DAY RESPECT	267	ALF'S ELEVENTH	23
LORD'S			
AND MEDITATE UPON THE LORD'S CONQUESTS.	246	MOYEN SENSUEL	228
LOSE			
I LOSE ALL WIT AND SENSE.	176	LANGUE D'OC: 3	69
LOSETH			
OR LOSETH POWER, E'EN LOST TO MEMORY.	249	DONNA MI PREGA	48
LOSS			
THE BALANCE FOR THIS LOSS IN IRE AND SADNESS!	37	THE YOUNG KING	16
MADE WITH NO LOSS OF TIME,	188	HUGH SELWYN: 2	10
LOST			
AND LOST MID-PAGE	15	FAMAM CANO	44
HA' WE LOST THE GOODLIEST FERE O' ALL	33	GOODLY FERE	1
WHO CALL'ST ABOUT MY GATES FOR SOME LOST ME;	51	THE FLAME	35
"POOR DEAR! HE HAS LOST HIS ILLUSIONS."	85	SALUTATION 2ND	15
THOUGH EVERY BRANCH HAVE BACK WHAT LAST YEAR LOST,	87	THE SPRING	11
TO THOSE WHO HAVE LOST THEIR INTEREST.	89	COMMISSION	27
A-STRAY, LOST IN THE VILLAGES,	92	THE REST	4
WILL YOU FIND YOUR LOST DEAD AMONG THEM?	103	CODA	3
TO MY DESIRE, WORTH YOURS WHOM I HAVE LOST,	105	DOMPNA POIS	9
WHOSE WHITE HEAD IS LOST FOR THIS PROVINCE?	139	SOUTH-FOLK	14
YOU, SOMETIMES, WILL LAMENT A LOST FRIEND,	219	SEXTUS PROP: 6	30
YOUR EYES! SINCE I LOST THEIR INCANDESCENCE	247	PIERROTS	1
OR LOSETH POWER, E'EN LOST TO MEMORY.	249	DONNA MI PREGA	48
LOT			
THE VICOMTE OF BEZIERS'S NOT SUCH A BAD LOT.	22	MARVOIL	6
WOEFUL IS THIS HUMAN LOT.	43	MR. HOUSMAN	9
A LOT OF ASSES PRAISE YOU BECAUSE YOU ARE "VIRILE,"	82	THE CONDOLENCE	2
BUT YOU, NEWEST SONG OF THE LOT,	94	INSTRUCTIONS	15
"HAVE YOU SEEN ANY OTHERS, ANY OF OUR LOT,	119	THE GYPSY	2
AND HE SAID, "HAVE YOU SEEN ANY OF OUR LOT?"	119	THE GYPSY	11
I'D SEEN A LOT OF HIS LOT ...	119	THE GYPSY	12
I'D SEEN A LOT OF HIS LOT ...	119	THE GYPSY	12
TIME'S TOOTH IS INTO THE LOT, AND WAR'S AND FATE'S TOO.	165	QUINTUS SEPTIM	17
DEATH HAS HIS TOOTH IN THE LOT,	223	SEXTUS PROP: 9	18
AVERNUS LUSTS FOR THE LOT OF THEM,	223	SEXTUS PROP: 9	19
AND THEY WERE NAKED, THE LOT OF THEM,	224	SEXTUS PROP:10	10
AND ONE OF THE LOT WAS GIVEN TO LUST.	224	SEXTUS PROP:10	11
SMEARED O'ER THE LOT IN EQUAL QUANTITIES.	244	MOYEN SENSUEL	174
AND A LOT OF SMALL STREET STENCHES.	270	OF 600 M.P.'S	16
COULD YEH SWAP TH' BRAINS OF ORL THIS LOT	270	OF 600 M.P.'S	19
"AS FOOTLIN' A LOT AS WAS EVER SPAWNED	270	OF 600 M.P.'S	23
LOTUS			
THE SONG OF THE LOTUS OF KUMI?	18	DE AEGYPTO	14
AS BUTEI OF KAN HAD MADE THE HIGH GOLDEN LOTUS	141	IDEA OF CHOAN	28
A BROWN, FAT BABE SITTING IN THE LOTUS,	147	POST MORTEM	1
LOUD			
AND A CLAMOUR LOUD	176	LANGUE D'OC: 3	77

LOUDER -- LOVE

	PAGE	TITLE	LINE
LOUDER			
NO, NO, THEY DANCED. THE MUSIC GREW MUCH LOUDER ...	243	MOYEN SENSUEL	131
LOUDNESS			
SEA-FOWLS' LOUDNESS WAS FOR ME LAUGHTER, ...	64	THE SEAFARER	21
LOUE			
OU NOUS AVIONS LOUE DES CHAISES	160	DANS OMNIBUS	22
LOUSY			
LOUSY TEN MILLION!	257	BREAD BRIGADE	16
LOVABLE			
TWO DEATHS--AND TO STOP LOVING AND BEING LOVABLE,	168	OF AROUET	27
LOVE			
VERY GLAD, FOR MY BRIDE HATH TOWARD ME A GREAT LOVE	5	LA FRAISNE	34
THAT IS SWEETER THAN THE LOVE OF WOMEN	5	LA FRAISNE	35
LEST LOVE RETURN WITH THE FOISON SUN	10	FOR THIS YULE	13
OF LOVE THAT LOVETH IN HELL'S DISDEIGN, ...	11	OF THE GIBBET	21
THESE THAT WE LOVED SHALL GOD LOVE LESS	12	OF THE GIBBET	39
FOR LOVE, OR HOPE, OR BEAUTY OR FOR POWER, ...	21	IN DURANCE	32
FOR THAT I LOVE YE AS THE WIND THE TREES	21	IN DURANCE	44
LO! THEY PAUSE NOT FOR LOVE NOR FOR SORROW, ...	25	THE WHITE STAG	2
TALK ME NO LOVE TALK, NO BOUGHT-CHEAP FIDDL'RY, ...	25	GUIDO INVITES	3
AND I LOVE TO SEE THE SUN RISE BLOOD-CRIMSON.	29	ALTAFORTE	19
SPEECH? WORDS? FAUGH! WHO TALKS OF WORDS AND LOVE?!	31	PIERE VIDAL	33
HOT IS SUCH LOVE AND SILENT, ...	31	PIERE VIDAL	34
LOVE TAKES HIS WAY AND HOLDS HIS JOY DECEITFUL, ...	37	THE YOUNG KING	26
O PALMS OF LOVE, THAT IN YOUR WONTED WAYS	41	HER MONUMENT	15
LOVE AND LAY THOU HAST FORGOTTEN FULLY, ...	44	FROM HEINE: 2	5
I KNOW NOT IF THE LOVE OR IF THE LAY WERE BETTER STUFF, ...	44	FROM HEINE: 2	7
TELL ME WHERE THY LOVELY LOVE IS, ...	45	FROM HEINE: 3	1
THEY SING OF LOVE THAT'S GROWN DESIROUS, ...	45	FROM HEINE: 5	9
OF LOVE, AND JOY THAT IS LOVE'S INMOST PART, ...	45	FROM HEINE: 5	10
HERE AM I COME PERFORCE MY LOVE OF HER, ...	49	OF SPLENDOUR	17
MEET THROUGH OUR VEILS AND WHISPER, AND OF LOVE.	50	THE FLAME	13
THE FLAME, THE AUTUMN, AND THE GREEN ROSE OF LOVE	51	THE ALTAR	2
SEARCH NOT MY LIPS, O LOVE, LET GO MY HANDS, ...	51	THE FLAME	37
AND I LOVED A LOVE ONCE, ...	53	AU JARDIN	15
I LOVED A LOVE ONCE, ...	53	AU JARDIN	17
O LOVE, COME NOW, THIS LAND TURNS EVIL SLOWLY.	69	THE NEEDLE	9
LOVE, YOU THE MUCH, THE MORE DESIRED!	70	THE PLUNGE	10
THIS MAN KNEW OUT THE SECRET WAYS OF LOVE, ...	73	JACOPO SELLAIO	1
FOR HERE WAS LOVE, WAS NOT TO BE DROWNED OUT.	73	THE PICTURE	2
AND NOW SHE TURNS TO ME SEEKING LOVE, ...	102	LADIES	3
I'LL HAVE NO OTHER LOVE AT ANY COST.	105	DOMPNA POIS	10
WHERE LOVE IS, ...	105	DOMPNA POIS	23
WITHOUT BLEMISH, FOR HER LOVE	106	DOMPNA POIS	45
THE BIRDS OF ETSU HAVE NO LOVE FOR EN, IN THE NORTH,	139	SOUTH FOLK	2
"MAENT, I LOVE YOU, YOU HAVE TURNED ME OUT.	151	NEAR PERIGORD	6
AND ALL MY HEART IS BOUND ABOUT WITH LOVE.	153	NEAR PERIGORD	73
IS IT A LOVE POEM? DID HE SING OF WAR?	153	NEAR PERIGORD	81
IN THE MID LOVE COURT, HE SINGS OUT THE CANZON, ...	154	NEAR PERIGORD	118
PLANTAGENET PUTS THE RIDDLE: "DID HE LOVE HER?" ...	155	NEAR PERIGORD	145
AND ARNAUT PARRIES: "DID HE LOVE YOUR SISTER?"	155	NEAR PERIGORD	146
'WHY DO YOU LOVE ME? WILL YOU ALWAYS LOVE ME?	157	NEAR PERIGORD	181
'WHY DO YOU LOVE ME? WILL YOU ALWAYS LOVE ME?	157	NEAR PERIGORD	181
BUT I AM LIKE THE GRASS, I CAN NOT LOVE YOU.'	157	NEAR PERIGORD	182
OR, 'LOVE, AND I LOVE AND LOVE YOU, ...	157	NEAR PERIGORD	183
OR, 'LOVE, AND I LOVE AND LOVE YOU, ...	157	NEAR PERIGORD	183
OR, 'LOVE, AND I LOVE AND LOVE YOU, ...	157	NEAR PERIGORD	183
SPANISH AND PARIS, LOVE OF THE ARTS PART OF YOUR GEISHA-CULTURE!	163	CABARET DANCER	52
THE GREEN STRETCHES WHERE LOVE IS AND THE GRAPES	167	OF AROUET	21
MY LOVE AND I KEEP STATE	171	LANGUE D'OC	EPI
OUR LOVE COMES OUT	173	LANGUE D'OC: 2	11
HER LOVE AND HER RING:	173	LANGUE D'OC: 2	20
THAT LOVE GOES OUT	174	LANGUE D'OC: 3	5
OF LOVE I HAVE NAUGHT	174	LANGUE D'OC: 3	7
WHERE MY LOVE IS, THERE IS A GLITTER OF SUN;	174	LANGUE D'OC: 3	16
'TILL I HAVE HER I LOVE	174	LANGUE D'OC: 3	18
FOR LOVE WILL GIVE	174	LANGUE D'OC: 3	22
FROM LOVE, AWAKE AND IN SWEVYN, ...	175	LANGUE D'OC: 3	29
WHEN HER LOVE LOOK STEALS ON ME.	175	LANGUE D'OC: 3	41

PAGE 239

LOVE -- LOVERS

	PAGE	TITLE	LINE
LOVE (CONTINUED)			
THE MAN WHOM LOVE HAD	175	LANGUE D'OC: 3	56
THE NOBLEST GIRLS MEN LOVE	176	LANGUE D'OC: 3	70
OUT OF MY LOVE WILL HER HEART NOT STIR.	177	LANGUE D'OC: 4	28
SOME FOR LOVE OF SLAUGHTER, IN IMAGINATION,	190	HUGH SELWYN: 4	8
SOME IN FEAR, LEARNING LOVE OF SLAUGHTER;	190	HUGH SELWYN: 4	10
IT IS NOBLE TO DIE OF LOVE, AND HONOURABLE TO REMAIN	218	SEXTUS PROP: 5	59
EYES ARE THE GUIDES OF LOVE,	220	SEXTUS PROP: 7	13
WHILE OUR FATES TWINE TOGETHER, SATE WE OUR EYES WITH LOVE;	220	SEXTUS PROP: 7	17
ERE LOVE KNOW MODERATIONS,	220	SEXTUS PROP: 7	26
AMOR STANDS UPON YOU, LOVE DRIVES UPON LOVERS,	226	SEXTUS PROP:11	11
LOVE INTERFERES WITH FIDELITIES;	227	SEXTUS PROP:12	2
AND SO NOW LOVE	236	MIDDLE-AGED	16
MY COUNTRY? I LOVE IT WELL, AND THOSE GOOD FELLOWS	238	MOYEN SENSUEL	3
AND TIMOROUS LOVE OF THE INNOCUOUS	240	MOYEN SENSUEL	63
WAS PURER IN ITS LOVE OF ONE LOCALITY,	245	MOYEN SENSUEL	212
AND IS SO OVERWEENING: LOVE BY NAME.	248	DONNA MI PREGA	3
LOVE IS CREATED, HATH A SENSATE NAME,	248	DONNA MI PREGA	22
NONE CAN IMAGINE LOVE	250	DONNA MI PREGA	62
THAT KNOWS NOT LOVE;	250	DONNA MI PREGA	63
LOVE DOTH NOT MOVE, BUT DRAWETH ALL TO HIM;	250	DONNA MI PREGA	64
LOVED			
THESE THAT WE LOVED SHALL GOD LOVE LESS	12	OF THE GIBBET	39
BUT AYE LOVED THE OPEN SEA.	33	GOODLY FERE	24
AND I LOVED A LOVE ONCE,	53	AU JARDIN	15
I LOVED A LOVE ONCE,	53	AU JARDIN	17
I HAVE LOVED A STREAM AND A SHADOW.	84	ORTUS	11
KNOW THEN THAT I LOVED YOU FROM AFORE-TIME,	96	DUM CAPITOLIUM	7
FU I LOVED THE HIGH CLOUD AND THE HILL,	117	EPITAPHS	1
HE LOVED THIS LADY IN CASTLE MONTAIGNAC?	152	NEAR PERIGORD	48
THINKING OF AELIS, WHOM HE LOVED HEART AND SOUL . . .	154	NEAR PERIGORD	110
"SAY THAT HE SAW THE CASTLES, SAY THAT HE LOVED MAENT!"	156	NEAR PERIGORD	155
"SAY THAT HE LOVED HER, DOES IT SOLVE THE RIDDLE?"	156	NEAR PERIGORD	156
FROM ONE I LOVED NEVER SO MUCH,	176	LANGUE D'OC: 3	61
LOVELIER			
VENUST THE LADY, AND NONE LOVELIER,	177	LANGUE D'OC: 4	26
LOVELIEST			
THAT HE ON DRY LAND LOVELIEST LIVETH,	64	THE SEAFARER	13
STRANDS OF LIGHT INWOVEN ABOUT IT, LOVELIEST	68	APPARUIT	18
LOVELINESS			
THY LOVELINESS IS HERE WRIT TILL,	9	NA AUDIART	35
UNTIL IS ITS LOVELINESS BECOME UNTO ME	26	NIGHT LITANY	7
LOVELY			
STATELY, TALL AND LOVELY TENDER	8	NA AUDIART	7
TELL ME WHERE THY LOVELY LOVE IS,	45	FROM HEINE: 3	1
"LOVELY THOU ART, TO HOLD ME CLOSE AND KISST,	177	LANGUE D'OC: 4	11
"ALL LOVELY WOMEN HAVE KNOWN THIS,"	226	SEXTUS PROP:11	22
LOVE-LYRICS			
YET YOU ASK ON WHAT ACCOUNT I WRITE SO MANY LOVE-LYRICS	217	SEXTUS PROP: 5	23
LOVER			
YET THEIR EYES ARE AS THE EYES OF A MAID TO HER LOVER,	25	THE WHITE STAG	3
AYE LOVER HE WAS OF BRAWNY MEN,	33	GOODLY FERE	3
WILL FIND THEE SUCH A LOVER	67	THE CLOAK	5
CANDIDIA HAS TAKEN A NEW LOVER	118	THREE POETS	1
SHE HAS HER LOVER TILL MORN,	177	LANGUE D'OC: 4	2
"WHERE A GIRL WAITS ALONE FOR HER LOVER;	210	SEXTUS PROP: 2	23
IF ANY MAN WOULD BE A LOVER	212	SEXTUS PROP: 3	17
A FOREIGN LOVER BROUGHT DOWN HELEN'S KINGDOM	227	SEXTUS PROP:11	25
LOVERS			
LOVERS OF BEAUTY, STARVED,	92	THE REST	6
MOVE AMONG THE LOVERS OF PERFECTION ALONE.	95	ITE	2
FOUR AND FORTY LOVERS HAD AGATHAS IN THE OLD DAYS,	102	LADIES	1
"OBVIOUSLY CROWNED LOVERS AT UNKNOWN DOORS,	211	SEXTUS PROP: 2	48
NOR IS THERE ANYONE TO WHOM LOVERS ARE NOT SACRED AT MIDNIGHT	212	SEXTUS PROP: 3	15
FOR THUS ARE TOMBS OF LOVERS MOST DESECRATED.	213	SEXTUS PROP: 3	34
"LET HER LOVERS SNORE AT HER IN THE MORNING!	215	SEXTUS PROP: 4	36

LOVERS -- LURE

	PAGE	TITLE	LINE
LOVERS (CONTINUED)			
TO-DAY WE TAKE THE GREAT BREATH OF LOVERS,	221	SEXTUS PROP: 7	31
I AM HUNG HERE, A SCARE-CROW FOR LOVERS.	226	SEXTUS PROP:11	3
AMOR STANDS UPON YOU, LOVE DRIVES UPON LOVERS,	226	SEXTUS PROP:11	11
LOVES			
THE GHOSTS OF DEAD LOVES EVERYONE	10	FOR THIS YULE	11
THAT LOVES AND KILLS,	14	FAMAM CANO	6
THIS IS ANOTHER OF OUR ANCIENT LOVES.	63	QUIES	1
A YOUNG MUSE WITH YOUNG LOVES CLUSTERED ABOUT HER	207	SEXTUS PROP: 1	13
HAPPY SELLING POOR LOVES FOR CHEAP APPLES.	229	SEXTUS PROP:12	45
LOVE'S			
'TIS MY TRUE LOVE'S SEPULCHRE.	45	FROM HEINE: 3	8
OF LOVE, AND JOY THAT IS LOVE'S INMOST PART,	45	FROM HEINE: 5	10
FOOL WHO WOULD SET A TERM TO LOVE'S MADNESS,	220	SEXTUS PROP: 7	22
I HAVE NO WILL TO PROVE LOVE'S COURSE	248	DONNA MI PREGA	11
LOVETH			
OF LOVE THAT LOVETH IN HELL'S DISDEIGN,	11	OF THE GIBBET	21
LOVING			
WELL, THERE'S NO USE YOUR LOVING ME	53	AU JARDIN	8
IF YOU'D HAVE ME GO ON LOVING YOU	167	OF AROUET	15
TWO DEATHS--AND TO STOP LOVING AND BEING LOVABLE,	168	OF AROUET	27
LOW			
AND THE WAX RUNS LOW.	35	THE EYES	7
HOW IF THE LOW DEAR SOUND WITHIN THY THROAT	40	GATIDMUG	14
LOW, PANEL-SHAPED, A-LEVEL WITH HER KNEES,	49	OF SPLENDOUR	11
TOMB HIDETH TROUBLE. THE BLADE IS LAYED LOW.	66	THE SEAFARER	90
GRASS, AND LOW FIELDS, AND HILLS,	70	THE PLUNGE	16
WHERE THE LOW DRONNE IS FILLED WITH WATER-LILIES.	152	NEAR PERIGORD	56
KNEW THE LOW FLOODED LANDS SQUARED OUT WITH POPLARS,	157	NEAR PERIGORD	174
THE CYTHAREAN BROUGHT LOW BY MARS' LECHERY	227	SEXTUS PROP:11	27
LOWELL			
"YOU REMEMBER MR. LOWELL,	182	MOEURS CON: 8	2
LOWER			
WHERE THE LOWER AND HIGHER HAVE ENDING;	196	HUGH SELWIN:12	16
THEN CUT THEIR SAVING TO THE HALF OR LOWER;	260	ALF'S FIFTH	3
LOWERING			
LOWERING MY HEAD, I LOOKED AT THE WALL.	130	RIVER-MER WIFE	9
LOWEST			
ITS LOWEST STONES JUST MEET THE VALLEY TIPS	152	NEAR PERIGORD	55
LOWLY			
UP, UP MY SOUL, FROM YOUR LOWLY CANTILATION,	216	SEXTUS PROP: 5	12
LOYAL			
AND I AM SLICED WITH LOYAL AESTHETICS.	247	PIERROTS	13
LOYALTY			
LOYALTY IS HARD TO EXPLAIN.	130	SOUTH FOLK	11
L'S			
STRIKING THE BOARD, FALLING IN STRONG L'S OF	120	GAME OF CHESS	2
LUC			
NO ONE HEARS SAVE ARRIMON LUC D'ESPARO--	154	NEAR PERIGORD	119
LUCID			
THE LUCID CASTALIAN SPRAY,	104	ANCORA	15
LUCK			
TRIED LAYU'S LUCK, OFFERED THE CHOYO SONG,	136	EXILE'S LETTER	66
OR LUCK, I MUST HAVE MY FILL.	173	LANGUE D'OC: 2	10
WAS GOT ABROAD, WHAT BETTER LUCK DO YOU WISH 'EM,	240	MOYEN SENSUEL	60
LUGETE			
LUGETE, VENERES! LUGETE, CUPIDINESQUE!	103	LADIES	14
LUGETE, VENERES! LUGETE, CUPIDINESQUE!	103	LADIES	14
LUINI			
LUINI IN PORCELAIN!	204	MEDALLION	1
LULLIN			
TO MADAME LULLIN	168	OF AROUET	ST
LUMINOUS			
LUMINOUS GREEN FROM THE ROOKS,	120	GAME OF CHESS	9
LUNAR			
NOR THE MODUS OF LUNAR ECLIPSES	228	SEXTUS PROP:12	26
LUNCH			
HE USED TO LUNCH WITH BALFOUR IN THOSE DAYS	265	ALF'S NINTH	22
AT ONE O'CLOCK I GO TO LUNCH,	266	ALF'S ELEVENTH	7
LURE			
LURE US BEYOND THE CLOUDY PEAK OF RIVA?	39	BLANDULA	15

		PAGE	TITLE	LINE
LURKING				
	LURKING, SERPENTINE, AMPHIBIOUS AND INSIDIOUS	244	MOYEN SENSUEL	170
LUSCIOUS				
	PIQUANTE, DELICIOUS, LUSCIOUS, CAPTIVATING:	241	MOYEN SENSUEL	84
LUST				
	MOANETH ALWAY MY MIND'S LUST	65	THE SEAFARER	37
	GO TO THOSE WHO HAVE DELICATE LUST,	88	COMMISSION	16
	AND ONE OF THE LOT WAS GIVEN TO LUST.	224	SEXTUS PROP:10	11
LUSTRE				
	HATH FOR BOSS THY LUSTRE GAY!	7	CINO	45
	PALLOR OF SILVER, PALE LUSTRE OF LATONA,	76	THE ALCHEMIST	58
	AND THE LUSTRE OF DIAMONDS,	167	OF AROUET	13
LUSTS				
	AVERNUS LUSTS FOR THE LOT OF THEM,	223	SEXTUS PROP: 9	19
LUSTY				
	DRINK WE THE LUSTY ROBBERS TWAIN,	11	OF THE GIBBET	17
LUTANY				
	BUT HIS ANSWER COMETH, AS WINDS AND AS LUTANY,	16	PRAISE YSOLT	5
LUTE-STRINGS				
	HATH AS FAINT LUTE-STRINGS IN ITS DIM ACCORD	43	SATIEMUS	15
LUTH				
	WOULD CINO OF THE LUTH WERE HERE!"	6	CINO	22
LUXURIOUS				
	THE LUXURIOUS AND IONIAN,	209	SEXTUS PROP: 1	55
LYCIA				
	MY VOTE COMING FROM THE TEMPLE OF PHOEBUS IN LYCIA, AT PATARA,	208	SEXTUS PROP: 1	38
LYCORIS				
	AND BUT NOW GALLUS HAD SUNG OF LYCORIS.	230	SEXTUS PROP:12	72
	FAIR, FAIREST LYCORIS--	230	SEXTUS PROP:12	73
LYGDAMUS				
	DIFFERENCE OF OPINION WITH LYGDAMUS	214	SEXTUS PROP: 4	SUB
	LYGDAMUS,	214	SEXTUS PROP: 4	2
	YOU, YOU LYGDAMUS	214	SEXTUS PROP: 4	16
	FOR WHICH THINGS YOU WILL GET A REWARD FROM ME, LYGDAMUS?	215	SEXTUS PROP: 4	27
	LYGDAMUS?	215	SEXTUS PROP: 4	39
LYING				
	OUT OF EREBUS, OUT OF THE FLAT WASTE OF AIR, LYING BENEATH THE WORLD;	76	THE ALCHEMIST	46
	WERE SEEN LYING ALONG THE UPPER SEATS	93	LES MILLWIN	3
	AND LYING;	167	OF AROUET	7
	HEAD FARMERS DO LIKEWISE, AND LYING WEARY AMID THEIR OATS	229	SEXTUS PROP:12	48
	LYING WITHIN PERFECTION POSTULATE	249	DONNA MI PREGA	34
	LET SOME NEW LYING ASS,	261	ALF'S SIXTH	1
LYMAN				
	MABIE, AND LYMAN ABBOT AND GEORGE WOODBERRY,	239	MOYEN SENSUEL	28
LYNCEUS				
	AND BESIDES, LYNCEUS,	228	SEXTUS PROP:12	8
	PREFERABLE, MY DEAR BOY, MY DEAR LYNCEUS,	228	SEXTUS PROP:12	13
	BUT IN ONE BED, IN ONE BED ALONE, MY DEAR LYNCEUS	228	SEXTUS PROP:12	15
LYRE				
	SHALL BE YAWNED OUT ON MY LYRE--WITH SUCH INDUSTRY.	210	SEXTUS PROP: 2	5
	IF SHE WITH IVORY FINGERS DRIVE A TUNE THROUGH THE LYRE,	217	SEXTUS PROP: 5	27
M.				
	WE WHO WENT OUT INTO THE FOUR A. M. OF THE WORLD	104	ANCORA	
	M. VEROG, OUT OF STEP WITH THE DECADE,	193	SIENA MI FE	1
	SONG OF SIX HUNDRED M. P.'S	270	OF 600 M.P.'S	
	STARTIN' IN ABOUT 6 A. M.	271	OLE KATE	1
	M. POM-POM	273	M. POM-POM	
	M. POM-POM ALLAIT EN GUERRE	273	M. POM-POM	
	M. POM-POM EST AU SENAT	273	M. POM-POM	
MA				
	AU DEDANS DE MA MEMOIRE	160	DANS OMNIBUS	
MA'				
	YOUR OWN MA' WARN'T NO BETTER	260	ALF'S FOURTH	1
MABIE				
	MABIE, AND LYMAN ABBOT AND GEORGE WOODBERRY,	239	MOYEN SENSUEL	2

MAC -- MADNESS

	PAGE	TITLE	LINE
MAC			
SOAPY SIME? SLIPP'RY MAC?	258	ALF'S THIRD	2
MACDONALD			
WHILE RAMSEY MACDONALD SLEEPS, SLEEPS.	265	ALF'S TENTH	8
MACERATIONS			
MADE WAY FOR MACERATIONS;	189	HUGH SELWYN: 3	7
MACH'			
MACH' ICH DIE KLEINEN LIEDER	97	THE BELLAIRES	EPI
MACHIAVELLI			
IN THE PARLANCE OF NICCOLO MACHIAVELLI:	178	MOEURS CON: 1	18
MAD			
TILL MEN SAY THAT I AM MAD;	4	LA FRAISNE	21
AND NOW MEN CALL ME MAD BECAUSE I HAVE THROWN	4	LA FRAISNE	27
THOUGH ALL MEN SAY THAT I AM MAD	5	LA FRAISNE	32
MAD AS A HATTER BUT SURELY NO MYOPE,	13	MESMERISM	11
THEN HOWL I MY HEART NIGH MAD WITH REJOICING.	28	ALTAFORTE	6
AND THE WINDS SHRIEK THROUGH THE CLOUDS MAD, OPPOSING,	28	ALTAFORTE	11
SOME OVERFLOWING RIVER IS RUN MAD,	32	PARACELSUS	12
NOW DO I KNOW THAT I AM MAD,	62	N. Y.	4
TO THE MAD CHASE THROUGH THE GARDENS.	132	AT TEN-SHIN	24
YOU EITHER DRIVE THEM MAD, OR ELSE YOU BLINK AT THEIR SUICIDES,	145	SALUTATION 3RD	22
BUT I WILL NOT GO MAD TO PLEASE YOU,	145	SALUTATION 3RD	25
JOY I HAVE NONE, IF SHE MAKE ME NOT MAD	173	LANGUE D'OC: 0	44
AND KEEP MAD DOGS OFF HIS ANKLES.	212	SEXTUS PROP: 3	23
MADAME			
TO MADAME DU CHATELET	167	OF AROUET	ST
TO MADAME LULLIN	168	OF AROUET	ST
MADE			
AND THE WANDERING OF MANY ROADS HATH MADE MY EYES	16	PRAISE YSOLT	12
WHEREFORE I MADE HER A SONG AND SHE WENT FROM ME	17	PRAISE YSOLT	31
MADE YOU YOUR PASS MOST VALIANTLY	19	FOR E. MCC	8
I MADE RIMES TO HIS LADY THIS THREE YEAR:	22	MARVOIL	7
WAS THERE SUCH FLESH MADE EVER AND UNMADE!	31	PIERE VIDAL	45
AND MADE MEN'S MOCK'RY IN MY ROTTEN SADNESS!	31	PIERE VIDAL	53
WHEN WE LAST MADE COMPANY,	33	GOODLY FERE	14
WHO MADE THE FREEST HAND SEEM COVETOUS.	37	THE YOUNG KING	14
ARCHES WORN OLD AND PALACES MADE COMMON,	40	ROME	3
TO BE A SIGN AND AN HOPE MADE SECURE	42	HER MONUMENT	33
A HOUSE NOT MADE WITH HANDS,	49	OF SPLENDOUR	2
ITS MIND WAS MADE UP IN "THE SEVENTIES,"	63	PHASELLUS ILLE	3
OUR DEFENCE IS NOT YET MADE SURE, NO ONE CAN LET HIS FRIEND RETURN.	127	BOWMEN OF SHU	8
AND THEY MADE NOTHING OF SEA-CROSSING OR OF MOUNTAIN-CROSSING,	134	EXILE'S LETTER	9
SHE MADE THE NAME FOR HERSELF: "GAUZE VEIL,"	140	MULBERRY ROAD	5
HER EARRINGS ARE MADE OF PEARL,	140	MULBERRY ROAD	12
AS BUTEI OF KAN HAD MADE THE HIGH GOLDEN LOTUS	141	IDEA OF CHOAN	28
THE HEADLESS TRUNK "THAT MADE ITS HEAD A LAMP,"	151	NEAR PERIGORD	23
THE TERM "VIRGO" BEING MADE MALE IN MEDIAEVAL LATINITY;	178	MOEURS CON: 1	6
MADE WITH NO LOSS OF TIME,	188	HUGH SELWYN: 2	10
MADE WAY FOR MACERATIONS;	189	HUGH SELWYN: 3	7
RED OVERWROUGHT WITH ORANGE AND ALL MADE	197	ENVOI (1919)	14
HE MADE NO IMMEDIATE APPLICATION	201	AGE DEMANDED	13
I HAD REHEARSED THE CURIAN BROTHERS, AND MADE REMARKS UPON THE HORATIAN JAVELIN	210	SEXTUS PROP: 2	8
OH COUCH MADE HAPPY BY MY LONG DELECTATIONS;	220	SEXTUS PROP: 7	2
WAS MADE TO INCUBATE SUCH MEDIOCRITIES,	239	MOYEN SENSUEL	24
THAT FIRST MADE HIM BELIEVE IN IMMORAL SUASION.	245	MOYEN SENSUEL	198
OH, WHAT A NOISE THEY MADE	261	ALF'S SIXTH	23
OH WHAT A FUSS THEY MADE	262	ALF'S SIXTH	25
BUT I HAVE MADE A RUDDY PILE	266	ALF'S ELEVENTH	15
BUT SHE NEVER MADE NO MENTION	271	OLE KATE	23
MADNESS			
AND TURN MY MIND UPON THAT SPLENDID MADNESS,	30	PIERE VIDAL	2
AND EVERY RUN-AWAY OF THE WOOD THROUGH THAT GREAT MADNESS,	31	PIERE VIDAL	51
FOOL WHO WOULD SET A TERM TO LOVE'S MADNESS,	220	SEXTUS PROP: 7	22

PAGE 243

MAD'ST -- MAIL

	PAGE	TITLE	LINE
MAD'ST			
GOD! THAT MAD'ST HER WELL REGARD HER,	72	DIEU! QU'IL	1
GOD! THAT MAD'ST HER WELL REGARD HER,	72	DIEU! QU'IL	7
GOD! THAT MAD'ST HER WELL REGARD HER.	72	DIEU! QU'IL	13
MAECENAS			
THUS MUCH THE FATES HAVE ALLOTTED ME, AND IF, MAECENAS,	217	SEXTUS PROP: 5	37
MAELIDS			
MAELIDS AND WATER-GIRLS,	87	THE SPRING	2
MAENSAC			
PIEIRE DE MAENSAC IS GONE.	123	PROVINC DESERT	75
MAENT			
AH, BELS SENHER, MAENT, AT LAST	106	DOMPNA POIS	6
"MAENT, I LOVE YOU, YOU HAVE TURNED ME OUT.	151	NEAR PERIGORD	
THINK YOU THAT MAENT LIVED AT MONTAIGNAC,	151	NEAR PERIGORD	1
AND MAENT FAILED HIM? OR SAW THROUGH THE SCHEME?	152	NEAR PERIGORD	5
AND EVERY ONE HALF JEALOUS OF MAENT?	153	NEAR PERIGORD	7
AND STILL THE KNOT, THE FIRST KNOT, OF MAENT?	153	NEAR PERIGORD	8
MAENT, MAENT, AND YET AGAIN MAENT,	154	NEAR PERIGORD	9
MAENT, MAENT, AND YET AGAIN MAENT,	154	NEAR PERIGORD	9
MAENT, MAENT, AND YET AGAIN MAENT,	154	NEAR PERIGORD	9
"SAY THAT HE SAW THE CASTLES, SAY THAT HE LOVED MAENT!"	156	NEAR PERIGORD	15
MAENT'S			
THE TEN GOOD MILES FROM THERE TO MAENT'S CASTLE,	153	NEAR PERIGORD	6
MAEONIA			
AND AMID ALL THE GLORIED AND STORIED BEAUTIES OF MAEONIA	222	SEXTUS PROP: 8	3
MAGAZINE			
THAT CANTING RAG CALLED EVERYBODY'S MAGAZINE,	241	MOYEN SENSUEL	9
MAGAZINES			
WHEN YOU CAME OUT IN THE MAGAZINES	114	EPILOGUE	
MAGIANS'			
(WHAT OF THE MAGIANS' SCENTED GEAR?)	10	FOR THIS YULE	
MAGIC			
THEY THAT COME MEWARDS, BEARING OLD MAGIC.	20	IN DURANCE	
OH, I HAVE PICKED UP MAGIC IN HER NEARNESS	71	A VIRGINAL	
AS ROSES MIGHT, IN MAGIC AMBER LAID,	197	ENVOI (1919)	
MAGICAL			
GONE AS WIND! THE CLOTH OF THE MAGICAL HANDS!	68	APPARUIT	
MAGNET			
OR TAKE HIS "MAGNET" SINGER SETTING OUT,	154	NEAR PERIGORD	1
MY MAGNET," BERTRANS HAD SAID.	154	NEAR PERIGORD	1
MAGNIFIED			
HOWE'ER IN MIRTH MOST MAGNIFIED,	66	THE SEAFARER	
MAGNITUDE			
"IN THINGS OF SIMILAR MAGNITUDE	216	SEXTUS PROP: 5	
MAGNOLIA			
THIS BOAT IS OF SHATO-WOOD, AND ITS GUNWALES ARE CUT MAGNOLIA,	128	THE RIVER SONG	
MAID			
YET THEIR EYES ARE AS THE EYES OF A MAID TO HER LOVER,	25	THE WHITE STAG	
THIS IS NO MAID.	62	N. Y.	
THOU ART A MAID WITH NO BREASTS,	62	N. Y.	
MAIDEN			
AND RELEASED THE MAIDEN ANDROMEDA.	237	ABU SALAMMAMM	
MAIDENS			
SHALL MAIDENS SCATTER ROSE LEAVES	24	THUS NINEVEH	
AND ALL THE MAIDENS OF ROME, AS MANY AS THEY WERE,	38	LADY'S LIFE	
AH! BOW YOUR HEADS, YE MAIDENS ALL,	72	PAN IS DEAD	
THY MAIDENS ARE WHITE LIKE PEBBLES;	91	DANCE FIGURE	
THERE COME FORTH MANY MAIDENS	108	CH'U YUAN	
AND ACCOST THE PROCESSION OF MAIDENS.	108	CH'U YUAN	
AND HOW TEN SINS CAN CORRUPT YOUNG MAIDENS;	229	SEXTUS PROP:12	
MAIGRE			
"CARMEN EST MAIGRE, UN TRAIT DE BISTRE	162	CABARET DANCER	
"PAUNVRE FEMME MAIGRE!" SHE SAYS.	163	CABARET DANCER	
MAIL			
STRAY GLEAMS ON HANGING MAIL, AN ARMOURER'S TORCH-FLARE	155	NEAR PERIGORD	

MAIL -- MALE

	PAGE	TITLE	LINE
MAIL (CONTINUED)			
ITS HOME MAIL IS STILL OPENED BY ITS MATERNAL PARENT	179	MOEURS CON: 4	2
AND ITS OFFICE MAIL MAY BE OPENED BY	179	MOEURS CON: 4	3
MAINTAIN			
OF POETRY; TO MAINTAIN "THE SUBLIME"	187	E. P. ODE	3
MAINTAINED			
AND THUS THE EMPIRE IS MAINTAINED.	178	MOEURS CON: 1	20
MAINTAINS			
MAINTAINS INTENTION REASON'S PEER AND MATE;	249	DONNA MI PREGA	37
MAITRE			
A-JUMBLING O' FIGURES FOR MAITRE JACQUES POLIN, ...	22	MARVOIL	4
MAITRE-DE-CAFE			
ARE THOSE OF A MAITRE-DE-CAFE.	114	EPILOGUE	11
MAJESTIES			
ANY BUT "MAJESTIES" AND ITALIAN NOBLES.	163	CABARET DANCER	66
MAKE			
MAKE THY LAUGH OUR WANDER-LIED;	7	CINO	47
THY SATINS MAKE UPON THE STAIR, ...	8	NA AUDIART	22
(CHRIST MAKE THE SHEPHERDS' HOMAGE DEAR!)	10	FOR THIS YULE	2
THAT MAKE THE STARK WINDS REEK WITH FEAR	10	FOR THIS YULE	12
TO MAKE HIM A MATE OF THE "HAULTE NOBLESSE"	11	OF THE GIBBET	10
MAKE CLEAN OUR HEARTS WITHIN US, ...	27	NIGHT LITANY	37
AND LET THE MUSIC OF THE SWORDS MAKE THEM CRIMSON!	29	ALTAFORTE	37
MAY NOT MAKE BOAST OF ANY BETTER THING	40	ERAT HORA	6
MAY MAKE MERRY MAN FARING NEEDY.	64	THE SEAFARER	27
THE TREASURE IS OURS, MAKE WE FAST LAND WITH IT.	69	THE NEEDLE	11
MAKE A CLEAR SOUND, ...	75	THE ALCHEMIST	4
GO! AND MAKE CAT CALLS!	86	SALUTATION 2ND	26
DANCE AND MAKE PEOPLE BLUSH, ...	86	SALUTATION 2ND	27
I MAKE A PACT WITH YOU, WALT WHITMAN--	89	A PACT	1
I AM OLD ENOUGH NOW TO MAKE FRIENDS.	89	A PACT	5
AND YOU MAY DECLINE TO MAKE THEM IMMORTAL, ...	99	SALVATIONISTS	7
TO MAKE ME A BORROWED LADY	105	DOMPNA POIS	19
TO MAKE THESE AVAIL	106	DOMPNA POIS	58
THE MONKEYS MAKE SORROWFUL NOISE OVERHEAD.	130	RIVER-MER WIFE	18
AND THE STREETS MAKE WAY FOR THEIR PASSAGE.	132	AT TEN-SHIN	17
HERE WE MUST MAKE SEPARATION	137	TAKING LEAVE	3
TAKE HIS OWN SPEECH, MAKE WHAT YOU WILL OF IT-- ...	153	NEAR PERIGORD	79
WITH HER VENUST AND NOBLEST TO MY MAKE	172	LANGUE D'OC: 1	27
JOY I HAVE NONE, IF SHE MAKE ME NOT MAD	175	LANGUE D'OC: 3	44
"MY PRETTY BOY, MAKE WE OUR PLAY AGAIN	177	LANGUE D'OC: 4	16
THOUGH YOU MAKE A HASH OF ANTIMACHUS, ...	228	SEXTUS PROP:12	21
MAKE WAY, YE ROMAN AUTHORS, ...	229	SEXTUS PROP:12	36
I WOULD MAKE VERSE IN YOUR FASHION, IF SHE SHOULD COMMAND IT.	229	SEXTUS PROP:12	60
AND MAKE THE TOUR ABROAD FOR THEIR WILD TILLAGE--	245	MOYEN SENSUEL	208
EH, MAKE IT UP?	248	PIERROTS	25
TO MAKE 'EM COSIER.	269	SAFE AND SOUND	16
TO MAKE THE PEOPLE PAY.	272	NATIONAL SONG	4
KER			
THE MAKER OF IT, SOME OTHER MOUTH, ...	197	ENVOI (1919)	20
KES			
MAKES HAY WITH THE THINGS IN HER HOUSE.	115	SOCIAL ORDER	10
WITH GREEN STRINGS SHE MAKES THE WARP OF HER BASKET,	140	MULBERRY ROAD	8
SHE MAKES THE SHOULDER-STRAPS OF HER BASKET	140	MULBERRY ROAD	9
THAT MAKES THE WORST MESS.	259	ALF'S FOURTH	7
KETH			
MAKETH ME CLEAR, AND THERE ARE POWERS IN THIS	49	OF SPLENDOUR	19
WHERE HE TAKES REST; WHO MAKETH HIM TO BE;	248	DONNA MI PREGA	13
DELIGHT MAKETH CERTAIN IN SEEMING	250	DONNA MI PREGA	71
KING			
WITH 2 AND 2 MAKING 4 IN REASON, ...	263	ALF'S EIGHTH	12
OF THE MAKING OF GUNS.	268	ANOTHER BIT	4
KYTH			
THEN MAKYTH MY HEART HIS YULE-TIDE CHEER	10	FOR THIS YULE	6
QUE ES M VOLS HAL.	9	NA AUDIART	57
E			
WE WERE IN ESPECIAL BORED WITH MALE STUPIDITY.	82	THE CONDOLENCE	8
HERE IS A FORMAL MALE GROUP:	104	THE SEEING EYE	4

PAGE 245

MALE -- MAN

	PAGE	TITLE	LINE
MALE (CONTINUED)			
THE TERM "VIRGO" BEING MADE MALE IN MEDIAEVAL LATINITY;	178	MOEURS CON: 1	6
BUT SURELY THE WORST OF YOUR OLD-WOMEN ARE THE MALE ONES.)	243	MOYEN SENSUEL	150
MALEMORT			
OF AUDIART AT MALEMORT,	106	DOMPNA POIS	40
ONE AT CHALAIS, ANOTHER AT MALEMORT	151	NEAR PERIGORD	12
AND MALEMORT KEEPS ITS CLOSE HOLD ON BRIVE,	153	NEAR PERIGORD	59
MALEMORT, GUESSES BENEATH, SENDS WORD TO COEUR-DE-LION:	155	NEAR PERIGORD	123
MALENESS			
OUR MALENESS LIFTS US OUT OF THE RUCK,	82	THE CONDOLENCE	5
MALES			
THOUGH MALES OF SEVENTY, WHO FEAR TRUTHS NAKED HARM US,	243	MOYEN SENSUEL	147
MALEVOLENCE			
BY THESE, FROM THE MALEVOLENCE OF THE DEW	76	THE ALCHEMIST	59
MALH			
TAN QUE I PUOSCH' OM GITAR AB MALH.	151	NEAR PERIGORD	EP
MALICE			
FRAME ON THE FAIR EARTH 'GAINST FOES HIS MALICE,	66	THE SEAFARER	76
MAMMON			
OF MAMMON	14	FAMAM CANO	3
MAN			
AND NO MAN TROUBLETH US.	5	LA FRAISNE	3
AYE YOU'RE A MAN THAT! YE OLD MESMERIZER	13	MESMERISM	
STRUCK OF THE BLADE THAT NO MAN PARRIETH;	19	FOR E. MCC	
FAITH! NO MAN TARRIETH,	19	FOR E. MCC	1
STRUCK OF THE BLADE THAT NO MAN PARRIETH	19	FOR E. MCC	2
IN THOSE DIM HALLS WHERE NO MAN TROUBLETH	24	THUS NINEVEH	1
THE MAN WHO FEARS WAR AND SQUATS OPPOSING	29	ALTAFORTE	2
NO MAN HATH HEARD THE GLORY OF MY DAYS:	32	PIERE VIDAL	5
NO MAN HATH DARED AND WON HIS DARE AS I:	32	PIERE VIDAL	5
WHEN THEY CAME WI' A HOST TO TAKE OUR MAN	33	GOODLY FERE	
BUT A MAN O' MEN WAS HE.	33	GOODLY FERE	
'TIS HOW A BRAVE MAN DIES ON THE TREE."	34	GOODLY FERE	3
LET EACH MAN VISAGE THIS YOUNG ENGLISH KING	37	THE YOUNG KING	2
THIS DELIGHTFUL YOUNG MAN	46	FROM HEINE: 6	
THAT MAN DOTH PASS THE NET OF DAYS AND HOURS.	50	THE FLAME	
THIS THING THAT MOVES AS MAN IS NO MORE MORTAL.	51	THE FLAME	8
ONE DULL MAN, DULLING AND UXORIOUS,	61	PORTRAIT FEMME	
MERE-WEARY MOOD. LEST MAN KNOW NOT	64	THE SEAFARER	
MAY MAKE MERRY MAN FARING NEEDY.	64	THE SEAFARER	
FOR THIS THERE'S NO MOOD-LOFTY MAN OVER EARTH'S MIDST,	65	THE SEAFARER	
ALL THIS ADMONISHETH MAN EAGER OF MOOD,	65	THE SEAFARER	
HE THE PROSPEROUS MAN--WHAT SOME PERFORM	65	THE SEAFARER	
NO MAN AT ALL GOING THE EARTH'S GAIT,	66	THE SEAFARER	
THIS MAN KNEW OUT THE SECRET WAYS OF LOVE,	73	JACOPO SELLAIO	
NO MAN COULD PAINT SUCH THINGS WHO DID NOT KNOW.	73	JACOPO SELLAIO	
LET US EXPRESS OUR ENVY OF THE MAN WITH A STEADY JOB AND NO WORRY ABOUT THE FUTURE.	94	INSTRUCTIONS	
AND YET THE MAN IS SO QUIET AND RESERVED IN DEMEANOUR	100	TEMPERAMENTS	
THAT MAN IS THE SUPERIOR ANIMAL.	102	MEDITATIO	
WHEN I CONSIDER THE CURIOUS HABITS OF MAN	102	MEDITATIO	
WITH A GARRULOUS OLD MAN AT THE INN.	121	PROVINC DESERT	
"HERE ONE MAN HASTENED HIS STEP.	122	PROVINC DESERT	
"A FAIR MAN AND A PLEASANT."	123	PROVINC DESERT	
WHO AMONG THEM IS A MAN LIKE HAN-REI	132	AT TEN-SHIN	
AND THERE CAME ALSO THE "TRUE MAN" OF SHI-YO TO MEET ME,	134	EXILE'S LETTER	
THE LONE MAN SITS WITH SHUT SPEECH,	139	SENNIN POEM	
I THINK OF TALKING AND MAN,	142	UNMOVING CLOUD	
TAKE THE WHOLE MAN, AND RAVEL OUT THE STORY.	152	NEAR PERIGORD	
TESTING HIS LIST OF RHYMES, A LEAN MAN? BILIOUS?	154	NEAR PERIGORD	
AND THEY DISCUSS THE DEAD MAN,	155	NEAR PERIGORD	
"YOU KNEW THE MAN."	155	NEAR PERIGORD	
"YOU KNEW THE MAN."	155	NEAR PERIGORD	
YOU'LL WONDER THAT AN OLD MAN OF EIGHTY	168	OF AROUET	
A MAN GO WHERE HE WILL.	173	LANGUE D'OC: 2	

PAGE 246

MAN -- MANNER

	PAGE	TITLE	LINE
MAN (CONTINUED)			
NO MAN CAN GET OR HAS GOT.	174	LANGUE D'OC: 3	12
THE MAN WHOM LOVE HAD	175	LANGUE D'OC: 3	56
TILL THE TRAIST MAN CRY OUT TO WARN	177	LANGUE D'OC: 4	3
"THERE WAS ONCE A MAN CALLED VOLTAIRE."	181	MOEURS CON: 7	16
WHAT GOD, MAN, OR HERO	189	HUGH SELWYN: 3	27
"I NEVER MENTIONED A MAN BUT WITH THE VIEW	194	MR. NIXON	14
"IT GIVES NO MAN A SINECURE.	194	MR. NIXON	17
IF ANY MAN WOULD BE A LOVER	212	SEXTUS PROP: 3	17
EACH MAN WHERE HE CAN, WEARING OUT THE DAY IN HIS MANNER.	218	SEXTUS PROP: 5	58
BEAUTY IS NOT ETERNAL, NO MAN HAS PERENNIAL FORTUNE,	223	SEXTUS PROP: 9	20
WHO, WHO WILL BE THE NEXT MAN TO ENTRUST HIS GIRL TO A FRIEND?	227	SEXTUS PROP:12	1
EACH MAN WANTS THE POMEGRANATE FOR HIMSELF;	227	SEXTUS PROP:12	4
AND YET ANOTHER, A "CHARMING MAN," "SWEET NATURE," BUT WAS GILDER,	240	MOYEN SENSUEL	57
STILL WE LOOK TOWARD THE DAY WHEN MAN, WITH UNCTION,	244	MOYEN SENSUEL	175
AND I CAN HEAR AN OLD MAN SAYING: "OH, THE RUB!	244	MOYEN SENSUEL	179
A TEMPERATE MAN, A THIN POTATIONIST, EACH DAY	245	MOYEN SENSUEL	199
THAT MAN WHO IS BASE IN HEART	248	DONNA MI PREGA	7
OR IF A MAN HAVE MIGHT	248	DONNA MI PREGA	17
NOR CAN MAN SAY HE HATH HIS LIFE BY CHANCE	249	DONNA MI PREGA	46
AND WILLS MAN LOOK INTO UNFORMED SPACE	250	DONNA MI PREGA	59
SO HATH MAN CRAFT FROM FEAR	250	DONNA MI PREGA	75
THOU ART SO FAIR ATTIRED THAT EVERY MAN AND EACH	250	DONNA MI PREGA	89
NEVER THE MAN INSIDE	258	ALF'S THIRD	5
"OH, WHAT A CHARMING MAN,"--	261	ALF'S SIXTH	13
THE UNSAFE SAFE, WHEREIN ALL ROTS, AND NO MAN CAN SAY HOW	261	ALF'S FIFTH	19
MY OLD MAN GOT NO INDEMNITY	263	ALF'S EIGHTH	24
"FIND US A HARPIST!! DAVID IS THE MAN!!"	264	ALF'S NINTH	16
DAVE WAS THE MAN TO SELL THE SHOT AND SHELL,	264	ALF'S NINTH	17
AND WOULD MY OLD MAN HAVE BEEN SMARTER	268	ANOTHER BIT	14
MANAGE			
SOON OUR HERO COULD MANAGE ONCE A WEEK,	243	MOYEN SENSUEL	141
MANCA			
"SE IL COR TI MANCA," BUT IT FAILED THEE NOT!	19	FOR E. MCC	12
MANDATE			
(ORCHID), MANDATE	200	MAUBERLEY: 2	32
MANDETTA			
VANNA, MANDETTA, VIERA, ALODETTA, PICARDA, MANUELA	76	THE ALCHEMIST	38
SELVAGGIA, GUISCARDA, MANDETTA,	76	THE ALCHEMIST	54
MANDRAKES			
PREGNANT WITH MANDRAKES, OR WITH SOMETHING ELSE	61	PORTRAIT FEMME	18
MANES			
LET THE MANES PUT OFF THEIR TERROR, LET THEM PUT OFF THEIR AQUEOUS BODIES WITH FIRE.	76	THE ALCHEMIST	51
MANHATTAN'S			
UPON MANHATTAN'S GORGEOUS PANOPLY,	245	MOYEN SENSUEL	188
MANHOOD			
MANHOOD OF ENGLAND,	258	ALF'S SECOND	1
MANIFEST			
UNDETERRED BY THE MANIFEST AGE OF MY TRAPPINGS?	114	SIMULACRA	6
THE MANIFEST UNIVERSE	202	AGE DEMANDED	30
MANIFESTATIONS			
BY VERBAL MANIFESTATIONS;	200	MAUBERLEY: 2	23
MAN-KIN'ARDS			
BROAD AS ALL OCEAN AND LEANIN' MAN-KIN'ARDS.	13	MESMERISM	12
MANKIND			
THE ARCANE SPIRIT OF THE WHOLE MANKIND	42	HER MONUMENT	44
MANNA			
OF INSUBSTANTIAL MANNA,	202	AGE DEMANDED	59
MANNER			
GO IN A FRIENDLY MANNER,	89	COMMISSION	22
HE WAS BORED WITH HIS MANNER OF LIFE,	100	ARIDES	3
LET COME THE GAY OF MANNER, THE INSOLENT AND THE EXULTING.	146	CANTILATIONS	10
I WITH MY BEAK HAULED ASHORE WOULD PROCEED IN A MORE STATELY MANNER,	216	SEXTUS PROP: 5	10

PAGE 247

MANNER -- MAPLE

	PAGE	TITLE	LINE
MANNER (CONTINUED)			
EACH MAN WHERE HE CAN, WEARING OUT THE DAY IN HIS MANNER.	218	SEXTUS PROP: 5	58
FORMED THERE IN MANNER AS A MIST OF LIGHT	248	DONNA MI PREGA	20
MANNERS			
THE OLD MEN WITH BEAUTIFUL MANNERS.	181	MOEURS CON: 7	2
OLD MEN WITH BEAUTIFUL MANNERS,	182	MOEURS CON: 7	23
BY HER PRETTY MANNERS,	215	SEXTUS PROP: 4	30
MAN'S			
LIFE IS THE LIVE MAN'S PART,	47	FROM HEINE: 7	18
THAT, ERE A MAN'S TIDE GO, TURN IT TO TWAIN.	66	THE SEAFARER	70
THE WALLS RISE IN A MAN'S FACE,	138	NEAR SHOKU	3
ONLY ANOTHER MAN'S NOTE:	159	PSYCHOLOG HOUR	42
GOD GRANT I DIE NOT BY ANY MAN'S STROKE	173	LANGUE D'OC: 2	21
MANTLE			
GREEN WAS HER MANTLE, CLOSE, AND WROUGHT	31	PIERE VIDAL	28
IN GILDED AND RUSSET MANTLE.	90	SURGIT FAMA	4
MANUELA			
VANNA, MANDETTA, VIERA, ALODETTA, PICARDA, MANUELA	76	THE ALCHEMIST	38
MANURE			
AND IT IS DOUBTFUL IF EVEN YOUR MANURE WILL BE RICH ENOUGH	146	MONUMENTUM AER	7
MANUS			
MANUS ANIMAM PINXIT,	18	DE AEGYPTO	9
MANY			
AND MANY A NEW THING UNDERSTOOD	3	THE TREE	11
"THERE BE MANY SINGERS GREATER THAN THOU."	16	PRAISE YSOLT	4
AND THE WANDERING OF MANY ROADS HATH MADE MY EYES	16	PRAISE YSOLT	12
MANY A SINGER PASS AND TAKE HIS PLACE	24	THUS NINEVEH	9
AND MANY A ONE HATH SUNG HIS SONGS	24	THUS NINEVEH	12
AND MANY A ONE NOW DOTH SURPASS	24	THUS NINEVEH	14
THAT HE SHOULD LIVE THAN MANY A LIVING DASTARD	37	THE YOUNG KING	23
SO MANY THOUSAND BEAUTIES ARE GONE DOWN TO AVERNUS,	38	LADY'S LIFE	3
AND ALL THE MAIDENS OF ROME, AS MANY AS THEY WERE,	38	LADY'S LIFE	9
SO MANY THOUSAND FAIR ARE GONE DOWN TO AVERNUS,	38	LADY'S LIFE	13
NOT ONCE BUT MANY A DAY	41	HER MONUMENT	16
THERE ARE THERE MANY ROOMS AND ALL OF GOLD,	49	OF SPLENDOUR	13
LO, THERE ARE MANY GODS WHOM WE HAVE SEEN,	50	THE FLAME	23
HOW MANY FACES I'D HAVE OUT OF MIND.	59	EXIT' CUIUSDAM	7
--EVEN THE RIVER MANY DAYS AGO,	60	TOMB AKR CAAR	16
KNOWN ON MY KEEL MANY A CARE'S HOLD,	64	THE SEAFARER	5
HATH OF PERFECT CHARMS SO MANY.	72	DIEU! QU'IL	11
LIKE SO MANY UNUSED BOAS.	93	LES MILLWIN	4
HOW MANY WILL COME AFTER ME	96	DUM CAPITOLIUM	1
THERE COME FORTH MANY MAIDENS	108	CH'U YUAN	5
MANY INSTRUMENTS, LIKE THE SOUND OF YOUNG PHOENIX BROODS.	135	EXILE'S LETTER	27
THOUGH MANY MOVE WITH SUSPICION,	146	SALUTATION 3RD	31
SO MANY HOURS WASTED!	158	PSYCHOLOG HOUR	9
FOR HER GREAT BEAUTY, MANY MEN LOOK ON HER,	177	LANGUE D'OC: 4	27
HOME TO MANY DECEITS,	190	HUGH SELWYN: 4	16
NINE GIRLS, FROM AS MANY COUNTRYSIDES	211	SEXTUS PROP: 2	33
TO SAY MANY THINGS IS EQUAL TO HAVING A HOME.	215	SEXTUS PROP: 4	28
YET YOU ASK ON WHAT ACCOUNT I WRITE SO MANY LOVE-LYRICS	217	SEXTUS PROP: 5	23
WE SHALL CONSTRUCT MANY ILIADS.	217	SEXTUS PROP: 5	34
HOW MANY WORDS TALKED OUT WITH ABUNDANT CANDLES;	220	SEXTUS PROP: 7	3
IN HOW MANY VARIED EMBRACES, OUR CHANGING ARMS,	220	SEXTUS PROP: 7	10
HER KISSES, HOW MANY, LINGERING ON MY LIPS.	220	SEXTUS PROP: 7	11
IF SHE GIVE ME MANY,	221	SEXTUS PROP: 7	39
THROUGH PERILS, (SO MANY) AND OF A VEXED LIFE,	222	SEXTUS PROP: 8	17
MANY AND MANY.	226	SEXTUS PROP:11	2
MANY AND MANY.	226	SEXTUS PROP:11	2
TESTED AND PRIED AND WORKED IN MANY FASHIONS,	235	TO WHISTLER	3
WITH SIGNS AS MANY, THAT SHALL REPRESENT 'EM	244	MOYEN SENSUEL	167
HOW MANY WEAK OF MIND, HOW MUCH TUBERCULOSIS	260	ALF'S FIFTH	13
MAPLE			
BRING THE RED GOLD OF THE MAPLE,	75	THE ALCHEMIST	10
FROM THE BRONZE OF THE MAPLE, FROM THE SAP IN THE BOUGH;	76	THE ALCHEMIST	34

MAQUERO'S -- MARSEILLES

	PAGE	TITLE	LINE
MAQUERO'S			
AT HER LAST MAQUERO'S	192	YEUX GLAUQUES	23
MARBLE			
HIGH WROUGHT OF MARBLE, AND THE PANTING BREATH	31	PIERE VIDAL	39
HIS PALACE IS WHITE LIKE MARBLE,	237	ABU SALAMMAMM	5
MARCH			
MARCH HAS COME TO THE BRIDGE HEAD,	131	AT TEN-SHIN	1
UNAFFECTED BY "THE MARCH OF EVENTS,"	187	E. P. ODE	17
IS, AT BOTTOM, DISTINGUISHED AND FRESH AS A MARCH HERB.	247	PIERROTS	18
MARCHERS			
MARCHERS, NOT GETTING FOR'ARDER,	265	ALF'S TENTH	7
MARCIAN			
NOR ARE MY CAVERNS STUFFED STIFF WITH A MARCIAN VINTAGE,	209	SEXTUS PROP: 1	56
MARE			
SUB MARE	69	SUB MARE	T
MAREMMA			
"SIENA MI FE'; DISFECEMI MAREMMA"	193	SIENA MI FE	T
MAREUIL			
MAREUIL TO THE NORTH-EAST,	121	PROVINC DESERT	22.
THERE ARE THREE KEEPS NEAR MAREUIL,	121	PROVINC DESERT	24
OF ARNAUT DE MAREUIL, I THOUGHT, "QU'IEU SUI AVINEN."	166	FISH & SHADOW	19
MARGINAL			
HATH LACKED A SOMETHING. 'TWAS BUT MARGINAL.	63	QUIES	4
MARGOT			
FRANCOIS AND MARGOT AND THEE AND ME,	11	OF THE GIBBET	2
FRANCOIS AND MARGOT AND THEE AND ME,	11	OF THE GIBBET	14
FRANCOIS AND MARGOT AND THEE AND ME,	12	OF THE GIBBET	26
FRANCOIS AND MARGOT AND THEE AND ME:	12	OF THE GIBBET	38
MARIA			
FROM THE STATUE OF THE INFANT CHRIST IN SANTA MARIA NOVELLA,	94	INSTRUCTIONS	20
MARIENNE			
DRINK WE TO MARIENNE YDOLE,	11	OF THE GIBBET	15
MARIUS			
MARIUS AND JUGURTHA TOGETHER,	218	SEXTUS PROP: 6	4
MARIUS AND JUGURTHA TOGETHER.	219	SEXTUS PROP: 6	12
MARK			
MARK HIM A CRAFTSMAN AND A STRATEGIST?	153	NEAR PERIGORD	85
MARKET			
FOR THE MARKET IN BRESCIA, AND HE	97	AESTHETICS	12
DECREED IN THE MARKET PLACE.	189	HUGH SELWYN: 3	16
I PUMP THE MARKET UP AND DOWN	266	ALF'S ELEVENTH	17
MARKS			
OF UGLY PRINT MARKS, BLACK	35	THE EYES	13
OH! I COULD GET ME OUT, DESPITE THE MARKS	60	TOMB AKR CAAR	29
"NIGHT DOGS, THE MARKS OF A DRUNKEN SCURRY,	211	SEXTUS PROP: 2	49
MARMALADE			
STIRRING THE MARMALADE	262	ALF'S SIXTH	26
MAR-NAN-OTHA			
BY THE STILL POOL OF MAR-NAN-OTHA	4	LA FRAISNE	13
MARRIED			
COME, LET US PITY THE MARRIED AND THE UNMARRIED.	83	THE GARRET	5
HAS MARRIED AN UGLY WIFE,	100	ARIDES	2
AND SHE HAS MARRIED A SOT,	128	BEAU TOILET	7
AT FOURTEEN I MARRIED MY LORD YOU.	130	RIVER-MER WIFE	7
A "BLUE" AND A CLIMBER OF MOUNTAINS, HAS MARRIED	178	MOEURS CON: 1	3
AND RESPECTABLY MARRIED TO PERSEUS,	222	SEXTUS PROP: 8	23
MARROW			
AND THE GOD STRIKES TO THE MARROW.	229	SEXTUS PROP:12	58
THEY HELD THE VERY MARROW OF THE IDEALS	241	MOYEN SENSUEL	95
MARS			
(SATURN AND MARS TO ZEUS DRAWN NEAR!)	10	FOR THIS YULE	18
"NOR MARS SHOUT YOU IN THE WOOD AT AEONIUM,	211	SEXTUS PROP: 2	44
UPON A DUSK THAT IS COME FROM MARS AND STAYS,	248	DONNA MI PREGA	21
MARS'			
THE CYTHAREAN BROUGHT LOW BY MARS' LECHERY	227	SEXTUS PROP:11	27
MARSEILLES			
BETWEEN MARSEILLES	98	THE BELLAIRES	39

MARSH-CRANBERRIES -- MATTER

```
                                                          PAGE    TITLE              LINE
MARSH-CRANBERRIES
     MARSH-CRANBERRIES, THE RIBBED AND ANGULAR PODS ....    162   CABARET DANCER       19
MARSHES
     UPON THE ACTIAN MARSHES VIRGIL IS PHOEBUS' CHIEF OF
        POLICE, .........................................  228   SEXTUS PROP:12       31
MARTIAN
     OUT-WEARIERS OF APOLLO WILL, AS WE KNOW, CONTINUE
        THEIR MARTIAN GENERALITIES, ....................    207   SEXTUS PROP: 1       10
MARTIN
     AND CABINETS AND CHESTS FROM MARTIN (ALMOST LACQUER),  167   OF AROUET            11
MARUS
     NOR OF WELSH MINES AND THE PROFIT MARUS HAD OUT OF
        THEM. ..........................................   217   SEXTUS PROP: 5       46
MARVEL
     THEE, A MARVEL, CARVEN IN SUBTLE STUFF, A .........    68    APPARUIT              2
MARVOIL
     MARVOIL ...........................................    22   MARVOIL               T
     THEY'LL KNOW MORE OF ARNAUT OF MARVOIL ............     22   MARVOIL              25
MARY
     AND HE TALKED ABOUT "THE GREAT MARY," .............    181   MOEURS CON: 7        10
MARY'S
     AND PRAY TO GOD THAT IS ST. MARY'S SON, ..........     172   LANGUE D'OC: 1       19
MA'S
     AND HIS POCKETS BY MA'S AID, THAT NIGHT WITH CASH
        FULL, ..........................................   242   MOYEN SENSUEL       126
MASEFIELD'S
     THAT WE, WITH MASEFIELD'S VEIN, IN THE NEXT SENTENCE   242   MOYEN SENSUEL       129
MASK
     'THOUT MASK OR GAUNTLET, AND ART LAID .............     19   FOR E. MCC           16
     THAT MASK AT PASSIONS AND DESIRE DESIRES, ........      32   PIERE VIDAL          61
MASS
     A HEAVY MASS ON FREE NECKS. ......................    226   SEXTUS PROP:11       12
     YOU AND ABE LINCOLN FROM THAT MASS OF DOLTS .......   235   TO WHISTLER          18
     HURL ME INTO SUCH A MASS OF DIVERGENT IMPRESSIONS.    248   PIERROTS             28
MASTER
     BERTRANS, MASTER OF HIS LAYS, ....................      9   NA AUDIART           30
     YOU, MASTER BOB BROWNING, SPITE YOUR APPAREL .....     13   MESMERISM             7
     "YE SHALL SEE ONE THING TO MASTER ALL: ...........     34   GOODLY FERE          31
     A MASTER OF MEN WAS THE GOODLY FERE, ..............    34   GOODLY FERE          49
     REST MASTER, FOR WE BE A-WEARY, WEARY ............     35   THE EYES              1
     DE MORTUIS VERUM, TRULY THE MASTER BUILDER? .......   240   MOYEN SENSUEL        58
MASTERPIECE
     "AND NO ONE KNOWS, AT SIGHT, A MASTERPIECE. .......   194   MR. NIXON            18
MATCH
     O WINDS, WHAT WIND CAN MATCH THE WEIGHT OF HIM! ...    39   FOR PSYCHE           10
     AND ROCHECOUART CAN MATCH IT, STRONGER YET, ......    152   NEAR PERIGORD        57
MATE
     TO MAKE HIM A MATE OF THE "HAULTE NOBLESSE" ......     11   OF THE GIBBET        10
     SILENT MY MATE CAME AS THE NIGHT WAS STILL. ......     31   PIERE VIDAL          32
     AH GOD, THE LOBA! AND MY ONLY MATE! ..............     31   PIERE VIDAL          44
     A MATE OF THE WIND AND SEA, .....................      34   GOODLY FERE          50
     I MATE WITH MY FREE KIND UPON THE CRAGS; .........     81   TENZONE              10
     WHIRL! CENTRIPETAL! MATE! KING DOWN IN THE VORTEX,   120   GAME OF CHESS        13
     WHEN THE NIGHTINGALE TO HIS MATE .................    171   LANGUE D'OC         EPI
     MAINTAINS INTENTION REASON'S PEER AND MATE; ......    249   DONNA MI PREGA       37
MATED
     GO TO THE UNLUCKILY MATED, ......................      88   COMMISSION           18
MATERNAL
     ITS HOME MAIL IS STILL OPENED BY ITS MATERNAL PARENT  179   MOEURS CON: 4         2
MATES
     'TIS NOT A GAME THAT PLAYS AT MATES AND MATING, ...    50   THE FLAME             1
     'TIS NOT A GAME THAT PLAYS AT MATES AND MATING, ...    50   THE FLAME            16
MATING
     'TIS NOT A GAME THAT PLAYS AT MATES AND MATING, ...    50   THE FLAME             1
     'TIS NOT A GAME THAT PLAYS AT MATES AND MATING, ...    50   THE FLAME            16
MATTER
     LET US LEAVE THIS MATTER, MY SONGS, ..............     82   THE CONDOLENCE        1
     WE MUST LOOK INTO THE MATTER. ....................    208   SEXTUS PROP: 1        4
     AND I ALSO WILL SING WAR WHEN THIS MATTER OF A GIRL
        IS EXHAUSTED. ..................................   216   SEXTUS PROP: 5
```

PAGE 250

MATTER -- MAYST

	PAGE	TITLE	LINE
MATTER (CONTINUED)			
THERE IS A VOLUME IN THE MATTER; IF HER EYELIDS SINK INTO SLEEP,	217	SEXTUS PROP: 5	31
BUT THIS HEAT IS NOT THE ROOT OF THE MATTER:	221	SEXTUS PROP: 8	5
OLD LECHER, LET NOT JUNO GET WIND OF THE MATTER,	222	SEXTUS PROP: 8	39
AND TO KEEP AN EYE ON THEIR READIN' MATTER	272	NATIONAL SONG	13
MATTERS			
WHY SHOULD ONE ALWAYS LIE ABOUT SUCH MATTERS?	113	TAME CAT	2
MATURIN			
MATURIN, GUILLAUME, JACQUES D'ALLMAIN,	12	OF THE GIBBET	29
MAUBERLEY			
HUGH SELWIN MAUBERLEY	185	HUGH SELWYN	T
MAUBERLEY 1920	198	MAUBERLEY 1920	T
MAUDLIN			
NOTHING, IN BRIEF, BUT MAUDLIN CONFESSION,	202	AGE DEMANDED	50
MAUPASSANT			
AND INNOCENT OF STENDHAL, FLAUBERT, MAUPASSANT AND FIELDING.	240	MOYEN SENSUEL	52
MAUSOLUS			
NOR THE MONUMENTAL EFFIGIES OF MAUSOLUS,	209	SEXTUS PROP: 1	68
MAUVE			
THE MAUVE AND GREENISH SOULS OF THE LITTLE MILLWINS	93	LES MILLWIN	2
MAXIM			
BEFORE THE "ARS POETICA" OF HIRAM MAXIM.	239	MOYEN SENSUEL	34
MAY			
MAY HER EYES AND HER CHEEK BE FAIR	23	MARVOIL	30
AND MAY I COME SPEEDILY TO BEZIERS	23	MARVOIL	32
MAY GOD DAMN FOR EVER ALL WHO CRY "PEACE!"	29	ALTAFORTE	36
MAY NOT MAKE BOAST OF ANY BETTER THING	40	ERAT HORA	6
AND, MAY BE, MORE TIMES,	53	AU JARDIN	18
OR GATHER MAY OF HARSH NORTHWINDISH TIME?	59	SILET	8
MAY I FOR MY OWN SELF SONG'S TRUTH RECKON,	64	THE SEAFARER	1
MAY MAKE MERRY MAN FARING NEEDY.	64	THE SEAFARER	27
NOR MAY HE THEN THE FLESH-COVER, WHOSE LIFE CEASETH,	66	THE SEAFARER	96
"THAT I MAY NOT SAY, LADIES.	72	PAN IS DEAD	8
THAT I MAY NOT SAY, LADIES.	72	PAN IS DEAD	10
SOME OTHERS MAY OVERHEAR THEM,	88	CAUSA	2
BUT THESE MAY NOT SUFFER ATTAINDER,	98	THE BELLAIRES	13
FOR THEY MAY NOT BELONG TO THE GOOD SQUIRE BELLAIRE	98	THE BELLAIRES	14
AND YOU MAY DECLINE TO MAKE THEM IMMORTAL,	99	SALVATIONISTS	7
SHE SAYS, "MAY MY POEMS BE PRINTED THIS WEEK?	110	TEMPORA	6
MAY MY POEMS BE PRINTED THIS WEEK?"	110	TEMPORA	8
AND ONE MAY HE HAD YOU SEND FOR ME,	135	EXILE'S LETTER	38
IT MAY LAST WELL IN THESE DARK NORTHERN CLIMATES,	163	CABARET DANCER	71
AND ITS OFFICE MAIL MAY BE OPENED BY	179	MOEURS CON: 4	3
MAY BE AS FAIR AS HERS,	197	ENVOI (1919)	21
WHERE BOLD HANDS MAY DO VIOLENCE TO MY PERSON?	212	SEXTUS PROP: 3	8
HE MAY WALK ON THE SCYTHIAN COAST,	212	SEXTUS PROP: 3	18
MAY A WOODY AND SEQUESTERED PLACE COVER ME WITH ITS FOLIAGE	213	SEXTUS PROP: 3	35
OR MAY I INTER BENEATH THE HUMMOCK	213	SEXTUS PROP: 3	36
AND MAY THE BOUGHT YOKE OF A MISTRESS LIE WITH	214	SEXTUS PROP: 4	3
"MAY THE GOUT CRAMP UP HER FEET!	215	SEXTUS PROP: 4	37
MAY THE FATES WATCH OVER MY DAY.	216	SEXTUS PROP: 5	22
NO, NOW WHILE IT MAY BE, LET NOT THE FRUIT OF LIFE CEASE	220	SEXTUS PROP: 7	28
YOU MAY FIND INTERMENT PLEASING,	222	SEXTUS PROP: 8	29
NOW YOU MAY BEAR FATE'S STROKE UNPERTURBED,	222	SEXTUS PROP: 8	37
OR JOVE, HARSH AS HE IS, MAY TURN ASIDE YOUR ULTIMATE DAY.	222	SEXTUS PROP: 8	38
OH MAY THE KING LIVE FOREVER!	237	ABU SALAMMAMM	26
OH MAY THE KING LIVE FOR A THOUSAND YEARS!	237	ABU SALAMMAMM	27
MAY WE REPEAT; THE CENTENNIAL EXPOSITION	240	MOYEN SENSUEL	54
TILL YOU MAY TAKE YOUR CHOICE: TO FEEL THE EDGE OF SATIRE OR	240	MOYEN SENSUEL	65
YBE			
(THAT, MAYBE, NEVER HAPPENED!)	152	NEAR PERIGORD	41
YHAP			
MAYHAP, RIGHT CLOSE AND KISSED.	107	DOMPNA POIS	68
YST			
WELL MAYST THOU BOAST THAT THOU THE BEST CHEVALIER	37	THE YOUNG KING	18

PAGE 251

MAY'ST -- MEET

```
                                                         PAGE     TITLE             LINE
MAY'ST
     SAFE MAY'ST THOU GO MY CANZON WHITHER THEE PLEASETH   250    DONNA MI PREGA     88
MCC
     FOR E. MCC  ..........................................  19  FOR E. MCC          T
ME (264)
MEAD-DRINK
     THE MEWS' SINGING ALL MY MEAD-DRINK.  ..............    64   THE SEAFARER       22
MEADOW
     SINGS IN THE OPEN MEADOW--AT LEAST THE KODAK SAYS
          SO--  ..........................................  161   CABARET DANCER      4
     NOW CRY THE BIRDS OUT, IN THE MEADOW MIST,  ........   177   LANGUE D'OC: 4     12
MEADOWS
     OVER FAIR MEADOWS,  ...............................   107   COMING OF WAR      16
MEALS
     THAT FED HIS SPIRIT; WERE HIS MENTAL MEALS.  .......   241   MOYEN SENSUEL      96
MEAN
     THE SINGER IS'T YOU MEAN?"  .......................     6   CINO               26
     THAT'S WHAT YOU MEAN YOU ADVERTISING SPADE,  .......   162   CABARET DANCER     34
     AND IN THE MEAN TIME MY SONGS WILL TRAVEL,  ........   208   SEXTUS PROP: 1     39
     AND THIS IS GOOD TO KNOW--FOR US, I MEAN,  .........   235   TO WHISTLER        11
     IN HIS EYE THERE IS DEATH,--I MEAN THE BANKER'S,--    263   ALF'S EIGHTH       15
MEANEST
     FROM COMSTOCK'S SELF, DOWN TO THE MEANEST RESIDENT,   239   MOYEN SENSUEL      15
MEANIN'
     TYIN' YOUR MEANIN' IN SEVENTY SWADELIN'S,  .........    13   MESMERISM           2
MEANS
     BY NO MEANS TOO SMALL,  ...........................   113   FORMIANUS LADY      2
     AND WITH A TONGUE BY NO MEANS TOO ELEGANT,  ........   113   FORMIANUS LADY      6
     TO SING ONE THING WHEN YOUR SONG MEANS ANOTHER,  ...   153   NEAR PERIGORD      89
     THE EDGE, UNCERTAIN, BUT A MEANS OF BLENDING  ......   196   HUGH SELWIN:12     14
MEANT
     WHEN IT TURNED OUT HE MEANT MRS. WARD.  ............   181   MOEURS CON: 7      12
MEASURE
     IS YOUR HATE, THEN, OF SUCH MEASURE?  ..............    44   FROM HEINE: 1       1
     WE TAKE THEIR MEASURE.  ............................   173   LANGUE D'OC: 2     28
     WHO HATH TAUGHT YOU SO SUBTLE A MEASURE,  ..........   207   SEXTUS PROP: 1      6
     IT TWISTS ITSELF FROM OUT ALL NATURAL MEASURE;  ....   249   DONNA MI PREGA     50
     RUDYARD THE FALSE MEASURE,  .......................   259   ALF'S FOURTH        2
MEAT
     AND GIVES YOU AUSTRALIAN ICED RABBITS' MEAT  .......   263   ALF'S EIGHTH       18
MEDALLION
     OF CURIOUS HEADS IN MEDALLION--  ...................   200   MAUBERLEY: 2       25
     MEDALLION  .........................................   204   MEDALLION           T
MEDIA
     AND STRETCHED AND TAMPERED WITH THE MEDIA.  ........   235   TO WHISTLER        17
MEDIAEVAL
     BEING FREE OF MEDIAEVAL SCHOLARSHIP,  ..............    98   THE BELLAIRES      24
     THE TERM "VIRGO" BEING MADE MALE IN MEDIAEVAL
          LATINITY;  ......................................  178   MOEURS CON: 1       6
MEDICAL
     "THE MEDICAL REPORT THIS WEEK DISCLOSES . . ."  ....   260   ALF'S FIFTH        15
MEDICINE
     BUT I REMEMBERED THE NAME OF HIS FEVER MEDICINE AND
          DIED.  ..........................................  165   QUINTUS SEPTIM    24
MEDIOCRITIES
     WAS MADE TO INCUBATE SUCH MEDIOCRITIES,  ...........   239   MOYEN SENSUEL      24
MEDITATE
     AND MEDITATE UPON THE LORD'S CONQUESTS.  ...........   246   MOYEN SENSUEL     228
MEDITATIO
     MEDITATIO  .........................................   102   MEDITATIO           T
MEDIUM
     REFINEMENT OF MEDIUM, ELIMINATION OF SUPERFLUITIES,   202   AGE DEMANDED        4
     ALL ONE CAN SAY OF THIS REFINING MEDIUM  ...........   239   MOYEN SENSUEL      3
MEET
     PRAISES MEET UNTO THY FASHION?  ....................     8   NA-AUDIART         1
     AND WOULD MEET KINDRED EVEN AS I AM,  ..............    20   IN DURANCE         2
     MY SOUL, I MEET THEE, WHEN THIS LIFE'S OUTRUN,  ....    39   BLANDULA
     SOUL, IF SHE MEET US THERE, WILL ANY RUMOUR  .......    39   BLANDULA            1
     MEET THROUGH OUR VEILS AND WHISPER, OF AND LOVE.          50   THE FLAME           1
     WHERE THESE HAVE BEEN, MEET 'TIS, THE GROUND IS HOLY.     51   THE ALTAR
     AND I WILL COME OUT TO MEET YOU  ..................   131   RIVER-MER WIFE     2
```

PAGE 252

MEET -- MEN

	PAGE	TITLE	LINE
MEET (CONTINUED)			
AND THERE CAME ALSO THE "TRUE MAN" OF SHI-YO TO MEET ME,	134	EXILE'S LETTER	24
WHOM WE MEET ON STRANGE ROADWAYS?	141	IDEA OF CHOAN	32
ITS LOWEST STONES JUST MEET THE VALLEY TIPS	152	NEAR PERIGORD	55
BELIEVING WE SHOULD MEET WITH LIPS AND HANDS,	157	NEAR PERIGORD	179
WILL MEET A DUCHESS AND AN EX-DIPLOMAT'S WIDOW	163	CABARET DANCER	64
'TIS MEET	173	LANGUE D'OC: 2	4
E'EN THOUGH HE MEET NOT WITH HATE	249	DONNA MI PREGA	43
AN' EVERY YEAR WE MEET TO LET	270	OF 600 M.P.'S	11
MEETETH			
OFTEN HIS POWER MEETETH WITH DEATH IN THE END	249	DONNA MI PREGA	39
MEETING			
AT THE MEETING OF HANDS.	3	THRENOS	10
AND THE SHEPHERDESS MEETING WITH GUIDO.	112	SHOP GIRL	4
A PLACE OF FELICITOUS MEETING.	141	IDEA OF CHOAN	25
MEETING-PLACE			
NO MORE FOR US THE MEETING-PLACE	3	THRENOS	16
MEETS			
AND THE SOIL MEETS HIS DISTRESS.	195	HUGH SELWIN:10	8
MEINEN			
AUS MEINEN GROSSEN SCHMERZEN	97	THE BELLAIRES	EPI
MELEAGAR			
NOW, QUENCHED AS THE BRAND OF MELEAGAR,	181	MOEURS CON: 6	3
MELLOWED			
WHAT WATER HAS MELLOWED YOUR WHISTLES?	207	SEXTUS PROP: 1	9
MELT			
LO, HOW THE LIGHT DOTH MELT US INTO SONG:	38	BALLATETTA	3
MELTING			
I HAVE SEEN IT MELTING ABOVE ME.	95	OF THE DEGREES	7
MELTING ON STEEL.	155	NEAR PERIGORD	135
MEMBRA			
NYMPHARUM MEMBRA DISJECTA	92	APRIL	EPI
MEMNON			
MEMNON, MEMNON, THAT LADY	102	LADIES	9
MEMNON, MEMNON, THAT LADY	102	LADIES	9
MEMOIRE			
AU DEDANS DE MA MEMOIRE	160	DANS OMNIBUS	7
MEMORABLE			
AS MEMORABLE BROKEN BLADES THAT BE	19	FOR E. MCC	17
MEMORIAL			
"OF" ROYAL AEMILIA, DRAWN ON THE MEMORIAL RAFT,	210	SEXTUS PROP: 2	10
MEMORIES			
AND SLAY THE MEMORIES THAT ME CHEER	10	FOR THIS YULE	14
TILL WE HAD NOTHING BUT THOUGHTS AND MEMORIES IN COMMON.	134	EXILE'S LETTER	15
THE HEAVY MEMORIES OF HOREB, SINAI AND THE FORTY YEARS,	193	BRENNBAUM	5
MEMORY			
SOLE GUARD OF MEMORY	41	HER MONUMENT	8
HE PASSED FROM MEN'S MEMORY IN L'AN TRENTIESME	187	E. P. ODE	18
FOR MEMORY OF THE FIRST WARM NIGHT STILL CAST A HAZE O'ER	245	MOYEN SENSUEL	195
OR LOSETH POWER, E'EN LOST TO MEMORY.	249	DONNA MI PREGA	48
MEMORY'S			
IN MEMORY'S LOCUS TAKETH HE HIS STATE	248	DONNA MI PREGA	10
MEN			
THE YOUNG MEN AT THE SWORD-PLAY;	4	LA FRAISNE	6
OF THE OLD WAYS OF MEN HAVE I CAST ASIDE.	4	LA FRAISNE	12
TILL MEN SAY THAT I AM MAD;	4	LA FRAISNE	21
BUT I HAVE SEEN THE SORROW OF MEN, AND AM GLAD,	4	LA FRAISNE	22
AND NOW MEN CALL ME MAD BECAUSE I HAVE THROWN	4	LA FRAISNE	27
TO LEAVE THE OLD BARREN WAYS OF MEN,	4	LA FRAISNE	29
THOUGH ALL MEN SAY THAT I AM MAD	5	LA FRAISNE	32
ONCE WHEN I WAS AMONG THE YOUNG MEN	5	LA FRAISNE	40
AND THEY SAID I WAS QUITE STRONG, AMONG THE YOUNG MEN,	5	LA FRAISNE	41
THEN CAME WHAT MIGHT COME, TO WIT: THREE MEN AND ONE WOMAN,	22	MARVOIL	11
TO ALL MEN EXCEPT THE KING OF ARAGON,	23	MARVOIL	31
AND MEN MYRTLES, ERE THE NIGHT	24	THUS NINEVEH	3

MEN -- MEN'S

	PAGE	TITLE	LINE
MEN (CONTINUED)			
SHALL ALL MEN SCATTER ROSE LEAVES	24	THUS NINEVEH	17
AS LESSER MEN DRINK WINE."	24	THUS NINEVEH	23
MEN HAVE I KNOWN AND MEN, BUT NEVER ONE	32	PARACELSUS	3
MEN HAVE I KNOWN AND MEN, BUT NEVER ONE	32	PARACELSUS	3
FLUIDS INTANGIBLE THAT HAVE BEEN MEN,	32	PARACELSUS	10
AYE LOVER HE WAS OF BRAWNY MEN,	33	GOODLY FERE	3
BUT A MAN O' MEN WAS HE.	33	GOODLY FERE	16
I HA' SEEN HIM DRIVE A HUNDRED MEN	33	GOODLY FERE	17
I HA' SEEN HIM COW A THOUSAND MEN.	34	GOODLY FERE	35
I HA' SEEN HIM COW A THOUSAND MEN	34	GOODLY FERE	41
A MASTER OF MEN WAS THE GOODLY FERE,	34	GOODLY FERE	49
THAT WAS MOST VALIANT 'MID ALL WORTHIEST MEN!	37	THE YOUNG KING	30
BLIND EYES AND SHADOWS THAT ARE FORMED AS MEN;	38	BALLATETTA	2
DEAD MEN STAY ALWAY DEAD MEN,	47	FROM HEINE: 7	17
DEAD MEN STAY ALWAY DEAD MEN,	47	FROM HEINE: 7	17
SO THAT ALL MEN SHALL HONOUR HIM AFTER	66	THE SEAFARER	78
LORDLY MEN, ARE TO EARTH O'ERGIVEN,	66	THE SEAFARER	95
ERI MEN HAI TE KUDONIAI--IBYCUS.	87	THE SPRING	EPI
THE YOUNG MEN LOOK UPON THEIR SENIORS,	104	THE SEEING EYE	5
YOUNG MEN RIDING IN THE STREET	111	IMAGE ORLEANS	1
"MEN HAVE GONE BY SUCH AND SUCH VALLEYS	122	PROVINC DESERT	57
TWO MEN TOSSING A COIN, ONE KEEPING A CASTLE,	122	PROVINC DESERT	66
BUT TO-DAY'S MEN ARE NOT THE MEN OF THE OLD DAYS,	131	AT TEN-SHIN	7
BUT TO-DAY'S MEN ARE NOT THE MEN OF THE OLD DAYS,	131	AT TEN-SHIN	7
NO LONGER THE MEN FOR OFFENCE AND DEFENCE.	133	FRONTIER GUARD	21
INTELLIGENT MEN CAME DRIFTING IN FROM THE SEA AND FROM THE WEST BORDER,	134	EXILE'S LETTER	6
AND WHEN MEN GOING BY LOOK ON RAFU	140	MULBERRY ROAD	15
AND MEN SAY THE SUN AND MOON KEEP ON MOVING	142	UNMOVING CLOUD	20
"IT IS NOT THAT THERE ARE NO OTHER MEN	142	UNMOVING CLOUD	24
I SEVERED MEN, MY HEAD AND HEART	156	NEAR PERIGORD	167
SAY "FORGET TO-MORROW," BEING OF ALL MEN	161	CABARET DANCER	7
THE NOBLEST GIRLS MEN LOVE	176	LANGUE D'OC: 3	70
FOR HER GREAT BEAUTY, MANY MEN LOOK ON HER,	177	LANGUE D'OC: 4	27
THE OLD MEN WITH BEAUTIFUL MANNERS.	181	MOEURS CON: 7	2
OLD MEN WITH BEAUTIFUL MANNERS,	182	MOEURS CON: 7	23
ALL MEN, IN LAW, ARE EQUALS.	189	HUGH SELWYN: 3	21
HIM OF ALL MEN, UNFIT	201	AGE DEMANDED	2
"THE WOUNDING OF AUSTERE MEN BY CHICANE."	211	SEXTUS PROP: 2	51
THIS CARE FOR PAST MEN,	219	SEXTUS PROP: 6	32
FROM THESE HE LEARNT. POE, WHITMAN, WHISTLER, MEN, THEIR RECOGNITION	240	MOYEN SENSUEL	59
OF LANGUAGE, BY MEN WHOLLY SOCIALIZED,	244	MOYEN SENSUEL	166
"AS FREE OF MOBS AS KINGS"? I'D HAVE MEN FREE OF THAT INVIDIOUS,	244	MOYEN SENSUEL	169
LEST IT SHOULD FAIL TO TREAT ALL MEN ALIKE.	244	MOYEN SENSUEL	178
SO RADWAY WALKED, QUITE LIKE THE OTHER MEN,	244	MOYEN SENSUEL	185
SOME MEN WILL LIVE AS PRUDES IN THEIR OWN VILLAGE	245	MOYEN SENSUEL	207
(SUCH CHANGES DON'T OCCUR IN MEN, OR RABBITS).	246	MOYEN SENSUEL	232
BUT YOU SHALL KNOW THAT THESE WERE THE MEN.	265	ALF'S NINTH	32
MY GREAT PRESS CLEAVES THE GUTS OF MEN,	266	ALF'S ELEVENTH	
MY SUFFERIN' FELLOW MEN,	269	SAFE AND SOUND	26
WE ARE SIX HUNDRED BEEFY MEN	270	OF 600 M.P.'S	
THAN MEN LIKE ME AND YOU,	272	THE BABY	
LIKE TO-DAY'S GREAT MEN IN BRITAIN.	272	THE BABY	1
MENCKEN			
FOR MENCKEN STATES SOMEWHERE, IN THIS CONNECTION:	238	MOYEN SENSUEL	16
MENDACITIES			
BETTER MENDACITIES	188	HUGH SELWYN: 2	
MENELAUS			
PARIS TOOK HELEN NAKED COMING FROM THE BED OF MENELAUS,	220	SEXTUS PROP: 7	1
A TROJAN AND ADULTEROUS PERSON CAME TO MENELAUS UNDER THE RITES OF HOSPITIUM,	227	SEXTUS PROP:12	
MENOETIUS			
WITHOUT IXION, AND WITHOUT THE SONS OF MENOETIUS AND THE ARGO AND WITHOUT JOVE'S GRAVE AND THE TITANS.	218	SEXTUS PROP: 5	5
MEN'S			
LIFE, ALL OF IT, MY SEA, AND ALL MEN'S STREAMS	25	GUIDO INVITES	
AND MADE MEN'S MOCK'RY IN MY ROTTEN SADNESS!	31	PIERE VIDAL	5

MEN'S -- MET

	PAGE	TITLE	LINE
MEN'S (CONTINUED)			
A-TREMBLE IN MEN'S VEINS; O LIP CURVED HIGH	41	HER MONUMENT	12
MEN'S FATES ARE ALREADY SET,	138	NEAR SHOKU	10
YOU'D HAVE MEN'S HEARTS UP FROM THE DUST	151	NEAR PERIGORD	1
WITH THE NOBLEST THAT STANDS IN MEN'S SIGHT,	174	LANGUE D'OC: 3	13
HE PASSED FROM MEN'S MEMORY IN L'AN TRENTIESME	187	E. P. ODE	18
BELIEVING IN OLD MEN'S LIES, THEN UNBELIEVING	190	HUGH SELWYN: 4	14
TO SHOW HIM VISIBLE TO MEN'S SIGHT.	248	DONNA MI PREGA	18
MENTAL			
THAT FED HIS SPIRIT; WERE HIS MENTAL MEALS.	241	MOYEN SENSUEL	96
IS HIGHER IN THE MENTAL SCALE	272	THE BABY	5
MENTION			
LET US THEREFORE MENTION THE FACT,	93	LES MILLWIN	13
IN THE HOPE OF HONOURABLE MENTION	264	ALF'S EIGHTH	32
BUT SHE NEVER MADE NO MENTION	271	OLE KATE	23
MENTIONED			
"I NEVER MENTIONED A MAN BUT WITH THE VIEW	194	MR. NIXON	14
HAPPY WHO ARE MENTIONED IN MY PAMPHLETS,	209	SEXTUS PROP: 1	63
MENTORS			
IN WHICH THEIR MENTORS PLACE SUCH WIDE RELIANCE.	244	MOYEN SENSUEL	164
MERCHANDISE			
MINE IS THE SHIP AND THINE THE MERCHANDISE,	25	GUIDO INVITES	4
MERCIFUL			
JOVE, BE MERCIFUL TO THAT UNFORTUNATE WOMAN	221	SEXTUS PROP: 8	1
MERCURY			
O GOD, O VENUS, O MERCURY, PATRON OF THIEVES,	117	THE LAKE ISLE	1
O GOD, O VENUS, O MERCURY, PATRON OF THIEVES,	117	THE LAKE ISLE	12
MERCY			
PERSEPHONE AND DIS, DIS, HAVE MERCY UPON HER,	223	SEXTUS PROP: 9	13
MERE			
I SKOAL TO THE EYES AS GREY-BLOWN MERE	10	FOR THIS YULE	22
INVITATION, MERE INVITATION TO PERCEPTIVITY	201	AGE DEMANDED	25
THE MERE WILL TO ACT IS SUFFICIENT."	216	SEXTUS PROP: 5	6
IT IS A MERE POSTPONEMENT OF YOUR DOMINATION.	216	SEXTUS PROP: 5	20
MERE-FLOOD			
MY MOOD 'MID THE MERE-FLOOD,	65	THE SEAFARER	60
MERE-WEARY			
MERE-WEARY MOOD. LEST MAN KNOW NOT	64	THE SEAFARER	12
MERGED			
IF I HAVE MERGED MY SOUL, OR UTTERLY	51	THE FLAME	32
MERRILY			
DRINK WE THE COMRADES MERRILY	11	OF THE GIBBET	3
MERRIMENT			
NOR FIND AUGHT NOVEL IN THY MERRIMENT?	43	SATIEMUS	10
BENEATH THEIR TRANSITORY STEP AND MERRIMENT,	236	MIDDLE-AGED	9
MERRY			
MAY MAKE MERRY MAN FARING NEEDY.	64	THE SEAFARER	27
MESMERISM			
MESMERISM	13	MESMERISM	T
MESMERIZER			
AYE YOU'RE A MAN THAT! YE OLD MESMERIZER	13	MESMERISM	1
MESS			
THAT MAKES THE WORST MESS.	259	ALF'S FOURTH	7
MESSAGE			
MR. HOUSMAN'S MESSAGE	43	MR. HOUSMAN	T
NO MESSAGE I GET;	173	LANGUE D'OC: 2	7
"MESSAGE TO GARCIA," MOSHER'S PROPAGANDAS	241	MOYEN SENSUEL	73
MESSALINA			
OF MESSALINA:	198	MAUBERLEY: 1	4
MESSENGER			
NO MESSENGER SHOULD COME WHOLLY EMPTY,	214	SEXTUS PROP: 4	8
MESSIRE			
AND TELL THEIR SECRETS, MESSIRE CINO,	151	NEAR PERIGORD	2
MET			
WHERE THY TONGUE AND LIMBS ARE MET	8	NA AUDIART	24
THOU TRUSTED'ST IN THYSELF AND MET THE BLADE	19	FOR E. MCC	15
MET TO DISCUSS THEIR AFFAIRS;	97	THE BELLAIRES	7
MET TO DISCUSS THEIR AFFAIRS,	98	THE BELLAIRES	29
WE MET, AND TRAVELLED INTO SEN-GO,	134	EXILE'S LETTER	17
AND IS NOT AGAIN TO BE MET WITH.	136	EXILE'S LETTER	64

MET -- MIDDLE-AGED

	PAGE	TITLE	LINE
MET (CONTINUED)			
AND ONCE AGAIN, LATER, WE MET AT THE SOUTH BRIDGEHEAD.	136	EXILE'S LETTER	70
WHEN LAST I MET HIM, HE WAS A PILLAR IN	246	MOYEN SENSUEL	229
"WE ARE 'ERE MET TOGETHER	270	OF 600 M.P.'S	1
WE ARE 'ERE MET TOGETHER	270	OF 600 M.P.'S	5
METAL			
GIVE LIGHT TO THE METAL.	75	THE ALCHEMIST	28
QUIET THIS METAL!	76	THE ALCHEMIST	50
LET THEM DRAW TOGETHER THE BONES OF THE METAL.	76	THE ALCHEMIST	53
QUIET THIS METAL.	76	THE ALCHEMIST	62
A THIN WAR OF METAL.	95	OF THE DEGREES	5
UPON HORSES WITH HEAD-TRAPPINGS OF YELLOW METAL,	132	AT TEN-SHIN	16
OF DRY AIR, AS CLEAR AS METAL.	146	CANTILATIONS	12
AND THE MOLTEN METAL OF YOUR SHOULDERS	170	PHANOPOEIA	19
FROM METAL, OR INTRACTABLE AMBER;	204	MEDALLION	12
METAMORPHOSIS			
CAUGHT IN METAMORPHOSIS, WERE	200	MAUBERLEY: 2	36
METAPHORS			
AND STREWS A MIND WITH PRECIOUS METAPHORS,	236	MIDDLE-AGED	18
METAPHYSICAL			
NATURE HERSELF'S TURNED METAPHYSICAL,	50	THE FLAME	27
METIERS			
"I AM AN ARTIST, YOU HAVE TRIED BOTH METIERS."	156	NEAR PERIGORD	152
METRES			
THEY HOWL. THEY COMPLAIN IN DELICATE AND EXHAUSTED METRES	148	FRATRES MINORE	5
METRO			
IN A STATION OF THE METRO	109	IN THE METRO	T
ME-WARD			
FOR HER HANDS HAVE NO KINDNESS ME-WARD,	212	SEXTUS PROP: 3	14
MEWARDS			
THEY THAT COME MEWARDS, BEARING OLD MAGIC.	20	IN DURANCE	22
MEWING			
AND WITH A PLAINTIVE, GENTLE MEWING,	115	SOCIAL ORDER	16
MEWS'			
THE MEWS' SINGING ALL MY MEAD-DRINK.	64	THE SEAFARER	22
MI			
MI BASTAN MIS PENSAMIENTOS.	82	THE CONDOLENCE	EPI
"SIENA MI FE'; DISFECEMI MAREMMA"	193	SIENA MI FE	T
DONNA MI PREGA	248	DONNA MI PREGA	T
MICA			
WE CAN'T PRESERVE THE ELUSIVE "MICA SALIS,"	163	CABARET DANCER	70
MICHAULT			
FOR MICHAULT LE BORGNE THAT WOULD CONFESS	12	OF THE GIBBET	34
MID			
WHAT IF MY THOUGHTS WERE TURNED IN THEIR MID REACH	43	SATIEMUS	9
NOR STIR HAND NOR THINK\IN MID HEART,	66	THE SEAFARER	9
IN THE MID LOVE COURT, HE SINGS OUT THE CANZON,	154	NEAR PERIGORD	11
'MID			
I HAVE CURLED 'MID THE BOLES OF THE ASH WOOD,	4	LA FRAISNE	
HERE 'MID THE ASH TREES.	5	LA FRAISNE	5
I HA' SEEN THEM 'MID THE CLOUDS ON THE HEATHER.	25	THE WHITE STAG	
THAT WAS MOST VALIANT 'MID ALL WORTHIEST MEN!	37	THE YOUNG KING	3
ABIDES 'MID BURGHERS SOME HEAVY BUSINESS,	64	THE SEAFARER	2
MY MOOD 'MID THE MERE-FLOOD,	65	THE SEAFARER	6
AND HIS LAUD BEYOND THEM REMAIN 'MID THE ENGLISH,	66	THE SEAFARER	7
DELIGHT 'MID THE DOUGHTY.	66	THE SEAFARER	8
'MID THESE THINGS OLDER THAN THE NAMES THEY HAVE,	69	SUB MARE	
'MID THE SILVER RUSTLING OF WHEAT,	75	THE ALCHEMIST	1
MID-CROWD			
"ANOTHER WHEEL, THE ARENA; MID-CROWD IS AS BAD AS MID-SEA."	210	SEXTUS PROP: 2	
MIDDLE			
GO TO THOSE WHO ARE THICKENED WITH MIDDLE AGE,	89	COMMISSION	
A TURMOIL OF WARS-MEN, SPREAD OVER THE MIDDLE KINGDOM,	133	FRONTIER GUARD	
AND ANOTHER SAID "GET HIM PLUMB IN THE MIDDLE!	224	SEXTUS PROP:10	
MIDDLE-AGED			
YES, SHE ALSO WILL TURN MIDDLE-AGED,	116	THE TEA SHOP	
SHE ALSO WILL TURN MIDDLE-AGED.	116	THE TEA SHOP	

MIDDLE-AGED -- MILES

	PAGE	TITLE	LINE
MIDDLE-AGED (CONTINUED)			
MIDDLE-AGED	236	MIDDLE-AGED	T
MIDDLE-AGEING			
WITH MIDDLE-AGEING CARE	158	PSYCHOLOG HOUR	3
MIDMOST			
AND WITHIN, THE MISTRESS, IN THE MIDMOST OF HER YOUTH,	128	BEAU TOILET	3
MIDNIGHT			
MIDNIGHT, AND A LETTER COMES TO ME FROM OUR MISTRESS:	212	SEXTUS PROP: 3	1
NOR IS THERE ANYONE TO WHOM LOVERS ARE NOT SACRED AT MIDNIGHT	212	SEXTUS PROP: 3	15
THE MIDNIGHT ACTIVITIES OF WHATS-HIS NAME,	264	ALF'S NINTH	2
MIDONS			
I ASK OF MIDONS AELIS (OF MONTFORT)	105	DOMPNA POIS	28
MIDONZ			
MIDONZ, WITH THE GOLD OF THE SUN, THE LEAF OF THE POPLAR, BY THE LIGHT OF THE AMBER,	75	THE ALCHEMIST	25
MIDONZ, DAUGHTER OF THE SUN, SHAFT OF THE TREE, SILVER OF THE LEAF, LIGHT OF THE YELLOW OF THE AMBER,	75	THE ALCHEMIST	26
MIDONZ, GIFT OF THE GOD, GIFT OF THE LIGHT, GIFT OF THE AMBER OF THE SUN,	75	THE ALCHEMIST	27
MID-PAGE			
AND LOST MID-PAGE	15	FAMAM CANO	44
MID-SEA			
"ANOTHER WHEEL, THE ARENA; MID-CROWD IS AS BAD AS MID-SEA."	210	SEXTUS PROP: 2	27
MIDST			
FOR THIS THERE'S NO MOOD-LOFTY MAN OVER EARTH'S MIDST,	65	THE SEAFARER	40
IN THE MIDST OF SHOKU, A PROUD CITY.	138	NEAR SHOKU	9
SHE WAS VEILED IN THE MIDST OF THAT PLACE,	214	SEXTUS PROP: 4	24
IN MIDST OF DARKNESS LIGHT LIGHT GIVETH FORTH	250	DONNA MI PREGA	85
MID-SUMMER			
WAITING HIS TURN IN THE MID-SUMMER EVENING,	154	NEAR PERIGORD	109
MIELS-DE-BEN			
UNTO LADY "MIELS-DE-BEN,"	8	NA AUDIART	13
I OF MIELS-DE-BEN DEMAND	106	DOMPNA POIS	47
MIGHT			
THAT THEY MIGHT DO THIS WONDER THING;	3	THE TREE	9
THEN CAME WHAT MIGHT COME, TO WIT: THREE MEN AND ONE WOMAN,	22	MARVOIL	11
HIS LONE MIGHT 'GAINST ALL DARKNESS OPPOSING.	29	ALTAFORTE	24
I WOULD THAT THE COOL WAVES MIGHT FLOW OVER MY MIND,	36	FRANCESCA	8
SO THAT I MIGHT FIND YOU AGAIN,	36	FRANCESCA	11
YE MIGHT LET ONE REMAIN ABOVE WITH US.	38	LADY'S LIFE	4
YE MIGHT LET ONE REMAIN ABOVE WITH US.	38	LADY'S LIFE	14
HOURS, WHERE SOMETHING MIGHT HAVE FLOATED UP.	61	PORTRAIT FEMME	12
THAT MIGHT PROVE USEFUL AND YET NEVER PROVES,	61	PORTRAIT FEMME	19
HATH SET ACQUAINTANCE WHERE MIGHT BE AFFECTIONS,	63	AN OBJECT	2
INDIFFERENT AND DISCOURAGED HE THOUGHT HE MIGHT AS	100	ARIDES	4
THAT I, MYSELF, MIGHT HAVE ENJOYED THEM.	101	AMITIES	5
LORD POWERFUL, ENGIRDLED ALL WITH MIGHT,	172	LANGUE D'OC: 1	2
AS ROSES MIGHT, IN MAGIC AMBER LAID,	197	ENVOI (1919)	13
MIGHT, IN NEW AGES, GAIN HER WORSHIPPERS,	197	ENVOI (1919)	22
TITYRUS MIGHT HAVE SUNG THE SAME VIXEN;	220	SEXTUS PROP:12	46
THE PROMINENT HAUNTS, WHERE ONE MIGHT RECOGNIZE HIM,	245	MOYEN SENSUEL	203
YOU MIGHT PARDON SUCH SLIPS.	247	PIERROTS	24
OR IF A MAN HAVE MIGHT	248	DONNA MI PREGA	17
MIGHT SAY, BE A SURPRISE	262	ALF'S SEVENTH	8
MIGHT CAUSE THOUGHT AND BE THEREFORE	262	ALF'S SEVENTH	19
MIGHT DO, TOO. MONTAGUE!	267	ALF'S TWELFTH	18
MIGHTY			
AND YET I MOCK YOU BY THE MIGHTY FIRES	32	PIERE VIDAL	63
MOUNTS, FROM OUR MIGHTY THOUGHTS AND FROM THE FOUNT	41	HER MONUMENT	27
MILDLY			
AND AT THIS I WAS MILDLY ABASHED.	97	AESTHETICS	22
MILDNESS			
MILDNESS, AMID THE NEO-NIETZSCHEAN CLATTER,	201	AGE DEMANDED	21
MILES			
AND SEND IT A THOUSAND MILES, THINKING.	136	EXILE'S LETTER	80

MILES -- MINDS

	PAGE	TITLE	LINE
MILES (CONTINUED)			
AND GO OUT THROUGH A THOUSAND MILES OF DEAD GRASS.	137	TAKING LEAVE	4
THE TEN GOOD MILES FROM THERE TO MAENT'S CASTLE,	153	NEAR PERIGORD	65
MILESIAN			
NO, "MILESIAN" IS AN EXAGGERATION.	195	HUGH SELWIN:11	5
MILESIEN			
"CONSERVATRIX OF MILESIEN"	195	HUGH SELWIN:11	1
MILK-WHITE			
LET THEM ASSUME THE MILK-WHITE BODIES OF AGATE. ...	76	THE ALCHEMIST	52
THE MILK-WHITE GIRLS	109	HEATHER	4
MILLENIA			
THESE FIVE MILLENIA, AND THY DEAD EYES	60	TOMB AKR CAAR	2
MILLION			
FOR HERE ARE A MILLION PEOPLE SURLY WITH TRAFFIC;	62	N. Y.	5
SLOUCHED THE TEN MILLION,	257	BREAD BRIGADE	4
DAMN THE TEN MILLION!	257	BREAD BRIGADE	8
LOUSY TEN MILLION!	257	BREAD BRIGADE	16
DAMN THE TEN MILLION.	257	BREAD BRIGADE	20
MILLWIN			
LES MILLWIN	93	LES MILLWIN	T
MILLWINS			
THE LITTLE MILLWINS ATTEND THE RUSSIAN BALLET.	93	LES MILLWIN	1
THE MAUVE AND GREENISH SOULS OF THE LITTLE MILLWINS	93	LES MILLWIN	2
AND THE LITTLE MILLWINS BEHELD THESE THINGS;	93	LES MILLWIN	11
MILORD			
WHILE MILORD BEAVERBROOK	257	BREAD BRIGADE	28
MIME			
REMAINS OF ROME. O WORLD, THOU UNCONSTANT MIME! ...	40	ROME	12
MINARETS			
SEEN THE LONG MINARETS, THE WHITE SHAFTS.	122	PROVINC DESERT	35
MIND			
AND BECAUSE I HAVE SMALL MIND TO SIT	22	MARVOIL	2
AND SO WERE MY MIND HOLLOW, DID SHE NOT FILL UTTERLY MY THOUGHT.	23	MARVOIL	39
AND TURN MY MIND UPON THAT SPLENDID MADNESS,	30	PIERE VIDAL	2
I WOULD THAT THE COOL WAVES MIGHT FLOW OVER MY MIND,	36	FRANCESCA	8
TO MIND ME OF SOME URN OF FULL DELIGHT,	41	HER MONUMENT	13
SWEPT FROM THE MIND WITH IT IN ITS DEPARTURE.	42	HER MONUMENT	40
SWEEP BACK UPON ME AND ENGULF MY MIND!	51	HORAE BEATAE	2
HOW MANY FACES I'D HAVE OUT OF MIND.	59	EXIT' CUIUSDAM	7
YOUR MIND AND YOU ARE OUR SARGASSO SEA,	61	PORTRAIT FEMME	1
ONE AVERAGE MIND--WITH ONE THOUGHT LESS, EACH YEAR.	61	PORTRAIT FEMME	10
ITS MIND WAS MADE UP IN "THE SEVENTIES,"	63	PHASELLUS ILLE	3
THEY CONSIDER THE ELDERLY MIND	104	THE SEEING EYE	6
OUR MIND IS FULL OF SORROW, WHO WILL KNOW OF OUR GRIEF?	127	BOWMEN OF SHU	24
MIND LIKE A FLOATING WIDE CLOUD,	137	TAKING LEAVE	5
MIND AND SPIRIT DRIVE ON THE FEATHERY BANNERS.	139	SOUTH-FOLK	9
AND HATE YOUR MIND, NOT YOU, YOUR SOUL, YOUR HANDS.'	157	NEAR PERIGORD	184
BEAUTY WOULD DRINK OF MY MIND.	158	PSYCHOLOG HOUR	28
HER MIND IS, AS EVER, UNCULTIVATED,	179	MOEURS CON: 2	6
TISSUE PRESERVED--THE PURE MIND	193	SIENA MI FE	11
HABITS OF MIND AND FEELING,	195	HUGH SELWIN:11	2
AND STREWS A MIND WITH PRECIOUS METAPHORS,	236	MIDDLE-AGED	18
THEY SET THEIR MIND (IT'S STILL IN THAT CONDITION)--	240	MOYEN SENSUEL	53
THE MIND OF RADWAY, WHENE'ER HE FOUND A PAIR OF PURPLE STAYS OR	245	MOYEN SENSUEL	196
HOW MANY WEAK OF MIND, HOW MUCH TUBERCULOSIS	260	ALF'S FIFTH	13
VEX NOT THOU THE BANKER'S MIND	263	ALF'S EIGHTH	1
VEX IT NOT, WILLIE, HIS MIND,	263	ALF'S EIGHTH	3
TO MIND THEIR "P'S" AND THEIR "Q'S" AND THEIR WAYS	263	ALF'S EIGHTH	27
UNTIL THE MIND OF THE OLD NATION GETS A LITTLE STRONGER.	266	ALF'S TENTH	16
MINDS			
GREAT MINDS HAVE SOUGHT YOU--LACKING SOMEONE ELSE.	61	PORTRAIT FEMME	6
SORROWFUL MINDS, SORROW IS STRONG, WE ARE HUNGRY AND THIRSTY.	127	BOWMEN OF SHU	7
AND WE ALL SPOKE OUT OUR HEARTS AND MINDS, AND WITHOUT REGRET.	134	EXILE'S LETTER	11
WITH MINDS STILL HOVERING ABOVE THEIR TESTICLES ...	148	FRATRES MINORE	1
FOR MINDS SO WHOLLY FOUNDED UPON QUOTATIONS ......, ..	239	MOYEN SENSUEL	29

MINDS -- MIRROR

	PAGE	TITLE	LINE
MINDS (CONTINUED)			
WHEN OUR MINDS ARE VERY BLEARY,	267	ALF'S TWELFTH	5
MIND'S			
MOANETH ALWAY MY MIND'S LUST	65	THE SEAFARER	37
MINE			
SHE HATH CALLED ME FROM MINE OLD WAYS	4	LA FRAISNE	16
SHE HATH DRAWN ME FROM MINE OLD WAYS,	4	LA FRAISNE	20
(SUCH AS I DRINK TO MINE FASHION)	10	FOR THIS YULE	15
WHERE ARE THE LIPS MINE LAY UPON,	10	FOR THIS YULE	19
MINE?	14	FAMAM CANO	17
BEHOLD MINE AUDIENCE,	14	FAMAM CANO	21
I AM HOMESICK AFTER MINE OWN KIND,	20	IN DURANCE	1
BUT I AM HOMESICK AFTER MINE OWN KIND.	20	IN DURANCE	3
OUT OF MINE OWN SOUL-KIN,	20	IN DURANCE	11
FOR I AM HOMESICK AFTER MINE OWN KIND	20	IN DURANCE	12
AFTER MINE OWN KIND THAT KNOW, AND FEEL	20	IN DURANCE	15
BUT FOR ALL THAT, I AM HOMESICK AFTER MINE OWN KIND	20	IN DURANCE	23
SO IS MY HEART HOLLOW WHEN SHE FILLETH NOT MINE EYES,	23	MARVOIL	38
"LO! THIS THING IS NOT MINE	24	THUS NINEVEH	5
MINE IS THE SHIP AND THINE THE MERCHANDISE,	25	GUIDO INVITES	4
LO, THOU HAST VOYAGED NOT! THE SHIP IS MINE."	25	GUIDO INVITES	11
HAVE I HIDDEN MINE EYES,	27	NIGHT LITANY	31
EVEN SO IS MINE HEART	27	NIGHT LITANY	47
MINE EYES UPON NEW COLOURS.	39	FOR PSYCHE	9
AS THEY WERE HIS AND MINE.	47	FROM HEINE: 7	14
BEHOLD MINE ADORATION	49	OF SPLENDOUR	18
THROUGH ALL THY VARIOUS MOOD I KNOW THEE MINE;	50	THE FLAME	31
HERE WE HAVE HAD OUR DAY, YOUR DAY AND MINE.	69	THE NEEDLE	5
OF SONG OF MINE."	172	LANGUE D'OC: 1	25
LET ME RETURN TO THIS BOLD THEME OF MINE,	246	MOYEN SENSUEL	226
MINES			
NOR OF WELSH MINES AND THE PROFIT MARUS HAD OUT OF THEM.	217	SEXTUS PROP: 5	46
MINGLE			
OR, AS OUR LAUGHTERS MINGLE EACH WITH EACH,	43	SATIEMUS	7
MINGLED			
YOU ARE MINGLED WITH THE ELEMENTS UNBORN;	84	ORTUS	10
MINGLED WITH A CURIOUS FEAR	101	AMITIES	4
I DESIRED MY DUST TO BE MINGLED WITH YOURS	130	RIVER-MER WIFE	12
MINOAN			
A MINOAN UNDULATION,	202	AGE DEMANDED	33
MINORES			
FRATRES MINORES	148	FRATRES MINORE	T
MINOS'			
SPUN IN KING MINOS' HALL	204	MEDALLION	11
MINSTREL			
OR WHEN THE MINSTREL, TALE HALF TOLD,	9	NA AUDIART	27
MINUSCULE			
JE VIS DES CANARDS SUR LE BORD D'UN LAC MINUSCULE,	160	DANS OMNIBUS	10
MINUTE			
THAT WE FIND MINUTE OBSERVATION.	104	THE SEEING EYE	10
AND A MINUTE CROWD OF SMALL BOYS CAME FROM OPPOSITE,	224	SEXTUS PROP:10	4
MINUTES			
LIFE GIVES US TWO MINUTES, TWO SEASONS--	168	OF AROUET	25
MIRALS			
MIRALS, OEMDELING, AUDIARDA,	75	THE ALCHEMIST	12
OF BELS MIRALS, THE REST,	106	DOMPNA POIS	56
MIRAL'S			
BEL MIRAL'S STATURE, THE VISCOUNTESS' THROAT,	151	NEAR PERIGORD	8
MIRE			
ABOVE THE BONES AND MIRE,	41	HER MONUMENT	4
ALL MIRE, MIST, ALL FOG,	70	THE PLUNGE	12
MIRROR			
THE MIST GOES FROM THE MIRROR AND I SEE.	32	PARACELSUS	6
MUTE MIRROR OF THE FLIGHT OF SPEEDING YEARS,	41	HER MONUMENT	6
IF THOU HAST SEEN THAT MIRROR OF ALL MOMENTS,	51	THE FLAME	40
CALL NOT THAT MIRROR ME, FOR I HAVE SLIPPED	51	THE FLAME	42
BY THE MIRROR OF BURNISHED COPPER,	76	THE ALCHEMIST	42
IT WAS NO GLIMPSE IN A MIRROR;	214	SEXTUS PROP: 4	18
AS HELD BEFORE HIM IN THAT UNSULLIED MIRROR	241	MOYEN SENSUEL	93

PAGE 259

MIRRORS -- MOBS

	PAGE	TITLE	LINE
MIRRORS			
MIRRORS UNSTILL OF THE ETERNAL CHANGE?	39	BLANDULA	12
A BROKEN BUNDLE OF MIRRORS . . . !	157	NEAR PERIGORD	192
MIRTH			
HOWE'ER IN MIRTH MOST MAGNIFIED,	66	THE SEAFARER	86
MIS			
MI BASTAN MIS PENSAMIENTOS.	82	THE CONDOLENCE	EPI
A MIS SOLEDADES VOY,	82	THE CONDOLENCE	EPI
DE MIS SOLEDADES VENGO,	82	THE CONDOLENCE	EPI
MISCHIEF			
YOU ARE NOT OLD ENOUGH TO HAVE DONE MUCH MISCHIEF,	94	INSTRUCTIONS	16
MISCONCEPTIONS			
IN HOPE TO SET SOME MISCONCEPTIONS RIGHT.	238	MOYEN SENSUEL	2
MISLAID			
I HAVE MISLAID THE "AD.," BUT NOTE THE TOUCH,	242	MOYEN SENSUEL	115
MISPLACEMENT			
CHURLISH AT SEEMED MISPLACEMENT,	9	NA AUDIART	43
MISS			
AS I? WILL THE NEW ROSES MISS THEE?	67	THE CLOAK	6
MISSED			
I SHALL HAVE MISSED NOTHING AT ALL,	105	DOMPNA POIS	26
MIST			
WELL THEN, SO CALL THEY, THE SWIRLERS OUT OF THE MIST OF MY SOUL,	20	IN DURANCE	21
BUT LIKE A MIST WHERETHROUGH HER WHITE FORM FOUGHT,	31	PIERE VIDAL	30
THE MIST GOES FROM THE MIRROR AND I SEE.	32	PARACELSUS	6
ALL MIRE, MIST, ALL FOG,	70	THE PLUNGE	12
PALE CARNAGE BENEATH BRIGHT MIST.	92	APRIL	5
AND MIST CLOTTED ABOUT THE TREES IN THE VALLEY,	119	THE GYPSY	8
THEIR CORDS TANGLE IN MIST, AGAINST THE BROCADE-LIKE PALACE.	129	THE RIVER SONG	26
THE TRAPPINGS ARE BORDERED WITH MIST.	141	IDEA OF CHOAN	12
THE HUNDRED CORDS OF MIST ARE SPREAD THROUGH	141	IDEA OF CHOAN	13
NOW CRY THE BIRDS OUT, IN THE MEADOW MIST,	177	LANGUE D'OC: 4	12
FORMED THERE IN MANNER AS A MIST OF LIGHT	248	DONNA MI PREGA	20
MISTRESS			
IS, FOR THE TIME BEING, THE MISTRESS OF MY FRIEND,	87	ALBATRE	2
AND WITHIN, THE MISTRESS, IN THE MIDMOST OF HER YOUTH,	128	BEAU TOILET	3
WHO DEPARTED ALONE WITH HIS MISTRESS,	132	AT TEN-SHIN	32
WITH A PLACID AND UNEDUCATED MISTRESS	195	HUGH SELWIN:10	6
THUS MISTRESS CALLIOPE,	211	SEXTUS PROP: 2	52
MIDNIGHT, AND A LETTER COMES TO ME FROM OUR MISTRESS:	212	SEXTUS PROP: 3	1
AND MAY THE BOUGHT YOKE OF A MISTRESS LIE WITH	214	SEXTUS PROP: 4	3
MISTRESSES			
AND EDWARD'S MISTRESSES STILL LIGHT THE STAGE,	163	CABARET DANCER	73
"YOU ARE A VERY EARLY INSPECTOR OF MISTRESSES.	225	SEXTUS PROP:10	34
MISTRUST			
FOR THOU SHOULDST MORE MISTRUST	67	THE CLOAK	9
WHY IS YOUR GLITTER FULL OF CURIOUS MISTRUST?	95	OF THE DEGREES	13
MISTRUSTED			
MISTRUSTED, SPOKEN-AGAINST,	92	THE REST	5
HATED, SHUT IN, MISTRUSTED:	93	THE REST	16
MISTS			
SAPPHIRE BENACUS, IN THY MISTS AND THEE	50	THE FLAME	26
MISVENTURE			
TO COME TO EARTH TO DRAW US FROM MISVENTURE,	37	THE YOUNG KING	34
MITRAILLEUSES			
DESTROYERS, BOMBS AND SPITTING MITRAILLEUSES.	265	ALF'S NINTH	21
MIXED			
THEIR SOUND IS MIXED IN THIS FLUTE,	130	THE RIVER SONG	39
SO HE "FACED LIFE" WITH RATHER MIXED INTENTIONS,	242	MOYEN SENSUEL	101
MNEMONIC			
ARE KEPT MNEMONIC OF THE STROKES THEY BORE,	19	FOR E. MCC	20
MOANETH			
MOANETH ALWAY MY MIND'S LUST	65	THE SEAFARER	37
MOBILE			
"LA DONNA E MOBILE."	163	CABARET DANCER	86
MOBS			
"AS FREE OF MOBS AS KINGS"? I'D HAVE MEN FREE OF THAT INVIDIOUS,	244	MOYEN SENSUEL	169

	PAGE	TITLE	LINE
MOCK			
BEHOLD ME SHRIVELLED, AND YOUR MOCK OF MOCKS;	32	PIERE VIDAL	62
AND YET I MOCK YOU BY THE MIGHTY FIRES	32	PIERE VIDAL	63
MOCK NOT THE FLOOD OF STARS, THE THING'S TO BE.	69	THE NEEDLE	8
MOCKED			
JUST THEN SHE WOKE AND MOCKED THE LESS KEEN BLADE.	31	PIERE VIDAL	43
MOCKERY			
HAVE THE EARTH IN MOCKERY, AND ARE KIND TO ALL,	20	IN DURANCE	27
MOCKETH			
AS A FOOL THAT MOCKETH HIS DRUE'S DISDEIGN.	11	OF THE GIBBET	12
MOCK'RY			
AND MADE MEN'S MOCK'RY IN MY ROTTEN SADNESS!	31	PIERE VIDAL	53
MOCKS			
AND THE RED SUN MOCKS MY SADNESS.	30	PIERE VIDAL	6
BEHOLD ME SHRIVELLED, AND YOUR MOCK OF MOCKS;	32	PIERE VIDAL	62
MODE			
NAY, NOR HIS VERY ESSENCE OR HIS MODE;	248	DONNA MI PREGA	15
MODEL			
SHE'D FIND A MODEL FOR ST. ANTHONY	63	PHASELLUS ILLE	13
ERINNA IS A MODEL PARENT,	103	THE PATTERNS	1
LALAGE IS ALSO A MODEL PARENT,	103	THE PATTERNS	3
MODELLED			
NOR HOUSES MODELLED UPON THAT OF JOVE IN EAST ELIS,	209	SEXTUS PROP: 1	67
MODERATE			
YOU ONCE DISCOVERED A MODERATE CHOP-HOUSE.	101	AMITIES	16
MODERATIONS			
ERE LOVE KNOW MODERATIONS,	220	SEXTUS PROP: 7	26
MODERN			
OF A MODERN AND ETHICAL CULT,	178	MOEURS CON: 1	12
SOMETHING FOR THE MODERN STAGE,	188	HUGH SELWYN: 2	3
MODERNITY			
(THUS FAR HATH MODERNITY BROUGHT US)	52	AU SALON	9
MODULATION			
A MODULATION TOWARD THE THEATRE,	196	HUGH SELWIN:12	18
MODUS			
NOR THE MODUS OF LUNAR ECLIPSES	228	SEXTUS PROP:12	26
HIS MODUS TAKES FROM SOUL, FROM HEART HIS WILL;	249	DONNA MI PREGA	23
MOEURS			
MOEURS CONTEMPORAINES	178	MOEURS CONTEMP	T
MOIETY			
ONE LEAN MOIETY OF HIS NAKEDNESS	12	OF THE GIBBET	31
MOLTEN			
FROM THE MOLTEN DYES OF THE WATER	75	THE ALCHEMIST	18
AND THE MOLTEN METAL OF YOUR SHOULDERS	170	PHANOPOEIA	19
MOLUCCAS			
SCATTERED MOLUCCAS	203	MAUBERLEY: 1	1
MOMENT			
FOR A MOMENT SHE RESTED AGAINST ME	112	SHOP GIRL	1
LIFE TO THE MOMENT,	197	ENVOI (1919)	11
AND MUCH OF LITTLE MOMENT, AND SOME FEW	235	TO WHISTLER	6
MOMENTOUS			
IN THIS MOMENTOUS HOWER,	270	OF 600 M.P.'S	2
MOMENTS			
MUST KNOW SUCH MOMENTS, THINKING ON THE GRASS;	43	SATIEMUS	11
DRINK OUR IMMORTAL MOMENTS; WE "PASS THROUGH."	50	THE FLAME	6
IF THOU HAST SEEN THAT MIRROR OF ALL MOMENTS,	51	THE FLAME	40
MON			
TE VOILA, MON BOURRIENNE, YOU ALSO SHALL BE IMMORTAL.	101	AMITIES	6
MON BEAU GRAND FRERE	273	M. POM-POM	3
MONARCH			
AND SHE SPOKE TO ME OF THE MONARCH,	180	MOEURS CON: 5	26
MONCEAU			
DU PARC MONCEAU,	160	DANS OMNIBUS	13
MONEY			
THE MONEY ROTTEN AND MORE ROTTEN YET,	260	ALF'S FIFTH	10
MONGOLS			
WE HAVE NO COMFORT BECAUSE OF THESE MONGOLS.	127	BOWMEN OF SHU	4
MONKEYS			
THE MONKEYS MAKE SORROWFUL NOISE OVERHEAD.	130	RIVER-MER WIFE	18
MONOTONY			
IN THIS EVER-FLOWING MONOTONY	35	THE EYES	12

	PAGE	TITLE	LINE
MONSIEUR			
SENATORIAL FAMILIES OF STRASBOURG, MONSIEUR VEROG.	193	SIENA MI FE	4
M'ONT			
M'ONT SALUE,	160	DANS OMNIBUS	2
ILS M'ONT SALUE	160	DANS OMNIBUS	5
M'ONT SALUE.	160	DANS OMNIBUS	31
MONTAGUE			
MONTAGUE, MONTAGUE!	267	ALF'S TWELFTH	3
MONTAGUE, MONTAGUE!	267	ALF'S TWELFTH	3
MONTAGUE, MONTAGUE!	267	ALF'S TWELFTH	6
MONTAGUE, MONTAGUE!	267	ALF'S TWELFTH	6
MONTAGUE, MONTAGUE!	267	ALF'S TWELFTH	9
MONTAGUE, MONTAGUE!	267	ALF'S TWELFTH	9
MONTAGUE, MONTAGUE!	267	ALF'S TWELFTH	12
MONTAGUE, MONTAGUE!	267	ALF'S TWELFTH	12
MONTAGUE, MONTAGUE!	267	ALF'S TWELFTH	15
MONTAGUE, MONTAGUE!	267	ALF'S TWELFTH	15
MIGHT DO, TOO. MONTAGUE!	267	ALF'S TWELFTH	18
MONTAGUE, MONTAGUE!	268	ALF'S TWELFTH	21
MONTAGUE, MONTAGUE!	268	ALF'S TWELFTH	21
MONTAIGNAC			
THINKING OF MONTAIGNAC, SOUTHWARD.	122	PROVINC DESERT	49
THINK YOU THAT MAENT LIVED AT MONTAIGNAC,	151	NEAR PERIGORD	11
TAIRIRAN HELD HALL IN MONTAIGNAC,	151	NEAR PERIGORD	16
HE LOVED THIS LADY IN CASTLE MONTAIGNAC?	152	NEAR PERIGORD	48
SOUTHWARD TOWARD MONTAIGNAC, AND HE BENDS AT A TABLE	154	NEAR PERIGORD	97
AND THE GREEN CAT'S-EYE LIFTS TOWARD MONTAIGNAC.	154	NEAR PERIGORD	103
MONT-AUSIER			
BEZIERS OFF AT MONT-AUSIER, I AND HIS LADY	22	MARVOIL	12
TIBORS ALL TONGUE AND TEMPER AT MONT-AUSIER,	22	MARVOIL	18
MONTFORT			
I ASK OF MIDONS AELIS (OF MONTFORT)	105	DOMPNA POIS	28
THE VOICE AT MONTFORT, LADY AGNES' HAIR,	151	NEAR PERIGORD	7
TO FIND HER HALF ALONE, MONTFORT AWAY,	154	NEAR PERIGORD	111
SIR ARRIMON COUNTS ON HIS FINGERS, MONTFORT,	155	NEAR PERIGORD	121
MONTH			
WE HAVE NO REST, THREE BATTLES A MONTH.	127	BOWMEN OF SHU	16
AND WE WERE DRUNK FOR MONTH ON MONTH, FORGETTING THE KINGS AND PRINCES.	134	EXILE'S LETTER	5
AND WE WERE DRUNK FOR MONTH ON MONTH, FORGETTING THE KINGS AND PRINCES.	134	EXILE'S LETTER	5
TO THE INDIVIDUAL, THE MONTH WAS MORE TEMPERATE ...	201	AGE DEMANDED	15
AND IT WILL LAST A TWELVE MONTH.	212	SEXTUS PROP: 3	13
MONTHLIES			
THE DAILY PRESS, AND MONTHLIES NINE CENTS DEARER.	241	MOYEN SENSUEL	94
MONTHS			
AND YOU HAVE BEEN GONE FIVE MONTHS.	130	RIVER-MER WIFE	17
IS AN INFANT, AGED ABOUT 14 MONTHS,	180	MOEURS CON: 5	11
"I ROSE IN EIGHTEEN MONTHS;	194	MR. NIXON	11
AFTER TWELVE MONTHS OF DISCOMFORT?	215	SEXTUS PROP: 4	42
MONTY			
MONTY HAS BLUNDER'D.	257	BREAD BRIGADE	12
MONUMENT			
ROME THAT ART ROME'S ONE SOLE LAST MONUMENT,	40	ROME	9
HER MONUMENT, THE IMAGE CUT THEREON	41	HER MONUMENT	T
MONUMENTAL			
NOR THE MONUMENTAL EFFIGIES OF MAUSOLUS,	209	SEXTUS PROP: 1	68
MONUMENTUM			
MONUMENTUM AERE, ETC.	146	MONUMENTUM AER	T
MOOD			
THROUGH ALL THY VARIOUS MOOD I KNOW THEE MINE;	50	THE FLAME	31
THAT NO SHIFT OF MOOD CAN SHAKE FROM US:	52	AU SALON	7
MERE-WEARY MOOD. LEST MAN KNOW NOT	64	THE SEAFARER	12
ALL THIS ADMONISHETH MAN EAGER OF MOOD,	65	THE SEAFARER	51
MY MOOD 'MID THE MERE-FLOOD,	65	THE SEAFARER	60
SO SPOKE THE AUTHOR OF "THE DORIAN MOOD,"	193	SIENA MI FE	16
AND THEN THESE SKETCHES IN THE MOOD OF GREECE?	235	TO WHISTLER	9
MOOD-LOFTY			
FOR THIS THERE'S NO MOOD-LOFTY MAN OVER EARTH'S MIDST,	65	THE SEAFARER	40

MOODS -- MORE

	PAGE	TITLE	LINE
MOODS			
BE IN ME AS THE ETERNAL MOODS	67	DORIA	1
FAINT IN THE MOST STRENUOUS MOODS,	202	AGE DEMANDED	38
MOOED			
IO MOOED THE FIRST YEARS WITH AVERTED HEAD,	222	SEXTUS PROP: 8	19
MOON			
AS THE MOON CALLETH THE TIDES,	16	PRAISE YSOLT	29
AS THE MOON DOTH FROM THE SEA,	17	PRAISE YSOLT	32
THE MOON IS UPON MY FOREHEAD,	18	DE AEGYPTO	19
THE MOON IS A GREAT PEARL IN THE WATERS OF SAPPHIRE,	18	DE AEGYPTO	21
OVER BEYOND THE MOON THERE,	53	AU JARDIN	16
HE TRIED TO EMBRACE A MOON	117	EPITAPHS	4
HANGS WITH THE SUN AND MOON.	128	THE RIVER SONG	10
AND THE MOON FALLS OVER THE PORTALS OF SEI-GO-YO,	131	AT TEN-SHIN	11
AND WATCH THE MOON THROUGH THE CLEAR AUTUMN.	132	JEWEL STAIRS'	4
AND MEN SAY THE SUN AND MOON KEEP ON MOVING	142	UNMOVING CLOUD	20
THE MOON WILL CARRY HIS CANDLE,	212	SEXTUS PROP: 3	20
THE MOON STILL DECLINED TO DESCEND OUT OF HEAVEN,	223	SEXTUS PROP: 9	3
MOONLIGHT			
AS MOONLIGHT CALLING,	16	PRAISE YSOLT	28
--EYEBROWS PAINTED GREEN ARE A FINE SIGHT IN YOUNG MOONLIGHT,	136	EXILE'S LETTER	57
MOP			
AN A-SLOSHIN' ROUND WITH 'ER MOP,	271	OLE KATE	10
MOPED			
AND I HAVE MOPED IN THE EMPEROR'S GARDEN, AWAITING AN ORDER-TO-WRITE!	129	THE RIVER SONG	19
MORAL			
"IT IS A MORAL NATION WE INFEST."	238	MOYEN SENSUEL	11
I FIND NO MORAL FOR A PERORATION,	246	MOYEN SENSUEL	241
MORALISTS			
OF RADWAY. O CLAP HAND YE MORALISTS!	246	MOYEN SENSUEL	227
MORALITY			
ALL THE WHILE THEY WERE TALKING THE NEW MORALITY	110	THE ENCOUNTER	1
MORALS			
(MY COUNTRY, I'VE SAID YOUR MORALS AND YOUR THOUGHTS ARE STALE ONES,	243	MOYEN SENSUEL	149
MORBID			
UPON FOND NATURE'S MORBID GRACE.	44	MR. HOUSMAN	14
MORE			
NO MORE FOR US THE LITTLE SIGHING.	3	THRENOS	1
NO MORE THE WINDS AT TWILIGHT TROUBLE US.	3	THRENOS	2
NO MORE DO I BURN.	3	THRENOS	4
NO MORE FOR US THE FLUTTERING OF WINGS	3	THRENOS	5
NO MORE DESIRE FLAYETH ME,	3	THRENOS	8
NO MORE FOR US THE TREMBLING	3	THRENOS	9
NO MORE FOR US THE WINE OF THE LIPS,	3	THRENOS	12
NO MORE FOR US THE KNOWLEDGE.	3	THRENOS	13
NO MORE THE TORRENT,	3	THRENOS	15
NO MORE FOR US THE MEETING-PLACE	3	THRENOS	16
IN ANOTHER FASHION THAT MORE SUITETH ME.	4	LA FRAISNE	8
I DO NOT LIKE TO REMEMBER THINGS ANY MORE.	5	LA FRAISNE	48
BEING UPON THE ROAD ONCE MORE,	6	CINO	11
THEY'LL KNOW MORE OF ARNAUT OF MARVOIL	22	MARVOIL	25
MORE CRAFTILY, MORE SUBTLE-SOULED THAN I;	24	THUS NINEVEH	13
MORE CRAFTILY, MORE SUBTLE-SOULED THAN I,	24	THUS NINEVEH	13
OR MORE SWEET IN TONE THAN ANY, BUT THAT I	24	THUS NINEVEH	21
ONE MOON FOOL'S VIGIL WITH THE HOLLYHOCKS.	31	PIERE VIDAL	25
WHOSE SMILE MORE AVAILETH	35	THE EYES	16
OF HAVENS MORE HIGH AND COURTS DESIRABLE	39	BLANDULA	14
THAT THERE'S NO THING MORE SWEET OR FALSE AT ALL.	44	FROM HEINE: 2	4
YET HIS TIES ARE MORE ADORNING,	46	FROM HEINE: 6	6
THIS THING THAT MOVES AS MAN IS NO MORE MORTAL.	51	THE FLAME	38
OTHERS ARE BEAUTIFUL, NONE MORE, SOME LESS.	52	AU SALON	EPI
SOME CIRCLE OF NOT MORE THAN THREE	52	AU SALON	18
AND, MAY BE, MORE TIMES,	53	AU JARDIN	18
FOR THOU SHOULDST MORE MISTRUST	67	THE CLOAK	9
LOVE, YOU THE MUCH, THE MORE DESIRED!	70	THE PLUNGE	10
ARE NOT MORE DELICATE THAN SHE IS,	87	ALBATRE	4
"ONCE MORE IN DELOS, ONCE MORE IS THE ALTAR A-QUIVER,	90	SURGIT FAMA	16
"ONCE MORE IN DELOS, ONCE MORE IS THE ALTAR A-QUIVER.	90	SURGIT FAMA	16

MORE -- MOSHER'S

	PAGE	TITLE	LINE
MORE (CONTINUED)			
ONCE MORE IS THE CHANT HEARD.	90	SURGIT FAMA	17
ONCE MORE ARE THE NEVER ABANDONED GARDENS	90	SURGIT FAMA	18
AND THERE WILL BE ONLY THE MORE CONFUSION,	98	THE BELLAIRES	26
THAT IN PLEASURE SHE RECEIVES MORE THAN SHE CAN GIVE;	103	PHYLLIDULA	3
IN THE STORIED HOUSES OF SAN-KO THEY GAVE US MORE SENNIN MUSIC,	135	EXILE'S LETTER	26
SLEEP THOU NO MORE. I SEE THE STAR UPLEAPING	172	LANGUE D'OC: 1	7
OR ANY MORE CHILDREN.	179	MOEURS CON: 2	9
THEY WILL COME NO MORE,	181	MOEURS CON: 7	1
TO THE INDIVIDUAL, THE MONTH WAS MORE TEMPERATE ...	201	AGE DEMANDED	15
UNDER A MORE TOLERANT, PERHAPS, EXAMINATION.	201	AGE DEMANDED	28
AND I NO MORE EXIST;	203	MAUBERLEY: 4	23
I WITH MY BEAK HAULED ASHORE WOULD PROCEED IN A MORE STATELY MANNER,	216	SEXTUS PROP: 5	10
MY GENIUS IS NO MORE THAN A GIRL.	217	SEXTUS PROP: 5	26
AND WITH MORE THAN ARABIAN ODOURS, •	225	SEXTUS PROP:10	20
STILL I'D RESPECT YOU MORE IF YOU COULD BURY	239	MOYEN SENSUEL	27
RADWAY? MY HERO, FOR IT WILL BE MORE INSPIRING	239	MOYEN SENSUEL	41
(WHICH PAYS HIM MORE PER WEEK THAN THE SUPERNAL).	240	MOYEN SENSUEL	46
AND HEARD A CLERGY THAT TRIES ON MORE WHEEZES	241	MOYEN SENSUEL	99
WHERE ONE GETS MORE CHANCES	242	MOYEN SENSUEL	103
FURNISH MORE DATE FOR A COMPILATION	243	MOYEN SENSUEL	153
AND, HEAVENLY, HOLY GODS! I CAN'T SAY MORE,	246	MOYEN SENSUEL	220
TEN MORE AND NOTHING DONE,	259	ALF'S THIRD	19
THE PIMPS OF WHITEHALL EVER MORE IN FEAR,	260	ALF'S FIFTH	7
THE MONEY ROTTEN AND MORE ROTTEN YET,	260	ALF'S FIFTH	10
HID MORE STATISTICS, MORE FEARED TO CONFESS	260	ALF'S FIFTH	11
HID MORE STATISTICS, MORE FEARED TO CONFESS	260	ALF'S FIFTH	11
FOR MORE THAN A DECADE.	262	ALF'S SIXTH	30
I DON'T QUITE SEE THE JOKE ANY MORE,	264	ALF'S EIGHTH	29
WHAT AIN'T GOT WORK NO MORE	269	SAFE AND SOUND	10
IF I HAD MORE GRUB TO EAT.	269	SAFE AND SOUND	24
A FEW MORE CANON.	273	M. POM-POM	11
MORN			
FOR IN THE MORN OF MY YEARS THERE CAME A WOMAN	16	PRAISE YSOLT	27
AND THE WHITE WIND BREAKS THE MORN.	25	THE WHITE STAG	5
SHE HAS HER LOVER TILL MORN,	177	LANGUE D'OC: 4	2
MORNING			
"ARE YOU FEELING WELL THIS MORNING?"	46	FROM HEINE: 6	8
AT MORNING THERE ARE FLOWERS TO CUT THE HEART,	131	AT TEN-SHIN	3
"BETWEEN THE NIGHT AND MORNING?"	158	PSYCHOLOG HOUR	27
SITTING IN THE ROW OF A MORNING;	182	MOEURS CON: 7	24
"LET HER LOVERS SNORE AT HER IN THE MORNING!	215	SEXTUS PROP: 4	36
AND IT WAS MORNING, AND I WANTED TO SEE IF SHE WAS ALONE, AND RESTING,	225	SEXTUS PROP:10	27
I SEE BY THE MORNING PAPERS	268	ANOTHER BIT	
THE MORNING PAPER TELLS ME	268	ANOTHER BIT	
MORROW			
AND ON THE MORROW, BY SOME LIGHTSOME TWIST,	42	HER MONUMENT	3
MORSUS			
"VACUOS EXERCET AERA MORSUS."	198	MAUBERLEY 1920 EP	
MORTAL			
GIVEN TO MORTAL STATE	42	HER MONUMENT	3
O MORTAL NATURE,	42	HER MONUMENT	4
THIS THING THAT MOVES AS MAN IS NO MORE MORTAL. ...	51	THE FLAME	3
MORTE			
TOWARDS THE NOEL THAT MORTE SAISON	10	FOR THIS YULE	
LES YEUX D'UNE MORTE	160	DANS OMNIBUS	
LES YEUX D'UNE MORTE	160	DANS OMNIBUS	3
MORTEM			
POST MORTEM CONSPECTU	147	POST MORTEM	
MORTMAIN			
BE AGAINST ALL SORTS OF MORTMAIN.	89	COMMISSION	3
MORTUIS			
DE MORTUIS VERUM, TRULY THE MASTER BUILDER?	240	MOYEN SENSUEL	5
MOSCOW			
TO BEAT PRAGUE, BUDAPESTH, VIENNA OR MOSCOW,	245	MOYEN SENSUEL	19
MOSHER'S			
"MESSAGE TO GARCIA," MOSHER'S PROPAGANDAS	241	MOYEN SENSUEL	

PAGE 264

MOSS -- MOULTED

	PAGE	TITLE	LINE
MOSS			
MOSS WORDS, LIP WORDS, WORDS OF SLOW STREAMS.	16	PRAISE YSOLT	22
MOSS YOU ARE,	62	A GIRL	7
BY THE GATE NOW, THE MOSS IS GROWN, THE DIFFERENT MOSSES,	131	RIVER-MER WIFE	20
MOSSES			
BY THE GATE NOW, THE MOSS IS GROWN, THE DIFFERENT MOSSES,	131	RIVER-MER WIFE	20
MOSSY			
THE MUSES CLINGING TO THE MOSSY RIDGES;	227	SEXTUS PROP:11	31
MOST			
DREW YOU YOUR SWORD MOST GALLANTLY	19	FOR E. MCC	7
MADE YOU YOUR PASS MOST VALIANTLY	19	FOR E. MCC	8
"QUASI KALOUN." S. T. SAYS BEAUTY IS MOST THAT, A "CALLING TO THE SOUL."	20	IN DURANCE	20
AS I HIDE MOST THE WHILE	21	IN DURANCE	30
THAT WAS MOST VALIANT 'MID ALL WORTHIEST MEN!	37	THE YOUNG KING	30
HIM DO WE PRAY AS TO A LORD MOST RIGHTEOUS	37	THE YOUNG KING	36
ONE HOUR WAS SUNLIT AND THE MOST HIGH GODS	40	ERAT HORA	5
SHAMEFUL, MOST SAD	41	HER MONUMENT	20
IS LIKE TO HEAVEN'S MOST 'LIVE IMAGINING.	41	HER MONUMENT	24
IN MOST SPIRITUEL POSITIONS,	46	FROM HEINE: 6	14
HOWE'ER IN MIRTH MOST MAGNIFIED,	66	THE SEAFARER	86
WHOE'ER LIVED IN LIFE MOST LORDLIEST,	66	THE SEAFARER	87
OLD FRIENDS THE MOST.--W. D. Y.	101	AMITIES	EPI
O MOST UNFORTUNATE AGE!	113	FORMIANUS LADY	10
THE MOST PRUDENT, ORDERLY, AND DECOROUS!	161	CABARET DANCER	8
HAVE YOU, OR I, SEEN MOST OF CABARETS, GOOD HEDGETHORN?	161	CABARET DANCER	17
WITH THE MOST BANK-CLERKLY OF ENGLISHMEN?	195	HUGH SELWIN:11	4
FAINT IN THE MOST STRENUOUS MOODS,	202	AGE DEMANDED	38
FOR THUS ARE TOMBS OF LOVERS MOST DESECRATED.	213	SEXTUS PROP: 3	34
THAT'S SENT TO HOLLAND, A MOST PARTICULAR FEATURE,	239	MOYEN SENSUEL	20
I RUSHED ABOUT IN THE MOST AGITATED WAY	247	PIERROTS	5
YET IS FOUND THE MOST	250	DONNA MI PREGA	56
BECAUSE I PRINT MOST LIES.	266	ALF'S ELEVENTH	4
MOST TIDILY AWAY	269	SAFE AND SOUND	18
MOSTLY			
. . . EH? . . . THEY MOSTLY HAD GREY EYES,	7	CINO	40
THE FOUR ROUND TOWERS, FOUR BROTHERS--MOSTLY FOOLS:	152	NEAR PERIGORD	35
(BUT MOSTLY GAS AND SUET)	270	OF 600 M.P.'S	10
MOTH			
BUT SHE DANCED LIKE A PINK MOTH IN THE SHRUBBERY.	53	AU JARDIN	19
MOTHER			
SO IS SHE THAT COMETH, THE MOTHER OF SONGS,	17	PRAISE YSOLT	50
THE CORN HAS AGAIN ITS MOTHER AND SHE, LEUCONOE,	90	SURGIT FAMA	5
UPON LEARNING THAT THE MOTHER WROTE VERSES,	179	MOEURS CON: 3	1
THE SMALL BIRDS OF THE CYTHAREAN MOTHER,	211	SEXTUS PROP: 2	31
THE MOTHER OF THE GREAT KING, IN A HOOP-SKIRT,	237	ABU SALAMMAMM	24
MOTHERS			
OH! THE LITTLE MOTHERS	14	FAMAM CANO	2
MOTHER'S			
SUCH WAS HE WHEN HE GOT HIS MOTHER'S LETTER	242	MOYEN SENSUEL	109
HIS MOTHER'S BIRTHDAY GIFT. (HOW PITIFUL	242	MOYEN SENSUEL	117
MOTION			
"TURN NOT VENUS INTO A BLINDED MOTION,	220	SEXTUS PROP: 7	12
MOTIONLESS			
MOTIONLESS, PLACED IN VAIN,	41	HER MONUMENT	5
MOTTOES			
RATHER THAN THE MOTTOES ON SUN-DIALS.	187	E. P. ODE	16
MOUCHIN'			
WE'LL SEND 'EM MOUCHIN' 'OME,	257	BREAD BRIGADE	7
MOUCHING			
SLOUCHING AND MOUCHING,	257	BREAD BRIGADE	15
GLOOMING AND MOUCHING!	257	BREAD BRIGADE	23
MOULD			
FINDS 'NEATH THIS ROCK FIT MOULD, FIT RESTING PLACE!	41	HER MONUMENT	21
THE "AGE DEMANDED" CHIEFLY A MOULD IN PLASTER,	188	HUGH SELWYN: 2	9
MOULTED			
"SHE STEWS PUFFED FROGS, SNAKE'S BONES, THE MOULTED FEATHERS OF SCREECH OWLS,	215	SEXTUS PROP: 4	33

PAGE 265

MOUNT -- MOVEMENTS

	PAGE	TITLE	LINE
MOUNT			
THE WIRE-LIKE BANDS OF COLOUR INVOLUTE MOUNT FROM MY FINGERS;	170	PHANOPOEIA	17
MOUNTAIN			
THEY WEAVE A WHOLE ROOF TO THE MOUNTAIN,	139	SENNIN POEM	5
AND YOU ON THAT GREAT MOUNTAIN OF A PALM--	152	NEAR PERIGORD	31
MOUNTAIN-CROSSING			
AND THEY MADE NOTHING OF SEA-CROSSING OR OF MOUNTAIN-CROSSING,	134	EXILE'S LETTER	9
MOUNTAINS			
O MOUNTAINS OF HELLAS!!	104	ANCORA	8
TINGEING THE MOUNTAINS,	122	PROVINC DESERT	53
AND WENT BACK TO THE EAST MOUNTAINS	136	EXILE'S LETTER	68
BLUE MOUNTAINS TO THE NORTH OF THE WALLS,	137	TAKING LEAVE	1
SHEER AS THE MOUNTAINS.	138	NEAR SHOKU	2
THE THREE MOUNTAINS FALL THROUGH THE FAR HEAVEN,	138	CITY OF CHOAN	8
A "BLUE" AND A CLIMBER OF MOUNTAINS, HAS MARRIED	178	MOEURS CON: 1	3
MOUNTS			
MOUNTS, FROM OUR MIGHTY THOUGHTS AND FROM THE FOUNT	41	HER MONUMENT	27
MOUNTS FROM THE FOUR HORNS OF MY BED-POSTS,	169	PHANOPOEIA	3
MOURNFUL			
"TELL ME NOT IN MOURNFUL WISH-WASH	241	MOYEN SENSUEL	89
MOURNING			
AND THREE POETS ARE GONE INTO MOURNING.	118	THREE POETS	2
CALVUS MOURNING QUINTILIA,	230	SEXTUS PROP:12	71
MOUSE			
NO MOUSE OF THE SCROLLS WAS THE GOODLY FERE	33	GOODLY FERE	23
MOUSSELINE			
SUPPLANTS THE MOUSSELINE OF COS,	189	HUGH SELWYN: 3	2
MOUSTACHES			
THEY STAND AND TWIRL THEIR MOUSTACHES.	140	MULBERRY ROAD	17
MOUTH			
MY MOUTH TO CHANT THE PURE SINGING!	18	DE AEGYPTO	12
WHO HATH THE MOUTH TO RECEIVE IT,	18	DE AEGYPTO	13
AND PRIES WIDE MY MOUTH WITH FAST MUSIC	29	ALTAFORTE	22
WITH FINGERS THAT ARE NOT LONG, AND WITH A MOUTH UNDRY,	113	FORMIANUS LADY	5
CHARM, SMILING AT THE GOOD MOUTH,	191	HUGH SELWYN: 5	5
THE MAKER OF IT, SOME OTHER MOUTH,	197	ENVOI (1919)	20
MY LITTLE MOUTH SHALL GOBBLE IN SUCH GREAT FOUNTAINS,	210	SEXTUS PROP: 2	6
AND WHENCE THIS SOFT BOOK COMES INTO MY MOUTH.	217	SEXTUS PROP: 5	24
HER LIPS UPON THEM; AND IT WAS HER MOUTH SAYING:	220	SEXTUS PROP: 7	8
MOUTH-ORGAN			
PLAYING ON A JEWELLED MOUTH-ORGAN.	135	EXILE'S LETTER	25
MOUTH-ORGANS			
WITH BOATS FLOATING, AND THE SOUND OF MOUTH-ORGANS AND DRUMS,	135	EXILE'S LETTER	51
MOUTHS			
MOUTHS BITING EMPTY AIR,	200	MAUBERLEY: 2	34
MOVE			
'TWOULD NOT MOVE IT ONE JOT FROM LEFT TO RIGHT.	63	PHASELLUS ILLE	11
MOVE WE AND TAKE THE TIDE, WITH ITS NEXT FAVOUR,	69	THE NEEDLE	12
AS YOU MOVE AMONG THE BRIGHT TREES;	75	THE ALCHEMIST	2
MOVE AMONG THE LOVERS OF PERFECTION ALONE.	95	ITE	2
MOVE OTHERS WITH IVORY CARS.	108	CH'U YUAN	4
BUT IF YOU MOVE OR SPEAK	109	THE FAUN	7
THOUGH MANY MOVE WITH SUSPICION,	146	SALUTATION 3RD	31
"CONTENT EVER TO MOVE WITH WHITE SWANS!	211	SEXTUS PROP: 2	40
THE FLOOD SHALL MOVE TOWARD THE FOUNTAIN	220	SEXTUS PROP: 7	25
AND HIS STRANGE PROPERTY SETS SIGHS TO MOVE	250	DONNA MI PREGA	58
LOVE DOTH NOT MOVE, BUT DRAWETH ALL TO HIM;	250	DONNA MI PREGA	64
MOVED			
WITH ALL THE ADMIRABLE CONCEPTS THAT MOVED FROM IT	42	HER MONUMENT	39
MOVED NOT, NOR EVER ANSWER MY DESIRE,	60	TOMB AKR CAAR	3
SHE, WHO MOVED HERE AMID THE CYCLAMEN,	87	THE SPRING	12
HE HAD MOVED AMID HER PHANTASMAGORIA,	199	MAUBERLEY: 2	5
MOVEMENT			
WITH THE MOVEMENT OF GODS,	107	COMING OF WAR	11
MOVEMENTS			
MOVEMENTS, AND THE SLOW FEET,	74	THE RETURN	2

PAGE 266

MOVES -- MUCH

	PAGE	TITLE	LINE
MOVES			
THIS THING THAT MOVES AS MAN IS NO MORE MORTAL. ...	51	THE FLAME	38
MOVES ONLY NOW A CLINGING TENUOUS GHOST.	87	THE SPRING	13
HE MOVES BEHIND ME	90	SURGIT FAMA	9
THE WIND MOVES ABOVE THE WHEAT--	95	OF THE DEGREES	3
THEIR MOVES BREAK AND REFORM THE PATTERN:	120	GAME OF CHESS	8
THE SEA'S COLOUR MOVES AT THE DAWN	131	AT TEN-SHIN	9
THE SALMON MOVES IN THE SUN-SHOT, BRIGHT SHALLOW SEA....	166	FISH & SHADOW	4
NEVER THEREAFTER, BUT MOVES CHANGING STATE, ...	249	DONNA MI PREGA	52
MOVES CHANGING COLOUR, OR TO LAUGH OR WEEP	250	DONNA MI PREGA	53
MOVING			
THOU AFAR, MOVING IN THE GLAMOROUS SUN, ...	68	APPARUIT	6
MOVING AMONG THE TREES, AND CLINGING	'92	GENTILDONNA	2
UNSTILL, EVER MOVING	107	COMING OF WAR	18
THE SWIFT MOVING, ...	139	SOUTH-FOLK	13
AND MEN SAY THE SUN AND MOON KEEP ON MOVING	142	UNMOVING CLOUD	20
HOW EASY THE MOVING FINGERS; IF HAIR IS MUSSED ON HER FOREHEAD, ...	217	SEXTUS PROP: 5	29
MOVING NAKED OVER ACHERON	218	SEXTUS PROP: 6	2
MOVING A NATION-WIDE	259	ALF'S THIRD	6
MOYEN			
L'HOMME MOYEN SENSUEL	238	MOYEN SENSUEL	T
MR.			
MR. HOUSMAN'S MESSAGE	43	MR. HOUSMAN	T
(TELL IT TO MR. STRACHEY)	86	SALUTATION 2ND	31
MR. STYRAX	178	MOEURS CON: 1	SUB
MR. HECATOMB STYRAX, THE OWNER OF A LARGE ESTATE ..	178	MOEURS CON: 1	1
AND EVEN NOW MR. STYRAX	178	MOEURS CON: 1	13
BUT THE SON-IN-LAW OF MR. H. STYRAX	178	MOEURS CON: 1	16
AND SAID: "MR. POUND IS SHOCKED AT MY LEVITY."	181	MOEURS CON: 7	11
"YOU REMEMBER MR. LOWELL, ...	182	MOEURS CON: 8	2
MR. NIXON	194	MR. NIXON	T
MR. NIXON ADVISED ME KINDLY, TO ADVANCE WITH FEWER	194	MR. NIXON	2
"ADVANCE ON ROYALTIES, FIFTY AT FIRST," SAID MR. NIXON, ...	194	MR. NIXON	7
DON'T GET A DISCOUNT LIKE MR. SELFRIDGE	262	ALF'S SEVENTH	11
WHEN FEEBLE MR. ASQUITH, GETTING OLD, ...	264	ALF'S NINTH	5
WHETHER MR. DUPONT AND THE GUN-SHARKS	268	ANOTHER BIT	7
MRS.			
WILL DINE NEXT WEEK WITH MRS. BASIL, ...	163	CABARET DANCER	63
WHEN IT TURNED OUT HE MEANT MRS. WARD.	181	MOEURS CON: 7	12
MUCH			
O'ER MUCH HATH TA'EN SIR DEATH THAT DEADLY WARRIOR	37	THE YOUNG KING	12
SHROPSHIRE IS MUCH PLEASANTER.	44	MR. HOUSMAN	12
LOVE, YOU THE MUCH, THE MORE DESIRED!	70	THE PLUNGE	10
I HAVE TALKED TO YOU SO MUCH THAT	94	INSTRUCTIONS	12
YOU ARE NOT OLD ENOUGH TO HAVE DONE MUCH MISCHIEF,	94	INSTRUCTIONS	16
O MY MUCH PRAISED BUT-NOT-ALTOGETHER-SATISFACTORY LADY.	100	THE BATH TUB	4
I WHO AM AS MUCH EMBITTERED	102	TO DIVES	2
AND LEAVES HER TOO MUCH ALONE.	128	BEAU TOILET	9
SO MUCH FOR THE GAGGED REVIEWERS, ...	145	SALUTATION 3RD	3
(ST. LEIDER HAD DONE AS MUCH AS POLHONAC, ...	153	NEAR PERIGORD	86
THAT MUCH WAS OMINOUS.	158	PSYCHOLOG HOUR	2
SO MUCH BARREN REGRET, ...	158	PSYCHOLOG HOUR	8
THERE IS NOT MUCH BUT ITS EVIL LEFT US.	168	OF AROUET	21
FROM ONE I LOVED NEVER SO MUCH, ...	176	LANGUE D'OC: 3	61
WERE MUCH TOO ABSTRUSE FOR HIS COMPREHENSION, ...	181	MOEURS CON: 7	9
"'CARE TOO MUCH FOR SOCIETY DINNERS?'	182	MOEURS CON: 8	11
MUCH CONVERSATION IS AS GOOD AS HAVING A HOME.	214	SEXTUS PROP: 4	10
THUS MUCH THE FATES HAVE ALLOTTED ME, AND IF, MAECENAS, ...	217	SEXTUS PROP: 5	37
GIVE THAT MUCH INSCRIPTION	219	SEXTUS PROP: 6	28
BITED THAT MUCH FOR HIS BAIL.	225	SEXTUS PROP:10	23
FOR A MUCH LARGER ILIAD IS IN THE COURSE OF CONSTRUCTION	229	SEXTUS PROP.12	68
AND THIS MUCH GIVES ME HEART TO PLAY THE GAME.	235	TO WHISTLER	4
AND MUCH OF LITTLE MOMENT, AND SOME FEW	235	TO WHISTLER	6
NO, NO, THEY DANCED. THE MUSIC GREW MUCH LOUDER ...	243	MOYEN SENSUEL	131
TO BE SO MUCH ALIKE THAT EVERY DOG THAT SMELLS 'EM,	244	MOYEN SENSUEL	172

	PAGE	TITLE	LINE
MUCH (CONTINUED)			
"AND RATE 'EM UP AT JUST SO MUCH PER HEAD,	244	MOYEN SENSUEL	181
AS NOTHING CAN RESTRAIN OR MUCH DISPARAGE. . . .	245	MOYEN SENSUEL	192
HOW MANY WEAK OF MIND, HOW MUCH TUBERCULOSIS	260	ALF'S FIFTH	13
MUD			
THEY HAVE TO STAND ABOUT IN MUD	266	ALF'S ELEVENTH	13
MUFFINS			
AS SHE BROUGHT US OUR MUFFINS	116	THE TEA SHOP	7
WITH MUFFINS AT HIS TEA.	272	NATIONAL SONG	8
MULBERRIES			
FOR SHE FEEDS MULBERRIES TO SILKWORMS.	140	MULBERRY ROAD	6
MULBERRY			
A BALLAD OF THE MULBERRY ROAD	140	MULBERRY ROAD	T
MUMMY			
HERE'S PEPITA, TALL AND SLIM AS AN EGYPTIAN MUMMY,	162	CABARET DANCER	18
MUMPODORUS			
BEGINNING WITH MUMPODORUS;	99	SALVATIONISTS	13
MUNDANE			
AND YOUR BUNDLE OF MUNDANE COMPLICATIONS.	247	PIERROTS	9
MUNDI			
SIC CRESCIT GLORIA MUNDI:	52	AU SALON	17
MURALH			
A PERIGORD, PRES DEL MURALH	151	NEAR PERIGORD	EPI
MURMUR			
AND MURMUR IN THE WIND,	74	THE RETURN	8
MURMURED			
ON HOW WHITE DOGWOODS MURMURED OVERHEAD	43	SATIEMUS	12
MURMURING			
MURMURING FOR HIS OWN SATISFACTION	97	AESTHETICS	19
MUSCLES			
AND OF LARGE MUSCLES,	178	MOEURS CON: 1	2
MUSE			
A YOUNG MUSE WITH YOUNG LOVES CLUSTERED ABOUT HER	207	SEXTUS PROP: 1	13
MY MUSE IS EAGER TO INSTRUCT ME IN A NEW GAMUT, OR GAMBETTO,	216	SEXTUS PROP: 5	11
HENRY VAN DYKE, WHO THINKS TO CHARM THE MUSE YOU PACK HER IN	239	MOYEN SENSUEL	21
MUSES			
GATHER ABOUT ME, O MUSES!	104	ANCORA	9
O MUSES WITH DELICATE SHINS,	104	ANCORA	12
O MUSES WITH DELECTABLE KNEE-JOINTS,	104	ANCORA	13
AND THERE IS NO HIGH-ROAD TO THE MUSES.	207	SEXTUS PROP: 1	15
YET THE COMPANIONS OF THE MUSES	209	SEXTUS PROP: 1	60
THE MUSES CLINGING TO THE MOSSY RIDGES;	227	SEXTUS PROP:11	31
MUSES'			
NO ADJUNCT TO THE MUSES' DIADEM.	187	E. P. ODE	20
MUSEUM			
THE EYES OF THE VERY LEARNED BRITISH MUSEUM ASSISTANT.	161	PAGANI'S NOV 8	3
MUSIC			
YOU WHORESON DOG, PAPIOLS, COME! LET'S TO MUSIC!	28	ALTAFORTE	2
AND THE FIERCE THUNDERS ROAR ME THEIR MUSIC	28	ALTAFORTE	10
WITH FAT BOARDS, BAWDS, WINE AND FRAIL MUSIC!	28	ALTAFORTE	17
AND PRIES WIDE MY MOUTH WITH FAST MUSIC	29	ALTAFORTE	22
YEA, I FILL ALL THE AIR WITH MY MUSIC.	29	ALTAFORTE	30
PAPIOLS, PAPIOLS, TO THE MUSIC!	29	ALTAFORTE	31
AND LET THE MUSIC OF THE SWORDS MAKE THEM CRIMSON!	29	ALTAFORTE	37
AND MUSIC FLOWING THROUGH ME SEEMED TO OPEN	39	FOR PSYCHE	8
THERE IS THE SUBTLER MUSIC, THE CLEAR LIGHT	50	THE FLAME	20
THEIR MUSIC ABOUT THEE!	91	DANCE FIGURE	22
ANCIENT MUSIC	116	ANCIENT MUSIC	T
IN THE STORIED HOUSES OF SAN-KO THEY GAVE US MORE SENNIN MUSIC,	135	EXILE'S LETTER	26
WITH THAT MUSIC PLAYING,	135	EXILE'S LETTER	30
WITH FORTY QUEENS, AND MUSIC TO REGALE	242	MOYEN SENSUEL	112
NO, NO, THEY DANCED. THE MUSIC GREW MUCH LOUDER	243	MOYEN SENSUEL	131
MUSICIANS			
MUSICIANS WITH JEWELLED FLUTES AND WITH PIPES OF GOLD	128	THE RIVER SONG	2
MUSIQUE			
S'ILS NE SENTENT PAS LA MUSIQUE, QU'EST CE	199	MAUBERLEY: 2	EPI

MUSSED -- NAKEDNESS

	PAGE	TITLE	LINE
MUSSED			
HOW EASY THE MOVING FINGERS; IF HAIR IS MUSSED ON HER FOREHEAD.	217	SEXTUS PROP: 5	29
MUST			
ONE MUST OF NEEDS BE A HANG'D EARLY RISER	13	MESMERISM	3
AH-EH! HE MUST BE RARE IF EVEN I HAVE NOT . . ."	15	FAMAM CANO	43
MUST KNOW SUCH MOMENTS, THINKING ON THE GRASS;	43	SATIEMUS	11
NAY, ON MY BREAST THOU MUST	47	FROM HEINE: 7	10
MUST BIDE ABOVE BRINE.	64	THE SEAFARER	31
THE ENEMY IS SWIFT, WE MUST BE CAREFUL.	127	BOWMEN OF SHU	20
HERE WE MUST MAKE SEPARATION	137	TAKING LEAVE	3
SHE MUST SPEAK OF THE TIME	166	FISH & SHADOW	18
OR LUCK, I MUST HAVE MY FILL.	173	LANGUE D'OC: 2	10
STILL SHE MUST KNOW IT.	175	LANGUE D'OC: 3	36
WE MUST LOOK INTO THE MATTER.	208	SEXTUS PROP: 1	48
"SOFT FIELDS MUST BE WORN BY SMALL WHEELS,	210	SEXTUS PROP: 2	21
ONE MUST HAVE RESONANCE, RESONANCE AND SONORITY . . . LIKE A GOOSE.	230	SEXTUS PROP:12	65
THIS YEAR PERFORCE I MUST WITH CIRCUMSPECTION--	238	MOYEN SENSUEL	9
MUST THINK TRUTH LOOKS AS THEY DO IN WOOL PYJAMAS.	243	MOYEN SENSUEL	148
MUTABILITY			
UPON THE MUTABILITY OF WOMAN,	118	THREE POETS	6
MUTE			
MUTE MIRROR OF THE FLIGHT OF SPEEDING YEARS,	41	HER MONUMENT	6
MUTILATED			
THE MUTILATED CHOIR BOYS	45	FROM HEINE: 5	1
MUVVER			
"O BRITAIN, MUVVER OF PARLIAMENTS,	270	OF 600 M.P.'S	17
MY (356)			
MYOPE			
MAD AS A HATTER BUT SURELY NO MYOPE,	13	MESMERISM	11
MYRIAD			
WHAT ANSWER? O YE MYRIAD	35	HIS OWN FACE	4
AND KISSED THEE WITH A MYRIAD GRASSY TONGUES;	60	TOMB AKR CAAR	7
THE SEED OF A MYRIAD HUES,	141	IDEA OF CHOAN	21
THERE DIED A MYRIAD,	191	HUGH SELWYN: 5	1
MYRRH			
HAVE I DRUNK A DRAUGHT, SWEETER THAN SCENT OF MYRRH.	177	LANGUE D'OC: 4	23
MYRTLES			
AND MEN MYRTLES, ERE THE NIGHT	24	THUS NINEVEH	3
MYSELF			
I WOULD BATHE MYSELF IN STRANGENESS:	70	THE PLUNGE	1
SAYING WITHIN HIS HEART, "I AM NO USE TO MYSELF,	100	ARIDES	6
THAT I, MYSELF, MIGHT HAVE ENJOYED THEM.	101	AMITIES	5
YOU SAY THAT I TAKE A GOOD DEAL UPON MYSELF;	146	MONUMENTUM AER	1
SHALL I ENTRUST MYSELF TO ENTANGLED SHADOWS,	212	SEXTUS PROP: 3	7
MYSTERY			
ALL, ALL OUR LIFE'S ETERNAL MYSTERY!	41	HER MONUMENT	25
N.			
N. Y.	62	N. Y.	T
THESE, AND YET GOD, AND DR. PARKHURST'S GOD, THE N. Y. JOURNAL	240	MOYEN SENSUEL	45
NA			
NA AUDIART	8	NA AUDIART	T
NAILED			
SIN' THEY NAILED HIM TO THE TREE.	31	GOODLY FERE	54
NAILS			
HE CRIED NO CRY WHEN THEY DRAVE THE NAILS	34	GOODLY FERE	37
NAKED			
HALF-SHEATHED, THEN NAKED FROM ITS SAFFRON SHEATH	31	PIERE VIDAL	41
GO, LITTLE NAKED AND IMPUDENT SONGS,	85	SALUTATION 2ND	16
CLEAR SPEAKERS, NAKED IN THE SUN, UNTRAMMELLED.	96	DUM CAPITOLIUM	8
MOVING NAKED OVER ACHERON	218	SEXTUS PROP: 6	2
PARIS TOOK HELEN NAKED COMING FROM THE BED OF MENELAUS,	220	SEXTUS PROP: 7	14
ENDYMION'S NAKED BODY, BRIGHT BAIT FOR DIANA,"	220	SEXTUS PROP: 7	15
AND THEY WERE NAKED, THE LOT OF THEM,	224	SEXTUS PROP:10	10
THOUGH MALES OF SEVENTY, WHO FEAR TRUTHS NAKED HARM US,	243	MOYEN SENSUEL	117
NAKEDNESS			
ONE LEAN MOIETY OF HIS NAKEDNESS	12	OF THE GIBBET	31

NAME -- NATIONAL

NAME	PAGE	TITLE	LINE
"AH-EH! THE STRANGE RARE NAME ...	15	FAMAM CANO	42
WAS ANGRY WHEN THEY SPOKE YOUR NAME	36	FRANCESCA	6
ROME'S NAME ALONE WITHIN THESE WALLS KEEPS HOME.	40	ROME	4
GARBLE A NAME WE DETEST, AND FOR PREJUDICE?	52	AU SALON	13
TO GIVE THESE ELEMENTS A NAME AND A CENTRE!	84	ORTUS	4
SHE HAS NO NAME, AND NO PLACE.	84	ORTUS	6
TO GIVE HER A NAME AND HER BEING!	84	ORTUS	8
I HEARD THE YOUNG DANTE, WHOSE LAST NAME I DO NOT KNOW--	96	AESTHETICS	7
WITH RIHOKU'S NAME FORGOTTEN,	133	FRONTIER GUARD	23
SHE MADE THE NAME FOR HERSELF: "GAUZE VEIL,"	140	MULBERRY ROAD	5
GOOD "HEDGETHORN," FOR WE'LL ANGLICIZE YOUR NAME	161	CABARET DANCER	1
BUT I REMEMBERED THE NAME OF HIS FEVER MEDICINE AND DIED.	165	QUINTUS SEPTIM	24
A NAME NOT TO BE WORN OUT WITH THE YEARS.	209	SEXTUS PROP: 1	73
"NOR WILL THE PUBLIC CRIERS EVER HAVE YOUR NAME	211	SEXTUS PROP: 2	42
AND TO NAME OVER THE CENSUS OF MY CHIEFS IN THE ROMAN CAMP.	216	SEXTUS PROP: 5	3
NOR WILL YOU BE WEARY OF CALLING MY NAME, NOR TOO WEARY	219	SEXTUS PROP: 6	23
BY NAME, IF NAMED." SO IT WAS PHRASED, OR RATHER SOMEWHAT SO	242	MOYEN SENSUEL	114
AND IS SO OVERWEENING: LOVE BY NAME.	248	DONNA MI PREGA	3
LOVE IS CREATED, HATH A SENSATE NAME,	248	DONNA MI PREGA	22
THE MIDNIGHT ACTIVITIES OF WHATS-HIS NAME,	264	ALF'S NINTH	2
MY NAME IS NUNTY CORMORANT	269	SAFE AND SOUND	1
NAMED			
FOR THEY HAVE A DAUGHTER NAMED RAFU,	140	MULBERRY ROAD	3
MY HERO, RADWAY, I HAVE NAMED, IN TRUTH,	241	MOYEN SENSUEL	77
BY NAME, IF NAMED." SO IT WAS PHRASED, OR RATHER SOMEWHAT SO	242	MOYEN SENSUEL	114
MY COUSIN'S NAMED BALDWIN	260	ALF'S FOURTH	14
NAMES			
'MID THESE THINGS OLDER THAN THE NAMES THEY HAVE,	69	SUB MARE	8
NAPKIN			
OF A JAPANESE PAPER NAPKIN.	110	THE ENCOUNTER	5
CAREFULLY KEPT FROM THE FLOOR BY A NAPKIN,	111	BLACK SLIPPERS	4
NARBONNE			
HAVE SEEN NARBONNE, AND CAHORS AND CHALUS,	122	PROVINC DESERT	40
NARROW			
NARROW NIGHTWATCH NIGH THE SHIP'S HEAD	64	THE SEAFARER	7
I LONG FOR THY NARROW BREASTS,	112	HIMERRO	6
THE NARROW STREETS CUT INTO THE WIDE HIGHWAY AT CHOAN,	141	IDEA OF CHOAN	1
WE, IN OUR NARROW BED, TURNING ASIDE FROM BATTLES:	218	SEXTUS PROP: 5	57
NARROWS			
IF YOU ARE COMING DOWN THROUGH THE NARROWS OF THE RIVER KIANG,	131	RIVER-MER WIFE	26
NARSTY			
UNTIL A NARSTY GERMAN TOLD THEM SO.	265	ALF'S NINTH	25
NASTY			
"WILL HE SAY NASTY THINGS AT MY FUNERAL?"	215	SEXTUS PROP: 4	40
NATHAT-IKANAIE			
O NATHAT-IKANAIE, "TREE-AT-THE-RIVER."	91	DANCE FIGURE	18
NATHLESS			
NATHLESS I HAVE BEEN A TREE AMID THE WOOD	3	THE TREE	10
CORN OF THE COLDEST. NATHLESS THERE KNOCKETH NOW	64	THE SEAFARER	34
NATION			
"IT IS A MORAL NATION WE INFEST."	238	MOYEN SENSUEL	11
THAN IF I TREAT THE NATION AS A WHOLE.	239	MOYEN SENSUEL	43
HE IS THE PROTOTYPE OF HALF THE NATION.	246	MOYEN SENSUEL	242
HOW THE WHOLE NATION SHOOK	257	BREAD BRIGADE	27
A PERIL TO SELFRIDGE AND THE NATION.	262	ALF'S SEVENTH	20
UNTIL THE MIND OF THE OLD NATION GETS A LITTLE STRONGER.	266	ALF'S TENTH	16
NATIONAL			
UPON THE NATIONAL BRAINS AND SET 'EM ACHIN'.	245	MOYEN SENSUEL	216
HATE TREMOLOS AND NATIONAL FRENETICS.	247	PIERROTS	14
NATIONAL SONG (E. C.)	272	NATIONAL SONG	1

PAGE 270

NATIONS -- 'NEATH

	PAGE	TITLE	LINE
NATIONS			
ARE NOT THE BEST OF PULSE FOR INFANT NATIONS.	239	MOYEN SENSUEL	30
NATION'S			
THAT ARE THE NATION'S BOTTS, COLLICKS AND GLANDERS.	241	MOYEN SENSUEL	74
WHAT WAS THE NATION'S, NOW BY NORMAN'S KIN	261	ALF'S FIFTH	20
NATION-WIDE			
MOVING A NATION-WIDE	259	ALF'S THIRD	6
NATURAL			
'GOT ON DESIROUS THOUGHT BY NATURAL VIRTUE,	42	HER MONUMENT	42
STILL SIGH OVER ESTABLISHED AND NATURAL FACT	148	FRATRES MINORE	3
IT TWISTS ITSELF FROM OUT ALL NATURAL MEASURE;	249	DONNA MI PREGA	50
NATURE			
BY THE IMMORTAL NATURE ON THIS QUICKSAND,	41	HER MONUMENT	30
O MORTAL NATURE,	42	HER MONUMENT	49
NATURE HERSELF'S TURNED METAPHYSICAL,	50	THE FLAME	27
BRING THE BURNISHED NATURE OF FIRE;	75	THE ALCHEMIST	19
"LIKE TO LIKE NATURE": THESE AGGLUTINOUS YELLOWS!	114	BEFORE A SHOP	2
NATURE RECEIVES HIM;	195	HUGH SELWIN:10	5
AND YET ANOTHER, A "CHARMING MAN," "SWEET NATURE,"			
BUT WAS GILDER,	240	MOYEN SENSUEL	57
NATURE'S			
UPON FOND NATURE'S MORBID GRACE.	44	MR. HOUSMAN	14
AND SAVE THEY KNOW'T ARIGHT FROM NATURE'S SOURCE	248	DONNA MI PREGA	10
NAUGHT			
NAUGHT BUT THE WIND THAT FLUTTERS IN THE LEAVES.	4	LA FRAISNE	19
THERE I HEARD NAUGHT SAVE THE HARSH SEA	64	THE SEAFARER	18
I ASK NAUGHT FROM YOU,	106	DOMPNA POIS	62
HERE IS THERE NAUGHT OF DEAD GODS	110	COITUS	3
WEEPING THAT WE CAN FOLLOW NAUGHT ELSE.	168	OF AROUET	34
OF LOVE I HAVE NAUGHT	174	LANGUE D'OC: 3	7
RECKING NAUGHT ELSE BUT THAT HER GRACES GIVE	197	ENVOI (1919)	10
NAUGHT BUT A SHIRT IS THERE	258	ALF'S THIRD	3
NAY			
NAY NO WHIT	8	NA AUDIART	18
WENT SWIFTLY FROM ME. NAY, WHATEVER COMES	40	ERAT HORA	4
NAY, ON MY BREAST THOU MUST	47	FROM HEINE: 7	10
NAY, SHOULD THE DEATHLESS VOICE OF ALL THE WORLD	63	PHASELLUS ILLE	9
NAY, NOR HIS VERY ESSENCE OR HIS MODE;	248	DONNA MI PREGA	15
NE			
S'ILS NE SENTENT PAS LA MUSIQUE, QU'EST CE	199	MAUBERLEY: 2	EPI
S'ILS NE COMPRENNENT PAS LA POESIE,	199	MAUBERLEY: 2	EPI
NE PEUT PLUS VOIR	273	M. POM-POM	4
NEAR			
(SATURN AND MARS TO ZEUS DRAWN NEAR!)	10	FOR THIS YULE	18
AND I AM NEAR MY DESIRE.	83	THE GARRET	8
UP ON THE WET ROAD NEAR CLERMONT.	119	THE GYPSY	0
THERE ARE THREE KEEPS NEAR MAREUIL,	121	PROVINC DESERT	24
LEAVE-TAKING NEAR SHOKU	138	NEAR SHOKU	T
NEAR PERIGORD	151	NEAR PERIGORD	T
"YOU WERE BORN NEAR HIM."	156	NEAR PERIGORD	153
NEAR THEM I NOTICED AN HARP	180	MOEURS CON: 5	22
(NEAR Q. H. FLACCUS' BOOK-STALL).	210	SEXTUS PROP: 2	9
WE WERE COMING NEAR TO THE HOUSE,	226	SEXTUS PROP:10	25
STILL WE WILL BRING OUR "FICTION AS NEAR TO FACT" AS	243	MOYEN SENSUEL	139
BEAUTY SO NEAR,	250	DONNA MI PREGA	73
NEARETH			
NEARETH NIGHTSHADE, SNOWETH FROM NORTH,	64	THE SEAFARER	32
NEARNESS			
OH, I HAVE PICKED UP MAGIC IN HER NEARNESS	71	A VIRGINAL	7
NEAT			
NOT A NEAT LEDGE, NOT FOIX BETWEEN ITS STREAMS,	152	NEAR PERIGORD	32
AND THE NEAT PILES OF UNOPENED, UNOPENING BOOKS,	180	MOEURS CON: 5	25
'NEATH			
AND YOU ALSO FOLLOW HIM "NEATH PHRYGIAN PINE SHADE:	229	SEXTUS PROP:12	41
'NEATH			
ONE WHO HATH SET THE WHOLE WORLD 'NEATH HER LAWS,	40	ROME	6
FINDS 'NEATH THIS ROCK FIT MOULD, FIT RESTING PLACE!	41	HER MONUMENT	21
'NEATH WHICH THE LAST YEAR LIES,	67	THE CLOAK	8
'NEATH THE DARK GLEAM OF THE SKY;	75	THE ALCHEMIST	7
'TILL I HAVE MY HAND 'NEATH HER CLOAK.	173	LANGUE D'OC: 2	22

NEATLY -- NET

	PAGE	TITLE	LINE
NEATLY			
PILED UP NEATLY UPON THE SHELVES	117	THE LAKE ISLE	4
NECK			
SO SPOKE. AND THE NOOSE WAS OVER MY NECK.	224	SEXTUS PROP:10	13
NECKS			
AND "IT IS, I THINK, INDIA WHICH NOW GIVES NECKS TO YOUR TRIUMPH,"	216	SEXTUS PROP: 5	17
A HEAVY MASS ON FREE NECKS.	226	SEXTUS PROP:11	12
AND THEIR NECKS SUNK INTO FUR	269	SAFE AND SOUND	14
NEED			
YOU GRABBED AT THE GOLD SURE; HAD NO NEED TO PACK CENTS	13	MESMERISM	19
THERE IS NO NEED OF ASKING DIVINERS.	138	NEAR SHOKU	11
THE CASTLE FLANKED HIM--HE HAD NEED OF IT.	152	NEAR PERIGORD	49
"YOU NEED, PROPERTIUS, NOT THINK	210	SEXTUS PROP: 2	19
THE INVITATION HAD NO NEED OF FINE AESTHETIC,	242	MOYEN SENSUEL	127
YOU CAN NOT GET CHEAP BOOKS, EVEN IF YOU NEED 'EM).	246	MOYEN SENSUEL	218
NEEDLE			
THE NEEDLE	69	THE NEEDLE	T
NOW! FOR THE NEEDLE TREMBLES IN MY SOUL!	69	THE NEEDLE	3
SAFES IN THREAD AND NEEDLE STREET.	269	SAFE AND SOUND	22
I WOULDN'T 'AVE THE NEEDLE	269	SAFE AND SOUND	23
OH THE NEEDLE IS YOUR PORTION,	269	SAFE AND SOUND	25
NEEDS			
ONE MUST OF NEEDS BE A HANG'D EARLY RISER	13	MESMERISM	3
WHERE ONE NEEDS ONE'S BRAINS ALL THE TIME.	117	THE LAKE ISLE	16
YET SENNIN NEEDS	128	THE RIVER SONG	6
NEEDY			
MAY MAKE MERRY MAN FARING NEEDY.	64	THE SEAFARER	27
NE'ER			
AS NE'ER HAD I OTHER, AND WHEN THE WIND BLOWS,	23	MARVOIL	35
(LET HIM REBUKE WHO NE'ER HAS KNOWN THE PURE PLATONIC GRAPPLE,	242	MOYEN SENSUEL	105
NEGLECTED			
NEGLECTED BY THE YOUNG,	193	SIENA MI FE	19
NEIGH			
OUR HORSES NEIGH TO EACH OTHER	137	TAKING LEAVE	8
NEIGHBOURS			
HOW WOULD YOU LIVE, WITH NEIGHBOURS SET ABOUT YOU--	152	NEAR PERIGORD	28
NEIGHS			
AND THE SHRILL NEIGHS OF DESTRIERS IN BATTLE REJOICING,	28	ALTAFORTE	14
THE DAI HORSE NEIGHS AGAINST THE BLEAK WIND OF ETSU,	139	SOUTH-FOLK	1
NEITHER (9)			
NELL			
NELL GWYNN'S STILL HERE, DESPITE THE REFORMATION,	163	CABARET DANCER	72
NEMESIANUS			
NEMESIANUS, EC. 4.	186	HUGH SELWYN	EP
NEO-COMMUNE			
THE NEO-COMMUNE	258	ALF'S SECOND	SU
NEO-NIETZSCHEAN			
MILDNESS, AMID THE NEO-NIETZSCHEAN CLATTER,	201	AGE DEMANDED	2
NEPHEW			
WHILE THE SECOND WIFE OF A NEPHEW	115	SOCIAL ORDER	
NEPHEWS			
AND I ALSO AMONG THE LATER NEPHEWS OF THIS CITY	208	SEXTUS PROP: 1	3
NEPTUNE			
THOUGH MY HOUSE IS NOT PROPPED UP BY TAENARIAN COLUMNS FROM LACONIA (ASSOCIATED WITH NEPTUNE AND CERBERUS),	208	SEXTUS PROP: 1	5
NERVES			
THAT THE TWITCHING OF THREE ABDOMINAL NERVES	148	FRATRES MINORE	
THE AMOROUS NERVES WILL GIVE WAY TO DIGESTIVE;	163	CABARET DANCER	6
MY NERVES STILL REGISTER THE SOUNDS OF CONTRA-BASS',	247	PIERROTS	1
NERVE-WRACKED			
GO ALSO TO THE NERVE-WRACKED, GO TO THE ENSLAVED-BY-CONVENTION,	88	COMMISSION	
NEST			
WITHIN HER NEST;	106	DOMPNA POIS	
NET			
THAT MAN DOTH PASS THE NET OF DAYS AND HOURS.	50	THE FLAME	

PAGE 272

NET-LIKE -- NEW

	PAGE	TITLE	LINE
NET-LIKE			
AND ALL HIS NET-LIKE THOUGHT OF NEW ALLIANCE?	152	NEAR PERIGORD	53
NET-WORK			
A NET-WORK OF ARBOURS AND PASSAGES AND COVERED WAYS,	141	IDEA OF CHOAN	22
BORDER THE NET-WORK OF WAYS:	141	IDEA OF CHOAN	24
NEUTRAL			
UNDER SOME NEUTRAL FORCE	69	THE NEEDLE	14
NEVER			
'CAUSE NEVER A FLAW WAS THERE	8	NA AUDIART	23
MEN HAVE I KNOWN AND MEN, BUT NEVER ONE	32	PARACELSUS	3
BUT NEVER A CRY CRIED HE.	34	GOODLY FERE	40
'LAS! NEVER WAS NOR WILL BE IN THIS WORLD	37	THE YOUNG KING	15
IN WILD-WOOD NEVER FAWN NOR FALLOW FARETH	38	BALLATETTA	6
HATH IT NEVER ONCE DISTRESSED YOU, ...	44	FROM HEINE: 1	6
BUT YOU NEVER STRING TWO DAYS UPON ONE WIRE	53	AU JARDIN	13
THAT MIGHT PROVE USEFUL AND YET NEVER PROVES, ...	61	PORTRAIT FEMME	19
THAT NEVER FITS A CORNER OR SHOWS USE, ...	61	PORTRAIT FEMME	20
THAT FAILED NEVER WOMEN, ...	90	SURGIT FAMA	6
ONCE MORE ARE THE NEVER ABANDONED GARDENS	90	SURGIT FAMA	18
FOR YOU SEEM NEVER TO HAVE DISCOVERED	101	AMITIES	8
HER CHILDREN HAVE NEVER DISCOVERED HER ADULTERIES.	103	THE PATTERNS	2
I WILL NEVER AGAIN GATHER	105	DOMPNA POIS	6
SEEING THAT TRISTAN'S LADY ISEUTZ HAD NEVER	106	DOMPNA POIS	37
UNSTILL, NEVER CEASING;	107	COMING OF WAR	9
WITH CARAVANS, BUT NEVER AN APE OR A BEAR.	119	THE GYPSY	16
I NEVER LAUGHED, BEING BASHFUL.	100	RIVER-MER WIFE	8
CALLED TO, A THOUSAND TIMES, I NEVER LOOKED BACK.	130	RIVER-MER WIFE	10
(THAT, MAYBE, NEVER HAPPENED!)	152	NEAR PERIGORD	41
SHE WHO COULD NEVER LIVE SAVE THROUGH ONE PERSON,	157	NEAR PERIGORD	189
SHE WHO COULD NEVER SPEAK SAVE TO ONE PERSON, ...	157	NEAR PERIGORD	190
FROM WEEHAWKEN--WHO HAS NEVER KNOWN	163	CABARET DANCER	65
FROM ONE I LOVED NEVER SO MUCH, ...	176	LANGUE D'OC: 3	61
I NEVER SAW HER AGAIN.	182	MOEURS CON: 8	15
DARING AS NEVER BEFORE, WASTAGE AS NEVER BEFORE.	190	HUGH SELWYN: 4	20
DARING AS NEVER BEFORE, WASTAGE AS NEVER BEFORE.	190	HUGH SELWYN: 4	20
FORTITUDE AS NEVER BEFORE	190	HUGH SELWYN: 4	23
FRANKNESS AS NEVER BEFORE, ...	190	HUGH SELWYN: 4	24
DISILLUSIONS AS NEVER TOLD IN THE OLD DAYS, ...	190	HUGH SELWYN: 4	25
NEVER RELAXING INTO GRACE;	193	BRENNBAUM	4
"I NEVER MENTIONED A MAN BUT WITH THE VIEW	194	MR. NIXON	14
KNOWING MY COAT HAS NEVER BEEN	196	HUGH SELWIN:12	5
BUT NEVER OF THE LADY VALENTINE'S VOCATION:	196	HUGH SELWIN:12	12
I HAD NEVER SEEN HER LOOKING SO BEAUTIFUL, ...	225	SEXTUS PROP:10	30
I'VE TOLD HIS TRAINING, HE WAS NEVER BASHFUL, ...	242	MOYEN SENSUEL	125
WAS NEVER ONE OF WHOM ONE SPEAKS AS "BRAZEN'D." ...	245	MOYEN SENSUEL	206
SPREADING ITS RAYS, IT TENDETH NEVER DOWN	249	DONNA MI PREGA	29
LEISURE'S ADORNMENT PUTS HE THEN NEVER ON, ...	249	DONNA MI PREGA	51
NEVER THEREAFTER, BUT MOVES CHANGING STATE, ...	249	DONNA MI PREGA	52
NEVER THE MAN INSIDE	258	ALF'S THIRD	5
NEVER AN HONEST WORD	262	ALF'S SIXTH	28
KNOWEST THOU NOT THE TRUTH IS NEVER IN SEASON	263	ALF'S EIGHTH	13
NEVER AT ALL WILL THEY DO	265	ALF'S TENTH	3
THE SIMPLE BRITONS NEVER KNEW HE WAS, ...	265	ALF'S NINTH	24
I NEVER HEERD HER SAY NOTHIN'	271	OLE KATE	7
AND DIDN'T SEEM NEVER TO STOP.	271	OLE KATE	12
NEVER GOT PROPERLY TANKED AS I SAW, ...	271	OLE KATE	15
AND NEVER GOT TOOK TO JAIL, ...	271	OLE KATE	10
BUT SHE NEVER MADE NO MENTION	271	OLE KATE	23
HAS NEVER UNTIL NOW	272	THE BABY	2
NEVERTHELESS			
BUT SAID IT WUZ GLORIOUS NEVERTHELESS	259	ALF'S FOURTH	5
NEW			
AND MANY A NEW THING UNDERSTOOD	0	THE TREE	11
SCORNING A NEW, WRY'D CASEMENT, ...	9	NA AUDIART	42
AS FLAME LEAVETH THE EMBERS SO WENT SHE UNTO NEW FORESTS	17	PRAISE YSOLT	43
MINE EYES UPON NEW COLOURS.	39	FOR PSYCHE	9
O THOU NEW COMER WHO SEEK'ST ROME IN ROME	40	ROME	1
AND THERE IS NO NEW THING IN ALL THIS PLACE.	60	TOMB AKR CAAR	11
STRANGE WOODS HALF SODDEN, AND NEW BRIGHTER STUFF:	61	PORTRAIT FEMME	26
AS I? WILL THE NEW ROSES MISS THEE?	67	THE CLOAK	6

PAGE 273

NEW -- NICCOLO

	PAGE	TITLE	LINE
NEW (CONTINUED)			
I BURN, I SCALD SO FOR THE NEW,	70	THE PLUNGE	3
NEW FRIENDS, NEW FACES,	70	THE PLUNGE	4
NEW FRIENDS, NEW FACES,	70	THE PLUNGE	4
--SAVE THE NEW.	70	THE PLUNGE	8
FOR MY SURROUNDING AIR HATH A NEW LIGHTNESS;	71	A VIRGINAL	3
CLAD IN NEW BRILLIANCIES.	87	THE SPRING	7
IT WAS YOU THAT BROKE THE NEW WOOD,	89	A PACT	6
BE EAGER TO FIND NEW EVILS AND NEW GOOD,	89	COMMISSION	24
BE EAGER TO FIND NEW EVILS AND NEW GOOD,	89	COMMISSION	24
AS NEW ALMONDS STRIPPED FROM THE HUSK.	91	DANCE FIGURE	13
THE NEW CAKE OF SOAP	99	CAKE OF SOAP	T
I WILL COME OUT FROM THE NEW THICKET	108	CH'U YUAN	9
ALL THE WHILE THEY WERE TALKING THE NEW MORALITY	110	THE ENCOUNTER	1
IN THE BRIGHT NEW SEASON	111	IMAGE ORLEANS	2
IN THE BRIGHT NEW SEASON.	111	IMAGE ORLEANS	8
CANDIDIA HAS TAKEN A NEW LOVER	118	THREE POETS	1
HE RETURNS BY WAY OF SEI ROCK, TO HEAR THE NEW NIGHTINGALES,	130	THE RIVER SONG	37
FOR THE GARDENS AT JO-RUN ARE FULL OF NEW NIGHTINGALES,	130	THE RIVER SONG	38
I PAT MY NEW CASK OF WINE.	142	UNMOVING CLOUD	7
ARE BURSTING OUT WITH NEW TWIGS,	142	UNMOVING CLOUD	18
THEY TRY TO STIR NEW AFFECTION,	142	UNMOVING CLOUD	19
COME, LET US ON WITH THE NEW DEAL,	145	SALUTATION 3RD	13
AND ALL HIS NET-LIKE THOUGHT OF NEW ALLIANCE?	152	NEAR PERIGORD	53
AND YOUR NEW SERVICE AT DINNER,	167	OF AROUET	9
THEIR NEW SONG IN THE LEAVES.	173	LANGUE D'OC: 2	3
HOME TO OLD LIES AND NEW INFAMY;	190	HUGH SELWYN: 4	17
MIGHT, IN NEW AGES, GAIN HER WORSHIPPERS,	197	ENVOI (1919)	22
HIS NEW FOUND ORCHID.	199	MAUBERLEY: 2	11
MY MUSE IS EAGER TO INSTRUCT ME IN A NEW GAMUT, OR GAMBETTO,	216	SEXTUS PROP: 5	11
THERE ARE NEW JOBS FOR THE AUTHOR;	217	SEXTUS PROP: 5	32
AND IN A NEW SIDONIAN NIGHT CAP,	225	SEXTUS PROP:10	19
THESE NEW CONCESSIONS	248	PIERROTS	27
LET SOME NEW LYING ASS,	261	ALF'S SIXTH	1
GET THE KID NICE NEW TOYS,	261	ALF'S SIXTH	5
THE BABY NEW TO EARTH AND SKY	272	THE BABY	1
"THE BABY NEW TO EARTH AND SKY,"	272	THE BABY	9
OF THE NEW ECONOMICAL THEORIES	273	NATIONAL SONG	15
NEWER			
GIVE T'OLD ONES A NEWER TWIST	261	ALF'S SIXTH	8
NEWEST			
BUT YOU, NEWEST SONG OF THE LOT,	94	INSTRUCTIONS	15
NEW-FANGLED			
A NEW-FANGLED CHARIOT FOLLOWS THE FLOWER-HUNG HORSES;	207	SEXTUS PROP: 1	12
NEW-LAID			
SEEKING E'ER THE NEW-LAID RAST-WAY	7	CINO	50
NEWLY			
AND YET AGAIN, AND NEWLY RUMOUR STRIKES ON MY EARS.	226	SEXTUS PROP:11	17
NEWMAN			
AROSE TOWARD NEWMAN AS THE WHISKEY WARMED.	193	SIENA MI FE	12
NEWNESS			
THESE ARE THEY WHO OBJECTED TO NEWNESS,	145	SALUTATION 3RD	5
NEWSPAPER			
SIR LAUNCELOT HAS A NEWSPAPER NOW	266	ALF'S ELEVENTH	SUB
NEXT			
MOVE WE AND TAKE THE TIDE, WITH ITS NEXT FAVOUR,	69	THE NEEDLE	12
YOU DO NEXT TO NOTHING AT ALL.	94	INSTRUCTIONS	7
SPOILING HIS VISIT, WITH A YEAR BEFORE THE NEXT ONE.	154	NEAR PERIGORD	113
END THE DISCUSSION, RICHARD GOES OUT NEXT DAY	156	NEAR PERIGORD	157
WILL DINE NEXT WEEK WITH MRS. BASIL,	163	CABARET DANCER	63
THE FIRST DAY'S END, IN THE NEXT NOON;	203	MAUBERLEY: 4	3
WHO, WHO WILL BE THE NEXT MAN TO ENTRUST HIS GIRL TO A FRIEND?	227	SEXTUS PROP:12	1
THAT WE, WITH MASEFIELD'S VEIN, IN THE NEXT SENTENCE	242	MOYEN SENSUEL	129
IS ONE DAY BLOWN UP LARGE, THE NEXT, SUCKED IN?	261	ALF'S FIFTH	21
NICCOLO			
IN THE PARLANCE OF NICCOLO MACHIAVELLI:	178	MOEURS CON: 1	18

NICE -- NIGHTINGALE

	PAGE	TITLE	LINE
NICE			
HE READ THE CENTURY AND THOUGHT IT NICE	245	MOYEN SENSUEL	201
GET THE KID NICE NEW TOYS,	261	ALF'S SIXTH	5
NOT THAT NICE BRITONS READ 'EM,	272	NATIONAL SONG	10
NICHARCUS			
NICHARCUS UPON PHIDON HIS DOCTOR	165	QUINTUS SEPTIM	ST
NIGGARDS			
WHAT DO YE OWN, YE NIGGARDS! THAT CAN BUY	32	PIERE VIDAL	57
NIGH			
THEN HOWL I MY HEART NIGH MAD WITH REJOICING.	28	ALTAFORTE	6
NARROW NIGHTWATCH NIGH THE SHIP'S HEAD	64	THE SEAFARER	7
NIGHT			
EYES, DREAMS, LIPS, AND THE NIGHT GOES.	6	CINO	10
WHOSE FRAMES HAVE THE NIGHT AND ITS WINDS IN FEE.	12	OF THE GIBBET	28
AND WHEN THE NIGHT	14	FAMAM CANO	4
AS A VAGUE CRYING UPON THE NIGHT	16	PRAISE YSOLT	6
AND MEN MYRTLES, ERE THE NIGHT	24	THUS NINEVEH	3
ERE THE NIGHT SLAY LIGHT	24	THUS NINEVEH	18
NIGHT LITANY	26	NIGHT LITANY	T
O GOD OF THE NIGHT,	26	NIGHT LITANY	14
FROM PIERE VIDAL'S REMEMBRANCE THAT BLUE NIGHT.	30	PIERE VIDAL	19
SILENT MY MATE CAME AS THE NIGHT WAS STILL.	31	PIERE VIDAL	32
ONE NIGHT, ONE BODY AND ONE WELDING FLAME!	32	PIERE VIDAL	56
YOU CAME IN OUT OF THE NIGHT	36	FRANCESCA	1
ALL NIGHT, AND AS THE WIND LIETH AMONG	39	FOR PSYCHE	1
NIGHT SONG	48	FROM HEINE: 8	SUB
YOU'VE GOT THE WHOLE NIGHT BEFORE YOU,	48	FROM HEINE: 8	5
IN AN UNINTERRUPTED NIGHT ONE CAN	48	FROM HEINE: 8	7
FROM AMBER LATTICES UPON THE COBALT NIGHT,	53	AU JARDIN	3
UNDER NIGHT, THE PEACOCK-THROATED,	75	THE ALCHEMIST	8
THE NIGHT ABOUT US IS RESTLESS.	110	COITUS	9
NIGHT AND DAY ARE GIVEN OVER TO PLEASURE	132	AT TEN-SHIN	25
NIGHT BIRDS, AND NIGHT WOMEN,	141	IDEA OF CHOAN	15
NIGHT BIRDS, AND NIGHT WOMEN,	141	IDEA OF CHOAN	15
FURTHER AND OUT OF REACH, THE PURPLE NIGHT,	155	NEAR PERIGORD	131
"BETWEEN THE NIGHT AND MORNING?"	158	PSYCHOLOG HOUR	27
THE FIRST NIGHT?	159	PSYCHOLOG HOUR	35
NIGHT AFTER NIGHT,	163	CABARET DANCER	84
NIGHT AFTER NIGHT,	163	CABARET DANCER	84
SINGS DAY-LONG AND NIGHT LATE	171	LANGUE D'OC	EPI
AND THE NIGHT	171	LANGUE D'OC	EPI
WHO STIRS NOT FORTH THIS NIGHT,	172	LANGUE D'OC: 1	4
THAT PLAINETH OF THE GOING OF THE NIGHT,	172	LANGUE D'OC: 1	12
WITH FROST AND HAIL AT NIGHT	173	LANGUE D'OC: 2	14
THEM. GOD HOW SWIFT THE NIGHT,	177	LANGUE D'OC: 4	4
O PLASMATOUR, THAT THOU END NOT THE NIGHT,	177	LANGUE D'OC: 4	6
'FORE GOD HOW SWIFT THE NIGHT,	177	LANGUE D'OC: 4	0
SO SWIFTLY GOES THE NIGHT	177	LANGUE D'OC: 4	14
AH GOD! HOW SWIFT THE NIGHT	177	LANGUE D'OC: 4	19
AH GOD! HOW SWIFT THE NIGHT.	177	LANGUE D'OC: 4	24
BY GOD, HOW SWIFT THE NIGHT.	177	LANGUE D'OC: 4	29
"NIGHT DOGS, THE MARKS OF A DRUNKEN SCURRY,	211	SEXTUS PROP: 2	49
ME HAPPY, NIGHT, NIGHT FULL OF BRIGHTNESS;	220	SEXTUS PROP: 7	1
ME HAPPY, NIGHT, NIGHT FULL OF BRIGHTNESS;	220	SEXTUS PROP: 7	1
FOR LONG NIGHT COMES UPON YOU	220	SEXTUS PROP: 7	18
PAY UP YOUR VOW OF NIGHT WATCHES	224	SEXTUS PROP: 9	25
AND IN A NEW SIDONIAN NIGHT CAP,	225	SEXTUS PROP:10	19
ALL THINGS ARE FORGIVEN FOR ONE NIGHT OF YOUR GAMES.	227	SEXTUS PROP:11	39
TO HIDING NIGHT OR TUNING "SYMPHONIES";	235	TO WHISTLER	15
AND HIS POCKETS BY MA'S AID, THAT NIGHT WITH CASH FULL,	242	MOYEN SENSUEL	126
FOR MEMORY OF THE FIRST WARM NIGHT STILL CAST A HAZE O'ER	245	MOYEN SENSUEL	195
BUT TURN TO RADWAY: THE FIRST NIGHT ON THE RIVER.	246	MOYEN SENSUEL	223
THERE GOES THE NIGHT BRIGADE,	257	BREAD BRIGADE	9
A SORT OF ARAB'S DREAM IN THE NIGHT	262	ALF'S SEVENTH	16
NIGHTINGALE			
WHEN THE NIGHTINGALE TO HIS MATE	171	LANGUE D'OC	EPI

PAGE 275

NIGHTINGALES -- NOBLENESS

	PAGE	TITLE	LINE
NIGHTINGALES			
AND HEARD THE FIVE-SCORE NIGHTINGALES AIMLESSLY SINGING.	129	THE RIVER SONG	22
HE RETURNS BY WAY OF SEI ROCK, TO HEAR THE NEW NIGHTINGALES,	130	THE RIVER SONG	37
FOR THE GARDENS AT JO-RUN ARE FULL OF NEW NIGHTINGALES,	130	THE RIVER SONG	38
NIGHTLY			
REST NIGHTLY UPON THE SOUL OF OUR DELICATE FRIEND FLORIALIS,	100	TEMPERAMENTS	2
NIGHTS			
RAVENS, NIGHTS, ALLUREMENT:	6	CINO	7
'TIS NOT "OF DAYS AND NIGHTS" AND TROUBLING YEARS,	50	THE FLAME	18
DIONE, YOUR NIGHTS ARE UPON US.	110	COITUS	7
IF SHE CONFER SUCH NIGHTS UPON ME,	221	SEXTUS PROP: 7	37
THE TEN NIGHTS OF YOUR COMPANY YOU HAVE	224	SEXTUS PROP: 9	28
SINCE THAT DAY I HAVE HAD NO PLEASANT NIGHTS.	225	SEXTUS PROP:10	43
THEN THERE CAME OTHER NIGHTS, CAME SLOW BUT CERTAIN	243	MOYEN SENSUEL	133
AND WERE SUCH NIGHTS THAT WE SHOULD "DRAW THE CURTAIN"	243	MOYEN SENSUEL	134
NIGHTSHADE			
NEARETH NIGHTSHADE, SNOWETH FROM NORTH,	64	THE SEAFARER	32
NIGHTWATCH			
NARROW NIGHTWATCH NIGH THE SHIP'S HEAD	64	THE SEAFARER	7
NIKOPTIS			
"I AM THY SOUL, NIKOPTIS. I HAVE WATCHED	60	TOMB AKR CAAR	1
NILE			
AND NOW DRINKS NILE WATER LIKE A GOD,	222	SEXTUS PROP: 8	20
NIMMIM			
BEGINNING WITH NIMMIM;	99	SALVATIONISTS	15
NINE			
NINE LAWYERS, FOUR COUNSELS, FIVE JUDGES AND THREE PROCTORS OF THE KING,	97	THE BELLAIRES	8
NINE LAWYERS, FOUR COUNSELS, ETC.,	98	THE BELLAIRES	24
NINE ADULTERIES, 12 LIAISONS, 64 FORNICATIONS AND SOMETHING APPROACHING A RAPE	100	TEMPERAMENTS	
NINE GIRLS, FROM AS MANY COUNTRYSIDES	211	SEXTUS PROP: 2	3
THE DAILY PRESS, AND MONTHLIES NINE CENTS DEARER.	241	MOYEN SENSUEL	9
NINETIES			
ACCEPT OPINION. THE "NINETIES" TRIED YOUR GAME	194	MR. NIXON	2
NINETY			
AND WROTE NINETY PETRARCHAN SONNETS.	118	CONTEMPORARIES	
NINETY-EIGHT			
HIS PALACE HAS NINETY-EIGHT WINDOWS,	237	ABU SALAMMAMM	
NINEVEH			
AND THUS IN NINEVEH	24	THUS NINEVEH	
AND HERE IN NINEVEH HAVE I BEHELD	24	THUS NINEVEH	
NINTH			
ALF'S NINTH BIT	264	ALF'S NINTH	
NIRVANA			
IS INCAPABLE OF PRODUCING A LASTING NIRVANA.	148	FRATRES MINORE	
NIXON			
MR. NIXON	194	MR. NIXON	
MR. NIXON ADVISED ME KINDLY, TO ADVANCE WITH FEWER	194	MR. NIXON	
"ADVANCE ON ROYALTIES, FIFTY AT FIRST," SAID MR. NIXON,	194	MR. NIXON	
NO (195)			
NO'			
THEY'LL NO' GET HIM A' IN A BOOK I THINK	33	GOODLY FERE	
NOBILITIES			
YOU DO NOT EVEN EXPRESS OUR INNER NOBILITIES,	94	INSTRUCTIONS	
NOBILITY			
AND WHATS-HIS-NAME ATTAINED NOBILITY.	264	ALF'S NINTH	
NOBLE			
NOBLE IN ANY PART	42	HER-MONUMENT	
IT IS NOBLE TO DIE OF LOVE, AND HONOURABLE TO REMAIN	218	SEXTUS PROP: 5	
TO FOLLOW A NOBLE SPIRIT,	250	DONNA MI PREGA	
NOBLENESS			
FOR THE NOBLENESS OF THE POPULACE BROOKS NOTHING BELOW ITS OWN ALTITUDE.	230	SEXTUS PROP:12	

PAGE 276

NOBLES -- NORTH

	PAGE	TITLE	LINE
NOBLES			
ANY BUT "MAJESTIES" AND ITALIAN NOBLES.	163	CABARET DANCER	66
NOBLESSE			
TO MAKE HIM A MATE OF THE "HAULTE NOBLESSE"	11	OF THE GIBBET	10
NOBLEST			
HOW IS THE NOBLEST OF THY SPEECH AND THOUGHT	42	HER MONUMENT	55
WITH HER VENUST AND NOBLEST TO MY MAKE	172	LANGUE D'OC: 1	27
WITH THE NOBLEST THAT STANDS IN MEN'S SIGHT,	174	LANGUE D'OC: 3	13
THE NOBLEST GIRLS MEN LOVE	176	LANGUE D'OC: 3	70
NOCTURNAL			
I SHALL BE PREY TO LAMENTATIONS WORSE THAN A NOCTURNAL ASSAILANT.	212	SEXTUS PROP: 3	11
NODIER			
"NODIER RACONTE . . ."	180	MOEURS CON: 5	SUB
NOEL			
TOWARDS THE NOEL THAT MORTE SAISON	10	FOR THIS YULE	1
NOIRS			
JE VIS LES CYGNES NOIRS,	160	DANS OMNIBUS	24
NOISE			
COMPLAIN ABOUT THE AWFUL NOISE	45	FROM HEINE: 5	3
THE MONKEYS MAKE SORROWFUL NOISE OVERHEAD.	130	RIVER-MER WIFE	18
"NOR WILL THE NOISE OF HIGH HORSES LEAD YOU EVER TO BATTLE;	211	SEXTUS PROP: 2	41
AND A QUERULOUS NOISE RESPONDED TO OUR SOLICITOUS REPROBATIONS.	215	SEXTUS PROP: 4	26
PAY FOR HIS WITLESS NOISE,	261	ALF'S SIXTH	4
OH, WHAT A NOISE THEY MADE	261	ALF'S SIXTH	23
MY GREAT NOISE DROWNS THEIR CRIES,	266	ALF'S ELEVENTH	2
NON			
"NON TI FIDAR," IT IS THE SWORD THAT SPEAKS	19	FOR E. MCC	13
NON "DULCE" NON "ET DECOR" . . .	190	HUGH SELWYN: 4	12
NON "DULCE" NON "ET DECOR" . . .	190	HUGH SELWYN: 4	12
NONCE			
I FOR THE NONCE TO THEM THAT KNOW IT CALL,	248	DONNA MI PREGA	5
NONE			
AND HAVE NONE ABOUT ME SAVE IN THE SHADOWS	20	IN DURANCE	18
AS FOR WILL AND TESTAMENT I LEAVE NONE,	22	MARVOIL	27
AND NONE FLED OVER LONG.	30	PIERE VIDAL	12
OTHERS ARE BEAUTIFUL, NONE MORE, SOME LESS.	52	AU SALON	EPI
THERE IS NONE LIKE THEE AMONG THE DANCERS,	91	DANCE FIGURE	4
NONE WITH SWIFT FEET.	91	DANCE FIGURE	5
THERE IS NONE LIKE THEE AMONG THE DANCERS;	91	DANCE FIGURE	23
NONE WITH SWIFT FEET.	91	DANCE FIGURE	24
SINGING AS WELL AS I SING, NONE BETTER;	96	DUM CAPITOLIUM	2
AND NOW THOU'LT NONE OF ME, AND WILT HAVE NONE	172	LANGUE D'OC: 1	24
AND NOW THOU'LT NONE OF ME, AND WILT HAVE NONE	172	LANGUE D'OC: 1	24
JOY I HAVE NONE, IF SHE MAKE ME NOT MAD	175	LANGUE D'OC: 3	44
VENUST THE LADY, AND NONE LOVELIER,	177	LANGUE D'OC: 4	26
THERE SHALL BE NONE IN A BETTER SEAT, NOT	222	SEXTUS PROP: 8	35
NONE CAN IMAGINE LOVE	250	DONNA MI PREGA	62
NON-ESTEEM			
NON-ESTEEM OF SELF-STYLED "HIS BETTERS"	202	AGE DEMANDED	58
NONSENSE			
"IS THIS," THEY SAY, "THE NONSENSE	85	SALUTATION 2ND	10
EVEN THOUGH WE TALK NOTHING BUT NONSENSE,	113	TAME CAT	5
NOON			
THE FIRST DAY'S END, IN THE NEXT NOON;	203	MAUBERLEY: 4	3
NOOSE			
SO SPOKE. AND THE NOOSE WAS OVER MY NECK.	224	SEXTUS PROP:10	13
NOR (91)			
NORMAL			
BUT FOR SOMETHING TO READ IN NORMAL CIRCUMSTANCES?	207	SEXTUS PROP: 1	19
NORMANDE			
NORMANDE COCOTTE	161	PAGANI'S NOV 8	2
NORMAN'S			
WHAT WAS THE NATION'S, NOW BY NORMAN'S KIN	261	ALF'S FIFTH	20
NORTH			
NEARETH NIGHTSHADE, SNOWETH FROM NORTH,	64	THE SEAFARER	32
KORE IS SEEN IN THE NORTH	90	SURGIT FAMA	2
FORK OUT TO SOUTH AND NORTH,	121	PROVINC DESERT	5
BY THE NORTH GATE, THE WIND BLOWS FULL OF SAND,	133	FRONTIER GUARD	1

PAGE 277

NORTH -- NOTHING

	PAGE	TITLE	LINE
NORTH (CONTINUED)			
AH, HOW SHALL YOU KNOW THE DREARY SORROW AT THE NORTH GATE,	133	FRONTIER GUARD	22
AND YOU TO THE NORTH OF RAKU-HOKU,	134	EXILE'S LETTER	14
IN THE CUTTING WIND FROM THE NORTH,	135	EXILE'S LETTER	43
AND THEN THE CROWD BROKE UP, YOU WENT NORTH TO SAN PALACE,	136	EXILE'S LETTER	71
BLUE MOUNTAINS TO THE NORTH OF THE WALLS,	137	TAKING LEAVE	1
THE BIRDS OF ETSU HAVE NO LOVE FOR EN, IN THE NORTH,	139	SOUTH-FOLK	2
NORTH-EAST			
MAREUIL TO THE NORTH-EAST,	121	PROVINC DESERT	22
NORTHERN			
IT MAY LAST WELL IN THESE DARK NORTHERN CLIMATES,	163	CABARET DANCER	71
NORTHWARD			
THEN THE WATERS OF HAN WOULD FLOW NORTHWARD.)	129	THE RIVER SONG	18
NORTHWINDISH			
OR GATHER MAY OF HARSH NORTHWINDISH TIME?	59	SILET	8
NOS			
O DIEU, PURIFIEZ NOS COEURS!	26	NIGHT LITANY	1
PURIFIEZ NOS COEURS!	26	NIGHT LITANY	2
PURIFIEZ NOS COEURS,	26	NIGHT LITANY	20
PURIFIEZ NOS COEURS,	26	NIGHT LITANY	21
PURIFIEZ NOS COEURS,	27	NIGHT LITANY	34
PURIFIEZ NOS COEURS,	27	NIGHT LITANY	35
PURIFIEZ NOS COEURS	27	NIGHT LITANY	49
PURIFIEZ NOS COEURS	27	NIGHT LITANY	51
NOSE			
ALL HAIL! YOUNG LADY WITH A NOSE	113	FORMIANUS LADY	1
WILL KEEP THEIR COLLECTIVE NOSE IN MY BOOKS,	209	SEXTUS PROP: 1	61
NOSES			
SALUTE THEM WITH YOUR THUMBS AT YOUR NOSES.	86	SALUTATION 2ND	22
NOT (244)			
NOTABLE			
THEIR DODDERING IGNORANCE IS WAXED SO NOTABLE	239	MOYEN SENSUEL	37
NOTE			
HER NOTE, THE LITTLE RABBIT FOLK	14	FAMAM CANO	8
TURNS HARDY PILOT . . . AND IF ONE WRONG NOTE	42	HER MONUMENT	45
ONLY ANOTHER MAN'S NOTE:	159	PSYCHOLOG HOUR	42
I HAVE MISLAID THE "AD.," BUT NOTE THE TOUCH,	242	MOYEN SENSUEL	11
NOTE, READER, NOTE THE SENTIMENTAL TOUCH:	242	MOYEN SENSUEL	11
NOTE, READER, NOTE THE SENTIMENTAL TOUCH:	242	MOYEN SENSUEL	11
NOTED			
WHICH ANAETHESIS, NOTED A YEAR LATE,	200	MAUBERLEY: 2	3
NOTES			
BRIGHT NOTES AGAINST THE EAR,	45	FROM HEINE: 5	
NOTHIN'			
I NEVER HEERD HER SAY NOTHIN'	271	OLE KATE	
NOTHING			
SITH NOTHING IS THAT UNTO WORTH PERTAINETH	37	THE YOUNG KING	2
FOR I'VE NOTHING BUT SONGS TO GIVE YOU.	53	AU JARDIN	1
NO! THERE IS NOTHING! IN THE WHOLE AND ALL,	61	PORTRAIT FEMME	2
NOTHING THAT'S QUITE YOUR OWN.	61	PORTRAIT FEMME	2
AND NOTHING NOW	63	AN OBJECT	
HERE THEY ARE WITH NOTHING ARCHAIC ABOUT THEM.	85	SALUTATION 2ND	
YOU DO NEXT TO NOTHING AT ALL.	94	INSTRUCTIONS	
BASTIDIDES, ON THE CONTRARY, WHO BOTH TALKS AND WRITES OF NOTHING SAVE COPULATION,	100	TEMPERAMENTS	
LADY, SINCE YOU CARE NOTHING FOR ME,	105	DOMPNA POIS	
I SHALL HAVE MISSED NOTHING AT ALL,	105	DOMPNA POIS	2
EVEN THOUGH WE TALK NOTHING BUT NONSENSE,	113	TAME CAT	
THERE WAS NOTHING AT CROSS PURPOSE,	134	EXILE'S LETTER	
AND THEY MADE NOTHING OF SEA-CROSSING OR OF MOUNTAIN-CROSSING,	134	EXILE'S LETTER	
TILL WE HAD NOTHING BUT THOUGHTS AND MEMORIES IN COMMON.	134	EXILE'S LETTER	
AND NOTHING IS GRIEVOUS	174	LANGUE D'OC: 3	
"THERE'S NOTHING IN IT."	194	MR. NIXON	
AND DIED, THERE'S NOTHING IN IT.	194	MR. NIXON	
NOTHING, IN BRIEF, BUT MAUDLIN CONFESSION,	202	AGE DEMANDED	
WE SHALL SPIN LONG YARNS OUT OF NOTHING.	217	SEXTUS PROP: 5	
YOU DO NOTHING, YOU PLOT INANE SCHEMES AGAINST ME,	226	SEXTUS PROP:11	

PAGE 278

NOTHING -- NOW

	PAGE	TITLE	LINE
NOTHING (CONTINUED)			
FOR THE NOBLENESS OF THE POPULACE BROOKS NOTHING BELOW ITS OWN ALTITUDE.	230	SEXTUS PROP:12	64
AS NOTHING CAN RESTRAIN OR MUCH DISPARAGE.	245	MOYEN SENSUEL	192
"NOTHING WILL PAY THEE, FRIEND, LIKE CHRISTIANITY."	246	MOYEN SENSUEL	236
TEN MORE AND NOTHING DONE,	259	ALF'S THIRD	19
NOTHINGNESS			
THAT PARADISE IS HURLED TO NOTHINGNESS.	42	HER MONUMENT	48
NOTICED			
NEAR THEM I NOTICED AN HARP	180	MOEURS CON: 5	22
NOTION			
TILL THE KING SHALL TAKE THE NOTION	269	SAFE AND SOUND	27
NOURISHED			
"WHICH THE HIGHEST CULTURES HAVE NOURISHED"	196	HUGH SELWIN:12	22
NOUS			
OU NOUS AVIONS LOUE DES CHAISES	160	DANS OMNIBUS	22
NO'US			
"DOMPNA POIS DE ME NO'US CAL"	105	DOMPNA POIS	T
NOVEL			
NOR FIND AUGHT NOVEL IN THY MERRIMENT?	43	SATIEMUS	19
AND THAT THE FRIEND OF THE SECOND DAUGHTER WAS UNDERGOING A NOVEL,	179	MOEURS CON: 3	4
NOVELIST			
AND IN THE HOME OF THE NOVELIST	180	MOEURS CON: 5	16
A NOVELIST, A PUBLISHER, TO PAY OLD SCORES,	239	MOYEN SENSUEL	18
A NOVELIST, A PUBLISHER AND A PREACHER,	239	MOYEN SENSUEL	19
NOVELLA			
FROM THE STATUE OF THE INFANT CHRIST IN SANTA MARIA NOVELLA,	94	INSTRUCTIONS	20
NOVEMBER			
PAGANI'S NOVEMBER 8	161	PAGANI'S NOV 8	T
NOW			
AND NOW MEN CALL ME MAD BECAUSE I HAVE THROWN	4	LA FRAISNE	27
AS NOW SEEMS IT SWEET,	9	NA AUDIART	45
AND MANY A ONE NOW DOTH SURPASS	24	THUS NINEVEH	14
NOW YOU WILL COME OUT OF A CONFUSION OF PEOPLE,	36	FRANCESCA	3
ALL-CONQUERING, NOW CONQUERED, BECAUSE	40	ROME	7
WHO ART NOW	41	HER MONUMENT	2
O GLANCE, WHEN THOU WAST STILL AS THOU ART NOW,	41	HER MONUMENT	10
THAT WHICH REMAINETH NOW	41	HER MONUMENT	19
BUT I KNOW NOW, THEY BOTH WERE GOOD ENOUGH.	44	FROM HEINE: 2	8
ALL THE FLAMES ARE DEAD AND SPED NOW	45	FROM HEINE: 3	5
AND NOW YOU PAY ONE. YES, YOU RICHLY PAY.	61	PORTRAIT FEMME	13
NOW DO I KNOW THAT I AM MAD,	62	N. Y.	4
AND NOTHING NOW	63	AN OBJECT	3
CORN OF THE COLDEST. NATHLESS THERE KNOCKETH NOW	64	THE SEAFARER	34
SO THAT BUT NOW MY HEART BURST FROM MY BREASTLOCK,	65	THE SEAFARER	59
THERE COME NOW NO KINGS NOR CAESARS	66	THE SEAFARER	84
NOW! FOR THE NEEDLE TREMBLES IN MY SOUL!	69	THE NEEDLE	3
COME NOW, BEFORE THIS POWER	69	THE NEEDLE	6
O LOVE, COME NOW, THIS LAND TURNS EVIL SLOWLY.	69	THE NEEDLE	9
AND NOW SHE'S GONE, WHO WAS HIS CYPRIAN,	73	JACOPO SELLAIO	3
AND NOW YOU HEAR WHAT IS SAID TO US:	82	THE CONDOLENCE	13
MOVES ONLY NOW A CLINGING TENUOUS GHOST.	87	THE SPRING	13
I AM OLD ENOUGH NOW TO MAKE FRIENDS.	89	A PACT	5
NOW IS A TIME FOR CARVING.	89	A PACT	7
FAILS NOT THE EARTH NOW,	00	SURGIT FAMA	7
SHE PASSED AND LEFT NO QUIVER IN THE VEINS, WHO NOW	92	GENTILDONNA	1
THAT NOW THERE IS NO ONE AT ALL	97	THE BELLAIRES	9
RESIDES NOW AT AGDE AND BIAUCAIRE.	98	THE BELLAIRES	35
AND NOW SHE TURNS TO ME SEEKING LOVE,	102	LADIES	3
AND NOW YOU GRUMBLE BECAUSE YOUR DRESS DOES NOT FIT	102	LADIES	7
IS NOW WEDDED	103	LADIES	12
NOW BEARS THE PALSIED CONTACT OF PHIDIPPUS.	111	SOCIETY	4
WALKED ONCE, AND NOW DOES NOT WALK	112	IONE, DEAD	8
AND NOW YOU ARE STALE AND WORN OUT,	114	EPILOGUE	5
IS NOW SURROUNDED	118	SOCIAL ORDER	1
WHO NOW GOES DRUNKENLY OUT	128	BEAU TOILET	8
IS NOW BUT BARREN HILL,	128	THE RIVER SONG	12
BY THE GATE NOW, THE MOSS IS GROWN, THE DIFFERENT MOSSES,	131	RIVER-MER WIFE	20

PAGE 279

NOW -- NUNTY

	PAGE	TITLE	LINE
NOW (CONTINUED)			
LONELY FROM THE BEGINNING OF TIME UNTIL NOW!	133	FRONTIER GUARD	2
NOW I REMEMBER THAT YOU BUILT ME A SPECIAL TAVERN	134	EXILE'S LETTER	2
AND NOW I SEE ONLY THE RIVER,	137	ON RIVER KIANG	4
ARE NOW THE BASE OF OLD HILLS.	138	CITY OF CHOAN	7
NOW THE HIGH CLOUDS COVER THE SUN	138	CITY OF CHOAN	11
AND NOW I WATCH, FROM THE WINDOW,	158	PSYCHOLOG HOUR	10
NOW THE THIRD DAY IS HERE--	159	PSYCHOLOG HOUR	39
COME NOW, MY DEAR PEPITA,	162	CABARET DANCER	32
NOW IN VENICE, 'STORANTE AL GIARDINO, I WENT EARLY,	163	CABARET DANCER	79
"NOT SO FAR, NO, NOT SO FAR NOW,	166	FISH & SHADOW	13
PHYLLIDULA NOW, WITH YOUR POWDERED SWISS FOOTMAN	167	OF AROUET	5
AND IF NOW WE CAN'T FIT WITH OUR TIME OF LIFE	168	OF AROUET	23
SLEEP NOT THOU NOW, I HEAR THE BIRD IN FLIGHT	172	LANGUE D'OC: 1	11
"COME NOW! OLD SWENKIN! RISE UP FROM THY BED,	172	LANGUE D'OC: 1	14
AND NOW THOU'LT NONE OF ME, AND WILT HAVE NONE	172	LANGUE D'OC: 1	24
IF SHE WON'T HAVE ME NOW, DEATH IS MY PORTION,	175	LANGUE D'OC: 3	37
NOW CRY THE BIRDS OUT, IN THE MEADOW MIST,	177	LANGUE D'OC: 4	12
SHE IS NOW THE HIGH-PRIESTESS	178	MOEURS CON: 1	11
AND EVEN NOW MR. STYRAX	178	MOEURS CON: 1	13
SHE NOW WRITES TO ME FROM A CONVENT;	179	MOEURS CON: 2	3
NOW, QUENCHED AS THE BRAND OF MELEAGAR,	181	MOEURS CON: 6	3
NUNC DIMITTIS, NOW LETTEST THOU THY SERVANT,	183	CANTICO SOLE	9
NOW LETTEST THOU THY SERVANT	183	CANTICO SOLE	10
NOW IF EVER IT IS TIME TO CLEANSE HELICON;	216	SEXTUS PROP: 5	1
OH AUGUST PIERIDES! NOW FOR A LARGE-MOUTHED PRODUCT.	216	SEXTUS PROP: 5	14
AND "IT IS, I THINK, INDIA WHICH NOW GIVES NECKS TO YOUR TRIUMPH,"	216	SEXTUS PROP: 5	17
TIGRIS AND EUPHRATES SHALL, FROM NOW ON, FLOW AT HIS BIDDING,	219	SEXTUS PROP: 6	7
"HE WHO IS NOW VACANT DUST	219	SEXTUS PROP: 6	26
NOW WITH BARED BREASTS SHE WRESTLED AGAINST ME,	220	SEXTUS PROP: 7	5
NO, NOW WHILE IT MAY BE, LET NOT THE FRUIT OF LIFE CEASE.	220	SEXTUS PROP: 7	28
AND NOW DRINKS NILE WATER LIKE A GOD,	222	SEXTUS PROP: 8	20
NOW YOU MAY BEAR FATE'S STROKE UNPERTURBED,	222	SEXTUS PROP: 8	37
GET ALONG NOW!"	225	SEXTUS PROP:10	24
AND BUT NOW GALLUS HAD SUNG OF LYCORIS.	230	SEXTUS PROP:12	72
AND NOW PROPERTIUS OF CYNTHIA, TAKING HIS STAND AMONG THESE,	230	SEXTUS PROP:12	75
NOW OVER AND SPENT,	236	MIDDLE-AGED	14
AND SO NOW LOVE	236	MIDDLE-AGED	16
WHO'S NOW THE EDITOR OF THE ATLANTIC,	239	MOYEN SENSUEL	14
OUT INTO THE CREPUSCULAR HALF-LIGHT, NOW AND THEN;	244	MOYEN SENSUEL	186
E'EN ITS DENIERS CAN NOW HEAR THE TRUTH,	248	DONNA MI PREGA	4
TIME FOR THAT QUESTION? AND THE TIME IS NOW.	260	ALF'S FIFTH	17
NOW THEY CAN'T FIRE HIM.	261	ALF'S SIXTH	16
WHAT WAS THE NATION'S, NOW BY NORMAN'S KIN	261	ALF'S FIFTH	20
SCARCELY A GENERAL NOW KNOWN TO FAME	264	ALF'S NINTH	3
SIR LAUNCELOT HAS A NEWSPAPER NOW	266	ALF'S ELEVENTH	SUB
HAS NEVER UNTIL NOW	272	THE BABY	2
NOWHERE			
FACT THAT LEADS NOWHERE; AND A TALE OR TWO,	61	PORTRAIT FEMME	17
NOYES			
"PROLIFIC NOYES" WITH OUTPUT UNDEFEATABLE).	240	MOYEN SENSUEL	50
NUKTIS			
NUKTIS 'AGALMA	199	MAUBERLEY: 2	7
NUMA			
MY CELLAR DOES NOT DATE FROM NUMA POMPILIUS,	209	SEXTUS PROP: 1	57
NUMBER			
BALLAD FOR THE TIMES' SPECIAL SILVER NUMBER	267	ALF'S TWELFTH	SUB
NUMERICAL			
AND I AM AFRAID OF NUMERICAL ESTIMATE,	224	SEXTUS PROP:10	6
NUMEROUS			
AND EVEN THIS INFAMY WOULD NOT ATTRACT NUMEROUS READERS	230	SEXTUS PROP:12	62
NUNC			
NUNC DIMITTIS, NOW LETTEST THOU THY SERVANT,	183	CANTICO SOLE	9
NUNTY			
MY NAME IS NUNTY CORMORANT	269	SAFE AND SOUND	1

NUT -- O

	PAGE	TITLE	LINE
NUT			
"THE HARDEST NUT I HAD TO CRACK	194	MR. NIXON	12
NYMPHARUM			
NYMPHARUM MEMBRA DISJECTA	92	APRIL	EPI
O			
O SINISTRO.	7	CINO	36
O HOLE IN THE WALL HERE! BE THOU MY JONGLEUR	23	MARVOIL	34
WHEREFORE, O HOLE IN THE WALL HERE, ...	23	MARVOIL	40
O HOLE IN THE WALL HERE, BE THOU MY JONGLEUR, ...	23	MARVOIL	45
O DIEU, PURIFIEZ NOS COEURS!	26	NIGHT LITANY	1
O GOD, WHAT GREAT KINDNESS	26	NIGHT LITANY	9
O GOD OF WATERS?	26	NIGHT LITANY	13
O GOD OF THE NIGHT, ...	26	NIGHT LITANY	14
O GOD OF SILENCE, ...	26	NIGHT LITANY	19
O GOD OF WATERS.	27	NIGHT LITANY	32
O GOD OF SILENCE, ...	27	NIGHT LITANY	33
O GOD OF WATERS, ...	27	NIGHT LITANY	36
O GOD OF WATERS, ...	27	NIGHT LITANY	44
O GOD OF THE SILENCE, ...	27	NIGHT LITANY	50
O GOD OF WATERS.	27	NIGHT LITANY	52
O AGE GONE LAX! O STUNTED FOLLOWERS, ...	32	PIERE VIDAL	60
O AGE GONE LAX! O STUNTED FOLLOWERS, ...	32	PIERE VIDAL	60
O STRANGE FACE THERE IN THE GLASS!	35	HIS OWN FACE	1
O RIBALD COMPANY, O SAINTLY HOST, ...	35	HIS OWN FACE	2
O RIBALD COMPANY, O SAINTLY HOST, ...	35	HIS OWN FACE	2
O SORROW-SWEPT MY FOOL, ...	35	HIS OWN FACE	3
WHAT ANSWER? O YE MYRIAD	35	HIS OWN FACE	4
O SKILLFUL DEATH AND FULL OF BITTERNESS, ...	37	THE YOUNG KING	17
WHAT HAST THOU, O MY SOUL, WITH PARADISE?	39	BLANDULA	1
O WINDS, WHAT WIND CAN MATCH THE WEIGHT OF HIM! ...	39	FOR PSYCHE	10
O THOU NEW COMER WHO SEEK'ST ROME IN ROME	40	ROME	1
REMAINS OF ROME. O WORLD, THOU UNCONSTANT MIME! ...	40	ROME	12
O GLANCE, WHEN THOU WAST STILL AS THOU ART NOW, ...	41	HER MONUMENT	10
A-TREMBLE IN MEN'S VEINS; O LIP CURVED HIGH	41	HER MONUMENT	12
O THROAT GIRT ROUND OF OLD WITH SWIFT DESIRE, ...	41	HER MONUMENT	14
O PALMS OF LOVE, THAT IN YOUR WONTED WAYS	41	HER MONUMENT	15
O MORTAL NATURE, ...	42	HER MONUMENT	49
O WOE, WOE, ...	43	MR. HOUSMAN	1
O YE LIPS THAT ARE UNGRATEFUL, ...	44	FROM HEINE: 1	5
O HARRY HEINE, CURSES BE, ...	46	TRANSLATOR	1
O WHAT COMFORT IS IT FOR ME	46	FROM HEINE: 6	17
O WOUNDED SORROWFULLY.	47	FROM HEINE: 7	8
O SMOKE AND SHADOW OF A DARKLING WORLD, ...	50	THE FLAME	14
O THOU DARK SECRET WITH A SHIMMERING FLOOR, ...	50	THE FLAME	30
THERE CANST THOU FIND ME, O THOU ANXIOUS THOU, ...	51	THE FLAME	34
SEARCH NOT MY LIPS, O LOVE, LET GO MY HANDS, ...	51	THE FLAME	37
O YOU AWAY HIGH THERE, ...	53	AU JARDIN	1
O THOU UNMINDFUL! HOW SHOULD I FORGET!	60	TOMB AKR CAAR	15
O LOVE, COME NOW, THIS LAND TURNS EVIL SLOWLY.	69	THE NEEDLE	9
O QUEEN OF CYPRESS, ...	76	THE ALCHEMIST	43
O MY FELLOW SUFFERERS, SONGS OF MY YOUTH, ...	82	THE CONDOLENCE	1
O MY FELLOW SUFFERERS, WE WENT OUT UNDER THE TREES,	82	THE CONDOLENCE	7
O GENERATION OF THE THOROUGHLY SMUG	85	SALUTATION	1
O BEWILDERED HEART, ...	87	THE SPRING	10
O WORLD, I AM SORRY FOR YOU, ...	88	CAUSA	3
O WOMAN OF MY DREAMS, ...	91	DANCE FIGURE	2
O NATHAT-IKANAIE, "TREE-AT-THE-RIVER."	91	DANCE FIGURE	18
O HELPLESS FEW IN MY COUNTRY, ...	92	THE REST	1
O REMNANT ENSLAVED!	92	THE REST	2
O GLASS SUBTLY EVIL, O CONFUSION OF COLOURS!	95	OF THE DEGREES	10
O GLASS SUBTLY EVIL, O CONFUSION OF COLOURS!	95	OF THE DEGREES	10
O LIGHT BOUND AND BENT IN, O SOUL OF THE CAPTIVE, .	95	OF THE DEGREES	11
O LIGHT BOUND AND BENT IN, O SOUL OF THE CAPTIVE, .	95	OF THE DEGREES	11
O GLASS SUBTLE AND CUNNING, O POWDERY GOLD!	95	OF THE DEGREES	14
O GLASS SUBTLE AND CUNNING, O POWDERY GOLD!, ...	95	OF THE DEGREES	14
O FILAMENTS OF AMBER, TWO-FACED IRIDESCENCE!	95	OF THE DEGREES	15
O MY UNNAMEABLE CHILDREN.	96	DUM CAPITOLIUM	6
O MY MUCH PRAISED BUT NOT ALTOGETHER-SATISFACTORY LADY.	100	THE BATH TUB	4
WHO AM I TO CONDEMN YOU, O DIVES.	102	TO DIVES	1
O MY SONGS, ...	103	CODA	1

PAGE 281

O -- OBJECTED

	PAGE	TITLE	LINE
O (CONTINUED)			
O CANZONETTI!	104	ANCORA	2
O MOUNTAINS OF HELLAS!!	104	ANCORA	8
GATHER ABOUT ME, O MUSES!	104	ANCORA	9
O MUSES WITH DELICATE SHINS,	104	ANCORA	12
O MUSES WITH DELECTABLE KNEE-JOINTS,	104	ANCORA	13
O FAN OF WHITE SILK,	108	FAN-PIECE	1
A PROCESSION, O GIULIO ROMANO,	110	COITUS	5
O ATTHIS,	112	HIMERRO	4
O MOST UNFORTUNATE AGE!	113	FORMIANUS LADY	10
O CHANSONS FOREGOING	114	EPILOGUE	1
O GOD, O VENUS, O MERCURY, PATRON OF THIEVES,	117	THE LAKE ISLE	1
O GOD, O VENUS, O MERCURY, PATRON OF THIEVES,	117	THE LAKE ISLE	1
O GOD, O VENUS, O MERCURY, PATRON OF THIEVES,	117	THE LAKE ISLE	1
O GOD, O VENUS, O MERCURY, PATRON OF THIEVES,	117	THE LAKE ISLE	12
O GOD, O VENUS, O MERCURY, PATRON OF THIEVES,	117	THE LAKE ISLE	12
O GOD, O VENUS, O MERCURY, PATRON OF 'THIEVES,	117	THE LAKE ISLE	12
THE GODS OF THE UNDERWORLD ATTEND ME, O ANNUBIS,	147	BEFORE SLEEP	6
WHITHER, O CITY, ARE YOUR PROFITS AND YOUR GILDED SHRINES,	165	QUINTUS SEPTIM	12
O PLASMATOUR AND TRUE CELESTIAL LIGHT,	172	LANGUE D'OC: 1	1
O PLASMATOUR, THAT THOU END NOT THE NIGHT,	177	LANGUE D'OC: 4	6
O BRIGHT APOLLO,	189	HUGH SELWYN: 3	25
SMALL TALK O ILION, AND O TROAD	208	SEXTUS PROP: 1	32
SMALL TALK O ILION, AND O TROAD	208	SEXTUS PROP: 1	32
AND YOU, O POLYPHEMUS? DID HARSH GALATEA ALMOST	208	SEXTUS PROP: 1	46
ESCAPE! THERE IS, O IDIOT, NO ESCAPE,	226	SEXTUS PROP:11	4
CLEAR THE STREET, O YE GREEKS,	229	SEXTUS PROP:12	37
CLEAR THE STREETS, O YE GREEKS!	229	SEXTUS PROP:12	40
EVOE, EVOE, EVOE BACCHO, O	231	CANTUS PLANUS	3
THE CONSTITUTION OF OUR LAND, O SOCRATES,	239	MOYEN SENSUEL	23
O STATE SANS SONG, SANS HOME-GROWN WINE, SANS REALIST!	241	MOYEN SENSUEL	88
OF RADWAY. O CLAP HAND YE MORALISTS!	246	MOYEN SENSUEL	227
"O BRITAIN, MUVVER OF PARLIAMENTS,	270	OF 600 M.P.'S	17
O'			
SHIELD O' STEEL-BLUE, TH' HEAVEN O'ER US	7	CINO	44
AND LAP O' THE SNOWS FOOD'S GUEREDON	10	FOR THIS YULE	5
BLACK IS THE PITCH O' THEIR WEDDING DRESS,	11	OF THE GIBBET	18
THAT PLUNDERED ST. HUBERT BACK O' THE FANE:	12	OF THE GIBBET	32
BUT GOD! WHAT A SIGHT YOU HA' GOT O' OUR IN'ARDS,	13	MESMERISM	10
SOUND IN YOUR WIND PAST ALL SIGNS O' CORRUPTION.	13	MESMERISM	16
HERE'S TO YOU, OLD HIPPETY-HOP O' THE ACCENTS,	13	MESMERISM	17
A-JUMBLING O' FIGURES FOR MAITRE JACQUES POLIN,	22	MARVOIL	4
HA' WE LOST THE GOODLIEST FERE O' ALL	33	GOODLY FERE	1
O' SHIPS AND THE OPEN SEA.	33	GOODLY FERE	4
BUT A MAN O' MEN WAS HE.	33	GOODLY FERE	16
WI' A BUNDLE O' CORDS SWUNG FREE,	33	GOODLY FERE	18
ON THE HILLS O' GALILEE,	34	GOODLY FERE	42
WI' HIS EYES LIKE THE GREY O' THE SEA,	34	GOODLY FERE	44
I HA' SEEN HIM EAT O' THE HONEY-COMB	34	GOODLY FERE	53
O' SUNDAYS.	53	AU JARDIN	22
FER 'ARFT A PINT O' BITTER?"	270	OF 600 M.P.'S	20
OAK			
I HAVE HIDDEN MY FACE WHERE THE OAK	4	LA FRAISNE	10
OAK'S			
BEHOLD ME SHRIVELLED AS AN OLD OAK'S TRUNK	31	PIERE VIDAL	52
OAR			
THEN ON AN OAR	203	MAUBERLEY: 4	20
"LET ANOTHER OAR CHURN THE WATER,	210	SEXTUS PROP: 2	26
OATS			
HEAD FARMERS DO LIKEWISE, AND LYING WEARY AMID THEIR OATS	229	SEXTUS PROP:12	48
OBEDIENCE			
YET IF I POSTPONE MY OBEDIENCE	212	SEXTUS PROP: 3	9
OBJECT			
AN OBJECT	63	AN OBJECT	7
SIX PENCE THE OBJECT FOR A CHANGE OF PASSION.	162	CABARET DANCER	30
OBJECTED			
THESE ARE THEY WHO OBJECTED TO NEWNESS,	145	SALUTATION 3RD	1

OBJECTS -- ODOUR

	PAGE	TITLE	LINE
OBJECTS			
OBJECTS TO PERFUMED CIGARETTES.	178	MOEURS CON: 1	17
OBLIVION			
SIFTINGS ON SIFTINGS IN OBLIVION,	197	ENVOI (1919)	24
OBLIVIONS			
WASHED IN THE COBALT OF OBLIVIONS;	203	MAUBERLEY: 4	9
OBSCURE			
HER LIFE IS OBSCURE AND TROUBLED;	179	MOEURS CON: 2	4
NOT, NOT CERTAINLY, THE OBSCURE REVERIES	188	HUGH SELWYN: 2	5
OBSEQUIES			
THERE WILL BE THREE BOOKS AT MY OBSEQUIES	219	SEXTUS PROP: 6	20
OBSERVATION			
THAT WE FIND MINUTE OBSERVATION.	104	THE SEEING EYE	10
OBSERVE			
OBSERVE THE IRRITATION IN GENERAL:	85	SALUTATION 2ND	9
THEY OBSERVE UNWIELDLY DIMENSIONS	104	THE SEEING EYE	2
AND OBSERVE ITS INEXPLICABLE CORRELATIONS.	104	THE SEEING EYE	7
YOU WILL OBSERVE THAT PURE FORM HAS ITS VALUE.	225	SEXTUS PROP:10	33
OBSERVED			
TO BE OBSERVED WITH DERISION,	145	SALUTATION 3RD	30
OBSERVED THE ELEGANCE OF CIRCE'S HAIR	187	E. P. ODE	15
OBSTINATE			
HE FISHED BY OBSTINATE ISLES;	187	E. P. ODE	14
OBSTRUCTIONIST			
YOU SLUT-BELLIED OBSTRUCTIONIST,	145	SALUTATION 3RD	10
OBVIOUS			
IN SPITE OF YOUR OBVIOUS FLAWS,	101	AMITIES	15
OBVIOUSLY			
"OBVIOUSLY CROWNED LOVERS AT UNKNOWN DOORS,	211	SEXTUS PROP: 2	48
OCCASION			
OR TO SUCH BASE OCCASION LIT AND QUENCHED?	42	HER MONUMENT	57
SOME OTHER QUAINT REMINDER OF THE OCCASION	245	MOYEN SENSUEL	197
OCCASIONAL			
AN' BE THANKFUL FOR OCCASIONAL HOLIDAYS.	263	ALF'S EIGHTH	28
OCCHI			
BLAGUEUR! "CON GLI OCCHI ONESTI E TARDI,"	181	MOEURS CON: 7	6
OCCUPANT			
OF USELESS RICHES FOR THE OCCUPANT,	236	MIDDLE-AGED	12
OCCUR			
(SUCH CHANGES DON'T OCCUR IN MEN, OR RABBITS).	246	MOYEN SENSUEL	232
OCEAN			
BROAD AS ALL OCEAN AND LEANIN' MAN-KIN'ARDS.	13	MESMERISM	12
O'ER TRACKS OF OCEAN; SEEING THAT ANYHOW	65	THE SEAFARER	65
THE SEA-CLEAR SAPPHIRE OF AIR, THE SEA-DARK CLARITY, STRETCHES BOTH SEA-CLIFF AND OCEAN	170	PHANOPOEIA	24
OCHAISOS			
SCRATCHED AND ERASED WITH AL AND OCHAISOS.	154	NEAR PERIGORD	100
OCHRE			
THEIR OCHRE CLINGS TO THE STONE.	108	TS'AI CHI'H	3
O'CLOCK			
AT ONE O'CLOCK I GO TO LUNCH,	266	ALF'S ELEVENTH	7
OCTOBER			
WE SAY: WILL WE BE LET TO GO BACK IN OCTOBER?	127	BOWMEN OF SHU	10
OCULISTS			
BEHIND THEM? WHAT'S THERE? HER SOUL'S AN AFFAIR FOR OCULISTS.	247	PIERROTS	12
ODD			
FOR FIRES AND ODD RISKS, COULD IN THIS SECTOR	243	MOYEN SENSUEL	152
ODDMENTS			
IDEAS, OLD GOSSIP, ODDMENTS OF ALL THINGS,	61	PORTRAIT FEMME	4
ODD'S			
TO CATCH YOU AT WORM TURNING. HOLY ODD'S BODYKINS!	13	MESMERISM	4
RECORD "ODD'S BLOOD! OUCH! OUCH!" A PRAYER, HIS SWIFT REPENTANCE.	243	MOYEN SENSUEL	130
ODE			
E. P. ODE POUR L'ELECTION DE SON SEPULCHRE	187	E. P. ODE	T
ODON			
AND CURIOUS IMPERFECTIONS OF ODOR.	104	THE SEEING EYE	3
ODOUR			
THE FAINT ODOUR OF YOUR PATCHOULI,	103	LADIES	18
"IN SACRED ODOUR"--(THAT'S APOCRYPHAL!)	156	NEAR PERIGORD	161

ODOURS -- OFFICER

	PAGE	TITLE	LINE
ODOURS			
AND WITH MORE THAN ARABIAN ODOURS,	225	SEXTUS PROP:10	20
OEIL			
CERNE SON OEIL DE GITANA"	162	CABARET DANCER	25
O'ER			
SHIELD O' STEEL-BLUE, TH' HEAVEN O'ER US	7	CINO	44
THAT HELL BRENN NOT HER O'ER CRUELLY.	11	OF THE GIBBET	16
O'ER MUCH HATH TA'EN SIR DEATH THAT DEADLY WARRIOR	37	THE YOUNG KING	12
AND ALL THE TIME THOU SAYEST THEM O'ER I SAID,	43	SATIEMUS	4
TURNED IN THEIR SAPPHIRE TIDE, COME FLOODING O'ER US!	51	HORAE BEATAE	4
O'ER TRACKS OF OCEAN; SEEING THAT ANYHOW	65	THE SEAFARER	65
SMEARED O'ER THE LOT IN EQUAL QUANTITIES.	244	MOYEN SENSUEL	174
FOR MEMORY OF THE FIRST WARM NIGHT STILL CAST A HAZE O'ER	245	MOYEN SENSUEL	195
O'ERGIVEN			
LORDLY MEN, ARE TO EARTH O'ERGIVEN,	66	THE SEAFARER	95
O'ERSHADOW			
THAT GLASS TO ALL THINGS THAT O'ERSHADOW IT,	51	THE FLAME	41
O'ERSHADOWED			
THE WORLD O'ERSHADOWED, SOILED AND OVERCAST,	36	THE YOUNG KING	7
OETIAN			
TWICE TAKEN BY OETIAN GODS,	208	SEXTUS PROP: 1	33
OF (1123)			
OFF			
AND SOME THE HILLS HOLD OFF,	21	IN DURANCE	38
BEZIERS OFF AT MONT-AUSIER, I AND HIS LADY	22	MARVOIL	12
TAKE YOUR HANDS OFF ME!	32	PIERE VIDAL	66
BUT WHERE'S THE OLD FRIEND HASN'T FALLEN OFF,	59	EXIT' CUIUSDAM	2
AND I FLOWED IN UPON THEE, BEAT THEM OFF;	60	TOMB AKR CAAR	20
LET THE MANES PUT OFF THEIR TERROR, LET THEM PUT OFF THEIR AQUEOUS BODIES WITH FIRE.	76	THE ALCHEMIST	51
LET THE MANES PUT OFF THEIR TERROR, LET THEM PUT OFF THEIR AQUEOUS BODIES WITH FIRE.	76	THE ALCHEMIST	51
COME, LET US PITY THOSE WHO ARE BETTER OFF THAN WE ARE.	83	THE GARRET	1
WE WHO SHOOK OFF OUR DEW WITH THE RABBITS,	104	ANCORA	5
WITH HER LITTLE SUEDE SLIPPERS OFF,	111	BLACK SLIPPERS	2
THE WIND BUNDLES ITSELF INTO A BLUISH CLOUD AND WANDERS OFF.	129	THE RIVER SONG	30
AND THEN I WAS SENT OFF TO SOUTH WEI,	134	EXILE'S LETTER	12
I HAD TO BE OFF TO SO, FAR AWAY OVER THE WATERS,	135	EXILE'S LETTER	34
LICK OFF THE BLACKING.	146	SALUTATION 3RD	3
AND KEEP MAD DOGS OFF HIS ANKLES.	212	SEXTUS PROP: 3	2
AND IF SHE PLAYS WITH ME WITH HER SHIRT OFF,	217	SEXTUS PROP: 5	3
AND YOU WILL NOT LEAVE OFF IMITATING AESCHYLUS.	228	SEXTUS PROP:12	2
THOUGH IT WILL, OF COURSE, PASS OFF WITH SOCIAL SCIENCE	244	MOYEN SENSUEL	16
A SILENT HUNTER OFF THE GREAT WHITE WAY,	245	MOYEN SENSUEL	20
YES, I HAVE RUBBED SHOULDERS AND KNOCKED OFF MY CHIPS	247	PIERROTS	2
IF YOU GIT OFF THE EMBANKMENT.	263	ALF'S EIGHTH	2
AND LICK THE DIRT OFF THE FLOOR	264	ALF'S EIGHTH	3
OFFENCE			
NO LONGER THE MEN FOR OFFENCE AND DEFENCE.	133	FRONTIER GUARD	2
OFFENDED			
AND ONE AMONG THEM LOOKED AT ME WITH FACE OFFENDED,	211	SEXTUS PROP: 2	3
OFFER			
ANOTHER BIT--AND AN OFFER	268	ANOTHER BIT	
OFFERED			
TRIED LAYU'S LUCK, OFFERED THE CHOYO SONG,	136	EXILE'S LETTER	6
ANDROMEDA WAS OFFERED TO A SEA-SERPENT	222	SEXTUS PROP: 8	2
SAW WHAT THE CITY OFFERED, CAST AN EYE	245	MOYEN SENSUEL	18
OFFERINGS			
BEARING HER OFFERINGS IN THEIR UNHARDENED HANDS,	211	SEXTUS PROP: 2	
OFFERS			
HE OFFERS SUCCULENT COOKING;	195	HUGH SELWIN:10	
OFFICE			
AND THAT THE YOUNGEST SON WAS IN A PUBLISHER'S OFFICE,	179	MOEURS CON: 3	
AND ITS OFFICE MAIL MAY BE OPENED BY	179	MOEURS CON: 4	
OFFICER			
IT IS AN OFFICER,	179	MOEURS CON: 4	

OFFICIAL -- OLD

	PAGE	TITLE	LINE
OFFICIAL			
THIS GOVERNMENT OFFICIAL	115	SOCIAL ORDER	1
OFFSPRING			
HER OFFSPRING ARE FAT AND HAPPY.	103	THE PATTERNS	4
THE PARENT RE-BEAMS AT ITS OFFSPRING.	180	MOEURS CON: 5	13
OFT			
HARDSHIP ENDURED OFT.	64	THE SEAFARER	3
AND DIRE SEA-SURGE, AND THERE I OFT SPENT	64	THE SEAFARER	6
IN ICY FEATHERS; FULL OFT THE EAGLE SCREAMED	64	THE SEAFARER	24
WEALTHY AND WINE-FLUSHED, HOW I WEARY OFT	64	THE SEAFARER	30
ON EARTH'S SHELTER COMETH OFT TO ME,	65	THE SEAFARER	62
OFTEN			
SHE WILL NOT BATHE TOO OFTEN, BUT HER JEWELS	161	CABARET DANCER	13
"YOUR PAMPHLETS WILL BE THROWN, THROWN OFTEN INTO A CHAIR	210	SEXTUS PROP: 2	22
OF AN AFFECT THAT COMES OFTEN AND IS FELL	248	DONNA MI PREGA	2
OFTEN HIS POWER MEETETH WITH DEATH IN THE END	249	DONNA MI PREGA	39
OGLING			
TO A WELSH SHIFTER WITH AN OGLING EYE,	264	ALF'S NINTH	7
OH			
"CINO?" "OH, EH, CINO POLNESI	6	CINO	25
(OH THEY ARE ALL ONE THESE VAGABONDS),	6	CINO	29
OH, TILL THOU COME AGAIN.	9	NA AUDIART	37
OH! THE LITTLE MOTHERS	14	FAMAM CANO	3
OH I KNOW THAT THERE ARE FOLK ABOUT ME, FRIENDLY FACES,	20	IN DURANCE	2
"THESE SELL OUR PICTURES"! OH WELL,	20	IN DURANCE	4
"THEE"? OH, "THEE" IS WHO COMETH FIRST	20	IN DURANCE	10
OH YE, MY FELLOWS: WITH THE SEAS BETWEEN US SOME BE,	21	IN DURANCE	35
OH WE DRUNK HIS "HALE" IN THE GOOD RED WINE	33	GOODLY FERE	13
OH, WOE, WOE, WOE, ETCETERA.	44	MR. HOUSMAN	15
OH, I KNOW YOU WOMEN FROM THE "OTHER FOLK,"	53	AU JARDIN	20
"TIME'S BITTER FLOOD"! OH, THAT'S ALL VERY WELL,	59	EXIT' CUIUSDAM	1
OH! I COULD GET ME OUT, DESPITE THE MARKS	60	TOMB AKR CAAR	29
OH, YOU ARE PATIENT, I HAVE SEEN YOU SIT	61	PORTRAIT FEMME	11
OH TO BE OUT OF THIS,	70	THE PLUNGE	6
OH, BUT FAR OUT OF THIS!	70	THE PLUNGE	15
OH, SUN ENOUGH!	70	THE PLUNGE	18
OH, I HAVE PICKED UP MAGIC IN HER NEARNESS	71	A VIRGINAL	7
OH HOW HIDEOUS IT IS	89	COMMISSION	29
OH, NO, SHE IS NOT CRYING: "TAMUZ."	110	TEMPORA	5
OH, NO, I WILL STICK IT OUT,	145	SALUTATION 3RD	27
OH, IS IT EASY ENOUGH?	151	NEAR PERIGORD	15
OH, THERE IS PRECEDENT, LEGAL TRADITION,	153	NEAR PERIGORD	88
OH, I KNOW WELL ENOUGH.	158	PSYCHOLOGY HOUR	17
OH WELL, HER PRESENT DULNESS	163	CABARET DANCER	78
WOMAN? OH, WOMAN IS A CONSUMMATE RAGE,	165	QUINTUS SEPTIM	20
"OH! ABELARD!" AS IF THE TOPIC	181	MOEURS CON: 7	8
OH WELL!	183	CANTICO SOLE	16
OH AUGUST PIERIDES! NOW FOR A LARGE-MOUTHED PRODUCT.	216	SEXTUS PROP: 5	14
OH COUCH MADE HAPPY BY MY LONG DELECTATIONS;	220	SEXTUS PROP: 7	2
OH, OH, AND ENOUGH OF THIS,	227	SEXTUS PROP:11	29
OH, OH, AND ENOUGH OF THIS,	227	SEXTUS PROP:11	29
OH HOW THE BIRD FLEW FROM TROJAN RAFTERS,	227	SEXTUS PROP:11	35
OH MAY THE KING LIVE FOREVER!	237	ABU SALAMMAMM	26
OH MAY THE KING LIVE FOR A THOUSAND YEARS!	237	ABU SALAMMAMM	27
AND I CAN HEAR AN OLD MAN SAYING: "OH, THE RUB!"	244	MOYEN SENSUEL	179
"OH, WHAT A CHARMING MAN,"--	261	ALF'S SIXTH	13
OH, WHAT A NOISE THEY MADE	261	ALF'S SIXTH	23
OH WHAT A FUSS THEY MADE	262	ALF'S SIXTH	25
WOT OH! MY BUXOM HEARTIES,	269	SAFE AND SOUND	9
OH THE NEEDLE IS YOUR PORTION,	269	SAFE AND SOUND	25
OISIN			
AND ALL THE TALES OF OISIN SAY BUT THIS:	50	THE FLAME	9
OLD			
AND THAT GOD-FEASTING COUPLE OLD	3	THE TREE	4
BEING IN ALL THINGS WISE, AND VERY OLD,	4	LA FRAISNE	2
THAT OLD AGE WEARETH FOR A CLOAK.	4	LA FRAISNE	4
OF THE OLD WAYS OF MEN HAVE I CAST ASIDE.	4	LA FRAISNE	12
SHE HATH CALLED ME FROM MINE OLD WAYS	4	LA FRAISNE	16
SHE HATH DRAWN ME FROM MINE OLD·WAYS,	4	LA FRAISNE	20

OLD

OLD (CONTINUED)

	PAGE	TITLE	LINE
TO LEAVE THE OLD BARREN WAYS OF MEN,	4	LA FRAISNE	29
STRANGE SPELLS OF OLD DEITY,	6	CINO	6
THAT TRAMP OLD WAYS BENEATH THE SUN-LIGHT,	6	CINO	21
"'POLLO PHOIBEE, OLD TIN PAN, YOU	7	CINO	42
UPON THY HANDS, AND THY OLD SOUL	9	NA AUDIART	41
AYE YOU'RE A MAN THAT! YE OLD MESMERIZER	13	MESMERISM	1
HERE'S TO YOU, OLD HIPPETY-HOP O' THE ACCENTS,	13	MESMERISM	17
THE WORDS ARE AS LEAVES, OLD BROWN LEAVES IN THE SPRING TIME	16	PRAISE YSOLT	19
KEPT AS BOLD TROPHIES OF OLD PAGEANTRY.	19	FOR E. MCC	18
AS OLD TOLEDOS PAST THEIR DAYS OF WAR	19	FOR E. MCC	19
THEY THAT COME MEWARDS, BEARING OLD MAGIC.	20	IN DURANCE	22
FOR THE CUSTOM IS FULL OLD,	24	THUS NINEVEH	7
PIERE VIDAL OLD	30	PIERE VIDAL	T
BEHOLD ME SHRIVELLED AS AN OLD OAK'S TRUNK	31	PIERE VIDAL	52
ARCHES WORN OLD AND PALACES MADE COMMON,	40	ROME	3
O THROAT GIRT ROUND OF OLD WITH SWIFT DESIRE,	41	HER MONUMENT	14
FOR THINE OLD LEGEND-LUST.	47	FROM HEINE: 7	12
BUT WHERE'S THE OLD FRIEND HASN'T FALLEN OFF,	59	EXIT' CUIUSDAM	2
IDEAS, OLD GOSSIP, ODDMENTS OF ALL THINGS,	61	PORTRAIT FEMME	4
THE TARNISHED, GAUDY, WONDERFUL OLD WORK;	61	PORTRAIT FEMME	22
I AM OLD ENOUGH NOW TO MAKE FRIENDS.	89	A PACT	5
IT IS LIKE AN OLD TREE WITH SHOOTS,	89	COMMISSION	31
FULL OF GOSSIP AND OLD TALES."	90	SURGIT FAMA	19
YOU ARE NOT OLD ENOUGH TO HAVE DONE MUCH MISCHIEF,	94	INSTRUCTIONS	16
OLD FRIENDS THE MOST.--W. B. Y.	101	AMITIES	EPI
YOU HAD THE SAME OLD AIR OF CONDESCENSION	101	AMITIES	3
FOUR AND FORTY LOVERS HAD AGATHAS IN THE OLD DAYS,	102	LADIES	1
THIS OLD LADY,	115	SOCIAL ORDER	5
WHO WAS "SO OLD THAT SHE WAS AN ATHEIST,"	115	SOCIAL ORDER	6
THINKING OF OLD DAYS.	121	PROVINC DESERT	8
OLD PENSIONERS AND OLD PROTECTED WOMEN	121	PROVINC DESERT	11
OLD PENSIONERS AND OLD PROTECTED WOMEN	121	PROVINC DESERT	11
I HAVE CREPT OVER OLD RAFTERS,	121	PROVINC DESERT	14
WITH A GARRULOUS OLD MAN AT THE INN.	121	PROVINC DESERT	20
AND AN OLD WOMAN,	121	PROVINC DESERT	25
WALKED OVER EN BERTRAN'S OLD LAYOUT,	122	PROVINC DESERT	39
I HAVE SAID: "THE OLD ROADS HAVE LAIN HERE.	122	PROVINC DESERT	56
WE GRUB THE OLD FERN-STALKS.	127	BOWMEN OF SHU	9
AND SHE WAS A COURTEZAN IN THE OLD DAYS,	128	BEAU TOILET	6
BUT TO-DAY'S MEN ARE NOT THE MEN OF THE OLD DAYS,	131	AT TEN-SHIN	7
SUNSET LIKE THE PARTING OF OLD ACQUAINTANCES	137	TAKING LEAVE	6
ARE NOW THE BASE OF OLD HILLS.	138	CITY OF CHOAN	7
OLD IDEA OF CHOAN BY ROSORIU	141	IDEA OF CHOAN	T
AND HAD HIS WAY WITH THE OLD ENGLISH KING,	151	NEAR PERIGORD	26
AND STIR OLD GRUDGES?	152	NEAR PERIGORD	37
BEFORE THE HARD OLD KING:	152	NEAR PERIGORD	43
THEY PROBE OLD SCANDALS, SAY DE BORN IS DEAD:	155	NEAR PERIGORD	137
OLD POPKOFF	163	CABARET DANCER	62
YOU'LL WONDER THAT AN OLD MAN OF EIGHTY	168	OF AROUET	35
"COME NOW! OLD SWENKIN! RISE UP FROM THY BED,	172	LANGUE D'OC: 1	14
WORN AND OLD.	176	LANGUE D'OC: 3	72
THE OLD MEN WITH BEAUTIFUL MANNERS.	181	MOEURS CON: 7	2
SHE WAS A VERY OLD LADY,	182	MOEURS CON: 8	14
OLD MEN WITH BEAUTIFUL MANNERS,	182	MOEURS CON: 7	23
IN THE OLD SENSE. WRONG FROM THE START--	187	E. P. ODE	4
BELIEVING IN OLD MEN'S LIES, THEN UNBELIEVING	190	HUGH SELWYN: 4	14
HOME TO OLD LIES AND NEW INFAMY;	190	HUGH SELWYN: 4	17
DISILLUSIONS AS NEVER TOLD IN THE OLD DAYS,	190	HUGH SELWYN: 4	25
FOR AN OLD BITCH GONE IN THE TEETH,	191	HUGH SELWYN: 5	3
OLD LECHER, LET NOT JUNO GET WIND OF THE MATTER,	222	SEXTUS PROP: 8	39
ZEUS' CLEVER RAPES, IN THE OLD DAYS,	227	SEXTUS PROP:11	33
A NOVELIST, A PUBLISHER, TO PAY OLD SCORES,	239	MOYEN SENSUEL	18
THAN SPANISH LADIES HAD IN OLD ROMANCES.	242	MOYEN SENSUEL	104
AND I CAN HEAR AN OLD MAN SAYING: "OH, THE RUB!	244	MOYEN SENSUEL	179
SEVERAL OLD SO'JERS KNOW	257	BREAD BRIGADE	11
MY OLD MAN GOT NO INDEMNITY	263	ALF'S EIGHTH	24
WHEN FEEBLE MR. ASQUITH, GETTING OLD,	264	ALF'S NINTH	5
OLD 'ERB WAS DOTING, SO THE RUMOUR RAN,	264	ALF'S NINTH	13
I'M GETTING TOO OLD FOR SUCH CAPERS.	264	ALF'S EIGHTH	35

PAGE 286

OLD -- ONCE

	PAGE	TITLE	LINE
OLD (CONTINUED)			
UNTIL THE MIND OF THE OLD NATION GETS A LITTLE STRONGER.	266	ALF'S TENTH	16
AND WOULD MY OLD MAN HAVE BEEN SMARTER	268	ANOTHER BIT	14
TER GRIND THE SAME OLD AXES	270	OF 600 M.P.'S	6
OLDER			
'MID THESE THINGS OLDER THAN THE NAMES THEY HAVE,	69	SUB MARE	8
THEY HURT ME. I GROW OLDER.	131	RIVER-MER WIFE	25
OLDER THAN THOSE HER GRANDMOTHER	195	HUGH SELWIN:11	7
OLDNESS			
DISEASE OR OLDNESS OR SWORD-HATE	66	THE SEAFARER	71
OLD-WOMEN			
BUT SURELY THE WORST OF YOUR OLD-WOMEN ARE THE MALE ONES.)	243	MOYEN SENSUEL	150
OLE			
OLE KATE	271	OLE KATE	T
OLE KATE WOULD GIT HER 'ARF A PINT	271	OLE KATE	3
OLIVE			
LETS DRIFT IN ON US THROUGH THE OLIVE LEAVES	39	BLANDULA	4
FROM THE WIDE EARTH AND THE OLIVE,	75	THE ALCHEMIST	21
TO WHERE THE OLIVE BOUGHS	92	APRIL	3
GREY OLIVE LEAVES BENEATH A RAIN-COLD SKY.	92	GENTILDONNA	5
OLYMPIAN			
BECAME AN OLYMPIAN APATHEIN	202	AGE DEMANDED	39
OLYMPUS			
SPIKED ONTO OLYMPUS,	217	SEXTUS PROP: 5	40
THERE WILL BE, IN ANY CASE, A STIR ON OLYMPUS.	222	SEXTUS PROP: 8	42
OM			
TAN QUE I PUOSCH' OM GITAR AB MALH.	151	NEAR PERIGORD	EPI
OMAKITSU			
(RIHAKU OR OMAKITSU)	137	OF DEPARTURE	EPI
'OME			
WE'LL SEND 'EM MOUCHIN' 'OME,	257	BREAD BRIGADE	7
OMINOUS			
THAT MUCH WAS OMINOUS.	158	PSYCHOLOG HOUR	2
BUT THE BLACK OMINOUS OWL HOOT WAS AUDIBLE.	223	SEXTUS PROP: 9	4
OMNIBUS			
DANS UN OMNIBUS DE LONDRES	160	DANS OMNIBUS	T
ON (198)			
ONCE			
ONCE WHEN I WAS AMONG THE YOUNG MEN	5	LA FRAISNE	40
ONCE THERE WAS A WOMAN	5	LA FRAISNE	42
I THINK SHE HURT ME ONCE, BUT	5	LA FRAISNE	46
BEING UPON THE ROAD ONCE MORE,	6	CINO	11
ONCE FOR WIND-RUNEING	6	CINO	14
ONCE, TWICE, A YEAR--	6	CINO	23
"AH YES, PASSED ONCE OUR WAY,	6	CINO	27
THOU WERT ONCE SHE	9	NA AUDIART	52
NOT ONCE BUT MANY A DAY	41	HER MONUMENT	16
THAT YE WERE ONCE! OF ALL THE GRACE YE HAD	41	HER MONUMENT	18
HATH IT NEVER ONCE DISTRESSED YOU,	44	FROM HEINE: 1	6
WHOM THOU ONCE DID SING SO SWEETLY,	45	FROM HEINE: 3	2
AND I LOVED A LOVE ONCE,	53	AU JARDIN	15
I LOVED A LOVE ONCE,	53	AU JARDIN	17
IT IS ENOUGH THAT WE ONCE CAME TOGETHER;	59	SILET	5
IT IS ENOUGH THAT WE ONCE CAME TOGETHER;	59	SILET	9
IT IS ENOUGH THAT WE ONCE CAME TOGETHER;	59	SILET	11
SPEAK ONCE AGAIN FOR ITS SOLE STIMULATION,	63	PHASELLUS ILLE	10
"ONCE MORE IN DELOS, ONCE MORE IS THE ALTAR A-QUIVER.	90	SURGIT FAMA	16
"ONCE MORE IN DELOS, ONCE MORE IS THE ALTAR A-QUIVER.	90	SURGIT FAMA	16
ONCE MORE IS THE CHANT HEARD.	90	SURGIT FAMA	17
ONCE MORE ARE THE NEVER ABANDONED GARDENS	90	SURGIT FAMA	18
YOU ONCE DISCOVERED A MODERATE CHOP-HOUSE.	101	AMITIES	16
WALKED ONCE, AND NOW DOES NOT WALK	112	IONE, DEAD	8
AND ONCE AGAIN, LATER, WE MET AT THE SOUTH BRIDGEHEAD.	136	EXILE'S LETTER	70
THERE WAS ONCE A MAN CALLED VOLTAIRE."	191	MOEURS CON: 7	16
LIKEWISE A FRIEND OF BLOUGHRAM'S ONCE ADVISED ME:	194	MR. NIXON	21
TELL HER THAT SANG ME ONCE THAT SONG OF LAWES:	197	ENVOI (1919)	2
AT ONCE!!	212	SEXTUS PROP: 3	3
"WAS ONCE THE SLAVE OF ONE PASSION:"	219	SEXTUS PROP: 6	27

ONCE -- ONE

	PAGE	TITLE	LINE
ONCE (CONTINUED)			
SO I, THE FIRES THAT LIT ONCE DREAMS	236	MIDDLE-AGED	13
OR HUGGED TWO GIRLS AT ONCE BEHIND A CHAPEL.)	242	MOYEN SENSUEL	106
SOON OUR HERO COULD MANAGE ONCE A WEEK,	243	MOYEN SENSUEL	141
AND WHERE HE ONCE SET FOOT, RIGHT THERE HE STAYED.	264	ALF'S NINTH	12
THE KING WAS ONCE THE BIGGEST THING	267	ALF'S ELEVENTH	21
ONE			
THAT PLAGUE AND BURN AND DRIVE ONE AWAY.	5	LA FRAISNE	36
I LIKE ONE LITTLE BAND OF WINDS THAT BLOW	5	LA FRAISNE	49
(OH THEY ARE ALL ONE THESE VAGABONDS),	6	CINO	29
BUT IT IS ALL ONE.	7	CINO	38
BUT IT IS ALL ONE, I WILL SING OF THE SUN.	7	CINO	41
BUT IT IS ALL ONE.	7	CINO	53
FOR WHOSE FAIRNESS ONE FORGAVE	9	NA AUDIART	54
ONE LEAN MOIETY OF HIS NAKEDNESS	12	OF THE GIBBET	31
ONE MUST OF NEEDS BE A HANG'D EARLY RISER	13	MESMERISM	3
SUCH AN ONE AS THE WORLD FEELS	14	FAMAM CANO	24
SUCH AN ONE AS WOMEN DRAW AWAY FROM	15	FAMAM CANO	33
SUCH AN ONE PICKING A RAGGED	15	FAMAM CANO	38
SUCH IS YOUR FENCE, ONE SAITH.	19	FOR E. MCC	5
ONE THAT HATH KNOWN YOU.	19	FOR E. MCC	6
ONE FLAME, THAT REACHES NOT BEYOND	20	IN DURANCE	7
AND YET MY SOUL SINGS "UP!" AND WE ARE ONE.	21	IN DURANCE	41
THEN CAME WHAT MIGHT COME, TO WIT: THREE MEN AND ONE WOMAN,	22	MARVOIL	11
AND ONE LEAN ARAGONESE CURSING THE SENESCHAL	22	MARVOIL	14
ALL FOR ONE HALF-BALD, KNOCK-KNEE'D KING OF THE ARAGONESE,	22	MARVOIL	21
AND MANY A ONE HATH SUNG HIS SONGS	24	THUS NINEVEH	12
AND MANY A ONE NOW DOTH SURPASS	24	THUS NINEVEH	14
BETTER ONE HOUR'S STOUR THAN A YEAR'S PEACE	28	ALTAFORTE	16
FOR THAT THE ONE IS DEAD	30	PIERE VIDAL	5
ONE MORE FOOL'S VIGIL WITH THE HOLLYHOCKS.	31	PIERE VIDAL	25
MEN HAVE I KNOWN AND MEN, BUT NEVER ONE	32	PARACELSUS	3
ONE NIGHT, ONE BODY AND ONE WELDING FLAME!	32	PIERE VIDAL	56
ONE NIGHT, ONE BODY AND ONE WELDING FLAME!	32	PIERE VIDAL	56
ONE NIGHT, ONE BODY AND ONE WELDING FLAME!	32	PIERE VIDAL	56
"YE SHALL SEE ONE THING TO MASTER ALL:	34	GOODLY FERE	31
FREE US, FOR THERE IS ONE	35	THE EYES	15
YE MIGHT LET ONE REMAIN ABOVE WITH US.	38	LADY'S LIFE	4
YE MIGHT LET ONE REMAIN ABOVE WITH US.	38	LADY'S LIFE	14
NOR HELD ME SAVE AS AIR THAT BRUSHETH BY ONE	39	FOR PSYCHE	3
ONE HOUR WAS SUNLIT AND THE MOST HIGH GODS	40	ERAT HORA	5
ONE WHO HATH SET THE WHOLE WORLD 'NEATH HER LAWS,	40	ROME	6
ROME THAT ART ROME'S ONE SOLE LAST MONUMENT,	40	ROME	9
TURNS HARDY PILOT . . . AND IF ONE WRONG NOTE	42	HER MONUMENT	45
"LO, ONE THERE WAS WHO BENT HER FAIR BRIGHT HEAD,	43	SATIEMUS	5
DIM TALES THAT BLIND ME, RUNNING ONE BY ONE	43	SATIEMUS	16
DIM TALES THAT BLIND ME, RUNNING ONE BY ONE	43	SATIEMUS	16
OF ANY ONE WHO EVER KISSED YOU?	44	FROM HEINE: 1	8
IN AN UNINTERRUPTED NIGHT ONE CAN	48	FROM HEINE: 8	7
ONE PLACE WHERE WE'D RATHER HAVE TEA	52	AU SALON	8
BUT YOU NEVER STRING TWO DAYS UPON ONE WIRE	53	AU JARDIN	13
ONE DULL MAN, DULLING AND UXORIOUS,	61	PORTRAIT FEMME	9
ONE AVERAGE MIND--WITH ONE THOUGHT LESS, EACH YEAR.	61	PORTRAIT FEMME	10
ONE AVERAGE MIND--WITH ONE THOUGHT LESS, EACH YEAR.	61	PORTRAIT FEMME	10
AND NOW YOU PAY ONE. YES, YOU RICHLY PAY.	61	PORTRAIT FEMME	13
YOU ARE A PERSON OF SOME INTEREST, ONE COMES TO YOU	61	PORTRAIT FEMME	14
NEITHER COULD I PLAY UPON ANY REED IF I HAD ONE.	62	N. Y.	7
'TWOULD NOT MOVE IT ONE JOT FROM LEFT TO RIGHT.	63	PHASELLUS ILLE	11
AND ONE GROPES IN THESE THINGS AS DELICATE	69	SUB MARE	5
SEE, THEY RETURN, ONE, AND BY ONE,	74	THE RETURN	5
SEE, THEY RETURN, ONE, AND BY ONE,	74	THE RETURN	5
SHE WOULD LIKE SOME ONE TO SPEAK TO HER,	83	THE GARDEN	10
WE HAVE ONE SAP AND ONE ROOT--	89	A PACT	8
WE HAVE ONE SAP AND ONE ROOT--	89	A PACT	8
TO SEE THREE GENERATIONS OF ONE HOUSE GATHERED TOGETHER!	89	COMMISSION	30
THAT NOW THERE IS NO ONE AT ALL	97	THE BELLAIRES	9
FROM LAWYERS TO WHOM NO ONE WAS INDEBTED,	98	THE BELLAIRES	33
TO ONE, ON RETURNING CERTAIN YEARS AFTER.	101	AMITIES	57

PAGE 288

ONE

	PAGE	TITLE	LINE
ONE (CONTINUED)			
NEITHER ONE SO FAIR, NOR OF SUCH HEART,	105	DOMPNA POIS	12
SHE HATH TO WELCOME ONE,	106	DOMPNA POIS	53
AND ONE SAID:	107	COMING OF WAR	13
WHY SHOULD ONE ALWAYS LIE ABOUT SUCH MATTERS?	113	TAME CAT	2
WHERE ONE NEEDS ONE'S BRAINS ALL THE TIME.	117	THE LAKE ISLE	16
HOLDING LINES IN ONE COLOUR.	120	GAME OF CHESS	5
GLAD TO LEND ONE DRY CLOTHING.	121	PROVINC DESERT	27
"HERE SUCH A ONE WALKED.	122	PROVINC DESERT	43
"HERE ONE MAN HASTENED HIS STEP.	122	PROVINC DESERT	46
"HERE ONE LAY PANTING."	122	PROVINC DESERT	47
TWO MEN TOSSING A COIN, ONE KEEPING A CASTLE,	122	PROVINC DESERT	66
ONE SET ON THE HIGHWAY TO SING.	122	PROVINC DESERT	67
OUR DEFENCE IS NOT YET MADE SURE, NO ONE CAN LET HIS FRIEND RETURN.	127	BOWMEN OF SHU	8
AND ONE MAY HE HAD YOU SEND FOR ME,	135	EXILE'S LETTER	38
ONE BIRD CASTS ITS GLEAM ON ANOTHER.	139	SENNIN POEM	3
ARE ALL FOLDED INTO ONE DARKNESS,	142	UNMOVING CLOUD	4
LET US DUMP OUR HATREDS INTO ONE BUNCH AND BE DONE WITH THEM,	146	CANTILATIONS	2
IN A FEW YEARS NO ONE WILL REMEMBER THE BUFFO,	146	MONUMENTUM AER	3
NO ONE WILL REMEMBER THE TRIVIAL PARTS OF ME,	146	MONUMENTUM AER	4
ONE AT CHALAIS, ANOTHER AT MALEMORT	151	NEAR PERIGORD	12
SPREAD LIKE THE FINGER-TIPS OF ONE FRAIL HAND;	152	NEAR PERIGORD	00
BUT ONE HUGE BACK HALF-COVERED UP WITH PINE,	152	NEAR PERIGORD	33
AND EVERY ONE HALF JEALOUS OF MAENT?	153	NEAR PERIGORD	76
TO SING ONE THING WHEN YOUR SONG MEANS ANOTHER,	153	NEAR PERIGORD	89
SPOILING HIS VISIT, WITH A YEAR BEFORE THE NEXT ONE.	154	NEAR PERIGORD	113
NO ONE HEARS SAVE ARRIMON LUC D'ESPARO--	154	NEAR PERIGORD	119
NO ONE HEARS AUGHT SAVE THE GRACIOUS SOUND OF COMPLIMENTS.	154	NEAR PERIGORD	120
OR NO ONE SEES IT, AND EN BERTRANS PROSPERED?	155	NEAR PERIGORD	126
SHE WHO COULD NEVER LIVE SAVE THROUGH ONE PERSON,	157	NEAR PERIGORD	189
SHE WHO COULD NEVER SPEAK SAVE TO ONE PERSON,	157	NEAR PERIGORD	190
BECAUSE ONE HAS JUST, AT LAST, FOUND THEM?	158	PSYCHOLOG HOUR	25
BUT YOUR SMILE PULLS ONE WAY	162	CABARET DANCER	41
THAT SOME ONE ELSE HAS PAID FOR,	163	CABARET DANCER	57
THERE IS A PLACE--BUT NO ONE ELSE KNOWS IT--	166	FISH & SHADOW	14
ONE TO BE DULL IN;	168	OF AROUET	26
I AM GONE FROM ONE JOY,	176	LANGUE D'OC: 3	60
FROM ONE I LOVED NEVER SO MUCH,	176	LANGUE D'OC: 3	61
SHE BY ONE TOUCH	176	LANGUE D'OC: 3	62
HAVE DRIVEN HIS WIFE FROM ONE RELIGIOUS EXCESS TO ANOTHER.	178	MOEURS CON: 1	8
"THE TIP'S A GOOD ONE, AS FOR LITERATURE	194	MR. NIXON	16
"AND NO ONE KNOWS, AT SIGHT, A MASTERPIECE,	194	MR. NIXON	18
ONE SUBSTANCE AND ONE COLOUR	197	ENVOI (1919)	15
ONE SUBSTANCE AND ONE COLOUR	197	ENVOI (1919)	15
AND ONE AMONG THEM LOOKED AT ME WITH FACE OFFENDED,	211	SEXTUS PROP: 2	38
UPON THE ONE RAFT, VICTOR AND CONQUERED TOGETHER,	218	SEXTUS PROP: 6	3
ONE TANGLE OF SHADOWS.	218	SEXTUS PROP: 6	5
ONE RAFT ON THE VEILED FLOOD OF ACHERON,	219	SEXTUS PROP: 6	11
"WAS ONCE THE SLAVE OF ONE PASSION:"	219	SEXTUS PROP: 6	27
ONE DENYING YOUR PRESTIGE,	222	SEXTUS PROP: 8	30
AND ONE RAFT BEARS OUR FATES	223	SEXTUS PROP: 9	5
AND ONE OF THE LOT WAS GIVEN TO LUST.	224	SEXTUS PROP:10	11
ALL THINGS ARE FORGIVEN FOR ONE NIGHT OF YOUR GAMES. . .	227	SEXTUS PROP:11	39
BUT IN ONE BED, IN ONE BED ALONE, MY DEAR LYNCEUS	228	SEXTUS PROP:12	15
BUT IN ONE BED, IN ONE BED ALONE, MY DEAR LYNCEUS	228	SEXTUS PROP:12	15
NOT ONE HAS ENQUIRED THE CAUSE OF THE WORLD,	228	SEXTUS PROP:12	25
ONE MUST HAVE RESONANCE, RESONANCE AND SONORITY . . . LIKE A GOOSE.	230	SEXTUS PROP:12	65
HAD NOT ONE STYLE FROM BIRTH, BUT TRIED AND PRIED	235	TO WHISTLER	16
ALL ONE CAN SAY OF THIS REFINING MEDIUM	239	MOYEN SENSUEL	35
WHERE ONE GETS MORE CHANCES	242	MOYEN SENSUEL	103
ONE OF THOSE FIRM-FACED INSPECTING WOMEN, WHO	243	MOYEN SENSUEL	156
ALAS, EHEU, ONE QUESTION THAT SORELY VEXES	244	MOYEN SENSUEL	161
THINKS ONE IDENTITY IS	244	MOYEN SENSUEL	173
THE PROMINENT HAUNTS, WHERE ONE MIGHT RECOGNIZE HIM,	245	MOYEN SENSUEL	203
WAS NEVER ONE OF WHOM ONE SPEAKS AS "BRAZEN'D."	245	MOYEN SENSUEL	206

ONE -- OPENING

	PAGE	TITLE	LINE
ONE (CONTINUED)			
WAS NEVER ONE OF WHOM ONE SPEAKS AS "BRAZEN'D." ...	245	MOYEN SENSUEL	206
I KNEW A TOURIST AGENT, ONE WHOSE ART IS	245	MOYEN SENSUEL	209
WAS PURER IN ITS LOVE OF ONE LOCALITY, ...	245	MOYEN SENSUEL	212
THOUGH I KNOW ONE, A VERY BASE DETRACTOR, ...	246	MOYEN SENSUEL	221
IS ONE DAY BLOWN UP LARGE, THE NEXT, SUCKED IN? ...	261	ALF'S FIFTH	21
ONE THING AMONG ALL THINGS YOU WILL NOT	265	ALF'S TENTH	11
AND SCARCELY HEED ONE WORD OF WHAT YOU HEAR.	265	ALF'S NINTH	28
AT ONE O'CLOCK I GO TO LUNCH, ...	266	ALF'S ELEVENTH	7
AT ONE AND THREE THE POUND.	269	SAFE AND SOUND	4
ONES			
OF TH' UNBOUNDED ONES, BUT YE, THAT HIDE	21	IN DURANCE	29
(MY COUNTRY, I'VE SAID YOUR MORALS AND YOUR THOUGHTS ARE STALE ONES, ...	243	MOYEN SENSUEL	149
BUT SURELY THE WORST OF YOUR OLD-WOMEN ARE THE MALE ONES.)	243	MOYEN SENSUEL	150
GIVE T'OLD ONES A NEWER TWIST	261	ALF'S SIXTH	8
ONE'S			
WHERE ONE NEEDS ONE'S BRAINS ALL THE TIME.	117	THE LAKE ISLE	16
ONESTI			
BLAGUEUR! "CON GLI OCCHI ONESTI E TARDI,"	181	MOEURS CON: 7	6
ONLY			
IT IS ONLY THAT I AM GLAD, ...	5	LA FRAISNE	33
AS THEN ONLY IN DREAMS, ...	9	NA AUDIART	47
AND BURST FORTH TO THE WINDOWS ONLY WHILES OR WHILES	21	IN DURANCE	31
BUT IS FIT ONLY TO ROT IN WOMANISH PEACE	29	ALTAFORTE	27
AH GOD, THE LOBA! AND MY ONLY MATE!	31	PIERE VIDAL	44
MOVES ONLY NOW A CLINGING TENUOUS GHOST.	87	THE SPRING	13
YOU WHO CAN ONLY SPEAK, ...	92	THE REST	11
AND SENT ME ONLY YOUR HANDMAIDS.	96	TO KALON	2
AND THERE WILL BE ONLY THE MORE CONFUSION, ...	98	THE BELLAIRES	26
IT IS ONLY IN SMALL DOGS AND THE YOUNG	104	THE SEEING EYE	9
ONLY EMOTION REMAINS.	114	EPILOGUE	9
TO "CHLORIS CHASTE AND COLD," HIS "ONLY CHLORIS."	118	THREE POETS	4
IF ONLY THEY COULD BE OF THAT FELLOWSHIP, ...	134	EXILE'S LETTER	10
AND NOW I SEE ONLY THE RIVER, ...	137	ON RIVER KIANG	4
HE WROTE THAT PRAISE ONLY TO SHOW HE HAD	155	NEAR PERIGORD	148
ONLY ANOTHER MAN'S NOTE:	159	PSYCHOLOG HOUR	42
WANTING ONLY WHAT	174	LANGUE D'OC: 3	11
SHOWED ONLY WHEN THE DAYLIGHT FELL	193	BRENNBAUM	6
THAT ONLY SENTIMENTAL STUFF WILL SELL!)	242	MOYEN SENSUEL	118
WILL LONG ONLY TO BE A SOCIAL FUNCTION, ...	244	MOYEN SENSUEL	176
WHEN I WAS ONLY A YOUNGSTER, ...	271	OLE KATE	1
ONTO (2)			
ONWARD			
THAT HE WILL WORK ERE HE PASS ONWARD, ...	66	THE SEAFARER	75
ONWARD TH' 'UNGRY BLOKES, ...	257	BREAD BRIGADE	5
ONYX			
WHEN THE SYRIAN ONYX IS BROKEN.	219	SEXTUS PROP: 6	25
OOT			
SING: TOODLE DOODLEDE OOT!	271	OLE KATE	2
OPAL			
THOU HOODED OPAL, THOU ETERNAL PEARL, ...	50	THE FLAME	29
OPEN			
O' SHIPS AND THE OPEN SEA.	33	GOODLY FERE	4
BUT AYE LOVED THE OPEN SEA.	33	GOODLY FERE	24
AND MUSIC FLOWING THROUGH ME SEEMED TO OPEN	39	FOR PSYCHE	8
OPEN LIES THE LAND, YET THE STEELY GOING	68	APPARUIT	10
GO WITH AN OPEN SPEECH.	89	COMMISSION	23
WHAT DOORS ARE OPEN TO FINE COMPLIMENT?"	153	NEAR PERIGORD	75
SINGS IN THE OPEN MEADOW--AT LEAST THE KODAK SAYS SO--	161	CABARET DANCER	4
SHE COULD SCARCELY KEEP HER EYES OPEN	225	SEXTUS PROP:10	22
OPENED			
THE SWIRLING SPHERE HAS OPENED	169	PHANOPOEIA	8
ITS HOME MAIL IS STILL OPENED BY ITS MATERNAL PARENT	179	MOEURS CON: 4	2
AND ITS OFFICE MAIL MAY BE OPENED BY	179	MOEURS CON: 4	3
OPENING			
AS ANADYOMENE IN THE OPENING	204	MEDALLION	7
AND SHE THEN OPENING MY EYELIDS FALLEN IN SLEEP,	220	SEXTUS PROP: 7	7

PAGE 290

OPERA -- ORE

	PAGE	TITLE	LINE
OPERA			
IN ROME, AFTER THE OPERA,	182	MOEURS CON: 7	18
OPINION			
GO OUT AND DEFY OPINION,	89	COMMISSION	33
TRUE, HE HAS PRAISED HER, BUT IN SOME OPINION	155	NEAR PERIGORD	147
ACCEPT OPINION. THE "NINETIES" TRIED YOUR GAME	194	MR. NIXON	23
DIFFERENCE OF OPINION WITH LYGDAMUS	214	SEXTUS PROP: 4	SUB
OPPOSING			
BUT AH! WHEN I SEE THE STANDARDS GOLD, VAIR, PURPLE, OPPOSING	28	ALTAFORTE	4
AND THE WINDS SHRIEK THROUGH THE CLOUDS MAD, OPPOSING,	28	ALTAFORTE	11
SPIKED BREAST TO SPIKED BREAST OPPOSING!	28	ALTAFORTE	15
HIS LONE MIGHT 'GAINST ALL DARKNESS OPPOSING.	29	ALTAFORTE	24
THE MAN WHO FEARS WAR AND SQUATS OPPOSING	29	ALTAFORTE	25
THERE'S NO SOUND LIKE TO SWORDS SWORDS OPPOSING,	29	ALTAFORTE	32
OPPOSITE			
ITS PARENT OF THE OPPOSITE GENDER.	179	MOEURS CON: 4	4
AND A MINUTE CROWD OF SMALL BOYS CAME FROM OPPOSITE,	224	SEXTUS PROP:10	4
OPPRESSION			
SPEAK AGAINST UNCONSCIOUS OPPRESSION,	88	COMMISSION	6
BE AGAINST ALL FORMS OF OPPRESSION.	89	COMMISSION	25
OPPRESSORS			
BEAR TO THEM MY CONTEMPT FOR THEIR OPPRESSORS.	88	COMMISSION	3
BEAR MY CONTEMPT OF OPPRESSORS.	88	COMMISSION	5
OPPROBRIUM			
LET US APPLY IT IN ALL ITS OPPROBRIUM	99	SALVATIONISTS	5
'OPS			
DID I 'EAR IT WHILE PICKIN' 'OPS;	262	ALF'S SEVENTH	3
OPULENT			
OPULENT SILENCE.	99	SALVATIONISTS	10
WILL BE A STUFFY, OPULENT SORT OF FUNGUS	161	CABARET DANCER	14
OR (136)			
ORANGE			
FLARE UP WITH SCARLET ORANGE ON STIFF STALKS	162	CABARET DANCER	20
RED OVERWROUGHT WITH ORANGE AND ALL MADE	197	ENVOI (1919)	14
ORANGE-COLOURED			
THE ORANGE-COLOURED ROSE-LEAVES,	108	TS'AI CHI'H	2
ORBAJOSA			
EUHENIA WILL HAVE A FONDA IN ORBAJOSA.	163	CABARET DANCER	67
ORCHARD			
IN ORCHARD UNDER THE HAWTHORNE	177	LANGUE D'OC: 4	1
HERE IN THE ORCHARD WHERE THE BIRDS COMPLAIN,	177	LANGUE D'OC: 4	17
ORCHARDS			
MY ORCHARDS DO NOT LIE LEVEL AND WIDE	209	SEXTUS PROP: 1	53
ORCHID			
HIS NEW FOUND ORCHID. . . .	199	MAUBERLEY: 2	11
(ORCHID), MANDATE	200	MAUBERLEY: 2	32
ORCHIDS			
FLASH BETWEEN THE ORCHIDS AND CLOVER,	139	SENNIN POEM	2
ORCUS			
THE SHADOWY FLOWERS OF ORCUS	67	DORIA	10
ORDER			
THOUGHTS OF HER ARE OF DREAM'S ORDER:	72	DIEU! QU'IL	12
THE SOCIAL ORDER	115	SOCIAL ORDER	T
WE HAVE KEPT OUR ERASERS IN ORDER.	207	SEXTUS PROP: 1	11
(AND TO IMPERIAL ORDER)	229	SEXTUS PROP:12	39
ORDERED			
"WHO HAS ORDERED A BOOK ABOUT HEROES?	210	SEXTUS PROP: 2	18
ORDERLY			
THE MOST PRUDENT, ORDERLY, AND DECOROUS!	161	CABARET DANCER	8
ORDER-TO-WRITE			
AND I HAVE MOPED IN THE EMPEROR'S GARDEN, AWAITING AN ORDER-TO-WRITE!	129	THE RIVER SONG	19
ORDINARY			
AND ORDINARY PEOPLE TOUCH ME NOT	20	IN DURANCE	13
IN ORDINARY PLACES.	36	FRANCESCA	7
ORE			
AND MY VENTRICLES DO NOT PALPITATE TO CAESARIAL OPE ROTUNDOS,	218	SEXTUS PROP: 5	53

PAGE 291

ORFEO -- OTHERS

	PAGE	TITLE	LINE
ORFEO			
ORFEO	206	SEXTUS PROP	EPI
ORFEVRERIE			
NO GAWDS ON HER SNOWY HANDS, NO ORFEVRERIE,	214	SEXTUS PROP: 4	19
ORGANIZATION			
AN ORGANIZATION FOR THE SUPPRESSION OF SIN.	246	MOYEN SENSUEL	230
ORGIES			
BRINGING THE GRECIAN ORGIES INTO ITALY,	207	SEXTUS PROP: 1	4
ORGIES OF VINTAGES, AN EARTHERN IMAGE OF SILENUS	211	SEXTUS PROP: 2	29
ORIEL			
STRAIGHT, THEN SHONE THINE ORIEL AND THE STUNNED LIGHT	68	APPARUIT	15
ORL			
COULD YEH SWAP TH' BRAINS OF ORL THIS LOT	270	OF 600 M.P.'S	19
ORNAMENT			
SHE WOULD SIT LIKE AN ORNAMENT ON MY PYRE.	213	SEXTUS PROP: 3	31
ORNAMENTAL			
OR AN ORNAMENTAL DEATH WILL BE HELD TO YOUR DEBIT,	221	SEXTUS PROP: 8	2
IS THE ORNAMENTAL GODDESS FULL OF ENVY?	221	SEXTUS PROP: 8	11
ORNAMENTED			
THE HORSES ARE WELL TRAINED, THE GENERALS HAVE IVORY ARROWS AND QUIVERS ORNAMENTED WITH FISH-SKIN.	127	BOWMEN OF SHU	19
ORPHEUS			
FOR ORPHEUS TAMED THE WILD BEASTS--	208	SEXTUS PROP: 1	42
ORTUS			
ORTUS	84	ORTUS	T
OSSA			
NEITHER WOULD I WARBLE OF TITANS, NOR OF OSSA	217	SEXTUS PROP: 5	39
OSTENDE			
"CONNAISSEZ-VOUS OSTENDE?"	111	BLACK SLIPPERS	6
OTHER			
WILL LAUGH YOUR VERSES TO EACH OTHER,	14	FAMAM CANO	11
THEIR ECHOES PLAY UPON EACH OTHER IN THE TWILIGHT	16	PRAISE YSOLT	9
AS NE'ER HAD I OTHER, AND WHEN THE WIND BLOWS,	23	MARVOIL	35
OH, I KNOW YOU WOMEN FROM THE "OTHER FOLK,"	53	AU JARDIN	20
I'LL HAVE NO OTHER LOVE AT ANY COST.	105	DOMPNA POIS	10
THE GURGLING ITALIAN LADY ON THE OTHER SIDE OF THE RESTAURANT	111	BLACK SLIPPERS	7
AND HIGH OVER THE WILLOWS, THE FINE BIRDS SING TO EACH OTHER, AND LISTEN,	129	THE RIVER SONG	28
AND THE GIRLS SINGING BACK AT EACH OTHER,	136	EXILE'S LETTER	59
OUR HORSES NEIGH TO EACH OTHER	137	TAKING LEAVE	8
"IT IS NOT THAT THERE ARE NO OTHER MEN	142	UNMOVING CLOUD	24
FOR AFTER DEATH THERE COMES NO OTHER CALAMITY.	164	QUINTUS SEPTIM	11
THE OTHER IS LITTLE BESIDE IT.	168	OF AROUET	29
AND THE OTHER WAS RATHER LIKE MY BUST BY GAUDIER,	181	MOEURS CON: 7	13
WITH OTHER STRATA	196	HUGH SELWIN:12	15
CONDUCT, ON THE OTHER HAND, THE SOUL	196	HUGH SELWIN:12	21
THE MAKER OF IT, SOME OTHER MOUTH,	197	ENVOI (1919)	20
AND THE OTHER WOMAN "HAS NOT ENTICED ME	215	SEXTUS PROP: 4	29
SUCH DERELICTIONS HAVE DESTROYED OTHER YOUNG LADIES AFORETIME,	221	SEXTUS PROP: 8	7
NOR CAN I SHIFT MY PAINS TO OTHER,	221	SEXTUS PROP: 7	35
READ BENNETT OR SOME OTHER FLACCID FLATTERER.	240	MOYEN SENSUEL	66
UPON A TALE, TO COMBAT OTHER TRACTS,	241	MOYEN SENSUEL	72
THEN THERE CAME OTHER NIGHTS, CAME SLOW BUT CERTAIN	243	MOYEN SENSUEL	133
SO RADWAY WALKED, QUITE LIKE THE OTHER MEN,	244	MOYEN SENSUEL	185
SOME OTHER QUAINT REMINDER OF THE OCCASION	245	MOYEN SENSUEL	197
TO STAND WITH OTHER	250	DONNA MI PREGA	92
WAS OTHER, OR THAT THIS CHEERFUL GIVER	263	ALF'S EIGHTH	6
MY SALES BEAT ALL THE OTHER TEN.	266	ALF'S ELEVENTH	3
SOME OTHER FELLER DO IT.	270	OF 600 M.P.'S	12
OTHERS			
OTHERS ARE BEAUTIFUL, NONE MORE, SOME LESS.	52	AU SALON	EPI
SOME OTHERS MAY OVERHEAR THEM,	88	CAUSA	2
MOVE OTHERS WITH IVORY CARS.	108	CH'U YUAN	4
"HAVE YOU SEEN ANY OTHERS, ANY OF OUR LOT,	119	THE GYPSY	2
WHEN ANYONE SAYS "RETURN," THE OTHERS ARE FULL OF SORROW.	127	BOWMEN OF SHU	6
AND OTHERS HELD ONTO ARROWS,	224	SEXTUS PROP:10	8

PAGE 292

OTHER'S -- OUT

	PAGE	TITLE	LINE
OTHER'S			
OR SOME OTHER'S THAT HE SINGS?	6	CINO	31
OU			
"EST-CE QUE VOUS AVEZ VU DES AUTRES--DES CAMARADES--AVEC DES SINGES OU DES OURS?"	119	THE GYPSY	EPI
OU NOUS AVIONS LOUE DES CHAISES	160	DANS OMNIBUS	22
OUCH			
RECORD "ODD'S BLOOD! OUCH! OUCH!" A PRAYER, HIS SWIFT REPENTANCE.	243	MOYEN SENSUEL	130
RECORD "ODD'S BLOOD! OUCH! OUCH!" A PRAYER, HIS SWIFT REPENTANCE.	243	MOYEN SENSUEL	130
OUR (103)			
OURS (3)			
OURSELVES			
WE SHALL GET OURSELVES RATHER DISLIKED.	99	SALVATIONISTS	2
'OUSE			
AND THINKS ABOUT A ROWTON 'OUSE	270	OF 600 M.P.'S	15
OUT			
AND ALL I KNEW WERE OUT, MY LORD, YOU	7	CINO	34
AND BADE HER BE OUT WITH ILL ADDRESS	11	OF THE GIBBET	11
GOD DAMN HIS HELL OUT SPEEDILY	12	OF THE GIBBET	42
SCRAWNY, BE-SPECTACLED, OUT AT HEELS, ...	14	FAMAM CANO	23
OUT OF MINE OWN SOUL,-KIN.	20	IN DURANCE	11
WELL THEN, SO CALL THEY, THE SWIRLERS OUT OF THE MIST OF MY SOUL, ...	20	IN DURANCE	21
THEY TAKE THE TROUBLE TO TEAR OUT THIS WALL HERE,	22	MARVOIL	24
HAVE SEEN THIS THING, OUT OF THEIR FAR COURSES	27	NIGHT LITANY	42
AYE HE SENT US OUT THROUGH THE CROSSED HIGH SPEARS	33	GOODLY FERE	9
THEY WHINED AS HE WALKED OUT CALM BETWEEN, ...	34	GOODLY FERE	43
YOU CAME IN OUT OF THE NIGHT	36	FRANCESCA	1
NOW YOU WILL COME OUT OF A CONFUSION OF PEOPLE, ...	36	FRANCESCA	3
OUT OF A TURMOIL OF SPEECH ABOUT YOU.	36	FRANCESCA	4
WHEN THE TRUMPET RANG OUT.	48	FROM HEINE: 7	32
BUT OUT SOMEWHERE BEYOND THE WORLDLY WAYS	49	OF SPLENDOUR	3
STRANGE WAYS AND WALLS ARE FASHIONED OUT OF IT. ...	49	OF SPLENDOUR	5
FOUGHT OUT THEIR STRIFE HERE, 'TIS A PLACE OF WONDER;	51	THE ALTAR	3
HOW MANY FACES I'D HAVE OUT OF MIND.	59	EXIT' CUIUSDAM	7
I HAVE READ OUT THE GOLD UPON THE WALL.	60	TOMB AKR CAAR	9
AND WEARIED OUT MY THOUGHT UPON THE SIGNS.	60	TOMB AKR CAAR	10
OH! I COULD GET ME OUT, DESPITE THE MARKS	60	TOMB AKR CAAR	29
OUT THROUGH THE GLASS-GREEN FIELDS. ...	60	TOMB AKR CAAR	31
THE BRANCHES GROW OUT OF ME, LIKE ARMS.	62	A GIRL	5
SEEK OUT A FOREIGN FASTNESS.	65	THE SEAFARER	39
BEATS OUT THE BREATH FROM DOOM-GRIPPED BODY.	66	THE SEAFARER	72
ALGAE REACH UP AND OUT, BENEATH	69	SUB MARE	6
OH TO BE OUT OF THIS, ...	70	THE PLUNGE	6
OH, BUT FAR OUT OF THIS!	70	THE PLUNGE	15
OUT, AND ALONE, AMONG SOME	70	THE PLUNGE	19
THIS MAN KNEW OUT THE SECRET WAYS OF LOVE, ...	73	JACOPO SELLAIO	1
FOR HERE WAS LOVE, WAS NOT TO BE DROWNED OUT.	73	THE PICTURE	2
AND HERE'S THE THING THAT LASTS THE WHOLE THING OUT:	73	JACOPO SELLAIO	5
OUT OF EREBUS, THE FLAT-LYING BREADTH, ...	76	THE ALCHEMIST	44
BREATH THAT IS STRETCHED OUT BENEATH THE WORLD: ...	76	THE ALCHEMIST	45
OUT OF EREBUS, OUT OF THE FLAT WASTE OF AIR, LYING BENEATH THE WORLD;	76	THE ALCHEMIST	46
OUT OF EREBUS, OUT OF THE FLAT WASTE OF AIR, LYING BENEATH THE WORLD;	76	THE ALCHEMIST	46
OUT OF THE BROWN LEAF-BROWN COLOURLESS	76	THE ALCHEMIST	47
OUR MALENESS LIFTS US OUT OF THE RUCK, ...	82	THE CONDOLENCE	5
O MY FELLOW SUFFERERS, WE WENT OUT UNDER THE TREES,	82	THE CONDOLENCE	7
GO OUT AND DEFY OPINION, ...	89	COMMISSION	33
YOU WHO CAN NOT WEAR YOURSELVES OUT	92	THE REST	9
WITH THEIR LARGE AND ANAEMIC EYES THEY LOOKED OUT UPON THIS CONFIGURATION.	93	LES MILLWIN	12
I HAVE BEATEN OUT MY EXILE.	93	THE REST	19
I WILL OUT YOU A GREEN COAT OUT OF CHINA;	94	INSTRUCTIONS	17
WHEN THE HOT WATER GIVES OUT OR GOES TEPID, ...	100	THE BATH TUB	2
WE WHO WENT OUT INTO THE FOUR A. M. OF THE WORLD	104	ANCORA	3
I WILL GO OUT A-SEARCHING, ...	105	DOMPNA POIS	17
ME OUT, KNOWING YOU HOLD ME SO FAST!	107	DOMPNA POIS	70
I WILL COME OUT FROM THE NEW THICKET	108	CH'U YUAN	9

PAGE 293

OUT

	PAGE	TITLE	LINE
OUT (CONTINUED)			
WHEN YOU CAME OUT IN THE MAGAZINES	114	EPILOGUE	3
AND NOW YOU ARE STALE AND WORN OUT,	114	EPILOGUE	5
SHE RUSHED OUT INTO THE SUNLIGHT AND SWARMED UP A COCOANUT PALM TREE,	118	CONTEMPORARIES	3
FORK OUT TO SOUTH AND NORTH.	121	PROVINC DESERT	5
WHEN WE SET OUT, THE WILLOWS WERE DROOPING WITH SPRING.	127	BOWMEN OF SHU	21
WHO NOW GOES DRUNKENLY OUT	128	BEAU TOILET	8
THE EMPEROR IN HIS JEWELLED CAR GOES OUT TO INSPECT HIS FLOWERS,	129	THE RIVER SONG	35
WHY SHOULD I CLIMB THE LOOK OUT?	130	RIVER-MER WIFE	14
HE GOES OUT TO HORI, TO LOOK AT THE WING-FLAPPING STORKS,	130	THE RIVER SONG	36
YOU DRAGGED YOUR FEET WHEN YOU WENT OUT.	131	RIVER-MER WIFE	19
AND I WILL COME OUT TO MEET YOU	131	RIVER-MER WIFE	28
TO WATCH OUT THE BARBAROUS LAND;	133	FRONTIER GUARD	5
AND WE ALL SPOKE OUT OUR HEARTS AND MINDS, AND WITHOUT REGRET.	134	EXILE'S LETTER	11
OUT CAME THE EAST OF KAN FOREMAN AND HIS COMPANY.	134	EXILE'S LETTER	23
AND YOU WOULD WALK OUT WITH ME TO THE WESTERN CORNER OF THE CASTLE,	135	EXILE'S LETTER	49
AND GO OUT THROUGH A THOUSAND MILES OF DEAD GRASS.	137	TAKING LEAVE	4
CLOUDS GROW OUT OF THE HILL	138	NEAR SHOKU	4
EMOTION IS BORN OUT OF HABIT.	139	SOUTH-FOLK	3
YESTERDAY WE WENT OUT OF THE WILD-GOOSE GATE,	139	SOUTH-FOLK	4
SPREAD OUT THEIR SOUNDS THROUGH THE GARDENS.	141	IDEA OF CHOAN	16
RIU'S HOUSE STANDS OUT ON THE SKY,	141	IDEA OF CHOAN	26
AND THE WIDE, FLAT ROAD STRETCHES OUT.	142	UNMOVING CLOUD	5
ARE BURSTING OUT WITH NEW TWIGS,	142	UNMOVING CLOUD	18
LET US GO OUT IN THE AIR A BIT.	145	SALUTATION 3RD	16
OH, NO, I WILL STICK IT OUT,	145	SALUTATION 3RD	27
UP AND OUT OF THEIR CARESSES.	147	BEFORE SLEEP	13
"MAENT, I LOVE YOU, YOU HAVE TURNED ME OUT.	151	NEAR PERIGORD	6
AND ALL THE WHILE YOU SING OUT THAT CANZONE,	151	NEAR PERIGORD	10
FOR SEPARATION WROUGHT OUT SEPARATION,	151	NEAR PERIGORD	24
TAKE THE WHOLE MAN, AND RAVEL OUT THE STORY.	152	NEAR PERIGORD	47
IS IT AN INTRIGUE TO RUN SUBTLY OUT,	153	NEAR PERIGORD	82
UP AND ABOUT AND IN AND OUT THE LAND,	153	NEAR PERIGORD	84
OR TAKE HIS "MAGNET" SINGER SETTING OUT,	154	NEAR PERIGORD	104
IN THE MID LOVE COURT, HE SINGS OUT THE CANZON,	154	NEAR PERIGORD	118
THE COMPACT, DE BORN SMOKED OUT, TREES FELLED	155	NEAR PERIGORD	124
ABOUT HIS CASTLE, CATTLE DRIVEN OUT!	155	NEAR PERIGORD	125
FURTHER AND OUT OF REACH, THE PURPLE NIGHT,	155	NEAR PERIGORD	131
AND THE "BEST CRAFTSMAN" SINGS OUT HIS FRIEND'S SONG,	155	NEAR PERIGORD	141
END THE DISCUSSION, RICHARD GOES OUT NEXT DAY	156	NEAR PERIGORD	157
AND OUR TWO HORSES HAD TRACED OUT THE VALLEYS;	157	NEAR PERIGORD	173
KNEW THE LOW FLOODED LANDS SQUARED OUT WITH POPLARS,	157	NEAR PERIGORD	174
I HAD LAID OUT JUST THE RIGHT BOOKS.	158	PSYCHOLOG HOUR	4
PEPITA HAS SUCH TO-MORROWS: WITH THE HANDS PUFFED OUT,	161	CABARET DANCER	10
PULLED BY THE KOHL AND ROUGE OUT OF RESEMBLANCE--	162	CABARET DANCER	29
TO BE LOOKING OUT ACROSS THE BRIGHT SEA,	164	QUINTUS SEPTIM	5
WHEN YOU COULD GO OUT IN A HIRED HANSOM	167	OF AROUET	2
TIME HAS DRIVEN ME OUT FROM THE FINE PLAISAUNCES,	167	OF AROUET	18
AND DELIA HERSELF FADING OUT,	168	OF AROUET	41
"AND THOU OUT HERE BENEATH THE PORCH OF STONE	172	LANGUE D'OC: 1	22
OUR LOVE COMES OUT	173	LANGUE D'OC: 2	11
THAT LOVE GOES OUT	174	LANGUE D'OC: 3	5
NOR WHEN I GO OUT.	174	LANGUE D'OC: 3	25
AND THOUGH I FEAR TO SPEAK OUT,	175	LANGUE D'OC: 3	35
OR TURN ME INSIDE OUT, AND ABOUT.	175	LANGUE D'OC: 3	47
TILL THE TRAIST MAN CRY OUT TO WARN	177	LANGUE D'OC: 4	3
NOW CRY THE BIRDS OUT, IN THE MEADOW MIST,	177	LANGUE D'OC: 4	12
"OUT OF THE WIND THAT BLOWS FROM HER,	177	LANGUE D'OC: 4	21
OUT OF MY LOVE WILL HER HEART NOT STIR.	177	LANGUE D'OC: 4	28
SHE WILL NEITHER STAY IN, NOR COME OUT.	179	MOEURS CON: 2	11
AND STICKING OUT ALL THE WAY ROUND;	181	MOEURS CON: 7	5
WHEN IT TURNED OUT HE MEANT MRS. WARD.	181	MOEURS CON: 7	12
FOR THREE YEARS, OUT OF KEY WITH HIS TIME,	187	E. P. ODE	1
IN A HALF SAVAGE COUNTRY, OUT OF DATE;	187	E. P. ODE	6

OUT -- OVER

	PAGE	TITLE	LINE
OUT (CONTINUED)			
CALIBAN CASTS OUT ARIEL.	189	HUGH SELWYN: 3	8
LAUGHTER OUT OF DEAD BELLIES.	190	HUGH SELWYN: 4	27
STILL DARTS OUT FAUN-LIKE FROM THE HALF-RUIN'D FACE,	192	YEUX GLAUQUES	18
M. VEROG, OUT OF STEP WITH THE DECADE,	193	SIENA MI FE	17
BUT SINGS NOT OUT THE SONG, NOR KNOWS	197	ENVOI (1919)	19
QUITE OUT OF PLACE AMID	201	AGE DEMANDED	23
WHAT FOOT BEAT OUT YOUR TIME-BAR,	207	SEXTUS PROP: 1	8
A NAME NOT TO BE WORN OUT WITH THE YEARS.	209	SEXTUS PROP: 1	73
SHALL BE YAWNED OUT ON MY LYRE--WITH SUCH INDUSTRY.	210	SEXTUS PROP: 2	5
"WHY WRENCH YOUR PAGE OUT OF ITS COURSE?	210	SEXTUS PROP: 2	24
THE STARS WILL POINT OUT THE STUMBLES,	212	SEXTUS PROP: 3	21
OUT WITH IT, TELL IT TO ME, ALL OF IT, FROM THE BEGINNING,	214	SEXTUS PROP: 4	11
WE SHALL SPIN LONG YARNS OUT OF NOTHING.	217	SEXTUS PROP: 5	36
NOR OF WELSH MINES AND THE PROFIT MARUS HAD OUT OF THEM.	217	SEXTUS PROP: 5	46
EACH MAN WHERE HE CAN, WEARING OUT THE DAY IN HIS MANNER.	218	SEXTUS PROP: 5	58
HOW MANY WORDS TALKED OUT WITH ABUNDANT CANDLES;	220	SEXTUS PROP: 7	3
INO IN HER YOUNG DAYS FLED PELLMELL OUT OF THEBES,	222	SEXTUS PROP: 8	21
THE MOON STILL DECLINED TO DESCEND OUT OF HEAVEN,	223	SEXTUS PROP: 9	3
AND TELL OUT THE LONG LIST OF HER TROUBLES.	223	SEXTUS PROP: 9	12
AND OUT OF TROAD, AND FROM THE CAMPANIA,	223	SEXTUS PROP: 9	17
LANGUIDLY YOU STRETCH OUT THE SNARE	226	SEXTUS PROP:11	15
OUT INTO THE CREPUSCULAR HALF-LIGHT, NOW AND THEN;	244	MOYEN SENSUEL	186
IT TWISTS ITSELF FROM OUT ALL NATURAL MEASURE;	249	DONNA MI PREGA	50
NOR TO SEEK OUT, SURELY,	250	DONNA MI PREGA	68
AND DAVID'S HARP LET OUT HEART-RENDING SQUEALS:	264	ALF'S NINTH	15
I GET THE KIDS OUT ON THE STREET	266	ALF'S ELEVENTH	5
AND THEN LENDS OUT THEIR PRINTED SLIPS	269	SAFE AND SOUND	19
OUTBLOTTED			
"YOUR GLORY IS NOT OUTBLOTTED BY VENOM,"	226	SEXTUS PROP:11	23
OUTCAST			
WEATHERED THE WINTER, WRETCHED OUTCAST	64	THE SEAFARER	15
OUTLAST			
SHALL OUTLAST OUR DAYS.	189	HUGH SELWYN: 3	12
OUTPUT			
"PROLIFIC NOYES" WITH OUTPUT UNDEFEATABLE).	240	MOYEN SENSUEL	50
OUTRIDERS			
DRAG ON THE SEVEN COACHES WITH OUTRIDERS.	141	IDEA OF CHOAN	3
OUTRIGHT			
THAT SHE GIVE ME OUTRIGHT	106	DOMPNA POIS	32
OUTRUN			
MY SOUL, I MEET THEE, WHEN THIS LIFE'S OUTRUN,	39	BLANDULA	6
AND THAT WHICH FLEETETH DOTH OUTRUN SWIFT TIME	40	ROME	14
OUTSIDE			
COMPLEYNT OF A GENTLEMAN WHO HAS BEEN WAITING OUTSIDE FOR SOME TIME	172	LANGUE D'OC: 1	SUB
OUTSIDE YOUR SET BUT, HAVING KEPT FAITH IN YOUR EYES,	247	PIERROTS	23
OUT-SPREAD			
RAN CRYING WITH OUT-SPREAD HAIR,	219	SEXTUS PROP: 6	34
OUTSTRETCHED			
I GUZZLE WITH OUTSTRETCHED EARS.	214	SEXTUS PROP: 4	12
OUT-WEARIERS			
OUT-WEARIERS OF APOLLO WILL, AS WE KNOW, CONTINUE THEIR MARTIAN GENERALITIES,	207	SEXTUS PROP: 1	10
OVER			
SPREAD HIS LEAVES OVER ME, AND THE YOKE	4	LA FRAISNE	11
AND NONE FLED OVER LONG.	30	PIERE VIDAL	12
OVER THE SHARPENED TEETH AND PURPLING LIPS!	30	PIERE VIDAL	15
UPON THESE LIDS THAT LIE OVER US	35	THE EYES	3
I WOULD THAT THE COOL WAVES MIGHT FLOW OVER MY MIND,	36	FRANCESCA	8
SEEMED OVER ME TO HOVER LIGHT AS LEAVES	39	FOR PSYCHE	6
WITH TIMES TOLD OVER AS WE TELL BY ROTE;	43	SATIEMUS	17
THY HEAD WILL I COVER OVER	47	FROM HEINE: 7	5
OVER BEYOND THE MOON THERE,	53	AU JARDIN	16
THE RIVER? THOU WAST OVER YOUNG.	60	TOMB AKR CAAR	17
FOR THIS THERE'S NO MOON-LOFTY MAN OVER EARTH'S MIDST,	65	THE SEAFARER	40
OVER THE WHALE'S ACRE, WOULD WANDER WIDE.	65	THE SEAFARER	61

PAGE 295

OVER -- OVERHEAD

	PAGE	TITLE	LINE
OVER (CONTINUED)			
TILL THE ROSE-TIME WILL BE OVER, ...	67	THE CLOAK	2
YOU, I WOULD HAVE FLOW OVER ME LIKE WATER, ...	70	THE PLUNGE	14
OVER FAIR MEADOWS, ...	107	COMING OF WAR	16
OVER THE COOL FACE OF THAT FIELD, ...	107	COMING OF WAR	17
DUST DRIFTS OVER THE COURT-YARD, ...	108	LIU CH'E	2
BEND OVER WITH HEAVY HEADS.	112	IONE, DEAD	4
I HAVE CREPT OVER OLD RAFTERS, ...	121	PROVINC DESERT	14
OVER THE DRONNE, ...	121	PROVINC DESERT	16
OVER A STREAM FULL OF LILIES.	121	PROVINC DESERT	17
I HAVE LOOKED BACK OVER THE STREAM	121	PROVINC DESERT	33
WALKED OVER EN BERTRAN'S OLD LAYOUT, ...	122	PROVINC DESERT	39
I HAVE WALKED OVER THESE ROADS;	123	PROVINC DESERT	80
AND HIGH OVER THE WILLOWS, THE FINE BIRDS SING TO EACH OTHER, AND LISTEN, ...	129	THE RIVER SONG	28
OVER A THOUSAND GATES, OVER A THOUSAND DOORS ARE THE SOUNDS OF SPRING SINGING, ...	129	THE RIVER SONG	31
OVER A THOUSAND GATES, OVER A THOUSAND DOORS ARE THE SOUNDS OF SPRING SINGING, ...	129	THE RIVER SONG	31
PEACH BOUGHS AND APRICOT BOUGHS HANG OVER A THOUSAND GATES, ...	131	AT TEN-SHIN	2
THOUGH THEY HANG IN THE SAME WAY OVER THE BRIDGERAIL.	131	AT TEN-SHIN	8
AND THE MOON FALLS OVER THE PORTALS OF SEI-GO-YO.	131	AT TEN-SHIN	11
OVER THE GRASS IN THE WEST GARDEN;	131	RIVER-MER WIFE	6
NIGHT AND DAY ARE GIVEN OVER TO PLEASURE	132	AT TEN-SHIN	25
A TURMOIL OF WARS-MEN, SPREAD OVER THE MIDDLE KINGDOM, ...	133	FRONTIER GUARD	15
AND MY SPIRIT SO HIGH IT WAS ALL OVER THE HEAVENS,	135	EXILE'S LETTER	32
I HAD TO BE OFF TO SO, FAR AWAY OVER THE WATERS,	135	EXILE'S LETTER	34
OVER ROADS TWISTED LIKE SHEEP'S GUTS.	135	EXILE'S LETTER	41
THE SMOKE-FLOWERS ARE BLURRED OVER THE RIVER.	137	ON RIVER KIANG	2
WHO BOW OVER THEIR CLASPED HANDS AT A DISTANCE. ...	137	TAKING LEAVE	7
COVER OVER THE DARK PATH	138	CITY OF CHOAN	4
LICE SWARM LIKE ANTS OVER OUR ACCOUTREMENTS.	139	SOUTH-FOLK	8
CROWD OVER THE THOUSAND GATES, ...	141	IDEA OF CHOAN	18
OVER YOUR GRAVE.	146	MONUMENTUM AER	9
STILL SIGH OVER ESTABLISHED AND NATURAL FACT	148	FRATRES MINORE	3
HARD OVER BRIVE--FOR EVERY LADY A CASTLE, ...	151	NEAR PERIGORD	13
LIE LITTLE STRIPS OF PARCHMENT COVERED OVER, ...	154	NEAR PERIGORD	99
ROSE OVER US; AND WE KNEW ALL THAT STREAM, ...	157	NEAR PERIGORD	172
THE SOUL OF THE SALMON-TROUT FLOATS OVER THE STREAM	166	FISH & SHADOW	2
THE PARKS WITH THE SWARDS ALL OVER DEW, ...	167	OF AROUET	19
TO RULE OVER US.	189	HUGH SELWYN: 3	24
WHEN THEY HAVE GOT OVER THE STRANGENESS, ...	208	SEXTUS PROP: 1	41
THE SONGS SHALL BE A FINE TOMB-STONE OVER THEIR BEAUTY.	209	SEXTUS PROP: 1	64
SADNESS HUNG OVER THE HOUSE, AND THE DESOLATED FEMALE ATTENDANTS	214	SEXTUS PROP: 4	22
AND TO NAME OVER THE CENSUS OF MY CHIEFS IN THE ROMAN CAMP.	216	SEXTUS PROP: 5	3
MAY THE FATES WATCH OVER MY DAY.	216	SEXTUS PROP: 5	22
NOR OF CAUSEWAYS OVER PELION, ...	217	SEXTUS PROP: 5	41
MOVING NAKED OVER ACHERON	218	SEXTUS PROP: 6	2
WHILE A BLACK VEIL WAS OVER HER STARS, ...	222	SEXTUS PROP: 8	26
SO SPOKE. AND THE NOOSE WAS OVER MY NECK.	224	SEXTUS PROP:10	13
THE WATERS OF STYX POURED OVER THE WOUND:	230	SEXTUS PROP:12	74
NOW OVER AND SPENT, ...	236	MIDDLE-AGED	14
OVER THE DYING HALF-WITS BLOW, ...	265	ALF'S TENTH	5
OVER THE EMPTY-HEADED, AND THE SLOW	265	ALF'S TENTH	6
AND LET THE BLIGHTERS START IT ALL OVER AGAIN. ...	265	ALF'S NINTH	30
OVERBLOTTED			
BEING BUT THIS OVERBLOTTED	203	MAUBERLEY: 4	15
OVERCAST			
THE WORLD O'ERSHADOWED, SOILED AND OVERCAST, ...	36	THE YOUNG KING	7
OVERFILLED			
AND THE WILLOWS HAVE OVERFILLED THE CLOSE GARDEN.	128	BEAU TOILET	2
OVERFLOWING			
SOME OVERFLOWING RIVER IS RUN MAD, ...	32	PARACELSUS	13
OVERHEAD			
ON HOW WHITE DOGWOODS MURMURED OVERHEAD	43	SATIEMUS	13
THE MONKEYS MAKE SORROWFUL NOISE OVERHEAD.	130	RIVER-MER WIFE	14

OVERHEAR -- PACES

	PAGE	TITLE	LINE
OVERHEAR			
SOME OTHERS MAY OVERHEAR THEM, ...	88	CAUSA	2
LEST THEY SHOULD OVERHEAR THE DISTRESSING CHATTER	272	NATIONAL SONG	14
OVERLORDS			
YOU READ TO-DAY, HOW LONG THE OVERLORDS OF PERIGORD,	152	NEAR PERIGORD	50
OVER-PREPARED			
I HAD OVER-PREPARED THE EVENT, ...	158	PSYCHOLOG HOUR	1
I HAD OVER-PREPARED THE EVENT--	158	PSYCHOLOG HOUR	20
OVERSKIRT			
HER OVERSKIRT IS THE SAME SILK DYED IN PURPLE, ...	140	MULBERRY ROAD	14
OVERWEENING			
AND IS SO OVERWEENING: LOVE BY NAME.	248	DONNA MI PREGA	3
OVERWROUGHT			
RED OVERWROUGHT WITH ORANGE AND ALL MADE	197	ENVOI (1919)	14
OVID			
LONG SINCE FULLY DISCUSSED BY OVID.	148	FRATRES MINORE	4
OWE			
FOR TO YOU WE OWE A REAL DEBT:	101	AMITIES	14
OWL			
BUT THE BLACK OMINOUS OWL HOOT WAS AUDIBLE.	223	SEXTUS PROP: 9	4
OWLS			
"SHE STEWS PUFFED FROGS, SNAKE'S BONES, THE MOULTED FEATHERS OF SCREECH OWLS, ...	215	SEXTUS PROP: 4	33
OWN			
PEOTE! 'TIS HIS OWN SONGS?	6	CINO	30
THOUGH IT SHOULD RUN FOR ITS OWN GETTING, ...	14	FAMAM CANO	28
I AM HOMESICK AFTER MINE OWN KIND, ...	20	IN DURANCE	1
BUT I AM HOMESICK AFTER MINE OWN KIND.	20	IN DURANCE	3
MY HEART'S OWN HEARTH, ...	20	IN DURANCE	8
OUT OF MINE OWN SOUL-KIN, ...	20	IN DURANCE	11
FOR I AM HOMESICK AFTER MINE OWN KIND	20	IN DURANCE	12
AFTER MINE OWN KIND THAT KNOW, AND FEEL	20	IN DURANCE	15
BUT FOR ALL THAT, I AM HOMESICK AFTER MINE OWN KIND	20	IN DURANCE	23
WHAT DO YE OWN, YE NIGGARDS! THAT CAN BUY	32	PIERE VIDAL	57
ON HIS OWN FACE IN A GLASS	35	HIS OWN FACE	T
NOTHING THAT'S QUITE YOUR OWN.	61	PORTRAIT FEMME	29
MAY I FOR MY OWN SELF SONG'S TRUTH RECKON, ...	64	THE SEAFARER	1
AND DO NOT EVEN OWN CLOTHING.	85	SALUTATION	10
MURMURING FOR HIS OWN SATISFACTION	97	AESTHETICS	19
FOR IT'S YOUR OWN, AND YOUR GLANCE	105	DOMPNA POIS	22
WITH HER HAIR UNBOUND, AND HE HIS OWN SKIFFSMAN!	132	AT TEN-SHIN	33
WHILE BORN, HIS OWN CLOSE PURSE, HIS RABBIT WARREN,	153	NEAR PERIGORD	60
TAKE HIS OWN SPEECH, MAKE WHAT YOU WILL OF IT--	153	NEAR PERIGORD	79
DISPRAISES HIS OWN SKILL?--THAT'S AS YOU WILL.	155	NEAR PERIGORD	143
ITS OWN HEAD SWINGING, GRIPPED BY THE DEAD HAIR,	156	NEAR PERIGORD	165
"OF SELLING MY OWN WORKS.	194	MR. NIXON	15
FOR THE NOBLENESS OF THE POPULACE BROOKS NOTHING BELOW ITS OWN ALTITUDE.	230	SEXTUS PROP:12	64
SOME MEN WILL LIVE AS PRUDES IN THEIR OWN VILLAGE	245	MOYEN SENSUEL	207
BY QUALITY, BUT IS ITS OWN EFFECT UNENDINGLY	249	DONNA MI PREGA	30
FOLLOWING HIS OWN EMANATION.	250	DONNA MI PREGA	83
YOUR OWN MA' WARN'T NO BETTER	260	ALF'S FOURTH	12
TO OWN HIS COIN AGAIN.	269	SAFE AND SOUND	28
THEY'RE ME OWN," SHE SEZ TO ME, ...	270	OF 600 M.P.'S	22
OWNER			
MR. HECATOMB STYRAX, THE OWNER OF A LARGE ESTATE	178	MOEURS CON: 1	1
OXEN			
DARK OXEN, WHITE HORSES, ...	141	IDEA OF CHOAN	2
AND YOUR BARBECUES OF GREAT OXEN, ...	165	QUINTUS SEPTIM	13
SAILOR, OF WINDS; A PLOWMAN, CONCERNING HIS OXEN;	218	SEXTUS PROP: 5	55
OXFORD			
AND THAT OXFORD STREET SITE	262	ALF'S SEVENTH	14
OYSTERS			
HE PROPITIATES ME WITH OYSTERS, ...	46	FROM HEINE: 6	3
E. P. ODE POUR L'ELECTION DE SON SEPULCHRE	187	E. P. ODE	T
PACE			
THE TROUBLE IN THE PACE AND THE UNCERTAIN	74	THE RETURN	3
AND AT THE PACE THEY KEEP	111	IMAGE ORLEANS	5
PACES			
AND THEN RADWAY BEGAN TO GO THE PACES:	243	MOYEN SENSUEL	144

PAGE 297

PACIFIC -- PALAVER

	PAGE	TITLE	LINE
PACIFIC			
CORACLE OF PACIFIC VOYAGES, ...	203	MAUBERLEY: 4	18
PACK			
YOU GRABBED AT THE GOLD SURE; HAD NO NEED TO PACK CENTS	13	MESMERISM	19
EVEN THE GREY PACK KNEW ME AND KNEW FEAR.	30	PIERE VIDAL	13
SET LOOSE THE WHOLE CONSUMMATE PACK	52	AU SALON	14
HENRY VAN DYKE, WHO THINKS TO CHARM THE MUSE YOU PACK HER IN	239	MOYEN SENSUEL	21
PACKING			
WERE PACKING THEM IN THE GREAT WOODEN BOXES	96	AESTHETICS	11
PACT			
A PACT	89	A PACT	T
I MAKE A PACT WITH YOU, WALT WHITMAN--	89	A PACT	1
PAGANI'S			
PAGANI'S NOVEMBER 8	161	PAGANI'S NoV 8	T
PAGE			
"WHY WRENCH YOUR PAGE OUT OF ITS COURSE?	210	SEXTUS PROP: 2	24
PAGEANTRY			
KEPT AS BOLD TROPHIES OF OLD PAGEANTRY.	19	FOR E. MCC	18
PAGES			
I HAD ALMOST TURNED DOWN THE PAGES.	158	PSYCHOLOG HOUR	5
PAGES OF REINACH.	204	MEDALLION	8
FOR A FEW PAGES BROUGHT DOWN FROM THE FORKED HILL UNSULLIED?	207	SEXTUS PROP: 1	20
AND IN THE DYED PAGES OF CALVUS, ...	230	SEXTUS PROP:12	70
PAID			
WITH YELLOW GOLD AND WHITE JEWELS, WE PAID FOR SONGS AND LAUGHTER	134	EXILE'S LETTER	4
THAT SOME ONE ELSE HAS PAID FOR, ...	163	CABARET DANCER	57
PAIL			
FELL PLUMP INTO HER PAIL.	271	OLE KATE	14
PAIN			
THAT STRIVETH TO OURS ACROSS THE PAIN.	11	OF THE GIBBET	24
ME NOT FROM PAIN, ...	175	LANGUE D'OC: 3	31
ALAS! WHO'ER IT PLEASE OR PAIN, ...	175	LANGUE D'OC: 3	58
PAINS			
NOR CAN I SHIFT MY PAINS TO OTHER, ...	221	SEXTUS PROP: 7	35
PAINT			
NO MAN COULD PAINT SUCH THINGS WHO DID NOT KNOW.	73	JACOPO SELLAIO	2
WHY PAINT THESE DAYS? AN INSURANCE INSPECTOR	243	MOYEN SENSUEL	151
PAINTED			
--EYEBROWS PAINTED GREEN ARE A FINE SIGHT IN YOUNG MOONLIGHT, ...	136	EXILE'S LETTER	57
GRACEFULLY PAINTED--	136	EXILE'S LETTER	58
AND YOUR PAINTED GRIN ANOTHER, ...	162	CABARET DANCER	42
PAINTERS			
PAINTERS AND ADULTERERS.	192	YEUX GLAUQUES	8
PAINTING			
PAINTING THE FRONT OF THAT CHURCH;	121	PROVINC DESERT	31
PAIR			
AND A PAIR OF SCALES NOT TOO GREASY, ...	117	THE LAKE ISLE	9
THE MIND OF RADWAY, WHENE'ER HE FOUND A PAIR OF PURPLE STAYS OR	245	MOYEN SENSUEL	196
PAIRED			
THE PAIRED BUTTERFLIES ARE ALREADY YELLOW WITH AUGUST	131	RIVER-MER WIFE	23
PALACE			
KING SO'S TERRACED PALACE	128	THE RIVER SONG	11
THEIR CORDS TANGLE IN MIST, AGAINST THE BROCADE-LIKE PALACE.	129	THE RIVER SONG	26
AND THEN THE CROWD BROKE UP, YOU WENT NORTH TO SAN PALACE, ...	136	EXILE'S LETTER	71
HIS PALACE IS WHITE LIKE MARBLE, ...	237	ABU SALAMMAMM	5
HIS PALACE HAS NINETY-EIGHT WINDOWS, ...	237	ABU SALAMMAMM	6
HIS PALACE IS LIKE A CUBE CUT IN THIRDS, ...	237	ABU SALAMMAMM	7
PALACES			
ARCHES WORN OLD AND PALACES MADE COMMON, ...	40	ROME	3
PALAVER			
THERE WILL BE A CROWD OF YOUNG WOMEN DOING HOMAGE TO MY PALAVER, ...	208	SEXTUS PROP: 1	5

PALE -- PAPERS

	PAGE	TITLE	LINE
PALE			
AND ALL HER ROBE WAS WOVEN OF PALE GOLD.	49	OF SPLENDOUR	12
PALE SLOW GREEN SURGINGS OF THE UNDERWAVE,	69	SUB MARE	7
PALLOR OF SILVER, PALE LUSTRE OF LATONA,	76	THE ALCHEMIST	58
PALE CARNAGE BENEATH BRIGHT MIST.	92	APRIL	5
AS COOL AS THE PALE WET LEAVES	109	ALBA	1
I HAVE SEEN THE FIELDS, PALE, CLEAR AS AN EMERALD,	122	PROVINC DESERT	54
THAT FALLS THROUGH THE PALE GREEN WATER.	166	FISH & SHADOW	21
A FADED, PALE BROWNISH PHOTOGRAPH,	180	MOEURS CON: 5	2
A PALE GOLD, IN THE AFORESAID PATTERN,	202	AGE DEMANDED	41
PALETH			
THE YELLOW FLAME PALETH	35	THE EYES	6
BUT AGE FARES AGAINST HIM, HIS FACE PALETH,	66	THE SEAFARER	93
PALLAS			
I AM UP TO FOLLOW THEE, PALLAS.	147	BEFORE SLEEP	12
I AM UP TO FOLLOW THEE, PALLAS.	147	BEFORE SLEEP	19
HAVE YOU DENIED PALLAS GOOD EYES?	221	SEXTUS PROP: 8	13
PALLID			
PALLID THE LEASH-MEN!	74	THE RETURN	20
PALLOR			
PALLOR OF SILVER, PALE LUSTRE OF LATONA,	76	THE ALCHEMIST	58
PALM			
SHE RUSHED OUT INTO THE SUNLIGHT AND SWARMED UP A COCOANUT PALM TREE,	118	CONTEMPORARIES	3
AND YOU ON THAT GREAT MOUNTAIN OF A PALM--	152	NEAR PERIGORD	31
PALMS			
O PALMS OF LOVE, THAT IN YOUR WONTED WAYS	41	HER MONUMENT	15
HAVE I NOT TOUCHED THY PALMS AND FINGER-TIPS,	60	TOMB AKR CAAR	22
THE UNEXPECTED PALMS	202	AGE DEMANDED	42
PALPITATE			
AND MY VENTRICLES DO NOT PALPITATE TO CAESARIAL ORE ROTUNDOS,	218	SEXTUS PROP: 5	53
PALSIED			
NOW BEARS THE PALSIED CONTACT OF PHIDIPPUS.	111	SOCIETY	4
PAMPHLETS			
HAPPY WHO ARE MENTIONED IN MY PAMPHLETS,	209	SEXTUS PROP: 1	63
"YOUR PAMPHLETS WILL BE THROWN, THROWN OFTEN INTO A CHAIR	210	SEXTUS PROP: 2	22
PAN			
"'POLLO PHOIBEE, OLD TIN PAN, YOU	7	CINO	42
PAN IS DEAD	72	PAN IS DEAD	T
"PAN IS DEAD. GREAT PAN IS DEAD.	72	PAN IS DEAD	1
"PAN IS DEAD. GREAT PAN IS DEAD.	72	PAN IS DEAD	1
THE GOD PAN IS AFRAID TO ASK YOU,	110	TEMPORA	7
STRENGTHENED WITH RUSHES, TEGAEAN PAN,	211	SEXTUS PROP: 2	30
PANDARS			
LET US BE DONE WITH PANDARS AND JOBBERY,	145	SALUTATION 3RD	14
PANEL-SHAPED			
LOW, PANEL-SHAPED, A-LEVEL WITH HER KNEES,	49	OF SPLENDOUR	11
PANOPLY			
UPON MANHATTAN'S GORGEOUS PANOPLY,	245	MOYEN SENSUEL	188
PANTH'			
HIDMEN GAR TOI PANTH', HOS' ENI TROIEI	187	E. P. ODE	9
PANTHER			
THE BLACK PANTHER TREADS AT MY SIDE,	109	HEATHER	1
THE BLACK PANTHER LIES UNDER HIS ROSE TREE	231	CANTUS PLANUS	1
THE BLACK PANTHER LIES UNDER HIS ROSE TREE.	231	CANTUS PLANUS	5
PANTING			
HIGH WROUGHT OF MARBLE, AND THE PANTING BREATH	31	PIERE VIDAL	39
"HERE ONE LAY PANTING."	122	PROVINC DESERT	47
PANTOSOCRACY			
HERE RADWAY GREW, THE FRUIT OF PANTOSOCRACY,	239	MOYEN SENSUEL	39
PANTS			
HOW HIS COAT AND PANTS ADORN HIM!	46	FROM HEINE: 6	5
THE DRY EARTH PANTS AGAINST THE CANICULAR HEAT,	221	SEXTUS PROP: 8	4
PAPER			
OF A JAPANESE PAPER NAPKIN.	110	THE ENCOUNTER	5
THE MORNING PAPER TELLS ME	268	ANOTHER BIT	5
PAPERS			
RADWAY HAD READ THE VARIOUS EVENING PAPERS	241	MOYEN SENSUEL	91
THAT THE PAPERS WERE GETTIN' TOGETHER	262	ALF'S SEVENTH	5

PAGE 299

PAPERS -- PARK

	PAGE	TITLE	LINE
PAPERS (CONTINUED)			
OR A BUYER OF SPACE IN THE PAPERS.	264	ALF'S EIGHTH	34
AND IF THE PAPERS SELDOM SANG HIS PRAISE,	265	ALF'S NINTH	23
TO SELL THE PAPERS EARLY,	266	ALF'S ELEVENTH	6
I SEE BY THE MORNING PAPERS	268	ANOTHER BIT	1
FOR THE FRENCH HAVE COMIC PAPERS--	272	NATIONAL SONG	9
PAPIER-MACHE			
THIS PAPIER-MACHE, WHICH YOU SEE, MY FRIENDS,	63	PHASELLUS ILLE	1
PAPIOL			
"PAPIOL,	153	NEAR PERIGORD	69
PAPIOLS			
YOU WHORESON DOG, PAPIOLS, COME! LET'S TO MUSIC!	28	ALTAFORTE	2
PAPIOLS, PAPIOLS, TO THE MUSIC!	29	ALTAFORTE	31
PAPIOLS, PAPIOLS, TO THE MUSIC!	29	ALTAFORTE	31
PAPYRUS			
PAPYRUS	112	PAPYRUS	T
PAR			
PAR JAQUEMART"	198	MAUBERLEY: 1	2
PARA			
PARA THINA POLYPHLOISBOIO THALASSES.	181	MOEURS CON: 6	5
PARACELSUS			
PARACELSUS IN EXCELSIS	32	PARACELSUS	T
PARADE			
EN ROBE DE PARADE.	83	THE GARDEN	EPI
PARADISE			
WHAT HAST THOU, O MY SOUL, WITH PARADISE?	39	BLANDULA	1
THAT PARADISE IS HURLED TO NOTHINGNESS.	42	HER MONUMENT	48
AS YOUR VOICES, UNDER THE LARCHES OF PARADISE	75	THE ALCHEMIST	3
PARAGON			
(WHO KNOWS WHOSE WAS THAT PARAGON?)	10	FOR THIS YULE	23
PARAPHRASE			
THAN THE CLASSICS IN PARAPHRASE!	188	HUGH SELWYN: 2	8
PARASITIC			
THAT YOUR RELATIONSHIP IS WHOLLY PARASITIC;	101	AMITIES	9
PARC			
DU PARC MONCEAU,	160	DANS OMNIBUS	13
JE VIS LE PARC,	160	DANS OMNIBUS	20
PARCH			
LEST THEY SHOULD PARCH TOO SWIFTLY, WHERE SHE PASSES.	38	BALLATETTA	10
PARCHMENT			
FOR EVEN AS THOU ART HOLLOW BEFORE I FILL THEE WITH THIS PARCHMENT,	23	MARVOIL	37
EVEN AS THOU SHALT SOON HAVE THIS PARCHMENT.	23	MARVOIL	44
UPON WHITE PARCHMENT.	35	THE EYES	14
LIE LITTLE STRIPS OF PARCHMENT COVERED OVER,	154	NEAR PERIGORD	99
THERE IS SONG IN THE PARCHMENT; CATULLUS THE HIGHLY INDECOROUS,	230	SEXTUS PROP:12	68
PARDON			
HE PLEASE TO PARDON, AS TRUE PARDON IS,	37	THE YOUNG KING	38
HE PLEASE TO PARDON, AS TRUE PARDON IS,	37	THE YOUNG KING	38
YOU MIGHT PARDON SUCH SLIPS.	247	PIERROTS	24
PARDONS			
AS HIS PARDONS THE HABIT,	15	FAMAM CANO	46
PARDONS THE BOWMAN, DIES,	156	NEAR PERIGORD	159
PARENT			
ERINNA IS A MODEL PARENT,	103	THE PATTERNS	1
LALAGE IS ALSO A MODEL PARENT,	103	THE PATTERNS	3
ITS HOME MAIL IS STILL OPENED BY ITS MATERNAL PARENT	179	MOEURS CON: 4	2
ITS PARENT OF THE OPPOSITE GENDER.	179	MOEURS CON: 4	4
THE INFANT BEAMS AT THE PARENT,	180	MOEURS CON: 5	12
THE PARENT RE-BEAMS AT ITS OFFSPRING.	180	MOEURS CON: 5	13
PARFUM			
EST GROSSIERE ET LE PARFUM DES VIOLETTES UN	199	MAUBERLEY: 2	EPI
PARIS			
SPANISH AND PARIS, LOVE OF THE ARTS PART OF YOUR GEISHA-CULTURE!	163	CABARET DANCER	52
THEIR DOOR-YARDS WOULD SCARCELY KNOW THEM, OR PARIS.	208	SEXTUS PROP: 1	31
PARIS TOOK HELEN NAKED COMING FROM THE BED OF MENELAUS,	220	SEXTUS PROP: 7	14
PARK			
AND LEAVES YOU A PARK BENCH TO SIT ON	263	ALF'S EIGHTH	20

	PAGE	TITLE	LINE
PARKHURST'S			
THESE, AND YET GOD, AND DR. PARKHURST'S GOD, THE N. Y. JOURNAL	240	MOYEN SENSUEL	45
PARKS			
THE PARKS WITH THE SWARDS ALL OVER DEW,	167	OF AROUET	19
PARLANCE			
IN THE PARLANCE OF NICCOLO MACHIAVELLI:	178	MOEURS CON: 1	18
PARLIAMENTARIANS			
THOSE PARLIAMENTARIANS.	261	ALF'S SIXTH	24
THESE PARLIAMENTARIANS	262	ALF'S SIXTH	27
PARLIAMENTS			
"O BRITAIN, MUVVER OF PARLIAMENTS,	270	OF 600 M.P.'S	17
PARRIES			
AND ARNAUT PARRIES: "DID HE LOVE YOUR SISTER?	155	NEAR PERIGORD	146
PARRIETH			
STRUCK OF THE BLADE THAT NO MAN PARRIETH;	19	FOR E. MCC	4
STRUCK OF THE BLADE THAT NO MAN PARRIETH	19	FOR E. MCC	23
PART			
--PART OF IT--OF THY SONG-LIFE.	14	FAMAM CANO	16
NOBLE IN ANY PART	42	HER MONUMENT	54
OF LOVE, AND JOY THAT IS LOVE'S INMOST PART,	45	FROM HEINE: 5	10
LIFE IS THE LIVE MAN'S PART,	47	FROM HEINE: 7	18
WHO COULD PART HIM FROM HER BORDERS	72	DIEU! QU'IL	5
FOR YOU ARE NO PART, BUT A WHOLE,	84	ORTUS	15
WHERE THE HILLS PART	121	PROVINC DESERT	2
SPANISH AND PARIS, LOVE OF THE ARTS PART OF YOUR GEISHA-CULTURE!	163	CABARET DANCER	52
HERE IS A PART THAT'S SLIGHT, AND PART GONE WRONG,	235	TO WHISTLER	5
HERE IS A PART THAT'S SLIGHT, AND PART GONE WRONG,	235	TO WHISTLER	5
CAN BEAR HIS PART OF WIT	248	DONNA MI PREGA	8
PARTED			
PARTED BEFORE THEE.	68	APPARUIT	12
PARTHIAN			
"THE EUPHRATES DENIES ITS PROTECTION TO THE PARTHIAN AND APOLOGIZES FOR CRASSUS,"	216	SEXTUS PROP: 5	16
PARTHIANS			
THE PARTHIANS SHALL GET USED TO OUR STATUARY	219	SEXTUS PROP: 6	9
PARTICULAR			
THERE WAS NO PARTICULAR HASTE,	48	FROM HEINE: 8	2
THERE'S NO PARTICULAR HASTE.	48	FROM HEINE: 8	4
THAT'S SENT TO HOLLAND, A MOST PARTICULAR FEATURE,	239	MOYEN SENSUEL	20
PARTIES			
TO RUN SUCH TOURS. HE CALLS 'EM. . . . HOUSE PARTIES.	245	MOYEN SENSUEL	210
PARTING			
AND IF YOU ASK HOW I REGRET THAT PARTING:	136	EXILE'S LETTER	72
SUNSET LIKE THE PARTING OF OLD ACQUAINTANCES	137	TAKING LEAVE	6
PARTS			
NO ONE WILL REMEMBER THE TRIVIAL PARTS OF ME,	146	MONUMENTUM AER	4
IN THEIR PARTS OF THE CITY	158	PSYCHOLOG HOUR	14
PARTY			
THE FAVOUR OF YOUR PARTY; HAD BEEN WELL RECEIVED."	155	NEAR PERIGORD	149
PAS			
S'ILS NE SENTENT PAS LA MUSIQUE, QU'EST CE	199	MAUBERLEY: 2	EPI
S'ILS NE COMPRENNENT PAS LA POESIE,	199	MAUBERLEY: 2	EPI
PASIPHAE			
WITH YOU IS EUROPA AND THE SHAMELESS PASIPHAE.	38	LADY'S LIFE	8
IOPE, AND TYRO, AND PASIPHAE, AND THE FORMAL GIRLS OF ACHAIA,	223	SEXTUS PROP: 9	16
PASS			
CLOUD AND RAIN-TEARS PASS THEY FLEET!	7	CINO	49
PASS I ON	8	NA AUDIART	12
MADE YOU YOUR PASS MOST VALIANTLY	19	FOR E. MCC	8
MANY A SINGER PASS AND TAKE HIS PLACE	24	THUS NINEVEH	9
THAT STRIVE AND PLAY AND PASS,	35	HIS OWN FACE	5
DRINK OUR IMMORTAL MOMENTS; WE "PASS THROUGH."	50	THE FLAME	6
THAT MAN DOTH PASS THE NET OF DAYS AND HOURS	50	THE FLAME	10
PASS AND BE SILENT, RULLUS, FOR THE DAY	63	QUIES	2
THAT HE WILL WORK ERE HE PASS ONWARD,	66	THE SEAFARER	75
WHO BROUGHT THIS TO PASS?	133	FRONTIER GUARD	10
BORN OF A JONGLEUR'S TONGUE, FREELY TO PASS	153	NEAR PERIGORD	83
YOU ENTER AND PASS HALL AFTER HALL,	180	MOEURS CON: 5	18

PASS -- PATCHED

```
                                                                PAGE      TITLE               LINE
PASS  (CONTINUED)
    THOUGH IT WILL, OF COURSE, PASS OFF WITH SOCIAL
        SCIENCE  .......................................          244     MOYEN SENSUEL        163
    I CAN WALK ABOUT WITHOUT FIDGETING WHEN PEOPLE PASS,           247     PIERROTS              20
PASSAGE
    AND THE STREETS MAKE WAY FOR THEIR PASSAGE.     .......        132     AT TEN-SHIN           17
PASSAGES
    A NET-WORK OF ARBOURS AND PASSAGES AND COVERED WAYS,           141     IDEA OF CHOAN         22
    BENDING YOUR PASSAGES FROM RIGHT TO LEFT AND FROM
        LEFT TO RIGHT   ................................           147     BEFORE SLEEP          15
PASSED
    "AH YES, PASSED ONCE OUR WAY,   .....................            6     CINO                  27
    THAN TO HAVE WATCHED THAT HOUR AS IT PASSED.    ......          40     ERAT HORA              7
    HATH LACKED A SOMETHING SINCE THIS LADY PASSED;   ...           63     QUIES                  3
    SHE PASSED AND LEFT NO QUIVER IN THE VEINS, WHO NOW             92     GENTILDONNA            1
    STOPPED IN THEIR PLAY AS SHE PASSED THEM   ..........           96     AESTHETICS             3
    "AND TWO SPRINGS HAVE PASSED US."    ................          166     FISH & SHADOW         12
    HE PASSED FROM MEN'S MEMORY IN L'AN TRENTIESME    ....         187     E. P. ODE             18
    HE HAD PASSED, INCONSCIENT, FULL GAZE,   .............         200     MAUBERLEY: 2          26
    BUT TO JAB A KNIFE IN MY VITALS, TO HAVE PASSED ON A
        SWIG OF POISON,   .............................           228     SEXTUS PROP:12        12
PASSES
    LEST THEY SHOULD PARCH TOO SWIFTLY, WHERE SHE PASSES.           38     BALLATETTA            10
    THAT HE PASSES FOR BOTH BLOODLESS AND SEXLESS.    ....         100     TEMPERAMENTS           4
    ALL PASSES, ANANGKE PREVAILS,    ....................          199     MAUBERLEY: 2           3
PASSING
    PASSING   ...........................................          103     LADIES                ST
    AND THE WHORES DROPPING IN FOR A WORD OR TWO IN
        PASSING,   ....................................           117     THE LAKE ISLE         10
    WHITE, WHITE OF FACE, HESITATES, PASSING THE DOOR.             128     BEAU TOILET            4
    HAUGHTY THEIR PASSING,   ............................          132     AT TEN-SHIN           18
PASSION
    LEUCIS, WHO INTENDED A GRAND PASSION,    .............          99     EPITAPH                1
    SO IS THE SLOW COOLING OF OUR CHIVALROUS PASSION,              100     THE BATH TUB           3
    SIX PENCE THE OBJECT FOR A CHANGE OF PASSION.    .....         162     CABARET DANCER        30
    A DURABLE PASSION;   ................................          196     HUGH SELWIN:12         8
    QU'ILS PEUVENT COMPRENDRE DE CETTE PASSION   ........          199     MAUBERLEY: 2         EPI
    --GIVEN THAT IS HIS "FUNDAMENTAL PASSION,"   ........          200     MAUBERLEY: 2          20
    "WAS ONCE THE SLAVE OF ONE PASSION:"    ..............         219     SEXTUS PROP: 6        27
    WERE THERE AN ERUDITE OR VIOLENT PASSION,    .........         230     SEXTUS PROP:12        63
    VARRO, OF HIS GREAT PASSION LEUCADIA,   ..............         230     SEXTUS PROP:12        67
PASSIONATE
    PASSIONATE CINO, OF THE WRINKLING EYES,    ...........           6     CINO                  17
PASSIONS
    THAT MASK AT PASSIONS AND DESIRE DESIRES,   .........           32     PIERE VIDAL           61
    COME, MY SONGS, LET US EXPRESS OUR BASER PASSIONS,              94     INSTRUCTIONS           1
PASSION'S
    WHOSE BLUBBERING YOWLS YOU TAKE FOR PASSION'S
        ESSENCE;   ....................................           240     MOYEN SENSUEL         68
PASSIVE
    QUESTING AND PASSIVE. . . .    ......................         192     YEUX GLAUQUES         19
PAST
    SOUND IN YOUR WIND PAST ALL SIGNS O' CORRUPTION.                13     MESMERISM             16
    AS OLD TOLEDOS PAST THEIR DAYS OF WAR    .............          19     FOR E. MCC            19
    HAVE WE DONE IN TIMES PAST    .......................           26     NIGHT LITANY          16
    DODGING HIS WAY PAST AUBETERRE, SINGING AT CHALAIS             154     NEAR PERIGORD        10
    THIS CARE FOR PAST MEN,   ...........................          219     SEXTUS PROP: 6         3
PASTIME
    BECAME A PASTIME FOR   ..............................          192     YEUX GLAUQUES
PAT
    I PAT MY NEW CASK OF WINE.    .......................         142     UNMOVING CLOUD
    LET US SPIT UPON THOSE WHO PAT THE BIG-BELLIES FOR
        PROFIT,   ....................................            145     SALUTATION 3RD         1
PATARA
    MY VOTE COMING FROM THE TEMPLE OF PHOEBUS IN LYCIA,
        AT PATARA,   .................................            208     SEXTUS PROP: 1         3
PATCH
    NOR WHETHER THERE BE ANY PATCH LEFT OF US    ........          228     SEXTUS PROP:12         2
PATCHED
    THE VERY SMALL CHILDREN IN PATCHED CLOTHING,   ......           96     AESTHETICS
```

PAGE 302

PATCHOULI -- PAY

	PAGE	TITLE	LINE
PATCHOULI			
THE FAINT ODOUR OF YOUR PATCHOULI,	103	LADIES	18
PATENT			
NOR IS IT EQUIPPED WITH A FRIGIDAIRE PATENT;	209	SEXTUS PROP: 1	59
PATH			
SHE WALKS BY THE RAILING OF A PATH IN KENSINGTON GARDENS,	83	THE GARDEN	2
COVER OVER THE DARK PATH	138	CITY OF CHOAN	4
A ROSY PATH, A SORT OF VERNAL INGRESS,	243	MOYEN SENSUEL	145
PATHETIC			
WITH A PATHETIC SOLICITUDE THEY ATTEND ME;	147	BEFORE SLEEP	8
PATHETICALLY			
THEY WORK PATHETICALLY IN MY FAVOUR,	147	BEFORE SLEEP	3
PATIENCE			
BUT I AWAIT WITH PATIENCE,	111	BLACK SLIPPERS	9
PATIENT			
OH, YOU ARE PATIENT, I HAVE SEEN YOU SIT	61	PORTRAIT FEMME	11
PATRIA			
DIED SOME, PRO PATRIA;	190	HUGH SELWYN: 4	11
PATRICIENNES			
DES PATRICIENNES,	160	DANS OMNIBUS	15
PATRIOT			
BUT RADWAY WAS A PATRIOT WHOSE VENALITY	245	MOYEN SENSUEL	211
PATRON			
O GOD, O VENUS, O MERCURY, PATRON OF THIEVES,	117	THE LAKE ISLE	1
O GOD, O VENUS, O MERCURY, PATRON OF THIEVES,	117	THE LAKE ISLE	12
PATS			
HE PURRS AND PATS THE CLEAR STRINGS.	139	SENNIN POEM	7
PATTERN			
THEIR MOVES BREAK AND REFORM THE PATTERN:	120	GAME OF CHESS	8
A PALE GOLD, IN THE AFORESAID PATTERN,	202	AGE DEMANDED	41
PATTERNED			
OF WOVEN WALLS DEEP PATTERNED, OF EMAIL,	49	OF SPLENDOUR	14
PATTERNS			
A BROWN ROBE, WITH THREADS OF GOLD WOVEN IN PATTERNS, HAST THOU GATHERED ABOUT THEE,	91	DANCE FIGURE	17
THE PATTERNS	103	THE PATTERNS	T
PATTERN-SILK			
HER UNDERSKIRT IS OF GREEN PATTERN-SILK,	140	MULBERRY ROAD	13
PAUNVRE			
"PAUNVRE FEMME MAIGRE!" SHE SAYS.	163	CABARET DANCER	55
PAUPER			
"QUIA PAUPER AMAVI."	206	SEXTUS PROP	EPI
PAUPER'S			
PERHAPS YOU WILL HAVE THE PLEASURE OF DEFILING MY PAUPER'S GRAVE;	145	SALUTATION 3RD	18
PAUSE			
LO! THEY PAUSE NOT FOR LOVE NOR FOR SORROW,	25	THE WHITE STAG	2
PAVED			
SWEET TREES ARE ON THE PAVED WAY OF THE SHIN.	138	NEAR SHOKU	6
PAVEMENTS			
LET ME BE FREE OF PAVEMENTS,	146	CANTILATIONS	4
PAVING			
THEIR TRUNKS BURST THROUGH THE PAVING,	138	NEAR SHOKU	7
PAVLOVA			
LIKE A GILDED PAVLOVA,	83	THE GARRET	7
PAWN			
FOR THEIR PAWN AND TREASURY.	33	GOODLY FERE	20
"PAWN YOUR CASTLES, LORDS!	152	NEAR PERIGORD	38
PAWNS			
"Y" PAWNS, CLEAVING, EMBANKING!	120	GAME OF CHESS	12
PAY			
AND NOW YOU PAY ONE. YES, YOU RICHLY PAY.	61	PORTRAIT FEMME	13
AND NOW YOU PAY ONE. YES, YOU RICHLY PAY.	61	PORTRAIT FEMME	13
WILL PAY NO ATTENTION TO THIS,	98	THE BELLAIRES	25
AND YOU CARING ENOUGH TO PAY IT.	135	EXILE'S LETTER	16
IT WILL PAY THEM WHEN THE WORMS ARE WRIGGLING IN THEIR VITALS;	145	SALUTATION 3RD	4
LET THE JEWS PAY."	152	NEAR PERIGORD	39
PAY UP YOUR VOW OF NIGHT WATCHES	224	SEXTUS PROP: 9	25
AND UNTO ME ALSO PAY DEBT:	224	SEXTUS PROP: 9	27

PAGE 303

PAY -- PENELOPE

	PAGE	TITLE	LINE
PAY (CONTINUED)			
A NOVELIST, A PUBLISHER, TO PAY OLD SCORES,	239	MOYEN SENSUEL	18
NOT THAT HIS PAY HAD RISEN, AND NO LEAK	243	MOYEN SENSUEL	142
"NOTHING WILL PAY THEE, FRIEND, LIKE CHRISTIANITY."	246	MOYEN SENSUEL	236
ALL DREW THEIR PAY, AND AS THE PAY GREW LESS,	260	ALF'S FIFTH	9
ALL DREW THEIR PAY, AND AS THE PAY GREW LESS,	260	ALF'S FIFTH	9
PAY FOR HIS WITLESS NOISE,	261	ALF'S SIXTH	4
TO MAKE THE PEOPLE PAY.	272	NATIONAL SONG	4
PAYS			
(WHICH PAYS HIM MORE PER WEEK THAN THE SUPERNAL).	240	MOYEN SENSUEL	46
"TENT PREACHIN' IS THE KIND THAT PAYS THE BEST."	246	MOYEN SENSUEL	238
PEACE			
DAMN IT ALL! ALL THIS OUR SOUTH STINKS PEACE.	28	ALTAFORTE	1
WHEN THE TEMPESTS KILL THE EARTH'S FOUL PEACE,	28	ALTAFORTE	8
BETTER ONE HOUR'S STOUR THAN A YEAR'S PEACE	28	ALTAFORTE	16
WHEN I SEE HIM SO SCORN AND DEFY PEACE,	29	ALTAFORTE	23
BUT IS FIT ONLY TO ROT IN WOMANISH PEACE	29	ALTAFORTE	27
MAY GOD DAMN FOR EVER ALL WHO CRY "PEACE!"	29	ALTAFORTE	36
HELL BLOT BLACK FOR ALWAY THE THOUGHT "PEACE"!	29	ALTAFORTE	39
TURMOIL GROWN VISIBLE BENEATH OUR PEACE,	32	PARACELSUS	8
DEPART IN PEACE.	183	CANTICO SOLE	11
PEACH			
PEACH BOUGHS AND APRICOT BOUGHS HANG OVER A THOUSAND GATES,	131	AT TEN-SHIN	2
PEACOCK'S			
THOUGH YOU WALK IN THE VIA SACRA, WITH A PEACOCK'S TAIL FOR A FAN.	227	SEXTUS PROP:11	40
PEACOCK-THROATED			
UNDER NIGHT, THE PEACOCK-THROATED,	75	THE ALCHEMIST	8
PEAK			
LURE US BEYOND THE CLOUDY PEAK OF RIVA?	39	BLANDULA	15
PEAKS			
SHARP PEAKS, HIGH SPURS, DISTANT CASTLES.	122	PROVINC DESERT	55
CAUSING THE FIVE PEAKS TO TREMBLE,	128	THE RIVER SONG	14
PEARL			
THE MOON IS A GREAT PEARL IN THE WATERS OF SAPPHIRE,	18	DE AEGYPTO	21
THOU HOODED OPAL, THOU ETERNAL PEARL,	50	THE FLAME	29
HER EARRINGS ARE MADE OF PEARL,	140	MULBERRY ROAD	12
PEBBLES			
THY MAIDENS ARE WHITE LIKE PEBBLES;	91	DANCE FIGURE	21
PECULIAR			
SOME CERTAIN PECULIAR THINGS,	52	AU SALON	24
PEER			
AND SINCE I COULD NOT FIND A PEER TO YOU,	105	DOMPNA POIS	11
MAINTAINS INTENTION REASON'S PEER AND MATE;	249	DONNA MI PREGA	37
PEERING			
PEERING DOWN	121	PROVINC DESERT	15
PEGASEAN			
THOUGH YOU HEAVE INTO THE AIR UPON THE GILDED PEGASEAN BACK,	226	SEXTUS PROP:11	7
PEIGNOIR			
THIS LADY IN THE WHITE BATH-ROBE WHICH SHE CALLS A PEIGNOIR,	87	ALBATRE	1
PELASGIAN			
HAVE YOU CONTEMPTED JUNO'S PELASGIAN TEMPLES,	221	SEXTUS PROP: 8	12
PELION			
NOR OF CAUSEWAYS OVER PELION,	217	SEXTUS PROP: 5	41
PELLMELL			
INO IN HER YOUNG DAYS FLED PELLMELL OUT OF THEBES,	222	SEXTUS PROP: 8	21
PEN			
MY PEN IS IN MY HAND	18	DE AEGYPTO	10
DRIPS FROM MY DEATHLESS PEN--AH, WELL-AWAY!	59	SILET	2
BUT I DRAW PEN ON THIS BARGE	128	THE RIVER SONG	13
PENATES			
CARI LARESQUE, PENATES,	52	AU SALON	25
PENAUTIER			
AS DID FIRST SCORN, THEN LIPS OF THE PENAUTIER!	30	PIERE VIDAL	17
PENCE			
SIX PENCE THE OBJECT FOR A CHANGE OF PASSION.	162	CABARET DANCER	30
PENELOPE			
HIS TRUE PENELOPE WAS FLAUBERT,	187	E. P. ODE	13

PENELOPE -- PERFECT

	PAGE	TITLE	LINE
PENELOPE (CONTINUED)			
"HIS TRUE PENELOPE	198	MAUBERLEY: 1	5
PENSAMIENTOS			
MI BASTAN MIS PENSAMIENTOS.	82	THE CONDOLENCE	EPI
PENSIONERS			
OLD PENSIONERS AND OLD PROTECTED WOMEN	121	PROVINC DESERT	11
PEOPLE			
AND ORDINARY PEOPLE TOUCH ME NOT.	20	IN DURANCE	13
NOW YOU WILL COME OUT OF A CONFUSION OF PEOPLE,	36	FRANCESCA	3
PEOPLE ARE BORN AND DIE,	43	MR. HOUSMAN	2
FOR HERE ARE A MILLION PEOPLE SURLY WITH TRAFFIC;	62	N. Y.	5
ALIEN PEOPLE!	70	THE PLUNGE	20
WILL PEOPLE ACCEPT THEM?	81	TENZONE	1
DANCE AND MAKE PEOPLE BLUSH,	86	SALUTATION 2ND	27
BUT, ABOVE ALL, GO TO PRACTICAL PEOPLE--	86	SALUTATION 2ND	34
I JOIN THESE WORDS FOR FOUR PEOPLE,	88	CAUSA	1
YOU DO NOT KNOW THESE FOUR PEOPLE.	88	CAUSA	4
ARE VERY CHARMING PEOPLE.	98	THE BELLAIRES	43
HOSTS OF AN ANCIENT PEOPLE,	107	COMING OF WAR	19
TWO SMALL PEOPLE, WITHOUT DISLIKE OR SUSPICION.	130	RIVER-MER WIFE	6
LET COME BEAUTIFUL PEOPLE	146	CANTILATIONS	6
FRIENDS? ARE PEOPLE LESS FRIENDS	158	PSYCHOLOG HOUR	24
ALL THESE PEOPLE.	163	CABARET DANCER	61
AMIABLE AND HARMONIOUS PEOPLE ARE PUSHED INCONTINENT INTO DUELS,	227	SEXTUS PROP:12	5
I CAN WALK ABOUT WITHOUT FIDGETING WHEN PEOPLE PASS,	247	PIERROTS	20
AND KEEP THE PEOPLE IN ITS PLACE	270	OF 600 M.P.'S	7
TO MAKE THE PEOPLE PAY.	272	NATIONAL SONG	4
PEOPLE'S			
WHY DO YOU LOOK SO EAGERLY AND SO CURIOUSLY INTO PEOPLE'S FACES,	103	CODA	2
PEPITA			
"PEPITA" HAS NO TO-MORROW, SO YOU WRITE.	161	CABARET DANCER	9
PEPITA HAS SUCH TO-MORROWS: WITH THE HANDS PUFFED OUT,	161	CABARET DANCER	10
HERE'S PEPITA, TALL AND SLIM AS AN EGYPTIAN MUMMY,	162	CABARET DANCER	18
AND SO PEPITA	162	CABARET DANCER	21
COME NOW, MY DEAR PEPITA,	162	CABARET DANCER	32
NO. PEPITA,	162	CABARET DANCER	38
SHE WILL BE DRUNK IN THE DITCH, BUT YOU, PEPITA,	162	CABARET DANCER	47
PRUDENT AND SVELTE PEPITA.	162	CABARET DANCER	50
PER			
(WHICH PAYS HIM MORE PER WEEK THAN THE SUPERNAL).	240	MOYEN SENSUEL	46
"AND RATE 'EM UP AT JUST 30 MUCH PER HEAD,	244	MOYEN SENSUEL	181
OF 25 PER CENT. ON THEIR ADS., AND THE WOODS	262	ALF'S SEVENTH	12
PER VENDERE CANNONI	273	M. POM-POM	2
PER VENDERE CANNONI.	273	M. POM-POM	5
PER VENDERE CANNONI	273	M. POM-POM	7
PERCEIVED			
YOU HAVE PERCEIVED THE BLADES OF THE FLAME	169	PHANOPOEIA	12
YOU HAVE PERCEIVED THE LEAVES OF THE FLAME.	169	PHANOPOEIA	16
PERCEPTION			
TO HIS PERCEPTION	201	AGE DEMANDED	7
PERCEPTIONS			
IN THE PRESENCE OF SELECTED PERCEPTIONS.	202	AGE DEMANDED	40
PERCEPTIVITY			
INVITATION, MERE INVITATION TO PERCEPTIVITY	201	AGE DEMANDED	25
PERDAMNATION			
I WOULD ARTICULATE YOUR PERDAMNATION.	238	MOYEN SENSUEL	8
PERENNIAL			
BEAUTY IS NOT ETERNAL, NO MAN HAS PERENNIAL FORTUNE,	223	SEXTUS PROP: 9	20
THESE AND A TASTE IN BOOKS THAT'S GROWN PERENNIAL	239	MOYEN SENSUEL	25
PERFECT			
THAT HATH NO PERFECT LIMNING, WHEN THE WARM	9	NA AUDIART	39
CLOTHED IN GOLDISH WEFT, DELICATELY PERFECT,	68	APPARUIT	21
HATH OF PERFECT CHARMS SO MANY	72	DIEU! QU'IL	11
IT WERE THROUGH A PERFECT GLAZE	201	AGE DEMANDED	12
PERFECT AS DURER!	235	TO WHISTLER	7
"ALL THE SAME STYLE, SAME CUT, WITH PERFECT LOATHING."	244	MOYEN SENSUEL	184

	PAGE	TITLE	LINE
PERFECTING			
ENGAGED IN PERFECTING THE CATALOGUE,	193	SIENA MI FE	2
PERFECTION			
WHICH BROUGHT THE HAIR-CLOTH CHAIR TO SUCH PERFECTION,	63	PHASELLUS ILLE	6
MOVE AMONG THE LOVERS OF PERFECTION ALONE.	95	ITE	2
COME, MY SONGS, LET US SPEAK OF PERFECTION--	99	SALVATIONISTS	1
A HOME-INDUSTRIOUS WORKER TO PERFECTION,	245	MOYEN SENSUEL	213
LYING WITHIN PERFECTION POSTULATE	249	DONNA MI PREGA	34
SAVE THAT PERFECTION FAILS, BE IT BUT A LITTLE;	249	DONNA MI PREGA	45
PERFECTION'S			
IT IS NOT VIRTU, BUT PERFECTION'S SOURCE	249	DONNA MI PREGA	33
PERFECTLY			
THUS ALL ROADS ARE PERFECTLY SAFE	212	SEXTUS PROP: 3	24
PERFORCE			
HERE AM I COME PERFORCE MY LOVE OF HER,	49	OF SPLENDOUR	17
THIS YEAR PERFORCE I MUST WITH CIRCUMSPECTION--	238	MOYEN SENSUEL	9
PERFORM			
HE THE PROSPEROUS MAN--WHAT SOME PERFORM	65	THE SEAFARER	57
PERFORMED			
AT THE AUTOPSY, PRIVATELY PERFORMED--	193	SIENA MI FE	10
PERFORMERS			
SAW THE PERFORMERS COME: HIM, HER, THE BABY,	163	CABARET DANCER	80
PERFORMING			
LIKE A TRAINED AND PERFORMING TORTOISE,	229	SEXTUS PROP:12	59
PERFUMED			
TO THE PERFUMED AIR AND GIRLS DANCING,	132	AT TEN-SHIN	21
THE COACHES ARE PERFUMED WOOD,	141	IDEA OF CHOAN	4
OBJECTS TO PERFUMED CIGARETTES.	178	MOEURS CON: 1	17
THE PERFUMED CLOTHS SHALL BE ABSENT.	219	SEXTUS PROP: 6	17
PERFUMES			
WITH THEIR PERFUMES IN LITTLE ALABASTER BOXES?	165	QUINTUS SEPTIM	15
PERGAMUS			
NOR OF HOMER'S REPUTATION IN PERGAMUS,	217	SEXTUS PROP: 5	43
PERHAPS			
OR PERHAPS I WILL DIE AT THIRTY?	145	SALUTATION 3RD	17
PERHAPS YOU WILL HAVE THE PLEASURE OF DEFILING MY PAUPER'S GRAVE;	145	SALUTATION 3RD	18
UNDER A MORE TOLERANT, PERHAPS, EXAMINATION.	201	AGE DEMANDED	28
OR PERHAPS JUNO HERSELF WILL GO UNDER,	222	SEXTUS PROP: 8	40
(YOU FEED A HEN ON GREASE, PERHAPS SHE'LL LAY	240	MOYEN SENSUEL	48
UNLESS PERHAPS I SHOULD HAVE RECOURSE TO	243	MOYEN SENSUEL	155
PERIGORD			
INTO PERIGORD,	121	PROVINC DESERT	29
NEAR PERIGORD	151	NEAR PERIGORD	T
A PERIGORD, PRES DEL MURALH	151	NEAR PERIGORD	EPI
IN PERIGORD, AND THIS GOOD UNION	151	NEAR PERIGORD	18
YOU READ TO-DAY, HOW LONG THE OVERLORDS OF PERIGORD,	152	NEAR PERIGORD	50
TO SNIFF THE TRAFFIC INTO PERIGORD.	153	NEAR PERIGORD	63
PERIL			
YOU ARE ESCAPED FROM GREAT PERIL,	224	SEXTUS PROP: 9	23
A PERIL TO SELFRIDGE AND THE NATION.	262	ALF'S SEVENTH	20
PERILOUS			
PERILOUS ASPECT;	107	COMING OF WAR	13
PERILS			
THROUGH PERILS, (SO MANY) AND OF A VEXED LIFE,	222	SEXTUS PROP: 8	1
PERISH			
FREE US, FOR WE PERISH	35	THE EYES	1
PERORATION			
I FIND NO MORAL FOR A PERORATION,	246	MOYEN SENSUEL	24
PERPETUAL			
WITH PERPETUAL ASCRIPTION OF GRACES?	222	SEXTUS PROP: 8	1
PERSEPHONE			
HERE LET THY CLEMENCY, PERSEPHONE, HOLD FIRM,	38	LADY'S LIFE	
HERE LET THY CLEMENCY, PERSEPHONE, HOLD FIRM,	38	LADY'S LIFE	1
WHICH I TAKE, MY NOT UNWORTHY GIFT, TO PERSEPHONE.	219	SEXTUS PROP: 6	2
PERSEPHONE AND DIS, DIS, HAVE MERCY UPON HER,	223	SEXTUS PROP: 9	
PERSEUS			
AND RESPECTABLY MARRIED TO PERSEUS,	222	SEXTUS PROP: 8	2
THOUGH YOU HAD THE FEATHERY SANDALS OF PERSEUS	226	SEXTUS PROP:11	

PERSIA -- PHIDON

	PAGE	TITLE	LINE
PERSIA			
AND CARPETS FROM SAVONNIER, AND FROM PERSIA,	167	OF AROUET	8
PERSISTING			
BY PERSISTING TO SUCCESSES,	92	THE REST	10
PERSON			
YOU ARE A PERSON OF SOME INTEREST, ONE COMES TO YOU	61	PORTRAIT FEMME	14
WE ARE COMPARED TO THAT SORT OF PERSON	82	THE CONDOLENCE	14
BUT SEEMS LIKE A PERSON JUST GONE.	112	IONE, DEAD	9
SHE WHO COULD NEVER LIVE SAVE THROUGH ONE PERSON,	157	NEAR PERIGORD	189
SHE WHO COULD NEVER SPEAK SAVE TO ONE PERSON,	157	NEAR PERIGORD	190
WHERE BOLD HANDS MAY DO VIOLENCE TO MY PERSON?	212	SEXTUS PROP: 3	8
A TROJAN AND ADULTEROUS PERSON CAME TO MENELAUS UNDER THE RITES OF HOSPITIUM,	227	SEXTUS PROP:12	6
COMRADE, COMRADE OF MY LIFE, OF MY PURSE, OF MY PERSON;	228	SEXTUS PROP:12	14
PERTAINETH			
SITH NOTHING IS THAT UNTO WORTH PERTAINETH	37	THE YOUNG KING	20
PERTURBATIONS			
MY SOUL'S ANTENNAE ARE PREY TO SUCH PERTURBATIONS,	247	PIERROTS	7
PESTE			
PESTE! 'TIS HIS OWN SONGS?	6	CINO	30
PETAL-LIKE			
THERE FLOAT THE PETAL-LIKE FLAMES.	109	HEATHER	3
PETALS			
CLOSE, AND AS THE PETALS OF FLOWERS IN FALLING	39	FOR PSYCHE	4
THE PETALS FALL IN THE FOUNTAIN,	108	TS'AI CHI'H	1
PETALS ON A WET, BLACK BOUGH.	109	IN THE METRO	2
PETALS ARE ON THE GONE WATERS AND ON THE GOING,	131	AT TEN-SHIN	5
DRY WREATHS DROP THEIR PETALS,	221	SEXTUS PROP: 7	29
PETIT			
AUPRES D'UN PETIT ENFANT GAI, BOSSU.	160	DANS OMNIBUS	11
IL ETAIT COMME UN TOUT PETIT GARCON	181	MOEURS CON: 7	3
PETITES			
ET DEUX PETITES FILLES GRACILES,	160	DANS OMNIBUS	14
PETRARCHAN			
AND WROTE NINETY PETRARCHAN SONNETS.	118	CONTEMPORARIES	5
PEUT			
NE PEUT PLUS VOIR	273	M. POM-POM	4
PEUVENT			
QU'EST CE QU'ILS PEUVENT COMPRENDRE?	199	MAUBERLEY: 2	EPI
QU'ILS PEUVENT COMPRENDRE DE CETTE PASSION	199	MAUBERLEY: 2	EPI
PHAECIA			
AS THE FORESTS OF PHAECIA,	209	SEXTUS PROP: 1	54
PHAETONA			
ALCYON, PHAETONA, ALCMENA,	76	THE ALCHEMIST	57
PHALANX			
AND THAT HARD PHALANX, THAT UNBROKEN LINE,	153	NEAR PERIGORD	64
PHALLIC			
PHALLIC AND AMBROSIAL	189	HUGH SELWYN: 3	6
PHALLUS			
DANCE THE DANCE OF THE PHALLUS	86	SALUTATION 2ND	28
CUPID, ASTRIDE A PHALLUS WITH TWO WINGS,	162	CABARET DANCER	36
PHALOI			
THE GILDED PHALOI OF THE CROCUSES	110	COITUS	1
PHANOPOEIA			
PHANOPOEIA	169	PHANOPOEIA	T
PHANTASMAGORIA			
HE HAD MOVED AMID HER PHANTASMAGORIA,	199	MAUBERLEY: 2	5
PHANTASMAL			
AUDITION OF THE PHANTASMAL SEA-SURGE,	202	AGE DEMANDED	45
PHANTOM			
THAT MY PHANTOM LACK NOT IN CUNNING.	105	DOMPNA POIS	30
THIS PHANTOM	106	DOMPNA POIS	64
PHASELLUS			
"PHASELLUS ILLE"	63	PHASELLUS ILLE	T
PHIDIPPUS			
NOW BEARS THE PALSIED CONTACT OF PHIDIPPUS.	111	SOCIETY	4
PHIDON			
NICHARCUS UPON PHIDON HIS DOCTOR	165	QUINTUS SEPTIM	ST
PHIDON NEITHER PURGED ME, NOR TOUCHED ME,	165	QUINTUS SEPTIM	23

PAGE 307

	PAGE	TITLE	LINE
PHILADELPHIA			
AND ANTEDATES THE PHILADELPHIA CENTENNIAL.	239	MOYEN SENSUEL	26
AT PHILADELPHIA, 1876?	240	MOYEN SENSUEL	55
PHILETAS			
SHADES OF CALLIMACHUS, COAN GHOSTS OF PHILETAS	207	SEXTUS PROP: 1	1
STIFFENED OUR FACE WITH THE BACKWASH OF PHILETAS THE COAN.	211	SEXTUS PROP: 2	54
PHILISTIA'S			
PHILISTIA'S POMP AND ART'S POMPOSITIES!	46	TRANSLATOR	4
PHOEBUS			
MY VOTE COMING FROM THE TEMPLE OF PHOEBUS IN LYCIA, AT PATARA,	208	SEXTUS PROP: 1	38
AND PHOEBUS LOOKING UPON ME FROM THE CASTALIAN TREE,	210	SEXTUS PROP: 2	16
"PHOEBUS OUR WITNESS, YOUR HANDS ARE UNSPOTTED."	226	SEXTUS PROP:11	24
PHOEBUS'			
UPON THE ACTIAN MARSHES VIRGIL IS PHOEBUS' CHIEF OF POLICE,	228	SEXTUS PROP:12	31
PHOENIX			
MANY INSTRUMENTS, LIKE THE SOUND OF YOUNG PHOENIX BROODS.	135	EXILE'S LETTER	27
THE PHOENIX ARE AT PLAY ON THEIR TERRACE.	138	CITY OF CHOAN	1
THE PHOENIX ARE GONE, THE RIVER FLOWS ON ALONE.	138	CITY OF CHOAN	2
PHOIBEE			
"'POLLO PHOIBEE, OLD TIN PAN, YOU	7	CINO	43
'POLLO PHOIBEE, TO OUR WAY-FARE	7	CINO	46
PHONETICS			
IN BRIEF, VIOLET IS THE GROUND TONE OF MY PHONETICS.	247	PIERROTS	1
PHOTOGRAPH			
AT A FRIEND OF MY WIFE'S THERE IS A PHOTOGRAPH,	180	MOEURS CON: 5	
A FADED, PALE BROWNISH PHOTOGRAPH,	180	MOEURS CON: 5	
PHOTOGRAPHS			
TRY PHOTOGRAPHS, WOLF DOWN THEIR ALE AND CAKES	236	MIDDLE-AGED	
PHRASE			
THIS IDENTICAL PHRASE:	97	AESTHETICS	2
WHO HAS THE PHRASE "AS IGNORANT AS AN ACTOR."	246	MOYEN SENSUEL	22
PHRASED			
BY NAME, IF NAMED." SO IT WAS PHRASED, OR RATHER SOMEWHAT SO	242	MOYEN SENSUEL	11
PHRASES			
HIS PHRASES INTERLARDING,	267	ALF'S TWELFTH	
PHRYGIAN			
NOR TO THE TUNE OF THE PHRYGIAN FATHERS.	218	SEXTUS PROP: 5	
AND YOU ALSO FOLLOW HIM "NEATH PHRYGIAN PINE SHADE:	229	SEXTUS PROP:12	
PHYLLIDULA			
PHYLLIDULA	103	PHYLLIDULA	
PHYLLIDULA IS SCRAWNY BUT AMOROUS,	103	PHYLLIDULA	
PHYLLIDULA AND THE SPOILS OF GOUVERNET	167	OF AROUET	
PHYLLIDULA NOW, WITH YOUR POWDERED SWISS FOOTMAN	167	OF AROUET	
PHYSICIST			
BEING A PHYSICIST	261	ALF'S SIXTH	
PIANIST			
PULLS UP A ROLL OF FAT FOR THE PIANIST,	163	CABARET DANCER	
PIANO			
THE GRAND PIANO	204	MEDALLION	
PIANOLA			
THE PIANOLA "REPLACES"	189	HUGH SELWYN: 3	
PICARDA			
VANNA, MANDETTA, VIERA, ALODETTA, PICARDA, MANUELA	76	THE ALCHEMIST	
PICKED			
OH, I HAVE PICKED UP MAGIC IN HER NEARNESS	71	A VIRGINAL	
PICKIN'			
DID I 'EAR IT WHILE PICKIN' 'OPS;	262	ALF'S SEVENTH	
PICKING			
SUCH AN ONE PICKING A RAGGED	15	FAMAM CANO	
HERE WE ARE, PICKING THE FIRST FERN-SHOOTS	127	BOWMEN OF SHU	
PICKINGS			
AND GET MY PICKINGS ON THE SIDE	266	ALF'S ELEVENTH	
PICKLED			
AMONG THE PICKLED FOETUSES AND BOTTLED BONES,	193	SIENA MI FE	
PICNICKING			
I HAVE SEEN FISHERMEN PICNICKING IN THE SUN,	85	SALUTATION	

PICTURE -- PINING

	PAGE	TITLE	LINE
PICTURE			
THE PICTURE	73	THE PICTURE	T
PICTURES			
"THESE SELL OUR PICTURES"! OH WELL,	20	IN DURANCE	4
PICTURESQUE			
"WHERE IS THE PICTURESQUE?"	85	SALUTATION 2ND	12
PIE			
THEIRS BUT TO BUY THE PIE,	257	BREAD BRIGADE	14
PIECE-MEAL			
AND SHE IS DYING PIECE-MEAL	83	THE GARDEN	3
PIECES			
THESE PIECES ARE LIVING IN FORM,	120	GAME OF CHESS	7
PIEIRE			
"PIEIRE KEPT THE SINGING--	123	PROVINC DESERT	72
PIEIRE DE MAENSAC IS GONE.	123	PROVINC DESERT	79
PIER			
PIER FRANCESCA,	198	MAUBERLEY: 1	14
PIERCE			
OR PIERCE ITS PRETENCE	263	ALF'S EIGHTH	4
PIERCED			
PIERCED OF THE POINT THAT TOUCHETH LASTLY ALL,	19	FOR E. MCC	24
PIERE			
PIERE VIDAL OLD	30	PIERE VIDAL	T
FROM PIERE VIDAL'S REMEMBRANCE THAT BLUE NIGHT.	30	PIERE VIDAL	10
FOR THAT RESTLESSNESS--PIERE SET TO KEEP	30	PIERE VIDAL	24
PIERIAN			
OF PIERIAN ROSES.	196	HUGH SELWIN:12	28
PIERIDES			
OH AUGUST PIERIDES! NOW FOR A LARGE-MOUTHED PRODUCT.	216	SEXTUS PROP: 5	14
PIERRE			
FAT PIERRE WITH THE HOOK GAUCHE-MAIN,	11	OF THE GIBBET	5
PIERROTS			
PIERROTS	247	PIERROTS	T
PIG			
UNTIL THE LAST SLUT'S HANGED AND THE LAST PIG DISEMBOWELED,	161	CABARET DANCER	2
PIGEONNES			
ET DES PIGEONNES	160	DANS OMNIBUS	17
PIG-HEADED			
WHO HAS HAD A PIG-HEADED FATHER;	89	A PACT	4
PILE			
BUT I HAVE MADE A RUDDY PILE	266	ALF'S ELEVENTH	15
PILED			
PILED UP NEATLY UPON THE SHELVES	117	THE LAKE ISLE	4
PILES			
AND SHE PILES HER HAIR UP ON THE LEFT SIDE OF HER HEAD-PIECE.	140	MULBERRY ROAD	11
AND THE NEAT PILES OF UNOPENED, UNOPENING BOOKS,	180	MOEURS CON: 5	25
PILGRIM			
THE YOUNG AMERICAN PILGRIM	179	MOEURS CON: 3	5
PILLAR			
WHEN LAST I MET HIM, HE WAS A PILLAR IN	246	MOYEN SENSUEL	229
PILLOW			
SEE, THE LIGHT GRASS SPRANG UP TO PILLOW THEE,	60	TOMB AKR CAAR	6
PILOT			
TURNS HARDY PILOT . . . AND IF ONE WRONG NOTE	42	HER MONUMENT	45
PIMPING			
PIMPING, CONCEITED, PLACID, EDITORIAL,	238	MOYEN SENSUEL	6
PIMPS			
THE PIMPS OF WHITEHALL EVER MORE IN FEAR,	260	ALF'S FIFTH	7
PINE			
A WOMAN AS FIRE UPON THE PINE WOODS	17	PRAISE YSOLT	39
I AM BELOW AMID THE PINE TREES,	53	AU JARDIN	4
AMID THE LITTLE PINE TREES, HEAR ME!	53	AU JARDIN	5
BUT ONE HUGE BACK HALF-COVERED UP WITH PINE,	152	NEAR PERIGORD	33
AND YOU ALSO FOLLOW HIM "NEATH PHRYGIAN PINE SHADE:	229	SEXTUS PROP:12	41
PINE-WINDS			
AND INTO TEN THOUSAND VALLEYS FULL OF VOICES AND PINE-WINDS.	134	EXILE'S LETTER	21
PINING			
IS WHAT HAS SET US PINING,	267	ALF'S TWELFTH	2

PAGE 309

PINION -- PLACE

	PAGE	TITLE	LINE
PINION			
WITH SPRAY ON HIS PINION.	64	THE SEAFARER	25
PINK			
BUT SHE DANCED LIKE A PINK MOTH IN THE SHRUBBERY.	53	AU JARDIN	19
PINNING			
PINNING THE GUISE THAT HAD BEEN FAIN	11	OF THE GIBBET	9
PINT			
FER 'ARFT A PINT O' BITTER?"	270	OF 600 M.P.'S	20
OLE KATE WOULD GIT HER 'ARF A PINT	271	OLE KATE	3
PINXIT			
MANUS ANIMAM PINXIT,	18	DE AEGYPTO	9
PIPES			
MUSICIANS WITH JEWELLED FLUTES AND WITH PIPES OF GOLD	128	THE RIVER SONG	2
THEIR VOICE IS IN THE TWELVE PIPES HERE.	130	THE RIVER SONG	40
PIQUANTE			
PIQUANTE, DELICIOUS, LUSCIOUS, CAPTIVATING:	241	MOYEN SENSUEL	84
PISANELLO			
PISANELLO LACKING THE SKILL	198	MAUBERLEY: 1	15
PISISTRATUS			
FREE OF PISISTRATUS,	189	HUGH SELWYN: 3	22
PISTIL			
HE BITES THROUGH THE FLOWER PISTIL	139	SENNIN POEM	9
PIT			
HE WROTE THE CATCH TO PIT THEIR JEALOUSIES	153	NEAR PERIGORD	77
PITCH			
BLACK IS THE PITCH O' THEIR WEDDING DRESS,	11	OF THE GIBBET	18
PITCHERS			
AMONG THE WOMEN WITH PITCHERS.	91	DANCE FIGURE	9
PITIFUL			
HIS MOTHER'S BIRTHDAY GIFT. (HOW PITIFUL	242	MOYEN SENSUEL	117
PITY			
BUT YOU "MY LORD," GOD'S PITY!	7	CINO	33
COME, LET US PITY THOSE WHO ARE BETTER OFF THAN WE ARE.	83	THE GARRET	1
COME, LET US PITY THE MARRIED AND THE UNMARRIED.	83	THE GARRET	5
PITYING			
LET US THEREFORE CEASE FROM PITYING THE DEAD	164	QUINTUS SEPTIM	10
PLACATION			
WHAT HIS PLACATION; WHY HE IS IN VERB,	248	DONNA MI PREGA	16
PLACE			
MANY A SINGER PASS AND TAKE HIS PLACE	24	THUS NINEVEH	9
GET US TO SOME CLEAR PLACE WHEREIN THE SUN	39	BLANDULA	3
FINDS 'NEATH THIS ROCK FIT MOULD, FIT RESTING PLACE!	41	HER MONUMENT	2
LONDON IS A WOEFUL PLACE,	44	MR. HOUSMAN	1
FOUGHT OUT THEIR STRIFE HERE, 'TIS A PLACE OF WONDER;	51	THE ALTAR	
ONE PLACE WHERE WE'D RATHER HAVE TEA	52	AU SALON	
AND THERE IS NO NEW THING IN ALL THIS PLACE.	60	TOMB AKR CAAR	1
AND NO SUN COMES TO REST ME IN THIS PLACE,	60	TOMB AKR CAAR	2
SINCE YOU HAVE COME THIS PLACE HAS HOVERED ROUND ME,	69	SUB MARE	
SHE HAS NO NAME, AND NO PLACE.	84	ORTUS	
THROUGHOUT THIS SYLVAN PLACE	87	THE SPRING	
GILT TURQUOISE AND SILVER ARE IN THE PLACE OF THY REST.	91	DANCE FIGURE	1
I HAVE KNOWN THE STONE-BRIGHT PLACE,	95	OF THE DEGREES	
THERE IS A PLACE OF TREES . . . GRAY WITH LICHEN.	121	PROVINC DESERT	
I KNOW THE ROADS IN THAT PLACE:	121	PROVINC DESERT	2
SOME LITTLE PRIZED PLACE IN AUVERGNAT:	122	PROVINC DESERT	6
A PLACE OF FELICITOUS MEETING.	141	IDEA OF CHOAN	2
EACH PLACE STRONG.	151	NEAR PERIGORD	1
THE TALLEYRANDS, HAVE HELD THE PLACE; IT WAS NO TRANSIENT FICTION.	152	NEAR PERIGORD	5
THIS PLACE IS THE CYPRIAN'S FOR SHE HAS EVER THE FANCY	164	QUINTUS SEPTIM	
THERE IS A PLACE--BUT NO ONE ELSE KNOWS IT--	166	FISH & SHADOW	
DECREED IN THE MARKET PLACE.	189	HUGH SELWYN: 3	
SHALL I PLACE A TIN WREATH UPON!	189	HUGH SELWYN: 3	
QUITE OUT OF PLACE AMID	201	AGE DEMANDED	
WHICH THESE PRESENTS PLACE	201	AGE DEMANDED	
HE HAD SPOKEN, AND POINTED ME A PLACE WITH HIS PLECTRUM:	211	SEXTUS PROP: 2	

PAGE 310

PLACE -- PLAYED

	PAGE	TITLE	LINE
PLACE (CONTINUED)			
MAY A WOODY AND SEQUESTERED PLACE COVER ME WITH ITS FOLIAGE	213	SEXTUS PROP: 3	35
SHE WAS VEILED IN THE MIDST OF THAT PLACE,	214	SEXTUS PROP: 4	24
TO PLACE THE LAST KISS ON MY LIPS	219	SEXTUS PROP: 6	24
IN WHICH THEIR MENTORS PLACE SUCH WIDE RELIANCE.	244	MOYEN SENSUEL	164
PLACE AND ABODE,	249	DONNA MI PREGA	27
YET IN THAT PLACE IT EVER IS UNSTILL,	249	DONNA MI PREGA	28
IN PLACE OF THE ROAST BEEF OF BRITAIN,	263	ALF'S EIGHTH	19
AND KEEP THE PEOPLE IN ITS PLACE	270	OF 600 M.P.'S	7
PLACED			
MOTIONLESS, PLACED IN VAIN,	41	HER MONUMENT	5
PLACES			
IN PLEASANT PLACES,	26	NIGHT LITANY	4
IN ORDINARY PLACES.	36	FRANCESCA	7
FOLK OF UNEARTHLY FASHION, PLACES SPLENDID,	50	THE FLAME	24
PLACES!	70	THE PLUNGE	5
AND LIARS IN PUBLIC PLACES.	190	HUGH SELWYN: 4	19
WAS FOUND IN HIS EMPLOYER'S CASH. HE LEARNED THE LAY OF CHEAPER PLACES,	243	MOYEN SENSUEL	143
PLACID			
AND A BROWN, PLACID, HATED WOMAN VISITING HER,	154	NEAR PERIGORD	112
WITH A PLACID AND UNEDUCATED MISTRESS	195	HUGH SELWIN:10	6
THE PLACID WATER	203	MAUBERLEY: 4	4
PLACID BENEATH WARM SUNS,	203	MAUBERLEY: 4	7
PIMPING, CONCEITED, PLACID, EDITORIAL,	238	MOYEN SENSUEL	6
PLAGUE			
THAT PLAGUE AND BURN AND DRIVE ONE AWAY.	5	LA FRAISNE	36
TO PLAGUE TO-MORROW WITH A TESTAMENT!	59	SILET	14
PLAGUES			
HE PLAGUES ME WITH JIBES AND STICKS,	237	ABU SALAMMAMM	29
PLAIN			
HAVE DAMP AND PLAIN TO BE OUR SHUTTING IN.	21	IN DURANCE	40
BETWEEN AUCTION AND PLAIN BRIDGE,	258	ALF'S SECOND	10
PLAINETH			
THAT PLAINETH OF THE GOING OF THE NIGHT,	172	LANGUE D'OC: 1	12
PLAINTIVE			
WITH PLAINTIVE, QUERULOUS CRYING.	110	TEMPORA	3
AND WITH A PLAINTIVE, GENTLE MEWING,	115	SOCIAL ORDER	16
PLAISAUNCES			
TIME HAS DRIVEN ME OUT FROM THE FINE PLAISAUNCES,	167	OF AROUET	18
PLANH			
PLANH FOR THE YOUNG ENGLISH KING	36	THE YOUNG KING	T
PLANTAGENET			
PLANTAGENET PUTS THE RIDDLE: "DID HE LOVE HER?"	155	NEAR PERIGORD	145
PLANUS			
CANTUS PLANUS	231	CANTUS PLANUS	T
PLASMATOUR			
O PLASMATOUR AND TRUE CELESTIAL LIGHT,	172	LANGUE D'OC: 1	1
O PLASMATOUR, THAT THOU END NOT THE NIGHT,	177	LANGUE D'OC: 4	6
PLASTER			
THE "AGE DEMANDED" CHIEFLY A MOULD IN PLASTER,	188	HUGH SELWYN: 2	9
PLATES			
AND PLATES FROM GERMAIN,	167	OF AROUET	10
PLATONIC			
(LET HIM REBUKE WHO NE'ER HAS KNOWN THE PURE PLATONIC GRAPPLE,	242	MOYEN SENSUEL	105
PLAUSIBILITIES			
AND A SLAVE SHOULD FEAR PLAUSIBILITIES;	214	SEXTUS PROP: 4	9
PLAY			
THEIR ECHOES PLAY UPON EACH OTHER IN THE TWILIGHT	16	PRAISE YSOLT	9
THAT STRIVE AND PLAY AND PASS,	35	HIS OWN FACE	5
THAT WE PREFER TO PLAY UP TO,	52	AU SALON	19
NEITHER COULD I PLAY UPON ANY REED IF I HAD ONE.	62	N. Y.	7
STOPPED IN THEIR PLAY AS SHE PASSED THEM	96	AESTHETICS	3
THE PHOENIX ARE AT PLAY ON THEIR TERRACE	100	CITY OF CHOAN	1
WHAT COULD HE DO BUT PLAY THE DESPERATE CHESS,	152	NEAR PERIGORD	36
"MY PRETTY BOY, MAKE WE OUR PLAY AGAIN	177	LANGUE D'OC: 4	16
AND THIS MUCH GIVES ME HEART TO PLAY THE GAME.	235	TO WHISTLER	4
PLAYED			
WHICH, PLAYED ON BY THE VIRTUES OF HER SOUL,	49	OF SPLENDOUR	20

PAGE 311

PLAYED -- PLEDGES

	PAGE	TITLE	LINE
PLAYED (CONTINUED)			
I PLAYED ABOUT THE FRONT GATE, PULLING FLOWERS. ...	130	RIVER-MER WIFE	2
THEY ARE PLAYED ON BY DIVERSE FORCES.	158	PSYCHOLOG HOUR	15
PLAYING			
YOU CAME BY ON BAMBOO STILTS, PLAYING HORSE, ...	130	RIVER-MER WIFE	3
YOU WALKED ABOUT MY SEAT, PLAYING WITH BLUE PLUMS.	130	RIVER-MER WIFE	4
PLAYING ON A JEWELLED MOUTH-ORGAN.	135	EXILE'S LETTER	25
WITH THAT MUSIC PLAYING, ...	135	EXILE'S LETTER	30
PLAYING, ...	180	MOEURS CON: 5	9
PLAYS			
STARK, KEEN, TRIUMPHANT, TILL IT PLAYS AT DEATH.	31	PIERE VIDAL	37
'TIS NOT A GAME THAT PLAYS AT MATES AND MATING, ...	50	THE FLAME	1
'TIS NOT A GAME THAT PLAYS AT MATES AND MATING, ...	50	THE FLAME	16
AND IF SHE PLAYS WITH ME WITH HER SHIRT OFF, ...	217	SEXTUS PROP: 5	33
PLEACHED			
IS A PLEACHED ARBOUR;	121	PROVINC DESERT	10
PLEAD			
HE WILL PLEAD	98	THE BELLAIRES	17
PLEASANT			
IN PLEASANT PLACES, ...	26	NIGHT LITANY	4
"A FAIR MAN AND A PLEASANT."	123	PROVINC DESERT	73
AS A PLEASANT TICKLE, ...	145	SALUTATION 3RD	29
SINCE THAT DAY I HAVE HAD NO PLEASANT NIGHTS.	225	SEXTUS PROP:10	43
PLEASANTER			
SHROPSHIRE IS MUCH PLEASANTER.	44	MR. HOUSMAN	12
THAT DANCING AND GENTLE IS AND THEREBY PLEASANTER,	177	LANGUE D'OC: 4	22
PLEASE			
HE PLEASE TO PARDON, AS TRUE PARDON IS, ...	37	THE YOUNG KING	38
SOME FEW WHOM WE'D RATHER PLEASE	52	AU SALON	20
(OR WITH TWO LIGHT FEET, IF IT PLEASE YOU!)	86	SALUTATION 2ND	18
PLEASE LET ME KNOW BEFOREHAND, ...	131	RIVER-MER WIFE	27
BUT I WILL NOT GO MAD TO PLEASE YOU, ...	145	SALUTATION 3RD	25
ALAS! WHO'ER IT PLEASE OR PAIN, ...	175	LANGUE D'OC: 3	58
PLEASED			
HIM, WHOM IT PLEASED FOR OUR GREAT BITTERNESS	37	THE YOUNG KING	33
THEODORUS WILL BE PLEASED AT MY DEATH, ...	164	QUINTUS SEPTIM	1
AND SOMEONE ELSE WILL BE PLEASED AT THE DEATH OF			
THEODORUS, ...	164	QUINTUS SEPTIM	2
PLEASES			
BUT DEAD, OR ASLEEP, SHE PLEASES.	165	QUINTUS SEPTIM	21
PLEASETH			
PLEASETH ME, AND IN LIKE WISE	52	AU SALON	EPI
SAFE MAY'ST THOU GO MY CANZON WHITHER THEE PLEASETH	250	DONNA MI PREGA	88
PLEASING			
WIT, NOR GOOD SPIRITS, NOR THE PLEASING ATTITUDES	101	AMITIES	11
YOU MAY FIND INTERMENT PLEASING, ...	222	SEXTUS PROP: 8	29
PLEASURABILITIES			
FOR I AM SWELLED UP WITH INANE PLEASURABILITIES ...	214	SEXTUS PROP: 4	5
PLEASURE			
AND BETTER WERE IT, SHOULD GOD GRANT HIS PLEASURE,	37	THE YOUNG KING	22
YOU TOOK NO PLEASURE AT ALL IN MY TRIUMPHS, ...	101	AMITIES	2
THAT IN PLEASURE SHE RECEIVES MORE THAN SHE CAN GIVE;	103	PHYLLIDULA	3
NIGHT AND DAY ARE GIVEN OVER TO PLEASURE	132	AT TEN-SHIN	25
PLEASURE LASTING, WITH COURTEZANS, GOING AND COMING			
WITHOUT HINDRANCE, ...	136	EXILE'S LETTER	53
PERHAPS YOU WILL HAVE THE PLEASURE OF DEFILING MY			
PAUPER'S GRAVE;	145	SALUTATION 3RD	18
SPOILERS OF PLEASURE, ...	173	LANGUE D'OC: 2	27
AND DANCED THEM INTO A BULWARK AT HIS PLEASURE, ...	208	SEXTUS PROP: 1	45
"THAT INCENSED FEMALE HAS CONSIGNED HIM TO OUR			
PLEASURE."	224	SEXTUS PROP:10	12
AIN'T ALWAYS A PLEASURE, ...	259	ALF'S FOURTH	4
PLEBEIAN			
A SMALL PLEBEIAN PROCESSION.	219	SEXTUS PROP: 6	18
PLECTRUM			
HE HAD SPOKEN, AND POINTED ME A PLACE WITH HIS			
PLECTRUM:	211	SEXTUS PROP: 2	28
PLED			
IN VAIN HAVE I PLED WITH HIM:	16	PRAISE YSOLT	25
PLEDGES			
OR GATHER FLORAL PLEDGES?"	72	PAN IS DEAD	7

PLENTY -- POET

	PAGE	TITLE	LINE
PLENTY			
ENOUGH, ENOUGH AND IN PLENTY	219	SEXTUS PROP: 6	19
PLENTY TO RIGHT OF 'EM,	257	BREAD BRIGADE	17
PLENTY TO LEFT OF 'EM,	257	BREAD BRIGADE	18
PLENTY TO RIGHT OF 'EM,	259	ALF'S THIRD	8
PLENTY TO LEFT OF 'EM,	259	ALF'S THIRD	9
"WE HAVE PLENTY, SO LET IT BE."	262	ALF'S SEVENTH	17
PLOT			
YOU DO NOTHING, YOU PLOT INANE SCHEMES AGAINST ME,	226	SEXTUS PROP:11	14
IF I SET FORTH A BAWDY PLOT LIKE BYRON	239	MOYEN SENSUEL	42
PLOTS			
CAESAR PLOTS AGAINST INDIA,	219	SEXTUS PROP: 6	6
PLOWMAN			
SAILOR, OF WINDS; A PLOWMAN, CONCERNING HIS OXEN;	218	SEXTUS PROP: 5	55
PLUMB			
AND ANOTHER SAID "GET HIM PLUMB IN THE MIDDLE!	224	SEXTUS PROP:10	14
PLUMB THE SPIKE OF THE TARGE.	250	DONNA MI PREGA	81
PLUM-COLOURED			
FROM THE PLUM-COLOURED LAKE, IN STILLNESS,	75	THE ALCHEMIST	17
PLUMP			
WILL BE QUITE RICH, QUITE PLUMP, WITH PUG-BITCH FEATURES,	162	CABARET DANCER	48
FELL PLUMP INTO HER PAIL.	271	OLE KATE	14
PLUMS			
YOU WALKED ABOUT MY SEAT, PLAYING WITH BLUE PLUMS.	130	RIVER-MER WIFE	4
PLUNDERED			
THAT PLUNDERED ST. HUBERT BACK O' THE FANE:	12	OF THE GIBBET	32
PLUNGE			
THE PLUNGE	70	THE PLUNGE	T
PLUS			
NE PEUT PLUS VOIR	273	M. POM-POM	4
PLUTO			
DO THOU, PLUTO, BRING HERE NO GREATER HARSHNESS.	38	LADY'S LIFE	2
DO THOU, PLUTO, BRING HERE NO GREATER HARSHNESS	38	LADY'S LIFE	12
PLUVIUS			
EAGLED AND THUNDERED AS JUPITER PLUVIUS,	13	MESMERISM	15
PLY			
HOW THE STAYS PLY BACK FROM IT;	8	NA AUDIART	15
THE EIGHT PLY OF THE HEAVENS	142	UNMOVING CLOUD	3
THE EIGHT PLY OF THE HEAVENS ARE DARKNESS,	142	UNMOVING CLOUD	11
PO			
LI PO	117	EPITAPHS	ST
AND LI PO ALSO DIED DRUNK.	117	EPITAPHS	3
POCKET-LOOKING-GLASS			
WITHOUT SMIRKING INTO A POCKET-LOOKING-GLASS.	247	PIERROTS	21
POCKETS			
AND HIS POCKETS BY MA'S AID, THAT NIGHT WITH CASH FULL,	242	MOYEN SENSUEL	126
PODS			
MARSH-CRANBERRIES, THE RIBBED AND ANGULAR PODS	162	CABARET DANCER	19
POE			
FROM THESE HE LEARNT. POE, WHITMAN, WHISTLER, MEN, THEIR RECOGNITION	240	MOYEN SENSUEL	59
POEM			
POEM BY THE BRIDGE AT TEN-SHIN	131	AT TEN-SHIN	T
SENNIN POEM BY KAKUHAKU	139	SENNIN POEM	T
IS IT A LOVE POEM? DID HE SING OF WAR?	153	NEAR PERIGORD	81
"WRITE ME A POEM."	162	CABARET DANCER	31
POEME			
"POETE, WRIT ME A POEME!"	162	CABARET DANCER	51
POEMS			
SHE SAYS, "MAY MY POEMS BE PRINTED THIS WEEK?	110	TEMPORA	6
MAY MY POEMS BE PRINTED THIS WEEK?"	110	TEMPORA	8
FOUR POEMS OF DEPARTURE	137	OF DEPARTURE	T
POESIE			
S'ILS NE COMPRENNENT PAS LA POESIE,	199	MAUBERLEY ?	EPI
POET			
"AYE! I AM A POET AND UPON MY TOMB	24	THUS NINEVEH	1
YET AM I POET, AND UPON MY TOMB	24	THUS NINEVEH	16
AM HERE A POET, THAT DOTH DRINK OF LIFE	24	THUS NINEVEH	22

PAGE 313

POETE -- POM-POM

	PAGE	TITLE	LINE
POETE			
"POETE, WRIT ME A POEME!"	162	CABARET DANCER	51
POETICA			
BEFORE THE "ARS POETICA" OF HIRAM MAXIM.	239	MOYEN SENSUEL	34
POETRY			
I SUPPOSE, WHEN POETRY COMES DOWN TO FACTS,	52	AU SALON	1
OF POETRY; TO MAINTAIN "THE SUBLIME"	187	E. P. ODE	3
POETRY, HER BORDER OF IDEAS,	196	HUGH SELWIN:12	13
POETS			
THAT WE EXPECT OF POETS?"	85	SALUTATION 2ND	11
THE THREE POETS	118	THREE POETS	T
AND THREE POETS ARE GONE INTO MOURNING.	118	THREE POETS	2
CERTAIN POETS HERE AND IN FRANCE	148	FRATRES MINORE	2
POICTIERS			
POICTIERS AND BRIVE, UNTAKEN ROCHECOUART,	152	NEAR PERIGORD	29
POIGNARD			
WHO GAVE THIS POIGNARD ITS PREMIER STAIN	11	OF THE GIBBET	8
POINT			
PIERCED OF THE POINT THAT TOUCHETH LASTLY ALL,	19	FOR E. MCC	24
THE STARS WILL POINT OUT THE STUMBLES,	212	SEXTUS PROP: 3	21
EDGE, THAT IS, AND POINT TO THE DART,	250	DONNA MI PREGA	78
POINTED			
HE HAD SPOKEN, AND POINTED ME A PLACE WITH HIS PLECTRUM:	211	SEXTUS PROP: 2	28
POIS			
"DOMPNA POIS DE ME NO'US CAL"	105	DOMPNA POIS	T
POISON			
"SHE HAS CAUGHT ME WITH HERBACEOUS POISON,	215	SEXTUS PROP: 4	31
BUT TO JAB A KNIFE IN MY VITALS, TO HAVE PASSED ON A SWIG OF POISON,	228	SEXTUS PROP:12	12
POKE-NOSE			
ALFONSO, QUATTRO, POKE-NOSE.	22	MARVOIL	22
POLE			
THAT BEARS US UP, SHALL TURN AGAINST THE POLE.	69	THE NEEDLE	7
POLHONAC			
(ST. LEIDER HAD DONE AS MUCH AS POLHONAC,	153	NEAR PERIGORD	86
POLICE			
UPON THE ACTIAN MARSHES VIRGIL IS PHOEBUS' CHIEF OF POLICE,	228	SEXTUS PROP:12	31
POLICEMEN			
TIBET SHALL BE FULL OF ROMAN POLICEMEN,	219	SEXTUS PROP: 6	8
POLIN			
A-JUMBLING O' FIGURES FOR MAITRE JACQUES POLIN,	22	MARVOIL	4
POLISHED			
WHO CAN DEMOLISH AT SUCH POLISHED EASE	46	TRANSLATOR	3
POLITICS			
OR WAR AND BROKEN HEAUMES AND POLITICS?	154	NEAR PERIGORD	93
POLLEN			
WHENCE THEIR SYMBOLICAL POLLEN HAS BEEN EXCERPTED,	180	MOEURS CON: 5	21
'POLLO			
"'POLLO PHOIBEE, OLD TIN PAN, YOU	7	CINO	42
'POLLO PHOIBEE, TO OUR WAY-FARE	7	CINO	46
POLNESI			
"CINO?" "OH, EH, CINO POLNESI	6	CINO	25
POLUPHLOIBOIOUS			
HE LIES BY THE POLUPHLOIBOIOUS SEA-COAST.	181	MOEURS CON: 6	4
POLYDMANTUS			
OR OF POLYDMANTUS, BY SCAMANDER, OR HELENUS AND DEIPHOIBOS?	208	SEXTUS PROP: 1	30
POLYPHEMUS			
AND YOU, O POLYPHEMUS? DID HARSH GALATEA ALMOST	208	SEXTUS PROP: 1	46
POLYPHLOISBOIO			
PARA THINA POLYPHLOISBOIO THALASSES.	181	MOEURS CON: 6	
POMEGRANATE			
EACH MAN WANTS THE POMEGRANATE FOR HIMSELF;	227	SEXTUS PROP:12	
POMP			
PHILISTIA'S POMP AND ART'S POMPOSITIES!	46	TRANSLATOR	
POMPILIUS			
MY CELLAR DOES NOT DATE FROM NUMA POMPILIUS,	209	SEXTUS PROP: 1	5
POM-POM			
M. POM-POM	273	M. POM-POM	

PAGE 314

POM-POM -- PORTRAITS

	PAGE	TITLE	LINE
POM-POM (CONTINUED)			
M. POM-POM ALLAIT EN GUERRE	273	M. POM-POM	1
M. POM-POM EST AU SENAT	273	M. POM-POM	6
POMPOSITIES			
PHILISTIA'S POMP AND ART'S POMPOSITIES!	46	TRANSLATOR	4
POMPS			
THE POMPS OF BUTCHERY, FINANCIAL POWER,	260	ALF'S FIFTH	1
THE POMPS OF FLEET ST., FESTERING YEAR ON YEAR,	260	ALF'S FIFTH	5
POND			
SOUTH OF THE POND THE WILLOW-TIPS ARE HALF-BLUE AND BLUER,	129	THE RIVER SONG	25
POOL			
BY THE STILL POOL OF MAR-NAN-OTHA	4	LA FRAISNE	13
IS A POOL OF THE WOOD, AND	5	LA FRAISNE	31
SHAKE UP THE STAGNANT POOL OF ITS CONVICTIONS;	63	PHASELLUS ILLE	8
POOLS			
"ANIENAN SPRING WATER FALLS INTO FLAT-SPREAD POOLS."	212	SEXTUS PROP: 3	5
POOR			
A POOR CLERK I, "ARNAUT THE LESS" THEY CALL ME,	22	MARVOIL	1
HOW CANST THOU REACH SO HIGH WITH THY POOR SENSE;	42	HER MONUMENT	52
OF THE FILTHY, STURDY, UNKILLABLE INFANTS OF THE VERY POOR.	83	THE GARDEN	6
"POOR DEAR! HE HAS LOST HIS ILLUSIONS."	85	SALUTATION 2ND	15
"AH, POOR JENNY'S CASE"	192	YEUX GLAUQUES	20
"I WAS AS POOR AS YOU ARE;	194	MR. NIXON	5
HAPPY SELLING POOR LOVES FOR CHEAP APPLES.	229	SEXTUS PROP:12	45
POOR IN DISCERNMENT, BEING THUS WEAKNESS' FRIEND,	249	DONNA MI PREGA	38
ARE ON THE POOR RELIEF.	269	SAFE AND SOUND	8
POPKOFF			
OLD POPKOFF	163	CABARET DANCER	62
POPLAR			
MIDONZ, WITH THE GOLD OF THE SUN, THE LEAF OF THE POPLAR, BY THE LIGHT OF THE AMBER,	75	THE ALCHEMIST	25
POPLARS			
FROM THE POPLARS WEEPING THEIR AMBER,	75	THE ALCHEMIST	22
CHALAIS IS HIGH, A-LEVEL WITH THE POPLARS.	152	NEAR PERIGORD	54
KNEW THE LOW FLOODED LANDS SQUARED OUT WITH POPLARS,	157	NEAR PERIGORD	174
POPPIES			
I HAVE FED YOUR LAR WITH POPPIES,	102	LADIES	5
POPPIES AND DAY'S EYES IN THE GREEN EMAIL	157	NEAR PERIGORD	171
POPULACE			
FOR THE NOBLENESS OF THE POPULACE BROOKS NOTHING BELOW ITS OWN ALTITUDE.	230	SEXTUS PROP:12	64
POR			
PORQUE POR ANDAR CONMIGO	82	THE CONDOLENCE	EPI
PORCELAIN			
AS A BATHTUB LINED WITH WHITE PORCELAIN,	100	THE BATH TUB	1
THE GLOW OF PORCELAIN	201	AGE DEMANDED	5
BURST IN UPON THE PORCELAIN REVERY:	201	AGE DEMANDED	18
LUINI IN PORCELAIN!	204	MEDALLION	1
PORCH			
"AND THOU OUT HERE BENEATH THE PORCH OF STONE	172	LANGUE D'OC: 1	22
PORQUE			
PORQUE POR ANDAR CONMIGO	82	THE CONDOLENCE	EPI
PORTAL			
GOLDEN ROSE THE HOUSE, IN THE PORTAL I SAW	68	APPARUIT	1
PORTALS			
AND THE MOON FALLS OVER THE PORTALS OF SEI-GO-YO,	131	AT TEN-SHIN	11
PORTENT			
PORTENT. LIFE DIED DOWN IN THE LAMP AND FLICKERED,	68	APPARUIT	3
PORTENTS			
FOR THEM THE YELLOW DOGS HOWL PORTENTS IN VAIN,	132	AT TEN-SHIN	28
PORTION			
NO PORTION, BUT A BEING.	84	ORTUS	16
IF SHE WON'T HAVE ME NOW, DEATH IS MY PORTION,	175	LANGUE D'OC: 3	37
OH THE NEEDLE IS YOUR PORTION	269	SAFE AND SOUND	20
PORTRAIT			
PORTRAIT D'UNE FEMME	61	PORTRAIT FEMME	T
PORTRAITS			
"IN THE STUDIO" AND THESE TWO PORTRAITS, IF I HAD MY CHOICE!	235	TO WHISTLER	8

POSITION -- PRAISE

	PAGE	TITLE	LINE
POSITION			
THE FAMILY POSITION WAS WANING,	111	SOCIETY	1
POSITIONS			
IN MOST SPIRITUEL POSITIONS,	46	FROM HEINE: 6	14
POSSIBLE			
A POSSIBLE FRIEND AND COMFORTER.	196	HUGH SELWIN:12	20
POSSIBLY			
POSSIBLY. BUT IN EALING	195	HUGH SELWIN:11	3
POST			
POST MORTEM CONSPECTU	147	POST MORTEM	T
POSTPONE			
YET IF I POSTPONE MY OBEDIENCE	212	SEXTUS PROP: 3	9
POSTPONEMENT			
IT IS A MERE POSTPONEMENT OF YOUR DOMINATION.	216	SEXTUS PROP: 5	20
POSTULATE			
LYING WITHIN PERFECTION POSTULATE	249	DONNA MI PREGA	34
POT			
AND IT WILL SURELY BOIL THE POT,	267	ALF'S TWELFTH	14
POTATIONIST			
A TEMPERATE MAN, A THIN POTATIONIST, EACH DAY	245	MOYEN SENSUEL	199
POTENTIAL			
AT SIXTEEN SHE WAS A POTENTIAL CELEBRITY	179	MOEURS CON: 2	1
POULARDES			
COMME DES POULARDES.	160	DANS OMNIBUS	19
POUND			
"DEAR POUND, I AM LEAVING ENGLAND."	159	PSYCHOLOG HOUR	43
AND SAID: "MR. POUND IS SHOCKED AT MY LEVITY."	181	MOEURS CON: 7	11
AT ONE AND THREE THE POUND.	269	SAFE AND SOUND	4
POUR			
POUR QUATRE SOUS.	160	DANS OMNIBUS	23
E. P. ODE POUR L'ELECTION DE SON SEPULCHRE	187	E. P. ODE	T
POUR VENDRE DES CANONS	273	M. POM-POM	8
POUR VENDRE DES CANONS	273	M. POM-POM	9
POURED			
THE WATERS OF STYX POURED OVER THE WOUND:	230	SEXTUS PROP:12	74
POVERTY			
WITH POVERTY	102	TO DIVES	3
POWDERED			
PHYLLIDULA NOW, WITH YOUR POWDERED SWISS FOOTMAN	167	OF AROUET	5
POWDERY			
O GLASS SUBTLE AND CUNNING, O POWDERY GOLD!	95	OF THE DEGREES	14
POWER			
WHEN COME THEY, SURGING OF POWER, "DAEMON,"	20	IN DURANCE	19
FOR LOVE, OR HOPE, OR BEAUTY OR FOR POWER,	21	IN DURANCE	32
COME NOW, BEFORE THIS POWER	69	THE NEEDLE	6
FROM THE POWER OF GRASS,	75	THE ALCHEMIST	30
HIS BROTHER-IN-LAW WAS ALL THERE WAS OF POWER	151	NEAR PERIGORD	17
LEAVING ME NO POWER TO HOLD HIM.	174	LANGUE D'OC: 3	6
AND WHEN HE COMES INTO POWER	238	ABU SALAMMAMM	30
POWER THAT COMPELS 'EM	244	MOYEN SENSUEL	171
OFTEN HIS POWER MEETETH WITH DEATH IN THE END	249	DONNA MI PREGA	39
OR LOSETH POWER, E'EN LOST TO MEMORY.	249	DONNA MI PREGA	48
THE POMPS OF BUTCHERY, FINANCIAL POWER,	260	ALF'S FIFTH	
THE POWER OF THE PRESS.	267	ALF'S ELEVENTH	24
AN' KEEP THE BANK IN POWER.	270	OF 600 M.P.'S	
POWERFUL			
LORD POWERFUL, ENGIRDLED ALL WITH MIGHT,	172	LANGUE D'OC: 1	
POWERS			
MAKETH ME CLEAR, AND THERE ARE POWERS IN THIS	49	OF SPLENDOUR	1
PRACTICAL			
BUT, ABOVE ALL, GO TO PRACTICAL PEOPLE--	86	SALUTATION 2ND	3
PRACTICE			
THE SUNDAY SCHOOL BRINGS VIRTUES INTO PRACTICE.	243	MOYEN SENSUEL	14
PRACTICES			
SUCH PRACTICES DILUTED RURAL BOREDOM	242	MOYEN SENSUEL	10
PRAGUE			
TO BEAT PRAGUE, BUDAPESTH, VIENNA OR MOSCOW,	245	MOYEN SENSUEL	19
PRAIRIES			
WANDERED THROUGH THE ARCADIAN PRAIRIES	222	SEXTUS PROP: 8	2
PRAISE			
BIDDING ME PRAISE	4	LA FRAISNE	1

PAGE 316

PRAISE -- PREFERRED

	PAGE	TITLE	LINE
PRAISE (CONTINUED)			
JUST A WORD IN THY PRAISE, GIRL,	8	NA AUDIART	20
SHALL BURST TO LILTING AT THE PRAISE	9	NA AUDIART	28
BERTRANS OF AULTAFORTE THY PRAISE	9	NA AUDIART	31
JUMP TO YOUR SENSE AND GIVE PRAISE AS WE'D LIEF DO.	13	MESMERISM	8
PRAISE OF YSOLT	16	PRAISE YSOLT	T
A LOT OF ASSES PRAISE YOU BECAUSE YOU ARE "VIRILE,"	82	THE CONDOLENCE	2
GO, MY SONGS, SEEK YOUR PRAISE FROM THE YOUNG AND FROM THE INTOLERANT,	95	ITE	1
HE WROTE THAT PRAISE ONLY TO SHOW HE HAD	155	NEAR PERIGORD	148
AND WILL NOT PRAISE HOMER	218	SEXTUS PROP: 5	62
THEY GET PRAISE FROM TOLERANT HAMADRYADS."	229	SEXTUS PROP:12	49
SHALL PRAISE THY SPEECH	250	DONNA MI PREGA	90
AND IF THE PAPERS SELDOM SANG HIS PRAISE,	265	ALF'S NINTH	23
PRAISED			
HAVING PRAISED THY GIRDLE'S SCOPE	8	NA AUDIART	14
AND PRAISED MY VERSES.	45	FROM HEINE: 4	4
YOU WERE PRAISED, MY BOOKS,	85	SALUTATION 2ND	1
O MY MUCH PRAISED BUT-NOT-ALTOGETHER-SATISFACTORY LADY.	100	THE BATH TUB	4
TRUE, HE HAS PRAISED HER, BUT IN SOME OPINION	155	NEAR PERIGORD	147
PRAISES			
PRAISES MEET UNTO THY FASHION?	8	NA AUDIART	10
A-MEAOWLING OUR PRAISES.	52	AU SALON	23
PRAISE-WORTHY			
IF I HAVE NOT THE FACULTY, "THE DARE ATTEMPT WOULD BE PRAISE-WORTHY."	216	SEXTUS PROP: 5	4
PRAY			
SKOAL!! TO THE GALLOWS! AND THEN PRAY WE:	12	OF THE GIBBET	41
HIM DO WE PRAY AS TO A LORD MOST RIGHTEOUS	37	THE YOUNG KING	36
AND WHAT, PRAY, DO YOU KNOW ABOUT	109	THE FAUN	3
AND PRAY TO GOD THAT IS ST. MARY'S SON,	172	LANGUE D'OC: 1	19
PRAYER			
PRAYER FOR HIS LADY'S LIFE	38	LADY'S LIFE	T
RECORD "ODD'S BLOOD! OUCH! OUCH!" A PRAYER, HIS SWIFT REPENTANCE.	243	MOYEN SENSUEL	130
PRAYERS			
AND ANSWER THEIR PRAYERS.	258	ALF'S SECOND	4
PREACHER			
"DELIGHT THY SOUL IN FATNESS," SAITH THE PREACHER.	163	CABARET DANCER	69
A NOVELIST, A PUBLISHER AND A PREACHER,	239	MOYEN SENSUEL	19
PREACHERS			
THESE HEAVY WEIGHTS, THESE DODGERS AND THESE PREACHERS,	241	MOYEN SENSUEL	79
PREACHIN'			
"TENT PREACHIN' IS THE KIND THAT PAYS THE BEST."	246	MOYEN SENSUEL	238
PRECEDED			
WHITHER MY DESIRE AND MY DREAM HAVE PRECEDED ME.	23	MARVOIL	33
PRECEDENT			
OH, THERE IS PRECEDENT, LEGAL TRADITION,	153	NEAR PERIGORD	88
AIN'T YEH GOT PRECEDENT?	259	ALF'S THIRD	17
PRECIOUS			
AND STREWS A MIND WITH PRECIOUS METAPHORS,	236	MIDDLE-AGED	18
PRECIPITATE			
DRIFTED . . . DRIFTED PRECIPITATE,	199	MAUBERLEY: 2	8
PRECIPITATION			
AMID THE PRECIPITATION, DOWN-FLOAT	202	AGE DEMANDED	52
PRECISELY			
OF PRECISELY THE FASHION	196	HUGH SELWIN:12	6
PREDESTINATION			
NOR IF THE THUNDER FALL FROM PREDESTINATION;	228	SEXTUS PROP:12	29
PREDILECTION			
DESPITE IT ALL, YOUR COMPOUND PREDILECTION	240	MOYEN SENSUEL	09
REFER			
THAT WE PREFER TO PLAY UP TO,	52	AU SALON	19
PREFER MY CLOAK UNTO THE CLOAK OF DUST	67	THE CLOAK	7
REFERABLE			
PREFERABLE, MY DEAR BOY, MY DEAR LYNCEUS,	228	SEXTUS PROP:12	13
REFERRED			
NO. YOU PREFERRED IT TO THE USUAL THING:	61	PORTRAIT FEMME	8

	PAGE	TITLE	LINE
PREGA			
DONNA MI PREGA	248	DONNA MI PREGA	T
PREGNANT			
PREGNANT WITH MANDRAKES, OR WITH SOMETHING ELSE ...	61	PORTRAIT FEMME	18
PREJUDICE			
GARBLE A NAME WE DETEST, AND FOR PREJUDICE?	52	AU SALON	13
PREMIER			
WHO GAVE THIS POIGNARD ITS PREMIER STAIN	11	OF THE GIBBET	8
PRES			
A PERIGORD, PRES DEL MURALH	151	NEAR PERIGORD	EPI
PRESCRIPTION			
GO ON, TO ASCRAEUS' PRESCRIPTION, THE ANCIENT, ...	229	SEXTUS PROP:12	50
PRESENCE			
IN THE PRESENCE OF SELECTED PERCEPTIONS.	202	AGE DEMANDED	40
PRESENT			
SHE OF THE SPEAR STANDS PRESENT.	147	BEFORE SLEEP	5
HER PRESENT DULNESS . . .	163	CABARET DANCER	77
OH WELL, HER PRESENT DULNESS . . .	163	CABARET DANCER	78
TO PRESENT THE SERIES	200	MAUBERLEY: 2	24
PRESENTED			
SUCH ASPECT WAS PRESENTED TO ME, ME RECENTLY EMERGED FROM MY VISIONS,	225	SEXTUS PROP:10	32
PRESENTLY			
BUT HE DIES ALSO, PRESENTLY.	43	MR. HOUSMAN	7
PRESENTS			
AND NO ISSUE PRESENTS ITSELF.	179	MOEURS CON: 2	7
DE SON EAGE; THE CASE PRESENTS	187	E. P. ODE	19
WHICH THESE PRESENTS PLACE	201	AGE DEMANDED	27
PRESERVE			
WE CAN'T PRESERVE THE ELUSIVE "MICA SALIS,"	163	CABARET DANCER	70
PRESERVED			
HAVE PRESERVED HER EYES;	192	YEUX GLAUQUES	10
TISSUE PRESERVED--THE PURE MIND	193	SIENA MI FE	11
PRESIDENT			
TILL UP AGAIN, RIGHT UP, WE REACH THE PRESIDENT,	239	MOYEN SENSUEL	16
PRESS			
AND SENSE THE TEETH THROUGH THE LIPS THAT PRESS ...	11	OF THE GIBBET	22
WE HAVE THE PRESS FOR WAFER;	189	HUGH SELWYN: 3	19
THE DAILY PRESS, AND MONTHLIES NINE CENTS DEARER.	241	MOYEN SENSUEL	94
STORMED AT BY PRESS AND ALL,	257	BREAD BRIGADE	21
THAT'S HOW THE PRESS BLURB RAN,--	261	ALF'S SIXTH	14
MY GREAT PRESS CLEAVES THE GUTS OF MEN,	266	ALF'S ELEVENTH	1
THE POWER OF THE PRESS.	267	ALF'S ELEVENTH	24
HAVE INFLUENCE WITH THE PRESS.	268	ANOTHER BIT	8
PRESSED			
KIDS FOR A BRIBE AND PRESSED UDDERS.	229	SEXTUS PROP:12	44
PRESSING			
HANG IN YELLOW-WHITE AND DARK CLUSTERS READY FOR PRESSING.	167	OF AROUET	22
PRESTIGE			
ONE DENYING YOUR PRESTIGE,	222	SEXTUS PROP: 8	36
PRETENCE			
OR PIERCE ITS PRETENCE	263	ALF'S EIGHTH	4
PRETEND			
PRETEND HUMANITY OR DON THE FRAIL ATTIRE?	32	PARACELSUS	2
PRETTY			
WE ALSO SHALL BE DEAD PRETTY SOON	43	MR. HOUSMAN	3
(PRETTY GIRL)	140	MULBERRY ROAD	4
"MY PRETTY BOY, MAKE WE OUR PLAY AGAIN	177	LANGUE D'OC: 4	16
BY HER PRETTY MANNERS,	215	SEXTUS PROP: 4	30
FIND PRETTY IRISH GIRLS IN CHINESE LAUNDRIES, ...	244	MOYEN SENSUEL	157
PREVAILS			
ALL PASSES, ANANGKE PREVAILS,	199	MAUBERLEY: 2	3
PREY			
SHE IS TIME'S PREY AND TIME CONSUMETH ALL.	40	ROME	8
I SHALL BE PREY TO LAMENTATIONS WORSE THAN A NOCTURNAL ASSAILANT.	212	SEXTUS PROP: 3	11
MY SOUL'S ANTENNAE ARE PREY TO SUCH PERTURBATIONS,	247	PIERROTS	7
PRIAMUS			
FROM THE SUNDERED REALMS, OF THEBES AND OF AGED PRIAMUS;	38	LADY'S LIFE	8

PRICE -- PROCEEDETH

	PAGE	TITLE	LINE
PRICE			
STRANGE SPARS OF KNOWLEDGE AND DIMMED WARES OF PRICE.	61	PORTRAIT FEMME	5
WOULD COUNT ON THE PRICE OF A GUN.	268	ANOTHER BIT	12
PRICKS			
DON'T KICK AGAINST THE PRICKS,	194	MR. NIXON	22
PRIDE			
BROKEN OF ANCIENT PRIDE,	9	NA AUDIART	49
BEHOLD HOW PRIDE AND RUIN CAN BEFALL	40	ROME	5
AGAINST HER; GIVE HER PRIDE IN THEM?	153	NEAR PERIGORD	78
PRIED			
TESTED AND PRIED AND WORKED IN MANY FASHIONS,	235	TO WHISTLER	3
HAD NOT ONE STYLE FROM BIRTH, BUT TRIED AND PRIED	235	TO WHISTLER	16
PRIES			
AND PRIES WIDE MY MOUTH WITH FAST MUSIC	29	ALTAFORTE	22
PRIEST			
NO CAPON PRIEST WAS THE GOODLY FERE	33	GOODLY FERE	15
PRIESTS			
FOR THE PRIESTS AND THE GALLOWS TREE?	33	GOODLY FERE	2
PRIG			
YET RADWAY WENT. A CIRCUMSPECTIOUS PRIG!	242	MOYEN SENSU.	119
PRIMAL			
I WHO HAVE SEEN YOU AMID THE PRIMAL THINGS	36	FRANCESCA	5
PRIMITIVE			
THE PRIMITIVE AGES SANG VENUS,	216	SEXTUS PROP: 5	7
PRINCE			
PRINCE: ASK ME NOT WHAT I HAVE DONE	10	FOR THIS YULE	25
FOR THE YOUNG PRINCE IS FOOLISH AND HEADSTRONG;	237	ABU SALAMMAMM	28
PRINCES			
AND THE PRINCES STILL STAND IN ROWS, ABOUT THE THRONE,	131	AT TEN-SHIN	10
AND WE WERE DRUNK FOR MONTH ON MONTH, FORGETTING THE KINGS AND PRINCES.	134	EXILE'S LETTER	5
PRINCESS			
I AM THE PRINCESS ILZA	47	FROM HEINE: 7	1
WHEN THE TAIHAITIAN PRINCESS	118	CONTEMPORARIES	1
A GLITTER OF GOLDEN SADDLES, AWAITING THE PRINCESS;	141	IDEA OF CHOAN	7
PRINT			
OF UGLY PRINT MARKS, BLACK	35	THE EYES	13
AS THE EDITOR OF THE CENTURY SAYS IN PRINT,	243	MOYEN SENSUEL	137
WHEN THOROUGHLY SOCIALIZED PRINTERS WANT TO PRINT 'EM.	244	MOYEN SENSUEL	168
BECAUSE I PRINT MOST LIES.	266	ALF'S ELEVENTH	4
PRINTED			
SHE SAYS, "MAY MY POEMS BE PRINTED THIS WEEK?	110	TEMPORA	6
MAY MY POEMS BE PRINTED THIS WEEK?"	110	TEMPORA	8
AND THEN LENDS OUT THEIR PRINTED SLIPS	269	SAFE AND SOUND	19
PRINTERS			
LET ME BE FREE OF THE PRINTERS.	146	CANTILATIONS	5
WHEN THOROUGHLY SOCIALIZED PRINTERS WANT TO PRINT 'EM.	244	MOYEN SENSUEL	168
PRIVATELY			
AT THE AUTOPSY, PRIVATELY PERFORMED--	193	SIENA MI FE	10
PRIV'LEGE			
ABOUT THE PRIV'LEGE OF LIBERTY.	271	OLE KATE	8
PRIZE			
'GAINST HER I PRIZE NOT AS A GLOVE	176	LANGUE D'OC: 3	71
PRIZED			
SOME LITTLE PRIZED PLACE IN AUVERGNAT:	122	PROVINC DESERT	65
DE GOURMONT SAYS THAT FIFTY GRUNTS ARE ALL THAT WILL BE PRIZED.	244	MOYEN SENSUEL	165
PRO			
PRO DOMO, IN ANY CASE	190	HUGH SELWYN. 4	9
DIED SOME, PRO PATRIA,	190	HUGH SELWYN: 4	11
PROBE			
THEY PROBE OLD GONZDALO, GAV DE DORN IS DEAD:	155	NEAR PERIGORD	137
PROCEED			
"THUS THINGS PROCEED IN THEIR CIRCLE";	178	MOEURS CON: 1	19
I WITH MY BEAK HAULED ASHORE WOULD PROCEED IN A MORE STATELY MANNER,	216	SEXTUS PROP: 5	10
PROCEEDETH			
WHO WELL PROCEEDETH, FORM NOT SEETH,	250	DONNA MI PREGA	82

PAGE 319

PROCESS -- PROPERTIUS

	PAGE	TITLE	LINE
PROCESS			
WE LOOK AT THE PROCESS.	217	SEXTUS PROP: 5	28
PROCESSION			
AND ACCOST THE PROCESSION OF MAIDENS.	108	CH'U YUAN	10
BUT A PROCESSION OF FESTIVAL,	110	COITUS	4
A PROCESSION, O GIULIO ROMANO,	110	COITUS	5
A SMALL PLEBEIAN PROCESSION.	219	SEXTUS PROP: 6	18
PROCTORS			
NINE LAWYERS, FOUR COUNSELS, FIVE JUDGES AND THREE PROCTORS OF THE KING,	97	THE BELLAIRES	5
PROCURE			
DO NOT SET ABOUT TO PROCURE ME AN AUDIENCE.	81	TENZONE	9
PRODUCED			
WHEN JOHN RUSKIN PRODUCED	192	YEUX GLAUQUES	2
PRODUCING			
IS INCAPABLE OF PRODUCING A LASTING NIRVANA.	148	FRATRES MINORE	7
PRODUCT			
OH AUGUST PIERIDES! NOW FOR A LARGE-MOUTHED PRODUCT.	216	SEXTUS PROP: 5	14
PROFANE			
UTTERS A PROFANE	204	MEDALLION	3
PROFESSION			
OR INSTALL ME IN ANY PROFESSION	117	THE LAKE ISLE	14
SAVE THIS DAMN'D PROFESSION OF WRITING,	117	THE LAKE ISLE	15
PROFESSOR			
CALL HIM "PROFESSOR."	261	ALF'S SIXTH	6
"PROFESSOR K---S IS."	261	ALF'S SIXTH	15
PROFFER			
I WISH YOU JOY, I PROFFER YOU ALL MY ASSISTANCE.	145	SALUTATION 3RD	19
PROFILE			
IN PROFILE;	198	MAUBERLEY: 1	12
PROFIT			
LET US SPIT UPON THOSE WHO PAT THE BIG-BELLIES FOR PROFIT,	145	SALUTATION 3RD	15
NOR OF WELSH MINES AND THE PROFIT MARUS HAD OUT OF THEM.	217	SEXTUS PROP: 5	46
PROFITABLE			
IN SPIRITUAL ASPIRATIONS, BUT HE FOUND IT PROFITABLE,	246	MOYEN SENSUEL	234
PROFITS			
WHITHER, O CITY, ARE YOUR PROFITS AND YOUR GILDED SHRINES,	165	QUINTUS SEPTIM	12
WHO ATE THE PROFITS, AND WHO LOCKED 'EM IN	260	ALF'S FIFTH	18
FROM PROFITS ON HOT AIR.	266	ALF'S ELEVENTH	16
PROGENY			
DO NOT YOU DISOWN YOUR PROGENY.	85	SALUTATION 2ND	6
PROGRAM			
NO CHANGE, NO CHANGE OF PROGRAM, "CHE!	163	CABARET DANCER	85
PROJECTION			
IN THE FLAT PROJECTION OF A SPIRAL.	147	BEFORE SLEEP	16
PROLETARIAT			
OF THIS HERE PROLETARIAT.	271	OLE KATE	24
PROLIFIC			
"PROLIFIC NOYES" WITH OUTPUT UNDEFEATABLE).	240	MOYEN SENSUEL	50
PROMINENT			
THE PROMINENT HAUNTS, WHERE ONE MIGHT RECOGNIZE HIM,	245	MOYEN SENSUEL	20
PROMISCUITY			
COULD YOU ENDURE SUCH PROMISCUITY?	228	SEXTUS PROP:12	1
PROMISED			
TWICE THEY PROMISED TO COME.	158	PSYCHOLOG HOUR	2
"BUT THEY PROMISED AGAIN:	159	PSYCHOLOG HOUR	3
PROMISED ME.	224	SEXTUS PROP: 9	2
PROMOTION			
AND GOT NO PROMOTION,	136	EXILE'S LETTER	6
PROPAGANDAS			
"MESSAGE TO GARCIA," MOSHER'S PROPAGANDAS	241	MOYEN SENSUEL	7
PROPERLY			
NEVER GOT PROPERLY TANKED AS I SAW,	271	OLE KATE	
PROPERTIUS			
"TROICA ROMA RESURGES."--PROPERTIUS	40	ROME	E
HOMAGE TO SEXTUS PROPERTIUS	205	SEXTUS PROP	
"YOU NEED, PROPERTIUS, NOT THINK	210	SEXTUS PROP: 2	

PAGE 320

	PAGE	TITLE	LINE
PROPERTIUS (CONTINUED)			
AND NOW PROPERTIUS OF CYNTHIA, TAKING HIS STAND AMONG THESE.	230	SEXTUS PROP:12	75
PROPERTY			
AND HIS STRANGE PROPERTY SETS SIGHS TO MOVE	250	DONNA MI PREGA	58
PROPHYLACTIC			
DOWN RODYHEAVER'S PROPHYLACTIC SPINE,	246	MOYEN SENSUEL	225
PROPITIATES			
HE PROPITIATES ME WITH OYSTERS,	46	FROM HEINE: 6	3
PROPPED			
THOUGH MY HOUSE IS NOT PROPPED UP BY TAENARIAN COLUMNS FROM LACONIA (ASSOCIATED WITH NEPTUNE AND CERBERUS),	208	SEXTUS PROP: 1	51
PROPRIETY			
CLINGS TO THE SKIRT IN STRICT (VIDE: "VOGUE") PROPRIETY.	241	MOYEN SENSUEL	86
PROSE			
KUTSU'S PROSE SONG	128	THE RIVER SONG	9
A PROSE KINEMA, NOT, NOT ASSUREDLY, ALABASTER	188	HUGH SELWYN: 2	11
PROSPERED			
OR NO ONE SEES IT, AND EN BERTRANS PROSPERED?	155	NEAR PERIGORD	126
PROSPEROUS			
HE THE PROSPEROUS MAN--WHAT SOME PERFORM	65	THE SEAFARER	57
PROTECTED			
OLD PENSIONERS AND OLD PROTECTED WOMEN	121	PROVINC DESERT	11
AND OF JOVE PROTECTED BY GEESE.	210	SEXTUS PROP: 2	15
PROTECTION			
"THE EUPHRATES DENIES ITS PROTECTION TO THE PARTHIAN AND APOLOGIZES FOR CRASSUS,"	216	SEXTUS PROP: 5	16
FOR IGNORANCE, ITS GROWTH AND ITS PROTECTION	241	MOYEN SENSUEL	70
A SENATORIAL JOBBER FOR PROTECTION,	245	MOYEN SENSUEL	214
PROTECTOR			
NOT ANY PROTECTOR	64	THE SEAFARER	26
PROTEST			
PROTEST WITH HER CLEAR SOPRANO.	204	MEDALLION	4
PROTOTYPE			
HE IS THE PROTOTYPE OF HALF THE NATION.	246	MOYEN SENSUEL	242
PROUD			
A PROUD THING I DO HERE,	105	DOMPNA POIS	24
IN THE MIDST OF SHOKU, A PROUD CITY.	138	NEAR SHOKU	9
PROVE			
THAT MIGHT PROVE USEFUL AND YET NEVER PROVES,	61	PORTRAIT FEMME	19
TO LIE WITH AND PROVE	174	LANGUE D'OC: 3	19
NOR DID DISGUST PROVE SUCH A STRONG EMETIC	242	MOYEN SENSUEL	138
I HAVE NO WILL TO PROVE LOVE'S COURSE	248	DONNA MI PREGA	11
PROVENCE			
PROVENCE KNEW;	50	THE FLAME	2
PROVENCE KNEW.	50	THE FLAME	4
PROVENCE KNEW;	50	THE FLAME	8
PROVES			
THAT MIGHT PROVE USEFUL AND YET NEVER PROVES,	61	PORTRAIT FEMME	19
PROVIDES			
HE PROVIDES ME WITH WOMEN AND DRINKS.	207	ABU SALAMMAMM	17
PROVINCE			
AND THEY CALL YOU BEAUTIFUL IN THE PROVINCE,	113	FORMIANUS LADY	8
WHOSE WHITE HEAD IS LOST FOR THIS PROVINCE?	139	SOUTH-FOLK	14
PROVINCIA			
PROVINCIA DESERTA	121	PROVINC DESERT	T
PROVISIONS			
IS DETAILED IN HIS PROVISIONS.	46	FROM HEINE: 6	12
PROVOSTS			
FROM THESE HE (RADWAY) LEARNT, FROM PROVOSTS AND FROM EDITORS UNYIELDING	240	MOYEN SENSUEL	51
PROWESSE			
SUCH BATTLE-GUERDON WITH HIS "PROWESSE HIGH"?	32	PIERE VIDAL	59
PRUDENT			
THE MOST PRUDENT, ORDERLY, AND DECOROUS!	161	CABARET DANCER	8
PRUDENT AND SVELTE PEPITA.	162	CABARET DANCER	50
THE PRUDENT WHORE IS NOT WITHOUT HER FUTURE,	163	CABARET DANCER	75
PRUDES			
RUFFLE THE SKIRTS OF PRUDES,	86	SALUTATION 2ND	32

PRUDES -- PURGED

	PAGE	TITLE	LINE
PRUDES (CONTINUED)			
SOME MEN WILL LIVE AS PRUDES IN THEIR OWN VILLAGE	245	MOYEN SENSUEL	207
P'S			
TO MIND THEIR "P'S" AND THEIR "Q'S" AND THEIR WAYS	263	ALF'S EIGHTH	27
P.'S			
SONG OF SIX HUNDRED M. P.'S	270	OF 600 M.P.'S	T
PSYCHE			
SPEECH FOR PSYCHE IN THE GOLDEN BOOK OF APULEIUS	39	FOR PSYCHE	T
PSYCHOLOGICAL			
VILLANELLE: THE PSYCHOLOGICAL HOUR	158	PSYCHOLOG HOUR	T
PUB			
BY FALLING FROM A HIGH STOOL IN A PUB . . .	193	SIENA MI FE	8
PUBLIC			
THAT SAME, THY PUBLIC IN MY SCREED	14	FAMAM CANO	19
AND LIARS IN PUBLIC PLACES.	190	HUGH SELWYN: 4	19
"NOR WILL THE PUBLIC CRIERS EVER HAVE YOUR NAME ...	211	SEXTUS PROP: 2	42
GODS' AID, LET NOT MY BONES LIE IN A PUBLIC LOCATION	213	SEXTUS PROP: 3	32
PUBLICATION			
OF PUBLICATION; "CIRCUMSTANCES,"	243	MOYEN SENSUEL	136
PUBLISHER			
A NOVELIST, A PUBLISHER, TO PAY OLD SCORES,	239	MOYEN SENSUEL	18
A NOVELIST, A PUBLISHER AND A PREACHER,	239	MOYEN SENSUEL	19
PUBLISHER'S			
AND THAT THE YOUNGEST SON WAS IN A PUBLISHER'S OFFICE,	179	MOEURS CON: 3	3
PUFFED			
PEPITA HAS SUCH TO-MORROWS: WITH THE HANDS PUFFED OUT,	161	CABARET DANCER	10
"SHE STEWS PUFFED FROGS, SNAKE'S BONES, THE MOULTED FEATHERS OF SCREECH OWLS,	215	SEXTUS PROP: 4	33
PUFFED SATIN, AND SILK STOCKINGS, WHERE THE KNEE	241	MOYEN SENSUEL	85
PUG-BITCH			
WILL BE QUITE RICH, QUITE PLUMP, WITH PUG-BITCH FEATURES,	162	CABARET DANCER	48
PUG-DOG'S			
THE PUG-DOG'S FEATURES ENCRUSTED WITH TALLOW	161	CABARET DANCER	11
PUI			
TO CARCASSONNE, PUI, AND ALAIS	98	THE BELLAIRES	36
PULLED			
PULLED BY THE KOHL AND ROUGE OUT OF RESEMBLANCE--	162	CABARET DANCER	29
PULLED DOWN BY A DEAL-WOOD HORSE;	208	SEXTUS PROP: 1	27
PULLING			
PULLING ON THEIR SHOES FOR THE DAY'S BUSINESS, ...	14	FAMAM CANO	12
I PLAYED ABOUT THE FRONT GATE, PULLING FLOWERS. ...	130	RIVER-MER WIFE	2
PULLS			
BUT YOUR SMILE PULLS ONE WAY	162	CABARET DANCER	41
PULLS UP A ROLL OF FAT FOR THE PIANIST,	163	CABARET DANCER	54
PULPING			
THE DASHING RUPERT OF THE PULPING TRADE,	264	ALF'S NINTH	9
PULSE			
ARE NOT THE BEST OF PULSE FOR INFANT NATIONS.	239	MOYEN SENSUEL	30
PUMP			
I PUMP THE MARKET UP AND DOWN	266	ALF'S ELEVENTH	17
PUNIC			
THEIR PUNIC FACES DYED IN THE GORGON'S LAKE;	211	SEXTUS PROP: 2	32
PUOSCH'			
TAN QUE I PUOSCH' OM GITAR AB MALH.	151	NEAR PERIGORD	EPI
PURE			
MY MOUTH TO CHANT THE PURE SINGING!	18	DE AEGYPTO	12
TISSUE PRESERVED--THE PURE MIND	193	SIENA MI FE	11
WHO SO INDECOROUS AS TO SHED THE PURE GORE OF A SUITOR?!	212	SEXTUS PROP: 3	26
YOU WILL OBSERVE THAT PURE FORM HAS ITS VALUE.	225	SEXTUS PROP:10	33
(LET HIM REBUKE WHO NE ER HAS KNOWN THE PURE PLATONIC GRAPPLE,	242	MOYEN SENSUEL	105
'TWAS AS A BUSINESS ASSET PURE AN' SIMPLE	246	MOYEN SENSUEL	239
PURER			
WAS PURER IN ITS LOVE OF ONE LOCALITY,	245	MOYEN SENSUEL	212
PURGED			
PHIDON NEITHER PURGED ME, NOR TOUCHED ME,	165	QUINTUS SEPTIM	23

PURIFIEZ -- PYPERS

	PAGE	TITLE	LINE
PURIFIEZ			
O DIEU, PURIFIEZ NOS COEURS!	26	NIGHT LITANY	1
PURIFIEZ NOS COEURS!	26	NIGHT LITANY	2
PURIFIEZ NOS COEURS,	26	NIGHT LITANY	20
PURIFIEZ NOS COEURS,	26	NIGHT LITANY	21
PURIFIEZ NOS COEURS,	27	NIGHT LITANY	34
PURIFIEZ NOS COEURS,	27	NIGHT LITANY	35
PURIFIEZ NOS COEURS	27	NIGHT LITANY	49
PURIFIEZ NOS COEURS	27	NIGHT LITANY	51
PURITY			
AND OF THE PURITY OF HER SOUL.	180	MOEURS CON: 5	27
PURPLE			
PURPLE AND SAPPHIRE FOR THE SILVER SHAFTS	21	IN DURANCE	36
BUT AH! WHEN I SEE THE STANDARDS GOLD, VAIR, PURPLE, OPPOSING	28	ALTAFORTE	4
GOD! BUT THE PURPLE OF THE SKY WAS DEEP!	30	PIERE VIDAL	20
THE PURPLE HOUSE AND THE CRIMSON ARE FULL OF SPRING SOFTNESS.	129	THE RIVER SONG	24
FIVE CLOUDS HANG ALOFT, BRIGHT ON THE PURPLE SKY,	129	THE RIVER SONG	33
HE RIDES THROUGH THE PURPLE SMOKE TO VISIT THE SENNIN,	140	SENNIN POEM	12
HER OVERSKIRT IS THE SAME SILK DYED IN PURPLE,	140	MULBERRY ROAD	14
FURTHER AND OUT OF REACH, THE PURPLE NIGHT,	155	NEAR PERIGORD	131
NO, NOT WHEN SHE WAS TUNICK'D IN PURPLE.	225	SEXTUS PROP:10	31
THE MIND OF RADWAY, WHENE'ER HE FOUND A PAIR OF PURPLE STAYS OR	245	MOYEN SENSUEL	196
PURPLING			
OVER THE SHARPENED TEETH AND PURPLING LIPS!	30	PIERE VIDAL	15
PURPOSE			
TO ALTER THEM TO HIS PURPOSE;	90	SURGIT FAMA	14
THERE WAS NOTHING AT CROSS PURPOSE,	134	EXILE'S LETTER	8
PURRING			
THE PURRING OF THE INVISIBLE ANTENNAE	113	TAME CAT	6
PURRS			
HE PURRS AND PATS THE CLEAR STRINGS.	139	SENNIN POEM	7
PURSE			
WHILE BORN, HIS OWN CLOSE PURSE, HIS RABBIT WARREN, COMRADE, COMRADE OF MY LIFE, OF MY PURSE, OF MY PERSON;	153 228	NEAR PERIGORD SEXTUS PROP:12	60 14
IN HIS PURSE THERE IS DECEIT,	263	ALF'S EIGHTH	16
PUSHED			
AMIABLE AND HARMONIOUS PEOPLE ARE PUSHED INCONTINENT INTO DUELS,	227	SEXTUS PROP:12	5
PUT			
BUT I HAVE PUT ASIDE THIS FOLLY AND THE COLD	4	LA FRAISNE	3
BUT I HAVE PUT ASIDE THIS FOLLY, BEING GAY	4	LA FRAISNE	7
AND I? I HAVE PUT ASIDE ALL FOLLY AND ALL GRIEF.	4	LA FRAISNE	24
LET THE MANES PUT OFF THEIR TERROR, LET THEM PUT OFF THEIR AQUEOUS BODIES WITH FIRE.	76	THE ALCHEMIST	51
LET THE MANES PUT OFF THEIR TERROR, LET THEM PUT OFF THEIR AQUEOUS BODIES WITH FIRE.	76	THE ALCHEMIST	51
WAS GOVERNOR IN HEI SHU, AND PUT DOWN THE BARBARIAN RABBLE.	135	EXILE'S LETTER	37
PUT ON A TIMELY VIGOUR.	216	SEXTUS PROP: 5	13
YOUR QUIET HOUR PUT FORWARD,	222	SEXTUS PROP: 8	28
YOUR EYES PUT ME UP TO IT.	247	PIERROT3	10
UNTO HIMSELF THE QUESTION PUT	272	THE BABY	3
PUTS			
SLENDER, SHE PUTS FORTH A SLENDER HAND;	128	BEAU TOILET	5
PLANTAGENET PUTS THE RIDDLE: "DID HE LOVE HER?"	155	NEAR PERIGORD	145
LEISURE'S ADORNMENT PUTS HE THEN NEVER ON,	249	DONNA MI PREGA	51
I READ THESE FELLERS PUTS IT	269	SAFE AND SOUND	17
PUTTING			
ALL FOLLY FROM ME, PUTTING IT ASIDE	4	LA FRAISNE	28
FOR PUTTING SILVER ON THE SPOT,	267	ALF'S TWELFTH	11
PUZZLED			
I CONFESS, MY FRIEND, I AM PUZZLED.	102	MEDITATIO	5
PYJAMAS			
MUST THINK TRUTH LOOKS AS THEY DO IN WOOL PYJAMAS.	243	MOYEN SENSUEL	148
PYPERS			
READIN' TH' PYPERS!	259	ALF'S THIRD	14

PYRAMID -- QUICK

	PAGE	TITLE	LINE
PYRAMID			
AND START TO INSPECT SOME FURTHER PYRAMID;	236	MIDDLE-AGED	7
PYRAMIDS			
NEITHER EXPENSIVE PYRAMIDS SCRAPING THE STARS IN THEIR ROUTE,	209	SEXTUS PROP: 1	66
PYRE			
SHE WOULD SIT LIKE AN ORNAMENT ON MY PYRE.	213	SEXTUS PROP: 3	31
Q.			
(NEAR Q. H. FLACCUS' BOOK-STALL).	210	SEXTUS PROP: 2	9
Q'S			
TO MIND THEIR "P'S" AND THEIR "Q'S" AND THEIR WAYS	263	ALF'S EIGHTH	27
QUAINT			
HERE THEY STAND WITHOUT QUAINT DEVICES,	85	SALUTATION 2ND	7
SOME OTHER QUAINT REMINDER OF THE OCCASION	245	MOYEN SENSUEL	197
QUALITY			
REGARDLESS OF QUALITY.	207	SEXTUS PROP: 1	25
BY QUALITY, BUT IS ITS OWN EFFECT UNENDINGLY	249	DONNA MI PREGA	30
QUANDARIES			
UP STAIRS, THE THIRD FLOOR UP, AND HAVE SUCH QUANDARIES	244	MOYEN SENSUEL	158
QUANTITIES			
SMEARED O'ER THE LOT IN EQUAL QUANTITIES.	244	MOYEN SENSUEL	174
QUARREL-BOLT			
AND GETS A QUARREL-BOLT SHOT THROUGH HIS VIZARD,	156	NEAR PERIGORD	158
QUARTERS			
IN THESE QUARTERS OR FLEET ST.?	263	ALF'S EIGHTH	14
QUASI			
"QUASI KALOUN." S. T. SAYS BEAUTY IS MOST THAT, A "CALLING TO THE SOUL."	20	IN DURANCE	20
QUATRE			
POUR QUATRE SOUS.	160	DANS OMNIBUS	23
QUATTRO			
ALFONSO, QUATTRO, POKE-NOSE.	22	MARVOIL	22
QUE			
QUE BE-M VOLS MAL.	9	NA AUDIART	57
"EST-CE QUE VOUS AVEZ VU DES AUTRES--DES CAMARADES--AVEC DES SINGES OU DES OURS?"	119	THE GYPSY	EPI
TAN QUE I PUOSCH' OM GITAR AB MALH.	151	NEAR PERIGORD	EPI
QUEEN			
O QUEEN OF CYPRESS,	76	THE ALCHEMIST	43
AND SEATED UPON IT IS THE LATE QUEEN, VICTORIA,	237	ABU SALAMMAMM	23
QUEENS			
RED KNIGHTS, BROWN BISHOPS, BRIGHT QUEENS,	120	GAME OF CHESS	1
CLASHING WITH X'S OF QUEENS,	120	GAME OF CHESS	10
WITH FORTY QUEENS, AND MUSIC TO REGALE	242	MOYEN SENSUEL	112
QUEERIES			
AND ASK INCONVENIENT QUEERIES.	273	NATIONAL SONG	16
QUENCHED			
OR TO SUCH BASE OCCASION LIT AND QUENCHED?	42	HER MONUMENT	57
NOW, QUENCHED AS THE BRAND OF MELEAGAR,	181	MOEURS CON: 6	3
QUERULOUS			
WITH PLAINTIVE, QUERULOUS CRYING.	110	TEMPORA	3
AND A QUERULOUS NOISE RESPONDED TO OUR SOLICITOUS REPROBATIONS.	215	SEXTUS PROP: 4	26
QU'EST			
S'ILS NE SENTENT PAS LA MUSIQUE, QU'EST CE	199	MAUBERLEY: 2	EPI
QU'EST CE QU'ILS PEUVENT COMPRENDRE?	199	MAUBERLEY: 2	EPI
"QU'EST CE QU'ILS SAVENT DE L'AMOUR, ET	199	MAUBERLEY: 2	EPI
QUESTING			
QUESTING AND PASSIVE....	192	YEUX GLAUQUES	19
QUESTION			
WHEN I QUESTION YOU;	84	ORTUS	14
ALAS; EHEU, ONE QUESTION THAT SORELY VEXES	244	MOYEN SENSUEL	161
"TIME FOR THAT QUESTION!" FRONT BENCH INTERPOSES.	260	ALF'S-FIFTH	16
TIME FOR THAT QUESTION? AND THE TIME IS NOW.	260	ALF'S FIFTH	17
UNTO HIMSELF THE QUESTION PUT	272	THE BABY	3
QUIA			
"QUIA PAUPER AMAVI."	206	SEXTUS PROP	EPI
QUICK			
GAY CINO, OF QUICK LAUGHTER,	6	CINO	18
SOME QUICK TO ARM,	190	HUGH SELWYN: 4	4

QUICK -- QUOTABLE

	PAGE	TITLE	LINE
QUICK (CONTINUED)			
QUICK EYES GONE UNDER EARTH'S LID,	191	HUGH SELWYN: 5	6
QUICKSAND			
BY THE IMMORTAL NATURE ON THIS QUICKSAND,	41	HER MONUMENT	30
QUIDEM			
VIR QUIDEM, ON DANCERS	161	CABARET DANCER	EPI
QUIES			
QUIES	63	QUIES	T
QUIET			
HER QUIET IRONIES.	52	AU SALON	EPI
YET IT IS QUIET HERE:	60	TOMB AKR CAAR	32
QUIET THIS METAL!	76	THE ALCHEMIST	50
QUIET THIS METAL.	76	THE ALCHEMIST	62
AND YET THE MAN IS SO QUIET AND RESERVED IN DEMEANOUR	100	TEMPERAMENTS	3
I STOP IN MY ROOM TOWARD THE EAST, QUIET, QUIET,	142	UNMOVING CLOUD	6
I STOP IN MY ROOM TOWARD THE EAST, QUIET, QUIET,	142	UNMOVING CLOUD	6
A QUIET AND RESPECTABLE-TAWDRY TRIO;	163	CABARET DANCER	81
QUIET TALKING IS ALL THAT IS LEFT US--	168	OF AROUET	31
OR SET ME QUIET, OR BID ME CHATTER.	175	LANGUE D'OC: 3	45
YOUR QUIET HOUR PUT FORWARD,	222	SEXTUS PROP: 8	28
QUIETEST			
AND IN THE QUIETEST SPACE	155	NEAR PERIGORD	136
QU'IEU			
QU'IEU SUI AVINEN,	166	FISH & SHADOW	16
OF ARNAUT DE MAREUIL, I THOUGHT, "QU'IEU SUI AVINEN."	166	FISH & SHADOW	19
QU'IL			
DIEU! QU'IL LA FAIT	72	DIEU! QU'IL	T
QU'ILS			
"QU'EST CE QU'ILS SAVENT DE L'AMOUR, ET	199	MAUBERLEY: 2	EPI
QU'EST CE QU'ILS PEUVENT COMPRENDRE?	199	MAUBERLEY: 2	EPI
QU'ILS PEUVENT COMPRENDE DE CETTE PASSION	199	MAUBERLEY: 2	EPI
QUINTILIA			
CALVUS MOURNING QUINTILIA,	230	SEXTUS PROP:12	71
QUINTUS			
HOMAGE TO QUINTUS SEPTIMIUS FLORENTIS CHRISTIANUS	164	QUINTUS SEPTIM	T
QUITE			
I WAS QUITE STRONG--AT LEAST THEY SAID SO--	4	LA FRAISNE	5
QUITE GAY, FOR I HAVE HER ALONE HERE	5	LA FRAISNE	38
AND THEY SAID I WAS QUITE STRONG, AMONG THE YOUNG MEN.	5	LA FRAISNE	41
FOR WE ARE QUITE ALONE	5	LA FRAISNE	51
NOTHING THAT'S QUITE YOUR OWN.	61	PORTRAIT FEMME	29
YOU WORE THE SAME QUITE CORRECT CLOTHING,	101	AMITIES	1
THE JEWELLED STEPS ARE ALREADY QUITE WHITE WITH DEW,	132	JEWEL STAIRS'	1
WILL BE QUITE RICH, QUITE PLUMP, WITH PUG-BITCH FEATURES,	162	CABARET DANCER	48
WILL BE QUITE RICH, QUITE PLUMP, WITH PUG-BITCH FEATURES,	162	CABARET DANCER	48
QUITE OUT OF PLACE AMID	201	AGE DEMANDED	23
QUITE ENOUGH BEAUTIFUL WOMEN,	223	SEXTUS PROP: 9	15
THE SOCIAL ITCH, THE ALMOST, ALL BUT, NOT QUITE, FASCINATING,	241	MOYEN SENSUEL	83
SO RADWAY WALKED, QUITE LIKE THE OTHER MEN,	244	MOYEN SENSUEL	185
NOT QUITE SNOWED UNDER.	261	ALF'S SIXTH	20
THEY CAN'T QUITE BRIBE HIM.	261	ALF'S SIXTH	22
I DON'T QUITE SEE THE JOKE ANY MORE,	264	ALF'S EIGHTH	29
QUIVER			
SHE PASSED AND LEFT NO QUIVER IN THE VEINS, WHO NOW	92	GENTILDONNA	1
I SHAKE AND BURN AND QUIVER	175	LANGUE D'OC: 3	28
QUIVERING			
THAT SEEMS TO BE SOME QUIVERING SPLENDOUR CAST	41	HER MONUMENT	29
QUIVERS			
THE HORSES ARE WELL TRAINED, THE GENERALS HAVE IVORY ARROWS AND QUIVERS ORNAMENTED WITH FISH-SKIN.	127	BOWMEN OF SHU	19
QUO'			
"FIRST LET THESE GO!" QUO' OUR GOODLY FERE,	33	GOODLY FERE	7
"I'LL GO TO THE FEAST," QUO' OUR GOODLY FERE,	33	GOODLY FERE	27
QUOD			
DEO LAUS, QUOD EST SEPULTUS,	101	AMITIES	10
QUOTABLE			
'TIS TIME THAT IT WAS CAPPED WITH SOMETHING QUOTABLE.	239	MOYEN SENSUEL	38

QUOTATIONS -- RAIN

	PAGE	TITLE	LINE
QUOTATIONS			
FOR MINDS SO WHOLLY FOUNDED UPON QUOTATIONS	239	MOYEN SENSUEL	29
RAANA			
"IT IS NOT, RAANA, THAT MY SONG RINGS HIGHEST	24	THUS NINEVEH	20
RABBIT			
HER NOTE, THE LITTLE RABBIT FOLK	14	FAMAM CANO	8
WHILE BORN, HIS OWN CLOSE PURSE, HIS RABBIT WARREN,	153	NEAR PERIGORD	60
RABBITS			
WE WHO SHOOK OFF OUR DEW WITH THE RABBITS,	104	ANCORA	5
(SUCH CHANGES DON'T OCCUR IN MEN, OR RABBITS).	246	MOYEN SENSUEL	232
RABBITS'			
AND GIVES YOU AUSTRALIAN ICED RABBITS' MEAT	263	ALF'S EIGHTH	18
RABBLE			
AND ROUND ABOUT THERE IS A RABBLE	83	THE GARDEN	5
WAS GOVERNOR IN HEI SHU, AND PUT DOWN THE BARBARIAN RABBLE.	135	EXILE'S LETTER	37
RACK			
THOUGH THE WHOLE WORLD RUN RACK	176	LANGUE D'OC: 3	73
AND THEY ALL GO TO RACK RUIN BENEATH THE THUD OF THE YEARS.	209	SEXTUS PROP: 1	71
RACONTE			
"NODIER RACONTE . . ."	180	MOEURS CON: 5	SUB
RADWAY			
HERE RADWAY GREW, THE FRUIT OF PANTOSOCRACY,	239	MOYEN SENSUEL	39
RADWAY? MY HERO, FOR IT WILL BE MORE INSPIRING	239	MOYEN SENSUEL	41
RADWAY GREW UP. THESE FORCES SHAPED HIS SOUL;	239	MOYEN SENSUEL	44
FROM THESE HE (RADWAY) LEARNT, FROM PROVOSTS AND FROM EDITORS UNYIELDING	240	MOYEN SENSUEL	51
MY HERO, RADWAY, I HAVE NAMED, IN TRUTH,	241	MOYEN SENSUEL	77
RADWAY HAD READ THE VARIOUS EVENING PAPERS	241	MOYEN SENSUEL	91
YET RADWAY WENT. A CIRCUMSPECTIOUS PRIG!	242	MOYEN SENSUEL	119
AND THEN RADWAY BEGAN TO GO THE PACES:	243	MOYEN SENSUEL	144
SO RADWAY WALKED, QUITE LIKE THE OTHER MEN,	244	MOYEN SENSUEL	185
THE MIND OF RADWAY, WHENE'ER HE FOUND A PAIR OF PURPLE STAYS OR	245	MOYEN SENSUEL	196
BUT RADWAY WAS A PATRIOT WHOSE VENALITY	245	MOYEN SENSUEL	211
RADWAY WAS IGNORANT AS AN EDITOR,	246	MOYEN SENSUEL	219
BUT TURN TO RADWAY: THE FIRST NIGHT ON THE RIVER,	246	MOYEN SENSUEL	223
OF RADWAY. O CLAP HAND YE MORALISTS!	246	MOYEN SENSUEL	227
THAT RADWAY JOINED THE BAPTIST BROADWAY TEMPLE.	246	MOYEN SENSUEL	240
RAFT			
"OF" ROYAL AEMILIA, DRAWN ON THE MEMORIAL RAFT,	210	SEXTUS PROP: 2	10
UPON THE ONE RAFT, VICTOR AND CONQUERED TOGETHER,	218	SEXTUS PROP: 6	3
ONE RAFT ON THE VEILED FLOOD OF ACHERON,	219	SEXTUS PROP: 6	11
AND ONE RAFT BEARS OUR FATES	223	SEXTUS PROP: 9	5
RAFTERS			
I HAVE CREPT OVER OLD RAFTERS,	121	PROVINC DESERT	14
OH HOW THE BIRD FLEW FROM TROJAN RAFTERS,	227	SEXTUS PROP:11	35
RAFU			
FOR THEY HAVE A DAUGHTER NAMED RAFU,	140	MULBERRY ROAD	3
AND WHEN MEN GOING BY LOOK ON RAFU	140	MULBERRY ROAD	15
RAG			
THAT CANTING RAG CALLED EVERYBODY'S MAGAZINE,	241	MOYEN SENSUEL	98
RAGE			
WOMAN? OH, WOMAN IS A CONSUMMATE RAGE,	165	QUINTUS SEPTIM	20
RAGGED			
SUCH AN ONE PICKING A RAGGED	15	FAMAM CANO	38
RAILING			
SHE WALKS BY THE RAILING OF A PATH IN KENSINGTON GARDENS,	83	THE GARDEN	2
RAILINGS			
VINE-STRINGS A HUNDRED FEET LONG HANG DOWN FROM CARVED RAILINGS,	129	THE RIVER SONG	27
RAIMENT			
GREEN AND GRAY IS HER RAIMENT,	18	DE AEGYPTO	5
RAIMONA			
RAIMONA, TIBORS, BERANGERE,	75	THE ALCHEMIST	6
RAIN			
WHAT IF THE WIND HAVE TURNED AGAINST THE RAIN?	59	SILET	10
RAIN FLAKES OF GOLD ON THE WATER	76	THE ALCHEMIST	55
THE WIND CAME, AND THE RAIN,	119	THE GYPSY	7

RAIN -- RATE

	PAGE	TITLE	LINE
RAIN (CONTINUED)			
AND SORROW, SORROW LIKE RAIN.	133	FRONTIER GUARD	17
AND BEFORE THE END OF THE DAY WE WERE SCATTERED LIKE STARS, OR RAIN.	135	EXILE'S LETTER	33
LIGHT RAIN IS ON THE LIGHT DUST	137	OF DEPARTURE	EPI
AND THE RAIN FALLS AND FALLS,	142	UNMOVING CLOUD	2
RAIN, RAIN, AND THE CLOUDS HAVE GATHERED,	142	UNMOVING CLOUD	10
RAIN, RAIN, AND THE CLOUDS HAVE GATHERED,	142	UNMOVING CLOUD	10
THE RAIN, THE WANDERING BUSSES.	158	PSYCHOLOG HOUR	11
FLAME BURNS, RAIN SINKS INTO THE CRACKS	209	SEXTUS PROP: 1	70
RAIN-COLD			
GREY OLIVE LEAVES BENEATH A RAIN-COLD SKY.	92	GENTILDONNA	5
RAINETH			
RAINETH DROP AND STAINETH SLOP,	116	ANCIENT MUSIC	3
RAINS			
AS GOLD THAT RAINS ABOUT SOME BURIED KING.	236	MIDDLE-AGED	2
RAINS DOWN AND SO ENRICHES SOME STIFF CASE,	236	MIDDLE-AGED	17
RAIN-TEARS			
CLOUD AND RAIN-TEARS PASS THEY FLEET!	7	CINO	49
RAKU-HOKU			
AND YOU TO THE NORTH OF RAKU-HOKU,	134	EXILE'S LETTER	14
RAKUYO			
TO SO-KIN OF RAKUYO, ANCIENT FRIEND, CHANCELLOR OF GEN.	134	EXILE'S LETTER	1
RAMBLING			
I HA' TAKEN TO RAMBLING THE SOUTH HERE.	22	MARVOIL	5
RAMM			
AND HOW THE WIND DOTH RAMM!	116	ANCIENT MUSIC	4
RAMSEY			
WHILE RAMSEY MACDONALD SLEEPS, SLEEPS.	265	ALF'S TENTH	8
RAN			
RAN CRYING WITH OUT-SPREAD HAIR,	219	SEXTUS PROP: 6	34
THAT'S HOW THE PRESS BLURB RAN,--	261	ALF'S SIXTH	14
OLD 'ERB WAS DOTING, SO THE RUMOUR RAN,	264	ALF'S NINTH	13
AND RUPERT RAN THE RUMOUR ROUND IN WHEELS,	264	ALF'S NINTH	14
RANAUS			
FLEE IF YOU LIKE INTO RANAUS,	226	SEXTUS PROP:11	5
RANCOUR			
SHE HATH HUSHED MY RANCOUR OF COUNCIL,	4	LA FRAISNE	17
RANG			
AND THE SCORN OF HIS LAUGH RANG FREE,	33	GOODLY FERE	10
WHEN THE TRUMPET RANG OUT.	48	FROM HEINE: 7	32
RANK			
THAT WAS RANK FOLLY TO MY HEAD BEFORE.	3	THE TREE	12
RAOUL			
FOR JEHAN AND RAOUL DE VALLERIE	12	OF THE GIDDET	27
RAPE			
NINE ADULTERIES, 12 LIAISONS, 64 FORNICATIONS AND SOMETHING APPROACHING A RAPE	100	TEMPERAMENTS	1
RAPES			
ZEUS' CLEVER RAPES, IN THE OLD DAYS,	227	SEXTUS PROP:11	33
RAPTURES			
WITH RAPTURES FOR BACCHUS, TERPSICHORE AND THE CHURCH.	193	SIENA MI FE	15
RARE			
"AH-EH! THE STRANGE RARE NAME . . .	16	FAMAM CANO	42
AH-EH! HE MUST BE RARE IF EVEN I HAVE NOT . . ."	15	FAMAM CANO	43
--RARE VISITOR--CAME NOT,--THE SAINTS I GUERDON	30	PIERE VIDAL	23
IDOLS AND AMBERGRIS AND RARE INLAYS,	61	PORTRAIT FEMME	23
BEAUTY IS SO RARE A THING.	158	PSYCHOLOG HOUR	6
BEAUTY IS SO RARE A THING	158	PSYCHOLOG HOUR	21
RASCAL			
"UP! THOU RASCAL, RISE,	171	LANGUE D'OC	EPI
RAST-WAY			
BEDDING O'ER THE NEW-LAID RAST-WAY	7	CINO	50
ATE			
NOT, AT ANY RATE, AN ATTIC GRACE;	188	HUGH SELWYN: 2	4
AT ANY RATE I SHALL NOT HAVE MY EPITAPH IN A HIGH ROAD.	213	SEXTUS PROP: 3	38
THERE COMES, IT SEEMS, AND AT ANY RATE	222	SEXTUS PROP: 8	16
"AND RATE 'EM UP AT JUST SO MUCH PER HEAD,	244	MOYEN SENSUEL	181

RATHER -- READIN'

	PAGE	TITLE	LINE
RATHER			
TELL US THIS THING RATHER, THEN WE'LL BELIEVE YOU,	13	MESMERISM	6
WILL WE NOT RATHER, WHEN OUR FREEDOM'S WON,	39	BLANDULA	2
ONE PLACE WHERE WE'D RATHER HAVE TEA	52	AU SALON	8
SOME FEW WHOM WE'D RATHER PLEASE	52	AU SALON	20
WE SHALL GET OURSELVES RATHER DISLIKED.	99	SALVATIONISTS	2
AND YET I'D RATHER	107	DOMPNA POIS	66
ANCIENT WISDOM, RATHER COSMIC	118	ANCIENT WISDOM	T
AND THE OTHER WAS RATHER LIKE MY BUST BY GAUDIER,	181	MOEURS CON: 7	13
RATHER THAN THE MOTTOES ON SUN-DIALS.	187	E. P. ODE	16
SO HE "FACED LIFE" WITH RATHER MIXED INTENTIONS,	242	MOYEN SENSUEL	101
BY NAME, IF NAMED." SO IT WAS PHRASED, OR RATHER SOMEWHAT SO	242	MOYEN SENSUEL	114
RAVEL			
TAKE THE WHOLE MAN, AND RAVEL OUT THE STORY.	152	NEAR PERIGORD	47
RAVENS			
RAVENS, NIGHTS, ALLUREMENT:	6	CINO	7
RAVVLES			
"SHE BINDS ME WITH RAVVLES OF SHROUDS.	215	SEXTUS PROP: 4	34
RAW			
WEARING RAW SILK OF GOOD COLOUR,	146	CANTILATIONS	7
RAY			
AND, AS THE RAY OF SUN ON HANGING FLOWERS	40	ERAT HORA	2
RAYS			
BENEATH HALF-WATT RAYS,	204	MEDALLION	15
SPREADING ITS RAYS, IT TENDETH NEVER DOWN	249	DONNA MI PREGA	29
RAZOR'S			
SHOWS RAZOR'S UNFAMILIARITY	15	FAMAM CANO	36
RE			
EMANUELE RE D' ITALIA,	182	MOEURS CON: 7	21
REACH			
THEY REACH ME NOT, TOUCH ME SOME EDGE OR THAT,	20	IN DURANCE	5
BUT REACH ME NOT AND ALL MY LIFE'S BECOME	20	IN DURANCE	6
HOW CANST THOU REACH SO HIGH WITH THY POOR SENSE;	42	HER MONUMENT	52
WHAT IF MY THOUGHTS WERE TURNED IN THEIR MID REACH	43	SATIEMUS	9
ALGAE REACH UP AND OUT, BENEATH	69	SUB MARE	6
FURTHER AND OUT OF REACH, THE PURPLE NIGHT,	155	NEAR PERIGORD	131
"BRIGHT TIPS REACH UP FROM TWIN TOWERS,	212	SEXTUS PROP: 3	4
TILL UP AGAIN, RIGHT UP, WE REACH THE PRESIDENT,	239	MOYEN SENSUEL	16
REACHES			
ONE FLAME, THAT REACHES NOT BEYOND	20	IN DURANCE	7
REACHING			
REACHING AND STRIKING IN ANGLES,	120	GAME OF CHESS	4
THE LONG KIANG, REACHING HEAVEN.	137	ON RIVER KIANG	5
READ			
THOUGH THOU HATE ME, READ IT SET	8	NA AUDIART	25
A BOOK IS KNOWN BY THEM THAT READ	14	FAMAM CANO	18
I HAVE READ OUT THE GOLD UPON THE WALL,	60	TOMB AKR CAAR	9
RIGHT ENOUGH? THEN READ BETWEEN THE LINES OF UC ST. CIRC,	151	NEAR PERIGORD	3
YOU READ TO-DAY, HOW LONG THE OVERLORDS OF PERIGORD,	152	NEAR PERIGORD	50
READ THIS:	203	MAUBERLEY: 4	21
BUT FOR SOMETHING TO READ IN NORMAL CIRCUMSTANCES?	207	SEXTUS PROP: 1	19
READ BENNETT OR SOME OTHER FLACCID FLATTERER.	240	MOYEN SENSUEL	66
RADWAY HAD READ THE VARIOUS EVENING PAPERS	241	MOYEN SENSUEL	91
ALSO, HE'D READ OF CHRISTIAN VIRTUES IN	241	MOYEN SENSUEL	97
"KNOW WHAT THEY THINK, AND JUST WHAT BOOKS THEY'VE READ,	244	MOYEN SENSUEL	182
HE READ THE CENTURY AND THOUGHT IT NICE	245	MOYEN SENSUEL	20
AND DON'T READ NO BOOKS;	260	ALF'S FOURTH	1
I READ THESE FELLERS PUTS IT	269	SAFE AND SOUND	1
TO READ HIS SMUTTY LITERATURE	272	NATIONAL SONG	
NOT THAT NICE BRITONS READ 'EM,	272	NATIONAL SONG	1
READER			
NOTE, READER, NOTE THE SENTIMENTAL TOUCH:	242	MOYEN SENSUEL	116
READERS			
AND EVEN THIS INFAMY WOULD NOT ATTRACT NUMEROUS READERS	230	SEXTUS PROP:12	6
READIN'			
READIN' TH' PYPERS!	259	ALF'S THIRD	1
AND TO KEEP AN EYE ON THEIR READIN' MATTER	272	NATIONAL SONG	1

READY -- RECORD

	PAGE	TITLE	LINE
READY			
AND ARE YOU NOT READY WHEN EVENING'S COME?	48	FROM HEINE: 8	3
EAGER AND READY, THE CRYING LONE-FLYER, ...	65	THE SEAFARER	63
READY ARE ALL FOLKS TO REWARD HER.	72	DIEU! QU'IL	4
SO YOU FOUND AN AUDIENCE READY.	85	SALUTATION 2ND	4
TILL I AGAIN FIND YOU READY.	105	DOMPNA POIS	20
LET COME THE READY OF WIT, ...	146	CANTILATIONS	9
HANG IN YELLOW-WHITE AND DARK CLUSTERS READY FOR PRESSING.	167	OF AROUET	22
AS IN A SUBJECT READY--	249	DONNA MI PREGA	26
REAL			
FOR TO YOU WE OWE A REAL DEBT:	101	AMITIES	14
THAT IS THE REAL DEATH, ...	168	OF AROUET	28
OR LIKE A REAL TEXAS COLONEL, ...	181	MOEURS CON: 7	14
REALIST			
O STATE SANS SONG, SANS HOME-GROWN WINE, SANS REALIST!	241	MOYEN SENSUEL	88
REALLY			
WHY DOES THE REALLY HANDSOME YOUNG WOMAN APPROACH ME IN SACKVILLE STREET	114	SIMULACRA	5
REALM			
THEIR REALM IS THE LATERAL COURSES.	147	BEFORE SLEEP	10
ALBA, YOUR KINGS, AND THE REALM YOUR FOLK	210	SEXTUS PROP: 2	3
REALMS			
FROM THE SUNDERED REALMS, OF THEBES AND OF AGED PRIAMUS;	38	LADY'S LIFE	8
REASON			
HOW SHOULD HE SHOW A REASON, ...	72	PAN IS DEAD	11
SPUR WITHOUT REASON, ...	111	IMAGE ORLEANS	3
AND FOR WHAT EARTHLY REASON THEY REMAIN.	244	MOYEN SENSUEL	160
NOT BY THE REASON, BUT 'TIS FELT, I SAY.	249	DONNA MI PREGA	35
THEIRS NOT TO REASON WHY, ...	257	BREAD BRIGADE	13
WITH 2 AND 2 MAKING 4 IN REASON, ...	263	ALF'S EIGHTH	12
REASON'S			
MAINTAINS INTENTION REASON'S PEER AND MATE;	249	DONNA MI PREGA	37
SO HE HAVE SENSE OR GLOW WITH REASON'S FIRE, ...	250	DONNA MI PREGA	91
RE-BEAMS			
THE PARENT RE-BEAMS AT ITS OFFSPRING.	180	MOEURS CON: 5	13
REBUKE			
(LET HIM REBUKE WHO NE'ER HAS KNOWN THE PURE PLATONIC GRAPPLE, ...	242	MOYEN SENSUEL	105
RECALLETH			
AND STILL WHEN FATE RECALLETH, ...	41	HER MONUMENT	22
RECEIVE			
WHO HATH THE MOUTH TO RECEIVE IT, ...	18	DE AEGYPTO	13
RECEIVED			
THE FAVOUR OF YOUR PARTY; HAD BEEN WELL RECEIVED."	155	NEAR PERIGORD	149
RECEIVES			
THAT IN PLEASURE SHE RECEIVES MORE THAN SHE CAN GIVE;	103	PHYLLIDULA	3
NATURE RECEIVES HIM;	195	HUGH SELWIN:10	5
RECENTLY			
SUCH ASPECT WAS PRESENTED TO ME, ME RECENTLY EMERGED FROM MY VISIONS, ...	225	SEXTUS PROP:10	32
RECEPTION			
AND WHAT A RECEPTION:	135	EXILE'S LETTER	46
RECESSES			
THE HIDDEN RECESSES	81	TENZONE	11
RECITING			
WALK DOWN LONGACRE RECITING SWINBURNE TO HERSELF, INAUDIBLY?	114	SIMULACRA	2
RECKING			
RECKING NAUGHT ELSE BUT THAT HER GRACES GIVE	197	ENVOI (1919)	10
RECKON			
MAY I FOR MY OWN SELF SONG'S TRUTH RECKON, ...	64	THE SEAFARER	1
RECOGNITION			
FROM THESE HE LEARNT. POE, WHITMAN, WHISTLER, HIM, THEIR RECOGNITION	240	MOYEN SENSUEL	59
RECOGNIZE			
THE PROMINENT HAUNTS, WHERE ONE MIGHT RECOGNIZE HIM,	245	MOYEN SENSUEL	203
RECORD			
FOR IT SEEMS TO US WORTHY OF RECORD.	93	LES MILLWIN	14

PAGE 329

RECORD -- REFORMING

	PAGE	TITLE	LINE
RECORD (CONTINUED)			
ANNALISTS WILL CONTINUE TO RECORD ROMAN REPUTATIONS,	207	SEXTUS PROP: 1	16
RECORD "ODD'S BLOOD! OUCH! OUCH!" A PRAYER, HIS SWIFT REPENTANCE.	243	MOYEN SENSUEL	130
RECOURSE			
UNLESS PERHAPS I SHOULD HAVE RECOURSE TO	243	MOYEN SENSUEL	155
RECUMBENT			
I HAD SEEN IN THE SHADE, RECUMBENT ON CUSHIONED HELICON,	210	SEXTUS PROP: 2	1
RED			
AND ITS AGE-LASTING WALLOW FOR RED GREED	14	FAMAM CANO	26
AS DARK RED CIRCLES FILLED WITH DUST.	16	PRAISE YSOLT	13
AND LITTLE RED ELF WORDS CRYING "A SONG,"	16	PRAISE YSOLT	15
AND THE RED SUN MOCKS MY SADNESS.	30	PIERE VIDAL	6
AND YET I CURSE THE SUN FOR HIS RED GLADNESS,	31	PIERE VIDAL	49
OH WE DRUNK HIS "HALE" IN THE GOOD RED WINE	33	GOODLY FERE	13
AND RED THE SUNLIGHT WAS, BEHIND IT ALL.	49	OF SPLENDOUR	8
BRING THE RED GOLD OF THE MAPLE,'	75	THE ALCHEMIST	10
FROM THE RED GLEAM OF COPPER,	76	THE ALCHEMIST	39
WE, YOU, I! WE ARE "RED BLOODS"!	82	THE CONDOLENCE	3
RED KNIGHTS, BROWN BISHOPS, BRIGHT QUEENS,	120	GAME OF CHESS	1
RED JADE CUPS, FOOD WELL SET ON A BLUE JEWELLED TABLE,	135	EXILE'S LETTER	47
THE RED AND GREEN KINGFISHERS	139	SENNIN POEM	1
SUNSET, THE RIBBON-LIKE ROAD LIES, IN RED CROSS-LIGHT,	154	NEAR PERIGORD	96
WITH A RED STRAGGLING BEARD?	154	NEAR PERIGORD	102
RED OVERWROUGHT WITH ORANGE AND ALL MADE	197	ENVOI (1919)	14
WITH RED CLOTHS ABOUT THEIR BUTTOCKS,	237	ABU SALAMMAMM	13
AND THEY HAVE RED FACES LIKE BRICKS.	237	ABU SALAMMAMM	14
DESPITE IT ALL, DESPITE YOUR RED BLOODS, FEBRILE CONCUPISCENCE	240	MOYEN SENSUEL	67
RED-BEAKED			
AS THE RED-BEAKED STEEDS OF	201	AGE DEMANDED	3
RED-PINE-TREE			
THE RED-PINE-TREE GOD LOOKS AT HIM AND WONDERS.	139	SENNIN POEM	11
REDUNDANCIES			
HUMAN REDUNDANCIES;	202	AGE DEMANDED	57
RED-WALLED			
THUS HE ESCHEWED THE BRIGHT RED-WALLED CAFES AND	245	MOYEN SENSUEL	205
REED			
DELICATELY UPON THE REED, ATTEND. ME!	62	N. Y.	3
NEITHER COULD I PLAY UPON ANY REED IF I HAD ONE.	62	N. Y.	7
THOU ART SLENDER AS A SILVER REED.	62	N. Y.	10
REEDS			
THYRSIS AND DAPHNIS UPON WHITTLED REEDS,	229	SEXTUS PROP:12	42
REEK			
THAT MAKE THE STARK WINDS REEK WITH FEAR	10	FOR THIS YULE	12
RE-ENTER			
TO SEE HOW CELESTINE WILL RE-ENTER HER SLIPPERS.	111	BLACK SLIPPERS	10
RE-ENTERS			
SHE RE-ENTERS THEM WITH A GROAN.	111	BLACK SLIPPERS	11
REFERENCE			
AND DECEIVED BY YOUR REFERENCE	214	SEXTUS PROP: 4	6
REFINEMENT			
REFINEMENT OF MEDIUM, ELIMINATION OF SUPERFLUITIES,	202	AGE DEMANDED	48
REFINING			
ALL ONE CAN SAY OF THIS REFINING MEDIUM	239	MOYEN SENSUEL	35
REFLECTING			
JUST REFLECTING THE SKY'S TINGE,	129	THE RIVER SONG	21
AND THE WATER, A HUNDRED FEET DEEP, REFLECTING GREEN EYEBROWS	136	EXILE'S LETTER	56
REFLECTIONS			
DISTURBETH HIS REFLECTIONS.	63	AN OBJECT	4
REFORM			
THEIR MOVES BREAK AND REFORM THE PATTERN:	120	GAME OF CHESS	8
REFORMATION			
NELL GWYNN'S STILL HERE, DESPITE THE REFORMATION,	163	CABARET DANCER	72
REFORMING			
BROUGHT NO REFORMING SENSE	201	AGE DEMANDED	

REFRAINS -- REMAIN

	PAGE	TITLE	LINE
REFRAINS			
OR IF THE COW REFRAINS FROM FOOD	272	THE BABY	7
REFT			
REFT ME AWAY;	176	LANGUE D'OC: 3	63
REFUSED			
ALL OF WHOM SHE REFUSED;	102	LADIES	2
REGALE			
WITH FORTY QUEENS, AND MUSIC TO REGALE	242	MOYEN SENSUEL	112
REGARD			
GOD! THAT MAD'ST HER WELL REGARD HER,	72	DIEU! QU'IL	1
GOD! THAT MAD'ST HER WELL REGARD HER,	72	DIEU! QU'IL	7
GOD! THAT MAD'ST HER WELL REGARD HER.	72	DIEU! QU'IL	13
REGARDLESS			
REGARDLESS OF QUALITY.	207	SEXTUS PROP: 1	25
REGISTER			
MY NERVES STILL REGISTER THE SOUNDS OF CONTRA-BASS',	247	PIERROTS	19
REGRET			
AND FOR ALL THIS I HAVE CONSIDERABLE REGRET,	98	THE BELLAIRES	41
AND WE ALL SPOKE OUT OUR HEARTS AND MINDS, AND WITHOUT REGRET.	134	EXILE'S LETTER	11
AND IF YOU ASK HOW I REGRET THAT PARTING:	136	EXILE'S LETTER	72
SO MUCH BARREN REGRET,	158	PSYCHOLOG HOUR	8
REHEARSED			
I HAD REHEARSED THE CURIAN BROTHERS, AND MADE REMARKS ON THE HORATIAN JAVELIN	210	SEXTUS PROP: 2	8
REIGNS			
REIGNS IN RESPECTABLE HEAVENS, . . .	227	SEXTUS PROP:11	28
REINACH			
PAGES OF REINACH.	204	MEDALLION	8
REINS			
AND WITH SILVER HARNESS AND REINS OF GOLD,	134	EXILE'S LETTER	22
DESPITE SUCH REINS AND CHECKS I'LL DO MY BEST,	238	MOYEN SENSUEL	12
REITERATION			
WHO CAN NOT STEEL YOURSELVES INTO REITERATION;	92	THE REST	12
REJOICER			
AND SHE THE REJOICER OF THE HEART IS BENEATH THEM:	108	LIU CH'E	5
REJOICING			
THEN HOWL I MY HEART NIGH MAD WITH REJOICING.	28	ALTAFORTE	6
IN HOT SUMMER HAVE I GREAT REJOICING	28	ALTAFORTE	7
AND THE SHRILL NEIGHS OF DESTRIERS IN BATTLE REJOICING,	28	ALTAFORTE	14
AND IT FILLS ALL MY HEART WITH REJOICING	29	ALTAFORTE	21
FOR THE DEATH OF SUCH SLUTS I GO REJOICING;	29	ALTAFORTE	29
NO CRY LIKE THE BATTLE'S REJOICING	29	ALTAFORTE	33
REJUVENATE			
GO! REJUVENATE THINGS!	86	SALUTATION 2ND	24
REJUVENATE EVEN "THE SPECTATOR."	86	SALUTATION 2ND	25
RELATION			
THIS URGE TO CONVEY THE RELATION	200	MAUBERLEY: 2	21
OF THIS TO RELATION OF THE STATE	201	AGE DEMANDED	14
RELATIONSHIP			
THAT YOUR RELATIONSHIP IS WHOLLY PARASITIC;	101	AMITIES	9
RELATIVES			
THE GODS HAVE BROUGHT SHAME ON THEIR RELATIVES;	227	SEXTUS PROP:12	3
RELAXING			
NEVER RELAXING INTO GRACE;	193	BRENNBAUM	4
RELEASED			
AND RELEASED THE MAIDEN ANDROMEDA.	237	ABU SALAMMAMM	9
RELIANCE			
IN WHICH THEIR MENTORS PLACE SUCH WIDE RELIANCE.	244	MOYEN SENSUEL	164
RELIEF			
ARE ON THE POOR RELIEF.	269	SAFE AND SOUND	8
RELIGION			
LET HER CHANGE HER RELIGION.	103	PHYLLIDULA	5
AND ACQUIRE A ROMAN RELIGION;	219	SEXTUS PROP: 6	10
RELIGIOUS			
HAVE DRIVEN HIS WIFE FROM ONE RELIGIOUS EXCESS TO ANOTHER,	178	MOEURS CON: 1	8
REMAIN			
YE MIGHT LET ONE REMAIN ABOVE WITH US.	38	LADY'S LIFE	4
YE MIGHT LET ONE REMAIN ABOVE WITH US.	38	LADY'S LIFE	14

REMAIN -- REPLIES

	PAGE	TITLE	LINE
REMAIN (CONTINUED)			
AND HIS LAUD BEYOND THEM REMAIN 'MID THE ENGLISH,	66	THE SEAFARER	79
IT IS NOBLE TO DIE OF LOVE, AND HONOURABLE TO REMAIN	218	SEXTUS PROP: 5	59
AND FOR WHAT EARTHLY REASON THEY REMAIN.	244	MOYEN SENSUEL	160
REMAINDER			
AND A FURTHER FREEDOM FOR THE REMAINDER	98	THE BELLAIRES	21
REMAINETH			
THAT WHICH REMAINETH NOW	41	HER MONUMENT	19
REMAINS			
REMAINS OF ROME. O WORLD, THOU UNCONSTANT MIME!	40	ROME	12
ONLY EMOTION REMAINS.	114	EPILOGUE	9
REMARKS			
I HAD REHEARSED THE CURIAN BROTHERS, AND MADE REMARKS ON THE HORATIAN JAVELIN	210	SEXTUS PROP: 2	8
REMEMBER			
. . . I DO NOT REMEMBER	5	LA FRAISNE	45
I DO NOT LIKE TO REMEMBER THINGS ANY MORE.	5	LA FRAISNE	48
REMEMBER THEE.	67	DORIA	11
REMEMBER THIS FIRE.	75	THE ALCHEMIST	13
REMEMBER THIS FIRE.	75	THE ALCHEMIST	24
COME, MY FRIEND, AND REMEMBER	83	THE GARRET	2
NOW I REMEMBER THAT YOU BUILT ME A SPECIAL TAVERN	134	EXILE'S LETTER	2
IN A FEW YEARS NO ONE WILL REMEMBER THE BUFFO,	146	MONUMENTUM AER	3
NO ONE WILL REMEMBER THE TRIVIAL PARTS OF ME,	146	MONUMENTUM AER	4
I REMEMBER THE YOUNG DAY	173	LANGUE D'OC: 2	17
"YOU REMEMBER MR. LOWELL,	182	MOEURS CON: 8	2
I SHOULD REMEMBER CAESAR'S AFFAIRS . . .	218	SEXTUS PROP: 5	47
REMEMBERED			
BUT I REMEMBERED THE NAME OF HIS FEVER MEDICINE AND DIED.	165	QUINTUS SEPTIM	24
REMEMBRANCE			
FROM PIERE VIDAL'S REMEMBRANCE THAT BLUE NIGHT.	30	PIERE VIDAL	19
REMINDER			
SOME OTHER QUAINT REMINDER OF THE OCCASION	245	MOYEN SENSUEL	197
REMISSION			
WITH HER HUSBAND ASKING A REMISSION OF SENTENCE,	230	SEXTUS PROP:12	61
REMNANT			
O REMNANT ENSLAVED!	92	THE REST	2
REMUER			
REMUER,	160	DANS OMNIBUS	8
REMUS			
NOR OF XERXES' TWO-BARRELED KINGDOM, NOR OF REMUS AND HIS ROYAL FAMILY,	217	SEXTUS PROP: 5	44
REND			
AND "REND LA FLAMME",	162	CABARET DANCER	26
RENDER			
WHO SHALL RENDER	8	NA AUDIART	8
RENEWAL			
BLOCKED LIGHTS WORKING IN. ESCAPES. RENEWAL OF CONTEST.	120	GAME OF CHESS	15
RENEWED			
WHEN SPELLS ARE ALWAY RENEWED ON HER?	72	DIEU! QU'IL	6
RENOWNED			
SHE WAS NOT RENOWNED FOR FIDELITY;	228	SEXTUS PROP:12	11
REPAYEST			
THAT THOU THUS REPAYEST US	26	NIGHT LITANY	17
REPEAT			
I REPEAT:	113	TAME CAT	3
AND THE BIRDS REPEAT	173	LANGUE D'OC: 2	2
MAY WE REPEAT; THE CENTENNIAL EXPOSITION	240	MOYEN SENSUEL	54
REPENTANCE			
RECORD "ODD'S BLOOD! OUCH! OUCH!" A PRAYER, HIS SWIFT REPENTANCE.	243	MOYEN SENSUEL	130
REPLACES			
THE PIANOLA "REPLACES"	189	HUGH SELWYN: 3	3
REPLEVIN			
REPLEVIN, ESTOPPEL, ESPAVIN AND WHAT NOT.	98	THE BELLAIRES	27
REPLIES			
AND SUCH REPLIES SHE LAVISHES	106	DOMPNA POIS	54
REPLIES WITH A CERTAIN HAUTEUR,	111	BLACK SLIPPERS	8

REPORT -- REST

	PAGE	TITLE	LINE
REPORT			
"THE MEDICAL REPORT THIS WEEK DISCLOSES . . ."	260	ALF'S FIFTH	15
REPORTS			
BY RIGGING STOCK REPORTS,	266	ALF'S ELEVENTH	18
REPRESENT			
IT WORKS TO REPRESENT THAT SCHOOL OF THOUGHT	63	PHASELLUS ILLE	5
WITH SIGNS AS MANY, THAT SHALL REPRESENT 'EM	244	MOYEN SENSUEL	167
REPROBATIONS			
AND A QUERULOUS NOISE RESPONDED TO OUR SOLICITOUS REPROBATIONS.	215	SEXTUS PROP: 4	26
REPUTATION			
"ABOUT ACQUIRING THAT SORT OF A REPUTATION.	210	SEXTUS PROP: 2	20
NOR OF HOMER'S REPUTATION IN PERGAMUS,	217	SEXTUS PROP: 5	43
REPUTATIONS			
ANNALISTS WILL CONTINUE TO RECORD ROMAN REPUTATIONS,	207	SEXTUS PROP: 1	16
RESEMBLANCE			
PULLED BY THE KOHL AND ROUGE OUT OF RESEMBLANCE--	162	CABARET DANCER	29
RESERVED			
AND YET THE MAN IS SO QUIET AND RESERVED IN DEMEANOUR	100	TEMPERAMENTS	3
RESIDENT			
FROM COMSTOCK'S SELF, DOWN TO THE MEANEST RESIDENT,	239	MOYEN SENSUEL	15
RESIDES			
RESIDES NOW AT AGDE AND BIAUCAIRE.	98	THE BELLAIRES	35
RESISTANCE			
RESISTANCE TO CURRENT EXACERBATIONS,	201	AGE DEMANDED	24
RESOLUTELY			
BENT RESOLUTELY ON WRINGING LILIES FROM THE ACORN;	187	E. P. ODE	7
RESONANCE			
ONE MUST HAVE RESONANCE, RESONANCE AND SONORITY . . . LIKE A GOOSE.	230	SEXTUS PROP:12	65
ONE MUST HAVE RESONANCE, RESONANCE AND SONORITY . . . LIKE A GOOSE.	230	SEXTUS PROP:12	65
RESPECT			
SHE DID NOT RESPECT ALL THE GODS;	221	SEXTUS PROP: 8	6
AN ART! YOU ALL RESPECT THE ARTS, FROM THAT INFANT TICK	239	MOYEN SENSUEL	13
STILL I'D RESPECT YOU MORE IF YOU COULD BURY	239	MOYEN SENSUEL	27
BUT KNIGHTS AND LORDS TO-DAY RESPECT	267	ALF'S ELEVENTH	23
RESPECTABILITY			
NOR OF THEBES IN ITS ANCIENT RESPECTABILITY,	217	SEXTUS PROP: 5	42
RESPECTABLE			
BECAUSE OF THIS RESPECTABLE TERROR,	212	SEXTUS PROP: 3	10
REIGNS IN RESPECTABLE HEAVENS, . . .	227	SEXTUS PROP:11	28
RESPECTABLE-TAWDRY			
A QUIET AND RESPECTABLE-TAWDRY TRIO;	163	CABARET DANCER	01
RESPECTABLY			
AND RESPECTABLY MARRIED TO PERSEUS,	222	SEXTUS PROP: 8	23
RESPECTED			
GLADSTONE WAS STILL RESPECTED,	192	YEUX GLAUQUES	1
RESPECTED, WORDSWORTHIAN:	229	SEXTUS PROP:12	51
RESPECTIVE			
TOGETHER WITH THE RESPECTIVE WIVES, HUSBANDS, SISTERS AND HETEROGENEOUS CONNECTIONS OF THE GOOD BELLAIRES,	97	THE BELLAIRES	6
RESPITE			
AS CRUSHED LIPS TAKE THEIR RESPITE FITFULLY,	43	SATIEMUS	8
ME NO RESPITE,	174	LANGUE D'OC: 3	23
RESPLENDENT			
AND VERY RESPLENDENT IS THIS FOUNTAIN.	237	ABU SALAMMAMM	19
RESPONDED			
AND A QUERULOUS NOISE RESPONDED TO OUR SOLICITOUS REPROBATIONS.	215	SEXTUS PROP: 4	26
REST			
THAT LEAVETH ME NO REST, SAYING EVER,	16	PRAISE YSOLT	7
REST MASTER FOR WE BE A-WEARY, WEARY	35	THE EYES	1
REST BROTHER, FOR LO! THE DAWN IS WITHOUT	35	THE EYES	5
FORGET AND REST AND DREAM THERE	47	FROM HEINE: 7	11
THESE, AND THE REST, AND ALL THE REST WE KNEW.	50	THE FLAME	15
THESE, AND THE REST, AND ALL THE REST WE KNEW.	50	THE FLAME	15
AND NO SUN COMES TO REST ME IN THIS PLACE,	60	TOMB AKR CAAR	25

PAGE 333

REST -- RETURNED

	PAGE	TITLE	LINE
REST (CONTINUED)			
GILT TURQUOISE AND SILVER ARE IN THE PLACE OF THY REST.	91	DANCE FIGURE	16
THE REST	92	THE REST	T
REST ME WITH CHINESE COLOURS,	95	OF THE DEGREES	1
REST NIGHTLY UPON THE SOUL OF OUR DELICATE FRIEND FLORIALIS,	100	TEMPERAMENTS	2
OF BELS MIRALS, THE REST,	106	DOMPNA POIS	56
WE HAVE NO REST, THREE BATTLES A MONTH.	127	BOWMEN OF SHU	16
THE BIRDS FLUTTER TO REST IN MY TREE,	142	UNMOVING CLOUD	22
ROCHECOUART, CHALAIS, THE REST, THE TACTIC,	155	NEAR PERIGORD	122
AND ALL THE REST OF HER A SHIFTING CHANGE,	157	NEAR PERIGORD	191
AND THE REST LAID THEIR CHAINS UPON ME,	224	SEXTUS PROP:10	9
WHERE HE TAKES REST; WHO MAKETH HIM TO BE;	248	DONNA MI PREGA	13
GOD REST HER SLOSHIN' SOUL.	271	OLE KATE	20
RESTAURANT			
THE GURGLING ITALIAN LADY ON THE OTHER SIDE OF THE RESTAURANT	111	BLACK SLIPPERS	7
AND DINE IN A SOGGY, CHEAP RESTAURANT?	167	OF AROUET	4
RESTED			
FOR A MOMENT SHE RESTED AGAINST ME	112	SHOP GIRL	1
RESTETH			
YEA, RESTETH LITTLE	250	DONNA MI PREGA	55
RESTING			
FINDS 'NEATH THIS ROCK FIT MOULD, FIT RESTING PLACE!	41	HER MONUMENT	21
AND IT WAS MORNING, AND I WANTED TO SEE IF SHE WAS ALONE, AND RESTING,	225	SEXTUS PROP:10	27
RESTLESS			
THE NIGHT ABOUT US IS RESTLESS.	110	COITUS	9
THOU RESTLESS, UNGATHERED.	112	HIMERRO	7
RESTLESSNESS			
FOR THAT RESTLESSNESS--PIERE SET TO KEEP	30	PIERE VIDAL	24
RESTORATION			
COULD I BUT SPEAK AS 'TWERE IN THE "RESTORATION"	238	MOYEN SENSUEL	7
RESTRAIN			
AS NOTHING CAN RESTRAIN OR MUCH DISPARAGE. . . .	245	MOYEN SENSUEL	192
RESTRAINT			
"COMPEL A CERTAIN SILENCE AND RESTRAINT."	243	MOYEN SENSUEL	138
RESTS			
"IT RESTS ME TO BE AMONG BEAUTIFUL WOMEN.	113	TAME CAT	1
IT RESTS ME TO CONVERSE WITH BEAUTIFUL WOMEN	113	TAME CAT	4
RESULT			
BUT THE SOLE RESULT WAS BILLS	98	THE BELLAIRES	30
RESURGES			
"TROICA ROMA RESURGES."--PROPERTIUS	40	ROME	EPI
RESURRECT			
AH YES, MY SONGS, LET US RESURRECT	99	SALVATIONISTS	3
RESUSCITATE			
HE STROVE TO RESUSCITATE THE DEAD ART	187	E. P. ODE	2
RETAIN			
SHE CAN ME RETAIN.	175	LANGUE D'OC: 3	59
RETROSPECT			
OF EROS, A RETROSPECT.	200	MAUBERLEY: 2	33
RETURN			
LEST LOVE RETURN WITH THE FOISON SUN	10	FOR THIS YULE	13
IN RETURN FOR THE FIRST KISS SHE GAVE ME."	23	MARVOIL	29
ALL THIS ANGELIC ASPECT CAN RETURN	42	HER MONUMENT	37
THE RETURN	74	THE RETURN	T
SEE, THEY RETURN; AH, SEE THE TENTATIVE	74	THE RETURN	1
SEE, THEY RETURN, ONE, AND BY ONE,	74	THE RETURN	5
AND RETURN TO THAT WHICH CONCERNS US.	82	THE CONDOLENCE	18
WHEN ANYONE SAYS "RETURN," THE OTHERS ARE FULL OF SORROW.	127	BOWMEN OF SHU	6
OUR DEFENCE IS NOT YET MADE SURE, NO ONE CAN LET HIS FRIEND RETURN.	127	BOWMEN OF SHU	8
OUR SORROW IS BITTER, BUT WE WOULD NOT RETURN TO OUR COUNTRY.	127	BOWMEN OF SHU	12
LET ME RETURN TO THIS BOLD THEME OF MINE,	246	MOYEN SENSUEL	226
RETURNED			
WHEN OUR SOULS ARE RETURNED TO THE GODS	52	AU SALON	2
BUT HE RETURNED TO THIS ISLAND	118	CONTEMPORARIES	4

PAGE 334

RETURNING -- RICH

	PAGE	TITLE	LINE
RETURNING			
TO ONE, ON RETURNING CERTAIN YEARS AFTER.	101	AMITIES	ST
SORROW TO GO, AND SORROW, SORROW RETURNING.	133	FRONTIER GUARD	18
AND I WAS DRUNK, AND HAD NO THOUGHT OF RETURNING.	135	EXILE'S LETTER	48
RETURNS			
HE RETURNS BY WAY OF SEI ROCK, TO HEAR THE NEW NIGHTINGALES,	130	THE RIVER SONG	37
AND A DAY WHEN NO DAY RETURNS.	220	SEXTUS PROP: 7	19
REVEALED			
AND WEIGHED, REVEALED HIS GREAT AFFECT,	200	MAUBERLEY: 2	31
REVERENCE			
KEEP SMALL WITH REVERENCE, BEHOLDING HER IMAGE.	164	QUINTUS SEPTIM	7
REVERIES			
NOT, NOT CERTAINLY, THE OBSCURE REVERIES	188	HUGH SELWYN: 2	5
BECAUSE OF THESE REVERIES.	193	SIENA MI FE	20
REVERY			
BURST IN UPON THE PORCELAIN REVERY:	201	AGE DEMANDED	18
REVIEWER			
"CAREFULLY THE REVIEWER.	194	MR. NIXON	4
REVIEWERS			
SO MUCH FOR THE GAGGED REVIEWERS,	145	SALUTATION 3RD	3
"BUTTER REVIEWERS. FROM FIFTY TO THREE HUNDRED	194	MR. NIXON	10
REVOLUTION			
ALSO, IN THE CASE OF REVOLUTION,	196	HUGH SELWIN:12	19
ROMANCE, REVOLUTION 1018!	258	ALF'S SECOND	11
REWARD			
THIS OUR REWARD FOR OUR WORKS,	52	AU SALON	16
READY ARE ALL FOLKS TO REWARD HER.	72	DIEU! QU'IL	4
HARD FIGHT GETS NO REWARD.	139	SOUTH-FOLK	10
FOR WHICH THINGS YOU WILL GET A REWARD FROM ME, LYGDAMUS?	215	SEXTUS PROP: 4	27
RHAPSODIZE			
COPHETUA TO RHAPSODIZE;	192	YEUX GLAUQUES	12
RHINE			
WITH RHINE WINE AND LIQUEURS.	46	FROM HEINE: 6	4
"NOR WHERE THE RHINE FLOWS WITH BARBAROUS BLOOD,	211	SEXTUS PROP: 2	46
RHODEZ			
EVER SINCE RHODEZ,	119	THE GYPSY	13
RHOMBS			
THE TWISTED RHOMBS CEASED THEIR CLAMOUR OF ACCOMPANIMENT;	223	SEXTUS PROP: 9	1
RHOMBUS			
SHE TWIDDLES THE SPIKED WHEEL OF A RHOMBUS.	215	SEXTUS PROP: 4	32
RHONE			
TORN, GREEN AND SILENT IN THE SWOLLEN RHONE,	31	PIERE VIDAL	27
RHYME			
OR THE "SCULPTURE" OF RHYME.	188	HUGH SELWYN: 2	12
RHYMERS'			
OF DOWSON; OF THE RHYMERS' CLUB;	193	SIENA MI FE	6
RHYMES			
TESTING HIS LIST OF RHYMES, A LEAN MAN? BILIOUS?	154	NEAR PERIGORD	101
RIBALD			
O RIBALD COMPANY, O SAINTLY HOST,	35	HIS OWN FACE	2
RIBBED			
MARSH-CRANBERRIES, THE RIBBED AND ANGULAR PODS	162	CABARET DANCER	19
RIBBON			
AND THE BLUE SATIN RIBBON,	180	MOEURS CON: 5	23
RIBBON-LIKE			
SUNSET, THE RIBBON-LIKE ROAD LIES, IN RED CROSS-LIGHT,	154	NEAR PERIGORD	96
RIBEYRAC			
I HAVE GONE IN RIBEYRAC	122	PROVINC DESERT	36
RIBS			
THE SHUDDER OF VAE SOLI GURGLES BENEATH MY RIBS.	247	PIERROTS	3
RICE-POWDER			
AS HE INHALED THE STILL FUMES OF RICE-POWDER.	140	HOYDEN ODNOVEL	122
RICH			
THAT THE RICH HAVE BUTLERS AND NO FRIENDS,	83	THE GARRET	3
JOY SO RICH, AND IF I FIND NOT EVER	105	DOMPNA POIS	7
IS RICH FOR A THOUSAND CUPS.	128	THE RIVER SONG	4

	PAGE	TITLE	LINE
RICH (CONTINUED)			
AND IT IS DOUBTFUL IF EVEN YOUR MANURE WILL BE RICH ENOUGH	146	MONUMENTUM AER	7
WILL BE QUITE RICH, QUITE PLUMP, WITH PUG-BITCH FEATURES,	162	CABARET DANCER	48
RICHARD			
ARNAUT AND RICHARD LODGE BENEATH CHALUS:	155	NEAR PERIGORD	128
RICHARD SHALL DIE TO-MORROW--LEAVE HIM THERE	155	NEAR PERIGORD	139
END THE DISCUSSION, RICHARD GOES OUT NEXT DAY	156	NEAR PERIGORD	157
RICHES			
THESE ARE YOUR RICHES, YOUR GREAT STORE; AND YET	61	PORTRAIT FEMME	24
AND ALL ARROGANCE OF EARTHEN RICHES,	66	THE SEAFARER	83
AS YOU ARE WITH USELESS RICHES?	102	TO DIVES	4
NOR WHERE ROME RUINS GERMAN RICHES,	211	SEXTUS PROP: 2	45
OF USELESS RICHES FOR THE OCCUPANT,	236	MIDDLE-AGED	12
RICHLY			
AND NOW YOU PAY ONE. YES, YOU RICHLY PAY.	61	PORTRAIT FEMME	13
RICKETY			
I HAVE CLIMBED RICKETY STAIRS, HEARD TALK OF CROY,	122	PROVINC DESERT	38
RID			
ASKING TIME TO BE RID OF . . .	199	MAUBERLEY: 2	9
RIDDLE			
SOLVE ME THE RIDDLE, FOR YOU KNOW THE TALE.	151	NEAR PERIGORD	4
PLANTAGENET PUTS THE RIDDLE: "DID HE LOVE HER?"	155	NEAR PERIGORD	145
"SAY THAT HE LOVED HER, DOES IT SOLVE THE RIDDLE?"	156	NEAR PERIGORD	156
RIDE			
WOULD FOLLOW THE WHITE GULLS OR RIDE THEM.	128	THE RIVER SONG	8
THEY RIDE UPON DRAGON-LIKE HORSES,	132	AT TEN-SHIN	15
RIDES			
HE RIDES THROUGH THE PURPLE SMOKE TO VISIT THE SENNIN,	140	SENNIN POEM	12
RIDGES			
THE MUSES CLINGING TO THE MOSSY RIDGES;	227	SEXTUS PROP:11	31
RIDING			
YOUNG MEN RIDING IN THE STREET	111	IMAGE ORLEANS	1
IT IS ADORNED WITH YOUNG GODS RIDING UPON DOLPHINS	237	ABU SALAMMAMM	20
RIGGING			
BY RIGGING STOCK REPORTS,	266	ALF'S ELEVENTH	18
RIGHT			
AND IT'LL ALL COME RIGHT,	53	AU JARDIN	21
'TWOULD NOT MOVE IT ONE JOT FROM LEFT TO RIGHT.	63	PHASELLUS ILLE	11
MAYHAP, RIGHT CLOSE AND KISSED.	107	DOMPNA POIS	68
HAVE THE RIGHT THERE--	121	PROVINC DESERT	12
BENDING YOUR PASSAGES FROM RIGHT TO LEFT AND FROM LEFT TO RIGHT	147	BEFORE SLEEP	15
BENDING YOUR PASSAGES FROM RIGHT TO LEFT AND FROM LEFT TO RIGHT	147	BEFORE SLEEP	15
RIGHT ENOUGH? THEN READ BETWEEN THE LINES OF UC ST. CIRC,	151	NEAR PERIGORD	3
I HAD LAID OUT JUST THE RIGHT BOOKS.	158	PSYCHOLOG HOUR	4
NOR DO I KNOW WHEN I TURN LEFT OR RIGHT	174	LANGUE D'OC: 3	24
IN HOPE TO SET SOME MISCONCEPTIONS RIGHT.	238	MOYEN SENSUEL	2
TILL UP AGAIN, RIGHT UP, WE REACH THE PRESIDENT,	239	MOYEN SENSUEL	16
PLENTY TO RIGHT OF 'EM,	257	BREAD BRIGADE	17
PLENTY TO RIGHT OF 'EM,	259	ALF'S THIRD	8
AND WHERE HE ONCE SET FOOT, RIGHT THERE HE STAYED.	264	ALF'S NINTH	12
RIGHTEOUS			
HIM DO WE PRAY AS TO A LORD MOST RIGHTEOUS	37	THE YOUNG KING	36
RIGOROUS			
THE RIGOROUS DEPUTATION FROM "SLADE"--	93	LES MILLWIN	6
RIHAKU			
(RIHAKU OR OMAKITSU)	137	OF DEPARTURE	EPI
RIHOKU'S			
WITH RIHOKU'S NAME FORGOTTEN,	133	FRONTIER GUARD	23
RILLET			
AS A RILLET AMONG THE SEDGE ARE THY HANDS UPON ME;	91	DANCE FIGURE	19
RIME			
WHAT IS THE USE OF SETTING IT TO RIME?	59	SILET	6
RIMES			
I MADE RIMES TO HIS LADY THIS THREE YEAR:	22	MARVOIL	7

RING -- RIVER

	PAGE	TITLE	LINE
RING			
RING DELICATE AND CLEAR.	45	FROM HEINE: 5	8
MY CRYSTAL HALLS RING CLEAR	47	FROM HEINE: 7	22
THEY SUPPORTED THE GAG AND THE RING:	145	SALUTATION 3RD	7
HER LOVE AND HER RING:	173	LANGUE D'OC: 2	20
NOT TIED TO THE RING AROUND,	261	ALF'S SIXTH	19
RING-HAVING			
HE HATH NOT HEART FOR HARPING, NOR IN RING-HAVING	65	THE SEAFARER	45
RINGS			
"IT IS NOT, RAANA, THAT MY SONG RINGS HIGHEST	24	THUS NINEVEH	20
RIOKUSHU			
AND WHAT ARE THEY COMPARED TO THE LADY RIOKUSHU,	132	AT TEN-SHIN	29
RIPPLES			
WITH RIPPLES LIKE DRAGON-SCALES, GOING GRASS GREEN ON THE WATER,	136	EXILE'S LETTER	52
AFTER WE CROSS THE INFERNAL RIPPLES,	228	SEXTUS PROP:12	28
RIQUIER			
"RIQUIER! GUIDO."	122	PROVINC DESERT	63
RISE			
AND I LOVE TO SEE THE SUN RISE BLOOD-CRIMSON.	29	ALTAFORTE	19
AND WE THAT ARE GROWN FORMLESS, RISE ABOVE--	32	PARACELSUS	9
RISE UP AND JUDGE US;	52	AU SALON	5
THE WALLS RISE IN A MAN'S FACE,	138	NEAR SHOKU	3
"UP! THOU RASCAL, RISE,	171	LANGUE D'OC	EPI
"COME NOW! OLD SWENKIN! RISE UP FROM THY BED,	172	LANGUE D'OC: 1	14
WHERE BANKS RISE DAY BY DAY,	272	NATIONAL SONG	2
RISEN			
NOT THAT HIS PAY HAD RISEN, AND NO LEAK	243	MOYEN SENSUEL	142
RISER			
ONE MUST OF NEEDS BE A HANG'D EARLY RISER	13	MESMERISM	3
RISES			
THE SUN RISES IN SOUTH EAST CORNER OF THINGS	140	MULBERRY ROAD	1
RISETH			
I AM FLAME THAT RISETH IN THE SUN,	18	DE AEGYPTO	17
RISHOGU			
WHO WILL BE SORRY FOR GENERAL RISHOGU,	139	SOUTH-FOLK	12
RISKS			
FOR FIRES AND ODD RISKS, COULD IN THIS SECTOR	243	MOYEN SENSUEL	152
RISQUE			
GOOD GOD! THEY SAY YOU ARE RISQUE,	104	ANCORA	1
RITES			
A TROJAN AND ADULTEROUS PERSON CAME TO MENELAUS UNDER THE RITES OF HOSPITIUM,	227	SEXTUS PROP:12	6
YOU WRITE OF ADRASTUS' HORSES AND THE FUNERAL RITES OF ACHENOR,	228	SEXTUS PROP:12	19
RITRATTO			
RITRATTO	182	MOEURS CON: 8	SUD
RIU'S			
RIU'S HOUSE STANDS OUT ON THE SKY,	141	IDEA OF CHOAN	26
RIVA			
LURE US BEYOND THE CLOUDY PEAK OF RIVA?	39	BLANDULA	15
RIVEN			
AND THROUGH ALL THE RIVEN SKIES GOD'S SWORDS CLASH.	28	ALTAFORTE	12
WORTH LIETH RIVEN AND YOUTH DOLOROUS,	36	THE YOUNG KING	6
RIVER			
SOME OVERFLOWING RIVER IS RUN MAD,	32	PARACELSUS	12
--EVEN THE RIVER MANY DAYS AGO,	60	TOMB AKR CAAR	16
THE RIVER? THOU WAST OVER YOUNG.	60	TOMB AKR CAAR	17
THY FACE AS A RIVER WITH LIGHTS.	91	DANCE FIGURE	11
FREEZETH RIVER, TURNETH LIVER,	116	ANCIENT MUSIC	8
IN THE YELLOW RIVER.	117	EPITAPHS	5
THE RIVER SONG	128	THE RIVER SONG	T
BLUE, BLUE IS THE GRASS ABOUT THE RIVER	128	BEAU TOILET	1
YOU WENT INTO FAR KU-TO-YEN, BY THE RIVER OF SWIRLING EDDIES,	130	RIVER-MER WIFE	16
IF YOU ARE COMING DOWN THROUGH THE NARROWS OF THE RIVER KIANG,	101	RIVER-MER WIFE	26
SEPARATION ON THE RIVER KIANG	137	ON RIVER KIANG	T
WHITE RIVER WINDING ABOUT THEM;	137	TAKING LEAVE	2
THE SMOKE-FLOWERS ARE BLURRED OVER THE RIVER.	137	ON RIVER KIANG	2
AND NOW I SEE ONLY THE RIVER,	137	ON RIVER KIANG	4

RIVER -- ROCK

	PAGE	TITLE	LINE
RIVER (CONTINUED)			
THE PHOENIX ARE GONE, THE RIVER FLOWS ON ALONE. ...	138	CITY OF CHOAN	2
THE FLAT LAND IS TURNED INTO RIVER.	142	UNMOVING CLOUD	12
AND HELD UP THE THREICIAN RIVER;	208	SEXTUS PROP: 1	43
BUT TURN TO RADWAY: THE FIRST NIGHT ON THE RIVER,	246	MOYEN SENSUEL	223
RIVER-BRIDGE			
YOU BACK TO YOUR RIVER-BRIDGE.	135	EXILE'S LETTER	35
RIVER-MERCHANT'S			
THE RIVER-MERCHANT'S WIFE: A LETTER	130	RIVER-MER WIFE	T
ROAD			
BEING UPON THE ROAD ONCE MORE, ...	6	CINO	11
SO TAKE I MY ROAD	106	DOMPNA POIS	34
UP ON THE WET ROAD NEAR CLERMONT.	119	THE GYPSY	6
EASTWARD THE ROAD LIES, ...	121	PROVINC DESERT	18
A BALLAD OF THE MULBERRY ROAD	140	MULBERRY ROAD	T
AND THE WIDE, FLAT ROAD STRETCHES OUT.	142	UNMOVING CLOUD	5
AND ALL THE ROAD TO CAHORS, TO TOULOUSE?	153	NEAR PERIGORD	67
SUNSET, THE RIBBON-LIKE ROAD LIES, IN RED CROSS-LIGHT, ...	154	NEAR PERIGORD	96
AT ANY RATE I SHALL NOT HAVE MY EPITAPH IN A HIGH ROAD.	213	SEXTUS PROP: 3	38
ROADS			
AND THE WANDERING OF MANY ROADS HATH MADE MY EYES	16	PRAISE YSOLT	12
I EVEN I, AM HE WHO KNOWETH THE ROADS	18	DE AEGYPTO	1
I, EVEN I, AM HE WHO KNOWETH THE ROADS	18	DE AEGYPTO	7
I, EVEN I, AM HE WHO KNOWETH THE ROADS	18	DE AEGYPTO	15
I, EVEN I, AM HE WHO KNOWETH THE ROADS	18	DE AEGYPTO	23
AND THREE VALLEYS, FULL OF WINDING ROADS, ...	121	PROVINC DESERT	4
I KNOW THE ROADS IN THAT PLACE:	121	PROVINC DESERT	21
I HAVE SAID: "THE OLD ROADS HAVE LAIN HERE.	122	PROVINC DESERT	56
I HAVE WALKED OVER THESE ROADS;	123	PROVINC DESERT	80
OVER ROADS TWISTED LIKE SHEEP'S GUTS.	135	EXILE'S LETTER	41
"SANSO, KING OF SHOKU, BUILT ROADS"	138	NEAR SHOKU	EPI
THEY SAY THE ROADS OF SANSO ARE STEEP, ...	138	NEAR SHOKU	1
A-BRISTLE WITH ANTENNAE TO FEEL ROADS, ...	153	NEAR PERIGORD	62
THUS ALL ROADS ARE PERFECTLY SAFE	212	SEXTUS PROP: 3	24
ROADWAYS			
WHOM WE MEET ON STRANGE ROADWAYS?	141	IDEA OF CHOAN	32
ROAR			
AND THE FIERCE THUNDERS ROAR ME THEIR MUSIC	28	ALTAFORTE	10
ROAST			
IN PLACE OF THE ROAST BEEF OF BRITAIN, ...	263	ALF'S EIGHTH	19
ROBBERS			
DRINK WE THE LUSTY ROBBERS TWAIN, ...	11	OF THE GIBBET	17
ROBE			
AND ALL HER ROBE WAS WOVEN OF PALE GOLD.	49	OF SPLENDOUR	12
EN ROBE DE PARADE.	83	THE GARDEN	EPI
A BROWN ROBE, WITH THREADS OF GOLD WOVEN IN PATTERNS, HAST THOU GATHERED ABOUT THEE, ...	91	DANCE FIGURE	17
ROBERT			
"AND A CAT'S IN THE WATER-BUTT."--ROBERT BROWNING	13	MESMERISM	EPI
ROBES			
AND ALL THY ROBES I HAVE KEPT SMOOTH ON THEE.	60	TOMB AKR CAAR	14
HER ROBES CAN BUT DO HER WRONG.	106	DOMPNA POIS	50
THAT I STRUT IN THE ROBES OF ASSUMPTION.	146	MONUMENTUM AER	2
ROCACOART			
ANHES OF ROCACOART, ARDENCA, AEMELIS, ...	75	THE ALCHEMIST	29
ROCAFIXADA			
I HAVE LAIN IN ROCAFIXADA, ...	122	PROVINC DESERT	50
ROCHECHOUART			
TO ROCHECHOUART, ...	106	DOMPNA POIS	35
ROCHECOART			
AT ROCHECOART, ...	121	PROVINC DESERT	
ROCHECOUART			
POICTIERS AND BRIVE, UNTAKEN ROCHECOUART, ...	152	NEAR PERIGORD	29
AND ROCHECOUART CAN MATCH IT, STRONGER YET, ...	152	NEAR PERIGORD	57
OR, BY A LICHENED TREE AT ROCHECOUART	154	NEAR PERIGORD	107
ROCHECOUART, CHALAIS, THE REST, THE TACTIC, ...	155	NEAR PERIGORD	122
ROCK			
FINDS 'NEATH THIS ROCK FIT MOULD, FIT RESTING PLACE!	41	HER MONUMENT	2
I HAVE SEEN FOIX ON ITS ROCK, SEEN TOULOUSE, AND	122	PROVINC DESERT	5

PAGE 338

ROCK -- ROSE

	PAGE	TITLE	LINE
ROCK (CONTINUED)			
HE RETURNS BY WAY OF SEI ROCK, TO HEAR THE NEW NIGHTINGALES,	130	THE RIVER SONG	37
ROCKET			
YOU WERE GONE UP AS A ROCKET,	147	BEFORE SLEEP	14
ROCKS			
GIVING THE ROCKS SMALL LEE-WAY	187	E. P. ODE	11
AND CITHARAON SHOOK UP THE ROCKS BY THEBES	208	SEXTUS PROP: 1	44
TO THE LEDGE OF THE ROCKS;	227	SEXTUS PROP:11	32
RODE			
AND BASIL WAS THE GREEK THAT RODE AROUND	264	ALF'S NINTH	18
RODYHEAVER'S			
DOWN RODYHEAVER'S PROPHYLACTIC SPINE,	246	MOYEN SENSUEL	225
ROGER			
TO BAY LIKE SIR ROGER DE COVERLEY'S	52	AU SALON	15
ROLL			
PULLS UP A ROLL OF FAT FOR THE PIANIST,	163	CABARET DANCER	54
ROLLS			
IT FALLS AND ROLLS TO YOUR FEET.	169	PHANOPOEIA	7
ROMA			
"TROICA ROMA RESURGES."--PROPERTIUS	40	ROME	EPI
ROMAN			
AND FIND'ST IN ROME NO THING THOU CANST CALL ROMAN;	40	ROME	2
ANNALISTS WILL CONTINUE TO RECORD ROMAN REPUTATIONS,	207	SEXTUS PROP: 1	16
CELEBRITIES FROM THE TRANS-CAUCASUS WILL BELAUD ROMAN CELEBRITIES	207	SEXTUS PROP: 1	17
OF LARES FLEEING THE "ROMAN SEAT" . . .	210	SEXTUS PROP: 2	12
AND TO NAME OVER THE CENSUS OF MY CHIEFS IN THE ROMAN CAMP.	216	SEXTUS PROP: 5	3
TIBET SHALL BE FULL OF ROMAN POLICEMEN,	219	SEXTUS PROP: 6	8
AND ACQUIRE A ROMAN RELIGION;	219	SEXTUS PROP: 6	10
MAKE WAY, YE ROMAN AUTHORS,	229	SEXTUS PROP:12	36
ROMANCE			
ROMANCE, REVOLUTION 1918!	258	ALF'S SECOND	11
ROMANCES			
THAN SPANISH LADIES HAD IN OLD ROMANCES.	242	MOYEN SENSUEL	104
ROMANO			
A PROCESSION, O GIULIO ROMANO,	110	COITUS	5
ROME			
AND ALL THE MAIDENS OF ROME, AS MANY AS THEY WERE,	38	LADY'S LIFE	9
ROME	40	ROME	T
O THOU NEW COMER WHO SEEK'ST ROME IN ROME	40	ROME	1
O THOU NEW COMER WHO SEEK'ST ROME IN ROME	40	ROME	1
AND FIND'ST IN ROME NO THING THOU CANST CALL ROMAN;	40	ROME	2
ROME THAT ART ROME'S ONE SOLE LAST MONUMENT,	40	ROME	9
ROME THAT ALONE HAST CONQUERED ROME THE TOWN,	40	ROME	10
ROME THAT ALONE HAST CONQUERED ROME THE TOWN,	40	ROME	10
REMAINS OF ROME. O WORLD, THOU UNCONSTANT MIME!	40	ROME	12
IN ROME, AFTER THE OPERA,	182	MOEURS CON: 7	18
NOR WHERE ROME RUINS GERMAN RICHES,	211	SEXTUS PROP: 2	45
ROME'S			
ROME'S NAME ALONE WITHIN THESE WALLS KEEPS HOME.	40	ROME	4
ROME THAT ART ROME'S ONE SOLE LAST MONUMENT,	40	ROME	9
ROOF			
THEY WEAVE A WHOLE ROOF TO THE MOUNTAIN,	139	SENNIN POEM	5
BENEATH THE GAGGING ROOF	195	HUGH SELWIN;10	1
STAMP ON HIS ROOF OR IN THE GLAZING LIGHT	236	MIDDLE-AGED	5
ROOFS			
DOUBLE TOWERS, WINGED ROOFS,	141	IDEA OF CHOAN	23
ROOKS			
LUMINOUS GREEN FROM THE ROOKS,	120	GAME OF CHESS	9
ROOM			
I STOP IN MY ROOM TOWARD THE EAST, QUIET, QUIET,	142	UNMOVING CLOUD	6
SHE CAME INTO THE LARGE ROOM BY THE STAIR,	166	FISH & SHADOW	7
ROOMS			
THERE AND THERE MANY ROOMS AND ALL OF GOLD,	49	OF SPLENDOUR	13
ROOT			
WE HAVE ONE SAP AND ONE ROOT--	89	A PACT	8
BUT THIS HEAT IS NOT THE ROOT OF THE MATTER:	221	SEXTUS PROP: 8	5
ROSE			
IN ROSE AND GOLD.	9	NA AUDIART	26

ROSE -- ROUND

```
                                                    PAGE   TITLE            LINE
ROSE (CONTINUED)
   SHALL MAIDENS SCATTER ROSE LEAVES   ..............    24   THUS NINEVEH        2
   SHALL ALL MEN SCATTER ROSE LEAVES   ..............    24   THUS NINEVEH       17
   THE FLAME, THE AUTUMN, AND THE GREEN ROSE OF LOVE     51   THE ALTAR           2
   GOLDEN ROSE THE HOUSE, IN THE PORTAL I SAW   ......    68   APPARUIT            1
   AUVERGNE ROSE TO THE SONG;   ......................   122   PROVINC DESERT    69
   ROSE OVER US; AND WE KNEW ALL THAT STREAM,   ......   157   NEAR PERIGORD    172
   ROSE WHITE, YELLOW, SILVER   ......................   169   PHANOPOEIA        ST
   "I ROSE IN EIGHTEEN MONTHS;   .....................   194   MR. NIXON         11
   EN COMPARAISON AVEC LAQUELLE LA ROSE   ............   199   MAUBERLEY: 2     EPI
   THE GREY AND ROSE   ...............................   203   MAUBERLEY: 4      11
   THE BLACK PANTHER LIES UNDER HIS ROSE TREE   ......   231   CANTUS PLANUS      1
   THE BLACK PANTHER LIES UNDER HIS ROSE TREE.   .....   231   CANTUS PLANUS      5
   THUS ROSE IN ALBION, AND TICKLED THE STATE   ......   264   ALF'S NINTH       11
ROSE-LEAF
   THOU KEEP'ST THY ROSE-LEAF   ......................    67   THE CLOAK          1
ROSE-LEAVES
   THE ORANGE-COLOURED ROSE-LEAVES,   ................   108   TS'AI CHI'H        2
ROSES
   AS I? WILL THE NEW ROSES MISS THEE?   .............    67   THE CLOAK          6
   CRIMSON, FROSTY WITH DEW, THE ROSES BEND WHERE  ...    68   APPARUIT           5
   THIS FABRICATION BUILT OF AUTUMN ROSES,   .........    69   SUB MARE           3
   THERE IS A TRELLIS FULL OF EARLY ROSES,   .........   153   NEAR PERIGORD     72
   OF PIERIAN ROSES.   ...............................   196   HUGH SELWIN:12    28
   AS ROSES MIGHT, IN MAGIC AMBER LAID,   ............   197   ENVOI (1919)      13
   ROSES TWINED IN HER HANDS.   ......................   211   SEXTUS PROP: 2    37
ROSE-TIME
   TILL THE ROSE-TIME WILL BE OVER,   ................    67   THE CLOAK          2
ROSORIU
   OLD IDEA OF CHOAN BY ROSORIU   ....................   141   IDEA OF CHOAN      T
ROSSETTI
   AND ROSSETTI STILL ABUSED.   ......................   192   YEUX GLAUQUES      4
ROSY
   A ROSY PATH, A SORT OF VERNAL INGRESS,   ..........   243   MOYEN SENSUEL    14
ROT
   BUT IS FIT ONLY TO ROT IN WOMANISH PEACE   ........    29   ALTAFORTE          2
   AS FOR YOU, YOU WILL ROT IN THE EARTH,   ..........   146   MONUMENTUM AER
   FESTER AND ROT, FESTER AND ROT,   .................   265   ALF'S TENTH
   FESTER AND ROT, FESTER AND ROT,   .................   265   ALF'S TENTH
ROTE
   WITH TIMES TOLD OVER AS WE TELL BY ROTE;   ........    43   SATIEMUS           1
ROTS
   THE UNSAFE SAFE, WHEREIN ALL ROTS, AND NO MAN CAN
      SAY HOW   ......................................   261   ALF'S FIFTH        1
ROTTED
   AND WITH SOME BRANCHES ROTTED AND FALLING.   ......    89   COMMISSION         3
ROTTEN
   AND MADE MEN'S MOCK'RY IN MY ROTTEN SADNESS!   ....    31   PIERE VIDAL        5
   THE MONEY ROTTEN AND MORE ROTTEN YET,   ...........   260   ALF'S FIFTH
   THE MONEY ROTTEN AND MORE ROTTEN YET,   ...........   260   ALF'S FIFTH
ROTUNDOS
   AND MY VENTRICLES DO NOT PALPITATE TO CAESARIAL ORE
      ROTUNDOS,   ....................................   218   SEXTUS PROP: 5
ROUGE
   PULLED BY THE KOHL AND ROUGE OUT OF RESEMBLANCE--     162   CABARET DANCER
ROUGH
   YOUR GRANDAD GOT THE ROUGH EDGE.   ................   259   ALF'S FOURTH
   ROUGH FROM THE VIRGIN FORESTS INVIOLATE,   ........   264   ALF'S NINTH
ROUND
   WE SEEM AS STATUES ROUND WHOSE HIGH-RISEN BASE ....    32   PARACELSUS
   O THROAT GIRT ROUND OF OLD WITH SWIFT DESIRE, .....    41   HER MONUMENT
   HEW MY HEART ROUND AND HUNGER BEGOT   .............    64   THE SEAFARER
   SINCE YOU HAVE COME THIS PLACE HAS HOVERED ROUND ME,   69   SUB MARE
   AND ROUND ABOUT THERE IS A RABBLE   ...............    83   THE GARDEN
   THE FOUR ROUND TOWERS, FOUR BROTHERS--MOSTLY FOOLS:   152   NEAR PERIGORD
   THE DULL ROUND TOWERS ENCROACHING ON THE FIELD, ...   155   NEAR PERIGORD
   I HAVE WRAPPED THE WIND ROUND YOUR SHOULDERS ......   170   PHANOPOEIA
   AND STICKING OUT ALL THE WAY ROUND;   .............   181   MOEURS CON: 7
   AND RUPERT RAN THE RUMOUR ROUND IN WHEELS,   ......   264   ALF'S NINTH
   AN A-SLOSHIN' ROUND WITH 'ER MOP,   ...............   271   OLE KATE
```

ROUSING -- RUN-AWAY

	PAGE	TITLE	LINE
ROUSING			
ROUSING THERE THIRST	250	DONNA MI PREGA	60
ROUTE			
NEITHER EXPENSIVE PYRAMIDS SCRAPING THE STARS IN THEIR ROUTE,	209	SEXTUS PROP: 1	66
ROW			
SITTING IN THE ROW OF A MORNING;	182	MOEURS CON: 7	24
ROWS			
FILL FULL THE SIDES IN ROWS, AND OUR WINE	128	THE RIVER SONG	3
AND THE PRINCES STILL STAND IN ROWS, ABOUT THE THRONE,	131	AT TEN-SHIN	10
ROWTON			
AND THINKS ABOUT A ROWTON 'OUSE	270	OF 600 M.P.'S	15
ROYAL			
THERE IS NO EASE IN ROYAL AFFAIRS, WE HAVE NO COMFORT.	127	BOWMEN OF SHU	11
BEFORE THE ROYAL LODGE:	141	IDEA OF CHOAN	6
"OF" ROYAL AEMILIA, DRAWN ON THE MEMORIAL RAFT,	210	SEXTUS PROP: 2	10
NOR OF XERXES' TWO-BARRELED KINGDOM, NOR OF REMUS AND HIS ROYAL FAMILY,	217	SEXTUS PROP: 5	44
ROYALTIES			
"ADVANCE ON ROYALTIES, FIFTY AT FIRST," SAID MR. NIXON,	194	MR. NIXON	7
RUB			
AND I CAN HEAR AN OLD MAN SAYING: "OH, THE RUB!	244	MOYEN SENSUEL	179
RUBAIYAT			
THE ENGLISH RUBAIYAT WAS STILL-BORN	192	YEUX GLAUQUES	15
RUBBED			
YES, I HAVE RUBBED SHOULDERS AND KNOCKED OFF MY CHIPS	247	PIERROTS	22
RUCK			
OUR MALENESS LIFTS US OUT OF THE RUCK,	82	THE CONDOLENCE	5
RUDDY			
BUT I HAVE MADE A RUDDY PILE	266	ALF'S ELEVENTH	15
RUDYARD			
RUDYARD THE DUD YARD,	259	ALF'S FOURTH	1
RUDYARD THE FALSE MEASURE,	259	ALF'S FOURTH	2
RUFFLE			
RUFFLE THE SKIRTS OF PRUDES,	86	SALUTATION 2ND	32
RUIN			
BEHOLD HOW PRIDE AND RUIN CAN BEFALL	40	ROME	5
AND THEY ALL GO TO RACK RUIN BENEATH THE THUD OF THE YEARS.	209	SEXTUS PROP: 1	71
RUINED			
I HAVE SEEN THE RUINED "DONATA."	122	PROVINC DESERT	61
RUINS			
NOR WHERE ROME RUINS GERMAN RICHES,	211	SEXTUS PROP: 2	45
RULE			
TO RULE OVER US.	189	HUGH SELWYN: 3	24
RULLUS			
PASS AND BE SILENT, RULLUS, FOR THE DAY	63	QUIES	2
RUMOUR			
SOUL, IF SHE MEET US THERE, WILL ANY RUMOUR	39	BLANDULA	13
EAGER TO SPREAD THEM WITH RUMOUR;	90	SURGIT FAMA	11
AND YET AGAIN, AND NEWLY RUMOUR STRIKES ON MY EARS,	226	SEXTUS PROP:11	17
AND NO GOOD RUMOUR AMONG THEM.	226	SEXTUS PROP:11	19
OLD 'ERB WAS DOTING, SO THE RUMOUR RAN,	264	ALF'S NINTH	13
AND RUPERT RAN THE RUMOUR ROUND IN WHEELS,	264	ALF'S NINTH	14
RUMOURS			
RUMOURS OF YOU THROUGHOUT THE CITY,	226	SEXTUS PROP:11	18
RUN			
THOUGH IT SHOULD RUN FOR ITS OWN GETTING,	14	FAMAM CANO	28
SOME OVERFLOWING RIVER IS RUN MAD,	32	PARACELSUS	12
THIS THING WILL RUN AT YOU	109	THE FAUN	8
IS IT AN INTRIGUE TO RUN SUBTLY OUT,	153	NEAR PERIGORD	82
FOR I KNOW HOW WORDS RUN LOOSE,	173	LANGUE D'OC: 2	25
GOD GIVE ME LIFE AND LET MY COURSE RUN	174	LANGUE D'OC: 3	17
THOUGH THE WHOLE WORLD RUN RACK	176	LANGUE D'OC: 3	73
TO RUN SUCH TOURS. HE CALLS 'EM. . . . HOUSE PARTIES.	245	MOYEN SENSUEL	210
RUN-AWAY			
AND EVERY RUN-AWAY OF THE WOOD THROUGH THAT GREAT MADNESS,	31	PIERE VIDAL	51

RUNNING -- SADNESS

	PAGE	TITLE	LINE
RUNNING			
DIM TALES THAT BLIND ME, RUNNING ONE BY ONE	43	SATIEMUS	16
RUNNING SO CLOSE TO "HELL" IT SENDS A SHIVER	246	MOYEN SENSUEL	224
RUNS			
AND THE WAX RUNS LOW.	35	THE EYES	7
THROUGH TRILLS AND RUNS LIKE CRYSTAL,	45	FROM HEINE: 5	7
RUPERT			
THE DASHING RUPERT OF THE PULPING TRADE,	264	ALF'S NINTH	9
AND RUPERT RAN THE RUMOUR ROUND IN WHEELS,	264	ALF'S NINTH	14
RURAL			
SUCH PRACTICES DILUTED RURAL BOREDOM	242	MOYEN SENSUEL	107
RUSH			
AND OUR CHARGES 'GAINST "THE LEOPARD'S" RUSH CLASH.	29	ALTAFORTE	35
RUSHED			
SHE RUSHED OUT INTO THE SUNLIGHT AND SWARMED UP A COCOANUT PALM TREE,	118	CONTEMPORARIES	3
I RUSHED ABOUT IN THE MOST AGITATED WAY	247	PIERROTS	5
RUSHES			
STRENGTHENED WITH RUSHES, TEGAEAN PAN,	211	SEXTUS PROP: 2	30
"A FLAT FIELD FOR RUSHES, GRAPES GROW ON THE SLOPE."	229	SEXTUS PROP:12	52
RUSKIN			
WHEN JOHN RUSKIN PRODUCED	192	YEUX GLAUQUES	2
RUSSET			
IN GILDED AND RUSSET MANTLE.	90	SURGIT FAMA	4
RUSSIA			
WANT RUSSIA TO SAVE 'EM	258	ALF'S SECOND	3
WANT RUSSIA TO SAVE 'EM,	258	ALF'S SECOND	5
RUSSIAN			
THE LITTLE MILLWINS ATTEND THE RUSSIAN BALLET.	93	LES MILLWIN	1
RUSTED			
BUT BURIED DUST AND RUSTED SKELETON.	41	HER MONUMENT	3
RUSTICUS			
THE VERY EXCELLENT TERM RUSTICUS.	99	SALVATIONISTS	4
RUSTLING			
THE SILKEN TRAINS GO RUSTLING,	47	FROM HEINE: 7	25
'MID THE SILVER RUSTLING OF WHEAT,	75	THE ALCHEMIST	15
YSAUT, YDONE, SLIGHT RUSTLING OF LEAVES,	76	THE ALCHEMIST	40
THE RUSTLING OF THE SILK IS DISCONTINUED,	108	LIU CH'E	1
S.			
"QUASI KALOUN." S. T. SAYS BEAUTY IS MOST THAT, A "CALLING TO THE SOUL.."	20	IN DURANCE	20
SACCHARINE			
A SORT OF STINKING DILIQUESCENT SACCHARINE.	239	MOYEN SENSUEL	22
SACKVILLE			
WHY DOES THE REALLY HANDSOME YOUNG WOMAN APPROACH ME IN SACKVILLE STREET	114	SIMULACRA	5
SACRA			
THOUGH YOU WALK IN THE VIA SACRA, WITH A PEACOCK'S TAIL FOR A FAN.	227	SEXTUS PROP:11	40
SACRED			
"IN SACRED ODOUR"--(THAT'S APOCRYPHAL!)	156	NEAR PERIGORD	161
NOR IS THERE ANYONE TO WHOM LOVERS ARE NOT SACRED AT MIDNIGHT	212	SEXTUS PROP: 3	15
SAD			
GRIEVING AND SAD AND FULL OF BITTERNESS	36	THE YOUNG KING	9
SHAMEFUL, MOST SAD	41	HER MONUMENT	20
AND I AM SAD.	138	CITY OF CHOAN	13
A SAD AND GREAT EVIL IS THE EXPECTATION OF DEATH-- SAVE TROUBLE AND SAD THOUGHT,	164	QUINTUS SEPTIM	8
SAD GARMENT DRAPED ON HER SLENDER ARMS.	174	LANGUE D'OC: 3	8
IN THE SEASON SAD AND WEARY	214	SEXTUS PROP: 4	20
TO CHEER THE BAD AND SAD,	267	ALF'S TWELFTH	4
SADDLES	268	ALF'S TWELFTH	20
A GLITTER OF GOLDEN SADDLES, AWAITING THE PRINCESS;	141	IDEA OF CHOAN	7
SADNESS			
"ALL THEY THAT WITH STRANGE SADNESS"	20	IN DURANCE	20
AND THE RED SUN MOCKS MY SADNESS.	30	PIERE VIDAL	0
AND MADE MEN'S MOCK'RY IN MY ROTTEN SADNESS!	31	PIERE VIDAL	5
VOID OF ALL JOY AND FULL OF IRE AND SADNESS.	36	THE YOUNG KING	
THE BALANCE FOR THIS LOSS IN IRE AND SADNESS!	37	THE YOUNG KING	10
THAT DOTH BUT WOUND THE GOOD WITH IRE AND SADNESS	37	THE YOUNG KING	20

SADNESS -- SAILORS

	PAGE	TITLE	LINE
SADNESS (CONTINUED)			
WHENCE HAVE WE GRIEF, DISCORD AND DEEPEST SADNESS.	37	THE YOUNG KING	32
THERE WHERE THERE IS NO GRIEF, NOR SHALL BE SADNESS.	37	THE YOUNG KING	40
SADNESS HUNG OVER THE HOUSE, AND THE DESOLATED FEMALE ATTENDANTS	214	SEXTUS PROP: 4	22
SAFE			
TO BRING THEE SAFE BACK, MY COMPANION.	172	LANGUE D'OC: 1	20
THUS ALL ROADS ARE PERFECTLY SAFE	212	SEXTUS PROP: 3	24
SAFE MAY'ST THOU GO MY CANZON WHITHER THEE PLEASETH	250	DONNA MI PREGA	88
THE UNSAFE SAFE, WHEREIN ALL ROTS, AND NO MAN CAN SAY HOW	261	ALF'S FIFTH	19
SAFE AND SOUND	269	SAFE AND SOUND	T
SAFES			
SAFES IN THREAD AND NEEDLE STREET.	269	SAFE AND SOUND	22
SAFFRON			
HALF-SHEATHED, THEN NAKED FROM ITS SAFFRON SHEATH	31	PIERE VIDAL	41
BURN NOT WITH ME NOR ANY SAFFRON THING.	60	TOMB AKR CAAR	5
SAFFRON-COLOURED			
BRING THE SAFFRON-COLOURED SHELL,	75	THE ALCHEMIST	9
SAGE			
SAGE HERACLEITUS SAYS:	189	HUGH SELWYN: 3	10
SAGGING			
BENEATH THE SAGGING ROOF	195	HUGH SELWIN:10	1
SAI			
IEU LO SAI."	166	FISH & SHADOW	17
SAID			
I WAS QUITE STRONG--AT LEAST THEY SAID SO--	4	LA FRAISNE	5
AND THEY SAID I WAS QUITE STRONG, AMONG THE YOUNG MEN.	5	LA FRAISNE	41
THAT SAID US, "TILL THEN" FOR THE GALLOWS TREE!	11	OF THE GIBBET	4
IN VAIN HAVE I SAID TO HIM	16	PRAISE YSOLT	3
AND ALL THE TIME THOU SAYEST THEM O'ER I SAID,	43	SATIEMUS	4
AND NOW YOU HEAR WHAT IS SAID TO US:	82	THE CONDOLENCE	13
SAID TSIN-TSU:	104	THE SEEING EYE	8
AND ONE SAID:	107	COMING OF WAR	13
THAT WAS THE TOP OF THE WALK, WHEN HE SAID:	119	THE GYPSY	1
AND HE SAID, "HAVE YOU SEEN ANY OF OUR LOT?"	119	THE GYPSY	11
I HAVE SAID:	122	PROVINC DESERT	42
I HAVE SAID: "THE OLD ROADS HAVE LAIN HERE.	122	PROVINC DESERT	56
I HAVE SAID:	122	PROVINC DESERT	62
MY MAGNET," BERTRANS HAD SAID.	154	NEAR PERIGORD	116
AND SAID SO FRANKLY.	159	PSYCHOLOG HOUR	33
AND HE SAID:	181	MOEURS CON: 7	7
AND SAID: "MR. POUND IS SHOCKED AT MY LEVITY."	181	MOEURS CON: 7	11
HE SAID: "WHY FLAY DEAD HORSES?	181	MOEURS CON: 7	15
AND SHE SAID:	182	MOEURS CON: 8	1
AND I SAID: "THAT WAS BEFORE I ARRIVED."	182	MOEURS CON: 8	4
AND SHE SAID:	182	MOEURS CON: 8	5
"AND SAID: 'DO I,	182	MOEURS CON: 8	9
AND HE SAID THEY USED TO CHEER VERDI,	182	MOEURS CON: 7	17
"ADVANCE ON ROYALTIES, FIFTY AT FIRST," SAID MR. NIXON,	194	MR. NIXON	7
SAID THEN "YOU IDIOT! WHAT ARE YOU DOING WITH THAT WATER:	210	SEXTUS PROP: 2	17
AND ANOTHER SAID "GET HIM PLUMB IN THE MIDDLE!	224	SEXTUS PROP:10	14
(I BURN, I FREEZE, I SWEAT, SAID THE FAIR GREEK	242	MOYEN SENSUEL	123
(MY COUNTRY, I'VE SAID YOUR MORALS AND YOUR THOUGHTS ARE STALE ONES,	243	MOYEN SENSUEL	149
FOR AS BEN FRANKLIN SAID, WITH SUCH URBANITY:	246	MOYEN SENSUEL	235
BUT SAID IT WUZ GLORIOUS NEVERTHELESS	259	ALF'S FOURTH	5
SAIL			
LO, I WOULD SAIL THE SEAS WITH THEE ALONE!	25	GUIDO INVITES	2
SAIL OF CLAUSTRA, AELIS, AZALAIS,	75	THE ALCHEMIST	1
SAIL OF CLAUSTRA, AELIS, AZALAIS,	75	THE ALCHEMIST	5
HIS LONE SAIL BLOTS THE FAR SKY.	137	ON RIVER KIANG	3
YET SAW AN "AD." "TO-NIGHT, THE HUDSON SAIL,	242	MOYEN SENSUEL	111
SAILOR			
SAILOR, OF WINDS; A PLOWMAN, CONCERNING HIS OXEN;	218	SEXTUS PROP: 5	55
SAILORS			
THEREFORE THE SAILORS ARE CHEERED, AND THE WAVES	164	QUINTUS SEPTIM	6

PAGE 343

SAILS -- SAME

	PAGE	TITLE	LINE
SAILS			
SAILS SPREAD ON CERULEAN WATERS, I WOULD SHED TEARS FOR TWO;	223	SEXTUS PROP: 9	7
SAINT			
NOT THAT HE WAS A SAINT, NOR WAS TOP-LOFTICAL	246	MOYEN SENSUEL	233
SAINTLY			
O RIBALD COMPANY, O SAINTLY HOST,	35	HIS OWN FACE	2
SAINTS			
--RARE VISITOR--CAME NOT,--THE SAINTS I GUERDON	30	PIERE VIDAL	23
SAINT'S			
NOR THE SAINT'S VISION.	189	HUGH SELWYN: 3	18
SAISON			
TOWARDS THE NOEL THAT MORTE SAISON	10	FOR THIS YULE	1
SAITH			
SUCH IS YOUR FENCE, ONE SAITH,	19	FOR E. MCC	5
SAITH 'TWAS THE WORTHIEST OF EDITORS.	63	PHASELLUS ILLE	2
"DELIGHT THY SOUL IN FATNESS," SAITH THE PREACHER.	163	CABARET DANCER	69
AND IN OUR DAY THUS SAITH THE EVANGELIST:	246	MOYEN SENSUEL	237
SAKE			
TRUE TO THE TRUTH'S SAKE AND CRAFTY DISSECTOR,	13	MESMERISM	18
SALAMMAMM			
ABU SALAMMAMM--A SONG OF EMPIRE	237	ABU SALAMMAMM	T
SALE			
THE SALE OF HALF-HOSE HAS	196	HUGH SELWIN:12	26
SALES			
MY SALES BEAT ALL THE OTHER TEN,	266	ALF'S ELEVENTH	3
SALIS			
WE CAN'T PRESERVE THE ELUSIVE "MICA SALIS,"	163	CABARET DANCER	70
SALMON			
THE SALMON MOVES IN THE SUN-SHOT, BRIGHT SHALLOW SEA...	166	FISH & SHADOW	4
SALMON-TROUT			
THE SALMON-TROUT DRIFTS IN THE STREAM,	166	FISH & SHADOW	1
THE SOUL OF THE SALMON-TROUT FLOATS OVER THE STREAM	166	FISH & SHADOW	2
SALON			
AU SALON	52	AU SALON	T
SALTUS			
SALTUS	169	PHANOPOEIA	ST
SALT-WAVY			
THE SALT-WAVY TUMULT TRAVERSE ALONE.	65	THE SEAFARER	36
SALUE			
M'ONT SALUE,	160	DANS OMNIBUS	2
ILS M'ONT SALUE	160	DANS OMNIBUS	5
M'ONT SALUE.	160	DANS OMNIBUS	31
SALUTATION			
SALUTATION THE SECOND	85	SALUTATION 2ND	T
SALUTATION	85	SALUTATION	T
SALUTATION THE THIRD	145	SALUTATION 3RD	T
SALUTE			
SALUTE THEM WITH YOUR THUMBS AT YOUR NOSES.	86	SALUTATION 2ND	22
SALVACIOUN			
WHO DRANK OF DEATH FOR OUR SALVACIOUN,	37	THE YOUNG KING	35
SALVATION			
BEYOND SALVATION, HOLDETH ITS JUDGING FORCE,	249	DONNA MI PREGA	36
SALVATIONISTS			
SALVATIONISTS	99	SALVATIONISTS	T
SAMAIN			
SAMAIN	83	THE GARDEN	EPI
SAME			
BUT IT IS ALL THE SAME;	6	CINO	2
THAT SAME. THY PUBLIC IN MY SCREED	14	FAMAM CANO	19
YOU WORE THE SAME QUITE CORRECT CLOTHING,	101	AMITIES	1
YOU HAD THE SAME OLD AIR OF CONDESCENSION	101	AMITIES	3
THOUGH THEY HANG IN THE SAME WAY OVER THE BRIDGERAIL.	131	AT TEN-SHIN	8
HER OVERSKIRT IS THE SAME SILK DYED IN PURPLE,	140	MULBERRY ROAD	14
THE THIN, CLEAR GAZE, THE SAME	192	YEUX GLAUQUES	17
TITYRUS MIGHT HAVE SUNG THE SAME VIXEN;	229	SEXTUS PROP:12	46
"ALL THE SAME STYLE, SAME CUT, WITH PERFECT LOATHING."	244	MOYEN SENSUEL	184
"ALL THE SAME STYLE, SAME CUT, WITH PERFECT LOATHING."	244	MOYEN SENSUEL	184

	PAGE	TITLE	LINE
SAME (CONTINUED)			
TER GRIND THE SAME OLD AXES	270	OF 600 M.P.'S	6
SAMOTHRACE			
DEFECTS--AFTER SAMOTHRACE;	189	HUGH SELWYN: 3	14
SAN			
AND THEN THE CROWD BROKE UP, YOU WENT NORTH TO SAN PALACE, ...	136	EXILE'S LETTER	71
SAND			
BY THE NORTH GATE, THE WIND BLOWS FULL OF SAND, ...	133	FRONTIER GUARD	1
THE CORAL ISLE, THE LION-COLOURED SAND	201	AGE DEMANDED	17
OF SOME AS YET UNCATALOGUED SAND;	213	SEXTUS PROP: 3	37
SANDALED			
IVORY SANDALED, ...	91	DANCE FIGURE	3
SANDALS			
WE WHO HAVE SEEN EVEN ARTEMIS A-BINDING HER SANDALS,	104	ANCONA	6
THE FLUTTER OF SHARP-EDGED SANDALS.	169	PHANOPOEIA	13
THOUGH YOU HAD THE FEATHERY SANDALS OF PERSEUS	226	SEXTUS PROP:11	8
SANE			
IT IS, AND IS NOT, I AM SANE ENOUGH, ...	69	SUB MARE	1
SANG			
FOR SHE I SANG OF HATH GONE FROM ME."	17	PRAISE YSOLT	37
HE SANG A WOMAN.	122	PROVINC DESERT	68
TELL HER THAT SANG ME ONCE THAT SONG OF LAWES:	197	ENVOI (1919)	2
THE PRIMITIVE AGES SANG VENUS, ...	216	SEXTUS PROP: 5	7
VARRO SANG JASON'S EXPEDITION, ...	230	SEXTUS PROP:12	66
AND IF THE PAPERS SELDOM SANG HIS PRAISE, ...	265	ALF'S NINTH	23
SANG-DE-DRAGON			
TEINTEES DE COULEUR SANG-DE-DRAGON, ...	160	DANS OMNIBUS	27
SAN-KO			
IN THE STORIED HOUSES OF SAN-KO THEY GAVE US MORE SENNIN MUSIC, ...	135	EXILE'S LETTER	26
SANS			
IF THOU HAST SEEN MY SHADE SANS CHARACTER, ...	51	THE FLAME	39
O STATE SANS SONG, SANS HOME-GROWN WINE, SANS REALIST!	241	MOYEN SENSUEL	88
O STATE SANS SONG, SANS HOME-GROWN WINE, SANS REALIST!	241	MOYEN SENSUEL	88
O STATE SANS SONG, SANS HOME-GROWN WINE, SANS REALIST!	241	MOYEN SENSUEL	88
SANSO			
"SANSO, KING OF SHOKU, BUILT ROADS"	138	NEAR SHOKU	EPI
THEY SAY THE ROADS OF SANSO ARE STEEP, ...	138	NEAR SHOKU	1
SANTA			
FROM THE STATUE OF THE INFANT CHRIST IN SANTA MARIA NOVELLA, ...	94	INSTRUCTIONS	20
SAP			
AS THE FLAME CRIETH UNTO THE SAP.	17	PRAISE YSOLT	41
THE SAP HAS ASCENDED MY ARMS, ...	62	A GIRL	2
FROM THE BRONZE OF THE MAPLE, FROM THE SAP IN THE BOUGH;	76	THE ALCHEMIST	34
WE HAVE ONE SAP AND ONE ROOT--	89	A PACT	8
SAPLING			
THINE ARMS ARE AS A YOUNG SAPLING UNDER THE BARK;	91	DANCE FIGURE	10
SAPPHIRE			
THE MOON IS A GREAT PEARL IN THE WATERS OF SAPPHIRE,	18	DE AEGYPTO	21
PURPLE AND SAPPHIRE FOR THE SILVER SHAFTS	21	IN DURANCE	36
CLEAR SAPPHIRE, COBALT, CYANINE, ...	39	BLANDULA	10
SAPPHIRE BENACUS, IN THY MISTS AND THEE	50	THE FLAME	26
TURNED IN THEIR SAPPHIRE TIDE, COME FLOODING O'ER US!	51	HORAE BEATAE	4
YOU ARE ENGLOBED IN MY SAPPHIRE.	169	PHANOPOEIA	10
THE SEA-CLEAR SAPPHIRE OF AIR, THE SEA-DARK CLARITY, STRETCHES BOTH SEA-CLIFF AND OCEAN.	170	PHANOPOEIA	24
SAPPHIRES			
WITH SIX GREAT SAPPHIRES HUNG ALONG THE WALL, ...	49	OF SPLENDOUR	10
SAPPHO'S			
SAPPHO'S BARBITOS	189	HUGH SELWYN: 3	4
SARCOPHAGUS			
DRIFTS THROUGH THE AIR, AND THE SARCOPHAGUS	236	MIDDLE-AGED	10
SARDINES			
AND THERE HAD BEEN A GREAT CATCH OF SARDINES, ...	96	AESTHETICS	9

SARGASSO -- SAVE

	PAGE	TITLE	LINE
SARGASSO			
YOUR MIND A. YOU ARE OUR SARGASSO SEA,	61	PORTRAIT FEMME	1
SARGENT			
YOU 'ARK TO THE SARGENT,	260	ALF'S FOURTH	16
SARLAT			
AND IN SARLAT,	122	PROVINC DESERT	37
SAT			
AND ALL THE ANGELS SAT ABOUT	45	FROM HEINE: 4	3
WHEN WE SAT UPON THE GRANITE BRINK IN HELICON	104	ANCORA	10
SATE			
WHILE OUR FATES TWINE TOGETHER, SATE WE OUR EYES WITH LOVE;	220	SEXTUS PROP: 7	17
SATIEMUS			
SATIEMUS	43	SATIEMUS	T
SATIETIES			
GROWN DELICATE WITH SATIETIES,	112	HIMERRO	2
SATIN			
THE BASKET IS LINED WITH SATIN,	180	MOEURS CON: 5	14
AND THE BLUE SATIN RIBBON,	180	MOEURS CON: 5	23
PUFFED SATIN, AND SILK STOCKINGS, WHERE THE KNEE	241	MOYEN SENSUEL	85
SATIN-LIKE			
THERE IS A SATIN-LIKE BOW ON THE HARP.	180	MOEURS CON: 5	15
THERE IS A SATIN-LIKE BOW ON AN HARP.	180	MOEURS CON: 5	17
SATINS			
THY SATINS MAKE UPON THE STAIR,	8	NA AUDIART	22
SATIRE			
TILL YOU MAY TAKE YOUR CHOICE: TO FEEL THE EDGE OF SATIRE OR	240	MOYEN SENSUEL	65
SATISFACTION			
MURMURING FOR HIS OWN SATISFACTION	97	AESTHETICS	19
SATURN			
(SATURN AND MARS TO ZEUS DRAWN NEAR!)	10	FOR THIS YULE	18
SAUCY			
A SAUCY FELLOW, BUT . . .	6	CINO	28
SAVAGE			
IN A HALF SAVAGE COUNTRY, OUT OF DATE;	187	E. P. ODE	6
SAVE			
AND HAVE NONE ABOUT ME SAVE IN THE SHADOWS	20	IN DURANCE	18
THAT 'THOUT HIM, SAVE THE ASPEN, WERE AS DUMB	21	IN DURANCE	47
SAVE THIS: "VERS AND CANZONE TO THE COUNTESS OF BEZIERS	22	MARVOIL	28
I HAVE NO LIFE SAVE WHEN THE SWORDS CLASH.	28	ALTAFORTE	3
NOR HELD ME SAVE AS AIR THAT BRUSHETH BY ONE	39	FOR PSYCHE	3
THERE I HEARD NAUGHT SAVE THE HARSH SEA	64	THE SEAFARER	18
NOR ANY WHIT ELSE SAVE THE WAVE'S SLASH,	65	THE SEAFARER	47
SAVE THERE BE SOMEWHAT CALAMITOUS	66	THE SEAFARER	69
--SAVE THE NEW. \	70	THE PLUNGE	8
BASTIDIDES, ON THE CONTRARY, WHO BOTH TALKS AND WRITES OF NOTHING SAVE COPULATION,	100	TEMPERAMENTS	5
SAVE THAT I HAVE SUCH HUNGER FOR	106	DOMPNA POIS	63
SAVE A SQUABBLE OF FEMALE CONNECTIONS.	115	SOCIAL ORDER	19
SAVE THIS DAMN'D PROFESSION OF WRITING,	117	THE LAKE ISLE	15
NO ONE HEARS SAVE ARRIMON LUC D'ESPARO--	154	NEAR PERIGORD	119
NO ONE HEARS AUGHT SAVE THE GRACIOUS SOUND OF COMPLIMENTS.	154	NEAR PERIGORD	120
SHE WHO HAD NOR EARS NOR TONGUE SAVE IN HER HANDS,	157	NEAR PERIGORD	187
SHE WHO COULD NEVER LIVE SAVE THROUGH ONE PERSON,	157	NEAR PERIGORD	189
SHE WHO COULD NEVER SPEAK SAVE TO ONE PERSON,	157	NEAR PERIGORD	190
SAVE YOUR DOUTH AND YOUR STORY.	165	QUINTUS SEPTIM	19
SAVE TROUBLE AND SAD THOUGHT,	174	LANGUE D'OC: 3	8
AND ALL THAT CAN SAVE ME.	174	LANGUE D'OC: 3	27
ALL THINGS SAVE BEAUTY ALONE.	197	ENVOI (1919)	26
GREAT ZEUS, SAVE THE WOMAN,	223	SEXTUS PROP: 9	10
AND SAVE THEY KNOW'T ARIGHT FROM NATURE'S SOURCE	248	DONNA MI PREGA	10
SAVE THAT PERFECTION FAILS, BE IT BUT A LITTLE;	249	DONNA MI PREGA	45
WANT RUSSIA TO SAVE 'EM	258	ALF'S SECOND	3
WANT RUSSIA TO SAVE 'EM,	258	ALF'S SECOND	5
LENIN TO SAVE 'EM, TROTSKY TO SAVE 'EM	258	ALF'S SECOND	6
LENIN TO SAVE 'EM, TROTSKY TO SAVE 'EM	258	ALF'S SECOND	6
GOD SAVE BRITANNIA!	259	ALF'S THIRD	20
TOLD 'EM TO DIE IN WAR, AND THEN TO SAVE,	260	ALF'S FIFTH	2

	PAGE	TITLE	LINE
SAVE (CONTINUED)			
WILL GIVE, SAVE TO THE BLIND.	263	ALF'S EIGHTH	7
SAVENT			
"QU'EST CE QU'ILS SAVENT DE L'AMOUR, ET	199	MAUBERLEY: 2	EPI
SAVING			
THEN CUT THEIR SAVING TO THE HALF OR LOWER;	260	ALF'S FIFTH	3
SAVONNIER			
AND CARPETS FROM SAVONNIER, AND FROM PERSIA,	167	OF AROUET	8
SAVOUR			
HATH OF THE TREES A LIKENESS OF THE SAVOUR:	71	A VIRGINAL	13
SAW			
GOLDEN ROSE THE HOUSE, IN THE PORTAL I SAW	68	APPARUIT	1
AND MAENT FAILED HIM? OR SAW THROUGH THE SCHEME?	152	NEAR PERIGORD	52
"SAY THAT HE SAW THE CASTLES, SAY THAT HE LOVED MAENT!"	156	NEAR PERIGORD	155
SURELY I SAW, AND STILL BEFORE MY EYES	156	NEAR PERIGORD	163
SAW THE PERFORMERS COME: HIM, HER, THE BABY,	163	CABARET DANCER	80
I NEVER SAW HER AGAIN.	182	MOEURS CON: 8	15
AND YOU SAW IT.	214	SEXTUS PROP: 4	14
SAW HER STRETCHED ON HER BED,--	214	SEXTUS PROP: 4	17
YET SAW AN "AD." "TO-NIGHT, THE HUDSON SAIL,	242	MOYEN SENSUEL	111
SAW WHAT THE CITY OFFERED, CAST AN EYE	245	MOYEN SENSUEL	187
NEVER GOT PROPERLY TANKED AS I SAW,	271	OLE KATE	15
SAY			
TILL MEN SAY THAT I AM MAD,	4	LA FRAISNE	21
THOUGH ALL MEN SAY THAT I AM MAD	5	LA FRAISNE	32
SIGHING, SAY, "WOULD CINO,	6	CINO	16
THAN HALF HIS CANZONI SAY OF HIM.	22	MARVOIL	26
THAT YOU CAN SAY SUCH AWFUL THINGS	44	FROM HEINE: 1	7
AND ALL THE TALES OF OISIN SAY BUT THIS:	50	THE FLAME	9
I SAY MY SOUL FLOWED BACK, BECAME TRANSLUCENT.	51	THE FLAME	36
TO SAY THAT LIFE IS, SOME WAY, A GAY THING,	53	AU JARDIN	12
THERE IS ENOUGH IN WHAT I CHANCE TO SAY,	59	SILET	4
AND NO LIGHT BEATS UPON ME, AND YOU SAY	60	TOMB AKR CAAR	27
"THAT I MAY NOT SAY, LADIES.	72	PAN IS DEAD	8
THAT I MAY NOT SAY, LADIES.	72	PAN IS DEAD	10
I BESEECH YOU LEARN TO SAY "I,"	84	ORTUS	13
"IS THIS," THEY SAY, "THE NONSENSE	85	SALUTATION 2ND	10
SAY THAT YOU DO NO WORK	86	SALUTATION 2ND	36
LEST THEY SAY WE ARE LACKING IN TASTE,	94	INSTRUCTIONS	21
AND WE SAY GOOD-BYE TO YOU ALSO,	101	AMITIES	7
AND BECAUSE I HAPPEN TO SAY SO.	102	LADIES	8
GOOD GOD! THEY SAY YOU ARE RISQUE,	104	ANCORA	1
WE SAY: WILL WE BE LET TO GO BACK IN OCTOBER?	127	BOWMEN OF SHU	10
AND WHAT WITH BROKEN WHEELS AND SO ON, I WON'T SAY IT WASN'T HARD GOING,	135	EXILE'S LETTER	40
THEY SAY THE ROADS OF SANSO ARE STEEP	100	NEAR SHOKU	1
AND MEN SAY THE SUN AND MOON KEEP ON MOVING	142	UNMOVING CLOUD	20
YOU SAY THAT I TAKE A GOOD DEAL UPON MYSELF;	146	MONUMENTUM AER	1
AFRAID TO SAY THAT THEY HATE YOU;	146	SALUTATION 3RD	32
END FACT. TRY FICTION. LET US SAY WE SEE	154	NEAR PERIGORD	94
THEY PROBE OLD SCANDALS, SAY DE BORN IS DEAD;	155	NEAR PERIGORD	137
"SAY THAT HE SAW THE CASTLES, SAY THAT HE LOVED MAENT!"	156	NEAR PERIGORD	155
"SAY THAT HE SAW THE CASTLES, SAY THAT HE LOVED MAENT!"	156	NEAR PERIGORD	155
"SAY THAT HE LOVED HER, DOES IT SOLVE THE RIDDLE?"	156	NEAR PERIGORD	160
SAY "FORGET TO-MORROW," BEING OF ALL MEN	161	CABARET DANCER	7
AND TIBULLUS COULD SAY OF HIS DEATH, IN HIS LATIN:	168	OF AROUET	39
I CAN NOT SAY MY SAY	176	LANGUE D'OC: 3	65
I CAN NOT SAY MY SAY	176	LANGUE D'OC: 3	65
"AND I WOULDN'T SAY THAT HE DIDN'T.	182	MOEURS CON: 8	12
TO SAY MANY THINGS IS EQUAL TO HAVING A HOME.	215	SEXTUS PROP: 4	28
"WILL HE SAY NASTY THINGS AT MY FUNERAL?"	215	SEXTUS PROP: 4	40
YOU WILL SAY THAT YOU SUCCUMBED TO A DANGER IDENTICAL,	222	SEXTUS PROP: 8	30
ALL ONE CAN SAY OF THIS REFINING MEDIUM	239	MOYEN SENSUEL	60
AND, HEAVENLY, HOLY GODS! I CAN'T SAY MORE,	246	MOYEN SENSUEL	220
CRYING: MY GOD, MY GOD, WHAT WILL SHE SAY?!	247	PIERROTS	6
OR SAY	248	DONNA MI PREGA	12
NOT BY THE REASON, BUT 'TIS FELT, I SAY.	249	DONNA MI PREGA	35

SAY -- SCARE-CROW

	PAGE	TITLE	LINE
SAY (CONTINUED)			
NOR CAN MAN SAY HE HATH HIS LIFE BY CHANCE	249	DONNA MI PREGA	46
THE UNSAFE SAFE, WHEREIN ALL ROTS, AND NO MAN CAN SAY HOW	261	ALF'S FIFTH	19
MIGHT SAY, BE A SURPRISE	262	ALF'S SEVENTH	8
IN ENGLAND? I'LL SAY YES!	267	ALF'S ELEVENTH	22
I NEVER HEERD HER SAY NOTHIN'	271	OLE KATE	7
SHE'D SAY TO HER TIBBY-CAT,	271	OLE KATE	22
SAYEST			
AND ALL THE TIME THOU SAYEST THEM O'ER I SAID,	43	SATIEMUS	4
SAYING			
THAT LEAVETH ME NO REST, SAYING EVER,	16	PRAISE YSOLT	7
SAYING "THE SOUL SENDETH US."	17	PRAISE YSOLT	34
SAYING WITHIN HIS HEART, "I AM NO USE TO MYSELF,	100	ARIDES	6
AND SAYING: WHEN SHALL WE GET BACK TO OUR COUNTRY?	127	BOWMEN OF SHU	2
AND I THINK I HAVE HEARD THEM SAYING,	142	UNMOVING CLOUD	23
HER LIPS UPON THEM; AND IT WAS HER MOUTH SAYING:	220	SEXTUS PROP: 7	8
AND I CAN HEAR AN OLD MAN SAYING: "OH, THE RUB!	244	MOYEN SENSUEL	179
SAYS			
"QUASI KALOUN." S. T. SAYS BEAUTY IS MOST THAT, A "CALLING TO THE SOUL."	20	IN DURANCE	20
"OR I'LL SEE YE DAMNED," SAYS HE.	33	GOODLY FERE	8
ALONE IN THE TOWN?" SAYS HE.	33	GOODLY FERE	12
AND WAKE THE DEAD," SAYS HE,	34	GOODLY FERE	30
SHE SAYS, "MAY MY POEMS BE PRINTED THIS WEEK?	110	TEMPORA	6
WHEN ANYONE SAYS "RETURN," THE OTHERS ARE FULL OF SORROW.	127	BOWMEN OF SHU	6
"WET SPRINGTIME," SAYS TO-EM-MEI, "WET SPRING IN THE GARDEN."	142	UNMOVING CLOUD	EPI
AND LIKE A SWINGING LAMP THAT SAYS, "AH ME!	156	NEAR PERIGORD	166
SINGS IN THE OPEN MEADOW--AT LEAST THE KODAK SAYS SO--	161	CABARET DANCER	4
"PAUNVRE FEMME MAIGRE!" SHE SAYS.	163	CABARET DANCER	55
SAGE HERACLEITUS SAYS:	189	HUGH SELWYN: 3	10
AND WHATEVER SHE DOES OR SAYS	217	SEXTUS PROP: 5	35
AS THE EDITOR OF THE CENTURY SAYS IN PRINT,	243	MOYEN SENSUEL	137
DE GOURMONT SAYS THAT FIFTY GRUNTS ARE ALL THAT WILL BE PRIZED.	244	MOYEN SENSUEL	165
I SAYS! 'AVE YOU SEEN 'EM?	258	ALF'S SECOND	13
SCALD			
I BURN, I SCALD SO FOR THE NEW,	70	THE PLUNGE	3
SCALE			
FOR THREE YEARS, DIABOLUS IN THE SCALE,	199	MAUBERLEY: 2	1
IS HIGHER IN THE MENTAL SCALE	272	THE BABY	5
SCALES			
AND A PAIR OF SCALES NOT TOO GREASY,	117	THE LAKE ISLE	9
SCAMANDER			
OR OF POLYDMANTUS, BY SCAMANDER, OR HELENUS AND DEIPHOIBOS?	208	SEXTUS PROP: 1	36
SCANDAL			
TALK OF THE LATEST SUCCESS, GIVE WING TO SOME SCANDAL,	52	AU SALON	1
SCANDALS			
THEY PROBE OLD SCANDALS, SAY DE BORN IS DEAD;	155	NEAR PERIGORD	13
SCANDET			
DUM CAPITOLIUM SCANDET	96	DUM CAPITOLIUM	
'SCAPED			
HOW I 'SCAPED IMMORTALITY.	15	FAMAM CANO	4
SCARCE			
OF SOME THIN SILK STUFF THAT'S SCARCE STUFF AT ALL,	31	PIERE VIDAL	2
SCARCE AND THIN, SCARCE AND THIN	265	ALF'S TENTH	
SCARCE AND THIN, SCARCE AND THIN	265	ALF'S TENTH	
SCARCELY			
THEIR DOOR-YARDS WOULD SCARCELY KNOW THEM, OR PARIS.	208	SEXTUS PROP: 1	
SHE COULD SCARCELY KEEP HER EYES OPEN	225	SEXTUS PROP:10	
SCARCELY A GENERAL NOW KNOWN TO FAME	264	ALF'S NINTH	
AND SCARCELY HEED ONE WORD OF WHAT YOU HEAR.	265	ALF'S NINTH	
SCARE			
AND SCARE ITSELF TO SPASMS."	109	THE FAUN	
SCARE-CROW			
I AM HUNG HERE, A SCARE-CROW FOR LOVERS.	226	SEXTUS PROP:11	

SCARIFIED -- SCREAMED

	PAGE	TITLE	LINE
SCARIFIED			
YOU WILL FOLLOW THE BARE SCARIFIED BREAST	219	SEXTUS PROP: 6	22
SCARLET			
I WILL GET YOU THE SCARLET SILK TROUSERS	94	INSTRUCTIONS	19
FLARE UP WITH SCARLET ORANGE ON STIFF STALKS	162	CABARET DANCER	20
SCATTER			
SHALL MAIDENS SCATTER ROSE LEAVES	24	THUS NINEVEH	2
SHALL ALL MEN SCATTER ROSE LEAVES	24	THUS NINEVEH	17
SCATTERED			
FOR THE TOBACCO ASHES SCATTERED ON HIS COAT	15	FAMAM CANO	34
AND BEFORE THE END OF THE DAY WE WERE SCATTERED LIKE STARS, OR RAIN.	135	EXILE'S LETTER	33
SCATTERED MOLUCCAS	203	MAUBERLEY: 4	1
WIND AND WAVE SCATTERED AWAY.	221	SEXTUS PROP: 8	9
SCENE			
AND THE GREAT SCENE--	152	NEAR PERIGORD	40
SCENT			
HA! THIS SCENT IS HOT!	32	PIERE VIDAL	67
HAVE I DRUNK A DRAUGHT, SWEETER THAN SCENT OF MYRRH.	177	LANGUE D'OC: 4	23
SCENTED			
(WHAT OF THE MAGIANS' SCENTED GEAR?)	10	FOR THIS YULE	10
SCHEME			
AND MAENT FAILED HIM? OR SAW THROUGH THE SCHEME?	152	NEAR PERIGORD	52
SCHEMES			
YOU DO NOTHING, YOU PLOT INANE SCHEMES AGAINST ME,	226	SEXTUS PROP:11	14
SCHMERZEN			
AUS MEINEN GROSSEN SCHMERZEN	97	THE BELLAIRES	EPI
SCHOLARSHIP			
BEING FREE OF MEDIAEVAL SCHOLARSHIP, ...	98	THE BELLAIRES	24
SCHOOL			
IT WORKS TO REPRESENT THAT SCHOOL OF THOUGHT	63	PHASELLUS ILLE	5
THE SUNDAY SCHOOL BRINGS VIRTUES INTO PRACTICE. ...	243	MOYEN SENSUEL	140
SCIENCE			
THOUGH IT WILL, OF COURSE, PASS OFF WITH SOCIAL SCIENCE	244	MOYEN SENSUEL	163
SCION			
I FOUND THE LAST SCION OF THE	193	SIENA MI FE	3
SCIRO			
AND IN THE VIA SCIRO.	212	SEXTUS PROP: 3	16
SCOPE			
HAVING PRAISED THY GIRDLE'S SCOPE	8	NA AUDIART	14
SCORCHED			
HOT WAS THAT HIND'S BLOOD YET IT SCORCHED ME NOT	30	PIERE VIDAL	16
THE SCORCHED LAUREL LAY IN THE FIRE-DUST;	223	SEXTUS PROP: 9	2
SCORE			
IS LISTED. WELL! SOME SCORE YEARS HENCE	14	FAMAM CANO	20
LONDON HAS SWEPT ABOUT YOU THIS SCORE YEARS	61	PORTRAIT FEMME	2
SCORES			
A NOVELIST, A PUBLISHER, TO PAY OLD SCORES, ...	239	MOYEN SENSUEL	18
SCORN			
WHEN I SEE HIM SO SCORN AND DEFY PEACE, ...	29	ALTAFORTE	23
AS DID FIRST SCORN, THEN LIPS OF THE PENAUTIER! ...	30	PIERE VIDAL	17
AND THE SCORN OF HIS LAUGH RANG FREE, ...	33	GOODLY FERE	10
SCORNING			
SCORNING A NEW, WRY'D CASEMENT, ...	9	NA AUDIART	42
SCORNS			
AND STILL A GIRL SCORNS THE GODS, ...	228	SEXTUS PROP:12	23
SCOUNDREL			
"AND SHE HAS BEEN WAITING FOR THE SCOUNDREL, ...	225	SEXTUS PROP:10	18
SCOWLING			
AT FIFTEEN I STOPPED SCOWLING, ...	130	RIVER-MER WIFE	11
SCRAPING			
NEITHER EXPENSIVE PYRAMIDS SCRAPING THE STARS IN THEIR ROUTE, ...	209	SEXTUS PROP: 1	66
SCRATCHED			
SCRATCHED AND ERASED WITH AL AND OCHAISOS.	154	NEAR PERIGORD	100
SCRAWNY			
SCRAWNY, BE-SPECTACLED, OUT AT HEELS, ...	14	FAMAM CANO	23
PHYLLIDULA IS SCRAWNY BUT AMOROUS, ...	103	PHYLLIDULA	1
SCREAMED			
IN ICY FEATHERS; FULL OFT THE EAGLE SCREAMED	64	THE SEAFARER	24

SCREECH -- SEA-FARE

	PAGE	TITLE	LINE
SCREECH			
"SHE STEWS PUFFED FROGS, SNAKE'S BONES, THE MOULTED FEATHERS OF SCREECH OWLS,	215	SEXTUS PROP: 4	33
SCREED			
THAT SAME. THY PUBLIC IN MY SCREED	14	FAMAM CANO	19
SCRIBBLING			
SCRIBBLING, SWEARING BETWEEN HIS TEETH; BY HIS LEFT HAND	154	NEAR PERIGORD	98
SCROLLS			
NO MOUSE OF THE SCROLLS WAS THE GOODLY FERE	33	GOODLY FERE	23
SCULPTORS			
WHERE IS THE WORK OF YOUR HOME-BORN SCULPTORS?	165	QUINTUS SEPTIM	16
SCULPTURE			
OR THE "SCULPTURE" OF RHYME.	188	HUGH SELWYN: 2	12
SCURRY			
SCURRY INTO HEAPS AND LIE STILL,	108	LIU CH'E	4
"NIGHT DOGS, THE MARKS OF A DRUNKEN SCURRY,	211	SEXTUS PROP: 2	49
SCUTTLES			
AND TOTIN' UP SCUTTLES OF COAL,	271	OLE KATE	18
SCYTHIAN			
HE MAY WALK ON THE SCYTHIAN COAST,	212	SEXTUS PROP: 3	18
SE			
"SE IL COR TI MANCA," BUT IT FAILED THEE NOT!	19	FOR E. MCC	12
SEA			
THE CLOUDS THAT ARE SPRAY TO ITS SEA.	7	CINO	56
AS THE MOON DOTH FROM THE SEA,	17	PRAISE YSOLT	32
LIFE, ALL OF IT, MY SEA, AND ALL MEN'S STREAMS	25	GUIDO INVITES	9
O' SHIPS AND THE OPEN SEA.	33	GOODLY FERE	4
BUT AYE LOVED THE OPEN SEA.	33	GOODLY FERE	24
WI' HIS EYES LIKE THE GREY O' THE SEA,	34	GOODLY FERE	44
LIKE THE SEA THAT BROOKS NO VOYAGING	34	GOODLY FERE	45
LIKE THE SEA THAT HE COWED AT GENSERET	34	GOODLY FERE	47
A MATE OF THE WIND AND SEA,	34	GOODLY FERE	50
YOUR MIND AND YOU ARE OUR SARGASSO SEA,	61	PORTRAIT FEMME	1
LIST HOW I, CARE-WRETCHED, ON ICE-COLD SEA,	64	THE SEAFARER	14
THERE I HEARD NAUGHT SAVE THE HARSH SEA	64	THE SEAFARER	18
SKIRTING THE BLUE-GRAY SEA	90	SURGIT FAMA	3
OR TAKES THE SEA AIR	98	THE BELLAIRES	38
LET US TAKE ARMS AGAINST THIS SEA OF STUPIDITIES--	99	SALVATIONISTS	12
AND AGAINST THIS SEA OF VULGARITIES--	99	SALVATIONISTS	14
AND AGAINST THIS SEA OF IMBECILES--	99	SALVATIONISTS	16
A SEA	107	COMING OF WAR	7
INTELLIGENT MEN CAME DRIFTING IN FROM THE SEA AND FROM THE WEST BORDER,	134	EXILE'S LETTER	6
SURPRISED. DESERT TURMOIL. SEA SUN.	139	SOUTH-FOLK	6
TO BE LOOKING OUT ACROSS THE BRIGHT SEA,	164	QUINTUS SEPTIM	5
THE SALMON MOVES IN THE SUN-SHOT, BRIGHT SHALLOW SEA. . . .	166	FISH & SHADOW	4
HE HURLED HIMSELF INTO A SEA OF SIX WOMEN.	181	MOEURS CON: 6	2
ON SEA AND LAND, WITH ALL CONVENIENCE FOUND	264	ALF'S NINTH	19
SEABOARD			
NOT THE HYRCANIAN SEABOARD, NOT IN SEEKING THE SHORE OF EOS.	227	SEXTUS PROP:11	38
SEA-CLEAR			
THE SEA-CLEAR SAPPHIRE OF AIR, THE SEA-DARK CLARITY, STRETCHES BOTH SEA-CLIFF AND OCEAN.	170	PHANOPOEIA	24
SEA-CLIFF			
THE SEA-CLEAR SAPPHIRE OF AIR, THE SEA-DARK CLARITY, STRETCHES BOTH SEA-CLIFF AND OCEAN.	170	PHANOPOEIA	24
SEACOAST			
IF ANY LAND SHRINK INTO A DISTANT SEACOAST,	216	SEXTUS PROP: 5	19
SEA-COAST			
HE LIES BY THE POLUPHLOIBOIOUS SEA-COAST.	181	MOEURS CON: 6	4
SEA-CROSSING			
AND THEY MADE NOTHING OF SEA-CROSSING OR OF MOUNTAIN-CROSSING,	134	EXILE'S LETTER	
SEA-DARK			
THE SEA-CLEAR SAPPHIRE OF AIR, THE SEA-DARK CLARITY, STRETCHES BOTH SEA-CLIFF AND OCEAN.	170	PHANOPOEIA	2
SEA-FARE			
BUT SHALL HAVE HIS SORROW FOR SEA-FARE	65	THE SEAFARER	4

SEAFARER -- SECRET

	PAGE	TITLE	LINE
SEAFARER			
THE SEAFARER	64	THE SEAFARER	T
SEA-FOWLS'			
SEA-FOWLS' LOUDNESS WAS FOR ME LAUGHTER,	64	THE SEAFARER	21
SEA-HOARD			
FOR ALL THIS SEA-HOARD OF DECIDUOUS THINGS,	61	PORTRAIT FEMME	25
SEAL			
TO SEAL THIS,	136	EXILE'S LETTER	79
SEALED			
I HAVE BEEN KIND. SEE, I HAVE LEFT THE JARS SEALED,	60	TOMB AKR CAAR	12
SEAMEN			
A YELLOW STORK FOR A CHARGER, AND ALL OUR SEAMEN	128	THE RIVER SONG	7
SEARCH			
SEARCH NOT MY LIPS, O LOVE, LET GO MY HANDS,	51	THE FLAME	37
I SEARCH THE FEATURES, THE AVARICIOUS FEATURES	162	CABARET DANCER	28
SEARCHES			
YOU HAD YOUR SEARCHES, YOUR UNCERTAINTIES,	235	TO WHISTLER	10
SEARETH			
EARTHLY GLORY AGETH AND SEARETH.	66	THE SEAFARER	91
SEAS			
OH YE, MY FELLOWS: WITH THE SEAS BETWEEN US SOME BE,	21	IN DURANCE	35
LO, I WOULD SAIL THE SEAS WITH THEE ALONE!	25	GUIDO INVITES	2
AND THE WISE CONCORD, WHENCE THROUGH DELICIOUS SEAS	42	HER MONUMENT	43
THE CHOPPED SEAS HELD HIM, THEREFORE, THAT YEAR.	187	E. P. ODE	12
SEA'S			
FROM HERE TO THERE TO THE SEA'S BORDER,	72	DIEU! QU'IL	9
THE SEA'S COLOUR MOVES AT THE DAWN	131	AT TEN-SHIN	9
SEA-SERPENT			
ANDROMEDA WAS OFFERED TO A SEA-SERPENT	222	SEXTUS PROP: 8	22
SEASON			
UPON SUCH HOLLOW SEASON?"	72	PAN IS DEAD	13
IN THE BRIGHT NEW SEASON	111	IMAGE ORLEANS	2
IN THE BRIGHT NEW SEASON.	111	IMAGE ORLEANS	8
UNCUCKOLDED FOR A SEASON.	218	SEXTUS PROP: 5	60
SLOW FOOT, OR SWIFT FOOT, DEATH DELAYS BUT FOR A SEASON.	223	SEXTUS PROP: 9	21
KNOWEST THOU NOT THE TRUTH IS NEVER IN SEASON	263	ALF'S EIGHTH	13
. IN THE SEASON SAD AND WEARY	267	ALF'S TWELFTH	4
SEASONS			
TAKE HER. SHE HAS TWO EXCELLENT SEASONS.	165	QUINTUS SEPTIM	22
LIFE GIVES US TWO MINUTES, TWO SEASONS--	168	OF AROUET	25
SEA-SURGE			
AND DIRE SEA-SURGE, AND THERE I OFT SPENT	64	THE SEAFARER	6
AUDITION OF THE PHANTASMAL SEA-SURGE,	202	AGE DEMANDED	45
SEAT			
YOU WALKED ABOUT MY SEAT, PLAYING WITH BLUE PLUMS,	130	RIVER MER WIFE	4
BECAUSE THEY CAN'T FIND A SOFT SEAT.	142	UNMOVING CLOUD	21
OF LARES FLEEING THE "ROMAN SEAT" . . .	210	SEXTUS PROP: 2	12
THERE SHALL BE NONE IN A BETTER SEAT, NOT	222	SEXTUS PROP: 8	35
SEATED			
AND SEATED UPON IT IS THE LATE QUEEN, VICTORIA,	237	ABU SALAMMAMM	23
SEATS			
WERE SEEN LYING ALONG THE UPPER SEATS	93	LES MILLWIN	3
I SEE THEIR 'IGH 'ATS ON THE SEATS	270	OF 600 M.P.'S	13
SEAWARD			
TIBER ALONE, TRANSIENT AND SEAWARD BENT,	40	ROME	11
SECOND			
YOU HAVE BEEN SECOND ALWAYS. TRAGICAL?	61	PORTRAIT FEMME	7
SALUTATION THE SECOND	85	SALUTATION 2ND	T
WHILE THE SECOND WIFE OF A NEPHEW	115	SOCIAL ORDER	9
THE SECOND HAS WRITTEN A SONNET	118	THREE POETS	5
I HAVE THOUGHT OF THE SECOND TROY,	122	PROVINC DESERT	64
THE SECOND EVENING?"	159	PSYCHOLOG HOUR	36
AND THAT THE FRIEND OF THE SECOND DAUGHTER WAS UNDERGOING A NOVEL,	179	MOEURS. CON: 3	4
HER SECOND HUSBAND WILL NOT DIVORCE HER;	179	MOEURS CON: 3	5
NO SIGNS OF A SECOND INCUMBENT.	225	SEXTUS PROP:10	37
ALF'S SECOND BIT	258	ALF'S SECOND	T
SECRET			
FLESH SHROUDED BEARING THE SECRET.	20	IN DURANCE	25
KEEP YET MY SECRET IN THY BREAST HERE;	23	MARVOIL	47

PAGE 351

SECRET -- SEEING

	PAGE	TITLE	LINE
SECRET (CONTINUED)			
O THOU DARK SECRET WITH A SHIMMERING FLOOR, ...	50	THE FLAME	30
THIS MAN KNEW OUT THE SECRET WAYS OF LOVE, ...	73	JACOPO SELLAIO	1
CRUSADERS, LECTURERS AND SECRET LECHERS, ...	241	MOYEN SENSUEL	80
SECRETS			
AND TELL THEIR SECRETS, MESSIRE CINO, ...	151	NEAR PERIGORD	2
SECTOR			
FOR FIRES AND ODD RISKS, COULD IN THIS SECTOR	243	MOYEN SENSUEL	152
SECURE			
TO BE A SIGN AND AN HOPE MADE SECURE	42	HER MONUMENT	33
SEDGE			
AS A RILLET AMONG THE SEDGE ARE THY HANDS UPON ME;	91	DANCE FIGURE	19
SEDGES			
AND WITHERED ARE THE SEDGES;	72	PAN IS DEAD	5
SEE			
HE ANALYSES FORM AND THOUGHT TO SEE	15	FAMAM CANO	47
TO THE END THAT YOU SEE, FRIENDS:	22	MARVOIL	15
BUT AH! WHEN I SEE THE STANDARDS GOLD, VAIR, PURPLE,			
OPPOSING	28	ALTAFORTE	4
AND I LOVE TO SEE THE SUN RISE BLOOD-CRIMSON.	29	ALTAFORTE	19
WHEN I SEE HIM SO SCORN AND DEFY PEACE, ...	29	ALTAFORTE	23
THE MIST GOES FROM THE MIRROR AND I SEE.	32	PARACELSUS	6
HIS SMILE WAS GOOD TO SEE, ...	33	GOODLY FERE	6
"OR I'LL SEE YE DAMNED," SAYS HE.	33	GOODLY FERE	8
"YE SHALL SEE ONE THING TO MASTER ALL:	34	GOODLY FERE	31
SEE, THE LIGHT GRASS SPRANG UP TO PILLOW THEE, ...	60	TOMB AKR CAAR	6
I HAVE BEEN KIND. SEE, I HAVE LEFT THE JARS SEALED.	60	TOMB AKR CAAR	12
THIS PAPIER-MACHE, WHICH YOU SEE, MY FRIENDS, ...	63	PHASELLUS ILLE	1
SEE, THEY RETURN; AH, SEE THE TENTATIVE	74	THE RETURN	1
SEE, THEY RETURN; AH, SEE THE TENTATIVE	74	THE RETURN	1
SEE, THEY RETURN, ONE, AND BY ONE, ...	74	THE RETURN	5
TO SEE THREE GENERATIONS OF ONE HOUSE GATHERED			
TOGETHER!	89	COMMISSION	30
I ALMOST SEE YOU ABOUT ME, ...	94	INSTRUCTIONS	13
AND SEE THE FAUN IN OUR GARDEN.	109	THE FAUN	6
TO SEE HOW CELESTINE WILL RE-ENTER HER SLIPPERS. ..	111	BLACK SLIPPERS	10
AND NOW I SEE ONLY THE RIVER, ...	137	ON RIVER KIANG	4
AND I CAN NOT SEE CHOAN AFAR	138	CITY OF CHOAN	12
END FACT. TRY FICTION. LET US SAY WE SEE	154	NEAR PERIGORD	94
YE SEE HERE SEVERED, MY LIFE'S COUNTERPART."	156	NEAR PERIGORD	168
I SEE THE WHITE	171	LANGUE D'OC	EPI
SLEEP THOU NO MORE. I SEE THE STAR UPLEAPING	172	LANGUE D'OC: 1	7
I SEE THE SIGNS UPON THE WELKIN SPREAD, ...	172	LANGUE D'OC: 1	15
BADEST ME TO SEE THAT A GOOD WATCH WAS DONE, ...	172	LANGUE D'OC: 1	23
WE SEE TO KALON	189	HUGH SELWYN: 3	15
AND IT WAS MORNING, AND I WANTED TO SEE IF SHE WAS			
ALONE, AND RESTING, ...	225	SEXTUS PROP:10	27
TO SEE THE BRIGHTNESS OF."	236	MIDDLE-AGED	23
TO SEE YOUR FORTY SELF-BAPTIZED IMMORTALS, ...	239	MOYEN SENSUEL	32
"I SEE THEM SITTING IN THE HARVARD CLUB, ...	244	MOYEN SENSUEL	180
SEE 'EM GO SLOUCHING THERE, ...	257	BREAD BRIGADE	24
SEE HOW THEY TAKE IT ALL, ...	259	ALF'S THIRD	12
I DON'T QUITE SEE THE JOKE ANY MORE, ...	264	ALF'S EIGHTH	29
I SEE BY THE MORNING PAPERS	268	ANOTHER BIT	1
I SEE THEIR 'IGH 'ATS ON THE SEATS	270	OF 600 M.P.'S	13
SEED			
YEA AS THE SUN CALLETH TO THE SEED, ...	17	PRAISE YSOLT	48
WHERE TIME IS SHRIVELLED DOWN TO TIME'S SEED CORN	50	THE FLAME	11
FROM THE WHITE, ALIVE IN THE SEED, ...	76	THE ALCHEMIST	31
FRUIT OF MY SEED, ...	96	DUM CAPITOLIUM	5
THE SEED OF A MYRIAD HUES, ...	141	IDEA OF CHOAN	21
SEED-POD			
OR AS A DANDELION SEED-POD AND BE SWEPT AWAY, ...	36	FRANCESCA	10
SEEING			
O'ER TRACKS OF OCEAN; SEEING THAT ANYHOW	65	THE SEAFARER	65
THE SEEING EYE	104	THE SEEING EYE	7
SEEING THAT TRISTAN'S LADY ISEUTZ HAD NEVER	106	DOMPNA POIS	37
SEEING YOUR WIFE IS CHARMING AND YOUR CHILD	161	CABARET DANCER	
NO, HARDLY, BUT SEEING HE HAD BEEN BORN	187	E. P. ODE	
SEEING THAT LONG STANDING INCREASES ALL THINGS	207	SEXTUS PROP: 1	24

PAGE 352

SEEK -- SEEN

	PAGE	TITLE	LINE
SEEK			
SEEK OUT A FOREIGN FASTNESS.	65	THE SEAFARER	39
GO, MY SONGS, SEEK YOUR PRAISE FROM THE YOUNG AND FROM THE INTOLERANT,	95	ITE	1
SEEK EVER TO STAND IN THE HARD SOPHOCLEAN LIGHT	95	ITE	3
THEY SEEK MY FINANCIAL GOOD.	147	BEFORE SLEEP	4
TWO YEARS, THREE YEARS I SEEK	175	LANGUE D'OC: 3	34
NOR TO SEEK OUT, SURELY,	250	DONNA MI PREGA	68
SEEKING			
SEEKING E'ER THE NEW-LAID RAST-WAY	7	CINO	50
SEEKING EVER A SONG.	16	PRAISE YSOLT	10
BLOWING THEY KNOW NOT WHITHER, SEEKING A SONG.	16	PRAISE YSOLT	20
AND NOW SHE TURNS TO ME SEEKING LOVE,	102	LADIES	3
I KNOW NOT WHERE TO GO SEEKING,	105	DOMPNA POIS	4
NOT THE HYRCANIAN SEABOARD, NOT IN SEEKING THE SHORE OF EOS.	227	SEXTUS PROP:11	38
SEEK'ST			
O THOU NEW COMER WHO SEEK'ST ROME IN ROME	40	ROME	1
SEEM			
WE SEEM AS STATUES ROUND WHOSE HIGH-RISEN BASE	32	PARACELSUS	11
WERE SET TOGETHER THEY WOULD SEEM BUT LIGHT	36	THE YOUNG KING	4
WHO MADE THE FREEST HAND SEEM COVETOUS.	37	THE YOUNG KING	14
WAVER AND SEEM NOT DRAWN TO EARTH, SO HE	39	FOR PSYCHE	5
FOR YOU SEEM NEVER TO HAVE DISCOVERED	101	AMITIES	8
A BASKET-WORK OF BRAIDS WHICH SEEM AS IF THEY WERE	204	MEDALLION.	10
AND DIDN'T SEEM NEVER TO STOP.	271	OLE KATE	12
SEEMED			
CHURLISH AT SEEMED MISPLACEMENT,	9	NA AUDIART	43
CLEAR, DEEP, TRANSLUCENT, SO THE STARS ME SEEMED	30	PIERE VIDAL	21
SEEMED OVER ME TO HOVER LIGHT AS LEAVES	39	FOR PSYCHE	6
AND MUSIC FLOWING THROUGH ME SEEMED TO OPEN	39	FOR PSYCHE	8
SEEMING			
DELIGHT MAKETH CERTAIN IN SEEMING	250	DONNA MI PREGA	71
SEEMS			
AS NOW SEEMS IT SWEET,	9	NA AUDIART	45
THAT SEEMS TO BE SOME QUIVERING SPLENDOUR CAST	41	HER MONUMENT	29
FOR IT SEEMS TO US WORTHY OF RECORD.	93	LES MILLWIN	14
BUT SEEMS LIKE A PERSON JUST GONE.	112	IONE, DEAD	9
IT SEEMS TO ME	176	LANGUE D'OC: 3	68
THERE COMES, IT SEEMS, AND AT ANY RATE	222	SEXTUS PROP: 8	16
SEEN			
BUT I HAVE SEEN THE SORROW OF MEN, AND AM GLAD,	4	LA FRAISNE	22
AS WE HAD SEEN HIM YESTERDAY.	14	FAMAM CANO	22
I HA' SEEN THEM 'MID THE CLOUDS ON THE HEATHER.	25	THE WHITE STAG	1
LO, I HAVE SEEN THEE BOUND ABOUT WITH DREAMS,	25	GUIDO INVITES	7
FOR WE HAVE SEEN	26	NIGHT LITANY	22
FOR I HAVE SEEN THE	27	NIGHT LITANY	38
HAVE SEEN THIS THING, OUT OF THEIR FAR COURSES	27	NIGHT LITANY	42
HAVE THEY SEEN THIS THING,	27	NIGHT LITANY	43
I HA' SEEN HIM DRIVE A HUNDRED MEN	33	GOODLY FERE	17
"YE HA' SEEN ME HEAL THE LAME AND BLIND,	34	GOODLY FERE	29
I HA' SEEN HIM COW A THOUSAND MEN.	34	GOODLY FERE	35
I HAVE SEEN HIM UPON THE TREE.	34	GOODLY FERE	36
I HA' SEEN HIM COW A THOUSAND MEN	34	GOODLY FERE	41
I HA' SEEN HIM EAT O' THE HONEY-COMB	34	GOODLY FERE	53
I WHO HAVE SEEN YOU AMID THE PRIMAL THINGS	36	FRANCESCA	5
AND I HAVE SEEN MY LADY IN THE SUN,	49	OF SPLENDOUR	6
AND I HAVE SEEN HER THERE WITHIN HER HOUSE,	49	OF SPLENDOUR	9
LO, THERE ARE MANY GODS WHOM WE HAVE SEEN,	50	THE FLAME	23
IF THOU HAST SEEN MY SHADE SANS CHARACTER,	51	THE FLAME	39
IF THOU HAST SEEN THAT MIRROR OF ALL MOMENTS,	51	THE FLAME	40
TIME HAS SEEN THIS, AND WILL NOT TURN AGAIN;	59	SILET	12
OH, YOU ARE PATIENT, I HAVE SEEN YOU SIT	61	PORTRAIT FEMME	11
I HAVE SEEN FISHERMEN PICNICKING IN THE SUN,	85	SALUTATION	3
I HAVE SEEN THEM WITH UNTIDY FAMILIES,	85	SALUTATION	4
I HAVE SEEN THEIR SMILES FULL OF TEETH	86	SALUTATION	5
KORE IS SEEN IN THE NORTH	90	SURGIT FAMA	2
WERE SEEN LYING ALONG THE UPPER SEATS	93	LES MILLWIN	3
I HAVE SEEN IT MELTING ABOVE ME.	95	OF THE DEGREES	7
WE WHO HAVE SEEN EVEN ARTEMIS A-BINDING HER SANDALS,	104	ANCORA	6
HA! SIR, I HAVE SEEN YOU SNIFFING AND SNOOZLING	109	THE FAUN	1

SEEN -- SELLING

```
                                                              PAGE    TITLE           LINE
SEEN (CONTINUED)
    "HAVE YOU SEEN ANY OTHERS, ANY OF OUR LOT,       ........   119   THE GYPSY          2
    AND HE SAID, "HAVE YOU SEEN ANY OF OUR LOT?"     ......     119   THE GYPSY         11
    I'D SEEN A LOT OF HIS LOT . . .     ......................  119   THE GYPSY         12
    I HAVE SEEN THE TORCH-FLAMES, HIGH-LEAPING,      .......    121   PROVINC DESERT    30
    AND SEEN THE HIGH BUILDING,     .......................     121   PROVINC DESERT    34
    SEEN THE LONG MINARETS, THE WHITE SHAFTS.        .........  122   PROVINC DESERT    35
    HAVE SEEN NARBONNE, AND CAHORS AND CHALUS,       ........   122   PROVINC DESERT    40
    HAVE SEEN EXCIDEUIL, CAREFULLY FASHIONED.        .........  122   PROVINC DESERT    41
    HAVE SEEN THE COPPER COME DOWN     ...................      122   PROVINC DESERT    52
    I HAVE SEEN THE FIELDS, PALE, CLEAR AS AN EMERALD,          122   PROVINC DESERT    54
    I HAVE SEEN FOIX ON ITS ROCK, SEEN TOULOUSE, AND            122   PROVINC DESERT    59
    I HAVE SEEN FOIX ON ITS ROCK, SEEN TOULOUSE, AND            122   PROVINC DESERT    59
    I HAVE SEEN THE RUINED "DORATA."     ..................     122   PROVINC DESERT    61
    HAVE YOU, OR I, SEEN MOST OF CABARETS, GOOD
      HEDGETHORN?     ........................................  161   CABARET DANCER    17
    I HAVE SEEN THROUGH THE CRUST.     .;..................     162   CABARET DANCER    39
    SEEN, WE ADMIT, AMID AMBROSIAL CIRCUMSTANCES     ......     202   AGE DEMANDED      34
    I HAD SEEN IN THE SHADE, RECUMBENT ON CUSHIONED
      HELICON,     .........................................    210   SEXTUS PROP: 2     1
    I HAD NEVER SEEN HER LOOKING SO BEAUTIFUL,       .........  225   SEXTUS PROP:10    30
    IN BOSTON, TO HENRY JAMES, THE GREATEST WHOM WE'VE
      SEEN LIVING.     .....................................    240   MOYEN SENSUEL     62
    YOU SHOULD HAVE SEEN ME AFTER THE AFFRAY,        .........  247   PIERROTS           4
    FROM FORM SEEN DOTH HE START, THAT, UNDERSTOOD,     ...     249   DONNA MI PREGA    24
    I SAYS! 'AVE YOU SEEN 'EM?     ........................     258   ALF'S SECOND      13
    'AVE YOU SEEN YER LARST SWEET LITTER?     ..............    270   OF 600 M.P.'S     18
SEES
    OR NO ONE SEES IT, AND EN BERTRANS PROSPERED?     .....     155   NEAR PERIGORD    126
SEETH
    WHO WELL PROCEEDETH, FORM NOT SEETH,     ..............     250   DONNA MI PREGA    82
SEI
    HE RETURNS BY WAY OF SEI ROCK, TO HEAR THE NEW
      NIGHTINGALES,     ...................................     130   THE RIVER SONG    37
SEIGNIORY
    OR THAT HE HATH NOT STABLISHED SEIGNIORY     ..........     249   DONNA MI PREGA    47
SEI-GO-YO
    AND THE MOON FALLS OVER THE PORTALS OF SEI-GO-YO,           131   AT TEN-SHIN       11
SEISMOGRAPH
    ULTIMATELY, HIS SEISMOGRAPH:     .....................      199   MAUBERLEY: 2      19
SELDOM
    AND IF THE PAPERS SELDOM SANG HIS PRAISE,        .........  265   ALF'S NINTH       23
SELECT
    THE SELECT COMPANY: BEAUTIES YOU ALL WOULD KNOW    ...      242   MOYEN SENSUEL    113
SELECTED
    IN THE PRESENCE OF SELECTED PERCEPTIONS.         ..........  202  AGE DEMANDED      40
SELF
    MAY I FOR MY OWN SELF SONG'S TRUTH RECKON,       ........    64   THE SEAFARER       1
    FROM COMSTOCK'S SELF, DOWN TO THE MEANEST RESIDENT,         239   MOYEN SENSUEL     15
SELF-BAPTIZED
    TO SEE YOUR FORTY SELF-BAPTIZED IMMORTALS,       ........   239   MOYEN SENSUEL     32
SELFRIDGE
    DON'T GET A DISCOUNT LIKE MR. SELFRIDGE     ...........     262   ALF'S SEVENTH     11
    A PERIL TO SELFRIDGE AND THE NATION.     ..............     262   ALF'S SEVENTH     20
    FROM A GREAT EMPLOYER LIKE SELFRIDGE     ..............     264   ALF'S EIGHTH      33
SELF-STYLED
    NON-ESTEEM OF SELF-STYLED "HIS BETTERS"     ...........     202   AGE DEMANDED      58
SELL
    "THESE SELL OUR PICTURES"! OH WELL,     ...............      20   IN DURANCE         4
    THAT ONLY SENTIMENTAL STUFF WILL SELL!)     ...........     242   MOYEN SENSUEL    118
    DAVE WAS THE MAN TO SELL THE SHOT AND SHELL,       ......   264   ALF'S NINTH       17
    TO SELL, TO SELL, TO SELL, THAT'S IT, TO SELL      ......   264   ALF'S NINTH       20
    TO SELL, TO SELL, TO SELL, THAT'S IT, TO SELL      ......   264   ALF'S NINTH       20
    TO SELL, TO SELL, TO SELL, THAT'S IT, TO SELL      ......   264   ALF'S NINTH       20
    TO SELL, TO SELL, TO SELL, THAT'S IT, TO SELL      ......   264   ALF'S NINTH       20
    TO SELL THE PAPERS EARLY,     ........................      266   ALF'S ELEVENTH     6
    TO SELL THE GOD DAMN'D FROGS     .....................      273   M. POM-POM        10
SELLAIO
    OF JACOPO DEL SELLAIO     ............................       73   JACOPO SELLAIO     T
SELLING
    "OF SELLING MY OWN WORKS.     .......................:..    194   MR. NIXON         15
```

SELLING -- SENT

	PAGE	TITLE	LINE
SELLING (CONTINUED)			
HAPPY SELLING POOR LOVES FOR CHEAP APPLES.	229	SEXTUS PROP:12	45
SELVAGGIA			
SELVAGGIA, GUISCARDA, MANDETTA, ...	76	THE ALCHEMIST	54
SELWIN			
HUGH SELWIN MAUBERLEY	185	HUGH SELWYN	T
SEMBLANCE			
EVEN THAT SEMBLANCE THAT APPEARS AMONGST US	41	HER MONUMENT	23
SEMELE'S			
CHARMINGLY IDENTICAL, WITH SEMELE'S, ...	222	SEXTUS PROP: 8	31
COMBUSTED SEMELE'S, OF IO STRAYED.	227	SEXTUS PROP:11	34
SENAT			
M. POM-POM EST AU SENAT	273	M. POM-POM	6
SENATE			
THEY HAVE ASKED THE SENATE TO GUESS	268	ANOTHER BIT	6
SENATORIAL			
SENATORIAL FAMILIES OF STRASBOURG, MONSIEUR VEROG.	193	SIENA MI FE	4
A SENATORIAL JOBBER FOR PROTECTION, ...	245	MOYEN SENSUEL	214
SEND			
AND ONE MAY HE HAD YOU SEND FOR ME, ...	135	EXILE'S LETTER	38
AND SEND IT A THOUSAND MILES, THINKING.	136	EXILE'S LETTER	80
WE'LL SEND 'EM MOUCHIN' 'OME, ...	257	BREAD BRIGADE	7
TO SEND ME TO WORK IN VICKERS	268	ANOTHER BIT	16
SENDETH			
SAYING "THE SOUL SENDETH US,"	17	PRAISE YSOLT	34
SENDS			
MALEMORT, GUESSES BENEATH, SENDS WORD TO			
COEUR-DE-LION:	155	NEAR PERIGORD	123
RUNNING SO CLOSE TO "HELL" IT SENDS A SHIVER	246	MOYEN SENSUEL	224
SENESCHAL			
AND ONE LEAN ARAGONESE CURSING THE SENESCHAL	22	MARVOIL	14
SEN-GO			
WE MET, AND TRAVELLED INTO SEN-GO, ...	134	EXILE'S LETTER	17
SENHER			
AH, BELS SENHER, MAENT, AT LAST	106	DOMPNA POIS	61
SENIOR			
WHOSE WIFE IS SEVERAL YEARS HIS SENIOR, ...	115	SOCIAL ORDER	2
SENIORS			
THE YOUNG MEN LOOK UPON THEIR SENIORS, ...	104	THE SEEING EYE	5
SENNIN			
YET SENNIN NEEDS	128	THE RIVER SONG	6
IN THE STORIED HOUSES OF SAN-KO THEY GAVE US MORE			
SENNIN MUSIC, ...	135	EXILE'S LETTER	26
SENNIN POEM BY KAKUHAKU	139	SENNIN POEM	T
HE RIDES THROUGH THE PURPLE SMOKE TO VISIT THE			
SENNIN, ...	140	SENNIN POEM	12
HE CLAPS HIS HAND ON THE BACK OF THE GREAT WATER			
SENNIN.	140	SENNIN POEM	14
SENSATE			
LOVE IS CREATED, HATH A SENSATE NAME, ...	248	DONNA MI PREGA	22
SENSE			
AND SENSE THE TEETH THROUGH THE LIPS THAT PRESS ...	11	OF THE GIBBET	22
JUMP TO YOUR SENSE AND GIVE PRAISE AS WE'D LIEF DO.	13	MESMERISM	8
OF SENSE UNTELLABLE, BEAUTY	41	HER MONUMENT	28
HOW CANST THOU REACH SO HIGH WITH THY POOR SENSE;	42	HER MONUMENT	52
YOU OF THE FINER SENSE,	90	THE REST	10
I LOSE ALL WIT AND SENSE.	176	LANGUE D'OC: 3	69
IN THE OLD SENSE. WRONG FROM THE START--	187	E. P. ODE	4
BROUGHT NO REFORMING SENSE	201	AGE DEMANDED	6
HIS SENSE OF GRADUATIONS,	201	AGE DEMANDED	22
SO HE HAVE SENSE OR GLOW WITH REASON'S FIRE, ...	250	DONNA MI PREGA	91
(HIS WHAT?) WITH A SHOW OF SENSE, ...	263	ALF'S EIGHTH	
SENSUEL			
L'HOMME MOYEN SENSUEL	238	MOYEN SENSUEL	T
SENT			
BUT MY SOUL SENT A WOMAN, A WOMAN OF THE WONDER-FOLK.	17	PRAISE YSOLT	38
TILL MY SOUL SENT A WOMAN AS THE SUN:	17	PRAISE YSOLT	47
AYE HE SENT US OUT THROUGH THE CROSSED HIGH SPEARS	33	GOODLY FERE	9
WHY AM I WARNED? WHY AM I SENT AWAY?	95	OF THE DEGREES	12
AND SENT ME ONLY YOUR HANDMAIDS.	96	TO KALON	2
AND THEN I WAS SENT OFF TO SOUTH WEI, ...	134	EXILE'S LETTER	12

PAGE 355

SENT -- SET

	PAGE	TITLE	LINE
SENT (CONTINUED)			
THAT'S SENT TO HOLLAND, A MOST PARTICULAR FEATURE,	239	MOYEN SENSUEL	20
SENTENCE			
WITH HER HUSBAND ASKING A REMISSION OF SENTENCE,	230	SEXTUS PROP:12	61
THAT WE, WITH MASEFIELD'S VEIN, IN THE NEXT SENTENCE	242	MOYEN SENSUEL	129
SENTENT			
S'ILS NE SENTENT PAS LA MUSIQUE, QU'EST CE	199	MAUBERLEY: 2	EPI
SENTIMENT			
AN ANXIOUS SENTIMENT WAS HIS EMPLOYMENT,	245	MOYEN SENSUEL	194
SENTIMENTAL			
NOTE, READER, NOTE THE SENTIMENTAL TOUCH:	242	MOYEN SENSUEL	116
THAT ONLY SENTIMENTAL STUFF WILL SELL!)	242	MOYEN SENSUEL	118
SEPARATION			
HOW HAVE I LABOURED TO BRING HER SOUL INTO SEPARATION;	84	ORTUS	7
AND THEN, WHEN SEPARATION HAD COME TO ITS WORST,	134	EXILE'S LETTER	16
SEPARATION ON THE RIVER KIANG	137	ON RIVER KIANG	T
HERE WE MUST MAKE SEPARATION	137	TAKING LEAVE	3
FOR SEPARATION WROUGHT OUT SEPARATION,	151	NEAR PERIGORD	24
FOR SEPARATION WROUGHT OUT SEPARATION,	151	NEAR PERIGORD	24
SEPTIMIUS			
HOMAGE TO QUINTUS SEPTIMIUS FLORENTIS CHRISTIANUS	164	QUINTUS SEPTIM	T
SEPULCHRE			
'TIS MY TRUE LOVE'S SEPULCHRE.	45	FROM HEINE: 3	8
E. P. ODE POUR L'ELECTION DE SON SEPULCHRE	187	E. P. ODE	T
WITH NO STONE UPON MY CONTEMPTIBLE SEPULCHRE;	208	SEXTUS PROP: 1	37
SEPULTUS			
DEO LAUS, QUOD EST SEPULTUS,	101	AMITIES	18
SEQUESTERED			
MAY A WOODY AND SEQUESTERED PLACE COVER ME WITH ITS FOLIAGE	213	SEXTUS PROP: 3	35
SERE			
AND MY HEART IS COLD AND SERE;	45	FROM HEINE: 3	6
SERIES			
TO PRESENT THE SERIES	200	MAUBERLEY: 2	24
SERIES	203	MAUBERLEY: 4	16
SERIOUS			
SERIOUS CHILD BUSINESS THAT THE WORLD	14	FAMAM CANO	13
THE SERIOUS SOCIAL FOLK IS "JUST WHAT SEX IS."	244	MOYEN SENSUEL	162
SERPENTINE			
LURKING, SERPENTINE, AMPHIBIOUS AND INSIDIOUS	244	MOYEN SENSUEL	170
SERVANT			
NUNC DIMITTIS, NOW LETTEST THOU THY SERVANT,	183	CANTICO SOLE	9
NOW LETTEST THOU THY SERVANT	183	CANTICO SOLE	10
AND NO SERVANT WAS LEADING ME,	224	SEXTUS PROP:10	3
SERVE			
AND IS DILIGENT TO SERVE ME,	46	FROM HEINE: 6	11
OUR "FANTASTIKON" DELIGHTED TO SERVE US.	82	THE CONDOLENCE	10
SERVICE			
AND YOUR NEW SERVICE AT DINNER,	167	OF AROUET	9
SESTINA			
SESTINA: ALTAFORTE	28	ALTAFORTE	T
SET			
THOUGH THOU HATE ME, READ IT SET	8	NA AUDIART	25
SET DEEP IN CRYSTAL; AND BECAUSE MY SLEEP	30	PIERE VIDAL	22
FOR THAT RESTLESSNESS--PIERE SET TO KEEP	30	PIERE VIDAL	24
WERE SET TOGETHER THEY WOULD SEEM BUT LIGHT	36	THE YOUNG KING	4
ONE WHO HATH SET THE WHOLE WORLD 'NEATH HER LAWS,	40	ROME	6
HOW HAST THOU SET THE FIRE	41	HER MONUMENT	11
SET TO SOME WEAVING, COMES THE AUREATE LIGHT.	49	OF SPLENDOUR	16
SET LOOSE THE WHOLE CONSUMMATE PACK	52	AU SALON	14
I AM SET WIDE UPON THE WORLD'S WAYS	53	AU JARDIN	11
HATH SET ACQUAINTANCE WHERE MIGHT BE AFFECTIONS,	63	AN OBJECT	2
DO NOT SET ABOUT TO PROCURE ME AN AUDIENCE.	81	TENZONE	9
TO SET UPON THEM HIS CHANGE	90	SURGIT FAMA	12
ONE SET ON THE HIGHWAY TO SING.	122	PROVINC DESERT	67
WHEN WE SET OUT, THE WILLOWS WERE DROOPING WITH SPRING,	127	BOWMEN OF SHU	21
RED JADE CUPS, FOOD WELL SET ON A BLUE JEWELLED TABLE,	135	EXILE'S LETTER	47
MEN'S FATES ARE ALREADY SET,	138	NEAR SHOKU	10

SET -- SHADES

	PAGE	TITLE	LINE
SET (CONTINUED)			
THEY SET DOWN THEIR BURDENS, ...	140	MULBERRY ROAD	16
SET ALL TOGETHER, ARE NOT WORTHY OF YOU. . . ." ...	151	NEAR PERIGORD	9
AND HE WHO SET THE STRIFE BETWEEN BROTHER AND BROTHER	151	NEAR PERIGORD	25
HOW WOULD YOU LIVE, WITH NEIGHBOURS SET ABOUT YOU--	152	NEAR PERIGORD	28
BUT FROM WHERE MY HEART IS SET	173	LANGUE D'OC: 2	6
WHEN WE SET STRIFE AWAY, ...	173	LANGUE D'OC: 2	18
OR SET ME QUIET, OR BID ME CHATTER.	175	LANGUE D'OC: 3	45
FOOL WHO WOULD SET A TERM TO LOVE'S MADNESS, ...	220	SEXTUS PROP: 7	22
YOU WERE NOT ALWAYS SURE, NOT ALWAYS SET	235	TO WHISTLER	14
IN HOPE TO SET SOME MISCONCEPTIONS RIGHT.	238	MOYEN SENSUEL	2
IF I SET FORTH A BAWDY PLOT LIKE BYRON	239	MOYEN SENSUEL	42
THEY SET THEIR MIND (IT'S STILL IN THAT CONDITION)--	240	MOYEN SENSUEL	53
UPON THE NATIONAL BRAINS AND SET 'EM ACHIN'.	245	MOYEN SENSUEL	216
OUTSIDE YOUR SET BUT, HAVING KEPT FAITH IN YOUR EYES,	247	PIERROTS	23
THERE, BEYOND COLOUR, ESSENCE SET APART, ...	250	DONNA MI PREGA	84
AND WHERE HE ONCE SET FOOT, RIGHT THERE HE STAYED.	264	ALF'S NINTH	12
IS WHAT HAS SET US PINING, ...	267	ALF'S TWELFTH	2
BUT SOME SILVER SET TO STEW	267	ALF'S TWELFTH	17
SETS			
SETS FORTH, AND THOUGH THOU HATE ME WELL, ...	9	NA AUDIART	32
IN EVENING COMPANY HE SETS HIS FACE	46	FROM HEINE: 6	13
AND HIS STRANGE PROPERTY SETS SIGHS TO MOVE	250	DONNA MI PREGA	58
SETTING			
WHAT IS THE USE OF SETTING IT TO RIME?	59	SILET	6
OR TAKE HIS "MAGNET" SINGER SETTING OUT, ...	154	NEAR PERIGORD	104
SUCH MY COHORT AND SETTING. AND SHE BOUND IVY TO HIS THYRSOS;	211	SEXTUS PROP: 2	35
S'EVEILLER			
S'EVEILLER.	160	DANS OMNIBUS	9
SEVEN			
YOU WERE A SEVEN DAYS' WONDER.	114	EPILOGUE	2
DRAG ON THE SEVEN COACHES WITH OUTRIDERS.	141	IDEA OF CHOAN	3
SEVENTH			
ALF'S SEVENTH BIT	262	ALF'S SEVENTH	T
SEVENTIES			
ITS MIND WAS MADE UP IN "THE SEVENTIES,"	63	PHASELLUS ILLE	3
SEVENTY			
TYIN' YOUR MEANIN' IN SEVENTY SWADELIN'S, ...	13	MESMERISM	2
TO THE DANCE OF THE SEVENTY COUPLES;	132	AT TEN-SHIN	23
THOUGH MALES OF SEVENTY, WHO FEAR TRUTHS NAKED HARM US, ...	243	MOYEN SENSUEL	147
SEVERAL			
WHOSE WIFE IS SEVERAL YEARS HIS SENIOR, ...	115	SOCIAL ORDER	2
SEVERAL OLD SO'JERS KNOW	257	BREAD BRIGADE	11
SEVERED			
IN THE AIR SHE SEVERED, ...	92	GENTILDONNA	3
I SEVERED MEN, MY HEAD AND HEART	156	NEAR PERIGORD	167
YE SEE HERE SEVERED, MY LIFE'S COUNTERPART."	156	NEAR PERIGORD	168
SEX			
WHO WANDERS ABOUT ANNOUNCING HIS SEX	82	THE CONDOLENCE	15
THE SERIOUS SOCIAL FOLK IS "JUST WHAT SEX IS." ...	244	MOYEN SENSUEL	162
SEXLESS			
THAT HE PASSES FOR BOTH BLOODLESS AND SEXLESS. ...	100	TEMPERAMENTS	4
SEXTUS			
HOMAGE TO SEXTUS PROPERTIUS	203	SEXTUS PROP	T
SEZ			
SEZ THE TIMES A SILVER LINING	267	ALF'S TWELFTH	1
"I COULDN'T," SHE SEZ, "AN' I AINT TRIED, ...	270	OF 600 M.P.'S	21
THEY'RE ME OWN," SHE SEZ TO ME, ...	270	OF 600 M.P.'S	22
SHADE			
STILL SHADE, AND BADE NO WHISPER SPEAK THE BIRDS OF HOW	21	IN DURANCE	48
IF THOU HAST SEEN MY SHADE SANS CHARACTER, ...	51	THE FLAME	39
I HAD SEEN IN THE SHADE RECUMBENT ON CUSHIONED HELICON, ...	210	SEXTUS PROP: 2	1
IN VAIN, YOU CALL BACK THE SHADE, ...	219	SEXTUS PROP: 6	35
AND YOU ALSO FOLLOW HIM "NEATH PHRYGIAN PINE SHADE:	229	SEXTUS PROP:12	41
SHADES			
SHADES OF CALLIMACHUS, COAN GHOSTS OF PHILETAS	207	SEXTUS PROP: 1	1

PAGE 357

SHADOW -- SHALL

	PAGE	TITLE	LINE
SHADOW			
THE GLORY OF THE SHADOW OF THE	26	NIGHT LITANY	23
YEA, THE GLORY OF THE SHADOW	26	NIGHT LITANY	25
UPON THE SHADOW OF THE WATERS	26	NIGHT LITANY	27
OF THE SHADOW OF THY HANDMAID	27	NIGHT LITANY	30
SHADOW OF THIS THY VENICE	27	NIGHT LITANY	39
O SMOKE AND SHADOW OF A DARKLING WORLD,	50	THE FLAME	14
I HAVE LOVED A STREAM AND A SHADOW.	84	ORTUS	11
FISH AND THE SHADOW	166	FISH & SHADOW	T
AS LIGHT AS THE SHADOW OF THE FISH	166	FISH & SHADOW	5
LIGHT AS THE SHADOW OF THE FISH	166	FISH & SHADOW	20
IN VAIN, CYNTHIA, VAIN CALL TO UNANSWERING SHADOW,	219	SEXTUS PROP: 6	36
SHADOWS			
AND HAVE NONE ABOUT ME SAVE IN THE SHADOWS	20	IN DURANCE	18
BLIND EYES AND SHADOWS THAT ARE FORMED AS MEN;	38	BALLATETTA	2
SHALL I ENTRUST MYSELF TO ENTANGLED SHADOWS,	212	SEXTUS PROP: 3	7
ONE TANGLE OF SHADOWS.	218	SEXTUS PROP: 6	5
SHADOWY			
THE SHADOWY FLOWERS OF ORCUS	67	DORIA	10
SHAFT			
MIDONZ, DAUGHTER OF THE SUN, SHAFT OF THE TREE, SILVER OF THE LEAF, LIGHT OF THE YELLOW OF THE AMBER,	75	THE ALCHEMIST	26
SHAFTS			
PURPLE AND SAPPHIRE FOR THE SILVER SHAFTS	21	IN DURANCE	36
SEEN THE LONG MINARETS, THE WHITE SHAFTS.	122	PROVINC DESERT	35
SHAG			
AND THE SHAG,	117	THE LAKE ISLE	6
SHAKE			
THAT NO SHIFT OF MOOD CAN SHAKE FROM US:	52	AU SALON	7
SHAKE UP THE STAGNANT POOL OF ITS CONVICTIONS;	63	PHASELLUS ILLE	8
I SHAKE AND BURN AND QUIVER	175	LANGUE D'OC: 3	28
SHAKEN			
"THEIR LITTLE COSMOS IS SHAKEN"--	158	PSYCHOLOG HOUR	12
SHAKES			
WHEN HE SHAKES HANDS WITH YOUNG LADIES.	115	SOCIAL ORDER	4
AND SO FORTH, AUGUSTUS. "VIRGIN ARABIA SHAKES IN HER INMOST DWELLING."	216	SEXTUS PROP: 5	18
HE SHAKES THE TROJAN WEAPONS OF AENEAS,	228	SEXTUS PROP:12	34
SHAKING			
OR SHAKING BETWEEN,	175	LANGUE D'OC: 3	53
SHALL			
WHO SHALL RENDER	8	NA AUDIART	8
SHALL BURST TO LILTING AT THE PRAISE	9	NA AUDIART	28
THESE THAT WE LOVED SHALL GOD LOVE LESS	12	OF THE GIBBET	39
BEHOLD THE SHIELD! HE SHALL NOT TAKE THEE ALL.	19	FOR E. MCC	26
SHALL MAIDENS SCATTER ROSE LEAVES	24	THUS NINEVEH	2
SHALL ALL MEN SCATTER ROSE LEAVES	24	THUS NINEVEH	17
"YE SHALL SEE ONE THING TO MASTER ALL:	34	GOODLY FERE	31
THERE WHERE THERE IS NO GRIEF, NOR SHALL BE SADNESS.	37	THE YOUNG KING	40
WE ALSO SHALL BE DEAD PRETTY SOON	43	MR. HOUSMAN	3
YET SHALL MY WHITE ARMS HOLD THEE,	48	FROM HEINE: 7	29
BUT SHALL HAVE HIS SORROW FOR SEA-FARE	65	THE SEAFARER	43
SO THAT ALL MEN SHALL HONOUR HIM AFTER	66	THE SEAFARER	78
THAT BEARS US UP, SHALL TURN AGAINST THE POLE.	69	THE NEEDLE	7
HOW SHALL WE WEAVE A CORONAL,	72	PAN IS DEAD	6
THEY SHALL INHERIT THE EARTH.	83	THE GARDEN	7
WE SHALL GET OURSELVES RATHER DISLIKED.	99	SALVATIONISTS	2
FOR WE SHALL CONSIDER THEM AND THEIR STATE	99	SALVATIONISTS	8
TE VOILA, MON BOURRIENNE, YOU ALSO SHALL BE IMMORTAL.	101	AMITIES	6
I SHALL HAVE MISSED NOTHING AT ALL,	105	DOMPNA POIS	26
AND SAYING: WHEN SHALL WE GET BACK TO OUR COUNTRY?	127	BOWMEN OF SHU	2
AH, HOW SHALL YOU KNOW THE DREARY SORROW AT THE NORTH GATE,	133	FRONTIER GUARD	22
HOW SHALL WE KNOW ALL THE FRIENDS	141	IDEA OF CHOAN	31
SO SHALL YOU BE ALSO,	145	SALUTATION 3RD	9
RICHARD SHALL DIE TO-MORROW--LEAVE HIM THERE	155	NEAR PERIGORD	139
SHALL OUTLAST OUR DAYS.	189	HUGH SELWYN: 3	12
SHALL I PLACE A TIN WREATH UPON!	189	HUGH SELWYN: 3	28
WHEN OUR TWO DUSTS WITH WALLER'S SHALL BE LAID,	197	ENVOI (1919)	23
I SHALL HAVE, DOUBTLESS, A BOOM AFTER MY FUNERAL,	207	SEXTUS PROP: 1	23

SHALL -- SHARP

	PAGE	TITLE	LINE
SHALL (CONTINUED)			
SHALL HAVE MY DOG'S DAY,	208	SEXTUS PROP: 1	36
THE SONGS SHALL BE A FINE TOMB-STONE OVER THEIR BEAUTY.	209	SEXTUS PROP: 1	64
SHALL BE YAWNED OUT ON MY LYRE--WITH SUCH INDUSTRY.	210	SEXTUS PROP: 2	5
MY LITTLE MOUTH SHALL GOBBLE IN SUCH GREAT FOUNTAINS,	210	SEXTUS PROP: 2	6
SHALL I ENTRUST MYSELF TO ENTANGLED SHADOWS,	212	SEXTUS PROP: 3	7
I SHALL BE PREY TO LAMENTATIONS WORSE THAN A NOCTURNAL ASSAILANT.	212	SEXTUS PROP: 3	11
AND I SHALL BE IN THE WRONG,	212	SEXTUS PROP: 3	12
AT ANY RATE I SHALL NOT HAVE MY EPITAPH IN A HIGH ROAD.	213	SEXTUS PROP: 3	38
AND I SHALL FOLLOW THE CAMP, I SHALL BE DULY CELEBRATED FOR SINGING THE AFFAIRS OF YOUR CAVALRY.	216	SEXTUS PROP: 5	21
AND I SHALL FOLLOW THE CAMP, I SHALL BE DULY CELEBRATED FOR SINGING THE AFFAIRS OF YOUR CAVALRY.	216	SEXTUS PROP: 5	21
WE SHALL CONSTRUCT MANY ILIADS.	217	SEXTUS PROP: 5	34
WE SHALL SPIN LONG YARNS OUT OF NOTHING.	217	SEXTUS PROP: 5	36
TIGRIS AND EUPHRATES SHALL, FROM NOW ON, FLOW AT HIS BIDDING,	219	SEXTUS PROP: 6	7
TIBET SHALL BE FULL OF ROMAN POLICEMEN,	219	SEXTUS PROP: 6	8
THE PARTHIANS SHALL GET USED TO OUR STATUARY	219	SEXTUS PROP: 6	9
NOR SHALL IT BE ON AN ATALIC BED;	219	SEXTUS PROP: 6	16
THE PERFUMED CLOTHS SHALL BE ABSENT.	219	SEXTUS PROP: 6	17
SO THAT NO DAY SHALL UNBIND THEM.	220	SEXTUS PROP: 7	21
FOR THE SUN SHALL DRIVE WITH BLACK HORSES,	220	SEXTUS PROP: 7	23
EARTH SHALL BRING WHEAT FROM BARLEY,	220	SEXTUS PROP: 7	24
THE FLOOD SHALL MOVE TOWARD THE FOUNTAIN	220	SEXTUS PROP: 7	25
THE FISH SHALL SWIM IN DRY STREAMS.	220	SEXTUS PROP: 7	27
THERE SHALL BE NONE IN A BETTER SEAT, NOT	222	SEXTUS PROP: 8	35
I SHALL LIVE, IF SHE CONTINUE IN LIFE,	223	SEXTUS PROP: 9	8
IF SHE DIES, I SHALL GO WITH HER.	223	SEXTUS PROP: 9	9
I SHALL TRIUMPH AMONG YOUNG LADIES OF INDETERMINATE CHARACTER,	229	SEXTUS PROP:12	55
I SHALL BE HONOURED WITH YESTERDAY'S WREATHS.	229	SEXTUS PROP:12	57
WITH SIGNS AS MANY, THAT SHALL REPRESENT 'EM	244	MOYEN SENSUEL	167
SHALL PRAISE THY SPEECH	250	DONNA MI PREGA	90
HOW SHALL WE DRESS 'EM ALL?	257	BREAD BRIGADE	22
LISTEN, MY CHILDREN, AND YOU SHALL HEAR	264	ALF'S NINTH	1
LISTEN, MY CHILDREN, AND YOU SHALL HEAR	265	ALF'S NINTH	26
BUT YOU SHALL KNOW THAT THESE WERE THE MEN.	265	ALF'S NINTH	32
TILL THE KING SHALL TAKE THE NOTION	269	SAFE AND SOUND	27
SHALLOW			
THE SALMON MOVES IN THE SUN-SHOT, BRIGHT SHALLOW ODA.	166	FISH & SHADOW	4
SHALT			
THOU SHALT THEN SOFTEN,	9	NA AUDIART	50
EVEN AS THOU SHALT SOON HAVE THIS PARCHMENT.	23	MARVOIL	44
AND THOU SHALT LIVE FOR EVER.	62	N. Y.	13
SHAME			
THE GODS HAVE BROUGHT SHAME ON THEIR RELATIVES;	227	SEXTUS PROP:12	3
SHAMED			
SHAMED AND YET BOWED NOT AND THAT WON AT LAST.	31	PIERE VIDAL	48
SHAMEFUL			
SHAMEFUL, MOST SAD	41	HER MONUMENT	20
SHAMEFUL IN SIGHT, ABJECT, ABOMINABLE	42	HER MONUMENT	36
SHAMELESS			
WITH YOU IS EUROPA AND THE SHAMELESS PASIPHAE,	38	LADY'S LIFE	6
INSOLENT LITTLE BEASTS, SHAMELESS, DEVOID OF CLOTHING!	94	INSTRUCTIONS	14
SHAMELESSLY			
GO AND DANCE SHAMELESSLY!	86	SALUTATION 2ND	19
SHAPED			
RADWAY GREW UP. THESE FORCES SHAPED HIS SOUL;	239	MOYEN SENSUEL	11
SHARKS			
HAVE BANK SHARKS TO BLEED 'EM	272	NATIONAL SONG	12
SHARP			
SHARP PEAKS, HIGH SPURS, DISTANT CASTLES.	122	PROVINC DESERT	55

PAGE 359

SHARP-EDGED -- SHE'S

	PAGE	TITLE	LINE
SHARP-EDGED			
THE FLUTTER OF SHARP-EDGED SANDALS.	169	PHANOPOEIA	13
SHARPENED			
OVER THE SHARPENED TEETH AND PURPLING LIPS!	30	PIERE VIDAL	15
SHATO-WOOD			
THIS BOAT IS OF SHATO-WOOD, AND ITS GUNWALES ARE CUT MAGNOLIA,	128	THE RIVER SONG	1
SHATTERED			
OF SUN AND SPRAY ALL SHATTERED AT THE BOWS;	21	IN DURANCE	37
SHAVE			
(AND VALETS TO SHAVE 'EM)	258	ALF'S SECOND	7
SHAW			
NOR WILL THE HORRID THREATS OF BERNARD SHAW	63	PHASELLUS ILLE	7
SHE (159)			
SHEAF			
HER HAIR WAS SPREAD ABOUT, A SHEAF OF WINGS,	49	OF SPLENDOUR	7
SHEATH			
HALF-SHEATHED, THEN NAKED FROM ITS SAFFRON SHEATH	31	PIERE VIDAL	41
I WILL NOT SPOIL MY SHEATH WITH LESSER BRIGHTNESS,	71	A VIRGINAL	2
SHEATHE			
TO SHEATHE ME HALF IN HALF THE THINGS THAT SHEATHE HER.	71	A VIRGINAL	8
TO SHEATHE ME HALF IN HALF THE THINGS THAT SHEATHE HER.	71	A VIRGINAL	8
SHED			
WHO SO INDECOROUS AS TO SHED THE PURE GORE OF A SUITOR?!	212	SEXTUS PROP: 3	26
SAILS SPREAD ON CERULEAN WATERS, I WOULD SHED TEARS FOR TWO;	223	SEXTUS PROP: 9	7
SHE'D (4)			
SHEDS			
TELL HER THAT SHEDS	197	ENVOI (1919)	8
SHEEP			
IDA HAS LAIN WITH A SHEPHERD, SHE HAS SLEPT BETWEEN SHEEP.	227	SEXTUS PROP:11	36
WHILE YOU STALWART SHEEP OF FREEDOM	269	SAFE AND SOUND	7
SHEEP-FEEDER			
SOLDIER, THE ENUMERATION OF WOUNDS; THE SHEEP-FEEDER, OF EWES;	218	SEXTUS PROP: 5	56
SHEEP'S			
OVER ROADS TWISTED LIKE SHEEP'S GUTS.	135	EXILE'S LETTER	41
SHEER			
SHEER AS THE MOUNTAINS.	138	NEAR SHOKU	2
SHEEREST			
THE VERY SPUR'S END, BUILT ON SHEEREST CLIFF,	153	NEAR PERIGORD	58
SHELF			
IT JUTS LIKE A SHELF BETWEEN THE JOWL AND CORSET.	161	CABARET DANCER	16
SHELL			
SWIFT AT COURAGE THOU IN THE SHELL OF GOLD, CASTING	68	APPARUIT	13
BRING THE SAFFRON-COLOURED SHELL,	75	THE ALCHEMIST	9
DAVE WAS THE MAN TO SELL THE SHOT AND SHELL,	264	ALF'S NINTH	17
SHE'LL			
(YOU FEED A HEN ON GREASE, PERHAPS SHE'LL LAY	240	MOYEN SENSUEL	48
SHELLEY			
"SHELLEY USED TO LIVE IN THIS HOUSE."	182	MOEURS CON: 8	13
SHELTER			
ON EARTH'S SHELTER COMETH OFT TO ME,	65	THE SEAFARER	62
THE STYLIST HAS TAKEN SHELTER,	195	HUGH SELWIN:10	2
THE HIGH TRACKS OF HERMES WOULD NOT AFFORD YOU SHELTER.	226	SEXTUS PROP:11	10
SHELVES			
PILED UP NEATLY UPON THE SHELVES	117	THE LAKE ISLE	4
SHEPHERD			
IDA HAS LAIN WITH A SHEPHERD, SHE HAS SLEPT BETWEEN SHEEP.	227	SEXTUS PROP:11	36
SHEPHERDESS			
AND THE SHEPHERDESS MEETING WITH GUIDO.	112	SHOP GIRL	4
SHEPHERDS'			
(CHRIST MAKE THE SHEPHERDS' HOMAGE DEAR!)	10	FOR THIS YULE	2
SHE'S (1)			

SHIELD -- SHORT

	PAGE	TITLE	LINE
SHIELD			
SHIELD O' STEEL-BLUE, TH' HEAVEN O'ER US	7	CINO	44
BEHOLD THE SHIELD! HE SHALL NOT TAKE THEE ALL.	19	FOR E. MCC	26
SHIFT			
THAT NO SHIFT OF MOOD CAN SHAKE FROM US:	52	AU SALON	7
NOR CAN I SHIFT MY PAINS TO OTHER,	221	SEXTUS PROP: 7	35
SHIFTER			
TO A WELSH SHIFTER WITH AN OGLING EYE,	264	ALF'S NINTH	7
SHIFTING			
AND ALL THE REST OF HER A SHIFTING CHANGE,	157	NEAR PERIGORD	191
SHIMMERING			
O THOU DARK SECRET WITH A SHIMMERING FLOOR,	50	THE FLAME	30
SHIN			
SWEET TREES ARE ON THE PAVED WAY OF THE SHIN,	138	NEAR SHOKU	6
THE BRIGHT CLOTHS AND BRIGHT CAPS OF SHIN	138	CITY OF CHOAN	6
TO LOOK ON THE TALL HOUSE OF THE SHIN	140	MULBERRY ROAD	2
SHINS			
O MUSES WITH DELICATE SHINS,	104	ANCORA	12
SHIP			
MINE IS THE SHIP AND THINE THE MERCHANDISE,	25	GUIDO INVITES	4
LO, THOU HAST VOYAGED NOT! THE SHIP IS MINE."	25	GUIDO INVITES	11
SHIPS			
O' SHIPS AND THE OPEN SEA.	33	GOODLY FERE	4
AND BRIGHT SHIPS LEFT YOU THIS OR THAT IN FEE:	61	PORTRAIT FEMME	3
HE CAN TABULATE CAESAR'S GREAT SHIPS.	228	SEXTUS PROP:12	32
SHIP'S			
NARROW NIGHTWATCH NIGH THE SHIP'S HEAD	64	THE SEAFARER	7
SHIRES			
DOUGTH OF THE SHIRES,	258	ALF'S SECOND	2
THE YOUTH OF THE SHIRES!	258	ALF'S SECOND	8
THE YOUTH OF THE SHIRES?	258	ALF'S SECOND	15
SHIRT			
AND IF SHE PLAYS WITH ME WITH HER SHIRT OFF,	217	SEXTUS PROP: 5	33
NAUGHT BUT A SHIRT IS THERE	258	ALF'S THIRD	3
SHIVER			
RUNNING SO CLOSE TO "HELL" IT SENDS A SHIVER	246	MOYEN SENSUEL	224
SHI-YO			
AND THERE CAME ALSO THE "TRUE MAN" OF SHI-YO TO MEET ME,	134	EXILE'S LETTER	24
SHOCKED			
AND SAID: "MR. POUND IS SHOCKED AT MY LEVITY."	181	MOEURS CON: 7	11
SHOE			
GODS OF THE WINGED SHOE!	74	THE RETURN	12
SHOES			
PULLING ON THEIR SHOES FOR THE DAY'S BUSINESS,	14	FAMAM CANO	12
AND SPATS ABOVE MY SHOES,	266	ALF'S ELEVENTH	10
SHOKU			
LEAVE-TAKING NEAR SHOKU	138	NEAR SHOKU	T
"SANSO, KING OF SHOKU, BUILT ROADS"	138	NEAR SHOKU	EPI
IN THE MIDST OF SHOKU, A PROUD CITY.	138	NEAR SHOKU	9
SHONE			
STRAIGHT, THEN SHONE THINE ORIEL AND THE STUNNED LIGHT	68	APPARUIT	15
SHOOK			
WE WHO SHOOK OFF OUR DEW WITH THE RABBITS,	104	ANCORA	5
AND CITHARAON SHOOK UP THE ROCKS BY THEBES	208	SEXTUS PROP: 1	11
AND SOME OF THEM SHOOK LITTLE TORCHES,	224	SEXTUS PROP:10	7
HOW THE WHOLE NATION SHOOK	257	BREAD BRIGADE	27
SHOOTS			
GREEN COME THE SHOOTS, AYE APRIL IN THE BRANCHES,	71	A VIRGINAL	11
IT IS LIKE AN OLD TREE WITH SHOOTS,	89	COMMISSION	31
SHOP			
SHOP GIRL	112	SHOP GIRL	T
WOMEN BEFORE A SHOP	114	BEFORE A SHOP	T
THE TEA SHOP	116	THE TEA SHOP	T
THE GIRL IN THE TEA SHOP	116	THE TEA SHOP	1
SHORE			
NOT THE HYRCANIAN SEABOARD, NOT IN SEEKING THE SHORE OF EOS.	227	SEXTUS PROP:11	38
SHORT			
EUHENIA, IN SHORT SKIRTS, SLAPS HER WIDE STOMACH,	163	CABARET DANCER	53

SHOT -- SHOWN

	PAGE	TITLE	LINE
SHOT			
SOME LADS GET HUNG, AND SOME GET SHOT.	43	MR. HOUSMAN	8
AND GETS A QUARREL-BOLT SHOT THROUGH HIS VIZARD,	156	NEAR PERIGORD	158
DAVE WAS THE MAN TO SELL THE SHOT AND SHELL,	264	ALF'S NINTH	17
SHOULD			
THOUGH IT SHOULD RUN FOR ITS OWN GETTING,	14	FAMAM CANO	28
"BEING NO LONGER HUMAN, WHY SHOULD I	32	PARACELSUS	1
AND THAT THE WORLD SHOULD DRY AS A DEAD LEAF,	36	FRANCESCA	9
AND BETTER WERE IT, SHOULD GOD GRANT HIS PLEASURE,	37	THE YOUNG KING	22
THAT HE SHOULD LIVE THAN MANY A LIVING DASTARD	37	THE YOUNG KING	23
LEST THEY SHOULD PARCH TOO SWIFTLY, WHERE SHE PASSES.	38	BALLATETTA	10
SHOULD NOT LACK FOR HONOURERS,	46	FROM HEINE: 6	2
WHY SHOULD WE STOP AT ALL FOR WHAT I THINK?	59	SILET	3
O THOU UNMINDFUL! HOW SHOULD I FORGET!	60	TOMB AKR CAAR	15
NAY, SHOULD THE DEATHLESS VOICE OF ALL THE WORLD	63	PHASELLUS ILLE	9
HOW SHOULD HE SHOW A REASON,	72	PAN IS DEAD	11
AS IF THE SNOW SHOULD HESITATE	74	THE RETURN	7
WHY SHOULD ONE ALWAYS LIE ABOUT SUCH MATTERS?	113	TAME CAT	2
HE WAS UNCERTAIN WHY HE SHOULD TRY TO FEEL LIKE ANYTHING ELSE,	118	ANCIENT WISDOM	3
WHY SHOULD I CLIMB THE LOOK OUT?	130	RIVER-MER WIFE	14
BELIEVING WE SHOULD MEET WITH LIPS AND HANDS,	157	NEAR PERIGORD	179
THEN WERE THERE CAUSE IN THEE THAT SHOULD CONDONE	197	ENVOI (1919)	5
NO MESSENGER SHOULD COME WHOLLY EMPTY,	214	SEXTUS PROP: 4	8
AND A SLAVE SHOULD FEAR PLAUSIBILITIES;	214	SEXTUS PROP: 4	9
I SHOULD REMEMBER CAESAR'S AFFAIRS . . .	218	SEXTUS PROP: 5	47
"YOU SHOULD NOT BELIEVE HOSTILE TONGUES.	226	SEXTUS PROP:11	20
I WOULD MAKE VERSE IN YOUR FASHION, IF SHE SHOULD COMMAND IT,	229	SEXTUS PROP:12	60
AND WERE SUCH NIGHTS THAT WE SHOULD "DRAW THE CURTAIN"	243	MOYEN SENSUEL	134
AND TRUTH SHOULD HERE BE CAREFUL OF HER THIN DRESS--	243	MOYEN SENSUEL	146
UNLESS PERHAPS I SHOULD HAVE RECOURSE TO	243	MOYEN SENSUEL	155
LEST IT SHOULD FAIL TO TREAT ALL MEN ALIKE.	244	MOYEN SENSUEL	178
YOU SHOULD HAVE SEEN ME AFTER THE AFFRAY,	247	PIERROTS	4
OR WHY WE SHOULD STAND TO ATTENTION	264	ALF'S EIGHTH	30
LEST THEY SHOULD OVERHEAR THE DISTRESSING CHATTER	272	NATIONAL SONG	14
SHOULDER			
HALF THE GRAVEN SHOULDER, THE THROAT AFLASH WITH	68	APPARUIT	17
SHOULDERS			
WHITE AS AN ALMOND ARE THY SHOULDERS;	91	DANCE FIGURE	12
I HAVE WRAPPED THE WIND ROUND YOUR SHOULDERS	170	PHANOPOEIA	18
AND THE MOLTEN METAL OF YOUR SHOULDERS	170	PHANOPOEIA	19
EQUITABLE WEIGHT ON YOUR SHOULDERS;	214	SEXTUS PROP: 4	4
YES, I HAVE RUBBED SHOULDERS AND KNOCKED OFF MY CHIPS	247	PIERROTS	22
SHOULDER-STRAPS			
SHE MAKES THE SHOULDER-STRAPS OF HER BASKET	140	MULBERRY ROAD	9
SHOULDST			
THAT THOU SHOULDST . . .	8	NA AUDIART	17
LEST THOU SHOULDST WAKE AND WHIMPER FOR THY WINE.	60	TOMB AKR CAAR	13
FOR THOU SHOULDST MORE MISTRUST	67	THE CLOAK	9
SHOUT			
"NOR MARS SHOUT YOU IN THE WOOD AT AEONIUM,	211	SEXTUS PROP: 2	44
SHOVE			
"SHOVE ALONG THERE, SHOVE ALONG!"	224	SEXTUS PROP:10	15
"SHOVE ALONG THERE, SHOVE ALONG!"	224	SEXTUS PROP:10	15
SHOW			
HOW SHOULD HE SHOW A REASON,	72	PAN IS DEAD	11
HE WROTE THAT PRAISE ONLY TO SHOW HE HAD	155	NEAR PERIGORD	148
AN HOUR LATER: A SHOW OF CALVES AND SPANGLES,	163	CABARET DANCER	82
SHOW US THERE'S CHANCE AT LEAST OF WINNING THROUGH.	235	TO WHISTLER	19
TO SHOW HIM VISIBLE TO MEN'S SIGHT.	248	DONNA MI PREGA	18
(HIS WHAT?) WITH A SHOW OF SENSE,	263	ALF'S EIGHTH	2
SHOWED			
SHOWED ONLY WHEN THE DAYLIGHT FELL	193	BRENNBAUM	6
BUT SHOWED NO TRACE OF ALCOHOL	193	SIENA MI FE	9
SHOWING			
GRASS SHOWING UNDER THE SNOW,	168	OF AROUET	37
SHOWN			
HAST THOU SHOWN UNTO ME	26	NIGHT LITANY	

PAGE 362

SHOWS -- SIENA

	PAGE	TITLE	LINE
SHOWS			
SHOWS RAZOR'S UNFAMILIARITY	15	FAMAM CANO	36
THAT NEVER FITS A CORNER OR SHOWS USE,	61	PORTRAIT FEMME	20
SHOWS NO SURPRISE	192	YEUX GLAUQUES	22
WHO SHOWS HIS TASTE IN HIS AMBASSADORS:	239	MOYEN SENSUEL	17
SHRIEK			
AND THE WINDS SHRIEK THROUGH THE CLOUDS MAD, OPPOSING,	28	ALTAFORTE	11
SHRILL			
AND THE SHRILL NEIGHS OF DESTRIERS IN BATTLE REJOICING,	28	ALTAFORTE	14
SHRINES			
WHITHER, O CITY, ARE YOUR PROFITS AND YOUR GILDED SHRINES,	165	QUINTUS SEPTIM	12
SHRINK			
AS LIPS SHRINK BACK WHEN WE FEEL THE STRAIN	11	OF THE GIBBET	20
IF ANY LAND SHRINK INTO A DISTANT SEACOAST,	216	SEXTUS PROP: 5	19
SHRINKETH			
SHRINKETH THE KISS OF THE DAWN	14	FAMAM CANO	5
SHRIVELLED			
BEHOLD ME SHRIVELLED AS AN OLD OAK'S TRUNK	31	PIERE VIDAL	52
BEHOLD ME SHRIVELLED, AND YOUR MOCK OF MOCKS;	32	PIERE VIDAL	62
WHERE TIME IS SHRIVELLED DOWN TO TIME'S SEED CORN	50	THE FLAME	11
SHROPSHIRE			
SHROPSHIRE IS MUCH PLEASANTER.	44	MR. HOUSMAN	12
SHROUDS			
"SHE BINDS ME WITH RAVVLES OF SHROUDS.	215	SEXTUS PROP: 4	34
SHRUBBERY			
BUT SHE DANCED LIKE A PINK MOTH IN THE SHRUBBERY.	53	AU JARDIN	19
SHRUNK			
LIPS SHRUNK BACK FOR THE WIND'S CARESS	11	OF THE GIBBET	19
SHU			
SONG OF THE BOWMEN OF SHU	127	BOWMEN OF SHU	T
WAS GOVERNOR IN HEI SHU, AND PUT DOWN THE BARBARIAN RABBLE.	135	EXILE'S LETTER	37
SHUDDER			
THE SHUDDER OF VAE SOLI GURGLES BENEATH MY RIBS.	247	PIERROTS	3
SHUT			
WE ARE NOT SHUT FROM ALL THE THOUSAND HEAVENS:	50	THE FLAME	22
HATED, SHUT IN, MISTRUSTED:	93	THE REST	16
AND SINCE YOU HAVE SHUT ME AWAY FROM YOU	105	DOMPNA POIS	2
THE LONE MAN SITS WITH SHUT SPEECH,	139	SENNIN POEM	6
THERE SHUT UP IN HIS CASTLE, TAIRIRAN'S,	157	NEAR PERIGORD	186
CLANKING THE DOOR SHUT,	167	OF AROUET	6
HER ESCRITOIRES LAY SHUT BY THE BED-FEET.	214	SEXTUS PROP: 4	21
SHUT-IN			
"THESE ARE YOUR IMAGES, AND FROM YOU THE SORCERIZING OF SHUT-IN YOUNG LADIES,	211	SEXTUS PROP: 2	50
SHUTS			
TO-MORROW FATE SHUTS US IN.	221	SEXTUS PROP: 7	32
SHUTTING			
HAVE DAMP AND PLAIN TO BE OUR SHUTTING IN.	21	IN DURANCE	40
SIC			
SIC CRESCIT GLORIA MUNDI:	52	AU SALON	17
SIDE			
THE BLACK PANTHER TREADS AT MY SIDE,	109	HEATHER	1
THE GURGLING ITALIAN LADY ON THE OTHER SIDE OF THE RESTAURANT	111	BLACK SLIPPERS	7
BY THE SOUTH SIDE OF THE BRIDGE AT TEN-SHIN.	134	EXILE'S LETTER	3
AND SHE PILES HER HAIR UP ON THE LEFT SIDE OF HER HEAD-PIECE.	140	MULBERRY ROAD	11
AND GET MY PICKINGS ON THE SIDE	266	ALF'S ELEVENTH	19
SIDES			
FILL FULL THE SIDES IN ROWS, AND OUR WINE	128	THE RIVER SONG	3
AND THE FAWNS COME TO SNIFF AT HIS SIDES:	231	CANTUS PLANUS	2
AND HOLDS HER SIDES WHERE SWELLING LAUGHTER CRACKS 'EM	239	MOYEN SENSUEL	33
SIDONIAN			
AND IN A NEW SIDONIAN NIGHT CAP,	225	SEXTUS PROP:10	19
SIENA			
"SIENA MI FE'; DISFECEMI MAREMMA"	193	SIENA MI FE	T

PAGE 363

SIEVE -- SILK

	PAGE	TITLE	LINE
SIEVE			
UNTIL HE FOUND HIS SIEVE	199	MAUBERLEY: 2	18
SIFT			
TO SIFT TO AGATHON FROM THE CHAFF	199	MAUBERLEY: 2	17
SIFTINGS			
SIFTINGS ON SIFTINGS IN OBLIVION, ...	197	ENVOI (1919)	24
SIFTINGS ON SIFTINGS IN OBLIVION, ...	197	ENVOI (1919)	24
SIGH			
WHEN THE WIND BLOWS SIGH THOU FOR MY SORROW	23	MARVOIL	41
STILL SIGH OVER ESTABLISHED AND NATURAL FACT	148	FRATRES MINORE	3
SIGHEST			
AND THOUGH THOU SIGHEST MY SORROW IN THE WIND, ...	23	MARVOIL	46
SIGHING			
NO MORE FOR US THE LITTLE SIGHING.	3	THRENOS	1
SIGHING, SAY, "WOULD CINO, ...	6	CINO	16
SIGHING AS THOU DOST THROUGH THE GOLDEN SPEECH."	43	SATIEMUS	6
SIGHS			
CHILL ITS CHAINS ARE; CHAFING SIGHS	64	THE SEAFARER	10
AND HIS STRANGE PROPERTY SETS SIGHS TO MOVE	250	DONNA MI PREGA	58
SIGHT			
BUT GOD! WHAT A SIGHT YOU HA' GOT O' OUR IN'ARDS,	13	MESMERISM	10
SHAMEFUL IN SIGHT, ABJECT, ABOMINABLE	42	HER MONUMENT	36
--EYEBROWS PAINTED GREEN ARE A FINE SIGHT IN YOUNG			
MOONLIGHT, ...	136	EXILE'S LETTER	57
WITH THE NOBLEST THAT STANDS IN MEN'S SIGHT, ...	174	LANGUE D'OC: 3	13
NOR TAKE MY BELOVED FROM MY SIGHT, ...	177	LANGUE D'OC: 4	7
"AND NO ONE KNOWS, AT SIGHT, A MASTERPIECE.	194	MR. NIXON	18
TO SHOW HIM VISIBLE TO MEN'S SIGHT.	248	DONNA MI PREGA	18
SIGHT'S			
CLEAR SIGHT'S ELECTOR!	13	MESMERISM	21
SIGN			
TO BE A SIGN AND AN HOPE MADE SECURE	42	HER MONUMENT	33
SIGNS			
SOUND IN YOUR WIND PAST ALL SIGNS O' CORRUPTION.	13	MESMERISM	16
AND WEARIED OUT MY THOUGHT UPON THE SIGNS.	60	TOMB AKR CAAR	10
I SEE THE SIGNS UPON THE WELKIN SPREAD, ...	172	LANGUE D'OC: 1	15
THERE WERE UPON THE BED NO SIGNS OF A VOLUPTUOUS			
ENCOUNTER, ...	225	SEXTUS PROP:10	36
NO SIGNS OF A SECOND INCUMBENT.	225	SEXTUS PROP:10	37
WITH SIGNS AS MANY, THAT SHALL REPRESENT 'EM	244	MOYEN SENSUEL	167
SILENCE			
O GOD OF SILENCE, ...	26	NIGHT LITANY	19
O GOD OF SILENCE, ...	27	NIGHT LITANY	33
O GOD OF THE SILENCE, ...	27	NIGHT LITANY	50
OPULENT SILENCE.	99	SALVATIONISTS	10
MY GOOD FELLOW, YOU, ON A CABARET SILENCE	161	CABARET DANCER	5
"COMPEL A CERTAIN SILENCE AND RESTRAINT."	243	MOYEN SENSUEL	138
SILENT			
SILENT UNTO US IN THEIR FAR-COURSING, ...	27	NIGHT LITANY	46
BECOME SILENT WITHIN ME.	27	NIGHT LITANY	48
TORN, GREEN AND SILENT IN THE SWOLLEN RHONE, ...	31	PIERE VIDAL	27
SILENT MY MATE CAME AS THE NIGHT WAS STILL.	31	PIERE VIDAL	32
HOT IS SUCH LOVE AND SILENT, ...	31	PIERE VIDAL	34
SILENT AS FATE IS, AND AS STRONG UNTIL	31	PIERE VIDAL	35
SO SILENT LIGHT; NO GOSSAMER IS SPUN	38	BALLATETTA	7
PASS AND BE SILENT, RULLUS, FOR THE DAY	63	QUIES	2
THE SILENT CORTEGE.	107	COMING OF WAR	20
A SILENT HUNTER OFF THE GREAT WHITE WAY, ...	245	MOYEN SENSUEL	200
SILENUS			
ORGIES OF VINTAGES, AN EARTHERN IMAGE OF SILENUS	211	SEXTUS PROP: 2	29
SILET			
SILET	59	SILET	T
SILK			
OF SOME THIN SILK STUFF THAT'S SCARCE STUFF AT ALL,	31	PIERE VIDAL	29
LIKE A SKEIN OF LOOSE SILK BLOWN AGAINST A WALL . . .	83	THE GARDEN	1
I WILL GET YOU THE SCARLET SILK TROUSERS	94	INSTRUCTIONS	19
O FAN OF WHITE SILK, ...	108	FAN-PIECE	1
THE RUSTLING OF THE SILK IS DISCONTINUED, ...	108	LIU CH'E	1
HER OVERSKIRT IS THE SAME SILK DYED IN PURPLE, ...	140	MULBERRY ROAD	14
WEARING RAW SILK OF GOOD COLOUR, ...	146	CANTILATIONS	7
SILK, STIFF AND LARGE ABOVE THE LACERTUS, ...	180	MOEURS CON: 5	4

SILK -- SINCE

	PAGE	TITLE	LINE
SILK (CONTINUED)			
AND ITS WATERS ARE WHITE LIKE SILK.	237	ABU SALAMMAMM	21
PUFFED SATIN, AND SILK STOCKINGS, WHERE THE KNEE	241	MOYEN SENSUEL	85
SILKEN			
THE SILKEN TRAINS GO RUSTLING,	47	FROM HEINE: 7	25
SILKWORMS			
FOR SHE FEEDS MULBERRIES TO SILKWORMS.	140	MULBERRY ROAD	6
S'ILS			
S'ILS NE SENTENT PAS LA MUSIQUE, QU'EST CE	199	MAUBERLEY: 2	EPI
S'ILS NE COMPRENNENT PAS LA POESIE,	199	MAUBERLEY: 2	EPI
SILVER			
PURPLE AND SAPPHIRE FOR THE SILVER SHAFTS	21	IN DURANCE	36
THOU ART SLENDER AS A SILVER REED.	62	N. Y.	10
WITH THEM THE SILVER HOUNDS,	74	THE RETURN	13
'MID THE SILVER RUSTLING OF WHEAT,	75	THE ALCHEMIST	15
MIDONZ, DAUGHTER OF THE SUN, SHAFT OF THE TREE, SILVER OF THE LEAF, LIGHT OF THE YELLOW OF THE AMBER,	75	THE ALCHEMIST	26
AZURE AND FLAKING SILVER OF WATER,	76	THE ALCHEMIST	56
PALLOR OF SILVER, PALE LUSTRE OF LATONA,	76	THE ALCHEMIST	58
GILT TURQUOISE AND SILVER ARE IN THE PLACE OF THY REST.	91	DANCE FIGURE	16
WITH A SILVER CRASHING,	93	OF THE DEGREES	4
BY THE SILVER BLUE FLOOD	108	CH'U YUAN	3
AND WITH SILVER HARNESS AND REINS OF GOLD,	134	EXILE'S LETTER	22
TERRACES TINGED WITH SILVER,	141	IDEA OF CHOAN	20
ROSE WHITE, YELLOW, SILVER	169	PHANOPOEIA	ST
THE SILVER BALL FORMS IN MY HAND,	169	PHANOPOEIA	6
AND THOSE BORN WITH A SILVER SPOON,	266	ALF'S TENTH	14
BALLAD FOR THE TIMES' SPECIAL SILVER NUMBER	267	ALF'S TWELFTH	SUB
SEZ THE TIMES A SILVER LINING	267	ALF'S TWELFTH	1
FOR PUTTING SILVER ON THE SPOT,	267	ALF'S TWELFTH	11
BUT SOME SILVER SET TO STEW	267	ALF'S TWELFTH	17
SIME			
SOAPY SIME? SLIPP'RY MAC?	258	ALF'S THIRD	2
SIMILAR			
"IN THINGS OF SIMILAR MAGNITUDE	216	SEXTUS PROP: 5	5
SIMOIS			
OR OF ACHILLES WITHSTAYING WATERS BY SIMOIS	208	SEXTUS PROP: 1	28
SIMOON			
UNBROKEN BY THE SIMOON;	203	MAUBERLEY: 4	5
SIMPLE			
(VIDE THE TARIFF), I WILL HANG SIMPLE FACTS	241	MOYEN SENSUEL	71
'TWAS AS A BUSINESS ASSET PURE AN' SIMPLE	246	MOYEN SENSUEL	239
THE SIMPLE BRITONS NEVER KNEW HE WAS,	265	ALF'S NINTH	24
SIMPLY			
SO SIMPLY ELEMENT AS WHAT I AM.	32	PARACELSUS	5
SIMULACRA			
SIMULACRA	114	SIMULACRA	T
SIN			
AN ORGANIZATION FOR THE SUPPRESSION OF SIN.	246	MOYEN SENSUEL	230
SIN'			
SIN' THEY NAILED HIM TO THE TREE.	34	GOODLY FERE	54
SINAI			
THE HEAVY MEMORIES OF HOREB, SINAI AND THE FORTY YEARS,	193	BRENNBAUM	5
SINCE			
HATH LACKED A SOMETHING SINCE THIS LADY PASSED;	63	QUIES	3
NOR HATH IT EVER SINCE CHANGED THAT CONCOCTION.	63	PHASELLUS ILLE	4
SINCE YOU HAVE COME THIS PLACE HAS HOVERED ROUND ME,	69	SUB MARE	2
LADY, SINCE YOU CARE NOTHING FOR ME,	105	DOMPNA POIS	1
AND SINCE YOU HAVE SHUT ME AWAY FROM YOU	105	DOMPNA POIS	2
AND SINCE I COULD NOT FIND A PEER TO YOU,	105	DOMPNA POIS	11
EVER SINCE RHODEZ,	119	THE GYPSY	13
LONG SINCE FULLY DISCUSSED BY OVID.	148	FRATRES MINORE	4
"YOUR SON, AH, SINCE HE DIED	152	NEAR PERIGORD	44
"AND HERE I AM SINCE GOING DOWN OF SUN,	172	LANGUE D'OC: 1	18
LONG SINCE SUPERSEDED THE CULTIVATION	196	HUGH SELWIN:12	27
SINCE ADONIS WAS GORED IN IDALIA, AND THE CYTHAREAN	219	SEXTUS PROP: 6	33
SINCE THAT DAY I HAVE HAD NO PLEASANT NIGHTS.	225	SEXTUS PROP:10	43
WHO, SINCE THEIR WIT'S UNKNOWN, ESCAPE THE GALLOWS.	238	MOYEN SENSUEL	4

SINCE -- SINGS

	PAGE	TITLE	LINE
SINCE (CONTINUED)			
YOUR EYES! SINCE I LOST THEIR INCANDESCENCE	247	PIERROTS	
SINECURE			
"IT GIVES NO MAN A SINECURE.	194	MR. NIXON	1
SING			
AND I WILL SING OF THE SUN.	6	CINO	
I WILL SING OF THE SUN.	7	CINO	3
BUT IT IS ALL ONE, I WILL SING OF THE SUN.	7	CINO	4
I WILL SING OF THE WHITE BIRDS	7	CINO	5
WILL SING THEM IN THE TWILIGHT, ...	14	FAMAM CANO	
SING THOU THE GRACE OF THE LADY OF BEZIERS, ...	23	MARVOIL	
WHOM THOU ONCE DID SING SO SWEETLY, ...	45	FROM HEINE: 3	
WHEN I BEGIN TO SING	45	FROM HEINE: 5	
THEY SING OF LOVE THAT'S GROWN DESIROUS, ...	45	FROM HEINE: 5	
SINGING AS WELL AS I SING, NONE BETTER;	96	DUM CAPITOLIUM	
LHUDE SING GODDAMM, ...	116	ANCIENT MUSIC	
SING: GODDAMM.	116	ANCIENT MUSIC	
DAMM YOU, SING: GODDAMM.	116	ANCIENT MUSIC	
SING GODDAMM, DAMM, SING GODDAMM, ...	116	ANCIENT MUSIC	1
SING GODDAMM, DAMM, SING GODDAMM, ...	116	ANCIENT MUSIC	1
SING GODDAMM, SING GODDAMM, DAMM.	116	ANCIENT MUSIC	1
SING GODDAMM, SING GODDAMM, DAMM.	116	ANCIENT MUSIC	1
ONE SET ON THE HIGHWAY TO SING.	122	PROVINC DESERT	6
AND HIGH OVER THE WILLOWS, THE FINE BIRDS SING TO EACH OTHER, AND LISTEN, ...	129	THE RIVER SONG	2
AND ALL THE WHILE YOU SING OUT THAT CANZONE, ...	151	NEAR PERIGORD	1
IS IT A LOVE POEM? DID HE SING OF WAR?	153	NEAR PERIGORD	8
TO SING ONE THING WHEN YOUR SONG MEANS ANOTHER, ...	153	NEAR PERIGORD	8
"HI! HARRY, HEAR ME, FOR I SING ARIGHT	172	LANGUE D'OC: 1	1
I SOUGH AND SING	174	LANGUE D'OC: 3	
AND I ALSO WILL SING WAR WHEN THIS MATTER OF A GIRL IS EXHAUSTED.	216	SEXTUS PROP: 5	
SING: TOODLE DOODLEDE OOT!	271	OLE KATE	
SINGER			
THE SINGER IS'T YOU MEAN?"	6	CINO	2
MANY A SINGER PASS AND TAKE HIS PLACE	24	THUS NINEVEH	
OR TAKE HIS "MAGNET" SINGER SETTING OUT, ...	154	NEAR PERIGORD	10
SINGERS			
"THERE BE MANY SINGERS GREATER THAN THOU."	16	PRAISE YSOLT	
SINGES			
"EST-CE QUE VOUS AVEZ VU DES AUTRES--DES CAMARADES--AVEC DES SINGES OU DES OURS?"	119	THE GYPSY	EP
SINGETH			
HE SINGETH SUMMERWARD, BODETH SORROW, ...	65	THE SEAFARER	5
SINGING			
MY MOUTH TO CHANT THE PURE SINGING!	18	DE AEGYPTO	1
AND CALLS THE UTMOST SINGING FROM THE BOUGHS	21	IN DURANCE	4
SINGING THE STARS IN THE TURRETS OF BEZIERS, ...	22	MARVOIL	1
THE MEWS' SINGING ALL MY MEAD-DRINK.	64	THE SEAFARER	2
SINGING AS WELL AS I SING, NONE BETTER;	96	DUM CAPITOLIUM	
"HERE WAS GOOD SINGING.	122	PROVINC DESERT	4
"PIEIRE KEPT THE SINGING--	123	PROVINC DESERT	7
WE CARRY SINGING GIRLS, DRIFT WITH THE DRIFTING WATER, ...	128	THE RIVER SONG	
AND HEARD THE FIVE-SCORE NIGHTINGALES AIMLESSLY SINGING.	129	THE RIVER SONG	2
OVER A THOUSAND GATES, OVER A THOUSAND DOORS ARE THE SOUNDS OF SPRING SINGING, ...	129	THE RIVER SONG	3
TO CLEAR FLUTES AND CLEAR SINGING;	132	AT TEN-SHIN	2
AND THE GIRLS SINGING BACK AT EACH OTHER, ...	136	EXILE'S LETTER	5
GO FORTHRIGHT SINGING--ANHES, CEMBELINS.	153	NEAR PERIGORD	7
SINGING A DIFFERENT STAVE, AS CLOSELY HIDDEN.)	153	NEAR PERIGORD	8
FOIX' COUNT KNEW THAT. WHAT IS SIR BERTRANS' SINGING?	153	NEAR PERIGORD	9
DODGING HIS WAY PAST AUBETERRE, SINGING AT CHALAIS	154	NEAR PERIGORD	10
BIRDS SINGING LATE IN THE YEAR!	168	OF AROUET	3
AND I SHALL FOLLOW THE CAMP, I SHALL BE DULY CELEBRATED FOR SINGING THE AFFAIRS OF YOUR CAVALRY.	216	SEXTUS PROP: 5	2
SINGS			
OR SOME OTHER'S THAT HE SINGS?	6	CINO	3
AND YET MY SOUL SINGS "UP!" AND WE ARE ONE.	21	IN DURANCE	4

PAGE 366

	PAGE	TITLE	LINE
SINGS (CONTINUED)			
IN THE MID LOVE COURT, HE SINGS OUT THE CANZON, ...	154	NEAR PERIGORD	118
AND THE "BEST CRAFTSMAN" SINGS OUT HIS FRIEND'S SONG,	155	NEAR PERIGORD	141
SINGS IN THE OPEN MEADOW--AT LEAST THE KODAK SAYS SO--	161	CABARET DANCER	4
SINGS DAY-LONG AND NIGHT LATE	171	LANGUE D'OC	EPI
BUT SINGS NOT OUT THE SONG, NOR KNOWS	197	ENVOI (1919)	19
THE LAST SINGS OF A TUMULT,	216	SEXTUS PROP: 5	8
SINISTRO			
O SINISTRO.	7	CINO	36
SINK			
"NO KEEL WILL SINK WITH YOUR GENIUS	210	SEXTUS PROP: 2	25
THERE IS A VOLUME IN THE MATTER; IF HER EYELIDS SINK INTO SLEEP,	217	SEXTUS PROP: 5	31
COULD FREUD OR JUNG UNFATHOM SUCH A SINK?	241	MOYEN SENSUEL	76
SINKS			
FLAME BURNS, RAIN SINKS INTO THE CRACKS	209	SEXTUS PROP: 1	70
SINS			
AND HOW TEN SINS CAN CORRUPT YOUNG MAIDENS;	229	SEXTUS PROP:12	43
SIR			
O'ER MUCH HATH TA'EN SIR DEATH THAT DEADLY WARRIOR	37	THE YOUNG KING	12
TO BAY LIKE SIR ROGER DE COVERLEY'S	52	AU SALON	15
HA! SIR, I HAVE SEEN YOU SNIFFING AND SNOOZLING	109	THE FAUN	1
BUT YOU, SIR, HAD BETTER TAKE WINE ERE YOUR DEPARTURE,	137	OF DEPARTURE	EPI
FOIX' COUNT KNEW THAT. WHAT IS SIR BERTRANS' SINGING?	153	NEAR PERIGORD	91
SIR ARRIMON COUNTS ON HIS FINGERS, MONTFORT,	155	NEAR PERIGORD	121
SIR LAUNCELOT HAS A NEWSPAPER NOW	266	ALF'S ELEVENTH	SUB
THERE IS SIR HEN. DETERDING	267	ALF'S TWELFTH	7
SIRMIO			
A LIQUID GLORY? IF AT SIRMIO,	39	BLANDULA	5
SIRMIONE			
FOR THERE ARE, IN SIRMIONE, TWENTY-EIGHT YOUNG DANTES AND THIRTY-FOUR CATULLI;	96	AESTHETICS	8
SISTE			
SISTE VIATOR.	181	MOEURS CON: 6	6
SISTER			
AND ARNAUT PARRIES: "DID HE LOVE YOUR SISTER?	155	NEAR PERIGORD	146
SISTERS			
TOGETHER WITH THE RESPECTIVE WIVES, HUSBANDS, SISTERS AND HETEROGENEOUS CONNECTIONS OF THE GOOD BELLAIRES,	97	THE BELLAIRES	6
SIT			
AND BECAUSE I HAVE SMALL MIND TO SIT	22	MARVOIL	2
OH, YOU ARE PATIENT, I HAVE SEEN YOU SIT	61	PORTRAIT FEMME	11
HAVE HIM SIT ON HIS KNEES HERE	136	EXILE'S LETTER	78
SHE WOULD SIT LIKE AN ORNAMENT ON MY PYRE.	213	SEXTUS PROP: 3	31
OR SHE WILL SIT BEFORE YOUR FEET IN A VEIL,	223	SEXTUS PROP: 9	11
AND LEAVES YOU A PARK BENCH TO SIT ON	263	ALF'S EIGHTH	20
I SIT ALONE IN THE TWILIGHT	268	ANOTHER BIT	9
SITE			
AND THAT OXFORD STREET SITE	262	ALF'S SEVENTH	14
SITH			
AND SITH HIS THROAT	15	FAMAM CANO	35
SITH NOTHING IS THAT UNTO WORTH PERTAINETH	37	THE YOUNG KING	20
SITH NO THING IS BUT TURNETH UNTO ANGUISH	37	THE YOUNG KING	27
SITS			
THE BIRD SITS ON THE HAWTHORN TREE	43	MR. HOUSMAN	6
AS SHE SITS IN THE GREAT CHAIR	87	ALBATRE	6
THE LONE MAN SITS WITH SHUT SPEECH,	139	SENNIN POEM	6
SHE SITS AT A HARP,	180	MOEURS CON: 5	8
SITTING			
A BROWN, FAT BABE SITTING IN THE LOTUS,	147	POST MORTEM	1
SITTING IN THE ROW OF A MORNING;	182	MOEURS CON: 7	24
"WHEREFROM FATHER ENNIUS, SITTING BEFORE I CAME, HATH DRUNK "	210	SEXTUS PROP: 2	7
"I SEE THEM SITTING IN THE HARVARD CLUB,	244	MOYEN SENSUEL	180
SITUATIONS			
WOUNDED BY YOUR INDIRECTNESS IN THESE SITUATIONS	247	PIERROTS	8
SIX			
WITH SIX GREAT SAPPHIRES HUNG ALONG THE WALL,	49	OF SPLENDOUR	10

PAGE 367

SIX -- SKY

	PAGE	TITLE	LINE
SIX (CONTINUED)			
BY SIX CANDLES AND A CRUCIFIX,	115	SOCIAL ORDER	8
AND WE'VE THE GOSSIP (SKIPPED SIX HUNDRED YEARS).	155	NEAR PERIGORD	138
SIX PENCE THE OBJECT FOR A CHANGE OF PASSION.	162	CABARET DANCER	30
HE HURLED HIMSELF INTO A SEA OF SIX WOMEN.	181	MOEURS CON: 6	2
SONG OF SIX HUNDRED M. P.'S	270	OF 600 M.P.'S	T
WE ARE SIX HUNDRED BEEFY MEN	270	OF 600 M.P.'S	9
SIXTEEN			
AT SIXTEEN YOU DEPARTED,	130	RIVER-MER WIFE	15
AT SIXTEEN SHE WAS A POTENTIAL CELEBRITY	179	MOEURS CON: 2	1
SIXTH			
OR THE SONG OF THE SIXTH COMPANION	11	OF THE GIBBET	SUB
ALF'S SIXTH BIT	261	ALF'S SIXTH	T
SIXTY			
THREE HUNDRED AND SIXTY THOUSAND,	133	FRONTIER GUARD	16
SKEIN			
LIKE A SKEIN OF LOOSE SILK BLOWN AGAINST A WALL	83	THE GARDEN	1
SKELETON			
BUT BURIED DUST AND RUSTED SKELETON.	41	HER MONUMENT	3
SKETCH			
SKETCH 48 B. 2	179	MOEURS CON: 4	SUB
SKETCHES			
AND THEN THESE SKETCHES IN THE MOOD OF GREECE?	235	TO WHISTLER	9
SKIDDETH			
SKIDDETH BUS AND SLOPPETH US,	116	ANCIENT MUSIC	6
SKIES			
AND THROUGH ALL THE RIVEN SKIES GOD'S SWORDS CLASH.	28	ALTAFORTE	12
AND YOU ARE CAUGHT UP TO THE SKIES,	169	PHANOPOEIA	9
SKIFFSMAN			
WITH HER HAIR UNBOUND, AND HE HIS OWN SKIFFSMAN!	132	AT TEN-SHIN	33
SKILL			
DISPRAISES HIS OWN SKILL?--THAT'S AS YOU WILL.	155	NEAR PERIGORD	143
PISANELLO LACKING THE SKILL	198	MAUBERLEY: 1	15
SKILLFUL			
O SKILLFUL DEATH AND FULL OF BITTERNESS,	37	THE YOUNG KING	17
SKIPPED			
AND WE'VE THE GOSSIP (SKIPPED SIX HUNDRED YEARS).	155	NEAR PERIGORD	138
SKIRT			
CLINGS TO THE SKIRT IN STRICT (VIDE: "VOGUE") PROPRIETY.	241	MOYEN SENSUEL	86
SKIRTING			
SKIRTING THE BLUE-GRAY SEA	90	SURGIT FAMA	3
SKIRTS			
RUFFLE THE SKIRTS OF PRUDES,	86	SALUTATION 2ND	32
EUHENIA, IN SHORT SKIRTS, SLAPS HER WIDE STOMACH,	163	CABARET DANCER	53
SKOAL			
(SKOAL! WITH THE DREGS IF THE CLEAR BE GONE!)	10	FOR THIS YULE	7
I SKOAL TO THE EYES AS GREY-BLOWN MERE	10	FOR THIS YULE	22
DRINK YE A SKOAL FOR THE GALLOWS TREE!	11	OF THE GIBBET	1
DRINK WE A SKOAL FOR THE GALLOWS TREE!	11	OF THE GIBBET	13
DRINK WE SKOAL TO THE GALLOWS TREE!	12	OF THE GIBBET	25
BUT DRINK WE SKOAL TO THE GALLOWS TREE!	12	OF THE GIBBET	37
SKOAL!! TO THE GALLOWS! AND THEN PRAY WE:	12	OF THE GIBBET	41
SKY			
THROUGH THE SKY, AND THE WIND THEREOF IS MY BODY.	18	DE AEGYPTO	2
THROUGH THE SKY, AND THE WIND THEREOF IS MY BODY.	18	DE AEGYPTO	8
THROUGH THE SKY, AND THE WIND THEREOF IS MY BODY.	18	DE AEGYPTO	16
THROUGH THE SKY, AND THE WIND THEREOF IS MY BODY.	18	DE AEGYPTO	24
GOD! BUT THE PURPLE OF THE SKY WAS DEEP!	30	PIERE VIDAL	20
THE HOUNDS OF THE CRIMSON SKY GAVE TONGUE	34	GOODLY FERE	39
'NEATH THE DARK GLEAM OF THE SKY;	75	THE ALCHEMIST	7
GREY OLIVE LEAVES BENEATH A RAIN-COLD SKY.	92	GENTILDONNA	5
FIVE CLOUDS HANG ALOFT, BRIGHT ON THE PURPLE SKY,	129	THE RIVER SONG	33
DESOLATE CASTLE, THE SKY, THE WIDE DESERT.	133	FRONTIER GUARD	6
HIS LONE SAIL BLOTS THE FAR SKY.	137	ON RIVER KIANG	3
HE THROWS HIS HEART UP THROUGH THE SKY,	139	SENNIN POEM	8
RIU'S HOUSE STANDS OUT ON THE SKY,	141	IDEA OF CHOAN	26
IN THE YOUNG DAYS WHEN THE DEEP SKY BEFRIENDED.	157	NEAR PERIGORD	175
THE BABY NEW TO EARTH AND SKY	272	THE BABY	1
"THE BABY NEW TO EARTH AND SKY,"	272	THE BABY	9

SKY-LIKE -- SLENDER

	PAGE	TITLE	LINE
SKY-LIKE			
THE SKY-LIKE LIMPID EYES,	193	BRENNBAUM	1
SKY'S			
JUST REFLECTING THE SKY'S TINGE,	129	THE RIVER SONG	21
SLACKED			
OR SLACKED HIS HAND-GRIP WHEN YOU FIRST GRIPPED FAME?	59	EXIT' CUIUSDAM	3
SLADE			
THE RIGOROUS DEPUTATION FROM "SLADE"--	93	LES MILLWIN	6
SLAIN			
"WHICH OF HIS BROTHERS HAD HE SLAIN?"	12	OF THE GIBBET	36
IF THEY THINK THEY HA' SLAIN OUR GOODLY FERE	34	GOODLY FERE	51
"HERE COEUR-DE-LION WAS SLAIN.	122	PROVINC DESERT	44
IT IS HE WHO HAS SLAIN THE DRAGON	237	ABU SALAMMAMM	8
SLANDER'S			
"BEAUTY IS SLANDER'S COCK-SHY.	226	SEXTUS PROP:11	21
SLAPS			
EUHENIA, IN SHORT SKIRTS, SLAPS HER WIDE STOMACH,	163	CABARET DANCER	53
SLASH			
NOR ANY WHIT ELSE SAVE THE WAVE'S SLASH,	65	THE SEAFARER	47
SLAUGHTER			
SOME FOR LOVE OF SLAUGHTER, IN IMAGINATION,	190	HUGH SELWYN: 4	8
SOME IN FEAR, LEARNING LOVE OF SLAUGHTER;	190	HUGH SELWYN: 4	10
SLAVE			
AND A SLAVE SHOULD FEAR PLAUSIBILITIES;	214	SEXTUS PROP: 4	9
"WAS ONCE THE SLAVE OF ONE PASSION:"	219	SEXTUS PROP: 6	27
SLAY			
AND SLAY THE MEMORIES THAT ME CHEER	10	FOR THIS YULE	14
ERE THE NIGHT SLAY LIGHT	24	THUS NINEVEH	18
SLAYS			
SLAYS DAY WITH HER DARK SWORD.	24	THUS NINEVEH	4
SLEEK			
THE SLEEK HEAD EMERGES	204	MEDALLION	5
SLEEP			
IN OUR HEART'S SWORD-RACK, THOUGH THY SWORD-ARM SLEEP.	19	FOR E. MCC	22
HIS SLEEP OR SONG.	24	THUS NINEVEH	11
SET DEEP IN CRYSTAL; AND BECAUSE MY SLEEP	30	PIERE VIDAL	22
AND I, WRAPPED IN BROCADE, WENT TO SLEEP WITH MY HEAD ON HIS LAP,	135	EXILE'S LETTER	31
BEFORE SLEEP	147	BEFORE SLEEP	T
THE GODS OF DRUGGED SLEEP ATTEND ME,	147	BEFORE SLEEP	17
YAWNING A LITTLE SHE CAME WITH THE SLEEP STILL UPON HER.	166	FISH & SHADOW	8
"I AM JUST FROM BED. THE SLEEP IS STILL IN MY EYES.	166	FISH & SHADOW	9
SLEEP THOU NO MORE. I SEE THE STAR UPLEAPING	172	LANGUE D'OC: 1	7
SLEEP NOT THOU NOW, I HEAR THE BIRD IN FLIGHT	172	LANGUE D'OC: 1	11
TROUBLES MY SLEEP,	183	CANTICO SOLE	3
TROUBLES MY SLEEP.	183	CANTICO SOLE	8
IT TROUBLES MY SLEEP.	183	CANTICO SOLE	17
"DOES HE LIKE ME TO SLEEP HERE ALONE,	215	SEXTUS PROP: 4	38
THERE IS A VOLUME IN THE MATTER; IF HER EYELIDS SINK INTO SLEEP,	217	SEXTUS PROP: 5	31
AND SHE THEN OPENING MY EYELIDS FALLEN IN SLEEP,	220	SEXTUS PROP: 7	7
THEY'LL TRICK YOU AGAIN AND AGAIN, AS YOU SLEEP;	265	ALF'S NINTH	31
SLEEPING			
"SST! MY GOOD FELLOW, ART AWAKE OR SLEEPING?	172	LANGUE D'OC: 1	6
SLEEPS			
WHILE RAMSEY MACDONALD SLEEPS, SLEEPS.	265	ALF'S TENTH	8
WHILE RAMSEY MACDONALD SLEEPS, SLEEPS.	265	ALF'S TENTH	8
SLEEVE			
HE TAKES "FLOATING HILL" BY THE SLEEVE,	140	SENNIN POEM	13
SLEEVES			
BECAUSE HIS LONG SLEEVES WOULDN'T KEEP STILL	135	EXILE'S LETTER	29
OF THE TIMES WHEN THE SLEEVES WERE LARGE,	180	MOEURS CON: 5	3
SLEIGHT			
AS WINTER'S WOUND WITH HER SLEIGHT HAND SHE STAUNCHES,	71	A VIRGINAL	12
SLENDER			
MY CITY, MY BELOVED, MY WHITE! AH, SLENDER,	62	N. Y.	1
THOU ART SLENDER AS A SILVER REED.	62	N. Y.	10
SLENDER, SHE PUTS FORTH A SLENDER HAND;	128	BEAU TOILET	5

PAGE 369

SLENDER -- SLUGGARD

	PAGE	TITLE	LINE
SLENDER (CONTINUED)			
SLENDER, SHE PUTS FORTH A SLENDER HAND;	128	BEAU TOILET	5
SAD GARMENT DRAPED ON HER SLENDER ARMS.	214	SEXTUS PROP: 4	20
SLEPT			
IDA HAS LAIN WITH A SHEPHERD, SHE HAS SLEPT BETWEEN SHEEP.	227	SEXTUS PROP:11	36
SLICED			
AND I AM SLICED WITH LOYAL AESTHETICS.	247	PIERROTS	13
SLIGHT			
THOU A SLIGHT THING, THOU IN ACCESS OF CUNNING	68	APPARUIT	23
SLIGHT ARE HER ARMS, YET THEY HAVE BOUND ME STRAITLY	71	A VIRGINAL	4
YSAUT, YDONE, SLIGHT RUSTLING OF LEAVES,	76	THE ALCHEMIST	40
HERE IS A PART THAT'S SLIGHT, AND PART GONE WRONG,	235	TO WHISTLER	5
GREAT KNOWLEDGE OR SLIGHT.	250	DONNA MI PREGA	69
SLIGHTEST			
AUGHT OF THE SLIGHTEST USE.	265	ALF'S TENTH	4
SLIGHTLY			
THEREON THE AMOROUS CALOR SLIGHTLY FROSTED HIM.	242	MOYEN SENSUEL	122
SLIM			
HERE'S PEPITA, TALL AND SLIM AS AN EGYPTIAN MUMMY,	162	CABARET DANCER	18
SLIP			
COME, OR THE STELLAR TIDE WILL SLIP AWAY.	69	THE NEEDLE	1
SLIPPED			
CALL NOT THAT MIRROR ME, FOR I HAVE SLIPPED	51	THE FLAME	42
SLIPPERS			
BLACK SLIPPERS: BELLOTTI	111	BLACK SLIPPERS	T
WITH HER LITTLE SUEDE SLIPPERS OFF,	111	BLACK SLIPPERS	2
TO SEE HOW CELESTINE WILL RE-ENTER HER SLIPPERS.	111	BLACK SLIPPERS	10
SLIPP'RY			
SOAPY SIME? SLIPP'RY MAC?	258	ALF'S THIRD	2
SLIPS			
YOU MIGHT PARDON SUCH SLIPS.	247	PIERROTS	24
AND THEN LENDS OUT THEIR PRINTED SLIPS	269	SAFE AND SOUND	19
SLITHER			
IF SHE GOES IN A GLEAM OF COS, IN A SLITHER OF DYED STUFF,	217	SEXTUS PROP: 5	30
SLITHERS			
OR SLITHERS ABOUT BETWEEN THE DISHONEST WAITERS--	162	CABARET DANCER	23
SLOP			
RAINETH DROP AND STAINETH SLOP,	116	ANCIENT MUSIC	3
SLOPE			
"A FLAT FIELD FOR RUSHES, GRAPES GROW ON THE SLOPE."	229	SEXTUS PROP:12	52
SLOPPETH			
SKIDDETH BUS AND SLOPPETH US,	116	ANCIENT MUSIC	6
SLOSHIN'			
JUST WENT ON A SLOSHIN'	271	OLE KATE	17
GOD REST HER SLOSHIN' SOUL.	271	OLE KATE	20
SLOT			
JUST DROP IT IN THE SLOT	267	ALF'S TWELFTH	13
SLOUCHED			
SLOUCHED THE TEN MILLION,	257	BREAD BRIGADE	4
SLOUCHING			
SLOUCHING AND MOUCHING,	257	BREAD BRIGADE	15
SEE 'EM GO SLOUCHING THERE,	257	BREAD BRIGADE	24
SLOW			
MOSS WORDS, LIP WORDS, WORDS OF SLOW STREAMS.	16	PRAISE YSOLT	22
IN THE SLOW FLOAT OF DIFFERING LIGHT AND DEEP,	61	PORTRAIT FEMME	27
PALE SLOW GREEN SURGINGS OF THE UNDERWAVE,	69	SUB MARE	7
MOVEMENTS, AND THE SLOW FEET,	74	THE RETURN	2
SLOW ON THE LEASH,	74	THE RETURN	19
SO IS THE SLOW COOLING OF OUR CHIVALROUS PASSION,	100	THE BATH TUB	3
SLOW FOOT, OR SWIFT FOOT, DEATH DELAYS BUT FOR A SEASON.	223	SEXTUS PROP: 9	21
THEN THERE CAME OTHER NIGHTS, CAME SLOW BUT CERTAIN	243	MOYEN SENSUEL	133
OVER THE EMPTY-HEADED, AND THE SLOW	265	ALF'S TENTH	6
SLOWLY			
O LOVE, COME NOW, THIS LAND TURNS EVIL SLOWLY.	69	THE NEEDLE	9
WE GO SLOWLY, WE ARE HUNGRY AND THIRSTY,	127	BOWMEN OF SHU	23
SLUGGARD			
SLUGGARD!	220	SEXTUS PROP: 7	

	PAGE	TITLE	LINE
SLUT-BELLIED			
YOU SLUT-BELLIED OBSTRUCTIONIST,	145	SALUTATION 3RD	10
SLUTS			
FOR THE DEATH OF SUCH SLUTS I GO REJOICING;	29	ALTAFORTE	29
SLUT'S			
UNTIL THE LAST SLUT'S HANGED AND THE LAST PIG DISEMBOWELED,	161	CABARET DANCER	2
SMALL			
AND BECAUSE I HAVE SMALL MIND TO SIT	22	MARVOIL	2
THY LITTLE HEART, SO SWEET AND FALSE AND SMALL	44	FROM HEINE: 2	3
SMALL HORN AND VIOLIN.	47	FROM HEINE: 7	28
THE VERY SMALL CHILDREN IN PATCHED CLOTHING,	96	AESTHETICS	1
THE SMALL DOGS LOOK AT THE BIG DOGS;	104	THE SEEING EYE	1
IT IS ONLY IN SMALL DOGS AND THE YOUNG	104	THE SEEING EYE	9
BY NO MEANS TOO SMALL,	113	FORMIANUS LADY	2
WHY DOES THE SMALL CHILD IN THE SOILED-WHITE IMITATION FUR COAT	114	SIMULACRA	3
TWO SMALL PEOPLE, WITHOUT DISLIKE OR SUSPICION.	130	RIVER-MER WIFE	6
THE CRACKLING OF SMALL FIRES, THE BANNERETS,	155	NEAR PERIGORD	132
KEEP SMALL WITH REVERENCE, BEHOLDING HER IMAGE.	164	QUINTUS SEPTIM	7
GIVING THE ROCKS SMALL LEE-WAY	187	E. P. ODE	11
SMALL TALK O ILION, AND O TROAD	208	SEXTUS PROP: 1	32
"SOFT FIELDS MUST BE WORN BY SMALL WHEELS,	210	SEXTUS PROP: 2	21
THE SMALL BIRDS OF THE CYTHAREAN MOTHER,	211	SEXTUS PROP: 2	31
A SMALL PLEBEIAN PROCESSION.	219	SEXTUS PROP: 6	18
SMALL TALK COMES FROM SMALL BONES.	219	SEXTUS PROP: 6	37
SMALL TALK COMES FROM SMALL BONES.	219	SEXTUS PROP: 6	37
AND A MINUTE CROWD OF SMALL BOYS CAME FROM OPPOSITE,	224	SEXTUS PROP:10	4
AND BEHOLD ME, SMALL FORTUNE LEFT IN MY HOUSE.	229	SEXTUS PROP:12	53
AND A LOT OF SMALL STREET STENCHES.	270	OF 600 M.P.'S	16
SMALL-BEER			
DRINK OF THE WINDS THEIR CHILL SMALL-BEER	10	FOR THIS YULE	4
SMARTER			
AND WOULD MY OLD MAN HAVE BEEN SMARTER	268	ANOTHER BIT	14
SMEARED			
GREEN ARSENIC SMEARED ON AN EGG-WHITE CLOTH,	113	L'ART, 1910	1
SMEARED O'ER THE LOT IN EQUAL QUANTITIES.	244	MOYEN SENSUEL	174
SMELLS			
TO BE SO MUCH ALIKE THAT EVERY DOG THAT SMELLS 'EM,	244	MOYEN SENSUEL	172
SMILE			
HIS SMILE WAS GOOD TO SEE,	33	GOODLY FERE	6
WHOSE SMILE MORE AVAILETH	35	THE EYES	16
THEN LET US SMILE A LITTLE SPACE	44	MR. HOUSMAN	13
BUT YOUR SMILE PULLS ONE WAY	162	CABARET DANCER	41
NOT THE FULL SMILE,	198	MAUBERLEY: 1	10
SMILES			
I HAVE SEEN THEIR SMILES FULL OF TEETH	85	SALUTATION	5
SMILING			
CHARM, SMILING AT THE GOOD MOUTH,	191	HUGH SELWYN: 5	5
SMIRKING			
WITHOUT SMIRKING INTO A POCKET-LOOKING-GLASS.	247	PIERROTS	21
SMITE			
AND SMITE ALWAYS AT THEIR FAIBLENESS?	12	OF THE GIBBET	40
SMITTEN			
BEING SMITTEN WITH AN UNUSUAL WISDOM,	96	AESTHETICS	2
SMOKE			
O SMOKE AND SHADOW OF A DARKLING WORLD,	50	THE FLAME	14
HE RIDES THROUGH THE PURPLE SMOKE TO VISIT THE SENNIN,	140	SENNIN POEM	12
THE SMOKE OF INCENSE	169	PHANOPOEIA	2
SMOKED			
THE COMPACT, DE BORN SMOKED OUT, TREES FELLED	155	NEAR PERIGORD	124
SMOKE-FLOWERS			
THE SMOKE FLOWERS ARE BLURRED OVER THE RIVER.	137	ON RIVER KIANG	2
SMOOTH			
AND ALL THY ROBES I HAVE KEPT SMOOTH ON THEE.	60	TOMB AKR CAAR	14
SMOTHER			
THESE COMFORTS HEAPED UPON ME, SMOTHER ME!	70	THE PLUNGE	2
SMOTHERED			
GO TO THE ADOLESCENT WHO ARE SMOTHERED IN FAMILY--	89	COMMISSION	28
SMOTHERED IN LAUREL GROVES,	134	EXILE'S LETTER	13

	PAGE	TITLE	LINE
SMOULDER			
THEN SMOULDER, WITH THE LIDS HALF CLOSED	21	IN DURANCE	33
SMUG			
O GENERATION OF THE THOROUGHLY SMUG	85	SALUTATION	1
SMUGNESS			
LET US DERIDE THE SMUGNESS OF "THE TIMES":	145	SALUTATION 3RD	1
SMUTTY			
CRACKIN' THEIR SMUTTY JOKES!	257	BREAD BRIGADE	6
TO READ HIS SMUTTY LITERATURE	272	NATIONAL SONG	7
SNAKE'S			
"SHE STEWS PUFFED FROGS, SNAKE'S BONES, THE MOULTED FEATHERS OF SCREECH OWLS,	215	SEXTUS PROP: 4	33
SNARE			
LIPS, WORDS, AND YOU SNARE THEM,	6	CINO	4
LANGUIDLY YOU STRETCH OUT THE SNARE	226	SEXTUS PROP:11	15
SNARED			
IF THEY THINK THEY HA' SNARED OUR GOODLY FERE	33	GOODLY FERE	25
SNATCH			
NO COIN, NO WILL TO SNATCH THE AFTERMATH	14	FAMAM CANO	31
SNATCHED			
WORKED FOR AND SNATCHED FROM THE STRING-PURSE OF BORN--	152	NEAR PERIGORD	34
SNATCHING			
LEAPT ABOUT, SNATCHING AT THE BRIGHT FISH	97	AESTHETICS	13
SNEER			
WILL TURN ASIDE TO SNEER AT	14	FAMAM CANO	29
SNIFF			
TO SNIFF THE TRAFFIC INTO PERIGORD.	153	NEAR PERIGORD	63
AND THE FAWNS COME TO SNIFF AT HIS SIDES:	231	CANTUS PLANUS	2
SNIFFING			
SNIFFING THE TRACE OF AIR!	74	THE RETURN	14
HA! SIR, I HAVE SEEN YOU SNIFFING AND SNOOZLING	109	THE FAUN	1
SNOOZLING			
HA! SIR, I HAVE SEEN YOU SNIFFING AND SNOOZLING	109	THE FAUN	1
SNORE			
"LET HER LOVERS SNORE AT HER IN THE MORNING!	215	SEXTUS PROP: 4	36
SNOW			
WHITE WORDS AS SNOW FLAKES BUT THEY ARE COLD,	16	PRAISE YSOLT	21
AS IF THE SNOW SHOULD HESITATE	74	THE RETURN	7
WE COME BACK IN THE SNOW,	127	BOWMEN OF SHU	2
WITH THE WILLOW FLAKES FALLING LIKE SNOW,	136	EXILE'S LETTER	5
FLYING SNOW BEWILDERS THE BARBARIAN HEAVEN.	139	SOUTH-FOLK	
GRASS SHOWING UNDER THE SNOW,	168	OF AROUET	3
IS FULL OF GILDED SNOW,	236	MIDDLE-AGED	2
SNOWED			
NOT QUITE SNOWED UNDER.	261	ALF'S SIXTH	2
SNOWETH			
NEARETH NIGHTSHADE, SNOWETH FROM NORTH,	64	THE SEAFARER	3
SNOWS			
AND LAP O' THE SNOWS FOOD'S GUEREDON	10	FOR THIS YULE	
SNOW-WHITE			
AND THEIR SNOW-WHITE LEOPARD	109	HEATHER	
SNOWY			
NO GAWDS ON HER SNOWY HANDS, NO ORFEVRERIE,	214	SEXTUS PROP: 4	1
SO			
I WAS QUITE STRONG--AT LEAST THEY SAID SO--	4	LA FRAISNE	
BEING SO YOUNG AND FAIR	9	NA AUDIART	4
AS FLAME LEAVETH THE EMBERS SO WENT SHE UNTO NEW FORESTS	17	PRAISE YSOLT	
SO IS SHE THAT COMETH, THE MOTHER OF SONGS,	17	PRAISE YSOLT	
SO ART THOU WITH US, BEING GOOD TO KEEP	19	FOR E. MCC	
WELL THEN, SO CALL THEY, THE SWIRLERS OUT OF THE MIST OF MY SOUL,	20	IN DURANCE	
SO IS MY HEART HOLLOW WHEN SHE FILLETH NOT MINE EYES,	23	MARVOIL	
AND SO WERE MY MIND HOLLOW, DID SHE NOT FILL UTTERLY MY THOUGHT.	23	MARVOIL	
EVEN SO IS MINE HEART	27	NIGHT LITANY	
WHEN I SEE HIM SO SCORN AND DEFY PEACE,	29	ALTAFORTE	
CLEAR, DEEP, TRANSLUCENT, SO THE STARS ME SEEMED	30	PIERE VIDAL	
WAS GROWN SO FREE AN ESSENCE, OR BECOME	32	PARACELSUS	
SO SIMPLY ELEMENT AS WHAT I AM.	32	PARACELSUS	

SO

		PAGE	TITLE	LINE
SO	(CONTINUED)			
	SO THAT I MIGHT FIND YOU AGAIN, ...	36	FRANCESCA	11
	SO MANY THOUSAND BEAUTIES ARE GONE DOWN TO AVERNUS,	38	LADY'S LIFE	3
	SO SILENT LIGHT; NO GOSSAMER IS SPUN	38	BALLATETTA	7
	SO DELICATE AS SHE IS, WHEN THE SUN	38	BALLATETTA	8
	SO MANY THOUSAND FAIR ARE GONE DOWN TO AVERNUS, ...	38	LADY'S LIFE	13
	WAVER AND SEEM NOT DRAWN TO EARTH, SO HE	39	FOR PSYCHE	5
	FRAIL AND SO VILE IN ALL, ...	42	HER MONUMENT	51
	HOW CANST THOU REACH SO HIGH WITH THY POOR SENSE;	42	HER MONUMENT	52
	SO LIGHTLY WROUGHT	42	HER MONUMENT	56
	SO THOU HAST FORGOTTEN FULLY	44	FROM HEINE: 2	1
	DO YOU, TRULY, SO DETEST ME?	44	FROM HEINE: 1	2
	THAT I SO LONG HELD THY HEART WHOLLY, ...	44	FROM HEINE: 2	2
	THY LITTLE HEART, SO SWEET AND FALSE AND SMALL	44	FROM HEINE: 2	3
	WHOM THOU ONCE DID SING SO SWEETLY, ...	45	FROM HEINE: 3	2
	DID HE SO?	53	AU JARDIN	7
	DID HE SO?	53	AU JARDIN	24
	A CHILD--SO HIGH--YOU ARE, ...	62	A GIRL	9
	THE HEART TURNS TO TRAVEL SO THAT HE THEN THINKS	65	THE SEAFARER	52
	SO THAT BUT NOW MY HEART BURST FROM MY BREASTLOCK,	65	THE SEAFARER	59
	SO THAT ALL MEN SHALL HONOUR HIM AFTER	66	THE SEAFARER	78
	I BURN, I SCALD SO FOR THE NEW, ...	70	THE PLUNGE	3
	AS WHITE THEIR BARK, SO WHITE THIS LADY'S HOURS.	71	A VIRGINAL	14
	HOW SHE IS SO FAIR AND BONNY;	72	DIEU! QU'IL	2
	HOW SHE IS SO FAIR AND BONNY.	72	DIEU! QU'IL	8
	HATH OF PERFECT CHARMS SO MANY.	72	DIEU! QU'IL	11
	SO YOU FOUND AN AUDIENCE READY.	85	SALUTATION 2ND	4
	LIKE SO MANY UNUSED BOAS.	93	LES MILLWIN	4
	I HAVE TALKED TO YOU SO MUCH THAT	94	INSTRUCTIONS	12
	IN FACT THEY UNDERSTOOD THEM SO BADLY	97	THE BELLAIRES	3
	BUT THE GOOD BELLAIRES HAVE SO LITTLE UNDERSTOOD			
	THEIR AFFAIRS	97	THE BELLAIRES	8
	SO IS THE SLOW COOLING OF OUR CHIVALROUS PASSION,	100	THE BATH TUB	3
	AND YET THE MAN IS SO QUIET AND RESERVED IN DEMEANOUR	100	TEMPERAMENTS	3
	AND BECAUSE I HAPPEN TO SAY GO.	102	LADIES	8
	WHY DO YOU LOOK SO EAGERLY AND SO CURIOUSLY INTO			
	PEOPLE'S FACES, ...	103	CODA	2
	WHY DO YOU LOOK SO EAGERLY AND SO CURIOUSLY INTO			
	PEOPLE'S FACES, ...	103	CODA	2
	JOY SO RICH, AND IF I FIND NOT EVER	105	DOMPNA POIS	7
	A LADY WITH LOOK SO SPEAKING	105	DOMPNA POIS	8
	NEITHER ONE SO FAIR, NOR OF SUCH HEART, ...	105	DOMPNA POIS	12
	SO EAGER AND ALERT, ...	105	DOMPNA POIS	13
	IN ATTIRE, NOR SO GAY	105	DOMPNA POIS	15
	NOR WITH GIFT SO BOUNTIFUL AND SO TRUE, ...	105	DOMPNA POIS	16
	NOR WITH GIFT SO BOUNTIFUL AND SO TRUE, ...	105	DOMPNA POIS	16
	SO TAKE I MY ROAD	106	DOMPNA POIS	34
	SO CUNNINGLY, ...	106	DOMPNA POIS	44
	SHE IS SO SUPPLE AND YOUNG, ...	106	DOMPNA POIS	49
	ME OUT, KNOWING YOU HOLD ME SO FAST!	107	DOMPNA POIS	70
	WHO WAS "SO OLD THAT SHE WAS AN ATHEIST."	115	SOCIAL ORDER	6
	IS NOT SO BEAUTIFUL AS SHE WAS, ...	116	THE TEA SHOP	2
	SHE DOES NOT GET UP THE STAIRS SO EAGERLY;	116	THE TEA SHOP	4
	SO 'GAINST THE WINTER'S BALM.	116	ANCIENT MUSIC	11
	SO ENDS THAT STORY.	123	PROVINC DESERT	77
	IT IS SO LATE THAT THE DEW SOAKS MY GAUZE STOCKINGS,	132	JEWEL STAIRS'	2
	AND MY SPIRIT SO HIGH IT WAS ALL OVER THE HEAVENS,	135	EXILE'S LETTER	32
	I HAD TO BE OFF TO SO, FAR AWAY OVER THE WATERS,	135	EXILE'S LETTER	34
	AND WHAT WITH BROKEN WHEELS AND SO ON, I WON'T SAY			
	IT WASN'T HARD GOING.	135	EXILE'S LETTER	40
	SO MUCH FOR THE GAGGED REVIEWERS, ...	145	SALUTATION 3RD	3
	SO SHALL YOU BE ALSO, ...	145	SALUTATION 3RD	9
	SO TO THIS LAST ESTRANGEMENT, TAIRIRAN!	157	NEAR PERIGORD	185
	BEAUTY IS SO RARE A THING.	158	PSYCHOLOG HOUR	6
	SO FEW DRINK OF MY FOUNTAIN.	158	PSYCHOLOG HOUR	7
	SO MUCH BARREN REGRET, ...	158	PSYCHOLOG HOUR	8
	SO MANY HOURS WASTED!	158	PSYCHOLOG HOUR	9
	BEAUTY IS SO RARE A THING	158	PSYCHOLOG HOUR	21
	SO FEW DRINK OF MY FOUNTAIN.	158	PSYCHOLOG HOUR	22
	("SPEAK UP! YOU HAVE DANCED SO STIFFLY?	159	PSYCHOLOG HOUR	31
	AND SAID SO FRANKLY.	159	PSYCHOLOG HOUR	33

SO -- SOCIALIZED

	PAGE	TITLE	LINE
SO (CONTINUED)			
SINGS IN THE OPEN MEADOW--AT LEAST THE KODAK SAYS SO--	161	CABARET DANCER	4
"PEPITA" HAS NO TO-MORROW, SO YOU WRITE.	161	CABARET DANCER	9
AND SO PEPITA	162	CABARET DANCER	21
"NOT SO FAR, NO, NOT SO FAR NOW,	166	FISH & SHADOW	13
"NOT SO FAR, NO, NOT SO FAR NOW,	166	FISH & SHADOW	13
FROM ONE I LOVED NEVER SO MUCH,	176	LANGUE D'OC: 3	61
SO DOTH BEWILDER ME	176	LANGUE D'OC: 3	64
SO SWIFTLY GOES THE NIGHT	177	LANGUE D'OC: 4	14
SO SPOKE THE AUTHOR OF "THE DORIAN MOOD,"	193	SIENA MI FE	16
WHO HATH TAUGHT YOU SO SUBTLE A MEASURE,	207	SEXTUS PROP: 1	6
WHO SO INDECOROUS AS TO SHED THE PURE GORE OF A SUITOR?!	212	SEXTUS PROP: 3	26
AND SO FORTH, AUGUSTUS. "VIRGIN ARABIA SHAKES IN HER INMOST DWELLING."	216	SEXTUS PROP: 5	18
YET YOU ASK ON WHAT ACCOUNT I WRITE SO MANY LOVE-LYRICS	217	SEXTUS PROP: 5	23
SO THAT NO DAY SHALL UNBIND THEM.	220	SEXTUS PROP: 7	21
THROUGH PERILS, (SO MANY) AND OF A VEXED LIFE,	222	SEXTUS PROP: 8	17
SO SPOKE. AND THE NOOSE WAS OVER MY NECK.	224	SEXTUS PROP:10	13
I HAD NEVER SEEN HER LOOKING SO BEAUTIFUL,	225	SEXTUS PROP:10	30
AND SO ON.	225	SEXTUS PROP:10	42
SO I, THE FIRES THAT LIT ONCE DREAMS	236	MIDDLE-AGED	13
AND SO NOW LOVE	236	MIDDLE-AGED	16
RAINS DOWN AND SO ENRICHES SOME STIFF CASE,	236	MIDDLE-AGED	17
AND SO THE SPACE	236	MIDDLE-AGED	19
FOR MINDS SO WHOLLY FOUNDED UPON QUOTATIONS	239	MOYEN SENSUEL	29
THEIR DODDERING IGNORANCE IS WAXED SO NOTABLE	239	MOYEN SENSUEL	37
SO HE "FACED LIFE" WITH RATHER MIXED INTENTIONS,	242	MOYEN SENSUEL	101
BY NAME, IF NAMED." SO IT WAS PHRASED, OR RATHER SOMEWHAT SO	242	MOYEN SENSUEL	114
BY NAME, IF NAMED." SO IT WAS PHRASED, OR RATHER SOMEWHAT SO	242	MOYEN SENSUEL	114
I SPEAK IN CONTRADICTIONS, SO TO SPEAK.)	242	MOYEN SENSUEL	124
TO BE SO MUCH ALIKE THAT EVERY DOG THAT SMELLS 'EM,	244	MOYEN SENSUEL	172
"AND RATE 'EM UP AT JUST SO MUCH PER HEAD,	244	MOYEN SENSUEL	181
SO RADWAY WALKED, QUITE LIKE THE OTHER MEN,	244	MOYEN SENSUEL	185
RUNNING SO CLOSE TO "HELL" IT SENDS A SHIVER	246	MOYEN SENSUEL	224
AND IS SO OVERWEENING: LOVE BY NAME.	248	DONNA MI PREGA	3
HE COMES TO BE AND IS WHEN WILL'S SO GREAT	249	DONNA MI PREGA	49
BEAUTY SO NEAR,	250	DONNA MI PREGA	73
SO HATH MAN CRAFT FROM FEAR	250	DONNA MI PREGA	75
THOU ART SO FAIR ATTIRED THAT EVERY MAN AND EACH	250	DONNA MI PREGA	89
SO HE HAVE SENSE OR GLOW WITH REASON'S FIRE,	250	DONNA MI PREGA	91
AIN'T IT ALWAYS BEEN SO?	259	ALF'S FOURTH	11
"WE HAVE PLENTY, SO LET IT BE."	262	ALF'S SEVENTH	17
WHO ON THE SO WELL-PAID GROUND	263	ALF'S EIGHTH	9
OLD 'ERB WAS DOTING, SO THE RUMOUR RAN,	264	ALF'S NINTH	13
UNTIL A NARSTY GERMAN TOLD THEM SO.	265	ALF'S NINTH	25
LOOKING SO BIG AND BURLY.	266	ALF'S ELEVENTH	8
SOAKS			
IT IS SO LATE THAT THE DEW SOAKS MY GAUZE STOCKINGS,	132	JEWEL STAIRS'	2
SOAP			
THE NEW CAKE OF SOAP	99	CAKE OF SOAP	1
SOAPY			
SOAPY SIME? SLIPP'RY MAC?	258	ALF'S THIRD	2
SOCIAL			
THE SOCIAL ORDER	115	SOCIAL ORDER	
OF THE SOCIAL INCONSEQUENCE.	201	AGE DEMANDED	
THE SOCIAL ITCH, THE ALMOST, ALL BUT, NOT QUITE, FASCINATING,	241	MOYEN SENSUEL	8
THE SERIOUS SOCIAL FOLK IS "JUST WHAT SEX IS."	244	MOYEN SENSUEL	16
THOUGH IT WILL, OF COURSE, PASS OFF WITH SOCIAL SCIENCE	244	MOYEN SENSUEL	16
WILL LONG ONLY TO BE A SOCIAL FUNCTION,	244	MOYEN SENSUEL	17
SOCIALIZED			
OF LANGUAGE, BY MEN WHOLLY SOCIALIZED,	244	MOYEN SENSUEL	16
WHEN THOROUGHLY SOCIALIZED PRINTERS WANT TO PRINT 'EM.	244	MOYEN SENSUEL	16

SOCIETY -- SOLID

	PAGE	TITLE	LINE
SOCIETY			
SOCIETY	111	SOCIETY	T
"'CARE TOO MUCH FOR SOCIETY DINNERS?'	182	MOEURS CON: 8	11
SOCRATES			
THE CONSTITUTION OF OUR LAND, O SOCRATES,	239	MOYEN SENSUEL	23
SODDEN			
SODDEN AND LEAD-HEAVY.	35	THE EYES	4
STRANGE WOODS HALF SODDEN, AND NEW BRIGHTER STUFF:	61	PORTRAIT FEMME	26
SOFT			
SOFT AS SPRING WIND THAT'S COME FROM BIRCHEN BOWERS.	71	A VIRGINAL	10
WE GRUB THE SOFT FERN-SHOOTS,	127	BOWMEN OF SHU	5
BECAUSE THEY CAN'T FIND A SOFT SEAT.	142	UNMOVING CLOUD	21
"SOFT FIELDS MUST BE WORN BY SMALL WHEELS,	210	SEXTUS PROP: 2	21
AND WHENCE THIS SOFT BOOK COMES INTO MY MOUTH.	217	SEXTUS PROP: 5	24
SOFTEN			
THOU SHALT THEN SOFTEN,	9	NA AUDIART	50
SOFTLY			
LET THE GODS SPEAK SOFTLY OF US	67	DORIA	8
GOD! HOW SOFTLY THIS KILLS!	175	LANGUE D'OC: 3	40
SOFTNESS			
THE PURPLE HOUSE AND THE CRIMSON ARE FULL OF SPRING SOFTNESS.	129	THE RIVER SONG	24
SOGGY			
AND DINE IN A SOGGY, CHEAP RESTAURANT?	107	OF AROUET	4
SOIL			
AND THE SOIL MEETS HIS DISTRESS.	195	HUGH SELWIN:10	8
SOILED			
THE WORLD O'ERSHADOWED, SOILED AND OVERCAST,	36	THE YOUNG KING	7
SOILED-WHITE			
WHY DOES THE SMALL CHILD IN THE SOILED-WHITE IMITATION FUR COAT	114	SIMULACRA	3
SOIREE			
SOIREE	179	MOEURS CON: 3	SUB
SOJER			
GO TO GOD LIKE A SOJER;	260	ALF'S FOURTH	18
SO'JERS			
SEVERAL OLD SO'JERS KNOW	257	BREAD BRIGADE	11
SO-KIN			
TO SO-KIN OF RAKUYO, ANCIENT FRIEND, CHANCELLOR OF GEN.	134	EXILE'S LETTER	1
SOLD			
THE DESTINIES OF ENGLAND WERE ALMOST SOLD	264	ALF'S NINTH	6
SOLDIER			
SOLDIER, THE ENUMERATION OF WOUNDS; THE SHEEP-FEEDER, OF EWES,	218	SEXTUS PROP: 5	56
SOLDIERS			
THE GENERALS ARE ON THEM, THE SOLDIERS ARE BY THEM.	127	BOWMEN OF SHU	18
HIS ARMY IS A THOUSAND AND FORTY-EIGHT SOLDIERS	237	ABU SALAMMAMM	12
SOLE			
ROME THAT ART ROME'S ONE SOLE LAST MONUMENT,	40	ROME	9
SOLE GUARD OF GRIEF	41	HER MONUMENT	7
SOLE GUARD OF MEMORY	41	HER MONUMENT	8
SPEAK ONCE AGAIN FOR ITS SOLE STIMULATION,	63	PHASELLUS ILLE	10
BUT THE SOLE RESULT WAS BILLS	98	THE BELLAIRES	30
CANTICO DEL SOLE	183	CANTICO SOLE	T
SOLEDADES			
DE MIS SOLEDADES VENGO,	82	THE CONDOLENCE	EPI
A MIS SOLEDADES VOY,	82	THE CONDOLENCE	EPI
SOLELY			
THAT IN HIM SOLELY IS COMPASSION BORN.	250	DONNA MI PREGA	87
SOLEMNITY			
THIS IS THE KIND OF TONE AND SOLEMNITY	263	ALF'S EIGHTH	22
SOLI			
THE SHUDDER OF VAE SOLI GURGLES BENEATH MY RIBS.	247	PIERROTS	3
SOLICITOUS			
AND A QUERULOUS NOISE RESPONDED TO OUR SOLICITOUS REPROBATIONS,	215	SEXTUS PROP: 4	26
SOLICITUDE			
WITH A PATHETIC SOLICITUDE THEY ATTEND ME;	147	BEFORE SLEEP	8
SOLID			
IS WOVEN AND GROWS SOLID BENEATH US;	170	PHANOPOEIA	23

PAGE 375

SOLID -- SOME

	PAGE	TITLE	LINE
SOLID (CONTINUED)			
GOLD, OF COURSE, IS SOLID TOO, ...	267	ALF'S TWELFTH	16
SOLVE			
SOLVE ME THE RIDDLE, FOR YOU KNOW THE TALE.	151	NEAR PERIGORD	4
"SAY THAT HE LOVED HER, DOES IT SOLVE THE RIDDLE?"	156	NEAR PERIGORD	156
SOLVED			
AM SOLVED AND BOUND IN, THROUGH AUGHT HERE ON EARTH,	51	THE FLAME	33
SOME			
THAT WAS A DOG-WOOD TREE SOME SYNE.	4	LA FRAISNE	15
OR SOME OTHER'S THAT HE SINGS?	6	CINO	31
THAT SOME CALL CHILDREN, ...	14	FAMAM CANO	9
IS LISTED. WELL! SOME SCORE YEARS HENCE	14	FAMAM CANO	20
THEY REACH ME NOT, TOUCH ME SOME EDGE OR THAT, ...	20	IN DURANCE	5
AND HAVE SOME BREATH FOR BEAUTY AND THE ARTS.	20	IN DURANCE	16
OH YE, MY FELLOWS: WITH THE SEAS BETWEEN US SOME BE,	21	IN DURANCE	35
AND SOME THE HILLS HOLD OFF, ...	21	IN DURANCE	38
OF SOME THIN SILK STUFF THAT'S SCARCE STUFF AT ALL,	31	PIERE VIDAL	29
GOD! SHE WAS WHITE THEN, SPLENDID AS SOME TOMB	31	PIERE VIDAL	38
SOME OVERFLOWING RIVER IS RUN MAD, ...	32	PARACELSUS	12
GET US TO SOME CLEAR PLACE WHEREIN THE SUN	39	BLANDULA	3
WILL WE NOT FIND SOME HEADLAND CONSECRATED	39	BLANDULA	7
TO MIND ME OF SOME URN OF FULL DELIGHT, ...	41	HER MONUMENT	13
THAT SEEMS TO BE SOME QUIVERING SPLENDOUR CAST	41	HER MONUMENT	29
AND ON THE MORROW, BY SOME LIGHTSOME TWIST, ...	42	HER MONUMENT	35
SOME LADS GET HUNG, AND SOME GET SHOT.	43	MR. HOUSMAN	8
SOME LADS GET HUNG, AND SOME GET SHOT.	43	MR. HOUSMAN	8
SET TO SOME WEAVING, COMES THE AUREATE LIGHT.	49	OF SPLENDOUR	16
WHO CALL'ST ABOUT MY GATES FOR SOME LOST ME;	51	THE FLAME	35
OTHERS ARE BEAUTIFUL, NONE MORE, SOME LESS.	52	AU SALON	EPI
TALK OF THE LATEST SUCCESS, GIVE WING TO SOME			
SCANDAL, ...	52	AU SALON	12
SOME CIRCLE OF NOT MORE THAN THREE	52	AU SALON	18
SOME FEW WHOM WE'D RATHER PLEASE	52	AU SALON	20
SOME CERTAIN PECULIAR THINGS, ...	52	AU SALON	24
SOME CERTAIN ACCUSTOMED FORMS, ...	52	AU SALON	26
TO SAY THAT LIFE IS, SOME WAY, A GAY THING, ...	53	AU JARDIN	12
YOU ARE A PERSON OF SOME INTEREST, ONE COMES TO YOU	61	PORTRAIT FEMME	14
TROPHIES FISHED UP; SOME CURIOUS SUGGESTION;	61	PORTRAIT FEMME	16
ABIDES 'MID BURGHERS SOME HEAVY BUSINESS, ...	64	THE SEAFARER	29
HE THE PROSPEROUS MAN--WHAT SOME PERFORM	65	THE SEAFARER	57
LAUD OF THE LIVING, BOASTETH SOME LAST WORD, ...	66	THE SEAFARER	74
UNDER SOME NEUTRAL FORCE	69	THE NEEDLE	14
OUT, AND ALONE, AMONG SOME	70	THE PLUNGE	19
SHE WOULD LIKE SOME ONE TO SPEAK TO HER, ...	83	THE GARDEN	10
SOME OTHERS MAY OVERHEAR THEM, ...	88	CAUSA	2
AND WITH SOME BRANCHES ROTTED AND FALLING.	89	COMMISSION	32
BUT HE ACCOMPLISHED THIS FEAT AT SOME COST;	100	TEMPERAMENTS	7
SOME LITTLE PRIZED PLACE IN AUVERGNAT:	122	PROVINC DESERT	65
GOBBLED ALL THE LAND, AND HELD IT LATER FOR SOME			
HUNDRED YEARS.	151	NEAR PERIGORD	19
TRUE, HE HAS PRAISED HER, BUT IN SOME OPINION	155	NEAR PERIGORD	147
THAT SOME ONE ELSE HAS PAID FOR, ...	163	CABARET DANCER	57
COMPLEYNT OF A GENTLEMAN WHO HAS BEEN WAITING			
OUTSIDE FOR SOME TIME	172	LANGUE D'OC: 1	SUB
AND SOME BELIEVING, ...	190	HUGH SELWYN: 4	2
SOME QUICK TO ARM, ...	190	HUGH SELWYN: 4	4
SOME FOR ADVENTURE, ...	190	HUGH SELWYN: 4	5
SOME FROM FEAR OF WEAKNESS, ...	190	HUGH SELWYN: 4	6
SOME FROM FEAR OF CENSURE, ...	190	HUGH SELWYN: 4	7
SOME FOR LOVE OF SLAUGHTER, IN IMAGINATION, ...	190	HUGH SELWYN: 4	8
SOME IN FEAR, LEARNING LOVE OF SLAUGHTER;	190	HUGH SELWYN: 4	10
DIED SOME, PRO PATRIA, ...	190	HUGH SELWYN: 4	11
THE MAKER OF IT, SOME OTHER MOUTH, ...	197	ENVOI (1919)	20
OF SOME AS YET UNCATALOGUED SAND;	213	SEXTUS PROP: 3	37
AND SOME OF THEM SHOOK LITTLE TORCHES, ...	224	SEXTUS PROP:10	7
AND MUCH OF LITTLE MOMENT, AND SOME FEW	235	TO WHISTLER	6
AS GOLD THAT RAINS ABOUT SOME BURIED KING.	236	MIDDLE-AGED	2
AND START TO INSPECT SOME FURTHER PYRAMID;	236	MIDDLE-AGED	7
RAINS DOWN AND SO ENRICHES SOME STIFF CASE, ...	236	MIDDLE-AGED	17
IN HOPE TO SET SOME MISCONCEPTIONS RIGHT.	238	MOYEN SENSUEL	2
READ BENNETT OR SOME OTHER FLACCID FLATTERER.	240	MOYEN SENSUEL	66

PAGE 376

SOME -- SONG

	PAGE	TITLE	LINE
SOME (CONTINUED)			
SOME FORCES AMONG THOSE WHICH "FORMED" HIS YOUTH:	241	MOYEN SENSUEL	78
THOUGH SOME APPROVED OF THEM, AND SOME DEPLORED 'EM.	242	MOYEN SENSUEL	108
THOUGH SOME APPROVED OF THEM, AND SOME DEPLORED 'EM.	242	MOYEN SENSUEL	108
SOME OTHER QUAINT REMINDER OF THE OCCASION	245	MOYEN SENSUEL	197
SOME MEN WILL LIVE AS PRUDES IN THEIR OWN VILLAGE	245	MOYEN SENSUEL	207
LET SOME NEW LYING ASS,	261	ALF'S SIXTH	1
BUT SOME SILVER SET TO STEW	267	ALF'S TWELFTH	17
SOME OTHER FELLER DO IT.	270	OF 600 M.P.'S	12
SOMEONE			
GREAT MINDS HAVE SOUGHT YOU--LACKING SOMEONE ELSE.	61	PORTRAIT FEMME	6
SOMEONE ADMIRED YOUR WORKS,	159	PSYCHOLOG HOUR	32
AND SOMEONE ELSE WILL BE PLEASED AT THE DEATH OF THEODORUS,	164	QUINTUS SEPTIM	2
HE WILL UNDOUBTEDLY CHAIN SOMEONE ELSE TO THIS FOUNTAIN,	238	ABU SALAMMAMM	31
SOMETHIN'			
TO THE CO-OPS, A ECHO OR SOMETHIN'?	262	ALF'S SEVENTH	9
SOMETHING			
HOURS, WHERE SOMETHING MIGHT HAVE FLOATED UP.	61	PORTRAIT FEMME	12
PREGNANT WITH MANDRAKES, OR WITH SOMETHING ELSE	61	PORTRAIT FEMME	18
HATH LACKED A SOMETHING SINCE THIS LADY PASSED;	63	QUIES	3
HATH LACKED A SOMETHING. 'TWAS BUT MARGINAL.	63	QUIES	4
NINE ADULTERIES, 12 LIAISONS, 64 FORNICATIONS AND SOMETHING APPROACHING A RAPE	100	TEMPERAMENTS	1
FOR THEM THERE IS SOMETHING AFOOT.	158	PSYCHOLOG HOUR	18
SOMETHING FOR THE MODERN STAGE,	188	HUGH SELWYN: 2	3
BUT FOR SOMETHING TO READ IN NORMAL CIRCUMSTANCES?	207	SEXTUS PROP: 1	19
'TIS TIME THAT IT WAS CAPPED WITH SOMETHING QUOTABLE.	239	MOYEN SENSUEL	38
CONSIDERING SOMETHING THAT WOULD, AS YOU	262	ALF'S SEVENTH	7
SOMETIMES			
YOU, SOMETIMES, WILL LAMENT A LOST FRIEND,	219	SEXTUS PROP: 6	30
SOMEWHAT			
SAVE THERE BE SOMEWHAT CALAMITOUS	66	THE SEAFARER	69
DOUBTFUL, SOMEWHAT, OF THE VALUE	196	HUGH SELWIN:12	9
BY NAME, IF NAMED." SO IT WAS PHRASED, OR RATHER SOMEWHAT SO	242	MOYEN SENSUEL	114
SOMEWHERE			
BUT OUT SOMEWHERE BEYOND THE WORLDLY WAYS	49	OF SPLENDOUR	3
FOR MENCKEN STATES SOMEWHERE, IN THIS CONNECTION:	238	MOYEN SENSUEL	10
THE CO-OPS WAS A GOIN' SOMEWHERE,	262	ALF'S SEVENTH	2
SON			
VERS AND CANZONE, TILL THAT DAMN'D SON OF ARAGON,	22	MARVOIL	8
A SON OF GOD WAS THE GOODLY FERE	34	GOODLY FERE	33
"YOUR SON, AH, SINCE HE DIED	152	NEAR PERIGORD	44
CERNE SON OEIL DE GITANA"	162	CABARET DANCER	25
AND PRAY TO GOD THAT IS ST. MARY'S SON,	172	LANGUE D'OC: 1	10
AND THAT THE YOUNGEST SON WAS IN A PUBLISHER'S OFFICE,	179	MOEURS CON: 3	3
E. P. ODE POUR L'ELECTION DE SON SEPULCHRE	187	E. P. ODE	T
DE SON EAGE; THE CASE PRESENTS	187	E. P. ODE	19
SONG			
HAVING BECOME THE SOULS OF SONG.	6	CINO	9
OR THE SONG OF THE SIXTH COMPANION	11	OF THE GIBBET	SUB
"SONG, A SONG."	16	PRAISE YSOLT	8
"SONG, A SONG."	16	PRAISE YSOLT	8
SEEKING EVER A SONG.	16	PRAISE YSOLT	10
AND LITTLE RED ELF WORDS CRYING "A SONG,"	16	PRAISE YSOLT	15
LITTLE GREY ELF WORDS CRYING FOR A SONG,	16	PRAISE YSOLT	16
LITTLE BROWN LEAF WORDS CRYING "A SONG,"	16	PRAISE YSOLT	17
LITTLE GREEN LEAF WORDS CRYING FOR A SONG.	16	PRAISE YSOLT	18
BLOWING THEY KNOW NOT WHITHER, SEEKING A SONG.	16	PRAISE YSOLT	20
"SONG, A SONG."	16	PRAISE YSOLT	30
"SONG, A SONG."	16	PRAISE YSOLT	30
WHEREFORE I MADE HER A SONG AND SHE WENT FROM ME	17	PRAISE YSOLT	31
"A SONG, A SONG!"	17	PRAISE YSOLT	35
"A SONG, A SONG!"	17	PRAISE YSOLT	35
AND IN VAIN I CRIED UNTO THEM "I HAVE NO SONG	17	PRAISE YSOLT	36
CRYING "SONG, A SONG."	17	PRAISE YSOLT	40
CRYING "SONG, A SONG."	17	PRAISE YSOLT	40
MY SONG WAS ABLAZE WITH HER AND SHE WENT FROM ME	17	PRAISE YSOLT	42

SONG -- SONNET

	PAGE	TITLE	LINE
SONG (CONTINUED)			
CRYING EVER "SONG, A SONG."	17	PRAISE YSOLT	45
CRYING EVER "SONG, A SONG."	17	PRAISE YSOLT	45
AND I "I HAVE NO SONG,"	17	PRAISE YSOLT	46
"SONG, A SONG."	17	PRAISE YSOLT	54
"SONG, A SONG."	17	PRAISE YSOLT	54
THE SONG OF THE LOTUS OF KUMI?	18	DE AEGYPTO	14
HIS SLEEP OR SONG.	24	THUS NINEVEH	11
"IT IS NOT, RAANA, THAT MY SONG RINGS HIGHEST	24	THUS NINEVEH	20
AND EVERY JONGLEUR KNEW ME IN HIS SONG,	30	PIERE VIDAL	10
LO, HOW THE LIGHT DOTH MELT US INTO SONG:	38	BALLATETTA	3
SONG FROM "DIE HARZREISE"	47	FROM HEINE: 7	SUB
NIGHT SONG	48	FROM HEINE: 8	SUB
BUT YOU, NEWEST SONG OF THE LOT,	94	INSTRUCTIONS	15
A SONG OF THE DEGREES	95	OF THE DEGREES	T
AUVERGNE ROSE TO THE SONG;	122	PROVINC DESERT	69
SONG OF THE BOWMEN OF SHU	127	BOWMEN OF SHU	T
THE RIVER SONG	128	THE RIVER SONG	T
KUTSU'S PROSE SONG	128	THE RIVER SONG	9
AND THE WIND LIFTING THE SONG, AND INTERRUPTING IT,	136	EXILE'S LETTER	61
TRIED LAYU'S LUCK, OFFERED THE CHOYO SONG,	136	EXILE'S LETTER	66
TO SING ONE THING WHEN YOUR SONG MEANS ANOTHER,	153	NEAR PERIGORD	89
AND THE "BEST CRAFTSMAN" SINGS OUT HIS FRIEND'S SONG,	155	NEAR PERIGORD	141
OF SONG OF MINE."	172	LANGUE D'OC: 1	25
THEIR NEW SONG IN THE LEAVES.	173	LANGUE D'OC: 2	3
'TILL THE TRAIST WATCHER HIS SONG UNREIN,	177	LANGUE D'OC: 4	18
TELL HER THAT SANG ME ONCE THAT SONG OF LAWES:	197	ENVOI (1919)	2
HADST THOU BUT SONG	197	ENVOI (1919)	3
WITH SONG UPON HER LIPS	197	ENVOI (1919)	18
BUT SINGS NOT OUT THE SONG, NOR KNOWS	197	ENVOI (1919)	19
FITTED SONG TO THE STRINGS;	211	SEXTUS PROP: 2	36
THERE IS SONG IN THE PARCHMENT; CATULLUS THE HIGHLY INDECOROUS,	230	SEXTUS PROP:12	68
ABU SALAMMAMM--A SONG OF EMPIRE	237	ABU SALAMMAMM	T
O STATE SANS SONG, SANS HOME-GROWN WINE, SANS REALIST!	241	MOYEN SENSUEL	88
SONG OF SIX HUNDRED M. P.'S	270	OF 600 M.P.'S	T
NATIONAL SONG (E. C.)	272	NATIONAL SONG	T
SONG-LIFE			
--PART OF IT--OF THY SONG-LIFE.	14	FAMAM CANO	16
SONGS			
PESTE! 'TIS HIS OWN SONGS?	6	CINO	30
YOUR SONGS?	14	FAMAM CANO	1
SO IS SHE THAT COMETH, THE MOTHER OF SONGS,	17	PRAISE YSOLT	50
AND MANY A ONE HATH SUNG HIS SONGS	24	THUS NINEVEH	12
FOR I'VE NOTHING BUT SONGS TO GIVE YOU.	53	AU JARDIN	10
(I. E. THESE SONGS).	81	TENZONE	2
O MY FELLOW SUFFERERS, SONGS OF MY YOUTH,	82	THE CONDOLENCE	1
LET US LEAVE THIS MATTER, MY SONGS,	82	THE CONDOLENCE	17
GO, LITTLE NAKED AND IMPUDENT SONGS,	85	SALUTATION 2ND	16
GO, MY SONGS, TO THE LONELY AND THE UNSATISFIED,	88	COMMISSION	1
COME, MY SONGS, LET US EXPRESS OUR BASER PASSIONS,	94	INSTRUCTIONS	1
YOU ARE VERY IDLE, MY SONGS.	94	INSTRUCTIONS	3
GO, MY SONGS, SEEK YOUR PRAISE FROM THE YOUNG AND FROM THE INTOLERANT,	95	ITE	1
COME, MY SONGS, LET US SPEAK OF PERFECTION--	99	SALVATIONISTS	1
AH YES, MY SONGS, LET US RESURRECT	99	SALVATIONISTS	3
COME, MY SONGS,	99	SALVATIONISTS	11
O MY SONGS,	103	CODA	1
WITH YELLOW GOLD AND WHITE JEWELS, WE PAID FOR SONGS AND LAUGHTER	134	EXILE'S LETTER	4
AND IN THE MEAN TIME MY SONGS WILL TRAVEL,	208	SEXTUS PROP: 1	39
THE SONGS SHALL BE A FINE TOMB-STONE OVER THEIR BEAUTY.	209	SEXTUS PROP: 1	64
SONG'S			
MAY I FOR MY OWN SELF SONG'S TRUTH RECKON,	64	THE SEAFARER	1
SON-IN-LAW			
BUT THE SON-IN-LAW OF MR. H. STYRAX	178	MOEURS CON: 1	16
SONNET			
THE SECOND HAS WRITTEN A SONNET	118	THREE POETS	5
AND THE DANCERS, YOU WRITE A SONNET;	161	CABARET DANCER	6

PAGE 378

SONNETS -- SORROW-SWEPT

	PAGE	TITLE	LINE
SONNETS			
AND WROTE NINETY PETRARCHAN SONNETS.	118	CONTEMPORARIES	5
SONORITY			
ONE MUST HAVE RESONANCE, RESONANCE AND SONORITY . . LIKE A GOOSE.	230	SEXTUS PROP:12	65
SONS			
WITHOUT IXION, AND WITHOUT THE SONS OF MENOETIUS AND THE ARGO AND WITHOUT JOVE'S GRAVE AND THE TITANS.	218	SEXTUS PROP: 5	52
THAT AMERICA'S STURDY SONS	268	ANOTHER BIT	2
SOON			
EVEN AS THOU SHALT SOON HAVE THIS PARCHMENT.	23	MARVOIL	44
HELL GRANT SOON WE HEAR AGAIN THE SWORDS CLASH! ...	28	ALTAFORTE	13
HELL GRANT SOON WE HEAR AGAIN THE SWORDS CLASH! ...	29	ALTAFORTE	38
WE ALSO SHALL BE DEAD PRETTY SOON	43	MR. HOUSMAN	3
THE WAVES BORE IN, SOON WILL THEY BEAR AWAY.	69	THE NEEDLE	10
SOON OUR HERO COULD MANAGE ONCE A WEEK,	243	MOYEN SENSUEL	141
ELECTION WILL NOT COME VERY SOON,	265	ALF'S TENTH	13
SOOTHING			
SYRUP AND SOOTHING DOPE,	259	ALF'S THIRD	15
SOOTHINGS			
SOOTHINGS, CONFESSIONS;	248	PIERROTS	26
SOPHIST			
COME NOT ANEAR THE DARK-BROWED SOPHIST	263	ALF'S EIGHTH	8
SOPHISTICATIONS			
THE HAVEN FROM SOPHISTICATIONS AND CONTENTIONS	195	HUGH SELWIN:10	9
SOPHOCLEAN			
SEEK EVER TO STAND IN THE HARD SOPHOCLEAN LIGHT ...	95	ITE	3
SOPRANO			
PROTEST WITH HER CLEAR SOPRANO.	204	MEDALLION	4
SORCERIZING			
"THESE ARE YOUR IMAGES, AND FROM YOU THE SORCERIZING OF SHUT-IN YOUNG LADIES,	211	SEXTUS PROP: 2	50
SORE			
TO KEEP YOUR FEELIN'S SORE,	260	SAFE AND SOUND	12
SORELY			
ALAS, EHEU, ONE QUESTION THAT SORELY VEXES	244	MOYEN SENSUEL	161
SORROW			
BUT I HAVE SEEN THE SORROW OF MEN, AND AM GLAD, ...	4	LA FRAISNE	22
WHEN THE WIND BLOWS SIGH THOU FOR MY SORROW	23	MARVOIL	41
AND THOUGH THOU SIGHEST MY SORROW IN THE WIND, ...	23	MARVOIL	46
LO! THEY PAUSE NOT FOR LOVE NOR FOR SORROW,	25	THE WHITE STAG	2
WHAT GREAT SORROW	26	NIGHT LITANY	15
TILL THOU FORGET THY SORROW,	47	FROM HEINE: 7	7
BUT THERE'LL COME SORROW OF IT.	53	AU JARDIN	14
BUT SHALL HAVE HIS SORROW FOR SEA-FARE	65	THE SEAFARER	43
HE SINGETH SUMMERWARD, BODETH SORROW,	66	THE SEAFARER	55
WHEN ANYONE SAYS "RETURN," THE OTHERS ARE FULL OF SORROW.	127	BOWMEN OF SHU	6
SORROWFUL MINDS, SORROW IS STRONG, WE ARE HUNGRY AND THIRSTY.	127	BOWMEN OF SHU	7
OUR SORROW IS BITTER, BUT WE WOULD NOT RETURN TO OUR COUNTRY.	127	BOWMEN OF SHU	12
OUR MIND IS FULL OF SORROW, WHO WILL KNOW OF OUR GRIEF?	127	BOWMEN OF SHU	24
AND SORROW, SORROW LIKE RAIN.	133	FRONTIER GUARD	17
AND SORROW, SORROW LIKE RAIN.	133	FRONTIER GUARD	17
SORROW TO GO, AND SORROW, SORROW RETURNING.	133	FRONTIER GUARD	18
SORROW TO GO, AND SORROW, SORROW RETURNING.	133	FRONTIER GUARD	18
SORROW TO GO, AND SORROW, SORROW RETURNING.	133	FRONTIER GUARD	18
AH, HOW SHALL YOU KNOW THE DREARY SORROW AT THE NORTH GATE,	133	FRONTIER GUARD	22
HE CAN NOT KNOW OF OUR SORROW."	142	UNMOVING CLOUD	27
SORROWFUL			
SORROWFUL MINDS, SORROW IS STRONG, WE ARE HUNGRY AND THIRSTY.	127	BOWMEN OF SHU	7
THE MONKEYS MAKE SORROWFUL NOISE OVERHEAD	130	RIVER-MER WIFE	19
SORROWFULLY			
O WOUNDED SORROWFULLY.	47	FROM HEINE: 7	8
SORROW-SWEPT			
O SORROW-SWEPT MY FOOL,	35	HIS OWN FACE	3

SORRY -- SOUL

	PAGE	TITLE	LINE
SORRY			
NOR EAT THE SWEET NOR FEEL THE SORRY,	66	THE SEAFARER	97
O WORLD, I AM SORRY FOR YOU,	88	CAUSA	3
WHO WILL BE SORRY FOR GENERAL RISHOGU,	139	SOUTH-FOLK	12
I, CERCLAMON, SORRY AND GLAD,	175	LANGUE D'OC: 3	55
SORT			
A SORT OF CURSE AGAINST ITS GUZZLING	14	FAMAM CANO	25
WE ARE COMPARED TO THAT SORT OF PERSON	82	THE CONDOLENCE	14
OF A SORT OF EMOTIONAL ANAEMIA.	83	THE GARDEN	4
A SORT OF CHLOROFORMED SUTTEE,	115	SOCIAL ORDER	13
WILL BE A STUFFY, OPULENT SORT OF FUNGUS	161	CABARET DANCER	14
"ABOUT ACQUIRING THAT SORT OF A REPUTATION.	210	SEXTUS PROP: 2	20
A SORT OF STINKING DILIQUESCENT SACCHARINE.	239	MOYEN SENSUEL	22
LIFE'S A SORT OF SUGARED DISH-WASH!"	241	MOYEN SENSUEL	90
A ROSY PATH, A SORT OF VERNAL INGRESS,	243	MOYEN SENSUEL	145
BUT MY SOUL, THE SORT WHICH HARSH SOUNDS DISTURB,	247	PIERROTS	17
A SORT OF ARAB'S DREAM IN THE NIGHT.	262	ALF'S SEVENTH	16
SORTS			
BE AGAINST ALL SORTS OF MORTMAIN.	89	COMMISSION	35
SO'S			
KING SO'S TERRACED PALACE	128	THE RIVER SONG	11
SO-SHU			
SO-SHU DREAMED,	118	ANCIENT WISDOM	1
SOT			
AND SHE HAS MARRIED A SOT,	128	BEAU TOILET	7
SOUGH			
I SOUGH AND SING	174	LANGUE D'OC: 3	4
SOUGHT			
GREAT MINDS HAVE SOUGHT YOU--LACKING SOMEONE ELSE.	61	PORTRAIT FEMME	6
SOUL			
UPON THY HANDS, AND THY OLD SOUL	9	NA AUDIART	41
TO TEACH MY SOUL TO BOW,	16	PRAISE YSOLT	24
SAYING "THE SOUL SENDETH US."	17	PRAISE YSOLT	34
BUT MY SOUL SENT A WOMAN, A WOMAN OF THE WONDER-FOLK,	17	PRAISE YSOLT	38
TILL MY SOUL SENT A WOMAN AS THE SUN:	17	PRAISE YSOLT	47
IN VAIN HAVE I STRIVEN WITH MY SOUL	17	PRAISE YSOLT	55
TO TEACH MY SOUL TO BOW.	17	PRAISE YSOLT	56
WHAT SOUL BOWETH	17	PRAISE YSOLT	57
"QUASI KALOUN." S. T. SAYS BEAUTY IS MOST THAT, A "CALLING TO THE SOUL."	20	IN DURANCE	20
WELL THEN, SO CALL THEY, THE SWIRLERS OUT OF THE MIST OF MY SOUL,	20	IN DURANCE	21
AND YET MY SOUL SINGS "UP!" AND WE ARE ONE.	21	IN DURANCE	41
WHAT HAST THOU, O MY SOUL, WITH PARADISE?	39	BLANDULA	1
MY SOUL, I MEET THEE, WHEN THIS LIFE'S OUTRUN,	39	BLANDULA	6
SOUL, IF SHE MEET US THERE, WILL ANY RUMOUR	39	BLANDULA	13
WHICH, PLAYED ON BY THE VIRTUES OF HER SOUL,	49	OF SPLENDOUR	20
IF I HAVE MERGED MY SOUL, OR UTTERLY	51	THE FLAME	32
I SAY MY SOUL FLOWED BACK, BECAME TRANSLUCENT.	51	THE FLAME	36
"I AM THY SOUL, NIKOPTIS. I HAVE WATCHED	60	TOMB AKR CAAR	1
LISTEN! LISTEN TO ME, AND I WILL BREATHE INTO THEE A SOUL.	62	N. Y.	2
AND I WILL BREATHE INTO THEE A SOUL,	62	N. Y.	12
NOW! FOR THE NEEDLE TREMBLES IN MY SOUL!	69	THE NEEDLE	3
TO BRING HER SOUL TO BIRTH,	84	ORTUS	3
HOW HAVE I LABOURED TO BRING HER SOUL INTO SEPARATION;	84	ORTUS	7
BRING CONFIDENCE UPON THE ALGAE AND THE TENTACLES OF THE SOUL.	88	COMMISSION	21
O LIGHT BOUND AND BENT IN, O SOUL OF THE CAPTIVE,	95	OF THE DEGREES	11
REST NIGHTLY UP THE SOUL OF OUR DELICATE FRIEND FLORIALIS,	100	TEMPERAMENTS	2
THY SOUL	112	HIMERRO	1
THINKING OF AELIS, WHOM HE LOVED HEART AND SOUL	154	NEAR PERIGORD	110
AND HATE YOUR MIND, NOT YOU, YOUR SOUL, YOUR HANDS.	157	NEAR PERIGORD	184
"DELIGHT THY SOUL IN FATNESS," SAITH THE PREACHER.	163	CABARET DANCER	69
THE SOUL OF THE SALMON-TROUT FLOATS OVER THE STREAM AND OF THE PURITY OF HER SOUL.	166	FISH & SHADOW	2
CONDUCT, ON THE OTHER HAND, THE SOUL	196	HUGH SELWIN:12	21
UP, UP MY SOUL, FROM YOUR LOWLY CANTILATION,	216	SEXTUS PROP: 5	12
RADWAY GREW UP. THESE FORCES SHAPED HIS SOUL;	239	MOYEN SENSUEL	44

SOUL -- SPACE

	PAGE	TITLE	LINE
SOUL (CONTINUED)			
WHO WROUGHT ABOUT HIS "SOUL" THEIR STALE INFECTION.	241	MOYEN SENSUEL	81
BUT MY SOUL, THE SORT WHICH HARSH SOUNDS DISTURB,	247	PIERROTS	17
HIS MODUS TAKES FROM SOUL, FROM HEART HIS WILL; ...	249	DONNA MI PREGA	23
GOD REST HER SLOSHIN' SOUL.	271	OLE KATE	20
SOUL-KIN			
OUT OF MINE OWN SOUL-KIN,	20	IN DURANCE	11
SOULS			
HAVING BECOME THE SOULS OF SONG.	6	CINO	9
AND BRING THEIR SOULS TO HIS "HAULTE CITEE."	12	OF THE GIBBET	43
"THERE BE GREATER SOULS THAN THOU."	16	PRAISE YSOLT	26
WHEN OUR SOULS ARE RETURNED TO THE GODS	52	AU SALON	2
AND THREE SOULS CAME UPON THEE--	60	TOMB AKR CAAR	18
THESE WERE THE SOULS OF BLOOD.	74	THE RETURN	18
THE MAUVE AND GREENISH SOULS OF THE LITTLE MILLWINS	93	LES MILLWIN	2
SOUL'S			
'GAINST OUR LIPS FOR THE SOUL'S DISTRESS	11	OF THE GIBBET	23
MY SOUL'S ANTENNAE ARE PREY TO SUCH PERTURBATIONS,	247	PIERROTS	7
BEHIND THEM? WHAT'S THERE? HER SOUL'S AN AFFAIR FOR OCULISTS.	247	PIERROTS	12
SOUND			
SOUND IN YOUR WIND PAST ALL SIGNS O' CORRUPTION.	13	MESMERISM	16
THERE'S NO SOUND LIKE TO SWORDS SWORDS OPPOSING,	29	ALTAFORTE	32
HOW IF THE LOW DEAR SOUND WITHIN THY THROAT	43	SATIEMUS	14
THE SPUR-CLINKS SOUND BETWEEN,	47	FROM HEINE: 7	26
MAKE A CLEAR SOUND,	75	THE ALCHEMIST	4
THERE IS NO SOUND OF FOOT-FALL, AND THE LEAVES ...	108	LIU CH'E	3
NO SOUND	115	SOCIAL ORDER	18
THEIR SOUND IS MIXED IN THIS FLUTE,	130	THE RIVER SONG	39
MANY INSTRUMENTS, LIKE THE SOUND OF YOUNG PHOENIX BROODS.	135	EXILE'S LETTER	27
WITH BOATS FLOATING, AND THE SOUND OF MOUTH ORGANS AND DRUMS,	135	EXILE'S LETTER	51
NO ONE HEARS AUGHT SAVE THE GRACIOUS SOUND OF COMPLIMENTS.	154	NEAR PERIGORD	120
SAFE AND SOUND	269	SAFE AND SOUND	T
AND MY FINANCE IS SOUND,	269	SAFE AND SOUND	2
SOUNDS			
OVER A THOUSAND GATES, OVER A THOUSAND DOORS ARE THE SOUNDS OF SPRING SINGING,	129	THE RIVER SONG	31
SPREAD OUT THEIR SOUNDS THROUGH THE GARDENS.	141	IDEA OF CHOAN	16
BUT MY SOUL, THE SORT WHICH HARSH SOUNDS DISTURB,	247	PIERROTS	17
MY NERVES STILL REGISTER THE SOUNDS OF CONTRA-BASS'	247	PIERROTS	19
SOURCE			
AND SAVE THEY KNOW'T ARIGHT FROM NATURE'S SOURCE	248	DONNA MI PREGA	10
IT IS NOT VIRTU, BUT PERFECTION'S SOURCE	249	DONNA MI PREGA	33
SOUS			
POUR QUATRE SOUS.	160	DANS OMNIBUS	23
SOUTH			
I HA' TAKEN TO RAMBLING THE SOUTH HERE.	22	MARVOIL	5
DAMN IT ALL! ALL THIS OUR SOUTH STINKS PEACE.	28	ALTAFORTE	1
FORK OUT TO SOUTH AND NORTH,	121	PROVINC DESERT	5
I HAVE LOOKED SOUTH FROM HAUTEFORT,	122	PROVINC DESERT	48
SOUTH OF THE POND THE WILLOW TIPS ARE HALF-BLUE AND BLUER,	129	THE RIVER SONG	25
BY THE SOUTH SIDE OF THE BRIDGE AT TEN-SHIN.	134	EXILE'S LETTER	3
AND THEN I WAS SENT OFF TO SOUTH WEI,	134	EXILE'S LETTER	12
AND ONCE AGAIN, LATER, WE MET AT THE SOUTH BRIDGEHEAD.	136	EXILE'S LETTER	70
THE SUN RISES IN SOUTH EAST CORNER OF THINGS	140	MULBERRY ROAD	1
SHE GETS THEM BY THE SOUTH WALL OF THE TOWN.	140	MULBERRY ROAD	7
SOUTH-FOLK			
SOUTH-FOLK IN COLD COUNTRY	139	SOUTH-FOLK	T
SOUTHWARD			
THINKING OF MONTAIGNAC, SOUTHWARD.	122	PROVINC DESERT	19
SOUTHWARD TOWARD MONTAIGNAC, AND HE BENDS AT A TABLE	154	NEAR PERIGORD	97
SPACE			
THEN LET US SMILE A LITTLE SPACE	44	HD. HOUSMAN	13
AND IN THE QUIETEST SPACE	155	NEAR PERIGORD	136
AND SO THE SPACE	236	MIDDLE-AGED	19
AND WILLS MAN LOOK INTO UNFORMED SPACE	250	DONNA MI PREGA	59

PAGE 381

SPACE -- SPEARS

```
                                                          PAGE    TITLE            LINE
SPACE  (CONTINUED)
    OR A BUYER OF SPACE IN THE PAPERS.    ...............   264   ALF'S EIGHTH       34
SPADE
    THAT'S WHAT YOU MEAN YOU ADVERTISING SPADE,   .......   162   CABARET DANCER     34
SPANGLES
    AN HOUR LATER: A SHOW OF CALVES AND SPANGLES,   .....   163   CABARET DANCER     82
SPANISH
    SPANISH AND PARIS, LOVE OF THE ARTS PART OF YOUR
       GEISHA-CULTURE!   ...............................    163   CABARET DANCER     52
    THAN SPANISH LADIES HAD IN OLD ROMANCES.  ..........    242   MOYEN SENSUEL     104
SPARKS
    WORDS THAT WERE WING'D AS HER SPARKS IN ERUPTION,        13   MESMERISM          14
    STRIKE SPARKS FROM THE COBBLED STREET   .............   111   IMAGE ORLEANS       7
SPARS
    STRANGE SPARS OF KNOWLEDGE AND DIMMED WARES OF PRICE.    61   PORTRAIT FEMME      5
SPASMS
    AND SCARE ITSELF TO SPASMS."   ......................   109   THE FAUN            9
SPATS
    THE STIFFNESS FROM SPATS TO COLLAR   ................   193   BRENNBAUM           3
    AND SPATS ABOVE MY SHOES,   .........................   266   ALF'S ELEVENTH     10
SPATTERING
    OR OF HECTOR SPATTERING WHEEL-RIMS,   ...............   208   SEXTUS PROP: 1     29
SPAWNED
    "AS FOOTLIN' A LOT AS WAS EVER SPAWNED   ...........    270   OF 600 M.P.'S      23
SPEAK
    STILL SHADE, AND BADE NO WHISPER SPEAK THE BIRDS OF
       HOW  .............................................    21   IN DURANCE         48
    AND IF THOU KNEW'ST I KNEW THEM WOULDST THOU SPEAK?      43   SATIEMUS            2
    SPEAK ONCE AGAIN FOR ITS SOLE STIMULATION,   ........    63   PHASELLUS ILLE     10
    LET THE GODS SPEAK SOFTLY OF US   ...................    67   DORIA               8
    THE EYES OF THIS DEAD LADY SPEAK TO ME,   ...........    73   THE PICTURE         1
    THE EYES OF THIS DEAD LADY SPEAK TO ME.   ...........    73   THE PICTURE         4
    THE EYES OF THIS DEAD LADY SPEAK TO ME.   ...........    73   JACOPO SELLAIO      6
    SHE WOULD LIKE SOME ONE TO SPEAK TO HER,   .........     83   THE GARDEN         10
    SPEAK OF THE INDECOROUS CONDUCT OF THE GODS!   ......    86   SALUTATION 2ND     30
    SPEAK OF THEIR KNEES AND ANKLES.   ..................    86   SALUTATION 2ND     33
    SPEAK AGAINST UNCONSCIOUS OPPRESSION,   ............     88   COMMISSION          6
    SPEAK AGAINST THE TYRANNY OF THE UNIMAGINATIVE,   ...    88   COMMISSION          7
    SPEAK AGAINST BONDS.   ..............................    88   COMMISSION          8
    BUT DO THOU SPEAK TRUE, EVEN TO THE LETTER:   .......    90   SURGIT FAMA        15
    YOU WHO CAN ONLY SPEAK,   ...........................    92   THE REST           11
    COME, MY SONGS, LET US SPEAK OF PERFECTION--   ......    99   SALVATIONISTS       1
    BUT IF YOU MOVE OR SPEAK   .........................    109   THE FAUN            7
    BUT HOWEVER WE LONG TO SPEAK   .....................    142   UNMOVING CLOUD     26
    WE SPEAK OF BURNISHED LAKES,   .....................    146   CANTILATIONS       11
    SHE WHO COULD NEVER SPEAK SAVE TO ONE PERSON,   .....   157   NEAR PERIGORD     190
    ("SPEAK UP! YOU HAVE DANCED SO STIFFLY?   ..........    159   PSYCHOLOG HOUR     31
    SHE MUST SPEAK OF THE TIME   .......................    166   FISH & SHADOW      18
    AND THOUGH I FEAR TO SPEAK OUT,   ..................    175   LANGUE D'OC: 3     35
    COULD I BUT SPEAK AS 'TWERE IN THE "RESTORATION"        238   MOYEN SENSUEL       7
    I SPEAK IN CONTRADICTIONS, SO TO SPEAK.)   .........    242   MOYEN SENSUEL     124
    I SPEAK IN CONTRADICTIONS, SO TO SPEAK.)   .........    242   MOYEN SENSUEL     124
SPEAKERS
    CLEAR SPEAKERS, NAKED IN THE SUN, UNTRAMMELLED.   ...    96   DUM CAPITOLIUM      8
    LET COME THE GRACEFUL SPEAKERS,   ..................    146   CANTILATIONS        8
SPEAKING
    AND FOR THIS, EVERY EARL WHATEVER, FOR THOSE
       SPEAKING AFTER--   ..............................     66   THE SEAFARER       73
    A LADY WITH LOOK SO SPEAKING   .....................    105   DOMPNA POIS         8
SPEAKS
    "NON TI FIDAR," IT IS THE SWORD THAT SPEAKS   ......     19   FOR E. MCC         13
    HE SPEAKS OF MY EXTENDED FAME,   ...................     46   FROM HEINE: 6       9
    AND YET EVERYONE SPEAKS EVIL OF DEATH.   ...........    164   QUINTUS SEPTIM      3
    AND SHE SPEAKS ILL OF LIGHT WOMEN,   ...............    218   SEXTUS PROP: 5     61
    WAS NEVER ONE OF WHOM ONE SPEAKS AS "BRAZEN'D."   ...   245   MOYEN SENSUEL     206
SPEAR
    SHE OF THE SPEAR STANDS PRESENT.   .................    147   BEFORE SLEEP        5
SPEARS
    AND I WATCH HIS SPEARS THROUGH THE DARK CLASH   ....     29   ALTAFORTE          20
    AYE HE SENT US OUT THROUGH THE CROSSED HIGH SPEARS       33   GOODLY FERE         9
```

PAGE 382

SPECIAL -- SPIRITS

```
                                                          PAGE    TITLE              LINE
SPECIAL
    NOW I REMEMBER THAT YOU BUILT ME A SPECIAL TAVERN      134    EXILE'S LETTER       2
    BALLAD FOR THE TIMES' SPECIAL SILVER NUMBER  .......   267    ALF'S TWELFTH      SUB
SPECIALIST
    LIES FROM THE SPECIALIST  .........................   261    ALF'S SIXTH          7
SPECTATOR
    REJUVENATE EVEN "THE SPECTATOR."  ..................    86    SALUTATION 2ND      25
SPED
    STANDETH THIS IMAGE OF THE BEAUTY SPED.  ..........    41    HER MONUMENT         9
    ALL THE FLAMES ARE DEAD AND SPED NOW  .............    45    FROM HEINE: 3        5
SPEECH
    SPEECH? WORDS? FAUGH! WHO TALKS OF WORDS AND LOVE?!    31    PIERE VIDAL         33
    OUT OF A TURMOIL OF SPEECH ABOUT YOU.  .............    36    FRANCESCA            4
    SPEECH FOR PSYCHE IN THE GOLDEN BOOK OF APULEIUS       39    FOR PSYCHE           T
    HOW IS THE NOBLEST OF THY SPEECH AND THOUGHT  ......    42    HER MONUMENT        55
    SIGHING AS THOU DOST THROUGH THE GOLDEN SPEECH."       43    SATIEMUS             6
    GO WITH AN OPEN SPEECH.  ..........................    89    COMMISSION          23
    HER STRAIGHT SPEECH FREE-RUNNING,  ................   105    DOMPNA POIS         29
    THE LONE MAN SITS WITH SHUT SPEECH,  ..............   139    SENNIN POEM          6
    YOU SWORN FOE TO FREE SPEECH AND GOOD LETTERS,  ...   145    SALUTATION 3RD      11
    TAKE HIS OWN SPEECH, MAKE WHAT YOU WILL OF IT--  ..   153    NEAR PERIGORD       79
    SHALL PRAISE THY SPEECH  ..........................   250    DONNA MI PREGA      90
SPEECHES
    WHAT IF I KNOW THY SPEECHES WORD BY WORD?  ........    43    SATIEMUS             1
    WHAT IF I KNOW THY SPEECHES WORD BY WORD,  ........    43    SATIEMUS             3
SPEED
    AND YET; FULL SPEED  ..............................    14    FAMAM CANO          27
SPEEDILY
    GOD DAMN HIS HELL OUT SPEEDILY  ...................    12    OF THE GIBBET       42
    AND MAY I COME SPEEDILY TO BEZIERS  ...............    23    MARVOIL             32
SPEEDING
    MUTE MIRROR OF THE FLIGHT OF SPEEDING YEARS,  .....    41    HER MONUMENT         6
SPELLS
    STRANGE SPELLS OF OLD DEITY,  .....................     6    CINO                 6
    WHEN SPELLS ARE ALWAY RENEWED ON HER?  ............    72    DIEU! QU'IL          6
SPENT
    AND DIRE SEA-SURGE, AND THERE I OFT SPENT  ........    64    THE SEAFARER         6
    NOW OVER AND SPENT,  ..............................   236    MIDDLE-AGED         14
SPHERE
    THE SWIRLING SPHERE HAS OPENED  ...................   169    PHANOPOEIA           8
SPHERES
    OF BLISSFUL KINGDOMS AND THE AUREATE SPHERES;  ....    42    HER MONUMENT        34
    AND THE SPHERES THEY BELONG IN,  ..................    52    AU SALON             3
SPIDERS
    "BLACK SPIDERS SPIN IN HER BED!  ..................   215    SEXTUS PROP: 4      35
SPIKE
    PLUMB THE SPIKE OF THE TARGE.  ....................   250    DONNA MI PREGA      81
SPIKED
    SPIKED BREAST TO SPIKED BREAST OPPOSING!  .........    28    ALTAFORTE           15
    SPIKED BREAST TO SPIKED BREAST OPPOSING!  .........    28    ALTAFORTE           15
    SHE TWIDDLES THE SPIKED WHEEL OF A RHOMBUS,  ......   215    SEXTUS PROP: 4      32
    SPIKED ONTO OLYMPUS,  .............................   217    SEXTUS PROP: 5      40
SPIN
    "BLACK SPIDERS SPIN IN HER BED!  ..................   215    SEXTUS PROP: 4      35
    WE SHALL SPIN LONG YARNS OUT OF NOTHING.  .........   217    SEXTUS PROP: 5      36
SPINE
    DOWN RODYHEAVER'S PROPHYLACTIC SPINE,  ............   246    MOYEN SENSUEL      225
SPIRAL
    IN THE FLAT PROJECTION OF A SPIRAL.  ..............   147    BEFORE SLEEP        16
SPIRIT
    AYE, I AM WISTFUL FOR MY KIN OF THE SPIRIT  .......    20    IN DURANCE          17
    THE ARCANE SPIRIT OF THE WHOLE MANKIND  ...........    42    HER MONUMENT        44
    FIT FOR YOUR SPIRIT TO DWELL IN.  .................   110    COITUS               6
    AND MY SPIRIT SO HIGH IT WAS ALL OVER THE HEAVENS,    135    EXILE'S LETTER      32
    MIND AND SPIRIT DRIVE ON THE FEATHERY BANNERS.  ...   139    SOUTH-FOLK           9
    DULNESS HERSELF, THAT ABJECT SPIRIT, CHORTLES  ....   000    MOYEN SENSUEL       31
    THAT FED HIS SPIRIT; WERE HIS MENTAL MEALS.  ......   241    MOYEN SENSUEL       90
    TO FOLLOW A NOBLE SPIRIT,  ........................   250    DONNA MI PREGA      77
SPIRITS
    VIERNA, JOCELYNN, DARING OF SPIRITS,  .............    76    THE ALCHEMIST       41
    THREE SPIRITS CAME TO ME  .........................    92    APRIL                1
```

PAGE 383

SPIRITS -- SPRAY

	PAGE	TITLE	LINE
SPIRITS (CONTINUED)			
WIT, NOR GOOD SPIRITS, NOR THE PLEASING ATTITUDES	101	AMITIES	11
AND IT IS TO BE HOPED THAT THEIR SPIRITS WILL WALK	115	SOCIAL ORDER	14
"THOUGH SPIRITS ARE CELEBRATED FOR ADULTERY.	225	SEXTUS PROP:10	40
SPIRITUAL			
IN SPIRITUAL ASPIRATIONS, BUT HE FOUND IT PROFITABLE,	246	MOYEN SENSUEL	234
SPIRITUEL			
IN MOST SPIRITUEL POSITIONS, ...	46	FROM HEINE: 6	14
SPIT			
LET US SPIT UPON THOSE WHO PAT THE BIG-BELLIES FOR PROFIT, ...	145	SALUTATION 3RD	15
SPITE			
YOU, MASTER BOB BROWNING, SPITE YOUR APPAREL	13	MESMERISM	7
IN SPITE OF YOUR OBVIOUS FLAWS, ...	101	AMITIES	15
SPITTING			
DESTROYERS, BOMBS AND SPITTING MITRAILLEUSES.	265	ALF'S NINTH	21
SPLASH			
IT IS GOOD TO SPLASH IN THE WATER	147	POST MORTEM	4
SPLASHED			
WHEN WE SPLASHED AND WERE SPLASHED WITH	104	ANCORA	14
WHEN WE SPLASHED AND WERE SPLASHED WITH	104	ANCORA	14
SPLENDID			
AND TURN MY MIND UPON THAT SPLENDID MADNESS, ...	30	PIERE VIDAL	2
GOD! SHE WAS WHITE THEN, SPLENDID AS SOME TOMB	31	PIERE VIDAL	38
IN ALL THEIR SPLENDID GEAR.	47	FROM HEINE: 7	24
FOLK OF UNEARTHLY FASHION, PLACES SPLENDID, ...	50	THE FLAME	24
SPLENDOUR			
THAT SEEMS TO BE SOME QUIVERING SPLENDOUR CAST	41	HER MONUMENT	29
THE HOUSE OF SPLENDOUR	49	OF SPLENDOUR	T
SPLENDOURS			
EXULTED, THEY BEHELD THE SPLENDOURS OF CLEOPATRA.	93	LES MILLWIN	10
SPLIT			
TO LIFT YOU UP THROUGH SPLIT AIR, ...	226	SEXTUS PROP:11	9
SPLITS			
SPLITS THE TWO STREAMS APART.	138	CITY OF CHOAN	10
SPLITTING			
SPLITTING ITS BEERY JOWL	52	AU SALON	22
SPOIL			
I WILL NOT SPOIL MY SHEATH WITH LESSER BRIGHTNESS,	71	A VIRGINAL	2
SPOILERS			
SPOILERS OF PLEASURE, ...	173	LANGUE D'OC: 2	27
SPOILING			
SPOILING HIS VISIT, WITH A YEAR BEFORE THE NEXT ONE.	154	NEAR PERIGORD	113
SPOILS			
PHYLLIDULA AND THE SPOILS OF GOUVERNET	167	OF AROUET	ST
SPOKE			
WAS ANGRY WHEN THEY SPOKE YOUR NAME	36	FRANCESCA	6
AND WE ALL SPOKE OUT OUR HEARTS AND MINDS, AND WITHOUT REGRET.	134	EXILE'S LETTER	11
AND SHE SPOKE TO ME OF THE MONARCH, ...	180	MOEURS CON: 5	26
SO SPOKE THE AUTHOR OF "THE DORIAN MOOD,"	193	SIENA MI FE	16
SO SPOKE. AND THE NOOSE WAS OVER MY NECK.	224	SEXTUS PROP:10	13
SPOKE'			
WI' TWEY WORDS SPOKE' SUDDENTLY.	34	GOODLY FERE	48
SPOKEN			
HE HAD SPOKEN, AND POINTED ME A PLACE WITH HIS PLECTRUM:	211	SEXTUS PROP: 2	28
SPOKEN-AGAINST			
MISTRUSTED, SPOKEN-AGAINST, ...	92	THE REST	5
SPOON			
AND THOSE BORN WITH A SILVER SPOON, ...	266	ALF'S TENTH	14
SPORTS			
FROM DRESS GOODS ADS, AND SPORTS.	266	ALF'S ELEVENTH	20
SPOT			
FOR PUTTING SILVER ON THE SPOT, ...	267	ALF'S TWELFTH	11
SPRANG			
SEE, THE LIGHT GRASS SPRANG UP TO PILLOW THEE, ...	60	TOMB AKR CAAR	6
SPRAWLING			
AN' THEM SPRAWLING ON THE BENCHES	270	OF 600 M.P.'S	14
SPRAY			
THE CLOUDS THAT ARE SPRAY TO ITS SEA.	7	CINO	56

PAGE 384

SPRAY -- SQUABBLE

	PAGE	TITLE	LINE
SPRAY (CONTINUED)			
OF SUN AND SPRAY ALL SHATTERED AT THE BOWS;	21	IN DURANCE	37
WITH SPRAY ON HIS PINION.	64	THE SEAFARER	25
THE LUCID CASTALIAN SPRAY,	104	ANCORA	15
SPRAYS			
AND BOTTICELLIAN SPRAYS IMPLIED	200	MAUBERLEY: 2	28
SPREAD			
SPREAD HIS LEAVES OVER ME, AND THE YOKE	4	LA FRAISNE	11
HER GOLD IS SPREAD, ABOVE, AROUND, INWOVEN;	49	OF SPLENDOUR	4
HER HAIR WAS SPREAD ABOUT, A SHEAF OF WINGS,	49	OF SPLENDOUR	7
EAGER TO SPREAD THEM WITH RUMOUR;	90	SURGIT FAMA	11
AND THE GLOW OF YOUTH THAT SHE SPREAD ABOUT US	116	THE TEA SHOP	6
WILL BE SPREAD ABOUT US NO LONGER.	116	THE TEA SHOP	8
A TURMOIL OF WARS-MEN, SPREAD OVER THE MIDDLE KINGDOM,	133	FRONTIER GUARD	15
THE HUNDRED CORDS OF MIST ARE SPREAD THROUGH	141	IDEA OF CHOAN	13
SPREAD OUT THEIR SOUNDS THROUGH THE GARDENS.	141	IDEA OF CHOAN	16
SPREAD LIKE THE FINGER-TIPS OF ONE FRAIL HAND;	152	NEAR PERIGORD	30
SPREAD ON BOTH HANDS AND ON THE UP-PUSHED-BOSOM--	161	CABARET DANCER	15
I SEE THE SIGNS UPON THE WELKIN SPREAD,	172	LANGUE D'OC: 1	15
TUNIC SPREAD IN DELAY;	220	SEXTUS PROP: 7	6
SAILS SPREAD ON CERULEAN WATERS, I WOULD SHED TEARS FOR TWO;	223	SEXTUS PROP: 9	7
SPREADING			
SPREADING ITS RAYS, IT TENDETH NEVER DOWN	249	DONNA MI PREGA	29
SPREADS			
SPREADS THE BRIGHT TIPS,	87	THE SPRING	5
SPRING			
THE WORDS ARE AS LEAVES, OLD BROWN LEAVES IN THE SPRING TIME	16	PRAISE YSOLT	19
AS THE SPRING UPON THE BOUGH	17	PRAISE YSOLT	49
WHEN IT IS AUTUMN DO WE GET SPRING WEATHER,	59	SILET	7
SOFT AS SPRING WIND THAT'S COME FROM BIRCHEN BOWERS.	71	A VIRGINAL	10
THE SPRING	87	THE SPRING	T
CYDONIAN SPRING WITH HER ATTENDANT TRAIN,	87	THE SPRING	1
ARE THRUSTING AT THE SPRING AIR.	110	COITUS	2
SPRING	112	PAPYRUS	1
WHEN WE SET OUT, THE WILLOWS WERE DROOPING WITH SPRING,	127	BOWMEN OF SHU	21
THE PURPLE HOUSE AND THE CRIMSON ARE FULL OF SPRING SOFTNESS.	129	THE RIVER SONG	24
OVER A THOUSAND GATES, OVER A THOUSAND DOORS ARE THE SOUNDS OF SPRING SINGING,	129	THE RIVER SONG	31
A GRACIOUS SPRING, TURNED TO BLOOD-RAVENOUS AUTUMN,	133	FRONTIER GUARD	14
"WET SPRINGTIME," SAYS TO-EM MEI, "WET SPRING IN THE GARDEN."	142	UNMOVING CLOUD EPI	
BEWILDERING SPRING, AND BY THE AUVEZERE	157	NEAR PERIGORD	170
"ANIENAN SPRING WATER FALLS INTO FLAT-SPREAD POOLS."	212	SEXTUS PROP: 3	5
SPRINGS			
"AND TWO SPRINGS HAVE PASSED US."	166	FISH & SHADOW	12
SPRING'S			
IT IS LIKE THE FLOWERS FALLING AT SPRING'S END	136	EXILE'S LETTER	73
SPRINGTIME			
"WET SPRINGTIME," SAYS TO-EM-MEI, "WET SPRING IN THE GARDEN."	142	UNMOVING CLOUD EPI	
WHEN THE SPRINGTIME IS SWEET	173	LANGUE D'OC: 2	1
SPUN			
SO SILENT LIGHT; NO GOSSAMER IS SPUN	38	BALLATETTA	7
SPUN IN KING MINOS' HALL	204	MEDALLION	11
SPUR			
SPUR WITHOUT REASON,	111	IMAGE ORLEANS	
SPUR-CLINKS			
THE SPUR-CLINKS SOUND BETWEEN,	47	FROM HEINE: 7	26
SPURS			
SHARP PEAKS, HIGH SPURS, DISTANT CASTLES.	122	PROVINC DESERT	55
SPUR'S			
THE VERY SPUR'S END, BUILT ON SHEEREST CLIFF,	153	NEAR PERIGORD	58
SPURTED			
GOD! HOW THE SWIFTEST HIND'S BLOOD SPURTED HOT	30	PIERE VIDAL	14
SQUABBLE			
SAVE A SQUABBLE OF FEMALE CONNECTIONS.	115	SOCIAL ORDER	19

PAGE 385

SQUARE -- STALKS

		PAGE	TITLE	LINE
SQUARE				
	THE SWIRL OF LIGHT FOLLOWS ME THROUGH THE SQUARE,	169	PHANOPOEIA	1
SQUARED				
	KNEW THE LOW FLOODED LANDS SQUARED OUT WITH POPLARS,	157	NEAR PERIGORD	174
SQUATS				
	THE MAN WHO FEARS WAR AND SQUATS OPPOSING	29	ALTAFORTE	25
SQUEALS				
	AND DAVID'S HARP LET OUT HEART-RENDING SQUEALS:	264	ALF'S NINTH	15
SQUIRE				
	THE GOOD SQUIRE BELLAIRE;	97	THE BELLAIRES	12
	FOR THEY MAY NOT BELONG TO THE GOOD SQUIRE BELLAIRE	98	THE BELLAIRES	14
	WHEREFORE THE GOOD SQUIRE BELLAIRE	98	THE BELLAIRES	34
S---'S				
	STILL DR. S---'S	261	ALF'S SIXTH	18
SST				
	"SST! MY GOOD FELLOW, ART AWAKE OR SLEEPING?	172	LANGUE D'OC: 1	6
ST.				
	THAT PLUNDERED ST. HUBERT BACK O' THE FANE:	12	OF THE GIBBET	32
	SHE'D FIND A MODEL FOR ST. ANTHONY	63	PHASELLUS ILLE	13
	OF ST. JOHN,	119	THE GYPSY	15
	RIGHT ENOUGH? THEN READ BETWEEN THE LINES OF UC ST. CIRC,	151	NEAR PERIGORD	3
	(ST. LEIDER HAD DONE AS MUCH AS POLHONAC,	153	NEAR PERIGORD	86
	AND PRAY TO GOD THAT IS ST. MARY'S SON,	172	LANGUE D'OC: 1	19
	TO FLEET ST. WHERE	196	HUGH SELWIN:12	23
	THE POMPS OF FLEET ST., FESTERING YEAR ON YEAR,	260	ALF'S FIFTH	5
	IN THESE QUARTERS OR FLEET ST.?	263	ALF'S EIGHTH	14
STA				
	AND IN VAIN THEY COMMANDED HIM TO STA FERMO!	97	AESTHETICS	15
STABLES				
	FOURTEEN HUNTERS STILL EAT IN THE STABLES OF	97	THE BELLAIRES	11
STABLISHED				
	OR THAT HE HATH NOT STABLISHED SEIGNIORY	249	DONNA MI PREGA	47
STAG				
	THE WHITE STAG	25	THE WHITE STAG	T
	"'TIS THE WHITE STAG, FAME, WE'RE A-HUNTING,	25	THE WHITE STAG	6
STAGE				
	FLARES ON THE CROWDED STAGE BEFORE OUR TABLES	162	CABARET DANCER	22
	AND EDWARD'S MISTRESSES STILL LIGHT THE STAGE,	163	CABARET DANCER	73
	SOMETHING FOR THE MODERN STAGE,	188	HUGH SELWYN: 2	3
STAGNANT				
	SHAKE UP THE STAGNANT POOL OF ITS CONVICTIONS;	63	PHASELLUS ILLE	8
STAGS				
	WHEN TALL STAGS FLED ME THROUGH THE ALDER BRAKES,	30	PIERE VIDAL	9
STAIN				
	WHO GAVE THIS POIGNARD ITS PREMIER STAIN	11	OF THE GIBBET	8
STAINETH				
	RAINETH DROP AND STAINETH SLOP,	116	ANCIENT MUSIC	3
STAINING				
	WITH A BLACK TINT STAINING YOUR CUTICLE,	162	CABARET DANCER	49
STAIR				
	THY SATINS MAKE UPON THE STAIR,	8	NA AUDIART	22
	SHE CAME INTO THE LARGE ROOM BY THE STAIR,	166	FISH & SHADOW	7
STAIRS				
	SHE DOES NOT GET UP THE STAIRS SO EAGERLY;	116	THE TEA SHOP	4
	I HAVE CLIMBED RICKETY STAIRS, HEARD TALK OF CROY,	122	PROVINC DESERT	38
	UP STAIRS, THE THIRD FLOOR UP, AND HAVE SUCH QUANDARIES	244	MOYEN SENSUEL	158
	"THEM STAIRS! THEM STAIRS, THEM GORDAM STAIRS	271	OLE KATE	5
	"THEM STAIRS! THEM STAIRS, THEM GORDAM STAIRS	271	OLE KATE	5
	"THEM STAIRS! THEM STAIRS, THEM GORDAM STAIRS	271	OLE KATE	5
STAIRS'				
	THE JEWEL STAIRS' GRIEVANCE	132	JEWEL STAIRS'	T
STALE				
	LAUGHS AT, AND GROWS STALE;	14	FAMAM CANO	14
	AND NOW YOU ARE STALE AND WORN OUT,	114	EPILOGUE	5
	WHO WROUGHT ABOUT HIS "SOUL" THEIR STALE INFECTION.	241	MOYEN SENSUEL	81
	(MY COUNTRY, I'VE SAID YOUR MORALS AND YOUR THOUGHTS ARE STALE ONES,	243	MOYEN SENSUEL	149
STALKS				
	FLARE UP WITH SCARLET ORANGE ON STIFF STALKS	162	CABARET DANCER	20

STALKS -- STARTIN'

	PAGE	TITLE	LINE
STALKS (CONTINUED)			
THEIR STALKS ARE WOVEN IN BASKETS,	221	SEXTUS PROP: 7	30
STALL			
BACKLESS COPY FROM THE STALL,	15	FAMAM CANO	39
STALWART			
WHILE YOU STALWART SHEEP OF FREEDOM	269	SAFE AND SOUND	7
STAMP			
STAMP ON HIS ROOF OR IN THE GLAZING LIGHT	236	MIDDLE-AGED	5
STAND			
HERE THEY STAND WITHOUT QUAINT DEVICES,	85	SALUTATION 2ND	7
YOU STAND ABOUT IN THE STREETS,	94	INSTRUCTIONS	5
SEEK EVER TO STAND IN THE HARD SOPHOCLEAN LIGHT	95	ITE	3
CRAWL IN THE VERY BLACK GUTTER BENEATH THE GRAPE STAND?	114	SIMULACRA	4
AND THE PRINCES STILL STAND IN ROWS, ABOUT THE THRONE,	131	AT TEN-SHIN	10
THEY STAND AND TWIRL THEIR MOUSTACHES.	140	MULBERRY ROAD	17
I BOW MY HEAD AND STAND STILL.	142	UNMOVING CLOUD	9
AND NOW PROPERTIUS OF CYNTHIA, TAKING HIS STAND AMONG THESE.	230	SEXTUS PROP:12	75
TO STAND WITH OTHER	250	DONNA MI PREGA	92
OR WHY WE SHOULD STAND TO ATTENTION	264	ALF'S EIGHTH	30
THEY HAVE TO STAND ABOUT IN MUD	266	ALF'S ELEVENTH	13
STANDARDS			
BUT AH! WHEN I SEE THE STANDARDS GOLD, VAIR, PURPLE, OPPOSING	28	ALTAFORTE	4
STANDETH			
STANDETH THIS IMAGE OF THE BEAUTY SPED.	41	HER MONUMENT	9
THAT ANY EARTH-WEAL ETERNAL STANDETH	66	THE SEAFARER	68
STANDING			
BREAK DOWN THE FOUR-SQUARE WALLS OF STANDING TIME.	49	OF SPLENDOUR	21
SEEING THAT LONG STANDING INCREASES ALL THINGS	207	SEXTUS PROP: 1	24
STANDS			
THAT WHICH STANDS FIRM IN THEE TIME BATTERS DOWN,	40	ROME	13
THE DRYAD STANDS IN MY COURT-YARD	110	TEMPORA	2
RIU'S HOUSE STANDS OUT ON THE SKY,	141	IDEA OF CHOAN	26
SHE OF THE SPEAR STANDS PRESENT.	147	BEFORE SLEEP	5
WITH THE NOBLEST THAT STANDS IN MEN'S SIGHT,	174	LANGUE D'OC: 3	13
WHERE SHE STANDS,	176	LANGUE D'OC: 3	76
STANDS GENIUS A DEATHLESS ADORNMENT,	209	SEXTUS PROP: 1	72
AMOR STANDS UPON YOU, LOVE DRIVES UPON LOVERS,	226	SEXTUS PROP:11	11
STAR			
SLEEP THOU NO MORE. I SEE THE STAR UPLEAPING	172	LANGUE D'OC: 1	7
STARK			
THAT MAKE THE STARK WINDS REEK WITH FEAR	10	FOR THIS YULE	12
STARK, KEEN, TRIUMPHANT, TILL IT PLAYS AT DEATH.	31	PIERE VIDAL	37
STARS			
SINGING THE STARS IN THE TURRETS OF BEZIERS,	22	MARVOIL	13
AND THY STARS	27	NIGHT LITANY	41
EVEN AS ARE THY STARS	27	NIGHT LITANY	45
CLEAR, DEEP, TRANSLUCENT, SO THE STARS ME SEEMED	30	PIERE VIDAL	21
MOCK NOT THE FLOOD OF STARS, THE THING'S TO BE.	69	THE NEEDLE	8
AND BEFORE THE END OF THE DAY WE WERE SCATTERED LIKE STARS, OR RAIN.	135	EXILE'S LETTER	33
NEITHER EXPENSIVE PYRAMIDS SCRAPING THE STARS IN THEIR ROUTE,	200	SEXTUS PROP: 1	66
THE STARS WILL POINT OUT THE STUMBLES,	212	SEXTUS PROP: 3	21
WHILE A BLACK VEIL WAS OVER HER STARS,	222	SEXTUS PROP: 8	26
START			
WHERE THY BODICE LACES START	8	NA AUDIART	3
IN THE OLD SENSE. WRONG FROM THE START--	187	E. P. ODE	4
AND START TO INSPECT SOME FURTHER PYRAMID;	236	MIDDLE-AGED	7
FROM FORM SEEN DOTH HE START, THAT, UNDERSTOOD,	249	DONNA MI PREGA	24
HOW THEY BETTER START TAKIN' CARE,	262	ALF'S SEVENTH	4
AND LET THE BLIGHTERS START IT ALL OVER AGAIN,	265	ALF'S NINTH	30
STARTED			
HAVE STARTED A INVESTIGATION	268	ANOTHER BIT	3
WAS I STARTED WRONG AS A KIDDIE,	268	ANOTHER BIT	13
STARTIN'			
STARTIN' IN ABOUT 6 A. M.	271	OLE KATE	11

STARVED -- STEEL-BLUE

	PAGE	TITLE	LINE
STARVED			
LOVERS OF BEAUTY, STARVED,	92	THE REST	6
STATE			
GIVEN TO MORTAL STATE	42	HER MONUMENT	32
FOR WE SHALL CONSIDER THEM AND THEIR STATE	99	SALVATIONISTS	8
MY LOVE AND I KEEP STATE	171	LANGUE D'OC	EPI
OF THIS TO RELATION OF THE STATE	201	AGE DEMANDED	14
O STATE SANS SONG, SANS HOME-GROWN WINE, SANS REALIST!	241	MOYEN SENSUEL	88
IN MEMORY'S LOCUS TAKETH HE HIS STATE	248	DONNA MI PREGA	19
NEVER THEREAFTER, BUT MOVES CHANGING STATE,	249	DONNA MI PREGA	52
THUS ROSE IN ALBION, AND TICKLED THE STATE	264	ALF'S NINTH	11
STATED			
IF HOMER HAD NOT STATED YOUR CASE!	208	SEXTUS PROP: 1	34
STATELY			
STATELY, TALL AND LOVELY TENDER	8	NA AUDIART	7
I WITH MY BEAK HAULED ASHORE WOULD PROCEED IN A MORE STATELY MANNER,	216	SEXTUS PROP: 5	10
STATES			
FOR MENCKEN STATES SOMEWHERE, IN THIS CONNECTION:	238	MOYEN SENSUEL	10
STATION			
IN A STATION OF THE METRO	109	IN THE METRO	T
TOLD HER WOULD FIT HER STATION.	195	HUGH SELWIN:11	8
THAN I CAN FROM THIS DISTANT LAND AND STATION,	243	MOYEN SENSUEL	154
STATISTICS			
HID HEALTH STATISTICS, DODGED THE LABOUR ACTS.	260	ALF'S FIFTH	8
HID MORE STATISTICS, MORE FEARED TO CONFESS	260	ALF'S FIFTH	11
STATUARY			
THE PARTHIANS SHALL GET USED TO OUR STATUARY	219	SEXTUS PROP: 6	9
STATUE			
FROM THE STATUE OF THE INFANT CHRIST IN SANTA MARIA NOVELLA,	94	INSTRUCTIONS	20
STATUES			
WE SEEM AS STATUES ROUND WHOSE HIGH-RISEN BASE	32	PARACELSUS	11
FOR TWO GROSS OF BROKEN STATUES,	191	HUGH SELWYN: 5	7
STATURE			
TALL STATURE AND GAIETY,	106	DOMPNA POIS	57
BEL MIRAL'S STATURE, THE VISCOUNTESS' THROAT,	151	NEAR PERIGORD	8
STAUNCHES			
AS WINTER'S WOUND WITH HER SLEIGHT HAND SHE STAUNCHES,	71	A VIRGINAL	12
STAVE			
SINGING A DIFFERENT STAVE, AS CLOSELY HIDDEN.)	153	NEAR PERIGORD	87
STAY			
DEAD MEN STAY ALWAY DEAD MEN,	47	FROM HEINE: 7	17
IF MY HEART STAY BELOW THERE,	47	FROM HEINE: 7	21
SHE WILL NEITHER STAY IN, NOR COME OUT.	179	MOEURS CON: 2	11
STAYED			
AND WHERE HE ONCE SET FOOT, RIGHT THERE HE STAYED.	264	ALF'S NINTH	12
STAYS			
HOW THE STAYS PLY BACK FROM IT;	8	NA AUDIART	15
THE MIND OF RADWAY, WHENE'ER HE FOUND A PAIR OF PURPLE STAYS OR	245	MOYEN SENSUEL	196
UPON A DUSK THAT IS COME FROM MARS AND STAYS.	248	DONNA MI PREGA	21
OR WRIES THE FACE WITH FEAR AND LITTLE STAYS,	250	DONNA MI PREGA	54
STEADY			
LET US EXPRESS OUR ENVY OF THE MAN WITH A STEADY JOB AND NO WORRY ABOUT THE FUTURE.	94	INSTRUCTIONS	2
THEY GOT NO STEADY TRADE,	257	BREAD BRIGADE	10
STEALS			
WHEN HER LOVE LOOK STEALS ON ME.	175	LANGUE D'OC: 3	41
STEAM			
IN THE CREAM GILDED CABIN OF HIS STEAM YACHT	194	MR. NIXON	1
STEEDS			
CAUSING THEIR STEEDS TO LEAP.	111	IMAGE ORLEANS	4
AS THE RED-BEAKED STEEDS OF	201	AGE DEMANDED	3
STEEL			
WHO CAN NOT STEEL YOURSELVES INTO REITERATION;	92	THE REST	12
MELTING ON STEEL.	155	NEAR PERIGORD	135
STEEL-BLUE			
SHIELD O' STEEL-BLUE, TH' HEAVEN O'ER US	7	CINO	44

STEELY -- STILL

	PAGE	TITLE	LINE
STEELY			
OPEN LIES THE LAND, YET THE STEELY GOING	68	APPARUIT	10
STEEP			
THEY SAY THE ROADS OF SANSO ARE STEEP,	138	NEAR SHOKU	1
STELE			
STELE	181	MOEURS CON: 6	SUB
STELLAR			
COME, OR THE STELLAR TIDE WILL SLIP AWAY.	69	THE NEEDLE	1
STENCHES			
AND A LOT OF SMALL STREET STENCHES.	270	OF 600 M.P.'S	16
STENDHAL			
AND INNOCENT OF STENDHAL, FLAUBERT, MAUPASSANT AND FIELDING.	240	MOYEN SENSUEL	52
STEP			
"HERE ONE MAN HASTENED HIS STEP.	122	PROVINC DESERT	46
M. VEROG, OUT OF STEP WITH THE DECADE,	193	SIENA MI FE	17
BENEATH THEIR TRANSITORY STEP AND MERRIMENT,	236	MIDDLE-AGED	9
STEPPING			
STEPPING BENEATH A BOISTEROUS WIND FROM THRACE,	87	THE SPRING	3
STEPS			
THE JEWELLED STEPS ARE ALREADY QUITE WHITE WITH DEW,	132	JEWEL STAIRS'	1
HAUGHTY THEIR STEPS AS THEY GO IN TO GREAT BANQUETS,	132	AT TEN-SHIN	19
STERILE			
THE STERILE EGG THAT IS STILL EATABLE:	240	MOYEN SENSUEL	49
STERN			
STORMS, ON THE STONE-CLIFFS BEATEN, FELL ON THE STERN	64	THE SEAFARER	23
STEW			
BUT SOME SILVER SET TO STEW	267	ALF'S TWELFTH	17
STEWS			
"SHE STEWS PUFFED FROGS, SNAKE'S BONES, THE MOULTED FEATHERS OF SCREECH OWLS,	215	SEXTUS PROP: 4	33
STICK			
OH, NO, I WILL STICK IT OUT,	145	SALUTATION 3RD	27
STICKING			
AND STICKING OUT ALL THE WAY ROUND;	181,	MOEURS CON: 7	5
STICKS			
HE PLAGUES ME WITH JIBES AND STICKS,	237	ABU SALAMMAMM	29
WHAT IT KNEW THEN, IT KNOWS, AND THERE IT STICKS.	240	MOYEN SENSUEL	56
STIFF			
FLARE UP WITH SCARLET ORANGE ON STIFF STALKS	162	CABARET DANCER	20
SILK, STIFF AND LARGE ABOVE THE LACERTUS,	180	MOEURS CON: 5	4
NOR ARE MY CAVERNS STUFFED STIFF WITH A MARCIAN VINTAGE,	209	SEXTUS PROP: 1	56
RAING DOWN AND SO ENRICHES SOME STIFF CASE,	236	MIDDLE-AGED	17
STIFFENED			
STIFFENED OUR FACE WITH THE BACKWASH OF PHILETAS THE COAN.	211	SEXTUS PROP: 2	54
STIFFLY			
("SPEAK UP! YOU HAVE DANCED SO STIFFLY?	159	PSYCHOLOG HOUR	31
STIFFNESS			
THE STIFFNESS FROM SPATS TO COLLAR	193	BRENNBAUM	3
STILL			
I STOOD STILL AND WAS A TREE AMID THE WOOD,	3	THE TREE	1
BY THE STILL POOL OF MAR-NAN-OTHA	4	LA FRAISNE	13
BUT STILL CAME THE LEAF WORDS, LITTLE BROWN ELF WORDS	17	PRAISE YSOLT	33
STILL SHADE, AND DADE NO WHISPER SPEAK THE BIRDS OF HOW	21	IN DURANCE	18
SILENT MY MATE CAME AS THE NIGHT WAS STILL.	31	PIERE VIDAL	32
O GLANCE, WHEN THOU WAST STILL AS THOU ART NOW,	41	HER MONUMENT	10
AND STILL WHEN FATE RECALLETH,	41	HER MONUMENT	22
NO, NO! GO FROM ME. I HAVE STILL THE FLAVOUR,	71	A VIRGINAL	9
FOURTEEN HUNTERS STILL EAT IN THE STABLES OF	97	THE BELLAIRES	11
SCURRY INTO HEAPS AND LIE STILL,	108	LIU CH'E	4
WHILE MY HAIR WAS STILL CUT STRAIGHT ACROSS MY FOREHEAD	130	RIVER-MER WIFE	1
AND THE PRINCES STILL STAND IN ROWS ABOUT THE THRONE,	131	AT TEN-SHIN	10
BECAUSE HIS LONG SLEEVES WOULDN'T KEEP STILL	135	EXILE'S LETTER	29
AND I WAS STILL GOING, LATE IN THE YEAR,	135	EXILE'S LETTER	42
I BOW MY HEAD AND STAND STILL.	142	UNMOVING CLOUD	9
WITH MINDS STILL HOVERING ABOVE THEIR TESTICLES	148	FRATRES MINORE	1

PAGE 389

STILL -- STOMACH

	PAGE	TITLE	LINE
STILL (CONTINUED)			
STILL SIGH OVER ESTABLISHED AND NATURAL FACT	148	FRATRES MINORE	3
AND STILL THE KNOT, THE FIRST KNOT, OF MAENT?	153	NEAR PERIGORD	80
SURELY I SAW, AND STILL BEFORE MY EYES	156	NEAR PERIGORD	163
NELL GWYNN'S STILL HERE, DESPITE THE REFORMATION,	163	CABARET DANCER	72
AND EDWARD'S MISTRESSES STILL LIGHT THE STAGE,	163	CABARET DANCER	73
YAWNING A LITTLE SHE CAME WITH THE SLEEP STILL UPON HER.	166	FISH & SHADOW	8
"I AM JUST FROM BED. THE SLEEP IS STILL IN MY EYES.	166	FISH & SHADOW	9
STILL SHE MUST KNOW IT.	175	LANGUE D'OC: 3	36
ITS HOME MAIL IS STILL OPENED BY ITS MATERNAL PARENT	179	MOEURS CON: 4	2
GLADSTONE WAS STILL RESPECTED,	192	YEUX GLAUQUES	1
AND ROSSETTI STILL ABUSED.	192	YEUX GLAUQUES	4
STILL, AT THE TATE, THEY TEACH	192	YEUX GLAUQUES	11
STILL DARTS OUT FAUN-LIKE FROM THE HALF-RUIN'D FACE,	192	YEUX GLAUQUES	18
THE STILL STONE DOGS,	200	MAUBERLEY: 2	35
THE MOON STILL DECLINED TO DESCEND OUT OF HEAVEN,	223	SEXTUS PROP: 9	3
AND STILL A GIRL SCORNS THE GODS,	228	SEXTUS PROP:12	23
OF MY STILL CONSCIOUSNESS	236	MIDDLE-AGED	20
STILL I'D RESPECT YOU MORE IF YOU COULD BURY	239	MOYEN SENSUEL	27
THE STERILE EGG THAT IS STILL EATABLE:	240	MOYEN SENSUEL	49
THEY SET THEIR MIND (IT'S STILL IN THAT CONDITION)--	240	MOYEN SENSUEL	53
AS HE INHALED THE STILL FUMES OF RICE-POWDER.	243	MOYEN SENSUEL	132
STILL WE WILL BRING OUR "FICTION AS NEAR TO FACT" AS	243	MOYEN SENSUEL	139
STILL WE LOOK TOWARD THE DAY WHEN MAN, WITH UNCTION,	244	MOYEN SENSUEL	175
STILL HE WAS NOT GIVEN UP TO BRUTE ENJOYMENT,	245	MOYEN SENSUEL	193
FOR MEMORY OF THE FIRST WARM NIGHT STILL CAST A HAZE O'ER	245	MOYEN SENSUEL	195
MY NERVES STILL REGISTER THE SOUNDS OF CONTRA-BASS',	247	PIERROTS	19
STILL DR. S---'S	261	ALF'S SIXTH	18
STILL-BORN			
THE ENGLISH RUBAIYAT WAS STILL-BORN	192	YEUX GLAUQUES	15
STILLNESS			
FROM THE PLUM-COLOURED LAKE, IN STILLNESS,	75	THE ALCHEMIST	17
STILTS			
YOU CAME BY ON BAMBOO STILTS, PLAYING HORSE,	130	RIVER-MER WIFE	3
STIMULATE			
TO STIMULATE, IN HER,	196	HUGH SELWIN:12	7
STIMULATING			
IS BOTH STIMULATING AND DELIGHTFUL."	113	TAME CAT	7
STIMULATION			
SPEAK ONCE AGAIN FOR ITS SOLE STIMULATION,	63	PHASELLUS ILLE	10
STINKING			
A SORT OF STINKING DILIQUESCENT SACCHARINE.	239	MOYEN SENSUEL	22
STINKS			
DAMN IT ALL! ALL THIS OUR SOUTH STINKS PEACE.	28	ALTAFORTE	1
STIR			
NOR STIR HAND NOR THINK IN MID HEART,	66	THE SEAFARER	98
BY THE STIR OF THE FIN,	76	THE ALCHEMIST	36
YOU CREATED CONSIDERABLE STIR IN CHICAGO,	114	EPILOGUE	4
THEY TRY TO STIR NEW AFFECTION,	142	UNMOVING CLOUD	19
AND STIR OLD GRUDGES?	152	NEAR PERIGORD	37
OUT OF MY LOVE WILL HER HEART NOT STIR.	177	LANGUE D'OC: 4	28
THERE WILL BE, IN ANY CASE, A STIR ON OLYMPUS.	222	SEXTUS PROP: 8	42
STIRRER-UP			
HUB OF THE WHEEL, THE STIRRER-UP OF STRIFE,	151	NEAR PERIGORD	21
STIRRING			
STIRRING THE MARMALADE	262	ALF'S SIXTH	26
STIRS			
WHO STIRS NOT FORTH THIS NIGHT,	172	LANGUE D'OC: 1	4
STOCK			
BY RIGGING STOCK REPORTS,	266	ALF'S ELEVENTH	18
STOCKINGS			
IT IS SO LATE THAT THE DEW SOAKS MY GAUZE STOCKINGS,	132	JEWEL STAIRS'	2
PUFFED SATIN, AND SILK STOCKINGS, WHERE THE KNEE	241	MOYEN SENSUEL	85
STODGY			
GREET THE GRAVE AND THE STODGY,	86	SALUTATION 2ND	21
STOLE			
STOLE HER AWAY FOR HIMSELF, KEPT HER AGAINST ARMED	123	PROVINC DESERT	75
STOMACH			
EUHENIA, IN SHORT SKIRTS, SLAPS HER WIDE STOMACH,	163	CABARET DANCER	53

STOMPED -- STRAIGHT

```
                                                       PAGE    TITLE              LINE
STOMPED
   "HE STOMPED INTO MY BEDROOM. . . .  . . . . . . . . . . . . .  182    MOEURS CON: 8       6
   ". . . STOMPED INTO MY BEDROOM. . . .  . . . . . . . . . . .   182    MOEURS CON: 8       8
STONE
   AND LEFT THEM UNDER A STONE   . . . . . . . . . . . . . . . . .   4    LA FRAISNE         26
   OF BEATEN WORK; AND THROUGH THE CLARET STONE,   . . . . .        49    OF SPLENDOUR       15
   THEIR OCHRE CLINGS TO THE STONE.   . . . . . . . . . . . . . .  108    TS'AI CHI'H         3
   "AND THOU OUT HERE BENEATH THE PORCH OF STONE   . . . . .       172    LANGUE D'OC: 1     22
   THE STILL STONE DOGS,   . . . . . . . . . . . . . . . . . . . . 200    MAUBERLEY: 2       35
   WITH NO STONE UPON MY CONTEMPTIBLE SEPULCHRE;   . . . . .       208    SEXTUS PROP: 1     37
STONE-BRIGHT
   I HAVE KNOWN THE STONE-BRIGHT PLACE,   . . . . . . . . . . . .   95    OF THE DEGREES      8
STONE-CLIFFS
   STORMS, ON THE STONE-CLIFFS BEATEN, FELL ON THE STERN            64    THE SEAFARER       23
STONES
   DO I NOT LOATHE ALL WALLS, STREETS, STONES,   . . . . . . .      70    THE PLUNGE         11
   ITS LOWEST STONES JUST MEET THE VALLEY TIPS   . . . . . . .     152    NEAR PERIGORD      55
STOOD
   I STOOD STILL AND WAS A TREE AMID THE WOOD,   . . . . . . .       3    THE TREE            1
STOOL
   DAY LONG, LONG DAY COOPED ON A STOOL   . . . . . . . . . . . .   22    MARVOIL             3
   BY FALLING FROM A HIGH STOOL IN A PUB . . .   . . . . . . .     193    SIENA MI FE         8
STOP
   WHY SHOULD WE STOP AT ALL FOR WHAT I THINK?   . . . . . . .      59    GILET               3
   I STOP IN MY ROOM TOWARD THE EAST, QUIET, QUIET,                142    UNMOVING CLOUD      6
   TWO DEATHS--AND TO STOP LOVING AND BEING LOVABLE,               168    OF AROUET          27
   AND THE GUARDS COULDN'T STOP THEM,   . . . . . . . . . . . . .  182    MOEURS CON: 7      19
   AND THE GUARDS COULDN'T STOP THEM.   . . . . . . . . . . . . .  182    MOEURS CON: 7      22
   AND DIDN'T SEEM NEVER TO STOP.   . . . . . . . . . . . . . . .  271    OLE KATE           12
STOPPED
   STOPPED IN THEIR PLAY AS SHE PASSED THEM   . . . . . . . . .     96    AESTHETICS          3
   AT FIFTEEN I STOPPED SCOWLING,   . . . . . . . . . . . . . . .  130    RIVER-MER WIFE     11
'STORANTE
   NOW IN VENICE, 'STORANTE AL GIARDINO, I WENT EARLY,             163    CABARET DANCER     79
STORE
   THESE ARE YOUR RICHES, YOUR GREAT STORE; AND YET                 61    PORTRAIT FEMME     24
STORES
   AND CASTS STORES ON LAVINIAN BEACHES.   . . . . . . . . . . .   228    SEXTUS PROP:12     35
   AND THE LARGER STORES WERE LIKEWISE   . . . . . . . . . . . .   262    ALF'S SEVENTH       6
STORIED
   IN THE STORIED HOUSES OF SAN-KO THEY GAVE US MORE
      SENNIN MUSIC,   . . . . . . . . . . . . . . . . . . . . . .  135    EXILE'S LETTER     26
   AND AMID ALL THE GLORIED AND STORIED BEAUTIES OF
      MAEONIA   . . . . . . . . . . . . . . . . . . . . . . . . .  222    SEXTUS PROP: 8     34
STORK
   A YELLOW STORK FOR A CHARGER, AND ALL OUR SEAMEN                128    THE RIVER SONG      7
STORKS
   HE GOES OUT TO HORI, TO LOOK AT THE WING-FLAPPING
      STORKS,   . . . . . . . . . . . . . . . . . . . . . . . . .  130    THE RIVER SONG     36
STORM
   I HAVE WEATHERED THE STORM,   . . . . . . . . . . . . . . . .    93    THE REST           18
STORMED
   STORMED AT BY PRESS AND ALL,   . . . . . . . . . . . . . . . .  257    BREAD BRIGADE      21
STORMS
   STORMS, ON THE STONE-CLIFFS BEATEN, FELL ON THE STERN            64    THE SEAFARER       23
STORY
   SO ENDS THAT STORY.   . . . . . . . . . . . . . . . . . . . .   123    PROVINC DESERT     77
   TAKE THE WHOLE MAN, AND RAVEL OUT THE STORY.   . . . . . .      152    NEAR PERIGORD      47
   SAVE YOUR DOUTH AND YOUR STORY.   . . . . . . . . . . . . . .   165    QUINTUS SEPTIM     19
   --SUCH AT LEAST IS THE STORY.   . . . . . . . . . . . . . . .   220    SEXTUS PROP: 7     16
STOUR
   BETTER ONE HOUR'S STOUR THAN A YEAR'S PEACE   . . . . . .        28    ALTAFORTE          16
   MY WORDS FOR STOUR, HATH NO BLOOD OF CRIMSON   . . . . . .       29    ALTAFORTE          26
STRACHEY
   (TELL IT TO MR. STRACHEY)   . . . . . . . . . . . . . . . . .    86    SALUTATION 2ND     31
STRAGGLING
   WITH A RED STRAGGLING BEARD?   . . . . . . . . . . . . . . .    154    NEAR PERIGORD     102
STRAIGHT
   STRAIGHT, THEN SHONE THINE ORIEL AND THE STUNNED
      LIGHT   . . . . . . . . . . . . . . . . . . . . . . . . . .   68    APPARUIT           15
   HER STRAIGHT SPEECH FREE-RUNNING,   . . . . . . . . . . . .     105    DOMPNA POIS        29
```

STRAIGHT -- STREET

	PAGE	TITLE	LINE
STRAIGHT (CONTINUED)			
HER STRAIGHT FRESH BODY, ...	106	DOMPNA POIS	48
CLASH, LEAPING OF BANDS, STRAIGHT STRIPS OF HARD COLOUR, ...	120	GAME OF CHESS	14
WHILE MY HAIR WAS STILL CUT STRAIGHT ACROSS MY FOREHEAD	130	RIVER-MER WIFE	1
STRAIN			
AS LIPS SHRINK BACK WHEN WE FEEL THE STRAIN	11	OF THE GIBBET	20
STRAIT			
TO THE STRAIT HEAD	198	MAUBERLEY: 1	3
STRAITLY			
SLIGHT ARE HER ARMS, YET THEY HAVE BOUND ME STRAITLY	71	A VIRGINAL	4
STRANDS			
STRANDS OF LIGHT INWOVEN ABOUT IT, LOVELIEST	68	APPARUIT	18
STRANGE			
STRANGE SPELLS OF OLD DEITY, ...	6	CINO	6
"AH-EH! THE STRANGE RARE NAME	15	FAMAM CANO	42
"ALL THEY THAT WITH STRANGE SADNESS"	20	IN DURANCE	26
O STRANGE FACE THERE IN THE GLASS!	35	HIS OWN FACE	1
STRANGE WAYS AND WALLS ARE FASHIONED OUT OF IT. ...	49	OF SPLENDOUR	5
STRANGE SPARS OF KNOWLEDGE AND DIMMED WARES OF PRICE.	61	PORTRAIT FEMME	5
AND TAKES STRANGE GAIN AWAY:	61	PORTRAIT FEMME	15
STRANGE WOODS HALF SODDEN, AND NEW BRIGHTER STUFF:	61	PORTRAIT FEMME	26
WHOM WE MEET ON STRANGE ROADWAYS?	141	IDEA OF CHOAN	32
AND HIS STRANGE PROPERTY SETS SIGHS TO MOVE	250	DONNA MI PREGA	58
STRANGENESS			
I WOULD BATHE MYSELF IN STRANGENESS:	70	THE PLUNGE	1
WHEN THEY HAVE GOT OVER THE STRANGENESS, ...	208	SEXTUS PROP: 1	41
STRASBOURG			
SENATORIAL FAMILIES OF STRASBOURG, MONSIEUR VEROG.	193	SIENA MI FE	4
STRATA			
WITH OTHER STRATA	196	HUGH SELWIN:12	15
STRATEGIST			
MARK HIM A CRAFTSMAN AND A STRATEGIST?	153	NEAR PERIGORD	85
STRATH			
I THAT HAVE KNOWN STRATH, GARTH, BRAKE, DALE, ...	31	PIERE VIDAL	50
STRAW			
"TILL I HAVE VIEWED STRAW HATS AND THEIR HABITUAL CLOTHING	244	MOYEN SENSUEL	183
STRAWBERRIES			
CRUSHED STRAWBERRIES! COME, LET US FEAST OUR EYES.	113	L'ART, 1910	2
STRAY			
A STRAY GIPSY--A. D. 1912	119	THE GYPSY	EPI
STRAY GLEAMS ON HANGING MAIL, AN ARMOURER'S TORCH-FLARE	155	NEAR PERIGORD	134
STRAYED			
COMBUSTED SEMELE'S, OF IO STRAYED.	227	SEXTUS PROP:11	34
STREAM			
I HAVE LOVED A STREAM AND A SHADOW.	84	ORTUS	11
THY FINGERS A FROSTED STREAM.	91	DANCE FIGURE	20
OVER A STREAM FULL OF LILIES.	121	PROVINC DESERT	17
I HAVE LOOKED BACK OVER THE STREAM	121	PROVINC DESERT	33
ROSE OVER US; AND WE KNEW ALL THAT STREAM, ...	157	NEAR PERIGORD	172
THE SALMON-TROUT DRIFTS IN THE STREAM, ...	166	FISH & SHADOW	1
THE SOUL OF THE SALMON-TROUT FLOATS OVER THE STREAM	166	FISH & SHADOW	2
STREAMS			
MOSS WORDS, LIP WORDS, WORDS OF SLOW STREAMS.	16	PRAISE YSOLT	22
LIFE, ALL OF IT, MY SEA, AND ALL MEN'S STREAMS	25	GUIDO INVITES	9
THE HEART'S THOUGHT THAT I ON HIGH STREAMS	65	THE SEAFARER	35
SPLITS THE TWO STREAMS APART.	138	CITY OF CHOAN	10
NOT A NEAT LEDGE, NOT FOIX BETWEEN ITS STREAMS, ...	152	NEAR PERIGORD	32
THE FISH SHALL SWIM IN DRY STREAMS.	220	SEXTUS PROP: 7	27
STREET			
YOUNG MEN RIDING IN THE STREET	111	IMAGE ORLEANS	1
STRIKE SPARKS FROM THE COBBLED STREET	111	IMAGE ORLEANS	7
WHY DOES THE REALLY HANDSOME YOUNG WOMAN APPROACH ME IN SACKVILLE STREET	114	SIMULACRA	5
CLEAR THE STREET, O YE GREEKS, ...	229	SEXTUS PROP:12	37
AND THAT OXFORD STREET SITE	262	ALF'S SEVENTH	14
I GET THE KIDS OUT ON THE STREET	266	ALF'S ELEVENTH	5
SAFES IN THREAD AND NEEDLE STREET.	269	SAFE AND SOUND	22

PAGE 392

STREET -- STRIPPED

	PAGE	TITLE	LINE
STREET (CONTINUED)			
AND A LOT OF SMALL STREET STENCHES.	270	OF 600 M.P.'S	16
STREETS			
DO I NOT LOATHE ALL WALLS, STREETS, STONES,	70	THE PLUNGE	11
YOU STAND ABOUT IN THE STREETS,	94	INSTRUCTIONS	5
AND THE STREETS MAKE WAY FOR THEIR PASSAGE.	132	AT TEN-SHIN	17
THE NARROW STREETS CUT INTO THE WIDE HIGHWAY AT CHOAN,	141	IDEA OF CHOAN	1
AND THE TALL WOMEN WALKING YOUR STREETS, IN GILT CLOTHES,	165	QUINTUS SEPTIM	14
CLEAR THE STREETS, O YE GREEKS!	229	SEXTUS PROP:12	40
STRENGTH			
LO! I DO CURSE MY STRENGTH	30	PIERE VIDAL	3
STRENGTHEN			
STRENGTHEN THE SUBTLE CORDS,	88	COMMISSION	20
STRENGTHENED			
STRENGTHENED HIM AGAINST	202	AGE DEMANDED	35
STRENGTHENED WITH RUSHES, TEGAEAN PAN,	211	SEXTUS PROP: 2	30
STRENUOUS			
FAINT IN THE MOST STRENUOUS MOODS,	202	AGE DEMANDED	38
STRETCH			
LANGUIDLY YOU STRETCH OUT THE SNARE	226	SEXTUS PROP:11	15
STRETCHED			
BREATH THAT IS STRETCHED OUT BENEATH THE WORLD:	76	THE ALCHEMIST	45
THOUGH IT IS NOT STRETCHED UPON GILDED BEAMS;	208	SEXTUS PROP: 1	52
SAW HER STRETCHED ON HER BED,--	214	SEXTUS PROP. 4	17
AND STRETCHED AND TAMPERED WITH THE MEDIA.	235	TO WHISTLER	17
STRETCHES			
AND THE WIDE, FLAT ROAD STRETCHES OUT.	142	UNMOVING CLOUD	5
THE GREEN STRETCHES WHERE LOVE IS AND THE GRAPES	167	OF AROUET	21
THE SEA-CLEAR SAPPHIRE OF AIR, THE SEA-DARK CLARITY, STRETCHES BOTH SEA-CLIFF AND OCEAN.	170	PHANOPOEIA	24
STRETCHES TOWARD ME HER LEAFY HANDS,"--	196	HUGH SELWIN:12	2
STREW			
AND THOUGH HE STREW THE GRAVE WITH GOLD,	66	THE SEAFARER	99
STREWS			
AND STREWS A MIND WITH PRECIOUS METAPHORS,	236	MIDDLE-AGED	18
STRICT			
CLINGS TO THE SKIRT IN STRICT (VIDE: "VOGUE") PROPRIETY.	241	MOYEN SENSUEL	86
STRIFE			
FOUGHT OUT THEIR STRIFE HERE, 'TIS A PLACE OF WONDER;	51	THE ALTAR	3
HUB OF THE WHEEL, THE STIRRER-UP OF STRIFE,	151	NEAR PERIGORD	21
AND HE WHO SET THE STRIFE BETWEEN BROTHER AND BROTHER	151	NEAR PERIGORD	25
WHEN WE SET STRIFE AWAY,	173	LANGUE D'OC: 2	18
STRIKE			
STRIKE THE TYMPANUM,	42	HER MONUMENT	46
STRIKE SPARKS FROM THE COBBLED STREET	111	IMAGE ORLEANS	7
AND EVEN ZEUS' WILD LIGHTNING FEAR TO STRIKE	244	MOYEN SENSUEL	177
STRIKES			
AND YET AGAIN, AND NEWLY RUMOUR STRIKES ON MY EARS.	226	SEXTUS PROP:11	17
AND THE GOD STRIKES TO THE MARROW.	229	SEXTUS PROP:12	58
STRIKING			
STRIKING THE BOARD, FALLING IN STRONG L'S OF	120	GAME OF CHESS	2
REACHING AND STRIKING IN ANGLES,	120	GAME OF CHESS	4
STRING			
BUT YOU NEVER STRING TWO DAYS UPON ONE WIRE	53	AU JARDIN	13
STRINGING			
STRINGING LONG VERSE FOR THE BURLATZ;	22	MARVOIL	20
STRING-PURSE			
WORKED FOR AND SNATCHED FROM THE STRING-PURSE OF BORN--	152	NEAR PERIGORD	34
STRINGS			
HE PURRS AND PATS THE CLEAR STRINGS.	139	SENNIN POEM	7
WITH GREEN STRINGS SHE MAKES THE WARP OF HER BASKET,	140	MULBERRY ROAD	8
FITTED SONG TO THE STRINGS;	211	SEXTUS PROP: 2	36
STRIPPED			
AS NEW ALMONDS STRIPPED FROM THE HUSK,	91	DANCE FIGURE	13
LAY STRIPPED UPON THE GROUND:	92	APRIL	4

PAGE 393

STRIPS -- STUFFED

STRIPS	PAGE	TITLE	LINE
CLASH, LEAPING OF BANDS, STRAIGHT STRIPS OF HARD COLOUR, ...	120	GAME OF CHESS	14
LIE LITTLE STRIPS OF PARCHMENT COVERED OVER, ...	154	NEAR PERIGORD	99
STRIVE			
THAT STRIVE AND PLAY AND PASS, ...	35	HIS OWN FACE	5
STRIVEN			
IN VAIN HAVE I STRIVEN, ...	16	PRAISE YSOLT	1
IN VAIN HAVE I STRIVEN	16	PRAISE YSOLT	23
IN VAIN HAVE I STRIVEN WITH MY SOUL	17	PRAISE YSOLT	55
STRIVETH			
THAT STRIVETH TO OURS ACROSS THE PAIN.	11	OF THE GIBBET	24
STROKE			
GOD GRANT I DIE NOT BY ANY MAN'S STROKE	173	LANGUE D'OC: 2	21
NOW YOU MAY BEAR FATE'S STROKE UNPERTURBED, ...	222	SEXTUS PROP: 8	37
STROKED			
HE STROKED THOSE WHICH WERE ALREADY ARRANGED, ...	97	AESTHETICS	18
STROKES			
ARE KEPT MNEMONIC OF THE STROKES THEY BORE, ...	19	FOR E. MCC	20
STRONG			
I WAS QUITE STRONG--AT LEAST THEY SAID SO--	4	LA FRAISNE	5
AND THEY SAID I WAS QUITE STRONG, AMONG THE YOUNG MEN.	5	LA FRAISNE	41
SWIFT AS THE KING WOLF WAS I AND AS STRONG	30	PIERE VIDAL	8
SILENT AS FATE IS, AND AS STRONG UNTIL	31	PIERE VIDAL	35
HAVE ME IN THE STRONG LONELINESS	67	DORIA	5
STRIKING THE BOARD, FALLING IN STRONG L'S OF	120	GAME OF CHESS	2
SORROWFUL MINDS, SORROW IS STRONG, WE ARE HUNGRY AND THIRSTY.	127	BOWMEN OF SHU	7
HORSES, HIS HORSES EVEN, ARE TIRED. THEY WERE STRONG.	127	BOWMEN OF SHU	15
EACH PLACE STRONG.	151	NEAR PERIGORD	14
NOR DID DISGUST PROVE SUCH A STRONG EMETIC	242	MOYEN SENSUEL	128
STRONGER			
AND ROCHECOUART CAN MATCH IT, STRONGER YET, ...	152	NEAR PERIGORD	57
UNTIL THE MIND OF THE OLD NATION GETS A LITTLE STRONGER.	266	ALF'S TENTH	16
STRONGEST			
FRAIL CINO, STRONGEST OF HIS TRIBE	6	CINO	20
STROVE			
HE STROVE TO RESUSCITATE THE DEAD ART	187	E. P. ODE	2
STRUCK			
STRUCK OF THE BLADE THAT NO MAN PARRIETH;	19	FOR E. MCC	4
STRUCK OF THE BLADE THAT NO MAN PARRIETH	19	FOR E. MCC	23
STRUGGLES			
STRUGGLES WHEN THE LIGHTS WERE TAKEN AWAY;	220	SEXTUS PROP: 7	4
STRUT			
THAT I STRUT IN THE ROBES OF ASSUMPTION.	146	MONUMENTUM AER	2
STUDENTS			
THE TURBULENT AND UNDISCIPLINED HOST OF ART STUDENTS--	93	LES MILLWIN	5
CROSSED IN GREAT FUTURISTIC X'S, THE ART STUDENTS	93	LES MILLWIN	9
STUDIO			
"IN THE STUDIO" AND THESE TWO PORTRAITS, IF I HAD MY CHOICE!	235	TO WHISTLER	8
STUDY			
THE STUDY IN AESTHETICS	96	AESTHETICS	T
STUFF			
OF SOME THIN SILK STUFF THAT'S SCARCE STUFF AT ALL,	31	PIERE VIDAL	29
OF SOME THIN SILK STUFF THAT'S SCARCE STUFF AT ALL,	31	PIERE VIDAL	29
I KNOW NOT IF THE LOVE OR IF THE LAY WERE BETTER STUFF, ...	44	FROM HEINE: 2	7
STRANGE WOODS HALF SODDEN, AND NEW BRIGHTER STUFF:	61	PORTRAIT FEMME	26
THEE, A MARVEL, CARVEN IN SUBTLE STUFF, A	68	APPARUIT	2
IF SHE GOES IN A GLEAM OF COS, IN A SLITHER OF DYED STUFF, ...	217	SEXTUS PROP: 5	30
THAT ONLY SENTIMENTAL STUFF WILL SELL!)	242	MOYEN SENSUEL	118
STUFFED			
NOR ARE MY CAVERNS STUFFED STIFF WITH A MARCIAN VINTAGE, ...	209	SEXTUS PROP: 1	56
DAMP WOOLLY HANDKERCHIEFS WERE STUFFED INTO HER UNDRYABLE EYES, ...	214	SEXTUS PROP: 4	25

STUFFED -- SUBTLE-SOULED

	PAGE	TITLE	LINE
STUFFED (CONTINUED)			
BUT YOU STUFFED COATS WHO'RE NEITHER TEPID NOR DISTINCTLY BOREAL,	238	MOYEN SENSUEL	5
STUFFED-SATIN			
SUBJECTIVELY. IN THE STUFFED-SATIN DRAWINGROOM	196	HUGH SELWIN:12	3
STUFFY			
WILL BE A STUFFY, OPULENT SORT OF FUNGUS	161	CABARET DANCER	14
STUMBLES			
THE STARS WILL POINT OUT THE STUMBLES,	212	SEXTUS PROP: 3	21
STUNNED			
STRAIGHT, THEN SHONE THINE ORIEL AND THE STUNNED LIGHT	68	APPARUIT	15
STUNTED			
O AGE GONE LAX! O STUNTED FOLLOWERS,	32	PIERE VIDAL	60
STUPEFIED			
I WAS STUPEFIED.	225	SEXTUS PROP:10	29
STUPIDE			
ENCHASSES DANS UN VISAGE STUPIDE	160	DANS OMNIBUS	3
STUPIDITIES			
LET US TAKE ARMS AGAINST THIS SEA OF STUPIDITIES--	99	SALVATIONISTS	12
STUPIDITY			
THEIR VIRGIN STUPIDITY IS UNTEMPTABLE.	81	TENZONE	7
WE WERE IN ESPECIAL BORED WITH MALE STUPIDITY,	82	THE CONDOLENCE	8
STURDY			
OF THE FILTHY, STURDY, UNKILLABLE INFANTS OF THE VERY POOR.	83	THE GARDEN	6
THAT AMERICA'S STURDY SONS	268	ANOTHER BIT	2
STYLE			
HAD NOT ONE STYLE FROM BIRTH, BUT TRIED AND PRIED	235	TO WHISTLER	16
"ALL THE SAME STYLE, SAME CUT, WITH PERFECT LOATHING."	244	MOYEN SENSUEL	184
STYLIST			
THE STYLIST HAS TAKEN SHELTER,	195	HUGH SELWIN:10	2
STYRAX			
MR. STYRAX	178	MOEURS CON: 1	SUB
MR. HECATOMB STYRAX, THE OWNER OF A LARGE ESTATE	178	MOEURS CON: 1	1
AND EVEN NOW MR. STYRAX	178	MOEURS CON: 1	13
BUT THE SON-IN-LAW OF MR. H. STYRAX	178	MOEURS CON: 1	16
STYX			
THE WATERS OF STYX POURED OVER THE WOUND:	230	SEXTUS PROP:12	74
SUASION			
THAT FIRST MADE HIM BELIEVE IN IMMORAL SUASION.	245	MOYEN SENSUEL	198
SUAVE			
DRIGHT IN ITS SUAVE BOUNDING-LINE, AS,	204	MEDALLION	14
SUB			
SUB MARE	69	SUB MARE	T
SUBJECT			
AS IN A SUBJECT READY--	249	DONNA MI PREGA	26
SUBJECTIVE			
OF HIS SUBJECTIVE HOSANNAH.	202	AGE DEMANDED	55
SUBJECTIVELY			
SUBJECTIVELY. IN THE STUFFED-SATIN DRAWINGROOM	196	HUGH SELWIN:12	3
SUBJECTS			
AS THOU HAST SUBJECTS KNOWN,	197	ENVOI (1919)	4
SUBLIME			
OF POETRY; TO MAINTAIN "THE SUBLIME"	187	E. P. ODE	3
SUBSTANCE			
ONE SUBSTANCE AND ONE COLOUR	197	ENVOI (1919)	15
SUBTERRANEAN			
HIS SUBTERRANEAN CHAMBER WITH A DOZEN DOORS,	153	NEAR PERIGORD	61
SUBTLE			
THEE, A MARVEL, CARVEN IN SUBTLE STUFF, A	68	APPARUIT	2
AS WITH SWEET LEAVES; AS WITH SUBTLE CLEARNESS.	71	A VIRGINAL	6
STRENGTHEN THE SUBTLE CORDS,	88	COMMISSION	20
CRAFTY AND SUBTLE,	90	SURGIT FAMA	13
O GLASS SUBTLE AND CUNNING, O POWDERY GOLD!	95	OF THE DEGREES	14
WHO HATH TAUGHT YOU SO SUBTLE A MEASURE,	207	SEXTUS PROP: 1	6
SUBTLER			
THERE IS THE SUBTLER MUSIC, THE CLEAR LIGHT	50	THE FLAME	20
SUBTLE-SOULED			
MORE CRAFTILY, MORE SUBTLE-SOULED THAN I;	24	THUS NINEVEH	13

PAGE 395

SUBTLY -- SUCH

	PAGE	TITLE	LINE
SUBTLY			
O GLASS SUBTLY EVIL, O CONFUSION OF COLOURS!	95	OF THE DEGREES	10
IS IT AN INTRIGUE TO RUN SUBTLY OUT,	153	NEAR PERIGORD	82
SUBURBS			
GO TO THE WOMEN IN SUBURBS.	88	COMMISSION	10
SUCCESS			
TALK OF THE LATEST SUCCESS, GIVE WING TO SOME SCANDAL,	52	AU SALON	12
SUCCESSES			
BY PERSISTING TO SUCCESSES,	92	THE REST	10
SUCCULENT			
HE OFFERS SUCCULENT COOKING;	195	HUGH SELWIN:10	11
SUCCUMBED			
YOU WILL SAY THAT YOU SUCCUMBED TO A DANGER IDENTICAL,	222	SEXTUS PROP: 8	30
SUCH			
(SUCH AS I DRINK TO MINE FASHION)	10	FOR THIS YULE	15
SUCH AS ARE UP AND WIDE,	14	FAMAM CANO	10
SUCH IS THE TALE	14	FAMAM CANO	15
SUCH AN ONE AS THE WORLD FEELS	14	FAMAM CANO	24
SUCH AN ONE AS WOMEN DRAW AWAY FROM	15	FAMAM CANO	33
SUCH AN ONE PICKING A RAGGED	15	FAMAM CANO	38
SUCH AGE	15	FAMAM CANO	45
SUCH IS YOUR FENCE, ONE SAITH,	19	FOR E. MCC	5
THE VICOMTE OF BEZIERS'S NOT SUCH A BAD LOT.	22	MARVOIL	6
FOR THE DEATH OF SUCH SLUTS I GO REJOICING;	29	ALTAFORTE	29
HOT IS SUCH LOVE AND SILENT,	31	PIERE VIDAL	34
WAS THERE SUCH FLESH MADE EVER AND UNMADE!	31	PIERE VIDAL	45
GOD CURSE THE YEARS THAT TURN SUCH WOMEN GREY!	31	PIERE VIDAL	46
SUCH GLORY OF THE EARTH? OR WHO WILL WIN	32	PIERE VIDAL	58
SUCH BATTLE-GUERDON WITH HIS "PROWESSE HIGH"?	32	PIERE VIDAL	59
SUCH WAST THOU,	41	HER MONUMENT	1
OR TO SUCH BASE OCCASION LIT AND QUENCHED?	42	HER MONUMENT	57
MUST KNOW SUCH MOMENTS, THINKING ON THE GRASS;	43	SATIEMUS	11
IS YOUR HATE, THEN, OF SUCH MEASURE?	44	FROM HEINE: 1	1
THAT YOU CAN SAY SUCH AWFUL THINGS	44	FROM HEINE: 1	7
TOWARD SUCH A WORK OF ART.	45	FROM HEINE: 5	12
WHO CAN DEMOLISH AT SUCH POLISHED EASE	46	TRANSLATOR	3
TO FIND HIM SUCH, WHEN THE DAYS BRING	46	FROM HEINE: 6	18
WHICH BROUGHT THE HAIR-CLOTH CHAIR TO SUCH PERFECTION,	63	PHASELLUS ILLE	6
WILL FIND THEE SUCH A LOVER	67	THE CLOAK	5
UPON SUCH HOLLOW SEASON?"	72	PAN IS DEAD	13
NO MAN COULD PAINT SUCH THINGS WHO DID NOT KNOW.	73	JACOPO SELLAIO	2
WITH SUCH GRACIOUS UNCERTAINITY,	103	LADIES	11
HAD WE EVER SUCH AN EPITHET CAST UPON US!!	104	ANCORA	16
NEITHER ONE SO FAIR, NOR OF SUCH HEART,	105	DOMPNA POIS	12
NOR WITH SUCH ART	105	DOMPNA POIS	14
SUCH GRACE OF LOCKS, I DO YE TO WIT,	106	DOMPNA POIS	38
AND SUCH REPLIES SHE LAVISHES	106	DOMPNA POIS	54
SAVE THAT I HAVE SUCH HUNGER FOR	106	DOMPNA POIS	63
AS I'VE FOR YOU, SUCH FLAME-LAP,	107	DOMPNA POIS	65
WHY SHOULD ONE ALWAYS LIE ABOUT SUCH MATTERS?	113	TAME CAT	2
HAS SUCH A CARESSING AIR	115	SOCIAL ORDER	3
"HERE SUCH A ONE WALKED.	122	PROVINC DESERT	43
"MEN HAVE GONE BY SUCH AND SUCH VALLEYS	122	PROVINC DESERT	57
"MEN HAVE GONE BY SUCH AND SUCH VALLEYS	122	PROVINC DESERT	57
VICED IN SUCH TORTURE FOR THE "COUNTERPASS."	151	NEAR PERIGORD	27
PEPITA HAS SUCH TO-MORROWS: WITH THE HANDS PUFFED OUT,	161	CABARET DANCER	10
"WAIT, MY GOOD FELLOW. FOR SUCH JOY I TAKE	172	LANGUE D'OC: 1	26
AND SHE GAVE ME SUCH GESNING,	173	LANGUE D'OC: 2	19
SUCH FEAR I HAVE SHE DELIVER	175	LANGUE D'OC: 3	30
SUCH TREASURE IN THE AIR,	197	ENVOI (1919)	9
HAVE CONSTRUCTED WITH SUCH INDUSTRY	210	SEXTUS PROP: 2	4
SHALL BE YAWNED OUT ON MY LYRE--WITH SUCH INDUSTRY.	210	SEXTUS PROP: 2	5
MY LITTLE MOUTH SHALL GOBBLE IN SUCH GREAT FOUNTAINS,	210	SEXTUS PROP: 2	6
SUCH MY COHORT AND SETTING. AND SHE BOUND IVY TO HIS THYRSOS;	211	SEXTUS PROP: 2	35
SUCH A DEATH IS WORTH DYING.	213	SEXTUS PROP: 3	29
--SUCH AT LEAST IS THE STORY.	220	SEXTUS PROP: 7	16

SUCH -- SUITABLE

	PAGE	TITLE	LINE
SUCH (CONTINUED)			
SUCH DERELICTIONS HAVE DESTROYED OTHER YOUNG LADIES AFORETIME,	221	SEXTUS PROP: 8	7
IF SHE CONFER SUCH NIGHTS UPON ME,	221	SEXTUS PROP: 7	37
SUCH ASPECT WAS PRESENTED TO ME, ME RECENTLY EMERGED FROM MY VISIONS,	225	SEXTUS PROP:10	32
COULD YOU ENDURE SUCH PROMISCUITY?	228	SEXTUS PROP:12	10
DESPITE SUCH REINS AND CHECKS I'LL DO MY BEST,	238	MOYEN SENSUEL	12
WAS MADE TO INCUBATE SUCH MEDIOCRITIES,	239	MOYEN SENSUEL	24
COULD FREUD OR JUNG UNFATHOM SUCH A SINK?	241	MOYEN SENSUEL	76
SUCH PRACTICES DILUTED RURAL BOREDOM	242	MOYEN SENSUEL	107
SUCH WAS HE WHEN HE GOT HIS MOTHER'S LETTER	242	MOYEN SENSUEL	109
NOR DID DISGUST PROVE SUCH A STRONG EMETIC	242	MOYEN SENSUEL	128
AND WERE SUCH NIGHTS THAT WE SHOULD "DRAW THE CURTAIN"	243	MOYEN SENSUEL	134
UP STAIRS, THE THIRD FLOOR UP, AND HAVE SUCH QUANDARIES	244	MOYEN SENSUEL	158
IN WHICH THEIR MENTORS PLACE SUCH WIDE RELIANCE.	244	MOYEN SENSUEL	164
SUCH ANIMAL INVIGORATING CARRIAGE	245	MOYEN SENSUEL	191
TO RUN SUCH TOURS. HE CALLS 'EM. . . . HOUSE PARTIES.	245	MOYEN SENSUEL	210
(SUCH CHANGES DON'T OCCUR IN MEN, OR RABBITS).	246	MOYEN SENSUEL	232
FOR AS BEN FRANKLIN SAID, WITH SUCH URBANITY:	246	MOYEN SENSUEL	235
MY SOUL'S ANTENNAE ARE PREY TO SUCH PERTURBATIONS,	247	PIERROTS	7
YOU MIGHT PARDON SUCH SLIPS.	247	PIERROTS	24
HURL ME INTO SUCH A MASS OF DIVERGENT IMPRESSIONS.	248	PIERROTS	28
IN SUCH HIS DESIRE	250	DONNA MI PREGA	76
SUCH AS THE FASCISTS WEAR,	258	ALF'S THIRD	4
I'M GETTING TOO OLD FOR SUCH CAPERS.	264	ALF'S EIGHTH	35
THERE IS NO SUCH LAND OF CASTLES	272	NATIONAL SONG	5
SUCKED			
IS ONE DAY BLOWN UP LARGE, THE NEXT, SUCKED IN?	261	ALF'S FIFTH	21
SUCKS			
HE SUCKS HIS CHOP BONE,	163	CABARET DANCER	56
JUST GOES AHEAD AND SUCKS A TEAT	272	THE BABY	11
SUDDENLY			
SUDDENLY DISCOVERING IN THE EYES OF THE VERY BEAUTIFUL	161	PAGANI'S NOV 8	1
SUDDENTLY			
WI' TWEY WORDS SPOKE' SUDDENTLY.	34	GOODLY FERE	48
SUEDE			
WITH HER LITTLE SUEDE SLIPPERS OFF,	111	BLACK SLIPPERS	2
SUET			
(BUT MOSTLY GAS AND SUET)	270	OF 600 M.P.'S	10
SUEVI			
AND FLOOD CARRIES WOUNDED SUEVI	211	SEXTUS PROP: 2	47
SUFFER			
BUT THESE MAY NOT SUFFER ATTAINDER,	98	THE DOLLAIRES	13
SUFFERERS			
O MY FELLOW SUFFERERS, SONGS OF MY YOUTH,	82	THE CONDOLENCE	1
IMAGINE IT, MY FELLOW SUFFERERS--	82	THE CONDOLENCE	4
O MY FELLOW SUFFERERS, WE WENT OUT UNDER THE TREES,	82	THE CONDOLENCE	7
SUFFERIN'			
MY SUFFERIN' FELLOW MEN,	269	SAFE AND SOUND	26
SUFFERS			
SUFFERS DESPITE	173	LANGUE D'OC: 2	15
SUFFICIENT			
THE MERE WILL TO ACT IS SUFFICIENT."	210	SEXTUS PROP: 5	6
SUGARED			
LIFE'S A SORT OF SUGARED DISH-WASH!"	241	MOYEN SENSUEL	90
SUGGESTION			
TROPHIES FISHED UP; SOME CURIOUS SUGGESTION;	61	PORTRAIT FEMME	16
SUI			
QU'IEU SUI AVINEN,	166	FISH & SHADOW	16
OF ARNAUT DE MAREUIL, I THOUGHT, "QU'IEU SUI AVINEN."	166	FISH & SHADOW	19
SUICIDES			
YOU EITHER DRIVE THEM MAD, OR ELSE YOU BLINK AT THEIR SUICIDES.	145	SALUTATION 3RD	22
SUITABLE			
GO BACK TO GREAT DIAN'S DANCES BEARING SUITABLE GIFTS,	224	SEXTUS PROP: 9	24

SUITED -- SUNG

	PAGE	TITLE	LINE
SUITED			
IS NOT SUITED TO CO-OPERATION--	262	ALF'S SEVENTH	15
SUITETH			
IN ANOTHER FASHION THAT MORE SUITETH ME.	4	LA FRAISNE	8
SUITOR			
WHO SO INDECOROUS AS TO SHED THE PURE GORE OF A			
SUITOR?!	212	SEXTUS PROP: 3	26
SUMMER			
IN HOT SUMMER HAVE I GREAT REJOICING	28	ALTAFORTE	7
"THERE IS NO SUMMER IN THE LEAVES, ...	72	PAN IS DEAD	4
SUMMERS			
WHO HAD LAUGHED ON EIGHTEEN SUMMERS, ...	111	SOCIETY	3
SUMMERWARD			
HE SINGETH SUMMERWARD, BODETH SORROW, ...	65	THE SEAFARER	55
SUMNER			
OR FROM THE FEATS OF SUMNER CULL IT? THINK, ...	241	MOYEN SENSUEL	75
SUN			
AND I WILL SING OF THE SUN.	6	CINO	3
I WILL SING OF THE SUN.	7	CINO	39
BUT IT IS ALL ONE, I WILL SING OF THE SUN.	7	CINO	41
TO THE GARDENS OF THE SUN	7	CINO	51
LEST LOVE RETURN WITH THE FOISON SUN	10	FOR THIS YULE	13
TILL MY SOUL SENT A WOMAN AS THE SUN:	17	PRAISE YSOLT	47
YEA AS THE SUN CALLETH TO THE SEED, ...	17	PRAISE YSOLT	48
I AM FLAME THAT RISETH IN THE SUN, ...	18	DE AEGYPTO	17
OF SUN AND SPRAY ALL SHATTERED AT THE BOWS;	21	IN DURANCE	37
AND I LOVE TO SEE THE SUN RISE BLOOD-CRIMSON.	29	ALTAFORTE	19
AND BLAME THE SUN HIS GLADNESS;	30	PIERE VIDAL	4
AND THE RED SUN MOCKS MY SADNESS.	30	PIERE VIDAL	6
AND YET I CURSE THE SUN FOR HIS RED GLADNESS, ...	31	PIERE VIDAL	49
SO DELICATE AS SHE IS, WHEN THE SUN	38	BALLATETTA	8
GET US TO SOME CLEAR PLACE WHEREIN THE SUN	39	BLANDULA	3
AND, AS THE RAY OF SUN ON HANGING FLOWERS	40	ERAT HORA	2
AND I HAVE SEEN MY LADY IN THE SUN, ...	49	OF SPLENDOUR	6
AND NO SUN COMES TO REST ME IN THIS PLACE, ...	60	TOMB AKR CAAR	25
THOU AFAR, MOVING IN THE GLAMOROUS SUN, ...	68	APPARUIT	6
AND SUN, ...	70	THE PLUNGE	17
OH, SUN ENOUGH!	70	THE PLUNGE	18
MIDONZ, WITH THE GOLD OF THE SUN, THE LEAF OF THE			
POPLAR, BY THE LIGHT OF THE AMBER, ...	75	THE ALCHEMIST	25
MIDONZ, DAUGHTER OF THE SUN, SHAFT OF THE TREE,			
SILVER OF THE LEAF, LIGHT OF THE YELLOW OF THE			
AMBER, ...	75	THE ALCHEMIST	26
MIDONZ, GIFT OF THE GOD, GIFT OF THE LIGHT, GIFT OF			
THE AMBER OF THE SUN, ...	75	THE ALCHEMIST	27
I HAVE SEEN FISHERMEN PICNICKING IN THE SUN, ...	85	SALUTATION	3
CLEAR SPEAKERS, NAKED IN THE SUN, UNTRAMMELLED. ...	96	DUM CAPITOLIUM	8
LO, HOW IT GLEAMS AND GLISTENS IN THE SUN	99	CAKE OF SOAP	1
HANGS WITH THE SUN AND MOON.	128	THE RIVER SONG	10
WITH HEAD GEAR GLITTERING AGAINST THE CLOUD AND SUN,	131	AT TEN-SHIN	13
NOW THE HIGH CLOUDS COVER THE SUN	138	CITY OF CHOAN	11
SURPRISED. DESERT TURMOIL. SEA SUN.	139	SOUTH-FOLK	6
THE SUN RISES IN SOUTH EAST CORNER OF THINGS	140	MULBERRY ROAD	1
DRINKS IN AND CASTS BACK THE SUN.	141	IDEA OF CHOAN	10
AND MEN SAY THE SUN AND MOON KEEP ON MOVING	142	UNMOVING CLOUD	20
HOT SUN, CLEAR WATER, FRESH WIND, ...	146	CANTILATIONS	3
"AND HERE I AM SINCE GOING DOWN OF SUN, ...	172	LANGUE D'OC: 1	18
'TILL THE SUN COME, AND THE GREEN LEAF ON THE BOUGH.	173	LANGUE D'OC: 2	16
WHERE MY LOVE IS, THERE IS A GLITTER OF SUN;	174	LANGUE D'OC: 3	16
FOR THE SUN SHALL DRIVE WITH BLACK HORSES, ...	220	SEXTUS PROP: 7	23
SUNDAY			
THE SUNDAY SCHOOL BRINGS VIRTUES INTO PRACTICE. ...	243	MOYEN SENSUEL	140
SUNDAYS			
O' SUNDAYS.	53	AU JARDIN	22
SUNDERED			
FROM THE SUNDERED REALMS, OF THEBES AND OF AGED			
PRIAMUS;	38	LADY'S LIFE	8
SUN-DIALS			
RATHER THAN THE MOTTOES ON SUN-DIALS.	187	E. P. ODE	16
SUNG			
BAH! I HAVE SUNG WOMEN IN THREE CITIES, ...	6	CINO	1

PAGE 398

SUNG -- SUR

	PAGE	TITLE	LINE
SUNG (CONTINUED)			
I HAVE SUNG WOMEN IN THREE CITIES.	7	CINO	37
I HAVE SUNG WOMEN IN THREE CITIES	7	CINO	52
AND MANY A ONE HATH SUNG HIS SONGS	24	THUS NINEVEH	12
I HAD SUNG OF ALL THESE	210	SEXTUS PROP: 2	13
NEITHER CALLIOPE NOR APOLLO SUNG THESE THINGS INTO MY EAR,	217	SEXTUS PROP: 5	25
TITYRUS MIGHT HAVE SUNG THE SAME VIXEN;	229	SEXTUS PROP:12	46
AND BUT NOW GALLUS HAD SUNG OF LYCORIS.	230	SEXTUS PROP:12	72
SUNK			
SUNK IN A FROWSY COLLAR--AN UNBRUSHED BLACK.	161	CABARET DANCER	12
AND THEIR NECKS SUNK INTO FUR	269	SAFE AND SOUND	14
SUNKEN			
OF CHEEKS GROWN SUNKEN AND GLAD HAIR GONE GRAY;	50	THE FLAME	19
SUNLESS			
OF SUNLESS CLIFFS	67	DORIA	6
SUNLIGHT			
THE BROKEN SUNLIGHT FOR A HEALM SHE BEARETH	38	BALLATETTA	4
AND RED THE SUNLIGHT WAS, BEHIND IT ALL.	49	OF SPLENDOUR	8
SHE IS BEAUTIFUL AS THE SUNLIGHT, AND AS FLUID.	84	ORTUS	5
CLOTHED IN THE TATTERED SUNLIGHT,	104	ANCORA	11
SHE RUSHED OUT INTO THE SUNLIGHT AND SWARMED UP A COCOANUT PALM TREE,	118	CONTEMPORARIES	3
SUN LIGHT			
THAT TRAMP OLD WAYS BENEATH THE SUN-LIGHT,	6	CINO	21
SUNLIT			
ONE HOUR WAS SUNLIT AND THE MOST HIGH GODS	40	ERAT HORA	5
SUNS			
PLACID BENEATH WARM SUNS,	203	MAUBERLEY: 4	7
SUNSET			
LEVEL WITH SUNSET,	122	PROVINC DESERT	51
AND THE VERMILIONED GIRLS GETTING DRUNK ABOUT SUNSET,	136	EXILE'S LETTER	55
SUNSET LIKE THE PARTING OF OLD ACQUAINTANCES	137	TAKING LEAVE	6
SUNSET, THE RIBBON-LIKE ROAD LIES, IN RED CROSS-LIGHT,	154	NEAR PERIGORD	96
SUN-SHOT			
THE SALMON MOVES IN THE SUN-SHOT, BRIGHT SHALLOW SEA. . .	166	FISH & SHADOW	4
SUP			
I LIVE TOO LATE TO SUP WITH THEE!	46	TRANSLATOR	2
SUPERB			
I AM NOT "THAT CHAP THERE" NOR YET "THE SUPERB"	247	PIERROTS	16
SUPERFLUITIES			
REFINEMENT OF MEDIUM, ELIMINATION OF SUPERFLUITIES,	202	AGE DEMANDED	48
SUPERIOR			
THAT MAN IS THE SUPERIOR ANIMAL.	102	MEDITATIO	3
SUPERNAL			
(WHICH PAYS HIM MORE PER WEEK THAN THE SUPERNAL).	240	MOYEN SENSUEL	46
SUPERSEDED			
LONG SINCE SUPERSEDED THE CULTIVATION	196	HUGH SELWIN:12	27
SUPERVENING			
UNADLE IN THE SUPERVENING BLANKNESS	199	MAUBERLEY: 2	16
SUPPLANTS			
SUPPLANTS THE MOUSSELINE OF COS,	189	HUGH SELWYN: 3	2
SUPPLE			
THE JOGLARS SUPPLE AND THE TROUBADOURS.	36	THE YOUNG KING	11
SHE IS SO SUPPLE AND YOUNG,	106	DOMPNA POIS	49
SUPPORTED			
THEY SUPPORTED THE GAG AND THE RING:	145	SALUTATION 3RD	7
SUPPOSE			
I SUPPOSE, WHEN POETRY COMES DOWN TO FACTS,	52	AU SALON	1
I SUPPOSE THERE ARE A FEW DOZEN VERITIES	52	AU SALON	6
SUPPOSED			
WERE UNCERTAIN WHO WAS SUPPOSED TO BE INDEBTED TO THEM.	98	THE BELLAIRES	33
SUPPOSITION			
ON THE SUPPOSITION THAT IT EVER	263	ALF'S EIGHTH	5
SUPPRESSION			
AN ORGANIZATION FOR THE SUPPRESSION OF SIN. . . .	246	MOYEN SENSUEL	230
SUR			
JE VIS DES CANARDS SUR LE BORD D'UN LAC MINUSCULE,	160	DANS OMNIBUS	10

SURE -- SWAP

	PAGE	TITLE	LINE
SURE			
YOU GRABBED AT THE GOLD SURE; HAD NO NEED TO PACK CENTS	13	MESMERISM	19
IN THIS THING'S SURE DECORUM AND BEHAVIOUR.	63	PHASELLUS ILLE	14
OUR DEFENCE IS NOT YET MADE SURE, NO ONE CAN LET HIS FRIEND RETURN.	127	BOWMEN OF SHU	8
HIGH, HIGH AND SURE . . . AND THEN THE COUNTERTHRUST:	157	NEAR PERIGORD	180
YOU WERE NOT ALWAYS SURE, NOT ALWAYS SET	235	TO WHISTLER	14
SURE, THEY CAN LIVE ON HOPE,	259	ALF'S THIRD	16
SURELY			
MAD AS A HATTER BUT SURELY NO MYOPE,	13	MESMERISM	11
SURELY YOU ARE BOUND AND ENTWINED,	84	ORTUS	9
SURELY I SAW, AND STILL BEFORE MY EYES	156	NEAR PERIGORD	163
BUT SURELY THE WORST OF YOUR OLD-WOMEN ARE THE MALE ONES.)	243	MOYEN SENSUEL	150
NOR TO SEEK OUT, SURELY,	250	DONNA MI PREGA	68
AND IT WILL SURELY BOIL THE POT,	267	ALF'S TWELFTH	14
SURGING			
WHEN COME THEY, SURGING OF POWER, "DAEMON,"	20	IN DURANCE	19
BORE US TOGETHER . . . SURGING . . . AND APART . . .	157	NEAR PERIGORD	178
SURGINGS			
PALE SLOW GREEN SURGINGS OF THE UNDERWAVE,	69	SUB MARE	7
SURGIT			
SURGIT FAMA	90	SURGIT FAMA	T
SURHUMAN			
AND BY SURHUMAN FATES	42	HER MONUMENT	31
SURLY			
FOR HERE ARE A MILLION PEOPLE SURLY WITH TRAFFIC;	62	N. Y.	5
SURPASS			
AND MANY A ONE NOW DOTH SURPASS	24	THUS NINEVEH	14
SURPRISE			
SHOWS NO SURPRISE	192	YEUX GLAUQUES	22
MIGHT SAY, BE A SURPRISE	262	ALF'S SEVENTH	8
SURPRISED			
SURPRISED. DESERT TURMOIL. SEA SUN.	139	SOUTH-FOLK	6
SURROUNDED			
IS NOW SURROUNDED	115	SOCIAL ORDER	7
SURROUNDING			
FOR MY SURROUNDING AIR HATH A NEW LIGHTNESS;	71	A VIRGINAL	3
SURVIVAL			
AND HIS DESIRE FOR SURVIVAL,	202	AGE DEMANDED	37
SURVIVED			
NO INSTINCT HAS SURVIVED IN HER	195	HUGH SELWIN:11	6
SUSPICION			
TWO SMALL PEOPLE, WITHOUT DISLIKE OR SUSPICION.	130	RIVER-MER WIFE	6
THOUGH MANY MOVE WITH SUSPICION,	146	SALUTATION 3RD	31
SUSURRUS			
LIFTING THE FAINT SUSURRUS	202	AGE DEMANDED	54
SUTTEE			
A SORT OF CHLOROFORMED SUTTEE,	115	SOCIAL ORDER	13
SVELTE			
PRUDENT AND SVELTE PEPITA.	162	CABARET DANCER	50
SWADELIN'S			
TYIN' YOUR MEANIN' IN SEVENTY SWADELIN'S,	13	MESMERISM	2
SWALLER'D			
BUT HE SWALLER'D HIS TONGUE.	263	ALF'S EIGHTH	25
SWALLOW			
WHAT TIMES THE SWALLOW FILLS	14	FAMAM CANO	7
LIKE A SWALLOW HALF BLOWN TO THE WALL,	112	SHOP GIRL	2
SWALLOWS			
I, EVEN I, WHO FLY WITH THE SWALLOWS.	18	DE AEGYPTO	4
I, EVEN I, WHO FLY WITH THE SWALLOWS.	18	DE AEGYPTO	18
SWAN			
AND ICE-COLD WAVE, AT WHILES THE SWAN CRIES,	64	THE SEAFARER	19
SWANKERS			
IT IS HE WHO BUYS GOLD-BRAID FOR THE SWANKERS	263	ALF'S EIGHTH	17
SWANS			
"CONTENT EVER TO MOVE WITH WHITE SWANS!	211	SEXTUS PROP: 2	40
SWAP			
COULD YEH SWAP TH' BRAINS OF ORL THIS LOT	270	OF 600 M.P.'S	19

	PAGE	TITLE	LINE
SWARDS			
THE PARKS WITH THE SWARDS ALL OVER DEW,	167	OF AROUET	19
SWARM			
LICE SWARM LIKE ANTS OVER OUR ACCOUTREMENTS.	139	SOUTH-FOLK	8
SWARMED			
SHE RUSHED OUT INTO THE SUNLIGHT AND SWARMED UP A COCOANUT PALM TREE,	118	CONTEMPORARIES	3
SWAY			
I CAME INTO HER SWAY.	175	LANGUE D'OC: 3	39
SWEARING			
SCRIBBLING, SWEARING BETWEEN HIS TEETH; BY HIS LEFT HAND	154	NEAR PERIGORD	98
SWEAT			
(I BURN, I FREEZE, I SWEAT, SAID THE FAIR GREEK,	242	MOYEN SENSUEL	123
SWEATIN'			
SHE'D COME A SWEATIN' UP WITH THE COALS	271	OLE KATE	9
SWEEP			
SWEEP BACK UPON ME AND ENGULF MY MIND!	51	HORAE BEATAE	2
SWEET			
AS NOW SEEMS IT SWEET,	9	NA AUDIART	45
OR MORE SWEET IN TONE THAN ANY, BUT THAT I	24	THUS NINEVEH	21
THY LITTLE HEART, SO SWEET AND FALSE AND SMALL	44	FROM HEINE: 2	3
THAT THERE'S NO THING MORE SWEET OR FALSE AT ALL.	44	FROM HEINE: 2	4
HER GRAVE, SWEET HAUGHTINESS	52	AU SALON	EPI
NOR EAT THE SWEET NOR FEEL THE SORRY,	66	THE SEAFARER	97
AS WITH SWEET LEAVES; AS WITH SUBTLE CLEARNESS.	71	A VIRGINAL	6
SWEET TREES ARE ON THE PAVED WAY OF THE SHIN,	138	NEAR SHOKU	6
WHEN THE SPRINGTIME IS SWEET	173	LANGUE D'OC: 2	1
WHEN THE SWEET AIR GOES BITTER,	174	LANGUE D'OC: 3	1
MY ILL DOTH SHE TURN SWEET.	175	LANGUE D'OC: 3	48
AND YET ANOTHER, A "CHARMING MAN," "SWEET NATURE," BUT WAS GILDER,	240	MOYEN SENSUEL	57
'AVE YOU SEEN YER LARST SWEET LITTER?	270	OF 600 M.P.'S	18
SWEETER			
THAT IS SWEETER THAN THE LOVE OF WOMEN	5	LA FRAISNE	35
HAVE I DRUNK A DRAUGHT, SWEETER THAN SCENT OF MYRRH.	177	LANGUE D'OC: 4	23
SWEETLY			
WHOM THOU ONCE DID SING SO SWEETLY,	45	FROM HEINE: 3	2
SWELLED			
FOR I AM SWELLED UP WITH INANE PLEASURABILITIES	214	SEXTUS PROP: 4	5
SWELLING			
AND HOLDS HER SIDES WHERE SWELLING LAUGHTER CRACKS 'EM	239	MOYEN SENSUEL	33
SWENKIN			
"COME NOW! OLD SWENKIN! RISE UP FROM THY BED,	172	LANGUE D'OC: 1	14
SWEPT			
BEHOLD! THE WORLD OF FORMS IS SWEPT BENEATH--	32	PARACELSUS	7
OR AS A DANDELION SEED-POD AND BE SWEPT AWAY,	36	FRANCESCA	10
SWEPT FROM THE MIND WITH IT IN ITS DEPARTURE.	42	HER MONUMENT	40
LONDON HAS SWEPT ABOUT YOU THIS SCORE YEARS	61	PORTRAIT FEMME	2
SWEVYN			
FROM LOVE, AWAKE AND IN SWEVYN,	175	LANGUE D'OC: 3	29
SWIFT			
SWIFT AS THE KING WOLF WAS I AND AS STRONG	30	PIERE VIDAL	8
SWIFT CAME THE LOBA, AS A BRANCH THAT'S CAUGHT,	31	PIERE VIDAL	26
AND THAT WHICH FLEETETH DOTH OUTRUN SWIFT TIME.	40	ROME	14
O THROAT GIRT ROUND OF OLD WITH SWIFT DESIRE,	41	HER MONUMENT	14
SWIFT AT COURAGE THOU IN THE SHELL OF GOLD, CASTING	68	APPARUIT	13
SWIFT IN DEPARTING.	68	APPARUIT	20
THESE WERE THE SWIFT TO HARRY;	74	THE RETURN	16
NONE WITH SWIFT FEET.	91	DANCE FIGURE	5
NONE WITH SWIFT FEET.	91	DANCE FIGURE	24
THE ENEMY IS SWIFT, WE MUST BE CAREFUL,	127	BOWMEN OF SHU	20
THE SWIFT MOVING,	139	SOUTH-FOLK	13
HOW SWIFT IT IS.	175	LANGUE D'OC: 3	49
THEM. GOD HOW SWIFT THE NIGHT,	177	LANGUE D'OC: 4	4
'FORE GOD, HOW SWIFT THE NIGHT,	177	LANGUE D'OC: 4	9
AH GOD! HOW SWIFT THE NIGHT	177	LANGUE D'OC: 4	19
AH GOD! HOW SWIFT THE NIGHT.	177	LANGUE D'OC: 4	24
BY GOD, HOW SWIFT THE NIGHT.	177	LANGUE D'OC: 4	29

SWIFT -- SWORE

		PAGE	TITLE	LINE
SWIFT (CONTINUED)				
	SLOW FOOT, OR SWIFT FOOT, DEATH DELAYS BUT FOR A SEASON.	223	SEXTUS PROP: 9	21
	RECORD "ODD'S BLOOD! OUCH! OUCH!" A PRAYER, HIS SWIFT REPENTANCE.	243	MOYEN SENSUEL	130
SWIFTEST				
	GOD! HOW THE SWIFTEST HIND'S BLOOD SPURTED HOT	30	PIERE VIDAL	14
SWIFT-FOOT				
	SWIFT-FOOT TO MY LADY ANHES,	106	DOMPNA POIS	36
SWIFTLY				
	LEST THEY SHOULD PARCH TOO SWIFTLY, WHERE SHE PASSES.	38	BALLATETTA	10
	WENT SWIFTLY FROM ME. NAY, WHATEVER COMES	40	ERAT HORA	4
	SO SWIFTLY GOES THE NIGHT	177	LANGUE D'OC: 4	14
SWIG				
	BUT TO JAB A KNIFE IN MY VITALS, TO HAVE PASSED ON A SWIG OF POISON,	228	SEXTUS PROP:12	12
SWIM				
	AND ALL THE LADIES SWIM THROUGH TEARS	45	FROM HEINE: 5	11
	AND THE FISH SWIM IN THE LAKE	85	SALUTATION	9
	THE FISH SHALL SWIM IN DRY STREAMS.	220	SEXTUS PROP: 7	27
SWINBURNE				
	WALK DOWN LONGACRE RECITING SWINBURNE TO HERSELF, INAUDIBLY?	114	SIMULACRA	2
	"KING'S TREASURIES"; SWINBURNE	192	YEUX GLAUQUES	3
SWINBURNE'S				
	AND THEY TALK OF SWINBURNE'S WOMEN,	112	SHOP GIRL	3
SWINGING				
	ITS OWN HEAD SWINGING, GRIPPED BY THE DEAD HAIR,	156	NEAR PERIGORD	165
	AND LIKE A SWINGING LAMP THAT SAYS, "AH ME!	156	NEAR PERIGORD	166
	SWINGING A CAT-O'-NINE-TAILS.	162	CABARET DANCER	37
SWIRL				
	JUST FOR THE SWIRL	8	NA AUDIART	21
	THE SWIRL OF LIGHT FOLLOWS ME THROUGH THE SQUARE,	169	PHANOPOEIA	1
SWIRLERS				
	WELL THEN, SO CALL THEY, THE SWIRLERS OUT OF THE MIST OF MY SOUL,	20	IN DURANCE	21
SWIRLING				
	YOU WENT INTO FAR KU-TO-YEN, BY THE RIVER OF SWIRLING EDDIES,	130	RIVER-MER WIFE	16
	THE SWIRLING SPHERE HAS OPENED	169	PHANOPOEIA	8
SWISS				
	PHYLLIDULA NOW, WITH YOUR POWDERED SWISS FOOTMAN	167	OF AROUET	5
SWOLLEN				
	TORN, GREEN AND SILENT IN THE SWOLLEN RHONE,	31	PIERE VIDAL	27
SWORD				
	DREW YOU YOUR SWORD MOST GALLANTLY	19	FOR E. MCC	7
	"NON TI FIDAR," IT IS THE SWORD THAT SPEAKS	19	FOR E. MCC	13
	SLAYS DAY WITH HER DARK SWORD.	24	THUS NINEVEH	4
	WITH HER BLUE SWORD.	24	THUS NINEVEH	19
SWORD-ARM				
	IN OUR HEART'S SWORD-RACK, THOUGH THY SWORD-ARM SLEEP.	19	FOR E. MCC	22
SWORD-HATE				
	DISEASE OR OLDNESS OR SWORD-HATE	66	THE SEAFARER	71
SWORD-PLAY				
	THE YOUNG MEN AT THE SWORD-PLAY;	4	LA FRAISNE	6
SWORD-RACK				
	IN OUR HEART'S SWORD-RACK, THOUGH THY SWORD-ARM SLEEP.	19	FOR E. MCC	22
SWORDS				
	I HAVE NO LIFE SAVE WHEN THE SWORDS CLASH.	28	ALTAFORTE	3
	AND THROUGH ALL THE RIVEN SKIES GOD'S SWORDS CLASH.	28	ALTAFORTE	12
	HELL GRANT SOON WE HEAR AGAIN THE SWORDS CLASH!	28	ALTAFORTE	13
	FAR FROM WHERE WORTH'S WON AND THE SWORDS CLASH	29	ALTAFORTE	28
	THERE'S NO SOUND LIKE TO SWORDS SWORDS OPPOSING,	29	ALTAFORTE	32
	THERE'S NO SOUND LIKE TO SWORDS SWORDS OPPOSING,	29	ALTAFORTE	32
	WHEN OUR ELBOWS AND SWORDS DRIP THE CRIMSON	29	ALTAFORTE	34
	AND LET THE MUSIC OF THE SWORDS MAKE THEM CRIMSON!	29	ALTAFORTE	37
	HELL GRANT SOON WE HEAR AGAIN THE SWORDS CLASH!	29	ALTAFORTE	38
SWORE				
	AND WHAT THEY SWORE IN THE CUPBOARD	221	SEXTUS PROP: 8	8

PAGE 402

SWORN -- TAKE

	PAGE	TITLE	LINE
SWORN			
YOU SWORN FOE TO FREE SPEECH AND GOOD LETTERS, ...	145	SALUTATION 3RD	11
SWUNG			
WI' A BUNDLE O' CORDS SWUNG FREE, ...	33	GOODLY FERE	18
SYLVAN			
THROUGHOUT THIS SYLVAN PLACE	87	THE SPRING	4
SYMBOLICAL			
LILIES LIFT THEIR WHITE SYMBOLICAL CUPS, ...	180	MOEURS CON: 5	20
WHENCE THEIR SYMBOLICAL POLLEN HAS BEEN EXCERPTED,	180	MOEURS CON: 5	21
SYMPHONIES			
TO HIDING NIGHT OR TUNING "SYMPHONIES";	235	TO WHISTLER	15
SYNE			
THAT WAS A DOG-WOOD TREE SOME SYNE.	4	LA FRAISNE	15
AND HE IS DEAD LANG SYNE.	47	FROM HEINE: 7	16
SYRIAN			
WHEN THE SYRIAN ONYX IS BROKEN.	219	SEXTUS PROP: 6	25
SYRUP			
SYRUP AND SOOTHING DOPE, ...	259	ALF'S THIRD	15
SYSTEM			
KEEP UP THE GRAND SYSTEM	259	ALF'S FOURTH	8
WHEN WILL THIS SYSTEM LIE DOWN IN ITS GRAVE?	260	ALF'S FIFTH	4
SYSTEMS			
THWARTED WITH SYSTEMS, ...	92	THE REST	7
T.			
"QUASI KALOUN." S. T. SAYS BEAUTY IS MOST THAT, A			
"CALLING TO THE SOUL."	20	IN DURANCE	20
TABLE			
AT THE TABLE BEYOND US	111	BLACK SLIPPERS	1
RED JADE CUPS, FOOD WELL SET ON A BLUE JEWELLED			
TABLE, ...	135	EXILE'S LETTER	47
SOUTHWARD TOWARD MONTAIGNAC, AND HE BENDS AT A TABLE	154	NEAR PERIGORD	97
TABLES			
FLARES ON THE CROWDED STAGE BEFORE OUR TABLES	162	CABARET DANCER	22
TABULATE			
HE CAN TABULATE CAESAR'S GREAT SHIPS.	228	SEXTUS PROP:12	32
TACTIC			
ROCHECOUART, CHALAIS, THE REST, THE TACTIC, ...	155	NEAR PERIGORD	122
TA'EN			
O'ER MUCH HATH TA'EN SIR DEATH THAT DEADLY WARRIOR	37	THE YOUNG KING	12
TAENARIAN			
THOUGH MY HOUSE IS NOT PROPPED UP BY TAENARIAN			
COLUMNS FROM LACONIA (ASSOCIATED WITH NEPTUNE AND			
CERBERUS), ...	208	SEXTUS PROP: 1	51
TAIHAITIAN			
WHEN THE TAIHAITIAN PRINCESS	118	CONTEMPORARIES	1
TAIL			
THOUGH YOU WALK IN THE VIA SACRA, WITH A PEACOCK'S			
TAIL FOR A FAN.	227	SEXTUS PROP:11	40
TAILS			
WITH THEIR TAILS UP, ...	115	SOCIAL ORDER	15
TAIRIRAN			
TAIRIRAN HELD HALL IN MONTAIGNAC, ...	151	NEAR PERIGORD	16
SO TO THIS LAST ESTRANGEMENT, TAIRIRAN!	157	NEAR PERIGORD	185
TAIRIRAN'S			
THERE SHUT UP IN HIS CASTLE, TAIRIRAN'S, ...	157	NEAR PERIGORD	186
TAKE			
BEHOLD THE SHIELD! HE SHALL NOT TAKE THEE ALL.	19	FOR E. MCC	26
THEY TAKE THE TROUBLE TO TEAR OUT THIS WALL HERE,	22	MARVOIL	24
MANY A SINGER PASS AND TAKE HIS PLACE	24	THUS NINEVEH	9
TAKE YOUR HANDS OFF ME!	32	PIERE VIDAL	66
WHEN THEY CAME WI' A HOST TO TAKE OUR MAN	33	GOODLY FERE	5
AS CRUSHED LIPS TAKE THEIR RESPITE FITFULLY, ...	43	SATIEMUS	8
MOVE WE AND TAKE THE TIDE, WITH ITS NEXT FAVOUR,	69	THE NEEDLE	12
TAKE THOUGHT:	93	THE REST	17
AND TAKE YOUR WOUNDS FROM IT GLADLY.	95	ITE	4
LET US TAKE ARMS AGAINST THIS SEA OF STUPIDITIES--	99	SALVATIONISTS	12
"LET HER, IF SHE WANTS ME, TAKE ME."	100	ARIDES	7
BELS CEMBELINS, I TAKE OF YOU YOUR COLOUR, ...	105	DOMPNA POIS	21
SO TAKE I MY ROAD	106	DOMPNA POIS	34
BUT YOU, SIR, HAD BETTER TAKE WINE ERE YOUR			
DEPARTURE, ...	137	OF DEPARTURE	EPI

	PAGE	TITLE	LINE
TAKE (CONTINUED)			
YOU SAY THAT I TAKE A GOOD DEAL UPON MYSELF;	146	MONUMENTUM AER	1
TAKE THE WHOLE MAN, AND RAVEL OUT THE STORY.	152	NEAR PERIGORD	47
TAKE HIS OWN SPEECH, MAKE WHAT YOU WILL OF IT--	153	NEAR PERIGORD	79
OR TAKE HIS "MAGNET" SINGER SETTING OUT,	154	NEAR PERIGORD	104
OR TAKE EN BERTRANS?	156	NEAR PERIGORD	169
OR TAKE THE INTAGLIO, MY FAT GREAT-UNCLE'S HEIRLOOM:	162	CABARET DANCER	35
TAKE HER. SHE HAS TWO EXCELLENT SEASONS.	165	QUINTUS SEPTIM	22
"WAIT, MY GOOD FELLOW. FOR SUCH JOY I TAKE	172	LANGUE D'OC: 1	26
WE TAKE THEIR MEASURE.	173	LANGUE D'OC: 2	28
NOR TAKE MY BELOVED FROM MY SIGHT,	177	LANGUE D'OC: 4	7
"FOLLOW ME, AND TAKE A COLUMN,	194	MR. NIXON	8
WHICH I TAKE, MY NOT UNWORTHY GIFT, TO PERSEPHONE.	219	SEXTUS PROP: 6	21
TO-DAY WE TAKE THE GREAT BREATH OF LOVERS,	221	SEXTUS PROP: 7	31
TILL YOU MAY TAKE YOUR CHOICE: TO FEEL THE EDGE OF SATIRE OR	240	MOYEN SENSUEL	65
WHOSE BLUBBERING YOWLS YOU TAKE FOR PASSION'S ESSENCE;	240	MOYEN SENSUEL	68
SEE HOW THEY TAKE IT ALL,	259	ALF'S THIRD	12
TILL THE KING SHALL TAKE THE NOTION	269	SAFE AND SOUND	27
TAKEN			
I HA' TAKEN TO RAMBLING THE SOUTH HERE.	22	MARVOIL	5
THAT ANY FOLK E'ER HAD, HAST FROM US TAKEN;	37	THE YOUNG KING	19
THAT HE HAS TAKEN OUR LORD AWAY	72	PAN IS DEAD	12
CANDIDIA HAS TAKEN A NEW LOVER	118	THREE POETS	1
ENVY HAS TAKEN YOUR ALL,	165	QUINTUS SEPTIM	18
HIS BROTHER HAS TAKEN TO GIPSIES,	178	MOEURS CON: 1	15
THE STYLIST HAS TAKEN SHELTER,	195	HUGH SELWIN:10	2
TWICE TAKEN BY OETIAN GODS,	208	SEXTUS PROP: 1	33
STRUGGLES WHEN THE LIGHTS WERE TAKEN AWAY;	220	SEXTUS PROP: 7	4
IF THE YOUNG LADY IS TAKEN?	222	SEXTUS PROP: 8	41
TAKES			
LOVE TAKES HIS WAY AND HOLDS HIS JOY DECEITFUL,	37	THE YOUNG KING	26
AND TAKES STRANGE GAIN AWAY:	61	PORTRAIT FEMME	15
OR TAKES THE SEA AIR	98	THE BELLAIRES	38
HE TAKES "FLOATING HILL" BY THE SLEEVE,	140	SENNIN POEM	13
WHERE HE TAKES REST; WHO MAKETH HIM TO BE;	248	DONNA MI PREGA	13
HIS MODUS TAKES FROM SOUL, FROM HEART HIS WILL;	249	DONNA MI PREGA	23
TAKETH			
BOSQUE TAKETH BLOSSOM, COMETH BEAUTY OF BERRIES,	65	THE SEAFARER	49
IN MEMORY'S LOCUS TAKETH HE HIS STATE	248	DONNA MI PREGA	19
TAKETH IN LATENT INTELLECT--	249	DONNA MI PREGA	25
TAKIN'			
HOW THEY BETTER START TAKIN' CARE,	262	ALF'S SEVENTH	4
TAKING			
IT FAINTS IN TAKING AND IN GIVING ALL.	31	PIERE VIDAL	36
IN TAKING FROM THEM THE YOUNG ENGLISH KING,	37	THE YOUNG KING	13
TAKING LEAVE OF A FRIEND	137	TAKING LEAVE	T
AND NOW PROPERTIUS OF CYNTHIA, TAKING HIS STAND AMONG THESE.	230	SEXTUS PROP:12	75
TALE			
OR WHEN THE MINSTREL, TALE HALF TOLD,	9	NA AUDIART	27
SUCH IS THE TALE	14	FAMAM CANO	15
FACT THAT LEADS NOWHERE; AND A TALE OR TWO,	61	PORTRAIT FEMME	17
SOLVE ME THE RIDDLE, FOR YOU KNOW THE TALE.	151	NEAR PERIGORD	4
UPON A TALE, TO COMBAT OTHER TRACTS,	241	MOYEN SENSUEL	72
TALENT			
MY TALENT ACCLAIMED IN THEIR BANQUETS,	229	SEXTUS PROP:12	56
TALENTS			
HE EXERCISES HIS TALENTS	195	HUGH SELWIN:10	7
TALES			
DIM TALES THAT BLIND ME, RUNNING ONE BY ONE	43	SATIEMUS	16
AND ALL THE TALES OF OISIN SAY BUT THIS:	50	THE FLAME	5
FULL OF GOSSIP AND OLD TALES."	90	SURGIT FAMA	15
TALK			
TALK ME NO LOVE TALK, NO BOUGHT-CHEAP FIDDL'RY,	25	GUIDO INVITES	1
TALK ME NO LOVE TALK, NO BOUGHT-CHEAP FIDDL'RY,	25	GUIDO INVITES	5
TALK OF THE LATEST SUCCESS, GIVE WING TO SOME SCANDAL,	52	AU SALON	1
AND THEY TALK OF SWINBURNE'S WOMEN,	112	SHOP GIRL	
EVEN THOUGH WE TALK NOTHING BUT NONSENSE,	113	TAME CAT	

TALK -- TARGE

	PAGE	TITLE	LINE
TALK (CONTINUED)			
I HAVE CLIMBED RICKETY STAIRS, HEARD TALK OF CROY,	122	PROVINC DESERT	38
AND TALK OF INSANITY AND GENIUS,	145	SALUTATION 3RD	24
AND WE CAN LEAVE THE TALK TILL DANTE WRITES:	156	NEAR PERIGORD	162
"DID YOU TALK LIKE A FOOL,	159	PSYCHOLOG HOUR	34
BIG TALK AND LITTLE USE.	173	LANGUE D'OC: 2	26
SMALL TALK O ILION, AND O TROAD	208	SEXTUS PROP: 1	32
SMALL TALK COMES FROM SMALL BONES.	219	SEXTUS PROP: 6	37
TALK ECONOMICS,	261	ALF'S SIXTH	3
TALKED			
I HAVE TALKED TO YOU SO MUCH THAT	94	INSTRUCTIONS	12
AND HE TALKED ABOUT "THE GREAT MARY,"	181	MOEURS CON: 7	10
FOR TWO HOURS HE TALKED OF GALLIFET;	193	SIENA MI FE	5
HOW MANY WORDS TALKED OUT WITH ABUNDANT CANDLES;	220	SEXTUS PROP: 7	3
TALKING			
ALL THE WHILE THEY WERE TALKING THE NEW MORALITY	110	THE ENCOUNTER	1
WHAT IS THE USE OF TALKING, AND THERE IS NO END OF TALKING,	136	EXILE'S LETTER	75
WHAT IS THE USE OF TALKING, AND THERE IS NO END OF TALKING,	136	EXILE'S LETTER	75
I THINK OF TALKING AND MAN,	142	UNMOVING CLOUD	15
TALKING OF TROBAR CLUS WITH DANIEL.	155	NEAR PERIGORD	140
QUIET TALKING IS ALL THAT IS LEFT US--	168	OF AROUET	31
GENTLE TALKING, NOT LIKE THE FIRST TALKING, LESS LIVELY;	168	OF AROUET	32
GENTLE TALKING, NOT LIKE THE FIRST TALKING, LESS LIVELY;	168	OF AROUET	32
TALKS			
SPEECH? WORDS? FAUGH! WHO TALKS OF WORDS AND LOVE?!	31	PIERE VIDAL	33
BASTIDIDES, ON THE CONTRARY, WHO BOTH TALKS AND WRITES OF NOTHING SAVE COPULATION,	100	TEMPERAMENTS	5
TALL			
STATELY, TALL AND LOVELY TENDER	8	NA AUDIART	7
WHEN TALL STAGS FLED ME THROUGH THE ALDER BRAKES,	30	PIERE VIDAL	9
TALL STATURE AND GAIETY,	106	DOMPNA POIS	57
TO LOOK ON THE TALL HOUSE OF THE SHIN	140	MULBERRY ROAD	2
HERE'S PEPITA, TALL AND SLIM AS AN EGYPTIAN MUMMY,	162	CABARET DANCER	18
AND THE TALL WOMEN WALKING YOUR STREETS, IN GILT CLOTHES,	165	QUINTUS SEPTIM	14
TALLEYRANDS			
THE TALLEYRANDS, HAVE HELD THE PLACE; IT WAS NO TRANSIENT FICTION.	152	NEAR PERIGORD	51
TALLOW			
THE PUG-DOG'S FEATURES ENCRUSTED WITH TALLOW	161	CABARET DANCER	11
TAME			
TAME CAT	113	TAME CAT	T
TAMED			
FOR ORPHEUS TAMED THE WILD BEASTS--	208	SEXTUS PROP: 1	42
TAMPERED			
AND STRETCHED AND TAMPERED WITH THE MEDIA.	235	TO WHISTLER	17
TAMUZ			
IO! IO! TAMUZ!	110	TEMPORA	1
(TAMUZ. IO! TAMUZ!)	110	TEMPORA	4
(TAMUZ. IO! TAMUZ!)	110	TEMPORA	4
OH, NO, SHE IS NOT CRYING: "TAMUZ."	110	TEMPORA	5
TAN			
TAN QUE I PUOSCH' OM GITAR AB MALH.	161	NEAR PERIGORD	EPI
TANGLE			
THEIR CORDS TANGLE IN MIST, AGAINST THE BROCADE-LIKE PALACE.	129	THE RIVER SONG	26
CONFUSED, WHIRLED IN A TANGLE.	136	EXILE'S LETTER	74
ONE TANGLE OF SHADOWS.	218	SEXTUS PROP: 6	5
TANKED			
NEVER GOT PROPERLY TANKED AS I SAW,	271	OLE KATE	15
TARDI			
DEAGUBURI "CON CLI OCCHI ONESTI E TARDI,"	181	MOEURS CON: 7	6
TARDILY			
"DEATH WHY TARDILY COME?"	219	SEXTUS PROP: 6	29
TARGE			
PLUMB THE SPIKE OF THE TARGE.	250	DONNA MI PREGA	81

PAGE 405

TARIFF -- TEETH

	PAGE	TITLE	LINE
TARIFF			
(VIDE THE TARIFF), I WILL HANG SIMPLE FACTS	241	MOYEN SENSUEL	71
TARNISHED			
THE TARNISHED, GAUDY, WONDERFUL OLD WORK;	61	PORTRAIT FEMME	22
TARRIETH			
FAITH! NO MAN TARRIETH, ...	19	FOR E. MCC	11
TASTE			
LEST THEY SAY WE ARE LACKING IN TASTE, ...	94	INSTRUCTIONS	21
THE TASTE OF MY BOOT?	146	SALUTATION 3RD	33
HERE IS THE TASTE OF MY BOOT, ...	146	SALUTATION 3RD	34
WHO SHOWS HIS TASTE IN HIS AMBASSADORS:	239	MOYEN SENSUEL	17
THESE AND A TASTE IN BOOKS THAT'S GROWN PERENNIAL	239	MOYEN SENSUEL	25
TASTES			
GONE WHILE YOUR TASTES WERE KEEN TO YOU, ...	19	FOR E. MCC	1
NOT THAT HE'D CHANGED HIS TASTES, NOR YET HIS HABITS,	246	MOYEN SENSUEL	231
TATE			
STILL, AT THE TATE, THEY TEACH	192	YEUX GLAUQUES	11
TATTERED			
CLOTHED IN THE TATTERED SUNLIGHT, ...	104	ANCORA	11
TAUGHT			
AS I HAVE TAUGHT THEM TO TELL IT;	96	DUM CAPITOLIUM	4
WHO HATH TAUGHT YOU SO SUBTLE A MEASURE, ...	207	SEXTUS PROP: 1	6
TAVERN			
NOW I REMEMBER THAT YOU BUILT ME A SPECIAL TAVERN	134	EXILE'S LETTER	2
TAWDRY			
BUT A TAWDRY CHEAPNESS	189	HUGH SELWYN: 3	11
TAWN			
TAWN FORE-SHORES	203	MAUBERLEY: 4	8
TAXES			
A'PAYIN' US THE TAXES.	270	OF 600 M.P.'S	8
TE			
ERI MEN HAI TE KUDONIAI--IBYCUS.	87	THE SPRING	EPI
TE VOILA, MON BOURRIENNE, YOU ALSO SHALL BE IMMORTAL.	101	AMITIES	6
TEA			
ONE PLACE WHERE WE'D RATHER HAVE TEA	52	AU SALON	8
"TEA" (DAMN YOU!)	52	AU SALON	10
HAVE TEA, DAMN THE CAESARS, ...	52	AU SALON	11
THE TEA SHOP	116	THE TEA SHOP	T
THE GIRL IN THE TEA SHOP	116	THE TEA SHOP	1
WITH MUFFINS AT HIS TEA.	272	NATIONAL SONG	8
TEACH			
TO TEACH MY HEART TO BOW;	16	PRAISE YSOLT	2
TO TEACH MY SOUL TO BOW, ...	16	PRAISE YSOLT	24
TO TEACH MY SOUL TO BOW.	17	PRAISE YSOLT	56
STILL, AT THE TATE, THEY TEACH	192	YEUX GLAUQUES	11
TEA-GOWN			
THE TEA-ROSE TEA-GOWN, ETC.	189	HUGH SELWYN: 3	1
TEAR			
THEY TAKE THE TROUBLE TO TEAR OUT THIS WALL HERE,	22	MARVOIL	24
TEA-ROSE			
THE TEA-ROSE TEA-GOWN, ETC.	189	HUGH SELWYN: 3	1
TEARS			
I WRAPPED MY TEARS IN AN ELLUM LEAF	4	LA FRAISNE	25
A THING OF TEARS.	26	NIGHT LITANY	8
AND ALL THE LADIES SWIM THROUGH TEARS	45	FROM HEINE: 5	11
SAILS SPREAD ON CERULEAN WATERS, I WOULD SHED TEARS FOR TWO;	223	SEXTUS PROP: 9	
TEAT			
JUST GOES AHEAD AND SUCKS A TEAT	272	THE BABY	1
TEA-TIME			
'TO-MORROW AT TEA-TIME.'")	159	PSYCHOLOG HOUR	3
TECHNIQUE			
ENVIES ITS VIGOUR . . . AND DEPLORES THE TECHNIQUE,	155	NEAR PERIGORD	14
TEEN			
ARE LEFT IN TEEN THE LIEGEMEN COURTEOUS, ...	36	THE YOUNG KING	1
TEETH			
AND SENSE THE TEETH THROUGH THE LIPS THAT PRESS ...	11	OF THE GIBBET	2
OVER THE SHARPENED TEETH AND PURPLING LIPS!	30	PIERE VIDAL	1
I HAVE SEEN THEIR SMILES FULL OF TEETH	85	SALUTATION	
HER WHITE TEETH, OF THE LADY FAIDITA	106	DOMPNA POIS	5

PAGE 406

TEETH -- TEN

	PAGE	TITLE	LINE
TEETH (CONTINUED)			
SCRIBBLING, SWEARING BETWEEN HIS TEETH; BY HIS LEFT HAND	154	NEAR PERIGORD	98
FOR AN OLD BITCH GONE IN THE TEETH,	191	HUGH SELWYN: 5	3
TEGAEAN			
STRENGTHENED WITH RUSHES, TEGAEAN PAN,	211	SEXTUS PROP: 2	30
TEINTEES			
TEINTEES DE COULEUR SANG-DE-DRAGON,	160	DANS OMNIBUS	27
TELL			
TELL US THIS THING RATHER, THEN WE'LL BELIEVE YOU,	13	MESMERISM	6
WITH TIMES TOLD OVER AS WE TELL BY ROTE;	43	SATIEMUS	17
TELL ME WHERE THY LOVELY LOVE IS,	45	FROM HEINE: 3	1
I KNOW YOUR CIRCLE AND CAN FAIRLY TELL	59	EXIT' CUIUSDAM	4
AND TELL ANECDOTES OF CYBELE!	86	SALUTATION 2ND	29
(TELL IT TO MR. STRACHEY)	86	SALUTATION 2ND	31
AS I HAVE TAUGHT THEM TO TELL IT;	96	DUM CAPITOLIUM	4
CAN YOU EVEN TELL THE AGE OF A TURTLE?	140	SENNIN POEM	16
AND TELL THEIR SECRETS, MESSIRE CINO,	151	NEAR PERIGORD	2
TELL HER THAT SANG ME ONCE THAT SONG OF LAWES:	197	ENVOI (1919)	2
TELL HER THAT SHEDS	197	ENVOI (1919)	8
TELL HER THAT GOES	197	ENVOI (1919)	17
TELL ME THE TRUTHS WHICH YOU HEAR OF OUR CONSTANT YOUNG LADY,	214	SEXTUS PROP: 4	1
OUT WITH IT, TELL IT TO ME, ALL OF IT, FROM THE BEGINNING,	214	SEXTUS PROP: 4	11
AND TELL OUT THE LONG LIST OF HER TROUBLES.	223	SEXTUS PROP: 9	12
"TELL ME NOT IN MOURNFUL WISH-WASH	241	MOYEN SENSUEL	89
BECAUSE A LADY ASKS ME, I WOULD TELL	248	DONNA MI PREGA	1
DON'T TELL WHAT YOU KNOW,	259	ALF'S FOURTH	9
THEY TELL ME THAT BRANDED GOODS	262	ALF'S SEVENTH	10
WILL CHEERFULLY TELL YOU A FIST IS NO FIST,	263	ALF'S EIGHTH	10
CAN TELL YOU OF THAT FAMOUS DAY AND YEAR.	264	ALF'S NINTH	4
TELLING			
TELLING THE HEART OF THEIR TRUTH	96	DUM CAPITOLIUM	3
TELLING ME TO COME TO TIBUR:	212	SEXTUS PROP: 3	2
TELLS			
THE MORNING PAPER TELLS ME	268	ANOTHER BIT	5
SHE DIED ON THE JOB THEY TELLS ME,	271	OLE KATE	13
TEMPER			
TIBORS ALL TONGUE AND TEMPER AT MONT-AUSIER,	22	MARVOIL	18
TEMPERAMENTS			
THE TEMPERAMENTS	100	TEMPERAMENTS	T
TEMPERATE			
TO THE INDIVIDUAL, THE MONTH WAS MORE TEMPERATE	201	AGE DEMANDED	15
A TEMPERATE MAN, A THIN POTATIONIST, EACH DAY	245	MOYEN SENSUEL	199
TEMPERED			
TEMPERED AS IF	201	AGE DEMANDED	11
TEMPESTS			
WHEN THE TEMPESTS KILL THE EARTH'S FOUL PEACE,	28	ALTAFORTE	8
TEMPLE			
TO THE DYNASTIC TEMPLE, WITH WATER ABOUT IT CLEAR AS BLUE JADE,	135	EXILE'S LETTER	50
MY VOTE COMING FROM THE TEMPLE OF PHOEBUS IN LYCIA, AT PATARA,	208	SEXTUS PROP: 1	38
"AND I AM GOING TO THE TEMPLE OF VESTA . . . "	225	SEXTUS PROP:10	41
THAT RADWAY JOINED THE BAPTIST BROADWAY TEMPLE.	246	MOYEN SENSUEL	240
TEMPLES			
HAVE YOU CONTEMPTED JUNO'S PELASGIAN TEMPLES,	221	SEXTUS PROP: 8	12
TEMPORA			
TEMPORA	110	TEMPORA	T
TEMPTED			
CORYDON TEMPTED ALEXIS.	229	SEXTUS PROP:12	47
TEN			
AND INTO TEN THOUSAND VALLEYS FULL OF VOICES AND PINE-WINDS.	134	EXILE'S LETTER	21
THE TEN GOOD MILES FROM THERE TO HAMDT'S CASTLE	153	NEAR PERIGORD	65
AND TEN YEARS AFTER, OR TWENTY, AS YOU WILL,	155	NEAR PERIGORD	127
TO-MORROW IN TEN YEARS AT THE LATEST,	162	CABARET DANCER	46
THE TEN NIGHTS OF YOUR COMPANY YOU HAVE	224	SEXTUS PROP: 9	28
AND HOW TEN SINS CAN CORRUPT YOUNG MAIDENS;	229	SEXTUS PROP:12	43
SLOUCHED THE TEN MILLION.	257	BREAD BRIGADE	4

PAGE 407

TEN -- TESTICLES

	PAGE	TITLE	LINE
TEN (CONTINUED)			
DAMN THE TEN MILLION!	257	BREAD BRIGADE	8
LOUSY TEN MILLION!	257	BREAD BRIGADE	16
DAMN THE TEN MILLION.	257	BREAD BRIGADE	20
TEN YEARS AND TWELVE YEARS GONE,	259	ALF'S THIRD	18
TEN MORE AND NOTHING DONE,	259	ALF'S THIRD	19
MY SALES BEAT ALL THE OTHER TEN,	266	ALF'S ELEVENTH	3
TENDER			
STATELY, TALL AND LOVELY TENDER	8	NA AUDIART	7
TENDETH			
SPREADING ITS RAYS, IT TENDETH NEVER DOWN	249	DONNA MI PREGA	29
TENNYSON			
AS TENNYSON HAS WRITTEN,	272	THE BABY	10
TEN-SHIN			
POEM BY THE BRIDGE AT TEN-SHIN	131	AT TEN-SHIN	T
BY THE SOUTH SIDE OF THE BRIDGE AT TEN-SHIN.	134	EXILE'S LETTER	3
TENT			
"TENT PREACHIN' IS THE KIND THAT PÁYS THE BEST."	246	MOYEN SENSUEL	238
TENTACLES			
BRING CONFIDENCE UPON THE ALGAE AND THE TENTACLES OF THE SOUL.	88	COMMISSION	21
TENTATIVE			
SEE, THEY RETURN; AH, SEE THE TENTATIVE	74	THE RETURN	1
TENTH			
ALF'S TENTH BIT	265	ALF'S TENTH	T
TENTS			
I HAVE NOT FOUND THEE IN THE TENTS,	91	DANCE FIGURE	6
THE TENTS TIGHT DRAWN, HORSES AT TETHER	155	NEAR PERIGORD	130
TENULLA			
"BLANDULA, TENULLA, VAGULA"	39	BLANDULA	T
TENUOUS			
MOVES ONLY NOW A CLINGING TENUOUS GHOST.	87	THE SPRING	13
TENZONE			
TENZONE	81	TENZONE	T
TEPID			
WHEN THE HOT WATER GIVES OUT OR GOES TEPID,	100	THE BATH TUB	2
BUT YOU STUFFED COATS WHO'RE NEITHER TEPID NOR DISTINCTLY BOREAL,	238	MOYEN SENSUEL	5
TER			
TER LICK TH' BANKERS' DIRTY BOOTS	270	OF 600 M.P.'S	3
TER GRIND THE SAME OLD AXES	270	OF 600 M.P.'S	6
TERGIVERSATE			
AND ANGLE AND TERGIVERSATE	265	ALF'S TENTH	10
TERM			
THE VERY EXCELLENT TERM RUSTICUS.	99	SALVATIONISTS	4
THE TERM "VIRGO" BEING MADE MALE IN MEDIAEVAL LATINITY;	178	MOEURS CON: 1	6
FOOL WHO WOULD SET A TERM TO LOVE'S MADNESS,	220	SEXTUS PROP: 7	22
TERPSICHORE			
WITH RAPTURES FOR BACCHUS, TERPSICHORE AND THE CHURCH.	193	SIENA MI FE	15
TERRACE			
THE PHOENIX ARE AT PLAY ON THEIR TERRACE.	138	CITY OF CHOAN	1
TERRACED			
KING SO'S TERRACED PALACE	128	THE RIVER SONG	11
TERRACES			
TERRACES TINGED WITH SILVER,	141	IDEA OF CHOAN	20
TERRENE			
BY AERY APOSTLES OF TERRENE DELIGHT,	39	BLANDULA	8
TERROR			
LET THE MANES PUT OFF THEIR TERROR, LET THEM PUT OFF THEIR AQUEOUS BODIES WITH FIRE.	76	THE ALCHEMIST	51
ALREADY THEY FLEE, HOWLING IN TERROR.	81	TENZONE	5
BECAUSE OF THIS RESPECTABLE TERROR,	212	SEXTUS PROP: 3	10
TESTAMENT			
AS FOR WILL AND TESTAMENT I LEAVE NONE,	22	MARVOIL	27
TO PLAGUE TO-MORROW WITH A TESTAMENT!	59	SILET	14
TESTED			
TESTED AND PRIED AND WORKED IN MANY FASHIONS,	235	TO WHISTLER	3
TESTICLES			
WITH MINDS STILL HOVERING ABOVE THEIR TESTICLES	148	FRATRES MINORE	1

		PAGE	TITLE	LINE
TESTING -- THAT'S				
TESTING				
	TESTING HIS LIST OF RHYMES, A LEAN MAN? BILIOUS?	154	NEAR PERIGORD	101
TETHER				
	THE TENTS TIGHT DRAWN, HORSES AT TETHER	155	NEAR PERIGORD	130
TEXAS				
	OR LIKE A REAL TEXAS COLONEL,	181	MOEURS CON: 7	14
TH'				
	SHIELD O' STEEL-BLUE, TH' HEAVEN O'ER US	7	CINO	44
	OF TH' UNBOUNDED ONES, BUT YE, THAT HIDE	21	IN DURANCE	29
	ALL THE BLIND EARTH KNOWS NOT TH' EMPRISE	25	GUIDO INVITES	5
	WHERE TIME BURNS BACK ABOUT TH' ETERNAL EMBERS.	50	THE FLAME	21
	ONWARD TH' 'UNGRY BLOKES,	257	BREAD BRIGADE	5
	READIN' TH' PYPERS!	259	ALF'S THIRD	14
	TER LICK TH' BANKERS' DIRTY BOOTS	270	OF 600 M.P.'S	3
	COULD YEH SWAP TH' BRAINS OF ORL THIS LOT	270	OF 600 M.P.'S	19
THALASSES				
	PARA THINA POLYPHLOISBOIO THALASSES.	181	MOEURS CON: 6	5
THAN				
	THAT IS SWEETER THAN THE LOVE OF WOMEN	5	LA FRAISNE	35
	"THERE BE MANY SINGERS GREATER THAN THOU."	16	PRAISE YSOLT	4
	"THERE BE GREATER SOULS THAN THOU."	16	PRAISE YSOLT	26
	THAN HALF HIS CANZONI SAY OF HIM.	22	MARVOIL	26
	MORE CRAFTILY, MORE SUBTLE-SOULED THAN I;	24	THUS NINEVEH	13
	OR MORE SWEET IN TONE THAN ANY, BUT THAT I	24	THUS NINEVEH	21
	BETTER ONE HOUR'S STOUR THAN A YEAR'S PEACE	28	ALTAFORTE	16
	THAN ALL THE AGE-OLD KNOWLEDGE OF THY BOOKS:	35	THE EYES	17
	THAT HE SHOULD LIVE THAN MANY A LIVING DASTARD	37	THE YOUNG KING	23
	AND EACH TO-DAY 'VAILS LESS THAN YESTERE'EN,	37	THE YOUNG KING	28
	AND CLOSER ME THAN AIR,	39	FOR PSYCHE	7
	THAN TO HAVE WATCHED THAT HOUR AS IT PASSED.	40	ERAT HORA	7
	SOME CIRCLE OF NOT MORE THAN THREE	52	AU SALON	18
	THAN HEAR THE WHOLE AEGRUM VULGUS	52	AU SALON	21
	TIME THAN MY EYES.	67	THE CLOAK	10
	'MID THESE THINGS OLDER THAN THE NAMES THEY HAVE,	69	SUB MARE	8
	COME, LET US PITY THOSE WHO ARE BETTER OFF THAN WE ARE.	83	THE GARRET	1
	THAN THIS HOUR OF CLEAR COOLNESS,	83	THE GARRET	10
	AND I AM HAPPIER THAN YOU ARE,	85	SALUTATION	7
	AND THEY WERE HAPPIER THAN I AM;	85	SALUTATION	8
	ARE NOT MORE DELICATE THAN SHE IS,	87	ALBATRE	4
	THAT IN PLEASURE SHE RECEIVES MORE THAN SHE CAN GIVE;	103	PHYLLIDULA	3
	HARSHER THAN GRANITE,	107	COMING OF WAR	8
	ASK OF YOU THAN HOLD ANOTHER,	107	DOMPNA POIS	67
	HAVE I DRUNK A DRAUGHT, SWEETER THAN SCENT OF MYRRH.	177	LANGUE D'OC: 4	23
	RATHER THAN THE MOTTOES ON SUN-DIALE.	187	E. P. ODE	16
	THAN THE CLASSICS IN PARAPHRASE!	188	HUGH SELWYN: 2	8
	DOWSON FOUND HARLOTS CHEAPER THAN HOTELS;	190	SIENA MI FE.	13
	OLDER THAN THOSE HER GRANDMOTHER	195	HUGH SELWIN:11	7
	I SHALL BE PREY TO LAMENTATIONS WORSE THAN A NOCTURNAL ASSAILANT.	212	SEXTUS PROP: 3	11
	MY GENIUS IS NO MORE THAN A GIRL.	217	SEXTUS PROP: 5	26
	AND WITH MORE THAN ARABIAN ODOURS,	225	SEXTUS PROP:10	20
	THAN IF I TREAT THE NATION AS A WHOLE.	239	MOYEN SENSUEL	43
	(WHICH PAYS HIM MORE PER WEEK THAN THE SUPERNAL).	240	MOYEN SENSUEL	46
	THAN E'ER WERE HEARD OF BY OUR LORD CH.... J....	241	MOYEN SENSUEL	100
	THAN SPANISH LADIES HAD IN OLD ROMANCES.	242	MOYEN SENSUEL	104
	THAN I CAN FROM THIS DISTANT LAND AND STATION,	243	MOYEN SENSUEL	154
	THAN THE DUCHESS OF KAUGH.	260	ALF'S FOURTH	13
	FOR MORE THAN A DECADE.	262	ALF'S SIXTH	30
	THAN MEN LIKE ME AND YOU,	272	THE BABY	6
THANK				
	"THANK YOU, WHATEVER COMES." AND THEN SHE TURNED	40	ERAT HORA	1
THANKFUL				
	AN' BE THANKFUL FOR OCCASIONAL HOLIDAYS.	263	ALF'S EIGHTH	28
THAT (396)				
THATCH				
	LEAKS THROUGH ITS THATCH;	195	HUGH SELWIN;10	10
THAT'S				
	SWIFT CAME THE LODA, AS A BRANCH THAT'S CAUGHT,	31	PIERE VIDAL	26
	OF SOME THIN SILK STUFF THAT'S SCARCE STUFF AT ALL,	31	PIERE VIDAL	29
	THEY SING OF LOVE THAT'S GROWN DESIROUS,	45	FROM HEINE: 5	9

PAGE 409

THAT'S -- THEE

	PAGE	TITLE	LINE
THAT'S (CONTINUED)			
"TIME'S BITTER FLOOD"! OH, THAT'S ALL VERY WELL,	59	EXIT' CUIUSDAM	1
NOTHING THAT'S QUITE YOUR OWN.	61	PORTRAIT FEMME	29
SOFT AS SPRING WIND THAT'S COME FROM BIRCHEN BOWERS.	71	A VIRGINAL	10
I'D HAVE HER FORM THAT'S LACED	106	DOMPNA POIS	43
DISPRAISES HIS OWN SKILL?--THAT'S AS YOU WILL.	155	NEAR PERIGORD	143
"IN SACRED ODOUR"--(THAT'S APOCRYPHAL!)	156	NEAR PERIGORD	161
THAT'S WHAT YOU MEAN YOU ADVERTISING SPADE,	162	CABARET DANCER	34
HERE IS A PART THAT'S SLIGHT, AND PART GONE WRONG,	235	TO WHISTLER	5
THAT'S SENT TO HOLLAND, A MOST PARTICULAR FEATURE,	239	MOYEN SENSUEL	20
THESE AND A TASTE IN BOOKS THAT'S GROWN PERENNIAL	239	MOYEN SENSUEL	25
ACCOSTED, THAT'S THE WORD, ACCOSTED HIM,	242	MOYEN SENSUEL	121
THAT'S HOW THE PRESS BLURB RAN,--	261	ALF'S SIXTH	14
TO SELL, TO SELL, TO SELL, THAT'S IT, TO SELL	264	ALF'S NINTH	20
THE (2417)			
THEATRE			
A MODULATION TOWARD THE THEATRE,	196	HUGH SELWIN:12	18
THEBES			
FROM THE SUNDERED REALMS, OF THEBES AND OF AGED PRIAMUS;	38	LADY'S LIFE	8
AND CITHARAON SHOOK UP THE ROCKS BY THEBES	208	SEXTUS PROP: 1	44
NOR OF THEBES IN ITS ANCIENT RESPECTABILITY,	217	SEXTUS PROP: 5	42
INO IN HER YOUNG DAYS FLED PELLMELL OUT OF THEBES,	222	SEXTUS PROP: 8	21
THEE			
FRANCOIS AND MARGOT AND THEE AND ME,	11	OF THE GIBBET	2
FRANCOIS AND MARGOT AND THEE AND ME,	11	OF THE GIBBET	14
FRANCOIS AND MARGOT AND THEE AND ME,	12	OF THE GIBBET	26
FRANCOIS AND MARGOT AND THEE AND ME:	12	OF THE GIBBET	38
"SE IL COR TI MANCA," BUT IT FAILED THEE NOT!	19	FOR E. MCC	12
BEHOLD THE SHIELD! HE SHALL NOT TAKE THEE ALL.	19	FOR E. MCC	26
OR HIDES AMONG THE ASHES THERE FOR THEE.	20	IN DURANCE	9
"THEE"? OH, "THEE" IS WHO COMETH FIRST	20	IN DURANCE	10
"THEE"? OH, "THEE" IS WHO COMETH FIRST	20	IN DURANCE	10
FOR EVEN AS THOU ART HOLLOW BEFORE I FILL THEE WITH THIS PARCHMENT,	23	MARVOIL	37
LO, I WOULD SAIL THE SEAS WITH THEE ALONE!	25	GUIDO INVITES	2
LO, I HAVE SEEN THEE BOUND ABOUT WITH DREAMS,	25	GUIDO INVITES	7
MY SOUL, I MEET THEE, WHEN THIS LIFE'S OUTRUN,	39	BLANDULA	6
THAT WHICH STANDS FIRM IN THEE TIME BATTERS DOWN,	40	ROME	13
THEE, AND HELD THY HEART COMPLETELY.	45	FROM HEINE: 3	4
I LIVE TOO LATE TO SUP WITH THEE!	46	TRANSLATOR	2
YET SHALL MY WHITE ARMS HOLD THEE,	48	FROM HEINE: 7	29
SAPPHIRE BENACUS, IN THY MISTS AND THEE	50	THE FLAME	26
THROUGH ALL THY VARIOUS MOOD I KNOW THEE MINE;	50	THE FLAME	31
SEE, THE LIGHT GRASS SPRANG UP TO PILLOW THEE,	60	TOMB AKR CAAR	6
AND KISSED THEE WITH A MYRIAD GRASSY TONGUES;	60	TOMB AKR CAAR	7
AND ALL THY ROBES I HAVE KEPT SMOOTH ON THEE.	60	TOMB AKR CAAR	14
AND THREE SOULS CAME UPON THEE--	60	TOMB AKR CAAR	18
AND I FLOWED IN UPON THEE, BEAT THEM OFF;	60	TOMB AKR CAAR	20
I HAVE BEEN INTIMATE WITH THEE, KNOWN THY WAYS.	60	TOMB AKR CAAR	21
FLOWED IN, AND THROUGH THEE AND ABOUT THY HEELS?	60	TOMB AKR CAAR	23
HOW 'CAME I IN'? WAS I NOT THEE AND THEE?	60	TOMB AKR CAAR	24
HOW 'CAME I IN'? WAS I NOT THEE AND THEE?	60	TOMB AKR CAAR	24
LISTEN! LISTEN TO ME, AND I WILL BREATHE INTO THEE A SOUL.	62	N. Y.	2
AND I WILL BREATHE INTO THEE A SOUL,	62	N. Y.	12
THINK'ST THOU THAT DEATH WILL KISS THEE?	67	THE CLOAK	3
WILL FIND THEE SUCH A LOVER	67	THE CLOAK	5
AS I? WILL THE NEW ROSES MISS THEE?	67	THE CLOAK	6
REMEMBER THEE.	67	DORIA	11
THEE, A MARVEL, CARVEN IN SUBTLE STUFF, A	68	APPARUIT	2
GOLDEN ABOUT THEE.	68	APPARUIT	8
PARTED BEFORE THEE.	68	APPARUIT	12
FADED ABOUT THEE.	68	APPARUIT	16
THERE IS NONE LIKE THEE AMONG THE DANCERS,	91	DANCE FIGURE	4
I HAVE NOT FOUND THEE IN THE TENTS,	91	DANCE FIGURE	6
I HAVE NOT FOUND THEE AT THE WELL-HEAD	91	DANCE FIGURE	8
THEY GUARD THEE NOT WITH EUNUCHS;	91	DANCE FIGURE	14
A BROWN ROBE, WITH THREADS OF GOLD WOVEN IN PATTERNS, HAST THOU GATHERED ABOUT THEE,	91	DANCE FIGURE	17
THEIR MUSIC ABOUT THEE!	91	DANCE FIGURE	22

THEE -- THEODORUS

	PAGE	TITLE	LINE
THEE (CONTINUED)			
THERE IS NONE LIKE THEE AMONG THE DANCERS;	91	DANCE FIGURE	23
I AM UP TO FOLLOW THEE, PALLAS.	147	BEFORE SLEEP	12
I AM UP TO FOLLOW THEE, PALLAS.	147	BEFORE SLEEP	19
TO BRING THEE SAFE BACK, MY COMPANION.	172	LANGUE D'OC: 1	20
THEN WERE THERE CAUSE IN THEE THAT SHOULD CONDONE	197	ENVOI (1919)	5
"NOTHING WILL PAY THEE, FRIEND, LIKE CHRISTIANITY."	246	MOYEN SENSUEL	236
SAFE MAY'ST THOU GO MY CANZON WHITHER THEE PLEASETH	250	DONNA MI PREGA	88
THEIR (134)			
THEIRS (3)			
THEM (97)			
THEME			
DESCANT ON A THEME BY CERCLAMON	174	LANGUE D'OC: 3	SUB
LET ME RETURN TO THIS BOLD THEME OF MINE,	246	MOYEN SENSUEL	226
THEN			
AS THEN ONLY IN DREAMS,	9	NA AUDIART	47
BEING THEN YOUNG AND WRY'D,	9	NA AUDIART	48
THOU SHALT THEN SOFTEN,	9	NA AUDIART	50
THEN WHEN THE GREY WOLVES EVERYCHONE	10	FOR THIS YULE	3
THEN MAKYTH MY HEART HIS YULE-TIDE CHEER	10	FOR THIS YULE	6
THAT SAID US, "TILL THEN" FOR THE GALLOWS TREE!	11	OF THE GIBBET	4
SKOAL!! TO THE GALLOWS! AND THEN PRAY WE:	12	OF THE GIBBET	41
TELL US THIS THING RATHER, THEN WE'LL BELIEVE YOU,	13	MESMERISM	6
WELL THEN, SO CALL THEY, THE SWIRLERS OUT OF THE MIST OF MY SOUL,	20	IN DURANCE	21
THEN SMOULDER, WITH THE LIDS HALF CLOSED	21	IN DURANCE	33
THEN CAME WHAT MIGHT COME, TO WIT: THREE MEN AND ONE WOMAN,	22	MARVOIL	11
THEN HOWL I MY HEART NIGH MAD WITH REJOICING.	28	ALTAFORTE	6
AS DID FIRST SCORN, THEN LIPS OF THE PENAUTIER!	30	PIERE VIDAL	17
GOD! SHE WAS WHITE THEN, SPLENDID AS SOME TOMB	31	PIERE VIDAL	38
CEASED UTTERLY. WELL, THEN I WAITED, DREW,	31	PIERE VIDAL	40
HALF-SHEATHED, THEN NAKED FROM ITS SAFFRON SHEATH	31	PIERE VIDAL	41
JUST THEN SHE WOKE AND MOCKED THE LESS KEEN BLADE.	31	PIERE VIDAL	43
"THANK YOU, WHATEVER COMES." AND THEN SHE TURNED	40	ERAT HORA	1
IS YOUR HATE, THEN, OF SUCH MEASURE?	44	FROM HEINE: 1	1
THEN LET US SMILE A LITTLE SPACE	44	MR. HOUSMAN	13
FROST FROZE THE LAND, HAIL FELL ON EARTH THEN,	64	THE SEAFARER	33
THE HEART TURNS TO TRAVEL SO THAT HE THEN THINKS	65	THE SEAFARER	52
NOR MAY HE THEN THE FLESH-COVER, WHOSE LIFE CEASETH,	66	THE SEAFARER	96
STRAIGHT, THEN SHONE THINE ORIEL AND THE STUNNED LIGHT	68	APPARUIT	15
THEN THERE'S A GOLDISH COLOUR, DIFFERENT.	69	SUB MARE	4
FANNING THE GRASS SHE WALKED ON THEN, ENDURES:	92	GENTILDONNA	4
KNOW THEN THAT I LOVED YOU FROM AFORE-TIME,	96	DUM CAPITOLIUM	7
THEN THE WATERS OF HAN WOULD FLOW NORTHWARD.)	129	THE RIVER SONG	18
AND THEN I WAS SENT OFF TO SOUTH WEI,	134	EXILE'S LETTER	12
AND THEN, WHEN SEPARATION HAD COME TO ITS WORST,	134	EXILE'S LETTER	16
AND THEN THE CROWD BROKE UP, YOU WENT NORTH TO SAN PALACE,	136	EXILE'S LETTER	71
RIGHT ENOUGH? THEN READ BETWEEN THE LINES OF UC ST. CIRC,	151	NEAR PERIGORD	3
HIGH, HIGH AND SURE . . . AND THEN THE COUNTERTHRUST:	157	NEAR PERIGORD	180
BELIEVING IN OLD MEN'S LIES, THEN UNBELIEVING	190	HUGH SELWYN: 4	14
THEN WERE THERE CAUSE IN THEE THAT SHOULD CONDONE	197	ENVOI (1919)	5
THEN ON AN OAR	203	MAUBERLEY: 4	20
SAID THEN "YOU IDIOT! WHAT ARE YOU DOING WITH THAT WATER:	210	SEXTUS PROP: 2	17
AND SHE THEN OPENING MY EYELIDS FALLEN IN SLEEP,	220	SEXTUS PROP: 7	7
AND THEN THESE SKETCHES IN THE MOOD OF GREECE?	235	TO WHISTLER	9
WHAT IT KNEW THEN, IT KNOWS, AND THERE IT STICKS.	240	MOYEN SENSUEL	56
AND THEN THAT WOMAN LIKE A GUINEA-PIG	242	MOYEN SENSUEL	120
THEN THERE CAME OTHER NIGHTS, CAME SLOW BUT CERTAIN	243	MOYEN SENSUEL	133
AND THEN RADWAY BEGAN TO GO THE PACES:	243	MOYEN SENSUEL	144
OUT INTO THE CREPUSCULAR HALF-LIGHT, NOW AND THEN;	244	MOYEN SENSUEL	186
LEISURE'S ADORNMENT PUTS HE THEN NEVER ON,	249	DONNA MI PREGA	51
TOLD 'EM TO DIE IN WAR, AND THEN TO DAVID,	260	ALF'S FIFTH	2
THEN CUT THEIR SAVING TO THE HALF OR LOWER;	260	ALF'S FIFTH	6
AND THEN LENDS OUT THEIR PRINTED SLIPS	269	SAFE AND SOUND	19
THEODORUS			
THEODORUS WILL BE PLEASED AT MY DEATH,	164	QUINTUS SEPTIM	1

PAGE 411

THEODORUS -- THERE

	PAGE	TITLE	LINE
THEODORUS (CONTINUED)			
AND SOMEONE ELSE WILL BE PLEASED AT THE DEATH OF THEODORUS,	164	QUINTUS SEPTIM	2
THEON			
TIN' ANDRA, TIN' HEROA, TINA THEON,	189	HUGH SELWYN: 3	26
THEORIES			
OF THE NEW ECONOMICAL THEORIES	273	NATIONAL SONG	15
THERE			
ONCE THERE WAS A WOMAN ...	5	LA FRAISNE	42
'CAUSE NEVER A FLAW WAS THERE	8	NA AUDIART	23
"THERE BE MANY SINGERS GREATER THAN THOU."	16	PRAISE YSOLT	4
YET THERE IS A TREMBLING UPON ME IN THE TWILIGHT,	16	PRAISE YSOLT	14
"THERE BE GREATER SOULS THAN THOU."	16	PRAISE YSOLT	26
FOR IN THE MORN OF MY YEARS THERE CAME A WOMAN	16	PRAISE YSOLT	27
OH I KNOW THAT THERE ARE FOLK ABOUT ME, FRIENDLY FACES,	20	IN DURANCE	2
OR HIDES AMONG THE ASHES THERE FOR THEE.	20	IN DURANCE	9
"BEYOND, BEYOND, BEYOND, THERE LIES ..."	21	IN DURANCE	49
WAS THERE SUCH FLESH MADE EVER AND UNMADE!	31	PIERE VIDAL	45
O STRANGE FACE THERE IN THE GLASS!	35	HIS OWN FACE	1
FREE US, FOR THERE IS ONE	35	THE EYES	15
AND THERE WERE FLOWERS IN YOUR HANDS,	36	FRANCESCA	2
THERE WHERE THERE IS NO GRIEF, NOR SHALL BE SADNESS.	37	THE YOUNG KING	40
THERE WHERE THERE IS NO GRIEF, NOR SHALL BE SADNESS.	37	THE YOUNG KING	40
SOUL, IF SHE MEET US THERE, WILL ANY RUMOUR	39	BLANDULA	13
"LO, ONE THERE WAS WHO BENT HER FAIR BRIGHT HEAD, AND WE'LL BE HAPPY THERE.	43	SATIEMUS	5
	47	FROM HEINE: 7	4
THOU WILT IN MY WHITE ARMS THERE,	47	FROM HEINE: 7	9
FORGET AND REST AND DREAM THERE	47	FROM HEINE: 7	11
MY LIPS AND MY HEART ARE THINE THERE	47	FROM HEINE: 7	13
IF MY HEART STAY BELOW THERE,	47	FROM HEINE: 7	21
THE DARK DWARFS BLOW AND BOW THERE	47	FROM HEINE: 7	27
THERE WAS NO PARTICULAR HASTE,	48	FROM HEINE: 8	2
AND I HAVE SEEN HER THERE WITHIN HER HOUSE,	49	OF SPLENDOUR	9
THERE ARE THERE MANY ROOMS AND ALL OF GOLD,	49	OF SPLENDOUR	13
THERE ARE THERE MANY ROOMS AND ALL OF GOLD,	49	OF SPLENDOUR	13
MAKETH ME CLEAR, AND THERE ARE POWERS IN THIS	49	OF SPLENDOUR	19
THERE IS THE SUBTLER MUSIC, THE CLEAR LIGHT	50	THE FLAME	20
LO, THERE ARE MANY GODS WHOM WE HAVE SEEN,	50	THE FLAME	23
THERE CANST THOU FIND ME, O THOU ANXIOUS THOU,	51	THE FLAME	34
I SUPPOSE THERE ARE A FEW DOZEN VERITIES	52	AU SALON	6
O YOU AWAY HIGH THERE,	53	AU JARDIN	1
OVER BEYOND THE MOON THERE,	53	AU JARDIN	16
THERE IS ENOUGH IN WHAT I CHANCE TO SAY.	59	SILET	4
AND THERE IS NO NEW THING IN ALL THIS PLACE.	60	TOMB AKR CAAR	11
NO! THERE IS NOTHING! IN THE WHOLE AND ALL,	61	PORTRAIT FEMME	28
AND DIRE SEA-SURGE, AND THERE I OFT SPENT	64	THE SEAFARER	6
THERE I HEARD NAUGHT SAVE THE HARSH SEA	64	THE SEAFARER	18
CORN OF THE COLDEST. NATHLESS THERE KNOCKETH NOW	64	THE SEAFARER	34
SAVE THERE BE SOMEWHAT CALAMITOUS	66	THE SEAFARER	69
THERE COME NOW NO KINGS NOR CAESARS	66	THE SEAFARER	84
GREEN THE WAYS, THE BREATH OF THE FIELDS IS THINE THERE,	68	APPARUIT	9
"THERE IS NO SUMMER IN THE LEAVES,	72	PAN IS DEAD	4
FROM HERE TO THERE TO THE SEA'S BORDER,	72	DIEU! QU'IL	9
AND ROUND ABOUT THERE IS A RABBLE	83	THE GARDEN	5
LET THERE BE COMMERCE BETWEEN US.	89	A PACT	9
THERE IS A TRUCE AMONG THE GODS,	90	SURGIT FAMA	1
THERE IS NONE LIKE THEE AMONG THE DANCERS,	91	DANCE FIGURE	4
THERE IS NONE LIKE THEE AMONG THE DANCERS;	91	DANCE FIGURE	23
OR THAT THERE IS NO CASTE IN THIS FAMILY.	94	INSTRUCTIONS	22
FOR THERE ARE, IN SIRMIONE, TWENTY-EIGHT YOUNG DANTES AND THIRTY-FOUR CATULLI;	96	AESTHETICS	8
AND THERE HAD BEEN A GREAT CATCH OF SARDINES,	96	AESTHETICS	9
THAT NOW THERE IS NO ONE AT ALL	97	THE BELLAIRES	9
AND THERE WILL BE ONLY THE MORE CONFUSION,	98	THE BELLAIRES	26
THERE IS NO SOUND OF FOOT-FALL, AND THE LEAVES	108	LIU CH'E	
THERE COME FORTH MANY MAIDENS	108	CH'U YUAN	
FOR THERE ARE LEOPARDS DRAWING THE CARS.	108	CH'U YUAN	
THERE FLOAT THE PETAL-LIKE FLAMES.	109	HEATHER	
HERE IS THERE NAUGHT OF DEAD GODS	110	COITUS	

PAGE 412

THERE

	PAGE	TITLE	LINE
THERE (CONTINUED)			
THERE IS A PLACE OF TREES . . . GRAY WITH LICHEN.	121	PROVINC DESERT	6
I HAVE WALKED THERE	121	PROVINC DESERT	7
HAVE THE RIGHT THERE--	121	PROVINC DESERT	12
THERE ARE THREE KEEPS NEAR MAREUIL,	121	PROVINC DESERT	24
THERE IS NO EASE IN ROYAL AFFAIRS, WE HAVE NO COMFORT.	127	BOWMEN OF SHU	11
AT MORNING THERE ARE FLOWERS TO CUT THE HEART,	131	AT TEN-SHIN	3
THERE IS NO WALL LEFT TO THIS VILLAGE.	133	FRONTIER GUARD	7
THERE WAS NOTHING AT CROSS PURPOSE,	134	EXILE'S LETTER	8
AND THERE CAME ALSO THE "TRUE MAN" OF SHI-YO TO MEET ME,	134	EXILE'S LETTER	24
WHAT IS THE USE OF TALKING, AND THERE IS NO END OF TALKING,	136	EXILE'S LETTER	75
THERE IS NO END OF THINGS IN THE HEART.	136	EXILE'S LETTER	76
THERE IS NO NEED OF ASKING DIVINERS.	138	NEAR SHOKU	11
"IT IS NOT THAT THERE ARE NO OTHER MEN	142	UNMOVING CLOUD	24
HIS BROTHER-IN-LAW WAS ALL THERE WAS OF POWER	151	NEAR PERIGORD	17
THE TEN GOOD MILES FROM THERE TO MAENT'S CASTLE,	153	NEAR PER'GORD	65
THERE IS A THROAT; AH, THERE ARE TWO WHITE HANDS;	153	NEAR PERIGORD	71
THERE IS A THROAT; AH, THERE ARE TWO WHITE HANDS;	153	NEAR PERIGORD	71
THERE IS A TRELLIS FULL OF EARLY ROSES,	153	NEAR PERIGORD	72
OH, THERE IS PRECEDENT, LEGAL TRADITION,	153	NEAR PERIGORD	88
RICHARD SHALL DIE TO-MORROW--LEAVE HIM THERE	155	NEAR PERIGORD	139
THERE SHUT UP IN HIS CASTLE, TAIRIRAN'S,	157	NEAR PERIGORD	186
FOR THEM THERE IS SOMETHING AFOOT.	158	PSYCHOLOG HOUR	18
AND THERE ARE ALSO THE INANE EXPENSES OF THE FUNERAL;	164	QUINTUS SEPTIM	9
FOR AFTER DEATH THERE COMES NO OTHER CALAMITY.	164	QUINTUS SEPTIM	11
THERE IS A PLACE--BUT NO ONE ELSE KNOWS IT--	166	FISH & SHADOW	14
THERE IS NOT MUCH BUT ITS EVIL LEFT US.	168	OF AROUET	24
WHERE MY LOVE IS, THERE IS A GLITTER OF SUN;	174	LANGUE D'OC: 3	16
AT A FRIEND OF MY WIFE'S THERE IS A PHOTOGRAPH,	180	MOEURS CON: 5	1
THERE IS A SATIN-LIKE BOW ON THE HARP.	180	MOEURS CON: 5	15
THERE IS A SATIN-LIKE BOW ON AN HARP.	180	MOEURS CON: 5	17
"THERE WAS ONCE A MAN CALLED VOLTAIRE."	181	MOEURS CON: 7	16
THERE DIED A MYRIAD,	191	HUGH SELWYN: 5	1
THEN WERE THERE CAUSE IN THEE THAT SHOULD CONDONE	197	ENVOI (1919)	5
AND THERE IS NO HIGH-ROAD TO THE MUSES.	207	SEXTUS PROP: 1	15
AND THERE IS NO HURRY ABOUT IT;	207	SEXTUS PROP: 1	22
THERE WILL BE A CROWD OF YOUNG WOMEN DOING HOMAGE TO MY PALAVER,	208	SEXTUS PROP: 1	50
NOR IS THERE ANYONE TO WHOM LOVERS ARE NOT SACRED AT MIDNIGHT	212	SEXTUS PROP: 3	15
THERE IS A VOLUME IN THE MATTER; IF HER EYELIDS SINK INTO SLEEP,	217	SEXTUS PROP: 5	31
THERE ARE NEW JOBS FOR THE AUTHOR;	217	SEXTUS PROP: 5	32
NOR AT MY FUNERAL EITHER WILL THERE BY ANY LONG TRAIL,	219	SEXTUS PROP: 6	13
THERE WILL BE THREE BOOKS AT MY OBSEQUIES	219	SEXTUS PROP: 6	20
THERE COMES, IT SEEMS, AND AT ANY RATE	222	SEXTUS PROP: 8	16
THERE SHALL BE NONE IN A BETTER SEAT, NOT	222	SEXTUS PROP: 8	35
THERE WILL BE, IN ANY CASE, A STIR ON OLYMPUS.	222	SEXTUS PROP: 8	42
THERE ARE ENOUGH WOMEN IN HELL,	223	SEXTUS PROP: 9	14
"SHOVE ALONG THERE, SHOVE ALONG!"	224	SEXTUS PROP:10	15
THERE WERE UPON THE BED NO SIGNS OF A VOLUPTUOUS ENCOUNTER,	225	SEXTUS PROP:10	36
ESCAPE! THERE IS, O IDIOT, NO ESCAPE,	226	SEXTUS PROP:11	4
EVEN THERE, NO ESCAPE	227	SEXTUS PROP:11	37
AND THERE WAS A CASE IN COLCHIS, JASON AND THAT WOMAN IN COLCHIS;	228	SEXTUS PROP:12	7
NOR WHETHER THERE BE ANY PATCH LEFT OF US	228	SEXTUS PROP:12	27
WERE THERE AN ERUDITE OR VIOLENT PASSION,	230	SEXTUS PROP:12	63
THERE IS SONG IN THE PARCHMENT; CATULLUS THE HIGHLY INDECOROUS,	230	SEXTUS PROP:12	68
WHAT IT KNEW THEN, IT KNOWS, AND THERE IT STICKS.	240	MOYEN SENSUEL	56
THEN THERE CAME OTHER NIGHTS, LAID SLOW BUT CERTAIN BEHIND THEM? WHAT'S THERE? HER SOUL'S AN AFFAIR FOR OCULISTS.	243	MOYEN SENSUEL	133
I AM NOT "THAT CHAP THERE" NOR YET "THE SUPERB"	247	PIERROTS	12
FORMED THERE IN MANNER AS A MIST OF LIGHT	247	PIERROTS	16
ROUSING THERE THIRST	248	DONNA MI PREGA	20
	250	DONNA MI PREGA	60

PAGE 413

THERE -- THIEVES

	PAGE	TITLE	LINE
THERE (CONTINUED)			
THERE, BEYOND COLOUR, ESSENCE SET APART,	250	DONNA MI PREGA	84
THERE GOES THE NIGHT BRIGADE,	257	BREAD BRIGADE	9
SEE 'EM GO SLOUCHING THERE,	257	BREAD BRIGADE	24
NAUGHT BUT A SHIRT IS THERE	258	ALF'S THIRD	3
DOWN THERE IN CAMBRIDGE	258	ALF'S SECOND	9
DOWN THERE IN CLERKENWALL	259	ALF'S THIRD	13
IN HIS EYE THERE IS DEATH,--I MEAN THE BANKER'S,--	263	ALF'S EIGHTH	15
IN HIS PURSE THERE IS DECEIT,	263	ALF'S EIGHTH	16
AND WHERE HE ONCE SET FOOT, RIGHT THERE HE STAYED.	264	ALF'S NINTH	12
THERE IS SIR HEN. DETERDING	267	ALF'S TWELFTH	7
THERE IS BLOKES IN AUTOMOBILES	269	SAFE AND SOUND	13
THERE IS NO LAND LIKE ENGLAND	272	NATIONAL SONG	1
THERE ARE NO BANKS LIKE ENGLISH BANKS	272	NATIONAL SONG	3
THERE IS NO SUCH LAND OF CASTLES	272	NATIONAL SONG	5
THEREAFTER			
NEVER THEREAFTER, BUT MOVES CHANGING STATE,	249	DONNA MI PREGA	52
THEREBY			
THAT DANCING AND GENTLE IS AND THEREBY PLEASANTER,	177	LANGUE D'OC: 4	22
THEREFORE			
THEREFORE LET US ACT AS IF WE WERE	43	MR. HOUSMAN	4
LET US THEREFORE MENTION THE FACT,	93	LES MILLWIN	13
THEREFORE THE SAILORS ARE CHEERED, AND THE WAVES	164	QUINTUS SEPTIM	6
LET US THEREFORE CEASE FROM PITYING THE DEAD	164	QUINTUS SEPTIM	10
THE CHOPPED SEAS HELD HIM, THEREFORE, THAT YEAR.	187	E. P. ODE	12
MIGHT CAUSE THOUGHT AND BE THEREFORE	262	ALF'S SEVENTH	19
THERE'LL			
BUT THERE'LL COME SORROW OF IT.	53	AU JARDIN	14
THEREOF			
THROUGH THE SKY, AND THE WIND THEREOF IS MY BODY.	18	DE AEGYPTO	2
THROUGH THE SKY, AND THE WIND THEREOF IS MY BODY.	18	DE AEGYPTO	8
THROUGH THE SKY, AND THE WIND THEREOF IS MY BODY.	18	DE AEGYPTO	16
THROUGH THE SKY, AND THE WIND THEREOF IS MY BODY.	18	DE AEGYPTO	24
THEREON			
AND WE WOULD LOOK THEREON.	35	THE EYES	18
HER MONUMENT, THE IMAGE CUT THEREON	41	HER MONUMENT	T
THEREON THE AMOROUS CALOR SLIGHTLY FROSTED HIM. ...	242	MOYEN SENSUEL	122
THERE'S			
BAH! THERE'S NO WINE LIKE THE BLOOD'S CRIMSON! ...	28	ALTAFORTE	18
THERE'S NO SOUND LIKE TO SWORDS SWORDS OPPOSING,	29	ALTAFORTE	32
THAT THERE'S NO THING MORE SWEET OR FALSE AT ALL.	44	FROM HEINE: 2	4
THERE'S NO PARTICULAR HASTE.	48	FROM HEINE: 8	4
WELL, THERE'S NO USE YOUR LOVING ME	53	AU JARDIN	8
FOR THIS THERE'S NO MOOD-LOFTY MAN OVER EARTH'S MIDST,	65	THE SEAFARER	40
THEN THERE'S A GOLDISH COLOUR, DIFFERENT.	69	SUB MARE	4
DAME NOR DAMSEL THERE'S NOT ANY	72	DIEU! QU'IL	10
"THERE'S NOTHING IN IT."	194	MR. NIXON	20
AND DIED, THERE'S NOTHING IN IT.	194	MR. NIXON	24
SHOW US THERE'S CHANCE AT LEAST OF WINNING THROUGH.	235	TO WHISTLER	19
THESE (68)			
THESEUS			
AND WITHOUT THESEUS,	218	SEXTUS PROP: 5	50
THEY (145)			
THEY'LL			
THEY'LL KNOW MORE OF ARNAUT OF MARVOIL	22	MARVOIL	25
THEY'LL NO' GET HIM A' IN A BOOK I THINK	33	GOODLY FERE	21
THEY'LL TRICK YOU AGAIN AND AGAIN, AS YOU SLEEP;	265	ALF'S NINTH	31
THEY'RE (1)			
THEY'VE (1)			
THICK			
AND CALL MY VOICE TOO THICK A THING.	45	FROM HEINE: 5	4
THICK FOLIAGE	203	MAUBERLEY: 4	6
THICKENED			
GO TO THOSE WHO ARE THICKENED WITH MIDDLE AGE, ...	89	COMMISSION	26
THICKET			
I WILL COME OUT FROM THE NEW THICKET	108	CH'U YUAN	9
THIEVES			
O GOD, O VENUS, O MERCURY, PATRON OF THIEVES,	117	THE LAKE ISLE	1
O GOD, O VENUS, O MERCURY, PATRON OF THIEVES,	117	THE LAKE ISLE	12

THIGHS -- THINGS

	PAGE	TITLE	LINE
THIGHS			
"DAPHNE WITH HER THIGHS IN BARK	196	HUGH SELWIN:12	1
THIN			
OF SOME THIN SILK STUFF THAT'S SCARCE STUFF AT ALL,	31	PIERE VIDAL	29
A THIN WAR OF METAL.	95	OF THE DEGREES	5
THIN LIKE BROOK-WATER, ...	192	YEUX GLAUQUES	13
THE THIN, CLEAR GAZE, THE SAME	192	YEUX GLAUQUES	17
AND TRUTH SHOULD HERE BE CAREFUL OF HER THIN DRESS--	243	MOYEN SENSUEL	146
A TEMPERATE MAN, A THIN POTATIONIST, EACH DAY	245	MOYEN SENSUEL	199
SCARCE AND THIN, SCARCE AND THIN	265	ALF'S TENTH	1
SCARCE AND THIN, SCARCE AND THIN	265	ALF'S TENTH	1
THINA			
PARA THINA POLYPHLOISBOIO THALASSES.	181	MOEURS CON: 6	5
THINE			
NOR THINE TO HINDER, ...	24	THUS NINEVEH	6
MINE IS THE SHIP AND THINE THE MERCHANDISE, ...	25	GUIDO INVITES	4
LIKENESS OF THINE HANDMAID, ...	26	NIGHT LITANY	24
FOR THINE OLD LEGEND-LUST.	47	FROM HEINE: 7	12
MY LIPS AND MY HEART ARE THINE THERE	47	FROM HEINE: 7	13
GREEN THE WAYS, THE BREATH OF THE FIELDS IS THINE THERE, ...	68	APPARUIT	9
STRAIGHT, THEN SHONE THINE ORIEL AND THE STUNNED LIGHT	68	APPARUIT	15
THINE ARMS ARE AS A YOUNG SAPLING UNDER THE DARK;	91	DANCE FIGURE	10
THING			
THAT THEY MIGHT DO THIS WONDER THING, ...	3	THE TREE	9
AND MANY A NEW THING UNDERSTOOD	3	THE TREE	11
TELL US THIS THING RATHER, THEN WE'LL BELIEVE YOU,	13	MESMERISM	6
"LO! THIS THING IS NOT MINE	24	THUS NINEVEH	5
A THING OF TEARS.	26	NIGHT LITANY	8
HAVE SEEN THIS THING, OUT OF THEIR FAR COURSES	27	NIGHT LITANY	42
HAVE THEY SEEN THIS THING, ...	27	NIGHT LITANY	43
"YE SHALL SEE ONE THING TO MASTER ALL:	34	GOODLY FERE	31
SITH NO THING IS BUT TURNETH UNTO ANGUISH	37	THE YOUNG KING	27
AND FIND'ST IN ROME NO THING THOU CANST CALL ROMAN;	40	ROME	2
MAY NOT MAKE BOAST OF ANY BETTER THING	40	ERAT HORA	6
THAT THERE'S NO THING MORE SWEET OR FALSE AT ALL.	44	FROM HEINE: 2	4
AND CALL MY VOICE TOO THICK A THING.	45	FROM HEINE: 5	4
THIS THING THAT MOVES AS MAN IS NO MORE MORTAL. ..	51	THE FLAME	38
TO SAY THAT LIFE IS, SOME WAY, A GAY THING, ...	53	AU JARDIN	12
BURN NOT WITH ME NOR ANY SAFFRON THING.	60	TOMB AKR CAAR	5
AND THERE IS NO NEW THING IN ALL THIS PLACE.	60	TOMB AKR CAAR	11
NO, YOU PREFERRED IT TO THE USUAL THING:	61	PORTRAIT FEMME	8
THIS THING, THAT HATH A CODE AND NOT A CORE, ...	63	AN OBJECT	7
THOU A SLIGHT THING, THOU IN ACCESS OF CUNNING ...	68	APPARUIT	23
AND HERE'S THE THING THAT LASTS THE WHOLE THING OUT:	73	JACOPO SELLAIO	5
AND HERE'S THE THING THAT LASTS THE WHOLE THING OUT:	73	JACOPO SELLAIO	5
A PROUD THING I DO HERE, ...	105	DOMPNA POIS	24
THIS THING WILL RUN AT YOU	109	THE FAUN	8
TO SING ONE THING WHEN YOUR SONG MEANS ANOTHER, ...	153	NEAR PERIGORD	89
BEAUTY IS SO RARE A THING.	158	PSYCHOLOG HOUR	6
BEAUTY IS SO RARE A THING	158	PSYCHOLOG HOUR	21
GIVE ME BACK THE TIME OF THE THING.	167	OF AROUET	16
AND WOULD NOT THINK A THING THAT COULD UPSET HER.	242	MOYEN SENSUEL	110
ONE THING AMONG ALL THINGS YOU WILL NOT	265	ALF'S TENTH	11
THE KING WAS ONCE THE BIGGEST THING	267	ALF'S ELEVENTH	21
THINGS			
KNOWING THE TRUTH OF THINGS UNSEEN BEFORE;	3	THE TREE	2
BEING IN ALL THINGS WISE, AND VERY OLD, ...	4	LA FRAISNE	2
I DO NOT LIKE TO REMEMBER THINGS ANY MORE.	5	LA FRAISNE	48
I WHO HAVE SEEN YOU AMID THE PRIMAL THINGS	36	FRANCESCA	5
INFINITE THINGS DESIRED, LOFTY VISIONS	42	HER MONUMENT	41
THAT YOU CAN SAY SUCH AWFUL THINGS	44	FROM HEINE: 1	7
ALL GOOD THINGS GO VANISHING.	46	FROM HEINE: 6	20
THAT GLADS ME ALL THINGS THAT O'ERSHADOW IT, ...	51	THE FLAME	41
SOME CERTAIN PECULIAR THINGS, ...	58	AU SALON	24
IDEAS, OLD GOSSIP, ODDMENTS OF ALL THINGS, ...	61	PORTRAIT FEMME	4
FOR ALL THIS SEA-HOARD OF DECIDUOUS THINGS, ...	61	PORTRAIT FEMME	25
AS TRANSIENT THINGS ARE--	67	DORIA	3
OF ALL THINGS, FRAIL ALABASTER, AH ME!	68	APPARUIT	19

THINGS -- THINKS

	PAGE	TITLE	LINE
THINGS (CONTINUED)			
AND ONE GROPES IN THESE THINGS AS DELICATE	69	SUB MARE	5
'MID THESE THINGS OLDER THAN THE NAMES THEY HAVE,	69	SUB MARE	8
THESE THINGS THAT ARE FAMILIARS OF THE GOD.	69	SUB MARE	9
TO SHEATHE ME HALF IN HALF THE THINGS THAT SHEATHE HER.	71	A VIRGINAL	8
NO MAN COULD PAINT SUCH THINGS WHO DID NOT KNOW.	73	JACOPO SELLAIO	2
GO! REJUVENATE THINGS!	86	SALUTATION 2ND	24
AND THE LITTLE MILLWINS BEHELD THESE THINGS;	93	LES MILLWIN	11
MAKES HAY WITH THE THINGS IN HER HOUSE.	115	SOCIAL ORDER	10
THERE IS NO END OF THINGS IN THE HEART.	136	EXILE'S LETTER	76
THE SUN RISES IN SOUTH EAST CORNER OF THINGS	140	MULBERRY ROAD	1
AND LAUGHTER IS THE END OF ALL THINGS.	147	POST MORTEM	5
"THUS THINGS PROCEED IN THEIR CIRCLE";	178	MOEURS CON: 1	19
ALL THINGS ARE A FLOWING,	189	HUGH SELWYN: 3	9
ALL THINGS SAVE BEAUTY ALONE.	197	ENVOI (1919)	26
SEEING THAT LONG STANDING INCREASES ALL THINGS	207	SEXTUS PROP: 1	24
TO THINGS WHICH YOU THINK I WOULD LIKE TO BELIEVE.	214	SEXTUS PROP: 4	7
FOR WHICH THINGS YOU WILL GET A REWARD FROM ME, LYGDAMUS?	215	SEXTUS PROP: 4	27
TO SAY MANY THINGS IS EQUAL TO HAVING A HOME.	215	SEXTUS PROP: 4	28
"WILL HE SAY NASTY THINGS AT MY FUNERAL?"	215	SEXTUS PROP: 4	40
"IN THINGS OF SIMILAR MAGNITUDE	216	SEXTUS PROP: 5	5
NEITHER CALLIOPE NOR APOLLO SUNG THESE THINGS INTO MY EAR,	217	SEXTUS PROP: 5	25
ALL THINGS ARE FORGIVEN FOR ONE NIGHT OF YOUR GAMES.	227	SEXTUS PROP:11	39
ONE THING AMONG ALL THINGS YOU WILL NOT	265	ALF'S TENTH	11
OF THINGS THAT HAPPENED VERY LONG AGO,	265	ALF'S NINTH	27
THING'S			
IN THIS THING'S SURE DECORUM AND BEHAVIOUR.	63	PHASELLUS ILLE	14
MOCK NOT THE FLOOD OF STARS, THE THING'S TO BE.	69	THE NEEDLE	8
THINK			
I THINK SHE HURT ME ONCE, BUT . .	5	LA FRAISNE	46
WHEN I BUT THINK UPON THE GREAT DEAD DAYS	30	PIERE VIDAL	1
AYE YE ARE FOOLS, IF YE THINK TIME CAN BLOT	30	PIERE VIDAL	18
THEY'LL NO' GET HIM A' IN A BOOK I THINK	33	GOODLY FERE	21
IF THEY THINK THEY HA' SNARED OUR GOODLY FERE	33	GOODLY FERE	25
IF THEY THINK THEY HA' SLAIN OUR GOODLY FERE	34	GOODLY FERE	51
WHY SHOULD WE STOP AT ALL FOR WHAT I THINK?	59	SILET	3
NOR STIR HAND NOR THINK IN MID HEART,	66	THE SEAFARER	98
FOR I THINK THE GLASS IS EVIL.	95	OF THE DEGREES	2
AND THEY THINK IT WILL LAST A THOUSAND AUTUMNS,	132	AT TEN-SHIN	26
I THINK OF TALKING AND MAN,	142	UNMOVING CLOUD	15
AND I THINK I HAVE HEARD THEM SAYING,	142	UNMOVING CLOUD	23
THINK YOU THAT MAENT LIVED AT MONTAIGNAC,	151	NEAR PERIGORD	11
"YOU NEED, PROPERTIUS, NOT THINK	210	SEXTUS PROP: 2	19
TO THINGS WHICH YOU THINK I WOULD LIKE TO BELIEVE.	214	SEXTUS PROP: 4	7
AND "IT IS, I THINK, INDIA WHICH NOW GIVES NECKS TO YOUR TRIUMPH,"	216	SEXTUS PROP: 5	17
"DO YOU THINK I HAVE ADOPTED YOUR HABITS?"	225	SEXTUS PROP:10	35
YOU THINK YOU ARE GOING TO DO HOMER.	228	SEXTUS PROP:12	22
OR FROM THE FEATS OF SUMNER CULL IT? THINK,	241	MOYEN SENSUEL	75
AND WOULD NOT THINK A THING THAT COULD UPSET HER. .	242	MOYEN SENSUEL	110
MUST THINK TRUTH LOOKS AS THEY DO IN WOOL PYJAMAS.	243	MOYEN SENSUEL	148
"KNOW WHAT THEY THINK, AND JUST WHAT BOOKS THEY'VE READ,	244	MOYEN SENSUEL	182
DO, THAT IS: THINK, BEFORE IT'S TOO LATE.	265	ALF'S TENTH	12
THINKING			
MUST KNOW SUCH MOMENTS, THINKING ON THE GRASS;	43	SATIEMUS	11
THINKING OF OLD DAYS.	121	PROVINC DESERT	8
THINKING OF MONTAIGNAC, SOUTHWARD.	122	PROVINC DESERT	49
AND THINKING HOW LITTLE YOU CARED FOR THE COST,	135	EXILE'S LETTER	44
AND SEND IT A THOUSAND MILES, THINKING.	136	EXILE'S LETTER	80
THINKING OF AELIS, WHOM HE LOVED HEART AND SOUL . . .	154	NEAR PERIGORD	110
THINKS			
THE HEART TURNS TO TRAVEL SO THAT HE THEN THINKS	65	THE SEAFARER	52
"HE THINKS THAT WE ARE NOT GODS."	224	SEXTUS PROP:10	17
HENRY VAN DYKE, WHO THINKS TO CHARM THE MUSE YOU PACK HER IN	239	MOYEN SENSUEL	21

PAGE 416

THINKS -- THOU

	PAGE	TITLE	LINE
THINKS (CONTINUED)			
THINKS ONE IDENTITY IS	244	MOYEN SENSUEL	173
AND THINKS ABOUT A ROWTON 'OUSE	270	OF 600 M.P.'S	15
THINK'ST			
THINK'ST THOU THAT DEATH WILL KISS THEE?	67	THE CLOAK	3
THINK'ST THOU THAT THE DARK HOUSE	67	THE CLOAK	4
THIRD			
AND THE THIRD WRITES AN EPIGRAM TO CANDIDIA.	118	THREE POETS	7
SALUTATION THE THIRD	145	SALUTATION 3RD	T
NOW THE THIRD DAY IS HERE--	159	PSYCHOLOG HOUR	39
UP STAIRS, THE THIRD FLOOR UP, AND HAVE SUCH QUANDARIES	244	MOYEN SENSUEL	158
ALF'S THIRD BIT	258	ALF'S THIRD	T
THIRDS			
HIS PALACE IS LIKE A CUBE CUT IN THIRDS,	237	ABU SALAMMAMM	7
THIRST			
ROUSING THERE THIRST	250	DONNA MI PREGA	60
THIRSTY			
SORROWFUL MINDS, SORROW IS STRONG, WE ARE HUNGRY AND THIRSTY.	127	BOWMEN OF SHU	7
WE GO SLOWLY, WE ARE HUNGRY AND THIRSTY,	127	BOWMEN OF SHU	23
THIRTY			
OR PERHAPS I WILL DIE AT THIRTY?	145	SALUTATION 3RD	17
THIRTY-FOUR			
FOR THERE ARE, IN SIRMIONE, TWENTY-EIGHT YOUNG DANTES AND THIRTY-FOUR CATULLI;	96	AESTHETICS	8
THIRTY-SIX			
THROUGH ALL THE THIRTY-SIX FOLDS OF THE TURNING AND TWISTING WATERS,	134	EXILE'S LETTER	18
THIS (177)			
THITHER			
DESIRE WILL FOLLOW YOU THITHER,	226	SEXTUS PROP:11	6
THOMAS			
THOMAS LARRON "EAR-THE-LESS,"	11	OF THE GIBBET	6
THOROUGHFARE			
BESIDE THIS THOROUGHFARE	196	HUGH SELWIN:12	25
THOROUGHLY			
AND HAVE YOU THOROUGHLY KISSED MY LIPS?	48	FROM HEINE: 8	1
O GENERATION OF THE THOROUGHLY SMUG	85	SALUTATION	1
AND THOROUGHLY UNCOMFORTABLE,	85	SALUTATION	2
THOROUGHLY BEAUTIFUL,	103	LADIES	16
WHEN THOROUGHLY SOCIALIZED PRINTERS WANT TO PRINT 'EM.	244	MOYEN SENSUEL	168
THOOD (21)			
THOU			
THOUGH THOU WELL DOST WISH ME ILL	8	NA AUDIART	1
THAT THOU SHOULDST . . .	8	NA AUDIART	17
THOUGH THOU HATE ME, READ IT SET	8	NA AUDIART	25
SETS FORTH, AND THOUGH THOU HATE ME WELL,	9	NA AUDIART	32
YEA THOUGH THOU WISH ME ILL,	9	NA AUDIART	33
OH, TILL THOU COME AGAIN.	9	NA AUDIART	37
THOU SHALT THEN SOFTEN,	9	NA AUDIART	50
THOU WERT ONCE SHE	9	NA AUDIART	52
"THERE BE MANY SINGERS GREATER THAN THOU."	16	PRAISE YSOLT	4
"THERE BE GREATER SOULS THAN THOU."	16	PRAISE YSOLT	26
WHILE IN HIS HEART ART THOU?	17	PRAISE YSOLT	58
THOU TRUSTED'ST IN THYSELF AND MET THE BLADE	19	FOR E. MCC	15
SO ART THOU WITH US, BEING GOOD TO KEEP	19	FOR E. MCC	21
YEA THOU, AND THOU, AND THOU, AND ALL MY KIN	21	IN DURANCE	42
YEA THOU, AND THOU, AND THOU, AND ALL MY KIN	21	IN DURANCE	42
YEA THOU, AND THOU, AND THOU, AND ALL MY KIN	21	IN DURANCE	42
O HOLE IN THE WALL HERE! BE THOU MY JONGLEUR	23	MARVOIL	34
SING THOU THE GRACE OF THE LADY OF BEZIERS,	23	MARVOIL	36
FOR EVEN AS THOU ART HOLLOW BEFORE I FILL THEE WITH THIS PARCHMENT,	23	MARVOIL	37
WHEN THE WIND BLOWS SIGH THOU FOR MY SORROW	23	MARVOIL	41
EVEN AS THOU SHALT SOON HAVE THIS PARCHMENT.	23	MARVOIL	44
O HOLE IN THE WALL HERE, BE THOU MY JONGLEUR,	23	MARVOIL	45
AND THOUGH THOU SIGHEST MY SORROW IN THE WIND,	23	MARVOIL	46
WHERETO THOU CALLEDST AND WHERETO I CALL.	25	GUIDO INVITES	6
LO, THOU HAST VOYAGED NOT! THE SHIP IS MINE."	25	GUIDO INVITES	11

PAGE 417

THOU

THOU (CONTINUED)

	PAGE	TITLE	LINE
YEA THE LINES HAST THOU LAID UNTO ME	26	NIGHT LITANY	3
HAST THOU SHOWN UNTO ME	26	NIGHT LITANY	6
THAT THOU GIVEST THIS WONDER UNTO US,	26	NIGHT LITANY	12
THAT THOU THUS REPAYEST US	26	NIGHT LITANY	17
WELL MAYST THOU BOAST THAT THOU THE BEST CHEVALIER	37	THE YOUNG KING	18
WELL MAYST THOU BOAST THAT THOU THE BEST CHEVALIER	37	THE YOUNG KING	18
DO THOU, PLUTO, BRING HERE NO GREATER HARSHNESS.	38	LADY'S LIFE	2
DO THOU, PLUTO, BRING HERE NO GREATER HARSHNESS.	38	LADY'S LIFE	12
WHAT HAST THOU, O MY SOUL, WITH PARADISE?	39	BLANDULA	1
O THOU NEW COMER WHO SEEK'ST ROME IN ROME	40	ROME	1
AND FIND'ST IN ROME NO THING THOU CANST CALL ROMAN;	40	ROME	2
REMAINS OF ROME. O WORLD, THOU UNCONSTANT MIME!	40	ROME	12
SUCH WAST THOU,	41	HER MONUMENT	1
O GLANCE, WHEN THOU WAST STILL AS THOU ART NOW,	41	HER MONUMENT	10
O GLANCE, WHEN THOU WAST STILL AS THOU ART NOW,	41	HER MONUMENT	10
HOW HAST THOU SET THE FIRE	41	HER MONUMENT	11
IF THOU ART	42	HER MONUMENT	50
HOW CANST THOU REACH SO HIGH WITH THY POOR SENSE;	42	HER MONUMENT	52
YET IF THOU ART	42	HER MONUMENT	53
AND IF THOU KNEW'ST I KNEW THEM WOULDST THOU SPEAK?	43	SATIEMUS	2
AND IF THOU KNEW'ST I KNEW THEM WOULDST THOU SPEAK?	43	SATIEMUS	2
AND ALL THE TIME THOU SAYEST THEM O'ER I SAID,	43	SATIEMUS	4
SIGHING AS THOU DOST THROUGH THE GOLDEN SPEECH."	43	SATIEMUS	6
SO THOU HAST FORGOTTEN FULLY	44	FROM HEINE: 2	1
LOVE AND LAY THOU HAST FORGOTTEN FULLY,	44	FROM HEINE: 2	5
WHOM THOU ONCE DID SING SO SWEETLY,	45	FROM HEINE: 3	2
TILL THOU FORGET THY SORROW,	47	FROM HEINE: 7	7
THOU WILT IN MY WHITE ARMS THERE,	47	FROM HEINE: 7	9
NAY, ON MY BREAST THOU MUST	47	FROM HEINE: 7	10
THOU HOODED OPAL, THOU ETERNAL PEARL,	50	THE FLAME	29
THOU HOODED OPAL, THOU ETERNAL PEARL,	50	THE FLAME	29
O THOU DARK SECRET WITH A SHIMMERING FLOOR,	50	THE FLAME	30
THERE CANST THOU FIND ME, O THOU ANXIOUS THOU,	51	THE FLAME	34
THERE CANST THOU FIND ME, O THOU ANXIOUS THOU,	51	THE FLAME	34
THERE CANST THOU FIND ME, O THOU ANXIOUS THOU,	51	THE FLAME	34
IF THOU HAST SEEN MY SHADE SANS CHARACTER,	51	THE FLAME	39
IF THOU HAST SEEN THAT MIRROR OF ALL MOMENTS,	51	THE FLAME	40
BUT NOT THOU ME.	60	TOMB AKR CAAR	8
LEST THOU SHOULDST WAKE AND WHIMPER FOR THY WINE.	60	TOMB AKR CAAR	13
O THOU UNMINDFUL! HOW SHOULD I FORGET!	60	TOMB AKR CAAR	15
THE RIVER? THOU WAST OVER YOUNG.	60	TOMB AKR CAAR	17
THOU ART A MAID WITH NO BREASTS,	62	N. Y.	9
THOU ART SLENDER AS A SILVER REED.	62	N. Y.	10
AND THOU SHALT LIVE FOR EVER.	62	N. Y.	13
THOU KEEP'ST THY ROSE-LEAF	67	THE CLOAK	1
THINK'ST THOU THAT DEATH WILL KISS THEE?	67	THE CLOAK	3
THINK'ST THOU THAT THE DARK HOUSE	67	THE CLOAK	4
FOR THOU SHOULDST MORE MISTRUST	67	THE CLOAK	9
THOU AFAR, MOVING IN THE GLAMOROUS SUN,	68	APPARUIT	6
DARKLY HAST THOU DARED AND THE DREADED AETHER	68	APPARUIT	11
SWIFT AT COURAGE THOU IN THE SHELL OF GOLD, CASTING	68	APPARUIT	13
THOU A SLIGHT THING, THOU IN ACCESS OF CUNNING	68	APPARUIT	23
THOU A SLIGHT THING, THOU IN ACCESS OF CUNNING	68	APPARUIT	23
BUT DO THOU SPEAK TRUE, EVEN TO THE LETTER:	90	SURGIT FAMA	15
A BROWN ROBE, WITH THREADS OF GOLD WOVEN IN PATTERNS, HAST THOU GATHERED ABOUT THEE,	91	DANCE FIGURE	17
THOU RESTLESS, UNGATHERED.	112	HIMERRO	7
"UP! THOU RASCAL, RISE,	171	LANGUE D'OC	EPI
SLEEP THOU NO MORE. I SEE THE STAR UPLEAPING	172	LANGUE D'OC: 1	7
SLEEP NOT THOU NOW, I HEAR THE BIRD IN FLIGHT	172	LANGUE D'OC: 1	11
IF THOU COME NOT, THE COST BE ON THY HEAD.	172	LANGUE D'OC: 1	16
"AND THOU OUT HERE BENEATH THE PORCH OF STONE	172	LANGUE D'OC: 1	22
O PLASMATOUR, THAT THOU END NOT THE NIGHT,	177	LANGUE D'OC: 4	6
"LOVELY THOU ART, TO HOLD ME CLOSE AND KISST,	177	LANGUE D'OC: 4	11
DESPITE THE CUCKOLD, DO THOU AS THOU LIST,	177	LANGUE D'OC: 4	13
DESPITE THE CUCKOLD, DO THOU AS THOU LIST,	177	LANGUE D'OC: 4	13
NUNC DIMITTIS, NOW LETTEST THOU THY SERVANT,	183	CANTICO SOLE	9
NOW LETTEST THOU THY SERVANT	183	CANTICO SOLE	10
HADST THOU BUT SONG	197	ENVOI (1919)	3
AS THOU HAST SUBJECTS KNOWN,	197	ENVOI (1919)	4

THOU -- THOUGHT

	PAGE	TITLE	LINE
THOU (CONTINUED)			
SAFE MAY'ST THOU GO MY CANZON WHITHER THEE PLEASETH	250	DONNA MI PREGA	88
THOU ART SO FAIR ATTIRED THAT EVERY MAN AND EACH	250	DONNA MI PREGA	89
HAST THOU NO DESIRE.	250	DONNA MI PREGA	93
VEX NOT THOU THE BANKER'S MIND	263	ALF'S EIGHTH	1
KNOWEST THOU NOT THE TRUTH IS NEVER IN SEASON	263	ALF'S EIGHTH	13
THOUGH			
THOUGH ALL MEN SAY THAT I AM MAD	5	LA FRAISNE	32
THOUGH THOU WELL DOST WISH ME ILL	8	NA AUDIART	1
THOUGH THOU HATE ME, READ IT SET	8	NA AUDIART	25
SETS FORTH, AND THOUGH THOU HATE ME WELL,	9	NA AUDIART	32
YEA THOUGH THOU WISH ME ILL,	9	NA AUDIART	33
THOUGH IT SHOULD RUN FOR ITS OWN GETTING,	14	FAMAM CANO	28
IN OUR HEART'S SWORD-RACK, THOUGH THY SWORD-ARM SLEEP.	19	FOR E. MCC	22
THE LITTLE HILLS TO EAST OF US, THOUGH HERE WE	21	IN DURANCE	39
AND THOUGH THOU SIGHEST MY SORROW IN THE WIND,	23	MARVOIL	46
THOUGH THEY WRITE IT CUNNINGLY;	33	GOODLY FERE	22
"THOUGH I GO TO THE GALLOWS TREE."	33	GOODLY FERE	28
NOT THOUGH HE BE GIVEN HIS GOOD, BUT WILL HAVE IN HIS YOUTH GREED;	65	THE SEAFARER	41
AND THOUGH HE STREW THE GRAVE WITH GOLD,	66	THE SEAFARER	99
THOUGH EVERY BRANCH HAVE BACK WHAT LAST YEAR LOST,	87	THE SPRING	11
THOUGH SHE WITH A FULL HEART	106	DOMPNA POIS	41
EVEN THOUGH WE TALK NOTHING BUT NONSENSE,	113	TAME CAT	5
THOUGH THEY HANG IN THE SAME WAY OVER THE BRIDGERAIL.	131	AT TEN CIIIN	8
THOUGH MANY MOVE WITH SUSPICION,	146	SALUTATION 3RD	31
THOUGH DAY BREAK."	172	LANGUE D'OC: 1	30
AND THOUGH I FEAR TO SPEAK OUT,	175	LANGUE D'OC: 3	35
THOUGH THE WHOLE WORLD RUN RACK	176	LANGUE D'OC: 3	73
THOUGH MY HOUSE IS NOT PROPPED UP BY TAENARIAN COLUMNS FROM LACONIA (ASSOCIATED WITH NEPTUNE AND CERBERUS),	208	SEXTUS PROP: 1	51
THOUGH IT IS NOT STRETCHED UPON GILDED BEAMS;	208	SEXTUS PROP: 1	52
THOUGH YOU GIVE ALL YOUR KISSES	221	SEXTUS PROP: 7	33
"THOUGH SPIRITS ARE CELEBRATED FOR ADULTERY.	225	SEXTUS PROP:10	40
THOUGH YOU HEAVE INTO THE AIR UPON THE GILDED PEGASEAN BACK,	226	SEXTUS PROP:11	7
THOUGH YOU HAD THE FEATHERY SANDALS OF PERSEUS	226	SEXTUS PROP:11	8
THOUGH YOU WALK IN THE VIA SACRA, WITH A PEACOCK'S TAIL FOR A FAN.	227	SEXTUS PROP:11	40
THOUGH YOU MAKE A HASH OF ANTIMACHUS,	228	SEXTUS PROP:12	21
THOUGH SOME APPROVED OF THEM, AND SOME DEPLORED 'EM.	242	MOYEN SENSUEL	108
THOUGH MALES OF SEVENTY, WHO FEAR TRUTHS NAKED HARM US,	243	MOYEN SENSUEL	147
THOUGH IT WILL, OF COURSE, PASS OFF WITH SOCIAL SCIENCE	244	MOYEN SENSUEL	163
THOUGH I KNOW ONE, A VERY BASE DETRACTOR,	246	MOYEN SENSUEL	221
E'EN THOUGH HE MEET NOT WITH HATE	249	DONNA MI PREGA	43
THOUGH FROM HER FACE INDISCERNIBLE;	250	DONNA MI PREGA	79
THOUGHT			
HE ANALYSES FORM AND THOUGHT TO SEE	15	FAMAM CANO	47
AND SO WERE MY MIND HOLLOW, DID SHE NOT FILL UTTERLY MY THOUGHT.	23	MARVOIL	39
HELL BLOT BLACK FOR ALWAY THE THOUGHT "PEACE"!	29	ALTAFORTE	39
'GOT ON DESIROUS THOUGHT BY NATURAL VIRTUE,	42	HER MONUMENT	42
HOW IS THE NOBLEST OF THY SPEECH AND THOUGHT	42	HER MONUMENT	55
AND WEARIED OUT MY THOUGHT UPON THE SIGNS.	60	TOMB AKR CAAR	10
ONE AVERAGE MIND--WITH ONE THOUGHT LESS, EACH YEAR.	61	PORTRAIT FEMME	10
IT WORKS TO REPRESENT THAT SCHOOL OF THOUGHT	63	PHASELLUS ILLE	5
THE HEART'S THOUGHT THAT I ON HIGH STREAMS	65	THE SEAFARER	35
TAKE THOUGHT:	93	THE REST	17
INDIFFERENT AND DISCOURAGED HE THOUGHT HE MIGHT AS I HAVE THOUGHT OF THE SECOND TROY,	100	ARIDES	4
I HAVE THOUGHT OF THEE LIVING	122	PROVINC DESERT	64
AND I WAS DRUNK, AND HAD NO THOUGHT OF RETURNING.	123	PROVINC DESERT	81
AND ALL HIS NET-LIKE THOUGHT OF NEW ALLIANCE?	135	EXILE'S LETTER	48
OF ARNAUT DE MAREUIL, I THOUGHT, "QU'IEU SUI AVINEN."	152	NEAR PERIGORD	50
SAVE TROUBLE AND SAD THOUGHT,	166	FISH & SHADOW	19
THE THOUGHT OF WHAT AMERICA WOULD BE LIKE	174	LANGUE D'OC: 3	8
THE THOUGHT OF WHAT AMERICA,	183	CANTICO SOLE	1
	183	CANTICO SOLE	4

PAGE 419

THOUGHT -- THREE

	PAGE	TITLE	LINE
THOUGHT (CONTINUED)			
THE THOUGHT OF WHAT AMERICA,	183	CANTICO SOLE	5
THE THOUGHT OF WHAT AMERICA WOULD BE LIKE	183	CANTICO SOLE	6
THE THOUGHT OF WHAT AMERICA,	183	CANTICO SOLE	12
THE THOUGHT OF WHAT AMERICA,	183	CANTICO SOLE	13
THE THOUGHT OF WHAT AMERICA WOULD BE LIKE	183	CANTICO SOLE	14
HE READ THE CENTURY AND THOUGHT IT NICE	245	MOYEN SENSUEL	201
I THOUGHT: YES, DIVINE, THESE EYES, BUT WHAT EXISTS	247	PIERROTS	11
NOT TO DELIGHT, BUT IN AN ARDOUR OF THOUGHT	249	DONNA MI PREGA	31
MIGHT CAUSE THOUGHT AND BE THEREFORE	262	ALF'S SEVENTH	19
THOUGHTS			
MOUNTS, FROM OUR MIGHTY THOUGHTS AND FROM THE FOUNT	41	HER MONUMENT	27
WHAT IF MY THOUGHTS WERE TURNED IN THEIR MID REACH	43	SATIEMUS	9
THOUGHTS OF HER ARE OF DREAM'S ORDER:	72	DIEU! QU'IL	12
WE WENT FORTH GATHERING DELICATE THOUGHTS,	82	THE CONDOLENCE	9
TILL WE HAD NOTHING BUT THOUGHTS AND MEMORIES IN COMMON.	134	EXILE'S LETTER	15
(MY COUNTRY, I'VE SAID YOUR MORALS AND YOUR THOUGHTS ARE STALE ONES,	243	MOYEN SENSUEL	149
THOUGHT'S			
"CAT'S I' THE WATER BUTT!" THOUGHT'S IN YOUR VERSE-BARREL,	13	MESMERISM	5
THOU'LT			
AND NOW THOU'LT NONE OF ME, AND WILT HAVE NONE	172	LANGUE D'OC: 1	24
THOUSAND			
I HA' SEEN HIM COW A THOUSAND MEN.	34	GOODLY FERE	35
I HA' SEEN HIM COW A THOUSAND MEN	34	GOODLY FERE	41
SO MANY THOUSAND BEAUTIES ARE GONE DOWN TO AVERNUS,	38	LADY'S LIFE	3
SO MANY THOUSAND FAIR ARE GONE DOWN TO AVERNUS,	38	LADY'S LIFE	13
WE ARE NOT SHUT FROM ALL THE THOUSAND HEAVENS:	50	THE FLAME	22
IS RICH FOR A THOUSAND CUPS.	128	THE RIVER SONG	4
OVER A THOUSAND GATES, OVER A THOUSAND DOORS ARE THE SOUNDS OF SPRING SINGING,	129	THE RIVER SONG	31
OVER A THOUSAND GATES, OVER A THOUSAND DOORS ARE THE SOUNDS OF SPRING SINGING,	129	THE RIVER SONG	31
CALLED TO, A THOUSAND TIMES, I NEVER LOOKED BACK.	130	RIVER-MER WIFE	10
PEACH BOUGHS AND APRICOT BOUGHS HANG OVER A THOUSAND GATES,	131	AT TEN-SHIN	2
AND THEY THINK IT WILL LAST A THOUSAND AUTUMNS,	132	AT TEN-SHIN	26
BONES WHITE WITH A THOUSAND FROSTS,	133	FRONTIER GUARD	8
THREE HUNDRED AND SIXTY THOUSAND,	133	FRONTIER GUARD	16
INTO A VALLEY OF THE THOUSAND BRIGHT FLOWERS,	134	EXILE'S LETTER	19
AND INTO TEN THOUSAND VALLEYS FULL OF VOICES AND PINE-WINDS.	134	EXILE'S LETTER	21
AND SEND IT A THOUSAND MILES, THINKING.	136	EXILE'S LETTER	80
AND GO OUT THROUGH A THOUSAND MILES OF DEAD GRASS.	137	TAKING LEAVE	4
CROWD OVER THE THOUSAND GATES,	141	IDEA OF CHOAN	18
FOR A FEW THOUSAND BATTERED BOOKS.	191	HUGH SELWYN: 5	8
HIS ARMY IS A THOUSAND AND FORTY-EIGHT SOLDIERS	237	ABU SALAMMAMM	12
OH MAY THE KING LIVE FOR A THOUSAND YEARS!	237	ABU SALAMMAMM	27
THREE THOUSAND CHORUS GIRLS AND ALL UNKISSED,	241	MOYEN SENSUEL	87
'THOUT			
'THOUT MASK OR GAUNTLET, AND ART LAID	19	FOR E. MCC	16
THAT 'THOUT HIM, SAVE THE ASPEN, WERE AS DUMB	21	IN DURANCE	47
THRACE			
STEPPING BENEATH A BOISTEROUS WIND FROM THRACE,	87	THE SPRING	3
THREAD			
SAFES IN THREAD AND NEEDLE STREET.	269	SAFE AND SOUND	22
THREADS			
A BROWN ROBE, WITH THREADS OF GOLD WOVEN IN PATTERNS, HAST THOU GATHERED ABOUT THEE,	91	DANCE FIGURE	17
THREATS			
NOR WILL THE HORRID THREATS OF BERNARD SHAW	63	PHASELLUS ILLE	7
THREE			
BAH! I HAVE SUNG WOMEN IN THREE CITIES,	6	CINO	1
I HAVE SUNG WOMEN IN THREE CITIES.	7	CINO	37
I HAVE SUNG WOMEN IN THREE CITIES	7	CINO	52
AND THREE DAYS' BEARD;	15	FAMAM CANO	37
I MADE RIMES TO HIS LADY THIS THREE YEAR:	22	MARVOIL	7
THEN CAME WHAT MIGHT COME, TO WIT: THREE MEN AND ONE WOMAN,	22	MARVOIL	11

PAGE 420

THREE -- THUNDERS

	PAGE	TITLE	LINE
THREE (CONTINUED)			
SOME CIRCLE OF NOT MORE THAN THREE	52	AU SALON	18
AND THREE SOULS CAME UPON THEE--	60	TOMB AKR CAAR	18
TO SEE THREE GENERATIONS OF ONE HOUSE GATHERED TOGETHER!	89	COMMISSION	30
THREE SPIRITS CAME TO ME	92	APRIL	1
BUT THREE YEARS AFTER THIS	96	AESTHETICS	6
NINE LAWYERS, FOUR COUNSELS, FIVE JUDGES AND THREE PROCTORS OF THE KING,	97	THE BELLAIRES	5
I HAVE ADORED YOU FOR THREE FULL YEARS;	102	LADIES	6
THE THREE POETS	118	THREE POETS	T
AND THREE POETS ARE GONE INTO MOURNING.	118	THREE POETS	2
IN THREE WAYS,	121	PROVINC DESERT	3
AND THREE VALLEYS, FULL OF WINDING ROADS,	121	PROVINC DESERT	4
THERE ARE THREE KEEPS NEAR MAREUIL,	121	PROVINC DESERT	24
WE HAVE NO REST, THREE BATTLES A MONTH.	127	BOWMEN OF SHU	16
THREE HUNDRED AND SIXTY THOUSAND,	133	FRONTIER GUARD	16
THE THREE MOUNTAINS FALL THROUGH THE FAR HEAVEN,	138	CITY OF CHOAN	8
THAT THE TWITCHING OF THREE ABDOMINAL NERVES	148	FRATRES MINORE	6
TWO YEARS, THREE YEARS I SEEK	175	LANGUE D'OC: 3	34
FOR THREE YEARS, OUT OF KEY WITH HIS TIME,	187	E. P. ODE	1
"BUTTER REVIEWERS, FROM FIFTY TO THREE HUNDRED	194	MR. NIXON	10
FOR THREE YEARS, DIABOLUS IN THE SCALE,	199	MAUBERLEY: 2	1
THERE WILL BE THREE BOOKS AT MY OBSEQUIES	219	SEXTUS PROP: 6	20
THREE THOUSAND CHORUS GIRLS AND ALL UNKISSED,	241	MOYEN SENSUEL	87
AND WONDER IF MY DAY'S THREE AND EIGHT-PENCE	268	ANOTHER BIT	11
AT ONE AND THREE THE POUND.	269	SAFE AND SOUND	4
THREICIAN			
AND HELD UP THE THREICIAN RIVER;	208	SEXTUS PROP: 1	43
THRENOS			
THRENOS	3	THRENOS	T
THRESHOLD			
A WET LEAF THAT CLINGS TO THE THRESHOLD.	108	LIU CH'E	6
THRILLS			
HE THRILLS TO ILIAN ARMS,	228	SEXTUS PROP:12	33
THROAT			
AND SITH HIS THROAT	15	FAMAM CANO	35
O THROAT GIRT ROUND OF OLD WITH SWIFT DESIRE,	41	HER MONUMENT	14
HOW IF THE LOW DEAR SOUND WITHIN THY THROAT	43	SATIEMUS	14
HALF THE GRAVEN SHOULDER, THE THROAT AFLASH WITH	68	APPARUIT	17
HER TWO HANDS AND HER THROAT,	106	DOMPNA POIS	33
BEL MIRAL'S STATURE, THE VISCOUNTESS' THROAT,	151	NEAR PERIGORD	8
THERE IS A THROAT; AH, THERE ARE TWO WHITE HANDS;	153	NEAR PERIGORD	71
THRONE			
AND THE PRINCES STILL STAND IN ROWS ABOUT THE THRONE,	131	AT TEN-SHIN	10
THROUGH (60)			
THROUGHOUT			
THROUGHOUT THIS SYLVAN PLACE	87	THE SPRING	4
RUMOURS OF YOU THROUGHOUT THE CITY,	226	SEXTUS PROP:11	18
THROWN			
AND NOW MEN CALL ME MAD BECAUSE I HAVE THROWN	4	LA FRAISNE	27
"YOUR PAMPHLETS WILL BE THROWN, THROWN OFTEN INTO A CHAIR	210	SEXTUS PROP: 2	22
"YOUR PAMPHLETS WILL BE THROWN, THROWN OFTEN INTO A CHAIR	210	SEXTUS PROP: 2	22
THROWS			
HE THROWS HIS HEART UP THROUGH THE SKY,	139	SENNIN POEM	8
THRUSTING			
ARE THRUSTING AT THE SPRING AIR.	110	COITUS	2
THUD			
AND THEY ALL GO TO RACK RUIN BENEATH THE THUD OF THE YEARS.	209	SEXTUS PROP: 1	71
THUMBS			
SALUTE THEM WITH YOUR THUMBS AT YOUR NOSES.	86	SALUTATION 2ND	22
THUNDER			
NOR IF THE THUNDER FALL FROM PREDESTINATION;	228	SEXTUS PROP:12	80
THUNDERED			
EAGLED AND THUNDERED AS JUPITER PLUVIUS.	13	MESMERISM	15
THUNDERS			
AND THE FIERCE THUNDERS ROAR ME THEIR MUSIC	28	ALTAFORTE	10

PAGE 421

THUS -- THY

	PAGE	TITLE	LINE
THUS			
VAGUELY THUS WORD THEY:	6	CINO	24
AND THUS IN NINEVEH	24	THUS NINEVEH	T
GUIDO INVITES YOU THUS	25	GUIDO INVITES	T
THAT THOU THUS REPAYEST US	26	NIGHT LITANY	17
(THUS FAR HATH MODERNITY BROUGHT US)	52	AU SALON	9
THUS HAVE THE GODS AWARDED HER,	103	PHYLLIDULA	2
"THUS THINGS PROCEED IN THEIR CIRCLE";	178	MOEURS CON: 1	19
AND THUS THE EMPIRE IS MAINTAINED.	178	MOEURS CON: 1	20
THUS, IF HER COLOUR	201	AGE DEMANDED	9
THUS MISTRESS CALLIOPE,	211	SEXTUS PROP: 2	52
DABBLING HER HANDS IN THE FOUNT, THUS SHE	211	SEXTUS PROP: 2	53
THUS ALL ROADS ARE PERFECTLY SAFE	212	SEXTUS PROP: 3	24
FOR THUS ARE TOMBS OF LOVERS MOST DESECRATED.	213	SEXTUS PROP: 3	34
THUS? SHE WEPT INTO UNCOMBED HAIR,	214	SEXTUS PROP: 4	13
THUS:	216	SEXTUS PROP: 5	15
THUS MUCH THE FATES HAVE ALLOTTED ME, AND IF, MAECENAS,	217	SEXTUS PROP: 5	37
THUS HE ESCHEWED THE BRIGHT RED-WALLED CAFES AND	245	MOYEN SENSUEL	205
AND IN OUR DAY THUS SAITH THE EVANGELIST:	246	MOYEN SENSUEL	237
POOR IN DISCERNMENT, BEING THUS WEAKNESS' FRIEND,	249	DONNA MI PREGA	38
THUS ROSE IN ALBION, AND TICKLED THE STATE	264	ALF'S NINTH	11
THWARTED			
GO TO THOSE WHOSE DELICATE DESIRES ARE THWARTED,	88	COMMISSION	17
THWARTED WITH SYSTEMS,	92	THE REST	7
THY			
HATH FOR BOSS THY LUSTRE GAY!	7	CINO	45
MAKE THY LAUGH OUR WANDER-LIED;	7	CINO	47
BID THY 'FULGENCE BEAR AWAY CARE.	7	CINO	48
WHERE THY BODICE LACES START	8	NA AUDIART	3
PRAISES MEET UNTO THY FASHION?	8	NA AUDIART	10
HAVING PRAISED THY GIRDLE'S SCOPE	8	NA AUDIART	14
JUST A WORD IN THY PRAISE, GIRL,	8	NA AUDIART	20
THY SATINS MAKE UPON THE STAIR,	8	NA AUDIART	22
WHERE THY TORSE AND LIMBS ARE MET	8	NA AUDIART	24
BERTRANS OF AULTAFORTE THY PRAISE	9	NA AUDIART	31
THY LOVELINESS IS HERE WRIT TILL,	9	NA AUDIART	35
UPON THY HANDS, AND THY OLD SOUL	9	NA AUDIART	41
UPON THY HANDS, AND THY OLD SOUL	9	NA AUDIART	41
--PART OF IT--OF THY SONG-LIFE.	14	FAMAM CANO	16
THAT SAME. THY PUBLIC IN MY SCREED	14	FAMAM CANO	19
IN OUR HEART'S SWORD-RACK, THOUGH THY SWORD-ARM SLEEP.	19	FOR E. MCC	22
KEEP YET MY SECRET IN THY BREAST HERE;	23	MARVOIL	47
LO, I HAVE KNOWN THY HEART AND ITS DESIRE;	25	GUIDO INVITES	8
AND THE BEAUTY OF THIS THY VENICE	26	NIGHT LITANY	5
OF THY BEAUTY HATH WALKED	26	NIGHT LITANY	26
IN THIS THY VENICE.	26	NIGHT LITANY	28
OF THE SHADOW OF THY HANDMAID	27	NIGHT LITANY	30
SHADOW OF THIS THY VENICE	27	NIGHT LITANY	39
AND THY STARS	27	NIGHT LITANY	41
EVEN AS ARE THY STARS	27	NIGHT LITANY	45
AH! CABARET! AH CABARET, THY HILLS AGAIN!	32	PIERE VIDAL	65
THAN ALL THE AGE-OLD KNOWLEDGE OF THY BOOKS:	35	THE EYES	17
HERE LET THY CLEMENCY, PERSEPHONE, HOLD FIRM,	38	LADY'S LIFE	1
HERE LET THY CLEMENCY, PERSEPHONE, HOLD FIRM,	38	LADY'S LIFE	11
HOW CANST THOU REACH SO HIGH WITH THY POOR SENSE;	42	HER MONUMENT	52
HOW IS THE NOBLEST OF THY SPEECH AND THOUGHT	42	HER MONUMENT	55
WHAT IF I KNOW THY SPEECHES WORD BY WORD?	43	SATIEMUS	1
WHAT IF I KNOW THY SPEECHES WORD BY WORD,	43	SATIEMUS	3
HOW IF THE LOW DEAR SOUND WITHIN THY THROAT	43	SATIEMUS	14
WHAT IF I KNOW THY LAUGHTER WORD BY WORD	43	SATIEMUS	18
NOR FIND AUGHT NOVEL IN THY MERRIMENT?	43	SATIEMUS	19
THAT I SO LONG HELD THY HEART WHOLLY,	44	FROM HEINE: 2	2
THY LITTLE HEART, SO SWEET AND FALSE AND SMALL	44	FROM HEINE: 2	3
TELL ME WHERE THY LOVELY LOVE IS,	45	FROM HEINE: 3	1
THEE, AND HELD THY HEART COMPLETELY.	45	FROM HEINE: 3	4
THY HEAD WILL I COVER OVER	47	FROM HEINE: 7	5
TILL THOU FORGET THY SORROW,	47	FROM HEINE: 7	7
SAPPHIRE BENACUS, IN THY MISTS AND THEE	50	THE FLAME	26
THROUGH ALL THY VARIOUS MOOD I KNOW THEE MINE;	50	THE FLAME	31

PAGE 422

THY -- TIED

	PAGE	TITLE	LINE
THY (CONTINUED)			
"I AM THY SOUL, NIKOPTIS. I HAVE WATCHED	60	TOMB AKR CAAR	1
THESE FIVE MILLENIA, AND THY DEAD EYES	60	TOMB AKR CAAR	2
AND THY LIGHT LIMBS, WHERETHROUGH I LEAPT AFLAME,	60	TOMB AKR CAAR	4
LEST THOU SHOULDST WAKE AND WHIMPER FOR THY WINE.	60	TOMB AKR CAAR	13
AND ALL THY ROBES I HAVE KEPT SMOOTH ON THEE.	60	TOMB AKR CAAR	14
I HAVE BEEN INTIMATE WITH THEE, KNOWN THY WAYS. ...	60	TOMB AKR CAAR	21
HAVE I NOT TOUCHED THY PALMS AND FINGER-TIPS, ...	60	TOMB AKR CAAR	22
FLOWED IN, AND THROUGH THEE AND ABOUT THY HEELS?	60	TOMB AKR CAAR	23
THOU KEEP'ST THY ROSE-LEAF	67	THE CLOAK	1
THY FACE AS A RIVER WITH LIGHTS.	91	DANCE FIGURE	11
WHITE AS AN ALMOND ARE THY SHOULDERS;	91	DANCE FIGURE	12
GILT TURQUOISE AND SILVER ARE IN THE PLACE OF THY REST.	91	DANCE FIGURE	16
AS A RILLET AMONG THE SEDGE ARE THY HANDS UPON ME;	91	DANCE FIGURE	19
THY FINGERS A FROSTED STREAM.	91	DANCE FIGURE	20
THY MAIDENS ARE WHITE LIKE PEBBLES;	91	DANCE FIGURE	21
THY SOUL	112	HIMERRO	1
I LONG FOR THY LIPS.	112	HIMERRO	5
I LONG FOR THY NARROW BREASTS, ...	112	HIMERRO	6
THESE ARE THEY OF THY COMPANY.	147	BEFORE SLEEP	7
"DELIGHT THY SOUL IN FATNESS," SAITH THE PREACHER.	163	CABARET DANCER	69
"COME NOW! OLD SWENKIN! RISE UP FROM THY BED, ...	172	LANGUE D'OC: 1	14
IF THOU COME NOT, THE COST BE ON THY HEAD.	172	LANGUE D'OC; 1	16
NUNC DIMITTIS, NOW LETTEST THOU THY SERVANT, ...	183	CANTICO SOLE	1
NOW LETTEST THOU THY SERVANT	183	CANTICO SOLE	9
SHALL PRAISE THY SPEECH	250	DONNA MI PREGA	90
THYRSIS			
THYRSIS AND DAPHNIS UPON WHITTLED REEDS, ...	229	SEXTUS PROP:12	42
THYRSOS			
SUCH MY COHORT AND SETTING. AND SHE BOUND IVY TO HIS THYRSOS;	211	SEXTUS PROP: 2	35
THYSELF			
BESPEAK THYSELF FOR ANYTHING.	8	NA AUDIART	19
THOU TRUSTED'ST IN THYSELF AND MET THE BLADE	19	FOR E. MCC	15
TI			
"SE IL COR TI MANCA," BUT IT FAILED THEE NOT!	19	FOR E. MCC	12
"NON TI FIDAR," IT IS THE SWORD THAT SPEAKS	19	FOR E. MCC	13
TIBBY-CAT			
SHE'D SAY TO HER TIBBY-CAT, ...	271	OLE KATE	22
TIBER			
TIBER ALONE, TRANSIENT AND SEAWARD BENT, ...	40	ROME	11
TIBET			
TIBET SHALL BE FULL OF ROMAN POLICEMEN, ...	219	SEXTUS PROP: 6	8
TIBORS			
TIBORS ALL TONGUE AND TEMPER AT MONT-AUSIER, ...	22	MARVOIL	18
RAIMONA, TIBORS, BERANGERE, ...	75	THE ALCHEMIST	6
TIBULLUS			
AND TIBULLUS COULD SAY OF HIS DEATH, IN HIS LATIN:	168	OF AROUET	39
TIBUR			
TELLING ME TO COME TO TIBUR:	212	SEXTUS PROP: 3	2
TICK			
AN ART! YOU ALL RESPECT THE ARTS, FROM THAT INFANT TICK	239	MOYEN SENSUEL	13
TICKLE			
AS A PLEASANT TICKLE, ...	145	SALUTATION 3RD	29
TICKLED			
THUS ROSE IN ALBION, AND TICKLED THE STATE	264	ALF'S NINTH	11
TIDE			
TURNED IN THEIR SAPPHIRE TIDE, COME FLOODING O'ER US!	51	HORAE BEATAE	4
THAT, ERE A MAN'S TIDE GO, TURN IT TO TWAIN.	66	THE SEAFARER	70
COME, OR THE STELLAR TIDE WILL SLIP AWAY.	69	THE NEEDLE	1
MOVE WE AND TAKE THE TIDE, WITH ITS NEXT FAVOUR, .	69	THE NEEDLE	12
TIDES			
AS THE MOON CALLETH THE TIDES, ...	16	PRAISE YSOLT	29
TIDILY			
MOST TIDILY AWAY	269	SAFE AND SOUND	18
TIDY			
FOR A FLIP WORD, AND TO TIDY THEIR HAIR A BIT.	117	THE LAKE ISLE	11
TIED			
NOT TIED TO THE RING AROUND, ...	261	ALF'S SIXTH	19

PAGE 423

TIES -- TIME

	PAGE	TITLE	LINE
TIES			
YET HIS TIES ARE MORE ADORNING, ...	46	FROM HEINE: 6	6
TIGERS			
AND WE GUARDSMEN FED TO THE TIGERS.	133	FRONTIER GUARD	24
TIGHT			
THE TENTS TIGHT DRAWN, HORSES AT TETHER	155	NEAR PERIGORD	130
TIGRIS			
TIGRIS AND EUPHRATES SHALL, FROM NOW ON, FLOW AT HIS BIDDING, ...	219	SEXTUS PROP: 6	7
TILL			
TILL MEN SAY THAT I AM MAD;	4	LA FRAISNE	21
THY LOVELINESS IS HERE WRIT TILL, ...	9	NA AUDIART	35
OH, TILL THOU COME AGAIN.	9	NA AUDIART	37
THAT SAID US, "TILL THEN" FOR THE GALLOWS TREE! ...	11	OF THE GIBBET	4
TILL MY SOUL SENT A WOMAN AS THE SUN:	17	PRAISE YSOLT	47
VERS AND CANZONE, TILL THAT DAMN'D SON OF ARAGON,	22	MARVOIL	8
STARK, KEEN, TRIUMPHANT, TILL IT PLAYS AT DEATH.	31	PIERE VIDAL	37
TILL THOU FORGET THY SORROW, ...	47	FROM HEINE: 7	7
TILL THE ROSE-TIME WILL BE OVER, ...	67	THE CLOAK	2
TILL I AGAIN FIND YOU READY.	105	DOMPNA POIS	20
TILL WE HAD NOTHING BUT THOUGHTS AND MEMORIES IN COMMON.	134	EXILE'S LETTER	15
AND WE CAN LEAVE THE TALK TILL DANTE WRITES:	156	NEAR PERIGORD	162
SHE HAS HER LOVER TILL MORN, ...	177	LANGUE D'OC: 4	2
TILL THE TRAIST MAN CRY OUT TO WARN	177	LANGUE D'OC: 4	3
TILL CHANGE HATH BROKEN DOWN	197	ENVOI (1919)	25
TILL UP AGAIN, RIGHT UP, WE REACH THE PRESIDENT,	239	MOYEN SENSUEL	16
TILL YOU MAY TAKE YOUR CHOICE: TO FEEL THE EDGE OF SATIRE OR	240	MOYEN SENSUEL	65
"TILL I HAVE VIEWED STRAW HATS AND THEIR HABITUAL CLOTHING	244	MOYEN SENSUEL	183
TILL THE KING SHALL TAKE THE NOTION	269	SAFE AND SOUND	27
TILL SHE FINDS WORK TO DO.	272	THE BABY	8
'TILL			
'TILL THE WATCHMAN ON THE TOWER	171	LANGUE D'OC	EPI
'TILL THE SUN COME, AND THE GREEN LEAF ON THE BOUGH.	173	LANGUE D'OC: 2	16
'TILL I HAVE MY HAND 'NEATH HER CLOAK.	173	LANGUE D'OC: 2	22
'TILL I HAVE HER I LOVE	174	LANGUE D'OC: 3	18
'TILL THE TRAIST WATCHER HIS SONG UNREIN, ...	177	LANGUE D'OC: 4	18
TILLAGE			
AND MAKE THE TOUR ABROAD FOR THEIR WILD TILLAGE--	245	MOYEN SENSUEL	208
TIME			
THE WORDS ARE AS LEAVES, OLD BROWN LEAVES IN THE SPRING TIME	16	PRAISE YSOLT	19
BEFORE THE TIME OF ITS COMING?	26	NIGHT LITANY	18
AYE YE ARE FOOLS, IF YE THINK TIME CAN BLOT	30	PIERE VIDAL	18
SHE IS TIME'S PREY AND TIME CONSUMETH ALL.	40	ROME	8
THAT WHICH STANDS FIRM IN THEE TIME BATTERS DOWN,	40	ROME	13
AND THAT WHICH FLEETETH DOTH OUTRUN SWIFT TIME. ...	40	ROME	14
AND ALL THE TIME THOU SAYEST THEM O'ER I SAID, ...	43	SATIEMUS	4
NO COMFORT, AT MY TIME OF LIFE WHEN	46	FROM HEINE: 6	19
BREAK DOWN THE FOUR-SQUARE WALLS OF STANDING TIME.	49	OF SPLENDOUR	21
WHERE TIME IS SHRIVELLED DOWN TO TIME'S SEED CORN	50	THE FLAME	11
WHERE TIME BURNS BACK ABOUT TH' ETERNAL EMBERS. ...	50	THE FLAME	21
OR GATHER MAY OF HARSH NORTHWINDISH TIME?	59	SILET	8
TIME HAS SEEN THIS, AND WILL NOT TURN AGAIN;	59	SILET	12
TIME THAN MY EYES.	67	THE CLOAK	10
IS, FOR THE TIME BEING, THE MISTRESS OF MY FRIEND,	87	ALBATRE	2
NOW IS A TIME FOR CARVING.	89	A PACT	7
GIVE ME IN DUE TIME, I BESEECH YOU, A LITTLE TOBACCO-SHOP, ...	117	THE LAKE ISLE	2
WHERE ONE NEEDS ONE'S BRAINS ALL THE TIME.	117	THE LAKE ISLE	16
LONELY FROM THE BEGINNING OF TIME UNTIL NOW!	133	FRONTIER GUARD	2
SHE MUST SPEAK OF THE TIME	166	FISH & SHADOW	18
GIVE ME BACK THE TIME OF THE THING.	167	OF AROUET	16
TIME HAS DRIVEN ME OUT FROM THE FINE PLAISAUNCES,	167	OF AROUET	18
AND IF NOW WE CAN'T FIT WITH OUR TIME OF LIFE	168	OF AROUET	23
COMPLEYNT OF A GENTLEMAN WHO HAS BEEN WAITING OUTSIDE FOR SOME TIME	172	LANGUE D'OC: 1	SUB
(BY THAT TIME SHE HAD GOT ON TO BROWNING.)	182	MOEURS CON: 8	7
FOR THREE YEARS, OUT OF KEY WITH HIS TIME, ...	187	E. P. ODE	1

PAGE 424

TIME -- TIREIS

	PAGE	TITLE	LINE
TIME (CONTINUED)			
MADE WITH NO LOSS OF TIME,	188	HUGH SELWYN: 2	10
BRAVING TIME.	197	ENVOI (1919)	16
ASKING TIME TO BE RID OF ...	199	MAUBERLEY: 2	9
(AMID AERIAL FLOWERS) . . . TIME FOR ARRANGEMENTS--	199	MAUBERLEY: 2	13
AND IN THE MEAN TIME MY SONGS WILL TRAVEL,	208	SEXTUS PROP: 1	39
NOW IF EVER IT IS TIME TO CLEANSE HELICON;	216	SEXTUS PROP: 5	1
THE TIME IS COME, THE AIR HEAVES IN TORRIDITY,	221	SEXTUS PROP: 8	3
GOD AM I FOR THE TIME.	221	SEXTUS PROP: 7	40
'TIS TIME THAT IT WAS CAPPED WITH SOMETHING QUOTABLE.	239	MOYEN SENSUEL	38
"TIME FOR THAT QUESTION!" FRONT BENCH INTERPOSES.	260	ALF'S FIFTH	16
TIME FOR THAT QUESTION? AND THE TIME IS NOW.	260	ALF'S FIFTH	17
TIME FOR THAT QUESTION? AND THE TIME IS NOW.	260	ALF'S FIFTH	17
TIME-BAR			
WHAT FOOT BEAT OUT YOUR TIME-BAR,	207	SEXTUS PROP: 1	8
TIMELY			
PUT ON A TIMELY VIGOUR.	216	SEXTUS PROP: 5	13
TIMES			
WHAT TIMES THE SWALLOW FILLS	14	FAMAM CANO	7
HAVE WE DONE IN TIMES PAST	26	NIGHT LITANY	10
WITH TIMES TOLD OVER AS WE TELL BY ROTE;	43	SATIEMUS	17
AND, MAY BE, MORE TIMES,	53	AU JARDIN	18
I WAS TWENTY YEARS BEHIND THE TIMES	85	SALUTATION 2ND	3
HE HAD TO BE FOUR TIMES CUCKOLD.	100	TEMPERAMENTS	8
CALLED TO, A THOUSAND TIMES, I NEVER LOOKED BACK.	130	RIVER-MER WIFE	10
LET US DERIDE THE SMUGNESS OF "THE TIMES":	145	SALUTATION 3RD	1
OF THE TIMES WHEN THE SLEEVES WERE LARGE,	180	MOEURS CON: 5	3
SEZ THE TIMES A SILVER LINING	267	ALF'S TWELFTH	1
TIME'S			
SHE IS TIME'S PREY AND TIME CONSUMETH ALL.	40	ROME	8
WHERE TIME IS SHRIVELLED DOWN TO TIME'S SEED CORN	50	THE FLAME	11
"TIME'S BITTER FLOOD"! OH, THAT'S ALL VERY WELL,	59	EXIT' CUIUSDAM	1
TIME'S TOOTH IS INTO THE LOT, AND WAR'S AND FATE'S TOO.	165	QUINTUS SEPTIM	17
TIMES'			
BALLAD FOR THE TIMES' SPECIAL SILVER NUMBER	267	ALF'S TWELFTH	SUB
TIMOROUS			
AS A TIMOROUS WENCH FROM A CENTAUR	81	TENZONE	3
AND TIMOROUS LOVE OF THE INNOCUOUS	240	MOYEN SENSUEL	63
TIN			
"'POLLO PHOIBEE, OLD TIN PAN, YOU	7	CINO	42
SHALL I PLACE A TIN WREATH UPON!	189	HUGH SELWYN: 3	28
TIN'			
TIN' ANDRA, TIN' HEROA, TINA THEON,	189	HUGH SELWYN: 3	26
TIN' ANDRA, TIN' HEROA, TINA THEON,	189	HUGH SELWYN: 3	26
TINA			
TIN' ANDRA, TIN' HEROA, TINA THEON,	189	HUGH SELWYN: 3	26
TINGE			
JUST REFLECTING THE SKY'S TINGE,	129	THE RIVER SONG	21
TINGED			
TERRACES TINGED WITH SILVER,	141	IDEA OF CHOAN	20
TINGEING			
TINGEING THE MOUNTAINS,	122	PROVINC DESERT	53
TINT			
WITH A BLACK TINT STAINING YOUR CUTICLE,	162	CABARET DANCER	49
TINTAGOEL			
TINTAGOEL.	3	THRENUS	18
TIPS			
SPREADS THE BRIGHT TIPS,	87	THE SPRING	5
ITS LOWEST STONES JUST MEET THE VALLEY TIPS	152	NEAR PERIGORD	55
"BRIGHT TIPS REACH UP FROM TWIN TOWERS,	212	SEXTUS PROP: 3	4
TIP'S			
"THE TIP'S A GOOD ONE, AS FOR LITERATURE	194	MR. NIXON	16
TIRED			
HORSES, HIS HORSES EVEN ARE TIRED. THEY WERE STRONG.	127	BOWMEN OF SHU	15
BY HEAVEN, HIS HORSES ARE TIRED.	127	BOWMEN OF SHU	17
BLOOD ON EACH TIRED FANG	261	ALF'S SIXTH	11
TIREIS			
ELAIN, TIREIS, ALCMENA,	75	THE ALCHEMIST	14
ELAIN, TIREIS, ALCMENA,	76	THE ALCHEMIST	49
ELAIN, TIREIS, ALLODETTA	76	THE ALCHEMIST	61

'TIS -- TOGETHER

	PAGE	TITLE	LINE
'TIS			
AIE-E! 'TIS TRUE THAT I AM GAY	5	LA FRAISNE	37
PESTE! 'TIS HIS OWN SONGS?	6	CINO	30
"'TIS THE WHITE STAG, FAME, WE'RE A-HUNTING,	25	THE WHITE STAG	6
'TIS HOW A BRAVE MAN DIES ON THE TREE."	34	GOODLY FERE	32
'TIS MY TRUE LOVE'S SEPULCHRE.	45	FROM HEINE: 3	8
'TIS EVANOE'S,	49	OF SPLENDOUR	1
'TIS NOT A GAME THAT PLAYS AT MATES AND MATING,	50	THE FLAME	1
'TIS NOT A GAME OF BARTER, LANDS AND HOUSES,	50	THE FLAME	3
'TIS NOT A GAME THAT PLAYS AT MATES AND MATING,	50	THE FLAME	16
'TIS NOT A GAME OF BARTER, LANDS AND HOUSES,	50	THE FLAME	17
'TIS NOT "OF DAYS AND NIGHTS" AND TROUBLING YEARS,	50	THE FLAME	18
FOUGHT OUT THEIR STRIFE HERE, 'TIS A PLACE OF WONDER;	51	THE ALTAR	3
WHERE THESE HAVE BEEN, MEET 'TIS, THE GROUND IS HOLY.	51	THE ALTAR	4
GODDAMM, GODDAMM, 'TIS WHY I AM, GODDAMM,	116	ANCIENT MUSIC	10
'TIS MEET	173	LANGUE D'OC: 2	4
'TIS BUT A VAGUE, INVARIOUS DELIGHT,	236	MIDDLE-AGED	1
'TIS OF MY COUNTRY THAT I WOULD ENDITE,	238	MOYEN SENSUEL	1
'TIS TIME THAT IT WAS CAPPED WITH SOMETHING QUOTABLE.	239	MOYEN SENSUEL	38
('TIS AN ANOMALY IN OUR LARGE LAND OF FREEDOM,	245	MOYEN SENSUEL	217
NOT BY THE REASON, BUT 'TIS FELT, I SAY.	249	DONNA MI PREGA	35
TISSUE			
DRINKST IN LIFE OF EARTH, OF THE AIR, THE TISSUE	68	APPARUIT	7
HER FINGERS WERE LIKE THE TISSUE	110	THE ENCOUNTER	4
THE WHIRLING TISSUE OF LIGHT	170	PHANOPOEIA	22
TISSUE PRESERVED--THE PURE MIND	193	SIENA MI FE	11
TITANS			
NEITHER WOULD I WARBLE OF TITANS, NOR OF OSSA	217	SEXTUS PROP: 5	39
WITHOUT IXION, AND WITHOUT THE SONS OF MENOETIUS AND THE ARGO AND WITHOUT JOVE'S GRAVE AND THE TITANS.	218	SEXTUS PROP: 5	52
TITYRUS			
TITYRUS MIGHT HAVE SUNG THE SAME VIXEN;	229	SEXTUS PROP:12	46
TO (658)			
TOBACCO			
FOR THE TOBACCO ASHES SCATTERED ON HIS COAT	15	FAMAM CANO	34
TOBACCO-SHOP			
GIVE ME IN DUE TIME, I BESEECH YOU, A LITTLE TOBACCO-SHOP,	117	THE LAKE ISLE	2
LEND ME A LITTLE TOBACCO-SHOP,	117	THE LAKE ISLE	13
TOC			
JE VIS LES COLONNES ANCIENNES EN "TOC"	160	DANS OMNIBUS	12
TO-DAY			
AND EACH TO-DAY 'VAILS LESS THAN YESTERE'EN,	37	THE YOUNG KING	28
TO-DAY, ON HIGH	41	HER MONUMENT	26
TO-DAY FROM THE DRAGON-PEN.	139	SOUTH-FOLK	5
YOU READ TO-DAY, HOW LONG THE OVERLORDS OF PERIGORD,	152	NEAR PERIGORD	50
TO-DAY WE TAKE THE GREAT BREATH OF LOVERS,	221	SEXTUS PROP: 7	31
BUT KNIGHTS AND LORDS TO-DAY RESPECT	267	ALF'S ELEVENTH	23
TO-DAY'S			
BUT TO-DAY'S MEN ARE NOT THE MEN OF THE OLD DAYS,	131	AT TEN-SHIN	7
LIKE TO-DAY'S GREAT MEN IN BRITAIN.	272	THE BABY	12
TO-EM-MEI			
"WET SPRINGTIME," SAYS TO-EM-MEI, "WET SPRING IN THE GARDEN."	142	UNMOVING CLOUD	EPI
TO-EM-MEI'S			
TO-EM-MEI'S "THE UNMOVING CLOUD"	142	UNMOVING CLOUD	T
TOFF			
AN' 'E LOOKS LIKE A TOFF.	260	ALF'S FOURTH	15
TOGETHER			
WERE SET TOGETHER THEY WOULD SEEM BUT LIGHT	36	THE YOUNG KING	4
IT IS ENOUGH THAT WE ONCE CAME TOGETHER;	59	SILET	5
IT IS ENOUGH THAT WE ONCE CAME TOGETHER;	59	SILET	9
IT IS ENOUGH THAT WE ONCE CAME TOGETHER;	59	SILET	11
LET THEM DRAW TOGETHER THE BONES OF THE METAL.	76	THE ALCHEMIST	53
THE HOUR OF WAKING TOGETHER.	83	THE GARRET	11
TO SEE THREE GENERATIONS OF ONE HOUSE GATHERED TOGETHER!	89	COMMISSION	30
TOGETHER WITH THE RESPECTIVE WIVES, HUSBANDS, SISTERS AND HETEROGENEOUS CONNECTIONS OF THE GOOD BELLAIRES,	97	THE BELLAIRES	6
"WHERE THE GREAT HALLS WERE CLOSER TOGETHER."	122	PROVINC DESERT	53

TOGETHER -- TONGUE

	PAGE	TITLE	LINE
TOGETHER (CONTINUED)			
SET ALL TOGETHER, ARE NOT WORTHY OF YOU. . . ." ...	151	NEAR PERIGORD	9
BORE US TOGETHER . . . SURGING . . . AND APART . . .	157	NEAR PERIGORD	178
UPON THE ONE RAFT, VICTOR AND CONQUERED TOGETHER,	218	SEXTUS PROP: 6	3
MARIUS AND JUGURTHA TOGETHER,	218	SEXTUS PROP: 6	4
MARIUS AND JUGURTHA TOGETHER.	219	SEXTUS PROP: 6	12
WHILE OUR FATES TWINE TOGETHER, SATE WE OUR EYES WITH LOVE;	220	SEXTUS PROP: 7	17
THAT THE PAPERS WERE GETTIN' TOGETHER	262	ALF'S SEVENTH	5
"WE ARE 'ERE MET TOGETHER	270	OF 600 M.P.'S	1
WE ARE 'ERE MET TOGETHER	270	OF 600 M.P.'S	5
TOI			
HIDMEN GAR TOI PANTH', HOS' ENI TROIEI	187	E. P. ODE	9
TOILET			
THE BEAUTIFUL TOILET	128	BEAU TOILET	T
TOISONS			
AUX TOISONS COULEUR DE LIN,	160	DANS OMNIBUS	16
TOLD			
OR WHEN THE MINSTREL, TALE HALF TOLD,	9	NA AUDIART	27
WITH TIMES TOLD OVER AS WE TELL BY ROTE;	43	SATIEMUS	17
DISILLUSIONS AS NEVER TOLD IN THE OLD DAYS,	190	HUGH SELWYN: 4	25
TOLD ME HOW JOHNSON (LIONEL) DIED	193	SIENA MI FE	7
TOLD HER WOULD FIT HER STATION.	193	HUGH SELWIN:11	8
WERE DESOLATED BECAUSE SHE HAD TOLD THEM HER DREAMS.	214	SEXTUS PROP: 4	23
I'VE TOLD HIS TRAINING, HE WAS NEVER BASHFUL,	242	MOYEN SENSUEL	125
TOLD 'EM THAT GLORY	259	ALF'S FOURTH	3
TOLD 'EM TO DIE IN WAR, AND THEN TO SAVE,	260	ALF'S FIFTH	2
LIKE ALL HIS CLASS WAS TOLD TO HOLD IT IN THOSE DAYS,	263	ALF'S EIGHTH	26
UNTIL A NARSTY GERMAN TOLD THEM SO.	265	ALF'S NINTH	25
T'OLD			
GIVE T'OLD ONES A NEWER TWIST	261	ALF'S SIXTH	8
TOLEDOS			
AS OLD TOLEDOS PAST THEIR DAYS OF WAR	19	FOR E. MCC	19
TOLERANT			
UNDER A MORE TOLERANT, PERHAPS, EXAMINATION.	201	AGE DEMANDED	28
THEY GET PRAISE FROM TOLERANT HAMADRYADS."	229	SEXTUS PROP:12	49
TOMB			
"AYE! I AM A POET AND UPON MY TOMB	24	THUS NINEVEH	1
YET AM I POET, AND UPON MY TOMB	24	THUS NINEVEH	16
GOD! SHE WAS WHITE THEN, SPLENDID AS SOME TOMB	31	PIERE VIDAL	38
THE TOMB AT AKR CAAR	60	TOMB AKR CAAR	T
TOMB HIDETH TROUBLE. THE BLADE IS LAYED LOW.	66	THE SEAFARER	90
SHE WOULD BRING FRANKINCENCE AND WREATHS TO MY TOMB,	213	SEXTUS PROP: 3	30
TOM-BOY			
THAT TOM-BOY WHO CAN'T EARN HER LIVING,	162	CABARET DANCER	44
TOMBS			
FOR THUS ARE TOMBS OF LOVERS MOST DESECRATED.	213	SEXTUS PROP: 3	34
TOMB STONE			
THE SONGS SHALL BE A FINE TOMB STONE OVER THEIR BEAUTY.	209	SEXTUS PROP: 1	64
TOMB-STONES			
HERE ARE THEIR TOMB-STONES.	145	SALUTATION 3RD	6
TO-MORROW			
TO PLAGUE TO-MORROW WITH A TESTAMENT!	59	SILET	14
RICHARD SHALL DIE TO-MORROW--LEAVE HIM THERE,	155	NEAR PERIGORD	139
'TO-MORROW AT TEA-TIME.'")	159	PSYCHOLOG HOUR	38
"BREATHE NOT THE WORD TO-MORROW IN HER EARS"	161	CABARET DANCER	EPI
SAY "FORGET TO-MORROW," BEING OF ALL MEN	161	CABARET DANCER	7
"PEPITA" HAS NO TO-MORROW, SO YOU WRITE.	161	CABARET DANCER	9
COME, COME TO-MORROW,	162	CABARET DANCER	45
TO-MORROW IN TEN YEARS AT THE LATEST,	162	CABARET DANCER	46
TO-MORROW FATE SHUTS US IN.	221	SEXTUS PROP: 7	32
TO-MORROWS			
PEPITA HAS SUCH TO-MORROWS: WITH THE HANDS PUFFED OUT,	161	CABARET DANCER	10
TONE			
OR MORE SWEET IN TONE THAN ANY, BUT THAT I	24	THUS NINEVEH	21
IN BRIEF, VIOLET IS THE GROUND TONE OF MY PHONETICS,	247	PIERROTS	15
THIS IS THE KIND OF TONE AND SOLEMNITY	263	ALF'S EIGHTH	22
TONGUE			
TIBORS ALL TONGUE AND TEMPER AT MONT-AUSIER,	22	MARVOIL	18

PAGE 427

TONGUE -- TORCH-FLAMES

```
                                                        PAGE      TITLE          LINE
TONGUE  (CONTINUED)
    THE HOUNDS OF THE CRIMSON SKY GAVE TONGUE  ........    34     GOODLY FERE      39
    AND WITH A TONGUE BY NO MEANS TOO ELEGANT,  ........   113     FORMIANUS LADY    6
    BORN OF A JONGLEUR'S TONGUE, FREELY TO PASS  .......   153     NEAR PERIGORD    83
    SHE WHO HAD NOR EARS NOR TONGUE SAVE IN HER HANDS,     157     NEAR PERIGORD   187
    OR IS IT MY TONGUE THAT WRONGS YOU  ................   222     SEXTUS PROP: 8   14
    BUT HE SWALLER'D HIS TONGUE.  .....................    263     ALF'S EIGHTH     25
TONGUES
    AND KISSED THEE WITH A MYRIAD GRASSY TONGUES;  .....    60     TOMB AKR CAAR     7
    "YOU SHOULD NOT BELIEVE HOSTILE TONGUES.  ..........   226     SEXTUS PROP:11   20
TO-NIGHT
    YET SAW AN "AD."  "TO-NIGHT, THE HUDSON SAIL,  .....   242     MOYEN SENSUEL   111
TONNERRE
    TONNERRE?"  .......................................   199     MAUBERLEY: 2    EPI
TOO
    TOO CHEAP FOR CATALOGUING,  .......................     15     FAMAM CANO       40
    "LAPPO I LEAVE BEHIND AND DANTE TOO,  .............     25     GUIDO INVITES     1
    LEST THEY SHOULD PARCH TOO SWIFTLY, WHERE SHE PASSES.   38     BALLATETTA       10
    AND CALL MY VOICE TOO THICK A THING.  .............     45     FROM HEINE: 5     4
    I LIVE TOO LATE TO SUP WITH THEE!  ................     46     TRANSLATOR        2
    TOO LONG . . . .  .................................    112     PAPYRUS           2
    BY NO MEANS TOO SMALL,  ...........................    113     FORMIANUS LADY    2
    AND WITH A TONGUE BY NO MEANS TOO ELEGANT,  ........   113     FORMIANUS LADY    6
    AND A PAIR OF SCALES NOT TOO GREASY,  .............    117     THE LAKE ISLE     9
    AND LEAVES HER TOO MUCH ALONE.  ...................    128     BEAU TOILET       9
    TOO DEEP TO CLEAR THEM AWAY!  .....................    131     RIVER-MER WIFE   21
    SHE WILL NOT BATHE TOO OFTEN, BUT HER JEWELS  .....    161     CABARET DANCER   13
    TIME'S TOOTH IS INTO THE LOT, AND WAR'S AND FATE'S
       TOO.  ..........................................   165     QUINTUS SEPTIM   17
    WERE MUCH TOO ABSTRUSE FOR HIS COMPREHENSION,  ....    181     MOEURS CON: 7     9
    "'CARE TOO MUCH FOR SOCIETY DINNERS?'  ............    182     MOEURS CON: 8    11
    WITH CROWDS TOO ASSIDUOUS IN THEIR CROSSING OF IT;     213     SEXTUS PROP: 3   33
    NOR WILL YOU BE WEARY OF CALLING MY NAME, NOR TOO
       WEARY  .........................................   219     SEXTUS PROP: 6   23
    TO BE NOT TOO WELL KNOWN IN HAUNTS OF VICE--  .....    245     MOYEN SENSUEL   202
    I'M GETTING TOO OLD FOR SUCH CAPERS.  .............    264     ALF'S EIGHTH     35
    DO, THAT IS: THINK, BEFORE IT'S TOO LATE.  ........    265     ALF'S TENTH      12
    GOLD, OF COURSE, IS SOLID TOO,  ...................    267     ALF'S TWELFTH    16
    MIGHT DO, TOO.  MONTAGUE!  ........................    267     ALF'S TWELFTH    18
TOODLE
    SING: TOODLE DOODLEDE OOT!  .......................    271     OLE KATE          2
TOOK
    ALFONSO THE HALF-BALD, TOOK TO HANGING  ...........     22     MARVOIL           9
    "WHY TOOK YE NOT ME WHEN I WALKED ABOUT  ..........     33     GOODLY FERE      11
    THAT THEY TOOK THE HIGH AND HOLY HOUSE  ...........     33     GOODLY FERE      19
    YOU TOOK NO PLEASURE AT ALL IN MY TRIUMPHS,  ......    101     AMITIES           2
    PARIS TOOK HELEN NAKED COMING FROM THE BED OF
       MENELAUS,  .....................................   220     SEXTUS PROP: 7   14
    AND NEVER GOT TOOK TO JAIL,  ......................    271     OLE KATE         16
TOOL
    AND HIS TOOL  .....................................    198     MAUBERLEY: 1      7
TOOTH
    TIME'S TOOTH IS INTO THE LOT, AND WAR'S AND FATE'S
       TOO.  ..........................................   165     QUINTUS SEPTIM   17
    DEATH HAS HIS TOOTH IN THE LOT,  ..................    223     SEXTUS PROP: 9   18
TOP
    THAT WAS THE TOP OF THE WALK, WHEN HE SAID:  ......    119     THE GYPSY         1
    ON THE TOP OF THE HAWTHORNE,  .....................    173     LANGUE D'OC: 2   13
TOPAZ
    THE EYES TURN TOPAZ.  .............................    204     MEDALLION        16
TOPIC
    "OH! ABELARD!" AS IF THE TOPIC  ...................    181     MOEURS CON: 7     8
TOP-LOFTICAL
    NOT THAT HE WAS A SAINT, NOR WAS TOP-LOFTICAL  ....    246     MOYEN SENSUEL   233
TORCH
    BY THE BRIGHT FLAME OF THE FISHING TORCH  .........     75     THE ALCHEMIST    23
TORCHES
    CUPID WILL CARRY LIGHTED TORCHES BEFORE HIM  ......    212     SEXTUS PROP: 3   22
    AND SOME OF THEM SHOOK LITTLE TORCHES,  ...........    224     SEXTUS PROP:10    7
TORCH-FLAMES
    I HAVE SEEN THE TORCH-FLAMES, HIGH-LEAPING,  ......    121     PROVINC DESERT   30
```

PAGE 428

	PAGE	TITLE	LINE
TORCH-FLARE			
STRAY GLEAMS ON HANGING MAIL, AN ARMOURER'S			
TORCH-FLARE	155	NEAR PERIGORD	134
TORN			
TORN, GREEN AND SILENT IN THE SWOLLEN RHONE,	31	PIERE VIDAL	27
AND I AM TORN AGAINST THE JAGGED DARK,	60	TOMB AKR CAAR	26
TORRENT			
NO MORE THE TORRENT,	3	THRENOS	15
TORRIDITY			
THE TIME IS COME, THE AIR HEAVES IN TORRIDITY,	221	SEXTUS PROP: 8	3
TORSE			
WHERE THY TORSE AND LIMBS ARE MET	8	NA AUDIART	24
TORTOISE			
LIKE A TRAINED AND PERFORMING TORTOISE,	229	SEXTUS PROP:12	59
TORTURE			
VICED IN SUCH TORTURE FOR THE "COUNTERPASS."	151	NEAR PERIGORD	27
TOSSED			
WHILE SHE TOSSED CLOSE TO CLIFFS. COLDLY AFFLICTED,	64	THE SEAFARER	8
TOSSING			
TWO MEN TOSSING A COIN, ONE KEEPING A CASTLE,	122	PROVINC DESERT	66
TOSSING IT UP UNDER THE CLOUDS.	136	EXILE'S LETTER	62
TOTIN'			
AND TOTIN' UP SCUTTLES OF COAL,	271	OLE KATE	18
TOUCH			
THEY REACH ME NOT. TOUCH ME SOME EDGE OR THAT,	20	IN DURANCE	5
AND ORDINARY PEOPLE TOUCH ME NOT.	20	IN DURANCE	13
SHE BY ONE TOUCH	176	LANGUE D'OC: 3	62
I HAVE MISLAID THE "AD.," BUT NOTE THE TOUCH,	242	MOYEN SENSUEL	115
NOTE, READER, NOTE THE SENTIMENTAL TOUCH:	242	MOYEN SENSUEL	116
TOUCHED			
HAVE I NOT TOUCHED THY PALMS AND FINGER-TIPS,	60	TOMB AKR CAAR	22
WILL THEY BE TOUCHED WITH THE VERISIMILITUDES?	81	TENZONE	6
PHIDON NEITHER PURGED ME, NOR TOUCHED ME,	165	QUINTUS SEPTIM	23
TOUCHETH			
PIERCED OF THE POINT THAT TOUCHETH LASTLY ALL,	19	FOR E. MCC	24
TOUCHING			
FELT HANDS TURN ICE A-SUDDEN, TOUCHING YE,	41	HER MONUMENT	17
TOULOUSE			
I HAVE SEEN FOIX ON ITS ROCK, SEEN TOULOUSE, AND	122	PROVINC DESERT	59
AND ALL THE ROAD TO CAHORS, TO TOULOUSE?	153	NEAR PERIGORD	67
TOUR			
LA TOUR,	121	PROVINC DESERT	23
AND MAKE THE TOUR ABROAD FOR THEIR WILD TILLAGE--	245	MOYEN SENSUEL	208
TOURIST			
I KNEW A TOURIST AGENT, ONE WHOSE ART IS	245	MOYEN SENSUEL	209
TOURISTS			
WHEN TOURISTS FROLICKING	236	MIDDLE-AGED	4
TOURS			
TO RUN SUCH TOURS. HE CALLS 'EM. . . . HOUSE PARTIES.	245	MOYEN SENSUEL	210
TOUS			
DONT TOUS LES AUTRES TRAITS ETAIENT BANALS,	160	DANS OMNIBUS	4
ET TOUS LES GAZONS DIVERS	160	DANS OMNIBUS	21
TOUT			
IL ETAIT COMME UN TOUT PETIT GARCON	181	MOEURS CON: 7	3
TOUTES			
ET TOUTES LES FLEURS	160	DANS OMNIBUS	28
TOWARD			
VERY GLAD, FOR MY BRIDE HATH TOWARD ME A GREAT LOVE	5	LA FRAISNE	34
TOWARD SUCH A WORK OF ART.	45	FROM HEINE: 5	12
I STOP IN MY ROOM TOWARD THE EAST, QUIET, QUIET,	142	UNMOVING CLOUD	6
SOUTHWARD TOWARD MONTAIGNAC, AND HE BENDS AT A TABLE	154	NEAR PERIGORD	97
AND THE GREEN CAT'S-EYE LIFTS TOWARD MONTAIGNAC.	154	NEAR PERIGORD	103
AROSE TOWARD NEWMAN AS THE WHISKEY WARMED.	193	SIENA MI FE	12
STRETCHES TOWARD ME HER LEAFY HANDS,"--	196	HUGH SELWIN:12	2
A MODULATION TOWARD THE THEATRE,	196	HUGH SELWIN:12	18
THE FLOOD SHALL MOVE TOWARD THE FOUNTAIN	220	SEXTUS PROP: 7	25
ON THE VEILED LAKE TOWARD AVERNUS	223	SEXTUS PROP: 9	6
STILL WE LOOK TOWARD THE DAY WHEN MAN, WITH UNCTION,	244	MOYEN SENSUEL	175
TOWARDS			
TOWARDS THE NOEL THAT MORTE SAISON	10	FOR THIS YULE	1

PAGE 429

TOWER -- TRAITORESS

	PAGE	TITLE	LINE
TOWER			
'TILL THE WATCHMAN ON THE TOWER	171	LANGUE D'OC	EPI
TOWER-MAN			
NOR I, NOR TOWER-MAN, LOOK ON DAYLIGHT,	177	LANGUE D'OC: 4	8
TOWER-ROOM			
EN BERTRANS, A TOWER-ROOM AT HAUTEFORT,	154	NEAR PERIGORD	95
TOWERS			
FORGETFUL IN THEIR TOWERS OF OUR TUNEING	6	CINO	13
I CLIMB THE TOWERS AND TOWERS	133	FRONTIER GUARD	4
I CLIMB THE TOWERS AND TOWERS	133	FRONTIER GUARD	4
DOUBLE TOWERS, WINGED ROOFS,	141	IDEA OF CHOAN	23
THE FOUR ROUND TOWERS, FOUR BROTHERS--MOSTLY FOOLS:	152	NEAR PERIGORD	35
THE DULL ROUND TOWERS ENCROACHING ON THE FIELD,	155	NEAR PERIGORD	129
AND WHO WOULD HAVE KNOWN THE TOWERS	208	SEXTUS PROP: 1	26
"BRIGHT TIPS REACH UP FROM TWIN TOWERS,	212	SEXTUS PROP: 3	4
TOWN			
ALONE IN THE TOWN?" SAYS HE.	33	GOODLY FERE	12
ROME THAT ALONE HAST CONQUERED ROME THE TOWN,	40	ROME	10
SHE GETS THEM BY THE SOUTH WALL OF THE TOWN.	140	MULBERRY ROAD	7
TOYS			
GET THE KID NICE NEW TOYS,	261	ALF'S SIXTH	5
TRACE			
SNIFFING THE TRACE OF AIR!	74	THE RETURN	14
WATCHES TO FOLLOW OUR TRACE.	109	HEATHER	7
BUT SHOWED NO TRACE OF ALCOHOL	193	SIENA MI FE	9
TRACED			
AND OUR TWO HORSES HAD TRACED OUT THE VALLEYS;	157	NEAR PERIGORD	173
TRACK			
WHAT IF UNDERTAKERS FOLLOW MY TRACK,	213	SEXTUS PROP: 3	28
TRACKS			
O'ER TRACKS OF OCEAN; SEEING THAT ANYHOW	65	THE SEAFARER	65
THE HIGH TRACKS OF HERMES WOULD NOT AFFORD YOU SHELTER.	226	SEXTUS PROP:11	10
TRACTS			
UPON A TALE, TO COMBAT OTHER TRACTS,	241	MOYEN SENSUEL	72
TRADE			
THEY GOT NO STEADY TRADE,	257	BREAD BRIGADE	10
THE DASHING RUPERT OF THE PULPING TRADE,	264	ALF'S NINTH	9
TRADITION			
OH, THERE IS PRECEDENT, LEGAL TRADITION,	153	NEAR PERIGORD	88
EMENDATION, CONSERVATION OF THE "BETTER TRADITION,"	202	AGE DEMANDED	47
TRAFFIC			
FOR HERE ARE A MILLION PEOPLE SURLY WITH TRAFFIC;	62	N. Y.	5
ALL WAYS OF TRAFFIC?	70	THE PLUNGE	13
TO SNIFF THE TRAFFIC INTO PERIGORD.	153	NEAR PERIGORD	63
TRAGICAL			
YOU HAVE BEEN SECOND ALWAYS. TRAGICAL?	61	PORTRAIT FEMME	7
TRAIL			
NOR AT MY FUNERAL EITHER WILL THERE BY ANY LONG TRAIL,	219	SEXTUS PROP: 6	13
TRAILING			
TRAILING ALONG THE WIND.	18	DE AEGYPTO	6
TRAIN			
CYDONIAN SPRING WITH HER ATTENDANT TRAIN,	87	THE SPRING	1
TRAINED			
THE HORSES ARE WELL TRAINED, THE GENERALS HAVE IVORY ARROWS AND QUIVERS ORNAMENTED WITH FISH-SKIN.	127	BOWMEN OF SHU	19
LIKE A TRAINED AND PERFORMING TORTOISE,	229	SEXTUS PROP:12	59
TRAINING			
I'VE TOLD HIS TRAINING, HE WAS NEVER BASHFUL,	242	MOYEN SENSUEL	125
TRAINS			
THE SILKEN TRAINS GO RUSTLING,	47	FROM HEINE: 7	25
TRAIST			
FOR I AM TRAIST AND LOOSE,	175	LANGUE D'OC: 3	50
TILL THE TRAIST MAN CRY OUT TO WARN	177	LANGUE D'OC: 4	3
'TILL THE TRAIST WATCHER HIS SONG UNREIN,	177	LANGUE D'OC: 4	18
TRAIT			
CULLING FROM EACH A FAIR TRAIT	105	DOMPNA POIS	18
"CARMEN EST MAIGRE, UN TRAIT DE BISTRE	162	CABARET DANCER	24
TRAITORESS			
IN "FAITH AND TROTH" TO A TRAITORESS,	12	OF THE GIBBET	35

	PAGE	TITLE	LINE
TRAITS			
DONT TOUS LES AUTRES TRAITS ETAIENT BANALS, ...	160	DANS OMNIBUS	4
TRAMP			
THAT TRAMP OLD WAYS BENEATH THE SUN-LIGHT, ...	6	CINO	21
TRANS-CAUCASUS			
CELEBRITIES FROM THE TRANS-CAUCASUS WILL BELAUD ROMAN CELEBRITIES	207	SEXTUS PROP: 1	17
TRANSIENT			
TIBER ALONE, TRANSIENT AND SEAWARD BENT, ...	40	ROME	11
AS TRANSIENT THINGS ARE--	67	DORIA	3
AN HOMELY, TRANSIENT ANTIQUITY.	114	EPILOGUE	8
THE TALLEYRANDS, HAVE HELD THE PLACE; IT WAS NO TRANSIENT FICTION.	152	NEAR PERIGORD	51
TRANSITORY			
BENEATH THEIR TRANSITORY STEP AND MERRIMENT, ...	236	MIDDLE-AGED	9
TRANSLATED			
TRANSLATOR TO TRANSLATED	46	TRANSLATOR	T
TRANSLATIONS			
TRANSLATIONS AND ADAPTATIONS FROM HEINE	44	FROM HEINE	T
TRANSLATOR			
TRANSLATOR TO TRANSLATED	46	TRANSLATOR	T
TRANSLUCENT			
CLEAR, DEEP, TRANSLUCENT, SO THE STARS ME SEEMED	30	PIERE VIDAL	21
I SAY MY SOUL FLOWED BACK, BECAME TRANSLUCENT.	51	THE FLAME	36
TRANSPARENT			
DANCING IN TRANSPARENT BROCADE, ...	136	EXILE'S LETTER	60
TRAPPINGS			
UNDETERRED BY THE MANIFEST AGE OF MY TRAPPINGS? ...	114	SIMULACRA	6
THE TRAPPINGS ARE BORDERED WITH MIST.	141	IDEA OF CHOAN	12
TRAVAIL			
LO, I AM WORN WITH TRAVAIL	16	PRAISE YSOLT	11
TRAVEL			
THE HEART TURNS TO TRAVEL SO THAT HE THEN THINKS	65	THE SEAFARER	52
AND IN THE MEAN TIME MY SONGS WILL TRAVEL, ...	208	SEXTUS PROP: 1	39
TRAVELLED			
WE MET, AND TRAVELLED INTO SEN-GO, ...	134	EXILE'S LETTER	17
TRAVERSE			
THE SALT-WAVY TUMULT TRAVERSE ALONE.	65	THE SEAFARER	36
TRE			
"UN E DUO FANNO TRE,"	163	CABARET DANCER	83
TREADS			
THE BLACK PANTHER TREADS AT MY SIDE, ...	109	HEATHER	1
TREASURE			
BE AN UNLIKELY TREASURE HOARD	66	THE SEAFARER	101
THE TREASURE IS OURS, MAKE WE FAST LAND WITH IT.	69	THE NEEDLE	11
SUCH TREASURE IN THE AIR, ...	197	ENVOI (1919)	9
TREASURIES			
"KING'S TREASURIES"; SWINBURNE	192	YEUX GLAUQUES	3
TREASURY			
FOR THEIR PAWN AND TREASURY.	33	GOODLY FERE	20
TREAT			
THAN IF I TREAT THE NATION AS A WHOLE.	239	MOYEN SENSUEL	43
LEST IT SHOULD FAIL TO TREAT ALL MEN ALIKE.	244	MOYEN SENSUEL	178
TREE			
THE TREE	3	THE TREE	T
I STOOD STILL AND WAS A TREE AMID THE WOOD, ...	3	THE TREE	1
NATHLESS I HAVE BEEN A TREE AMID THE WOOD	3	THE TREE	10
THAT WAS A DOG-WOOD TREE SOME SYNE.	4	LA FRAISNE	15
DRINK YE A SKOAL FOR THE GALLOWS TREE!	11	OF THE GIBBET	1
THAT SAID US, "TILL THEN" FOR THE GALLOWS TREE! ...	11	OF THE GIBBET	4
DRINK WE A SKOAL FOR THE GALLOWS TREE!	11	OF THE GIBBET	13
DRINK WE SKOAL FOR THE GALLOWS TREE!	12	OF THE GIBBET	25
AIE! THE LEAN BARE TREE IS WIDOWED AGAIN	12	OF THE GIBBET	33
BUT DRINK WE SKOAL TO THE GALLOWS TREE!	12	OF THE GIBBET	37
FOR THE PRIESTS AND THE GALLOWS TREE?	33	GOODLY FERE	2
"THOUGH I GO TO THE GALLOWS TREE."	33	GOODLY FERE	29
'TIS HOW A BRAVE MAN DIES ON THE TREE,"	34	GOODLY FERE	32
I HAVE SEEN HIM UPON THE TREE.	34	GOODLY FERE	36
SIN' THEY NAILED HIM TO THE TREE.	34	GOODLY FERE	54
THE BIRD SITS ON THE HAWTHORN TREE	43	MR. HOUSMAN	6
THE TREE HAS ENTERED MY HANDS, ...	62	A GIRL	1

TREE -- TRIES

	PAGE	TITLE	LINE
TREE (CONTINUED)			
THE TREE HAS GROWN IN MY BREAST--	62	A GIRL	3
TREE YOU ARE, ...	62	A GIRL	6
BRING THE LIGHT OF THE BIRCH TREE IN AUTUMN	75	THE ALCHEMIST	11
MIDONZ, DAUGHTER OF THE SUN, SHAFT OF THE TREE, SILVER OF THE LEAF, LIGHT OF THE YELLOW OF THE AMBER, ...	75	THE ALCHEMIST	26
IT IS LIKE AN OLD TREE WITH SHOOTS, ...	89	COMMISSION	31
SHE RUSHED OUT INTO THE SUNLIGHT AND SWARMED UP A COCOANUT PALM TREE, ...	118	CONTEMPORARIES	3
THE BIRDS FLUTTER TO REST IN MY TREE, ...	142	UNMOVING CLOUD	22
OR, BY A LICHENED TREE AT ROCHECOUART	154	NEAR PERIGORD	107
AND PHOEBUS LOOKING UPON ME FROM THE CASTALIAN TREE,	210	SEXTUS PROP: 2	16
THE BLACK PANTHER LIES UNDER HIS ROSE TREE	231	CANTUS PLANUS	1
THE BLACK PANTHER LIES UNDER HIS ROSE TREE.	231	CANTUS PLANUS	5
TREE-AT-THE-RIVER			
O NATHAT-IKANAIE, "TREE-AT-THE-RIVER."	91	DANCE FIGURE	18
TREES			
IN THE ASH TREES HERE:	5	LA FRAISNE	50
HERE 'MID THE ASH TREES.	5	LA FRAISNE	52
FOR THAT I LOVE YE AS THE WIND THE TREES	21	IN DURANCE	44
AND COOLNESS BENEATH THE TREES.	35	THE EYES	10
THE CYPRESS TREES, HE LAY, ...	39	FOR PSYCHE	2
I AM BELOW AMID THE PINE TREES, ...	53	AU JARDIN	4
AMID THE LITTLE PINE TREES, HEAR ME!	53	AU JARDIN	5
HATH OF THE TREES A LIKENESS OF THE SAVOUR:	71	A VIRGINAL	13
AS YOU MOVE AMONG THE BRIGHT TREES;	75	THE ALCHEMIST	2
O MY FELLOW SUFFERERS, WE WENT OUT UNDER THE TREES,	82	THE CONDOLENCE	7
MOVING AMONG THE TREES, AND CLINGING	92	GENTILDONNA	2
AND MIST CLOTTED ABOUT THE TREES IN THE VALLEY, ...	119	THE GYPSY	8
THERE IS A PLACE OF TREES . . . GRAY WITH LICHEN.	121	PROVINC DESERT	6
TREES FALL, THE GRASS GOES YELLOW WITH AUTUMN.	133	FRONTIER GUARD	3
HIGH HEAPS, COVERED WITH TREES AND GRASS;	133	FRONTIER GUARD	9
SWEET TREES ARE ON THE PAVED WAY OF THE SHIN, ...	138	NEAR SHOKU	6
AND DOUBLE THE TREES, ...	141	IDEA OF CHOAN	14
TREES THAT GLITTER LIKE JADE, ...	141	IDEA OF CHOAN	19
THE TREES IN MY EAST-LOOKING GARDEN	142	UNMOVING CLOUD	17
THE COMPACT, DE BORN SMOKED OUT, TREES FELLED	155	NEAR PERIGORD	124
TRELLIS			
THERE IS A TRELLIS FULL OF EARLY ROSES, ...	153	NEAR PERIGORD	72
TREMBLE			
DREW FULL THIS DAGGER THAT DOTH TREMBLE HERE.	31	PIERE VIDAL	42
CAUSING THE FIVE PEAKS TO TREMBLE, ...	128	THE RIVER SONG	14
TREMBLES			
NOW! FOR THE NEEDLE TREMBLES IN MY SOUL!	69	THE NEEDLE	3
TREMBLING			
NO MORE FOR US THE TREMBLING	3	THRENOS	9
YET THERE IS A TREMBLING UPON ME IN THE TWILIGHT, .	16	PRAISE YSOLT	14
TREMOLOS			
HATE TREMOLOS AND NATIONAL FRENETICS.	247	PIERROTS	14
TRENCH			
HYSTERIAS, TRENCH CONFESSIONS, ...	190	HUGH SELWYN: 4	26
TRENTIESME			
HE PASSED FROM MEN'S MEMORY IN L'AN TRENTIESME	187	E. P. ODE	18
TRIBE			
FRAIL CINO, STRONGEST OF HIS TRIBE	6	CINO	20
TRICK			
THEY'LL TRICK YOU AGAIN AND AGAIN, AS YOU SLEEP;	265	ALF'S NINTH	31
TRICKSOME			
THE TRICKSOME HERMES IS HERE;	90	SURGIT FAMA	8
TRIED			
HE TRIED TO EMBRACE A MOON	117	EPITAPHS	4
TRIED LAYU'S LUCK, OFFERED THE CHOYO SONG, ...	136	EXILE'S LETTER	66
"I AM AN ARTIST, YOU HAVE TRIED BOTH METIERS."	156	NEAR PERIGORD	152
ACCEPT OPINION. THE "NINETIES" TRIED YOUR GAME	194	MR. NIXON	23
HAD TRIED ALL WAYS;	235	TO WHISTLER	2
HAD NOT ONE STYLE FROM BIRTH, BUT TRIED AND PRIED	235	TO WHISTLER	16
"I COULDN'T," SHE SEZ, "AN' I AINT TRIED, ...	270	OF 600 M.P.'S	21
TRIES			
AND HEARD A CLERGY THAT TRIES ON MORE WHEEZES	241	MOYEN SENSUEL	99

TRILLS -- TROY

	PAGE	TITLE	LINE
TRILLS			
THROUGH TRILLS AND RUNS LIKE CRYSTAL,	45	FROM HEINE: 5	7
TRIO			
A QUIET AND RESPECTABLE-TAWDRY TRIO;	163	CABARET DANCER	81
TRISTAN'S			
SEEING THAT TRISTAN'S LADY ISEUTZ HAD NEVER	106	DOMPNA POIS	37
TRIUMPH			
AND "IT IS, I THINK, INDIA WHICH NOW GIVES NECKS TO YOUR TRIUMPH,"	216	SEXTUS PROP: 5	17
I SHALL TRIUMPH AMONG YOUNG LADIES OF INDETERMINATE CHARACTER,	229	SEXTUS PROP:12	55
TRIUMPHANT			
STARK, KEEN, TRIUMPHANT, TILL IT PLAYS AT DEATH.	31	PIERE VIDAL	37
TRIUMPHS			
YOU TOOK NO PLEASURE AT ALL IN MY TRIUMPHS,	101	AMITIES	2
TRIUNE			
ON TRIUNE AZURES, THE IMPALPABLE	39	BLANDULA	11
TRIVIAL			
NO ONE WILL REMEMBER THE TRIVIAL PARTS OF ME,	146	MONUMENTUM AER	4
TROAD			
SMALL TALK O ILION, AND O TROAD	208	SEXTUS PROP: 1	32
AND OUT OF TROAD, AND FROM THE CAMPANIA,	223	SEXTUS PROP: 9	17
TROBAR			
TALKING OF TROBAR CLUS WITH DANIEL.	155	NEAR PERIGORD	140
TROICA			
"TROICA ROMA RESURGES."--PROPERTIUS	40	ROME	EPI
TROIEI			
HIDMEN GAR TOI PANTH', HOS' ENI TROIEI	187	E. P. ODE	9
TROJAN			
A TROJAN AND ADULTEROUS PERSON CAME TO MENELAUS UNDER THE RITES OF HOSPITIUM,	227	SEXTUS PROP:12	6
OH HOW THE BIRD FLEW FROM TROJAN RAFTERS,	227	SEXTUS PROP:11	35
HE SHAKES THE TROJAN WEAPONS OF AENEAS,	228	SEXTUS PROP:12	34
TROPHIES			
KEPT AS BOLD TROPHIES OF OLD PAGEANTRY.	19	FOR E. MCC	18
TROPHIES FISHED UP; SOME CURIOUS SUGGESTION;	61	PORTRAIT FEMME	16
TROTH			
IN "FAITH AND TROTH" TO A TRAITORESS,	12	OF THE GIBBET	35
TROTSKY			
LENIN TO SAVE 'EM, TROTSKY TO SAVE 'EM	258	ALF'S SECOND	6
TROUBADOURS			
THE JOGLARS SUPPLE AND THE TROUBADOURS.	36	THE YOUNG KING	11
TROUBLE			
NO MORE THE WINDS AT TWILIGHT TROUBLE US.	3	THRENOS	2
THEY TAKE THE TROUBLE TO TEAR OUT THIS WALL HERE,	22	MARVOIL	24
TOMB HIDETH TROUBLE. THE BLADE IS LAYED LOW.	66	THE SEAFARER	90
THE TROUBLE IN THE PACE AND THE UNCERTAIN	74	THE RETURN	3
SAVE TROUBLE AND SAD THOUGHT,	174	LANGUE D'OC: 3	8
TROUBLED			
HER LIFE IS OBSCURE AND TROUBLED;	179	MOEURS CON: 2	4
TROUBLES			
TROUBLES MY SLEEP,	183	CANTICO SOLE	3
TROUBLES MY SLEEP.	183	CANTICO SOLE	8
IT TROUBLES MY SLEEP.	183	CANTICO SOLE	17
AND TELL OUT THE LONG LIST OF HER TROUBLES.	223	SEXTUS PROP: 9	12
TROUBLETH			
AND NO MAN TROUBLETH US.	5	LA FRAISNE	30
IN THOSE DIM HALLS WHERE NO MAN TROUBLETH	24	THUS NINEVEH	10
TROUBLING			
'TIS NOT "OF DAYS AND NIGHTS" AND TROUBLING YEARS,	50	THE FLAME	18
IMPETUOUS TROUBLING	201	AGE DEMANDED	19
TROUSERS			
I WILL GET YOU THE SCARLET SILK TROUSERS	94	INSTRUCTIONS	19
TROUT			
BY THE TROUT ASLEEP IN THE GRAY-GREEN OF WATER;	76	THE ALCHEMIST	37
CAPANEUS; TROUT FOR FACTITIOUS BAIT;	187	E. P. ODE	8
TROY			
AND ALL THE FAIR FROM TROY AND ALL FROM ACHAIA,	38	LADY'S LIFE	7
I HAVE THOUGHT OF THE SECOND TROY,	123	PROVINC DESERT	64
TROY	165	QUINTUS SEPTIM	ST

PAGE 433

TRUCE -- TUNE

	PAGE	TITLE	LINE
TRUCE			
THERE IS A TRUCE AMONG THE GODS, ...	90	SURGIT FAMA	1
TRUE			
AIE-E! 'TIS TRUE THAT I AM GAY	5	LA FRAISNE	37
TRUE TO THE TRUTH'S SAKE AND CRAFTY DISSECTOR, ...	13	MESMERISM	18
HE PLEASE TO PARDON, AS TRUE PARDON IS, ...	37	THE YOUNG KING	38
'TIS MY TRUE LOVE'S SEPULCHRE.	45	FROM HEINE: 3	8
BUT DO THOU SPEAK TRUE, EVEN TO THE LETTER:	90	SURGIT FAMA	15
NOR WITH GIFT SO BOUNTIFUL AND SO TRUE, ...	105	DOMPNA POIS	16
AND THERE CAME ALSO THE "TRUE MAN" OF SHI-YO TO MEET ME, ...	134	EXILE'S LETTER	24
TRUE, HE HAS PRAISED HER, BUT IN SOME OPINION	155	NEAR PERIGORD	147
O PLASMATOUR AND TRUE CELESTIAL LIGHT, ...	172	LANGUE D'OC: 1	1
I AM TRUE, OR A LIAR, ...	175	LANGUE D'OC: 3	51
HIS TRUE PENELOPE WAS FLAUBERT, ...	187	E. P. ODE	13
"HIS TRUE PENELOPE	198	MAUBERLEY: 1	5
OR FROM TRUE COURSE	249	DONNA MI PREGA	41
TRULY			
DO YOU, TRULY, SO DETEST ME?	44	FROM HEINE: 1	2
DE MORTUIS VERUM, TRULY THE MASTER BUILDER?	240	MOYEN SENSUEL	58
TRUMPET			
WHEN THE TRUMPET RANG OUT.	48	FROM HEINE: 7	32
TRUMPETS			
NO TRUMPETS FILLED WITH MY EMPTINESS, ...	219	SEXTUS PROP: 6	15
TRUNK			
BEHOLD ME SHRIVELLED AS AN OLD OAK'S TRUNK	31	PIERE VIDAL	52
THE HEADLESS TRUNK "THAT MADE ITS HEAD A LAMP," ...	151	NEAR PERIGORD	23
GOES ON THAT HEADLESS TRUNK, THAT BEARS FOR LIGHT	156	NEAR PERIGORD	164
TRUNKS			
THEIR TRUNKS BURST THROUGH THE PAVING, ...	138	NEAR SHOKU	7
TRUSTED'ST			
THOU TRUSTED'ST IN THYSELF AND MET THE BLADE	19	FOR E. MCC	15
TRUTH			
KNOWING THE TRUTH OF THINGS UNSEEN BEFORE;	3	THE TREE	2
MAY I FOR MY OWN SELF SONG'S TRUTH RECKON, ...	64	THE SEAFARER	1
TELLING THE HEART OF THEIR TRUTH	96	DUM CAPITOLIUM	3
MY HERO, RADWAY, I HAVE NAMED, IN TRUTH, ...	241	MOYEN SENSUEL	77
AND TRUTH SHOULD HERE BE CAREFUL OF HER THIN DRESS--	243	MOYEN SENSUEL	146
MUST THINK TRUTH LOOKS AS THEY DO IN WOOL PYJAMAS,	243	MOYEN SENSUEL	148
E'EN ITS DENIERS CAN NOW HEAR THE TRUTH, ...	248	DONNA MI PREGA	4
HID TRUTH AND LIED, AND LIED AND HID THE FACTS, ...	260	ALF'S FIFTH	6
KNOWEST THOU NOT THE TRUTH IS NEVER IN SEASON	263	ALF'S EIGHTH	13
TRUTHS			
TELL ME THE TRUTHS WHICH YOU HEAR OF OUR CONSTANT YOUNG LADY, ...	214	SEXTUS PROP: 4	1
THOUGH MALES OF SEVENTY, WHO FEAR TRUTHS NAKED HARM US, ...	243	MOYEN SENSUEL	147
TRUTH'S			
TRUE TO THE TRUTH'S SAKE AND CRAFTY DISSECTOR, ...	13	MESMERISM	18
TRY			
HE WAS UNCERTAIN WHY HE SHOULD TRY TO FEEL LIKE ANYTHING ELSE, ...	118	ANCIENT WISDOM	3
THEY TRY TO STIR NEW AFFECTION, ...	142	UNMOVING CLOUD	19
END FACT. TRY FICTION. LET US SAY WE SEE	154	NEAR PERIGORD	94
AND TRY TO WRENCH HER IMPULSE INTO ART.	235	TO WHISTLER	13
TRY PHOTOGRAPHS, WOLF DOWN THEIR ALE AND CAKES	236	MIDDLE-AGED	6
TS'AI			
TS'AI CHI'H	108	TS'AI CHI'H	T
TSIN-TSU			
SAID TSIN-TSU:	104	THE SEEING EYE	8
TUB			
THE BATH TUB	100	THE BATH TUB	T
TUBERCULOSIS			
HOW MANY WEAK OF MIND, HOW MUCH TUBERCULOSIS	260	ALF'S FIFTH	13
TUMULT			
THE SALT-WAVY TUMULT TRAVERSE ALONE.	65	THE SEAFARER	36
THE LAST SINGS OF A TUMULT, ...	216	SEXTUS PROP: 5	8
TUNE			
TURN TO YOUR DRIPPING HORSES, BECAUSE OF A TUNE, UNDER AETNA?	208	SEXTUS PROP: 1	47

PAGE 434

TUNE -- TURNING

	PAGE	TITLE	LINE
TUNE (CONTINUED)			
AND WEARY WITH HISTORICAL DATA, THEY WILL TURN TO MY DANCE TUNE.	209	SEXTUS PROP: 1	62
IF SHE WITH IVORY FINGERS DRIVE A TUNE THROUGH THE LYRE,	217	SEXTUS PROP: 5	27
NOR TO THE TUNE OF THE PHRYGIAN FATHERS.	218	SEXTUS PROP: 5	54
TUNEING			
FORGETFUL IN THEIR TOWERS OF OUR TUNEING	6	CINO	13
TUNIC			
TUNIC SPREAD IN DELAY;	220	SEXTUS PROP: 7	6
TUNICK'D			
NO, NOT WHEN SHE WAS TUNICK'D IN PURPLE.	225	SEXTUS PROP:10	31
TUNING			
TO HIDING NIGHT OR TUNING "SYMPHONIES";	235	TO WHISTLER	15
TURBULENT			
THE TURBULENT AND UNDISCIPLINED HOST OF ART STUDENTS--	93	LES MILLWIN	5
TURMOIL			
TURMOIL GROWN VISIBLE BENEATH OUR PEACE,	32	PARACELSUS	8
OUT OF A TURMOIL OF SPEECH ABOUT YOU.	36	FRANCESCA	4
A TURMOIL OF WARS-MEN, SPREAD OVER THE MIDDLE KINGDOM,	133	FRONTIER GUARD	15
SURPRISED, DESERT TURMOIL, SEA SUN.	139	SOUTH-FOLK	6
TURN			
WILL TURN ASIDE TO SNEER AT	14	FAMAM CANO	29
AND THE BROAD FIELDS BENEATH THEM TURN CRIMSON,	28	ALTAFORTE	5
AND TURN MY MIND UPON THAT SPLENDID MADNESS,	30	PIERE VIDAL	2
GOD CURSE THE YEARS THAT TURN SUCH WOMEN GREY!	31	PIERE VIDAL	46
FELT HANDS TURN ICE A-SUDDEN, TOUCHING YE,	41	HER MONUMENT	17
TIME HAS SEEN THIS, AND WILL NOT TURN AGAIN;	59	SILET	12
THAT, ERE A MAN'S TIDE GO, TURN IT TO TWAIN.	66	THE SEAFARER	70
THAT BEARS US UP, SHALL TURN AGAINST THE POLE.	69	THE NEEDLE	7
AND HALF TURN BACK;	74	THE RETURN	9
YES, SHE ALSO WILL TURN MIDDLE-AGED,	116	THE TEA SHOP	5
SHE ALSO WILL TURN MIDDLE-AGED.	116	THE TEA SHOP	9
WAITING HIS TURN IN THE MID-SUMMER EVENING,	154	NEAR PERIGORD	109
BENDS INTO THE TURN OF THE WIND,	170	PHANOPOEIA	20
NOR DO I KNOW WHEN I TURN LEFT OR RIGHT	174	LANGUE D'OC: 3	24
OR TURN ME INSIDE OUT, AND ABOUT.	175	LANGUE D'OC: 3	47
MY ILL DOTH SHE TURN SWEET.	175	LANGUE D'OC: 3	48
THE EYES TURN TOPAZ.	204	MEDALLION	16
TURN TO YOUR DRIPPING HORSES, BECAUSE OF A TUNE, UNDER AETNA?	208	SEXTUS PROP: 1	47
AND WEARY WITH HISTORICAL DATA, THEY WILL TURN TO MY DANCE TUNE.	209	SEXTUS PROP: 1	62
"TURN NOT VENUS INTO A BLINDED MOTION	220	SEXTUS PROP. 7	12
OR JOVE, HARSH AS HE IS, MAY TURN ASIDE YOUR ULTIMATE DAY.	222	SEXTUS PROP: 8	38
BUT TURN TO RADWAY: THE FIRST NIGHT ON THE RIVER,	246	MOYEN SENSUEL	223
NOR DOTH HE TURN	250	DONNA MI PREGA	65
TURNED			
"THANK YOU, WHATEVER COMES." AND THEN SHE TURNED	40	ERAT HORA	1
WHAT IF MY THOUGHTS WERE TURNED IN THEIR MID REACH	43	SATIEMUS	9
NATURE HERSELF'S TURNED METAPHYSICAL,	50	THE FLAME	27
TURNED IN THEIR SAPPHIRE TIDE, COME FLOODING O'ER US!	51	HORAE BEATAE	4
WHAT IF THE WIND HAVE TURNED AGAINST THE RAIN?	59	SILET	10
A GRACIOUS SPRING, TURNED TO BLOOD-RAVENOUS AUTUMN,	133	FRONTIER GUARD	14
THE FLAT LAND IS TURNED INTO RIVER.	142	UNMOVING CLOUD	12
"MAENT, I LOVE YOU, YOU HAVE TURNED ME OUT."	151	NEAR PERIGORD	6
I HAD ALMOST TURNED DOWN THE PAGES.	158	PSYCHOLOG HOUR	5
WHEN IT TURNED OUT HE MEANT MRS. WARD.	181	MOEURS CON: 7	12
TURNED FROM THE "EAU-FORTE	198	MAUBERLEY: 1	1
TURNETH			
SITH NO THING IS BUT TURNETH UNTO ANGUISH	37	THE YOUNG KING	27
UNTIL THIS COURSE TURNETH ASIDE.	69	THE NEEDLE	15
FREEZETH RIVER, TURNETH LIVER,	116	ANCIENT MUSIC	8
TURNING			
TO CATCH YOU AT WORM TURNING. HOLY ODD'S BODYKINS!	13	MESMERISM	4
AND HER HAIR ALSO IS TURNING.	102	LADIES	4
NO CHANGE NOR TURNING ASIDE.	106	DOMPNA POIS	60

PAGE 435

TURNING -- TWINE

	PAGE	TITLE	LINE
TURNING (CONTINUED)			
THROUGH ALL THE THIRTY-SIX FOLDS OF THE TURNING AND TWISTING WATERS,	134	EXILE'S LETTER	18
WE, IN OUR NARROW BED, TURNING ASIDE FROM BATTLES:	218	SEXTUS PROP: 5	57
TURNS			
TURNS HARDY PILOT . . . AND IF ONE WRONG NOTE	42	HER MONUMENT	45
THE HEART TURNS TO TRAVEL SO THAT HE THEN THINKS	65	THE SEAFARER	52
O LOVE, COME NOW, THIS LAND TURNS EVIL SLOWLY.	69	THE NEEDLE	9
AND NOW SHE TURNS TO ME SEEKING LOVE,	102	LADIES	3
BREAKS NOT NOR TURNS ASIDE.	106	DOMPNA POIS	46
LIKE THE BRANCH THAT TURNS ABOUT	173	LANGUE D'OC: 2	12
TURQUOISE			
GILT TURQUOISE AND SILVER ARE IN THE PLACE OF THY REST.	91	DANCE FIGURE	16
THE GEW-GAWS OF FALSE AMBER AND FALSE TURQUOISE ATTRACT THEM.	114	BEFORE A SHOP	1
TURRETS			
SINGING THE STARS IN THE TURRETS OF BEZIERS,	22	MARVOIL	13
TURTLE			
CAN YOU EVEN TELL THE AGE OF A TURTLE?	140	SENNIN POEM	16
TWAIN			
DRINK WE THE LUSTY ROBBERS TWAIN,	11	OF THE GIBBET	17
HOW WILL THESE HOURS, WHEN WE TWAIN ARE GRAY,	51	HORAE BEATAE	3
THAT, ERE A MAN'S TIDE GO, TURN IT TO TWAIN.	66	THE SEAFARER	70
'TWAS			
'TWAS NOT UNTIL THE GODS HAD BEEN	3	THE TREE	6
SAITH 'TWAS THE WORTHIEST OF EDITORS.	63	PHASELLUS ILLE	2
HATH LACKED A SOMETHING. 'TWAS BUT MARGINAL.	63	QUIES	4
'TWAS AS A BUSINESS ASSET PURE AN' SIMPLE	246	MOYEN SENSUEL	239
TWELFTH			
ALF'S TWELFTH BIT	267	ALF'S TWELFTH	T
TWELVE			
FOR TWELVE HORSES AND ALSO FOR TWELVE BOARHOUNDS	98	THE BELLAIRES	19
FOR TWELVE HORSES AND ALSO FOR TWELVE BOARHOUNDS	98	THE BELLAIRES	19
THEIR VOICE IS IN THE TWELVE PIPES HERE.	130	THE RIVER SONG	40
AND IT WILL LAST A TWELVE MONTH,	212	SEXTUS PROP: 3	13
AFTER TWELVE MONTHS OF DISCOMFORT?	215	SEXTUS PROP: 4	42
TEN YEARS AND TWELVE YEARS GONE,	259	ALF'S THIRD	18
TWENTY			
I WAS TWENTY YEARS BEHIND THE TIMES	85	SALUTATION 2ND	3
AND TEN YEARS AFTER, OR TWENTY, AS YOU WILL,	155	NEAR PERIGORD	127
TWENTY-EIGHT			
FOR THERE ARE, IN SIRMIONE, TWENTY-EIGHT YOUNG DANTES AND THIRTY-FOUR CATULLI;	96	AESTHETICS	8
'TWERE			
COULD I BUT SPEAK AS 'TWERE IN THE "RESTORATION"	238	MOYEN SENSUEL	7
C.3, C.4, 'TWERE BETTER TO FORGET	260	ALF'S FIFTH	12
TWEY			
WI' TWEY WORDS SPOKE' SUDDENTLY.	34	GOODLY FERE	48
TWICE			
ONCE, TWICE, A YEAR--	6	CINO	25
TWICE THEY PROMISED TO COME.	158	PSYCHOLOG HOUR	26
TWICE TAKEN BY OETIAN GODS,	208	SEXTUS PROP: 1	35
TWIDDLES			
SHE TWIDDLES THE SPIKED WHEEL OF A RHOMBUS,	215	SEXTUS PROP: 4	35
TWIG			
WHERE THE LEAF FALLS FROM THE TWIG,	174	LANGUE D'OC: 3	
TWIGS			
ARE BURSTING OUT WITH NEW TWIGS,	142	UNMOVING CLOUD	14
TWILIGHT			
NO MORE THE WINDS AT TWILIGHT TROUBLE US.	3	THRENOS	
WILL SING THEM IN THE TWILIGHT,	14	FAMAM CANO	
THEIR ECHOES PLAY UPON EACH OTHER IN THE TWILIGHT	16	PRAISE YSOLT	
YET THERE IS A TREMBLING UPON ME IN THE TWILIGHT,	16	PRAISE YSOLT	1
AND GREAT WINGS BEAT ABOVE US IN THE TWILIGHT.	157	NEAR PERIGORD	17
I SIT ALONE IN THE TWILIGHT	268	ANOTHER BIT	
TWIN			
"BRIGHT TIPS REACH UP FROM TWIN TOWERS,	212	SEXTUS PROP: 3	
TWINE			
WHILE OUR FATES TWINE TOGETHER, SATE WE OUR EYES WITH LOVE;	220	SEXTUS PROP: 7	

TWINED -- TYRO

	PAGE	TITLE	LINE
TWINED			
ROSES TWINED IN HER HANDS.	211	SEXTUS PROP: 2	37
TWINS			
HAS BECOME THE FATHER OF TWINS,	100	TEMPERAMENTS	6
TWIRL			
THEY STAND AND TWIRL THEIR MOUSTACHES.	140	MULBERRY ROAD	17
TWIST			
AND ON THE MORROW, BY SOME LIGHTSOME TWIST,	42	HER MONUMENT	35
GIVE T'OLD ONES A NEWER TWIST	261	ALF'S SIXTH	8
TWISTED			
OVER ROADS TWISTED LIKE SHEEP'S GUTS.	135	EXILE'S LETTER	41
THE TWISTED RHOMBS CEASED THEIR CLAMOUR OF ACCOMPANIMENT;	223	SEXTUS PROP: 9	1
TWISTING			
THROUGH ALL THE THIRTY-SIX FOLDS OF THE TURNING AND TWISTING WATERS,	134	EXILE'S LETTER	18
TWISTS			
IT TWISTS ITSELF FROM OUT ALL NATURAL MEASURE;	249	DONNA MI PREGA	50
TWITCHING			
THAT THE TWITCHING OF THREE ABDOMINAL NERVES	148	FRATRES MINORE	6
TWITTER			
AND THE COLD BIRDS TWITTER	174	LANGUE D'OC: 3	2
TWO			
BUT YOU NEVER STRING TWO DAYS UPON ONE WIRE	53	AU JARDIN	13
FACT THAT LEADS NOWHERE; AND A TALE OR TWO,	61	PORTRAIT FEMME	17
(OR WITH TWO LIGHT FEET, IF IT PLEASE YOU!)	86	SALUTATION 2ND	18
BETWEEN THE TWO INDOLENT CANDLES.	87	ALBATRE	7
HER TWO HANDS AND HER THROAT,	106	DOMPNA POIS	33
HER TWO CATS	115	SOCIAL ORDER	11
AND THE WHORES DROPPING IN FOR A WORD OR TWO IN PASSING,	117	THE LAKE ISLE	10
TWO MEN TOSSING A COIN, ONE KEEPING A CASTLE,	122	PROVINC DESERT	66
TWO SMALL PEOPLE, WITHOUT DISLIKE OR SUSPICION.	130	RIVER-MER WIFE	6
SPLITS THE TWO STREAMS APART.	138	CITY OF CHOAN	10
THERE IS A THROAT; AH, THERE ARE TWO WHITE HANDS;	153	NEAR PERIGORD	71
AND OUR TWO HORSES HAD TRACED OUT THE VALLEYS;	157	NEAR PERIGORD	173
TWO FRIENDS: A BREATH OF THE FOREST . . .	158	PSYCHOLOG HOUR	23
CUPID, ASTRIDE A PHALLUS WITH TWO WINGS,	162	CABARET DANCER	36
TAKE HER. SHE HAS TWO EXCELLENT SEASONS.	165	QUINTUS SEPTIM	22
"AND TWO SPRINGS HAVE PASSED US."	166	FISH & SHADOW	12
LIFE GIVES US TWO MINUTES, TWO SEASONS--	168	OF AROUET	25
LIFE GIVES US TWO MINUTES, TWO SEASONS--	168	OF AROUET	25
TWO DEATHS--AND TO STOP LOVING AND BEING LOVABLE,	168	OF AROUET	27
TWO YEARS, THREE YEARS I SEEK	175	LANGUE D'OC: 3	34
FOR TWO GROSS OF BROKEN STATUES,	191	HUGH SELWYN: 5	7
FOR TWO HOURS HE TALKED OF GALLIFET;	193	SIENA MI FE	5
WHEN OUR TWO DUSTS WITH WALLER'S SHALL BE LAID,	197	ENVOI (1919)	20
SAILS SPREAD ON CERULEAN WATERS, I WOULD SHED TEARS FOR TWO;	223	SEXTUS PROP: 9	7
"IN THE STUDIO" AND THESE TWO PORTRAITS, IF I HAD MY CHOICE!	235	TO WHISTLER	8
OR HUGGED TWO GIRLS AT ONCE BEHIND A CHAPEL.)	242	MOYEN SENSUEL	106
WO-BARRELED			
NOR OF XERXES' TWO-BARRELED KINGDOM, NOR OF REMUS AND HIS ROYAL FAMILY,	217	SEXTUS PROP: 5	44
WO-FACED			
O FILAMENTS OF AMBER, TWO-FACED IRIDESCENCE!	95	OF THE DEGREES	15
TWOULD			
'TWOULD NOT MOVE IT ONE JOT FROM LEFT TO RIGHT.	63	PHASELLUS ILLE	11
YBALDE			
TYBALDE AND THAT ARMOURESS	11	OF THE GIBBET	7
YIN'			
TYIN' YOUR MEANIN' IN SEVENTY SWADELIN'S,	13	MESMERISM	2
TYMPANUM			
STRIKE THE TYMPANUM,	42	HER MONUMENT	46
TRANNY			
SPEAK AGAINST THE TYRANNY OF THE UNIMAGINATIVE,	88	COMMISSION	7
RO			
WITH YOU IS IOPE, WITH YOU THE WHITE-GLEAMING TYRO,	38	LADY'S LIFE	5
IOPE, AND TYRO, AND PASIPHAE, AND THE FORMAL GIRLS OF ACHAIA,	223	SEXTUS PROP: 9	16

UC -- UNCOMBED

	PAGE	TITLE	LINE
UC			
RIGHT ENOUGH? THEN READ BETWEEN THE LINES OF UC ST.			
CIRC,	151	NEAR PERIGORD	3
UDDERS			
KIDS FOR A BRIBE AND PRESSED UDDERS,	229	SEXTUS PROP:12	44
UGLY			
OF UGLY PRINT MARKS, BLACK	35	THE EYES	13
HAS MARRIED AN UGLY WIFE,	100	ARIDES	2
ULTIMATE			
ULTIMATE AFFRONTS TO	202	AGE DEMANDED	56
THE GENTLER HOUR OF AN ULTIMATE DAY.	222	SEXTUS PROP: 8	18
OR JOVE, HARSH AS HE IS, MAY TURN ASIDE YOUR			
ULTIMATE DAY.	222	SEXTUS PROP: 8	38
ULTIMATELY			
ULTIMATELY, HIS SEISMOGRAPH:	199	MAUBERLEY: 2	19
UMBRAM			
"VOCAT AESTUS IN UMBRAM"	186	HUGH SELWYN	EPI
UM-HUM			
HALF A LOAF? UM-HUM?	257	BREAD BRIGADE	2
UN			
DANS UN OMNIBUS DE LONDRES	160	DANS OMNIBUS	T
ENCHASSES DANS UN VISAGE STUPIDE	160	DANS OMNIBUS	3
"CARMEN EST MAIGRE, UN TRAIT DE BISTRE	162	CABARET DANCER	24
"UN E DUO FANNO TRE,"	163	CABARET DANCER	83
IL ETAIT COMME UN TOUT PETIT GARCON	181	MOEURS CON: 7	3
EST GROSSIERE ET LE PARFUM DES VIOLETTES UN	199	MAUBERLEY: 2	EPI
UNABLE			
UNABLE IN THE SUPERVENING BLANKNESS	199	MAUBERLEY: 2	16
UNAFFECTED			
UNAFFECTED BY "THE MARCH OF EVENTS,"	187	E. P. ODE	17
UNANSWERING			
IN VAIN, CYNTHIA. VAIN CALL TO UNANSWERING SHADOW,	219	SEXTUS PROP: 6	36
UNBEAUTIFUL			
WITH A FOOT UNBEAUTIFUL,	113	FORMIANUS LADY	3
UNBELIEVING			
BELIEVING IN OLD MEN'S LIES, THEN UNBELIEVING	190	HUGH SELWYN: 4	14
UNBEND			
UNBEND FROM THE HOLLY-TREES,	109	HEATHER	5
UNBIND			
SO THAT NO DAY SHALL UNBIND THEM.	220	SEXTUS PROP: 7	21
UNBORN			
YOU ARE MINGLED WITH THE ELEMENTS UNBORN;	84	ORTUS	10
UNBOUND			
WITH HER HAIR UNBOUND, AND HE HIS OWN SKIFFSMAN!	132	AT TEN-SHIN	33
UNBOUNDED			
OF TH' UNBOUNDED ONES, BUT YE, THAT HIDE	21	IN DURANCE	29
UNBROKEN			
AND THAT HARD PHALANX, THAT UNBROKEN LINE,	153	NEAR PERIGORD	64
UNBROKEN BY THE SIMOON;	203	MAUBERLEY: 4	5
UNBRUSHED			
SUNK IN A FROWSY COLLAR--AN UNBRUSHED BLACK.	161	CABARET DANCER	12
UNCATALOGUED			
OF SOME AS YET UNCATALOGUED SAND;	213	SEXTUS PROP: 3	37
UNCELEBRATED			
UNPAID, UNCELEBRATED,	195	HUGH SELWIN:10	3
UNCERTAIN			
THE TROUBLE IN THE PACE AND THE UNCERTAIN	74	THE RETURN	3
WERE UNCERTAIN WHO WAS SUPPOSED TO BE INDEBTED TO			
THEM.	98	THE BELLAIRES	33
HE WAS UNCERTAIN WHY HE SHOULD TRY TO FEEL LIKE			
ANYTHING ELSE,	118	ANCIENT WISDOM	4
THE EDGE, UNCERTAIN, BUT A MEANS OF BLENDING	196	HUGH SELWIN:12	14
IN WRITING FICTION ON UNCERTAIN CHANCES	243	MOYEN SENSUEL	13
BOOZY, UNCERTAIN.	259	ALF'S THIRD	1
UNCERTAINITY			
WITH SUCH GRACIOUS UNCERTAINITY,	103	LADIES	1
UNCERTAINTIES			
YOU HAD YOUR SEARCHES, YOUR UNCERTAINTIES,	235	TO WHISTLER	1
UNCOMBED			
THUS? SHE WEPT INTO UNCOMBED HAIR,	214	SEXTUS PROP: 4	1

UNCOMFORTABLE -- UNDRY

	PAGE	TITLE	LINE
UNCOMFORTABLE			
AND THOROUGHLY UNCOMFORTABLE,	85	SALUTATION	2
UNCONSCIOUS			
SPEAK AGAINST UNCONSCIOUS OPPRESSION,	88	COMMISSION	6
UNCONSTANT			
REMAINS OF ROME. O WORLD, THOU UNCONSTANT MIME! ...	40	ROME	12
UNCTION			
STILL WE LOOK TOWARD THE DAY WHEN MAN, WITH UNCTION,	244	MOYEN SENSUEL	175
UNCUCKOLDED			
UNCUCKOLDED FOR A SEASON.	218	SEXTUS PROP: 5	60
UNCULTIVATED			
HER MIND IS, AS EVER, UNCULTIVATED,	179	MOEURS CON: 2	6
UNDEFEATABLE			
"PROLIFIC NOYES" WITH OUTPUT UNDEFEATABLE).	240	MOYEN SENSUEL	50
UNDER			
AND LEFT THEM UNDER A STONE	4	LA FRAISNE	26
THE WINDS ARE UNDER MY LIPS.	18	DE AEGYPTO	20
UNDER SOME NEUTRAL FORCE	69	THE NEEDLE	14
AS YOUR VOICES, UNDER THE LARCHES OF PARADISE	75	THE ALCHEMIST	3
UNDER NIGHT, THE PEACOCK-THROATED,	75	THE ALCHEMIST	8
O MY FELLOW SUFFERERS, WE WENT OUT UNDER THE TREES,	82	THE CONDOLENCE	7
THINE ARMS ARE AS A YOUNG SAPLING UNDER THE BARK;	91	DANCE FIGURE	10
LOOSE UNDER THE BRIGHT GLASS CASES,	117	THE LAKE ISLE	8
HEARD, UNDER THE DARK, WHIRLING LAUGHTER.	121	PROVINC DESERT	32
TOSSING IT UP UNDER THE CLOUDS.	136	EXILE'S LETTER	62
GRASS SHOWING UNDER THE SNOW,	168	OF AROUET	37
IN ORCHARD UNDER THE HAWTHORNE	177	LANGUE D'OC: 4	1
QUICK EYES GONE UNDER EARTH'S LID,	191	HUGH SELWYN: 5	6
UNDER A MORE TOLERANT, PERHAPS, EXAMINATION.	201	AGE DEMANDED	28
TURN TO YOUR DRIPPING HORSES, BECAUSE OF A TUNE,			
UNDER AETNA?	208	SEXTUS PROP: 1	47
OR PERHAPS JUNO HERSELF WILL GO UNDER,	222	SEXTUS PROP: 8	40
A TROJAN AND ADULTEROUS PERSON CAME TO MENELAUS			
UNDER THE RITES OF HOSPITIUM,	227	SEXTUS PROP;12	6
THE BLACK PANTHER LIES UNDER HIS ROSE TREE	231	CANTUS PLANUS	1
THE BLACK PANTHER LIES UNDER HIS ROSE TREE.	231	CANTUS PLANUS	5
NOT QUITE SNOWED UNDER.	261	ALF'S SIXTH	20
UNDERGOING			
AND THAT THE FRIEND OF THE SECOND DAUGHTER WAS			
UNDERGOING A NOVEL,	179	MOEURS CON: 3	4
UNDERSKIRT			
HER UNDERSKIRT IS OF GREEN PATTERN-SILK,	140	MULBERRY ROAD	13
UNDERSTAND			
DO NOT UNDERSTAND THE CONDUCT OF THIS WORLD S			
AFFAIRS.	97	THE BELLAIRES	2
WHO CAN UNDERSTAND ANY AFFAIR OF THEIRS. YET	97	THE BELLAIRES	10
UNDERSTOOD			
AND MANY A NEW THING UNDERSTOOD	3	THE TREE	11
IN FACT THEY UNDERSTOOD THEM SO BADLY	97	THE BELLAIRES	3
BUT THE GOOD BELLAIRES HAVE SO LITTLE UNDERSTOOD			
THEIR AFFAIRS	97	THE BELLAIRES	8
FROM FORM SEEN DOTH HE START, THAT, UNDERSTOOD, ...	249	DONNA MI PREGA	24
UNDERTAKERS			
WHAT IF UNDERTAKERS FOLLOW MY TRACK,	213	SEXTUS PROP: 3	28
UNDERWAVE			
PALE SLOW GREEN SURGINGS OF THE UNDERWAVE,	60	SUB MARE	7
UNDERWORLD			
THE GODS OF THE UNDERWORLD ATTEND ME, O ANNUBIS,	147	BEFORE SLEEP	6
UNDETERRED			
UNDETERRED BY THE MANIFEST AGE OF MY TRAPPINGS? ...	114	SIMULACRA	6
UNDISCIPLINED			
THE TURBULENT AND UNDISCIPLINED HOST OF ART			
STUDENTS--	93	LES MILLWIN	5
UNDOUBTEDLY			
HE WILL UNDOUBTEDLY CHAIN SOMEONE ELSE TO THIS			
FOUNTAIN,	000	ABU SALAMMAMM	31
UNDRY			
WITH FINGERS THAT ARE NOT LONG, AND WITH A MOUTH			
UNDRY,	113	FORMIANUS LADY	5

PAGE 439

UNDRYABLE -- UNMADE

	PAGE	TITLE	LINE
UNDRYABLE			
DAMP WOOLLY HANDKERCHIEFS WERE STUFFED INTO HER UNDRYABLE EYES,	214	SEXTUS PROP: 4	25
UNDULATION			
A MINOAN UNDULATION,	202	AGE DEMANDED	33
UNDULENT			
UNDULENT,	147	BEFORE SLEEP	9
UNDULY			
AND MY HEART WORKED AT THEM UNDULY.	44	FROM HEINE: 2	6
UNDURABLE			
DREAR ALL THIS EXCELLENCE, DELIGHTS UNDURABLE!	66	THE SEAFARER	88
UNEARTHLY			
FOLK OF UNEARTHLY FASHION, PLACES SPLENDID,	50	THE FLAME	24
UNEDUCATED			
WITH A PLACID AND UNEDUCATED MISTRESS	195	HUGH SELWIN:10	6
UNENDINGLY			
BY QUALITY, BUT IS ITS OWN EFFECT UNENDINGLY	249	DONNA MI PREGA	30
UNEXPECTED			
THE UNEXPECTED PALMS	202	AGE DEMANDED	42
UNFAMILIARITY			
SHOWS RAZOR'S UNFAMILIARITY	15	FAMAM CANO	36
UNFATHOM			
COULD FREUD OR JUNG UNFATHOM SUCH A SINK?	241	MOYEN SENSUEL	76
UNFIT			
HIM OF ALL MEN, UNFIT	201	AGE DEMANDED	2
UNFORECASTED			
THE UNFORECASTED BEACH;	203	MAUBERLEY: 4	19
UNFORMED			
AND WILLS MAN LOOK INTO UNFORMED SPACE	250	DONNA MI PREGA	59
UNFORTUNATE			
O MOST UNFORTUNATE AGE!	113	FORMIANUS LADY	10
JOVE, BE MERCIFUL TO THAT UNFORTUNATE WOMAN	221	SEXTUS PROP: 8	1
UNGAINLY			
AND HEARD UNGAINLY LAUGHTER.	85	SALUTATION	6
UNGATHERED			
THOU RESTLESS, UNGATHERED.	112	HIMERRO	7
UNGRATEFUL			
O YE LIPS THAT ARE UNGRATEFUL,	44	FROM HEINE: 1	5
'UNGRY			
ONWARD TH' 'UNGRY BLOKES,	257	BREAD BRIGADE	5
UNHARDENED			
BEARING HER OFFERINGS IN THEIR UNHARDENED HANDS,	211	SEXTUS PROP: 2	34
UNIMAGINATIVE			
SPEAK AGAINST THE TYRANNY OF THE UNIMAGINATIVE,	88	COMMISSION	7
UNIMPORTANT			
THE ABSOLUTE UNIMPORTANT.	52	AU SALON	27
UNINTERRUPTED			
IN AN UNINTERRUPTED NIGHT ONE CAN	48	FROM HEINE: 8	7
UNION			
IN PERIGORD, AND THIS GOOD UNION	151	NEAR PERIGORD	18
UNIVERSE			
THE MANIFEST UNIVERSE	202	AGE DEMANDED	30
UNKILLABLE			
OF THE FILTHY, STURDY, UNKILLABLE INFANTS OF THE VERY POOR.	83	THE GARDEN	6
UNKISSED			
THREE THOUSAND CHORUS GIRLS AND ALL UNKISSED,	241	MOYEN SENSUEL	87
UNKNOWN			
"OBVIOUSLY CROWNED LOVERS AT UNKNOWN DOORS,	211	SEXTUS PROP: 2	48
WHO, SINCE THEIR WIT'S UNKNOWN, ESCAPE THE GALLOWS.	238	MOYEN SENSUEL	4
UNLEASHED			
WITH THE WINDS UNLEASHED AND FREE,	34	GOODLY FERE	46
UNLESS			
UNLESS PERHAPS I SHOULD HAVE RECOURSE TO	243	MOYEN SENSUEL	155
UNLIKELY			
BE AN UNLIKELY TREASURE HOARD.	66	THE SEAFARER	101
UNLUCKILY			
GO TO THE UNLUCKILY MATED,	88	COMMISSION	13
UNMADE			
WAS THERE SUCH FLESH MADE EVER AND UNMADE!	31	PIERE VIDAL	45

UNMARRIED -- UNTIL

	PAGE	TITLE	LINE
UNMARRIED			
COME, LET US PITY THE MARRIED AND THE UNMARRIED.	83	THE GARRET	5
UNMENTIONABLE			
WHY DOES THE HORSE-FACED LADY OF JUST THE UNMENTIONABLE AGE	114	SIMULACRA	1
UNMINDFUL			
O THOU UNMINDFUL! HOW SHOULD I FORGET!	60	TOMB AKR CAAR	15
UNMOVING			
TO-EM-MEI'S "THE UNMOVING CLOUD"	142	UNMOVING CLOUD	T
UNNAMEABLE			
O MY UNNAMEABLE CHILDREN.	96	DUM CAPITOLIUM	6
UNO			
ED ERAN DUE IN UNO, ED UNO IN DUE;	157	NEAR PERIGORD	EPI
ED ERAN DUE IN UNO, ED UNO IN DUE;	157	NEAR PERIGORD	EPI
UNOPENED			
AND THE NEAT PILES OF UNOPENED, UNOPENING BOOKS,	180	MOEURS CON: 5	25
UNOPENING			
AND THE NEAT PILES OF UNOPENED, UNOPENING BOOKS,	180	MOEURS CON: 5	25
UNPAID			
UNPAID, UNCELEBRATED,	195	HUGH SELWIN:10	3
UNPERTURBED			
NOW YOU MAY BEAR FATE'S STROKE UNPERTURBED,	222	SEXTUS PROP: 8	37
UNREACHABLE			
GONE--AH, GONE--UNTOUCHED, UNREACHABLE!	157	NEAR PERIGORD	188
UNREIN			
'TILL THE TRAIST WATCHER HIS SONG UNREIN,	177	LANGUE D'OC: 4	18
UNSAFE			
THE UNSAFE SAFE, WHEREIN ALL ROTS, AND NO MAN CAN SAY HOW	261	ALF'S FIFTH	19
UNSATISFIED			
GO, MY SONGS, TO THE LONELY AND THE UNSATISFIED,	88	COMMISSION	1
UNSEEN			
KNOWING THE TRUTH OF THINGS UNSEEN BEFORE;	3	THE TREE	2
UNSPOTTED			
"PHOEBUS OUR WITNESS, YOUR HANDS ARE UNSPOTTED."	226	SEXTUS PROP:11	24
UNSTILL			
MIRRORS UNSTILL OF THE ETERNAL CHANGE?	39	BLANDULA	12
UNSTILL, NEVER CEASING;	107	COMING OF WAR	9
UNSTILL, EVER MOVING	107	COMING OF WAR	18
YET IN THAT PLACE IT EVER IS UNSTILL,	249	DONNA MI PREGA	28
UNSTOPPED			
CAUGHT IN THE UNSTOPPED EAR;	187	E. P. ODE	10
UNSUITABLE			
BECAUSE HELEN'S CONDUCT IS "UNSUITABLE."	218	SEXTUS PROP: 5	63
UNSULLIED			
FOR A FEW PAGES BROUGHT DOWN FROM THE FORKED HILL UNSULLIED?	207	SEXTUS PROP: 1	20
AS HELD BEFORE HIM IN THAT UNSULLIED MIRROR	241	MOYEN SENSUEL	93
UNTAKEN			
POICTIERS AND BRIVE, UNTAKEN ROCHECOUART,	152	NEAR PERIGORD	29
UNTELLABLE			
OF SENSE UNTELLABLE, BEAUTY	41	HER MONUMENT	28
UNTEMPTABLE			
THEIR VIRGIN STUPIDITY IS UNTEMPTABLE.	81	TENZONE	7
UNTIDY			
I HAVE SEEN THEM WITH UNTIDY FAMILIES,	85	SALUTATION	4
UNTIE			
HARDER TO UNTIE.	261	ALF'S SIXTH	9
UNTIL			
'TWAS NOT UNTIL THE GODS HAD BEEN	3	THE TREE	6
UNTIL IS ITS LOVELINESS BECOME UNTO ME	26	NIGHT LITANY	7
SILENT AS FATE IS, AND AS STRONG UNTIL	31	PIERE VIDAL	35
UNTIL THIS COURSE TURNETH ASIDE.	69	THE NEEDLE	15
LONELY FROM THE BEGINNING OF TIME UNTIL NOW!	133	FRONTIER GUARD	2
UNTIL THE LAST SLUT'S HANGED AND THE LAST PIG DISEMBOWELED,	161	CABARET DANCER	2
UNTIL HE FOUND HIS SIEVE . . .	199	MAUBERLEY! 2	18
UNTIL A NARSTY GERMAN TOLD THEM SO.	265	ALF'S NINTH	25
UNTIL THE MIND OF THE OLD NATION GETS A LITTLE STRONGER.	266	ALF'S TENTH	16
HAS NEVER UNTIL NOW	272	THE BABY	2

PAGE 441

UNTO -- UP

	PAGE	TITLE	LINE
UNTO			
UNTO THE HEARTH OF THEIR HEART'S HOME	3	THE TREE	8
PRAISES MEET UNTO THY FASHION?	8	NA AUDIART	10
UNTO LADY "MIELS-DE-BEN,"	8	NA AUDIART	13
AND IN VAIN I CRIED UNTO THEM "I HAVE NO SONG	17	PRAISE YSOLT	36
AS THE FLAME CRIETH UNTO THE SAP.	17	PRAISE YSOLT	41
AS FLAME LEAVETH THE EMBERS SO WENT SHE UNTO NEW FORESTS	17	PRAISE YSOLT	43
THAT CALL EVER UNTO ME,	17	PRAISE YSOLT	53
YEA THE LINES HAST THOU LAID UNTO ME	26	NIGHT LITANY	3
HAST THOU SHOWN UNTO ME	26	NIGHT LITANY	6
UNTIL IS ITS LOVELINESS BECOME UNTO ME	26	NIGHT LITANY	7
THAT THOU GIVEST THIS WONDER UNTO US,	26	NIGHT LITANY	12
COMETH UNTO US,	26	NIGHT LITANY	16
SILENT UNTO US IN THEIR FAR-COURSING,	27	NIGHT LITANY	46
SITH NOTHING IS THAT UNTO WORTH PERTAINETH	37	THE YOUNG KING	20
SITH NO THING IS BUT TURNETH UNTO ANGUISH	37	THE YOUNG KING	27
PREFER MY CLOAK UNTO THE CLOAK OF DUST	67	THE CLOAK	7
AND UNTO ME ALSO PAY DEBT:	224	SEXTUS PROP: 9	27
UNTO HIMSELF THE QUESTION PUT	272	THE BABY	3
UNTOUCHED			
AND ARE UNTOUCHED BY ECHOES OF THE WORLD.	21	IN DURANCE	34
GONE--AH, GONE--UNTOUCHED, UNREACHABLE!	157	NEAR PERIGORD	188
UNTRAMMELLED			
CLEAR SPEAKERS, NAKED IN THE SUN, UNTRAMMELLED.	96	DUM CAPITOLIUM	8
UNUSED			
LIKE SO MANY UNUSED BOAS.	93	LES MILLWIN	4
UNUSUAL			
BEING SMITTEN WITH AN UNUSUAL WISDOM,	96	AESTHETICS	2
UNWEARYING			
UNWEARYING AUTUMNS.	132	AT TEN-SHIN	27
UNWIELDLY			
THEY OBSERVE UNWIELDLY DIMENSIONS	104	THE SEEING EYE	2
UNWORTHY			
WHICH I TAKE, MY NOT UNWORTHY GIFT, TO PERSEPHONE.	219	SEXTUS PROP: 6	21
UNYIELDING			
FROM THESE HE (RADWAY) LEARNT, FROM PROVOSTS AND FROM EDITORS UNYIELDING	240	MOYEN SENSUEL	51
UP			
SUCH AS ARE UP AND WIDE,	14	FAMAM CANO	10
AND YET MY SOUL SINGS "UP!" AND WE ARE ONE.	21	IN DURANCE	41
WHEN LIGHT THEIR VOICES LIFT THEM UP,	45	FROM HEINE: 5	5
RISE UP AND JUDGE US;	52	AU SALON	5
THAT WE PREFER TO PLAY UP TO,	52	AU SALON	19
SEE, THE LIGHT GRASS SPRANG UP TO PILLOW THEE,	60	TOMB AKR CAAR	6
HOURS, WHERE SOMETHING MIGHT HAVE FLOATED UP.	61	PORTRAIT FEMME	12
TROPHIES FISHED UP; SOME CURIOUS SUGGESTION;	61	PORTRAIT FEMME	16
ITS MIND WAS MADE UP IN "THE SEVENTIES,"	63	PHASELLUS ILLE	3
SHAKE UP THE STAGNANT POOL OF ITS CONVICTIONS;	63	PHASELLUS ILLE	8
ALGAE REACH UP AND OUT, BENEATH	69	SUB MARE	6
THAT BEARS US UP, SHALL TURN AGAINST THE POLE.	69	THE NEEDLE	7
OH, I HAVE PICKED UP MAGIC IN HER NEARNESS	71	A VIRGINAL	7
AND CRIED UP FROM THEIR COBBLES:	96	AESTHETICS	4
WITH THEIR TAILS UP,	115	SOCIAL ORDER	15
SHE DOES NOT GET UP THE STAIRS SO EAGERLY;	116	THE TEA SHOP	4
PILED UP NEATLY UPON THE SHELVES	117	THE LAKE ISLE	4
SHE RUSHED OUT INTO THE SUNLIGHT AND SWARMED UP A COCOANUT PALM TREE,	118	CONTEMPORARIES	3
UP ON THE WET ROAD NEAR CLERMONT.	119	THE GYPSY	6
TOSSING IT UP UNDER THE CLOUDS.	136	EXILE'S LETTER	62
I WENT UP TO THE COURT FOR EXAMINATION,	136	EXILE'S LETTER	65
AND THEN THE CROWD BROKE UP, YOU WENT NORTH TO SAN PALACE,	136	EXILE'S LETTER	71
HE THROWS HIS HEART UP THROUGH THE SKY,	139	SENNIN POEM	8
AND BRINGS UP A FINE FOUNTAIN.	139	SENNIN POEM	10
AND SHE PILES HER HAIR UP ON THE LEFT SIDE OF HER HEAD-PIECE.	140	MULBERRY ROAD	11
THE JEWELLED CHAIR IS HELD UP AT THE CROSSWAY,	141	IDEA OF CHOAN	5
I AM UP TO FOLLOW THEE, PALLAS.	147	BEFORE SLEEP	12
UP AND OUT OF THEIR CARESSES.	147	BEFORE SLEEP	13
YOU WERE GONE UP AS A ROCKET,	147	BEFORE SLEEP	14

PAGE 442

UP -- UPON

	PAGE	TITLE	LINE
UP (CONTINUED)			
I AM UP TO FOLLOW THEE, PALLAS.	147	BEFORE SLEEP	19
YOU'D HAVE MEN'S HEARTS UP FROM THE DUST	151	NEAR PERIGORD	1
BUT ONE HUGE BACK HALF-COVERED UP WITH PINE,	152	NEAR PERIGORD	33
UP AND ABOUT AND IN AND OUT THE LAND,	153	NEAR PERIGORD	84
THERE SHUT UP IN HIS CASTLE, TAIRIRAN'S,	157	NEAR PERIGORD	186
("SPEAK UP! YOU HAVE DANCED SO STIFFLY?	159	PSYCHOLOG HOUR	31
FLARE UP WITH SCARLET ORANGE ON STIFF STALKS	162	CABARET DANCER	20
PULLS UP A ROLL OF FAT FOR THE PIANIST,	163	CABARET DANCER	54
GRINS UP AN AMIABLE GRIN,	163	CABARET DANCER	58
THE WATER-JET OF GOLD LIGHT BEARS US UP THROUGH THE CEILINGS;	169	PHANOPOEIA	4
AND YOU ARE CAUGHT UP TO THE SKIES,	169	PHANOPOEIA	9
"UP! THOU RASCAL, RISE,	171	LANGUE D'OC	EPI
"COME NOW! OLD SWENKIN! RISE UP FROM THY BED,	172	LANGUE D'OC: 1	14
FOETID BUCHANAN LIFTED UP HIS VOICE	192	YEUX GLAUQUES	5
"AND GIVE UP VERSE, MY BOY,	194	MR. NIXON	19
AND HELD UP THE THREICIAN RIVER;	208	SEXTUS PROP: 1	43
AND CITHARAON SHOOK UP THE ROCKS BY THEBES	208	SEXTUS PROP: 1	44
THOUGH MY HOUSE IS NOT PROPPED UP BY TAENARIAN COLUMNS FROM LACONIA (ASSOCIATED WITH NEPTUNE AND CERBERUS),	208	SEXTUS PROP: 1	51
"BRIGHT TIPS REACH UP FROM TWIN TOWERS,	212	SEXTUS PROP: 3	4
FOR I AM SWELLED UP WITH INANE PLEASURABILITIES	214	SEXTUS PROP: 4	5
"MAY THE GOUT CRAMP UP HER FEET!	215	SEXTUS PROP: 4	37
UP, UP MY SOUL, FROM YOUR LOWLY CANTILATION,	216	SEXTUS PROP: 5	12
UP, UP MY SOUL, FROM YOUR LOWLY CANTILATION,	216	SEXTUS PROP: 5	12
PAY UP YOUR VOW OF NIGHT WATCHES	224	SEXTUS PROP: 9	25
TO LIFT YOU UP THROUGH SPLIT AIR,	226	SEXTUS PROP:11	9
TILL UP AGAIN, RIGHT UP, WE REACH THE PRESIDENT,	239	MOYEN SENSUEL	16
TILL UP AGAIN, RIGHT UP, WE REACH THE PRESIDENT,	239	MOYEN SENSUEL	16
RADWAY GREW UP, THESE FORCES SHAPED HIS SOUL;	239	MOYEN SENSUEL	44
UP STAIRS, THE THIRD FLOOR UP, AND HAVE SUCH QUANDARIES	244	MOYEN SENSUEL	158
UP STAIRS, THE THIRD FLOOR UP, AND HAVE SUCH QUANDARIES	244	MOYEN SENSUEL	158
"AND RATE 'EM UP AT JUST SO MUCH PER HEAD,	244	MOYEN SENSUEL	181
STILL HE WAS NOT GIVEN UP TO BRUTE ENJOYMENT,	245	MOYEN SENSUEL	193
YOUR EYES PUT ME UP TO IT.	247	PIERROTS	10
EH, MAKE IT UP?	248	PIERROTS	25
KEEP UP THE GRAND SYSTEM	259	ALF'S FOURTH	8
IS ONE DAY BLOWN UP LARGE, THE NEXT, SUCKED IN?	261	ALF'S FIFTH	21
I PUMP THE MARKET UP AND DOWN	266	ALF'S ELEVENTH	17
SHE'D COME A SWEATIN' UP WITH THE COALS	271	OLE KATE	9
AND TOTIN' UP SCUTTLES OF COAL,	271	OLE KATE	18
UPLEAPING			
SLEEP THOU NO MORE. I SEE THE STAR UPLEAPING	172	LANGUE D'OC: 1	7
UPLIFT			
HEADLAM FOR UPLIFT; IMAGE IMPARTIALLY IMBUED	193	SIENA MI FE	14
UPON			
BEING UPON THE ROAD ONCE MORE,	6	CINO	11
THY SATINS MAKE UPON THE STAIR,	8	NA AUDIART	22
UPON THY HANDS, AND THY OLD SOUL	9	NA AUDIART	41
ASK YE WHAT GHOSTS I DREAM UPON?	10	FOR THIS YULE	9
WHERE ARE THE LIPS MINE LAY UPON	10	FOR THIS YULE	19
AS A VAGUE CRYING UPON THE NIGHT	16	PRAISE YSOLT	6
THEIR ECHOES PLAY UPON EACH OTHER IN THE TWILIGHT	16	PRAISE YSOLT	9
YET THERE IS A TREMBLING UPON ME IN THE TWILIGHT,	16	PRAISE YSOLT	14
A WOMAN AS FIRE UPON THE PINE WOODS	17	PRAISE YSOLT	39
AS THE SPRING UPON THE BOUGH	17	PRAISE YSOLT	49
THE MOON IS UPON MY FOREHEAD,	18	DE AEGYPTO	19
"AYE! I AM A POET AND UPON MY TOMB	24	THUS NINEVEH	1
YET AM I POET, AND UPON MY TOMB	24	THUS NINEVEH	16
UPON THE SHADOW OF THE WATERS	26	NIGHT LITANY	27
FLOATING UPON THE WATERS,	27	NIGHT LITANY	40
WHEN I BUT THINK UPON THE GREAT DEAD DAYS	30	PIERE VIDAL	1
AND TURN MY MIND UPON THAT SPLENDID MADNESS,	30	PIERE VIDAL	2
I HAVE SEEN HIM UPON THE TREE.	34	GOODLY FERE	36
UPON THESE LIDS THAT LIE OVER US	35	THE EYES	3
UPON WHITE PARCHMENT,	35	THE EYES	14
THAT EVER CAME UPON THIS GRIEVING WORLD	36	THE YOUNG KING	3

PAGE 443

UPON

	PAGE	TITLE	LINE
UPON (CONTINUED)			
MINE EYES UPON NEW COLOURS.	39	FOR PSYCHE	9
UPON FOND NATURE'S MORBID GRACE.	44	MR. HOUSMAN	14
SWEEP BACK UPON ME AND ENGULF MY MIND!	51	HORAE BEATAE	2
FROM AMBER LATTICES UPON THE COBALT NIGHT,	53	AU JARDIN	3
I AM SET WIDE UPON THE WORLD'S WAYS	53	AU JARDIN	11
BUT YOU NEVER STRING TWO DAYS UPON ONE WIRE	53	AU JARDIN	13
I HAVE READ OUT THE GOLD UPON THE WALL,	60	TOMB AKR CAAR	9
AND WEARIED OUT MY THOUGHT UPON THE SIGNS.	60	TOMB AKR CAAR	10
AND THREE SOULS CAME UPON THEE--	60	TOMB AKR CAAR	18
AND I FLOWED IN UPON THEE, BEAT THEM OFF;	60	TOMB AKR CAAR	20
AND NO LIGHT BEATS UPON ME, AND YOU SAY	60	TOMB AKR CAAR	27
AND ALL THEIR CRAFTY WORK UPON THE DOOR,	60	TOMB AKR CAAR	30
OR FINDS ITS HOUR UPON THE LOOM OF DAYS:	61	PORTRAIT FEMME	21
DELICATELY UPON THE REED, ATTEND ME!	62	N. Y.	3
NEITHER COULD I PLAY UPON ANY REED IF I HAD ONE.	62	N. Y.	7
YET LONGING COMES UPON HIM TO FARE FORTH ON THE WATER.	65	THE SEAFARER	48
THESE COMFORTS HEAPED UPON ME, SMOTHER ME!	70	THE PLUNGE	2
FOR THE GREAT CHARMS THAT ARE UPON HER	72	DIEU! QU'IL	3
UPON SUCH HOLLOW SEASON?"	72	PAN IS DEAD	13
I MATE WITH MY FREE KIND UPON THE CRAGS;	81	TENZONE	10
GO LIKE A BLIGHT UPON THE DULNESS OF THE WORLD;	88	COMMISSION	18
BRING CONFIDENCE UPON THE ALGAE AND THE TENTACLES OF THE SOUL.	88	COMMISSION	21
TO SET UPON THEM HIS CHANGE	90	SURGIT FAMA	12
AS A RILLET AMONG THE SEDGE ARE THY HANDS UPON ME;	91	DANCE FIGURE	19
LAY STRIPPED UPON THE GROUND:	92	APRIL	4
WITH THEIR LARGE AND ANAEMIC EYES THEY LOOKED OUT UPON THIS CONFIGURATION.	93	LES MILLWIN	12
WITH DRAGONS WORKED UPON IT,	94	INSTRUCTIONS	18
REST NIGHTLY UPON THE SOUL OF OUR DELICATE FRIEND FLORIALIS,	100	TEMPERAMENTS	2
THE YOUNG MEN LOOK UPON THEIR SENIORS,	104	THE SEEING EYE	5
WHEN WE SAT UPON THE GRANITE BRINK IN HELICON	104	ANCORA	10
HAD WE EVER SUCH AN EPITHET CAST UPON US!!	104	ANCORA	16
DIONE, YOUR NIGHTS ARE UPON US.	110	COITUS	7
THE DEW IS UPON THE LEAF.	110	COITUS	8
PILED UP NEATLY UPON THE SHELVES	117	THE LAKE ISLE	4
UPON THE MUTABILITY OF WOMAN,	118	THREE POETS	6
THEY RIDE UPON DRAGON-LIKE HORSES,	132	AT TEN-SHIN	15
UPON HORSES WITH HEAD-TRAPPINGS OF YELLOW METAL,	132	AT TEN-SHIN	16
AND NO CHILDREN OF WARFARE UPON THEM,	133	FRONTIER GUARD	20
LET US SPIT UPON THOSE WHO PAT THE BIG-BELLIES FOR PROFIT,	145	SALUTATION 3RD	15
YOU SAY THAT I TAKE A GOOD DEAL UPON MYSELF;	146	MONUMENTUM AER	1
NICHARCUS UPON PHIDON HIS DOCTOR	165	QUINTUS SEPTIM	ST
YAWNING A LITTLE SHE CAME WITH THE SLEEP STILL UPON HER.	166	FISH & SHADOW	8
I SEE THE SIGNS UPON THE WELKIN SPREAD,	172	LANGUE D'OC: 1	15
UPON LEARNING THAT THE MOTHER WROTE VERSES,	179	MOEURS CON: 3	1
SHALL I PLACE A TIN WREATH UPON!	189	HUGH SELWYN: 3	28
EVEN MY FAULTS THAT HEAVY UPON ME LIE,	197	ENVOI (1919)	6
WITH SONG UPON HER LIPS	197	ENVOI (1919)	18
BURST IN UPON THE PORCELAIN REVERY:	201	AGE DEMANDED	18
WITH NO STONE UPON MY CONTEMPTIBLE SEPULCHRE;	208	SEXTUS PROP: 1	37
THOUGH IT IS NOT STRETCHED UPON GILDED BEAMS;	208	SEXTUS PROP: 1	52
NOR HOUSES MODELLED UPON THAT OF JOVE IN EAST ELIS,	209	SEXTUS PROP: 1	67
AND PHOEBUS LOOKING UPON ME FROM THE CASTALIAN TREE,	210	SEXTUS PROP: 2	16
UPON THE ONE RAFT, VICTOR AND CONQUERED TOGETHER,	218	SEXTUS PROP: 6	3
HER LIPS UPON ᾽ᴀEM; AND IT WAS HER MOUTH SAYING:	220	SEXTUS PROP: 7	8
FOR LONG NIGHT COMES UPON YOU	220	SEXTUS PROP: 7	18
LET THE GODS LAY CHAINS UPON US	220	SEXTUS PROP: 7	20
IF SHE CONFER SUCH NIGHTS UPON ME,	221	SEXTUS PROP: 7	37
PERSEPHONE AND DIS, DIS, HAVE MERCY UPON HER,	223	SEXTUS PROP: 9	13
AND THE REST LAID THEIR CHAINS UPON ME,	224	SEXTUS PROP:10	9
AND ANOTHER BROKE IN UPON THIS:	224	SEXTUS PROP:10	16
THERE WERE UPON THE BED NO SIGNS OF A VOLUPTUOUS ENCOUNTER,	225	SEXTUS PROP:10	36
THOUGH YOU HEAVE INTO THE AIR UPON THE GILDED PEGASEAN BACK,	226	SEXTUS PROP:11	7

UPON -- UTTERANCE

	PAGE	TITLE	LINE
UPON (CONTINUED)			
AMOR STANDS UPON YOU, LOVE DRIVES UPON LOVERS, ...	226	SEXTUS PROP:11	11
AMOR STANDS UPON YOU, LOVE DRIVES UPON LOVERS, ...	226	SEXTUS PROP:11	11
UPON THE ACTIAN MARSHES VIRGIL IS PHOEBUS' CHIEF OF POLICE, ...	228	SEXTUS PROP:12	31
THYRSIS AND DAPHNIS UPON WHITTLED REEDS, ...	229	SEXTUS PROP:12	42
IT IS ADORNED WITH YOUNG GODS RIDING UPON DOLPHINS	237	ABU SALAMMAMM	20
AND SEATED UPON IT IS THE LATE QUEEN, VICTORIA, ...	237	ABU SALAMMAMM	23
FOR MINDS SO WHOLLY FOUNDED UPON QUOTATIONS	239	MOYEN SENSUEL	29
UPON A TALE, TO COMBAT OTHER TRACTS, ...	241	MOYEN SENSUEL	72
UPON MANHATTAN'S GORGEOUS PANOPLY, ...	245	MOYEN SENSUEL	188
THE FLOOD OF LIMBS UPON EIGHTH AVENUE	245	MOYEN SENSUEL	189
UPON THE NATIONAL BRAINS AND SET 'EM ACHIN'.	245	MOYEN SENSUEL	216
AND MEDITATE UPON THE LORD'S CONQUESTS.	246	MOYEN SENSUEL	228
UPON A DUSK THAT IS COME FROM MARS AND STAYS.	248	DONNA MI PREGA	21
UPPER			
WERE SEEN LYING ALONG THE UPPER SEATS	93	LES MILLWIN	3
THAT IS, THE UPPER ARM, ...	180	MOEURS CON: 5	5
UP-PUSHED-BOSOM			
SPREAD ON BOTH HANDS AND ON THE UP-PUSHED-BOSOM--	161	CABARET DANCER	15
UPSET			
AND WOULD NOT THINK A THING THAT COULD UPSET HER.	242	MOYEN SENSUEL	110
UPSTANDING			
--A BROWN UPSTANDING FELLOW	119	THE GYPSY	4
URBANITY			
FOR AS BEN FRANKLIN SAID, WITH SUCH URBANITY:	246	MOYEN SENSUEL	235
URGE			
THIS URGE TO CONVEY THE RELATION	200	MAUBERLEY: 2	21
DESTROYING, CERTAINLY, THE ARTIST'S URGE, ...	202	AGE DEMANDED	43
URN			
TO MIND ME OF SOME URN OF FULL DELIGHT, ...	41	HER MONUMENT	13
BEHOLD THIS BOOK, THE URN OF ASHES, ...	45	FROM HEINE: 3	7
US (104)			
USE			
WELL, THERE'S NO USE YOUR LOVING ME	53	AU JARDIN	
WHAT IS THE USE OF SETTING IT TO RIME?	59	SILET	6
THAT NEVER FITS A CORNER OR SHOWS USE, ...	61	PORTRAIT FEMME	20
SAYING WITHIN HIS HEART, "I AM NO USE TO MYSELF, ..	100	ARIDES	6
WHAT IS THE USE OF TALKING, AND THERE IS NO END OF TALKING, ...	136	EXILE'S LETTER	75
BIG TALK AND LITTLE USE.	173	LANGUE D'OC: 2	26
AUGHT OF THE SLIGHTEST USE.	265	ALF'S TENTH	4
USED			
WHO USED TO WALK ABOUT AMONGST US	102	LADIES	10
"SHELLEY USED TO LIVE IN THIS HOUSE."	182	MOEURS CON: 8	13
AND HE SAID THEY USED TO CHEER VERDI, ...	182	MOEURS CON: 7	17
THE PARTHIANS SHALL GET USED TO OUR STATUARY	219	SEXTUS PROP: 6	9
THAT USED TO BE USED ON THE YOUNG, ...	263	ALF'S EIGHTH	23
THAT USED TO BE USED ON THE YOUNG, ...	263	ALF'S EIGHTH	23
HE USED TO LUNCH WITH BALFOUR IN THOSE DAYS	265	ALF'S NINTH	22
USEFUL			
THAT MIGHT PROVE USEFUL AND YET NEVER PROVES, ...	61	PORTRAIT FEMME	19
USELESS			
AS YOU ARE WITH USELESS RICHES?	102	TO DIVES	4
OF USELESS RICHES FOR THE OCCUPANT, ...	236	MIDDLE-AGED	12
US-TOWARD			
THEY DREAM US-TOWARD AND	6	CINO	15
USUAL			
NO. YOU PREFERRED IT TO THE USUAL THING:	61	PORTRAIT FEMME	8
USURY			
USURY AGE-OLD AND AGE-THICK	190	HUGH SELWYN: 4	18
THAT KEEP ON GETTIN' USURY	269	SAFE AND SOUND	15
UTMOST			
AND CALLS THE UTMOST SINGING FROM THE BOUGHS	21	IN DURANCE	46
UTTER			
AGAINST UTTER CONSTERNATION, ...	202	AGE DEMANDED	32
UTTERANCE			
INCAPABLE OF THE LEAST UTTERANCE OR COMPOSITION, ..	202	AGE DEMANDED	46

UTTERLY -- VALLEYS

	PAGE	TITLE	LINE
UTTERLY			
AND SO WERE MY MIND HOLLOW, DID SHE NOT FILL UTTERLY MY THOUGHT.	23	MARVOIL	39
CEASED UTTERLY. WELL, THEN I WAITED, DREW,	31	PIERE VIDAL	40
IF I HAVE MERGED MY SOUL, OR UTTERLY	51	THE FLAME	32
UTTERS			
UTTERS A PROFANE	204	MEDALLION	3
UXORIOUS			
ONE DULL MAN, DULLING AND UXORIOUS,	61	PORTRAIT FEMME	9
VACANT			
WITH A VACANT GAZE.	192	YEUX GLAUQUES	14
"HE WHO IS NOW VACANT DUST	219	SEXTUS PROP: 6	26
VACUOS			
"VACUOS EXERCET AERA MORSUS."	198	MAUBERLEY 1920	EPI
VAE			
THE SHUDDER OF VAE SOLI GURGLES BENEATH MY RIBS.	247	PIERROTS	3
VAGABONDS			
(OH THEY ARE ALL ONE THESE VAGABONDS),	6	CINO	29
VAGUE			
AS A VAGUE CRYING UPON THE NIGHT	16	PRAISE YSOLT	6
HER AMBITION IS VAGUE AND INDEFINITE,	179	MOEURS CON: 2	10
'TIS BUT A VAGUE, INVARIOUS DELIGHT	236	MIDDLE-AGED	1
VAGUELY			
VAGUELY THUS WORD THEY:	6	CINO	24
VAGULA			
"BLANDULA, TENULLA, VAGULA"	39	BLANDULA	T
'VAILS			
AND EACH TO-DAY 'VAILS LESS THAN YESTERE'EN,	37	THE YOUNG KING	28
VAIN			
IN VAIN HAVE I STRIVEN,	16	PRAISE YSOLT	1
IN VAIN HAVE I SAID TO HIM	16	PRAISE YSOLT	3
IN VAIN HAVE I STRIVEN	16	PRAISE YSOLT	23
IN VAIN HAVE I PLED WITH HIM:	16	PRAISE YSOLT	25
AND IN VAIN I CRIED UNTO THEM "I HAVE NO SONG	17	PRAISE YSOLT	36
IN VAIN HAVE I STRIVEN WITH MY SOUL	17	PRAISE YSOLT	55
MOTIONLESS, PLACED IN VAIN,	41	HER MONUMENT	5
AND IN VAIN THEY COMMANDED HIM TO STA FERMO!	97	AESTHETICS	15
THEY BEND IN VAIN.	112	IONE, DEAD	5
FOR THEM THE YELLOW DOGS HOWL PORTENTS IN VAIN,	132	AT TEN-SHIN	28
IN VAIN, YOU CALL BACK THE SHADE,	219	SEXTUS PROP: 6	35
IN VAIN, CYNTHIA. VAIN CALL TO UNANSWERING SHADOW,	219	SEXTUS PROP: 6	36
IN VAIN, CYNTHIA. VAIN CALL TO UNANSWERING SHADOW,	219	SEXTUS PROP: 6	36
VAIR			
BUT AH! WHEN I SEE THE STANDARDS GOLD, VAIR, PURPLE, OPPOSING	28	ALTAFORTE	4
VALE			
DOWN THROUGH THE VALE OF GLOOM	257	BREAD BRIGADE	3
VALENTINE'S			
I AWAIT THE LADY VALENTINE'S COMMANDS,	196	HUGH SELWIN:12	4
BUT NEVER OF THE LADY VALENTINE'S VOCATION:	196	HUGH SELWIN:12	12
VALETS			
(AND VALETS TO SHAVE 'EM)	258	ALF'S SECOND	7
VALIANT			
THAT WAS MOST VALIANT 'MID ALL WORTHIEST MEN!	37	THE YOUNG KING	30
VALIANTLY			
MADE YOU YOUR PASS MOST VALIANTLY	19	FOR E. MCC	8
VALLERIE			
FOR JEHAN AND RAOUL DE VALLERIE	12	OF THE GIBBET	27
VALLEY			
AND MIST CLOTTED ABOUT THE TREES IN THE VALLEY,	119	THE GYPSY	8
INTO A VALLEY OF THE THOUSAND BRIGHT FLOWERS,	134	EXILE'S LETTER	19
THAT WAS THE FIRST VALLEY;	134	EXILE'S LETTER	20
ITS LOWEST STONES JUST MEET THE VALLEY TIPS	152	NEAR PERIGORD	55
A FIELD IN A VALLEY . . .	166	FISH & SHADOW	15
VALLEYS			
AND THREE VALLEYS, FULL OF WINDING ROADS,	121	PROVINC DESERT	4
"MEN HAVE GONE BY SUCH AND SUCH VALLEYS	122	PROVINC DESERT	57
AND INTO TEN THOUSAND VALLEYS FULL OF VOICES AND PINE-WINDS.	134	EXILE'S LETTER	21
AIMLESSLY WATCHING A HAWK ABOVE THE VALLEYS,	154	NEAR PERIGORD	108
ᴺᴰ OUR TWO HORSES HAD TRACED OUT THE VALLEYS;	157	NEAR PERIGORD	173

VALLIS -- VENGO

	PAGE	TITLE	LINE
VALLIS			
CONCAVA VALLIS	170	PHANOPOEIA	ST
VALOUR			
THAT BADE MY HEART HIS VALOUR DON?	10	FOR THIS YULE	21
VALUE			
DOUBTFUL, SOMEWHAT, OF THE VALUE	196	HUGH SELWIN:12	9
YOU WILL OBSERVE THAT PURE FORM HAS ITS VALUE.	225	SEXTUS PROP:10	33
VAN			
HENRY VAN DYKE, WHO THINKS TO CHARM THE MUSE YOU PACK HER IN	239	MOYEN SENSUEL	21
VANISHING			
ALL GOOD THINGS GO VANISHING.	46	FROM HEINE: 6	20
VANNA			
VANNA, MANDETTA, VIERA, ALODETTA, PICARDA, MANUELA	76	THE ALCHEMIST	38
VANTAGE			
HERE HAVE WE HAD OUR VANTAGE, THE GOOD HOUR.	69	THE NEEDLE	4
VARIED			
IN HOW MANY VARIED EMBRACES, OUR CHANGING ARMS,	220	SEXTUS PROP: 7	10
VARIOUS			
THROUGH ALL THY VARIOUS MOOD I KNOW THEE MINE;	50	THE FLAME	31
RADWAY HAD READ THE VARIOUS EVENING PAPERS	241	MOYEN SENSUEL	91
VARRO			
VARRO SANG JASON'S EXPEDITION,	230	SEXTUS PROP:12	66
VARRO, OF HIS GREAT PASSION LEUCADIA,	230	SEXTUS PROP:12	67
VASES			
AND YOUR WHITE VASES FROM JAPAN,	167	OF AROUET	12
VAST			
VAST WATERS FLOWED FROM HER EYES?	214	SEXTUS PROP: 4	15
VAULTED			
IN THE VAULTED HALL,	154	NEAR PERIGORD	106
VAULTS			
FROM THEIR VAULTS AND COMBINATION	269	SAFE AND SOUND	21
VECCHII			
I VECCHII	181	MOEURS CON: 7	SUB
VEGA			
LOPE DE VEGA.	82	THE CONDOLENCE	EPI
VEGETABLE			
GO AGAINST THIS VEGETABLE BONDAGE OF THE BLOOD.	89	COMMISSION	34
VEHEMENCE			
FOR HE WAS LACKING IN VEHEMENCE;	178	MOEURS CON: 1	10
VEIL			
SHE MADE THE NAME FOR HERSELF: "GAUZE VEIL,"	140	MULBERRY ROAD	5
WHILE A BLACK VEIL WAS OVER HER STARS,	222	SEXTUS PROP: 8	26
OR SHE WILL SIT BEFORE YOUR FEET IN A VEIL,	223	SEXTUS PROP: 9	11
VEILED			
SHE WAS VEILED IN THE MIDST OF THAT PLACE,	214	SEXTUS PROP: 4	24
ONE RAFT ON THE VEILED FLOOD OF ACHERON,	219	SEXTUS PROP: 6	11
ON THE VEILED LAKE TOWARD AVERNUS	223	SEXTUS PROP: 9	6
VEILS			
MEET THROUGH OUR VEILS AND WHISPER, AND OF LOVE.	50	THE FLAME	13
VEIN			
THAT WE, WITH MASEFIELD'S VEIN, IN THE NEXT SENTENCE	242	MOYEN SENSUEL	129
VEINS			
A-TREMBLE IN MEN'S VEINS; O LIP CURVED HIGH	41	HER MONUMENT	12
SHE PASSED AND LEFT NO QUIVER IN THE VEINS, WHO NOW	92	GENTILDONNA	1
VENALITY			
BUT RADWAY WAS A PATRIOT WHOSE VENALITY	245	MOYEN SENSUEL	211
VENDERE			
PER VENDERE CANNONI	273	M. POM-POM	2
PER VENDERE CANNONI	273	M. POM-POM	5
PER VENDERE CANNONI	273	M. POM-POM	7
VENDOR			
YOU ARE THE FRIEND OF FORMIANUS, THE VENDOR OF COSMETICS,	113	FORMIANUS LADY	7
VENDRE			
POUR VENDRE DES CANONS	273	M. POM-POM	8
POUR VENDRE DES CANONS	273	M. POM-POM	9
VENERES			
LUGETE, VENERES! LUGETE, CUPIDINESQUE!	103	LADIES	14
VENGO			
DE MIS SOLEDADES VENGO,	82	THE CONDOLENCE	EPI

VENICE -- VERY

	PAGE	TITLE	LINE
VENICE			
AND THE BEAUTY OF THIS THY VENICE	26	NIGHT LITANY	5
IN THIS THY VENICE.	26	NIGHT LITANY	28
SHADOW OF THIS THY VENICE	27	NIGHT LITANY	39
NOW IN VENICE, 'STORANTE AL GIARDINO, I WENT EARLY,	163	CABARET DANCER	79
VENOM			
"YOUR GLORY IS NOT OUTBLOTTED BY VENOM,"	226	SEXTUS PROP:11	23
VENTADOUR			
WE CAME TO VENTADOUR	154	NEAR PERIGORD	117
VENTRICLES			
AND MY VENTRICLES DO NOT PALPITATE TO CAESARIAL ORE ROTUNDOS,	218	SEXTUS PROP: 5	53
VENUS			
O GOD, O VENUS, O MERCURY, PATRON OF THIEVES,	117	THE LAKE ISLE	1
O GOD, O VENUS, O MERCURY, PATRON OF THIEVES,	117	THE LAKE ISLE	12
THE PRIMITIVE AGES SANG VENUS,	216	SEXTUS PROP: 5	7
"TURN NOT VENUS INTO A BLINDED MOTION,	220	SEXTUS PROP: 7	12
WAS VENUS EXACERBATED BY THE EXISTENCE OF A COMPARABLE EQUAL?	221	SEXTUS PROP: 8	10
VENUST			
WITH HER VENUST AND NOBLEST TO MY MAKE	172	LANGUE D'OC: 1	27
VENUST THE LADY, AND NONE LOVELIER,	177	LANGUE D'OC: 4	26
VERB			
WHAT HIS PLACATION; WHY HE IS IN VERB,	248	DONNA MI PREGA	16
VERBAL			
BY VERBAL MANIFESTATIONS;	200	MAUBERLEY: 2	23
VERDI			
AND HE SAID THEY USED TO CHEER VERDI,	182	MOEURS CON: 7	17
VERGIER			
VERGIER	177	LANGUE D'OC: 4	SUB
VERISIMILITUDES			
WILL THEY BE TOUCHED WITH THE VERISIMILITUDES?	81	TENZONE	6
VERITIES			
I SUPPOSE THERE ARE A FEW DOZEN VERITIES	52	AU SALON	6
VERMES			
VERMES HABENT EIUS VULTUM	101	AMITIES	19
VERMILIONED			
AND THE VERMILIONED GIRLS GETTING DRUNK ABOUT SUNSET,	136	EXILE'S LETTER	55
VERNAL			
A ROSY PATH, A SORT OF VERNAL INGRESS,	243	MOYEN SENSUEL	145
VEROG			
SENATORIAL FAMILIES OF STRASBOURG, MONSIEUR VEROG.	193	SIENA MI FE	4
M. VEROG, OUT OF STEP WITH THE DECADE,	193	SIENA MI FE	17
VERS			
VERS AND CANZONE, TILL THAT DAMN'D SON OF ARAGON,	22	MARVOIL	8
SAVE THIS: "VERS AND CANZONE TO THE COUNTESS OF BEZIERS	22	MARVOIL	28
VERSE			
STRINGING LONG VERSE FOR THE BURLATZ;	22	MARVOIL	20
"AND GIVE UP VERSE, MY BOY,	194	MR. NIXON	19
I WOULD MAKE VERSE IN YOUR FASHION, IF SHE SHOULD COMMAND IT,	229	SEXTUS PROP:12	60
VERSE-BARREL			
"CAT'S I' THE WATER BUTT!" THOUGHT'S IN YOUR VERSE-BARREL,	13	MESMERISM	5
VERSES			
WILL LAUGH YOUR VERSES TO EACH OTHER,	14	FAMAM CANO	11
AND PRAISED MY VERSES.	45	FROM HEINE: 4	4
YOU KNOW THE DEATHLESS VERSES.	162	CABARET DANCER	27
CAN GO ON WRITING YOU VERSES.	168	OF AROUET	36
UPON LEARNING THAT THE MOTHER WROTE VERSES,	179	MOEURS CON: 3	1
AND THAT THE FATHER WROTE VERSES,	179	MOEURS CON: 3	2
VERSICLES			
INTO YOUR VERSICLES.	13	MESMERISM	20
VERTIGO			
"WHERE IS THE VERTIGO OF EMOTION?"	85	SALUTATION 2ND	13
VERUM			
DE MORTUIS VERUM, TRULY THE MASTER BUILDER?	240	MOYEN SENSUEL	58
VERY			
BEING IN ALL THINGS WISE, AND VERY OLD,	4	LA FRAISNE	2
VERY GLAD, FOR MY BRIDE HATH TOWARD ME A GREAT LOVE	5	LA FRAISNE	34

VERY -- VIDAL'S

	PAGE	TITLE	LINE
VERY (CONTINUED)			
THAT WAS VERY LONG AGO.	5	LA FRAISNE	47
"TIME'S BITTER FLOOD"! OH, THAT'S ALL VERY WELL,	59	EXIT' CUIUSDAM	1
I KNOW MY CIRCLE AND KNOW VERY WELL	59	EXIT' CUIUSDAM	6
OF THE FILTHY, STURDY, UNKILLABLE INFANTS OF THE VERY POOR.	83	THE GARDEN	6
YOU ARE VERY IDLE, MY SONGS.	94	INSTRUCTIONS	3
YOU WILL COME TO A VERY BAD END.	94	INSTRUCTIONS	9
THE VERY SMALL CHILDREN IN PATCHED CLOTHING,	96	AESTHETICS	1
ARE VERY CHARMING PEOPLE.	98	THE BELLAIRES	43
THE VERY EXCELLENT TERM RUSTICUS.	99	SALVATIONISTS	4
CRAWL IN THE VERY BLACK GUTTER BENEATH THE GRAPE STAND?	114	SIMULACRA	4
YOU'RE A VERY DEPLETED FASHION,	114	EPILOGUE	6
THE VERY SPUR'S END, BUILT ON SHEEREST CLIFF,	153	NEAR PERIGORD	58
SUDDENLY DISCOVERING IN THE EYES OF THE VERY BEAUTIFUL	161	PAGANI'S NOV 8	1
THE EYES OF THE VERY LEARNED BRITISH MUSEUM ASSISTANT.	161	PAGANI'S NOV 8	3
SHE WAS A VERY OLD LADY,	182	MOEURS CON: 8	14
"YOU ARE A VERY EARLY INSPECTOR OF MISTRESSES.	225	SEXTUS PROP:10	34
AND VERY RESPLENDENT IS THIS FOUNTAIN.	237	ABU SALAMMAMM	19
THE VERY FAIREST FLOWER OF THEIR GYNOCRACY.	239	MOYEN SENSUEL	40
THEY HELD THE VERY MARROW OF THE IDEALS	241	MOYEN SENSUEL	95
THOUGH I KNOW ONE, A VERY BASE DETRACTOR,	246	MOYEN SENSUEL	221
NAY, NOR HIS VERY ESSENCE OR HIS MODE;	248	DONNA MI PREGA	15
ELECTION WILL NOT COME VERY SOON,	265	ALF'S TENTH	13
OF THINGS THAT HAPPENED VERY LONG AGO,	265	ALF'S NINTH	27
WHEN OUR MINDS ARE VERY BLEARY,	267	ALF'S TWELFTH	3
VESTA			
"AND I AM GOING TO THE TEMPLE OF VESTA . . ."	225	SEXTUS PROP:10	41
VESUVIUS			
HEART THAT WAS BIG AS THE BOWELS OF VESUVIUS,	13	MESMERISM	13
VEX			
VEX NOT THOU THE BANKER'S MIND	263	ALF'S EIGHTH	1
VEX IT NOT, WILLIE, HIS MIND,	263'	ALF'S EIGHTH	3
VEXED			
THROUGH PERILS, (SO MANY) AND OF A VEXED LIFE,	222	SEXTUS PROP: 8	17
VEXES			
ALAS, EHEU, ONE QUESTION THAT SORELY VEXES	244	MOYEN SENSUEL	161
VIA			
AND IN THE VIA SCIRO.	212	SEXTUS PROP: 3	16
THOUGH YOU WALK IN THE VIA SACRA, WITH A PEACOCK'S TAIL FOR A FAN.	227	SEXTUS PROP:11	40
VIATOR			
SISTE VIATOR.	181	MOEURS CON: 6	6
VIBRATIONS			
THE LATERAL VIBRATIONS CARESS ME,	147	BEFORE SLEEP	1
VICAR			
SHE HAS ABANDONED THE VICAR	178	MOEURS CON: 1	9
VICE			
TO BE NOT TOO WELL KNOWN IN HAUNTS OF VICE--	245	MOYEN SENSUEL	202
VICED			
VICED IN SUCH TORTURE FOR THE "COUNTERPASS."	151	NEAR PERIGORD	27
VICKERS			
TO SEND ME TO WORK IN VICKERS	268	ANOTHER BIT	15
VICOMTE			
THE VICOMTE OF BEZIERS'S NOT SUCH A BAD LOT.	22	MARVOIL	6
VICTOR			
UPON THE ONE RAFT, VICTOR AND CONQUERED TOGETHER,	218	SEXTUS PROP: 6	3
VICTORIA			
AND SEATED UPON IT IS THE LATE QUEEN, VICTORIA,	237	ABU SALAMMAMM	23
VICTORIOUS			
"OF" THE VICTORIOUS DELAY OF FABIUS, AND THE LEFT-HANDED BATTLE AT CANNAE,	210	SEXTUS PROP: 2	11
VIDAL			
PIERE VIDAL OLD	30	PIERE VIDAL	T
BEHOLD ME VIDAL, THAT WAS FOOL OF FOOLS!	30	PIERE VIDAL	7
BEHOLD HERE VIDAL, THAT WAS HUNTED, PLATED,	31	PIERE VIDAL	47
VIDAL'S			
FROM PIERE VIDAL'S REMEMBRANCE THAT BLUE NIGHT.	30	PIERE VIDAL	19

PAGE 449

VIDE -- VIRGIN

	PAGE	TITLE	LINE
VIDE			
(VIDE THE TARIFF), I WILL HANG SIMPLE FACTS	241	MOYEN SENSUEL	71
CLINGS TO THE SKIRT IN STRICT (VIDE: "VOGUE") PROPRIETY.	241	MOYEN SENSUEL	86
VIENNA			
TO BEAT PRAGUE, BUDAPESTH, VIENNA OR MOSCOW,	245	MOYEN SENSUEL	190
VIERA			
VANNA, MANDETTA, VIERA, ALODETTA, PICARDA, MANUELA	76	THE ALCHEMIST	38
VIERNA			
VIERNA, JOCELYNN, DARING OF SPIRITS,	76	THE ALCHEMIST	41
VIEW			
"I NEVER MENTIONED A MAN BUT WITH THE VIEW	194	MR. NIXON	14
VIEWED			
"TILL I HAVE VIEWED STRAW HATS AND THEIR HABITUAL CLOTHING	244	MOYEN SENSUEL	183
VIGIL			
ONE MORE FOOL'S VIGIL WITH THE HOLLYHOCKS.	31	PIERE VIDAL	25
VIGOUR			
ENVIES ITS VIGOUR . . . AND DEPLORES THE TECHNIQUE,	155	NEAR PERIGORD	142
PUT ON A TIMELY VIGOUR.	216	SEXTUS PROP: 5	13
VILE			
FRAIL AND SO VILE IN ALL,	42	HER MONUMENT	51
ALL VILE, OR ALL GENTLE,	175	LANGUE D'OC: 3	52
VILLAGE			
AND WE WENT ON LIVING IN THE VILLAGE OF CHOKAN:	130	RIVER-MER WIFE	5
THERE IS NO WALL LEFT TO THIS VILLAGE.	133	FRONTIER GUARD	7
SOME MEN WILL LIVE AS PRUDES IN THEIR OWN VILLAGE	245	MOYEN SENSUEL	207
VILLAGES			
A-STRAY, LOST IN THE VILLAGES,	92	THE REST	4
VILLANELLE			
VILLANELLE: THE PSYCHOLOGICAL HOUR	158	PSYCHOLOG HOUR	T
VILLEINY			
OR VILLEINY	249	DONNA MI PREGA	44
VILLONAUD			
VILLONAUD FOR THIS YULE	10	FOR THIS YULE	T
A VILLONAUD: BALLAD OF THE GIBBET	11	OF THE GIBBET	T
VINES			
GREEN VINES HANG THROUGH THE HIGH FOREST,	139	SENNIN POEM	4
VINE-STOCK			
AND EVERY VINE-STOCK IS	87	THE SPRING	6
VINE-STRINGS			
VINE-STRINGS A HUNDRED FEET LONG HANG DOWN FROM CARVED RAILINGS,	129	THE RIVER SONG	27
VINTAGE			
NOR ARE MY CAVERNS STUFFED STIFF WITH A MARCIAN VINTAGE,	209	SEXTUS PROP: 1	56
VINTAGES			
ORGIES OF VINTAGES, AN EARTHERN IMAGE OF SILENUS	211	SEXTUS PROP: 2	29
VIOLENCE			
WHERE BOLD HANDS MAY DO VIOLENCE TO MY PERSON?	212	SEXTUS PROP: 3	8
VIOLENT			
WERE THERE AN ERUDITE OR VIOLENT PASSION,	230	SEXTUS PROP:12	63
VIOLET			
IN BRIEF, VIOLET IS THE GROUND TONE OF MY PHONETICS.	247	PIERROTS	15
VIOLETS			
YOU ARE VIOLETS WITH WIND ABOVE THEM.	62	A GIRL	8
VIOLETTES			
EST GROSSIERE ET LE PARFUM DES VIOLETTES UN	199	MAUBERLEY: 2	EPI
VIOLIN			
SMALL HORN AND VIOLIN.	47	FROM HEINE: 7	28
VIR			
ISTE FUIT VIR INCULTUS,	101	AMITIES	17
VIR QUIDEM, ON DANCERS	161	CABARET DANCER	EPI
VIRGIL			
UPON THE ACTIAN MARSHES VIRGIL IS PHOEBUS' CHIEF OF POLICE,	228	SEXTUS PROP:12	31
VIRGIN			
THEIR VIRGIN STUPIDITY IS UNTEMPTABLE.	81	TENZONE	7
HE BEING AT THAT AGE A VIRGIN,	178	MOEURS CON: 1	5
AND SO FORTH, AUGUSTUS. "VIRGIN ARABIA SHAKES IN HER INMOST DWELLING."	216	SEXTUS PROP: 5	18

VIRGIN -- VOGUE

	PAGE	TITLE	LINE
VIRGIN (CONTINUED)			
ROUGH FROM THE VIRGIN FORESTS INVIOLATE,	264	ALF'S NINTH	10
VIRGINAL			
A VIRGINAL	71	A VIRGINAL	T
VIRGINIA			
AND THE BRIGHT VIRGINIA	117	THE LAKE ISLE	7
VIRGINS			
TO DIAN GODDESS OF VIRGINS.	224	SEXTUS PROP: 9	26
VIRGO			
THE TERM "VIRGO" BEING MADE MALE IN MEDIAEVAL LATINITY;	178	MOEURS CON: 1	6
VIRILE			
A LOT OF ASSES PRAISE YOU BECAUSE YOU ARE "VIRILE,"	82	THE CONDOLENCE	2
VIRTU			
OR WHAT HIS ACTIVE VIRTU IS, OR WHAT HIS FORCE;	248	DONNA MI PREGA	14
IT IS NOT VIRTU, BUT PERFECTION'S SOURCE	249	DONNA MI PREGA	33
VIRTUE			
'GOT ON DESIROUS THOUGHT BY NATURAL VIRTUE,	42	HER MONUMENT	42
VIRTUES			
WHICH, PLAYED ON BY THE VIRTUES OF HER SOUL,	49	OF SPLENDOUR	20
ALSO, HE'D READ OF CHRISTIAN VIRTUES IN	241	MOYEN SENSUEL	97
THE SUNDAY SCHOOL BRINGS VIRTUES INTO PRACTICE.	243	MOYEN SENSUEL	140
VIS			
ET ALORS JE VIS BIEN DES CHOSES	160	DANS OMNIBUS	6
JE VIS DES CANARDS SUR LE BORD D'UN LAC MINUSCULE,	160	DANS OMNIBUS	10
JE VIS LES COLONNES ANCIENNES EN "TOC"	160	DANS OMNIBUS	12
JE VIS LE PARC,	160	DANS OMNIBUS	20
JE VIS LES CYGNES NOIRS,	160	DANS OMNIBUS	24
VISAGE			
LET EACH MAN VISAGE THIS YOUNG ENGLISH KING	37	THE YOUNG KING	29
ENCHASSES DANS UN VISAGE STUPIDE	160	DANS OMNIBUS	3
VISCOUNTESS			
AT CHALAIS OF THE VISCOUNTESS, I WOULD	106	DOMPNA POIS	31
VISCOUNTESS'			
BEL MIRAL'S STATURE, THE VISCOUNTESS' THROAT,	151	NEAR PERIGORD	8
VISIBLE			
TURMOIL GROWN VISIBLE BENEATH OUR PEACE,	32	PARACELSUS	8
TO SHOW HIM VISIBLE TO MEN'S SIGHT.	248	DONNA MI PREGA	18
VISION			
NOR THE SAINT'S VISION.	189	HUGH SELWYN: 3	18
VISIONS			
INFINITE THINGS DESIRED, LOFTY VISIONS	42	HER MONUMENT	41
SUCH ASPECT WAS PRESENTED TO ME, ME RECENTLY EMERGED FROM MY VISIONS,	225	SEXTUS PROP:10	32
VISIT			
HE RIDES THROUGH THE PURPLE SMOKE TO VISIT THE SENNIN,	140	SENNIN POEM	12
SPOILING HIS VISIT, WITH A YEAR BEFORE THE NEXT ONE.	154	NEAR PERIGORD	113
VISITING			
AND A BROWN, PLACID, HATED WOMAN VISITING HER,	154	NEAR PERIGORD	112
VISITOR			
--RARE VISITOR--CAME NOT,--THE SAINTS I GUERDON	30	PIERE VIDAL	23
VITALS			
IT WILL PAY THEM WHEN THE WORMS ARE WRIGGLING IN THEIR VITALS;	145	SALUTATION 3RD	4
BUT TO JAB A KNIFE IN MY VITALS, TO HAVE PASSED ON A SWIG OF POISON,	228	SEXTUS PROP:12	12
VITTORIO			
AND THAT WAS AN ANAGRAM FOR VITTORIO	182	MOEURS CON: 7	20
VIXEN			
TITYRUS MIGHT HAVE SUNG THE SAME VIXEN;	229	SEXTUS PROP:12	46
VIZARD			
AND GETS A QUARREL-BOLT SHOT THROUGH HIS VIZARD,	156	NEAR PERIGORD	158
VOCAT			
"VOCAT AESTUS IN UMBRAM"	186	HUGH SELWYN	EPI
VOCATION			
BUT NEVER OF THE LADY VALENTINE'S VOCATION:	196	HUGH SELWIN:12	12
VOGUE			
CLINGS TO THE SKIRT IN STRICT (VIDE: "VOGUE") PROPRIETY.	241	MOYEN SENSUEL	86

PAGE 451

VOICE -- WAITING

	PAGE	TITLE	LINE
VOICE			
AND CALL MY VOICE TOO THICK A THING.	45	FROM HEINE: 5	4
NAY, SHOULD THE DEATHLESS VOICE OF ALL THE WORLD	63	PHASELLUS ILLE	9
THEIR VOICE IS IN THE TWELVE PIPES HERE.	130	THE RIVER SONG	40
THE VOICE AT MONTFORT, LADY AGNES' HAIR,	151	NEAR PERIGORD	7
FOETID BUCHANAN LIFTED UP HIS VOICE	192	YEUX GLAUQUES	5
VOICES			
WHEN LIGHT THEIR VOICES LIFT THEM UP,	45	FROM HEINE: 5	5
AS YOUR VOICES, UNDER THE LARCHES OF PARADISE	75	THE ALCHEMIST	3
AND INTO TEN THOUSAND VALLEYS FULL OF VOICES AND PINE-WINDS.	134	EXILE'S LETTER	21
VOID			
VOID OF ALL JOY AND FULL OF IRE AND SADNESS.	36	THE YOUNG KING	8
VOILA			
TE VOILA, MON BOURRIENNE, YOU ALSO SHALL BE IMMORTAL.	101	AMITIES	6
VOIR			
NE PEUT PLUS VOIR	273	M. POM-POM	4
VOLS			
QUE BE-M VOLS MAL.	9	NA AUDIART	57
VOLTAIRE			
IMPRESSIONS OF FRANCOIS-MARIE AROUET (DE VOLTAIRE)	167	OF AROUET	T
"THERE WAS ONCE A MAN CALLED VOLTAIRE."	181	MOEURS CON: 7	16
VOLUME			
THERE IS A VOLUME IN THE MATTER; IF HER EYELIDS SINK INTO SLEEP,	217	SEXTUS PROP: 5	31
VOLUPTUOUS			
THERE WERE UPON THE BED NO SIGNS OF A VOLUPTUOUS ENCOUNTER,	225	SEXTUS PROP:10	36
VORTEX			
WHIRL! CENTRIPETAL! MATE! KING DOWN IN THE VORTEX,	120	GAME OF CHESS	13
VOTE			
MY VOTE COMING FROM THE TEMPLE OF PHOEBUS IN LYCIA, AT PATARA,	208	SEXTUS PROP: 1	38
VOUS			
"EST-CE QUE VOUS AVEZ VU DES AUTRES--DES CAMARADES--AVEC DES SINGES OU DES OURS?"	119	THE GYPSY	EPI
VOW			
PAY UP YOUR VOW OF NIGHT WATCHES	224	SEXTUS PROP: 9	25
VOY			
A MIS SOLEDADES VOY,	82	THE CONDOLENCE	EPI
VOYAGED			
LO, THOU HAST VOYAGED NOT! THE SHIP IS MINE."	25	GUIDO INVITES	11
VOYAGES			
CORACLE OF PACIFIC VOYAGES,	203	MAUBERLEY: 4	18
VOYAGING			
LIKE THE SEA THAT BROOKS NO VOYAGING	34	GOODLY FERE	45
VU			
"EST-CE QUE VOUS AVEZ VU DES AUTRES--DES CAMARADES--AVEC DES SINGES OU DES OURS?"	119	THE GYPSY	EPI
VULGARITIES			
AND AGAINST THIS SEA OF VULGARITIES--	99	SALVATIONISTS	14
VULGUS			
THAN HEAR THE WHOLE AEGRUM VULGUS	52	AU SALON	21
VULTUM			
VERMES HABENT EIUS VULTUM	101	AMITIES	19
W.			
OLD FRIENDS THE MOST.--W. B. Y.	101	AMITIES	EPI
WAFER			
LIKE A LITTLE WAFER OF LIGHT.	166	FISH & SHADOW	3
WE HAVE THE PRESS FOR WAFER;	189	HUGH SELWYN: 3	19
WAILING			
FOR I KNOW THAT THE WAILING AND BITTERNESS ARE A FOLLY.	4	LA FRAISNE	23
WAIT			
"WAIT, MY GOOD FELLOW. FOR SUCH JOY I TAKE	172	LANGUE D'OC: 1	26
WAITED			
CEASED UTTERLY. WELL, THEN I WAITED, DREW,	31	PIERE VIDAL	40
WAITERS			
OR SLITHERS ABOUT BETWEEN THE DISHONEST WAITERS--	162	CABARET DANCER	23
WAITING			
WAITING HIS TURN IN THE MID-SUMMER EVENING,	154	NEAR PERIGORD	109

PAGE 452

WAITING -- WALLOW

	PAGE	TITLE	LINE
WAITING (CONTINUED)			
COMPLEYNT OF A GENTLEMAN WHO HAS BEEN WAITING OUTSIDE FOR SOME TIME	172	LANGUE D'OC: 1	SUB
"AND SHE HAS BEEN WAITING FOR THE SCOUNDREL,	225	SEXTUS PROP:10	18
WAITS			
"WHERE A GIRL WAITS ALONE FOR HER LOVER;	210	SEXTUS PROP: 2	23
WAKE			
AND WAKE THE DEAD," SAYS HE,	34	GOODLY FERE	30
LEST THOU SHOULDST WAKE AND WHIMPER FOR THY WINE.	60	TOMB AKR CAAR	13
WAKES			
MY HEART ALL WAKES AND GRIEVES;	173	LANGUE D'OC: 2	8
WAKING			
THE HOUR OF WAKING TOGETHER.	83	THE GARRET	11
WALDORF			
AND YEARNED TO IMITATE THE WALDORF CAPERS	241	MOYEN SENSUEL	92
WALK			
WHO USED TO WALK ABOUT AMONGST US	102	LADIES	10
WHERE THE GODS WALK GARLANDED IN WISTARIA,	108	CH'U YUAN	2
I WILL WALK IN THE GLADE,	108	CH'U YUAN	8
WALKED ONCE, AND NOW DOES NOT WALK	112	IONE, DEAD	8
WALK DOWN LONGACRE RECITING SWINBURNE TO HERSELF, INAUDIBLY?	114	SIMULACRA	2
AND IT IS TO BE HOPED THAT THEIR SPIRITS WILL WALK	115	SOCIAL ORDER	14
THAT WAS THE TOP OF THE WALK, WHEN HE SAID:	119	THE GYPSY	1
AND YOU WOULD WALK OUT WITH ME TO THE WESTERN CORNER OF THE CASTLE,	135	EXILE'S LETTER	49
IT IS IN YOUR GROVE I WOULD WALK,	207	SEXTUS PROP: 1	2
HE MAY WALK ON THE SCYTHIAN COAST,	212	SEXTUS PROP: 3	18
THOUGH YOU WALK IN THE VIA SACRA, WITH A PEACOCK'S TAIL FOR A FAN.	227	SEXTUS PROP:11	40
I CAN WALK ABOUT WITHOUT FIDGETING WHEN PEOPLE PASS,	247	PIERROTS	20
WALKED			
OF THY BEAUTY HATH WALKED	26	NIGHT LITANY	26
"WHY TOOK YE NOT ME WHEN I WALKED ABOUT	33	GOODLY FERE	11
THEY WHINED AS HE WALKED OUT CALM BETWEEN,	34	GOODLY FERE	43
"THE JESTER WALKED IN THE GARDEN."	53	AU JARDIN	6
"THE JESTER WALKED IN THE GARDEN."	53	AU JARDIN	23
FANNING THE GRASS SHE WALKED ON THEN, ENDURES:	92	GENTILDONNA	4
WALKED ONCE, AND NOW DOES NOT WALK	112	IONE, DEAD	8
I HAVE WALKED THERE	121	PROVINC DESERT	7
I HAVE WALKED	121	PROVINC DESERT	28
WALKED OVER EN BERTRAN'S OLD LAYOUT,	122	PROVINC DESERT	39
"HERE SUCH A ONE WALKED.	122	PROVINC DESERT	43
I HAVE WALKED OVER THESE ROADS;	123	PROVINC DESERT	80
YOU WALKED ABOUT MY SEAT, PLAYING WITH BLUE PLUMS.	130	RIVER-MER WIFE	4
WALKED EYE-DEEP IN HELL	190	HUGH SELWYN: 4	13
SO RADWAY WALKED, QUITE LIKE THE OTHER MEN,	244	MOYEN SENSUEL	185
WALKING			
AND THE TALL WOMEN WALKING YOUR STREETS, IN GILT CLOTHES,	165	QUINTUS SEPTIM	14
WALKING ON THE CHELSEA EMBANKMENT.	182	MOEURS CON: 7	25
WALKS			
SHE WALKS BY THE RAILING OF A PATH IN KENSINGTON GARDENS,	83	THE GARDEN	2
AND IN HIS DAILY WALKS DULY CAPSIZE HIM.	245	MOYEN SENSUEL	204
WALL			
THEY TAKE THE TROUBLE TO TEAR OUT THIS WALL HERE,	22	MARVOIL	24
O HOLE IN THE WALL HERE! BE THOU MY JONGLEUR	23	MARVOIL	34
WHEREFORD, O HOLE IN THE WALL HERE,	23	MARVOIL	40
O HOLE IN THE WALL HERE, BE THOU MY JONGLEUR,	23	MARVOIL	45
WITH SIX GREAT SAPPHIRES HUNG ALONG THE WALL,	49	OF SPLENDOUR	10
I HAVE READ OUT THE GOLD UPON THE WALL,	60	TOMB AKR CAAR	9
LIKE A SKEIN OF LOOSE SILK BLOWN AGAINST A WALL	83	THE GARDEN	1
LIKE A SWALLOW HALF BLOWN TO THE WALL,	112	SHOP GIRL	2
LOWERING MY HEAD, I LOOKED AT THE WALL.	130	RIVER-MER WIFE	9
THERE IS NO WALL LEFT TO THIS VILLAGE.	133	FRONTIER GUARD	7
SHE GETS THEM BY THE SOUTH WALL OF THE TOWN.	140	MULBERRY ROAD	7
WALLER'S			
WHEN OUR TWO DUSTS WITH WALLER'S SHALL BE LAID,	197	ENVOI (1919)	23
WALLOW			
AND ITS AGE-LASTING WALLOW FOR RED GREED	11	FAMAM CANO	20

PAGE 453

WALLOW -- WARM

	PAGE	TITLE	LINE
WALLOW (CONTINUED)			
AS CAUGHT BY DANTE IN THE LAST WALLOW OF HELL-- ...	151	NEAR PERIGORD	22
WALLS			
ROME'S NAME ALONE WITHIN THESE WALLS KEEPS HOME.	40	ROME	4
STRANGE WAYS AND WALLS ARE FASHIONED OUT OF IT. ...	49	OF SPLENDOUR	5
OF WOVEN WALLS DEEP PATTERNED, OF EMAIL, ...	49	OF SPLENDOUR	14
BREAK DOWN THE FOUR-SQUARE WALLS OF STANDING TIME.	49	OF SPLENDOUR	21
DO I NOT LOATHE ALL WALLS, STREETS, STONES, ...	70	THE PLUNGE	11
AND CLINGS TO THE WALLS AND THE GATE-TOP.	131	AT TEN-SHIN	12
BLUE MOUNTAINS TO THE NORTH OF THE WALLS, ...	137	TAKING LEAVE	1
THE WALLS RISE IN A MAN'S FACE, ...	138	NEAR SHOKU	3
LIE DEAD WITHIN FOUR WALLS	236	MIDDLE-AGED	15
WALT			
I MAKE A PACT WITH YOU, WALT WHITMAN--	89	A PACT	1
WANDER			
OVER THE WHALE'S ACRE, WOULD WANDER WIDE.	65	THE SEAFARER	61
WANDERED			
WANDERED THROUGH THE ARCADIAN PRAIRIES	222	SEXTUS PROP: 8	25
WANDERING			
AND THE WANDERING OF MANY ROADS HATH MADE MY EYES	16	PRAISE YSOLT	12
WHERE WANDERING THEM WIDEST DRAWETH.	65	THE SEAFARER	58
THE RAIN, THE WANDERING BUSSES.	158	PSYCHOLOG HOUR	11
LIGHT, LIGHT OF MY EYES, AT AN EXCEEDING LATE HOUR I WAS WANDERING, ...	224	SEXTUS PROP:10	1
WANDER-LIED			
MAKE THY LAUGH OUR WANDER-LIED;	7	CINO	47
WANDERS			
WHO WANDERS ABOUT ANNOUNCING HIS SEX	82	THE CONDOLENCE	15
THE WIND BUNDLES ITSELF INTO A BLUISH CLOUD AND WANDERS OFF.	129	THE RIVER SONG	30
WANETH			
WANETH THE WATCH, BUT THE WORLD HOLDETH.	66	THE SEAFARER	89
WANING			
THE FAMILY POSITION WAS WANING, ...	111	SOCIETY	1
WANT			
WHEN THOROUGHLY SOCIALIZED PRINTERS WANT TO PRINT 'EM.	244	MOYEN SENSUEL	168
WANT RUSSIA TO SAVE 'EM	258	ALF'S SECOND	3
WANT RUSSIA TO SAVE 'EM, ...	258	ALF'S SECOND	5
WANTED			
THIS THAT IS ALL I WANTED	70	THE PLUNGE	7
AND IT WAS MORNING, AND I WANTED TO SEE IF SHE WAS ALONE, AND RESTING, ...	225	SEXTUS PROP:10	27
WANTING			
WANTING ONLY WHAT	174	LANGUE D'OC: 3	11
WANTS			
"LET HER, IF SHE WANTS ME, TAKE ME."	100	ARIDES	7
EACH MAN WANTS THE POMEGRANATE FOR HIMSELF;	227	SEXTUS PROP:12	4
WAR			
AS OLD TOLEDOS PAST THEIR DAYS OF WAR ....,....	19	FOR E. MCC	19
THE MAN WHO FEARS WAR AND SQUATS OPPOSING	29	ALTAFORTE	25
A THIN WAR OF METAL.	95	OF THE DEGREES	5
THE COMING OF WAR: ACTAEON	107	COMING OF WAR	T
IS IT A LOVE POEM? DID HE SING OF WAR?	153	NEAR PERIGORD	81
OR WAR AND BROKEN HEAUMES AND POLITICS?	154	NEAR PERIGORD	93
AND I ALSO WILL SING WAR WHEN THIS MATTER OF A GIRL IS EXHAUSTED.	216	SEXTUS PROP: 5	9
TOLD 'EM TO DIE IN WAR, AND THEN TO SAVE, ...	260	ALF'S FIFTH	2
WARBLE			
NEITHER WOULD I WARBLE OF TITANS, NOR OF OSSA	217	SEXTUS PROP: 5	39
WARD			
WHEN IT TURNED OUT HE MEANT MRS. WARD.	181	MOEURS CON: 7	12
WARES			
STRANGE SPARS OF KNOWLEDGE AND DIMMED WARES OF PRICE.	61	PORTRAIT FEMME	5
WARFARE			
AND NO CHILDREN OF WARFARE UPON THEM, ...	133	FRONTIER GUARD	20
WARM			
THAT HATH NO PERFECT LIMNING, WHEN THE WARM	9	NA AUDIART	39
TO WHOM MY BREAST AND ARMS ARE EVER WARM, ...	21	IN DURANCE	43
PLACID BENEATH WARM SUNS, ...	203	MAUBERLEY: 4	7

WARM -- WATER

	PAGE	TITLE	LINE
WARM (CONTINUED)			
FOR MEMORY OF THE FIRST WARM NIGHT STILL CAST A HAZE O'ER	245	MOYEN SENSUEL	195
WARMED			
AROSE TOWARD NEWMAN AS THE WHISKEY WARMED.	193	SIENA MI FE	12
WARN			
TILL THE TRAIST MAN CRY OUT TO WARN	177	LANGUE D'OC: 4	3
WARNED			
WHY AM I WARNED? WHY AM I SENT AWAY?	95	OF THE DEGREES	12
WARN'T			
YOUR OWN MA' WARN'T NO BETTER	260	ALF'S FOURTH	12
WARP			
WITH GREEN STRINGS SHE MAKES THE WARP OF HER BASKET,	140	MULBERRY ROAD	8
WARREN			
WHILE BORN, HIS OWN CLOSE PURSE, HIS RABBIT WARREN,	153	NEAR PERIGORD	60
WARRIOR			
O'ER MUCH HATH TA'EN SIR DEATH THAT DEADLY WARRIOR	37	THE YOUNG KING	12
WAR'S			
TIME'S TOOTH IS INTO THE LOT, AND WAR'S AND FATE'S TOO.	165	QUINTUS SEPTIM	17
WARS-MEN			
A TURMOIL OF WARS-MEN, SPREAD OVER THE MIDDLE KINGDOM,	133	FRONTIER GUARD	15
WAS (156)			
WASHED			
WASHED IN THE COBALT OF OBLIVIONS;	203	MAUDERLEY: 4	9
WASN'T (1)			
WAST			
SUCH WAST THOU,	41	HER MONUMENT	1
O GLANCE, WHEN THOU WAST STILL AS THOU ART NOW,	41	HER MONUMENT	10
THE RIVER? THOU WAST OVER YOUNG.	60	TOMB AKR CAAR	17
WASTAGE			
DARING AS NEVER BEFORE, WASTAGE AS NEVER BEFORE.	190	HUGH SELWYN: 4	20
WASTE			
OUT OF EREBUS, OUT OF THE FLAT WASTE OF AIR, LYING BENEATH THE WORLD;	76	THE ALCHEMIST	46
WASTED			
SO MANY HOURS WASTED!	158	PSYCHOLOG HOUR	9
WATCH			
AND I WATCH HIS SPEARS THROUGH THE DARK CLASH	29	ALTAFORTE	20
WANETH THE WATCH, BUT THE WORLD HOLDETH.	66	THE SEAFARER	89
AND WATCH THE MOON THROUGH THE CLEAR AUTUMN.	132	JEWEL STAIRS'	4
TO WATCH OUT THE BARBAROUS LAND:	133	FRONTIER GUARD	5
AND NOW I WATCH, FROM THE WINDOW,	158	PSYCHOLOG HOUR	10
BADEST ME TO SEE THAT A GOOD WATCH WAS DONE,	172	LANGUE D'OC: 1	23
MAY THE FATES WATCH OVER MY DAY.	216	SEXTUS PROP: 5	22
WATCHED			
THAN TO HAVE WATCHED THAT HOUR AS IT PASSED.	40	ERAT HORA	7
"I AM THY SOUL, NIKOPTIS. I HAVE WATCHED	60	TOMB AKR CAAR	1
WATCHER			
'TILL THE TRAIST WATCHER HIS SONG UNREIN,	177	LANGUE D'OC: 4	18
WATCHES			
WATCHES TO FOLLOW OUR TRACE.	109	HEATHER	7
PAY UP YOUR VOW OF NIGHT WATCHES	224	SEXTUS PROP: 9	25
WATCHING			
AIMLESSLY WATCHING A HAWK ABOVE THE VALLEYS,	154	NEAR PERIGORD	108
WATCHMAN			
'TILL THE WATCHMAN ON THE TOWER	171	LANGUE D'OC	EPI
WATER			
"CAT'S I' THE WATER BUTT!" THOUGHT'S IN YOUR VERSE-BARREL,	13	MESMERISM	5
YET LONGING COMES UPON HIM TO FARE FORTH ON THE WATER.	65	THE SEAFARER	48
YOU, I WOULD HAVE FLOW OVER ME LIKE WATER,	70	THE PLUNGE	14
FROM THE MOLTEN DYES OF THE WATER	75	THE ALCHEMIST	18
BY THE TROUT ASLEEP IN THE GRAY-GREEN OF WATER;	76	THE ALCHEMIST	37
RAIN FLAKES OF GOLD ON THE WATER	76	THE ALCHEMIST	55
AZURE AND FLAKING SILVER OF WATER,	76	THE ALCHEMIST	56
GO AS A GREAT WAVE OF COOL WATER,	88	COMMISSION	4
WHEN THE HOT WATER GIVES OUT OR GOES TEPID,	100	THE BATH TUB	2

WATER -- WAVES

	PAGE	TITLE	LINE
WATER (CONTINUED)			
WE CARRY SINGING GIRLS, DRIFT WITH THE DRIFTING WATER,	128	THE RIVER SONG	5
I LOOKED AT THE DRAGON-POND, WITH ITS WILLOW-COLOURED WATER	129	THE RIVER SONG	20
TO THE DYNASTIC TEMPLE, WITH WATER ABOUT IT CLEAR AS BLUE JADE,	135	EXILE'S LETTER	50
WITH RIPPLES LIKE DRAGON-SCALES, GOING GRASS GREEN ON THE WATER,	136	EXILE'S LETTER	52
AND THE WATER, A HUNDRED FEET DEEP, REFLECTING GREEN EYEBROWS	136	EXILE'S LETTER	56
HE CLAPS HIS HAND ON THE BACK OF THE GREAT WATER SENNIN.	140	SENNIN POEM	14
HOT SUN, CLEAR WATER, FRESH WIND,	146	CANTILATIONS	3
IT IS GOOD TO SPLASH IN THE WATER	147	POST MORTEM	4
THAT FALLS THROUGH THE WATER,	166	FISH & SHADOW	6
THAT FALLS THROUGH THE PALE GREEN WATER.	166	FISH & SHADOW	21
THE PLACID WATER	203	MAUBERLEY: 4	4
WHAT WATER HAS MELLOWED YOUR WHISTLES?	207	SEXTUS PROP: 1	9
THE WATER DRIPPING FROM BELLEROPHON'S HORSE,	210	SEXTUS PROP: 2	2
SAID THEN "YOU IDIOT! WHAT ARE YOU DOING WITH THAT WATER:	210	SEXTUS PROP: 2	17
"LET ANOTHER OAR CHURN THE WATER,	210	SEXTUS PROP: 2	26
"ANIENAN SPRING WATER FALLS INTO FLAT-SPREAD POOLS."	212	SEXTUS PROP: 3	5
AND NOW DRINKS NILE WATER LIKE A GOD,	222	SEXTUS PROP: 8	20
WATER-BUTT			
"AND A CAT'S IN THE WATER-BUTT."--ROBERT BROWNING	13	MESMERISM	EPI
WATER-GIRLS			
MAELIDS AND WATER-GIRLS,	87	THE SPRING	2
WATER-JET			
THE WATER-JET OF GOLD LIGHT BEARS US UP THROUGH THE CEILINGS;	169	PHANOPOEIA	4
WATER-LILIES			
WHERE THE LOW DRONNE IS FILLED WITH WATER-LILIES.	152	NEAR PERIGORD	56
WATERS			
IN THE BLUE WATERS OF HEAVEN,	7	CINO	55
THE MOON IS A GREAT PEARL IN THE WATERS OF SAPPHIRE,	18	DE AEGYPTO	21
COOL TO MY FINGERS THE FLOWING WATERS.	18	DE AEGYPTO	22
O GOD OF WATERS?	26	NIGHT LITANY	13
UPON THE SHADOW OF THE WATERS	26	NIGHT LITANY	27
O GOD OF WATERS.	27	NIGHT LITANY	32
O GOD OF WATERS,	27	NIGHT LITANY	36
FLOATING UPON THE WATERS,	27	NIGHT LITANY	40
O GOD OF WATERS,	27	NIGHT LITANY	44
O GOD OF WATERS.	27	NIGHT LITANY	52
AND OF GREY WATERS.	67	DORIA	7
THEN THE WATERS OF HAN WOULD FLOW NORTHWARD.)	129	THE RIVER SONG	18
AND EVENING DRIVES THEM ON THE EASTWARD-FLOWING WATERS.	131	AT TEN-SHIN	4
PETALS ARE ON THE GONE WATERS AND ON THE GOING,	131	AT TEN-SHIN	5
THROUGH ALL THE THIRTY-SIX FOLDS OF THE TURNING AND TWISTING WATERS,	134	EXILE'S LETTER	18
I HAD TO BE OFF TO SO, FAR AWAY OVER THE WATERS,	135	EXILE'S LETTER	34
OR OF ACHILLES WITHSTAYING WATERS BY SIMOIS	208	SEXTUS PROP: 1	28
VAST WATERS FLOWED FROM HER EYES?	214	SEXTUS PROP: 4	15
SAILS SPREAD ON CERULEAN WATERS, I WOULD SHED TEARS FOR TWO;	223	SEXTUS PROP: 9	7
THE WATERS OF STYX POURED OVER THE WOUND:	230	SEXTUS PROP:12	74
AND ITS WATERS ARE WHITE LIKE SILK.	237	ABU SALAMMAMM	21
WAVE			
AND ICE-COLD WAVE, AT WHILES THE SWAN CRIES,	64	THE SEAFARER	19
GO AS A GREAT WAVE OF COOL WATER,	88	COMMISSION	4
WIND AND WAVE SCATTERED AWAY.	221	SEXTUS PROP: 8	9
WAVER			
WAVER AND SEEM NOT DRAWN TO EARTH, SO HE	39	FOR PSYCHE	5
WAVERING			
WAVERING!	74	THE RETURN	4
WAVES			
I WOULD THAT THE COOL WAVES MIGHT FLOW OVER MY MIND,	36	FRANCESCA	8
WILL NOT OUR CULT BE FOUNDED ON THE WAVES,	39	BLANDULA	9
THE WAVES BORE IN, SOON WILL THEY BEAR AWAY.	69	THE NEEDLE	10

PAGE 456

	PAGE	TITLE	LINE
WAVES (CONTINUED)			
THEREFORE THE SAILORS ARE CHEERED, AND THE WAVES	164	QUINTUS SEPTIM	6
WAVE'S			
NOR ANY WHIT ELSE SAVE THE WAVE'S SLASH, ...	65	THE SEAFARER	47
WAVES'			
WITH MY WAVES' CLARITY	47	FROM HEINE: 7	6
WAVE-WORN			
MY WAVE-WORN BEAUTY WITH HIS WIND OF FLOWERS, ...	24	THUS NINEVEH	15
WAX			
AND THE WAX RUNS LOW.	35	THE EYES	7
WAXED			
THEIR DODDERING IGNORANCE IS WAXED SO NOTABLE	239	MOYEN SENSUEL	37
WAY			
"AH YES, PASSED ONCE OUR WAY, ...	6	CINO	27
LOVE TAKES HIS WAY AND HOLDS HIS JOY DECEITFUL, ...	37	THE YOUNG KING	26
THAT WAY, LADY;	53	AU JARDIN	9
TO SAY THAT LIFE IS, SOME WAY, A GAY THING, ...	53	AU JARDIN	12
HE RETURNS BY WAY OF SEI ROCK, TO HEAR THE NEW NIGHTINGALES, ...	130	THE RIVER SONG	37
THOUGH THEY HANG IN THE SAME WAY OVER THE BRIDGERAIL.	131	AT TEN-SHIN	8
AND THE STREETS MAKE WAY FOR THEIR PASSAGE.	132	AT TEN-SHIN	17
SWEET TREES ARE ON THE PAVED WAY OF THE SHIN, ...	138	NEAR SHOKU	6
AND HAD HIS WAY WITH THE OLD ENGLISH KING, ...	151	NEAR PERIGORD	26
DODGING HIS WAY PAST AUBETERRE, SINGING AT CHALAIS	154	NEAR PERIGORD	105
BUT YOUR SMILE PULLS ONE WAY	162	CABARET DANCER	41
THE AMOROUS NERVES WILL GIVE WAY TO DIGESTIVE; .	163	CABARET DANCER	68
AND STICKING OUT ALL THE WAY ROUND;	181	MOEURS CON: 7	5
MADE WAY FOR MACERATIONS;	189	HUGH SELWYN: 3	7
MAKE WAY, YE ROMAN AUTHORS, ...	229	SEXTUS PROP:12	36
A SILENT HUNTER OFF THE GREAT WHITE WAY, ...	245	MOYEN SENSUEL	200
I RUSHED ABOUT IN THE MOST AGITATED WAY	247	PIERROTS	5
WAY-FARE			
'POLLO PHOIBEE, TO OUR WAY-FARE	7	CINO	46
WAYS			
OF THE OLD WAYS OF MEN HAVE I CAST ASIDE.	4	LA FRAISNE	12
SHE HATH CALLED ME FROM MINE OLD WAYS	4	LA FRAISNE	16
SHE HATH DRAWN ME FROM MINE OLD WAYS, ...	4	LA FRAISNE	20
TO LEAVE THE OLD BARREN WAYS OF MEN, ...	4	LA FRAISNE	29
THAT TRAMP OLD WAYS BENEATH THE SUN-LIGHT, ...	6	CINO	21
O PALMS OF LOVE, THAT IN YOUR WONTED WAYS	41	HER MONUMENT	15
BUT OUT SOMEWHERE BEYOND THE WORLDLY WAYS	49	OF SPLENDOUR	3
STRANGE WAYS AND WALLS ARE FASHIONED OUT OF IT. ...	49	OF SPLENDOUR	5
I AM SET WIDE UPON THE WORLD'S WAYS	53	AU JARDIN	11
I HAVE BEEN INTIMATE WITH THEE, KNOWN THY WAYS. ...	60	TOMB AKR CAAR	21
GREEN THE WAYS, THE BREATH OF THE FIELDS IS THINE THERE, ...	68	APPARUIT	9
ALL WAYS OF TRAFFIC?	70	THE PLUNGE	13
THIS MAN KNEW OUT THE SECRET WAYS OF LOVE, ...	73	JACOPO SELLAIO	1
AND GETTING IN BOTH OF THEIR WAYS;	97	AESTHETICS	14
EMPTY ARE THE WAYS, ...	112	IONE, DEAD	1
EMPTY ARE THE WAYS OF THIS LAND	112	IONE, DEAD	2
EMPTY ARE THE WAYS OF THIS LAND	112	IONE, DEAD	6
AND I'D THE LONG WAYS BEHIND ME, ...	119	THE GYPSY	9
IN THREE WAYS, ...	121	PROVINC DESERT	3
A NET-WORK OF ARBOURS AND PASSAGES AND COVERED WAYS,	141	IDEA OF CHOAN	22
BORDER THE NET-WORK OF WAYS:	141	IDEA OF CHOAN	24
HAD TRIED ALL WAYS:	235	TO WHISTLER	2
TO MIND THEIR "P'S" AND THEIR "Q'S" AND THEIR WAYS	263	ALF'S EIGHTH	27
WE (157)			
WEAK			
HOW MANY WEAK OF MIND, HOW MUCH TUBERCULOSIS	260	ALF'S FIFTH	13
WEAKNESS			
SOME FROM FEAR OF WEAKNESS, ...	190	HUGH SELWYN: 4	6
WEAKNESS'			
POOR IN DISCERNMENT, BEING THUS WEAKNESS' FRIEND,	249	DONNA MI PREGA	38
WEALTHY			
WEALTHY AND WINE-FLUSHED, HOW I WEARY OFT	64	THE SEAFARER	30
WEAPONS			
HE SHAKES THE TROJAN WEAPONS OF AENEAS, ..	220	SEXTUS PROP:12	34
WEAR			
YOU WHO CAN NOT WEAR YOURSELVES OUT	92	THE REST	9

	PAGE	TITLE	LINE
WEAR (CONTINUED)			
SUCH AS THE FASCISTS WEAR,	258	ALF'S THIRD	4
I WEAR A FINE FUR COAT AND GLOVES,	266	ALF'S ELEVENTH	9
WEARETH			
THAT OLD AGE WEARETH FOR A CLOAK.	4	LA FRAISNE	4
WEARIED			
AND WEARIED OUT MY THOUGHT UPON THE SIGNS.	60	TOMB AKR CAAR	10
WEARING			
WEARING RAW SILK OF GOOD COLOUR,	146	CANTILATIONS	7
EACH MAN WHERE HE CAN, WEARING OUT THE DAY IN HIS MANNER.	218	SEXTUS PROP: 5	58
WEARY			
REST MASTER, FOR WE BE A-WEARY, WEARY	35	THE EYES	1
WEALTHY AND WINE-FLUSHED, HOW I WEARY OFT	64	THE SEAFARER	30
AND WEARY WITH HISTORICAL DATA, THEY WILL TURN TO MY DANCE TUNE.	209	SEXTUS PROP: 1	62
NOR WILL YOU BE WEARY OF CALLING MY NAME, NOR TOO WEARY	219	SEXTUS PROP: 6	23
NOR WILL YOU BE WEARY OF CALLING MY NAME, NOR TOO WEARY	219	SEXTUS PROP: 6	23
HEAD FARMERS DO LIKEWISE, AND LYING WEARY AMID THEIR OATS	229	SEXTUS PROP:12	48
IN THE SEASON SAD AND WEARY	267	ALF'S TWELFTH	4
WEATHER			
WHEN IT IS AUTUMN DO WE GET SPRING WEATHER,	59	SILET	7
WEATHERED			
WEATHERED THE WINTER, WRETCHED OUTCAST	64	THE SEAFARER	15
I HAVE WEATHERED THE STORM,	93	THE REST	18
WEAVE			
AND WEAVE YE HIM HIS CORONAL."	72	PAN IS DEAD	3
HOW SHALL WE WEAVE A CORONAL,	72	PAN IS DEAD	6
THEY WEAVE A WHOLE ROOF TO THE MOUNTAIN,	139	SENNIN POEM	5
WEAVING			
SET TO SOME WEAVING, COMES THE AUREATE LIGHT.	49	OF SPLENDOUR	16
WE'D (3)			
WEDDED			
GO TO THE HIDEOUSLY WEDDED,	88	COMMISSION	11
IS NOW WEDDED	103	LADIES	12
WEDDING			
BLACK IS THE PITCH O' THEIR WEDDING DRESS,	11	OF THE GIBBET	18
WEEHAWKEN			
FROM WEEHAWKEN--WHO HAS NEVER KNOWN	163	CABARET DANCER	65
WEEK			
SHE SAYS, "MAY MY POEMS BE PRINTED THIS WEEK?	110	TEMPORA	6
MAY MY POEMS BE PRINTED THIS WEEK?"	110	TEMPORA	8
WILL DINE NEXT WEEK WITH MRS. BASIL,	163	CABARET DANCER	63
(WHICH PAYS HIM MORE PER WEEK THAN THE SUPERNAL).	240	MOYEN SENSUEL	46
SOON OUR HERO COULD MANAGE ONCE A WEEK,	243	MOYEN SENSUEL	141
"THE MEDICAL REPORT THIS WEEK DISCLOSES . . ."	260	ALF'S FIFTH	15
WEEP			
MOVES CHANGING COLOUR, OR TO LAUGH OR WEEP	250	DONNA MI PREGA	53
WEEPING			
FROM THE POPLARS WEEPING THEIR AMBER,	75	THE ALCHEMIST	22
WEEPING THAT WE CAN FOLLOW NAUGHT ELSE.	168	OF AROUET	34
WEFT			
CLOTHED IN GOLDISH WEFT, DELICATELY PERFECT,	68	APPARUIT	21
WEI			
AND THEN I WAS SENT OFF TO SOUTH WEI,	134	EXILE'S LETTER	12
WEIGHED			
AND WEIGHED, REVEALED HIS GREAT AFFECT,	200	MAUBERLEY: 2	31
WEIGHT			
O WINDS, WHAT WIND CAN MATCH THE WEIGHT OF HIM!	39	FOR PSYCHE	10
EQUITABLE WEIGHT ON YOUR SHOULDERS;	214	SEXTUS PROP: 4	4
WEIGHTS			
THESE HEAVY WEIGHTS, THESE DODGERS AND THESE PREACHERS,	241	MOYEN SENSUEL	79
WELCOME			
SHE HATH TO WELCOME ONE,	106	DOMPNA POIS	53
WELDING			
ONE NIGHT, ONE BODY AND ONE WELDING FLAME!	32	PIERE VIDAL	56

WELKIN -- WENT

	PAGE	TITLE	LINE
WELKIN			
I SEE THE SIGNS UPON THE WELKIN SPREAD,	172	LANGUE D'OC: 1	15
WELL			
THOUGH THOU WELL DOST WISH ME ILL	8	NA AUDIART	1
SETS FORTH, AND THOUGH THOU HATE ME WELL,	9	NA AUDIART	32
IS LISTED. WELL! SOME SCORE YEARS HENCE	14	FAMAM CANO	20
"THESE SELL OUR PICTURES"! OH WELL,	20	IN DURANCE	4
WELL THEN, SO CALL THEY, THE SWIRLERS OUT OF THE MIST OF MY SOUL,	20	IN DURANCE	21
CEASED UTTERLY. WELL, THEN I WAITED, DREW,	31	PIERE VIDAL	40
WELL MAYST THOU BOAST THAT THOU THE BEST CHEVALIER	37	THE YOUNG KING	18
"ARE YOU FEELING WELL THIS MORNING?"	46	FROM HEINE: 6	8
WELL, THERE'S NO USE YOUR LOVING ME	53	AU JARDIN	8
"TIME'S BITTER FLOOD"! OH, THAT'S ALL VERY WELL,	59	EXIT' CUIUSDAM	1
I KNOW MY CIRCLE AND KNOW VERY WELL	59	EXIT' CUIUSDAM	6
GOD! THAT MAD'ST HER WELL REGARD HER,	72	DIEU! QU'IL	1
GOD! THAT MAD'ST HER WELL REGARD HER,	72	DIEU! QU'IL	7
GOD! THAT MAD'ST HER WELL REGARD HER.	72	DIEU! QU'IL	13
SINGING AS WELL AS I SING, NONE BETTER;	96	DUM CAPITOLIUM	2
WELL DO THIS AS ANYTHING ELSE.	100	ARIDES	5
SHE KNOWETH WELL, BETIDE	106	DOMPNA POIS	59
THE HORSES ARE WELL TRAINED, THE GENERALS HAVE IVORY ARROWS AND QUIVERS ORNAMENTED WITH FISH-SKIN.	127	BOWMEN OF SHU	19
RED JADE CUPS, FOOD WELL SET ON A BLUE JEWELLED TABLE,	135	EXILE'S LETTER	47
WISHING ME WELL;	147	BEFORE SLEEP	18
THE FAVOUR OF YOUR PARTY; HAD BEEN WELL RECEIVED."	155	NEAR PERIGORD	149
OH, I KNOW WELL ENOUGH.	158	PSYCHOLOG HOUR	17
IT MAY LAST WELL IN THESE DARK NORTHERN CLIMATES,	163	CABARET DANCER	71
OH WELL, HER PRESENT DULNESS . . .	163	CABARET DANCER	78
OH WELL!	183	CANTICO SOLE	16
LEADING, AS HE WELL KNEW,	202	AGE DEMANDED	59
MY COUNTRY? I LOVE IT WELL, AND THOSE GOOD FELLOWS	238	MOYEN SENSUEL	3
WHEN WRITING WELL HAS NOT YET BEEN FORGIVEN	240	MOYEN SENSUEL	61
TO BE NOT TOO WELL KNOWN IN HAUNTS OF VICE--	245	MOYEN SENSUEL	202
WHO WELL PROCEEDETH, FORM NOT SEETH,	250	DONNA MI PREGA	82
BURY IT ALL, BURY IT ALL WELL DEEP,	265	ALF'S NINTH	29
WE'LL			
TELL US THIS THING RATHER, THEN WE'LL BELIEVE YOU,	13	MESMERISM	6
AND WE'LL BE HAPPY THERE.	47	FROM HEINE: 7	4
GOOD "HEDGETHORN," FOR WE'LL ANGLICIZE YOUR NAME	161	CABARET DANCER	1
WE'LL SEND 'EM MOUCHIN' 'OME,	257	BREAD BRIGADE	7
WELL-AWAY			
DRIPS FROM MY DEATHLESS PEN--AH, WELL-AWAY!	59	SILET	2
WELL-GOWNED			
OF WELL-GOWNED APPROBATION	196	HUGH SELWIN:12	10
WELL-HEAD			
I HAVE NOT FOUND THEE AT THE WELL-HEAD	91	DANCE FIGURE	8
WELL-PAID			
WHO ON THE SO WELL-PAID GROUND	263	ALF'S EIGHTH	9
WELSH			
NOR OF WELSH MINES AND THE PROFIT MARUS HAD OUT OF THEM.	217	SEXTUS PROP: 5	46
TO A WELSH SHIFTER WITH AN OGLING EYE,	264	ALF'S NINTH	7
WELTER			
AT LAST FROM THE WORLD'S WELTER	195	HUGH SELWIN:10	4
WENCH			
AS A TIMOROUS WENCH FROM A CENTAUR	81	TENZONE	3
WENT			
WHEREFORE I MADE HER A SONG AND SHE WENT FROM ME	17	PRAISE YSOLT	31
MY SONG WAS ABLAZE WITH HER AND SHE WENT FROM ME	17	PRAISE YSOLT	42
AS FLAME LEAVETH THE EMBERS SO WENT SHE UNTO NEW FORESTS	17	PRAISE YSOLT	43
WENT SWIFTLY FROM ME. NAY, WHATEVER COMES	40	ERAT HORA	4
O MY FELLOW SUFFERERS, WE WENT OUT UNDER THE TREES,	82	THE CONDOLENCE	7
WE WENT FORTH GATHERING DELICATE THOUGHTS,	82	THE CONDOLENCE	9
HE WENT TO HIS DOOM.	100	ARIDES	8
WE WHO WENT OUT INTO THE FOUR A. M. OF THE WORLD	104	ANCORA	3
AND WE WENT ON LIVING IN THE VILLAGE OF CHOKAN-	190	RIVER-MER WIFE	5
YOU WENT INTO FAR KU TO YEN, BY THE RIVER OF SWIRLING EDDIES,	130	RIVER-MER WIFE	10

PAGE 459

WENT -- WHAT

	PAGE	TITLE	LINE
WENT (CONTINUED)			
YOU DRAGGED YOUR FEET WHEN YOU WENT OUT.	131	RIVER-MER WIFE	19
AND I, WRAPPED IN BROCADE, WENT TO SLEEP WITH MY HEAD ON HIS LAP,	135	EXILE'S LETTER	31
I WENT UP TO THE COURT FOR EXAMINATION,	136	EXILE'S LETTER	65
AND WENT BACK TO THE EAST MOUNTAINS	136	EXILE'S LETTER	68
AND THEN THE CROWD BROKE UP, YOU WENT NORTH TO SAN PALACE,	136	EXILE'S LETTER	71
YESTERDAY WE WENT OUT OF THE WILD-GOOSE GATE,	139	SOUTH-FOLK	4
NOW IN VENICE, 'STORANTE AL GIARDINO, I WENT EARLY,	163	CABARET DANCER	79
YET RADWAY WENT. A CIRCUMSPECTIOUS PRIG!	242	MOYEN SENSUEL	119
JUST WENT ON A SLOSHIN'	271	OLE KATE	17
WEPT			
THUS? SHE WEPT INTO UNCOMBED HAIR,	214	SEXTUS PROP: 4	13
WERE (65)			
WE'RE (1)			
WERT			
THOU WERT ONCE SHE	9	NA AUDIART	52
WEST			
OVER THE GRASS IN THE WEST GARDEN;	131	RIVER-MER WIFE	24
INTELLIGENT MEN CAME DRIFTING IN FROM THE SEA AND FROM THE WEST BORDER,	134	EXILE'S LETTER	6
KO-JIN GOES WEST FROM KO-KAKU-RO,	137	ON RIVER KIANG	1
WESTERN			
AND YOU WOULD WALK OUT WITH ME TO THE WESTERN CORNER OF THE CASTLE,	135	EXILE'S LETTER	49
WET			
A WET LEAF THAT CLINGS TO THE THRESHOLD.	108	LIU CH'E	6
AS COOL AS THE PALE WET LEAVES	109	ALBA	1
PETALS ON A WET, BLACK BOUGH.	109	IN THE METRO	2
UP ON THE WET ROAD NEAR CLERMONT.	119	THE GYPSY	6
"WET SPRINGTIME," SAYS TO-EM-MEI, "WET SPRING IN THE GARDEN."	142	UNMOVING CLOUD	EPI
"WET SPRINGTIME," SAYS TO-EM-MEI, "WET SPRING IN THE GARDEN."	142	UNMOVING CLOUD	EPI
WE'VE (2)			
WHALE-PATH			
WHETS FOR THE WHALE-PATH THE HEART IRRESISTIBLY,	65	THE SEAFARER	64
WHALE'S			
OVER THE WHALE'S ACRE, WOULD WANDER WIDE.	65	THE SEAFARER	61
WHAT			
ASK YE WHAT GHOSTS I DREAM UPON?	10	FOR THIS YULE	9
(WHAT OF THE MAGIANS' SCENTED GEAR?)	10	FOR THIS YULE	10
PRINCE: ASK ME NOT WHAT I HAVE DONE	10	FOR THIS YULE	25
NOR WHAT GOD HATH THAT CAN ME CHEER	10	FOR THIS YULE	26
BUT GOD! WHAT A SIGHT YOU HA' GOT O' OUR IN'ARDS,	13	MESMERISM	10
WHAT TIMES THE SWALLOW FILLS	14	FAMAM CANO	7
WHAT SOUL BOWETH	17	PRAISE YSOLT	57
THEN CAME WHAT MIGHT COME, TO WIT: THREE MEN AND ONE WOMAN,	22	MARVOIL	11
O GOD, WHAT GREAT KINDNESS	26	NIGHT LITANY	9
WHAT GREAT SORROW	26	NIGHT LITANY	15
SO SIMPLY ELEMENT AS WHAT I AM.	32	PARACELSUS	5
WHAT DO YE OWN, YE NIGGARDS! THAT CAN BUY	32	PIERE VIDAL	57
WHAT ANSWER? O YE MYRIAD	35	HIS OWN FACE	4
WHAT HAST THOU, O MY SOUL, WITH PARADISE?	39	BLANDULA	1
O WINDS, WHAT WIND CAN MATCH THE WEIGHT OF HIM!	39	FOR PSYCHE	10
AND BE BUT WHAT IT WAS	42	HER MONUMENT	38
WHAT IF I KNOW THY SPEECHES WORD BY WORD?	43	SATIEMUS	1
WHAT IF I KNOW THY SPEECHES WORD BY WORD,	43	SATIEMUS	3
WHAT IF MY THOUGHTS WERE TURNED IN THEIR MID REACH	43	SATIEMUS	9
WHAT IF I KNOW THY LAUGHTER WORD BY WORD	43	SATIEMUS	18
O WHAT COMFORT IS IT FOR ME	46	FROM HEINE: 6	17
WHY SHOULD WE STOP AT ALL FOR WHAT I THINK?	59	SILET	3
THERE IS ENOUGH IN WHAT I CHANCE TO SAY.	59	SILET	4
WHAT YOU HAVE KEPT AND WHAT YOU'VE LEFT BEHIND:	59	EXIT' CUIUSDAM	5
WHAT YOU HAVE KEPT AND WHAT YOU'VE LEFT BEHIND:	59	EXIT' CUIUSDAM	5
WHAT IS THE USE OF SETTING IT TO RIME?	59	SILET	6
WHAT IF THE WIND HAVE TURNED AGAINST THE RAIN?	59	SILET	10
HE THE PROSPEROUS MAN--WHAT SOME PERFORM	65	THE SEAFARER	57
AND NOW YOU HEAR WHAT IS SAID TO US:	82	THE CONDOLENCE	13

WHAT -- WHATEVER

	PAGE	TITLE	LINE
WHAT (CONTINUED)			
THOUGH EVERY BRANCH HAVE BACK WHAT LAST YEAR LOST,	87	THE SPRING	11
REPLEVIN, ESTOPPEL, ESPAVIN AND WHAT NOT.	98	THE BELLAIRES	27
AND WHAT, PRAY, DO YOU KNOW ABOUT	109	THE FAUN	3
WHAT FLOWER HAS COME INTO BLOSSOM?	127	BOWMEN OF SHU	13
AND WHAT ARE THEY COMPARED TO THE LADY RIOKUSHU,	132	AT TEN-SHIN	29
AND WHAT WITH BROKEN WHEELS AND SO ON, I WON'T SAY IT WASN'T HARD GOING, ...	135	EXILE'S LETTER	40
AND WHAT A RECEPTION:	135	EXILE'S LETTER	46
WHAT IS THE USE OF TALKING, AND THERE IS NO END OF TALKING, ...	136	EXILE'S LETTER	75
WHAT COULD HE DO BUT PLAY THE DESPERATE CHESS, ...	152	NEAR PERIGORD	36
"IN THE FULL FLARE OF GRIEF. DO WHAT YOU WILL." ...	152	NEAR PERIGORD	46
WHAT WOULD HE DO WITHOUT HER?	153	NEAR PERIGORD	68
WHAT DOORS ARE OPEN TO FINE COMPLIMENT?"	153	NEAR PERIGORD	75
TAKE HIS OWN SPEECH, MAKE WHAT YOU WILL OF IT-- ...	153	NEAR PERIGORD	79
FOIX' COUNT KNEW THAT. WHAT IS SIR BERTRANS' SINGING?	153	NEAR PERIGORD	91
THAT'S WHAT YOU MEAN YOU ADVERTISING SPADE, ...	162	CABARET DANCER	34
I DON'T KNOW WHAT YOU LOOK LIKE	162	CABARET DANCER	40
WANTING ONLY WHAT	174	LANGUE D'OC: 3	11
THE THOUGHT OF WHAT AMERICA WOULD BE LIKE	183	CANTICO SOLE	1
THE THOUGHT OF WHAT AMERICA, ...	183	CANTICO SOLE	4
THE THOUGHT OF WHAT AMERICA, ...	183	CANTICO SOLE	5
THE THOUGHT OF WHAT AMERICA WOULD BE LIKE	183	CANTICO SOLE	6
THE THOUGHT OF WHAT AMERICA, ...	183	CANTICO SOLE	12
THE THOUGHT OF WHAT AMERICA, ...	183	CANTICO SOLE	10
THE THOUGHT OF WHAT AMERICA WOULD BE LIKE	183	CANTICO SOLE	14
WHAT GOD, MAN, OR HERO	189	HUGH SELWYN: 3	27
IN WHAT HALL HAVE YOU HEARD IT;	207	SEXTUS PROP: 1	7
WHAT FOOT BEAT OUT YOUR TIME-BAR, ...	207	SEXTUS PROP: 1	8
WHAT WATER HAS MELLOWED YOUR WHISTLES?	207	SEXTUS PROP: 1	9
SAID THEN "YOU IDIOT! WHAT ARE YOU DOING WITH THAT WATER:	210	SEXTUS PROP: 2	17
WHAT IS TO BE DONE ABOUT IT?	212	SEXTUS PROP: 3	6
WHAT IF UNDERTAKERS FOLLOW MY TRACK, ...	213	SEXTUS PROP: 3	28
YET YOU ASK ON WHAT ACCOUNT I WRITE SO MANY LOVE-LYRICS	217	SEXTUS PROP: 5	23
AND WHAT THEY SWORE IN THE CUPBOARD	221	SEXTUS PROP: 8	8
WHAT IF YOUR FATES ARE ACCELERATED, ...	222	SEXTUS PROP: 8	27
I DO NOT KNOW WHAT BOYS, ...	224	SEXTUS PROP:10	5
WHAT IT KNEW THEN, IT KNOWS, AND THERE IT STICKS.	240	MOYEN SENSUEL	56
WAS GOT ABROAD, WHAT BETTER LUCK DO YOU WISH 'EM,	240	MOYEN SENSUEL	60
AND FOR WHAT EARTHLY REASON THEY REMAIN.	244	MOYEN SENSUEL	160
THE SERIOUS SOCIAL FOLK IS "JUST WHAT SEX IS."	244	MOYEN SENSUEL	162
"KNOW WHAT THEY THINK, AND JUST WHAT BOOKS THEY'VE READ, ...	244	MOYEN SENSUEL	182
"KNOW WHAT THEY THINK, AND JUST WHAT BOOKS THEY'VE READ, ...	244	MOYEN SENSUEL	182
SAW WHAT THE CITY OFFERED, CAST AN EYE ,..	245	MOYEN SENSUEL	187
CRYING: MY GOD, MY GOD, WHAT WILL SHE SAY?!	247	PIERROTS	6
I THOUGHT: YES, DIVINE, THESE EYES, BUT WHAT EXISTS	247	PIERROTS	11
OR WHAT HIS ACTIVE VIRTU IS, OR WHAT HIS FORCE; ...	248	DONNA MI PREGA	14
OR WHAT HIS ACTIVE VIRTU IS, OR WHAT HIS FORCE; ...	248	DONNA MI PREGA	14
WHAT HIS PLACATION; WHY HE IS IN VERB, ...	248	DONNA MI PREGA	16
DON'T TELL WHAT YOU KNOW, ...	259	ALF'S FOURTH	9
YEH! WHAT IS LEFT OF 'EM, ...	259	ALF'S THIRD	10
WHAT COUNTS IS THE LOOKS	260	ALF'S FOURTH	19
WHO KNOWS NOT WHAT IS OR WAS, ...	261	ALF'S SIXTH	2
"OH, WHAT A CHARMING MAN,"--	261	ALF'S SIXTH	13
WHAT WAS THE NATION'S, NOW BY NORMAN'S KIN	261	ALF'S FIFTH	20
OH, WHAT A NOISE THEY MADE	261	ALF'S SIXTH	23
OH WHAT A FUSS THEY MADE	262	ALF'S SIXTH	25
(HIS WHAT?) WITH A SHOW OF SENSE, ...	263	ALF'S EIGHTH	2
AND SCARCELY HEED ONE WORD OF WHAT YOU HEAR.	265	ALF'S NINTH	28
IS WHAT HAS SET US PINING, ...	267	ALF'S TWELFTH	2
WITH THE THIS AND THAT AND WHAT	267	ALF'S TWELFTH	5
WHAT AIN'T GOT WORK NO MORE	269	SAFE AND SOUND	10
AND DON'T KNOW WHAT BUG IS A-BITIN'	269	SAFE AND SOUND	11
WHATEVER			
"THANK YOU WHATEVER COMES. AND THEN SHE TURNED	40	ERAT HORA	1
WENT SWIFTLY FROM ME. NAY, WHATEVER COMES	40	ERAT HORA	4

PAGE 461

WHATEVER -- WHEN

```
                                                    PAGE    TITLE              LINE
WHATEVER (CONTINUED)
  WHATEVER HIS LORD WILL. ..........................  65    THE SEAFARER         44
  AND FOR THIS, EVERY EARL WHATEVER, FOR THOSE
    SPEAKING AFTER-- ...............................  66    THE SEAFARER         73
  AND WHATEVER SHE DOES OR SAYS ..................... 217    SEXTUS PROP: 5       35
  I DO WHATEVER I CHOOSE. ........................... 266    ALF'S ELEVENTH       12
WHAT'S
  BEHIND THEM? WHAT'S THERE? HER SOUL'S AN AFFAIR FOR
    OCULISTS. ...................................... 247    PIERROTS             12
WHATS-HIS
  THE MIDNIGHT ACTIVITIES OF WHATS-HIS NAME, ........ 264    ALF'S NINTH           2
WHATS-HIS-NAME
  AND WHATS-HIS-NAME ATTAINED NOBILITY. ............. 264    ALF'S NINTH           8
WHEAT
  'MID THE SILVER RUSTLING OF WHEAT, ................  75    THE ALCHEMIST        15
  THE WIND MOVES ABOVE THE WHEAT-- ..................  95    OF THE DEGREES        3
  EARTH SHALL BRING WHEAT FROM BARLEY, .............. 220    SEXTUS PROP: 7       24
WHEEL
  HUB OF THE WHEEL, THE STIRRER-UP OF STRIFE, ....... 151    NEAR PERIGORD        21
  "ANOTHER WHEEL, THE ARENA; MID-CROWD IS AS BAD AS
    MID-SEA." ...................................... 210    SEXTUS PROP: 2       27
  SHE TWIDDLES THE SPIKED WHEEL OF A RHOMBUS, ....... 215    SEXTUS PROP: 4       32
WHEEL-RIMS
  OR OF HECTOR SPATTERING WHEEL-RIMS, ............... 208    SEXTUS PROP: 1       29
WHEELS
  AND WHAT WITH BROKEN WHEELS AND SO ON, I WON'T SAY
    IT WASN'T HARD GOING, .......................... 135    EXILE'S LETTER       40
  AND THE GREAT WHEELS IN HEAVEN  ................... 157    NEAR PERIGORD       177
  "SOFT FIELDS MUST BE WORN BY SMALL WHEELS, ........ 210    SEXTUS PROP: 2       21
  AND RUPERT RAN THE RUMOUR ROUND IN WHEELS, ........ 264    ALF'S NINTH          14
WHEEZE
  YOU WHEEZE AS A HEAD-COLD LONG-TONSILLED CALLIOPE,  13    MESMERISM             9
WHEEZES
  AND HEARD A CLERGY THAT TRIES ON MORE WHEEZES ..... 241    MOYEN SENSUEL        99
WHEN
  ONCE WHEN I WAS AMONG THE YOUNG MEN . . . .........   5    LA FRAISNE           40
  OR WHEN THE MINSTREL, TALE HALF TOLD, .............   9    NA AUDIART           27
  THAT HATH NO PERFECT LIMNING, WHEN THE WARM .......   9    NA AUDIART           39
  THEN WHEN THE GREY WOLVES EVERYCHONE ..............  10    FOR THIS YULE         3
  AS LIPS SHRINK BACK WHEN WE FEEL THE STRAIN .......  11    OF THE GIBBET        20
  AND WHEN THE NIGHT ................................  14    FAMAM CANO            4
  WHEN COME THEY, SURGING OF POWER, "DAEMON," .......  20    IN DURANCE           19
  AND IF WHEN I AM DEAD .............................  22    MARVOIL              23
  AS NE'ER HAD I OTHER, AND WHEN THE WIND BLOWS, ....  23    MARVOIL              35
  SO IS MY HEART HOLLOW WHEN SHE FILLETH NOT MINE EYES, 23   MARVOIL              38
  WHEN THE WIND BLOWS SIGH THOU FOR MY SORROW .......  23    MARVOIL              41
  WHEN THE WHITE HART BREAKS HIS COVER ..............  25    THE WHITE STAG        4
  I HAVE NO LIFE SAVE WHEN THE SWORDS CLASH. ........  28    ALTAFORTE             3
  BUT AH! WHEN I SEE THE STANDARDS GOLD, VAIR, PURPLE,
    OPPOSING ....................................... 28    ALTAFORTE             4
  WHEN THE TEMPESTS KILL THE EARTH'S FOUL PEACE, ....  28    ALTAFORTE             8
  WHEN I SEE HIM SO SCORN AND DEFY PEACE, ...........  29    ALTAFORTE            23
  WHEN OUR ELBOWS AND SWORDS DRIP THE CRIMSON .......  29    ALTAFORTE            34
  WHEN I BUT THINK UPON THE GREAT DEAD DAYS .........  30    PIERE VIDAL           1
  WHEN TALL STAGS FLED ME THROUGH THE ALDER BRAKES, .  30    PIERE VIDAL           9
  WHEN THEY CAME WI' A HOST TO TAKE OUR MAN .........  33    GOODLY FERE           5
  "WHY TOOK YE NOT ME WHEN I WALKED ABOUT ...........  33    GOODLY FERE          11
  WHEN WE LAST MADE COMPANY, ........................  33    GOODLY FERE          14
  HE CRIED NO CRY WHEN THEY DRAVE THE NAILS .........  34    GOODLY FERE          37
  WAS ANGRY WHEN THEY SPOKE YOUR NAME ...............  36    FRANCESCA             6
  SO DELICATE AS SHE IS, WHEN THE SUN ...............  38    BALLATETTA            8
  WILL WE NOT RATHER, WHEN OUR FREEDOM'S WON, .......  39    BLANDULA              2
  MY SOUL, I MEET THEE, WHEN THIS LIFE'S OUTRUN, ....  39    BLANDULA              6
  FADES WHEN THE WIND HATH LIFTED THEM ASIDE, .......  40    ERAT HORA             3
  O GLANCE, WHEN THOU WAST STILL AS THOU ART NOW, ...  41    HER MONUMENT         10
  AND STILL WHEN FATE RECALLETH, ....................  41    HER MONUMENT         22
  WHEN I BEGIN TO SING ..............................  45    FROM HEINE: 5         2
  WHEN THE FAIRY FLAMES ENSHROUDED ..................  45    FROM HEINE: 3         3
  WHEN LIGHT THEIR VOICES LIFT THEM UP, .............  45    FROM HEINE: 5         5
  TO FIND HIM SUCH, WHEN THE DAYS BRING .............  46    FROM HEINE: 6        18
  NO COMFORT, AT MY TIME OF LIFE WHEN ...............  46    FROM HEINE: 6        19
```

WHEN

	PAGE	TITLE	LINE
WHEN (CONTINUED)			
AND ARE YOU NOT READY WHEN EVENING'S COME?	48	FROM HEINE: 8	3
WHEN THE TRUMPET RANG OUT.	48	FROM HEINE: 7	32
HOW WILL THIS BEAUTY, WHEN I AM FAR HENCE,	51	HORAE BEATAE	1
HOW WILL THESE HOURS, WHEN WE TWAIN ARE GRAY,	51	HORAE BEATAE	3
I SUPPOSE, WHEN POETRY COMES DOWN TO FACTS,	52	AU SALON	1
WHEN OUR SOULS ARE RETURNED TO THE GODS	52	AU SALON	2
WHEN I BEHOLD HOW BLACK, IMMORTAL INK	59	SILET	1
OR SLACKED HIS HAND-GRIP WHEN YOU FIRST GRIPPED FAME?	59	EXIT' CUIUSDAM	3
WHEN IT IS AUTUMN DO WE GET SPRING WEATHER,	59	SILET	7
WHEN SPELLS ARE ALWAY RENEWED ON HER?	72	DIEU! QU'IL	6
WHEN I QUESTION YOU;	84	ORTUS	14
AND WHEN THEY WOULD NOT LET HIM ARRANGE	97	AESTHETICS	16
WHEN THE HOT WATER GIVES OUT OR GOES TEPID,	100	THE BATH TUB	2
WHEN I CAREFULLY CONSIDER THE CURIOUS HABITS OF DOGS	102	MEDITATIO	1
WHEN I CONSIDER THE CURIOUS HABITS OF MAN	102	MEDITATIO	4
WHEN WE SAT UPON THE GRANITE BRINK IN HELICON	104	ANCORA	10
WHEN WE SPLASHED AND WERE SPLASHED WITH	104	ANCORA	11
AND WHEN I AROSE TO GO	110	THE ENCOUNTER	3
WHEN YOU CAME OUT IN THE MAGAZINES	114	EPILOGUE	3
WHEN HE SHAKES HANDS WITH YOUNG LADIES.	115	SOCIAL ORDER	4
WHEN THE TAIHAITIAN PRINCESS	118	CONTEMPORARIES	1
THAT WAS THE TOP OF THE WALK, WHEN HE SAID:	119	THE GYPSY	1
AND SAYING: WHEN SHALL WE GET BACK TO OUR COUNTRY?	127	BOWMEN OF SHU	2
WHEN ANYONE SAYS "RETURN," THE OTHERS ARE FULL OF SORROW	127	BOWMEN OF SHU	6
WHEN WE SET OUT, THE WILLOWS WERE DROOPING WITH SPRING,	127	BOWMEN OF SHU	21
YOU DRAGGED YOUR FEET WHEN YOU WENT OUT.	131	RIVER-MER WIFE	19
AND THEN, WHEN SEPARATION HAD COME TO ITS WORST,	134	EXILE'S LETTER	16
WHEN YOU COME TO THE GATES OF GO.	137	OF DEPARTURE	EPI
AND WHEN MEN GOING BY LOOK ON RAFU	140	MULBERRY ROAD	15
IT WILL PAY THEM WHEN THE WORMS ARE WRIGGLING IN THEIR VITALS;	145	SALUTATION 3RD	4
TO SING ONE THING WHEN YOUR SONG MEANS ANOTHER,	153	NEAR PERIGORD	89
IN THE YOUNG DAYS WHEN THE DEEP SKY BEFRIENDED.	157	NEAR PERIGORD	175
WHEN YOU COULD GO OUT IN A HIRED HANSOM	167	OF AROUET	2
WHEN THE NIGHTINGALE TO HIS MATE	171	LANGUE D'OC	EPI
WHEN THE SPRINGTIME IS SWEET	173	LANGUE D'OC: 2	1
WHEN WE SET STRIFE AWAY,	173	LANGUE D'OC: 2	18
WHEN THE SWEET AIR GOES BITTER,	174	LANGUE D'OC: 3	1
NOR DO I KNOW WHEN I TURN LEFT OR RIGHT	174	LANGUE D'OC: 3	24
NOR WHEN I GO OUT.	174	LANGUE D'OC: 3	25
WHEN HER LOVE LOOK STEALS ON ME.	175	LANGUE D'OC: 3	41
AND WHEN SHE LOOKS ON ME	176	LANGUE D'OC: 3	67
OF THE TIMES WHEN THE SLEEVES WERE LARGE,	180	MOEURS CON: 5	3
WHEN IT TURNED OUT HE MEANT MRS. WARD.	181	MOEURS CON: 7	12
WHEN JOHN RUSKIN PRODUCED	192	YEUX GLAUQUES	2
WHEN THAT FAUN'S HEAD OF HERS	192	YEUX GLAUQUES	6
SHOWED ONLY WHEN THE DAYLIGHT FELL	193	BRENNBAUM	6
"WHEN I BEGAN I GOT, OF COURSE,	194	MR. NIXON	6
WHEN OUR TWO DUSTS WITH WALLER'S SHALL BE LAID,	197	ENVOI (1919)	23
WHEN THEY HAVE GOT OVER THE STRANGENESS,	208	SEXTUS PROP: 1	41
AND I ALSO WILL SING WAR WHEN THIS MATTER OF A GIRL IS EXHAUSTED.	216	SEXTUS PROP: 5	9
WHEN , WHEN, AND WHENEVER DEATH CLOSES OUR EYELIDS,	218	SEXTUS PROP: 6	1
WHEN , WHEN, AND WHENEVER DEATH CLOSES OUR EYELIDS,	218	SEXTUS PROP: 6	1
WHEN THE SYRIAN ONYX IS BROKEN.	219	SEXTUS PROP: 6	25
STRUGGLES WHEN THE LIGHTS WERE TAKEN AWAY;	220	SEXTUS PROP: 7	4
AND A DAY WHEN NO DAY RETURNS.	220	SEXTUS PROP: 7	19
NO, NOT WHEN SHE WAS TUNICK'D IN PURPLE.	225	SEXTUS PROP:10	31
WHEN TOURISTS FROLICKING	236	MIDDLE-AGED	4
AND WHEN HE COMES INTO POWER	238	ABU SALAMMAMM	30
WHEN WRITING WELL HAS NOT YET BEEN FORGIVEN	240	MOYEN SENSUEL	61
SUCH WAS HE WHEN HE GOT HIS MOTHER'S LETTER	242	MOYEN SENSUEL	109
WHEN THOROUGHLY SOCIALIZED PRINTERS WANT TO PRINT 'EM.	244	MOYEN SENSUEL	168
STILL WE LOOK TOWARD THE DAY WHEN MAN WITH UNOTION,	244	MOYEN SENSUEL	175
WHEN LAST I MET HIM, HE WAS A PILLAR IN	246	MOYEN SENSUEL	229
I CAN WALK ABOUT WITHOUT FIDGETING WHEN PEOPLE PASS,	247	PIERROTS	20
HE COMES TO BE AND IS WHEN WILL'S SO GREAT	249	DONNA MI PREGA	49

PAGE 463

WHEN -- WHERE

	PAGE	TITLE	LINE
WHEN (CONTINUED)			
WHEN WILL THIS SYSTEM LIE DOWN IN ITS GRAVE?	260	ALF'S FIFTH	4
WHEN FEEBLE MR. ASQUITH, GETTING OLD,	264	ALF'S NINTH	5
WHEN OUR MINDS ARE VERY BLEARY,	267	ALF'S TWELFTH	5
WHEN I WAS ONLY A YOUNGSTER,	271	OLE KATE	1
WHENCE			
WHENCE HAVE WE GRIEF, DISCORD AND DEEPEST SADNESS.	37	THE YOUNG KING	32
AND THE WISE CONCORD, WHENCE THROUGH DELICIOUS SEAS	42	HER MONUMENT	43
WHENCE THEIR SYMBOLICAL POLLEN HAS BEEN EXCERPTED,	180	MOEURS CON: 5	21
AND WHENCE THIS SOFT BOOK COMES INTO MY MOUTH.	217	SEXTUS PROP: 5	24
WHENE'ER			
THE MIND OF RADWAY, WHENE'ER HE FOUND A PAIR OF PURPLE STAYS OR	245	MOYEN SENSUEL	196
WHENEVER			
WHEN , WHEN, AND WHENEVER DEATH CLOSES OUR EYELIDS,	218	SEXTUS PROP: 6	1
WHERE			
I HAVE HIDDEN MY FACE WHERE THE OAK	4	LA FRAISNE	10
WHERE THY BODICE LACES START	8	NA AUDIART	3
WHERE THY TORSE AND LIMBS ARE MET	8	NA AUDIART	24
WHERE ARE THE JOYS MY HEART HAD WON?	10	FOR THIS YULE	17
WHERE ARE THE LIPS MINE LAY UPON,	10	FOR THIS YULE	19
AYE! WHERE ARE THE GLANCES FEAT AND CLEAR	10	FOR THIS YULE	20
BUT YE ASK FIRST WHERE THE WINDS ARE GONE	10	FOR THIS YULE	27
GONE WHERE THE GREY WINDS CALL TO YOU,	19	FOR E. MCC	2
IN THOSE DIM HALLS WHERE NO MAN TROUBLETH	24	THUS NINEVEH	10
FAR FROM WHERE WORTH'S WON AND THE SWORDS CLASH	29	ALTAFORTE	28
THERE WHERE THERE IS NO GRIEF, NOR SHALL BE SADNESS.	37	THE YOUNG KING	40
LEST THEY SHOULD PARCH TOO SWIFTLY, WHERE SHE PASSES.	38	BALLATETTA	10
TELL ME WHERE THY LOVELY LOVE IS,	45	FROM HEINE: 3	1
WHERE TIME IS SHRIVELLED DOWN TO TIME'S SEED CORN	50	THE FLAME	11
WHERE TIME BURNS BACK ABOUT TH' ETERNAL EMBERS.	50	THE FLAME	21
WHERE THESE HAVE BEEN, MEET 'TIS, THE GROUND IS HOLY.	51	THE ALTAR	4
HERE IN THE EVERY-DAY WHERE OUR ACTS	52	AU SALON	4
ONE PLACE WHERE WE'D RATHER HAVE TEA	52	AU SALON	8
HOURS, WHERE SOMETHING MIGHT HAVE FLOATED UP.	61	PORTRAIT FEMME	12
HATH SET ACQUAINTANCE WHERE MIGHT BE AFFECTIONS,	63	AN OBJECT	2
HUNG WITH HARD ICE-FLAKES, WHERE HAIL-SCUR FLEW,	64	THE SEAFARER	17
WHERE WANDERING THEM WIDEST DRAWETH.	65	THE SEAFARER	58
CRIMSON, FROSTY WITH DEW, THE ROSES BEND WHERE	68	APPARUIT	5
"WHERE IS THE PICTURESQUE?"	85	SALUTATION 2ND	12
"WHERE IS THE VERTIGO OF EMOTION?"	85	SALUTATION 2ND	13
TO WHERE THE OLIVE BOUGHS	92	APRIL	3
I KNOW NOT WHERE TO GO SEEKING,	105	DOMPNA POIS	4
WHERE LOVE IS,	105	DOMPNA POIS	23
WHERE THE GODS WALK GARLANDED IN WISTARIA,	108	CH'U YUAN	2
WHERE IONE	112	IONE, DEAD	7
WHERE ONE NEEDS ONE'S BRAINS ALL THE TIME.	117	THE LAKE ISLE	16
WHERE THE HILLS PART	121	PROVINC DESERT	2
"WHERE THE GREAT HALLS WERE CLOSER TOGETHER."	122	PROVINC DESERT	58
WHERE LAY THE DYNASTIC HOUSE OF THE GO.	138	CITY OF CHOAN	5
WHERE THE LOW DRONNE IS FILLED WITH WATER-LILIES.	152	NEAR PERIGORD	56
WHERE AM I COME WITH COMPOUND FLATTERIES--	153	NEAR PERIGORD	74
WHERE IS THE WORK OF YOUR HOME-BORN SCULPTORS?	165	QUINTUS SEPTIM	16
WHERE, LADY, ARE THE DAYS	167	OF AROUET	1
THE GREEN STRETCHES WHERE LOVE IS AND THE GRAPES	167	OF AROUET	21
A MAN GO WHERE HE WILL.	173	LANGUE D'OC: 2	5
BUT FROM WHERE MY HEART IS SET	173	LANGUE D'OC: 2	6
WHERE THE LEAF FALLS FROM THE TWIG,	174	LANGUE D'OC: 3	3
WHERE MY LOVE IS, THERE IS A GLITTER OF SUN;	174	LANGUE D'OC: 3	16
WHERE SHE STANDS,	176	LANGUE D'OC: 3	76
HERE IN THE ORCHARD WHERE THE BIRDS COMPLAIN,	177	LANGUE D'OC: 4	17
WHERE THE LOWER AND HIGHER HAVE ENDING;	196	HUGH SELWIN:12	16
TO FLEET ST. WHERE	196	HUGH SELWIN:12	23
"WHERE A GIRL WAITS ALONE FOR HER LOVER;	210	SEXTUS PROP: 2	23
NOR WHERE ROME RUINS GERMAN RICHES,	211	SEXTUS PROP: 2	45
"NOR WHERE THE RHINE FLOWS WITH BARBAROUS BLOOD,	211	SEXTUS PROP: 2	46
WHERE BOLD HANDS MAY DO VIOLENCE TO MY PERSON?	212	SEXTUS PROP: 3	8
EACH MAN WHERE HE CAN, WEARING OUT THE DAY IN HIS MANNER.	218	SEXTUS PROP: 5	58
GOD KNOWS WHERE HE HAS BEEN.	225	SEXTUS PROP:10	21

	PAGE	TITLE	LINE
WHERE (CONTINUED)			
AND HOLDS HER SIDES WHERE SWELLING LAUGHTER CRACKS 'EM	239	MOYEN SENSUEL	33
PUFFED SATIN, AND SILK STOCKINGS, WHERE THE KNEE	241	MOYEN SENSUEL	85
WHERE ONE GETS MORE CHANCES	242	MOYEN SENSUEL	103
THE PROMINENT HAUNTS, WHERE ONE MIGHT RECOGNIZE HIM,	245	MOYEN SENSUEL	203
WHERE HE TAKES REST; WHO MAKETH HIM TO BE;	248	DONNA MI PREGA	13
WHERE FOLK OF WORTH BE HOST.	250	DONNA MI PREGA	57
IS WHERE THE CO-OPS ARE GOIN' TO,	262	ALF'S SEVENTH	13
AND WHERE HE ONCE SET FOOT, RIGHT THERE HE STAYED.	264	ALF'S NINTH	12
WHERE BANKS RISE DAY BY DAY,	272	NATIONAL SONG	2
WHERE AN ENGLISHMAN IS FREE	272	NATIONAL SONG	6
WHEREBY			
AS TO HOW AND WHY AND WHEREBY THEY GOT IN	244	MOYEN SENSUEL	159
WHEREFORE			
WHEREFORE I MADE HER A SONG AND SHE WENT FROM ME	17	PRAISE YSOLT	31
WHEREFORE, O HOLE IN THE WALL HERE,	23	MARVOIL	40
WHEREFORE THE GOOD SQUIRE BELLAIRE	98	THE BELLAIRES	34
WHEREFROM			
"WHEREFROM FATHER ENNIUS, SITTING BEFORE I CAME, HATH DRUNK."	210	SEXTUS PROP: 2	7
WHEREIN			
GET US TO SOME CLEAR PLACE WHEREIN THE SUN	39	BLANDULA	3
THE UNSAFE SAFE, WHEREIN ALL ROTS, AND NO MAN CAN SAY HOW	261	ALF'S FIFTH	19
WHERE'S			
BUT WHERE'S THE OLD FRIEND HASN'T FALLEN OFF,	59	EXIT' CUIUSDAM	2
WHERETHROUGH			
BUT LIKE A MIST WHERETHROUGH HER WHITE FORM FOUGHT,	31	PIERE VIDAL	30
AND THY LIGHT LIMBS, WHERETHROUGH I LEAPT AFLAME,	60	TOMB AKR CAAR	4
WHERETO			
WHERETO THOU CALLEDST AND WHERETO I CALL.	25	GUIDO INVITES	6
WHERETO THOU CALLEDST AND WHERETO I CALL.	25	GUIDO INVITES	6
WHETHER			
NOR WHETHER THERE BE ANY PATCH LEFT OF US	228	SEXTUS PROP:12	27
WHETHER MR. DUPONT AND THE GUN-SHARKS	268	ANOTHER BIT	7
WHETS			
WHETS FOR THE WHALE-PATH THE HEART IRRESISTIBLY,	65	THE SEAFARER	64
WHICH			
"WHICH OF HIS BROTHERS HAD HE SLAIN?"	12	OF THE GIBBET	36
THAT WHICH STANDS FIRM IN THEE TIME BATTERS DOWN,	40	ROME	13
AND THAT WHICH FLEETETH DOTH OUTRUN SWIFT TIME.	40	ROME	14
THAT WHICH REMAINETH NOW	41	HER MONUMENT	19
WHICH, PLAYED ON BY THE VIRTUES OF HER SOUL,	49	OF SPLENDOUR	20
THIS PAPIER-MACHE, WHICH YOU SEE, MY FRIENDS,	63	PHASELLUS ILLE	1
WHICH BROUGHT THE HAIR-CLOTH CHAIR TO SUCH PERFECTION,	63	PHASELLUS ILLE	6
'NEATH WHICH THE LAST YEAR LIES,	67	THE CLOAK	8
AND RETURN TO THAT WHICH CONCERNS US.	82	THE CONDOLENCE	18
THIS LADY IN THE WHITE BATH-ROBE WHICH SHE CALLS A PEIGNOIR,	87	ALBATRE	1
HE STROKED THOSE WHICH WERE ALREADY ARRANGED,	97	AESTHETICS	18
BEFORE IT ANOTHER HOUSE WHICH I DO NOT KNOW:	141	IDEA OF CHOAN	30
"WHICH THE HIGHEST CULTURES HAVE NOURISHED"	196	HUGH SELWIN:12	22
WHICH ANAETHESIS, NOTED A YEAR LATE,	200	MAUBERLEY: 2	30
WHICH THESE PRESENTS PLACE	201	AGE DEMANDED	27
A BASKET WORK OF BRAIDS WHICH SEEM AS IF THEY WERE	204	MEDALLION	10
I ASK A WREATH WHICH WILL NOT CRUSH MY HEAD.	207	SEXTUS PROP: 1	21
TELL ME THE TRUTHS WHICH YOU HEAR OF OUR CONSTANT YOUNG LADY,	214	SEXTUS PROP: 4	1
TO THINGS WHICH YOU THINK I WOULD LIKE TO BELIEVE.	214	SEXTUS PROP: 4	7
FOR WHICH THINGS YOU WILL GET A REWARD FROM ME, LYGDAMUS?	215	SEXTUS PROP: 4	27
AND "IT IS, I THINK, INDIA WHICH NOW GIVES NECKS TO YOUR TRIUMPH,"	216	SEXTUS PROP: 5	17
WHICH I TAKE, MY NOT UNWORTHY GIFT, TO PERSEPHONE.	219	SEXTUS PROP 6	21
WITH WHICH I AM ALREADY FAMILIAR,	226	SEXTUS PROP:11	16
THE WHICH, NO CAT HAS EYES ENOUGH	236	MIDDLE AGED	22
(WHICH PAYS HIM MORE PER WEEK THAN THE SUPERNAL).	240	MOYEN SENSUEL	46
BONE FORCES AMONG THOSE WHICH "FORMED" HIS YOUTH:	241	MOYEN SENSUEL	78
IN WHICH THEIR MENTORS PLACE SUCH WIDE RELIANCE.	244	MOYEN SENSUEL	164

WHICH -- WHITE

	PAGE	TITLE	LINE
WHICH (CONTINUED)			
BUT MY SOUL, THE SORT WHICH HARSH SOUNDS DISTURB,	247	PIERROTS	17
WHILE			
WHILE IN HIS HEART ART THOU?	17	PRAISE YSOLT	58
GONE WHILE YOUR TASTES WERE KEEN TO YOU,	19	FOR E. MCC	1
AS I HIDE MOST THE WHILE	21	IN DURANCE	30
WHILE SHE TOSSED CLOSE TO CLIFFS, COLDLY AFFLICTED,	64	THE SEAFARER	8
ALL THE WHILE THEY WERE TALKING THE NEW MORALITY	110	THE ENCOUNTER	1
WHILE THE SECOND WIFE OF A NEPHEW	115	SOCIAL ORDER	9
WHILE MY HAIR WAS STILL CUT STRAIGHT ACROSS MY FOREHEAD	130	RIVER-MER WIFE	1
AND ALL THE WHILE YOU SING OUT THAT CANZONE,	151	NEAR PERIGORD	10
WHILE BORN, HIS OWN CLOSE PURSE, HIS RABBIT WARREN,	153	NEAR PERIGORD	60
WHILE THAT CROPPED FOOL,	162	CABARET DANCER	43
WHILE OUR FATES TWINE TOGETHER, SATE WE OUR EYES WITH LOVE;	220	SEXTUS PROP: 7	17
NO, NOW WHILE IT MAY BE, LET NOT THE FRUIT OF LIFE CEASE.	220	SEXTUS PROP: 7	28
WHILE A BLACK VEIL WAS OVER HER STARS,	222	SEXTUS PROP: 8	26
WHILE MILORD BEAVERBROOK	257	BREAD BRIGADE	28
DID I 'EAR IT WHILE PICKIN' 'OPS;	262	ALF'S SEVENTH	3
WHILE RAMSEY MACDONALD SLEEPS, SLEEPS.	265	ALF'S TENTH	8
WHILE YOU STALWART SHEEP OF FREEDOM	269	SAFE AND SOUND	7
WHILES			
AND BURST FORTH TO THE WINDOWS ONLY WHILES OR WHILES	21	IN DURANCE	31
AND BURST FORTH TO THE WINDOWS ONLY WHILES OR WHILES	21	IN DURANCE	31
AND ICE-COLD WAVE, AT WHILES THE SWAN CRIES,	64	THE SEAFARER	19
WHIM			
FOR A WHIM	250	DONNA MI PREGA	66
WHIMPER			
LEST THOU SHOULDST WAKE AND WHIMPER FOR THY WINE.	60	TOMB AKR CAAR	13
WHINED			
THEY WHINED AS HE WALKED OUT CALM BETWEEN,	34	GOODLY FERE	43
WHIRL			
WHIRL! CENTRIPETAL! MATE! KING DOWN IN THE VORTEX,	120	GAME OF CHESS	13
WHIRLED			
CONFUSED, WHIRLED IN A TANGLE.	136	EXILE'S LETTER	74
WHIRLING			
HEARD, UNDER THE DARK, WHIRLING LAUGHTER.	121	PROVINC DESERT	32
THE WHIRLING TISSUE OF LIGHT	170	PHANOPOEIA	22
WHIRRED			
THAT WHIRRED IN THE AIR ABOVE US.	3	THRENOS	6
WHISKEY			
AROSE TOWARD NEWMAN AS THE WHISKEY WARMED.	193	SIENA MI FE	12
WHISPER			
STILL SHADE, AND BADE NO WHISPER SPEAK THE BIRDS OF HOW	21	IN DURANCE	48
MEET THROUGH OUR VEILS AND WHISPER, AND OF LOVE.	50	THE FLAME	13
WHISPERING			
WHISPERING AMONG THEM, "THE FAIR DEAD	43	SATIEMUS	10
WHISTLER			
TO WHISTLER, AMERICAN	235	TO WHISTLER	T
FROM THESE HE LEARNT. POE, WHITMAN, WHISTLER, MEN, THEIR RECOGNITION	240	MOYEN SENSUEL	59
WHISTLES			
WHAT WATER HAS MELLOWED YOUR WHISTLES?	207	SEXTUS PROP: 1	9
WHIT			
NAY NO WHIT	8	NA AUDIART	18
NOR ANY WHIT ELSE SAVE THE WAVE'S SLASH,	65	THE SEAFARER	47
WHITE			
I WILL SING OF THE WHITE BIRDS	7	CINO	54
WHITE WORDS AS SNOW FLAKES BUT THEY ARE COLD,	16	PRAISE YSOLT	21
THE WHITE STAG	25	THE WHITE STAG	T
WHEN THE WHITE HART BREAKS HIS COVER	25	THE WHITE STAG	4
AND THE WHITE WIND BREAKS THE MORN.	25	THE WHITE STAG	5
"'TIS THE WHITE STAG, FAME, WE'RE A-HUNTING,	25	THE WHITE STAG	6
BUT LIKE A MIST WHERETHROUGH HER WHITE FORM FOUGHT,	31	PIERE VIDAL	30
GOD! SHE WAS WHITE THEN, SPLENDID AS SOME TOMB	31	PIERE VIDAL	38
UPON WHITE PARCHMENT.	35	THE EYES	14
ON HOW WHITE DOGWOODS MURMURED OVERHEAD	43	SATIEMUS	12
THOU WILT IN MY WHITE ARMS THERE,	47	FROM HEINE: 7	9

WHITE -- WHO

	PAGE	TITLE	LINE
WHITE (CONTINUED)			
YET SHALL MY WHITE ARMS HOLD THEE,	48	FROM HEINE: 7	29
MY CITY, MY BELOVED, MY WHITE! AH, SLENDER,	62	N. Y.	1
AS WHITE THEIR BARK, SO WHITE THIS LADY'S HOURS.	71	A VIRGINAL	14
AS WHITE THEIR BARK, SO WHITE THIS LADY'S HOURS.	71	A VIRGINAL	14
FROM THE WHITE, ALIVE IN THE SEED,	76	THE ALCHEMIST	31
THIS LADY IN THE WHITE BATH-ROBE WHICH SHE CALLS A PEIGNOIR,	87	ALBATRE	1
AND THE DELICATE WHITE FEET OF HER LITTLE WHITE DOG	87	ALBATRE	3
AND THE DELICATE WHITE FEET OF HER LITTLE WHITE DOG	87	ALBATRE	3
WHITE AS AN ALMOND ARE THY SHOULDERS;	91	DANCE FIGURE	12
THY MAIDENS ARE WHITE LIKE PEBBLES;	91	DANCE FIGURE	21
AS A BATHTUB LINED WITH WHITE PORCELAIN,	100	THE BATH TUB	1
HER WHITE TEETH, OF THE LADY FAIDITA	106	DOMPNA POIS	51
O FAN OF WHITE SILK,	108	FAN-PIECE	1
SEEN THE LONG MINARETS, THE WHITE SHAFTS.	122	PROVINC DESERT	35
WHITE, WHITE OF FACE, HESITATES, PASSING THE DOOR.	128	BEAU TOILET	4
WHITE, WHITE OF FACE, HESITATES, PASSING THE DOOR.	128	BEAU TOILET	4
WOULD FOLLOW THE WHITE GULLS OR RIDE THEM.	128	THE RIVER SONG	8
THE JEWELLED STEPS ARE ALREADY QUITE WHITE WITH DEW,	132	JEWEL STAIRS'	1
BONES WHITE WITH A THOUSAND FROSTS,	133	FRONTIER GUARD	8
WITH YELLOW GOLD AND WHITE JEWELS, WE PAID FOR SONGS AND LAUGHTER	134	EXILE'S LETTER	4
WHITE RIVER WINDING ABOUT THEM;	137	TAKING LEAVE	2
THE ISLE OF WHITE HERON	138	CITY OF CHOAN	0
WHOSE WHITE HEAD IS LOST FOR THIS PROVINCE?	139	SOUTH-FOLK	14
DARK OXEN, WHITE HORSES,	141	IDEA OF CHOAN	2
THERE IS A THROAT; AH, THERE ARE TWO WHITE HANDS;	153	NEAR PERIGORD	71
AND YOUR WHITE VASES FROM JAPAN,	167	OF AROUET	12
ROSE WHITE, YELLOW, SILVER	169	PHANOPOEIA	ST
I SEE THE WHITE	171	LANGUE D'OC	EPI
LILIES LIFT THEIR WHITE SYMBOLICAL CUPS,	180	MOEURS CON: 5	20
"CONTENT EVER TO MOVE WITH WHITE SWANS!	211	SEXTUS PROP: 2	40
HIS PALACE IS WHITE LIKE MARBLE,	237	ABU SALAMMAMM	5
AND ITS WATERS ARE WHITE LIKE SILK.	237	ABU SALAMMAMM	21
A SILENT HUNTER OFF THE GREAT WHITE WAY,	245	MOYEN SENSUEL	200
WHITE-GLEAMING			
WITH YOU IS IOPE, WITH YOU THE WHITE-GLEAMING TYRO,	38	LADY'S LIFE	5
WHITEHALL			
THE PIMPS OF WHITEHALL EVER MORE IN FEAR,	260	ALF'S FIFTH	7
WHITE-HEADED			
WHITE-HEADED.	136	EXILE'S LETTER	69
WHITENESS			
NOR WOULD GAUTIER HIMSELF HAVE DESPISED THEIR CONTRASTS IN WHITENESS	87	ALBATRE	5
WHITE-STOCKING'D			
WITH HER WHITE-STOCKING'D FEET	111	BLACK SLIPPERS	3
WHITHER			
BLOWING THEY KNOW NOT WHITHER, SEEKING A SONG.	16	PRAISE YSOLT	20
WHITHER MY DESIRE AND MY DREAM HAVE PRECEDED ME.	23	MARVOIL	33
WHITHER, O CITY, ARE YOUR PROFITS AND YOUR GILDED SHRINES,	165	QUINTUS SEPTIM	12
SAFE MAY'ST THOU GO MY CANZON WHITHER THEE PLEASETH	250	DONNA MI PREGA	88
WHITMAN			
I MAKE A PACT WITH YOU, WALT WHITMAN--	89	A PACT	1
FROM THESE HE LEARNT. POE, WHITMAN, WHISTLER, MEN, THEIR RECOGNITION	240	MOYEN SENSUEL	59
WHITTLED			
THYRSIS AND DAPHNIS UPON WHITTLED REEDS,	229	SEXTUS PROP:12	42
WHO			
WHO SHALL RENDER	8	NA AUDIART	8
(WHO KNOWS WHOSE WAS THAT PARAGON?)	10	FOR THIS YULE	23
WHO GAVE THIS POIGNARD ITS PREMIER STAIN	11	OF THE GIBBET	8
I EVEN I, AM HE WHO KNOWETH THE ROADS	18	DE AEGYPTO	1
I, EVEN I, WHO FLY WITH THE SWALLOWS.	18	DE AEGYPTO	4
I, EVEN I, AM HE WHO KNOWETH THE ROADS	18	DE AEGYPTO	7
WHO HATH THE MOUTH TO RECEIVE IT,	18	DE AEGYPTO	13
I, EVEN I, AM HE WHO KNOWETH THE ROADS	18	DE AEGYPTO	15
I, EVEN I, WHO FLY WITH THE SWALLOWS.	18	DE AEGYPTO	18
I, EVEN I, AM HE WHO KNOWETH THE ROADS	18	DE AEGYPTO	23
"THEE"? OH, "THEE" IS WHO COMETH FIRST	20	IN DURANCE	10

PAGE 467

WHO

	PAGE	TITLE	LINE
WHO (CONTINUED)			
THE MAN WHO FEARS WAR AND SQUATS OPPOSING	29	ALTAFORTE	25
MAY GOD DAMN FOR EVER ALL WHO CRY "PEACE!"	29	ALTAFORTE	36
SPEECH? WORDS? FAUGH! WHO TALKS OF WORDS AND LOVE?!	31	PIERE VIDAL	33
SUCH GLORY OF THE EARTH? OR WHO WILL WIN	32	PIERE VIDAL	58
I WHO HAVE SEEN YOU AMID THE PRIMAL THINGS	36	FRANCESCA	5
WHO MADE THE FREEST HAND SEEM COVETOUS.	37	THE YOUNG KING	14
WHO DRANK OF DEATH FOR OUR SALVACIOUN,	37	THE YOUNG KING	35
WHO HATH MY HEART IN JURISDICTION.	38	BALLATETTA	5
O THOU NEW COMER WHO SEEK'ST ROME IN ROME	40	ROME	1
ONE WHO HATH SET THE WHOLE WORLD 'NEATH HER LAWS,	40	ROME	6
WHO ART NOW	41	HER MONUMENT	2
"LO, ONE THERE WAS WHO BENT HER FAIR BRIGHT HEAD,	43	SATIEMUS	5
OF ANY ONE WHO EVER KISSED YOU?	44	FROM HEINE: 1	8
WHO CAN DEMOLISH AT SUCH POLISHED EASE	46	TRANSLATOR	3
WE WHO ARE WISE BEYOND YOUR DREAM OF WISDOM,	50	THE FLAME	5
WHO CAN LOOK ON THAT BLUE AND NOT BELIEVE?	50	THE FLAME	28
WHO CALL'ST ABOUT MY GATES FOR SOME LOST ME;	51	THE FLAME	35
AND WHO ARE WE, WHO KNOW THAT LAST INTENT,	59	SILET	13
AND WHO ARE WE, WHO KNOW THAT LAST INTENT,	59	SILET	13
THIS HE LITTLE BELIEVES, WHO AYE IN WINSOME LIFE	64	THE SEAFARER	28
WHO COULD PART HIM FROM HER BORDERS	72	DIEU! QU'IL	5
NO MAN COULD PAINT SUCH THINGS WHO DID NOT KNOW.	73	JACOPO SELLAIO	2
AND NOW SHE'S GONE, WHO WAS HIS CYPRIAN,	73	JACOPO SELLAIO	3
AND YOU ARE HERE, WHO ARE "THE ISLES" TO ME.	73	JACOPO SELLAIO	4
WHO WANDERS ABOUT ANNOUNCING HIS SEX	82	THE CONDOLENCE	15
COME, LET US PITY THOSE WHO ARE BETTER OFF THAN WE ARE.	83	THE GARRET	1
SHE, WHO MOVED HERE AMID THE CYCLAMEN,	87	THE SPRING	12
GO TO THE BOURGEOISE WHO IS DYING OF HER ENNUIS,	88	COMMISSION	9
GO TO THOSE WHO HAVE DELICATE LUST,	88	COMMISSION	16
WHO HAS HAD A PIG-HEADED FATHER;	89	A PACT	4
GO TO THOSE WHO ARE THICKENED WITH MIDDLE AGE,	89	COMMISSION	26
TO THOSE WHO HAVE LOST THEIR INTEREST.	89	COMMISSION	27
GO TO THE ADOLESCENT WHO ARE SMOTHERED IN FAMILY--	89	COMMISSION	28
SHE PASSED AND LEFT NO QUIVER IN THE VEINS, WHO NOW	92	GENTILDONNA	1
YOU WHO CAN NOT WEAR YOURSELVES OUT	92	THE REST	9
YOU WHO CAN ONLY SPEAK,	92	THE REST	11
WHO CAN NOT STEEL YOURSELVES INTO REITERATION;	92	THE REST	12
YOU WHO CAN KNOW AT FIRST HAND,	93	THE REST	15
WHO CAN UNDERSTAND ANY AFFAIR OF THEIRS. YET	97	THE BELLAIRES	10
WERE UNCERTAIN WHO WAS SUPPOSED TO BE INDEBTED TO THEM.	98	THE BELLAIRES	33
LEUCIS, WHO INTENDED A GRAND PASSION,	99	EPITAPH	1
BASTIDIDES, ON THE CONTRARY, WHO BOTH TALKS AND WRITES OF NOTHING SAVE COPULATION,	100	TEMPERAMENTS	5
WHO AM I TO CONDEMN YOU, O DIVES,	102	TO DIVES	1
I WHO AM AS MUCH EMBITTERED	102	TO DIVES	2
WHO USED TO WALK ABOUT AMONGST US	102	LADIES	10
WE WHO WENT OUT INTO THE FOUR A. M. OF THE WORLD	104	ANCORA	3
WE WHO SHOOK OFF OUR DEW WITH THE RABBITS,	104	ANCORA	5
WE WHO HAVE SEEN EVEN ARTEMIS A-BINDING HER SANDALS,	104	ANCORA	6
WHO HAD LAUGHED ON EIGHTEEN SUMMERS,	111	SOCIETY	3
WHO WAS "SO OLD THAT SHE WAS AN ATHEIST,"	115	SOCIAL ORDER	6
OUR MIND IS FULL OF SORROW, WHO WILL KNOW OF OUR GRIEF?	127	BOWMEN OF SHU	24
WHO NOW GOES DRUNKENLY OUT	128	BEAU TOILET	8
WHO AMONG THEM IS A MAN LIKE HAN-REI	132	AT TEN-SHIN	31
WHO DEPARTED ALONE WITH HIS MISTRESS,	132	AT TEN-SHIN	32
WHO BROUGHT THIS TO PASS?	133	FRONTIER GUARD	10
WHO HAS BROUGHT THE FLAMING IMPERIAL ANGER?	133	FRONTIER GUARD	11
WHO HAS BROUGHT THE ARMY WITH DRUMS AND WITH KETTLE-DRUMS?	133	FRONTIER GUARD	12
AND YOUR FATHER, WHO WAS BRAVE AS A LEOPARD,	135	EXILE'S LETTER	36
WHO BOW OVER THEIR CLASPED HANDS AT A DISTANCE.	137	TAKING LEAVE	7
WHO WILL BE SORRY FOR GENERAL RISHOGU,	139	SOUTH-FOLK	12
THESE ARE THEY WHO OBJECTED TO NEWNESS,	145	SALUTATION 3RD	5
LET US SPIT UPON THOSE WHO PAT THE BIG-BELLIES FOR PROFIT,	145	SALUTATION 3RD	15
AND HE WHO SET THE STRIFE BETWEEN BROTHER AND BROTHER	151	NEAR PERIGORD	25
SHE WHO HAD NOR EARS NOR TONGUE SAVE IN HER HANDS,	157	NEAR PERIGORD	187

PAGE 468

WHO -- WHOLLY

	PAGE	TITLE	LINE
WHO (CONTINUED)			
SHE WHO COULD NEVER LIVE SAVE THROUGH ONE PERSON,	157	NEAR PERIGORD	189
SHE WHO COULD NEVER SPEAK SAVE TO ONE PERSON,	157	NEAR PERIGORD	190
THAT TOM-BOY WHO CAN'T EARN HER LIVING,	162	CABARET DANCER	44
FROM WEEHAWKEN--WHO HAS NEVER KNOWN	163	CABARET DANCER	65
COMPLEYNT OF A GENTLEMAN WHO HAS BEEN WAITING OUTSIDE FOR SOME TIME	172	LANGUE D'OC: 1	SUB
WHO STIRS NOT FORTH THIS NIGHT,	172	LANGUE D'OC: 1	4
WHO HAVE COME BETWEEN ME AND MY CHARMER,	173	LANGUE D'OC: 2	24
WHO KNOW NOT HOW TO ASK HER;	175	LANGUE D'OC: 3	32
WHO CAN NOT.	175	LANGUE D'OC: 3	33
I WHO COME FIRST FROM THE CLEAR FONT	207	SEXTUS PROP: 1	3
WHO HATH TAUGHT YOU SO SUBTLE A MEASURE,	207	SEXTUS PROP: 1	6
AND WHO WOULD HAVE KNOWN THE TOWERS	208	SEXTUS PROP: 1	26
HAPPY WHO ARE MENTIONED IN MY PAMPHLETS,	209	SEXTUS PROP: 1	63
"WHO HAS ORDERED A BOOK ABOUT HEROES?	210	SEXTUS PROP: 2	18
WHO SO INDECOROUS AS TO SHED THE PURE GORE OF A SUITOR?!	212	SEXTUS PROP: 3	26
"HE WHO IS NOW VACANT DUST	219	SEXTUS PROP: 6	26
FOOL WHO WOULD SET A TERM TO LOVE'S MADNESS,	220	SEXTUS PROP: 7	22
WHO, WHO WILL BE THE NEXT MAN TO ENTRUST HIS GIRL TO A FRIEND?	227	SEXTUS PROP:12	1
WHO, WHO WILL BE THE NEXT MAN TO ENTRUST HIS GIRL TO A FRIEND?	227	SEXTUS PROP:12	1
AND YOU WRITE OF ACHELOUS, WHO CONTENDED WITH HERCULES,	228	SEXTUS PROP:12	18
ME, WHO HAD NO GENERAL FOR A GRANDFATHER!	229	SEXTUS PROP:12	54
WHO BEAR THE BRUNT OF OUR AMERICA	235	TO WHISTLER	12
IT IS HE WHO HAS SLAIN THE DRAGON	237	ABU SALAMMAMM	8
WHO, SINCE THEIR WIT'S UNKNOWN, ESCAPE THE GALLOWS.	238	MOYEN SENSUEL	4
WHO SHOWS HIS TASTE IN HIS AMBASSADORS:	239	MOYEN SENSUEL	17
HENRY VAN DYKE, WHO THINKS TO CHARM THE MUSE YOU PACK HER IN	239	MOYEN SENSUEL	21
WHO WROUGHT ABOUT HIS "SOUL" THEIR STALE INFECTION.	241	MOYEN SENSUEL	81
(LET HIM REBUKE WHO NE'ER HAS KNOWN THE PURE PLATONIC GRAPPLE,	242	MOYEN SENSUEL	105
THOUGH MALES OF SEVENTY, WHO FEAR TRUTHS NAKED HARM US,	243	MOYEN SENSUEL	147
ONE OF THOSE FIRM-FACED INSPECTING WOMEN, WHO	243	MOYEN SENSUEL	156
WHO HAS THE PHRASE "AS IGNORANT AS AN ACTOR."	246	MOYEN SENSUEL	222
THAT MAN WHO IS BASE IN HEART	248	DONNA MI PREGA	7
WHERE HE TAKES REST; WHO MAKETH HIM TO BE;	248	DONNA MI PREGA	13
WHO WELL PROCEEDETH, FORM NOT SEETH,	250	DONNA MI PREGA	82
WHO ATE THE PROFITS, AND WHO LOCKED 'EM IN	260	ALF'S FIFTH	18
WHO ATE THE PROFITS, AND WHO LOCKED 'EM IN	260	ALF'S FIFTH	18
WHO KNOWS NOT WHAT IS OR WAS,	261	ALF'S SIXTH	2
WHO ON THE SO WELL-PAID GROUND	263	ALF'S EIGHTH	9
IT IS HE WHO BUYS GOLD-BRAID FOR THE SWANKERS	263	ALF'S EIGHTH	17
WHO'D			
WHO'D HAVE FORESEEN IT?	82	THE CONDOLENCE	6
WHOE'ER			
WHOE'ER LIVED IN LIFE MOST LORDLIEST,	66	THE SEAFARER	87
WHO'ER			
ALAS! WHO'ER IT PLEASE OR PAIN,	175	LANGUE D'OC: 3	58
WHOLE			
ONE WHO HATH SET THE WHOLE WORLD 'NEATH HER LAWS,	40	ROME	6
THE ARCANE SPIRIT OF THE WHOLE MANKIND	42	HER MONUMENT	44
YOU'VE GOT THE WHOLE NIGHT BEFORE YOU,	48	FROM HEINE: 8	5
SET LOOSE THE WHOLE CONSUMMATE PACK	52	AU SALON	14
THAN HEAR THE WHOLE AEGRUM VULGUS	52	AU SALON	21
NO! THERE IS NOTHING! IN THE WHOLE AND ALL,	61	PORTRAIT FEMME	28
AND HERE'S THE THING THAT LASTS THE WHOLE THING OUT:	73	JACOPO SELLAIO	5
FOR YOU ARE NO PART, BUT A WHOLE,	84	ORTUS	15
THEY WEAVE A WHOLE ROOF TO THE MOUNTAIN,	139	SENNIN POEM	5
TAKE THE WHOLE MAN, AND RAVEL OUT THE STORY,	152	NEAR PERIGORD	47
THOUGH THE WHOLE WORLD RUN RACK	176	LANGUE D'OC: 3	73
THAN IF I TREAT THE NATION AS A WHOLE.	239	MOYEN SENSUEL	43
HOW THE WHOLE NATION SHOOK	257	BREAD BRIGADE	??
WHOLLY			
THAT I SO LONG HELD THY HEART WHOLLY,	44	FROM HEINE: 2	2
THAT YOUR RELATIONSHIP IS WHOLLY PARASITIC;	101	AMITIES	5

PAGE 469

WHOLLY -- WHY

	PAGE	TITLE	LINE
WHOLLY (CONTINUED)			
NO MESSENGER SHOULD COME WHOLLY EMPTY,	214	SEXTUS PROP: 4	8
FOR MINDS SO WHOLLY FOUNDED UPON QUOTATIONS	239	MOYEN SENSUEL	29
OF LANGUAGE, BY MEN WHOLLY SOCIALIZED,	244	MOYEN SENSUEL	166
WHOM			
TO WHOM MY BREAST AND ARMS ARE EVER WARM,	21	IN DURANCE	43
HIM, WHOM IT PLEASED FOR OUR GREAT BITTERNESS	37	THE YOUNG KING	33
WHOM HEAVENLY JOY IMMERSES,	45	FROM HEINE: 4	2
WHOM THOU ONCE DID SING SO SWEETLY,	45	FROM HEINE: 3	2
LO, THERE ARE MANY GODS WHOM WE HAVE SEEN,	50	THE FLAME	23
SOME FEW WHOM WE'D RATHER PLEASE	52	AU SALON	20
FROM LAWYERS TO WHOM NO ONE WAS INDEBTED,	98	THE BELLAIRES	31
TO THOSE TO WHOM IT APPLIES.	99	SALVATIONISTS	6
ALL OF WHOM SHE REFUSED;	102	LADIES	2
TO MY DESIRE, WORTH YOURS WHOM I HAVE LOST,	105	DOMPNA POIS	9
WHOM WE MEET ON STRANGE ROADWAYS?	141	IDEA OF CHOAN	32
THINKING OF AELIS, WHOM HE LOVED HEART AND SOUL . . .	154	NEAR PERIGORD	110
THE MAN WHOM LOVE HAD	175	LANGUE D'OC: 3	56
NOR IS THERE ANYONE TO WHOM LOVERS ARE NOT SACRED AT			
MIDNIGHT	212	SEXTUS PROP: 3	15
IN BOSTON, TO HENRY JAMES, THE GREATEST WHOM WE'VE			
SEEN LIVING.	240	MOYEN SENSUEL	62
WAS NEVER ONE OF WHOM ONE SPEAKS AS "BRAZEN'D." . . .	245	MOYEN SENSUEL	206
WHOM CAN THESE DUDS ATTACK?	258	ALF'S THIRD	1
WHORE			
THE PRUDENT WHORE IS NOT WITHOUT HER FUTURE,	163	CABARET DANCER	75
WHO'RE			
BUT YOU STUFFED COATS WHO'RE NEITHER TEPID NOR			
DISTINCTLY BOREAL,	238	MOYEN SENSUEL	5
WHORES			
AND THE WHORES DROPPING IN FOR A WORD OR TWO IN			
PASSING,	117	THE LAKE ISLE	10
WHORESON			
YOU WHORESON DOG, PAPIOLS, COME! LET'S TO MUSIC!	28	ALTAFORTE	2
WHO'S			
WHO'S NOW THE EDITOR OF THE ATLANTIC,	239	MOYEN SENSUEL	14
WHOSE			
FOR WHOSE FAIRNESS ONE FORGAVE	9	NA AUDIART	54
(WHO KNOWS WHOSE WAS THAT PARAGON?)	10	FOR THIS YULE	23
WHOSE FRAMES HAVE THE NIGHT AND ITS WINDS IN FEE.	12	OF THE GIBBET	28
WE SEEM AS STATUES ROUND WHOSE HIGH-RISEN BASE	32	PARACELSUS	11
WHOSE SMILE MORE AVAILETH	35	THE EYES	16
NOR MAY HE THEN THE FLESH-COVER, WHOSE LIFE CEASETH,	66	THE SEAFARER	96
GO TO THEM WHOSE FAILURE IS CONCEALED,	88	COMMISSION	12
GO TO THOSE WHOSE DELICATE DESIRES ARE THWARTED,	88	COMMISSION	17
I HEARD THE YOUNG DANTE, WHOSE LAST NAME I DO NOT			
KNOW--	96	AESTHETICS	7
WHOSE WIFE IS SEVERAL YEARS HIS SENIOR,	115	SOCIAL ORDER	2
WHOSE CHARIOT? THE GENERAL'S.	127	BOWMEN OF SHU	14
WHOSE WHITE HEAD IS LOST FOR THIS PROVINCE?	139	SOUTH-FOLK	14
WHOSE BLUBBERING YOWLS YOU TAKE FOR PASSION'S			
ESSENCE;	240	MOYEN SENSUEL	68
I KNEW A TOURIST AGENT, ONE WHOSE ART IS	245	MOYEN SENSUEL	209
BUT RADWAY WAS A PATRIOT WHOSE VENALITY	245	MOYEN SENSUEL	211
WHY			
"BEING NO LONGER HUMAN, WHY SHOULD I	32	PARACELSUS	1
"WHY TOOK YE NOT ME WHEN I WALKED ABOUT	33	GOODLY FERE	11
HIS? WHY THE GOOD KING HARRY'S,	47	FROM HEINE: 7	15
WHY SHOULD WE STOP AT ALL FOR WHAT I THINK?	59	SILET	3
WHY AM I WARNED? WHY AM I SENT AWAY?	95	OF THE DEGREES	12
WHY AM I WARNED? WHY AM I SENT AWAY?	95	OF THE DEGREES	12
WHY IS YOUR GLITTER FULL OF CURIOUS MISTRUST?	95	OF THE DEGREES	13
WHY DO YOU LOOK SO EAGERLY AND SO CURIOUSLY INTO			
PEOPLE'S FACES,	103	CODA	2
AH, LADY, WHY HAVE YOU CAST	107	DOMPNA POIS	69
WHY SHOULD ONE ALWAYS LIE ABOUT SUCH MATTERS?	113	TAME CAT	2
WHY DOES THE HORSE-FACED LADY OF JUST THE			
UNMENTIONABLE AGE	114	SIMULACRA	1
WHY DOES THE SMALL CHILD IN THE SOILED-WHITE			
IMITATION FUR COAT	114	SIMULACRA	3

WHY -- WILD-WOOD

	PAGE	TITLE	LINE
WHY (CONTINUED)			
WHY DOES THE REALLY HANDSOME YOUNG WOMAN APPROACH ME IN SACKVILLE STREET	114	SIMULACRA	5
GODDAMM, GODDAMM, 'TIS WHY I AM, GODDAMM,	116	ANCIENT MUSIC	10
HE WAS UNCERTAIN WHY HE SHOULD TRY TO FEEL LIKE ANYTHING ELSE,	118	ANCIENT WISDOM	3
WHY SHOULD I CLIMB THE LOOK OUT?	130	RIVER-MER WIFE	14
'WHY DO YOU LOVE ME? WILL YOU ALWAYS LOVE ME?	157	NEAR PERIGORD	181
HE SAID: "WHY FLAY DEAD HORSES?	181	MOEURS CON: 7	15
"WHY WRENCH YOUR PAGE OUT OF ITS COURSE?	210	SEXTUS PROP: 2	24
"DEATH WHY TARDILY COME?"	219	SEXTUS PROP: 6	29
WHY PAINT THESE DAYS? AN INSURANCE INSPECTOR	243	MOYEN SENSUEL	151
AS TO HOW AND WHY AND WHEREBY THEY GOT IN	244	MOYEN SENSUEL	159
WHAT HIS PLACATION; WHY HE IS IN VERB,	248	DONNA MI PREGA	16
THEIRS NOT TO REASON WHY,	257	BREAD BRIGADE	13
OR WHY WE SHOULD STAND TO ATTENTION	264	ALF'S EIGHTH	30
WI'			
WHEN THEY CAME WI' A HOST TO TAKE OUR MAN	33	GOODLY FERE	5
WI' A BUNDLE O' CORDS SWUNG FREE,	33	GOODLY FERE	18
WI' HIS EYES LIKE THE GREY O' THE SEA,	34	GOODLY FERE	44
WI' TWEY WORDS SPOKE' SUDDENTLY.	34	GOODLY FERE	48
WIDE			
SUCH AS ARE UP AND WIDE,	14	FAMAM CANO	10
AND PRIZE WIDE MY MOUTH WITH FAST MUSIC	29	ALTAFORTE	22
I AM SET WIDE UPON THE WORLD'S WAYS	53	AU JARDIN	11
OVER THE WHALE'S ACRE, WOULD WANDER WIDE.	65	THE SEAFARER	61
FROM THE WIDE EARTH AND THE OLIVE,	75	THE ALCHEMIST	21
DESOLATE CASTLE, THE SKY, THE WIDE DESERT.	133	FRONTIER GUARD	6
MIND LIKE A FLOATING WIDE CLOUD,	137	TAKING LEAVE	5
THE NARROW STREETS CUT INTO THE WIDE HIGHWAY AT CHOAN,	141	IDEA OF CHOAN	1
AND THE WIDE, FLAT ROAD STRETCHES OUT.	142	UNMOVING CLOUD	5
EUHENIA, IN SHORT SKIRTS, SLAPS HER WIDE STOMACH,	163	CABARET DANCER	53
IF THE CLASSICS HAD A WIDE CIRCULATION	183	CANTICO SOLE	2
IF THE CLASSICS HAD A WIDE CIRCULATION	183	CANTICO SOLE	7
IF THE CLASSICS HAD A WIDE CIRCULATION . . .	183	CANTICO SOLE	15
MY ORCHARDS DO NOT LIE LEVEL AND WIDE	209	SEXTUS PROP: 1	53
IN WHICH THEIR MENTORS PLACE SUCH WIDE RELIANCE.	244	MOYEN SENSUEL	164
WIDE-BANDED			
THE WIDE-BANDED IRIDES	200	MAUBERLEY: 2	27
WIDEST			
WHERE WANDERING THEM WIDEST DRAWETH.	65	THE SEAFARER	58
WIDOW			
WILL MEET A DUCHESS AND AN EX-DIPLOMAT'S WIDOW	163	CABARET DANCER	64
WIDOWED			
AIE! THE LEAN BARE TREE IS WIDOWED AGAIN	12	OF THE GIBBET	33
WIFE			
NOR WINSOMENESS TO WIFE, NOR WORLD'S DELIGHT	65	THE SEAFARER	46
GO TO THE BOUGHT WIFE,	88	COMMISSION	14
BUT TO HIS WIFE.	98	THE BELLAIRES	15
ON THE CONTRARY, IF THEY DO NOT BELONG TO HIS WIFE,	98	THE BELLAIRES	16
HAS MARRIED AN UGLY WIFE,	100	ARIDES	2
WHOSE WIFE IS SEVERAL YEARS HIS SENIOR,	115	SOCIAL ORDER	2
WHILE THE SECOND WIFE OF A NEPHEW	115	SOCIAL ORDER	9
THE RIVER-MERCHANT'S WIFE: A LETTER	130	RIVER-MER WIFE	T
SEEING YOUR WIFE IS CHARMING AND YOUR CHILD	161	CABARET DANCER	3
HAVE DRIVEN HIS WIFE FROM ONE RELIGIOUS EXCESS TO ANOTHER.	178	MOEURS CON: 1	8
WIFE'S			
AT A FRIEND OF MY WIFE'S THERE IS A PHOTOGRAPH,	180	MOEURS CON: 5	1
WILD			
AND WILD DESIRE	87	THE SPRING	8
FOR ORPHEUS TAMED THE WILD BEASTS--	208	SEXTUS PROP: 1	42
AND EVEN ZEUS' WILD LIGHTNING FEAR TO STRIKE	244	MOYEN SENSUEL	177
AND MAKE THE TOUR ABROAD FOR THEIR WILD TILLAGE--	245	MOYEN SENSUEL	208
WILD-CRUEL			
NOT YET WILD-CRUEL AS DAPHNE,	250	DONNA MI PREGA	74
WILD-GOOSE			
YESTERDAY WE WENT OUT OF THE WILD-GOOSE GATE,	139	SOUTH-FOLK	4
WILD-WOOD			
IN WILD-WOOD NEVER FAWN NOR FALLOW FARETH	38	BALLATETTA	6

PAGE 471

WILL

	PAGE	TITLE	LINE
WILL			
. . . I HOPE SHE WILL NOT COME AGAIN.	5	LA FRAISNE	44
AND I WILL SING OF THE SUN.	6	CINO	3
I WILL SING OF THE SUN.	7	CINO	39
BUT IT IS ALL ONE, I WILL SING OF THE SUN.	7	CINO	41
I WILL SING OF THE WHITE BIRDS	7	CINO	54
WILL SING THEM IN THE TWILIGHT,	14	FAMAM CANO	3
WILL LAUGH YOUR VERSES TO EACH OTHER,	14	FAMAM CANO	11
WILL TURN ASIDE TO SNEER AT	14	FAMAM CANO	29
NO COIN, NO WILL TO SNATCH THE AFTERMATH	14	FAMAM CANO	31
AS FOR WILL AND TESTAMENT I LEAVE NONE,	22	MARVOIL	27
SUCH GLORY OF THE EARTH? OR WHO WILL WIN	32	PIERE VIDAL	58
NOW YOU WILL COME OUT OF A CONFUSION OF PEOPLE,	36	FRANCESCA	3
'LAS! NEVER WAS NOR WILL BE IN THIS WORLD	37	THE YOUNG KING	15
WILL WE NOT RATHER, WHEN OUR FREEDOM'S WON,	39	BLANDULA	2
WILL WE NOT FIND SOME HEADLAND CONSECRATED	39	BLANDULA	7
WILL NOT OUR CULT BE FOUNDED ON THE WAVES,	39	BLANDULA	9
SOUL, IF SHE MEET US THERE, WILL ANY RUMOUR	39	BLANDULA	13
THROUGH ALL THE WORLD WILL I COMPLAIN	44	FROM HEINE: 1	3
THY HEAD WILL I COVER OVER	47	FROM HEINE: 7	5
HOW WILL THIS BEAUTY, WHEN I AM FAR HENCE,	51	HORAE BEATAE	1
HOW WILL THESE HOURS, WHEN WE TWAIN ARE GRAY,	51	HORAE BEATAE	3
TIME HAS SEEN THIS, AND WILL NOT TURN AGAIN;	59	SILET	12
LISTEN! LISTEN TO ME, AND I WILL BREATHE INTO THEE A SOUL.	62	N. Y.	2
AND I WILL BREATHE INTO THEE A SOUL,	62	N. Y.	12
NOR WILL THE HORRID THREATS OF BERNARD SHAW	63	PHASELLUS ILLE	7
NOT THOUGH HE BE GIVEN HIS GOOD, BUT WILL HAVE IN HIS YOUTH GREED;	65	THE SEAFARER	41
WHATEVER HIS LORD WILL.	65	THE SEAFARER	44
THAT HE WILL WORK ERE HE PASS ONWARD,	66	THE SEAFARER	75
TILL THE ROSE-TIME WILL BE OVER,	67	THE CLOAK	2
THINK'ST THOU THAT DEATH WILL KISS THEE?	67	THE CLOAK	3
WILL FIND THEE SUCH A LOVER	67	THE CLOAK	5
AS I? WILL THE NEW ROSES MISS THEE?	67	THE CLOAK	6
COME, OR THE STELLAR TIDE WILL SLIP AWAY.	69	THE NEEDLE	1
THE WAVES BORE IN, SOON WILL THEY BEAR AWAY.	69	THE NEEDLE	10
I WILL NOT SPOIL MY SHEATH WITH LESSER BRIGHTNESS,	71	A VIRGINAL	2
WILL PEOPLE ACCEPT THEM?	81	TENZONE	1
WILL THEY BE TOUCHED WITH THE VERISIMILITUDES?	81	TENZONE	6
WILL COMMIT THAT INDISCRETION.	83	THE GARDEN	12
AND THAT YOU WILL LIVE FOREVER.	86	SALUTATION 2ND	37
I FEAR YOU WILL COME TO A BAD END.	94	INSTRUCTIONS	4
YOU WILL COME TO A VERY BAD END.	94	INSTRUCTIONS	9
I WILL GET YOU A GREEN COAT OUT OF CHINA	94	INSTRUCTIONS	17
I WILL GET YOU THE SCARLET SILK TROUSERS	94	INSTRUCTIONS	19
HOW MANY WILL COME AFTER ME	96	DUM CAPITOLIUM	1
HE WILL PLEAD	98	THE BELLAIRES	17
WILL PAY NO ATTENTION TO THIS,	98	THE BELLAIRES	25
AND THERE WILL BE ONLY THE MORE CONFUSION,	98	THE BELLAIRES	26
WILL YOU FIND YOUR LOST DEAD AMONG THEM?	103	CODA	3
I WILL NEVER AGAIN GATHER	105	DOMPNA POIS	6
I WILL GO OUT A-SEARCHING,	105	DOMPNA POIS	17
I WILL GET ME TO THE WOOD	108	CH'U YUAN	1
I WILL WALK IN THE GLADE,	108	CH'U YUAN	8
I WILL COME OUT FROM THE NEW THICKET	108	CH'U YUAN	9
THIS THING WILL RUN AT YOU	109	THE FAUN	2
TO SEE HOW CELESTINE WILL RE-ENTER HER SLIPPERS.	111	BLACK SLIPPERS	10
AND IT IS TO BE HOPED THAT THEIR SPIRITS WILL WALK	115	SOCIAL ORDER	14
YES, SHE ALSO WILL TURN MIDDLE-AGED,	116	THE TEA SHOP	5
WILL BE SPREAD ABOUT US NO LONGER.	116	THE TEA SHOP	8
SHE ALSO WILL TURN MIDDLE-AGED.	116	THE TEA SHOP	9
WE SAY: WILL WE BE LET TO GO BACK IN OCTOBER?	127	BOWMEN OF SHU	10
OUR MIND IS FULL OF SORROW, WHO WILL KNOW OF OUR GRIEF?	127	BOWMEN OF SHU	24
AND I WILL COME OUT TO MEET YOU	131	RIVER-MER WIFE	28
AND THEY THINK IT WILL LAST A THOUSAND AUTUMNS,	132	AT TEN-SHIN	26
WILL BE GOING GREENER AND GREENER,	137	OF DEPARTURE	EPI
FOR YOU WILL HAVE NO FRIENDS ABOUT YOU	137	OF DEPARTURE	EPI
WHO WILL BE SORRY FOR GENERAL RISHOGU,	139	SOUTH-FOLK	12

WILL (CONTINUED)

	PAGE	TITLE	LINE
IT WILL PAY THEM WHEN THE WORMS ARE WRIGGLING IN THEIR VITALS;	145	SALUTATION 3RD	4
OR PERHAPS I WILL DIE AT THIRTY?	145	SALUTATION 3RD	17
PERHAPS YOU WILL HAVE THE PLEASURE OF DEFILING MY PAUPER'S GRAVE;	145	SALUTATION 3RD	18
BUT I WILL NOT GO MAD TO PLEASE YOU,	145	SALUTATION 3RD	25
I WILL NOT FLATTER YOU WITH AN EARLY DEATH,	145	SALUTATION 3RD	26
OH, NO, I WILL STICK IT OUT,	145	SALUTATION 3RD	27
IN A FEW YEARS NO ONE WILL REMEMBER THE BUFFO,	146	MONUMENTUM AER	3
NO ONE WILL REMEMBER THE TRIVIAL PARTS OF ME,	146	MONUMENTUM AER	4
THE COMIC DETAIL WILL BE ABSENT.	146	MONUMENTUM AER	5
AS FOR YOU, YOU WILL ROT IN THE EARTH,	146	MONUMENTUM AER	6
AND IT IS DOUBTFUL IF EVEN YOUR MANURE WILL BE RICH ENOUGH	146	MONUMENTUM AER	7
"IN THE FULL FLARE OF GRIEF. DO WHAT YOU WILL."	152	NEAR PERIGORD	46
TAKE HIS OWN SPEECH, MAKE WHAT YOU WILL OF IT--	153	NEAR PERIGORD	79
AND TEN YEARS AFTER, OR TWENTY, AS YOU WILL,	155	NEAR PERIGORD	127
DISPRAISES HIS OWN SKILL?--THAT'S AS YOU WILL.	155	NEAR PERIGORD	143
'WHY DO YOU LOVE ME? WILL YOU ALWAYS LOVE ME?	157	NEAR PERIGORD	181
SHE WILL NOT BATHE TOO OFTEN, BUT HER JEWELS	161	CABARET DANCER	13
WILL BE A STUFFY, OPULENT SORT OF FUNGUS	161	CABARET DANCER	14
SHE WILL BE DRUNK IN THE DITCH, BUT YOU, PEPITA,	162	CABARET DANCER	47
WILL BE QUITE RICH, QUITE PLUMP, WITH PUG-BITCH FEATURES,	162	CABARET DANCER	48
WILL DINE NEXT WEEK WITH MRS. BASIL,	163	CABARET DANCER	63
WILL MEET A DUCHESS AND AN EX-DIPLOMAT'S WIDOW	163	CABARET DANCER	64
EUHENIA WILL HAVE A FONDA IN ORBAJOSA.	163	CABARET DANCER	67
THE AMOROUS NERVES WILL GIVE WAY TO DIGESTIVE;	163	CABARET DANCER	68
THEODORUS WILL BE PLEASED AT MY DEATH,	164	QUINTUS SEPTIM	1
AND SOMEONE ELSE WILL BE PLEASED AT THE DEATH OF THEODORUS,	164	QUINTUS SEPTIM	2
WILL YOU GIVE ME DAWN LIGHT AT EVENING?	167	OF AROUET	17
TO HOLD EMBRACED, AND WILL NOT HER FORSAKE	172	LANGUE D'OC: 1	28
A MAN GO WHERE HE WILL.	173	LANGUE D'OC: 2	5
FOR LOVE WILL GIVE	174	LANGUE D'OC: 3	22
OUT OF MY LOVE WILL HER HEART NOT STIR.	177	LANGUE D'OC: 4	28
HER SECOND HUSBAND WILL NOT DIVORCE HER;	179	MOEURS CON: 2	5
SHE WILL NEITHER STAY IN, NOR COME OUT.	179	MOEURS CON: 2	11
THEY WILL COME NO MORE,	181	MOEURS CON: 7	1
OUT-WEARIERS OF APOLLO WILL, AS WE KNOW, CONTINUE THEIR MARTIAN GENERALITIES,	207	SEXTUS PROP: 1	10
ANNALISTS WILL CONTINUE TO RECORD ROMAN REPUTATIONS,	207	SEXTUS PROP: 1	16
CELEBRITIES FROM THE TRANS-CAUCASUS WILL BELAUD ROMAN CELEBRITIES	207	SEXTUS PROP: 1	17
I ASK A WREATH WHICH WILL NOT CRUSH MY HEAD.	207	SEXTUS PROP: 1	21
AND IN THE MEAN TIME, MY SONGS WILL TRAVEL,	208	SEXTUS PROP: 1	39
AND THE DEVIRGINATED YOUNG LADIES WILL ENJOY THEM	208	SEXTUS PROP: 1	40
THERE WILL BE A CROWD OF YOUNG WOMEN DOING HOMAGE TO MY PALAVER,	208	SEXTUS PROP: 1	50
WILL KEEP THEIR COLLECTIVE NOSE IN MY BOOKS,	209	SEXTUS PROP: 1	61
AND WEARY WITH HISTORICAL DATA, THEY WILL TURN TO MY DANCE TUNE.	209	SEXTUS PROP: 1	62
"YOUR PAMPHLETS WILL BE THROWN, THROWN OFTEN INTO A CHAIR	210	SEXTUS PROP: 2	22
"NO KEEL WILL SINK WITH YOUR GENIUS	210	SEXTUS PROP: 2	25
"NOR WILL THE NOISE OF HIGH HORSES LEAD YOU EVER TO BATTLE;	211	SEXTUS PROP: 2	41
"NOR WILL THE PUBLIC CRIERS EVER HAVE YOUR NAME	211	SEXTUS PROP: 2	42
AND IT WILL LAST A TWELVE MONTH,	212	SEXTUS PROP: 3	13
THE MOON WILL CARRY HIS CANDLE,	212	SEXTUS PROP: 3	20
THE STARS WILL POINT OUT THE STUMBLES,	212	SEXTUS PROP: 3	21
CUPID WILL CARRY LIGHTED TORCHES BEFORE HIM	212	SEXTUS PROP: 3	22
FOR WHICH THINGS YOU WILL GET A REWARD FROM ME, LYGDAMUS?	215	SEXTUS PROP: 4	27
"WILL HE SAY NASTY THINGS AT MY FUNERAL?"	215	SEXTUS PROP: 4	40
THE MERE WILL TO ACT IS SUFFICIENT "	216	SEXTUS PROP: 5	8
AND I ALSO WILL SING WAR WHEN THIS MATTER OF A GIRL IS EXHAUSTED.	216	SEXTUS PROP: 5	9
AND WILL NOT PRAISE HOMER,	218	SEXTUS PROP: 5	62

WILL -- WILL'S

	PAGE	TITLE	LINE
WILL (CONTINUED)			
NOR AT MY FUNERAL EITHER WILL THERE BY ANY LONG TRAIL,	219	SEXTUS PROP: 6	13
THERE WILL BE THREE BOOKS AT MY OBSEQUIES	219	SEXTUS PROP: 6	20
YOU WILL FOLLOW THE BARE SCARIFIED BREAST	219	SEXTUS PROP: 6	22
NOR WILL YOU BE WEARY OF CALLING MY NAME, NOR TOO WEARY	219	SEXTUS PROP: 6	23
YOU, SOMETIMES, WILL LAMENT A LOST FRIEND,	219	SEXTUS PROP: 6	30
OR AN ORNAMENTAL DEATH WILL BE HELD TO YOUR DEBIT,	221	SEXTUS PROP: 8	2
HERS WILL I BE DEAD,	221	SEXTUS PROP: 7	36
YOU WILL SAY THAT YOU SUCCUMBED TO A DANGER IDENTICAL,	222	SEXTUS PROP: 8	30
AND BELIEVE IT, AND SHE ALSO WILL BELIEVE IT,	222	SEXTUS PROP: 8	32
OR PERHAPS JUNO HERSELF WILL GO UNDER,	222	SEXTUS PROP: 8	40
THERE WILL BE, IN ANY CASE, A STIR ON OLYMPUS.	222	SEXTUS PROP: 8	42
OR SHE WILL SIT BEFORE YOUR FEET IN A VEIL,	223	SEXTUS PROP: 9	11
YOU WILL OBSERVE THAT PURE FORM HAS, ITS VALUE.	225	SEXTUS PROP:10	33
DESIRE WILL FOLLOW YOU THITHER,	226	SEXTUS PROP:11	6
WHO, WILL BE THE NEXT MAN TO ENTRUST HIS GIRL TO A FRIEND?	227	SEXTUS PROP:12	1
AND YOU WILL NOT LEAVE OFF IMITATING AESCHYLUS.	228	SEXTUS PROP:12	20
HE WILL UNDOUBTEDLY CHAIN SOMEONE ELSE TO THIS FOUNTAIN,	238	ABU SALAMMAMM	31
AND MY GLORY WILL	238	ABU SALAMMAMM	32
RADWAY? MY HERO, FOR IT WILL BE MORE INSPIRING	239	MOYEN SENSUEL	41
(VIDE THE TARIFF), I WILL HANG SIMPLE FACTS	241	MOYEN SENSUEL	71
THAT ONLY SENTIMENTAL STUFF WILL SELL!)	242	MOYEN SENSUEL	118
STILL WE WILL BRING OUR "FICTION AS NEAR TO FACT" AS THOUGH IT WILL, OF COURSE, PASS OFF WITH SOCIAL SCIENCE	243	MOYEN SENSUEL	139
	244	MOYEN SENSUEL	163
DE GOURMONT SAYS THAT FIFTY GRUNTS ARE ALL THAT WILL BE PRIZED.	244	MOYEN SENSUEL	165
WILL LONG ONLY TO BE A SOCIAL FUNCTION,	244	MOYEN SENSUEL	176
SOME MEN WILL LIVE AS PRUDES IN THEIR OWN VILLAGE	245	MOYEN SENSUEL	207
"NOTHING WILL PAY THEE, FRIEND, LIKE CHRISTIANITY."	246	MOYEN SENSUEL	236
CRYING: MY GOD, MY GOD, WHAT WILL SHE SAY?!	247	PIERROTS	6
I HAVE NO WILL TO PROVE LOVE'S COURSE	248	DONNA MI PREGA	11
HIS MODUS TAKES FROM SOUL, FROM HEART HIS WILL;	249	DONNA MI PREGA	23
WHEN WILL THIS SYSTEM LIE DOWN IN ITS GRAVE?	260	ALF'S FIFTH	4
WILL GIVE, SAVE TO THE BLIND.	263	ALF'S EIGHTH	7
WILL CHEERFULLY TELL YOU A FIST IS NO FIST,	263	ALF'S EIGHTH	10
NEVER AT ALL WILL THEY DO	265	ALF'S TENTH	3
ONE THING AMONG ALL THINGS YOU WILL NOT	265	ALF'S TENTH	11
ELECTION WILL NOT COME VERY SOON,	265	ALF'S TENTH	13
WILL KEEP IT A LITTLE LONGER,	266	ALF'S TENTH	15
AND IT WILL SURELY BOIL THE POT,	267	ALF'S TWELFTH	14
WILL BE THE DEATH OF ME."	271	OLE KATE	6
WILLIE			
VEX IT NOT, WILLIE, HIS MIND,	263	ALF'S EIGHTH	3
WILLINGNESS-TO-OBLIGE			
ENDS WITH A WILLINGNESS-TO-OBLIGE.	99	EPITAPH	2
WILLOW			
WITH THE WILLOW FLAKES FALLING LIKE SNOW,	136	EXILE'S LETTER	54
WILLOW-COLOURED			
I LOOKED AT THE DRAGON-POND, WITH ITS WILLOW-COLOURED WATER	129	THE RIVER SONG	20
WILLOWS			
WHEN WE SET OUT, THE WILLOWS WERE DROOPING WITH SPRING,	127	BOWMEN OF SHU	21
AND THE WILLOWS HAVE OVERFILLED THE CLOSE GARDEN.	128	BEAU TOILET	2
AND HIGH OVER THE WILLOWS, THE FINE BIRDS SING TO EACH OTHER, AND LISTEN,	129	THE RIVER SONG	28
THE WILLOWS OF THE INN-YARD	137	OF DEPARTURE	EPI
WILLOW-TIPS			
SOUTH OF THE POND THE WILLOW-TIPS ARE HALF-BLUE AND BLUER,	129	THE RIVER SONG	25
WILLS			
AND WILLS MAN LOOK INTO UNFORMED SPACE	250	DONNA MI PREGA	59
WILL'S			
HE COMES TO BE AND IS WHEN WILL'S SO GREAT	249	DONNA MI PREGA	49

```
                                                    PAGE       TITLE         LINE
WILT
     THOU WILT IN MY WHITE ARMS THERE, ..............  47    FROM HEINE: 7    9
     AND NOW THOU'LT NONE OF ME, AND WILT HAVE NONE ..  172   LANGUE D'OC: 1  24
WIN
     SUCH GLORY OF THE EARTH? OR WHO WILL WIN .........  32   PIERE VIDAL     58
WIND
     NAUGHT BUT THE WIND THAT FLUTTERS IN THE LEAVES.    4    LA FRAISNE      19
     SOUND IN YOUR WIND PAST ALL SIGNS O' CORRUPTION.   13    MESMERISM       16
     THROUGH THE SKY, AND THE WIND THEREOF IS MY BODY.  18    DE AEGYPTO       2
     TRAILING ALONG THE WIND. ........................  18    DE AEGYPTO       6
     THROUGH THE SKY, AND THE WIND THEREOF IS MY BODY.  18    DE AEGYPTO       8
     THROUGH THE SKY, AND THE WIND THEREOF IS MY BODY.  18    DE AEGYPTO      16
     THROUGH THE SKY, AND THE WIND THEREOF IS MY BODY.  18    DE AEGYPTO      24
     FOR THAT I LOVE YE AS THE WIND THE TREES .........  21   IN DURANCE      44
     AS NE'ER HAD I OTHER, AND WHEN THE WIND BLOWS, ...  23   MARVOIL         35
     WHEN THE WIND BLOWS SIGH THOU FOR MY SORROW .....   23   MARVOIL         41
     AND THOUGH THOU SIGHEST MY SORROW IN THE WIND, ..   23   MARVOIL         46
     MY WAVE-WORN BEAUTY WITH HIS WIND OF FLOWERS, ...   24   THUS NINEVEH    15
     AND THE WHITE WIND BREAKS THE MORN. .............   25   THE WHITE STAG   5
     A MATE OF THE WIND AND SEA, .....................   34   GOODLY FERE     50
     AND WOULD FEEL THE FINGERS OF THE WIND ..........   35   THE EYES         2
     ALL NIGHT, AND AS THE WIND LIETH AMONG ..........   39   FOR PSYCHE       1
     O WINDS, WHAT WIND CAN MATCH THE WEIGHT OF HIM! .   39   FOR PSYCHE      10
     FADES WHEN THE WIND HATH LIFTED THEM ASIDE, .....   40   ERAT HORA        3
     WHAT IF THE WIND HAVE TURNED AGAINST THE RAIN? ..   59   SILET           10
     YOU ARE VIOLETS WITH WIND ABOVE THEM. ...........   62   A GIRL           8
     OF THE BLEAK WIND, AND NOT ......................   67   DORIA            2
     GONE AS WIND! THE CLOTH OF THE MAGICAL HANDS! ...   68   APPARUIT        22
     SOFT AS SPRING WIND THAT'S COME FROM BIRCHEN BOWERS. 71  A VIRGINAL      10
     AND MURMUR IN THE WIND, .........................   74   THE RETURN       8
     STEPPING BENEATH A BOISTEROUS WIND FROM THRACE, .   87   THE SPRING       3
     THE WIND MOVES ABOVE THE WHEAT-- ................   95   OF THE DEGREES   3
     AND HOW THE WIND DOTH RAMM! .....................  116   ANCIENT MUSIC    4
     THE WIND CAME, AND THE RAIN, ....................  119   THE GYPSY        7
     THE EASTERN WIND BRINGS THE GREEN COLOUR INTO THE
         ISLAND GRASSES AT YEI-SHU, ..................  129   THE RIVER SONG  23
     CRYING--"KWAN, KUAN," FOR THE EARLY WIND, AND THE
         FEEL OF IT. .................................  129   THE RIVER SONG  29
     THE WIND BUNDLES ITSELF INTO A BLUISH CLOUD AND
         WANDERS OFF. ................................  129   THE RIVER SONG  30
     THE LEAVES FALL EARLY THIS AUTUMN, IN WIND. .....  131   RIVER-MER WIFE   2
     BY THE NORTH GATE, THE WIND BLOWS FULL OF SAND, .  133   FRONTIER GUARD
     IN THE CUTTING WIND FROM THE NORTH, .............  135   EXILE'S LETTER   4
     AND THE WIND LIFTING THE SONG, AND INTERRUPTING IT, 136  EXILE'S LETTER   6
     THE DAI HORSE NEIGHS AGAINST THE BLEAK WIND OF ETSU, 139 SOUTH-FOLK       1
     HOT SUN, CLEAR WATER, FRESH WIND, ...............  146   CANTILATIONS     3
     I HAVE WRAPPED THE WIND ROUND YOUR SHOULDERS ....  170   PHANOPOEIA       8
     BENDS INTO THE TURN OF THE WIND, ................  170   PHANOPOEIA      20
     "OUT OF THE WIND THAT BLOWS FROM HER, ...........  177   LANGUE D'OC: 4  21
     WIND AND WAVE SCATTERED AWAY. ...................  221   SEXTUS PROP: 8   9
     OLD LECHER, LET NOT JUNO GET WIND OF THE MATTER, . 222   SEXTUS PROP: 8  39
     WIND ............................................  265   ALF'S TENTH    SUB
WINDING
     AND THREE VALLEYS, FULL OF WINDING ROADS, .......  121   PROVINC DESERT   4
     WHITE RIVER WINDING ABOUT THEM; .................  137   TAKING LEAVE     2
WINDOW
     I DRINK BY MY EASTERN WINDOW. ...................  142   UNMOVING CLOUD  14
     AND NOW I WATCH, FROM THE WINDOW, ...............  158   PSYCHOLOG HOU   10
WINDOWS
     AND BURST FORTH TO THE WINDOWS ONLY WHILES OR WHILES 21  IN DURANCE      31
     HIS PALACE HAS NINETY-EIGHT WINDOWS, ............  237   ABU SALAMMAMM    6
WIND-RUNEING
     ONCE FOR WIND-RUNEING ...........................    6   CINO            14
WINDS
     NO MORE THE WINDS AT TWILIGHT TROUBLE US. .......    3   THRENOS          2
     I LIKE ONE LITTLE BAND OF WINDS THAT BLOW .......    5   LA FRAISNE      49
     DRINK OF THE WINDS THEIR CHILL SMALL-BEER .......   10   FOR THIS YULE    4
     THAT MAKE THE STARK WINDS REEK WITH FEAR ........   10   FOR THIS YULE   12
     BUT YE ASK FIRST WHERE THE WINDS ARE GONE .......   10   FOR THIS YULE   27
     WHOSE FRAMES HAVE THE NIGHT AND ITS WINDS IN FEE.   12   OF THE GIBBET   28
     BUT HIS ANSWER COMETH, AS WINDS AND AS LUTANY, ..   16   PRAISE YSOLT     5
```

WINDS -- WIRE

	PAGE	TITLE	LINE
WINDS (CONTINUED)			
THE WINDS ARE UNDER MY LIPS.	18	DE AEGYPTO	20
GONE WHERE THE GREY WINDS CALL TO YOU,	19	FOR E. MCC	2
AND THE WINDS SHRIEK THROUGH THE CLOUDS MAD,			
OPPOSING,	28	ALTAFORTE	11
WITH THE WINDS UNLEASHED AND FREE,	34	GOODLY FERE	46
O WINDS, WHAT WIND CAN MATCH THE WEIGHT OF HIM!	39	FOR PSYCHE	10
SAILOR, OF WINDS; A PLOWMAN, CONCERNING HIS OXEN;	218	SEXTUS PROP: 5	55
WIND'S			
LIPS SHRUNK BACK FOR THE WIND'S CARESS	11	OF THE GIBBET	19
WINE			
NO MORE FOR US THE WINE OF THE LIPS,	3	THRENOS	12
AS LESSER MEN DRINK WINE."	24	THUS NINEVEH	23
WITH FAT BOARDS, BAWDS, WINE AND FRAIL MUSIC!	28	ALTAFORTE	17
BAH! THERE'S NO WINE LIKE THE BLOOD'S CRIMSON!	28	ALTAFORTE	18
OH WE DRUNK HIS "HALE" IN THE GOOD RED WINE	33	GOODLY FERE	13
WITH RHINE WINE AND LIQUEURS.	46	FROM HEINE: 6	4
LEST THOU SHOULDST WAKE AND WHIMPER FOR THY WINE.	60	TOMB AKR CAAR	13
FILL FULL THE SIDES IN ROWS, AND OUR WINE	128	THE RIVER SONG	3
BUT YOU, SIR, HAD BETTER TAKE WINE ERE YOUR			
DEPARTURE,	137	OF DEPARTURE	EPI
I PAT MY NEW CASK OF WINE.	142	UNMOVING CLOUD	7
"WINE, WINE, HERE IS WINE!"	142	UNMOVING CLOUD	13
"WINE, WINE, HERE IS WINE!"	142	UNMOVING CLOUD	13
"WINE, WINE, HERE IS WINE!"	142	UNMOVING CLOUD	13
NOR BRISTLE WITH WINE JARS,	209	SEXTUS PROP: 1	58
HE FEEDS ME WITH BEEF-BONES AND WINE.	237	ABU SALAMMAMM	3
O STATE SANS SONG, SANS HOME-GROWN WINE, SANS			
REALIST!	241	MOYEN SENSUEL	88
WINE-FLUSHED			
WEALTHY AND WINE-FLUSHED, HOW I WEARY OFT	64	THE SEAFARER	30
WING			
TALK OF THE LATEST SUCCESS, GIVE WING TO SOME			
SCANDAL,	52	AU SALON	12
BIRDS WITH FLOWERY WING, HOVERING BUTTERFLIES	141	IDEA OF CHOAN	17
WING'D			
WORDS THAT WERE WING'D AS HER SPARKS IN ERUPTION,	13	MESMERISM	14
WING'D-WITH-AWE			
THESE WERE THE "WING'D-WITH-AWE,"	74	THE RETURN	10
WINGED			
GODS OF THE WINGED SHOE!	74	THE RETURN	12
DOUBLE TOWERS, WINGED ROOFS,	141	IDEA OF CHOAN	23
WING-FLAPPING			
HE GOES OUT TO HORI, TO LOOK AT THE WING-FLAPPING			
STORKS,	130	THE RIVER SONG	36
WINGS			
NO MORE FOR US THE FLUTTERING OF WINGS	3	THRENOS	5
HER HAIR WAS SPREAD ABOUT, A SHEAF OF WINGS,	49	OF SPLENDOUR	7
AND GREAT WINGS BEAT ABOVE US IN THE TWILIGHT,	157	NEAR PERIGORD	176
CUPID, ASTRIDE A PHALLUS WITH TWO WINGS,	162	CABARET DANCER	36
WINING			
WINING THE GHOSTS OF YESTER-YEAR.	10	FOR THIS YULE	8
WINING THE GHOSTS OF YESTER-YEAR.	10	FOR THIS YULE	16
WINING THE GHOSTS OF YESTER-YEAR.	10	FOR THIS YULE	24
WINING THE GHOSTS OF YESTER-YEAR.	10	FOR THIS YULE	28
WINNING			
SHOW US THERE'S CHANCE AT LEAST OF WINNING THROUGH.	235	TO WHISTLER	19
WINSOME			
THIS HE LITTLE BELIEVES, WHO AYE IN WINSOME LIFE	64	THE SEAFARER	28
WINSOMENESS			
NOR WINSOMENESS TO WIFE, NOR WORLD'S DELIGHT	65	THE SEAFARER	46
WINTER			
WEATHERED THE WINTER, WRETCHED OUTCAST	64	THE SEAFARER	15
WINTER IS ICUMMEN IN,	116	ANCIENT MUSIC	1
WINTER'S			
AS WINTER'S WOUND WITH HER SLEIGHT HAND SHE			
STAUNCHES,	71	A VIRGINAL	12
SO 'GAINST THE WINTER'S BALM.	116	ANCIENT MUSIC	11
WIRE			
BUT YOU NEVER STRING TWO DAYS UPON ONE WIRE	53	AU JARDIN	13

PAGE 476

WIRE-LIKE -- WITHOUT

	PAGE	TITLE	LINE
WIRE-LIKE			
THE WIRE-LIKE BANDS OF COLOUR INVOLUTE MOUNT FROM MY FINGERS;	170	PHANOPOEIA	17
WISDOM			
WE WHO ARE WISE BEYOND YOUR DREAM OF WISDOM,	50	THE FLAME	5
BEING SMITTEN WITH AN UNUSUAL WISDOM,	96	AESTHETICS	2
ANCIENT WISDOM, RATHER COSMIC	118	ANCIENT WISDOM	T
WISE			
BEING IN ALL THINGS WISE, AND VERY OLD,	4	LA FRAISNE	2
AND THE WISE CONCORD, WHENCE THROUGH DELICIOUS SEAS	42	HER MONUMENT	43
WE WHO ARE WISE BEYOND YOUR DREAM OF WISDOM,	50	THE FLAME	5
PLEASETH ME, AND IN LIKE WISE	52	AU SALON	EPI
WISH			
THOUGH THOU WELL DOST WISH ME ILL	8	NA AUDIART	1
YEA THOUGH THOU WISH ME ILL,	9	NA AUDIART	33
WISH ME ILL,	106	DOMPNA POIS	42
I WISH YOU JOY, I PROFFER YOU ALL MY ASSISTANCE.	145	SALUTATION 3RD	19
WAS GOT ABROAD, WHAT BETTER LUCK DO YOU WISH 'EM,	240	MOYEN SENSUEL	60
WISHING			
WISHING ME WELL;	147	BEFORE SLEEP	18
WISH-WASH			
"TELL ME NOT IN MOURNFUL WISH-WASH	241	MOYEN SENSUEL	89
WISTARIA			
WHERE THE GODS WALK GARLANDED IN WISTARIA,	108	CH'U YUAN	2
WISTFUL			
AYE, I AM WISTFUL FOR MY KIN OF THE SPIRIT	20	IN DURANCE	17
WIT			
THEN CAME WHAT MIGHT COME, TO WIT: THREE MEN AND ONE WOMAN,	22	MARVOIL	11
MY WIT, CHARM, DEFINITIONS,	46	FROM HEINE: 6	10
WIT, NOR GOOD SPIRITS, NOR THE PLEASING ATTITUDES	101	AMITIES	11
SUCH GRACE OF LOCKS, I DO YE TO WIT,	106	DOMPNA POIS	38
LET COME THE READY OF WIT,	146	CANTILATIONS	9
"MY WIT AND WORTH ARE COBWEBS BRUSHED ASIDE	152	NEAR PERIGORD	45
I LOSE ALL WIT AND SENSE.	176	LANGUE D'OC: 3	69
CAN BEAR HIS PART OF WIT	248	DONNA MI PREGA	8
WITH (375)			
WITHERED			
AND WITHERED ARE THE SEDGES;	72	PAN IS DEAD	5
WITHIN			
KINDLY ENTREATED, AND BEEN BROUGHT WITHIN	3	THE TREE	7
SHE THAT HOLDETH THE WONDER WORDS WITHIN HER EYES	17	PRAISE YSOLT	51
MAKE CLEAN OUR HEARTS WITHIN US,	27	NIGHT LITANY	37
BECOME SILENT WITHIN ME.	27	NIGHT LITANY	48
ROME'S NAME ALONE WITHIN THESE WALLS KEEPS HOME.	40	ROME	4
HOW IF THE LOW DEAR SOUND WITHIN THY THROAT	43	SATIEMUS	14
AND I HAVE SEEN HER THERE WITHIN HER HOUSE,	49	OF SPLENDOUR	9
SAYING WITHIN HIS HEART, "I AM NO USE TO MYSELF,	100	ARIDES	6
WITHIN HER NEST;	106	DOMPNA POIS	55
AND WITHIN, THE MISTRESS, IN THE MIDMOST OF HER YOUTH,	128	BEAU TOILET	3
LIE DEAD WITHIN FOUR WALLS	236	MIDDLE-AGED	15
LYING WITHIN PERFECTION POSTULATE	249	DONNA MI PREGA	34
WITHOUT			
REST BROTHER, FOR LO! THE DAWN IS WITHOUT!	35	THE EYES	5
FREE US, FOR WITHOUT BE GOODLY COLOURS,	35	THE EYES	8
HERE THEY STAND WITHOUT QUAINT DEVICES,	85	SALUTATION 2ND	7
WITHOUT BLEMISH, FOR HER LOVE	106	DOMPNA POIS	43
SPUR WITHOUT REASON,	111	IMAGE ORLEANS	3
TWO SMALL PEOPLE, WITHOUT DISLIKE OR SUSPICION.	130	RIVER-MER WIFE	6
AND WE ALL SPOKE OUT OUR HEARTS AND MINDS, AND WITHOUT REGRET.	134	EXILE'S LETTER	11
PLEASURE LASTING, WITH COURTEZANS, GOING AND COMING WITHOUT HINDRANCE,	136	EXILE'S LETTER	53
ALL OF HIS FLANK--HOW COULD HE DO WITHOUT HER?	153	NEAR PERIGORD	66
WHAT WOULD HE DO WITHOUT HER?	153	NEAR PERIGORD	68
THE PRUDENT WHORE IS NOT WITHOUT HER FUTURE,	163	CABARET DANCER	75
WITHOUT FOOTMEN AND EQUIPMENTS?	167	OF ANGELS	
ALTHOUGH CALLIMACHUS DID WITHOUT THEM,	218	SEXTUS PROP: 5	49
AND WITHOUT THEODAS,	218	SEXTUS PROP: 5	50

PAGE 477

WITHOUT -- WOMAN

	PAGE	TITLE	LINE
WITHOUT (CONTINUED)			
WITHOUT AN INFERNO, WITHOUT ACHILLES ATTENDED OF GODS,	218	SEXTUS PROP: 5	51
WITHOUT AN INFERNO, WITHOUT ACHILLES ATTENDED OF GODS,	218	SEXTUS PROP: 5	51
WITHOUT IXION, AND WITHOUT THE SONS OF MENOETIUS AND THE ARGO AND WITHOUT JOVE'S GRAVE AND THE TITANS.	218	SEXTUS PROP: 5	52
WITHOUT IXION, AND WITHOUT THE SONS OF MENOETIUS AND THE ARGO AND WITHOUT JOVE'S GRAVE AND THE TITANS.	218	SEXTUS PROP: 5	52
WITHOUT IXION, AND WITHOUT THE SONS OF MENOETIUS AND THE ARGO AND WITHOUT JOVE'S GRAVE AND THE TITANS.	218	SEXTUS PROP: 5	52
I CAN WALK ABOUT WITHOUT FIDGETING WHEN PEOPLE PASS,	247	PIERROTS	20
WITHOUT SMIRKING INTO A POCKET-LOOKING-GLASS.	247	PIERROTS	21
WITHSTAYED			
BE HE WITHSTAYED	249	DONNA MI PREGA	40
WITHSTAYING			
OR OF ACHILLES WITHSTAYING WATERS BY SIMOIS	208	SEXTUS PROP: 1	28
WITLESS			
PAY FOR HIS WITLESS NOISE,	261	ALF'S SIXTH	4
WITNESS			
"PHOEBUS OUR WITNESS, YOUR HANDS ARE UNSPOTTED."	226	SEXTUS PROP:11	24
WIT'S			
WHO, SINCE THEIR WIT'S UNKNOWN, ESCAPE THE GALLOWS.	238	MOYEN SENSUEL	4
WIVES			
TOGETHER WITH THE RESPECTIVE WIVES, HUSBANDS, SISTERS AND HETEROGENEOUS CONNECTIONS OF THE GOOD BELLAIRES,	97	THE BELLAIRES	6
WOE			
IF ALL THE GRIEF AND WOE AND BITTERNESS,	36	THE YOUNG KING	1
O WOE, WOE,	43	MR. HOUSMAN	1
O WOE, WOE,	43	MR. HOUSMAN	1
WOE! WOE, ETCETERA.	43	MR. HOUSMAN	10
WOE! WOE, ETCETERA.	43	MR. HOUSMAN	10
OH, WOE, WOE, WOE, ETCETERA.	44	MR. HOUSMAN	15
OH, WOE, WOE, WOE, ETCETERA.	44	MR. HOUSMAN	15
OH, WOE, WOE, WOE, ETCETERA.	44	MR. HOUSMAN	15
WOEFUL			
WOEFUL IS THIS HUMAN LOT.	43	MR. HOUSMAN	9
LONDON IS A WOEFUL PLACE,	44	MR. HOUSMAN	11
WOKE			
JUST THEN SHE WOKE AND MOCKED THE LESS KEEN BLADE.	31	PIERE VIDAL	43
WOLD			
THAT GREW ELM-OAK AMID THE WOLD.	3	THE TREE	5
WOLF			
SWIFT AS THE KING WOLF WAS I AND AS STRONG	30	PIERE VIDAL	8
TRY PHOTOGRAPHS, WOLF DOWN THEIR ALE AND CAKES	236	MIDDLE-AGED	6
TO KEEP THE WOLF AWAY	269	SAFE AND SOUND	20
WOLVES			
THEN WHEN THE GREY WOLVES EVERYCHONE	10	FOR THIS YULE	3
WOMAN			
ONCE THERE WAS A WOMAN	5	LA FRAISNE	42
FOR IN THE MORN OF MY YEARS THERE CAME A WOMAN	16	PRAISE YSOLT	27
BUT MY SOUL SENT A WOMAN, A WOMAN OF THE WONDER-FOLK,	17	PRAISE YSOLT	38
BUT MY SOUL SENT A WOMAN, A WOMAN OF THE WONDER-FOLK,	17	PRAISE YSOLT	38
A WOMAN AS FIRE UPON THE PINE WOODS	17	PRAISE YSOLT	39
TILL MY SOUL SENT A WOMAN AS THE SUN:	17	PRAISE YSOLT	47
THEN CAME WHAT MIGHT COME, TO WIT: THREE MEN AND ONE WOMAN,	22	MARVOIL	11
GO TO THE WOMAN ENTAILED.	88	COMMISSION	15
O WOMAN OF MY DREAMS,	91	DANCE FIGURE	2
WHY DOES THE REALLY HANDSOME YOUNG WOMAN APPROACH ME IN SACKVILLE STREET	114	SIMULACRA	5
UPON THE MUTABILITY OF WOMAN,	118	THREE POETS	6
AND AN OLD WOMAN,	121	PROVINC DESERT	25
HE SANG A WOMAN.	122	PROVINC DESERT	68
AND A BROWN, PLACID, HATED WOMAN VISITING HER,	154	NEAR PERIGORD	112
WOMAN? OH, WOMAN IS A CONSUMMATE RAGE,	165	QUINTUS SEPTIM	20
WOMAN? OH, WOMAN IS A CONSUMMATE RAGE,	165	QUINTUS SEPTIM	20
FOR I WOULD NOT LOOK ON A WOMAN.	175	LANGUE D'OC: 3	43
AND THE OTHER WOMAN "HAS NOT ENTICED ME	215	SEXTUS PROP: 4	29
JOVE, BE MERCIFUL TO THAT UNFORTUNATE WOMAN	221	SEXTUS PROP: 8	1

WOMAN -- WOOD

	PAGE	TITLE	LINE
WOMAN (CONTINUED)			
GREAT ZEUS, SAVE THE WOMAN,	223	SEXTUS PROP: 9	10
AND THERE WAS A CASE IN COLCHIS, JASON AND THAT WOMAN IN COLCHIS;	228	SEXTUS PROP:12	7
LIKE A WOMAN HEAVY WITH CHILD.	237	ABU SALAMMAMM	25
"I HATE A DUMPY WOMAN"	238	MOYEN SENSUEL	EPI
AND THEN THAT WOMAN LIKE A GUINEA-PIG	242	MOYEN SENSUEL	120
WOMANISH			
BUT IS FIT ONLY TO ROT IN WOMANISH PEACE	29	ALTAFORTE	27
WOMEN			
THAT IS SWEETER THAN THE LOVE OF WOMEN	5	LA FRAISNE	35
BAH! I HAVE SUNG WOMEN IN THREE CITIES,	6	CINO	1
I HAVE SUNG WOMEN IN THREE CITIES.	7	CINO	37
I HAVE SUNG WOMEN IN THREE CITIES	7	CINO	52
SUCH AN ONE AS WOMEN DRAW AWAY FROM	15	FAMAM CANO	33
GOD CURSE THE YEARS THAT TURN SUCH WOMEN GREY!	31	PIERE VIDAL	46
OH, I KNOW YOU WOMEN FROM THE "OTHER FOLK,"	53	AU JARDIN	20
WE WERE NOT EXASPERATED WITH WOMEN,	82	THE CONDOLENCE	11
GO TO THE WOMEN IN SUBURBS.	88	COMMISSION	10
THAT FAILED NEVER WOMEN,	90	SURGIT FAMA	6
AMONG THE WOMEN WITH PITCHERS.	91	DANCE FIGURE	9
AND THEY TALK OF SWINBURNE'S WOMEN,	112	SHOP GIRL	3
"IT RESTS ME TO BE AMONG BEAUTIFUL WOMEN.	113	TAME CAT	1
IT RESTS ME TO CONVERSE WITH BEAUTIFUL WOMEN	113	TAME CAT	4
WOMEN BEFORE A SHOP	114	BEFORE A SHOP	T
OLD PENSIONERS AND OLD PROTECTED WOMEN	121	PROVINC DESERT	11
NIGHT BIRDS, AND NIGHT WOMEN,	141	IDEA OF CHOAN	15
AND THE TALL WOMEN WALKING YOUR STREETS, IN GILT CLOTHES,	165	QUINTUS SEPTIM	14
HE HURLED HIMSELF INTO A SEA OF SIX WOMEN.	181	MOEURS CON: 6	2
THERE WILL BE A CROWD OF YOUNG WOMEN DOING HOMAGE TO MY PALAVER,	208	SEXTUS PROP: 1	50
AND SHE SPEAKS ILL OF LIGHT WOMEN,	218	SEXTUS PROP: 5	61
THERE ARE ENOUGH WOMEN IN HELL,	223	SEXTUS PROP: 9	14
QUITE ENOUGH BEAUTIFUL WOMEN,	223	SEXTUS PROP: 9	15
"ALL LOVELY WOMEN HAVE KNOWN THIS,"	226	SEXTUS PROP:11	22
OF ALL THESE YOUNG WOMEN	228	SEXTUS PROP:12	24
HE PROVIDES ME WITH WOMEN AND DRINKS.	237	ABU SALAMMAMM	17
ONE OF THOSE FIRM-FACED INSPECTING WOMEN, WHO	243	MOYEN SENSUEL	156
WON			
WHERE ARE THE JOYS MY HEART HAD WON?	10	FOR THIS YULE	17
FAR FROM WHERE WORTH'S WON AND THE SWORDS CLASH	29	ALTAFORTE	28
SHAMED AND YET BOWED NOT AND THAT WON AT LAST.	31	PIERE VIDAL	48
NO MAN HATH DARED AND WON HIS DARE AS I:	32	PIERE VIDAL	55
WILL WE NOT RATHER, WHEN OUR FREEDOM'S WON,	39	BLANDULA	2
HE WON THE LADY,	123	PROVINC DESERT	74
WONDER			
THAT THEY MIGHT DO THIS WONDER THING,	3	THE TREE	9
SHE THAT HOLDETH THE WONDER WORDS WITHIN HER EYES	17	PRAISE YSOLT	51
THAT THOU GIVEST THIS WONDER UNTO US,	26	NIGHT LITANY	12
FOUGHT OUT THEIR STRIFE HERE, 'TIS A PLACE OF WONDER;	51	THE ALTAR	3
CAUGHT AT THE WONDER.	68	APPARUIT	4
YOU WERE A SEVEN DAYS' WONDER.	114	EPILOGUE	2
YOU'LL WONDER THAT AN OLD MAN OF EIGHTY	168	OF AROUET	35
AND WONDER IF MY DAY'S THREE AND EIGHT-PENCE	268	ANOTHER BIT	11
WONDER-FOLK			
BUT MY SOUL SENT A WOMAN, A WOMAN OF THE WONDER-FOLK,	17	PRAISE YSOLT	38
WONDERFUL			
THE TARNISHED, GAUDY, WONDERFUL OLD WORK;	61	PORTRAIT FEMME	22
WONDERS			
THE RED-PINE-TREE GOD LOOKS AT HIM AND WONDERS.	139	SENNIN POEM	11
WON'T			
AND WHAT WITH BROKEN WHEELS AND SO ON, I WON'T SAY IT WASN'T HARD GOING,	135	EXILE'S LETTER	40
IF SHE WON'T HAVE ME NOW, DEATH IS MY PORTION,	175	LANGUE D'OC: 3	37
NO! THEY WON'T HIRE HIM.	261	ALF'S SIXTH	17
WONTED			
O PALMS OF LOVE, THAT IN YOUR WONTED WAYS	41	HER MONUMENT	15
WOOD			
I STOOD STILL AND WAS A TREE AMID THE WOOD,	3	THE TREE	1
NATHLESS I HAVE BEEN A TREE AMID THE WOOD	3	THE TREE	10

WOOD -- WORDS

	PAGE	TITLE	LINE
WOOD (CONTINUED)			
I HAVE CURLED 'MID THE BOLES OF THE ASH WOOD,	4	LA FRAISNE	9
IS A POOL OF THE WOOD, AND	5	LA FRAISNE	31
AND EVERY RUN-AWAY OF THE WOOD THROUGH THAT GREAT MADNESS,	31	PIERE VIDAL	51
IT WAS YOU THAT BROKE THE NEW WOOD,	89	A PACT	6
I WILL GET ME TO THE WOOD	108	CH'U YUAN	1
THE COACHES ARE PERFUMED WOOD,	141	IDEA OF CHOAN	4
AND I: "THAT WOOD?	166	FISH & SHADOW	11
"NOR MARS SHOUT YOU IN THE WOOD AT AEONIUM,	211	SEXTUS PROP: 2	44
WOODBERRY			
MABIE, AND LYMAN ABBOT AND GEORGE WOODBERRY,	239	MOYEN SENSUEL	28
WOODEN			
WERE PACKING THEM IN THE GREAT WOODEN BOXES	96	AESTHETICS	11
WOOD-MOSS			
GREEN OF THE WOOD-MOSS AND FLOWER COLOURS,	35	THE EYES	9
WOOD-PULP			
WITH A LIVELY WOOD-PULP "AD."	268	ALF'S TWELFTH	19
WOODS			
A WOMAN AS FIRE UPON THE PINE WOODS	17	PRAISE YSOLT	39
STRANGE WOODS HALF SODDEN, AND NEW BRIGHTER STUFF:	61	PORTRAIT FEMME	26
OF 25 PER CENT. ON THEIR ADS., AND THE WOODS	262	ALF'S SEVENTH	12
WOODY			
MAY A WOODY AND SEQUESTERED PLACE COVER ME WITH ITS FOLIAGE	213	SEXTUS PROP: 3	35
WOOL			
MUST THINK TRUTH LOOKS AS THEY DO IN WOOL PYJAMAS.	243	MOYEN SENSUEL	148
WOOLLY			
DAMP WOOLLY HANDKERCHIEFS WERE STUFFED INTO HER UNDRYABLE EYES,	214	SEXTUS PROP: 4	25
WORD			
VAGUELY THUS WORD THEY:	6	CINO	24
HERE A WORD KISS!	8	NA AUDIART	11
JUST A WORD IN THY PRAISE, GIRL,	8	NA AUDIART	20
TO WRITE THE ACCEPTABLE WORD. . . .	18	DE AEGYPTO	11
WHAT IF I KNOW THY SPEECHES WORD BY WORD?	43	SATIEMUS	1
WHAT IF I KNOW THY SPEECHES WORD BY WORD?	43	SATIEMUS	1
WHAT IF I KNOW THY SPEECHES WORD BY WORD,	43	SATIEMUS	3
WHAT IF I KNOW THY SPEECHES WORD BY WORD,	43	SATIEMUS	3
WHAT IF I KNOW THY LAUGHTER WORD BY WORD	43	SATIEMUS	18
WHAT IF I KNOW THY LAUGHTER WORD BY WORD	43	SATIEMUS	18
NO WORD, DAY AFTER DAY.	60	TOMB AKR CAAR	28
LAUD OF THE LIVING, BOASTETH SOME LAST WORD,	66	THE SEAFARER	74
AND THE WHORES DROPPING IN FOR A WORD OR TWO IN PASSING,	117	THE LAKE ISLE	10
FOR A FLIP WORD, AND TO TIDY THEIR HAIR A BIT.	117	THE LAKE ISLE	11
MALEMORT, GUESSES BENEATH, SENDS WORD TO COEUR-DE-LION:	155	NEAR PERIGORD	123
NO WORD FROM EITHER;	159	PSYCHOLOG HOUR	40
NO WORD FROM HER NOR HIM,	159	PSYCHOLOG HOUR	41
"BREATHE NOT THE WORD TO-MORROW IN HER EARS"	161	CABARET DANCER	EPI
ACCOSTED, THAT'S THE WORD, ACCOSTED HIM,	242	MOYEN SENSUEL	121
NEVER AN HONEST WORD	262	ALF'S SIXTH	28
AND SCARCELY HEED ONE WORD OF WHAT YOU HEAR.	265	ALF'S NINTH	28
WORDS			
LIPS, WORDS, AND YOU SNARE THEM,	6	CINO	4
DREAMS, WORDS, AND THEY ARE AS JEWELS,	6	CINO	5
WORDS THAT WERE WING'D AS HER SPARKS IN ERUPTION,	13	MESMERISM	14
AND LITTLE RED ELF WORDS CRYING "A SONG,"	16	PRAISE YSOLT	15
LITTLE GREY ELF WORDS CRYING FOR A SONG,	16	PRAISE YSOLT	16
LITTLE BROWN LEAF WORDS CRYING "A SONG,"	16	PRAISE YSOLT	17
LITTLE GREEN LEAF WORDS CRYING FOR A SONG.	16	PRAISE YSOLT	18
THE WORDS ARE AS LEAVES, OLD BROWN LEAVES IN THE SPRING TIME	16	PRAISE YSOLT	19
WHITE WORDS AS SNOW FLAKES BUT THEY ARE COLD,	16	PRAISE YSOLT	21
MOSS WORDS, LIP WORDS, WORDS OF SLOW STREAMS.	16	PRAISE YSOLT	22
MOSS WORDS, LIP WORDS, WORDS OF SLOW STREAMS.	16	PRAISE YSOLT	22
MOSS WORDS, LIP WORDS, WORDS OF SLOW STREAMS.	16	PRAISE YSOLT	22
BUT STILL CAME THE LEAF WORDS, LITTLE BROWN ELF WORDS	17	PRAISE YSOLT	33
BUT STILL CAME THE LEAF WORDS, LITTLE BROWN ELF WORDS	17	PRAISE YSOLT	33
AND THE WORDS WERE WITH ME	17	PRAISE YSOLT	44

WORDS -- WORLD

	PAGE	TITLE	LINE
WORDS (CONTINUED)			
SHE THAT HOLDETH THE WONDER WORDS WITHIN HER EYES	17	PRAISE YSOLT	51
THE WORDS, LITTLE ELF WORDS	17	PRAISE YSOLT	52
THE WORDS, LITTLE ELF WORDS	17	PRAISE YSOLT	52
MY WORDS FOR STOUR, HATH NO BLOOD OF CRIMSON	29	ALTAFORTE	26
SPEECH? WORDS? FAUGH! WHO TALKS OF WORDS AND LOVE?!	31	PIERE VIDAL	33
SPEECH? WORDS? FAUGH! WHO TALKS OF WORDS AND LOVE?!	31	PIERE VIDAL	33
WI' TWEY WORDS SPOKE' SUDDENTLY.	34	GOODLY FERE	48
I JOIN THESE WORDS FOR FOUR PEOPLE,	88	CAUSA	1
EAGER TO CATCH MY WORDS,	90	SURGIT FAMA	10
AND I HAVE JOY IN THESE WORDS	129	THE RIVER SONG	15
FOR I KNOW HOW WORDS RUN LOOSE,	173	LANGUE D'OC: 2	25
HOW MANY WORDS TALKED OUT WITH ABUNDANT CANDLES;	220	SEXTUS PROP: 7	3
WORDSWORTHIAN			
RESPECTED, WORDSWORTHIAN:	229	SEXTUS PROP:12	51
WORE			
YOU WORE THE SAME QUITE CORRECT CLOTHING,	101	AMITIES	1
WORK			
TOWARD SUCH A WORK OF ART.	45	FROM HEINE: 5	12
OF BEATEN WORK; AND THROUGH THE CLARET STONE,	49	OF SPLENDOUR	15
AND ALL THEIR CRAFTY WORK UPON THE DOOR,	60	TOMB AKR CAAR	30
THE TARNISHED, GAUDY, WONDERFUL OLD WORK;	61	PORTRAIT FEMME	22
THAT HE WILL WORK ERE HE PASS ONWARD,	66	THE SEAFARER	75
"NO! HIS FIRST WORK WAS THE BEST."	85	SALUTATION 2ND	14
SAY THAT YOU DO NO WORK	80	SALUTATION 2ND	36
THEY WORK PATHETICALLY IN MY FAVOUR,	147	BEFORE SLEEP	3
WHERE IS THE WORK OF YOUR HOME-BORN SCULPTORS?	165	QUINTUS SEPTIM	16
"EVEN IF YOU HAVE TO WORK FREE.	194	MR. NIXON	9
THEY HAVE TO DO THE DIRTY WORK,	266	ALF'S ELEVENTH	11
AFTER MY WORK IS DONE	268	ANOTHER BIT	10
TO SEND ME TO WORK IN VICKERS	268	ANOTHER BIT	15
WHAT AIN'T GOT WORK NO MORE	269	SAFE AND SOUND	10
TILL SHE FINDS WORK TO DO.	272	THE BABY	8
WORKED			
AND MY HEART WORKED AT THEM UNDULY.	44	FROM HEINE: 2	6
WITH DRAGONS WORKED UPON IT,	94	INSTRUCTIONS	18
WORKED FOR AND SNATCHED FROM THE STRING-PURSE OF BORN--	152	NEAR PERIGORD	34
TESTED AND PRIED AND WORKED IN MANY FASHIONS,	235	TO WHISTLER	3
WORKER			
A HOME-INDUSTRIOUS WORKER TO PERFECTION,	245	MOYEN SENSUEL	213
WORKING			
BLOCKED LIGHTS WORKING IN. ESCAPES. RENEWAL OF CONTEST.	120	GAME OF CHESS	15
WORKS			
THIS OUR REWARD FOR OUR WORKS,	52	AU SALON	16
IT WORKS TO REPRESENT THAT SCHOOL OF THOUGHT	63	PHASELLUS ILLE	3
SOMEONE ADMIRED YOUR WORKS,	159	PSYCHOLOG HOUR	32
"OF SELLING MY OWN WORKS.	194	MR. NIXON	15
WORLD			
SERIOUS CHILD BUSINESS THAT THE WORLD	14	FAMAM CANO	13
SUCH AN ONE AS THE WORLD FEELS	14	FAMAM CANO	24
AND ARE UNTOUCHED BY ECHOES OF THE WORLD.	21	IN DURANCE	34
BEHOLD! THE WORLD OF FORMS IS SWEPT BENEATH--	32	PARACELSUS	7
THAT EVER CAME UPON THIS GRIEVING WORLD	36	THE YOUNG KING	3
THE WORLD O'ERSHADOWED, SOILED AND OVERCAST,	36	THE YOUNG KING	7
AND THAT THE WORLD SHOULD DRY AS A DEAD LEAF,	36	FRANCESCA	9
'LAS! NEVER WAS NOR WILL BE IN THIS WORLD	37	THE YOUNG KING	15
FROM THIS FAINT WORLD, HOW FULL OF BITTERNESS	37	THE YOUNG KING	25
ONE WHO HATH SET THE WHOLE WORLD 'NEATH HER LAWS,	40	ROME	6
REMAINS OF ROME. O WORLD, THOU UNCONSTANT MIME!	40	ROME	12
THROUGH ALL THE WORLD WILL I COMPLAIN	44	FROM HEINE: 1	3
O SMOKE AND SHADOW OF A DARKLING WORLD,	50	THE FLAME	14
AND ALL THIS IS FOLLY TO THE WORLD.	62	A GIRL	10
NAY, SHOULD THE DEATHLESS VOICE OF ALL THE WORLD	63	PHASELLUS ILLE	9
WANETH THE WATCH, BUT THE WORLD HOLDETH.	66	THE SEAFARER	89
BREATH THAT IS STRETCHED OUT BENEATH THE WORLD:	76	THE ALCHEMIST	45
OUT OF EREBUS, OUT OF THE FLAT WASTE OF AIR LYING BENEATH THE WORLD,	76	THE ALCHEMIST	46
O WORLD, I AM SORRY FOR YOU,	88	CAUSA	3
GO LIKE A BLIGHT UPON THE DULNESS OF THE WORLD;	88	COMMISSION	18

PAGE 481

WORLD -- WOULD

	PAGE	TITLE	LINE
WORLD (CONTINUED)			
WE WHO WENT OUT INTO THE FOUR A. M. OF THE WORLD	104	ANCORA	3
WITH A LAUGHTER NOT OF THIS WORLD.	147	POST MORTEM	3
IF ALL THE WORLD BE IN DESPITE	174	LANGUE D'OC: 3	14
THOUGH THE WHOLE WORLD RUN RACK	176	LANGUE D'OC: 3	73
BEWILDERED THAT A WORLD	192	YEUX GLAUQUES	21
EXCLUSION FROM THE WORLD OF LETTERS.	202	AGE DEMANDED	61
NOT ONE HAS ENQUIRED THE CAUSE OF THE WORLD,	228	SEXTUS PROP:12	25
WORLDLY			
BUT OUT SOMEWHERE BEYOND THE WORLDLY WAYS	49	OF SPLENDOUR	3
WORLD'S			
BID THE WORLD'S HOUNDS COME TO HORN!"	25	THE WHITE STAG	7
I AM SET WIDE UPON THE WORLD'S WAYS	53	AU JARDIN	11
NOR WINSOMENESS TO WIFE, NOR WORLD'S DELIGHT	65	THE SEAFARER	46
DO NOT UNDERSTAND THE CONDUCT OF THIS WORLD'S			
AFFAIRS.	97	THE BELLAIRES	2
AT LAST FROM THE WORLD'S WELTER	195	HUGH SELWIN:10	4
WORM			
TO CATCH YOU AT WORM TURNING. HOLY ODD'S BODYKINS!	13	MESMERISM	4
WORMS			
IT WILL PAY THEM WHEN THE WORMS ARE WRIGGLING IN			
THEIR VITALS;	145	SALUTATION 3RD	4
WORN			
LO, I AM WORN WITH TRAVAIL	16	PRAISE YSOLT	11
ARCHES WORN OLD AND PALACES MADE COMMON,	40	ROME	3
AND NOW YOU ARE STALE AND WORN OUT,	114	EPILOGUE	5
THE AUGUST HAS WORN AGAINST HER.	116	THE TEA SHOP	3
WORN AND OLD.	176	LANGUE D'OC: 3	72
A NAME NOT TO BE WORN OUT WITH THE YEARS.	209	SEXTUS PROP: 1	73
"SOFT FIELDS MUST BE WORN BY SMALL WHEELS,	210	SEXTUS PROP: 2	21
WORRY			
LET US EXPRESS OUR ENVY OF THE MAN WITH A STEADY JOB			
AND NO WORRY ABOUT THE FUTURE.	94	INSTRUCTIONS	2
WORSE			
I SHALL BE PREY TO LAMENTATIONS WORSE THAN A			
NOCTURNAL ASSAILANT.	212	SEXTUS PROP: 3	11
WORSHIPPERS			
MIGHT, IN NEW AGES, GAIN HER WORSHIPPERS,	197	ENVOI (1919)	22
WORST			
AND THEN, WHEN SEPARATION HAD COME TO ITS WORST,	134	EXILE'S LETTER	16
BUT SURELY THE WORST OF YOUR OLD-WOMEN ARE THE MALE			
ONES.)	243	MOYEN SENSUEL	150
THAT MAKES THE WORST MESS.	259	ALF'S FOURTH	7
WORTH			
WORTH LIETH RIVEN AND YOUTH DOLOROUS,	36	THE YOUNG KING	6
SITH NOTHING IS THAT UNTO WORTH PERTAINETH	37	THE YOUNG KING	20
TO MY DESIRE, WORTH YOURS WHOM I HAVE LOST,	105	DOMPNA POIS	9
"MY WIT AND WORTH ARE COBWEBS BRUSHED ASIDE	152	NEAR PERIGORD	45
SUCH A DEATH IS WORTH DYING.	213	SEXTUS PROP: 3	29
WHERE FOLK OF WORTH BE HOST.	250	DONNA MI PREGA	57
WORTHIEST			
THAT WAS MOST VALIANT 'MID ALL WORTHIEST MEN!	37	THE YOUNG KING	30
SAITH 'TWAS THE WORTHIEST OF EDITORS.	63	PHASELLUS ILLE	2
WORTH'S			
FAR FROM WHERE WORTH'S WON AND THE SWORDS CLASH	29	ALTAFORTE	28
WORTHY			
FOR IT SEEMS TO US WORTHY OF RECORD.	93	LES MILLWIN	14
SET ALL TOGETHER, ARE NOT WORTHY OF YOU. . . . "	151	NEAR PERIGORD	9
BEYOND ALL FALSITY, WORTHY OF FAITH, ALONE	250	DONNA MI PREGA	86
WOT			
YES, WOT IS LEFT OF 'EM,	257	BREAD BRIGADE	19
WOT OH! MY BUXOM HEARTIES,	269	SAFE AND SOUND	9
WOULD			
SIGHING, SAY, "WOULD CINO,	6	CINO	16
WOULD CINO OF THE LUTH WERE HERE!"	6	CINO	22
FOR MICHAULT LE BORGNE THAT WOULD CONFESS	12	OF THE GIBBET	34
AND WOULD MEET KINDRED EVEN AS I AM,	20	IN DURANCE	24
LO, I WOULD SAIL THE SEAS WITH THEE ALONE!	25	GUIDO INVITES	2
AND WOULD FEEL THE FINGERS OF THE WIND	35	THE EYES	2
AND WE WOULD LOOK THEREON.	35	THE EYES	18
WERE SET TOGETHER THEY WOULD SEEM BUT LIGHT	36	THE YOUNG KING	4

PAGE 482

WOULD -- WOULDST

	PAGE	TITLE	LINE
WOULD (CONTINUED)			
I WOULD THAT THE COOL WAVES MIGHT FLOW OVER MY MIND.	36	FRANCESCA	8
OVER THE WHALE'S ACRE, WOULD WANDER WIDE.	65	THE SEAFARER	61
I WOULD BATHE MYSELF IN STRANGENESS:	70	THE PLUNGE	1
YOU, I WOULD HAVE FLOW OVER ME LIKE WATER, ...	70	THE PLUNGE	14
SHE WOULD LIKE SOME ONE TO SPEAK TO HER, ...	83	THE GARDEN	10
NOR WOULD GAUTIER HIMSELF HAVE DESPISED THEIR			
CONTRASTS IN WHITENESS	87	ALBATRE	5
AND WHEN THEY WOULD NOT LET HIM ARRANGE	97	AESTHETICS	16
AT CHALAIS OF THE VISCOUNTESS, I WOULD	106	DOMPNA POIS	31
OUR SORROW IS BITTER, BUT WE WOULD NOT RETURN TO OUR			
COUNTRY.	127	BOWMEN OF SHU	12
WOULD FOLLOW THE WHITE GULLS OR RIDE THEM.	128	THE RIVER SONG	8
THEN THE WATERS OF HAN WOULD FLOW NORTHWARD.)	129	THE RIVER SONG	15
AND YOU WOULD WALK OUT WITH ME TO THE WESTERN CORNER			
OF THE CASTLE, ...	135	EXILE'S LETTER	49
HOW WOULD YOU LIVE, WITH NEIGHBOURS SET ABOUT YOU	152	NEAR PERIGORD	28
WHAT WOULD HE DO WITHOUT HER?	153	NEAR PERIGORD	
BEAUTY WOULD DRINK OF MY MIND.	158	PSYCHOLOG	
YOUTH WOULD AWHILE FORGET	158	PSYCHOLOG HOUR	29
"DELIA, I WOULD LOOK ON YOU, DYING."	168	OF AROUET	40
WOULD I HAD DIED THAT DAY	175	LANGUE D'OC: 3	38
FOR I WOULD NOT LOOK ON A WOMAN.	175	LANGUE D OC: 3	43
THE THOUGHT OF WHAT AMERICA WOULD BE LIKE	183	CANTICO SOLE	1
THE THOUGHT OF WHAT AMERICA WOULD BE LIKE	183	CANTICO SOLE	6
THE THOUGHT OF WHAT AMERICA WOULD BE LIKE	183	CANTICO SOLE	14
TOLD HER WOULD FIT HER STATION.	195	HUGH SELWIN:11	8
I WOULD BID THEM LIVE	197	ENVOI (1919)	12
IT IS IN YOUR GROVE I WOULD WALK, ...	207	SEXTUS PROP: 1	2
AND WHO WOULD HAVE KNOWN THE TOWERS	208	SEXTUS PROP: 1	26
THEIR DOOR-YARDS WOULD SCARCELY KNOW THEM, OR PARIS.	208	SEXTUS PROP: 1	31
IF ANY MAN WOULD BE A LOVER	212	SEXTUS PROP: 3	17
NO BARBARISM WOULD GO TO THE EXTENT OF DOING HIM			
HARM.	212	SEXTUS PROP: 3	19
SHE WOULD BRING FRANKINCENSE AND WREATHS TO MY TOMB,	213	SEXTUS PROP: 3	30
SHE WOULD SIT LIKE AN ORNAMENT ON MY PYRE.	213	SEXTUS PROP: 3	31
TO THINGS WHICH YOU THINK I WOULD LIKE TO BELIEVE.	214	SEXTUS PROP: 4	7
IF I HAVE NOT THE FACULTY, "THE BARE ATTEMPT WOULD			
BE PRAISE-WORTHY."	216	SEXTUS PROP: 5	4
I WITH MY BEAK HAULED ASHORE WOULD PROCEED IN A MORE			
STATELY MANNER, ...	216	SEXTUS PROP: 5	10
I WERE ABLE TO LEAD HEROES INTO ARMOUR, I WOULD NOT,	217	SEXTUS PROP: 5	38
NEITHER WOULD I WARBLE OF TITANS, NOR OF OSSA	217	SEXTUS PROP: 5	39
FOOL WHO WOULD SET A TERM TO LOVE'S MADNESS, ...	220	SEXTUS PROP: 7	22
SAILS SPREAD ON CERULEAN WATERS, I WOULD SHED TEARS			
FOR TWO;	333	SEXTUS PROP: 9	7
THE HIGH TRACKS OF HERMES WOULD NOT AFFORD YOU			
SHELTER.	226	SEXTUS PROP:11	10
I WOULD ASK A LIKE BOON OF JOVE.	228	SEXTUS PROP:12	17
I WOULD MAKE VERSE IN YOUR FASHION, IF SHE SHOULD			
COMMAND IT, ...	229	SEXTUS PROP:12	60
AND EVEN THIS INFAMY WOULD NOT ATTRACT NUMEROUS			
READERS	230	SEXTUS PROP:12	62
'TIS OF MY COUNTRY THAT I WOULD ENDITE, ...	238	MOYEN SENSUEL	1
I WOULD ARTICULATE YOUR PERDAMNATION, ...	238	MOYEN SENSUEL	8
AND WOULD NOT THINK A THING THAT COULD UPSET HER. .			
....	242	MOYEN SENSUEL	110
THE SELECT COMPANY: BEAUTIES YOU ALL WOULD KNOW ..	242	MOYEN SENSUEL	113
BECAUSE A LADY ASKS ME, I WOULD TELL	248	DONNA MI PREGA	1
CONSIDERING SOMETHING THAT WOULD, AS YOU	262	ALF'S SEVENTH	7
WOULD COUNT ON THE PRICE OF A GUN.	268	ANOTHER BIT	12
AND WOULD MY OLD MAN HAVE BEEN SMARTER	268	ANOTHER BIT	
OLE KATE WOULD GIT HER 'ARF A PINT	271	OLE KATE	8
WOULDN'T			
BECAUSE HIS LONG SLEEVES WOULDN'T KEEP STILL	135	EXILE'S LETTER	29
"AND I WOULDN'T SAY THAT HE DIDN'T.	182	MOEURS CON: 8	12
I WOULDN'T 'AVE THE NEEDLE	269	SAFE AND SOUND	23
AND WOULDN'T GIV' A DAMN HOOT	271	OLE KATE	4
WOULDST			
AND IF THOU KNEW'ST I KNEW THEM WOULDST THOU SPEAK?	43	SATIEMUS	2

PAGE 483

	PAGE	TITLE	LINE

WOUND
- THAT DOTH BUT WOUND THE GOOD WITH IRE AND SADNESS. — 37 — THE YOUNG KING — 24
- AS WINTER'S WOUND WITH HER SLEIGHT HAND SHE STAUNCHES, — 71 — A VIRGINAL — 12
- THE WATERS OF STYX POURED OVER THE WOUND: — 230 — SEXTUS PROP:12 — 74

WOUNDED
- O WOUNDED SORROWFULLY. — 47 — FROM HEINE: 7 — 8
- AND FLOOD CARRIES WOUNDED SUEVI. — 211 — SEXTUS PROP: 2 — 47
- WOUNDED BY YOUR INDIRECTNESS IN THESE SITUATIONS — 247 — PIERROTS — 8

WOUNDING
- "THE WOUNDING OF AUSTERE MEN BY CHICANE." — 211 — SEXTUS PROP: 2 — 51

WOUNDS
- AND TAKE YOUR WOUNDS FROM IT GLADLY. — 95 — ITE — 4
- SOLDIER, THE ENUMERATION OF WOUNDS; THE SHEEP-FEEDER, OF EWES; — 218 — SEXTUS PROP: 5 — 56

WOVEN
- AND ALL HER ROBE WAS WOVEN OF PALE GOLD. — 49 — OF SPLENDOUR — 12
- OF WOVEN WALLS DEEP PATTERNED, OF EMAIL, — 49 — OF SPLENDOUR — 14
- A BROWN ROBE, WITH THREADS OF GOLD WOVEN IN PATTERNS, HAST THOU GATHERED ABOUT THEE, — 91 — DANCE FIGURE — 17
- IS WOVEN AND GROWS SOLID BENEATH US; — 170 — PHANOPOEIA — 23
- THEIR STALKS ARE WOVEN IN BASKETS, — 221 — SEXTUS PROP: 7 — 30

WRAPPED
- I WRAPPED MY TEARS IN AN ELLUM LEAF — 4 — LA FRAISNE — 25
- AND I, WRAPPED IN BROCADE, WENT TO SLEEP WITH MY HEAD ON HIS LAP, — 135 — EXILE'S LETTER — 31
- I HAVE WRAPPED THE WIND ROUND YOUR SHOULDERS — 170 — PHANOPOEIA — 18

WREATH
- SHALL I PLACE A TIN WREATH UPON! — 189 — HUGH SELWYN: 3 — 28
- I ASK A WREATH WHICH WILL NOT CRUSH MY HEAD. — 207 — SEXTUS PROP: 1 — 21

WREATHS
- SHE WOULD BRING FRANKINCENSE AND WREATHS TO MY TOMB, — 213 — SEXTUS PROP: 3 — 30
- DRY WREATHS DROP THEIR PETALS, — 221 — SEXTUS PROP: 7 — 29
- I SHALL BE HONOURED WITH YESTERDAY'S WREATHS. — 229 — SEXTUS PROP:12 — 57

WRENCH
- "WHY WRENCH YOUR PAGE OUT OF ITS COURSE? — 210 — SEXTUS PROP: 2 — 24
- AND TRY TO WRENCH HER IMPULSE INTO ART. — 235 — TO WHISTLER — 13

WRESTLED
- NOW WITH BARED BREASTS SHE WRESTLED AGAINST ME, — 220 — SEXTUS PROP: 7 — 5

WRETCHED
- WEATHERED THE WINTER, WRETCHED OUTCAST — 64 — THE SEAFARER — 15

WRIES
- OR WRIES THE FACE WITH FEAR AND LITTLE STAYS, — 250 — DONNA MI PREGA — 54

WRIGGLING
- IT WILL PAY THEM WHEN THE WORMS ARE WRIGGLING IN THEIR VITALS; — 145 — SALUTATION 3RD — 4
- FEEL YOUR HATES WRIGGLING ABOUT MY FEET — 145 — SALUTATION 3RD — 28

WRINGING
- BENT RESOLUTELY ON WRINGING LILIES FROM THE ACORN; — 187 — E. P. ODE — 7

WRINKLED
- AND BEING BENT AND WRINKLED, IN A FORM — 9 — NA AUDIART — 38

WRINKLING
- PASSIONATE CINO, OF THE WRINKLING EYES, — 6 — CINO — 17

WRIT
- THY LOVELINESS IS HERE WRIT TILL, — 9 — NA AUDIART — 35
- "POETE, WRIT ME A POEME!" — 162 — CABARET DANCER — 51

WRITE
- TO WRITE THE ACCEPTABLE WORD.... — 18 — DE AEGYPTO — 11
- THOUGH THEY WRITE IT CUNNINGLY; — 33 — GOODLY FERE — 22
- AND THE DANCERS, YOU WRITE A SONNET; — 161 — CABARET DANCER — 6
- "PEPITA" HAS NO TO-MORROW, SO YOU WRITE. — 161 — CABARET DANCER — 9
- "WRITE ME A POEM." — 162 — CABARET DANCER — 31
- YET YOU ASK ON WHAT ACCOUNT I WRITE SO MANY LOVE-LYRICS — 217 — SEXTUS PROP: 5 — 23
- AND YOU WRITE OF ACHELOUS, WHO CONTENDED WITH HERCULES, — 228 — SEXTUS PROP:12 — 18
- YOU WRITE OF ADRASTUS' HORSES AND THE FUNERAL RITES OF ACHENOR, — 228 — SEXTUS PROP:12 — 19

WRITERS
- TO DO AWAY WITH GOOD WRITERS, — 145 — SALUTATION 3RD — 21

PAGE 484

WRITES -- YAWNING

	PAGE	TITLE	LINE
WRITES			
BASTIDIDES, ON THE CONTRARY, WHO BOTH TALKS AND WRITES OF NOTHING SAVE COPULATION,	100	TEMPERAMENTS	5
AND THE THIRD WRITES AN EPIGRAM TO CANDIDIA.	118	THREE POETS	7
AND WE CAN LEAVE THE TALK TILL DANTE WRITES:	156	NEAR PERIGORD	162
SHE NOW WRITES TO ME FROM A CONVENT;	179	MOEURS CON: 2	3
WRITING			
SAVE THIS DAMN'D PROFESSION OF WRITING,	117	THE LAKE ISLE	15
TO A FRIEND WRITING ON CABARET DANCERS	161	CABAR T DANCER	T
CAN GO ON WRITING YOU VERSES. . . .	168	OF AROUET	36
WHEN WRITING WELL HAS NOT YET BEEN FORGIVEN	240	MOYEN SENSUEL	61
IN WRITING FICTION ON UNCERTAIN CHANCES	243	MOYEN SENSUEL	135
WRITTEN			
THE FIRST HAS WRITTEN A LONG ELEGY TO "CHLORIS,"	118	THREE POETS	3
THE SECOND HAS WRITTEN A SONNET	118	THREE POETS	5
AS TENNYSON HAS WRITTEN,	272	THE BABY	10
WRONG			
TURNS HARDY PILOT . . . AND IF ONE WRONG NOTE	42	HER MONUMENT	45
HER ROBES CAN BUT DO HER WRONG.	106	DOMPNA POIS	50
IN THE OLD SENSE. WRONG FROM THE START--	187	E. P. ODE	4
AND I SHALL BE IN THE WRONG,	212	SEXTUS PROP: 3	12
HERE IS A PART THAT'S SLIGHT, AND PART GONE WRONG,	235	TO WHISTLER	5
WAS I STARTED WRONG AS A KIDDIE,	268	ANOTHER BIT	13
WRONGS			
OR IS IT MY TONGUE THAT WRONGS YOU	222	SEXTUS PROP: 8	14
WROTE			
AND WROTE NINETY PETRARCHAN SONNETS.	118	CONTEMPORARIES	5
HE WROTE THE CATCH TO PIT THEIR JEALOUSIES	153	NEAR PERIGORD	77
HE WROTE THAT PRAISE ONLY TO SHOW HE HAD	155	NEAR PERIGORD	148
UPON LEARNING THAT THE MOTHER WROTE VERSES,	179	MOEURS CON: 3	1
AND THAT THE FATHER WROTE VERSES,	179	MOEURS CON: 3	2
WROUGHT			
GREEN WAS HER MANTLE, CLOSE, AND WROUGHT	31	PIERE VIDAL	28
HIGH WROUGHT OF MARBLE, AND THE PANTING BREATH	31	PIERE VIDAL	39
SO LIGHTLY WROUGHT	42	HER MONUMENT	56
FOR SEPARATION WROUGHT OUT SEPARATION,	151	NEAR PERIGORD	24
WHO WROUGHT ABOUT HIS "SOUL" THEIR STALE INFECTION.	241	MOYEN SENSUEL	81
WRY'D			
SCORNING A NEW, WRY'D CASEMENT,	9	NA AUDIART	42
BEING THEN YOUNG AND WRY'D,	9	NA AUDIART	48
WUZ			
BUT SAID IT WUZ GLORIOUS NEVERTHELESS	259	ALF'S FOURTH	5
XERXES'			
NOR OF XERXES' TWO-BARRELED KINGDOM, NOR OF REMUS AND HIS ROYAL FAMILY,	217	SEXTUS PROP: 5	44
X'S			
CROSSED IN GREAT FUTURISTIC X'S, THE ART STUDENTS	93	LES MILLWIN	9
CLASHING WITH X'S OF QUEENS,	120	GAME OF CHESS	10
Y			
"Y" PAWNS, CLEAVING, EMBANKING!	120	GAME OF CHESS	12
Y.			
N. Y.	62	N. Y.	T
OLD FRIENDS THE MOST.--W. B. Y.	101	AMITIES	EPI
THESE, AND YET GOD, AND DR. PARKHURST'S GOD, THE N. Y. JOURNAL	240	MOYEN SENSUEL	45
YACHT			
IN THE CREAM GILDED CABIN OF HIS STEAM YACHT	194	MR. NIXON	1
YAMMER			
FOR YAMMER OF THE CUCKOLD,	172	LANGUE D'OC: 1	29
YANK			
AND THEY GAVE ANOTHER YANK TO MY CLOAK,	225	SEXTUS PROP:10	26
YARD			
RUDYARD THE DUD YARD,	259	ALF'S FOURTH	1
YARNS			
WE SHALL SPIN LONG YARNS OUT OF NOTHING.	217	SEXTUS PROP: 5	36
YAWNED			
SHALL BE YAWNED OUT ON MY LYRE--WITH SUCH INDUSTRY.	210	SEXTUS PROP: 2	5
YAWNING			
YAWNING A LITTLE SHE CAME WITH THE SLEEP STILL UPON HER.	166	FISH & SHADOW	8

YDOLE -- YEARS

YDOLE

	PAGE	TITLE	LINE
DRINK WE TO MARIENNE YDOLE, ...	11	OF THE GIBBET	15

YDONE

YSAUT, YDONE, SLIGHT RUSTLING OF LEAVES, ...	76	THE ALCHEMIST	40

YE

ASK YE WHAT GHOSTS I DREAM UPON?	10	FOR THIS YULE	9
BUT YE ASK FIRST WHERE THE WINDS ARE GONE	10	FOR THIS YULE	27
DRINK YE A SKOAL FOR THE GALLOWS TREE!	11	OF THE GIBBET	1
AYE YOU'RE A MAN THAT! YE OLD MESMERIZER	13	MESMERISM	1
OF TH' UNBOUNDED ONES, BUT YE, THAT HIDE	21	IN DURANCE	29
OH YE, MY FELLOWS: WITH THE SEAS BETWEEN US SOME BE,	21	IN DURANCE	35
FOR THAT I LOVE YE AS THE WIND THE TREES	21	IN DURANCE	44
AYE YE ARE FOOLS, IF YE THINK TIME CAN BLOT	30	PIERE VIDAL	18
AYE YE ARE FOOLS, IF YE THINK TIME CAN BLOT	30	PIERE VIDAL	18
WHAT DO YE OWN, YE NIGGARDS! THAT CAN BUY	32	PIERE VIDAL	57
WHAT DO YE OWN, YE NIGGARDS! THAT CAN BUY	32	PIERE VIDAL	57
"OR I'LL SEE YE DAMNED," SAYS HE.	33	GOODLY FERE	8
"WHY TOOK YE NOT ME WHEN I WALKED ABOUT	33	GOODLY FERE	11
"YE HA' SEEN ME HEAL THE LAME AND BLIND, ...	34	GOODLY FERE	29
"YE SHALL SEE ONE THING TO MASTER ALL:	34	GOODLY FERE	31
WHAT ANSWER? O YE MYRIAD	35	HIS OWN FACE	4
AND YE?	35	HIS OWN FACE	8
YE MIGHT LET ONE REMAIN ABOVE WITH US.	38	LADY'S LIFE	4
YE MIGHT LET ONE REMAIN ABOVE WITH US.	38	LADY'S LIFE	14
FELT HANDS TURN ICE A-SUDDEN, TOUCHING YE, ...	41	HER MONUMENT	17
THAT YE WERE ONCE! OF ALL THE GRACE YE HAD	41	HER MONUMENT	18
THAT YE WERE ONCE! OF ALL THE GRACE YE HAD	41	HER MONUMENT	18
O YE LIPS THAT ARE UNGRATEFUL, ...	44	FROM HEINE: 1	5
AH! BOW YOUR HEADS, YE MAIDENS ALL, ...	72	PAN IS DEAD	2
AND WEAVE YE HIM HIS CORONAL."	72	PAN IS DEAD	3
SUCH GRACE OF LOCKS, I DO YE TO WIT, ...	106	DOMPNA POIS	38
YE SEE HERE SEVERED, MY LIFE'S COUNTERPART."	156	NEAR PERIGORD	168
MAKE WAY, YE ROMAN AUTHORS, ...	229	SEXTUS PROP:12	36
CLEAR THE STREET, O YE GREEKS, ...	229	SEXTUS PROP:12	37
CLEAR THE STREETS, O YE GREEKS!	229	SEXTUS PROP:12	40
OF RADWAY. O CLAP HAND YE MORALISTS!	246	MOYEN SENSUEL	227

YEA

YEA THOUGH THOU WISH ME ILL, ...	9	NA AUDIART	33
YEA AS THE SUN CALLETH TO THE SEED, ...	17	PRAISE YSOLT	48
YEA THOU, AND THOU, AND THOU, AND ALL MY KIN	21	IN DURANCE	42
YEA THE LINES HAST THOU LAID UNTO ME	26	NIGHT LITANY	3
YEA, THE GLORY OF THE SHADOW	26	NIGHT LITANY	25
YEA, I FILL ALL THE AIR WITH MY MUSIC.	29	ALTAFORTE	30
YEA, RESTETH LITTLE	250	DONNA MI PREGA	55

YEAR

ONCE, TWICE, A YEAR--	6	CINO	23
I MADE RIMES TO HIS LADY THIS THREE YEAR:	22	MARVOIL	7
ONE AVERAGE MIND--WITH ONE THOUGHT LESS, EACH YEAR.	61	PORTRAIT FEMME	10
'NEATH WHICH THE LAST YEAR LIES, ...	67	THE CLOAK	8
THOUGH EVERY BRANCH HAVE BACK WHAT LAST YEAR LOST,	87	THE SPRING	11
"IONE, DEAD THE LONG YEAR"	112	IONE, DEAD	T
AND I WAS STILL GOING, LATE IN THE YEAR, ...	135	EXILE'S LETTER	42
SPOILING HIS VISIT, WITH A YEAR BEFORE THE NEXT ONE.	154	NEAR PERIGORD	113
BIRDS SINGING LATE IN THE YEAR!	168	OF AROUET	38
THE CHOPPED SEAS HELD HIM, THEREFORE, THAT YEAR.	187	E. P. ODE	12
WHICH ANAETHESIS, NOTED A YEAR LATE, ...	200	MAUBERLEY: 2	30
THIS YEAR PERFORCE I MUST WITH CIRCUMSPECTION-- ...	238	MOYEN SENSUEL	9
THE POMPS OF FLEET ST., FESTERING YEAR ON YEAR,	260	ALF'S FIFTH	5
THE POMPS OF FLEET ST., FESTERING YEAR ON YEAR,	260	ALF'S FIFTH	5
CAN TELL YOU OF THAT FAMOUS DAY AND YEAR.	264	ALF'S NINTH	4
AN' EVERY YEAR WE MEET TO LET	270	OF 600 M.P.'S	11

YEARNED

AND YEARNED TO IMITATE THE WALDORF CAPERS	241	MOYEN SENSUEL	92

YEARS

IS LISTED. WELL! SOME SCORE YEARS HENCE	14	FAMAM CANO	20
FOR IN THE MORN OF MY YEARS THERE CAME A WOMAN ...	16	PRAISE YSOLT	27
GOD CURSE THE YEARS THAT TURN SUCH WOMEN GREY!	31	PIERE VIDAL	46
MUTE MIRROR OF THE FLIGHT OF SPEEDING YEARS, ...	41	HER MONUMENT	6
'TIS NOT "OF DAYS AND NIGHTS" AND TROUBLING YEARS,	50	THE FLAME	18
LONDON HAS SWEPT ABOUT YOU THIS SCORE YEARS	61	PORTRAIT FEMME	2
I WAS TWENTY YEARS BEHIND THE TIMES	85	SALUTATION 2ND	3

PAGE 486

YEARS -- YESTERDAY'S

	PAGE	TITLE	LINE
YEARS (CONTINUED)			
BUT THREE YEARS AFTER THIS	96	AESTHETICS	6
TO ONE, ON RETURNING CERTAIN YEARS AFTER.	101	AMITIES	ST
I HAVE ADORED YOU FOR THREE FULL YEARS;	102	LADIES	6
WHOSE WIFE IS SEVERAL YEARS HIS SENIOR,	115	SOCIAL ORDER	2
IN A FEW YEARS NO ONE WILL REMEMBER THE BUFFO,	146	MONUMENTUM AER	3
GOBBLED ALL THE LAND, AND HELD IT LATER FOR SOME HUNDRED YEARS.	151	NEAR PERIGORD	19
AND TEN YEARS AFTER, OR TWENTY, AS YOU WILL,	155	NEAR PERIGORD	127
AND WE'VE THE GOSSIP (SKIPPED SIX HUNDRED YEARS).	155	NEAR PERIGORD	138
TO-MORROW IN TEN YEARS AT THE LATEST,	162	CABARET DANCER	46
TWO YEARS, THREE YEARS I SEEK	175	LANGUE D'OC: 3	34
TWO YEARS, THREE YEARS I SEEK	175	LANGUE D'OC: 3	34
AFTER YEARS OF CONTINENCE	181	MOEURS CON: 6	1
FOR THREE YEARS, OUT OF KEY WITH HIS TIME,	187	E. P. ODE	1
THE HEAVY MEMORIES OF HOREB, SINAI AND THE FORTY YEARS,	193	BRENNBAUM	5
FOR THREE YEARS, DIABOLUS IN THE SCALE,	199	MAUBERLEY: 2	1
AND THEY ALL GO TO RACK RUIN BENEATH THE THUD OF THE YEARS.	209	SEXTUS PROP: 1	71
A NAME NOT TO BE WORN OUT WITH THE YEARS.	209	SEXTUS PROP: 1	73
LONG IS MY LIFE, LONG IN YEARS,	221	SEXTUS PROP: 7	38
IO MOOED THE FIRST YEARS WITH AVERTED HEAD,	222	SEXTUS PROP: 8	19
OH MAY THE KING LIVE FOR A THOUSAND YEARS!	237	ABU SALAMMAMM	27
TEN YEARS AND TWELVE YEARS GONE,	259	ALF'S THIRD	18
TEN YEARS AND TWELVE YEARS GONE,	259	ALF'S THIRD	18
YEAR'S			
BETTER ONE HOUR'S STOUR THAN A YEAR'S PEACE	28	ALTAFORTE	16
YEH			
YEH! WHAT IS LEFT OF 'EM,	259	ALF'S THIRD	10
AIN'T YEH GOT PRECEDENT?	259	ALF'S THIRD	17
COULD YEH SWAP TH' BRAINS OF ORL THIS LOT	270	OF 600 M.P.'S	19
YEI-SHU			
THE EASTERN WIND BRINGS THE GREEN COLOUR INTO THE ISLAND GRASSES AT YEI-SHU,	129	THE RIVER SONG	23
YELLOW			
THE YELLOW FLAME PALETH	35	THE EYES	6
MIDONZ, DAUGHTER OF THE SUN, SHAFT OF THE TREE, SILVER OF THE LEAF, LIGHT OF THE YELLOW OF THE AMBER,	75	THE ALCHEMIST	26
IN THE YELLOW RIVER.	117	EPITAPHS	5
A YELLOW STORK FOR A CHARGER, AND ALL OUR SEAMEN	128	THE RIVER SONG	7
THE PAIRED BUTTERFLIES ARE ALREADY YELLOW WITH AUGUST	131	RIVER-MER WIFE	23
UPON HORSES WITH HEAD-TRAPPINGS OF YELLOW METAL,	132	AT TEN-SHIN	16
FOR THEM THE YELLOW DOGS HOWL PORTENTS IN VAIN,	132	AT TEN SHIN	28
TREES FALL, THE GRASS GOES YELLOW WITH AUTUMN.	133	FRONTIER GUARD	3
WITH YELLOW GOLD AND WHITE JEWELS, WE PAID FOR SONGS AND LAUGHTER	134	EXILE'S LETTER	4
ROSE WHITE, YELLOW, SILVER	169	PHANOPOEIA	ST
YELLOWS			
"LIKE TO LIKE NATURE": THESE AGGLUTINOUS YELLOWS!	114	BEFORE A SHOP	2
YELLOW-WHITE			
HANG IN YELLOW-WHITE AND DARK CLUSTERS READY FOR PRESSING.	167	OF AROUET	22
YER			
'AVE YOU SEEN YER LARST SWEET LITTER?	270	OF 600 M.P.'S	18
YES			
"AH YES, PASSED ONCE OUR WAY,	6	CINO	27
AND NOW YOU PAY ONE. YES, YOU RICHLY PAY.	61	PORTRAIT FEMME	13
AH YES, MY SONGS, LET US RESURRECT	99	SALVATIONISTS	3
YES, SHE ALSO WILL TURN MIDDLE-AGED,	116	THE TEA SHOP	5
I THOUGHT: YES, DIVINE, THESE EYES, BUT WHAT EXISTS	247	PIERROTS	11
YES, I HAVE RUBBED SHOULDERS AND KNOCKED OFF MY CHIPS	247	PIERROTS	22
YES, WOT IS LEFT OF 'EM,	257	BREAD BRIGADE	19
IN ENGLAND? I'LL SAY YES!	267	ALF'S ELEVENTH	22
YESTERDAY			
AS WE HAD SEEN HIM YESTERDAY.	11	PAHAM CANO	22
YESTERDAY WE WENT OUT OF THE WILD-GOOSE GATE,	139	SOUTH-FOLK	4
YESTERDAY'S			
I SHALL BE HONOURED WITH YESTERDAY'S WREATHS.	229	SEXTUS PROP:12	57

YESTERE'EN -- YOKE

	PAGE	TITLE	LINE
YESTERE'EN			
AND EACH TO-DAY 'VAILS LESS THAN YESTERE'EN,	37	THE YOUNG KING	28
YESTER-YEAR			
WINING THE GHOSTS OF YESTER-YEAR.	10	FOR THIS YULE	8
WINING THE GHOSTS OF YESTER-YEAR.	10	FOR THIS YULE	16
WINING THE GHOSTS OF YESTER-YEAR.	10	FOR THIS YULE	24
WINING THE GHOSTS OF YESTER-YEAR.	10	FOR THIS YULE	28
YET			
AND YET; FULL SPEED	14	FAMAM CANO	27
YET THERE IS A TREMBLING UPON ME IN THE TWILIGHT,	16	PRAISE YSOLT	14
AND YET MY SOUL SINGS "UP!" AND WE ARE ONE.	21	IN DURANCE	41
KEEP YET MY SECRET IN THY BREAST HERE;	23	MARVOIL	47
YET AM I POET, AND UPON MY TOMB	24	THUS NINEVEH	16
YET THEIR EYES ARE AS THE EYES OF A MAID TO HER LOVER,	25	THE WHITE STAG	3
HOT WAS THAT HIND'S BLOOD YET IT SCORCHED ME NOT	30	PIERE VIDAL	16
SHAMED AND YET BOWED NOT AND THAT WON AT LAST.	31	PIERE VIDAL	48
AND YET I CURSE THE SUN FOR HIS RED GLADNESS,	31	PIERE VIDAL	49
AND YET I MOCK YOU BY THE MIGHTY FIRES	32	PIERE VIDAL	63
YET IF THOU ART	42	HER MONUMENT	53
YET HIS TIES ARE MORE ADORNING,	46	FROM HEINE: 6	6
YET SHALL MY WHITE ARMS HOLD THEE,	48	FROM HEINE: 7	29
YET IT IS QUIET HERE:	60	TOMB AKR CAAR	32
THAT MIGHT PROVE USEFUL AND YET NEVER PROVES,	61	PORTRAIT FEMME	19
THESE ARE YOUR RICHES, YOUR GREAT STORE; AND YET	61	PORTRAIT FEMME	24
YET THIS IS YOU.	61	PORTRAIT FEMME	30
YET LONGING COMES UPON HIM TO FARE FORTH ON THE WATER.	65	THE SEAFARER	48
OPEN LIES THE LAND, YET THE STEELY GOING	68	APPARUIT	10
SLIGHT ARE HER ARMS, YET THEY HAVE BOUND ME STRAITLY	71	A VIRGINAL	4
WHO CAN UNDERSTAND ANY AFFAIR OF THEIRS, YET	97	THE BELLAIRES	10
AND YET THE MAN IS SO QUIET AND RESERVED IN DEMEANOUR	100	TEMPERAMENTS	3
YET TO OUR FEASTS YOU BRING NEITHER	101	AMITIES	10
AND YET I'D RATHER	107	DOMPNA POIS	66
OUR DEFENCE IS NOT YET MADE SURE, NO ONE CAN LET HIS FRIEND RETURN.	127	BOWMEN OF SHU	8
YET SENNIN NEEDS	128	THE RIVER SONG	6
AND ROCHECOUART CAN MATCH IT, STRONGER YET,	152	NEAR PERIGORD	57
MAENT, MAENT, AND YET AGAIN MAENT,	154	NEAR PERIGORD	92
AND YET EVERYONE SPEAKS EVIL OF DEATH.	164	QUINTUS SEPTIM	3
YET THE COMPANIONS OF THE MUSES	209	SEXTUS PROP: 1	60
YET IF I POSTPONE MY OBEDIENCE	212	SEXTUS PROP: 3	9
OF SOME AS YET UNCATALOGUED SAND;	213	SEXTUS PROP: 3	37
YET YOU ASK ON WHAT ACCOUNT I WRITE SO MANY LOVE-LYRICS	217	SEXTUS PROP: 5	23
AND YET AGAIN, AND NEWLY RUMOUR STRIKES ON MY EARS.	226	SEXTUS PROP:11	17
GAINS YET ANOTHER CRUST	236	MIDDLE-AGED	11
THESE, AND YET GOD, AND DR. PARKHURST'S GOD, THE N. Y. JOURNAL	240	MOYEN SENSUEL	45
AND YET ANOTHER, A "CHARMING MAN," "SWEET NATURE," BUT WAS GILDER,	240	MOYEN SENSUEL	57
WHEN WRITING WELL HAS NOT YET BEEN FORGIVEN	240	MOYEN SENSUEL	61
YET SAW AN "AD." "TO-NIGHT, THE HUDSON SAIL,	242	MOYEN SENSUEL	111
YET RADWAY WENT. A CIRCUMSPECTIOUS PRIG!	242	MOYEN SENSUEL	119
NOT THAT HE'D CHANGED HIS TASTES, NOR YET HIS HABITS,	246	MOYEN SENSUEL	231
I AM NOT "THAT CHAP THERE" NOR YET "THE SUPERB"	247	PIERROTS	16
YET IN THAT PLACE IT EVER IS UNSTILL,	249	DONNA MI PREGA	28
YET IS FOUND THE MOST	250	DONNA MI PREGA	56
NOT YET WILD-CRUEL AS DARTS,	250	DONNA MI PREGA	74
THE MONEY ROTTEN AND MORE ROTTEN YET,	260	ALF'S FIFTH	10
YEUX			
LES YEUX D'UNE MORTE	160	DANS OMNIBUS	1
LES YEUX D'UNE MORTE	160	DANS OMNIBUS	30
YEUX GLAUQUES	192	YEUX GLAUQUES	T
YIELDED			
YIELDED AN ARMOUR	202	AGE DEMANDED	31
YOGA			
AND THE COPY OF "HATHA YOGA"	180	MOEURS CON: 5	24
YOKE			
SPREAD HIS LEAVES OVER ME, AND THE YOKE	4	LA FRAISNE	11
AND MAY THE BOUGHT YOKE OF A MISTRESS LIE WITH	214	SEXTUS PROP: 4	3

PAGE 488

YOU -- YOUR

	PAGE	TITLE	LINE
YOU (358)			
YOU'D (2)			
YOU'LL			
YOU'LL WONDER THAT AN OLD MAN OF EIGHTY	168	OF AROUET	35
YOUNG			
THE YOUNG MEN AT THE SWORD-PLAY;	4	LA FRAISNE	6
ONCE WHEN I WAS AMONG THE YOUNG MEN . . .	5	LA FRAISNE	40
AND THEY SAID I WAS QUITE STRONG, AMONG THE YOUNG MEN.	5	LA FRAISNE	41
BEING SO YOUNG AND FAIR	9	NA AUDIART	46
BEING THEN YOUNG AND WRY'D,	9	NA AUDIART	48
PLANH FOR THE YOUNG ENGLISH KING	36	THE YOUNG KING	T
AGAINST THE DEATH OF THE YOUNG ENGLISH KING.	36	THE YOUNG KING	5
IN TAKING FROM THEM THE YOUNG ENGLISH KING,	37	THE YOUNG KING	13
BUT HAD ITS LIFE IN THE YOUNG ENGLISH KING	37	THE YOUNG KING	21
LET EACH MAN VISAGE THIS YOUNG ENGLISH KING	37	THE YOUNG KING	29
AND HUMBLE EKE, THAT THE YOUNG ENGLISH KING	37	THE YOUNG KING	37
THIS DELIGHTFUL YOUNG MAN	46	FROM HEINE: 6	1
THE RIVER? THOU WAST OVER YOUNG.	60	TOMB AKR CAAR	17
THINE ARMS ARE AS A YOUNG SAPLING UNDER THE BARK;	91	DANCE FIGURE	10
GO, MY SONGS, SEEK YOUR PRAISE FROM THE YOUNG AND FROM THE INTOLERANT,	95	ITE	1
I HEARD THE YOUNG DANTE, WHOSE LAST NAME I DO NOT KNOW--	96	AESTHETICS	7
FOR THERE ARE, IN SIRMIONE, TWENTY-EIGHT YOUNG DANTES AND THIRTY-FOUR CATULLI;	96	AESTHETICS	8
YOUNG LADY	102	LADIES	ST
THE YOUNG MEN LOOK UPON THEIR SENIORS,	104	THE SEEING EYE	5
IT IS ONLY IN SMALL DOGS AND THE YOUNG	104	THE SEEING EYE	9
SHE IS SO SUPPLE AND YOUNG,	106	DOMPNA POIS	49
YOUNG MEN RIDING IN THE STREET	111	IMAGE ORLEANS	1
TO FORMIANUS' YOUNG LADY FRIEND	113	FORMIANUS LADY	T
ALL HAIL! YOUNG LADY WITH A NOSE	113	FORMIANUS LADY	1
WHY DOES THE REALLY HANDSOME YOUNG WOMAN APPROACH ME IN SACKVILLE STREET	114	SIMULACRA	5
WHEN HE SHAKES HANDS WITH YOUNG LADIES.	115	SOCIAL ORDER	4
MANY INSTRUMENTS, LIKE THE SOUND OF YOUNG PHOENIX BROODS.	135	EXILE'S LETTER	27
--EYEBROWS PAINTED GREEN ARE A FINE SIGHT IN YOUNG MOONLIGHT,	136	EXILE'S LETTER	57
IN THE YOUNG DAYS WHEN THE DEEP SKY BEFRIENDED. ...	157	NEAR PERIGORD	175
I REMEMBER THE YOUNG DAY	173	LANGUE D'OC: 2	17
THE YOUNG AMERICAN PILGRIM	179	MOEURS CON: 3	5
YOUNG BLOOD AND HIGH BLOOD,	190	HUGH SELWYN: 4	21
NEGLECTED BY THE YOUNG,	193	SIENA MI FE	19
A YOUNG MUSE WITH YOUNG LOVES CLUSTERED ABOUT HER	207	SEXTUS PROP: 1	13
A YOUNG MUSE WITH YOUNG LOVES CLUSTERED ABOUT HER	207	SEXTUS PROP: 1	13
AND THE DEVIRGINATED YOUNG LADIES WILL ENJOY THEM	208	SEXTUS PROP: 1	40
THERE WILL BE A CROWD OF YOUNG WOMEN DOING HOMAGE TO MY PALAVER,	208	SEXTUS PROP: 1	50
"THESE ARE YOUR IMAGES, AND FROM YOU THE SORCERIZING OF SHUT-IN YOUNG LADIES,	211	SEXTUS PROP: 2	50
TELL ME THE TRUTHS WHICH YOU HEAR OF OUR CONSTANT YOUNG LADY,	214	SEXTUS PROP: 4	1
SUCH DERELICTIONS HAVE DESTROYED OTHER YOUNG LADIES AFORETIME,	221	SEXTUS PROP: 8	7
INO IN HER YOUNG DAYS FLED PELLMELL OUT OF THEBES,	222	SEXTUS PROP: 8	21
IF THE YOUNG LADY IS TAKEN?	222	SEXTUS PROP: 8	41
OF ALL THESE YOUNG WOMEN	228	SEXTUS PROP:12	24
AND HOW TEN SINS CAN CORRUPT YOUNG MAIDENS;	229	SEXTUS PROP:12	43
I SHALL TRIUMPH AMONG YOUNG LADIES OF INDETERMINATE CHARACTER,	229	SEXTUS PROP:12	55
IT IS ADORNED WITH YOUNG GODS RIDING UPON DOLPHINS	237	ABU SALAMMAMM	20
FOR THE YOUNG PRINCE IS FOOLISH AND HEADSTRONG; ...	237	ABU SALAMMAMM	28
THAT USED TO BE USED ON THE YOUNG,	263	ALF'S EIGHTH	23
YOUNGEST			
AND THAT THE YOUNGEST SON WAS IN A PUBLISHER'S OFFICE,	179	MOEURS CON: 3	3
YOUNGSTER			
WHEN I WAS ONLY A YOUNGSTER,	271	OLE KATE	1
YOUR (151)			

PAGE 489

YOU'RE -- ZUT

	PAGE	TITLE	LINE
YOU'RE (2)			
YOURS (3)			
YOURSELF			
EVEN IN MY DREAMS YOU HAVE DENIED YOURSELF TO ME	96	TO KALON	1
YOURSELVES			
YOU WHO CAN NOT WEAR YOURSELVES OUT	92	THE REST	9
WHO CAN NOT STEEL YOURSELVES INTO REITERATION;	92	THE REST	12
YOUTH			
YOUTH DEW IS COLD	9	NA AUDIART	40
WORTH LIETH RIVEN AND YOUTH DOLOROUS.	36	THE YOUNG KING	6
NOT THOUGH HE BE GIVEN HIS GOOD, BUT WILL HAVE IN HIS YOUTH GREED;	65	THE SEAFARER	41
O MY FELLOW SUFFERERS, SONGS OF MY YOUTH,	82	THE CONDOLENCE	1
AND THE GLOW OF YOUTH THAT SHE SPREAD ABOUT US	116	THE TEA SHOP	6
AND WITHIN, THE MISTRESS, IN THE MIDMOST OF HER YOUTH,	128	BEAU TOILET	3
YOUTH WOULD AWHILE FORGET	158	PSYCHOLOG HOUR	29
MY YOUTH IS GONE FROM ME.	158	PSYCHOLOG HOUR	30
A GLAMOUR OF CLASSIC YOUTH IN THEIR DEPORTMENT.	163	CABARET DANCER	74
SOME FORCES AMONG THOSE WHICH "FORMED" HIS YOUTH:	241	MOYEN SENSUEL	78
THE YOUTH OF THE SHIRES!	258	ALF'S SECOND	8
THE YOUTH OF THE SHIRES?	258	ALF'S SECOND	15
YOU'VE (2)			
YOWLS			
WHOSE BLUBBERING YOWLS YOU TAKE FOR PASSION'S ESSENCE;	240	MOYEN SENSUEL	68
YSAUT			
YSAUT, YDONE, SLIGHT RUSTLING OF LEAVES,	76	THE ALCHEMIST	40
YSOLT			
PRAISE OF YSOLT	16	PRAISE YSOLT	T
YUAN			
AFTER CH'U YUAN	108	CH'U YUAN	T
YULE			
VILLONAUD FOR THIS YULE	10	FOR THIS YULE	T
YULE-TIDE			
THEN MAKYTH MY HEART HIS YULE-TIDE CHEER	10	FOR THIS YULE	6
ZAGREUS			
ZAGREUS, ZAGREUS, ZAGREUS,	231	CANTUS PLANUS	4
ZAGREUS, ZAGREUS, ZAGREUS,	231	CANTUS PLANUS	4
ZAGREUS, ZAGREUS, ZAGREUS,	231	CANTUS PLANUS	4
ZEUS			
(SATURN AND MARS TO ZEUS DRAWN NEAR!)	10	FOR THIS YULE	18
GREAT ZEUS, SAVE THE WOMAN,	223	SEXTUS PROP: 9	10
ZEUS'			
GLORY TO ZEUS' AEGIS-DAY,	7	CINO	43
ZEUS' CLEVER RAPES, IN THE OLD DAYS,	227	SEXTUS PROP:11	33
AND EVEN ZEUS' WILD LIGHTNING FEAR TO STRIKE	244	MOYEN SENSUEL	177
ZUT			
IS "ZUT! CINQUE LETTRES!" A BANISHED GALLIC IDIOM,	239	MOYEN SENSUEL	36

12 -- 8

	PAGE	TITLE	LINE
12			
NINE ADULTERIES, 12 LIAISONS, 64 FORNICATIONS AND SOMETHING APPROACHING A RAPE	100	TEMPERAMENTS	1
125			
INFERNO, 28, 125	157	NEAR PERIGORD	EPI
14			
IS AN INFANT, AGED ABOUT 14 MONTHS,	180	MOEURS CON: 5	11
1876			
AT PHILADELPHIA, 1876?	240	MOYEN SENSUEL	55
1910			
L'ART, 1910	113	L'ART, 1910	T
1912			
A STRAY GIPSY--A. D. 1912	119	THE GYPSY	EPI
1918			
ROMANCE, REVOLUTION 1918!	258	ALF'S SECOND	11
1919			
ENVOI (1919)	197	ENVOI (1919)	T
1920			
MAUBERLEY 1920	198	MAUBERLEY 1920	T
2			
SKETCH 48 B. 2	179	MOEURS CON: 4	SUB
WITH 2 AND 2 MAKING 4 IN REASON,	263	ALF'S EIGHTH	12
WITH 2 AND 2 MAKING 4 IN REASON,	263	ALF'S EIGHTH	12
25			
OF 25 PER CENT. ON THEIR ADS., AND THE WOODS	262	ALF'S SEVENTH	12
27			
AT THE AGE OF 27	179	MOEURS CON: 4	1
28			
INFERNO, 28, 125	157	NEAR PERIGORD	EPI
AT THE AGE OF 28,	178	MOEURS CON: 1	4
4			
NEMESIANUS, EC. 4.	186	HUGH SELWYN	EPI
WITH 2 AND 2 MAKING 4 IN REASON,	263	ALF'S EIGHTH	12
48			
SKETCH 48 B. 2	179	MOEURS CON: 4	SUB
6			
STARTIN' IN ABOUT 6 A. M.	271	OLE KATE	11
64			
NINE ADULTERIES, 12 LIAISONS, 64 FORNICATIONS AND SOMETHING APPROACHING A RAPE	100	TEMPERAMENTS	1
8			
PAGANI'S NOVEMBER 8	161	PAGANI'S NOV 8	T

A -- BASS'

```
                                                    PAGE    TITLE              LINE
A (22)
AEGIS
     GLORY TO ZEUS' AEGIS-DAY,  ......................   7    CINO                43
AFORE
     KNOW THEN THAT I LOVED YOU FROM AFORE-TIME,  .......  96  DUM CAPITOLIUM       7
AGAINST
     MISTRUSTED, SPOKEN-AGAINST,  ......................  92  THE REST             5
AGE
     AND ITS AGE-LASTING WALLOW FOR RED GREED  ..........  14  FAMAM CANO          26
     THAN ALL THE AGE-OLD KNOWLEDGE OF THY BOOKS:  ......  35  THE EYES            17
     USURY AGE-OLD AND AGE-THICK  ...................... 190  HUGH SELWYN: 4      18
     USURY AGE-OLD AND AGE-THICK  ...................... 190  HUGH SELWYN: 4      18
AGED
     YES, SHE ALSO WILL TURN MIDDLE-AGED,  .............. 116  THE TEA SHOP        5
     SHE ALSO WILL TURN MIDDLE-AGED.  ................... 116  THE TEA SHOP        9
     MIDDLE-AGED  ....................................... 236  MIDDLE-AGED         T
AGEING
     WITH MIDDLE-AGEING CARE  ........................... 158  PSYCHOLOG HOUR      3
AH
     "AH-EH! THE STRANGE RARE NAME . . .  ...............  15  FAMAM CANO         42
     AH-EH! HE MUST BE RARE IF EVEN I HAVE NOT . . ."      15  FAMAM CANO         43
AIE
     AIE-E! 'TIS TRUE THAT I AM GAY  ....................   5  LA FRAISNE         37
ALL
     ALL-CONQUERING, NOW CONQUERED, BECAUSE  ............  40  ROME                7
     HEART'S-ALL-BELOVED-MY-OWN;  .......................  48  FROM HEINE: 8       6
ALTOGETHER
     O MY MUCH PRAISED BUT-NOT-ALTOGETHER-SATISFACTORY
          LADY.  ......................................... 100  THE BATH TUB        4
ARM
     IN OUR HEART'S SWORD-RACK, THOUGH THY SWORD-ARM
          SLEEP.  ........................................  19  FOR E. MCC         22
ARMS
     WITH ARMS EXALTED, WITH FORE-ARMS  .................  93  LES MILLWIN         8
AT (1)
AUSIER
     BEZIERS OFF AT MONT-AUSIER, I AND HIS LADY  ........  22  MARVOIL            12
     TIBORS ALL TONGUE AND TEMPER AT MONT-AUSIER,  ......  22  MARVOIL            18
AWAKENED
     WITH FEAR, AS HALF-AWAKENED;  ......................  74  THE RETURN          6
AWAY
     AND EVERY RUN-AWAY OF THE WOOD THROUGH THAT GREAT
          MADNESS,  ......................................  31  PIERE VIDAL        51
     DRIPS FROM MY DEATHLESS PEN--AH, WELL-AWAY!  .......  59  SILET               2
AWE
     THESE WERE THE "WING'D-WITH-AWE,"  .................  74  THE RETURN         10
BACK
     AND ON THE BACK-SWIRLING EDDIES,  .................. 131  AT TEN-SHIN         6
BALD
     ALFONSO THE HALF-BALD, TOOK TO HANGING  ............  22  MARVOIL             9
     ALL FOR ONE HALF-BALD, KNOCK-KNEE'D KING OF THE
          ARAGONESE,  ....................................  22  MARVOIL           21
BANDED
     THE WIDE-BANDED IRIDES  ............................ 200  MAUBERLEY: 2       27
BANK
     WITH THE MOST BANK-CLERKLY OF ENGLISHMEN?  ......... 195  HUGH SELWIN:11      4
BAPTIZED
     TO SEE YOUR FORTY SELF-BAPTIZED IMMORTALS,  ........ 239  MOYEN SENSUEL      32
BAR
     WHAT FOOT BEAT OUT YOUR TIME-BAR,  ................. 207  SEXTUS PROP: 1      8
BARREL
     "CAT'S I' THE WATER BUTT!" THOUGHT'S IN YOUR
          VERSE-BARREL,  .................................  13  MESMERISM          5
BARRELED
     NOR OF XERXES' TWO-BARRELED KINGDOM, NOR OF REMUS
          AND HIS ROYAL FAMILY,  ......................... 217  SEXTUS PROP: 5     44
BASKET
     A BASKET-WORK OF BRAIDS WHICH SEEM AS IF THEY WERE   204  MEDALLION          10
BASS'
     MY NERVES STILL REGISTER THE SOUNDS OF CONTRA-BASS'. 247  PIERROTS           19
```

BATH -- BOUNDING

		PAGE	TITLE	LINE
BATH				
	THIS LADY IN THE WHITE BATH-ROBE WHICH SHE CALLS A PEIGNOIR.	87	ALBATRE	1
BATTLE				
	SUCH BATTLE-GUERDON WITH HIS "PROWESSE HIGH"?	32	PIERE VIDAL	59
BE (2)				
BEAKED				
	AS THE RED-BEAKED STEEDS OF	201	AGE DEMANDED	3
BEAMS				
	THE PARENT RE-BEAMS AT ITS OFFSPRING.	180	MOEURS CON: 5	13
BED				
	MOUNTS FROM THE FOUR HORNS OF MY BED-POSTS,	169	PHANOPOEIA	3
	HER ESCRITOIRES LAY SHUT BY THE BED-FEET.	214	SEXTUS PROP: 4	21
BEEF				
	HE FEEDS ME WITH BEEF-BONES AND WINE.	237	ABU SALAMMAMM	3
BEER				
	DRINK OF THE WINDS THEIR CHILL SMALL-BEER	10	FOR THIS YULE	4
BELLIED				
	YOU SLUT-BELLIED OBSTRUCTIONIST.	145	SALUTATION 3RD	10
BELLIES				
	LET US SPIT UPON THOSE WHO PAT THE BIG-BELLIES FOR PROFIT.	145	SALUTATION 3RD	15
BELLS				
	GO! JANGLE THEIR DOOR-BELLS!	86	SALUTATION 2ND	35
BELOVED				
	HEART'S-ALL-BELOVED-MY-OWN;	48	FROM HEINE: 8	6
BEN				
	UNTO LADY "MIELS-DE-BEN,"	8	NA AUDIART	13
	I OF MIELS-DE-BEN DEMAND	106	DOMPNA POIS	47
BIG				
	LET US SPIT UPON THOSE WHO PAT THE BIG-BELLIES FOR PROFIT,	145	SALUTATION 3RD	15
BINDING				
	WE WHO HAVE SEEN EVEN ARTEMIS A-BINDING HER SANDALS,	104	ANCORA	6
BITCH				
	WILL BE QUITE RICH, QUITE PLUMP, WITH PUG-BITCH FEATURES,	162	CABARET DANCER	48
BITIN'				
	AND DON'T KNOW WHAT BUG IS A-BITIN'	269	SAFE AND SOUND	11
BLADE				
	CLEAR AS FROST ON THE GRASS-BLADE,	108	FAN-PIECE	2
BLAST				
	AYE, FOR EVER, A LASTING LIFE'S-BLAST,	66	THE SEAFARER	80
BLOOD				
	AND I LOVE TO SEE THE SUN RISE BLOOD-CRIMSON.	29	ALTAFORTE	19
	A GRACIOUS SPRING, TURNED TO BLOOD-RAVENOUS AUTUMN,	133	FRONTIER GUARD	14
BLOWN				
	I SKOAL TO THE EYES AS GREY-BLOWN MERE	10	FOR THIS YULE	22
BLUE				
	SHIELD O' STEEL-BLUE, TH' HEAVEN O'ER US	7	CINO	44
	SKIRTING THE BLUE-GRAY SEA	90	SURGIT FAMA	3
	SOUTH OF THE POND THE WILLOW-TIPS ARE HALF-BLUE AND BLUER,	129	THE RIVER SONG	25
BOLT				
	AND GETS A QUARREL-BOLT SHOT THROUGH HIS VIZARD,	156	NEAR PERIGORD	158
BONE				
	OF EYE-LID AND CHEEK-BONE	200	MAUBERLEY: 2	22
BONES				
	HE FEEDS ME WITH BEEF-BONES AND WINE.	237	ABU SALAMMAMM	3
BOOK				
	(NEAR Q. H. FLACCUS' BOOK-STALL).	210	SEXTUS PROP: 2	9
BORN				
	WHERE IS THE WORK OF YOUR HOME-BORN SCULPTORS?	165	QUINTUS SEPTIM	16
	THE ENGLISH RUBAIYAT WAS STILL-BORN	192	YEUX GLAUQUES	15
	GO, DUMB-BORN BOOK,	197	ENVOI (1919)	1
BOSOM				
	SPREAD ON BOTH HANDS AND ON THE UP-PUSHED-BOSOM--	161	CABARET DANCER	15
BOUGHT				
	TALK ME NO LOVE TALK, NO BOUGHT-CHEAP FIDDL'RY,	25	GUIDO INVITES	3
BOUNDING				
	BRIGHT IN ITS SUAVE BOUNDING-LINE, AS,	204	MEDALLION	14

PAGE 493

BOY -- CLIFF

	PAGE	TITLE	LINE
BOY			
THAT TOM-BOY WHO CAN'T EARN HER LIVING,	162	CABARET DANCER	44
BRAID			
IT IS HE WHO BUYS GOLD-BRAID FOR THE SWANKERS	263	ALF'S EIGHTH	17
BREAST			
BITTER BREAST-CARES HAVE I ABIDED,	64	THE SEAFARER	4
BRIDGE			
YOU BACK TO YOUR RIVER-BRIDGE.	135	EXILE'S LETTER	35
BRIGHT			
I HAVE KNOWN THE STONE-BRIGHT PLACE,	95	OF THE DEGREES	8
BRISTLE			
A-BRISTLE WITH ANTENNAE TO FEEL ROADS,	153	NEAR PERIGORD	62
BROCADE			
THEIR CORDS TANGLE IN MIST, AGAINST THE BROCADE-LIKE PALACE.	129	THE RIVER SONG	26
BROOK			
THIN LIKE BROOK-WATER,	192	YEUX GLAUQUES	13
BROTHER			
HIS BROTHER-IN-LAW WAS ALL THERE WAS OF POWER	151	NEAR PERIGORD	17
BROWED			
COME NOT ANEAR THE DARK-BROWED SOPHIST	263	ALF'S EIGHTH	8
BROWN			
OUT OF THE BROWN LEAF-BROWN COLOURLESS	76	THE ALCHEMIST	47
BROWS			
THESE ARE THE HIGH-BROWS, AND TO THIS COLLECTION	241	MOYEN SENSUEL	82
BURNE			
THE BURNE-JONES CARTONS	192	YEUX GLAUQUES	9
BUS			
YOU LOITER AT THE CORNERS AND BUS-STOPS,	94	INSTRUCTIONS	6
BUT (1)			
BUTT			
"AND A CAT'S IN THE WATER-BUTT."--ROBERT BROWNING	13	MESMERISM	EPI
BY (1)			
BYE			
AND WE SAY GOOD-BYE TO YOU ALSO,	101	AMITIES	7
CAFE			
ARE THOSE OF A MAITRE-DE-CAFE.	114	EPILOGUE	11
CARE			
LIST HOW I, CARE-WRETCHED, ON ICE-COLD SEA,	64	THE SEAFARER	14
CARES			
BITTER BREAST-CARES HAVE I ABIDED,	64	THE SEAFARER	4
CASTES			
NOT LIKE THE HALF-CASTES,	119	THE GYPSY	5
CAT			
SWINGING A CAT-O'-NINE-TAILS.	162	CABARET DANCER	37
SHE'D SAY TO HER TIBBY-CAT,	271	OLE KATE	22
CAT'S			
AND THE GREEN CAT'S-EYE LIFTS TOWARD MONTAIGNAC.	154	NEAR PERIGORD	103
CAUCASUS			
CELEBRITIES FROM THE TRANS-CAUCASUS WILL BELAUD ROMAN CELEBRITIES	207	SEXTUS PROP: 1	17
CE			
"EST-CE QUE VOUS AVEZ VU DES AUTRES--DES CAMARADES--AVEC DES SINGES OU DES OURS?"	119	THE GYPSY	EPI
CHEAP			
TALK ME NO LOVE TALK, NO BOUGHT-CHEAP FIDDL'RY,	25	GUIDO INVITES	3
CHEEK			
OF EYE-LID AND CHEEK-BONE	200	MAUBERLEY: 2	22
CHO			
AS FAR AS CHO-FU-SA.	131	RIVER-MER WIFE	29
CHOP			
YOU ONCE DISCOVERED A MODERATE CHOP-HOUSE.	101	AMITIES	16
CLEAR			
THE SEA-CLEAR SAPPHIRE OF AIR, THE SEA-DARK CLARITY, STRETCHES BOTH SEA-CLIFF AND OCEAN.	170	PHANOPOEIA	24
CLERKLY			
WITH THE MOST BANK-CLERKLY OF ENGLISHMEN?	195	HUGH SELWIN:11	4
CLIFF			
THE SEA-CLEAR SAPPHIRE OF AIR, THE SEA-DARK CLARITY, STRETCHES BOTH SEA-CLIFF AND OCEAN.	170	PHANOPOEIA	24

	PAGE	TITLE	LINE
CLIFFS			
STORMS, ON THE STONE-CLIFFS BEATEN, FELL ON THE STERN	64	THE SEAFARER	23
CLINKS			
THE SPUR-CLINKS SOUND BETWEEN,	47	FROM HEINE: 7	26
CLOTH			
WHICH BROUGHT THE HAIR-CLOTH CHAIR TO SUCH			
PERFECTION,	63	PHASELLUS ILLE	6
CO			
THE CO-OPS WAS A GOIN' SOMEWHERE,	262	ALF'S SEVENTH	2
TO THE CO-OPS, A ECHO OR SOMETHIN'?	262	ALF'S SEVENTH	9
IS WHERE THE CO-OPS ARE GOIN' TO,	262	ALF'S SEVENTH	13
IS NOT SUITED TO CO-OPERATION--	262	ALF'S SEVENTH	15
COAST			
HE LIES BY THE POLUPHLOIBOIOUS SEA-COAST.	181	MOEURS CON: 6	4
COCK			
"BEAUTY IS SLANDER'S COCK-SHY.	226	SEXTUS PROP:11	21
COEUR			
"HERE COEUR-DE-LION WAS SLAIN.	122	PROVINC DESERT	44
MALEMORT, GUESSES BENEATH, SENDS WORD TO			
COEUR-DE-LION:	155	NEAR PERIGORD	123
COLD			
YOU WHEEZE AS A HEAD-COLD LONG-TONSILLED CALLIOPE,	13	MESMERISM	9
LIST HOW I, CARE-WRETCHED, ON ICE-COLD SEA,	64	THE SEAFARER	14
AND ICE-COLD WAVE, AT WHILES THE SWAN CRIES,	64	THE SEAFARER	19
GREY OLIVE LEAVES BENEATH A RAIN-COLD SKY.	92	GENTILDONNA	5
COLOURED			
BRING THE SAFFRON-COLOURED SHELL,	75	THE ALCHEMIST	9
FROM THE PLUM-COLOURED LAKE, IN STILLNESS,	75	THE ALCHEMIST	17
THE ORANGE-COLOURED ROSE-LEAVES,	108	TS'AI CHI'H	2
I LOOKED AT THE DRAGON-POND, WITH ITS			
WILLOW-COLOURED WATER	129	THE RIVER SONG	20
LAPPED IN THE GOLD-COLOURED FLAME I DESCEND THROUGH			
THE AETHER.	169	PHANOPOEIA	5
THE CORAL ISLE, THE LION-COLOURED SAND	201	AGE DEMANDED	17
COMB			
I HA' SEEN HIM EAT O' THE HONEY-COMB	34	GOODLY FERE	53
COMMUNE			
THE NEO-COMMUNE	258	ALF'S SECOND	SUB
CONNAISSEZ			
"CONNAISSEZ-VOUS OSTENDE?"	111	BLACK SLIPPERS	6
CONQUERING			
ALL-CONQUERING, NOW CONQUERED, BECAUSE	40	ROME	7
CONTRA			
MY NERVES STILL REGISTER THE SOUNDS OF CONTRA-BASS',	247	PIERROTS	19
CONVENTION			
GO ALSO TO THE NERVE-WRACKED, GO TO THE			
ENSLAVED-BY-CONVENTION,	88	COMMISSION	2
COURSING			
SILENT UNTO US IN THEIR FAR-COURSING,	27	NIGHT LITANY	46
COURT			
DUST DRIFTS OVER THE COURT-YARD,	108	LIU CH'E	2
THE DRYAD STANDS IN MY COURT-YARD	110	TEMPORA	2
COVER			
NOR MAY HE THEN THE FLESH-COVER, WHOSE LIFE CEASETH,	66	THE SEAFARER	96
COVERED			
BUT ONE HUGE BACK HALF-COVERED UP WITH PINE,	152	NEAR PERIGORD	33
CRANBERRIES			
MARSH-CRANBERRIES, THE RIBBED AND ANGULAR PODS	162	CABARET DANCER	19
CRIMSON			
AND I LOVE TO SEE THE SUN RISE BLOOD-CRIMSON.	29	ALTAFORTE	19
CROSS			
SUNSET, THE RIBBON-LIKE ROAD LIES, IN RED			
CROSS-LIGHT,	154	NEAR PERIGORD	96
CROSSING			
AND THEY MADE NOTHING OF SEA-CROSSING OR OF			
MOUNTAIN-CROSSING,	134	EXILE'S LETTER	9
AND THEY MADE NOTHING OF SEA-CROSSING OR OF			
MOUNTAIN-CROSSING,	134	EXILE'S LETTER	9
CROW			
I AM HUNG HERE, A SCARE-CROW FOR LOVERS.	226	SEXTUS PROP:11	3

CROWD -- DRINK

	PAGE	TITLE	LINE
CROWD			
"ANOTHER WHEEL, THE ARENA; MID-CROWD IS AS BAD AS MID-SEA."	210	SEXTUS PROP: 2	27
CRUEL			
NOT YET WILD-CRUEL AS DARTS,	250	DONNA MI PREGA	74
CUDDLE			
"GIMME A KISSY-CUDDLE"	271	OLE KATE	21
CULTURE			
SPANISH AND PARIS, LOVE OF THE ARTS PART OF YOUR GEISHA-CULTURE!	163	CABARET DANCER	52
DARK			
THE SEA-CLEAR SAPPHIRE OF AIR, THE SEA-DARK CLARITY, STRETCHES BOTH SEA-CLIFF AND OCEAN.	170	PHANOPOEIA	24
COME NOT ANEAR THE DARK-BROWED SOPHIST	263	ALF'S EIGHTH	8
DAWN			
OR THROUGH DAWN-MIST	203	MAUBERLEY: 4	10
DAY			
GLORY TO ZEUS' AEGIS-DAY,	7	CINO	43
AND EACH TO-DAY 'VAILS LESS THAN YESTERE'EN,	37	THE YOUNG KING	28
TO-DAY, ON HIGH	41	HER MONUMENT	26
HERE IN THE EVERY-DAY WHERE OUR ACTS	52	AU SALON	4
TO-DAY FROM THE DRAGON-PEN.	139	SOUTH-FOLK	5
YOU READ TO-DAY, HOW LONG THE OVERLORDS OF PERIGORD,	152	NEAR PERIGORD	50
SINGS DAY-LONG AND NIGHT LATE	171	LANGUE D'OC	EPI
TO-DAY WE TAKE THE GREAT BREATH OF LOVERS,	221	SEXTUS PROP: 7	31
BUT KNIGHTS AND LORDS TO-DAY RESPECT	267	ALF'S ELEVENTH	23
DAY'S			
BUT TO-DAY'S MEN ARE NOT THE MEN OF THE OLD DAYS,	131	AT TEN-SHIN	7
LIKE TO-DAY'S GREAT MEN IN BRITAIN.	272	THE BABY	12
DE			
UNTO LADY "MIELS-DE-BEN,"	8	NA AUDIART	13
I OF MIELS-DE-BEN DEMAND	106	DOMPNA POIS	47
ARE THOSE OF A MAITRE-DE-CAFE.	114	EPILOGUE	11
"HERE COEUR-DE-LION WAS SLAIN.	122	PROVINC DESERT	44
MALEMORT, GUESSES BENEATH, SENDS WORD TO COEUR-DE-LION:	155	NEAR PERIGORD	123
TEINTEES DE COULEUR SANG-DE-DRAGON,	160	DANS OMNIBUS	27
DEAL			
PULLED DOWN BY A DEAL-WOOD HORSE;	208	SEXTUS PROP: 1	27
DEEP			
WALKED EYE-DEEP IN HELL	190	HUGH SELWYN: 4	13
DEW			
BY DEW-SPREAD CAVERNS,	227	SEXTUS PROP:11	30
DIALS			
RATHER THAN THE MOTTOES ON SUN-DIALS.	187	E. P. ODE	16
DIPLOMAT'S			
WILL MEET A DUCHESS AND AN EX-DIPLOMAT'S WIDOW	163	CABARET DANCER	64
DISH			
LIFE'S A SORT OF SUGARED DISH-WASH!"	241	MOYEN SENSUEL	90
DOG			
THAT WAS A DOG-WOOD TREE SOME SYNE.	4	LA FRAISNE	15
DOG'S			
THE PUG-DOG'S FEATURES ENCRUSTED WITH TALLOW	161	CABARET DANCER	11
DOOM			
BEATS OUT THE BREATH FROM DOOM-GRIPPED BODY.	66	THE SEAFARER	72
DOOR			
GO! JANGLE THEIR DOOR-BELLS!	86	SALUTATION 2ND	35
THEIR DOOR-YARDS WOULD SCARCELY KNOW THEM, OR PARIS.	208	SEXTUS PROP: 1	31
DOWN			
AMID THE PRECIPITATION, DOWN-FLOAT	202	AGE DEMANDED	52
DRAGON			
I LOOKED AT THE DRAGON-POND, WITH ITS WILLOW-COLOURED WATER	129	THE RIVER SONG	20
THEY RIDE UPON DRAGON-LIKE HORSES,	132	AT TEN-SHIN	15
WITH RIPPLES LIKE DRAGON-SCALES, GOING GRASS GREEN ON THE WATER,	136	EXILE'S LETTER	52
TO-DAY FROM THE DRAGON-PEN.	139	SOUTH-FOLK	5
TEINTEES DE COULEUR SANG-DE-DRAGON,	160	DANS OMNIBUS	27
DRINK			
THE MEWS' SINGING ALL MY MEAD-DRINK.	64	THE SEAFARER	22

DRUMS -- FACED

	PAGE	TITLE	LINE
DRUMS			
WHO HAS BROUGHT THE ARMY WITH DRUMS AND WITH KETTLE-DRUMS?	133	FRONTIER GUARD	12
DUMB			
GO, DUMB-BORN BOOK,	197	ENVOI (1919)	1
DUST			
THE SCORCHED LAUREL LAY IN THE FIRE-DUST;	223	SEXTUS PROP: 9	2
E			
AIE-E! 'TIS TRUE THAT I AM GAY	5	LA FRAISNE	37
EAR			
THOMAS LARRON "EAR-THE-LESS,"	11	OF THE GIBBET	6
EARTH			
THAT ANY EARTH-WEAL ETERNAL STANDETH	66	THE SEAFARER	68
EAST			
MAREUIL TO THE NORTH-EAST,	121	PROVINC DESERT	22
THE TREES IN MY EAST-LOOKING GARDEN	142	UNMOVING CLOUD	17
EASTWARD			
AND EVENING DRIVES THEM ON THE EASTWARD-FLOWING WATERS.	131	AT TEN-SHIN	4
EAU			
TURNED FROM THE "EAU-FORTE	198	MAUBERLEY: 1	1
EDGED			
THE FLUTTER OF SHARP-EDGED SANDALS.	169	PHANOPOEIA	13
EGG			
GREEN ARSENIC SMEARED ON AN EGG-WHITE CLOTH,	113	L'ART, 1910	1
EH			
"AH-EH! THE STRANGE RARE NAME . . .	15	FAMAM CANO	42
AH-EH! HE MUST BE RARE IF EVEN I HAVE NOT . . ."	15	FAMAM CANO	43
EIGHT			
FOR THERE ARE, IN SIRMIONE, TWENTY-EIGHT YOUNG DANTES AND THIRTY-FOUR CATULLI;	96	AESTHETICS	8
HIS PALACE HAS NINETY-EIGHT WINDOWS,	237	ABU SALAMMAMM	6
HIS ARMY IS A THOUSAND AND FORTY-EIGHT SOLDIERS	237	ABU SALAMMAMM	12
AND WONDER IF MY DAY'S THREE AND EIGHT-PENCE	268	ANOTHER BIT	11
ELM			
THAT GREW ELM-OAK AMID THE WOLD.	3	THE TREE	5
EM			
TO-EM-MEI'S "THE UNMOVING CLOUD"	142	UNMOVING CLOUD	T
"WET SPRINGTIME," SAYS TO-EM-MEI, "WET SPRING IN THE GARDEN."	142	UNMOVING CLOUD	EPI
EMPTY			
OVER THE EMPTY-HEADED, AND THE SLOW	265	ALF'S TENTH	6
ENSLAVED			
GO ALSO TO THE NERVE-WRACKED, GO TO THE ENSLAVED-BY-CONVENTION,	88	COMMISSION	2
ENTER			
TO SEE HOW CELESTINE WILL RE-ENTER HER SLIPPERS.	111	BLACK SLIPPERS	10
ENTERS			
SHE RE-ENTERS THEM WITH A GROAN.	111	BLACK SLIPPERS	11
EST			
"EST-CE QUE VOUS AVEZ VU DES AUTRES--DES CAMARADES--AVEC DES SINGES OU DES OURS?"	119	THE GYPSY	EPI
ESTEEM			
NON-ESTEEM OF SELF-STYLED "HIS BETTERS"	202	AGE DEMANDED	58
EVER			
IN THIS EVER-FLOWING MONOTONY	35	THE EYES	12
WE OF THE EVER-LIVING IN THAT LIGHT	50	THE FLAME	12
EVERY			
HERE IN THE EVERY-DAY WHERE OUR ACTS	52	AU SALON	4
EX			
WILL MEET A DUCHESS AND AN EX-DIPLOMAT'S WIDOW	163	CABARET DANCER	64
EYE			
AND THE GREEN CAT'S-EYE LIFTS TOWARD MONTAIGNAC.	154	NEAR PERIGORD	103
WALKED EYE-DEEP IN HELL	190	HUGH SELWYN: 4	13
OF EYE-LID AND CHEEK-BONE	200	MAUBERLEY: 2	22
FACE			
HONEY-RED, CLOSING THE FACE OVAL,	204	MEDALLION	9
THE FACE-OVAL BENEATH THE GLAZE,	204	MEDALLION	13
FACED			
O FILAMENTS OF AMBER, TWO-FACED IRIDESCENCE!	95	OF THE DEGREES	15

FACED -- FLOWERS

	PAGE	TITLE	LINE
FACED (CONTINUED)			
WHY DOES THE HORSE-FACED LADY OF JUST THE UNMENTIONABLE AGE	114	SIMULACRA	1
ONE OF THOSE FIRM-FACED INSPECTING WOMEN, WHO	243	MOYEN SENSUEL	156
FALL			
THERE IS NO SOUND OF FOOT-FALL, AND THE LEAVES	108	LIU CH'E	3
FAN			
FAN-PIECE, FOR HER IMPERIAL LORD	108	FAN-PIECE	T
FANGLED			
A NEW-FANGLED CHARIOT FOLLOWS THE FLOWER-HUNG HORSES;	207	SEXTUS PROP: 1	12
FAR			
SILENT UNTO US IN THEIR FAR-COURSING,	27	NIGHT LITANY	46
FARE			
'POLLO PHOIBEE, TO OUR WAY-FARE	7	CINO	46
BUT SHALL HAVE HIS SORROW FOR SEA-FARE	65	THE SEAFARER	43
FAUN			
STILL DARTS OUT FAUN-LIKE FROM THE HALF-RUIN'D FACE,	192	YEUX GLAUQUES	18
FEASTING			
AND THAT GOD-FEASTING COUPLE OLD	3	THE TREE	4
FEEDER			
SOLDIER, THE ENUMERATION OF WOUNDS; THE SHEEP-FEEDER, OF EWES;	218	SEXTUS PROP: 5	56
FEET			
HER ESCRITOIRES LAY SHUT BY THE BED-FEET.	214	SEXTUS PROP: 4	21
FELLOW			
GIVE MY GOOD-FELLOW AID IN FOOLS' DESPITE	172	LANGUE D'OC: 1	3
FERN			
HERE WE ARE, PICKING THE FIRST FERN-SHOOTS	127	BOWMEN OF SHU	1
WE GRUB THE SOFT FERN-SHOOTS,	127	BOWMEN OF SHU	5
WE GRUB THE OLD FERN-STALKS.	127	BOWMEN OF SHU	9
FINGER			
HAVE I NOT TOUCHED THY PALMS AND FINGER-TIPS,	60	TOMB AKR CAAR	22
SPREAD LIKE THE FINGER-TIPS OF ONE FRAIL HAND;	152	NEAR PERIGORD	30
FIRE			
THE SCORCHED LAUREL LAY IN THE FIRE-DUST;	223	SEXTUS PROP: 9	2
FIRM			
ONE OF THOSE FIRM-FACED INSPECTING WOMEN, WHO	243	MOYEN SENSUEL	156
FISH			
THE HORSES ARE WELL TRAINED, THE GENERALS HAVE IVORY ARROWS AND QUIVERS ORNAMENTED WITH FISH-SKIN.	127	BOWMEN OF SHU	19
FIVE			
AND HEARD THE FIVE-SCORE NIGHTINGALES AIMLESSLY SINGING.	129	THE RIVER SONG	22
FLAKES			
HUNG WITH HARD ICE-FLAKES, WHERE HAIL-SCUR FLEW,	64	THE SEAFARER	17
FLAME			
AS I'VE FOR YOU, SUCH FLAME-LAP,	107	DOMPNA POIS	65
FLAMES			
I HAVE SEEN THE TORCH-FLAMES, HIGH-LEAPING,	121	PROVINC DESERT	30
FLAPPING			
HE GOES OUT TO HORI, TO LOOK AT THE WING-FLAPPING STORKS,	130	THE RIVER SONG	36
FLARE			
STRAY GLEAMS ON HANGING MAIL, AN ARMOURER'S TORCH-FLARE	155	NEAR PERIGORD	134
FLAT			
OUT OF EREBUS, THE FLAT-LYING BREADTH,	76	THE ALCHEMIST	44
"ANIENAN SPRING WATER FALLS INTO FLAT-SPREAD POOLS."	212	SEXTUS PROP: 3	5
FLESH			
FLESH-SHROUDED BEARING THE SECRET.	20	IN DURANCE	25
NOR MAY HE THEN THE FLESH-COVER, WHOSE LIFE CEASETH,	66	THE SEAFARER	96
FLOAT			
AMID THE PRECIPITATION, DOWN-FLOAT	202	AGE DEMANDED	52
FLOOD			
ON FLOOD-WAYS TO BE FAR DEPARTING.	65	THE SEAFARER	53
MY MOOD 'MID THE MERE-FLOOD,	65	THE SEAFARER	60
FLOWER			
A NEW-FANGLED CHARIOT FOLLOWS THE FLOWER-HUNG HORSES;	207	SEXTUS PROP: 1	12
FLOWERS			
THE SMOKE-FLOWERS ARE BLURRED OVER THE RIVER.	137	ON RIVER KIANG	2

	PAGE	TITLE	LINE
FLOWING			
IN THIS EVER-FLOWING MONOTONY	35	THE EYES	12
AND EVENING DRIVES THEM ON THE EASTWARD-FLOWING WATERS.	131	AT TEN-SHIN	4
FLUSHED			
WEALTHY AND WINE-FLUSHED, HOW I WEARY OFT	64	THE SEAFARER	30
FLYER			
EAGER AND READY, THE CRYING LONE-FLYER,	65	THE SEAFARER	63
FOLK			
BUT MY SOUL SENT A WOMAN, A WOMAN OF THE WONDER-FOLK,	17	PRAISE YSOLT	38
SOUTH-FOLK IN COLD COUNTRY	139	SOUTH-FOLK	T
FOOT			
SWIFT-FOOT TO MY LADY ANHES,	106	DOMPNA POIS	36
THERE IS NO SOUND OF FOOT-FALL, AND THE LEAVES	108	LIU CH'E	3
FORE			
WITH ARMS EXALTED, WITH FORE-ARMS	93	LES MILLWIN	8
TAWN FORE-SHORES	203	MAUBERLEY: 4	8
FORTE			
TURNED FROM THE "EAU-FORTE	198	MAUBERLEY: 1	1
FORTY			
HIS ARMY IS A THOUSAND AND FORTY-EIGHT SOLDIERS	237	ABU SALAMMAMM	12
FOUR			
BREAK DOWN THE FOUR SQUARE WALLS OF STANDING TIME.	49	OF SPLENDOUR	21
FOR THERE ARE, IN SIRMIONE, TWENTY-EIGHT YOUNG DANTES AND THIRTY-FOUR CATULLI;	96	AESTHETICS	8
FOWLS'			
SEA-FOWLS' LOUDNESS WAS FOR ME LAUGHTER,	64	THE SEAFARER	21
FRANCOIS			
IMPRESSIONS OF FRANCOIS-MARIE AROUET (DE VOLTAIRE)	167	OF AROUET	T
FREE			
HER STRAIGHT SPEECH FREE-RUNNING,	105	DOMPNA POIS	29
FU			
AS FAR AS CHO-FU-SA.	131	RIVER-MER WIFE	29
GATE			
AND CLINGS TO THE WALLS AND THE GATE-TOP.	131	AT TEN-SHIN	12
GAUCHE			
FAT PIERRE WITH THE HOOK GAUCHE-MAIN,	11	OF THE GIBBET	5
GAWS			
THE GEW-GAWS OF FALSE AMBER AND FALSE TURQUOISE ATTRACT THEM.	114	BEFORE A SHOP	1
GEISHA			
SPANISH AND PARIS, LOVE OF THE ARTS PART OF YOUR GEISHA-CULTURE!	163	CABARET DANCER	52
GEW			
THE GEW-GAWS OF FALSE AMBER AND FALSE TURQUOISE ATTRACT THEM.	114	BEFORE A SHOP	1
GIRLS			
MAELIDS AND WATER-GIRLS,	87	THE SPRING	2
GIVING			
NOR GOLD-GIVING LORDS LIKE THOSE GONE.	66	THE SEAFARER	85
GLASS			
OUT THROUGH THE GLASS-GREEN FIELDS.	60	TOMB AKR CAAR	31
WITHOUT SMIRKING INTO A POCKET-LOOKING-GLASS.	247	PIERROTS	21
GLEAMING			
WITH YOU IS IOPE, WITH YOU THE WHITE-GLEAMING TYRO,	38	LADY'S LIFE	5
THE IMPERIAL GUARDS COME FORTH FROM THE GOLDEN HOUSE WITH THEIR ARMOUR A-GLEAMING.	129	THE RIVER SONG	31
GO			
AND THE MOON FALLS OVER THE PORTALS OF SEI-GO-YO,	131	AT TEN-SHIN	11
WE MET, AND TRAVELLED INTO SEN-GO,	134	EXILE'S LETTER	17
GOD			
AND THAT GOD-FEASTING COUPLE OLD	3	THE TREE	4
MY GOD-LIKE COMPOSITIONS.	40	FROM HEINE: 6	16
GOLD			
NOR GOLD-GIVING LORDS LIKE THOSE GONE.	66	THE SEAFARER	85
LAPPED IN THE GOLD-COLOURED FLAME I DESCEND THROUGH THE AETHER.	169	PHANOPOEIA	3
FROM THE GOLD-YELLOW FROCK	204	MEDALLION	6
IT IS HE WHO BUYS GOLD-BRAID FOR THE SWANKERS	263	ALF'S EIGHTH	17
GOOD			
AND WE SAY GOOD-BYE TO YOU ALSO,	101	AMITIES	7

	PAGE	TITLE	LINE

GOOD (CONTINUED)
GIVE MY GOOD-FELLOW AID IN FOOLS' DESPITE .... 172 LANGUE D'OC: 1   3
GOOSE
YESTERDAY WE WENT OUT OF THE WILD-GOOSE GATE, ... 139 SOUTH-FOLK   4
GOWN
THE TEA-ROSE TEA-GOWN, ETC. .... 189 HUGH SELWYN: 3   1
GOWNED
OF WELL-GOWNED APPROBATION .... 196 HUGH SELWIN:12 10
GRASS
CLEAR AS FROST ON THE GRASS-BLADE, ... 108 FAN-PIECE   2
GRAY
BY THE TROUT ASLEEP IN THE GRAY-GREEN OF WATER; ... 76 THE ALCHEMIST 37
SKIRTING THE BLUE-GRAY SEA .... 90 SURGIT FAMA   3
GREAT
OR TAKE THE INTAGLIO, MY FAT GREAT-UNCLE'S HEIRLOOM: 162 CABARET DANCER 35
GREEN
OUT THROUGH THE GLASS-GREEN FIELDS. ... . 60 TOMB AKR CAAR 31
BY THE TROUT ASLEEP IN THE GRAY-GREEN OF WATER; ... 76 THE ALCHEMIST 37
GREY
I SKOAL TO THE EYES AS GREY-BLOWN MERE .... 10 FOR THIS YULE 22
GREY-HAIRED HE GROANETH, KNOWS GONE COMPANIONS, ... 66 THE SEAFARER 94
GRIP
OR SLACKED HIS HAND-GRIP WHEN YOU FIRST GRIPPED FAME? 59 EXIT' CUIUSDAM   3
GRIPPED
BEATS OUT THE BREATH FROM DOOM-GRIPPED BODY. ...... 66 THE SEAFARER 72
GROWN
O STATE SANS SONG, SANS HOME-GROWN WINE, SANS
REALIST! .... 241 MOYEN SENSUEL 88
GUERDON
SUCH BATTLE-GUERDON WITH HIS "PROWESSE HIGH"? ..... 32 PIERE VIDAL 59
GUINEA
AND THEN THAT WOMAN LIKE A GUINEA-PIG .... 242 MOYEN SENSUEL 120
GUN
WHETHER MR. DUPONT AND THE GUN-SHARKS .... 268 ANOTHER BIT   7
HAIL
HUNG WITH HARD ICE-FLAKES, WHERE HAIL-SCUR FLEW,   64 THE SEAFARER 17
HAIR
WHICH BROUGHT THE HAIR-CLOTH CHAIR TO SUCH
PERFECTION, ... 63 PHASELLUS ILLE   6
HAIRED
GREY-HAIRED HE GROANETH, KNOWS GONE COMPANIONS, ... 66 THE SEAFARER 94
HALF
ALFONSO THE HALF-BALD, TOOK TO HANGING .... 22 MARVOIL   9
ALL FOR ONE HALF-BALD, KNOCK-KNEE'D KING OF THE
ARAGONESE, ... 22 MARVOIL 21
HALF-SHEATHED, THEN NAKED FROM ITS SAFFRON SHEATH   31 PIERE VIDAL 41
WITH FEAR, AS HALF-AWAKENED; .... 74 THE RETURN   6
NOT LIKE THE HALF-CASTES, ... 119 THE GYPSY   5
SOUTH OF THE POND THE WILLOW-TIPS ARE HALF-BLUE AND
BLUER, ... 129 THE RIVER SONG 25
BUT ONE HUGE BACK HALF-COVERED UP WITH PINE, ... 152 NEAR PERIGORD 33
STILL DARTS OUT FAUN-LIKE FROM THE HALF-RUIN'D FACE, 192 YEUX GLAUQUES 18
THE SALE OF HALF-HOSE HAS .... 196 HUGH SELWIN:12 26
BENEATH HALF-WATT RAYS, ... 204 MEDALLION 15
OUT INTO THE CREPUSCULAR HALF-LIGHT, NOW AND THEN; 244 MOYEN SENSUEL 186
OVER THE DYING HALF-WITS BLOW, ... 265 ALF'S TENTH   5
HAN
WHO AMONG THEM IS A MAN LIKE HAN-REI .... 132 AT TEN-SHIN 31
HAND
OR SLACKED HIS HAND-GRIP WHEN YOU FIRST GRIPPED FAME? 59 EXIT' CUIUSDAM   3
HANDED
"OF" THE VICTORIOUS DELAY OF FABIUS, AND THE
LEFT-HANDED BATTLE AT CANNAE, ... 210 SEXTUS PROP: 2 11
HATE
DISEASE OR OLDNESS OR SWORD-HATE .... 66 THE SEAFARER 71
HAVING
HE HATH NOT HEART FOR HARPING, NOR IN RING-HAVING   65 THE SEAFARER 45
HEAD
YOU WHEEZE AS A HEAD-COLD LONG-TONSILLED CALLIOPE,   13 MESMERISM   9
I HAVE NOT FOUND THEE AT THE WELL-HEAD .... 91 DANCE FIGURE   8
UPON HORSES WITH HEAD-TRAPPINGS OF YELLOW METAL, 132 AT TEN-SHIN 16

	PAGE	TITLE	LINE
HEAD (CONTINUED)			
AND SHE PILES HER HAIR UP ON THE LEFT SIDE OF HER HEAD-PIECE.	140	MULBERRY ROAD	11
HEADED			
WHO HAS HAD A PIG-HEADED FATHER;	89	A PACT	4
WHITE-HEADED.	136	EXILE'S LETTER	69
OVER THE EMPTY-HEADED, AND THE SLOW	265	ALF'S TENTH	6
HEART			
AND DAVID'S HARP LET OUT HEART-RENDING SQUEALS:	264	ALF'S NINTH	15
HEART'S			
HEART'S-ALL-BELOVED-MY-OWN;	48	FROM HEINE: 8	6
HEAVY			
SODDEN AND LEAD-HEAVY.	35	THE EYES	4
HIGH			
WE SEEM AS STATUES ROUND WHOSE HIGH-RISEN BASE	32	PARACELSUS	11
I HAVE SEEN THE TORCH-FLAMES, HIGH-LEAPING,	121	PROVINC DESERT	30
SHE IS NOW THE HIGH-PRIESTESS	178	MOEURS CON: 1	11
AND THERE IS NO HIGH-ROAD TO THE MUSES.	207	SEXTUS PROP: 1	15
THESE ARE THE HIGH-BROWS, AND TO THIS COLLECTION	241	MOYEN SENSUEL	82
HIPPETY			
HERE'S TO YOU, OLD HIPPETY-HOP O' THE ACCENTS,	13	MESMERISM	17
HIS (2)			
HOARD			
FOR ALL THIS SEA-HOARD OF DECIDUOUS THINGS,	61	PORTRAIT FEMME	25
HOKU			
AND YOU TO THE NORTH OF RAKU-HOKU,	134	EXILE'S LETTER	14
HOLLY			
UNBEND FROM THE HOLLY-TREES,	109	HEATHER	5
HOME			
WHERE IS THE WORK OF YOUR HOME-BORN SCULPTORS?	165	QUINTUS SEPTIM	16
O STATE SANS SONG, SANS HOME-GROWN WINE, SANS REALIST!	241	MOYEN SENSUEL	88
A HOME-INDUSTRIOUS WORKER TO PERFECTION,	245	MOYEN SENSUEL	213
HONEY			
I HA' SEEN HIM EAT O' THE HONEY-COMB	34	GOODLY FERE	53
HONEY-RED, CLOSING THE FACE-OVAL,	204	MEDALLION	9
HOOP			
A HOOP-SKIRT, A CALASH,	114	EPILOGUE	7
THE MOTHER OF THE GREAT KING, IN A HOOP-SKIRT,	237	ABU SALAMMAMM	24
HOP			
HERE'S TO YOU, OLD HIPPETY-HOP O' THE ACCENTS,	13	MESMERISM	17
HORSE			
WHY DOES THE HORSE-FACED LADY OF JUST THE UNMENTIONABLE AGE	114	SIMULACRA	1
HOSE			
THE SALE OF HALF-HOSE HAS	196	HUGH SELWIN:12	26
HOUSE			
YOU ONCE DISCOVERED A MODERATE CHOP-HOUSE.	101	AMITIES	16
HUM			
HALF A LOAF? UM-HUM?	257	BREAD BRIGADE	2
HUNG			
A NEW-FANGLED CHARIOT FOLLOWS THE FLOWER-HUNG HORSES;	207	SEXTUS PROP: 1	12
HUNTING			
"'TIS THE WHITE STAG, FAME, WE'RE A-HUNTING,	25	THE WHITE STAG	6
ICE			
LIST HOW I, CARE-WRETCHED, ON ICE-COLD SEA,	64	THE SEAFARER	14
HUNG WITH HARD ICE-FLAKES, WHERE HAIL-SCUR FLEW,	64	THE SEAFARER	17
AND ICE-COLD WAVE, AT WHILES THE SWAN CRIES,	64	THE SEAFARER	19
IKANAIE			
O NATHAT-IKANAIE, "TREE-AT-THE-RIVER."	91	DANCE FIGURE	18
IN (3)			
INDUSTRIOUS			
A HOME-INDUSTRIOUS WORKER TO PERFECTION,	245	MOYEN SENSUEL	213
INN			
THE WILLOWS OF THE INN-YARD	137	OF DEPARTURE	EPI
JET			
THE WATER JET OF COLD LIGHT BEARS US UP THROUGH THE CEILINGS;	169	PHANOPOEIA	4
JIN			
KO-JIN GOES WEST FROM KO-KAKU-RO,	137	ON RIVER KIANG	1

	PAGE	TITLE	LINE
JO			
FOR THE GARDENS AT JO-RUN ARE FULL OF NEW NIGHTINGALES,	130	THE RIVER SONG	38
JOINTS			
O MUSES WITH DELECTABLE KNEE-JOINTS,	104	ANCORA	13
JONES			
THE BURNE-JONES CARTONS	192	YEUX GLAUQUES	9
JUMBLING			
A-JUMBLING O' FIGURES FOR MAITRE JACQUES POLIN,	22	MARVOIL	4
KAKU			
KO-JIN GOES WEST FROM KO-KAKU-RO,	137	ON RIVER KIANG	1
KEEN			
THESE THE KEEN-SCENTED;	74	THE RETURN	17
KEN			
HERE WE ARE BECAUSE WE HAVE THE KEN-NIN FOR OUR FOEMEN,	127	BOWMEN OF SHU	3
KETTLE			
WHO HAS BROUGHT THE ARMY WITH DRUMS AND WITH KETTLE-DRUMS?	133	FRONTIER GUARD	12
KIN			
OUT OF MINE OWN SOUL-KIN,	20	IN DURANCE	11
TO SO-KIN OF RAKUYO, ANCIENT FRIEND, CHANCELLOR OF GEN.	134	EXILE'S LETTER	1
KIN'ARDS			
BROAD AS ALL OCEAN AND LEANIN' MAN-KIN'ARDS.	13	MESMERISM	12
KISSY			
"GIMME A KISSY-CUDDLE"	271	OLE KATE	21
KNEE			
O MUSES WITH DELECTABLE KNEE-JOINTS,	104	ANCORA	13
KNEE'D			
ALL FOR ONE HALF-BALD, KNOCK-KNEE'D KING OF THE ARAGONESE,	22	MARVOIL	21
KNIGHT			
LOOPED WITH THE KNIGHT-LEAPS.	120	GAME OF CHESS	11
KNOCK			
ALL FOR ONE HALF-BALD, KNOCK-KNEE'D KING OF THE ARAGONESE,	22	MARVOIL	21
KO			
IN THE STORIED HOUSES OF SAN-KO THEY GAVE US MORE SENNIN MUSIC,	135	EXILE'S LETTER	26
KO-JIN GOES WEST FROM KO-KAKU-RO,	137	ON RIVER KIANG	1
KO-JIN GOES WEST FROM KO-KAKU-RO,	137	ON RIVER KIANG	1
KU			
YOU WENT INTO FAR KU-TO-YEN, BY THE RIVER OF SWIRLING EDDIES,	130	RIVER-MER WIFE	16
LACK			
WERE LACK-LAND CINO, E'EN AS I AM,	7	CINO	35
LAID			
SEEKING E'ER THE NEW-LAID RAST-WAY	7	CINO	50
LAND			
WERE LACK-LAND CINO, E'EN AS I AM,	7	CINO	35
LAP			
AS I'VE FOR YOU, SUCH FLAME-LAP,	107	DOMPNA POIS	65
LARGE			
OH AUGUST PIERIDES! NOW FOR A LARGE-MOUTHED PRODUCT.	216	SEXTUS PROP: 5	14
LASTING			
AND ITS AGE-LASTING WALLOW FOR RED GREED	14	FAMAM CANO	26
LAW			
HIS BROTHER-IN-LAW WAS ALL THERE WAS OF POWER	151	NEAR PERIGORD	17
BUT THE SON-IN-LAW OF MR. H. STYRAX	178	MOEURS CON: 1	16
LEAD			
SODDEN AND LEAD-HEAVY.	35	THE EYES	4
LEAF			
THOU KEEP'ST THY ROSE-LEAF	67	THE CLOAK	1
OUT OF THE BROWN LEAF-BROWN COLOURLESS	76	THE ALCHEMIST	47
LEAPING			
I HAVE SEEN THE TORCH-FLAMES, HIGH-LEAPING,	121	PROVINC DESERT	30
LEAPS			
LOOPED WITH THE KNIGHT-LEAPS.	120	GAME OF CHESS	11
LEASH			
PALLID THE LEASH-MEN!	74	THE RETURN	20

LEAVE -- LOOKING

	PAGE	TITLE	LINE
LEAVE			
LEAVE-TAKING NEAR SHOKU	138	NEAR SHOKU	T
LEAVES			
THE ORANGE-COLOURED ROSE-LEAVES,	108	TS'AI CHI'H	2
LEE			
GIVING THE ROCKS SMALL LEE-WAY	187	E. P. ODE	11
LEFT			
"OF" THE VICTORIOUS DELAY OF FABIUS, AND THE LEFT-HANDED BATTLE AT CANNAE,	210	SEXTUS PROP: 2	11
LEGEND			
FOR THINE OLD LEGEND-LUST.	47	FROM HEINE: 7	12
LESS			
THOMAS LARRON "EAR-THE-LESS,"	11	OF THE GIBBET	6
LEVEL			
LOW, PANEL-SHAPED, A-LEVEL WITH HER KNEES,	49	OF SPLENDOUR	11
CHALAIS IS HIGH, A-LEVEL WITH THE POPLARS.	152	NEAR PERIGORD	54
LID			
OF EYE-LID AND CHEEK-BONE	200	MAUBERLEY: 2	22
LIED			
MAKE THY LAUGH OUR WANDER-LIED;	7	CINO	47
LIFE			
--PART OF IT--OF THY SONG-LIFE.	14	FAMAM CANO	16
LIFE'S			
AYE, FOR EVER, A LASTING LIFE'S-BLAST,	66	THE SEAFARER	80
LIGHT			
THAT TRAMP OLD WAYS BENEATH THE SUN-LIGHT,	6	CINO	21
SUNSET, THE RIBBON-LIKE ROAD LIES, IN RED CROSS-LIGHT,	154	NEAR PERIGORD	96
OUT INTO THE CREPUSCULAR HALF-LIGHT, NOW AND THEN;	244	MOYEN SENSUEL	186
IKE			
MY GOD-LIKE COMPOSITIONS.	46	FROM HEINE: 6	16
THERE FLOAT THE PETAL-LIKE FLAMES.	109	HEATHER	3
THEIR CORDS TANGLE IN MIST, AGAINST THE BROCADE-LIKE PALACE.	129	THE RIVER SONG	26
THEY RIDE UPON DRAGON-LIKE HORSES,	132	AT TEN-SHIN	15
AND ALL HIS NET-LIKE THOUGHT OF NEW ALLIANCE?	152	NEAR PERIGORD	53
SUNSET, THE RIBBON-LIKE ROAD LIES, IN RED CROSS-LIGHT,	154	NEAR PERIGORD	96
THE WIRE-LIKE BANDS OF COLOUR INVOLUTE MOUNT FROM MY FINGERS;	170	PHANOPOEIA	17
THERE IS A SATIN-LIKE BOW ON THE HARP.	180	MOEURS CON: 5	15
THERE IS A SATIN-LIKE BOW ON AN HARP.	180	MOEURS CON: 5	17
STILL DARTS OUT FAUN-LIKE FROM THE HALF-RUIN'D FACE,	192	YEUX GLAUQUES	18
THE SKY-LIKE, LIMPID EYES,	193	BRENNBAUM	1
LILIES			
WHERE THE LOW DRONNE IS FILLED WITH WATER-LILIES,	152	NEAR PERIGORD	56
LILY			
OF LILY-OF-THE-VALLEY	109	ALBA	2
LINE			
BRIGHT IN ITS SUAVE BOUNDING-LINE, AS,	204	MEDALLION	14
LION			
"HERE COEUR-DE-LION WAS SLAIN.	122	PROVINC DESERT	44
MALEMORT, GUESSES BENEATH, SENDS WORD TO COEUR-DE-LION:	155	NEAR PERIGORD	123
THE CORAL ISLE, THE LION-COLOURED SAND	201	AGE DEMANDED	17
LIP			
COVERED WITH LIP-STICK.	261	ALF'S SIXTH	12
LIVING			
WE OF THE EVER-LIVING, IN THAT LIGHT	50	THE FLAME	12
LOFTICAL			
NOT THAT HE WAS A SAINT, NOR WAS TOP-LOFTICAL	246	MOYEN SENSUEL	233
LOFTY			
FOR THIS THERE'S NO MOOD-LOFTY MAN OVER EARTH'S MIDST,	65	THE SEAFARER	40
LONE			
EAGER AND READY, THE CRYING LONE-FLYER,	65	THE SEAFARER	63
LONG			
YOU WHEEZE AS A HEAD-COLD LONG-TONSILLED CALLIOPE,	13	MESMERISM	9
SINGS DAY-LONG AND NIGHT LATE	171	LANGUE D'OC	EPI
LOOKING			
THE TREES IN MY EAST-LOOKING GARDEN	142	UNMOVING CLOUD	17

PAGE 503

	PAGE	TITLE	LINE
LOOKING (CONTINUED)			
WITHOUT SMIRKING INTO A POCKET-LOOKING-GLASS.	247	PIERROTS	21
LOOSE			
A-LOOSE THE CLOAK OF THE BODY, CAMEST	68	APPARUIT	14
LOVE			
YET YOU ASK ON WHAT ACCOUNT I WRITE SO MANY LOVE-LYRICS	217	SEXTUS PROP: 5	23
LUST			
FOR THINE OLD LEGEND-LUST.	47	FROM HEINE: 7	12
LUTE			
HATH AS FAINT LUTE-STRINGS IN ITS DIM ACCORD	43	SATIEMUS	15
LYING			
OUT OF EREBUS, THE FLAT-LYING BREADTH,	76	THE ALCHEMIST	44
LYRICS			
YET YOU ASK ON WHAT ACCOUNT I WRITE SO MANY LOVE-LYRICS	217	SEXTUS PROP: 5	23
M			
QUE BE-M VOLS MAL.	9	NA AUDIART	57
MACHE			
THIS PAPIER-MACHE, WHICH YOU SEE, MY FRIENDS,	63	PHASELLUS ILLE	1
MAIN			
FAT PIERRE WITH THE HOOK GAUCHE-MAIN,	11	OF THE GIBBET	5
MAITRE			
ARE THOSE OF A MAITRE-DE-CAFE.	114	EPILOGUE	11
MAN			
BROAD AS ALL OCEAN AND LEANIN' MAN-KIN'ARDS.	13	MESMERISM	12
NOR I, NOR TOWER-MAN, LOOK ON DAYLIGHT,	177	LANGUE D'OC: 4	8
MAR			
BY THE STILL POOL OF MAR-NAN-OTHA	4	LA FRAISNE	13
MARIE			
IMPRESSIONS OF FRANCOIS-MARIE AROUET (DE VOLTAIRE)	167	OF AROUET	T
MARSH			
MARSH-CRANBERRIES, THE RIBBED AND ANGULAR PODS	162	CABARET DANCER	19
ME (1)			
MEAD			
THE MEWS' SINGING ALL MY MEAD-DRINK.	64	THE SEAFARER	22
MEAL			
AND SHE IS DYING PIECE-MEAL	83	THE GARDEN	3
MEAOWLING			
A-MEAOWLING OUR PRAISES.	52	AU SALON	23
MEETING			
NO MORE FOR US THE MEETING-PLACE	3	THRENOS	16
MEI			
"WET SPRINGTIME," SAYS TO-EM-MEI, "WET SPRING IN THE GARDEN."	142	UNMOVING CLOUD	EPI
MEI'S			
TO-EM-MEI'S "THE UNMOVING CLOUD"	142	UNMOVING CLOUD	T
MEN			
PALLID THE LEASH-MEN!	74	THE RETURN	20
A-A-A-A--A-MEN.	101	AMITIES	20
A TURMOIL OF WARS-MEN, SPREAD OVER THE MIDDLE KINGDOM,	133	FRONTIER GUARD	15
MERCHANT'S			
THE RIVER-MERCHANT'S WIFE: A LETTER	130	RIVER-MER WIFE	T
MERE			
MERE-WEARY MOOD. LEST MAN KNOW NOT	64	THE SEAFARER	12
MY MOOD 'MID THE MERE-FLOOD,	65	THE SEAFARER	60
MID			
AND LOST MID-PAGE	15	FAMAM CANO	44
WAITING HIS TURN IN THE MID-SUMMER EVENING,	154	NEAR PERIGORD	109
"ANOTHER WHEEL, THE ARENA; MID-CROWD IS AS BAD AS MID-SEA."	210	SEXTUS PROP: 2	27
"ANOTHER WHEEL, THE ARENA; MID-CROWD IS AS BAD AS MID-SEA."	210	SEXTUS PROP: 2	27
MIDDLE			
YES, SHE ALSO WILL TURN MIDDLE-AGED,	116	THE TEA SHOP	5
SHE ALSO WILL TURN MIDDLE-AGED.	116	THE TEA SHOP	9
WITH MIDDLE-AGEING CARE	158	PSYCHOLOG HOUR	3
MIDDLE-AGED	236	MIDDLE-AGED	T
MIELS			
UNTO LADY "MIELS-DE-BEN,"	8	NA AUDIART	13

	PAGE	TITLE	LINE
MIELS (CONTINUED)			
I OF MIELS-DE-BEN DEMAND	106	DOMPNA POIS	47
MILK			
LET THEM ASSUME THE MILK-WHITE BODIES OF AGATE. ...	76	THE ALCHEMIST	52
THE MILK-WHITE GIRLS	109	HEATHER	4
MIST			
OR THROUGH DAWN-MIST	203	MAUBERLEY: 4	10
MONT			
BEZIERS OFF AT MONT-AUSIER, I AND HIS LADY	22	MARVOIL	12
TIBORS ALL TONGUE AND TEMPER AT MONT-AUSIER,	22	MARVOIL	18
MOOD			
FOR THIS THERE'S NO MOOD-LOFTY MAN OVER EARTH'S MIDST,	65	THE SEAFARER	40
MORROW			
TO PLAGUE TO-MORROW WITH A TESTAMENT!	59	SILET	14
RICHARD SHALL DIE TO-MORROW--LEAVE HIM THERE	155	NEAR PERIGORD	139
'TO-MORROW AT TEA-TIME.'")	159	PSYCHOLOG HOUR	38
"BREATHE NOT THE WORD TO-MORROW IN HER EARS"	161	CABARET DANCER	EPI
SAY "FORGET TO-MORROW," BEING OF ALL MEN	161	CABARET DANCER	7
"PEPITA" HAS NO TO-MORROW, SO YOU WRITE.	161	CABARET DANCER	9
COME, COME TO-MORROW,	162	CABARET DANCER	45
TO-MORROW IN TEN YEARS AT THE LATEST,	162	CABARET DANCER	46
TO-MORROW FATE SHUTS US IN.	221	SEXTUS PROP: 7	32
MORROWS			
PEPITA HAS SUCH TO-MORROWS! WITH THE HANDS PUFFED OUT,	161	CABARET DANCER	10
MOSS			
GREEN OF THE WOOD-MOSS AND FLOWER COLOURS,	35	THE EYES	9
MOUNTAIN			
AND THEY MADE NOTHING OF SEA-CROSSING OR OF MOUNTAIN-CROSSING,	134	EXILE'S LETTER	9
MOUTH			
PLAYING ON A JEWELLED MOUTH-ORGAN.	135	EXILE'S LETTER	25
WITH BOATS FLOATING, AND THE SOUND OF MOUTH-ORGANS AND DRUMS,	135	EXILE'S LETTER	51
MOUTHED			
OH AUGUST PIERIDES! NOW FOR A LARGE-MOUTHED PRODUCT.	216	SEXTUS PROP: 5	14
MY (1)			
NAME			
AND WHATS-HIS-NAME ATTAINED NOBILITY.	264	ALF'S NINTH	8
NAN			
BY THE STILL POOL OF MAR-NAN-OTHA	4	LA FRAISNE	13
NATHAT			
O NATHAT-IKANAIE, "TREE-AT-THE-RIVER."	91	DANCE FIGURE	18
NATION			
MOVING A NATION-WIDE	259	ALF'S THIRD	6
NEO			
MILDNESS, AMID THE NEO-NIETZSCHEAN CLATTER,	201	AGE DEMANDED	21
THE NEO-COMMUNE	258	ALF'S SECOND	SUB
NERVE			
GO ALSO TO THE NERVE-WRACKED, GO TO THE ENSLAVED-BY-CONVENTION,	88	COMMISSION	2
NET			
A NET-WORK OF ARBOURS AND PASSAGES AND COVERED WAYS,	141	IDEA OF CHOAN	22
BORDER THE NET-WORK OF WAYS:	141	IDEA OF CHOAN	24
AND ALL HIS NET-LIKE THOUGHT OF NEW ALLIANCE?	152	NEAR PERIGORD	53
NEW			
SEEKING E'ER THE NEW-LAID RAST-WAY	7	CINO	50
A NEW-FANGLED CHARIOT FOLLOWS THE FLOWER-HUNG HORSES;	207	SEXTUS PROP: 1	12
NIETZSCHEAN			
MILDNESS, AMID THE NEO-NIETZSCHEAN CLATTER,	201	AGE DEMANDED	21
NIGHT			
YET SAW AN "AD." "TO-NIGHT, THE HUDSON SAIL,	242	MOYEN SENSUEL	111
NIN			
HERE WE ARE BECAUSE WE HAVE THE KEN-NIN FOR OUR FOEMEN,	127	BOWMEN OF SHU	3
NINE			
SWINGING A CAT O "NINE-TAILS.	162	CABARET DANCER	37
NINETY			
HIS PALACE HAS NINETY-EIGHT WINDOWS,	207	ADU GALAHHAMM	6

PAGE 505

NON -- PIECE

	PAGE	TITLE	LINE
NON			
NON-ESTEEM OF SELF-STYLED "HIS BETTERS"	202	AGE DEMANDED	58
NORTH			
MAREUIL TO THE NORTH-EAST,	121	PROVINC DESERT	22
NOSE			
ALFONSO, QUATTRO, POKE-NOSE.	22	MARVOIL	22
NOT (1)			
O'			
SWINGING A CAT-O'-NINE-TAILS.	162	CABARET DANCER	37
OAK			
THAT GREW ELM-OAK AMID THE WOLD.	3	THE TREE	5
OBLIGE			
ENDS WITH A WILLINGNESS-TO-OBLIGE.	99	EPITAPH	2
OF (1)			
OLD			
THAN ALL THE AGE-OLD KNOWLEDGE OF THY BOOKS:	35	THE EYES	17
USURY AGE-OLD AND AGE-THICK	190	HUGH SELWYN: 4	18
BUT SURELY THE WORST OF YOUR OLD-WOMEN ARE THE MALE ONES.)	243	MOYEN SENSUEL	150
OPERATION			
IS NOT SUITED TO CO-OPERATION--	262	ALF'S SEVENTH	15
OPS			
THE CO-OPS WAS A GOIN' SOMEWHERE,	262	ALF'S SEVENTH	2
TO THE CO-OPS, A ECHO OR SOMETHIN'?	262	ALF'S SEVENTH	9
IS WHERE THE CO-OPS ARE GOIN' TO,	262	ALF'S SEVENTH	13
ORANGE			
THE ORANGE-COLOURED ROSE-LEAVES,	108	TS'AI CHI'H	2
ORDER			
AND I HAVE MOPED IN THE EMPEROR'S GARDEN, AWAITING AN ORDER-TO-WRITE!	129	THE RIVER SONG	19
ORGAN			
PLAYING ON A JEWELLED MOUTH-ORGAN.	135	EXILE'S LETTER	25
ORGANS			
WITH BOATS FLOATING, AND THE SOUND OF MOUTH-ORGANS AND DRUMS,	135	EXILE'S LETTER	51
OTHA			
BY THE STILL POOL OF MAR-NAN-OTHA	4	LA FRAISNE	13
OUT			
OUT-WEARIERS OF APOLLO WILL, AS WE KNOW, CONTINUE THEIR MARTIAN GENERALITIES,	207	SEXTUS PROP: 1	10
RAN CRYING WITH OUT-SPREAD HAIR,	219	SEXTUS PROP: 6	34
OVAL			
HONEY-RED, CLOSING THE FACE-OVAL,	204	MEDALLION	9
THE FACE-OVAL BENEATH THE GLAZE,	204	MEDALLION	13
OVER			
I HAD OVER-PREPARED THE EVENT,	158	PSYCHOLOG HOUR	1
I HAD OVER-PREPARED THE EVENT--	158	PSYCHOLOG HOUR	20
OWN			
HEART'S-ALL-BELOVED-MY-OWN;	48	FROM HEINE: 8	6
PAGE			
AND LOST MID-PAGE	15	FAMAM CANO	44
PAID			
WHO ON THE SO WELL-PAID GROUND	263	ALF'S EIGHTH	9
PANEL			
LOW, PANEL-SHAPED, A-LEVEL WITH HER KNEES,	49	OF SPLENDOUR	11
PAPIER			
THIS PAPIER-MACHE, WHICH YOU SEE, MY FRIENDS.	63	PHASELLUS ILLE	1
PATH			
WHETS FOR THE WHALE-PATH THE HEART IRRESISTIBLY,	65	THE SEAFARER	64
PATTERN			
HER UNDERSKIRT IS OF GREEN PATTERN-SILK,	140	MULBERRY ROAD	13
PEACOCK			
UNDER NIGHT, THE PEACOCK-THROATED,	75	THE ALCHEMIST	8
PEN			
TO-DAY FROM THE DRAGON-PEN.	139	SOUTH-FOLK	5
PENCE			
AND WONDER IF MY DAY'S THREE AND EIGHT-PENCE	268	ANOTHER BIT	11
PETAL			
THERE FLOAT THE PETAL-LIKE FLAMES.	109	HEATHER	3
PIECE			
AND SHE IS DYING PIECE-MEAL	83	THE GARDEN	3

PIECE -- RAST

	PAGE	TITLE	LINE
PIECE (CONTINUED)			
FAN-PIECE, FOR HER IMPERIAL LORD	108	FAN-PIECE	T
AND SHE PILES HER HAIR UP ON THE LEFT SIDE OF HER			
HEAD-PIECE.	140	MULBERRY ROAD	11
PIG			
WHO HAS HAD A PIG HEADED FATHER;	89	A PACT	4
AND THEN THAT WOMAN LIKE A GUINEA-PIG	242	MOYEN SENSUEL	120
PINE			
AND INTO TEN THOUSAND VALLEYS FULL OF VOICES AND			
PINE-WINDS.	134	EXILE'S LETTER	21
THE RED-PINE-TREE GOD LOOKS AT HIM AND WONDERS. ...	139	SENNIN POEM	11
PLACE			
NO MORE FOR US THE MEETING-PLACE	3	THRENOS	16
PLAY			
THE YOUNG MEN AT THE SWORD-PLAY;	4	LA FRAISNE	6
PLUM			
FROM THE PLUM-COLOURED LAKE, IN STILLNESS, ...	75	THE ALCHEMIST	17
POCKET			
WITHOUT SMIRKING INTO A POCKET-LOOKING-GLASS.	247	PIERROTS	21
POD			
OR AS A DANDELION SEED-POD AND BE SWEPT AWAY, ...	36	FRANCESCA	10
POKE			
ALFONSO, QUATTRO, POKE-NOSE.	22	MARVOIL	22
POM			
M. POM-POM	273	M. POM-POM	T
M. POM-POM	273	M. POM-POM	T
M. POM-POM ALLAIT EN GUERRE	273	M. POM-POM	1
M. POM-POM ALLAIT EN GUERRE	273	M. POM-POM	1
M. POM-POM EST AU SENAT	273	M. POM-POM	6
M. POM-POM EST AU SENAT	273	M. POM-POM	6
POND			
I LOOKED AT THE DRAGON-POND, WITH ITS			
WILLOW-COLOURED WATER	129	THE RIVER SONG	20
POSTS			
MOUNTS FROM THE FOUR HORNS OF MY BED-POSTS, ...	169	PHANOPOEIA	3
POWDER			
AS HE INHALED THE STILL FUMES OF RICE-POWDER.	243	MOYEN SENSUEL	132
PRAISE			
IF I HAVE NOT THE FACULTY, "THE BARE ATTEMPT WOULD			
BE PRAISE-WORTHY."	216	SEXTUS PROP: 5	4
PREPARED			
I HAD OVER-PREPARED THE EVENT, ...	158	PSYCHOLOG HOUR	1
I HAD OVER-PREPARED THE EVENT--	158	PSYCHOLOG HOUR	20
PRIESTESS			
SHE IS NOW THE HIGH-PRIESTESS	178	MOEURS CON: 1	11
PUG			
THE PUG-DOG'S FEATURES ENCRUSTED WITH TALLOW	161	CABARET DANCER	11
WILL BE QUITE RICH, QUITE PLUMP, WITH PUG-BITCH			
FEATURES, ...	162	CABARET DANCER	48
PULP			
WITH A LIVELY WOOD-PULP "AD."	268	ALF'S TWELFTH	19
PURSE			
WORKED FOR AND SNATCHED FROM THE STRING-PURSE OF			
BORN--	152	NEAR PERIGORD	34
PUSHED			
SPREAD ON BOTH HANDS AND ON THE UP PUSHED BOSOM	161	CABARET DANCER	15
QUARREL			
AND GETS A QUARREL-BOLT SHOT THROUGH HIS VIZARD,	156	NEAR PERIGORD	158
QUIVER			
"ONCE MORE IN DELOS, ONCE MORE IS THE ALTAR A-QUIVER.	90	SURGIT FAMA	16
RACK			
IN OUR HEART'S SWORD-RACK, THOUGH THY SWORD-ARM			
SLEEP.	19	FOR E. MCC	22
RAIN			
CLOUD AND RAIN-TEARS PASS THEY FLEET!	7	CINO	49
GREY OLIVE LEAVES BENEATH A RAIN-COLD SKY.	55	QUITTILBOINIA	8
RAKU			
AND YOU TO THE NORTH OF RAKU-HOKU.	134	EXILE'S LETTER	14
RAST			
SEEKING E'ER THE NEW-LAID RAST-WAY	7	CINO	50

RAVENOUS -- SANG

		PAGE	TITLE	LINE
RAVENOUS				
	A GRACIOUS SPRING, TURNED TO BLOOD-RAVENOUS AUTUMN,	133	FRONTIER GUARD	14
RE				
	TO SEE HOW CELESTINE WILL RE-ENTER HER SLIPPERS.	111	BLACK SLIPPERS	10
	SHE RE-ENTERS THEM WITH A GROAN.	111	BLACK SLIPPERS	11
	THE PARENT RE-BEAMS AT ITS OFFSPRING.	180	MOEURS CON: 5	13
RED				
	THE RED-PINE-TREE GOD LOOKS AT HIM AND WONDERS. ...	139	SENNIN POEM	11
	AS THE RED-BEAKED STEEDS OF	201	AGE DEMANDED	3
	HONEY-RED, CLOSING THE FACE-OVAL, ...	204	MEDALLION	9
	THUS HE ESCHEWED THE BRIGHT RED-WALLED CAFES AND	245	MOYEN SENSUEL	205
REI				
	WHO AMONG THEM IS A MAN LIKE HAN-REI	132	AT TEN-SHIN	31
RENDING				
	AND DAVID'S HARP LET OUT HEART-RENDING SQUEALS: ...	264	ALF'S NINTH	15
RESPECTABLE				
	A QUIET AND RESPECTABLE-TAWDRY TRIO;	163	CABARET DANCER	81
RIBBON				
	SUNSET, THE RIBBON-LIKE ROAD LIES, IN RED CROSS-LIGHT, ...	154	NEAR PERIGORD	96
RICE				
	AS HE INHALED THE STILL FUMES OF RICE-POWDER.	243	MOYEN SENSUEL	132
RIMS				
	OR OF HECTOR SPATTERING WHEEL-RIMS, ...	208	SEXTUS PROP: 1	29
RING				
	HE HATH NOT HEART FOR HARPING, NOR IN RING-HAVING	65	THE SEAFARER	45
RISEN				
	WE SEEM AS STATUES ROUND WHOSE HIGH-RISEN BASE	32	PARACELSUS	11
RIVER				
	O NATHAT-IKANAIE, "TREE-AT-THE-RIVER."	91	DANCE FIGURE	18
	THE RIVER-MERCHANT'S WIFE: A LETTER	130	RIVER-MER WIFE	T
	YOU BACK TO YOUR RIVER-BRIDGE.	135	EXILE'S LETTER	35
RO				
	KO-JIN GOES WEST FROM KO-KAKU-RO, ...	137	ON RIVER KIANG	1
ROAD				
	AND THERE IS NO HIGH-ROAD TO THE MUSES.	207	SEXTUS PROP: 1	15
ROBE				
	THIS LADY IN THE WHITE BATH-ROBE WHICH SHE CALLS A PEIGNOIR, ...	87	ALBATRE	1
ROOM				
	EN BERTRANS, A TOWER-ROOM AT HAUTEFORT, ...	154	NEAR PERIGORD	95
ROSE				
	THOU KEEP'ST THY ROSE-LEAF	67	THE CLOAK	1
	TILL THE ROSE-TIME WILL BE OVER, ...	67	THE CLOAK	2
	THE ORANGE-COLOURED ROSE-LEAVES, ...	108	TS'AI CHI'H	2
	THE TEA-ROSE TEA-GOWN, ETC.	189	HUGH SELWYN: 3	1
RUIN'D				
	STILL DARTS OUT FAUN-LIKE FROM THE HALF-RUIN'D FACE,	192	YEUX GLAUQUES	18
RUN				
	AND EVERY RUN-AWAY OF THE WOOD THROUGH THAT GREAT MADNESS, ...	31	PIERE VIDAL	51
	FOR THE GARDENS AT JO-RUN ARE FULL OF NEW NIGHTINGALES, ...	130	THE RIVER SONG	38
RUNEING				
	ONCE FOR WIND-RUNEING	6	CINO	14
RUNNING				
	HER STRAIGHT SPEECH FREE-RUNNING, ...	105	DOMPNA POIS	29
SA				
	AS FAR AS CHO-FU-SA.	131	RIVER-MER WIFE	29
SAFFRON				
	BRING THE SAFFRON-COLOURED SHELL, ...	75	THE ALCHEMIST	9
SALMON				
	THE SALMON-TROUT DRIFTS IN THE STREAM, ...	166	FISH & SHADOW	1
	THE SOUL OF THE SALMON-TROUT FLOATS OVER THE STREAM	166	FISH & SHADOW	2
SALT				
	THE SALT-WAVY TUMULT TRAVERSE ALONE.	65	THE SEAFARER	36
SAN				
	IN THE STORIED HOUSES OF SAN-KO THEY GAVE US MORE SENNIN MUSIC, ...	135	EXILE'S LETTER	26
SANG				
	TEINTEES DE COULEUR SANG-DE-DRAGON,˙	160	DANS OMNIBUS	27

SATIN -- SHIN

	PAGE	TITLE	LINE
SATIN			
THERE IS A SATIN-LIKE BOW ON THE HARP.	180	MOEURS CON: 5	15
THERE IS A SATIN-LIKE BOW ON AN HARP.	180	MOEURS CON: 5	17
SUBJECTIVELY. IN THE STUFFED-SATIN DRAWINGROOM	196	HUGH SELWIN:12	3
SATISFACTORY			
O MY MUCH PRAISED BUT-NOT-ALTOGETHER-SATISFACTORY LADY.	100	THE BATH TUB	4
SCALES			
WITH RIPPLES LIKE DRAGON-SCALES, GOING GRASS GREEN ON THE WATER,	136	EXILE'S LETTER	52
SCARE			
I AM HUNG HERE, A SCARE-CROW FOR LOVERS.	226	SEXTUS PROP:11	3
SCENTED			
THESE THE KEEN-SCENTED;	74	THE RETURN	17
SCORE			
AND HEARD THE FIVE-SCORE NIGHTINGALES AIMLESSLY SINGING.	129	THE RIVER SONG	22
SCUR			
HUNG WITH HARD ICE-FLAKES, WHERE HAIL-SCUR FLEW,	64	THE SEAFARER	17
SEA			
FOR ALL THIS SEA-HOARD OF DECIDUOUS THINGS,	61	PORTRAIT FEMME	25
AND DIRE SEA-SURGE, AND THERE I OFT SPENT	64	THE SEAFARER	6
SEA-FOWLS' LOUDNESS WAS FOR ME LAUGHTER,	64	THE SEAFARER	21
BUT SHALL HAVE HIS SORROW FOR SEA-FARE	65	THE SEAFARER	43
AND THEY MADE NOTHING OF SEA-CROSSING OR OF MOUNTAIN-CROSSING,	134	EXILE'S LETTER	9
THE SEA-CLEAR SAPPHIRE OF AIR, THE SEA-DARK CLARITY, STRETCHES BOTH SEA-CLIFF AND OCEAN.	170	PHANOPOEIA	24
THE SEA-CLEAR SAPPHIRE OF AIR, THE SEA-DARK CLARITY, STRETCHES BOTH SEA-CLIFF AND OCEAN.	170	PHANOPOEIA	24
THE SEA-CLEAR SAPPHIRE OF AIR, THE SEA-DARK CLARITY, STRETCHES BOTH SEA-CLIFF AND OCEAN.	170	PHANOPOEIA	24
HE LIES BY THE POLUPHLOIBOIOUS SEA-COAST.	181	MOEURS CON: 6	4
AUDITION OF THE PHANTASMAL SEA-SURGE,	202	AGE DEMANDED	45
"ANOTHER WHEEL, THE ARENA; MID-CROWD IS AS BAD AS MID-SEA."	210	SEXTUS PROP: 2	27
ANDROMEDA WAS OFFERED TO A SEA-SERPENT	222	SEXTUS PROP: 8	22
SEARCHING			
I WILL GO OUT A-SEARCHING,	105	DOMPNA POIS	17
SEED			
OR AS A DANDELION SEED-POD AND BE SWEPT AWAY,	36	FRANCESCA	10
SEI			
AND THE MOON FALLS OVER THE PORTALS OF SEI-GO YO,	131	AT TEN-SHIN	11
SELF			
NON ESTEEM OF SELF-STYLED "HIS BETTERS"	202	AGE DEMANDED	58
TO SEE YOUR FORTY SELF-BAPTIZED IMMORTALS,	239	MOYEN SENSUEL	32
SEN			
WE MET, AND TRAVELLED INTO SEN-GO,	134	EXILE'S LETTER	17
SERPENT			
ANDROMEDA WAS OFFERED TO A SEA-SERPENT	222	SEXTUS PROP: 8	22
SHAPED			
LOW, PANEL-SHAPED, A-LEVEL WITH HER KNEES,	49	OF SPLENDOUR	11
SHARKS			
WHETHER MR. DUPONT AND THE GUN-SHARKS	268	ANOTHER BIT	7
SHARP			
THE FLUTTER OF SHARP-EDGED SANDALS.	169	PHANOPOEIA	13
SHATO			
THIS BOAT IS OF SHATO-WOOD, AND ITS GUNWALES ARE CUT MAGNOLIA,	128	THE RIVER SONG	1
SHEATHED			
HALF-SHEATHED, THEN NAKED FROM ITS SAFFRON SHEATH	31	PIERE VIDAL	41
SHEEP			
SOLDIER, THE ENUMERATION OF WOUNDS; THE SHEEP-FEEDER, OF EWES;	218	SEXTUS PROP: 5	56
SHI			
AND THERE CAME ALSO THE "TRUE MAN" OF SHI-YO TO MEET ME,	134	EXILE'S LETTER	24
SHIN			
POEM BY THE BRIDGE AT TEN-SHIN	131	AT TEN-SHIN	T
BY THE SOUTH SIDE OF THE BRIDGE AT TEN-SHIN.	134	EXILE'S LETTER	3

SHOOTS -- SPOKEN

	PAGE	TITLE	LINE
SHOOTS			
HERE WE ARE, PICKING THE FIRST FERN-SHOOTS	127	BOWMEN OF SHU	1
WE GRUB THE SOFT FERN-SHOOTS,	127	BOWMEN OF SHU	5
SHOP			
GIVE ME IN DUE TIME, I BESEECH YOU, A LITTLE TOBACCO-SHOP,	117	THE LAKE ISLE	2
LEND ME A LITTLE TOBACCO-SHOP,	117	THE LAKE ISLE	13
SHORES			
TAWN FORE-SHORES	203	MAUBERLEY: 4	8
SHOT			
THE SALMON MOVES IN THE SUN-SHOT, BRIGHT SHALLOW SEA...	166	FISH & SHADOW	4
SHOULDER			
SHE MAKES THE SHOULDER-STRAPS OF HER BASKET	140	MULBERRY ROAD	9
SHROUDED			
FLESH-SHROUDED BEARING THE SECRET.	20	IN DURANCE	25
SHU			
SO-SHU DREAMED,	118	ANCIENT WISDOM	1
THE EASTERN WIND BRINGS THE GREEN COLOUR INTO THE ISLAND GRASSES AT YEI-SHU,	129	THE RIVER SONG	23
SHUT			
"THESE ARE YOUR IMAGES, AND FROM YOU THE SORCERIZING OF SHUT-IN YOUNG LADIES,	211	SEXTUS PROP: 2	50
SHY			
"BEAUTY IS SLANDER'S COCK-SHY.	226	SEXTUS PROP:11	21
SILK			
HER UNDERSKIRT IS OF GREEN PATTERN-SILK,	140	MULBERRY ROAD	13
SIX			
THROUGH ALL THE THIRTY-SIX FOLDS OF THE TURNING AND TWISTING WATERS,	134	EXILE'S LETTER	18
SKIN			
THE HORSES ARE WELL TRAINED, THE GENERALS HAVE IVORY ARROWS AND QUIVERS ORNAMENTED WITH FISH-SKIN.	127	BOWMEN OF SHU	19
SKIRT			
A HOOP-SKIRT, A CALASH,	114	EPILOGUE	7
THE MOTHER OF THE GREAT KING, IN A HOOP-SKIRT,	237	ABU SALAMMAMM	24
SKY			
THE SKY-LIKE LIMPID EYES,	193	BRENNBAUM	1
SLOSHIN'			
AN A-SLOSHIN' ROUND WITH 'ER MOP,	271	OLE KATE	10
SLUT			
YOU SLUT-BELLIED OBSTRUCTIONIST,	145	SALUTATION 3RD	10
SMALL			
DRINK OF THE WINDS THEIR CHILL SMALL-BEER	10	FOR THIS YULE	4
SMOKE			
THE SMOKE-FLOWERS ARE BLURRED OVER THE RIVER.	137	ON RIVER KIANG	2
SNOW			
AND THEIR SNOW-WHITE LEOPARD	109	HEATHER	6
SO			
SO-SHU DREAMED,	118	ANCIENT WISDOM	1
TO SO-KIN OF RAKUYO, ANCIENT FRIEND, CHANCELLOR OF GEN.	134	EXILE'S LETTER	1
SOILED			
WHY DOES THE SMALL CHILD IN THE SOILED-WHITE IMITATION FUR COAT	114	SIMULACRA	3
SON			
BUT THE SON-IN-LAW OF MR. H. STYRAX	178	MOEURS CON: 1	16
SONG			
--PART OF IT--OF THY SONG-LIFE.	14	FAMAM CANO	16
SORROW			
O SORROW-SWEPT MY FOOL,	35	HIS OWN FACE	3
SOUL			
OUT OF MINE OWN SOUL-KIN,	20	IN DURANCE	11
SOULED			
MORE CRAFTILY, MORE SUBTLE-SOULED THAN I;	24	THUS NINEVEH	13
SOUTH			
SOUTH-FOLK IN COLD COUNTRY	139	SOUTH-FOLK	T
SPECTACLED			
SCRAWNY, BE-SPECTACLED, OUT AT HEELS,	14	FAMAM CANO	23
SPOKEN			
MISTRUSTED, SPOKEN-AGAINST,	92	THE REST	5

SPREAD -- SWORD

	PAGE	TITLE	LINE
SPREAD			
"ANIENAN SPRING WATER FALLS INTO FLAT-SPREAD POOLS."	212	SEXTUS PROP: 3	5
RAN CRYING WITH OUT-SPREAD HAIR,	219	SEXTUS PROP: 6	34
BY DEW-SPREAD CAVERNS,	227	SEXTUS PROP:11	30
SPUR			
THE SPUR-CLINKS SOUND BETWEEN,	47	FROM HEINE: 7	26
SQUARE			
BREAK DOWN THE FOUR-SQUARE WALLS OF STANDING TIME.	49	OF SPLENDOUR	21
STALKS			
WE GRUB THE OLD FERN-STALKS.	127	BOWMEN OF SHU	9
STALL			
(NEAR Q. H. FLACCUS' BOOK-STALL).	210	SEXTUS PROP: 2	9
STEEL			
SHIELD O' STEEL-BLUE, TH' HEAVEN O'ER US	7	CINO	44
STICK			
COVERED WITH LIP-STICK.	261	ALF'S SIXTH	12
STILL			
THE ENGLISH RUBAIYAT WAS STILL-BORN	192	YEUX GLAUQUES	15
STIRRER			
HUB OF THE WHEEL, THE STIRRER-UP OF STRIFE,	151	NEAR PERIGORD	21
STOCK			
AND EVERY VINE-STOCK IS	87	THE SPRING	6
STOCKING'D			
WITH HER WHITE-STOCKING'D FEET	111	BLACK SLIPPERS	3
STONE			
STORMS, ON THE STONE-CLIFFS BEATEN, FELL ON THE STERN	64	THE SEAFARER	23
I HAVE KNOWN THE STONE-BRIGHT PLACE,	95	OF THE DEGREES	8
THE SONGS SHALL BE A FINE TOMB-STONE OVER THEIR BEAUTY.	209	SEXTUS PROP: 1	64
STONES			
HERE ARE THEIR TOMB-STONES.	145	SALUTATION 3RD	6
STOPS			
YOU LOITER AT THE CORNERS AND BUS-STOPS,	94	INSTRUCTIONS	6
STRAPS			
SHE MAKES THE SHOULDER-STRAPS OF HER BASKET	140	MULBERRY ROAD	9
STRAY			
A-STRAY, LOST IN THE VILLAGES,	92	THE REST	4
STRING			
WORKED FOR AND SNATCHED FROM THE STRING-PURSE OF BORN--	152	NEAR PERIGORD	34
STRINGS			
HATH AS FAINT LUTE-STRINGS IN ITS DIM ACCORD	43	SATIEMUS	15
VINE-STRINGS A HUNDRED FEET LONG HANG DOWN FROM CARVED RAILINGS,	129	THE RIVER SONG	27
STUFFED			
SUBJECTIVELY. IN THE STUFFED-SATIN DRAWINGROOM	196	HUGH SELWIN.12	3
STYLED			
NON-ESTEEM OF SELF-STYLED "HIS BETTERS"	202	AGE DEMANDED	58
SUBTLE			
MORE CRAFTILY, MORE SUBTLE-SOULED THAN I;	24	THUS NINEVEH	13
SUDDEN			
FELT HANDS TURN ICE A-SUDDEN, TOUCHING YE,	41	HER MONUMENT	17
SUMMER			
WAITING HIS TURN IN THE MID-SUMMER EVENING,	154	NEAR PERIGORD	109
SUN			
THAT TRAMP OLD WAYS BENEATH THE SUN LIGHT,	6	CINO	21
THE SALMON MOVES IN THE SUN-SHOT, BRIGHT SHALLOW SEA...	166	FISH & SHADOW	4
RATHER THAN THE MOTTOES ON SUN-DIALS.	187	E. P. ODE	16
SURGE			
AND DIRE SEA-SURGE, AND THERE I OFT SPENT	64	THE SEAFARER	6
AUDITION OF THE PHANTASMAL SEA-SURGE,	202	AGE DEMANDED	45
SWEPT			
O SORROW-SWEPT MY FOOL,	35	HIS OWN FACE	3
SWIFT			
SWIFT FOOT TO MY LADY AGNES,	108	DONNA TOTO	80
SWIRLING			
AND ON THE BACK-SWIRLING EDDIES,	131	AT TEN-SHIN	6
SWORD			
THE YOUNG MEN AT THE SWORD-PLAY;	4	LA FRAISNE	6

SWORD -- TOWER

	PAGE	TITLE	LINE
SWORD (CONTINUED)			
IN OUR HEART'S SWORD-RACK, THOUGH THY SWORD-ARM SLEEP.	19	FOR E. MCC	22
IN OUR HEART'S SWORD-RACK, THOUGH THY SWORD-ARM SLEEP.	19	FOR E. MCC	22
DISEASE OR OLDNESS OR SWORD-HATE	66	THE SEAFARER	71
TAILS			
SWINGING A CAT-O'-NINE-TAILS.	162	CABARET DANCER	37
TAKING			
LEAVE-TAKING NEAR SHOKU	138	NEAR SHOKU	T
TAWDRY			
A QUIET AND RESPECTABLE-TAWDRY TRIO;	163	CABARET DANCER	81
TEA			
'TO-MORROW AT TEA-TIME.'")	159	PSYCHOLOG HOUR	38
THE TEA-ROSE TEA-GOWN, ETC.	189	HUGH SELWYN: 3	1
THE TEA-ROSE TEA-GOWN, ETC.	189	HUGH SELWYN: 3	1
TEARS			
CLOUD AND RAIN-TEARS PASS THEY FLEET!	7	CINO	49
TEN			
POEM BY THE BRIDGE AT TEN-SHIN	131	AT TEN-SHIN	T
BY THE SOUTH SIDE OF THE BRIDGE AT TEN-SHIN.	134	EXILE'S LETTER	3
THE (3)			
THICK			
USURY AGE-OLD AND AGE-THICK	190	HUGH SELWYN: 4	18
THIRTY			
FOR THERE ARE, IN SIRMIONE, TWENTY-EIGHT YOUNG DANTES AND THIRTY-FOUR CATULLI;	96	AESTHETICS	8
THROUGH ALL THE THIRTY-SIX FOLDS OF THE TURNING AND TWISTING WATERS.	134	EXILE'S LETTER	18
THROATED			
UNDER NIGHT, THE PEACOCK-THROATED,	75	THE ALCHEMIST	8
TIBBY			
SHE'D SAY TO HER TIBBY-CAT,	271	OLE KATE	22
TIDE			
THEN MAKYTH MY HEART HIS YULE-TIDE CHEER	10	FOR THIS YULE	6
TIME			
TILL THE ROSE-TIME WILL BE OVER,	67	THE CLOAK	2
KNOW THEN THAT I LOVED YOU FROM AFORE-TIME,	96	DUM CAPITOLIUM	7
'TO-MORROW AT TEA-TIME.'")	159	PSYCHOLOG HOUR	38
WHAT FOOT BEAT OUT YOUR TIME-BAR,	207	SEXTUS PROP: 1	8
TIPS			
HAVE I NOT TOUCHED THY PALMS AND FINGER-TIPS,	60	TOMB AKR CAAR	22
SOUTH OF THE POND THE WILLOW-TIPS ARE HALF-BLUE AND BLUER,	129	THE RIVER SONG	25
SPREAD LIKE THE FINGER-TIPS OF ONE FRAIL HAND;	152	NEAR PERIGORD	30
TO (24)			
TOBACCO			
GIVE ME IN DUE TIME, I BESEECH YOU, A LITTLE TOBACCO-SHOP.	117	THE LAKE ISLE	2
LEND ME A LITTLE TOBACCO-SHOP,	117	THE LAKE ISLE	13
TOM			
THAT TOM-BOY WHO CAN'T EARN HER LIVING,	162	CABARET DANCER	44
TOMB			
HERE ARE THEIR TOMB-STONES.	145	SALUTATION 3RD	6
THE SONGS SHALL BE A FINE TOMB-STONE OVER THEIR BEAUTY.	209	SEXTUS PROP: 1	64
TONSILLED			
YOU WHEEZE AS A HEAD-COLD LONG-TONSILLED CALLIOPE,	13	MESMERISM	9
TOP			
AND CLINGS TO THE WALLS AND THE GATE-TOP.	131	AT TEN-SHIN	12
NOT THAT HE WAS A SAINT, NOR WAS TOP-LOFTICAL	246	MOYEN SENSUEL	233
TORCH			
I HAVE SEEN THE TORCH-FLAMES, HIGH-LEAPING,	121	PROVINC DESERT	30
STRAY GLEAMS ON HANGING MAIL, AN ARMOURER'S TORCH-FLARE	155	NEAR PERIGORD	134
TOWARD			
THEY DREAM US-TOWARD AND	6	CINO	15
TOWER			
EN BERTRANS, A TOWER-ROOM AT HAUTEFORT,	154	NEAR PERIGORD	95
NOR I, NOR TOWER-MAN, LOOK ON DAYLIGHT,	177	LANGUE D'OC: 4	8

TRANS -- WAVY

	PAGE	TITLE	LINE
TRANS			
CELEBRITIES FROM THE TRANS-CAUCASUS WILL BELAUD ROMAN CELEBRITIES	207	SEXTUS PROP: 1	17
TRAPPINGS			
UPON HORSES WITH HEAD-TRAPPINGS OF YELLOW METAL,	132	AT TEN-SHIN	16
TREE			
O NATHAT-IKANAIE, "TREE-AT-THE-RIVER."	91	DANCE FIGURE	18
THE RED-PINE-TREE GOD LOOKS AT HIM AND WONDERS.	139	SENNIN POEM	11
TREES			
UNBEND FROM THE HOLLY-TREES,	109	HEATHER	5
TREMBLE			
A-TREMBLE IN MEN'S VEINS; O LIP CURVED HIGH	41	HER MONUMENT	12
TROUT			
THE SALMON-TROUT DRIFTS IN THE STREAM,	166	FISH & SHADOW	1
THE SOUL OF THE SALMON-TROUT FLOATS OVER THE STREAM	166	FISH & SHADOW	2
TSIN			
SAID TSIN-TSU:	104	THE SEEING EYE	8
TSU			
SAID TSIN-TSU:	104	THE SEEING EYE	8
TWENTY			
FOR THERE ARE, IN SIRMIONE, TWENTY-EIGHT YOUNG DANTES AND THIRTY-FOUR CATULLI;	96	AESTHETICS	8
TWO			
O FILAMENTS OF AMBER, TWO-FACED IRIDESCENCE!	95	OF THE DEGREES	15
NOR OF XERXES' TWO-BARRELED KINGDOM, NOR OF REMUS AND HIS ROYAL FAMILY,	217	SEXTUS PROP: 5	44
UM			
HALF A LOAF? UM-HUM?	257	BREAD BRIGADE	2
UNCLE'S			
OR TAKE THE INTAGLIO, MY FAT GREAT-UNCLE'S HEIRLOOM:	162	CABARET DANCER	35
UP			
HUB OF THE WHEEL, THE STIRRER-UP OF STRIFE,	151	NEAR PERIGORD	21
SPREAD ON BOTH HANDS AND ON THE UP-PUSHED-BOSOM--	161	CABARET DANCER	15
US (1)			
VALLEY			
OF LILY-OF-THE-VALLEY	109	ALBA	2
VERSE			
"CAT'S I' THE WATER BUTT!" THOUGHT'S IN YOUR VERSE-BARREL,	13	MESMERISM	5
VINE			
AND EVERY VINE-STOCK IS	87	THE SPRING	6
VINE-STRINGS A HUNDRED FEET LONG HANG DOWN FROM CARVED RAILINGS,	129	THE RIVER SONG	27
VOUS			
"CONNAISSEZ-VOUS OSTENDE?"	111	BLACK SLIPPERS	6
WALLED			
THUS HE ESCHEWED THE BRIGHT RED-WALLED CAFES AND	245	MOYEN SENSUEL	205
WANDER			
MAKE THY LAUGH OUR WANDER-LIED;	7	CINO	47
WARD			
FOR HER HANDS HAVE NO KINDNESS ME-WARD,	212	SEXTUS PROP: 3	14
WARS			
A TURMOIL OF WARS-MEN, SPREAD OVER THE MIDDLE KINGDOM,	133	FRONTIER GUARD	15
WASH			
"TELL ME NOT IN MOURNFUL WISH-WASH	241	MOYEN SENSUEL	89
LIFE'S A SORT OF SUGARED DISH-WASH!"	241	MOYEN SENSUEL	90
WATER			
"AND A CAT'S IN THE WATER-BUTT."--ROBERT BROWNING	13	MESMERISM	EPI
MAELIDS AND WATER-GIRLS,	87	THE SPRING	2
WHERE THE LOW DRONNE IS FILLED WITH WATER-LILIES.	152	NEAR PERIGORD	56
THE WATER-JET OF GOLD LIGHT BEARS US UP THROUGH THE CEILINGS;	169	PHANOPOEIA	4
THIN LIKE BROOK-WATER,	192	YEUX GLAUQUES	13
WATT			
BENEATH HALF-WATT RAYS,	204	MEDALLION	16
WAVE			
MY WAVE-WORN BEAUTY WITH HIS WIND OF FLOWERS,	24	THUS NINEVEH	15
WAVY			
THE SALT-WAVY TUMULT TRAVERSE ALONE.	65	THE SEAFARER	36

WAY -- WITH

	PAGE	TITLE	LINE
WAY			
'POLLO PHOIBEE, TO OUR WAY-FARE	7	CINO	46
SEEKING E'ER THE NEW-LAID RAST-WAY	7	CINO	50
GIVING THE ROCKS SMALL LEE-WAY	187	E. P. ODE	11
WAYS			
ON FLOOD-WAYS TO BE FAR DEPARTING.	65	THE SEAFARER	53
WEAL			
THAT ANY EARTH-WEAL ETERNAL STANDETH	66	THE SEAFARER	68
WEARIERS			
OUT-WEARIERS OF APOLLO WILL, AS WE KNOW, CONTINUE THEIR MARTIAN GENERALITIES,	207	SEXTUS PROP: 1	10
WEARY			
REST MASTER, FOR WE BE A-WEARY, WEARY	35	THE EYES	1
MERE-WEARY MOOD. LEST MAN KNOW NOT	64	THE SEAFARER	12
WELL			
DRIPS FROM MY DEATHLESS PEN--AH, WELL-AWAY!	59	SILET	2
I HAVE NOT FOUND THEE AT THE WELL-HEAD	91	DANCE FIGURE	8
OF WELL-GOWNED APPROBATION	196	HUGH SELWIN:12	10
WHO ON THE SO WELL-PAID GROUND	263	ALF'S EIGHTH	9
WHALE			
WHETS FOR THE WHALE-PATH THE HEART IRRESISTIBLY,	65	THE SEAFARER	64
WHATS			
THE MIDNIGHT ACTIVITIES OF WHATS-HIS NAME,	264	ALF'S NINTH	2
AND WHATS-HIS-NAME ATTAINED NOBILITY.	264	ALF'S NINTH	8
WHEEL			
OR OF HECTOR SPATTERING WHEEL-RIMS,	208	SEXTUS PROP: 1	29
WHITE			
WITH YOU IS IOPE, WITH YOU THE WHITE-GLEAMING TYRO,	38	LADY'S LIFE	5
LET THEM ASSUME THE MILK-WHITE BODIES OF AGATE.	76	THE ALCHEMIST	52
THE MILK-WHITE GIRLS	109	HEATHER	4
AND THEIR SNOW-WHITE LEOPARD	109	HEATHER	6
WITH HER WHITE-STOCKING'D FEET	111	BLACK SLIPPERS	3
GREEN ARSENIC SMEARED ON AN EGG-WHITE CLOTH,	113	L'ART, 1910	1
WHY DOES THE SMALL CHILD IN THE SOILED-WHITE IMITATION FUR COAT	114	SIMULACRA	3
WHITE-HEADED.	136	EXILE'S LETTER	69
HANG IN YELLOW-WHITE AND DARK CLUSTERS READY FOR PRESSING.	167	OF AROUET	22
WIDE			
THE WIDE-BANDED IRIDES	200	MAUBERLEY: 2	27
MOVING A NATION-WIDE	259	ALF'S THIRD	6
WILD			
IN WILD-WOOD NEVER FAWN NOR FALLOW FARETH	38	BALLATETTA	6
YESTERDAY WE WENT OUT OF THE WILD-GOOSE GATE,	139	SOUTH-FOLK	4
NOT YET WILD-CRUEL AS DARTS,	250	DONNA MI PREGA	74
WILLINGNESS			
ENDS WITH A WILLINGNESS-TO-OBLIGE.	99	EPITAPH	2
WILLOW			
I LOOKED AT THE DRAGON-POND, WITH ITS WILLOW-COLOURED WATER	129	THE RIVER SONG	20
SOUTH OF THE POND THE WILLOW-TIPS ARE HALF-BLUE AND BLUER,	129	THE RIVER SONG	25
WIND			
ONCE FOR WIND-RUNEING	6	CINO	14
WINDS			
AND INTO TEN THOUSAND VALLEYS FULL OF VOICES AND PINE-WINDS.	134	EXILE'S LETTER	21
WINE			
WEALTHY AND WINE-FLUSHED, HOW I WEARY OFT	64	THE SEAFARER	30
WING			
HE GOES OUT TO HORI, TO LOOK AT THE WING-FLAPPING STORKS,	130	THE RIVER SONG	36
WING'D			
THESE WERE THE "WING'D-WITH-AWE,"	74	THE RETURN	10
WIRE			
THE WIRE-LIKE BANDS OF COLOUR INVOLUTE MOUNT FROM MY FINGERS;	170	PHANOPOEIA	17
WISH			
"TELL ME NOT IN MOURNFUL WISH-WASH	241	MOYEN SENSUEL	89
WITH (1)			

	PAGE	TITLE	LINE
WITS			
OVER THE DYING HALF-WITS BLOW,	265	ALF'S TENTH	5
WOMEN			
BUT SURELY THE WORST OF YOUR OLD-WOMEN ARE THE MALE ONES.)	243	MOYEN SENSUEL	150
WONDER			
BUT MY SOUL SENT A WOMAN, A WOMAN OF THE WONDER FOLK,	17	PRAISE YSOLT	38
WOOD			
THAT WAS A DOG-WOOD TREE SOME SYNE.	4	LA FRAISNE	15
GREEN OF THE WOOD-MOSS AND FLOWER COLOURS,	35	THE EYES	9
IN WILD-WOOD NEVER FAWN NOR FALLOW FARETH	38	BALLATETTA	6
THIS BOAT IS OF SHATO-WOOD, AND ITS GUNWALES ARE CUT MAGNOLIA,	128	THE RIVER SONG	1
PULLED DOWN BY A DEAL-WOOD HORSE;	208	SEXTUS PROP: 1	27
WITH A LIVELY WOOD-PULP "AD."	268	ALF'S TWELFTH	19
WORK			
A NET-WORK OF ARBOURS AND PASSAGES AND COVERED WAYS,	141	IDEA OF CHOAN	22
BORDER THE NET-WORK OF WAYS:	141	IDEA OF CHOAN	24
A BASKET-WORK OF BRAIDS WHICH SEEM AS IF THEY WERE	204	MEDALLION	10
WORN			
MY WAVE-WORN BEAUTY WITH HIS WIND OF FLOWERS,	24	THUS NINEVEH	15
WORTHY			
IF I HAVE NOT THE FACULTY, "THE BARE ATTEMPT WOULD BE PRAISE-WORTHY."	216	SEXTUS PROP. 5	4
WRACKED			
GO ALSO TO THE NERVE-WRACKED, GO TO THE ENSLAVED-BY-CONVENTION,	88	COMMISSION	2
WRETCHED			
LIST HOW I, CARE-WRETCHED, ON ICE-COLD SEA,	64	THE SEAFARER	14
WRITE			
AND I HAVE MOPED IN THE EMPEROR'S GARDEN, AWAITING AN ORDER-TO-WRITE!	129	THE RIVER SONG	19
YARD			
DUST DRIFTS OVER THE COURT-YARD,	108	LIU CH'E	2
THE DRYAD STANDS IN MY COURT-YARD	110	TEMPORA	2
THE WILLOWS OF THE INN-YARD	137	OF DEPARTURE	EPI
YARDS			
THEIR DOOR-YARDS WOULD SCARCELY KNOW THEM, OR PARIS.	208	SEXTUS PROP: 1	31
YEAR			
WINING THE GHOSTS OF YESTER-YEAR.	10	FOR THIS YULE	8
WINING THE GHOSTS OF YESTER-YEAR.	10	FOR THIS YULE	16
WINING THE GHOSTS OF YESTER-YEAR.	10	FOR THIS YULE	24
WINING THE GHOSTS OF YESTER-YEAR.	10	FOR THIS YULE	28
YEI			
THE EASTERN WIND BRINGS THE GREEN COLOUR INTO THE ISLAND GRASSES AT YEI-SHU,	129	THE RIVER SONG	23
YELLOW			
HANG IN YELLOW-WHITE AND DARK CLUSTERS READY FOR PRESSING.	167	OF AROUET	22
FROM THE GOLD-YELLOW FROCK	204	MEDALLION	6
YEN			
YOU WENT INTO FAR KU-TO-YEN, BY THE RIVER OF SWIRLING EDDIES,	130	RIVER-MER WIFE	16
YESTER			
WINING THE GHOSTS OF YESTER-YEAR.	10	FOR THIS YULE	8
WINING THE GHOSTS OF YESTER-YEAR.	10	FOR THIS YULE	16
WINING THE GHOSTS OF YESTER-YEAR.	10	FOR THIS YULE	24
WINING THE GHOSTS OF YESTER-YEAR.	10	FOR THIS YULE	28
YO			
AND THE MOON FALLS OVER THE PORTALS OF SEI-GO-YO,	131	AT TEN-SHIN	11
AND THERE CAME ALSO THE "TRUE MAN" OF SHI-YO TO MEET ME,	134	EXILE'S LETTER	24
YULE			
THEN MAKYTH MY HEART HIS YULE-TIDE CHEER	10	FOR THIS YULE	6

TABLE OF WORD FREQUENCIES

FREQUENCY: 5 -- 4

SHOULDERS	BRITAIN	FLOW	PHYLLIDULA
SIDE	BROTHER	FLOWED	PLAYS
SLENDER	BUILT	FOLLOWS	PLEASANT
SLIGHT	BUSINESS	FORCE	POEM
SMILE	CABARET	FORGOTTEN	POETS
SOFT	CALLED	FORTY	PORCELAIN
SPACE	CALLIOPE	FRANCOIS	POUR
SPEAKS	CALLS	FREEDOM	PRAY
SPIRITS	CANZONE	FROST	PRESENT
SPOKE	CAREFULLY	FURTHER	PRINT
STRAIGHT	CARESS	GENERAL	PROCESSION
SUNLIGHT	CARRY	GENIUS	PROPERTIUS
TALE	CASTLES	GENTLE	PROVE
TASTE	CASTS	GLEAM	PUBLIC
THINKS	CAT	GRAND	PUTS
THIRD	CAUSE	GRANT	RAFT
THOROUGHLY	CHAIR	GREATER	RAN
TILL	CHARMING	GROUND	RATE
TOUCH	CHEAP	GROW	REGRET
TROUBLE	CHOAN	HARRY	RESPECT
TRY	CIRCLE	HENCE	REWARD
TURNING	CLAMOUR	HERO	ROCHECOUART
VALLEY	CLASSICS	HIDDEN	ROT
VALLEYS	CLINGS	HOLLOW	ROYAL
VENUS	COMFORT	HOLY	RUSTLING
VIS	COMPLAIN	HOMAGE	SAITH
VOICE	CONDUCT	HORSE	SANS
WHOLLY	CORDS	HOST	SAP
WISH	COST	HOUNDS	SCARCELY
WORLD'S	COW	HUMAN	SCATTERED
WOVEN	CRIED	IMPERIAL	SEAS
WRITING	CRYSTAL	ITSELF	SEAT
WROTE	CURSE	I'VE	SEEMED
WROUGHT	DAMN'D	IVORY	SEND
	DANTE	LAUGH	SHADOWS
(4)	DAPING	LAWYERS	SHE'D
ACROSS	DAY'S	LE	SHOOK
AELIS	DEATHLESS	LEND	SHOP
AETHER	DIES	LICK	SHOWS
AFRAID	DIM	LINES	SITS
AIN'T	DISCOVERED	LIST	SITTING
ALWAY	DISTANT	LONGER	SLAIN
AMOROUS	DOOR	LOOKING	SOMEONE
ANHES	DOORS	LOVELY	SORRY
ANSWER	DR.	LOVE'S	SOUNDS
ANYTHING	DRIFTED	MAKES	SPIKED
APART	DYED	MALE	SPLENDID
APOLLO	E.	MALEMORT	SPRAY
ARAGON	EAT	MARGOT	STALE
ASH	E'EN	MEANS	STAYS
AU	ELF	MEMORY	STIFF
AUGUST	ENDS	MERE	STORY
BABY	ESCAPE	MIDST	STRETCHED
BADE	ESSENCE	MONTFORT	STRETCHES
BALLAD	EST	MONTHS	STRIFE
BASKET	FAITH	MOVED	STRAX
BEATEN	FAMILY	MYRIAD	SUNSET
BECAME	FAVOUR	NAMED	SWEPT
BEGINNING	FEATURES	NARROW	SWORD
BEHELD	FED	NOBLEST	TAKING
BIG	FEMALE	OBSERVE	TALKED
BLOWS	FICTION	OFTEN	TAMUZ
BODIES	FIELD	OLIVE	TEACH
BORDER	FILLED	ONES	TEARS
BOUGH	FINDS	OPINION	TEMPLE
BOXES	FIRES	ORDER	THEBES
BOY	FLAGES	PACK	THEREOF
BREAK	FLAMES	PAGES	TIDE
BREATHE	FLEET	PASSING	TIME'S
BRIDGE	FLOATING	PERFUMED	TISSUE
BRIGHTNESS	FLOOR	PERSEPHONE	TRANSIENT

PAGE 521

FREQUENCY: 4 -- 3

TROUBLES	BESIDE	DEAL	GRUB
TUNE	BLOW	DEL	GUARDS
TURMOIL	BLOWN	DELAY	GUIDO
'TWAS	BOLD	DEMANDED	HABIT
UNDERSTOOD	BORDERS	DEPARTING	HAIL
UNSTILL	BORE	DEPARTURE	HANGING
VENICE	BORED	DESIRED	HEADS
VIRGIN	BOYS	DESIROUS	HEARTS
WANDERING	BRAINS	DESOLATE	HEAT
WARM	BRANCH	DIFFERENT	HEDGETHORN
WAVES	BRANCHES	DISCUSS	HEELS
WE'LL	BREAKS	DOG	HELICON
WHEELS	BREASTS	DOING	HENRY
WHENCE	BRIDE	DRIFTS	HERE'S
WHITHER	BRINGS	DRINKS	HERS
WI'	BRITONS	DRIVEN	HESPER
WILD	BRIVE	DRIVES	HOLDETH
WILLOWS	BROKE	DROP	HOLDS
WINGS	BROWNING	DUE	HOLE
WINING	BUNDLE	DULL	HOMER
WISE	BURIED	D'UNE	HOWL
WORKED	BURNISHED	EAR	IDENTICAL
WORKS	BURY	EASTWARD	INANE
WOULDN'T	CALLETH	EDITOR	INDECOROUS
WRITES	CALLING	E'ER	INVITATION
YESTER-YEAR	CALM	EH	IRE
	CANDLES	EITHER	ISLE
(3)	CANNONI	ELAIN	IT'S
A.	CANST	EMOTION	JADE
ACHAIA	CE	EMPIRE	JEWELS
ACTAEON	CEMBELINS	ENGLISHMEN	JONGLEUR
ACTS	CERTAINLY	ENTER	KAN
AD.	CHAINS	ENVY	KEEN
ADEST	CHANCES	EQUAL	KEEPS
ADULTERIES	CHANGING	ETC.	KIANG
AFAR	CHARM	EVOE	KIN
AGO	CHLORIS	EXPRESS	KINGDOM
AID	CHRIST	EYELIDS	KNEES
ALABASTER	CHRISTIAN	FACTS	LABOURED
ALAS	CIRCULATION	FAILED	LAIN
ALBA	CIRCUMSTANCES	FARE	LAMP
ALCMENA	CITIES	FAST	LANDS
ALIVE	CLIFFS	FATE	LASTING
ALTAR	CLINGING	FELLOWS	LAUREL
ANTENNAE	CLOTHS	FENCER	LEAD
ARMOUR	COBALT	FIFTY	LEARNING
ARMY	COIN	FIRM	LEOPARDS
AROUND	COMPANIONS	FLAUBERT	LESBIA
ARTS	COMPARED	FLEE	LEVEL
ASHES	CONFESS	FLOWING	LIFT
ASKING	CONFUSION	FOOD	LIGHTS
ASPECT	CONTINUE	FORCES	LIKENESS
ATTENTION	CO-OPS	FOREHEAD	LIKEWISE
AUDIENCE	CORN	FORESTS	LILIES
'AVE	CORNER	FORMED	LIMBS
BANKS	COULDN'T	FOUGHT	LOAF
BARBAROUS	COUNT	FOURTH	LONE
BARE	COURT	FRESH	LOTUS
BARK	CRAFTY	FRIENDLY	LOVING
BARREN	CROSS	FRONT	LUCK
BASHFUL	CRUSHED	FRUIT	LUST
BATTLE	CUCKOLD	FULLY	LUSTRE
BEAUTIES	CUNNING	FUR	LYNCEUS
BELIEVING	CUPS	GAUZE	MADNESS
BELLAIRE	CYNTHIA	GEAR	MAD'ST
BELONG	CYTHAREAN	GLOW	MAGIC
BELOVED	DAILY	GOSSIP	MAID
BELOW	DAMM	GRACIOUS	MAIL
BELS	DANCING	GRAPES	MAKETH
BEND	DATE	GRASSES	MANNERS
BESEECH	DAUGHTER	GREED	MARCH

FREQUENCY: 3 -- 2

MAREUIL	POETRY	SLIPPERS	WORST
MARKET	POINT	SMOKE	WORTHY
MARKS	POM-POM	SOMEWHAT	WOUND
MARS	POOL	SOMEWHERE	WOUNDED
MASS	POPLARS	SOUL'S	WRAPPED
MEETING	PORTION	SQUIRE	WREATHS
MEMORIES	POUND	STAGE	WRITTEN
MENTION	PRESENTS	STATION	Y.
MESSAGE	PREY	STAY	YEH
MI	PRIDE	STEP	YEUX
MID	PRINCESS	STRIKE	YOURS
MIDDLE	PRINTED	STRINGS	ZAGREUS
MIDDLE-AGED	PROFITS	STRIVEN	ZEUS'
MIDNIGHT	PROMISED	STUFFED	
MIDONZ	PROTECTION	SUFFERERS	(2)
MILES	PROVENCE	SWIFTLY	AB
MILLWINS	PRUDENT	SWIM	ABANDONED
MINGLED	PUFFED	SWINGING	ABJECT
MIS	PURSE	TABLE	ABROAD
MOCK	QUE	TAKETH	ABSENT
MODEL	QUEENS	TALES	ACCELERATED
MOMENT	QU'EST	TANGLE	ACCEPT
MOMENTS	QUICK	TERM	ACCOSTED
M'ONT	QU'ILS	TERROR	ACCOUNT
MORN	REAL	THEIRS	ACHERON
MORTAL	RECORD	THEREON	ACHILLES
MORTE	REED	THEY'LL	ACT
MOSS	REGARD	THROWN	ADORNMENT
MOSTLY	REPEAT	TIPS	ADVANCE
MUSE	RETURNING	TIRED	ADVISED
NATIONAL	RICHARD	TIREIS	AESTHETICS
NATURAL	RIDDLE	TONE	AFFAIR
NE	ROBE	TOUCHED	AFFECT
NECKS	ROBES	TOWN	AGATHAS
NEEDS	ROCK	TRACE	AGED
NERVES	ROCKS	TRAFFIC	AGE-OLD
NICE	ROOF	TRAIST	AGES
NIGHTINGALES	ROTTEN	TREASURE	AH-EH
NIXON	SALUE	TROJAN	AIMLESSLY
NOBLE	SALUTATION	TROY	AL
NON	SAND	TRUNK	ALCOHOL
NOVELIST	SANDALS	TURNETH	A-LEVEL
OCEAN	SATIN	TWAIN	ALFONSO
OFFERED	SCARCE	TWICE	ALGAE
OLDER	SCORN	ULTIMATE	ALIKE
OPENED	SELFRIDGE	UTTERLY	AMBROSIAL
OURS	SEPULCHRE	VAGUE	AMERICAN
OXEN	SERVANT	VEIL	AMIABLE
PAIN	SETS	VEILED	AMONGST
PAINTED	SETTING	VENDERE	ANDROMEDA
PALLAS	SEVENTY	VERSE	ANIMAL
PALMS	SEVERED	VIDAL	ANKLES
PANTHER	SEZ	VILLAGE	ANXIOUS
PAPIOLS	SHAKE	VIRTUES	ANYONE
PARADISE	SHAKES	VOICES	APPLES
PARDON	SHALT	WAITING	APRIL
PARIS	SHELL	WANT	ARAGONESE
PARTICULAR	SHELTER	WAST	ARDENCA
PASSES	SHIN	WAVE	'ARF
PATH	SHIPS	WEAR	ARIDES
PEARL	SHIRES	WEAVE	ARIGHT
PEN	SHOKU	WE'D	ARLES
PHOEBUS	SHOT	WEST	ARM
PHOENIX	SHOULDST	WHEAT	AROSE
PIERE	SHRIVELLED	WHEEL	ARRIMON
PITY	SIDES	WHEREFORE	ARROWS
PLAYED	SIGHING	WHILES	ASKED
PLEASED	SIMPLE	WISDOM	ASLEEP
PLY	SINGER	WOLF	ASSUME
POEMS	SINK	WON'T	ATTAINDER
POET	SITH	WOODS	ATTENDED

PAGE 523

FREQUENCY: 2

ATTHIS	BURSTING	COMME	DINE
ATTIRE	BUTLERS	COMMON	DIRTY
ATTRACT	BUTTERFLIES	COMPANION	DIS
AUBETERRE	BUY	COMPOUND	DISCUSSION
AUREATE	BYRON	COMPRENDRE	DISDEIGN
AUTHOR	CAESARS	COMRADE	DISGUST
AUTRES	CAESAR'S	CONCERNS	DISOWN
AUTUMNS	CAHORS	CONDONE	DISTANCE
AVEC	CALLIMACHUS	CONFESSIONS	DISTRESS
AVINEN	CALVUS	CONNECTIONS	DIVES
AWAIT	CAMBRIDGE	CONSCIOUSNESS	DOLE
AWAITING	CAMP	CONSERVATORY	DON
AWAKE	CANDIDIA	CONSIDERABLE	DONNA
AWFUL	CANONS	CONSTANT	DOST
AZALAIS	CANTILATIONS	CONSUMMATE	DOUBLE
B.	CANZON	CONTEMPORARIES	DOUBTFUL
BACCHUS	CAPERS	CONTEMPT	DOWSON
BAH	CAREFUL	CONTRARY	DOZEN
BAIT	CARESSES	COOLNESS	DRAGONS
BANDS	CARRIAGE	COPY	DRANK
BANK	CARS	CORONAL	DRAWETH
BANKER'S	CASH	COS	DREAMED
BANQUETS	CASTALIAN	COULEUR	DRIFT
BARBARIAN	CAT'S	COUNSELS	DRIFTING
BARTER	'CAUSE	COUNTESS	DRIPPING
BASIL	CAUSING	COUNTS	DRONNE
BATHE	CAVERNS	COURSES	DRUMS
BATTLES	CEASE	COURTS	DU
BAWDY	CEASED	COURT-YARD	DUCHESS
BE'A	CELEBRATED	COWED	DULY
BEAMS	CELEBRITIES	CRACKS	D'UN
BEARD	CENTENNIAL	CRAFTSMAN	DURABLE
BEASTS	CENTS	CREATED	DYNASTIC
BEATS	CENTURY	CRIES	EAGERLY
BEDROOM	CERCLAMON	CROSSED	'EAR
BEEF	CH'	CRUST	EARTHLY
BEGAN	CHAIN	CULT	EASE
BELL	CHAINED	CUNNINGLY	EASTERN
BENCH	CHALUS	CUPID	EASY
BENDS	CHANGED	CURE	ECHO
BEWILDERED	CHANT	CURSING	ECHOES
BIAUCAIRE	CHARACTER	CURTAIN	ED
BIDDING	CHARIOT	CUSTOM	EDDIES
BIRTH	CHARMS	CYPRESS	EDITORS
BLADES	CHATTER	DAMP	EIGHT
BLEAK	CHEAPER	DANS	EIGHTEEN
BLOKES	CHEEK	DAPHNE	EIGHTH
BLOODS	CHEEKS	DARE	ELEMENT
BLOSSOM	CHESS	DARED	ELEMENTS
BLOT	CHILL	DARTS	ELIMINATION
BOARD	CHINESE	DAYLIGHT	EMAIL
BOAST	CHOICE	DAYS'	EMBANKMENT
BOAT	CHOOSE	DEBT	EMBERS
BONDS	CHURCH	DECADE	EMPEROR
BONNY	CLARITY	DECLINE	ENCOUNTER
BOOT	CLASSIC	DEFENCE	ENTRUST
BOOTS	CLAUSTRA	DEFY	ENVOI
BOREDOM	CLEMENCY	DELIA	EPITAPH
BOUGHT	CLEVER	DELICATELY	'ERE
BRAVE	CLIMB	DELICIOUS	EREBUS
BRENNBAUM	CLOSER	DELIGHTED	ESPECIALLY
BRIBE	CLOTH	DELIGHTFUL	ESTRANGEMENT
BRIEF	CLOTHED	DENIED	ETSU
BRIGADE	CLUB	DEPARTED	EUHENIA
BRITISH	COACHES	DESCEND	EUPHRATES
BROAD	COAN	DESERT	EVENT
BROCADE	COEUR-DE-LION	DESIRES	EVERYONE
BROOKS	COLCHIS	DESOLATED	EXAMINATION
BUILD	COLLAR	DETEST	EXCELLENT
BUNCH	COLOURLESS	DIDN'T	EXHAUSTED
BURNS	COMIC	DIEU	EXPECT

FREQUENCY: 7 -- 5

GRIEF	ERE	SUBTLE	FUNERAL
HALL	FALLING	SURE	GATES
HANG	FALSE	SURELY	GATHERED
HARSH	FAT	TAKES	GAZE
HEAVY	FLAT	TALL	GETS
HILLS	FLOWER	TEA	GLITTER
I'D	FOOL	TEETH	GREW
ILL	FOREVER	THEREFORE	GUARD
IO	FRAIL	THINKING	HABITS
LAID	GARDENS	THOUGHTS	HALLS
LOOKED	GATE	TO-DAY	HARP
M.	GATHER	TOMB	HEART'S
MAIDENS	GAVE	TOOK	HEAVENS
MATTER	GEORGE	TURNS	HERSELF
MIRROR	GETTING	TWELVE	HID
MISTRESS	GIFT	TWILIGHT	HILL
MOOD	GIVEN	UN	HOMESICK
MOUNTAINS	GIVES	UNCERTAIN	HOUSES
NATURE	GRAY	VERSES	HUNG
NOISE	HAPPY	WEEK	I'LL
PAPERS	HIMSELF	WET	IMMORTAL
RISE	HOURS	WHATEVER	INFANT
ROSES	JEWELLED	WON	JE
SAPPHIRE	KNOWLEDGE	WORTH	JOVE
SAYING	LISTEN	WRONG	KINGS
SEASON	LOOSE		KISS
SEEM	LYING	(5)	KISSED
SENT	MANNER	AUGHT	KNOWETH
SHUT	MARRIED	AVERNUS	KNOWING
SIGHT	MASTER	BAD	LACKING
SIT	MINDS	BEARING	LAKE
SIX	MONTAIGNAC	BEAT	LATER
SKOAL	MUSES	BELLAIRES	LEAN
SNOW	NATION	BENT	LEAST
SOON	NEED	BID	LETTER
SOULS	NOTE	BIRD	LIFE'S
STIR	OPPOSING	BLADE	LOOKS
STREAM	OTHERS	BLIND	LORDS
STUFF	PALACE	BOUGHS	LOVES
THROAT	PAN	BROTHERS	LYGDAMUS
TONGUE	PARENT	BURST	MAN'S
TRIED	PER	CATCH	MEAN
USE	PERFECT	CHANCE	MEASURE
USED	PERFECTION	CHEER	MILLION
WATCH	PERHAPS	CONQUERED	MONTH
WEARY	PERIGORD	CONSIDER	MOTHER
WORN	PLACES	COPPER	MYSELF
YEA	PLEASE	COVER	NAY
	PLENTY	COVERED	'NEATH
(6)	PURE	DANCED	NEEDLE
ALONG	RARE	DANCERS	NINE
ATTEND	REASON	DRAW	OFT
BASE	REJOICING	DRESS	PARCHMENT
BEARS	RUMOUR	DREW	PAST
BECOME	SANG	DULNESS	PETALS
BITTERNESS	SEEING	DYING	PINE
BURN	SEEK	E	PLACID
CAST	SEEKING	EARTH'S	PLAYING
CHALAIS	SEEME	EMPTY	PRAISED
CHILD	SEPARATION	ETCETERA	PRETTY
CLOTHING	SHOW	EYE	QUESTION
COLOURS	SIGNS	FALL	REMAIN
COMETH	SILENCE	FAME	RICH
CROWD	SOCIAL	FATHER	RICHES
DARKNESS	SOLE	FELL	RING
DRAWN	STAIRS	FIFTH	SAFE
DRIVE	START	FILL	SAIL
EARS	STONE	FIVE	SHOULD
EAST	STOP	FLED	SEED
EDGE	STREAMS	FOOLS	SENNIN
ENGLAND	STREETS	FORMS	SHADE

FREQUENCY: 13 -- 7

WHOLE	(10)	LESS	NAUGHT
WINDS	BELIEVE	MEN'S	NIGHTS
	BEZIERS	METAL	NOS
(12)	BOW	MOUTH	O'ER
AYE	CLOSE	MOVES	OPEN
BEHOLD	COUNTRY	NEITHER	PEPITA
BLOOD	DELIGHT	NEXT	PERSON
BOOKS	DRUNK	PALE	PRESS
BORN	ENGLISH	PASSED	PURIFIEZ
BROKEN	FEEL	PASSION	REACH
DIED	FELLOW	PEACE	READY
FOUR	FERE	PLAY	ROMAN
GLORY	FOUNTAIN	POOR	RUN
GREY	GIRL	ROAD	SAD
HOLD	GODDAMM	SADNESS	SINGS
JOY	GOODLY	SELL	SIR
LADIES	GROWN	SLOW	SON
LEAF	HUNDRED	ST.	SPIRIT
LIE	KIND	STARS	STANDS
LIES	LAUGHTER	SWORDS	STATE
LORD	LOVERS	TO-MORROW	STREET
LOVED	MAENT	TRUTH	SUNG
MOON	MET	WALLS	TALKING
NEAR	'MID		TH'
REMEMBER	NORTH	(8)	THIN
WALK	PLEASURE	ALWAYS	THINE
WITHIN	PURPLE	AMERICA	TOWERS
YOUTH	PUT	ANCIENT	WAR
	SECOND	BEHIND	WIT
(11)	SILENT	BEST	WOE
ALF'S	SILK	BOTH	WONDER
BED	SOMETHING	BOUND	WRITE
BODY	SOUTH	BREATH	YES
CASTLE	STRANGE	CARE	
CERTAIN	STRONG	CAUGHT	(7)
CINO	TAKEN	CLASH	AFFAIRS
CITY	TIMES	COEURS	ALREADY
DESPITE	UNTIL	COLD	AN'
DONE	WIFE	COMING	ARNAUT
EN	WOOD	CURIOUS	BITTER
EVERY	YELLOW	CUT	BONES
FEW		DAMN	BOOK
FINGERS	(9)	DEAR	BREAST
GIRLS	ALMOST	DEW	CAN'T
GOLDEN	AMBER	DIE	CLOAK
HA'	AUTUMN	DOGS	CLOUD
HOME	BEAR	DON'T	COAT
HOT	BERTRANS	DREAMS	COMPANY
KNOWS	BROWN	EARLY	COOL
MIST	CASE	FIT	CRY
MOVE	CHANGE	FOLK	DAWN
PART	CHILDREN	FORM	DREAM
QUIET	CLOUDS	'GAINST	DRY
RAIN	COURSE	GAY	EAGER
RATHER	CRIMSON	GILDED	ETERNAL
RETURN	DANCE	GRAVE	EVENING
ROME	DEEP	HAVING	EVIL
ROUND	DUST	HEAVEN	FACES
SAME	ET	HOPE	FACT
SAW	FALLS	LA	FAINT
SENSE	FIELDS	LARGE	FASHION
SHADOW	FIRE	LEAVE	FATES
SORT	GALLOWS	LES	FISH
SPEECH	GARDEN	LEST	FLOOD
STAND	GLAD	LIVING	FOLLY
THERE'S	HARD	LOVER	FOOT
TOLD	HATE	LOW	FORGET
TOWARD	HELL	MATE	GAME
TURNED	IMAGE	MORNING	GHOSTS
WALL	KEPT	MOVING	GLASS
	LATE	NAKED	GRACE

FREQUENCY: 38 → 13

(38)	HANDS	ANOTHER	WINE
AGAINST	LAST	BLACK	YEAR
TIME	WOMEN	EARTH	
	WORDS	FIND	(15)
(37)	WORLD	FRIEND	BETTER
SEE		HOUSE	BIT
THINGS	(26)	LAND	COLOUR
	AFTER	LEAVES	CRYING
(36)	BENEATH	PEOPLE	DARK
GONE	BRIGHT	SONGS	FLAME
MAY	SING	SORROW	FLOWERS
	SPEAK	THUS	FOUND
(35)	TWO	TILL	HAST
LONG	VERY	'TIS	HEAR
ONCE	WATER	TREES	LIVE
THOUGH		UNDER	MEET
	(25)		MUSIC
(34)	FAIR	(19)	MUST
ANY	GREEN	BETWEEN	NONE
CAME	MINE	FREE	PAY
DOWN	WHY	HORSES	RADWAY
'EM		KNEW	SAYS
FULL	(24)	LO	SINCE
PLACE	AGAIN	RED	SPRING
SET	ALONE	REST	WALKED
	ART	SILVER	WHOSE
(33)	BEAUTY	SWIFT	WIDE
BEFORE	DE	WENT	WORK
	GIVE		
(32)	MOST	(18)	(14)
COMES	NOTHING	ABOVE	ASIDE
HIGH	SEA	END	BEAUTIFUL
MAKE	WOMAN	HALF	BEYOND
SAVE		JUST	BLUE
	(23)	RIVER	DOTH
(31)	AH	SINGING	ELSE
EVER	ALSO	TOGETHER	FINE
MADE	AWAY	UNTO	FORTH
TAKE	BEEN		FRIENDS
THING	BEING	(17)	GOING
WELL	GODS	AUDIART	HELD
YE	THINK	BRING	MR.
	TURN	CALL	PASS
(30)	WAYS	DESIRE	RIGHT
AIR		DID	ROADS
CLEAR	(22)	EACH	ROSE
DEATH	BECAUSE	GOES	SPREAD
KING	COULD	GOT	
LIFE	ENOUGH	KNOWN	(13)
SAID	FIRST	LOT	ARMS
THREE	KEEP	O'	BIRDS
	LIPS	SLEEP	BROUGHT
(29)	MIGHT	WAY	DELICATE
BACK	OFF	WHILE	DES
OWN	THOUSAND	WHOM	DOES
SHOULD	TOO		FOLLOW
YEARS		(16)	HAIR
	(21)	AGE	HAND
(28)	GOLD	AMID	HOUR
AMONG	HEAD	ASK	LAY
LEFT	LOOK	DRINK	LOST
MIND	NAME	FACE	MAD
MUCH	ONLY	FAR	MONTAGUE
OTHER	SMALL	FEAR	POWER
THOUGHT	TELL	FEET	PRAISE
TREE	THOSE	GRASS	SOUND
WHICH	WATERS	HEARD	SWEET
	WITHOUT	QUITE	TALK
(27)	WORD	READ	TEN
DAYS		SKY	TRUE
GET	(20)	THAT'S	VAIN

PAGE 518

FREQUENCY: 2417 -- 38

(2417) THE	(192) ALL	(96) UPON	(60) THROUGH
(1421) AND	(187) HE	(92) LIKE	(59) KNOW
(1123) OF	(177) THIS	(91) IF NOR	(59) WOULD
(683) A	(163) BUT	(90) WHAT	(56) GOD
(658) TO	(161) WILL	(89) AN	(54) LIGHT SONG
(651) IN	(159) SHE	(84) NOW	(53) GREAT SEEN
(610) I	(157) WE	(79) COME HAD HAS	(52) CAN NIGHT
(396) THAT	(156) AT WAS	(78) LOVE OLD	(51) NEVER THEE
(393) IS	(151) YOUR	(76) GO SUCH	(50) LITTLE
(375) WITH	(145) THEY	(75) HERE	(49) DAY SAY
(358) YOU	(139) OUT	(73) HOW	(48) EYES THEN YOUNG
(356) MY	(136) OR	(72) MAN	
(302) FOR	(134) ONE THEIR	(69) THY	(46) YET
(264) ME	(133) THERE	(68) ABOUT AM SOME THESE UP	(45) HEART NEW
(258) HAVE	(130) BE		(44) GOOD WHITE
(244) NOT	(123) SO		
(239) AS	(114) WHO	(67) HIM	(43) HATH STILL WIND
(224) HIS	(108) BY	(65) DO WERE	
(218) HER	(104) US WHEN	(64) INTO LET MEN	(42) LADY
(214) ARE	(103) OUR		(41) OH
(203) IT	(99) THOU	(63) OVER WHERE	(40) DEAD EVEN THAN
(200) FROM	(97) O THEM	(62) ITS MORE SHALL	(39) MANY SOUL SUN
(198) ON			
(195) NO			

PAGE 517

FREQUENCY: 2

EXQUISITE	GETTIN'	HUNGRY	LEARNED
EYEBROWS	GILT	HURLED	LEARNT
FACE-OVAL	GIT	HURT	LEAVETH
FADED	GIVING	HUSBAND	LEAVING
FAILS	GLADNESS	ICE	LED
FAIREST	GLANCE	ICE-COLD	LEDGE
FAIRNESS	GLAZE	IDEA	LEOPARD
FALLEN	GLEAMS	IDEAS	LESSER
FAMILIES	GLOVE	IDIOT	LETTERS
FAN	GODDESS	IGNORANCE	LETTEST
FARES	GOD'S	IGNORANT	LEVITY
FARETH	GOIN'	IL	LI
FASHIONED	GOLDISH	IMAGES	LIANOR
FATE'S	GOODS	IMAGINE	LIDS
FAUN	GRACES	IMPRESSIONS	LIED
FAUN'S	GRANITE	INCAPABLE	LIETH
FEARED	GREATLY	INDEBTED	LIFTED
FEAST	GREEK	INDIA	LIFTING
FEAT	GREEKS	INDUSTRY	LIFTS
FEATHERS	GREENER	INFAMY	LIGHTNING
FEATHERY	GRIEVING	INFERNO	LINED
FEE	GRIN	INMOST	LIP
FEEDS	GRIPPED	INN	LIT
FEELING	GROWS	INSIDE	LITERATURE
FELT	GUARDA	INSOLENT	LIVED
FEMME	GUTS	INSPECT	LIVELY
FER	H.	INSPECTOR	LOBA
FERN-SHOOTS	HA	INTEREST	LODGE
FESTER	HAIE	INWOVEN	LOFTY
FILLS	HALF-BALD	IONE	LOICA
FINAL	HANDMAID	IOPE	LONDON
FINANCIAL	HAPPENED	ISLAND	LONELY
FINGER-TIPS	HAPPIER	ISLES	LOSS
FISHED	HARLOTS	ITALIAN	LOVELIEST
FIST	HARM	ITALY	LOVELINESS
FLARE	HARSHNESS	IVY	LOWER
FLASH	HASTE	JACQUES	LUGETE
FLESH	HATED	JARS	LUNCH
FLEW	HAUGHTY	JESTER	LYCORIS
FLIGHT	HAULTE	JOB	LYRE
FLOAT	HAUNTS	JOHN	MADAME
FLOWS	HAUTEFORT	JOHNSON	MAGNET
FLUTES	HAWTHORNE	JOWL	MAIGRE
FLUTTER	HEADLESS	JUDGES	MAKING
FLY	HEAPS	JUGURTHA	MANDETTA
FOIX	HEARS	JUNO	MANIFEST
FOLIAGE	HEARTH	KALON	MANTLE
FOREIGN	HEATHER	KATE	MAPLE
FOREMAN	HEAVENLY	KEEL	MARBLE
FOREST	HE'D	KEEPING	MARIUS
FORGETTING	HEINE	KIDS	MARROW
FORGIVEN	HELEN	KILLS	MARVOIL
FORMAL	HELEN'S	KINDLY	MASK
FORTUNE	HELPLESS	KINDNESS	MATCH
FORWARD	HERMES	KISSES	MATES
FOUNDED	HEROES	KNIGHTS	MATING
FOUNT	HIDE	KNOT	MAUDERLEY
FOURTEEN	HIGHER	LACK	MEADOW
FRANCESCA	HIGHEST	LACKED	MEDALLION
FRIENDSHIP	HIGHWAY	LADY'S	MEDIAEVAL
FROGS	HIND'S	LAMENT	MEDIUM
FROSTED	HIRED	LAP	MELTING
FU	HONOURABLE	LARES	MEMNON
FUNGUS	HONOURED	LARGER	MENELAUS
FUTURE	HOOK	LATERAL	MENTAL
GAIETY	HOOP-SKIRT	LATEST	MENTIONED
GAIN	HOOT	LAUD	MERCURY
GAMES	HORN	LAUGHED	MERRIMENT
GENERALS	HORNS	LEADING	MIELS-DE-BEN
GENTLEMAN	HOVERING	LEAP	MIGHTY
GERMAN	HUNGER	LEAPT	MILK-WHITE

PAGE 525

FREQUENCY: 2

MINUTE	OVER-PREPARED	PRECEDENT	RIDING
MIRALS	PACE	PREFER	RIPPLES
MIRE	PACT	PRESERVED	RITES
MIRRORS	PAID	PRICE	RIVEN
MISTRESSES	PAINT	PRIED	ROME'S
MISTRUST	PAIR	PRINCE	ROOM
MISTRUSTED	PALETH	PRINCES	ROOT
MIXED	PALM	PRINTERS	ROUGH
MOCKS	PAMPHLETS	PRIZED	ROWS
MODERN	PANTING	PRO	RUDYARD
MODUS	PANTS	PROCEED	RUIN
MOLTEN	PAPER	PROFESSION	RUNNING
MON	PARC	PROFESSOR	RUNS
MONT-AUSIER	PARDONS	PROFIT	RUPERT
MONUMENT	PARLIAMENTARIANS	PROSE	RUSHED
MOODS	PARRIETH	PROTECTED	RUSHES
MOONLIGHT	PARTING	PROUD	RUSSIA
MORAL	PARTS	PROVINCE	SACRED
MOTHER'S	PAS	PRUDES	SAFFRON
MOUCHING	PASIPHAE	PUBLISHER	SALMON-TROUT
MOULD	PASSAGES	PULLED	SANSO
MOUNTAIN	PASSIONS	PULLING	SAT
MOUNTS	PAT	PULLS	SATIN-LIKE
MOURNING	PATRON	PURPOSE	SCALE
MRS.	PATTERN	PUTTING	SCARLET
MUFFINS	PATTERNS	QUAINT	SCATTER
N.	PAWN	QUALITY	SCENT
NAPKIN	PAYS	QUEEN	SCHOOL
NATHLESS	PEAKS	QUENCHED	SCORCHED
NATION'S	PEER	QUERULOUS	SCORE
NATURE'S	PENELOPE	QU'IEU	SCRAWNY
NEAT	PERCEIVED	QUIVER	SCURRY
NE'ER	PERENNIAL	QUO'	SEARCH
NEIGHS	PERFORCE	RABBIT	SEA'S
NET-WORK	PERIL	RABBITS	SEASONS
NIGH	PERSEUS	RABBLE	SEA-SURGE
NINEVEH	PETIT	RACK	SEATS
NONSENSE	PEUVENT	RAFTERS	SELF
NOSE	PHALLUS	RAFU	SELLING
NOVEL	PHANTOM	RAINS	SEMELE'S
OAR	PHIDON	RANG	SENATORIAL
OBJECT	PHILADELPHIA	RAYS	SENDS
OBSCURE	PHILETAS	REACHING	SENTENCE
OBSERVED	PHOIBEE	READIN'	SENTIMENTAL
OCCASION	PHOTOGRAPH	REALM	SERIES
ODD'S	PHRASE	REASON'S	SERIOUS
ODOUR	PHRYGIAN	RECEIVES	SERVE
OFFICE	PICKING	REFLECTING	SEVEN
OFFSPRING	PIEIRE	REINS	SEVERAL
OLE	PILES	REJUVENATE	SEX
OLYMPUS	PINT	RELATION	SHAFTS
OMINOUS	PIPES	RELIGION	SHAMEFUL
ONTO	PLAGUE	REMAINS	SHAMELESS
ONWARD	PLAIN	REPLIES	SHEATH
OPENING	PLAINTIVE	REPRESENT	SHEATHE
OPPOSITE	PLASMATOUR	REPUTATION	SHED
OPPRESSION	PLEASANTER	RESONANCE	SHEEP
OPPRESSORS	PLEASETH	RESPECTABLE	SHIELD
OPULENT	PLEASING	RESPECTED	SHIFT
ORANGE	PLOT	RESPITE	SHIP
ORCHARD	PLUMB	RESTAURANT	SHIRT
ORCHID	PLUMP	RESTING	SHOES
ORDINARY	PLUTO	RESTLESS	SHOOTS
ORGIES	PO	RESTS	SHOVE
ORNAMENTAL	POISON	RETURNED	SHOWED
OU	'POLLO	RETURNS	SHRINK
OUCH	POMPS	REVERIES	SHU
OUTRUN	POPPIES	REVIEWERS	SIFTINGS
OUTSIDE	PRAISES	REVOLUTION	SIGH
OVERHEAD	PRAYER	RHINE	SIGHS
OVERHEAR	PREACHER	RIDE	S'ILS

PAGE 526

FREQUENCY: 2 -- 1

SIXTEEN	STOOL	TONGUES	VOLTAIRE
SIXTH	STOPPED	TOOTH	WAFER
SKIES	STORES	TOP	WAKE
SKILL	STORIED	TORCHES	WALKING
SKIRTS	STOUR	TORN	WALKS
SLAUGHTER	STRANGENESS	TOSSING	WALLOW
SLAVE	STRAY	TOULOUSE	WANDERS
SLAY	STRENGTHENED	TOUR	WANTED
SLEEPS	STRIKES	TOUS	WANTS
SLEEVES	STRIKING	TRACKS	WATCHED
SLIPS	STRIPPED	TRADE	WATCHES
SLOSHIN'	STRIPS	TRADITION	WEARING
SLOUCHING	STROKE	TRAINED	WEATHERED
SLOWLY	STRONGER	TRAIT	WEDDED
SMEARED	STRUCK	TRANSLUCENT	WEEPING
SMOTHERED	STUDENTS	TRAPPINGS	WEIGHT
SMUTTY	STUPIDITY	TRAVEL	WELSH
SNARE	STURDY	TREAT	WE'VE
SNIFF	STYLE	TREMBLE	WHEREIN
SNIFFING	SUBTLY	TREMBLING	WHERETHROUGH
SOCIALIZED	SUCKS	TRIUMPH	WHERETO
SOCIETY	SUI	TROAD	WHETHER
SODDEN	SUMMER	TROPHIES	WHIRLING
SOFTLY	SUNK	TROUBLETH	WHISPER
SOLDIERS	SUPPLE	TROUBLING	WHISTLER
SOLEDADES	SUPPOSE	TROUT	WHIT
SOLID	SURGING	TRULY	WHITMAN
SOLVE	SURPRISE	TRUTHS	WILT
SONNET	SUSPICION	TUMULT	WINDING
SONS	SWALLOW	TURQUOISE	WINDOW
SORROWFUL	SWALLOWS	TWENTY	WINDOWS
SOURCE	SWEETER	'TWERE	WING
SOUTHWARD	SWINBURNE	TWIST	WINGED
SPANISH	SWIRL	TWISTED	WINTER
SPARKS	SWIRLING	TYRO	WINTER'S
SPATS	SYMBOLICAL	UGLY	WOEFUL
SPEAKERS	SYNE	UNBROKEN	WORTHIEST
SPEAKING	SYSTEM	UNDERSTAND	WOT
SPEARS	TAIRIRAN	UNFORTUNATE	WOUNDS
SPECIAL	TALKS	UNKNOWN	WREATH
SPED	TASTES	UNO	WRENCH
SPEECHES	TAUGHT	UNSULLIED	WRIGGLING
SPEEDILY	TE	UNTOUCHED	WRIT
SPELLS	TELLING	UPPER	WRY'D
SPENT	TELLS	URGE	X'S
SPHERES	TEMPERATE	URN	YESTERDAY
SPIN	TEN-SHIN	USELESS	YOKE
SPITE	TENTS	USURY	YOU'D
SPLASHED	TEPID	VACANT	YOU'RE
SPLENDOUR	TER	VALENTINE'S	YOURSELVES
SPRINGTIME	TESTAMENT	VALUE	YOU'VE
SPUN	THEME	VARIOUS	ZEUS
STAG	THEODORUS	VARRO	
STAIR	THICK	VEINS	(1)
STALKS	THIEVES	VENDRE	A'
STANDETH	THING'S	VENUST	A-A-A-A
STANDING	THINK'ST	VEROG	ABASHED
STARK	THIRSTY	VERS	ABBOT
STARTED	'THOUT	VEX	ABDOMINAL
STATELY	THROUGHOUT	VIA	ABE
STATISTICS	THWARTED	VIDE	ABELARD
STATUES	THYSELF	VIGOUR	ABIDE
STATURE	TI	VILE	ABIDED
STEADY	TIBORS	VILLONAUD	ABIDES
STEEDS	TIMOROUS	VIR	A-BINDING
STEEL	TIN	VIRTU	A-BITIN'
STEPS	TIN'	VISAGE	ADLAZE
STICKS	TITANS	VISIBLE	ABLE
STOCKINGS	TOBACCO-SHOP	VISIONS	ABODE
STOMPED	TO-DAY'S	VISIT	ABOMINABLE
STONES	TOLERANT	VITALS	A-BRISTLE

FREQUENCY: 1

ABSOLUTE	AFFLICTED	AMBASSADOR	AQUEOUS
ABSTRUSE	AFFORD	AMBASSADORS	A-QUIVER
ABU	AFFRAY	AMBERGRIS	ARABIA
ABUNDANT	AFFRONTS	AMBITION	ARABIAN
ABUSED	AFIELD	AMBROSIA	ARAB'S
ACCENTS	AFLAME	A-MEAOWLING	ARBOUR
ACCEPTABLE	AFLASH	A-MEN	ARBOURS
ACCESS	AFOOT	AMERICA'S	ARCADIA
ACCLAIMED	AFORESAID	AMIC	ARCADIAN
ACCOMPANIMENT	AFORETIME	AMITIES	ARCANE
ACCOMPLISHED	AFORE-TIME	AMOR	ARCHAIC
ACCORD	AFTERMATH	AMPHIBIOUS	ARCHES
ACCOST	'AGALMA	ANADYOMENE	ARCHITECT
ACCOUTREMENTS	AGATE	ANAEMIA	ARDOUR
ACCUSTOMED	AGATHON	ANAEMIC	ARENA
ACHE	AGDE	ANAETHESIS	'ARFT
ACHELOUS	AGE-LASTING	ANAGRAM	ARGO
ACHENOR	AGENT	ANALYSES	ARIEL
ACHIN'	AGETH	ANANGKE	'ARK
ACORN	AGE-THICK	ANCESTRAL	ARMED
ACQUAINTANCE	AGGLUTINOUS	ANCIENNES	ARMOURED
ACQUAINTANCES	AGGRESSION	ANCORA	ARMOURER'S
ACQUIRE	AGILITY	ANDAR	ARMOURESS
ACQUIRING	AGITATED	ANDRA	AROUET
ACRE	A-GLEAMING	ANEAR	ARRANGE
ACTIAN	AGNES'	ANECDOTES	ARRANGED
ACTIVE	AGRADIVA	ANGELIC	ARRANGEMENTS
ACTIVITIES	AGUE	ANGELS	ARRIVED
ACTOR	AHEAD	ANGER	ARROGANCE
ADAPTATIONS	AHI	ANGLE	ARS
ADDRESS	A-HUNTING	ANGLES	ARSENIC
ADDRESSED	AIE	ANGLICIZE	ARTEMIS
ADJUNCT	AIE-E	ANGRY	ARTICULATE
ADMIRABLE	AILES	ANGUISH	ARTIST
ADMIRED	AINT	ANGULAR	ARTISTS
ADMIT	A-JUMBLING	ANIENAN	ARTIST'S
ADMONISHETH	AKR	ANIMAM	ART'S
ADO	ALAIS	ANNALISTS	ASCENDED
ADOLESCENT	ALBAS	ANNOUNCING	ASCENDS
ADONIS	ALBATRE	ANNUBIS	ASCRAEUS'
ADOPTED	ALBION	ANOMALY	ASCRIPTION
ADORATION	ALBIRAR	ANTEDATES	A-SEARCHING
ADORED	ALCHEMIST	ANTHONY	ASHORE
ADORN	ALCYON	ANTIMACHUS	ASKS
ADORNED	ALDER	ANTIQUITY	A-SLOSHIN'
ADORNING	ALE	ANTS	ASPEN
ADRASTUS'	ALEMBIC	ANYHOW	ASPIRATIONS
ADS	ALERT	AOI	ASQUITH
ADS.	ALEXIS	APATHEIN	ASS
ADULTERERS	ALI	A'PAYIN'	ASSAILANT
ADULTEROUS	ALIEN	APE	ASSAILS
ADULTERY	ALLAIT	APELIOTA	ASSES
ADVENTURE	ALL-CONQUERING	APES	ASSET
ADVERTISING	ALLEYS	APHRODITE	ASSIDUOUS
AEGIS-DAY	ALLIANCE	APOCRYPHAL	ASSISTANCE
AEGRUM	ALIODETTA	APOLOGIZES	ASSISTANT
AEGYPTO	ALLOTTED	APOSTLES	ASSOCIATED
AEMELIS	ALLUREMENT	APPAREL	ASSUMPTION
AEMILIA	ALMOND	APPARITION	ASSUREDLY
AENEAS	ALMONDS	APPARUIT	ASTHETICS
AEONIUM	ALODETTA	APPEARS	A-STRAY
AERA	ALOFT	APPLICATION	ASTRIDE
AERE	A-LOOSE	APPLIES	A-SUDDEN
AERIAL	ALORS	APPLY	ATALIC
AERY	ALTAFORT	APPROACH	ATE
AESCHYLUS	ALTAFORTE	APPROACHES	ATHEIST
AESTHETIC	ALTER	APPROACHING	ATLANTIC
AESTUS	ALTERED	APPROBATION	A'TOP
AETNA	ALTHOUGH	APPROVED	A-TREMBLE
AFFECTION	ALTITUDE	APRICOT	'ATS
AFFECTIONS	AMAVI	APULEIUS	ATTACK

PAGE 528

FREQUENCY: 1

ATTAINED	BANNERETS	BE-SPECTACLED	BOMBS
ATTEMPT	BANNERS	BETIDE	BONDAGE
ATTENDANCE	BAPTIST	BETTERS	BONE
ATTENDANT	BARBARISM	BEWILDER	BONITA
ATTENDANTS	BARBECUES	BEWILDERING	BOOK-STALL
ATTIC	BARBITOS	BEWILDERMENT	BOOM
ATTIRED	BARED	BEWILDERS	BOON
ATTITUDES	BAREFOOT	BEWRAYED	BOOZY
ATTRACTION	BARGE	BEZIERS'S	BORD
AUCTION	BARLEY	BIDE	BORDERED
AUDIARDA	BARONS	BIEN	BORDON
AUDIBLE	BARS	BIG-BELLIES	BOREAL
AUDITION	BASER	BIGGEST	BORGNE
AUGUSTUS	BASKETS	BILIOUS	BORROWED
AULTAFORTE	BASKET-WORK	BILLS	BOS
AUPRES	BASTAN	BINDS	BOSQUE
AURELIA	BASTIDIDES	BIRCH	BOSS
AUS	BATH	BIRCHEN	BOSSU
AUSTER	BATH-ROBE	BIRTHDAY	BOSTON
AUSTERE	BATHTUB	BISHOPS	BOTCHED
AUSTORS	BATTERED	BISTRE	BOTTICELLIAN
AUSTRALIAN	BATTERS	BITCH	BOTTLED
AUTEM	BATTLE-GUERDON	BITES	BOTTOM
AUTHORS	BATTLE'S	BITING	BOTTS
AUTOMOBILES	BAUDELAIRE	BLACKING	BOUGHT-CHEAP
AUTOPSY	BAWDS	BLAGUEUR	BOUNDING-LINE
AUVERGNAT	BAY	BLAME	BOUNTIFUL
AUVERGNE	BEACH	BLANDULA	BOURGEOIS
AUVEZERE	BEACHES	BLANKNESS	BOURGEOISE
AUX	BEAK	BLEARY	BOURRIENNE
AVAIL	BEARETH	BLEED	BOWED
AVAILETH	BEATAE	BLEMISH	BOWELS
AVARICIOUS	BEAU	BLENDING	BOWER
AVENUE	BEAVERBROOK	BLESS	BOWERS
AVERAGE	BED-FEET	BLESSED	BOWETH
AVERTED	BED-POSTS	BLIGHT	BOWMAN
AVEZ	BEE	BLIGHTERS	BOWMEN
AVIGNON	BEEF-BONES	BLINDED	BOWS
AVIONS	BEEFY	BLINK	BOX
AVOID	BEERY	BLISSFUL	BRAIDS
AVRIL	BEFALL	BLOCKED	BRAINLESS
AWARDED	BEFOREHAND	BLOKE	BRAKE
A-WEARY	BEFRIENDED	BLOOD-CRIMSON	BRAKES
AWHILE	BEG	BLOODLESS	BRAND
AXES	BEGIN	BLOOD-RAVENOUS	BRANDED
AZURE	BEGOT	BLOOD'S	BRAVING
AZURES	BEHAVIOUR	BLOSSOMS	BRAWNY
BABE	BEHOLDING	BLOTS	BRAZEN'D
BACCHO	BEL	BLOUGHRAM'S	BREAD
BACKED	BELAUD	BLOUSE	BREADTH
BACKGROUND	BELIEVES	BLOWING	BREAKETH
BACKLESS	BELLEROPHON'S	BLUBBERING	BREAST-CARES
BACK-SWIRLING	BELLIES	BLUE-GRAY	BREASTLOCK
BACKWASH	BELLOTTI	BLUER	BREATHLESS
BADEST	BELLS	BLUISH	BREEDING
BADLY	BE-M	BLUNDER'D	BRENN
DAIL	BEN	BLURB	BRESCIA
BALANCE	BENACUS	BLURRED	BRICKS
BALDWIN	BENCHES	BLUSH	BRIDEGHEAD
BALFOUR	BENDED	BOARDS	BRIDGERAIL
BALL	BENDING	BOARHOUNDS	BRIDLE
BALLATETTA	BENNETT	BOAS	BRIGHTER
BALLET	BENUMBED	BOASTETH	BRILLIANCIES
BALM	BERANGERE	BOATS	BRINE
BAMBOO	BERNARD	BOB	BRINGING
BANALS	BERRIES	BODETH	BRINK
DAUB	BERTRAN'S	BODICE	BRISEIS
BANISHED	BERTRANS'	BODYKINS	BRISKER
BANK-CLERKLY	BERYL	BOIL	BRISTLE
BANKERS'	BESIDES	BOISTEROUS	BRITANNIA
BANNER	BESPEAK	BOLES	BROADWAY

PAGE 529

FREQUENCY: 1

BROCADE-LIKE	CANICULAR	CENTRIPETAL	CICERONE
BRONZE	CANNAE	CENTURION	CIGARETTES
BROODS	CANO	CERBERUS	CINQUE
BROOK-WATER	CANON	CERNE	CIRC
BROTHER-IN-LAW	CANOPY	CERULEAN	CIRCE'S
BROWNISH	CANTICO	CETTE	CIRCLES
BRUNT	CANTILATION	CH	CIRCULAR
BRUSHED	CANTING	CHAFF	CIRCUMCISION
BRUSHETH	CANTUS	CHAFING	CIRCUMSPECTION
BRUTE	CANZONETTI	CHAISES	CIRCUMSPECTIOUS
BUCHANAN	CANZONI	CHALLENGE	CITEE
BUD	CAP	CHAMBER	CITHARAON
BUDAPESTH	CAPANEUS	CHANCELLOR	CIVILIZATION
BUFFO	CAPITOLIUM	CHANGES	CLAD
BUG	CAPON	CHANNEL	CLANKING
BUILDER	CAPPED	CHANSONS	CLAP
BUILDING	CAPRIPED	CHAP	CLAPS
BULMENIAN	CAPS	CHAPEL	CLARA
BULWARK	CAPSIZE	CHARACTERS	CLARET
BULWARKS	CAPTIVATING	CHARGE	CLASHING
BUNDLES	CAPTIVE	CHARGER	CLASPED
BURDENS	CAR	CHARGES	CLASS
BURGHER	CARAVANS	CHARITY	CLATTER
BURGHERS	CARCASSONNE	CHARLES	CLEAN
BURLATZ	CARED	CHARMER	CLEANSE
BURLY	CARE'S	CHARMINGLY	CLEARNESS
BURNE-JONES	CARESSING	CHASE	CLEAVES
BURNT	CARE-WRETCHED	CHASTE	CLEAVING
BUS	CARI	CHATELET	CLEOPATRA
BUSSES	CARING	CHE	CLERGY
BUS-STOPS	CARMEN	CH'E	CLERK
BUST	CARNAGE	CHEAPNESS	CLERKENWALL
BUSY	CARPETS	CHECKS	CLERMONT
BUTCHERY	CARRIES	CHEEK-BONE	CLIFF
BUTEI	CARTER	CHEERED	CLIMATES
BUT-NOT-	CARTHAGINIAN	CHEERFUL	CLIMBED
ALTOGETHER-	CARTONS	CHEERFULLY	CLIMBER
SATISFACTORY	CARVED	CHELSEA	CLOAKED
BUTT	CARVEN	CHESTERTON	CLOSED
BUTTER	CARVING	CHESTS	CLOSELY
BUTTERFLY	CASEMENT	CHEVALIER	CLOSES
BUTTOCKS	CASES	CHICAGO	CLOSING
BUXOM	CASK	CHICANE	CLOTHES
BUYER	CASTE	CHIEF	CLOTTED
BUYS	CASTING	CHIEFLY	CLOUDY
C.	CATALOGUE	CHIEFS	CLOVER
CAAR	CATALOGUING	CHI'H	CLUS
CABARETS	CAT-O'-NINE-TAILS	CHIN	CLUSTERED
CABIN	CATS	CHINA	CLUSTERS
CABINETS	CAT'S-EYE	CHIPS	CLUTCHING
CAESAR	CATTLE	CHIQUITA	COAL
CAESARIAL	CATULLI	CHIVALROUS	COALS
CAFES	CATULLUS	CHLOROFORMED	COAST
CAID	CAUSA	CHO-FU-SA	COATS
CAKE	CAUSELESSLY	CHOIR	COBBLED
CAKES	CAUSEWAYS	CHOKAN	COBBLES
CAL	CAVALRY	CHOP	COBWEBS
CALAMITOUS	CAVENDISH	CHOP-HOUSE	COCK-SHY
CALAMITY	CEASETH	CHOPPED	COCOANUT
CALASH	CEASING	CHORTLES	COCOTTE
CALIBAN	CEILINGS	CHORUS	CODA
CALLEDST	CELEBRITY	CHOSES	CODE
CALLISTO	CELESTIAL	CHOYO	COHORT
CALL'ST	CELESTINE	CHRISTIANITY	COITUS
CALOR	CELL	CHRISTIANUS	COLDEST
CALVES	CELLAR	CHRYSOPHRASE	COLDLY
CAMARADES	CENSURE	CHU	COLLECTION
CAMEST	CENSUS	CH'U	COLLECTIVE
CAMPANIA	CENT.	CHURL	COLLICKS
CANARDS	CENTAUR	CHURLISH	COLONEL
CANDLE	CENTRE	CHURN	COLONNES

PAGE 530

FREQUENCY: 1

COLUMN	CONSTRUCTION	COVERT	D'
COLUMNS	CONSUMERS	COVETOUS	DABBLING
COMBAT	CONSUMES	COWER	DAEMON
COMBINATION	CONSUMETH	CRACK	DAGGER
COMBUSTED	CONTACT	CRACKED	DAI
COMER	CONTAINS	CRACKIN'	DALE
COMFORTER	CONTEMPORAINES	CRACKLING	D'ALLMAIN
COMFORTS	CONTEMPTED	CRAFT	DAM'D
COMMAND	CONTEMPTIBLE	CRAFTILY	DAME
COMMANDED	CONTENDED	CRAGS	DAMNED
COMMANDS	CONTENT	CRAMP	DAMSEL
COMMERCE	CONTENTIONS	CRASHING	DANCES
COMMISSION	CONTENTMENT	CRASSUS	DANDELION
COMMIT	CONTEST	CRAWL	DANGER
COMPACT	CONTINENCE	CREAKING	DANGERS
COMPARABLE	CONTINUED	CREAM	DANIEL
COMPARAISON	CONTINUOUS	CREPT	DANTES
COMPASSION	CONTRA-BASS'	CREPUSCULAR	DAPHNIS
COMPEL	CONTRADICTIONS	CRESCIT	DAR'DST
COMPELLED	CONTRASTS	CREVICES	DARK-BROWED
COMPELS	CONTROL	CRIERS	DARKLING
COMPILATION	CONTUBERNALIS	CRIETH	DARKLY
COMPLETE	CONVENIENCE	CRITICS	D'ARMENONVILLE
COMPLETELY	CONVENT	CROCUSES	DARN'D
COMPLEYNT	CONVENTIONS	CROPPED	DART
COMPLICATIONS	CONVERGATION	CROSSING	DASHING
COMPLIMENT	CONVERSE	CROSS-LIGHT	DASTARD
COMPLIMENTS	CONVERSES	CROSSWAY	DATA
COMPOSING	CONVEY	CROUCHING	DAUPHIN
COMPOSITION	CONVICTIONS	CROWDED	DAVE
COMPOSITIONS	COOKING	CROWDS	DAVID
COMPREHENSION	COOLING	CROWNED	DAVID'S
COMPRENNENT	COOPED	CROY	DAWN-MIST
COMRADES	COOPERATION	CRUCIFIX	DAY-LONG
COMSTOCK'S	CO-OPERATION	CRUELLY	DEADLY
CON	COPHETUA	CRUELTY	DEAL-WOOD
CONCAVA	COPULATION	CRUSADERS	DEARER
CONCEALED	COR	CRUSH	DEATHS
CONCEITED	CORACLE	CUBE	DEBIT
CONCENTRATION	CORAL	CUCKOO	DECEIT
CONCEPTS	CORE	CUIUSDAM	DECEITFUL
CONCERNING	CORMORANT	CULDOU	DECEITS
CONCESSIONS	CORNERS	CULL	DECEIVED
CONCLUDE	CORRECT	CULLING	DECIDED
CONCOCTION	CORRELATIONS	CULTIVATION	DECIDUOUS
CONCORD	CORRUPT	CULTURES	DECLAIMS
CONCUPISCENCE	CORRUPTION	CUM	DECLINED
CONDEMN	CORSET	CUPBOARD	DECOLLETE
CONDESCENSION	CORTEGE	CUPIDINESQUE	DECOR
CONDITION	CORYDON	CURIAN	DECORATIONS
CONDOLENCE	COSIER	CURIOUSLY	DECOROUS
CONFER	COSMETICS	CURLED	DECORUM
CONFESSION	COSMIC	CURRENT	DECREED
CONFETTI	COSMOS	CURSES	DEDANS
CONFIDENCE	COUCH	CURVED	DEED
CONFIGURATION	COUNCIL	CUSHIONED	DEEMS
CONFUSED	COUNCILLOR	CUTICLE	DEEPEST
CONMIGO	COUNTERLIE	CUTTING	DEER
CONNAISSEZ-VOUS	COUNTERPART	CYANINE	DEFEAT
CONNECTION	COUNTERPASS	CYBELE	DEFECTS
CONQUESTS	COUNTERTHRUST	CYCLADES	DEFEND
CONSECRATED	COUNTRYSIDES	CYCLAMEN	DEFERRED
CONSERVATION	COUPLE	CYDONIAN	DEFILING
CONSERVATRIX	COUPLES	CYGNES	DEFINITIONS
CONSIDERING	COURAGE	CYPRIAN	DEGREE
CONSIGNED	COURTEOUS	CYPRIAN'S	DEGREES
CONSPECTU	COURTESY	CYPRIS	DEIPNOIDES
CONSTERNATION	COURTEZAN	CYTHERAEAN	DEITY
CONSTITUTION	COURTEZANS	C.3	DELAYS
CONSTRUCT	COUSIN'S	C.4	DELECTABLE
CONSTRUCTED	COVERLEY'S	D.	DELECTATIONS

PAGE 531

FREQUENCY: 1

DELIGHTS	DISC	DOUBTLESS	EARN
DELIVER	DISCERNMENT	DOUGHTY	EARRINGS
DELOS	DISCIPLESHIP	DOUGTH	EAR-THE-LESS
DEMAND	DISCLOSES	DOUTH	EARTHEN
DEMEANOUR	DISCOMFORT	DOWN-FLOAT	EARTHERN
DEMOCRACY	DISCONTINUED	DOWNWARD	EARTH-WEAL
DEMOLISH	DISCORD	DOZE	EAST-LOOKING
DENIERS	DISCOUNT	DRAG	EASTWARD-FLOWING
DENIES	DISCOURAGED	DRAGGED	EATABLE
DENYING	DISCOURAGING	DRAGON	EAU-FORTE
DEO	DISCOVERING	DRAGON-LIKE	EC.
DEPART	DISCUSSED	DRAGON-PEN	ECLIPSES
DEPLETED	DISEASE	DRAGON-POND	ECONOMICAL
DEPLORED	DISEMBOWELED	DRAGON-SCALES	ECONOMICS
DEPLORES	DISFECEMI	DRAPED	EDDY
DEPORTMENT	DISGUISED	DRAUGHT	EDITORIAL
DEPRECATE	DISHONEST	DRAVE	EDWARD'S
DEPRIVED	DISH-WASH	DRAWING	EFFECT
DEPUTATION	DISILLUSIONS	DRAWINGROOM	EFFIGIES
DERELICTIONS	DISJECTA	DREADED	EFFORT
DERIDE	DISJUNCT	DREAM'S	EGG
DERISION	DISLIKE	DREAMT	EGG-WHITE
DESCANT	DISLIKED	DREAR	EGO
DESECRATED	DISPARAGE	DREARY	EGYPTIAN
DESERTA	DISPRAISES	DREGS	EHEU
DESIGNATE	DISSECTOR	DRINKST	EIGHT-PENCE
DESIRABLE	DISTASTE	DRIP	EIGHTY
DESPAIR	DISTENTIONS	DRIPS	EIUS
D'ESPARO	DISTINCTLY	DROOPING	EKE
DESPERATE	DISTINGUISHED	DROPPING	ELBOWS
DESPISED	DISTRESSED	DROWNED	ELDERLY
DESTINIES	DISTRESSING	DROWNS	ELDERS
DESTRIERS	DISTURB	DRUE'S	ELECTION
DESTROYED	DISTURBETH	DRUGGED	ELECTOR
DESTROYERS	DITCH	DRUGS	ELEGANCE
DESTROYING	DIVERGENT	DRUNKEN	ELEGANT
DETACHED	DIVERS	DRUNKENLY	ELEGY
DETAIL	DIVERSE	DRYAD	ELEVENTH
DETAILED	DIVERSION	DUCTILE	ELIS
DETERDING	DIVINE	DUD	ELLUM
DETESTED	DIVINERS	DUDS	ELM-OAK
DETRACTOR	DIVORCE	DUELS	ELUCIDATION
DEUX	D'OC	DULCE	ELUDED
DEVICES	DOCTOR	DULLARDS	ELUSIVE
DEVIRGINATED	DOCTRINE	DULLING	EMANATION
DEVOID	DODDERING	DUM	EMANUELE
DEWS	DODGED	DUMB	EMATHIAN
DEW-SPREAD	DODGERS	DUMB-BORN	EMBANKING
DIABOLUS	DODGING	DUMP	EMBITTERED
DIADEM	DOG'S	DUMPED	EMBRACE
DIAMONDS	DOG-WOOD	DUMPY	EMBRACED
DIAN	DOGWOODS	DUNDAS	EMBRACES
DIANA	DOLOROUS	DUNDERING	EMBROIDERED
DIAN'S	DOLOUR	DUO	EMENDATION
DIASTASIS	DOLPHINS	DUPONT	EMERALD
DIFFERENCE	DOLTS	DURANCE	EMERALDS
DIFFERING	DOMINATION	DURER	EMERGED
DIGESTIVE	DOMO	DUSK	EMERGES
DIGNIFIED	DOMPNA	DUSTS	EMETIC
DILIGENT	DONT	DWARFS	EMOTIONAL
DILIQUESCENT	DOODLEDE	DWELL	EMOTIONS
DILUTED	DOOM	DWELLING	EMPEROR'S
DIMENSIONS	DOOM-GRIPPED	DWELT	EMPLOYER
DIMITTIS	DOOR-BELLS	DYES	EMPLOYER'S
DIMMED	DOOR-YARDS	DYKE	EMPLOYMENT
DINNER	DOPE	'E	EMPRISE
DINNERS	DORATA	EAGE	EMPTINESS
DIONE	DORIA	EAGLE	EMPTY-HEADED
DIONYSUS	DORIAN	EAGLED	ENCHASSES
DIRE	D'ORLEANS	EALING	ENCROACHING
DIRT	DOTING	EARL	ENCRUSTED

PAGE 532

FREQUENCY: 1

ENDEAVOUR	ETAIT	FAIL	FILAMENTS
ENDING	ETERNALLY	FAILURE	FILLES
ENDITE	ETHICAL	FAIN	FILLETH
ENDURE	EUNUCH	FAINTS	FILTHY
ENDURED	EUNUCHS	FAIRLY	FIN
ENDURES	EUROPA	FAIRY	FINANCE
ENDYMION'S	EVANGELIST	FAIT	FIND'ST
ENEMY	EVANOE'S	FAITHFUL	FINER
ENFANT	EVENING'S	FALLETH	FIRE-DUST
ENGAGED	EVENTS	FALLOW	FIRM-FACED
ENGIRDLED	EVER-FLOWING	FALSITY	FIRMNESS
ENGLISHMAN	EVER-LIVING	FAMA	FISHERMEN
ENGLOBED	EVERYBODY'S	FAMAM	FISHING
ENGRAVER'S	EVERYCHONE	FAMILIAR	FISH-SKIN
ENGULF	EVERY-DAY	FAMILIARS	FITFULLY
ENGULPHS	EVILS	FAMOUS	FITS
ENI	EWES	FANCY	FITTED
ENJOY	EXACERBATED	FANE	FIVE-SCORE
ENJOYED	EXACERBATIONS	FANG	FLACCID
ENJOYMENT	EXAGGERATION	FANNING	FLACCUS'
ENNIUS	EXALTED	FANNO	FLAKING
ENNUIS	EXAMPLE	FAN-PIECE	FLAME-LAP
ENQUIRED	EXASPERATED	FANTASTIKON	FLAMING
ENRICHES	EXCEEDING	FAR-COURSING	FLAMINGOES
ENSHROUDED	EXCELLENCE	FARING	FLAMME
ENSLAVED	EXCELSIS	FARMERS	FLANK
ENSLAVED-BY-	EXCEPT	FASCINATING	FLANKED
CONVENTION	EXCERPTED	FASCISTS	FLARES
ENTAILED	EXCESS	FASHIONS	FLAT-LYING
ENTANGLED	EXCESSIVE	FASTNESS	FLAT-SPREAD
ENTERED	EXCIDEUIL	FATHERS	FLATTER
ENTERS	EXCLAIMED	FATNESS	FLATTERER
ENTICED	EXCLUSION	FAUGH	FLATTERIES
ENTREATED	EXCUSE	FAULTS	FLAVOUR
ENTWINED	EX-DIPLOMAT'S	FAUN-LIKE	FLAW
ENUMERATION	EXERCET	FAWN	FLAWLESS
ENVIES	EXERCISES	FAWNS	FLAWS
EOS	EXILE	FE'	FLAY
EPIGRAM	EXILE'S	FEARS	FLAYED
EPILOGUE	EXIST	FEASTS	FLAYETH
EPILOGUES	EXISTENCE	FEATS	FLEEING
EPITAPHS	EXISTS	FEATURE	FLEETETH
EPITHET	EXITUM	FEBRILE	FLESH-COVER
EQUALS	EXPECTATION	FEEBLE	FLESH-SHROUDED
EQUIPMENTS	EXPEDITION	FEED	FLEURS
EQUIPPED	EXPENSES	FEELIN'S	FLICKERED
EQUITABLE	EXPENSIVE	FEELS	FLIES
'ER	EXPERIENCE	FELICITOUS	FLIP
ERAN	EXPERT	FELLED	FLOATED
ERASED	EXPLAIN	FELLER	FLOATS
ERASERS	EXPLAINS	FELLERS	FLOODED
ERAT	EXPLORED	FELLOWSHIP	FLOODING
'ERB	EXPOSITION	FEMINA	FLOOD-WAYS
ERI	EXPOUND	FENCE	FLORAL
ERINNA	EXTENDED	FERMO	FLORENTIS
EROS	EXTENT	FERN-STALKS	FLORIALIS
ERUDITE	EXTINCTION	FESTERING	FLOURISHED
ERUPTION	EXULTED	FESTIVAL	FLOUT
ESCAPED	EXULTING	FEVER	FLOWER-HUNG
ESCAPES	EYED	FEWER	FLOWERY
ESCHEWED	EYE-DEEP	FIDAR	FLUID
ESCRITOIRES	EYE-LID	FIDDL'RY	FLUIDS
ESPAVIN	FABIUS	FIDELITIES	FLUTE
ESPECIAL	FABRICATION	FIDELITY	FLUTTERING
ESTABLISHED	FACED	FIDGETING	FLUTTERS
ESTATE	FACTITIOUS	FIELDING	FLYING
ESTEUE	FACULTY	FIERCE	FOE
ESTIMATE	FADES	FIFTEEN	FOEMEN
ESTOPPEL	FADING	FIGHT	FOES
ESTRANGED	FAIBLENESS	FIGURE	FOETID
ETAIENT	FAIDITA	FIGURES	FOETUSES

FREQUENCY: 1

FOG	FRONTIER	GILDER	GRADUATIONS
FOISON	FROSTS	GIMME	GRANDAD
FOIX'	FROSTY	GIPSIES	GRANDFATHER
FOLDED	FROWSY	GIPSY	GRANDMOTHER
FOLDING	FROZE	GIRDLE'S	GRAPE
FOLDS	FUIT	GIRT	GRAPPLE
FOLKS	'FULGENCE	GITANA	GRASP
FOLLIES	FUMES	GITAR	GRASS-BLADE
FOLLOWERS	FUNCTION	GIULIO	GRASSY
FOLLOWING	FUNDAMENTAL	GIV'	GRAVEN
FOND	FURNISH	GIVER	GRAY-GREEN
FONDA	FUSED	GIVEST	GREASE
FONT	FUSS	GIVETH	GREASY
FOOD'S	FUTURES	GLADE	GREATEST
FOOLISH	FUTURISTIC	GLADLY	GREAT-UNCLE'S
FOOL'S	GAG	GLADSTONE	GREAVES
FOOLS'	GAGGED	GLAMOROUS	GRECIAN
FOOT-FALL	GAI	GLAMOUR	GREECE
FOOTLIN'	GAINS	GLANCES	GREENISH
FOOTMAN	GAIT	GLANDERS	GREET
FOOTMEN	GALATEA	GLASS-GREEN	GREY-BLOWN
FOR'ARDER	GALAXIES	GLASSY	GREY-HAIRED
'FORE	GALILEE	GLAUQUES	GRIEVANCE
FORE-ARMS	GALLANTLY	GLAZING	GRIEVES
FOREGOING	GALLIC	GLI	GRIEVOUS
FORESEEN	GALLIFET	GLIMPSE	GRIMACE
FORE-SHORES	GALLUS	GLISTENS	GRIND
FORGAVE	GAMBETTO	GLITTERING	GRINS
FORGE	GAMUT	GLOOM	GROAN
FORGETFUL	GANG	GLOOMING	GROANETH
FORK	GANGRENE	GLOOMY	GROPES
FORKED	GANNET'S	GLORIA	GROSS
FORMIANUS	GAR	GLORIED	GROSSEN
FORMIANUS	GARBLE	GLORIES	GROSSIERE
FORMLESS	GARCIA	GLORIOUS	GROUP
FORNICATIONS	GARCON	GLOVES	GROVE
FORSAKE	GARLANDED	GNATS	GROVES
FORTHRIGHT	GARMENT	GOBBLE	GROWTH
FORTITUDE	GARRET	GOBBLED	GRUDGES
FORTY-EIGHT	GARRULOUS	GOD-FEASTING	GRUMBLE
FOUL	GARTH	GODLET	GRUNTS
FOUNTAINS	GAS	GOD-LIKE	GT.
FOUR-SQUARE	GATE-TOP	GODS'	GUARDSMEN
FRAGRANT	GATHERING	GOLD-BRAID	GUERDON
FRAISNE	GAUCHE-MAIN	GOLD-COLOURED	GUEREDON
FRAME	GAUDERO	GOLD-GIVING	GUERRE
FRAMES	GAUDIER	GOLD-YELLOW	GUESS
FRANCE	GAUDY	GONGULA	GUESSES
FRANCHISE	GAUNT	GOOD-BYE	GUFFAW
FRANCOIS-MARIE	GAUNTLET	GOOD-FELLOW	GUIDES
FRANKINCENSE	GAUTIER	GOODLIEST	GUILLAUME
FRANKLIN	GAWDS	GOOSE	GUINEA-PIG
FRANKLY	GAZONS	GORDAM	GUISCARDA
FRANKNESS	GEESE	GORDON	GUISE
FRATRES	GEISHA-CULTURE	GORE	GULLS
FREEDOM'S	GEN	GORED	GUN
FREELY	GENDER	GORGEOUS	GUNS
FREE-RUNNING	GENERALITIES	GORGON'S	GUN-SHARKS
FREEST	GENERAL'S	GOSSAMER	GUNWALES
FREEZE	GENERATION	'GOT	GURGLES
FREEZETH	GENERATIONS	GOURMONT	GURGLING
FRENCH	GENSERET	GOUT	GUSHED
FRENETICS	GENTILDONNA	GOUVERNET	GUST
FRERE	GENTLER	GOVERNMENT	GUTTER
FRESHETS	GERMAIN	GOVERNMENT'S	GUZZLE
FREUD	GESNING	GOVERNOR	GUZZLING
FRIEND'S	GEW-GAWS	GRABBED	GWYNN'S
FRIGIDAIRE	GHOST	GRACEFUL	GYNOCRACY
FROCK	GIARDINO	GRACEFULLY	GYPSY
FROLIC	GIBBET	GRACILES	HABENT
FROLICKING	GIFTS	GRADUALLY	HABITUAL

PAGE 534

FREQUENCY: 1

HADST	HEART-RENDING	HONOURERS	ILLUSIONS
HAI	HEART'S-ALL-	HOODED	ILS
HAIL-SCUR	BELOVED-MY-OWN	HOPED	ILSENSTEIN
HAIR-CLOTH	HEAUMES	HORA	ILZA
HALE	HEAVE	HORAE	I'M
HALF-AWAKENED	HEAVEN'S	HORATIAN	IMAGERY
HALF-BLUE	HEAVES	HOREB	IMAGINARY
HALF-CASTES	HEAV'N	HORI	IMAGINATION
HALF-COVERED	HECATOMB	HORRID	IMAGINING
HALF-HOSE	HECTOR	HORSE-FACED	IMBECILES
HALF-LIGHT	HEDONIST	HORSE'S	IMBUED
HALF-RUIN'D	HEED	HORSES'	IMITATE
HALF-SHEATHED	HEERD	HORTICULTURE	IMITATING
HALF-WATT	HEI	HOS'	IMITATION
HALF-WITS	HEIRLOOM	HOSANNAH	IMMEDIATE
HAM	HELENUS	HOSPITIUM	IMMERSES
HAMADRYADS	HELLAS	HOSTILE	IMMORAL
HAN	HELL'S	HOSTS	IMMORTALITY
HAND-GRIP	HELMET	HOTELS	IMMORTALS
HANDKERCHIEFS	HEN	HOUR'S	IMPALPABLE
HANDMAIDS	HEN.	HOUSEHOLDER	IMPARTIALLY
HANDSOME	HERACLEITUS	HOUSMAN'S	IMPECCABLE
HANG'D	HERB	HOVER	IMPERCEPTIBLE
HANGED	HERBACEOUS	HOVERED	IMPERFECTIONS
HANGS	HERCULES	HOWE'ER	IMPERTINENT
HANNIBAL	HEREAFTER	HOWER	IMPETUOUS
HAN-REI	HEROA	HOWEVER	IMPLIED
HANSOM	HERON	HOWLING	IMPORTANCE
HAPPEN	HERSELF'S	HUB	IMPUDENT
HARDER	HESITATE	HUBERT	IMPULSE
HARDEST	HESITATES	HUDSON	IN'ARDS
HARDLY	HETEROGENEOUS	HUES	INAUDIBLY
HARDSHIP	HEW	HUGE	INCANDESCENCE
HARDY	HI	HUGGED	INCENSE
HARMONIOUS	HIDEOUS	HUGH	INCENSED
HARNESS	HIDEOUSLY	HUMANITY	INCH
HARPING	HIDES	HUMBLE	INCONSCIENT
HARPIST	HIDETH	HUMMOCK	INCONSEQUENCE
HARRY'S	HIDING	HUNTED	INCONTINENT
HARSHER	HIDMEN	HUNTER	INCONVENIENT
HART	HIGH-BROWS	HUNTERS	INCREASES
HARVARD	HIGH-LEAPING	HURL	INCUBATE
HARZREISE	HIGHLY	HURRY	INCUBUS
HASH	HIGH-PRIESTESS	HUSBANDS	INCULTUS
HASN'T	HIGH-RISEN	HUGHED	INCUMBENT
HASTENED	HIGH-ROAD	HUSK	INDEFINITE
HATES	HIMERRO	HYRCANIAN	INDEMNITY
HATHA	HINDER	HYSTERIAS	INDETERMINATE
HATREDS	HINDRANCE	I.	INDIFFERENT
HATS	HIPPETY-HOP	I'	INDIRECTNESS
HATTER	HIRAM	IBYCUS	INDISCERNIBLE
HAUGHTINESS	HIRE	ICED	INDISCRETION
HAULED	HISTORICAL	ICE-FLAKES	INDIVIDUAL
HAUTEUR	HOARD	ICH	INDOLENT
HAVEN	HOGWASH	ICUMMEN	INEPTITUDES
HAVENS	HOKUM	ICY	INEXPLICABLE
HAWK	HOLDING	IDA	INFANTE
HAWTHORN	HOLIDAYS	IDALIA	INFANT'S
HAY	HOLINESS	IDEALS	INFECTION
HAZE	HOLLAND	IDENTITY	INFERNAL
HEAD-COLD	HOLLYHOCKS	IDIOM	INFEST
HEADLAM	HOLLY-TREES	IDLE	INFINITE
HEADLAND	HOME DORN	IDOLS	INFLUENCE
HEAD-PIECE	HOME-GROWN	IEU	INGRESS
HEADSTRONG	HOME-INDUSTRIOUS	'IGH	INHALED
HEAD-TRAPPINGS	HOMELY	ILIAD	INHERIT
HEAL	HOMER'S	ILIADS	IHH
HEALM	HONEST	ILIAN	INLAYS
HEALTH	HONEY-COMB	ILION	INNER
HEAPED	HONEY-RED	ILLA	INNOCENT
HEARTIES	HONOUR	ILLE	INNOCUOUS

FREQUENCY: 1

INN-YARD	JAGGED	KING'S	LATTICES
INO	JAIL	KINSMEN	LAUGHING
INSANITY	JAMES	KISSIN'	LAUGHS
INSCRIPTIO	JANE'S	KISSING	LAUGHTERS
INSCRIPTION	JANGLE	KISST	LAUNCELOT
INSIDIOUS	JAPAN	KISSY-CUDDLE	LAUNDRIES
INSPECTING	JAPANESE	KLEINEN	LAUS
INSPIRING	JAPONAIS	KNAVE	LAVINIAN
INSTALL	JAQUEMART	KNEE	LAVISHES
INSTANTLY	JARDIN	KNEE-JOINTS	LAW
INSTEAD	JARGON	KNEW'ST	LAWES
INSTINCT	JASON	KNIFE	LAWS
INSTRUCT	JASON'S	KNIGHT-LEAPS	LAX
INSTRUCTIONS	JAVELIN	KNOCKED	LAYED
INSTRUMENTS	JEALOUS	KNOCKETH	LAYOUT
INSUBSTANTIAL	JEALOUSIES	KNOCK-KNEE'D	LAYS
INSURANCE	JEHAN	KNOWEST	LAYU'S
INTAGLIO	JENNY'S	KNOW'T	LAZY
INTANGIBLE	JEST	KO	LEAD-HEAVY
INTELLECT	JEWEL	KODAK	LEADS
INTELLIGENT	JEWS	KOHL	LEAF-BROWN
INTENDED	JIBE	KO-JIN	LEAFY
INTENT	JIBES	KO-KAKU-RO	LEAK
INTENTION	JIBS	KORE	LEAKS
INTENTIONS	JOBBER	K---S	LEANIN'
INTER	JOBBERY	KUAN	LEAPING
INTERFERES	JOBS	KUDONIAI	LEARN
INTERLARDING	JOCELYNN	KUMI	LEASH
INTERMENT	JOCUNDA	KU-TO-YEN	LEASH-MEN
INTERMITTENCES	JOGLARS	KUTSU'S	LEAVE-TAKING
INTERPOSES	JOIN	KWAN	LECHER
INTERRUPTING	JOINED	LABOUR	LECHERS
INTIMATE	JOKE	LAC	LECHERY
INTOLERANT	JOKES	LACED	LECTURERS
INTOXICATED	JONGLEUR'S	LACERTUS	LEE-WAY
INTRACTABLE	JO-RUN	LACES	LEFT-HANDED
INTRIGUE	JOT	LACK-LAND	LEGAL
INVARIOUS	JOURNAL	LACONIA	LEGEND-LUST
INVESTIGATION	JOURNEY'S	LACQUER	LEGION
INVIDIOUS	JOVE'S	LADS	LEIDER
INVIGORATING	JOVIALIS	LAKES	LEISURE'S
INVIOLABLE	JOYS	LALAGE	L'ELECTION
INVIOLATE	JUDGE	LAME	LENDS
INVISIBLE	JUDGING	LAMENTATIONS	LENIN
INVITES	JUMP	L'AMOUR	LEOPARD'S
INVOLUTE	JUNG	L'AN	LETHE
INWARD	JUNO'S	LANG	LETS
IOANNA	JUPITER	LANGUAGE	LET'S
IONIAN	JURIDICAL	LANGUE	LETTRES
IRIDES	JURISDICTION	LANGUIDLY	LEUCADIA
IRIDESCENCE	JUTS	LAPPED	LEUCIS
IRISH	KAKUHAKU	LAPPING	LEUCONOE
IRONIES	KALOUN	LAPPO	LEURS
IRRESISTIBLY	KATSURA	LAQUELLE	L'HOMME
IRRESPONSE	KAUGH	LAR	LHUDE
IRRITATION	KEEN-SCENTED	LARCHES	LIAISONS
ISEUTZ	KEEP'ST	LARESQUE	LIAR
ISLANDS	KEN-NIN	LARGE-MOUTHED	LIARS
ISOLATION	KENSINGTON	LARGEST	LIBERTY
ISSUE	KETTLE-DRUMS	LARRON	LIBROSQUE
IS'T	KEY	LARST	LICE
ISTE	KICK	L'ART	LICHEN
-ITA	KID	'LAS	LICHENED
ITALIA	KIDDIE	LASTLY	LID
ITCH	KILL	LASTS	LIEDER
ITE	KILLED	LATCH	LIEF
IT'LL	KINDLETH	LATELY	LIEGEMEN
IXION	KINDRED	LATENT	LIFE'S-BLAST
J	KINEMA	LATIN	LIGHTED
JAB	KINGDOMS	LATINITY	LIGHTLY
JACOPO	KINGFISHERS	LATONA	LIGHTNESS

PAGE 536

FREQUENCY: 1

LIGHTNINGS	LUMINOUS	MARK	MESSENGER
LIGHTSOME	LUNAR	MARMALADE	MESSIRE
LILTING	LURE	MAR-NAN-OTHA	METAMORPHOSIS
LILY-OF-THE-VALLEY	LURKING	MARS'	METAPHORS
LIMNING	LUSCIOUS	MARSEILLES	METAPHYSICAL
LIMPID	LUSTS	MARSH-CRANBERRIES	METIERS
LIN	LUSTY	MARSHES	METRES
LINCOLN	LUTANY	MARTIAN	METRO
LINE	LUTE-STRINGS	MARTIN	ME-WARD
LINGERING	LUTH	MARUS	MEWARDS
LINING	LUXURIOUS	MARVEL	MEWING
LION-COLOURED	LYCIA	MARY	MEWS'
LIONEL	LYMAN	MARY'S	MICA
LIP-STICK	MA	MA'S	MICHAULT
LIQUEURS	MA'	MASEFIELD'S	MID-CROWD
LIQUID	MABIE	MASTERPIECE	MIDDLE-AGEING
LISTED	MAC	MATED	MIDMOST
LITANY	MACDONALD	MATERNAL	MIDONS
LITERARY	MACERATIONS	MATTERS	MID-PAGE
LITERATI	MACH'	MATURIN	MID-SEA
LITTER	MACHIAVELLI	MAUDLIN	MID-SUMMER
LIU	MAECENAS	MAUPASSANT	MILDLY
'LIVE	MAELIDS	MAUSOLUS	MILDNESS
LIVER	MAENSAC	MAUVE	MILESIAN
LIVETH	MAENT'S	MAXIM	MILESIEN
LOAN	MAEONIA	MAYBE	MILLENIA
LOATHE	MAGAZINE	MAYHAP	MILLWIN
LOATHING	MAGAZINES	MAYST	MILORD
LOCALITY	MAGIANS'	MAY'ST	MIME
LOCATION	MAGICAL	MCC	MINARETS
LOCKED	MAGNIFIED	MEAD-DRINK	MIND'S
LOCKS	MAGNITUDE	MEADOWS	MINES
LOCUS	MAGNOLIA	MEALS	MINGLE
LOITER	MAIDEN	MEANEST	MINOAN
LONDRES	MAINTAIN	MEANIN'	MINORES
LONE-FLYER	MAINTAINED	MEANT	MINOS'
LONELINESS	MAINTAINS	MEAT	MINSTREL
LONGACRE	MAITRE	MEDIA	MINUSCULE
LONGEVITY	MAITRE-DE-CAFE	MEDICAL	MINUTES
LONGING	MAJESTIES	MEDICINE	MIRAL'S
LONG-TONSILLED	MAKER	MEDIOCRITIES	MIRTH
LOOM	MAKYTH	MEDITATE	MISCHIEF
LOOPED	MAL	MEDITATIO	MISCONCEPTIONS
LOPE	MALENESS	MEETETH	MISLAID
LOQUITUR	MALES	MEETING-PLACE	MISPLACEMENT
LOR	MALEVOLENCE	MEETS	MISS
LORDLIEST	MALH	MEINEN	MISSED
LORDLY	MALICE	MELEAGAR	MISTS
LORD'S	MAMMON	MELLOWED	MISVENTURE
LOSE	MANAGE	MELT	MITRAILLEUSES
LOSETH	MANCA	MEMBRA	MNEMONIC
LOUD	MANDATE	MEMOIRE	MOANETH
LOUDER	MANDRAKES	MEMORABLE	MOBILE
LOUDNESS	MANES	MEMORIAL	MOBS
LOUE	MANHATTAN'S	MEMORY'S	MOCKED
LOUSY	MANHOOD	MENCKEN	MOCKERY
LOVABLE	MANIFESTATIONS	MENDACITIES	MOCKETH
LOVELIER	MAN-KIN'ARDS	MENOETIUS	MOCK'RY
LOVE-LYRICS	MANKIND	MENTORS	MODE
LOVETH	MANNA	MERCHANDISE	MODELLED
LOWELL	MANUELA	MERCIFUL	MODERATE
LOWERING	MANURE	MERCY	MODERATIONS
LOWEST	MANUS	MERE-FLOOD	MODERNITY
LOWLY	MAQUERO'S	MERE-WEARY	MODULATION
LOYAL	MARCHERS	MERGED	MOEURS
LOYALTY	MARCIAN	MERRILY	MOIETY
L S	MARE	MERRY	MOLUCCAS
LUC	MAREMMA	MESMERISM	MOMENTOUS
LUCID	MARGINAL	MESMERIZER	MONARCH
LUINI	MARIA	MESS	MONCEAU
LULLIN	MARIENNE	MESSALINA	MONEY

PAGE 537

FREQUENCY: 1

MONGOLS	NAILS	NORMAN'S	OLDNESS
MONKEYS	NAKEDNESS	NORTH-EAST	OLD-WOMEN
MONOTONY	NAMES	NORTHERN	OLYMPIAN
MONSIEUR	NARBONNE	NORTHWARD	OM
MONTHLIES	NARROWS	NORTHWINDISH	OMAKITSU
MONTY	NARSTY	NOSES	'OME
MONUMENTAL	NASTY	NOTABLE	OMNIBUS
MONUMENTUM	NATHAT-IKANAIE	NOTED	ONE'S
MOOD-LOFTY	NATIONS	NOTES	ONESTI
MOOED	NATION-WIDE	NOTHIN'	ONYX
MOP	NEARETH	NOTHINGNESS	OOT
MOPED	NEARNESS	NOTICED	OPAL
MORALISTS	NEATH	NOTION	OPERA
MORALITY	NEATLY	NOURISHED	OPPROBRIUM
MORALS	NECK	NOUS	'OPS
MORBID	NEEDY	NO'US	ORANGE-COLOURED
MORROW	NEGLECTED	NOVELLA	ORBAJOSA
MORSUS	NEIGH	NOVEMBER	ORCHARDS
MORTEM	NEIGHBOURS	NOWHERE	ORCHIDS
MORTMAIN	NELL	NOYES	ORCUS
MORTUIS	NEMESIANUS	NUKTIS	ORDERED
MOSCOW	NEO-COMMUNE	NUMA	ORDERLY
MOSHER'S	NEO-NIETZSCHEAN	NUMBER	ORDER-TO-WRITE
MOSSES	NEPHEW	NUMERICAL	ORE
MOSSY	NEPHEWS	NUMEROUS	ORFEO
MOTH	NEPTUNE	NUNC	ORFEVRERIE
MOTHERS	NERVE-WRACKED	NUNTY	ORGANIZATION
MOTION	NEST	NUT	ORIEL
MOTIONLESS	NET	NYMPHARUM	ORL
MOTTOES	NET-LIKE	OAK	ORNAMENT
MOUCHIN	NEUTRAL	OAK'S	ORNAMENTED
MOULTED	NEVERTHELESS	OATS	ORPHEUS
MOUNT	NEWER	OBEDIENCE	ORTUS
MOUNTAIN-CROSSING	NEWEST	OBJECTED	OSSA
MOURNFUL	NEW-FANGLED	OBJECTS	OSTENDE
MOUSE	NEW-LAID	OBLIVION	OTHER'S
MOUSSELINE	NEWLY	OBLIVIONS	OURSELVES
MOUSTACHES	NEWMAN	OBSEQUIES	'OUSE
MOUTH-ORGAN	NEWNESS	OBSERVATION	OUTBLOTTED
MOUTH-ORGANS	NEWSPAPER	OBSTINATE	OUTCAST
MOUTHS	NICCOLO	OBSTRUCTIONIST	OUTLAST
MOVEMENT	NICHARCUS	OBVIOUS	OUTPUT
MOVEMENTS	NIGGARDS	OBVIOUSLY	OUTRIDERS
MOYEN	NIGHTINGALE	OCCASIONAL	OUTRIGHT
MUD	NIGHTLY	OCCHI	OUT-SPREAD
MULBERRIES	NIGHTSHADE	OCCUPANT	OUTSTRETCHED
MULBERRY	NIGHTWATCH	OCCUR	OUT-WEARIERS
MUMMY	NIKOPTIS	OCHAISOS	OVERBLOTTED
MUMPODORUS	NILE	OCHRE	OVERCAST
MUNDANE	NIMMIM	O'CLOCK	OVERFILLED
MUNDI	NINETIES	OCTOBER	OVERFLOWING
MURALH	NINETY	OCULISTS	OVERLORDS
MURMUR	NINETY-EIGHT	ODD	OVERSKIRT
MURMURED	NINTH	ODDMENTS	OVERWEENING
MURMURING	NIRVANA	ODE	OVERWROUGHT
MUSCLES	NO'	ODOR	OVID
MUSES'	NOBILITIES	ODOURS	OWE
MUSEUM	NOBILITY	OEIL	OWL
MUSICIANS	NOBLENESS	O'ERGIVEN	OWLS
MUSIQUE	NOBLES	O'ERSHADOW	OWNER
MUSSED	NOBLESSE	O'ERSHADOWED	OXFORD
MUTABILITY	NOCTURNAL	OETIAN	OYSTERS
MUTE	NODIER	OFFENCE	P.
MUTILATED	NOEL	OFFENDED	PACES
MUVVER	NOIRS	OFFER	PACIFIC
MYOPE	NONCE	OFFERINGS	PACKING
MYRRH	NON-ESTEEM	OFFERS	PAGANI'S
MYRTLES	NOON	OFFICER	PAGE
MYSTERY	NOOSE	OFFICIAL	PAGEANTRY
NA	NORMAL	OGLING	PAIL
NAILED	NORMANDE	OISIN	PAINS

FREQUENCY: 1

PAINTERS	PECULIAR	PIECES	POICTIERS
PAINTING	PEERING	PIER	POIGNARD
PAIRED	PEGASEAN	PIERCE	POINTED
PALACES	PEIGNOIR	PIERCED	POIS
PALAVER	PELASGIAN	PIERIAN	POKE-NOSE
PALLID	PELION	PIERIDES	POLE
PALLOR	PELLMELL	PIERRE	POLHONAC
PALPITATE	PENATES	PIERROTS	POLICE
PALSIED	PENAUTIER	PIG	POLICEMEN
PANDARS	PENCE	PIGEONNES	POLIN
PANEL-SHAPED	PENSAMIENTOS	PIG-HEADED	POLISHED
PANOPLY	PENSIONERS	PILE	POLITICS
PANTH'	PEOPLE'S	PILED	POLLEN
PANTOSOCRACY	PERCEPTION	PILGRIM	POLNESI
PAPIER-MACHE	PERCEPTIONS	PILLAR	POLUPHLOIBOIOUS
PAPIOL	PERCEPTIVITY	PILLOW	POLYDMANTUS
PAPYRUS	PERDAMNATION	PILOT	POLYPHEMUS
PAR	PERFECTING	PIMPING	POLYPHLOISBOIO
PARA	PERFECTION'S	PIMPS	POMEGRANATE
PARACELSUS	PERFECTLY	PINE-WINDS	POMP
PARADE	PERFORM	PINING	POMPILIUS
PARAGON	PERFORMED	PINION	POMPOSITIES
PARAPHRASE	PERFORMERS	PINK	POND
PARASITIC	PERFORMING	PINNING	POOLS
PARCH	PERFUMES	PINXIT	POPKOFF
PARFUM	PERGAMUS	PIQUANTE	POPLAR
PARK	PERILOUS	PISANELLO	POPULACE
PARKHURST'S	PERILS	PISISTRATUS	POR
PARKS	PERISH	PISTIL	PORCH
PARLANCE	PERORATION	PIT	PORQUE
PARLIAMENTS	PERPETUAL	PITCH	PORTAL
PARRIES	PERSIA	PITCHERS.	PORTALS
PARTED	PERSISTING	PITIFUL	PORTENT
PARTHIAN	PERTAINETH	PITYING	PORTENTS
PARTHIANS	PERTURBATIONS	PLACATION	PORTRAIT
PARTIES	PESTE	PLACED	PORTRAITS
PARTY	PETAL-LIKE	PLAGUES	POSITION
PASSAGE	PETITES	PLAINETH	POSITIONS
PASSIONATE	PETRARCHAN	PLAISAUNCES	POSSIBLE
PASSION'S	PEUT	PLANH	POSSIBLY
PASSIVE	PHAECIA	PLANTAGENET	POST
PASTIME	PHAETONA	PLANUS	POSTPONE
PATARA	PHALANX	PLASTER	POSTPONEMENT
PATCH	PHALLIC	PLATES	POSTULATE
PATCHED	PHALOI	PLATONIC	POT
PATCHOULI	PHANOPOEIA	PLAUSIBILITIES	POTATIONIST
PATENT	PHANTASMAGORIA	PLEACHED	POTENTIAL
PATHETIC	PHANTASMAL	PLEAD	POULARDES
PATHETICALLY	PHASELLUS	PLEASES	POURED
PATIENCE	PHIDIPPUS	PLEASURABILITIES	POVERTY
PATIENT	PHILISTIA'S	PLEBEIAN	POWDERED
PATRIA	PHOEBUS'	PLECTRUM	POWDERY
PATRICIENNES	PHONETICS	PLED	POWERFUL
PATRIOT	PHOTOGRAPHS	PLEDGES	POWERS
PATS	PHRASED	PLOTS	PRACTICAL
PATTERNED	PHRASES	PLOWMAN	PRACTICE
PATTERN-SILK	PHYSICIST	PLUM-COLOURED	PRACTICES
PAUNVRE	PIANIST	PLUMS	PRAGUE
PAUPER	PIANO	PLUNDERED	PRAIRIES
PAUPER'S	PIANOLA	PLUNGE	PRAISE-WORTHY
PAUSE	PICARDA	PLUS	PRAYERS
PAVED	PICKED	PLUVIUS	PREACHERS
PAVEMENTS	PICKIN'	POCKET-LOOKING-	PREACHIN'
PAVING	PICKINGS	GLASS	PRECEDED
PAVLOVA	PICKLED	POCKETS	PRECIOUS
PAWNS	PICNICKING	PODS	PRECIPITATE
PEACH	PICTURE	POE	PRECIPITATION
PEACOCK'S	PICTURES	POEME	PRECISELY
PEACOCK-THROATED	PICTURESQUE	POESIE	PREDESTINATION
PEAK	PIE	POETE	PREDILECTION
PEBBLES	PIECE-MEAL	POETICA	PREFERABLE

PAGE 539

FREQUENCY: 1

PREFERRED	PUB	RAPES	REMISSION
PREGA	PUBLICATION	RAPTURES	REMNANT
PREGNANT	PUBLISHER'S	RASCAL	REMUER
PREJUDICE	PUG-BITCH	RAST-WAY	REMUS
PREMIER	PUG-DOG'S	RAVEL	REND
PRES	PUI	RAVENS	RENDER
PRESCRIPTION	PULPING	RAVVLES	RENEWAL
PRESENCE	PULSE	RAW	RENEWED
PRESENTED	PUMP	RAY	RENOWNED
PRESENTLY	PUNIC	RAZOR'S	REPAYEST
PRESERVE	PUOSCH'	RE	REPENTANCE
PRESIDENT	PURER	REACHES	REPLACES
PRESSED	PURGED	READER	REPLEVIN
PRESSING	PURITY	READERS	REPORT
PRESTIGE	PURPLING	REALIST	REPORTS
PRETENCE	PURRING	REALLY	REPROBATIONS
PRETEND	PURRS	REALMS	REPUTATIONS
PREVAILS	PUSHED	RE-BEAMS	RESEMBLANCE
PRIAMUS	PUZZLED	REBUKE	RESERVED
PRICKS	PYJAMAS	RECALLETH	RESIDENT
PRIES	PYPERS	RECEIVE	RESIDES
PRIEST	PYRAMID	RECEIVED	RESISTANCE
PRIESTS	PYRAMIDS	RECENTLY	RESOLUTELY
PRIG	PYRE	RECEPTION	RESPECTABILITY
PRIMAL	Q.	RECESSES	RESPECTABLE-TAWDRY
PRIMITIVE	Q'S	RECITING	RESPECTABLY
PRIVATELY	QUANDARIES	RECKING	RESPECTIVE
PRIV'LEGE	QUANTITIES	RECKON	RESPLENDENT
PRIZE	QUARREL-BOLT	RECOGNITION	RESPONDED
PROBE	QUARTERS	RECOGNIZE	RESTED
PROCEEDETH	QUASI	RECOURSE	RESTETH
PROCESS	QUATRE	RECUMBENT	RESTLESSNESS
PROCTORS	QUATTRO	RED-BEAKED	RESTORATION
PROCURE	QUEERIES	RED-PINE-TREE	RESTRAIN
PRODUCED	QUESTING	REDUNDANCIES	RESTRAINT
PRODUCING	QUIA	RED-WALLED	RESULT
PRODUCT	QUICKSAND	REEDS	RESURGES
PROFANE	QUIDEM	REEK	RESURRECT
PROFFER	QUIES	RE-ENTER	RESUSCITATE
PROFILE	QUIETEST	RE-ENTERS	RETAIN
PROFITABLE	QU'IL	REFERENCE	RETROSPECT
PROGENY	QUINTILIA	REFINEMENT	REVEALED
PROGRAM	QUINTUS	REFINING	REVERENCE
PROJECTION	QUIVERING	REFLECTIONS	REVERY
PROLETARIAT	QUIVERS	REFORM	REVIEWER
PROLIFIC	QUOD	REFORMATION	RHAPSODIZE
PROMINENT	QUOTABLE	REFORMING	RHODEZ
PROMISCUITY	QUOTATIONS	REFRAINS	RHOMBS
PROMOTION	RAANA	REFT	RHOMBUS
PROPAGANDAS	RABBITS'	REFUSED	RHONE
PROPERLY	RACONTE	REGALE	RHYME
PROPERTY	RAG	REGARDLESS	RHYMERS'
PROPHYLACTIC	RAGE	REGISTER	RHYMES
PROPITIATES	RAGGED	REHEARSED	RIBALD
PROPPED	RAILING	REIGNS	RIBBED
PROPRIETY	RAILINGS	REINACH	RIBBON
PROSPERED	RAIMENT	REITERATION	RIBBON-LIKE
PROSPEROUS	RAIMONA	REJOICER	RIBEYRAC
PROTECTOR	RAIN-COLD	RELATIONSHIP	RIBS
PROTEST	RAINETH	RELATIVES	RICE-POWDER
PROTOTYPE	RAIN-TEARS	RELAXING	RICHLY
PROVES	RAKU-HOKU	RELEASED	RICKETY
PROVIDES	RAKUYO	RELIANCE	RID
PROVINCIA	RAMBLING	RELIEF	RIDES.
PROVISIONS	RAMM	RELIGIOUS	RIDGES
PROVOSTS	RAMSEY	REMAINDER	RIGGING
PROWESSE	RANAUS	REMAINETH	RIGHTEOUS
P.'S	RANCOUR	REMARKS	RIGOROUS
P'S	RANK	REMEMBERED	RIHAKU
PSYCHE	RAOUL	REMEMBRANCE	RIHOKU'S
PSYCHOLOGICAL	RAPE	REMINDER	RILLET

PAGE 540

FREQUENCY: 1

RIME	RUSSET	'SCAPED	SELWIN
RIMES	RUSSIAN	SCARE	SEMBLANCE
RING-HAVING	RUSTED	SCARE-CROW	SENAT
RINGS	RUSTICUS	SCARIFIED	SENATE
RIOKUSHU	S.	SCENE	SENDETH
RIQUIER	SACCHARINE	SCENTED	SENESCHAL
RISEN	SACKVILLE	SCHEME	SEN-GO
RISER	SACRA	SCHEMES	SENHER
RISES	SADDLES	SCHMERZEN	SENIOR
RISETH	SAFES	SCHOLARSHIP	SENIORS
RISHOGU	SAFFRON-COLOURED	SCIENCE	SENSATE
RISKS	SAGE	SCION	SENSUEL
RISQUE	SAGGING	SCIRO	SENTENT
RITRATTO	SAI	SCOPE	SENTIMENT
RIU'S	SAILOR	SCORES	SEPTIMIUS
RIVA	SAILORS	SCORNING	SEPULTUS
RIVER-BRIDGE	SAILS	SCORNS	SEQUESTERED
RIVER-MERCHANT'S	SAINT	SCOUNDREL	SERE
ROADWAYS	SAINTLY	SCOWLING	SERPENTINE
ROAR	SAINTS	SCRAPING	SERVICE
ROAST	SAINT'S	SCRATCHED	SESTINA
ROBBERS	SAISON	SCREAMED	S'EVEILLER
ROBERT	SAKE	SCREECH	SEVENTH
ROCACOART	SALAMMAMM	SCREED	SEVENTIES
ROCAFIXADA	SALE	SCRIBBLING	SEXLESS
ROCHECHOUART	SALES	SCROLLS	SEXTUS
ROCHECOART	SALIS	SCULPTORS	SHADES
ROCKET	SALMON	SCULPTURE	SHADOWY
RODE	SALON	SCUTTLES	SHAFT
RODYHEAVER'S	SALTUS	SCYTHIAN	SHAG
ROGER	SALT-WAVY	SE	SHAKEN
ROLL	SALUTE	SEABOARD	SHAKING
ROLLS	SALVACIOUN	SEA-CLEAR	SHALLOW
ROMA	SALVATION	SEA-CLIFF	SHAME
ROMANCE	SALVATIONISTS	SEACOAST	SHAMED
ROMANCES	SAMAIN	SEA-COAST	SHAMELESSLY
ROMANO	SAMOTHRACE	SEA-CROSSING	SHAPED
ROOFS	SAN	SEA-DARK	SHARKS
ROOKS	SANDALED	SEA-FARE	SHARP
ROOMS	SANE	SEAFARER	SHARP-EDGED
ROSE-LEAF	SANG-DE-DRAGON	SEA-FOWLS	SHARPENED
ROSE-LEAVES	SAN-KO	SEA-HOARD	SHATO-WOOD
ROSE-TIME	SANTA	SEAL	SHATTERED
ROSORIU	SAPLING	SEALED	SHAVE
ROSSETTI	SAPPHIRES	SEAMEN	SHAW
ROSY	SAPPHO'S	SEARCHES	SHEAF
ROTE	SARCOPHAGUS	SEARETH	SHEDS
ROTS	SARDINES	SEA-SERPENT	SHEEP-FEEDER
ROTTED	SARGASSO	SEATED	SHEEP'S
ROTUNDOS	SARGENT	SEAWARD	SHEER
ROUGE	SARLAT	SECRETS	SHEEREST
ROUSING	SATE	SECTOR	SHELF
ROUTE	SATIEMUS	SECURE	SHE'LL
ROW	SATIETIES	SEDGE	SHELLEY
ROWTON	SATINS	SEDGES	SHELVES
ROYALTIES	SATIRE	SEED-POD	SHEPHERD
RUB	SATISFACTION	SEEK'ST	SHEPHERDESS
RUBAIYAT	SATURN	SEEMING	SHEPHERDS'
RUBBED	SAUCY	SEES	SHE'S
RUCK	SAVAGE	SEETH	SHIFTER
RUDDY	SAVENT	SEI	SHIFTING
RUFFLE	SAVING	SEIGNIORY	SHIMMERING
RUINED	SAVONNIER	SEI-GO-YO	SHINS
RUINS	SAVOUR	SEISMOGRAPH	SHIP'S
RULE	SAYEST	SELDOM	SHIVER
RULES	SCALD	SELECT	SHI-YO
RUMOURS	SCALES	SELECTED	SHOCKED
RUN-AWAY	SCAMANDER	SELF-BAPTIZED	SHOE
RURAL	SCANDAL	SELF-STYLED	SHONE
RUSH	SCANDALS	SELLAIO	SHORE
RUSKIN	SCANDET	SELVAGGIA	SHORT

PAGE 541

FREQUENCY: 1

SHOULDER	SLEEK	SOLICITUDE	SPUR
SHOULDER-STRAPS	SLEEPING	SOLVED	SPUR-CLINKS
SHOUT	SLEEVE	SOMETHIN'	SPURS
SHOWING	SLEIGHT	SOMETIMES	SPUR'S
SHOWN	SLEPT	SONG-LIFE	SPURTED
SHRIEK	SLICED	SONG'S	SQUABBLE
SHRILL	SLIGHTEST	SON-IN-LAW	SQUARE
SHRINES	SLIGHTLY	SONNETS	SQUARED
SHRINKETH	SLIM	SONORITY	SQUATS
SHROPSHIRE	SLIP	SOOTHING	SQUEALS
SHROUDS	SLIPPED	SOOTHINGS	S---'S
SHRUBBERY	SLIPP'RY	SOPHIST	SST
SHRUNK	SLITHER	SOPHISTICATIONS	STA
SHUDDER	SLITHERS	SOPHOCLEAN	STABLES
SHUT-IN	SLOP	SOPRANO	STABLISHED
SHUTS	SLOPE	SORCERIZING	STAGNANT
SHUTTING	SLOPPETH	SORE	STAGS
SIC	SLOT	SORELY	STAIN
SIDONIAN	SLOUCHED	SORROWFULLY	STAINETH
SIENA	SLUGGARD	SORROW-SWEPT	STAINING
SIEVE	SLUT-BELLIED	SORTS	STAIRS'
SIFT	SLUTS	SO'S	STALL
SIGHEST	SLUT'S	SO-SHU	STALWART
SIGHT'S	SMALL-BEER	SOT	STAMP
SIGN	SMARTER	SOUGH	STANDARDS
SILENUS	SMELLS	SOUGHT	STAR
SILET	SMILES	SOUL-KIN	STARTIN'
SILKEN	SMILING	SOUS	STARVED
SILKWORMS	SMIRKING	SOUTH-FOLK	STATED
SIME	SMITE	SPADE	STATES
SIMILAR	SMITTEN	SPANGLES	STATUARY
SIMOIS	SMOKED	SPARS	STATUE
SIMOON	SMOKE-FLOWERS	SPASMS	STAUNCHES
SIMPLY	SMOOTH	SPATTERING	STAVE
SIMULACRA	SMOTHER	SPAWNED	STAYED
SIN	SMOULDER	SPEAR	STEALS
SIN'	SMUG	SPECIALIST	STEAM
SINAI	SMUGNESS	SPECTATOR	STEEL-BLUE
SINECURE	SNAKE'S	SPEED	STEELY
SINGERS	SNARED	SPEEDING	STEEP
SINGES	SNATCH	SPHERE	STELE
SINGETH	SNATCHED	SPIDERS	STELLAR
SINISTRO	SNATCHING	SPIKE	STENCHES
SINKS	SNEER	SPINE	STENDHAL
SINS	SNOOZLING	SPIRAL	STEPPING
SIRMIO	SNORE	SPIRITUAL	STERILE
SIRMIONE	SNOWED	SPIRITUEL	STERN
SISTE	SNOWETH	SPIT	STEW
SISTER	SNOWS	SPITTING	STEWS
SISTERS	SNOW-WHITE	SPLASH	STICK
SITE	SNOWY	SPLENDOURS	STICKING
SITUATIONS	SOAKS	SPLIT	STIFFENED
SIXTY	SOAP	SPLITS	STIFFLY
SKEIN	SOAPY	SPLITTING	STIFFNESS
SKELETON	SOCRATES	SPOIL	STILL-BORN
SKETCH	SOFTEN	SPOILERS	STILLNESS
SKETCHES	SOFTNESS	SPOILING	STILTS
SKIDDETH	SOGGY	SPOILS	STIMULATE
SKIFFSMAN	SOIL	SPOKE'	STIMULATING
SKILLFUL	SOILED	SPOKEN	STIMULATION
SKIPPED	SOILED-WHITE	SPOKEN-AGAINST	STINKING
SKIRT	SOIREE	SPOON	STINKS
SKIRTING	SOJER	SPORTS	STIRRER-UP
SKY-LIKE	SO'JERS	SPOT	STIRRING
SKY'S	SO-KIN	SPRANG	STIRS
SLACKED	SOLD	SPRAWLING	STOCK
SLADE	SOLDIER	SPRAYS	STODGY
SLANDER'S	SOLELY	SPREADING	STOLE
SLAPS	SOLEMNITY	SPREADS	STOMACH
SLASH	SOLI	SPRINGS	STONE-BRIGHT
SLAYS	SOLICITOUS	SPRING'S	STONE-CLIFFS

PAGE 542

FREQUENCY: 1

STOOD	SUEDE	SWEVYN	TENT
'STORANTE	SUET	SWIFTEST	TENTACLES
STORE	SUEVI	SWIFT-FOOT	TENTATIVE
STORK	SUFFER	SWIG	TENTH
STORKS	SUFFERIN'	SWINBURNE'S	TENULLA
STORM	SUFFERS	SWIRLERS	TENUOUS
STORMED	SUFFICIENT	SWISS	TENZONE
STORMS	SUGARED	SWOLLEN	TERGIVERSATE
STRACHEY	SUGGESTION	SWORD-ARM	TERPSICHORE
STRAGGLING	SUICIDES	SWORD-HATE	TERRACE
STRAIN	SUITABLE	SWORD-PLAY	TERRACED
STRAIT	SUITED	SWORD-RACK	TERRACES
STRAITLY	SUITETH	SWORE	TERRENE
STRANDS	SUITOR	SWORN	TESTED
STRASBOURG	SUMMERS	SWUNG	TESTICLES
STRATA	SUMMERWARD	SYLVAN	TESTING
STRATEGIST	SUMNER	SYMPHONIES	TETHER
STRATH	SUNDAY	SYRIAN	TEXAS
STRAW	SUNDAYS	SYRUP	THALASSES
STRAWBERRIES	SUNDERED	SYSTEMS	THANK
STRAYED	SUN-DIALS	T.	THANKFUL
STRENGTH	SUNKEN	TABLES	THATCH
STRENGTHEN	SUNLESS	TABULATE	THEATRE
STRENUOUS	SUN-LIGHT	TACTIC	THEON
STRETCH	SUNLIT	TA'EN	THEORIES
STREW	SUNS	TAENARIAN	THEREAFTER
STREWS	SUN-SHOT	TAIHAITIAN	THEREBY
STRICT	SUP	TAIL	THERE'LL
STRING	SUPERB	TAILS	THESEUS
STRINGING	SUPERFLUITIES	TAIRIRAN'S	THEY'RE
STRING-PURSE	SUPERIOR	TAKIN'	THEY'VE
STRIVE	SUPERNAL	TALENT	THICKENED
STRIVETH	SUPERSEDED	TALENTS	THICKET
STROKED	SUPERVENING	TALLEYRANDS	THIGHS
STROKES	SUPPLANTS	TALLOW	THINA
STRONGEST	SUPPORTED	TAME	THIRDS
STROVE	SUPPOSED	TAMED	THIRST
STRUGGLES	SUPPOSITION	TAMPERED	THIRTY
STRUT	SUPPRESSION	TAN	THIRTY-FOUR
STUDIO	SUR	TANKED	THIRTY-SIX
STUDY	SURGINGS	TARDI	THITHER
STUFFED-SATIN	SURGIT	TARDILY	THOMAS
STUFFY	SURHUMAN	TARGE	THOROUGHFARE
STUMBLES	SURLY	TARIFF	THOUGHT'S
STUNNED	SURPASS	TARNISHED	THOU'LT
STUNTED	SURPRISED	TARRIETH	THRACE
STUPEFIED	SURROUNDED	TATE	THREAD
STUPIDE	SURROUNDING	TATTERED	THREADS
STUPIDITIES	SURVIVAL	TAVERN	THREATS
STYLIST	SURVIVED	TAWDRY	THREICIAN
STYX	SUSURRUS	TAWN	THRENOS
SUASION	SUTTEE	TAXES	THRESHOLD
SUAVE	SVELTE	TEA-GOWN	THRILLS
SUB	SWADELIN'S	TEAR	THRONE
SUBJECT	SWALLER'D	TEA-ROSE	THROWS
SUBJECTIVE	SWAN	TEAT	THRUSTING
SUBJECTIVELY	SWANKERS	TEA-TIME	THUD
SUBJECTS	SWANS	TECHNIQUE	THUMBS
SUBLIME	SWAP	TEEN	THUNDER
SUBSTANCE	SWARDS	TEGAEAN	THUNDERED
SUBTERRANEAN	SWARM	TEINTEES	THUNDERS
SUBTLER	SWARMED	TEMPER	THYRSIS
SUBTLE-SOULED	SWAY	TEMPERAMENTS	THYRSOS
SUBURBS	SWEARING	TEMPERED	TIBBY-CAT
SUCCESS	SWEAT	TEMPESTS	TIBER
SUCCESSES	SWEATIN'	TEMPLES	TIBET
SUCCULENT	SWEEP	TEMPORA	TIBULLUS
SUCCUMBED	SWEETLY	TEMPTED	TIBUR
SUCKED	SWELLED	TENDER	TICK
SUDDENLY	SWELLING	TENDETH	TICKLE
SUDDENTLY	SWENKIN	TENNYSON	TICKLED

PAGE 543

FREQUENCY: 1

TIDES	TRAINING	TWISTING	UNIVERSE
TIDILY	TRAINS	TWISTS	UNKILLABLE
TIDY	TRAITORESS	TWITCHING	UNKISSED
TIED	TRAITS	TWITTER	UNLEASHED
TIES	TRAMP	TWO-BARRELED	UNLESS
TIGERS	TRANS-CAUCASUS	TWO-FACED	UNLIKELY
TIGHT	TRANSITORY	'TWOULD	UNLUCKILY
TIGRIS	TRANSLATED	TYBALDE	UNMADE
TILLAGE	TRANSLATIONS	TYIN'	UNMARRIED
TIME-BAR	TRANSLATOR	TYMPANUM	UNMENTIONABLE
TIMELY	TRANSPARENT	TYRANNY	UNMINDFUL
TIMES'	TRAVAIL	UC	UNMOVING
TINA	TRAVELLED	UDDERS	UNNAMEABLE
TINGE	TRAVERSE	ULTIMATELY	UNOPENED
TINGED	TRE	UMBRAM	UNOPENING
TINGEING	TREADS	UM-HUM	UNPAID
TINT	TREASURIES	UNABLE	UNPERTURBED
TINTAGOEL	TREASURY	UNAFFECTED	UNREACHABLE
TIP'S	TREE-AT-THE-RIVER	UNANSWERING	UNREIN
TITYRUS	TRELLIS	UNBEAUTIFUL	UNSAFE
TOBACCO	TREMBLES	UNBELIEVING	UNSATISFIED
TOC	TREMOLOS	UNBEND	UNSEEN
TO-EM-MEI	TRENCH	UNBIND	UNSPOTTED
TO-EM-MEI'S	TRENTIESME	UNBORN	UNSTOPPED
TOFF	TRIBE	UNBOUND	UNSUITABLE
TOI	TRICK	UNBOUNDED	UNTAKEN
TOILET	TRICKSOME	UNBRUSHED	UNTELLABLE
TOISONS	TRIES	UNCATALOGUED	UNTEMPTABLE
T'OLD	TRILLS	UNCELEBRATED	UNTIDY
TOLEDOS	TRIO	UNCERTAINITY	UNTIE
TOM-BOY	TRISTAN'S	UNCERTAINTIES	UNTRAMMELLED
TOMBS	TRIUMPHANT	UNCOMBED	UNUSED
TOMB-STONE	TRIUMPHS	UNCOMFORTABLE	UNUSUAL
TOMB-STONES	TRIUNE	UNCONSCIOUS	UNWEARYING
TO-MORROWS	TRIVIAL	UNCONSTANT	UNWIELDLY
TO-NIGHT	TROBAR	UNCTION	UNWORTHY
TONNERRE	TROICA	UNCUCKOLDED	UNYIELDING
TOODLE	TROIEI	UNCULTIVATED	UPLEAPING
TOOL	TROTH	UNDEFEATABLE	UPLIFT
TOPAZ	TROTSKY	UNDERGOING	UP-PUSHED-BOSOM
TOPIC	TROUBADOURS	UNDERSKIRT	UPSET
TOP-LOFTICAL	TROUBLED	UNDERTAKERS	UPSTANDING
TORCH	TROUSERS	UNDERWAVE	URBANITY
TORCH-FLAMES	TRUCE	UNDERWORLD	USEFUL
TORCH-FLARE	TRUMPET	UNDETERRED	US-TOWARD
TORRENT	TRUMPETS	UNDISCIPLINED	USUAL
TORRIDITY	TRUNKS	UNDOUBTEDLY	UTMOST
TORSE	TRUSTED'ST	UNDRY	UTTER
TORTOISE	TRUTH'S	UNDRYABLE	UTTERANCE
TORTURE	TS'AI	UNDULATION	UTTERS
TOSSED	TSIN-TSU	UNDULENT	UXORIOUS
TOTIN'	TUB	UNDULY	VACUOS
TOUCHETH	TUBERCULOSIS	UNDURABLE	VAE
TOUCHING	TUNEING	UNEARTHLY	VAGABONDS
TOURIST	TUNIC	UNEDUCATED	VAGUELY
TOURISTS	TUNICK'D	UNENDINGLY	VAGULA
TOURS	TUNING	UNEXPECTED	'VAILS
TOUT	TURBULENT	UNFAMILIARITY	VAIR
TOUTES	TURRETS	UNFATHOM	VALE
TOWARDS	TURTLE	UNFIT	VALETS
TOWER	TWELFTH	UNFORECASTED	VALIANT
TOWER-MAN	TWENTY-EIGHT	UNFORMED	VALIANTLY
TOWER-ROOM	TWEY	UNGAINLY	VALLERIE
TOYS	TWIDDLES	UNGATHERED	VALLIS
TRACED	TWIG	UNGRATEFUL	VALOUR
TRACK	TWIGS	'UNGRY	VAN
TRACTS	TWIN	UNHARDENED	VANISHING
TRAGICAL	TWINE	UNIMAGINATIVE	VANNA
TRAIL	TWINED	UNIMPORTANT	VANTAGE
TRAILING	TWINS	UNINTERRUPTED	VARIED
TRAIN	TWIRL	UNION	VASES

FREQUENCY: 1

VAST	VISCOUNTESS	WAVER	WHORES
VAULTED	VISCOUNTESS	WAVERING	WHORESON
VAULTS	VISION	WAVE'S	WHO'S
VECCHII	VISITING	WAVES'	WIDE-BANDED
VEGA	VISITOR	WAVE-WORN	WIDEST
VEGETABLE	VITTORIO	WAX	WIDOW
VEHEMENCE	VIXEN	WAXED	WIDOWED
VEILS	VIZARD	WAY-FARE	WIFE'S
VEIN	VOCAT	WEAK	WILD-CRUEL
VENALITY	VOCATION	WEAKNESS	WILD-GOOSE
VENDOR	VOGUE	WEAKNESS'	WILD-WOOD
VENERES	VOID	WEALTHY	WILLIE
VENGO	VOILA	WEAPONS	WILLINGNESS-TO-
VENOM	VOIR	WEARETH	OBLIGE
VENTADOUR	VOLS	WEARIED	WILLOW
VENTRICLES	VOLUME	WEATHER	WILLOW-COLOURED
VERB	VOLUPTUOUS	WEAVING	WILLOW-TIPS
VERBAL	VORTEX	WEDDING	WILLS
VERDI	VOTE	WEEHAWKEN	WILL'S
VERGIER	VOUS	WEEP	WIN
VERISIMILITUDES	VOW	WEFT	WIND-RUNEING
VERITIES	VOY	WEI	WIND'S
VERMES	VOYAGED	WEIGHED	WINE-FLUSHED
VERMILIONED	VOYAGES	WEIGHTS	WING'D
VERNAL	VOYAGING	WELCOME	WING'D-WITH-AWE
VERSE-BARREL	VU	WELDING	WING-FLAPPING
VERSICLES	VULGARITIES	WELKIN	WINNING
VERTIGO	VULGUS	WELL-AWAY	WINSOME
VERUM	VULTUM	WELL-GOWNED	WINSOMENESS
VESTA	W.	WELL-HEAD	WIRE
VESUVIUS	WAILING	WELL-PAID	WIRE-LIKE
VEXED	WAIT	WELTER	WISHING
VEXES	WAITED	WENCH	WISH-WASH
VIATOR	WAITERS	WEPT	WISTARIA
VIBRATIONS	WAITS	WE'RE	WISTFUL
VICAR	WAKES	WERT	WITHERED
VICE	WAKING	WESTERN	WITHSTAYED
VICED	WALDORF	WHALE-PATH	WITHSTAYING
VICKERS	WALLER'S	WHALE'S	WITLESS
VICOMTE	WALT	WHAT'S	WITNESS
VICTOR	WANDER	WHATS-HIS	WIT'S
VICTORIA	WANDERED	WHATS-HIS-NAME	WIVES
VICTORIOUS	WANDER-LIED	WHEEL-RIMS	WOKE
VIDAL'S	WANETH	WHEEZE	WOLD
VIENNA	WANING	WHEEZES	WOLVES
VIERA	WANTING	WHENE'ER	WOMANISH
VIERNA	WARBLE	WHENEVER	WONDER-FOLK
VIEW	WARD	WHEREBY	WONDERFUL
VIEWED	WARES	WHEREFROM	WONDERS
VIGIL	WARFARE	WHERE'S	WONTED
VILLAGES	WARMED	WHETS	WOODBERRY
VILLANELLE	WARN	WHIM	WOODEN
VILLEINY	WARNED	WHIMPER	WOOD-MOSS
VINES	WARN'T	WHINED	WOOD-PULP
VINE-STOCK	WARP	WHIRL	WOODY
VINE-STRINGS	WARREN	WHIRLED	WOOL
VINTAGE	WARRIOR	WHIRRED	WOOLLY
VINTAGES	WAR'S	WHISKEY	WORDGWORTHIAN
VIOLENCE	WARS-MEN	WHISPERING	WORE
VIOLENT	WASHED	WHISTLES	WORKER
VIOLET	WASN'T	WHITE-GLEAMING	WORKING
VIOLETS	WASTAGE	WHITEHALL	WORLDLY
VIOLETTES	WASTE	WHITE-HEADED	WORM
VIOLIN	WASTED	WHITENESS	WORMS
VIRGIL	WATCHER	WHITE-STOCKING'D	WORRY
VIRGINAL	WATCHING	WHITTLED	WORSE
VIRGINIA	WATCHMAN	WHO'D	WORSHIPPERS
VIRGINS	WATER-BUTT	WHOE'ER	WORTH'S
VIRGO	WATER-GIRLS	WHO'ER	WOULDST
VIRILE	WATER-JET	WHORE	WOUNDING
VIRTUE	WATER-LILIES	WHO'RE	WRESTLED

FREQUENCY: 1

WRETCHED
WRIES
WRINGING
WRINKLED
WRINKLING
WRITERS
WRONGS
WUZ
XERXES
Y
YACHT
YAMMER
YANK
YARD
YARNS
YAWNED
YAWNING
YDOLE
YDONE
YEARNED
YEAR'S
YEI-SHU
YELLOWS
YELLOW-WHITE
YER
YESTERDAY'S
YESTERE'EN
YIELDED
YOGA
YOU'LL
YOUNGEST
YOUNGSTER
YOURSELF
YOWLS
YSAUT
YSOLT
YUAN
YULE
YULE-TIDE

PAGE 546